Microsoft® Official Academic Course

Administering Windows Server® 2012 Exam 70-411

Patrick Regan

WILEY

Credits

VP & PUBLISHER	Don Fowley
EXECUTIVE EDITOR	John Kane
DIRECTOR OF SALES	Mitchell Beaton
EXECUTIVE MARKETING MANAGER	Chris Ruel
MICROSOFT PRODUCT MANAGER	Gene R. Longo of Microsoft Learning
ASSISTANT EDITOR	Jennifer Lartz
TECHNICAL EDITORS	Jeff T. Parker
	Brien Posey
	Kenneth Hess
ASSISTANT MARKETING MANAGER	Debbie Martin
SENIOR PRODUCTION & MANUFACTURING MANAGER	Janis Soo
ASSOCIATE PRODUCTION MANAGER	Joel Balbin
CREATIVE DIRECTOR	Harry Nolan
COVER DESIGNER	Georgina Smith
SENIOR PRODUCT DESIGNER	Thomas Kulesa
CONTENT EDITOR	Wendy Ashenberg
PRODUCTION EDITOR	Eugenia Lee

This book was set in Garamond by Aptara, Inc. and printed and bound by Bind-Rite Robbinsville. The covers were printed by Bind-Rite Robbinsville.

ISBN 978-1-118-51161-9

Printed in the United States of America

10 9 8 7 6 5 4

www.wiley.com/college/microsoft *or*
call the MOAC Toll-Free Number: 1+(888) 764-7001 (U.S. & Canada only)

Foreword from the Publisher

Wiley's publishing vision for the Microsoft Official Academic Course series is to provide students and instructors with the skills and knowledge they need to use Microsoft technology effectively in all aspects of their personal and professional lives. Quality instruction is required to help both educators and students get the most from Microsoft's software tools and to become more productive. Thus, our mission is to make our instructional programs trusted educational companions for life.

To accomplish this mission, Wiley and Microsoft have partnered to develop the highest-quality educational programs for information workers, IT professionals, and developers. Materials created by this partnership carry the brand name "Microsoft Official Academic Course," assuring instructors and students alike that the content of these textbooks is fully endorsed by Microsoft and that they provide the highest-quality information and instruction on Microsoft products. The Microsoft Official Academic Course textbooks are "Official" in still one more way—they are the officially sanctioned courseware for Microsoft IT Academy members.

The Microsoft Official Academic Course series focuses on *workforce development*. These programs are aimed at those students seeking to enter the workforce, change jobs, or embark on new careers as information workers, IT professionals, and developers. Microsoft Official Academic Course programs address their needs by emphasizing authentic workplace scenarios with an abundance of projects, exercises, cases, and assessments.

The Microsoft Official Academic Courses are mapped to Microsoft's extensive research and job-task analysis, the same research and analysis used to create the Microsoft Certified Solutions Associate (MCSA) exam. The textbooks focus on real skills for real jobs. As students work through the projects and exercises in the textbooks and labs, they enhance their level of knowledge and their ability to apply the latest Microsoft technology to everyday tasks. These students also gain resume-building credentials that can assist them in finding a job, keeping their current job, or furthering their education.

The concept of life-long learning is today an utmost necessity. Job roles, and even whole job categories, are changing so quickly that none of us can stay competitive and productive without continuously updating our skills and capabilities. The Microsoft Official Academic Course offerings, and their focus on Microsoft certification exam preparation, provide a means for people to acquire and effectively update their skills and knowledge. Wiley supports students in this endeavor through the development and distribution of these courses as Microsoft's official academic publisher.

Today educational publishing requires attention to providing quality print and robust electronic content. By integrating Microsoft Official Academic Course products, MOAC Labs Online, and Microsoft certifications, we are better able to deliver efficient learning solutions for students and teachers alike.

Joseph Heider

General Manager and Senior Vice President

Preface

Welcome to the Microsoft Official Academic Course (MOAC) program for becoming a Microsoft Certified Solutions Associate for Windows Server 2012. MOAC represents the collaboration between Microsoft Learning and John Wiley & Sons, Inc. Microsoft and Wiley teamed up to produce a series of textbooks that deliver compelling and innovative teaching solutions to instructors and superior learning experiences for students. Infused and informed by in-depth knowledge from the creators of Windows Server 2012, and crafted by a publisher known worldwide for the pedagogical quality of its products, these textbooks maximize skills transfer in minimum time. Students are challenged to reach their potential by using their new technical skills as highly productive members of the workforce.

Because this knowledgebase comes directly from Microsoft, architect of Windows Server 2012 and creator of the Microsoft Certified Solutions Associate exams, you are sure to receive the topical coverage that is most relevant to students' personal and professional success. Microsoft's direct participation not only assures you that MOAC textbook content is accurate and current, it also means that students will receive the best instruction possible to enable their success on certification exams and in the workplace.

■ The Microsoft Official Academic Course Program

The Microsoft Official Academic Course series is a complete program for instructors and institutions to prepare and deliver great courses on Microsoft software technologies. With MOAC, we recognize that because of the rapid pace of change in the technology and curriculum developed by Microsoft, there is an ongoing set of needs beyond classroom instruction tools for an instructor to be ready to teach the course. The MOAC program endeavors to provide solutions for all these needs in a systematic manner in order to ensure a successful and rewarding course experience for both instructor and student, including technical and curriculum training for instructor readiness with new software releases; the software itself for student use at home for building hands-on skills, assessment, and validation of skill development; and a great set of tools for delivering instruction in the classroom and lab. All are important to the smooth delivery of an interesting course on Microsoft software, and all are provided with the MOAC program. We think about the model below as a gauge for ensuring that we completely support you in your goal of teaching a great course. As you evaluate your instructional materials options, you may wish to use the model for comparison purposes with available products.

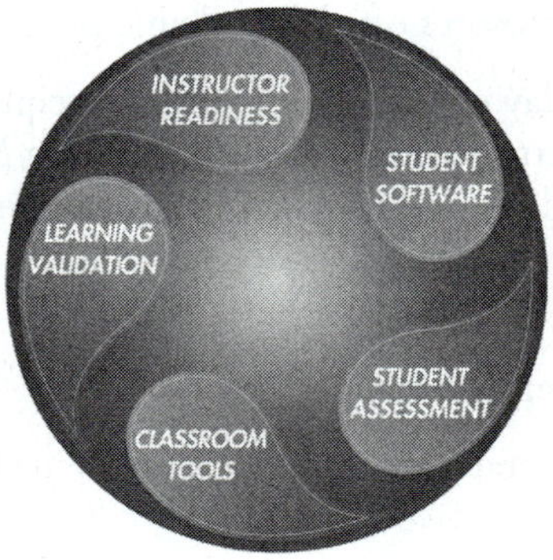

Illustrated Book Tour

■ Textbook Organization

This textbook is organized in 22 lessons, with each lesson corresponding to a particular exam objective for the 70-411 Administering Windows Server 2012 exam. This MOAC textbook covers all the learning objectives for the 70-411 certification exam, which is the second of three exams needed in order to obtain a Microsoft Certified Solutions Associate (MCSA) certification. The exam objectives are highlighted throughout the textbook.

■ Pedagogical Features

Many pedagogical features have been developed specifically for Microsoft Official Academic Course programs.

Presenting the extensive procedural information and technical concepts woven throughout the textbook raises challenges for the student and instructor alike. The Illustrated Book Tour that follows provides a guide to the rich features contributing to Microsoft Official Academic Course program's pedagogical plan. Following is a list of key features in each lesson designed to prepare students for success on the certification exams and in the workplace:

- Each lesson begins with an overview of the skills covered in the lesson. More than a standard list of learning objectives, the overview correlates skills to the certification exam objective.
- Illustrations: Screen images provide visual feedback as students work through the exercises. The images reinforce key concepts, provide visual clues about the steps, and allow students to check their progress.
- Key Terms: Important technical vocabulary is listed at the beginning of the lesson. When these terms are used later in the lesson, they appear in bold italic type and are defined.
- Engaging point-of-use reader aids, located throughout the lessons, tell students why this topic is relevant (*The Bottom Line*), provide students with helpful hints (*Take Note*), or show cross-references to where content is covered in greater detail (*X Ref*). Reader aids also provide additional relevant or background information that adds value to the lesson.
- Certification Ready features throughout the text signal students where a specific certification objective is covered. They provide students with a chance to check their understanding of that particular exam objective and, if necessary, review the section of the lesson where it is covered.
- Using Windows PowerShell: ***Windows PowerShell*** is a Windows command-line shell that can be utilized with many Windows Server 2012 functions. The Using Windows PowerShell sidebar provides Windows PowerShell-based alternatives to graphical user interface (GUI) functions or procedures. These sidebars begin with a brief description of what the Windows PowerShell commands can do, and they contain any parameters needed to perform the task at hand. When needed, explanations are provided for the functions of individual parameters.

- Knowledge Assessments provide lesson-ending activities that test students' comprehension and retention of the material taught, presented using some of the question types that they'll see on the certification exam.
- An important supplement to this textbook is the accompanying lab work. Labs are available via a Lab Manual and also by MOAC Labs Online. MOAC Labs Online provides students with the ability to work on the actual software simply by connecting through their Internet Explorer web browser. Either way, the labs use real-world scenarios to help students learn workplace skills associated with administering a Windows Server 2012 infrastructure in an enterprise environment.

■ Lesson Features

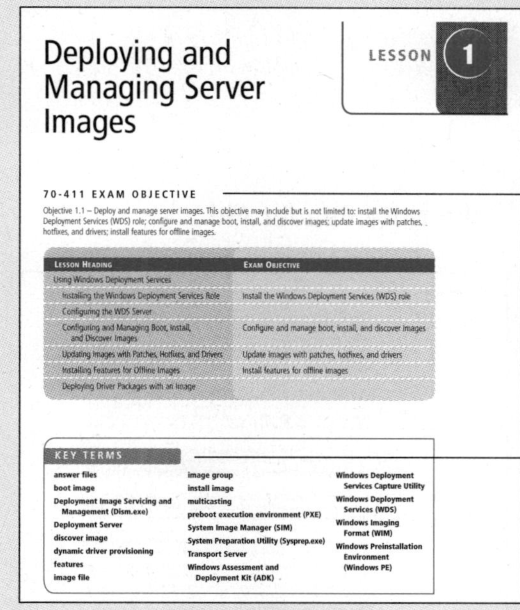

Deploying and Managing Server Images

LESSON 1

70-411 EXAM OBJECTIVE

Objective 1.1 – Deploy and manage server images. This objective may include but is not limited to: install the Windows Deployment Services (WDS) role; configure and manage boot, install, and discover images; update images with patches, hotfixes, and drivers; install features for offline images.

Lesson Heading	Exam Objective
Using Windows Deployment Services	
Installing the Windows Deployment Services Role	Install the Windows Deployment Services (WDS) role
Configuring the WDS Server	
Configuring and Managing Boot, Install, and Discover Images	Configure and manage boot, install, and discover images
Updating Images with Patches, Hotfixes, and Drivers	Update images with patches, hotfixes, and drivers
Installing Features for Offline Images	Install features for offline images
Deploying Driver Packages with an Image	

KEY TERMS

answer files
boot image
Deployment Image Servicing and Management (Dism.exe)
Deployment Server
discover image
dynamic driver provisioning
features
image file
image group
install image
multicasting
preboot execution environment (PXE)
System Image Manager (SIM)
System Preparation Utility (Sysprep.exe)
Transport Server
Windows Assessment and Deployment Kit (ADK)
Windows Deployment Services Capture Utility
Windows Deployment Services (WDS)
Windows Imaging Format (WIM)
Windows Preinstallation Environment (Windows PE)

Exam Objective

Key Terms

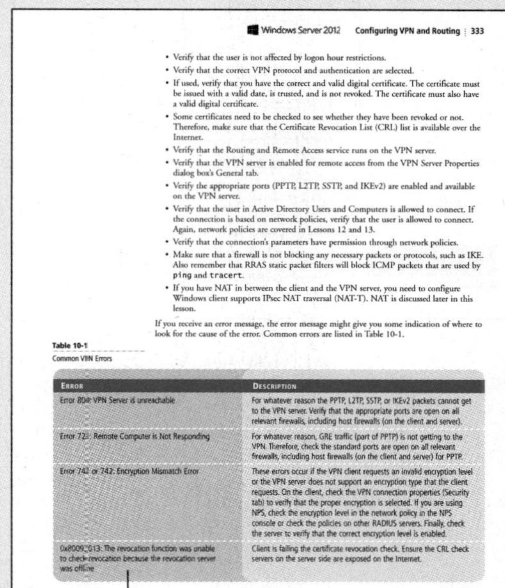

Windows Server 2012 Configuring VPN and Routing | 333

- Verify that the user is not affected by logon hour restrictions.
- Verify that the correct VPN protocol and authentication are selected.
- If used, verify that you have the correct and valid digital certificate. The certificate must be issued with a valid date, is trusted, and is not revoked. The certificate must also have a valid digital certificate.
- Some certificates need to be checked to see whether they have been revoked or not. Therefore, make sure that the Certificate Revocation List (CRL) list is available over the Internet.
- Verify that the Routing and Remote Access service runs on the VPN server.
- Verify that the VPN server is enabled for remote access from the VPN Server Properties dialog box's General tab.
- Verify the appropriate ports (PPTP, L2TP, SSTP, and IKEv2) are enabled and available on the VPN server.
- Verify that the user in Active Directory Users and Computers is allowed to connect. If the connection is based on network policies, verify that the user is allowed to connect. Again, network policies are covered in Lessons 12 and 13.
- Verify that the connection's parameters have permission through network policies.
- Make sure that a firewall is not blocking any necessary packets or protocols, such as IKE. Also remember that RRAS static packet filters will block ICMP packets that are used by ping and tracert.
- If you have NAT in between the client and the VPN server, you need to configure Windows client supports IPsec NAT traversal (NAT-T). NAT is discussed later in this lesson.

If you receive an error message, the error message might give you some indication of where to look for the cause of the error. Common errors are listed in Table 10-1.

Table 10-1
Common VPN Errors

Error	Description
Error 800: VPN Server is unreachable	For whatever reason the PPTP, L2TP, SSTP, or IKEv2 packets cannot get to the VPN server. Verify that the appropriate ports are open on all relevant firewalls, including host firewalls (on the client and server).
Error 721: Remote Computer is Not Responding	For whatever reason, GRE traffic (part of PPTP) is not getting to the VPN. Therefore, check the standard ports are open on all relevant firewalls, including host firewalls (on the client and server) for PPTP.
Error 741 or 742: Encryption Mismatch Error	These errors occur if the VPN client requests an invalid encryption level or the VPN server does not support an encryption type that the client requests. On the client, check the VPN connection properties (Security tab) to verify that the proper encryption is selected. If you are using NPS, check the encryption level in the network policy in the NPS console or check the policies on other RADIUS servers. Finally, check the server to verify that the correct encryption level is enabled.
0x80092013: The revocation function was unable to check revocation because the revocation server was offline	Client is failing the certificate revocation check. Ensure the CRL check servers on the server side are exposed on the Internet.

Easy-to-Read Tables

Bottom Line Reader Aid

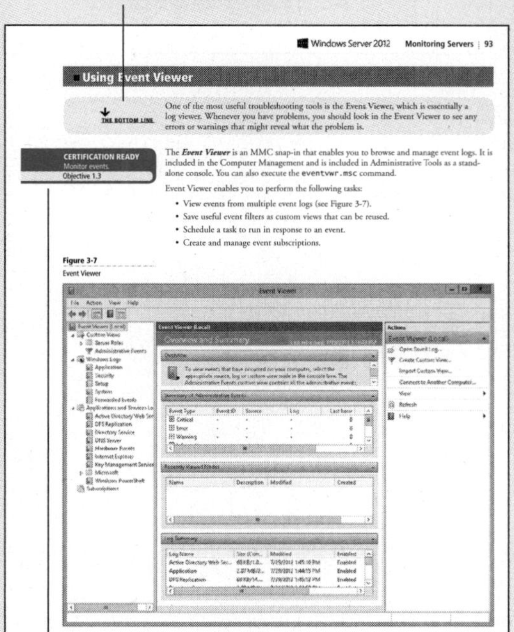

Windows Server 2012 Monitoring Servers | 93

■ Using Event Viewer

THE BOTTOM LINE: One of the most useful troubleshooting tools is the Event Viewer, which is essentially a log viewer. Whenever you have problems, you should look in the Event Viewer to see any errors or warnings that might reveal what the problem is.

CERTIFICATION READY
Monitor events.
Objective 1.3

The *Event Viewer* is an MMC snap-in that enables you to browse and manage event logs. It is included in the Computer Management and is included in Administrative Tools as a stand-alone console. You can also execute the eventvwr.msc command.

Event Viewer enables you to perform the following tasks:

- View events from multiple event logs (see Figure 3-7).
- Save useful event filters as custom views that can be reused.
- Schedule a task to run in response to an event.
- Create and manage event subscriptions.

Figure 3-7
Event Viewer

Certification Ready Alert

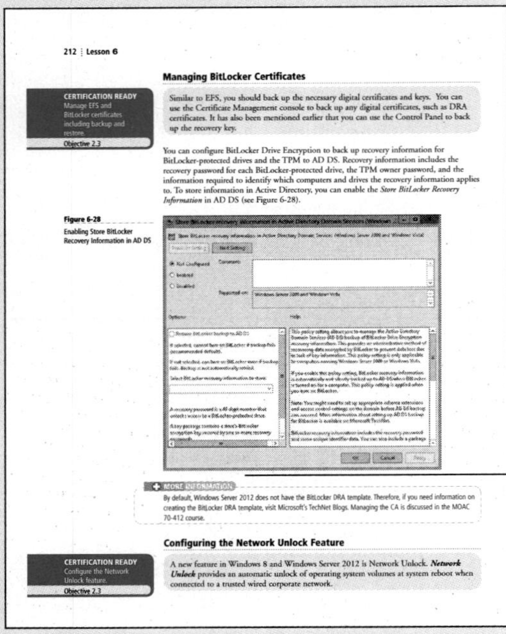

More Information Reader Aid

Take Note Reader Aid

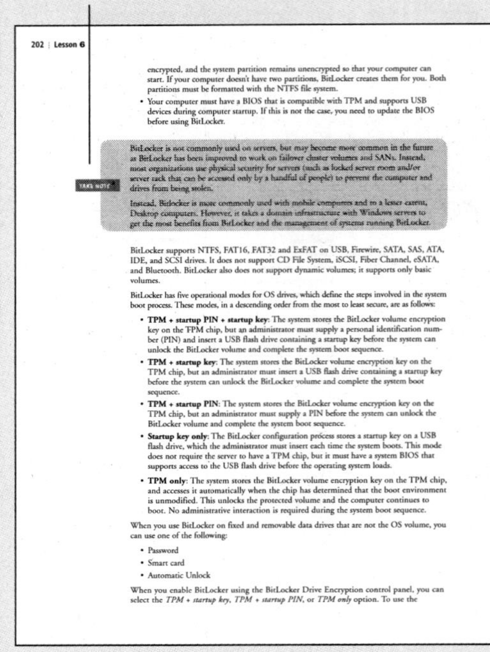

Warning Reader Aid

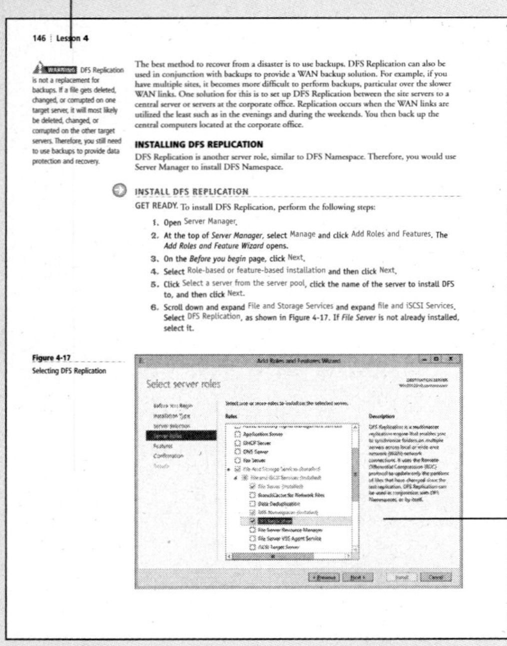

Screen Images

www.wiley.com/college/microsoft ***or***
call the MOAC Toll-Free Number: 1+(888) 764-7001 (U.S. & Canada only)

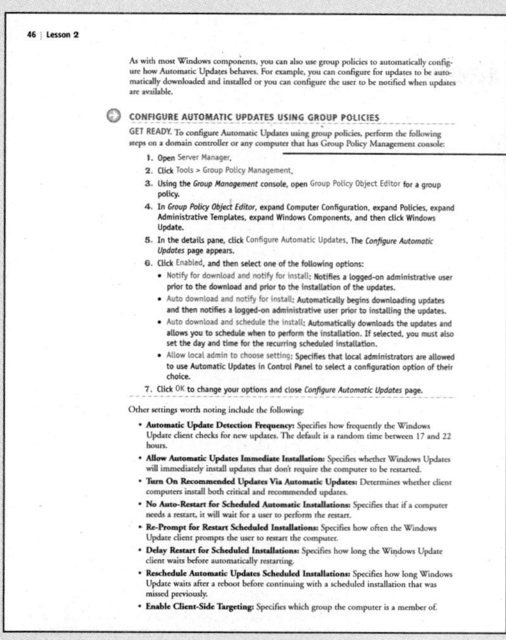

46 | Lesson 2

As with most Windows components, you can also use group policies to automatically configure how Automatic Updates behaves. For example, you can configure for updates to be automatically downloaded and installed or you can configure the user to be notified when updates are available.

CONFIGURE AUTOMATIC UPDATES USING GROUP POLICIES

GET READY. To configure Automatic Updates using group policies, perform the following steps on a domain controller or any computer that has Group Policy Management console:

1. Open Server Manager.
2. Click Tools > Group Policy Management.
3. Using the Group Management console, open Group Policy Object Editor for a group policy.
4. In Group Policy Object Editor, expand Computer Configuration, expand Policies, expand Administrative Templates, expand Windows Components, and then click Windows Update.
5. In the details pane, click Configure Automatic Updates. The Configure Automatic Updates page appears.
6. Click Enabled, and then select one of the following options:
   - Notify for download and notify for install: Notifies a logged-on administrative user prior to the download and prior to the installation of the updates.
   - Auto download and notify for install: Automatically begins downloading updates and then notifies a logged-on administrative user prior to installing the updates.
   - Auto download and schedule the install: Automatically downloads the updates and allows you to schedule when to perform the installation. If selected, you must also set the day and time for the recurring scheduled installation.
   - Allow local admin to choose setting: Specifies that local administrators are allowed to use Automatic Updates in Control Panel to select a configuration option of their choice.
7. Click OK to change your options and close Configure Automatic Updates page.

Other settings worth noting include the following:

- **Automatic Update Detection Frequency:** Specifies how frequently the Windows Update client checks for new updates. The default is a random time between 17 and 22 hours.
- **Allow Automatic Updates Immediate Installation:** Specifies whether Windows Updates will immediately install updates that don't require the computer to be restarted.
- **Turn On Recommended Updates Via Automatic Updates:** Determines whether client computers install both critical and recommended updates.
- **No Auto-Restart for Scheduled Automatic Installations:** Specifies that if a computer needs a restart, it will wait for a user to perform the restart.
- **Re-Prompt for Restart Scheduled Installations:** Specifies how often the Windows Update client prompts the user to restart the computer.
- **Delay Restart for Scheduled Installations:** Specifies how long the Windows Update client waits before automatically restarting.
- **Reschedule Automatic Updates Scheduled Installations:** Specifies how long Windows Update waits after a reboot before continuing with a scheduled installation that was missed previously.
- **Enable Client-Side Targeting:** Specifies which group the computer is a member of.

Step-by-Step Exercises

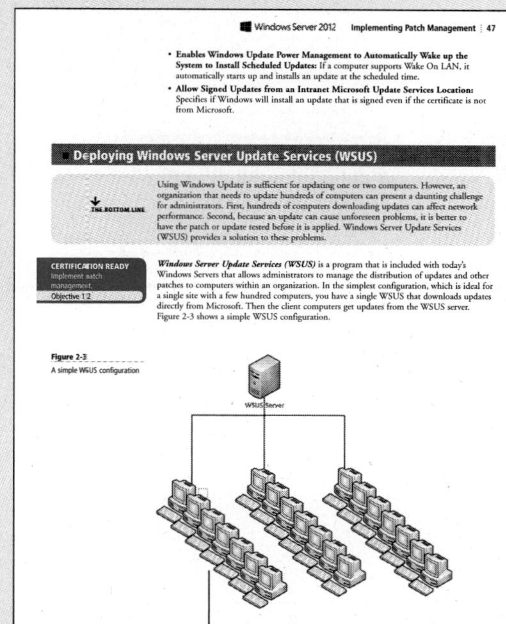

Windows Server 2012 | Implementing Patch Management | 47

- **Enables Windows Update Power Management to Automatically Wake up the System to Install Scheduled Updates:** If a computer supports Wake On LAN, it automatically starts up and installs an update at the scheduled time.
- **Allow Signed Updates from an Intranet Microsoft Update Services Location:** Specifies if Windows will install an update that is signed even if the certificate is not from Microsoft.

Deploying Windows Server Update Services (WSUS)

THE BOTTOM LINE: Using Windows Update is sufficient for updating one or two computers. However, an organization that needs to update hundreds of computers can present a daunting challenge for administrators. First, hundreds of computers downloading updates can affect network performance. Second, because an update can cause unforeseen problems, it is better to have the patch or update tested before it is applied. Windows Server Update Services (WSUS) provides a solution to these problems.

CERTIFICATION READY: Implement patch management. Objective 1.2

Windows Server Update Services (WSUS) is a program that is included with today's Windows Servers that allows administrators to manage the distribution of updates and other patches to computers within an organization. In the simplest configuration, which is ideal for a single site with a few hundred computers, you have a single WSUS that downloads updates directly from Microsoft. Then the client computers get updates from the WSUS server. Figure 2-3 shows a simple WSUS configuration.

Figure 2-3
A simple WSUS configuration

WSUS Server

Informative Diagrams

X Ref Reader Aid

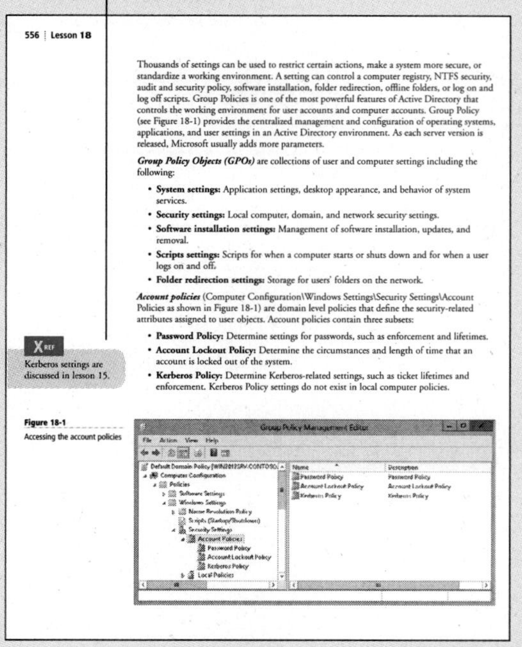

556 | Lesson 18

Thousands of settings can be used to restrict certain actions, make a system more secure, or standardize a working environment. A setting can control a computer registry, NTFS security, audit and security policy, software installation, folder redirection, offline folders, or log on and log off scripts. Group Policies is one of the most powerful features of Active Directory that controls the working environment for user accounts and computer accounts. Group Policy (see Figure 18-1) provides the centralized management and configuration of operating systems, applications, and user settings in an Active Directory environment. As each server version is released, Microsoft usually adds more parameters.

Group Policy Objects (GPOs) are collections of user and computer settings including the following:

- **System settings:** Application settings, desktop appearance, and behavior of system services.
- **Security settings:** Local computer, domain, and network security settings.
- **Software installation settings:** Management of software installation, updates, and removal.
- **Scripts settings:** Scripts for when a computer starts or shuts down and for when a user logs on and off.
- **Folder redirection settings:** Storage for users' folders on the network.

Account policies (Computer Configuration\Windows Settings\Security Settings\Account Policies as shown in Figure 18-1) are domain level policies that define the security-related attributes assigned to user objects. Account policies contain three subsets:

- **Password Policy:** Determine settings for passwords, such as enforcement and lifetimes.
- **Account Lockout Policy:** Determine the circumstances and length of time that an account is locked out of the system.
- **Kerberos Policy:** Determine Kerberos-related settings, such as ticket lifetimes and enforcement. Kerberos Policy settings do not exist in local computer policies.

X REF: Kerberos settings are discussed in lesson 15.

Figure 18-1
Accessing the account policies

www.wiley.com/college/microsoft *or*
call the MOAC Toll-Free Number: 1+(888) 764-7001 (U.S. & Canada only)

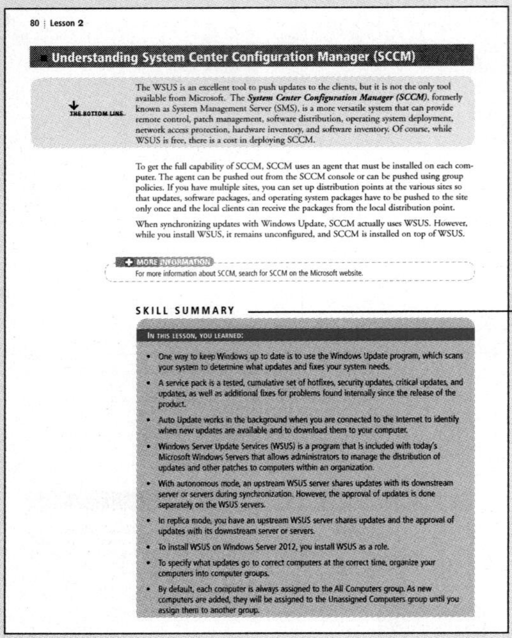
80 | Lesson 2

■ Understanding System Center Configuration Manager (SCCM)

THE BOTTOM LINE

The WSUS is an excellent tool to push updates to the clients, but it is not the only tool available from Microsoft. The ***System Center Configuration Manager (SCCM)***, formerly known as System Management Server (SMS), is a more versatile system that can provide remote control, patch management, software distribution, operating system deployment, network access protection, hardware inventory, and software inventory. Of course, while WSUS is free, there is a cost in deploying SCCM.

To get the full capability of SCCM, SCCM uses an agent that must be installed on each computer. The agent can be pushed out from the SCCM console or can be pushed using group policies. If you have multiple sites, you can set up distribution points at the various sites so that updates, software packages, and operating system packages have to be pushed to the site only once and the local clients can receive the packages from the local distribution point.

When synchronizing updates with Windows Update, SCCM actually uses WSUS. However, while you install WSUS, it remains unconfigured, and SCCM is installed on top of WSUS.

+ MORE INFORMATION
For more information about SCCM, search for SCCM on the Microsoft website.

SKILL SUMMARY

IN THIS LESSON, YOU LEARNED:

- One way to keep Windows up to date is to use the Windows Update program, which scans your system to determine what updates and fixes your system needs.
- A service pack is a tested, cumulative set of hotfixes, security updates, critical updates, and updates, as well as additional fixes for problems found internally since the release of the product.
- Auto Update works in the background when you are connected to the Internet to identify when new updates are available and to download them to your computer.
- Windows Server Update Services (WSUS) is a program that is included with today's Microsoft Windows Servers that allows administrators to manage the distribution of updates and other patches to computers within an organization.
- With autonomous mode, an upstream WSUS server shares updates with its downstream server or servers during synchronization. However, the approval of updates is done separately on the WSUS servers.
- In replica mode, you have an upstream WSUS server shares updates and the approval of updates with its downstream server or servers.
- To install WSUS on Windows Server 2012, you install WSUS as a role.
- To specify what updates go to correct computers at the correct time, organize your computers into computer groups.
- By default, each computer is always assigned to the All Computers group. As new computers are added, they will be assigned to the Unassigned Computers group until you assign them to another group.

Skill Summary

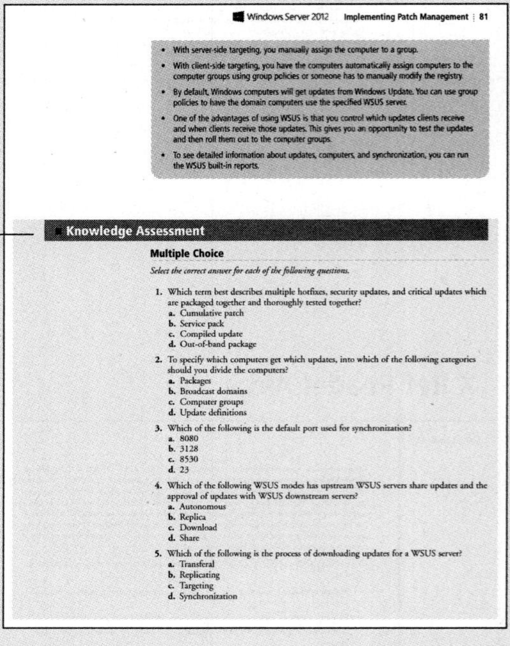
Windows Server 2012 Implementing Patch Management | 81

- With server-side targeting, you manually assign the computer to a group.
- With client-side targeting, you have the computers automatically assign computers to the computer groups using group policies or someone has to manually modify the registry.
- By default, Windows computers will get updates from Windows Update. You can use group policies to have the domain computers use the specified WSUS server.
- One of the advantages of using WSUS is that you control which updates clients receive and when clients receive those updates. This gives you an opportunity to test the updates and then roll them out to the computer groups.
- To see detailed information about updates, computers, and synchronization, you can run the WSUS built-in reports.

■ Knowledge Assessment

Multiple Choice

Select the correct answer for each of the following questions.

1. Which term best describes multiple hotfixes, security updates, and critical updates which are packaged together and thoroughly tested together?
   a. Cumulative patch
   b. Service pack
   c. Compiled update
   d. Out-of-band package
2. To specify which computers get which updates, into which of the following categories should you divide the computers?
   a. Packages
   b. Broadcast domains
   c. Computer groups
   d. Update definitions
3. Which of the following is the default port used for synchronization?
   a. 8080
   b. 3128
   c. 8530
   d. 23
4. Which of the following WSUS modes has upstream WSUS servers share updates and the approval of updates with WSUS downstream servers?
   a. Autonomous
   b. Replica
   c. Download
   d. Share
5. Which of the following is the process of downloading updates for a WSUS server?
   a. Transferal
   b. Replicating
   c. Targeting
   d. Synchronization

Knowledge Assessment

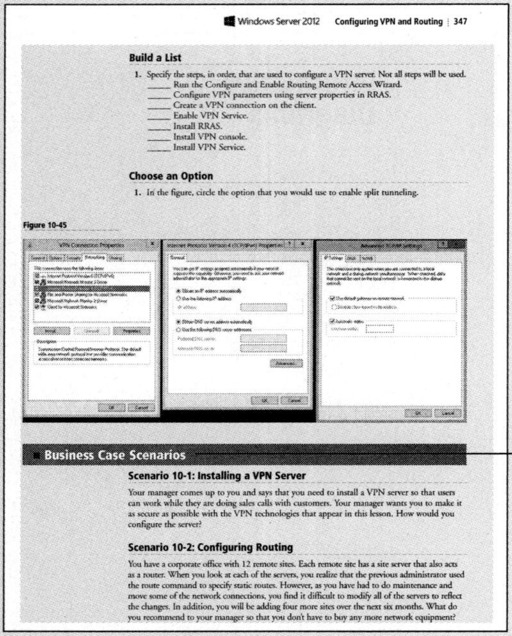
Windows Server 2012 Configuring VPN and Routing | 347

Build a List

1. Specify the steps, in order, that are used to configure a VPN server. Not all steps will be used.
   _____ Run the Configure and Enable Routing Remote Access Wizard.
   _____ Configure VPN parameters using server properties in RRAS.
   _____ Create a VPN connection on the client.
   _____ Enable VPN Service.
   _____ Install RRAS.
   _____ Install VPN console.
   _____ Install VPN Service.

Choose an Option

1. In the figure, circle the option that you would use to enable split tunneling.

Figure 10-45

■ Business Case Scenarios

Scenario 10-1: Installing a VPN Server

Your manager comes up to you and says that you need to install a VPN server so that users can work while they are doing sales calls with customers. Your manager wants you to make it as secure as possible with the VPN technologies that appear in this lesson. How would you configure the server?

Scenario 10-2: Configuring Routing

You have a corporate office with 12 remote sites. Each remote site has a site server that also acts as a router. When you look at each of the servers, you realize that the previous administrator used the route command to specify static routes. However, as you have had to do maintenance and move some of the network connections, you find it difficult to modify all of the servers to reflect the changes. In addition, you will be adding four more sites over the next six months. What do you recommend to your manager so that you don't have to buy any more network equipment?

Business Case Scenarios

www.wiley.com/college/microsoft ***or***
call the MOAC Toll-Free Number: 1+(888) 764-7001 (U.S. & Canada only)

Conventions and Features Used in This Book

This book uses particular fonts, symbols, and heading conventions to highlight important information or to call your attention to special steps. For more information about the features in each lesson, refer to the Illustrated Book Tour section.

CONVENTION	MEANING
THE BOTTOM LINE	This feature provides a brief summary of the material to be covered in the section that follows.
CERTIFICATION READY	This feature signals the point in the text where a specific certification objective is covered. It provides you with a chance to check your understanding of that particular exam objective and, if necessary, review the section of the lesson where it is covered.
TAKE NOTE* MORE INFORMATION	Reader aids appear in shaded boxes found in your text. *Take Note and More Information* provide helpful hints related to particular tasks or topics.
USING WINDOWS POWERSHELL	The Using Windows PowerShell sidebar provides Windows PowerShell-based alternatives to graphical user interface (GUI) functions or procedures.
WARNING	*Warning* points out instances when error or misuse could cause damage to the computer or network.
X REF	These *X Ref* notes provide pointers to information discussed elsewhere in the textbook or describe interesting features of Windows Server that are not directly addressed in the current topic or exercise.
A ***shared printer*** can be used by many individuals on a network.	Key terms appear in bold italic.
`cd\windows\system32\ServerMigrationTools`	Commands that are to be typed are shown in a special font.
Click Install Now.	Any button on the screen you are supposed to click on or select will appear in blue.

Instructor Support Program

The Microsoft Official Academic Course programs are accompanied by a rich array of resources that incorporate the extensive textbook visuals to form a pedagogically cohesive package. These resources provide all the materials instructors need to deploy and deliver their courses. Resource information available at www.wiley.com/college/microsoft includes:

- **DreamSpark Premium** is designed to provide the easiest and most inexpensive developer tools, products, and technologies available to faculty and students in labs, classrooms, and on student PCs. A free 3-year membership is available to qualified MOAC adopters.

  Note: Windows Server 2012 can be downloaded from DreamSpark Premium for use in this course.
- **Instructor's Guide.** The Instructor's Guide contains solutions to all the textbook exercises as well as chapter summaries and lecture notes. The Instructor's Guide and Syllabi for various term lengths are available from the Instructor's Book Companion site.
- **Test Bank.** The Test Bank contains hundreds of questions organized by lesson in multiple-choice, best answer, build a list, and essay formats and is available to download from the Instructor's Book Companion site. A complete answer key is provided.
- **PowerPoint Presentations.** A complete set of PowerPoint presentations is available on the Instructor's Book Companion site to enhance classroom presentations. Tailored to the text's topical coverage, these presentations are designed to convey key Windows Server 2012 concepts addressed in the text.
- **Available Textbook Figures.** All figures from the text are on the Instructor's Book Companion site. By using these visuals in class discussions, you can help focus students' attention on key elements of Windows Server and help them understand how to use it effectively in the workplace.
- **MOAC Labs Online.** MOAC Labs Online is a cloud-based environment that enables students to conduct exercises using real Microsoft products. These are not simulations but instead are live virtual machines where faculty and students can perform any activities they would on a local virtual machine. MOAC Labs Online relieves the need for local setup, configuration, and most troubleshooting tasks. This represents an opportunity to lower costs, eliminate the hassle of lab setup, and support and improve student access and portability. Contact your Wiley rep about including MOAC Labs Online with your course offering.
- **Lab Answer Keys.** Answer keys for review questions found in the lab manuals and MOAC Labs Online are available on the Instructor's Book Companion site.
- **Lab Worksheets.** The review questions found in the lab manuals and MOAC Labs Online are gathered in Microsoft Word documents for students to use. These are available on the Instructor's Book Companion site.
- **Sharing with Fellow Faculty Members.** When it comes to improving the classroom experience, there is no better source of ideas and inspiration than your colleagues teaching the same material. The Wiley Faculty Network connects teachers with technology, facilitates the exchange of best practices, and helps to enhance instructional efficiency and effectiveness. Faculty Network activities include technology training and tutorials, virtual seminars, peer-to-peer exchanges of experiences and ideas, personal consulting, and sharing of resources. For details visit www.WhereFacultyConnect.com.

Wiley Faculty Network

DREAMSPARK PREMIUM—FREE 3-YEAR MEMBERSHIP AVAILABLE TO QUALIFIED ADOPTERS!

DreamSpark Premium is designed to provide the easiest and most inexpensive way for schools to make the latest Microsoft developer tools, products, and technologies available in labs, classrooms, and on student PCs. DreamSpark Premium is an annual membership program for departments teaching Science, Technology, Engineering, and Mathematics (STEM) courses. The membership provides a complete solution to keep academic labs, faculty, and students on the leading edge of technology.

Software available through the DreamSpark Premium program is provided at no charge to adopting departments through the Wiley and Microsoft publishing partnership.

Contact your Wiley rep for details.

For more information about the DreamSpark Premium program, go to Microsoft's DreamSpark website.

Note: Windows Server 2012 can be downloaded from DreamSpark Premium for use by students in this course.

■ Important Web Addresses and Phone Numbers

To locate the Wiley Higher Education Rep in your area, go to http://www.wiley.com/college and click on the "*Contact Us*" link at the top of the page, or call the MOAC Toll Free Number: 1 + (888) 764-7001 (U.S. & Canada only).

To learn more about becoming a Microsoft Certified Solutions Associate and exam availability, visit Microsoft's Training & Certification website.

Student Support Program

Book Companion Website (www.wiley.com/college/microsoft)

The students' book companion site for the MOAC series includes any resources, exercise files, and web links that will be used in conjunction with this course.

Wiley E-Text: Powered by VitalSource

Wiley E-Texts: Powered by VitalSource are innovative, electronic versions of printed textbooks. Students can buy Wiley E-Texts for around 50% off the U.S. price of the printed text and get the added value of permanence and portability. Wiley E-Texts provide students with numerous additional benefits that are not available with other e-text solutions.

Wiley E-Texts are NOT subscriptions; students download the Wiley E-Text to their computer desktops. Students own the content they buy to keep for as long as they want. Once a Wiley E-Text is downloaded to the computer desktop, students have instant access to all of the content without being online. Students can also print the sections they prefer to read in hard copy. Students also have access to fully integrated resources within their Wiley E-Text. From highlighting their e-text to taking and sharing notes, students can easily personalize their Wiley E-Text as they are reading or following along in class.

Microsoft Windows Server Software

Windows Server 2012 software is available through a DreamSpark student membership. DreamSpark is a Microsoft program that provides students with free access to Microsoft software for learning, teaching, and research purposes. Students can download full versions of Windows Server 2012 and other types of software at no cost by visiting Microsoft's DreamSpark website.

■ Microsoft Certification

Microsoft Certification has many benefits and enables you to keep your skills relevant, applicable, and competitive. In addition, Microsoft Certification is an industry standard that is recognized worldwide—which helps open doors to potential job opportunities. After you earn your Microsoft Certification, you have access to a number of benefits, which can be found on the Microsoft Certified Professional member site.

Microsoft Learning has reinvented the Microsoft Certification Program by building cloud-related skills validation into the industry's most recognized certification program. Microsoft Certified Solutions Expert (MCSE) and Microsoft Certified Solutions Developer (MCSD) are Microsoft's flagship certifications for professionals who want to lead their IT organization's journey to the cloud. These certifications recognize IT professionals with broad and deep skill sets across Microsoft solutions. The Microsoft Certified Solutions Associate (MCSA) is the certification for aspiring IT professionals and is also the prerequisite certification necessary to earn an MCSE. These new certifications integrate cloud-related and on-premise skills validation in order to support organizations and recognize individuals who have the skills required to be productive using Microsoft technologies.

On-premise or in the cloud, Microsoft training and certification empowers technology professionals to expand their skills and gain knowledge directly from the source. Securing these essential skills will allow you to grow your career and make yourself indispensable as the industry shifts to the cloud. Cloud computing ultimately enables IT to focus on more mission-critical activities, raising the bar of required expertise for IT professionals and developers. These reinvented certifications test on a deeper set of skills that map to real-world business context. Rather than testing only on a feature of a technology, Microsoft Certifications now validate more advanced skills and a deeper understanding of the platform.

Microsoft Certified Solutions Associate (MCSA)

The Microsoft Certified Solutions Associate (MCSA) certification is for students preparing to get their first jobs in Microsoft technology. Whether in the cloud or on-premise, this certification validates the core platform skills needed in an IT environment. The MCSA certifications are a requirement to achieve Microsoft's flagship Microsoft Certified Solutions Expert (MCSE) and Microsoft Certified Solutions Developer (MCSD) certifications.

The MCSA Windows Server 2012 certification shows that you have the primary set of Windows Server skills that are relevant across multiple solution areas in a business environment. The MCSA Windows Server 2012 certification is a prerequisite for earning the MCSE Server Infrastructure certification, the MCSE Desktop Infrastructure certification, or the MCSE Private Cloud certification.

Exam 70-411, Administering Windows Server 2012, is part two of a series of three exams that validate the skills and knowledge necessary to implement a core Windows Server 2012 Infrastructure into an existing enterprise environment. This exam will validate the administration tasks necessary to maintain a Windows Server 2012 infrastructure, such as user and group management, network access, and data security. This exam along with the other two exams will collectively validate the skills and knowledge necessary for implementing, managing, maintaining, and provisioning services and infrastructure in a Windows Server 2012 environment.

If you are a student new to IT who may not yet be ready for MCSA, the Microsoft Technology Associate (MTA) certification is an optional starting point that may be available through your school.

You can learn more about the MCSA certification at the Microsoft Training & Certification website.

Preparing to Take an Exam

Unless you are a very experienced user, you will need to use test preparation materials to prepare to complete the test correctly and within the time allowed. The Microsoft Official Academic Course series is designed to prepare you with a strong knowledge of all exam topics, and with some additional review and practice on your own, you should feel confident in your ability to pass the appropriate exam.

After you decide which exam to take, review the list of objectives for the exam. You can easily identify tasks that are included in the objective list by locating the exam objective overview at the start of each lesson and the Certification Ready sidebars in the margin of the lessons in this book.

To register for the 70-411 exam, visit Microsoft Training & Certifications Registration webpage for directions on how to register with Prometric, the company that delivers the MCSA exams. Keep in mind these important items about the testing procedure:

- **What to expect.** Microsoft Certification testing labs typically have multiple workstations, which may or may not be occupied by other candidates. Test center administrators strive to provide a quiet and comfortable environment for all test takers.
- **Plan to arrive early.** It is recommended that you arrive at the test center at least 30 minutes before the test is scheduled to begin.
- **Bring your identification.** To take your exam, you must bring the identification (ID) that was specified when you registered for the exam. If you are unclear about which forms of ID are required, contact the exam sponsor identified in your registration information. Although requirements vary, you typically must show two valid forms of ID, one with a photo, both with your signature.
- **Leave personal items at home.** The only item allowed into the testing area is your identification, so leave any backpacks, laptops, briefcases, and other personal items at home. If you have items that cannot be left behind (such as purses), the testing center might have small lockers available for use.
- **Nondisclosure agreement.** At the testing center, Microsoft requires that you accept the terms of a nondisclosure agreement (NDA) and complete a brief demographic survey before taking your certification exam.

About the Author

Patrick Regan has been a PC technician, network administrator/engineer, design architect, and security analyst for the past 23 years since graduating with a bachelor's degree in physics from the University of Akron. He has taught many computer and network classes at Sacramento local colleges (Heald Colleges and MTI Colleges) and participated in and led many projects (Heald Colleges, Intel Corporation, Miles Consulting Corporation, and Pacific Coast Companies). For his teaching accomplishments, he received the Teacher of the Year award from Heald Colleges and he has received several recognition awards from Intel. Previously, he worked as a product support engineer for the Intel Corporation Customer Service, a senior network engineer for Virtual Alert supporting the BioTerrorism Readiness suite and as a senior design architect/engineer and training coordinator for Miles Consulting Corporation (MCC), a premiere Microsoft Gold partner and consulting firm.

He is currently a senior network engineer and consultant supporting a large enterprise network at Pacific Coast Companies, which is also a Microsoft Gold Partner and consulting firm. As a senior system administrator, he supports approximately 120 servers and 1,500 users spread over 5 subsidiaries and 70 sites. He has designed, implemented, and managed systems running Exchange Server 2010, SharePoint 2010, and SQL Server 2008 R2. To manage the servers and client computers, Pat and his team use group policies, SCOM, SCCM, and Symantec server.

He has earned several certifications, including Microsoft's MCSE, MCSA, and MCT; CompTIA's A+, Network+, Server+, Linux+, and Security+; Cisco's CCNA; and Novell's CNE and CWNP Certified Wireless Network Administrator (CWNA).

Over the past several years, he has written several textbooks for Prentice Hall, including *Troubleshooting the PC, Networking with Windows 2000 and 2003, Linux, Local Area Networks, Wide Area Networks*, and the Acing Series (*Acing the A+*, *Acing the Network+*, *Acing the Security+*, and *Acing the Linux+*). For Que Publishing has written several Exam Cram books for Windows Server 2008 certification tracks. For Wiley Publishing, he has written books on SharePoint 2010, Windows 7, and Windows Server 2012.

Acknowledgments

We thank the MOAC faculty and instructors who have assisted us in building the Microsoft Official Academic Course courseware. These elite educators have acted as our sounding board on key pedagogical and design decisions leading to the development of the MOAC courseware for future Information Technology workers. They have provided invaluable advice in the service of quality instructional materials, and we truly appreciate their dedication to technology education.

Brian Bridson, Baker College of Flint

David Chaulk, Baker College Online

Ron Handlon, Remington College – Tampa Campus

Katherine James, Seneca College of Applied Arts & Technology

Wen Liu, ITT Educational Services

Zeshan Sattar, Pearson in Practice

Jared Spencer, Westwood College Online

David Vallerga, MTI College

Bonny Willy, Ivy Tech State College

We also thank Microsoft Learning's Lutz Ziob, Don Field, Tim Sneath, Moorthy Uppaluri, Keith Loeber, Rob Linsky, Anne Hamilton, Shelby Grieve, Christine Yoshida, Gene Longo, Mike Mulcare, Paul Schmitt, Martin DelRe, Colin Klein, Julia Stasio, and Josh Barnhill for their encouragement and support in making the Microsoft Official Academic Course programs the finest academic materials for mastering the newest Microsoft technologies for both students and instructors.

Brief Contents

Contents

Lesson 4: Configuring Distributed File System (DFS) 133

Lesson 5: Configuring File Server Resource Manager (FSRM) 165

Lesson 6: Configuring File Services and Disk Encryption 188

Lesson 7: Configuring Advanced Audit Policies 218

Lesson 8: Configuring DNS Zones 255

Lesson 9: Configuring DNS Records 286

Lesson 10: Configuring VPN and Routing 309

Lesson 11: Configuring Direct Access 348

Lesson 22: Configuring Group Policy Preferences 646

LESSON 1

Deploying and Managing Server Images

70-411 EXAM OBJECTIVE

Objective 1.1 – Deploy and manage server images. This objective may include but is not limited to: install the Windows Deployment Services (WDS) role; configure and manage boot, install, and discover images; update images with patches, hotfixes, and drivers; install features for offline images.

Lesson Heading	Exam Objective
Using Windows Deployment Services	
Installing the Windows Deployment Services Role	Install the Windows Deployment Services (WDS) role
Configuring the WDS Server	
Configuring and Managing Boot, Install, and Discover Images	Configure and manage boot, install, and discover images
Updating Images with Patches, Hotfixes, and Drivers	Update images with patches, hotfixes, and drivers
Installing Features for Offline Images	Install features for offline images
Deploying Driver Packages with an Image	

KEY TERMS

answer files
boot image
Deployment Image Servicing and Management (Dism.exe)
Deployment Server
discover image
dynamic driver provisioning
features
image file
image group
install image
multicasting
preboot execution environment (PXE)
System Image Manager (SIM)
System Preparation Utility (Sysprep.exe)
Transport Server
Windows Assessment and Deployment Kit (ADK)
Windows Deployment Services Capture Utility
Windows Deployment Services (WDS)
Windows Imaging Format (WIM)
Windows Preinstallation Environment (Windows PE)

TAKE NOTE*

Before beginning this course, you should have some experience installing Windows, including installing Windows Server 2012. In an enterprise environment, many administrators will need to install Windows numerous times. In addition, administrators in many enterprise environments will have a need to deploy servers to remote site. Therefore, as a server administrator, you must be familiar with the various methods to install and deploy Windows.

Using Windows Deployment Services

THE BOTTOM LINE

In the 70-410 course, you learned how to install Windows from a Windows installation disk. It is not difficult to figure out that installing 100 computers using an installation disk is a daunting task. In these situations, rather than do a manual install on each computer, you can use Windows Deployment Services to automatically deploy Windows to multiple computers. While Windows Deployment Services takes a little bit of work up front, it can save you a lot of work later.

Windows Deployment Services (WDS) is a software platform and technology that allows you to perform automated network-based installations based on network-based boot and installation media. In other words, you can perform an installation over a network with no operating system or local boot device on it. The WDS server will store the installation files and help you manage the boot and operating system image files used in the network installations. Although WDS is included with later versions of Windows Server, including Windows Server 2012, it can be used to deploy Windows XP, Windows Vista, Windows 7, Windows 8, Windows Server 2003, Windows Server 2008, and Windows Server 2012.

An ***image file*** is basically a snapshot of a computer's hard drive taken at a particular moment in time. The image file is sometimes referred to as an install image and is used to install an operating system. It contains the following:

- All of the operating system files on the computer
- Any updates and drives that have been applied
- Any applications that have been installed
- Any configuration changes that have been made

For client computers to communicate with a WDS server without an operating system, the client computer must have support ***preboot execution environment (PXE)***, pronounced "pixie." PXE is a technology that boots computers using the network interface without a data storage device, such as a hard drive or an installed operating system. For a computer to perform a PXE boot, you must configure the BIOS setup program to perform a network boot. Depending on your system, you must enable the PXE boot and/or change the boot order so that the PXE boot occurs before the system tries other boot devices to boot from.

When PXE is used with WDS, the client computer downloads a boot image that loads ***Windows Preinstallation Environment (Windows PE)***. Windows PE is a minimal Windows operating system with limited services. Windows PE is then used to install the operating system using an operating system image file. Windows PE 4.0 is based on the Windows 8 operating system.

Installing the Windows Deployment Services Role

WDS is a server role that is included with Windows Server 2012. Therefore, before you can use WDS, you must install the WDS role and configure the services. Then you need to create and add the images that you want to deploy.

CERTIFICATION READY
Install the Windows Deployment Services (WDS) role.
Objective 1.1

WDS is a standard server role that can be installed using the Server Manager console and includes the following two role services:

- ***Deployment Server:*** Provides full functionality of WDS. It includes an image repository (including boot images, install images, and other files necessary for remote installation over a network), PXE server for remote computers to boot, and a Trivial File Transfer Protocol (TFTP) server to transfer files over the network. TFTP is similar to FTP, but uses User Datagram Protocol (UDP) instead of Transmission Control Protocol (TCP) for less overhead (simpler packets that can be processed faster than TCP packets because UDP does not require the use of acknowledgments). In addition, the Deployment Server includes tools to create and customize images.
- ***Transport Server:*** While required by the Deployment Server, the Transport Server role is a subset of WDS functionality, but can also be used for custom solutions. The Transport Server can also use ***multicasting***, which allows one set of packets to be sent to multiple computers simultaneously.

DEPLOY WDS

GET READY. To deploy WDS on Windows Server 2012, perform the following steps:

1. Open Server Manager by clicking the Server Manager button on the task bar. The *Server Manager* opens.
2. At the top of *Server Manager*, click Manage and then click Add Roles and Features. The Add Roles and Feature Wizard opens.
3. On the *Before you begin* page, click Next.
4. Select Role-based or feature-based installation, and then click Next.
5. Click Select a server from the server pool, click the name of the server to install WDS to, and then click Next.
6. Scroll down and select Windows Deployment Services (see Figure 1-1).

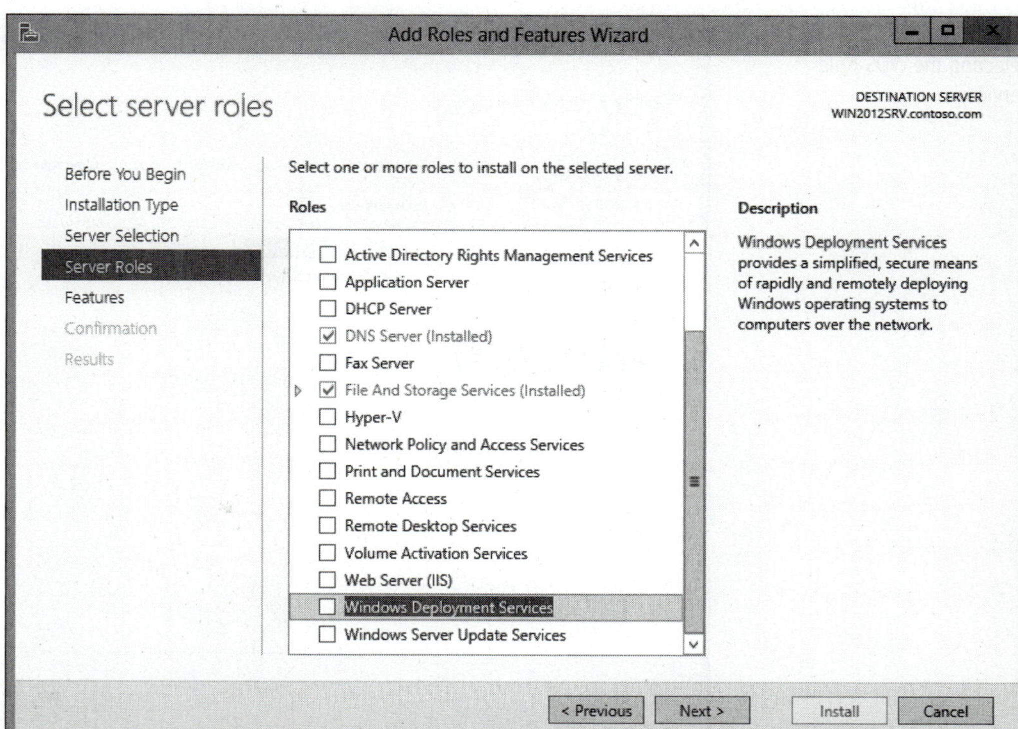

Figure 1-1
Selecting Windows Deployment Services

7. When the *Add Roles and Features Wizard* dialog box opens, click Add Features (see Figure 1-2).

Figure 1-2
Adding Required Features for WDS

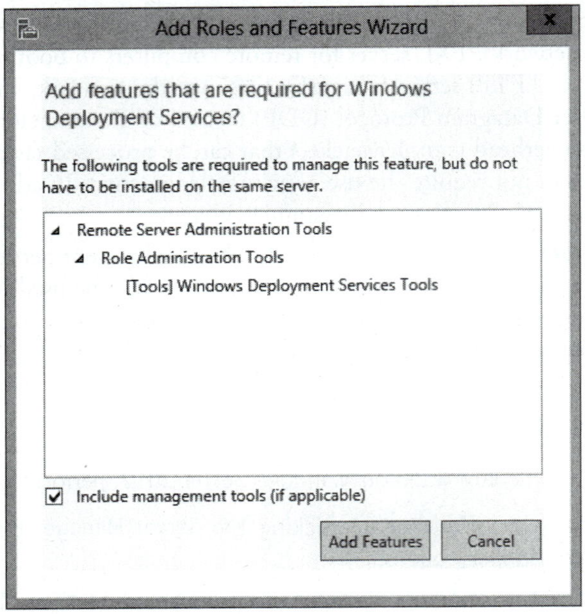

8. Click Next.
9. Back on the *Select server roles* page, click Next.
10. On the *Select features* page, click Next.
11. On the *WDS* page, click Next.
12. On the *Select role services* page, make sure that the Deployment Server option and the Transport Server option are selected (see Figure 1-3), and then click Next.

Figure 1-3
Selecting the WDS Role Services

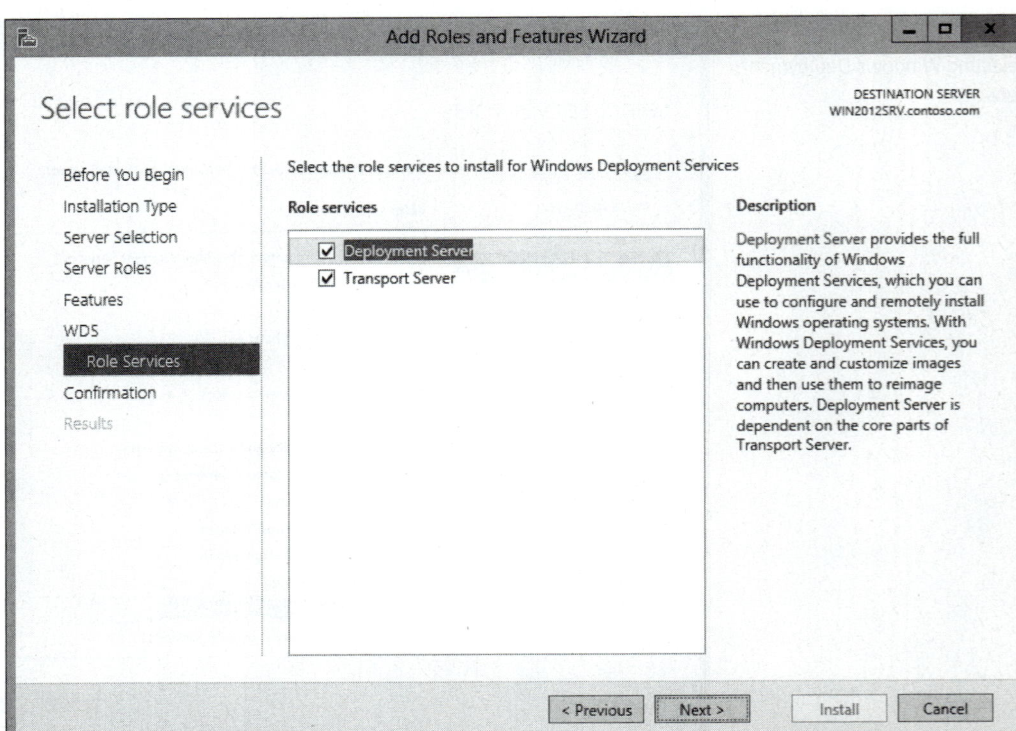

13. On the *Confirm installation selections* page, click Install.
14. When the installation finishes, click Close.

Configuring the WDS Server

Before you can use WDS, you must configure the WDS server, including performing the initial server configuration, adding a default startup and install images, and configuring a boot menu.

WDS is inactive until you perform the initial configuration of the service and add images to the server. To use WDS, your system must meet the following requirements:

- The server is a member of an Active Directory Domain Services (AD DS) domain, or a domain controller for an AD DS domain.
- There is an active DHCP server on the network.
- There is an active DNS server on your network.
- The WDS server has an NTFS file system partition to store images.

PERFORMING THE INITIAL CONFIGURATION OF WDS

Before you can use WDS, you must configure WDS by determining if the server will be part of Active Directory, determining where the boot and install images will be stored, and configuring the DHCP server so that clients can boot to the WDS server. To perform the initial configuration using the Windows Deployment Services Configuration Wizard, open the Windows Deployment Services console, right-click the WDS server, and then select Configure Server.

PERFORM THE INITIAL CONFIGURATION OF WDS

GET READY. To perform the initial configuration of WDS on Windows Server 2012, perform the following steps:

1. Open Server Manager by clicking the Server Manager button on the task bar. The *Server Manager* opens.
2. At the top of *Server Manager*, click Tools > Windows Deployment Services (see Figure 1-4). The *Windows Deployment Services* console opens.
3. Expand Servers, right-click the WDS server, and then select Configure Server (see Figure 1-5).

Figure 1-4

Opening the Windows Deployment Services console

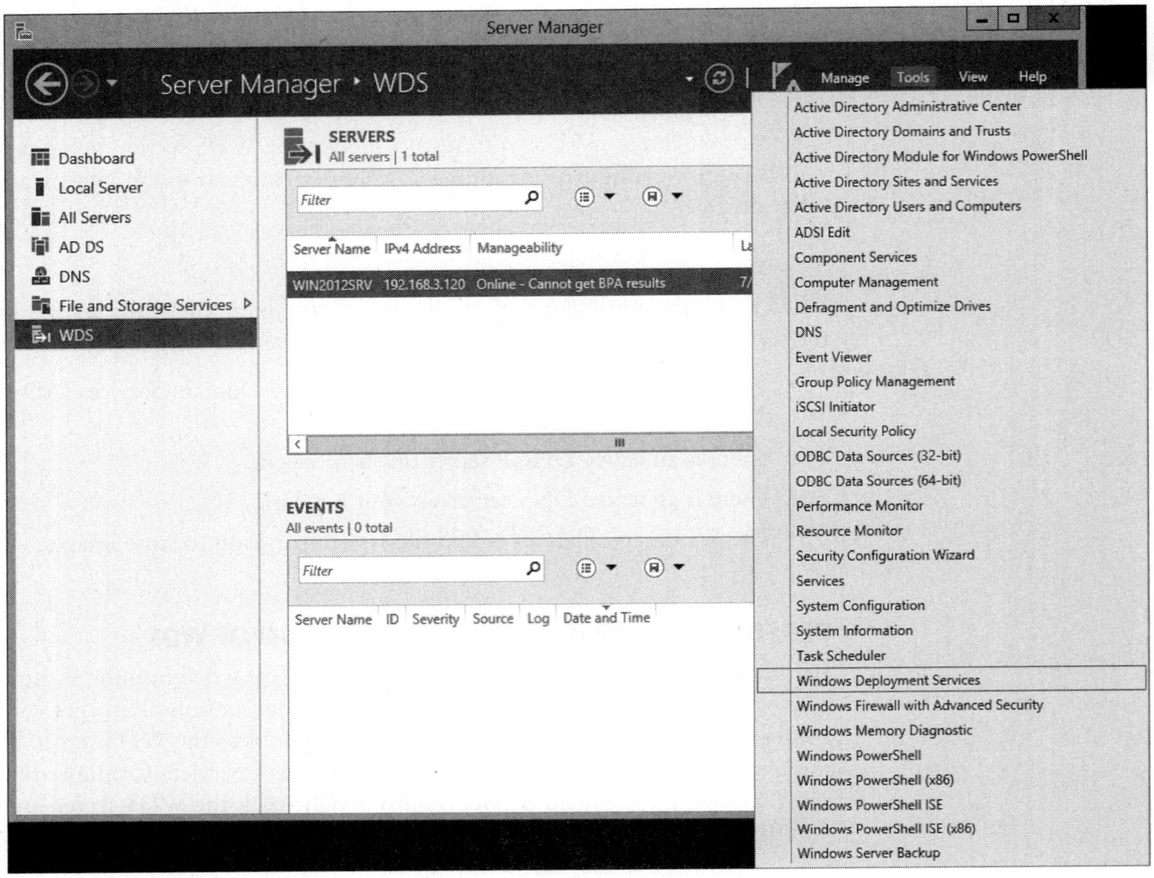

Figure 1-5

Starting the Initial Configuration Wizard for WDS

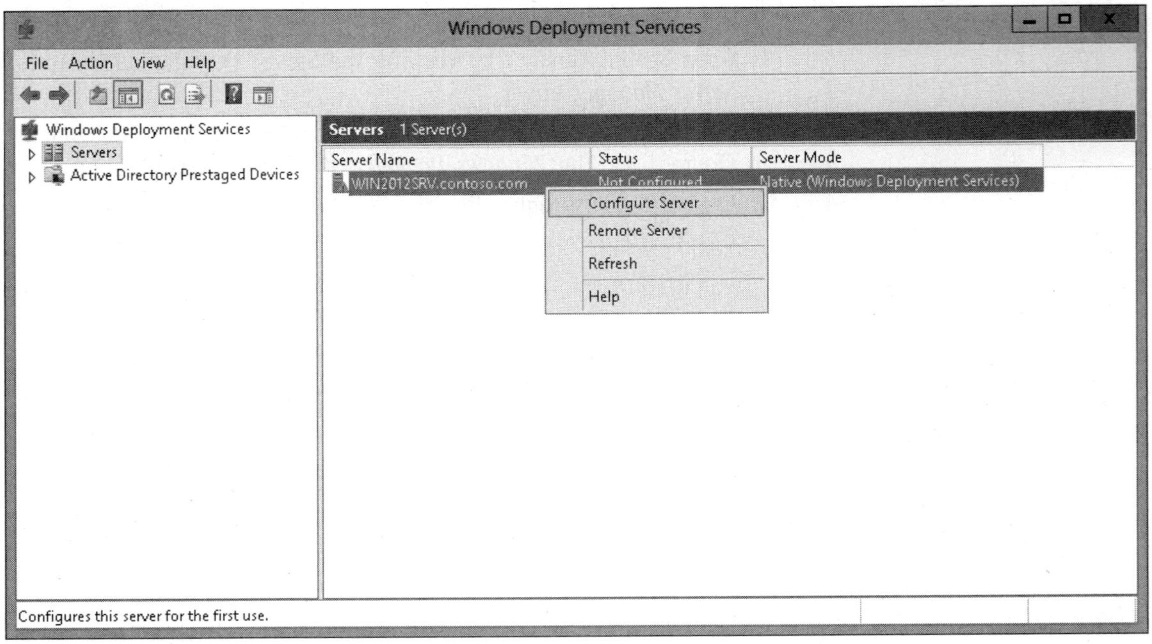

4. When the *Before You Begin* page appears, click Next.
5. On the *Install Options* page, select the Integrated with Active Directory option (see Figure 1-6), and then click Next.

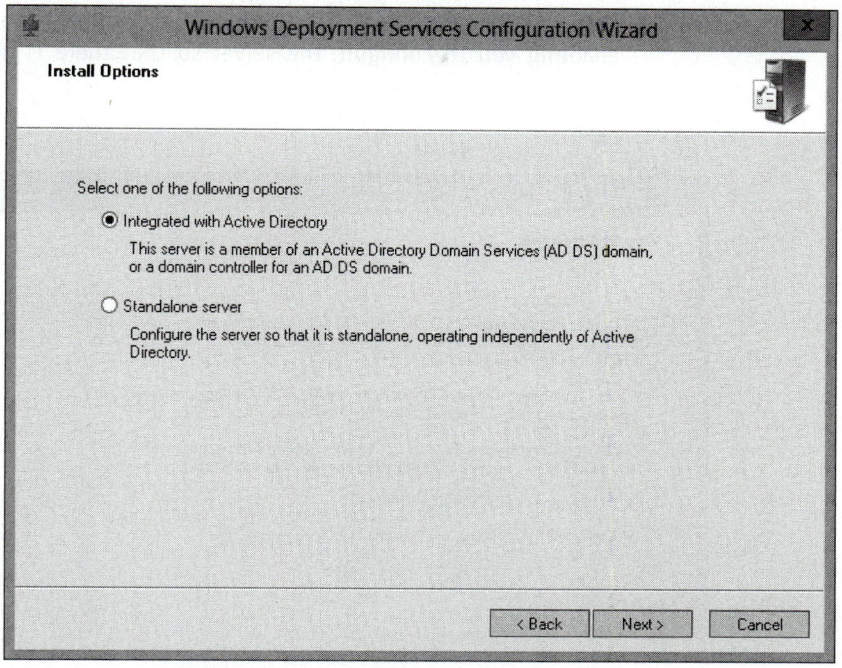

Figure 1-6
Selecting the *Integrated with Active Directory* option

6. On the *Remote Installation Folder Location* page, specify the location of the remote installation folder (see Figure 1-7) and then click Next.

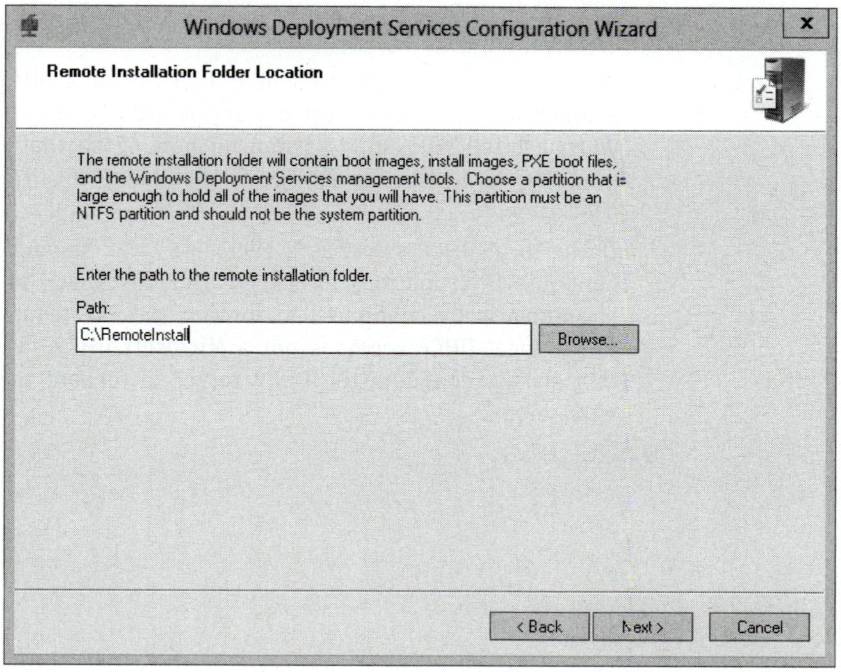

Figure 1-7
Specifying the location of the remote installation folder

7. If you use the C drive, you will be warned that you have selected the Windows system volume and that you should use a separate volume. To continue, click Yes. Of course, in a production environment, for performance and system reliability, you should create a separate volume to store the WDS images.
8. If your WDS server is also a DHCP server, another page appears (see Figure 1-8), enabling you to configure the server so that there is not a port conflict.

Figure 1-8

Specifying the DHCP Server options

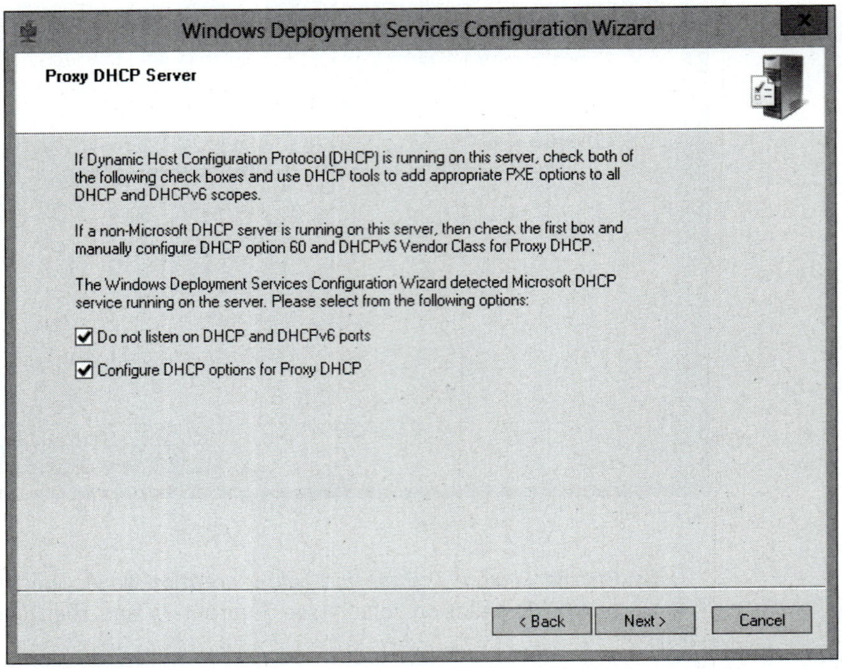

By default, when a DHCP client is looking for a DHCP server, it will perform a broadcast using UDP port 67. If the WDS server is also the DHCP server, you must tell WDS not to listen on port 67 so that DHCP can function properly. To do this, select the Do not listen on DHCP and DHCPv6 ports check box.

If the local DHCP server is a Microsoft DHCP server, you should select the Configure DHCP options for Proxy DHCP check box so that the DHCP server is automatically configured to forward the PXE requests to the WDS server. If the local DHCP server is not a Microsoft DHCP server, you will have to manually configure the DHCP server to forward the request to the WDS server.

9. Click Next.

10. On the *PXE Server Initial Settings* page (see Figure 1-9), select the appropriate options:
    - **Do not respond to any client computers:** By selecting this option, WDS cannot perform installations. You would typically use this option to keep WDS disabled until you are ready to use it.
    - **Respond only to known client computers:** A known client computer is a computer that has a computer account pre-staged or created in Active Directory before you perform the installation. By selecting this option, WDS responds to computers that you have prestaged; it does not respond to unstaged or rogue systems. This option is selected by default.
    - **Respond to all client computers (known and unknown):** By selecting this option, WDS responds to any client system that makes an installation request. Because it responds to any computer that attempts a PXE boot, it is the least secure option.

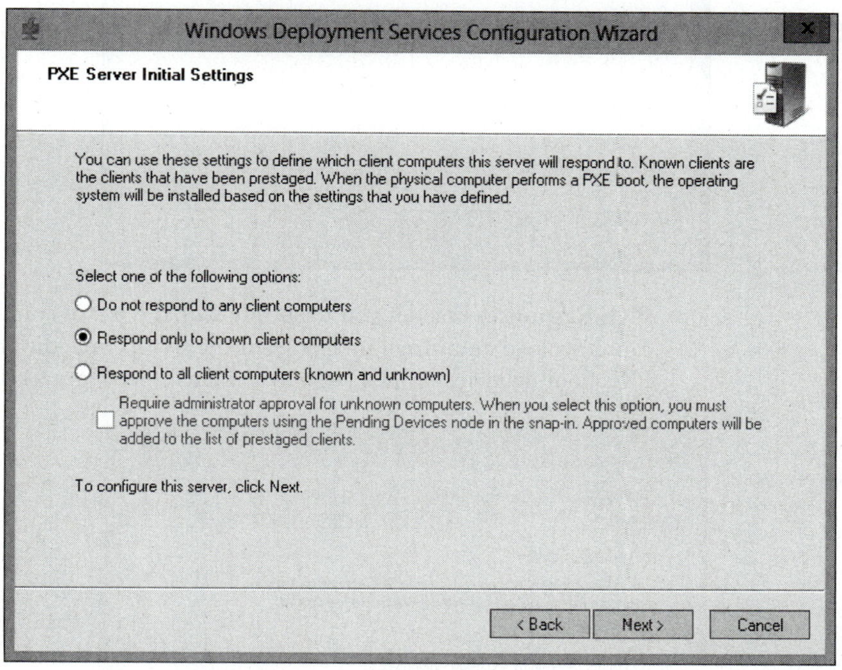

Figure 1-9

Specifying how WDS/PXE Server responds to clients

11. Click Next.
12. When the task is completed, click Finish.

CONFIGURING THE WDS PROPERTIES

After you perform the initial configuration, you must reconfigure the WDS server by accessing the WDS Properties (right-click the server in the Windows Deployment Services console and then select Properties). The WDS properties include the following tabs:

- **General:** Displays server name, mode, and location of the remote installation folder where images are stored. (See Figure 1-10.)

Figure 1-10

Viewing the General tab

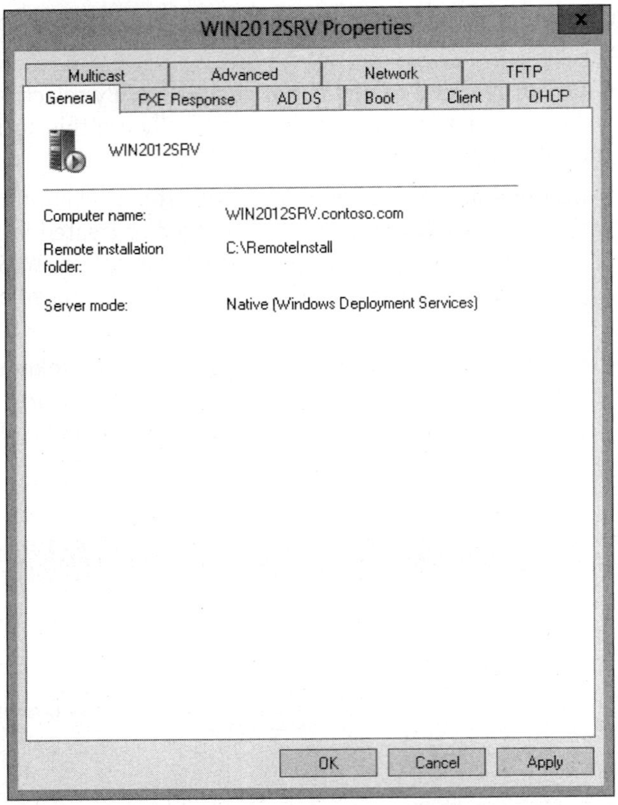

- **PXE Response:** Enables you to specify which types of computers (known or unknown) can download and install images from the server. In addition, you can determine the PXE boot delay in seconds (zero by default). (See Figure 1-11.)

Figure 1-11

Viewing the PXE Response tab

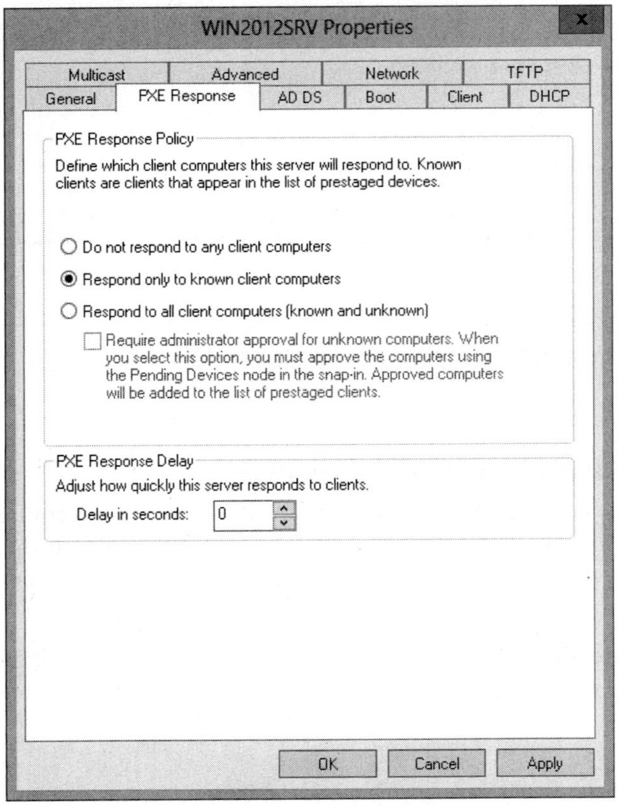

- **AD DS:** Allows you to determine the automatic naming format for WDS clients in AD DS that are not prestaged, and it allows you to specify where the computer account will be created in Active Directory. (See Figure 1-12.)

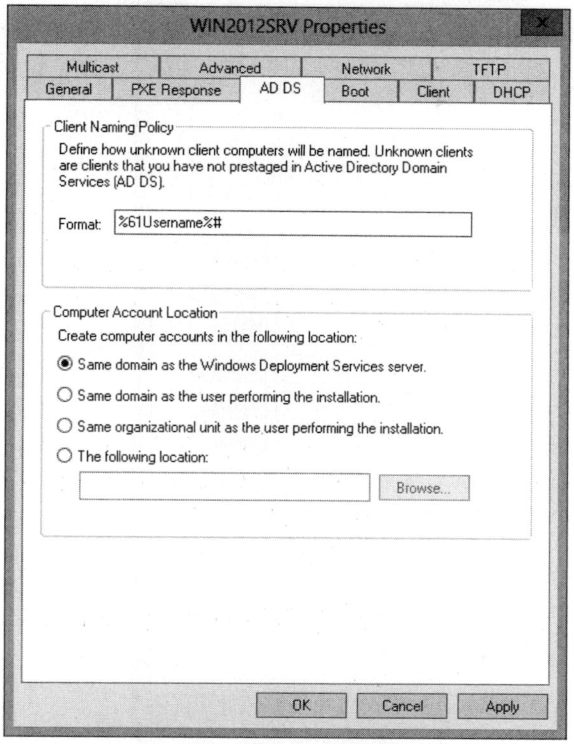

Figure 1-12
Viewing the AD DS tab

- **Boot:** Allows you to specify the default network boot image for each architecture type (x86, x64, and ia64) and the PXE Boot Policy settings for known and unknown clients. It also allows you to specify if a user must press F12 to continue the PXE boot. (See Figure 1-13.)

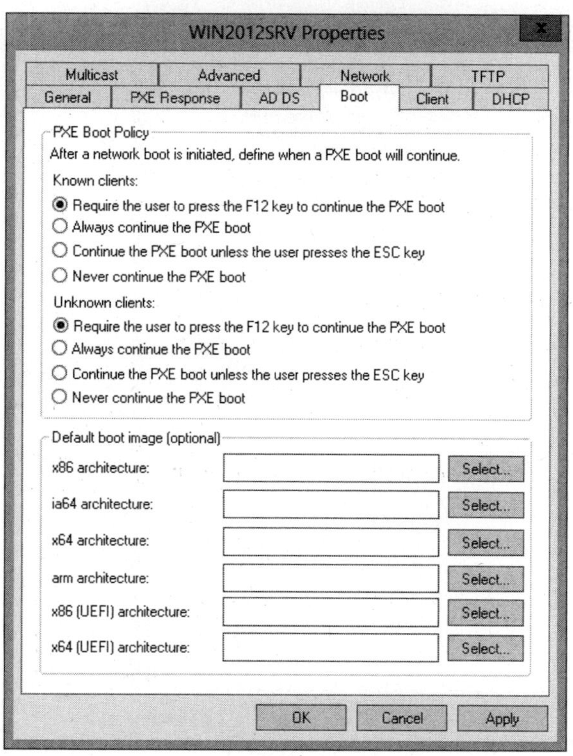

Figure 1-13
Viewing the Boot tab

- **Client:** Allows you to enable and configure unattended installations of the WDS clients. In addition, if you do not want to add a computer to the domain, you can select the *Do not join the client to a domain after an installation* option. (See Figure 1-14.)

Figure 1-14

Viewing the Client tab

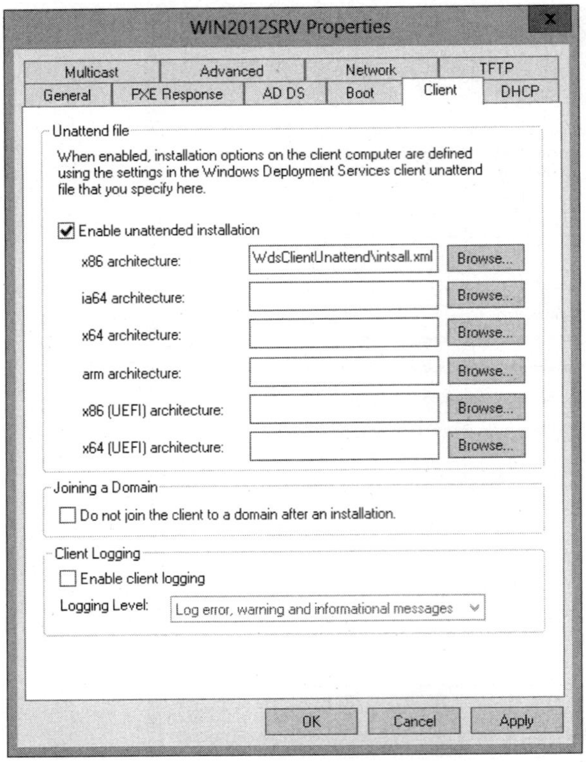

- **DHCP:** Allows you to enable or disable if a server listens on the DHCP ports (port 67) and to automatically configure DHCP option 60 on a DHCP server. (See Figure 1-15.)

Figure 1-15

Viewing the DHCP tab

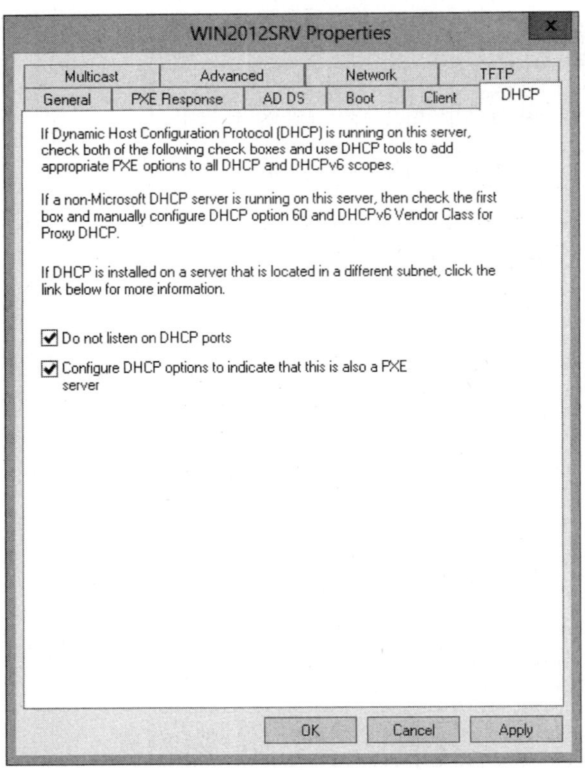

- **Multicast:** Allows you to use one set of packets to install operating systems on multiple computers simultaneously. As a result, you minimize network traffic. The Multicast tab also allows you to configure Transfer Settings. (See Figure 1-16.)

Figure 1-16
Viewing the Multicast tab

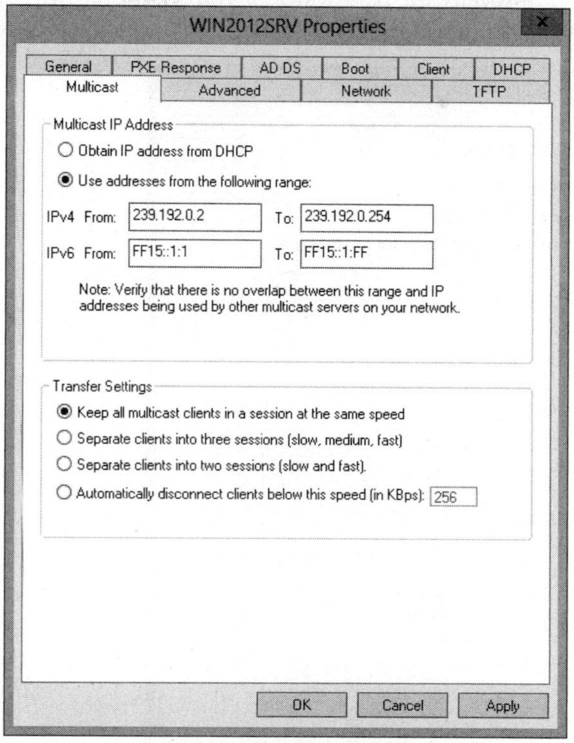

- **Advanced:** Allows you to authorize your WDS server in DHCP. It also allows you to specify a domain controller and global catalog or to allow WDS to discover them on its own. (See Figure 1-17.)

Figure 1-17
Viewing the Advanced tab

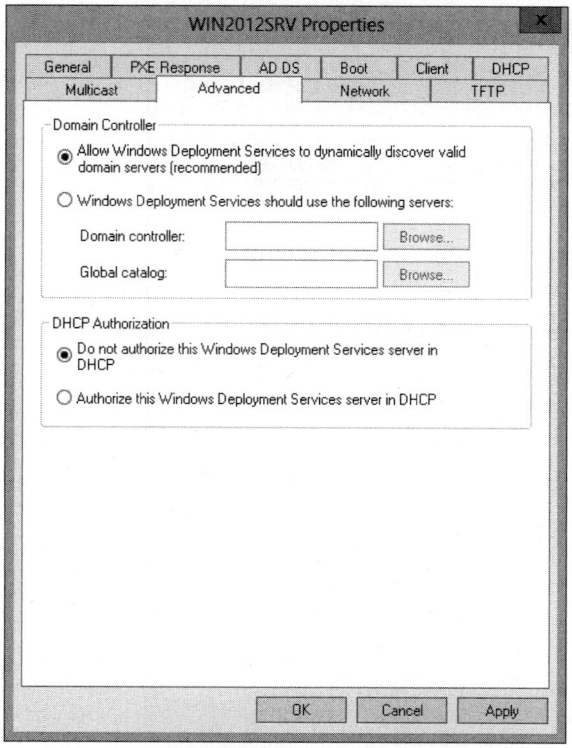

- **Network:** Allows you to specify the UDP port ranges WDS uses. Typically, you would leave the default setting (*Obtain dynamic ports from Winsock*) selected. You should note that the Network profile option is grayed out in Windows Server 2012, which would allow you to specify the bandwidth of your network. Instead, the bandwidth is determined automatically. (See Figure 1-18.)

Figure 1-18

Viewing the Network tab

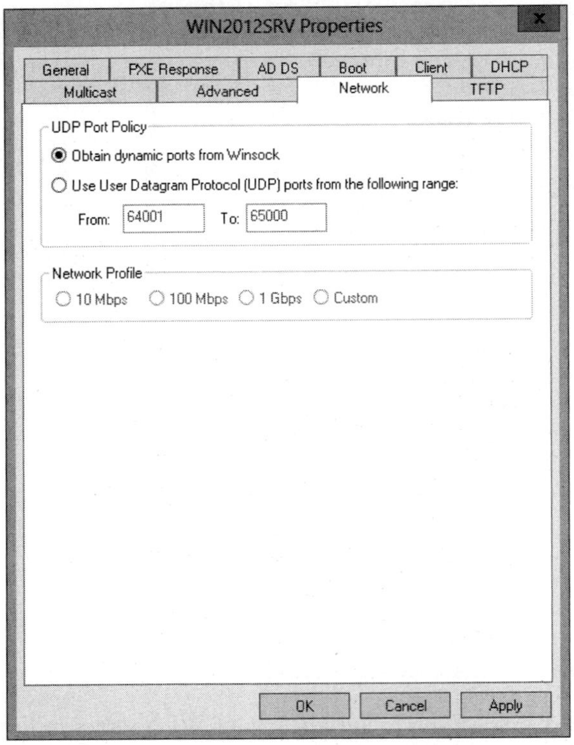

- **TFTP:** Allows you to configure the maximum block size used for FTP transfers. The TFTP option is new to Windows Server 2012. (See Figure 1-19.)

Figure 1-19

Viewing the TFTP tab

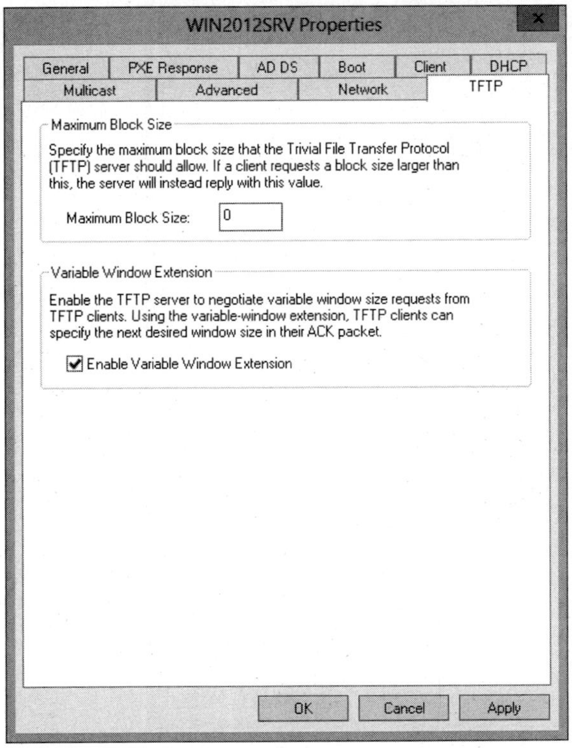

STARTING WDS

After you perform the initial configuration, you reconfigure the WDS server by accessing the WDS Properties. To access the WDS Properties, right-click the server in the Windows Deployment Services console, choose All Tasks, and then choose Start (see Figure 1-20). Then you will need to add the images that you want to deploy, which is discussed in the next section.

Figure 1-20

Starting WDS

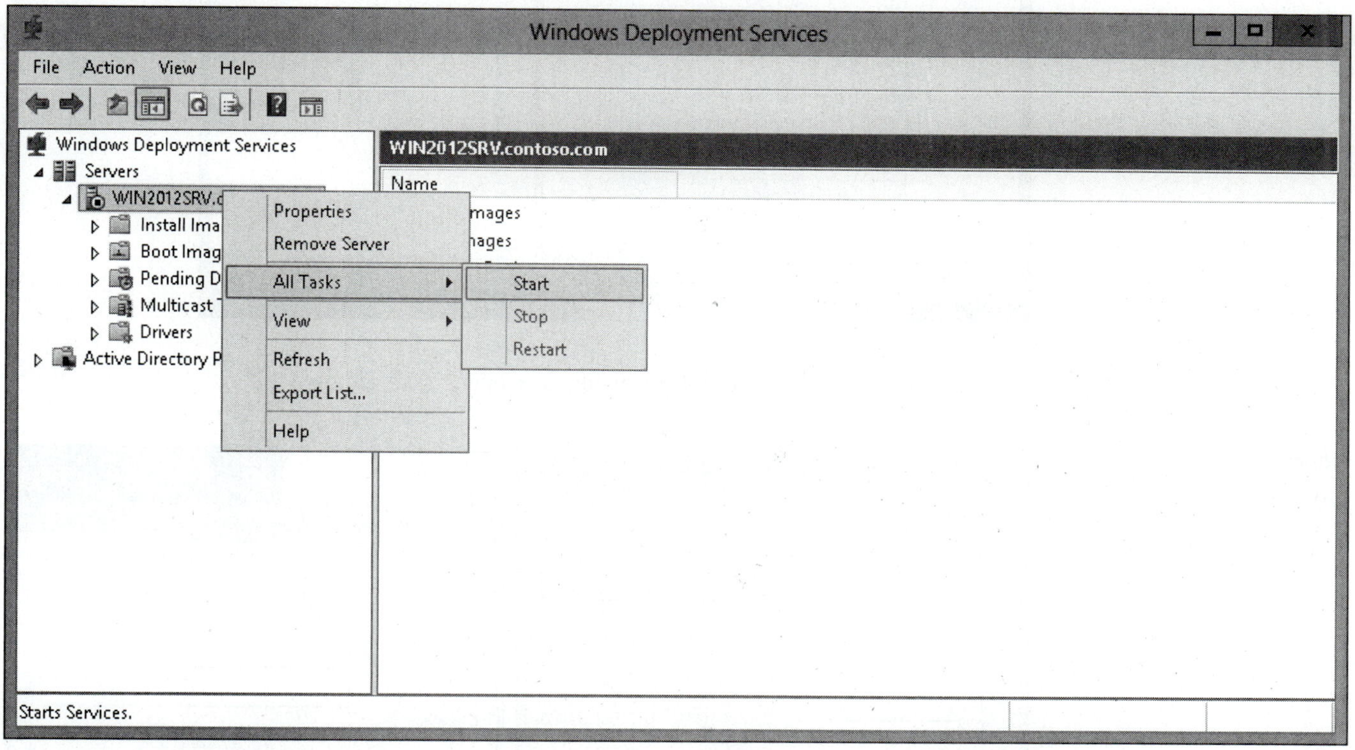

CONFIGURING THE CUSTOM DHCP OPTION

As previously mentioned, if you have a separate server that is running the DHCP server, you must configure it manually to include the custom option that provides the WDS clients with the name of the WDS Server via DHCP. If this option is not performed, the WDS clients will not be able to find the WDS server to boot from.

CONFIGURE THE CUSTOM DHCP OPTION

GET READY. To configure the custom DHCP Option on the DHCP server, perform the following steps:

1. Open the Server Manager by clicking the Server Manager button on the task bar. The *Server Manager* opens.
2. Click Tools > DHCP. The DHCP console opens.
3. Expand the server node.
4. Right-click IPv4 and then select Set Predefined Options (see Figure 1-21). The *Predefined Options and Values* dialog box appears.

Figure 1-21

Selecting Set Predefined Options

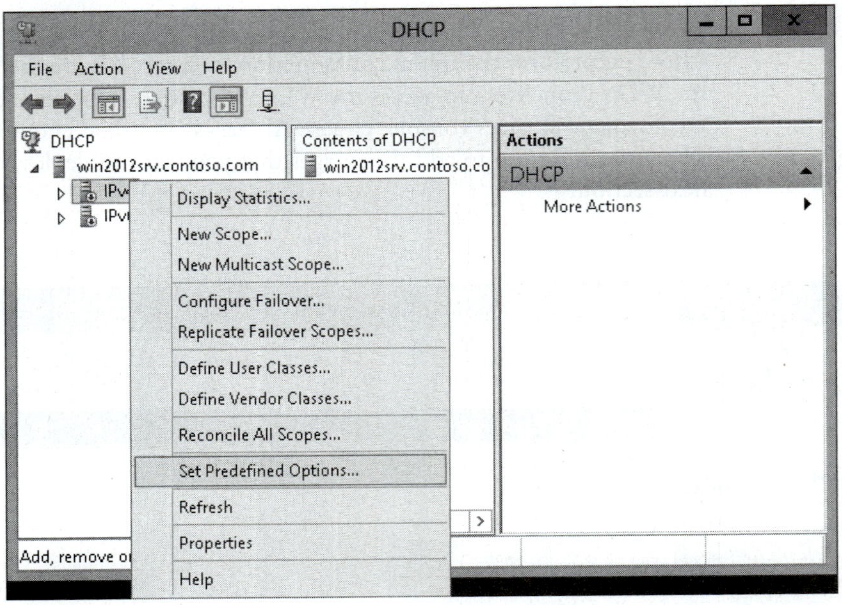

5. Click Add. The *Option Type* dialog box opens (see Figure 1-22).

Figure 1-22

Setting option types

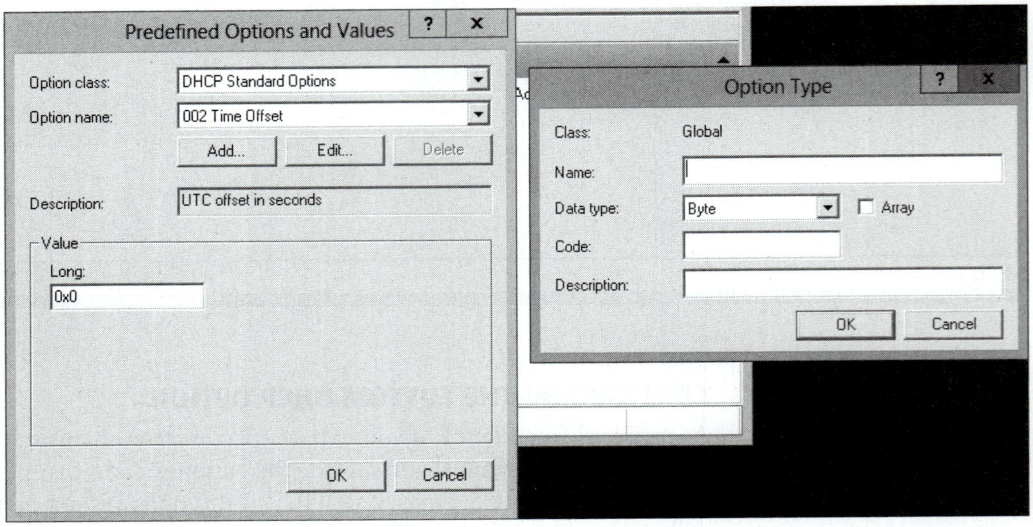

6. In the *Name* text box, type PXEClient.
7. For the *Data* type, select String.
8. In the *Code* text box, type 060 (see Figure 1-23).

Figure 1-23

Specifying the PXE Client Option 060

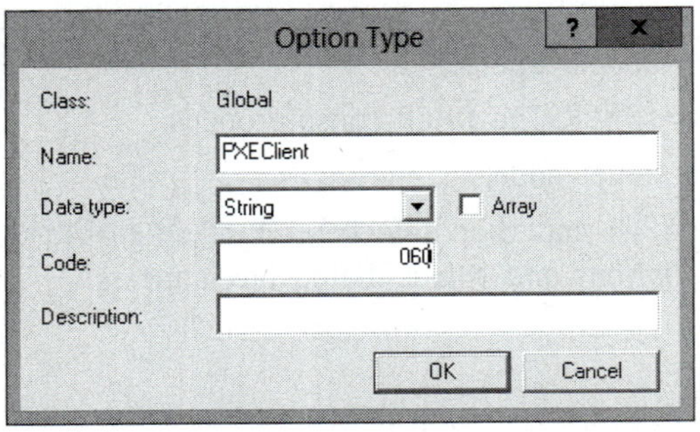

9. Click OK to accept your settings.
10. Click OK to close the *Predefined Options and Values* dialog box.
11. Expand the IPv4 node, and then click Server Options.
12. Find and then click the 060 PXEClient option.
13. In the *String value* text box, type the name or IP address of your WDS server (see Figure 1-24).

Figure 1-24

Typing the name of your WDS server

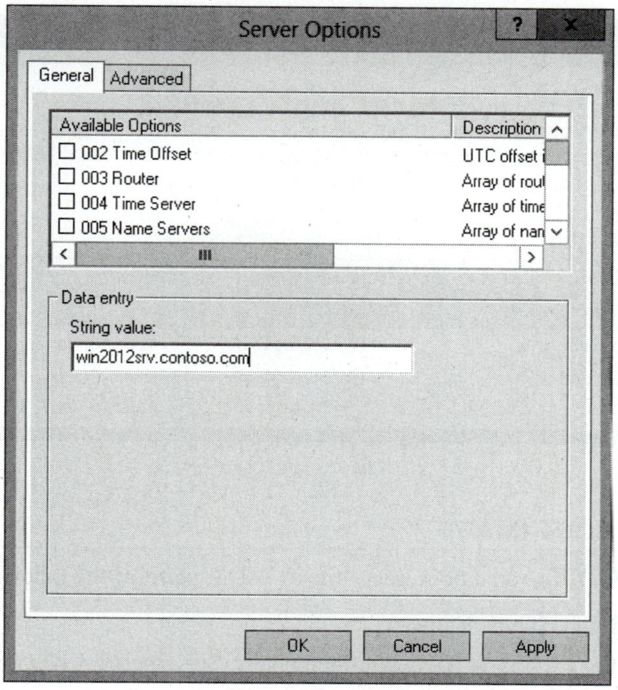

14. Click OK to accept your settings and to close the *Server Options* dialog box.

Configuring and Managing Boot, Install, and Discover Images

To deploy Windows, you must create two types of images: a boot image and an install image. Just as the name implies, the boot image boots the computer. In addition, the ***boot image*** starts the operating system installation. The ***install image*** contains the operating system that WDS installs.

CERTIFICATION READY
Configure and manage boot, install, and discover images.
Objective 1.1

There are two types of image formats:

- ***Sector-based image formats***, whereby each sector is stored within the file and each sector is the smallest unit of information. One common example of a disk image is the .ISO file used for a CD image and a DVD image.
- ***File-based image formats***, whereby each file is the smallest unit. The advantage of using a file-based image is that it is hardware-independent and a file can be referenced multiple times within the file system tree. A common example is a WIM image used with WDS.

The boot images and the install images use the ***Windows Imaging Format (WIM)***, a file format that allows a file structure (folders and files) to be stored inside a single WIM database. By using a database, the system does not have to open and close several individual files during the data transfer.

ADDING BOOT IMAGES

The Windows Server 2012 installation DVD includes a boot image file named *boot.wim*, located in the *\sources* folder (see Figure 1-25), which loads Windows PE 4.0 on the client computer. Since it is used to boot the computer and start the installation of an operating system, it can be used for virtually any operating system deployment without modification.

Figure 1-25

Viewing the sources folder

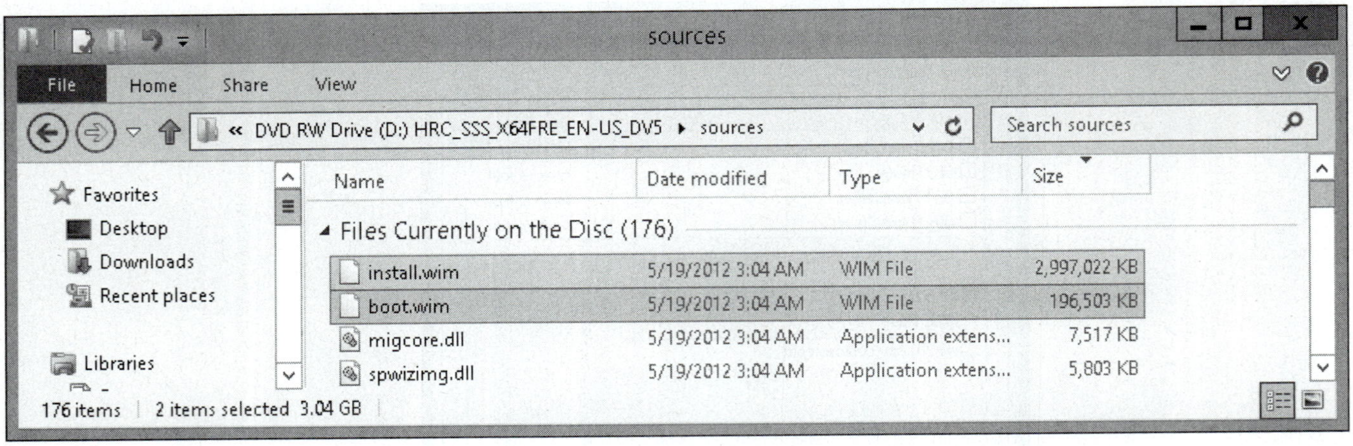

ADD A BOOT IMAGE

GET READY. To add a boot image file to WDS, perform the following steps:

1. Open Server Manager.
2. Click Tools > Windows Deployment Services. The *Windows Deployment Services* console opens.
3. Expand Servers and then expand the server so that you can see the *Install Images* folder and the *Boot Images* folder (see Figure 1-26).

Figure 1-26

Viewing the Install Images folder and the Boot Images folder

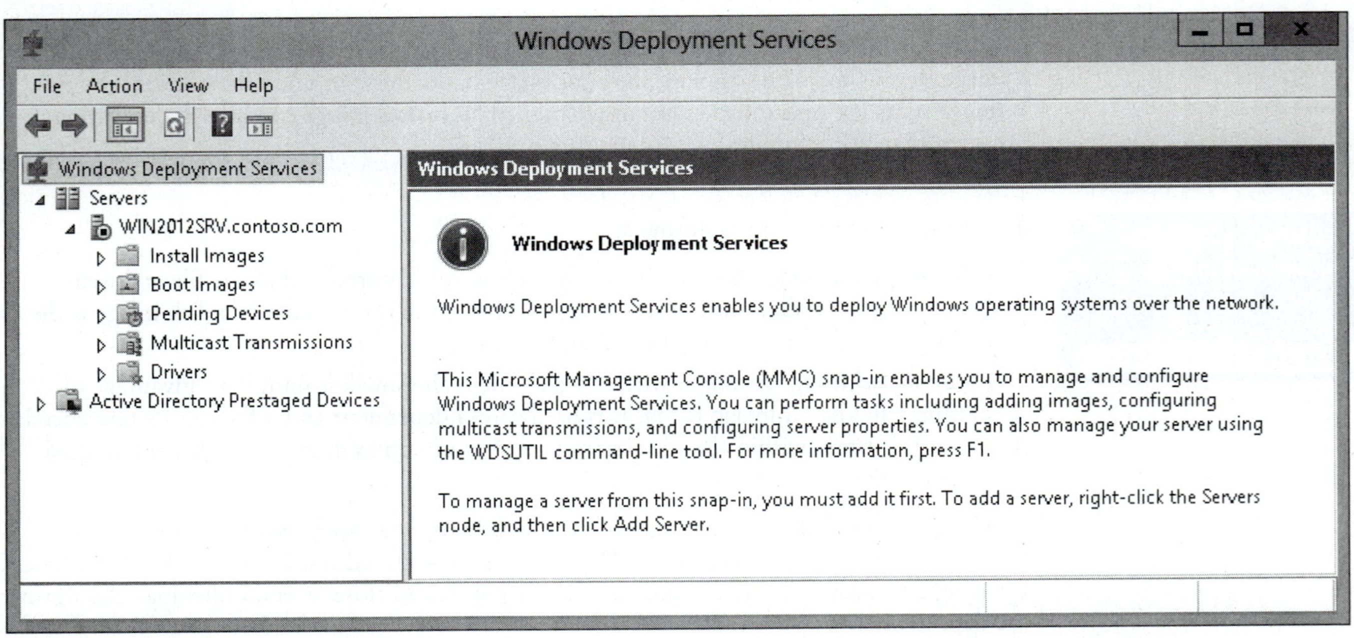

4. To add a boot image, right-click the *Boot Images* folder and choose Add Boot Image. The *Add Image Wizard* opens.

5. Browse to the location of the image file (such as the *Sources* folder located on the installation DVD), click the boot.wim file (see Figure 1-27), and then click Open.

Figure 1-27

Opening the Boot.wim file

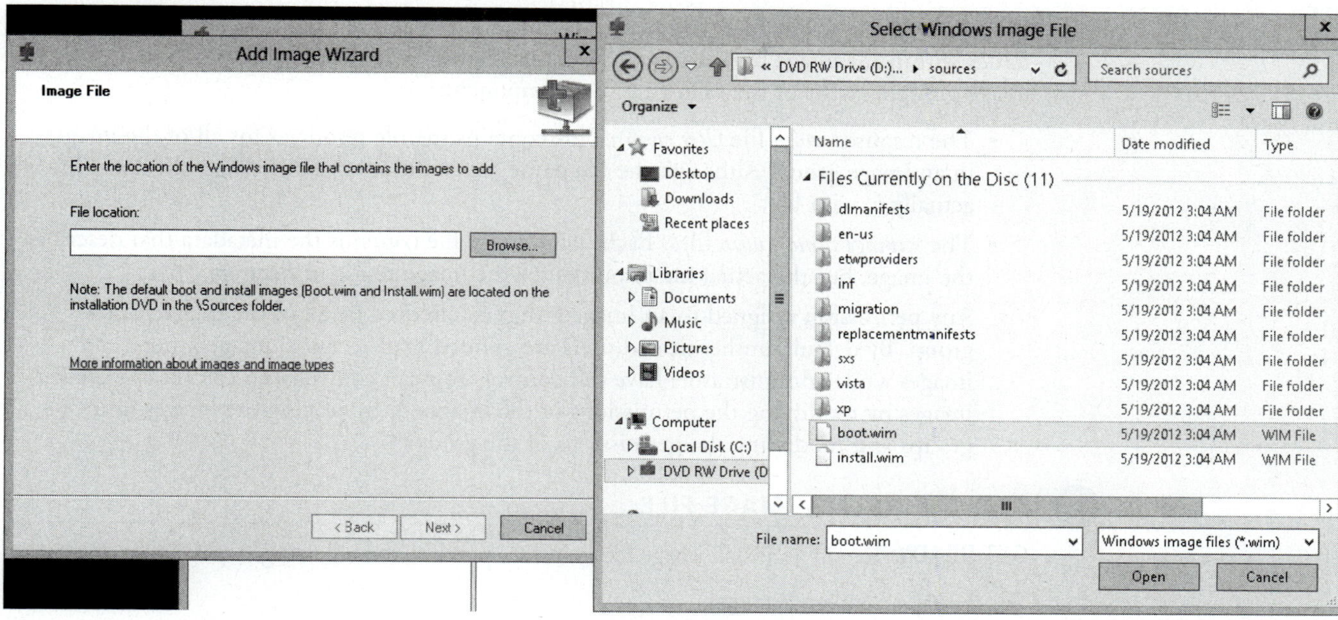

6. On the *Image File* page, click Next.

7. On the *Image Metadata* page, type a name and description of the image and then click Next. Most of the time, you can use the default values shown in Figure 1-28.

Figure 1-28

Specifying the image name and description

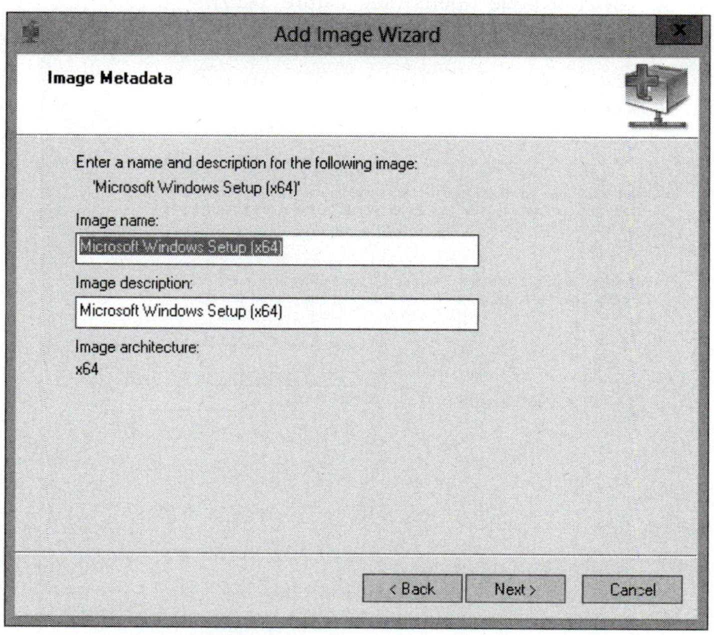

8. On the *Summary* page, click Next.

9. When the image is added to the server, click Finish.

ADDING IMAGE FILES

As previously mentioned, the image file contains the operating system that WDS will install on the client computer. Included in the Sources folder on the Windows Server 2012 installation disk is an *install.wim* file for Windows Server 2012 that allows you to perform a standard Windows Server 2012 installation similar to performing a manual installation from disk.

When you create image files, you place the image file in an image group. An ***image group*** is a folder within the image repository of WDS that shares security options and file resources. The image group consists of the following two components:

- The resource *.wim* file (*Res.rwm*). This contains the file resources for all of the images in an image group. Although the file name seems to indicate otherwise, the .rwm file is actually a .wim file.
- The *<imagename>.wim* files. Each *.wim* image file contains the metadata that describes the image, but the actual file resources for the image reside in *Res.rwm*.

  Any permission assigned to an image group is inherited by all of the images in the group. By default, authenticated users are granted read access to image groups and images while administrators have full control. You can control who can receive specific images by modifying the permissions of the images or by placing the images in image groups and modifying the permissions of the groups.

ADD AN INSTALL IMAGE FILE

GET READY. To add an install image file to WDS, perform the following steps:

1. Open Server Manager.
2. Click Tools > Windows Deployment Services. The *Windows Deployment Services* console opens.
3. Expand *Servers* and then expand the server so that you can see the *Install Images* folder and the *Boot Images* folder (see Figure 1-26).
4. Right-click the *Install Images* folder and select Add Install Image. The *Add Image Wizard* page opens (see Figure 1-29).

Figure 1-29

Creating an Image Group

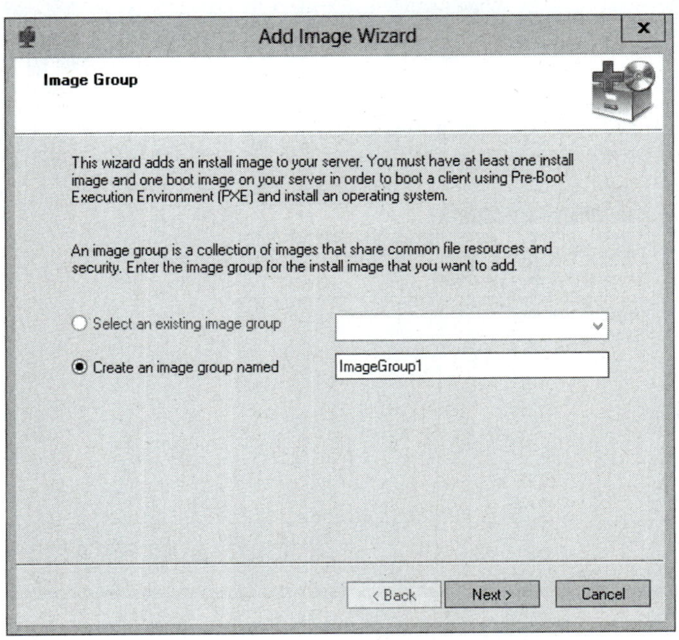

5. On the *Image Group* page, the Create an image group named option is selected. If desired, type a different name of the image group and then click Next.

6. Browse to the location of the image file (such as the *Sources* folder located on the installation DVD), select the install.wim file, and then click Open.
7. On the *Image File* page, click Next.
8. On the *Available Images* page, select the images you want to include (see Figure 1-30), and then click Next.

Figure 1-30

Specifying the images you want to include

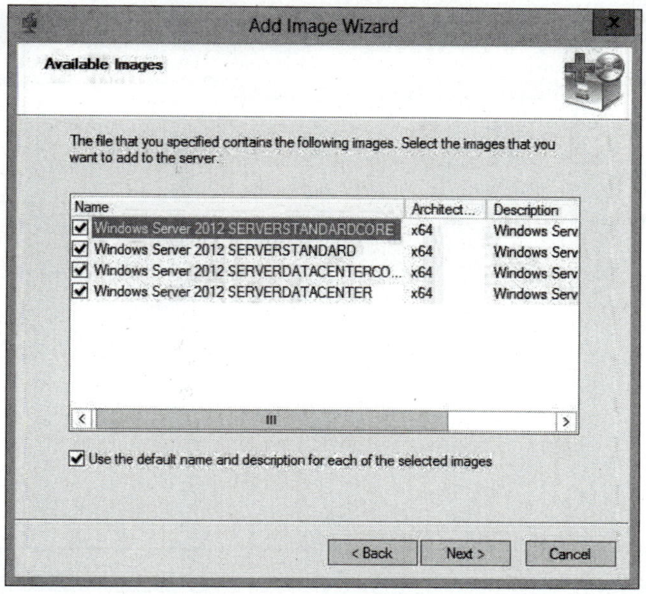

9. On the *Summary* page, click Next.
10. When the images are added to the server, click Finish.

CREATING AN IMAGE FILE WITH WDS

The install images that are included on a Windows installation disk are images of a basic Windows installation, with no patches, updates, or additional drivers. If you would like to create your own image files, you must first set up a master computer with all of the patches, drivers, applications, and configurations applied. Then use WDS to create your own image file by modifying an existing boot image, booting the master computer with the modified boot image, and running the ***Windows Deployment Services Capture Utility***. The Windows Deployment Services Capture Utility will create an image file and write it to the computer's drive, which will eventually be copied to the WDS server. You can then use it to be deployed to other computers.

CREATE AN IMAGE FILE

GET READY. To create an image file, perform the following steps:

1. Open Server Manager.
2. Click Tools > Windows Deployment Services. The *Windows Deployment Services* console opens.
3. Expand Servers and then expand the server so that you can see the *Install Images* folder and the *Boot Images* folder.
4. If you have not done so already, add the Windows Server 2012 boot.wim image to the Boot Images store by following the steps provided in the Add a Boot Image exercise.

5. Right-click the boot image and choose Create Capture Image (see Figure 1-31). The *Create Capture Image Wizard* opens.

Figure 1-31

Starting the Create Capture Image Wizard

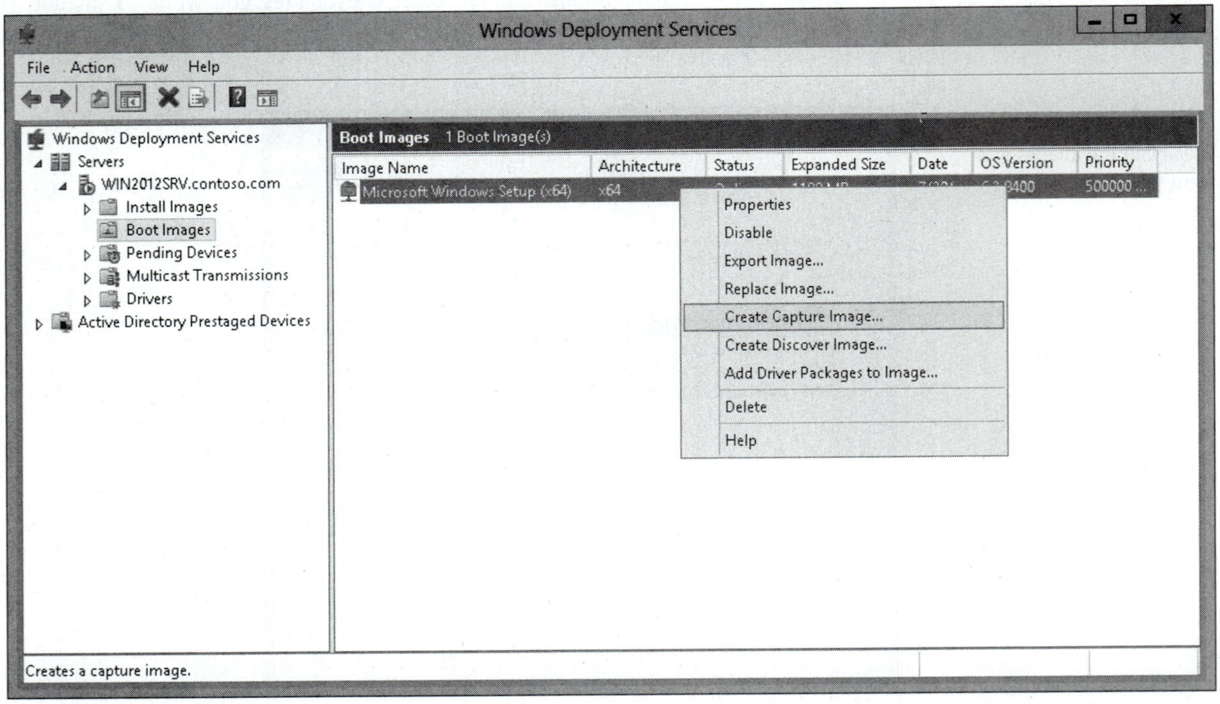

6. Specify a name and description for the new image. Then specify the Location and file name for the new image file (see Figure 1-32). Click Next.

Figure 1-32

Specifying the location and file name

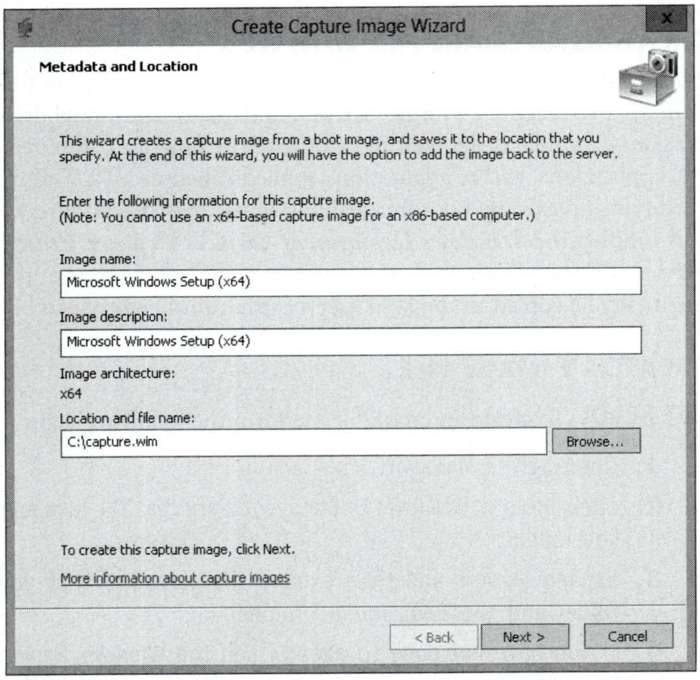

7. When the task is complete, you can select Add image to the Windows Deployment Server now (if desired). Then click Finish.

Before capturing a computer with WDS, you must prepare a master or reference computer with the Sysprep.exe utility and reboot the computer using the capture image. Microsoft's ***System Preparation Utility (Sysprep.exe)*** prepares a Windows computer for cloning by removing specific computer information such as the computer name and Security Identifier (SID). On Windows Server 2012, the Sysprep.exe is located in the C:\Windows\System32\Sysprep folder. When you reboot the computer with the capture image, a Wizard guides you through the process of capturing an image of the computer and uploading it to the WDS server.

When running `sysprep` on the master computer, use the following syntax:

```
sysprep /generalize /oobe
```

The `/generalize` parameter removes the unique values, such as the computer name and the SID, so that they are not captured in the image file and replicated to the target workstations. The `/oobe` parameter configures Windows to present the Windows Welcome Wizard the next time the computer starts. The Windows Welcome Wizard allows you to name the computer and generate a SID and any other required unique information.

CREATING A DISCOVER IMAGE

If you have a computer that does not support a PXE boot, you can boot the computer from disk using a discover image. A ***discover image*** is an image file that you can burn to a CD-ROM or other boot medium. When you boot the client computer using the discover image disk, the computer loads Windows PE, connects to a specified WDS server, and proceeds with the operating system installation process.

CREATE A DISCOVER IMAGE

GET READY. To create a discover image file, perform the following steps:

1. Open Server Manager.
2. Click Tools > Windows Deployment Services. The *Windows Deployment Services* console appears.
3. Expand Servers and then expand the server so that you can see the *Install Images* folder and the *Boot Images* folder.
4. To create a discover boot image, right-click a boot image in the *Windows Deployment Services* console and choose Create Discover Image (see Figure 1-33). Click Next.

Figure 1-33

Creating a discover image

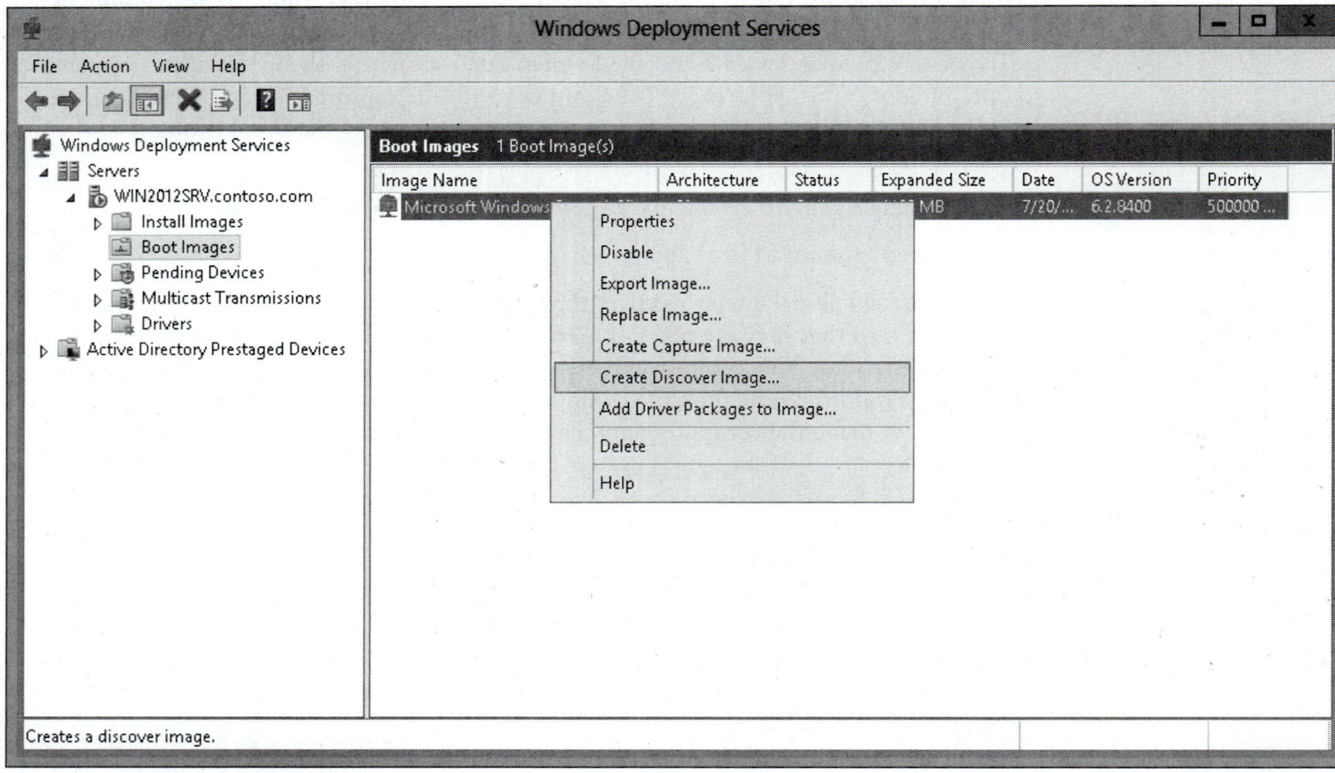

5. On the *Metadata and Location* page, leave the default Image name and Image description as-is. Then specify where you want to store the discover image file. In addition, you can *Enter the name of the Windows Deployment Services server...* (see Figure 1-34). Click Next.

Figure 1-34

Specifying the image name, the image description, and where to store the discover image file

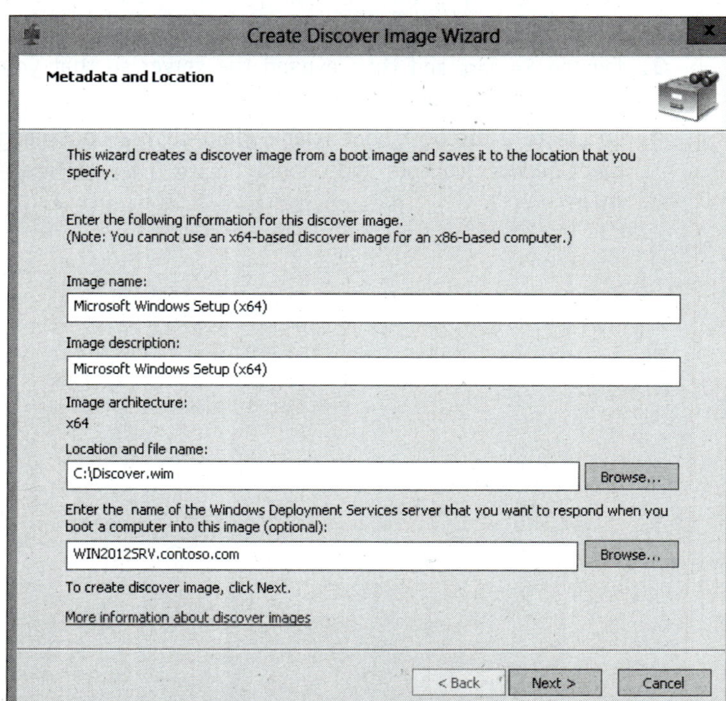

6. On the *Summary* page, click Next.
7. When the images are added to the server, click Finish.

To convert the discover image to a bootable .ISO image, you first must download and install the ***Windows Assessment and Deployment Kit (ADK)*** for Windows 8. ADK is a set of tools provided by Microsoft to customize, assess, and deploy a Windows operating system to new computers. It is located at Microsoft's Download Center. Then use the oscdimg.exe command to create the .ISO image.

INSTALL THE WINDOWS ASSESSMENT AND DEPLOYMENT KIT (ADK)

GET READY. To install the ADK, perform the following steps:

1. Start the Windows Assessment and Deployment Kit by double-clicking adksetup.exe.
2. On the *Specify Location* page, leave the default settings, and then click Next.
3. When you are prompted to join the *Customer Experience Improvement Program (CEIP)*, click Next.
4. On the *License Agreement* page, click Accept.
5. With the *Deployment Tools and Windows Preinstallation Environment (Windows PE)* already selected, click Install.
6. When the installation is complete, click Close.

CREATE A BOOTABLE ISO IMAGE

GET READY. After you have installed the ADK for Windows 8, perform the following steps to create a bootable ISO Image:

1. Create a folder named C:\WinPE_x64\ISO.
2. Copy the contents of the C:\Program Files (x86)\Windows Kits\8.0\Assessment and Deployment Kit\Windows Preinstallation Environment\amd64\Media folder to C:\WinPE_x64\ISO.
3. Create the C:\WinPE_x64\ISO\Sources folder.
4. Copy the discover image to the C:\WinPE_x64\ISO\Sources folder.
5. Rename the discover.wim file in the C:\WinPE_x64\ISO\Sources folder to boot.wim.
6. Copy the etfsboot.com file from the C:\Program Files (x86)\Windows Kits\8.0\Assessment and Deployment Kit\Deployment and Imaging Tools\amd64\Oscdimg folder to the C:\WinPE_x64 folder.
7. Create the bootable ISO by running the following command:

```
oscdimg -b"c:\WinPE_X64\etfsboot.com" -n C:\WinPE_X64\ISO C:\
WinPE_X64\WinPE_X64.iso
```

USING WDSUTIL

Different from most of the components that are included with Windows, you cannot install and configure Windows Deployment Services by using Windows PowerShell. Instead, the wdsutil command is used for managing the Windows Deployment Services server. To use the wdsutil command line, you will need to open a Command Prompt as an administrator.

The wdsutil commands include:

- **/add** – Adds prestaged computers, images, or image groups.
- **/approve-AutoAddDevices** – Approves computers that are pending administrator approval.

- **/convert-RiprepImage** – Converts an existing Remote Installation Preparation (RIPrep) image to a Windows Image (.wim) file.
- **/copy** – Copies an image or a driver group.
- **/delete-AutoAddDevices** – Deletes computers that are in the Auto-Add database (which stores information about the computers on the server).
- **/disable** – Disables all services for Windows Deployment Services.
- **/disconnect-Client** – Disconnects a client from a multicast transmission or namespace.
- **/enable** – Enables all services for Windows Deployment Services.
- **/export-Image** – Exports an image from the image store to a .wim file.
- **/get** – Retrieves properties and attributes about the specified object.
- **/initialize-Server** – Configures a Windows Deployment Services server for initial use.
- **/new** – Creates new capture and discover images, multicast transmissions, and namespaces.
- **/progress** – Displays the progress status while a command is being executed.
- **/reject-AutoAddDevices** – Rejects computers that are pending administrator approval.
- **/remove** – Removes objects.
- **/replace-Image** – Replaces a boot or installation image with a new version of that image.
- **/set** – Sets properties and attributes on the specified object.
- **/start** – Starts all services on the Windows Deployment Services server, including multicast transmissions, namespaces, and the Transport Server.
- **/stop** – Stops all services on the Windows Deployment Services server.
- **/uninitialize-Server** – Reverts changes made during server initialization.
- **/update-ServerFiles** – Updates server files on the RemoteInstall share.
- **/verbose** – Displays verbose output for the specified command.

For example, to show the WDS configuration, you can use one of the following commands:

```
wdsutil /get-server /show configure
wdsutil /get-server /show:all /detailed
```

To show the WDS configuration, you can use one of the following commands:

```
wdsutil /get-server /show configure
wdsutil /get-server /show:all /detailed
```

To stop or start the WDS server, use the following commands:

```
wdsutil /stop-server
wdsutil /start-server
```

To show the WDS configuration, you can use one of the following commands:

```
wdsutil /get-server /show configure
wdsutil /get-server /show:all /detailed
```

To show the WDS configuration, you can use one of the following commands:

```
wdsutil /get-server /show configure
wdsutil /get-server /show:all /detailed
```

To add a computer by using a MAC address, you would use the following command:

```
wdsutil /Add-Device /Device:PC1 /ID:00-C1-46-8A-1F-EB
```

To add a boot image, use the following command:

```
wdsutil /Add-Image /ImageFile:"C:\Data\Boot.wim" /ImageType:Boot
```

To add an install image, use the following command:

```
Wdsutil /Add-Image /ImageFile:"C:\Data\Install.wim" /ImageType:Install
```

PERFORMING AN UNATTENDED INSTALLATION

So far, we've discussed deploying Windows over the network. However, the installations covered thus far have been a manual process whereby you have to step through the installation Wizard. To streamline the installation process, you need to automate the Windows installation by using ***answer files***, which provide responses to the prompts that would normally appear during the Windows installation. Besides clicking the standard Next button used on most screens, the answer file can also be used to partition and format disk, install additional device drivers, and specify what Windows features to install.

You can create an answer file with a text editor or XML editor, but Microsoft recommends that you use the ***System Image Manager (SIM)***, a tool used to create and manage unattended Windows setup answer files using a graphical interface. SIM can also be used to check answer files. SIM is also part of the Windows Assessment and Deployment Kit.

CREATE AN ANSWER FILE

GET READY. To create an answer file, log on to the computer where you installed the ADK and then perform the following steps:

1. Click Start > All Ap ps > Windows System Image Manager. The *Windows System Image Manager* console opens (see Figure 1-35).

Figure 1-35

Viewing the Windows System Image Manager console

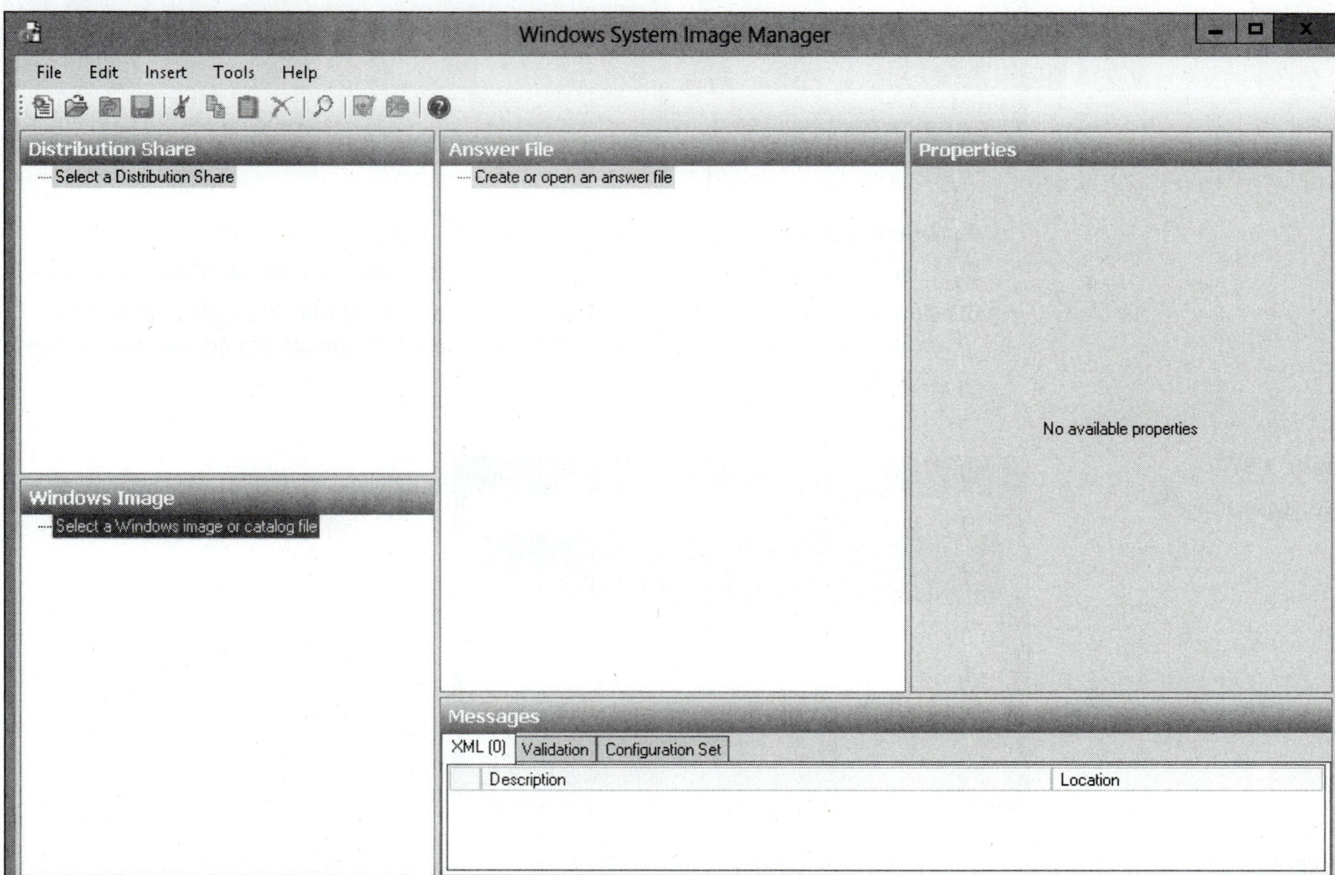

2. Click Tools > Create Distribution Share. The *Create Distribution Share* dialog box opens.
3. Browse to the folder where you want to create the distribution share and then click Open. The distribution share subfolders appear in the *Distribution Share* pane (see Figure 1-36).

Figure 1-36

Viewing the distribution share subfolders in the Distribution Share pane

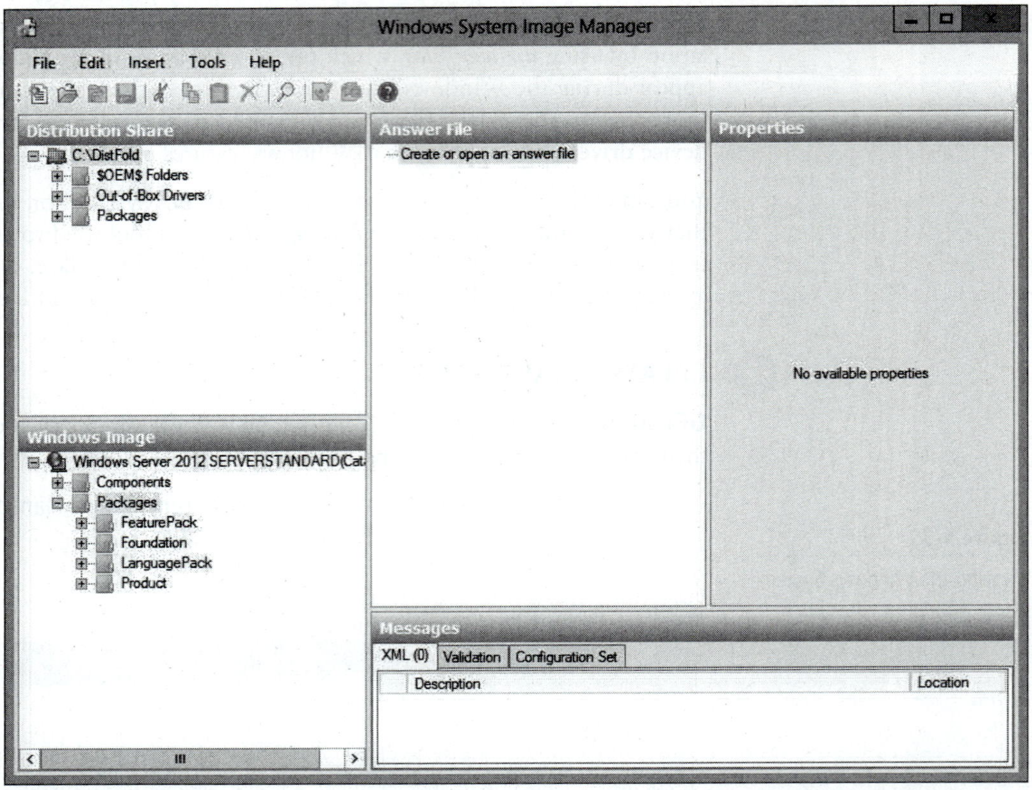

4. Insert a Windows 2012 installation disk into the computer's DVD drive.
5. Click File > Select Windows Image. The Select a *Windows Image* dialog box opens.
6. Browse to the folder where you are storing an *install.wim* file, select the install .wim image file, and then click Open. The *Select an Image* dialog box opens (see Figure 1-37).

Figure 1-37

Selecting an Image

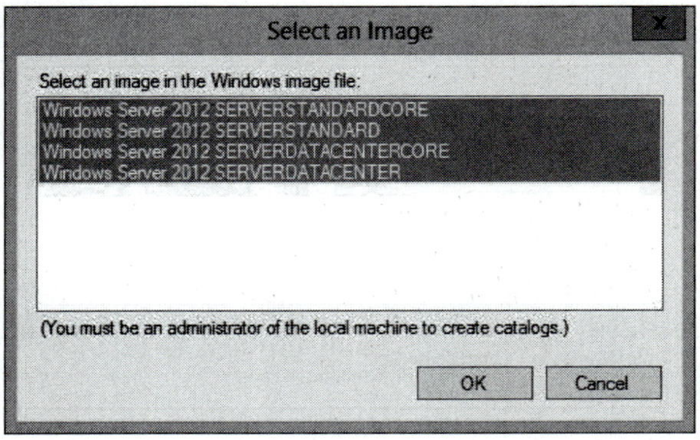

7. Select the image that you want to use, and then click OK.
8. If you are prompted to create a catalog file, click Yes.
9. Click File > New Answer File. The answer file elements appear in the *Answer File* pane (see Figure 1-38).

Figure 1-38

Viewing elements in the Answer File pane

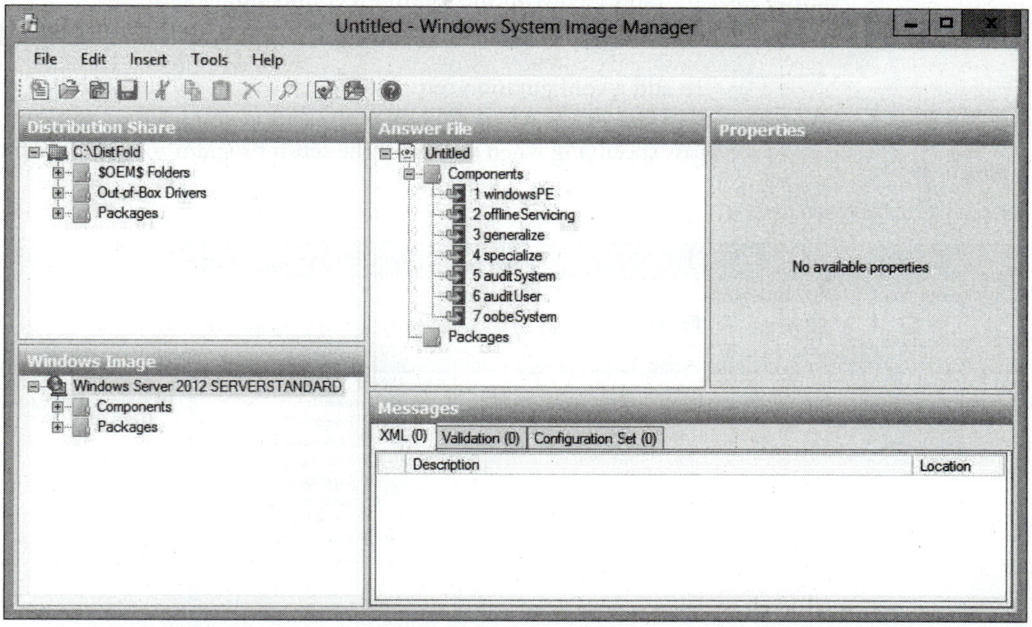

After you create the answer file, you are ready to start configuring the elements or settings that you want to include in the answer file. As Windows is installed, the installation is divided into seven configuration passes. Each pass specifies what actions can occur during the installation process. For example, if you need to partition and format your disk, you must do that at the very beginning of the installation process, which happens to be the Windows PE pass.

The seven configuration passes in an answer file are as follows:

- `windowsPE`: Configures Windows PE options and basic Windows Setup, including the initial boot options. Options can include specifying the product key and configuring a disk (partitioning and formatting).
- `offlineServicing`: Applies updates to a Windows image using DISM.exe, including software fixes, language packs, and other security updates.
- `generalize`: If you used the `sysprep /generalize` command, `generalize` removes system-specific information, such as computer name and security ID.

- `specialize`: Creates and applies system-specific information, such as network settings, international settings, and domain information (including joining a computer to the domain).
- `auditSystem`: Applies settings to the system if the computer is started in audit mode as specified with the `sysprep` command.
- `auditUser`: Applies settings to the user if the computer is started in audit mode as specified with the `sysprep` command.
- `oobeSystem`: Applies settings to Windows before the Windows Welcome starts.

To add a configuration setting to the answer file, browse through the available settings in the *Windows Image* pane, right-click the setting you want to add, and then select the configuration pass specifying when you want the setup program to configure the setting (see Figure 1-39).

Figure 1-39

Selecting a configuration pass

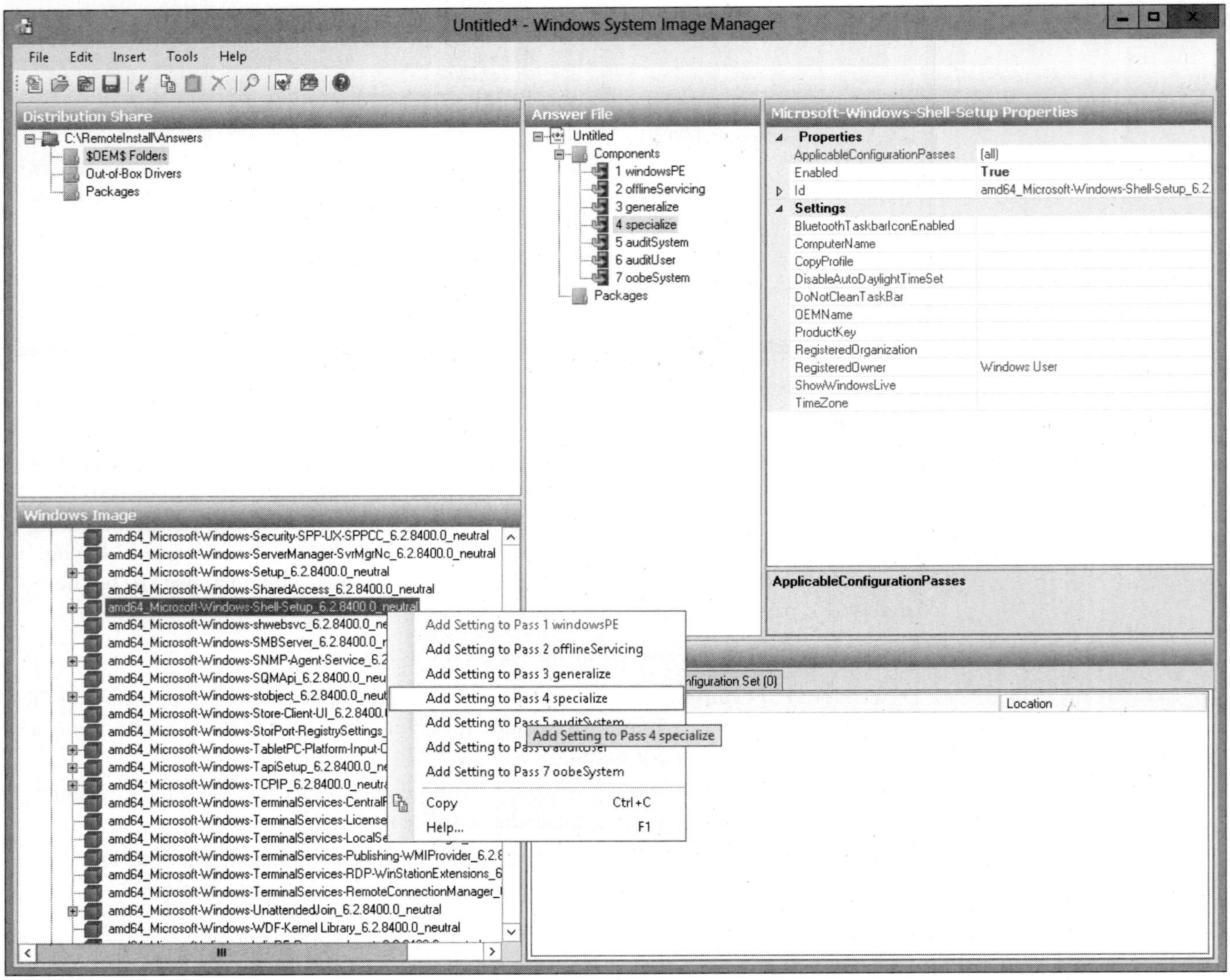

The setting then appears in the Answer File pane and the properties specific to that setting appear in the adjacent Properties pane (see Figure 1-40). After the setting has been added, you modify the values in the properties. If you need clarification on a setting, press F1 while a property or setting is highlighted to open the Unattended Windows Setup Reference Guide (see Figure 1-41).

Figure 1-40

Configuring setting properties

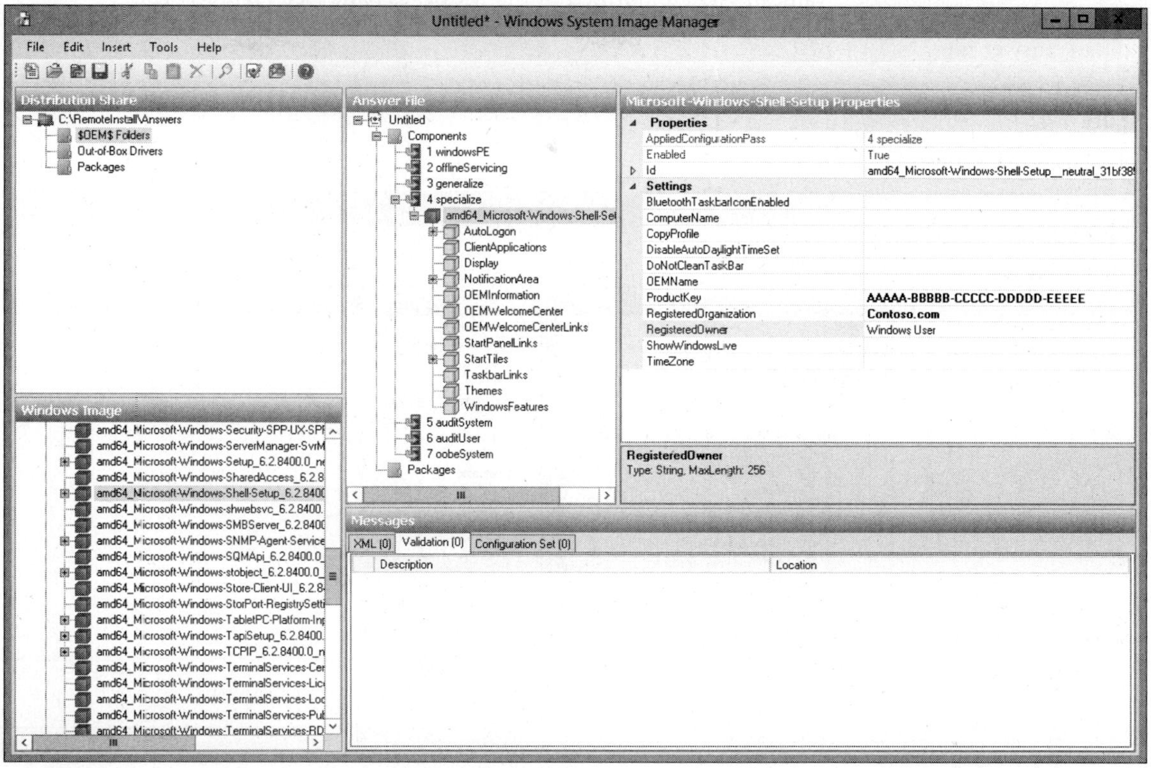

Figure 1-41

Opening the Unattended Windows Setup Reference Guide

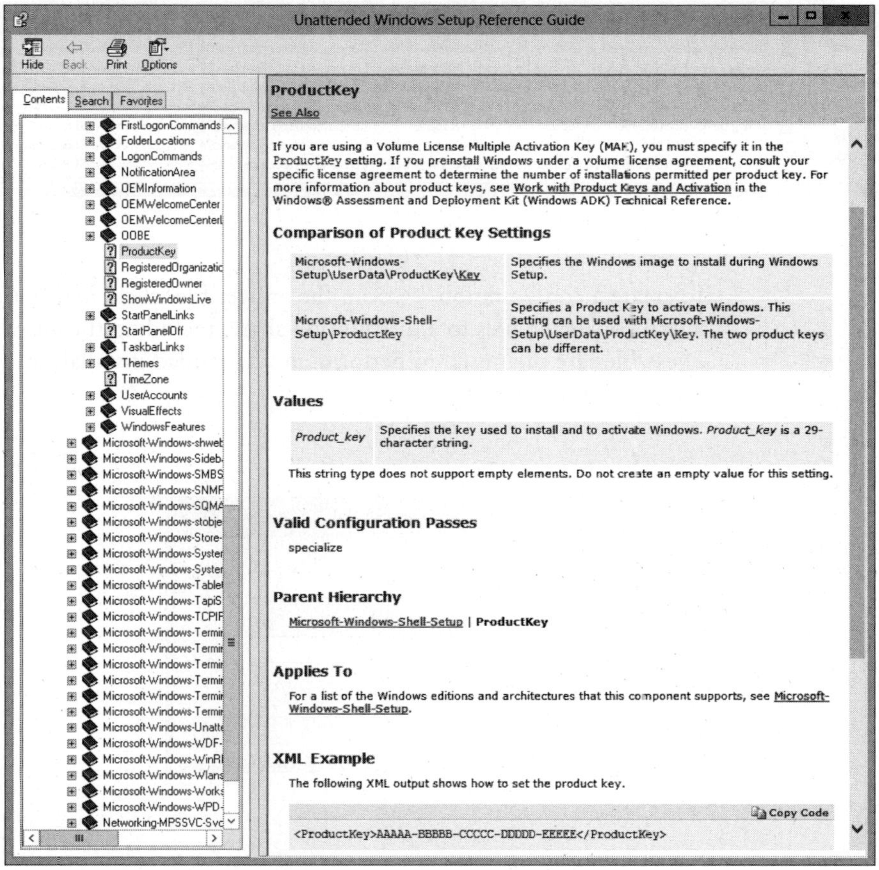

TAKE NOTE*

Microsoft recommends using SIM to create and validate answer files.

After you configure the answer files, you can validate the answer file by clicking *Tools > Validate Answer file*. If SIM finds any discrepancies (such as incorrect values or omitted values), you are notified in the Messages pane (see Figure 1-42).

Figure 1-42

Validating an answer file

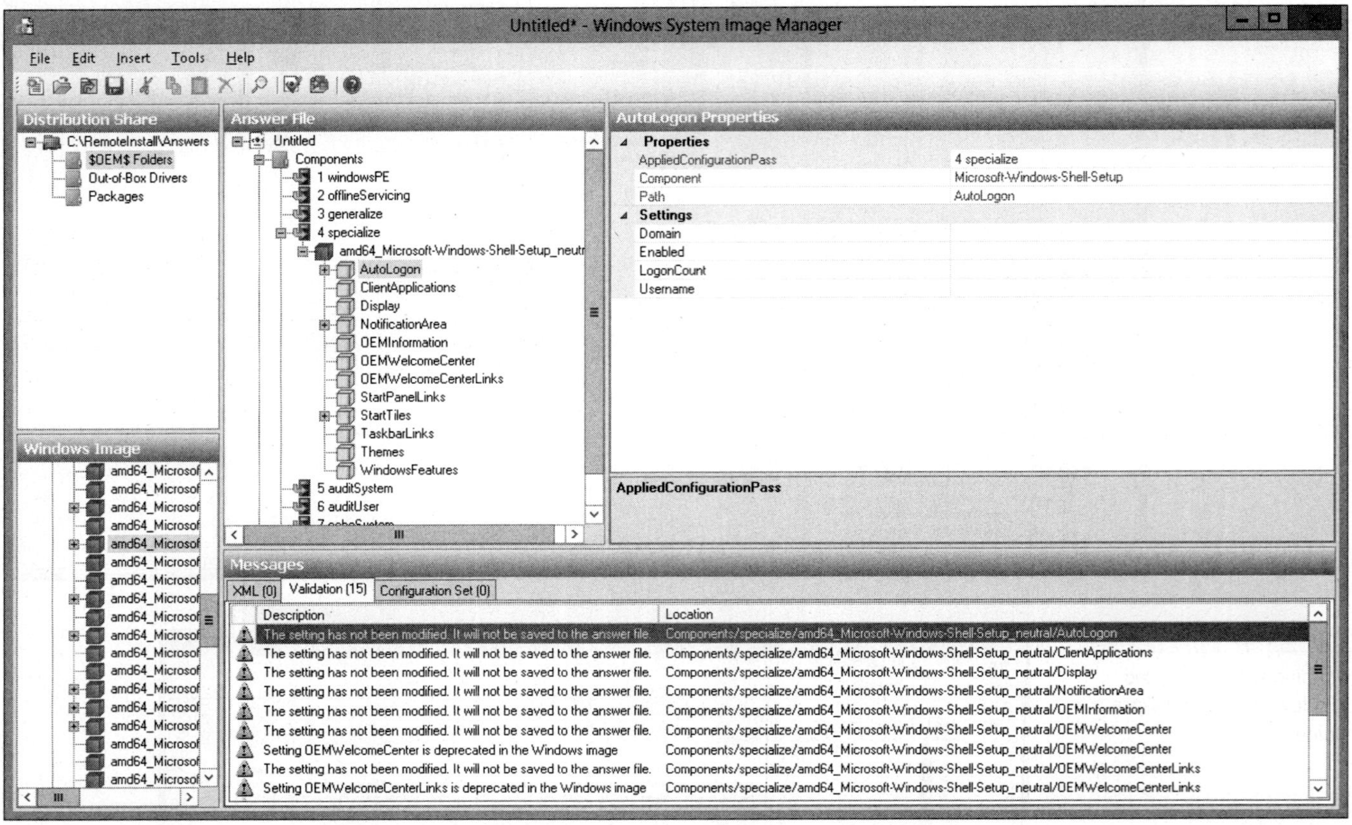

To create a configuration set from the answer file, click *Tools > Create Configuration Set*. This action copies the files to a distribution share, including the answer file (Autounattend.xml). These files are then used to perform an unattended installation. Figure 1-43 shows the Create Configuration Set dialog box.

Figure 1-43

Creating a configuration set

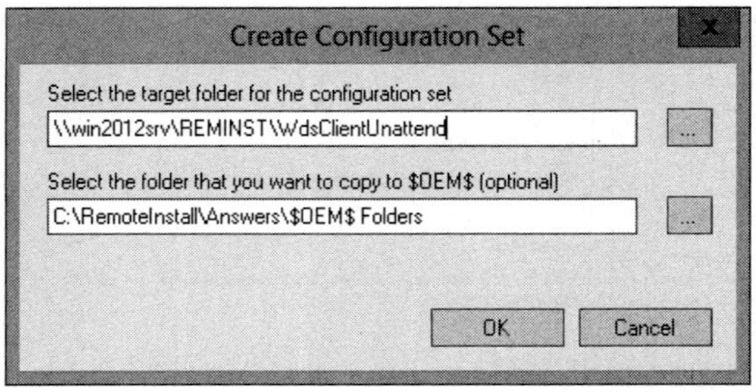

The configuration set could be copied to a removable medium, such as a CD-ROM, a DVD-ROM, or a USB flash drive. To perform an unattended installation, boot the computer from a Windows installation disk. Once the system has begun to boot from the disk, insert the removable medium containing the configuration set. The Windows Setup program automatically scans all of the removable drives on the computer for an answer file. If it finds the answer file, it will use the answer file to perform the installation. If you are performing a network installation using the Windows PE command prompt, you can specify the location of the answer file at the command prompt:

```
setup.exe /unattend:\\server\share\configset
```

By using the standard Windows image files and boot files, you will only be performing a standard operating system installation over the network through the WDS server. Unfortunately, this installation is still a manual installation whereby you have to go through the installation wizard. If you have hundreds of installations, the easiest and quickest way to install all of the computers the same way is to perform an unattended installation, whereby you boot the computer and it automatically starts and completes the installation.

To install an operating system on a client using WDS with no interactivity, you must have the following two unattend files:

- WDS client unattend file: This unattend file automates the WDS client procedure that begins when the client computer loads the boot image file.
- Operating system unattend file: This is an unattend file for a standard operating system installation, containing responses to all of the prompts that display after the client computer loads the install image file.

DEPLOY A SERVER USING AN UNATTEND FILE

GET READY. To deploy a server using an unattended installation, perform the following steps:

1. Open Server Manager.
2. Click Tools > Windows Deployment Services. The Windows Deployment Services console opens.
3. Expand the Servers node.
4. Right-click the node for your server and choose Properties. The server's *Properties* dialog box opens.
5. Click the Client tab.
6. Select the Enable unattended installation checkbox.
7. Click the Browse button corresponding to the processor architecture of the client computer, and then browse to your unattend file. Click Open.
8. Click OK to close the server's *Properties* sheet.
9. Expand the *Install Images* node.
10. Right-click the image for which you want to perform an unattended installation and then choose Properties. The *Image Properties* dialog box opens (see Figure 1-44).

Figure 1-44

Viewing the Image Properties dialog box

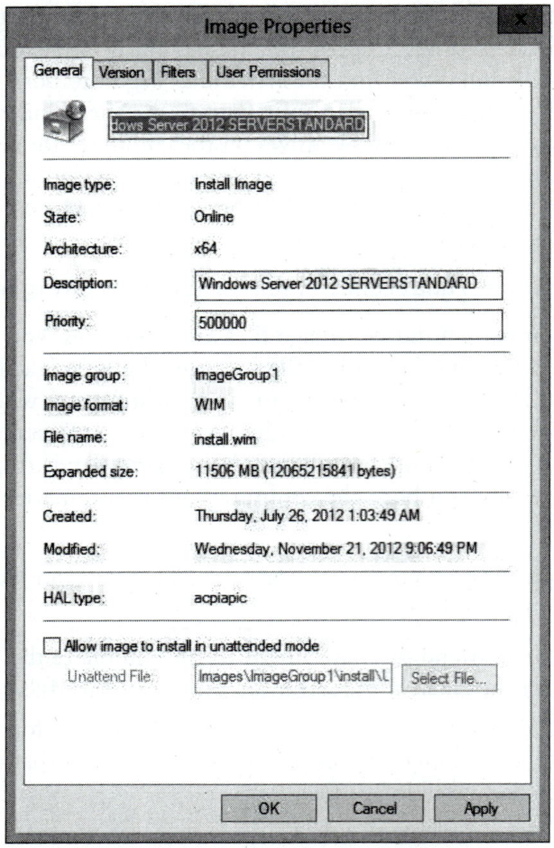

11. Select the *Allow image to install in unattended mode* checkbox.
12. Click Select File. The *Select Unattend File* dialog box opens.
13. Browse to the unattend file you want to use, and then click OK.
14. Click OK to accept your settings and to close the *Image Properties* dialog box.

Updating Images with Patches, Hotfixes, and Drivers

CERTIFICATION READY
Update images with patches, hotfixes, and drivers.
Objective 1.1

When you create an image file, you install Windows on a master computer, update and configure the computer, and then install any applications – all of which can take many hours to get everything just right. When Microsoft releases updates that you want to include in the new image, instead of going through the entire process of creating and setting up a new master computer, you can update the image file using Deployment Image Servicing and Management (Dism.exe).

Deployment Image Servicing and Management (Dism.exe) is a command-line tool that can be used to service a Windows image or to prepare a Windows PE image. With Dism, you can mount an image offline and then add, remove, update, or list the features, packages, drivers, or international settings stored on that image. Dism.exe is not included with Windows.

To make changes to an image, you must mount the Windows image in the Windows file structure using the `Mount-Wim` option. To mount the *D:\RemoteInstall\install.wim* file to the *C:\Offline* folder, use the following command:

```
Dism /Mount-Wim /WimFile: D:\RemoteInstall\install.wim /index:1 /
MountDir:C:\Offline
```

After you make changes to the image, you need to commit the changes by using the /Commit-Wim option:

```
Dism /Commit-Wim /MountDir:C:\Offline
```

To unmount the image, use the /Unmount-Wim option. If you want to commit the changes while you unmount the image, add the /Commit option. To discard the changes, use the /Discard option. For example, to unmount the image mounted to the *C:\Offline folder* while saving the changes, execute the following command:

```
Dism /Unmount-Wim /MountDir:C:\offline /commit
```

To get information about an image or WIM file, use the /Get-WimInfo option. For example, in the previous WIM file, execute the following command:

```
Dism /Get-WimInfo /WimFile:C:\offline\install.wim /index:1
```

Packages are used by Microsoft to distribute software patches, hotfixes, service packs, language packages, and Windows features. If a Windows package is provided as a cabinet (*.cab*) file or as a Windows Update Stand-alone Installer (*.msu*) file, you can add the package using the /Add-Package command. For example, to add the *C:\Update\Update.cab* file, execute the following command:

```
Dism /image:C:\offline /Add-Package /Packagepath:C:\Update\Update.cab
```

To remove a package, use the /Remove-Package option. For example, to remove the *update.cab* file, execute the following command:

```
Dism /image:C:\offline /Remove-Package /PackagePath:C:\Update\Update.cab
```

You can use the /Add-Driver option to add third-party driver packages that include a valid INF file. For example, to add *mydriver* to the Windows image, execute the following command:

```
Dism /image:C:\offline /Add-Driver /driver:C:\Drivers\mydriver.INF
```

If you point to a path and use /Recurse, all subfolders will be checked for valid drivers. For example, to add drivers from the *C:\Drivers* folder, execute the following command:

```
Dism /image:C:\offline /Add-Driver /driver:C:\drivers /recurse
```

To remove a third-party device driver, use the /Remove-Driver option to specify the name of a device driver (such as *oem0.inf*, *oem1.inf*, and so on). For example, to remove the second third-party driver (*oem1.inf*) that has been added to the system, execute the following command:

```
Dism /image:C:\offline /Remove-Driver /driver:oem1.inf
```

Installing Features for Offline Images

Features are a set of Windows programs that can be enabled or disabled by an administrator and are included with Windows. Examples of features include FreeCell, Hearts, Solitaire, FTP Server, World Wide Web Service, and Microsoft .NET Framework 3.5. To add or remove features in Windows Server 2012, you would use Server Manager. To add or remove features in Windows 8, you would use *Control Panel > Programs and Features*. Similarly, you can use Dism.exe to add to or remove features from of offline image.

CERTIFICATION READY
Install features for offline images.
Objective 1.1

Similar to adding or removing packages, you can use Dism.exe to mount an image offline and then use Dism.exe to add, remove, update, or list the Windows feature. For example, to list the features, execute the following command:

```
Dism /image:C:\offline /Get-Features
```

To enable a feature, use the /Enable-Feature option. For example, to install the Hearts game, execute the following command:

```
Dism /image:C:\offline /Enable-Feature /FeatureName:Hearts
```

To remove the Hearts game, use the `/Disable-Features` option. For example, to remove the Hearts game, execute the following command:

```
Dism /Image:C:\offline /Disable-Feature /FeatureName:Hearts
```

`Of course, after you add or remove features, remember to commit the changes with the Dism /Commit-Wim` command that was discussed previously.

Deploying Driver Packages with an Image

Starting with Windows Server 2008 R2, WDS includes ***dynamic driver provisioning***, which allows you to add driver packages to WDS and then deploy them when you deploy an image.

Using dynamic driver provisioning requires the following:

- The boot image from either Windows 7, Windows 8, Windows Server 2008 R2, or Windows Server 2012 (from \Sources\Boot.wim on the DVD).
- The install images for Windows Vista SP1, Windows 7, Windows 8, Windows Server 2008, Windows 7, Windows Server 2008 R2, or Windows Server 2012.

To deploy drivers based on the plug-and-play hardware of the client, you must extract the drives; they cannot be an *.msi* file or an *.exe* file.

CREATE A BOOTABLE ISO IMAGE

GET READY. To add drivers to an image, perform the following steps:

1. Open Server Manager.
2. Click Tools > Windows Deployment Services. The *Windows Deployment Services* console opens.
3. Expand the server node.
4. Right-click the Drivers node and then choose Add Driver Package (see Figure 1-45).

Figure 1-45

Selecting the Add Driver Package option

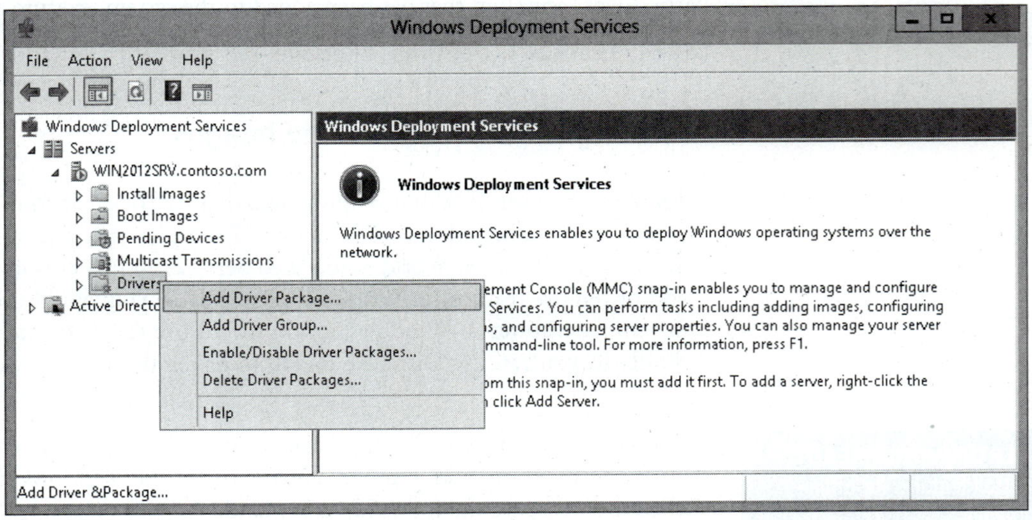

5. On the *Driver Package Location* page, select either the Select driver packages from an .inf file option or the Select all driver packages from a folder option. Specify the location of the .inf file or folder, and then click Next.

6. On the *Available Driver Packages* page, select the drivers that you want to include (see Figure 1-46), and then click Next.

Figure 1-46

Selecting driver packages

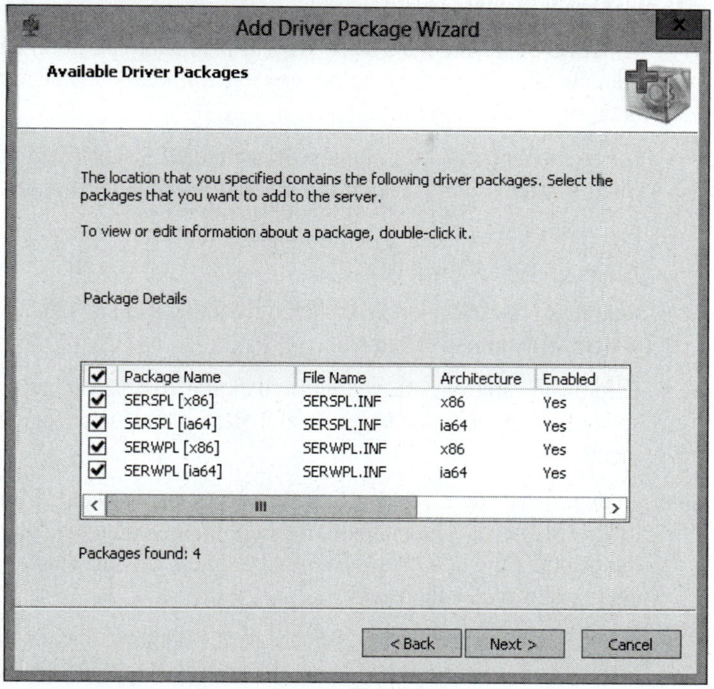

7. On the *Summary* page, click Next.
8. When the tasks are completed, click Next.
9. Select a current driver group or create a new driver group (see Figure 1-47), and then click Next.

Figure 1-47

Selecting a driver group

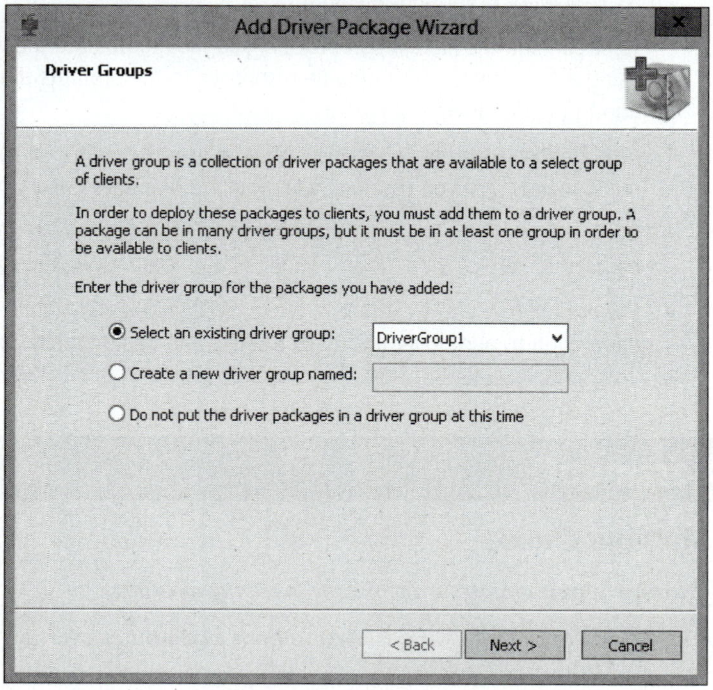

10. On the *Tasks Complete* page, click Finish.

SKILL SUMMARY

IN THIS LESSON, YOU LEARNED:

- Windows Deployment Services (WDS) is a software platform and technology that allows administrators to perform automated network-based installations based on network-based boot and installation media.
- For client computers to communicate with a WDS server without an operating system, the client computer must support the preboot execution environment (PXE).
- PXE (pronounced "pixie") is a technology that boots computers using the network interface without a data storage device, such as a hard drive or an installed operating system.
- Windows Preinstallation Environment (Windows PE) is a minimal Windows operating system with limited services.
- Before you can use WDS, you must configure WDS server, including performing the initial server configuration, adding a default startup and install images, and configuring a boot menu.
- To deploy Windows, you must create two types of images: a boot image and an install image. Just as its name implies, the boot image boots the computer. In addition, the boot image starts the operating system installation. The install image contains the operating system that WDS will install.
- The boot images and install images use the Windows Imaging Format (WIM). While the architecture is file-based, the files are actually stored inside a single WIM database.
- The Microsoft's System Preparation Utility (Sysprep.exe) prepares a Windows computer for cloning by removing specific computer information such as the computer name and Security Identifier (SID).
- If you have a computer that does not support a PXE boot, you can boot the computer from a disk using a discover image. A discover image is an image file that you can burn to a CD-ROM or other boot medium.
- To streamline the installation process, you must automate the Windows installation by using answer files, which provide responses to the prompts that would normally display during the Windows installation.
- Although you can create an answer file with a text editor or XML editor, Microsoft recommends that you use the System Image Manager (SIM) to generate the answer file.
- Deployment Image Servicing and Management (Dism.exe) is a command-line tool that can be used to service a Windows image or to prepare a Windows PE image.
- Starting with Windows Server 2008 R2, WDS includes dynamic driver provisioning, which allows you to add driver packages to WDS and deploy them when you deploy an image.

Knowledge Assessment

Multiple Choice

Select the correct answer for each of the following questions.

1. Which of the following is used to boot a computer over the network?
   a. Multicast Transmitter
   b. System Preparation Utility
   c. PXE
   d. Answer File

2. Which of the following is used to load a minimum version of Windows to troubleshooting and installation?
   a. PXE
   b. Windows PE
   c. System Preparation Utility
   d. WDS Server
3. Which two roles are available in WDS? (Choose two answers.)
   a. Deployment server
   b. Boot Server
   c. File Archive Server
   d. Transport Server
4. Which of the following are necessary for deploying WDS? (Choose all that apply.)
   a. AD DS
   b. FAT32 or NTFS
   c. DHCP
   d. DNS
5. The answer file is made as a(n) _____ file.
   a. XLS
   b. SIM
   c. XML
   d. RTF
6. Which of the following allows you to package drivers together and deploy them with images?
   a. DISM
   b. SIM
   c. PXE
   d. Dynamic Driver Provisioning
7. Which command allows you to modify an offline image?
   a. DISM
   b. SIM
   c. PXE
   d. Dynamic Driver Provisioning
8. Which program is used to remove the computer name and SID from a computer?
   a. PXE
   b. Windows PE
   c. System Preparation Utility
   d. WDS Server
9. Which of the following is the filename extension for install images and boot images?
   a. WIM
   b. FTP
   c. TIP
   d. XML
10. Which of the following is used to convert a master computer to an image file?
   a. Deployment Image Servicing and Managing utility
   b. Discover Utility
   c. System Preparation utility
   d. Windows Deployment Service Capture utility

Best Answer

Choose the letter that corresponds to the best answer. More than one answer choice may achieve the goal. Select the BEST answer.

1. You are an administrator of several regional offices. You install WDS on *Server1* and create three images for each regional office. You want to deploy the images using WDS, but you want to ensure that the administrator for each regional office can view only the images for his or her regional office. Which of the following actions should you perform?
   a. Grant each administrator administrative permissions to the images assigned to the regional office.
   b. Create an OU for each regional office and place the computers in the appropriate regional OU.
   c. Place the images for each regional office into a separate image group on the WDS server. Then grant each administrator permission to his or her regional office's image group.
   d. Add all images to an image group and assign administrator permissions to the image group.
2. Which of the following is used to convert a discover image to an ISO file?
   a. oscdimg.exe
   b. sim.exe
   c. oobe.exe
   d. sysprep.exe
3. Which term best describes computers that have computer accounts created in Active Directory before the installation is completed with WDS?
   a. dynamic computers
   b. sysprep computers
   c. MAC-defined computers
   d. prestaged computers
4. You are preparing 30 computers for classroom instruction. Which of the following is the quickest way to redeploy all 30 computers?
   a. Use WDS to deploy each computer at a time.
   b. Use WDS to deploy all of the computers at once while using unicast transmissions.
   c. Use WDS to deploy all of the computers while using multicasting.
   d. Use TFTP to copy the image to each computer manually.
5. You are administering a computer that does not support PXE boot. Which action should be taken to start the computer and install an image using WDS?
   a. Use a boot image.
   b. Use an install image.
   c. Use a discover image.
   d. Boot with a DOS floppy disk.
6. Which of the following ports is used by a DHCP client to contact a DHCP server?
   a. 23
   b. 67
   c. 341
   d. 387

Matching and Identification

1. Match the configuration pass with its respective function when creating an answer file with Windows SIM.

_______ a) `Specialize`
_______ b) `Windows PE`
_______ c) `Generalize`
_______ d) `OobeSystem`
_______ e) `OfflineServicing`

1. Includes initial boot options including specifying the product and key and configuring a disk
2. Applies updates using DISM.exe
3. Applies settings to Windows before the Windows Welcome starts
4. Configures network settings and join a computer to a domain
5. Removes the system-specific information, such as computer name and security ID

2. Write the DISM command that is used to perform each respective function.

_________ a) Remove a package.
_________ b) Mount a WIM image.
_________ c) Add a driver.
_________ d) Commit the changes to the image.
_________ e) Unmounts a WIM image.

Build a List

1. Specify the correct order in which to prepare a WDS server to deploy Windows to multiple computers. (Not all steps will be used.)

_____ Install an image to a DVD image.
_____ Add an image file.
_____ Create an WDS Client unattend file.
_____ Run DISM to deploy the image.
_____ Add a boot image.
_____ Create a system unattend file.
_____ Boot the computer using a PXE boot.

2. Specify the correct order in which to create an image file.

_____ Run the `sysprep` command.
_____ Boot the master computer with the modified boot image.
_____ Use the WDS Capture Utility.
_____ Install all Windows patches, applications, and drivers.
_____ Install Windows.
_____ Modify a boot image.

Business Case Scenarios

Scenario 1-1: Deploying Servers Using WDS

Your organization decides to build a second data center to be used as a backup site. You need to deploy roughly 150 servers. What steps will you need to take to deploy 150 servers at the new data center?

Scenario 1-2: Adding a Service Pack to WDS Install Image

Several months ago, you deployed a WDS server to deploy computers running Windows 2012. Service Pack 2 was just released and you need to add Service Pack 2 to your image so that future installations will automatically have the service pack. What steps will you need to take to make this happen?

2 LESSON

Implementing Patch Management

70-411 EXAM OBJECTIVE

Objective 1.2 – Implement patch management. This objective may include but is not limited to: install and configure the Windows Server Update Services (WSUS) role; configure group policies for updates; configure client-side targeting; configure WSUS synchronization; configure WSUS groups.

Lesson Heading	Exam Objective
Understanding Windows Updates and Automatic Updates	
Deploying Windows Server Update Services (WSUS)	Implement patch management
Installing WSUS	Install and configure the Windows Server Update Services (WSUS) role
Configuring WSUS	Install and configure the Windows Server Update Services (WSUS) role Configure WSUS synchronization Configure WSUS groups Configure group policies for updates Configure client-side targeting
Approving Updates	
Viewing Reports	
Administrating WSUS with Commands	
Troubleshooting Problems with Installing Updates	
Understanding System Center Configuration Manager (SCCM)	

KEY TERMS

Automatic Update
autonomous mode
client-side targeting
computer groups
critical update
cumulative patch
hotfix
out-of-band patches
out-of-band updates
Patch Tuesday
replica mode
security update
server-side targeting
service pack
System Center Configuration Manager (SCCM)
Windows Server Update Services (WSUS)
Windows Update

Take Note*

Now that you know how to install Windows using various methods, you need to know how to update Windows. Coming into this lesson, you already know how to update a Windows using the Control Panel's Windows Update. Updating Windows 8 and Windows Server 2012 is the same as updating Windows 7 and Windows Server 2008.

Understanding Windows Updates and Automatic Updates

THE BOTTOM LINE

Windows is a complicated system with many components and files. To keep Windows reliable and secure, you must check whether Microsoft has released any Windows updates, including fixes, patches, service packs, and updated device drivers. If updates are available, you should apply them to your Windows system. By adding fixes and patches, you'll keep Windows stable and secure.

One way to keep Windows up to date is to use the ***Windows Update*** program, which scans your system to determine the updates and fixes your system needs. You then have the opportunity to select, download, and install each update.

Administrators of corporate networks can also use Windows Server Update Services (WSUS) or System Center Configuration Manager (SCCM)—each covered in more detail later in this lesson—to keep your systems updated. The advantage of using one of these systems is that it allows you to test the patch, schedule updates, and prioritize client updates. Once you determine a patch is safe, you can enable the patch for deployment.

Microsoft routinely releases security updates on the second Tuesday of each month, commonly known as ***Patch Tuesday***. While most updates are released on Patch Tuesday, there might be occasional patches (known as ***out-of-band patches***) released at other times when the patches are deemed critical or time-sensitive.

Most other updates are released as needed; these are known as ***out-of-band updates***. Because computers are often used as production systems, you should test any updates to make sure they do not cause problems for you. Although Microsoft performs intensive testing, occasionally problems do occur, either as a bug or as a compatibility issue with third-party software. Therefore, always be sure you have a good backup of your system and data files before you install patches so that you have a back-out plan if necessary.

Microsoft classifies updates as Important, Recommended, or Optional:

- **Important updates:** These updates offer significant benefits, such as improved security, privacy, and reliability. They should be installed as they become available and can be installed automatically with Windows Update.
- **Recommended updates:** These updates address noncritical problems or help enhance your computing experience. Although these updates do not address fundamental issues with your computer or Windows software, they can offer meaningful improvements.
- **Optional updates:** These include updates, drivers, or new software from Microsoft to enhance your computing experience. You need to install these manually.

Depending on the type of update, Windows Update can deliver the following:

- **Security updates:** A ***security update*** is a broadly released fix for a product-specific, security-related vulnerability. Security vulnerabilities are rated based on their severity, which is indicated in the Microsoft security bulletin as critical, important, moderate, or low.
- **Critical updates:** A ***critical update*** is a broadly released fix for a specific problem addressing a critical, non-security related bug.

- **Service packs:** A ***service pack*** is a tested, cumulative set of hotfixes, security updates, critical updates, and updates, as well as additional fixes for problems found internally since the release of the product. Service packs might also contain a limited number of customer-requested design changes or features. After an operating system is released, many corporations consider the first service pack as the time when the operating system has matured enough to be used throughout the organization.

Not all updates can be retrieved through Windows Update. Sometimes, Microsoft might offer the fix for a specific problem in the form of a hotfix or cumulative patch that you can install. A ***hotfix*** is a single, cumulative package that includes one or more files that are used to address a problem in a software product, such as a software bug. Typically, hotfixes are made to address a specific customer situation, and they often have not gone through the same extensive testing as patches retrieved through Windows Updates. A ***cumulative patch*** is multiple hotfixes combined into a single package.

For small environments, you can configure your system to run ***Automatic Updates*** to ensure that critical updates, security updates, and compatibility updates are made available for installation automatically without significantly affecting your regular use of the Internet. Auto Update works in the background when you are connected to the Internet to identify when new updates are available and to download them to your computer. When Automatic Updates are downloaded in the background, the download is using Background Intelligent Transfer Service (BITS), which performs the download when the computer's network bandwidth is idle. When a download is complete, you are notified and prompted to install the update. At this point, you can install the update, get more details about what is included in the update, or let Windows remind you about the update at a later time. Some updates require you to reboot, but some do not.

UPDATE WINDOWS SERVER 2012

GET READY. To update Windows 2012, perform the following steps:

1. Click Start > Control Panel.
2. If you are in *Category* view, click System and Security > Windows Update. If you are in *Icon* view, double-click Windows Update. The *Windows Update* page opens (see Figure 2-1).

Figure 2-1

Checking for updates

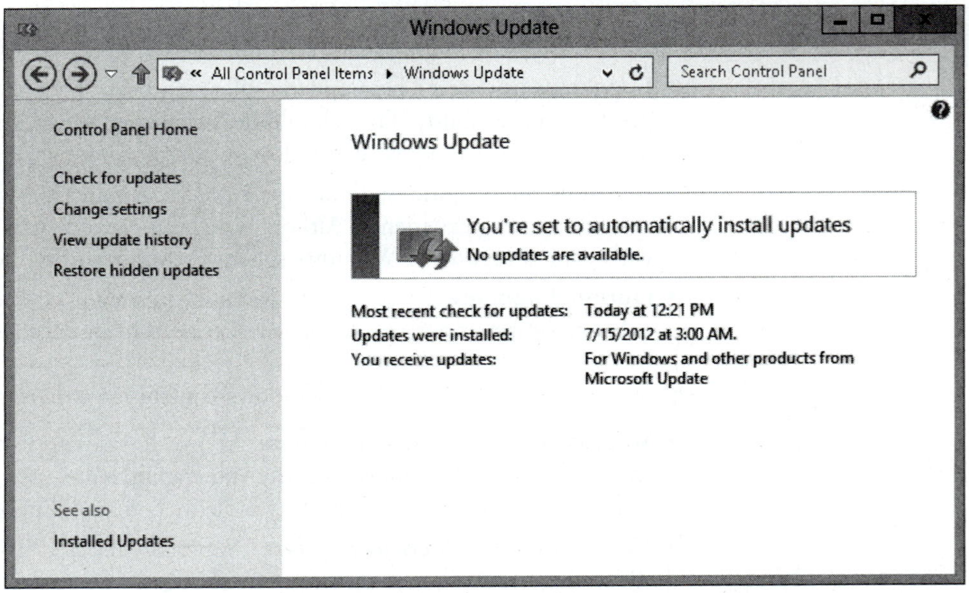

3. In the left pane, click Check for updates.
4. To view a list of updates, click the xx important updates are available link or the xx optional updates are available link. On the *Select the updates you want to install* page, select the updates that you want to install and deselect the updates you don't want to install. Click OK.
5. To download and install the updates, click Install updates.
6. When the installation is done, click Close. Note that depending on which updates are installed, you might be prompted to reboot the computer.

To change your Windows Update settings, click the *Change settings* option in the left pane of the Windows Update window. On the Change settings page (see Figure 2-2), you can specify which types of updates you want to download and install automatically or you can disable Windows Update all together. You can also specify whether Windows Update will check for updates for other Microsoft products and/or install any other software Microsoft recommends.

Figure 2-2

Changing Windows Update settings

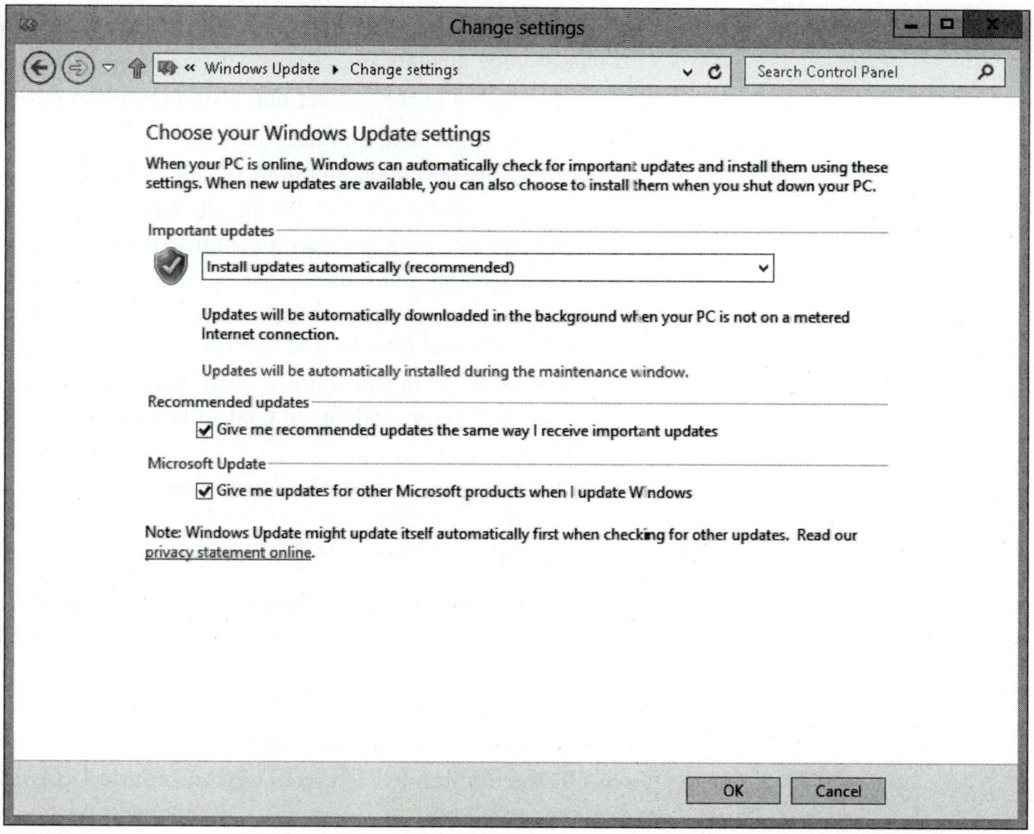

If Windows Update fails to retrieve any updates, you should check your proxy settings in Internet Explorer to see whether the program can get through your proxy server (if any) or firewall. You should also make sure that you can access the Internet, such as by going to the Microsoft website.

To see all updates that have been installed, click View update history on the main screen of Windows Update. If you suspect a problem with a specific update, you can then click Installed Updates at the top of the screen to open the Control Panel's programs. From there, you will see all installed programs and updates. If the option is available, you can then remove the update.

As with most Windows components, you can also use group policies to automatically configure how Automatic Updates behaves. For example, you can configure for updates to be automatically downloaded and installed or you can configure the user to be notified when updates are available.

CONFIGURE AUTOMATIC UPDATES USING GROUP POLICIES

GET READY. To configure Automatic Updates using group policies, perform the following steps on a domain controller or any computer that has Group Policy Management console:

1. Open Server Manager.
2. Click Tools > Group Policy Management.
3. Using the *Group Management* console, open Group Policy Object Editor for a group policy.
4. In *Group Policy Object Editor*, expand Computer Configuration, expand Policies, expand Administrative Templates, expand Windows Components, and then click Windows Update.
5. In the details pane, click Configure Automatic Updates. The *Configure Automatic Updates* page appears.
6. Click Enabled, and then select one of the following options:
   - Notify for download and notify for install: Notifies a logged-on administrative user prior to the download and prior to the installation of the updates.
   - Auto download and notify for install: Automatically begins downloading updates and then notifies a logged-on administrative user prior to installing the updates.
   - Auto download and schedule the install: Automatically downloads the updates and allows you to schedule when to perform the installation. If selected, you must also set the day and time for the recurring scheduled installation.
   - Allow local admin to choose setting: Specifies that local administrators are allowed to use Automatic Updates in Control Panel to select a configuration option of their choice.
7. Click OK to change your options and close *Configure Automatic Updates* page.

Other settings worth noting include the following:

- **Automatic Update Detection Frequency:** Specifies how frequently the Windows Update client checks for new updates. The default is a random time between 17 and 22 hours.
- **Allow Automatic Updates Immediate Installation:** Specifies whether Windows Updates will immediately install updates that don't require the computer to be restarted.
- **Turn On Recommended Updates Via Automatic Updates:** Determines whether client computers install both critical and recommended updates.
- **No Auto-Restart for Scheduled Automatic Installations:** Specifies that if a computer needs a restart, it will wait for a user to perform the restart.
- **Re-Prompt for Restart Scheduled Installations:** Specifies how often the Windows Update client prompts the user to restart the computer.
- **Delay Restart for Scheduled Installations:** Specifies how long the Windows Update client waits before automatically restarting.
- **Reschedule Automatic Updates Scheduled Installations:** Specifies how long Windows Update waits after a reboot before continuing with a scheduled installation that was missed previously.
- **Enable Client-Side Targeting:** Specifies which group the computer is a member of.

- **Enables Windows Update Power Management to Automatically Wake up the System to Install Scheduled Updates:** If a computer supports Wake On LAN, it automatically starts up and installs an update at the scheduled time.
- **Allow Signed Updates from an Intranet Microsoft Update Services Location:** Specifies if Windows will install an update that is signed even if the certificate is not from Microsoft.

Deploying Windows Server Update Services (WSUS)

THE BOTTOM LINE

Using Windows Update is sufficient for updating one or two computers. However, an organization that needs to update hundreds of computers can present a daunting challenge for administrators. First, hundreds of computers downloading updates can affect network performance. Second, because an update can cause unforeseen problems, it is better to have the patch or update tested before it is applied. Windows Server Update Services (WSUS) provides a solution to these problems.

CERTIFICATION READY
Implement patch management.
Objective 1.2

Windows Server Update Services (WSUS) is a program that is included with today's Windows Servers that allows administrators to manage the distribution of updates and other patches to computers within an organization. In the simplest configuration, which is ideal for a single site with a few hundred computers, you have a single WSUS that downloads updates directly from Microsoft. Then the client computers get updates from the WSUS server. Figure 2-3 shows a simple WSUS configuration.

Figure 2-3
A simple WSUS configuration

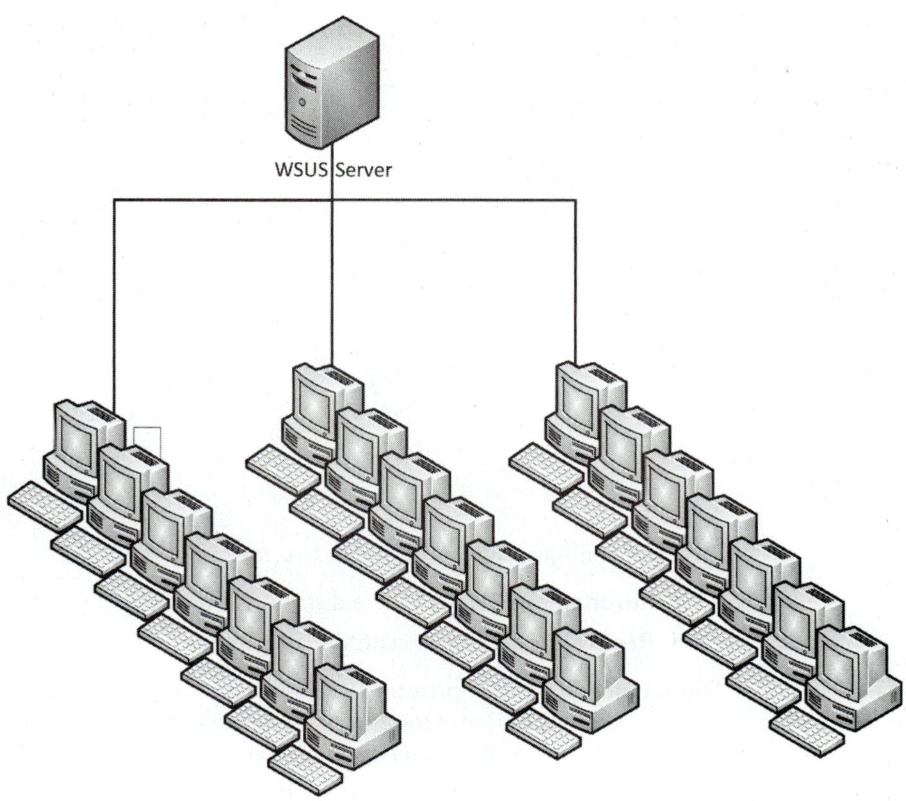

If you administer more than a few hundred computers or you administer multiple sites, you can create a hierarchy of WSUS servers (see Figure 2-4). The number of WSUS servers will be determined by the number of sites, the speed and load of the links between sites, and the number of clients that you must support.

WSUS can retrieve updates directly from Microsoft Update or from another WSUS server on your network. If you have two WSUS servers connected with a high-speed link, one server can get the updates from the Microsoft Update while the other gets from the first server. If you have multiple sites that are linked together through a VPN, you can place a WSUS server at each site and have each WSUS server get the updates from Microsoft Update.

Figure 2-4

The WSUS hierarchy

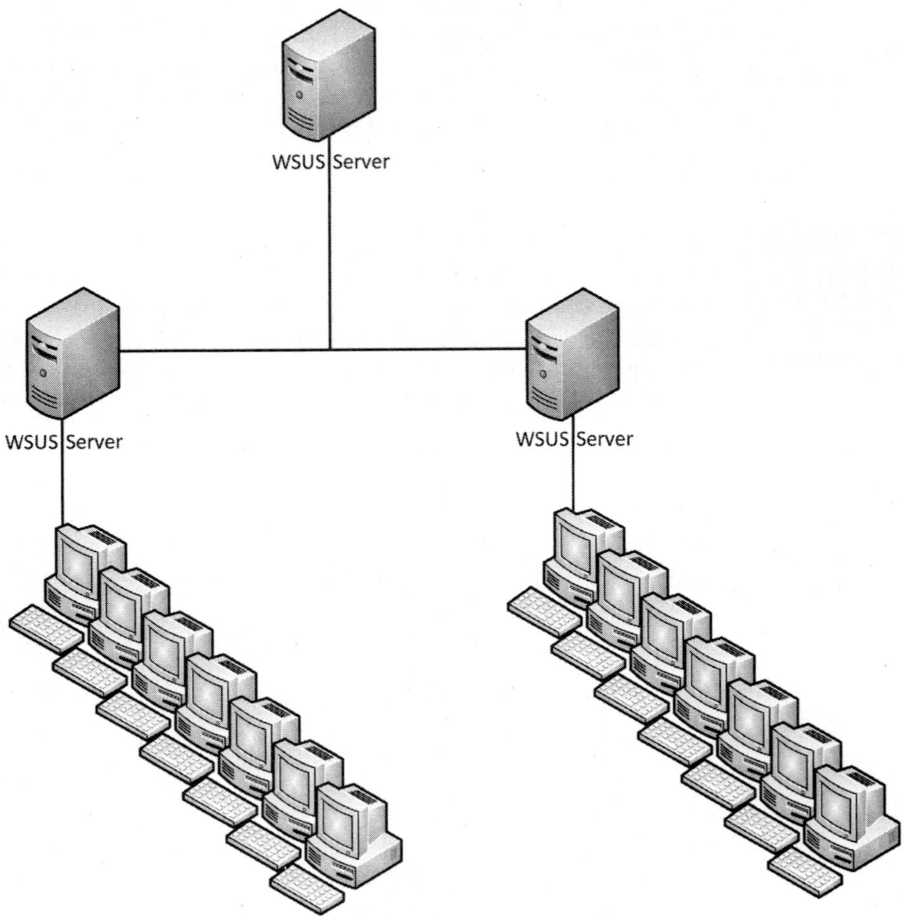

You can configure WSUS in one of two modes:

- **Autonomous mode:** Offers distributed management
- **Replica mode:** Offers central management

Both modes have the upstream WSUS servers share updates with the downstream servers during synchronization. However, with ***autonomous mode***, approval of updates is done on each WSUS server. With ***replica mode***, you approve the updates on the upstream server and those approvals are replicated to the downstream servers.

Installing WSUS

WSUS has been part of the Windows Server operating systems for quite some time. To install WSUS on Windows Server 2012, you must install WSUS as a role.

CERTIFICATION READY
Install and configure the Windows Server Update Services (WSUS) role.
Objective 1.2

As with most network services, you should perform a little bit of planning before deploying WSUS. To implement WSUS, the minimum hardware and software requirements for WSUS 3.0 SP2 are as follows:

- Windows Server 2012, Windows Server 2008 R2, Windows Server 2008 Service Pack 1 (SP1) or newer, Windows Server 2003 SP1 or newer, Windows Small Business Server 2008, or Windows Small Business Server 2003
- Internet Information Services (IIS) 6.0 or newer
- Microsoft .NET Framework 2.0 or newer
- Microsoft Management Console (MMC) 3.0
- Microsoft Report Viewer Redistributable 2008 or later
- SQL Server 2012, SQL Server 2008, SQL Server 2005 SP2, or Windows Internal Database
- A WSUS server requires about 10 gigabytes (GB) of disk space for WSUS to run and 2 GB minimum to store the database. You will also need at least 30 GB to store the updates locally; however, depending on how many updates you need to store, you will most likely need much more.

A single WSUS server can support thousands of clients. A single WSUS server with 4 GB of RAM and dual quad-core processor can support up to 100,000 clients. However, most organizations of that size will have multiple WSUS servers to reduce the load on wide area network (WAN) links.

Lastly, the WSUS server or servers will need to communicate with Microsoft Update. Therefore, if you are having problems communicating with Microsoft Update, you might need to check the firewalls of an organization.

INSTALL WSUS

GET READY. To install WSUS on Windows Server 2012, perform the following steps:

1. On the C drive, create an Updates folder.
2. Open Server Manager.
3. At the top of *Server Manager*, click Manage > Add Roles and Features. The *Add Roles and Feature Wizard* appears.
4. On the *Before you begin* page, click Next.
5. Select Role-based or feature-based installation and then click Next.
6. Click Select a server from the server pool, click the name of the server to install WSUS to, and then click Next.
7. Scroll down and select Windows Server Update Services (see Figure 2-5).

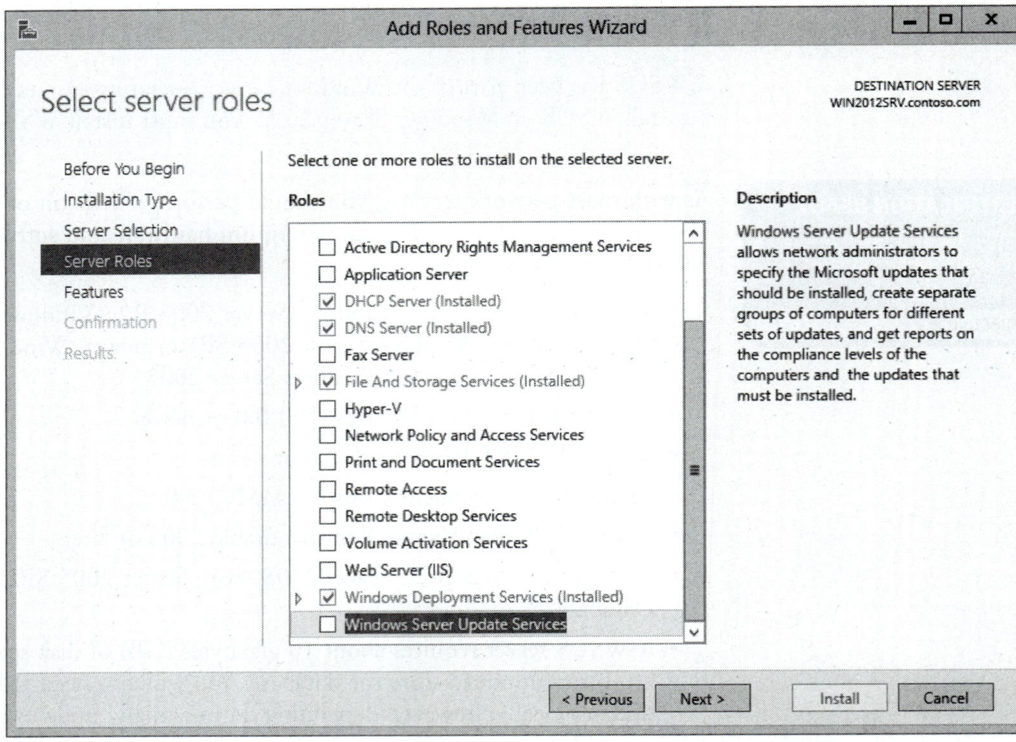

Figure 2-5

Selecting Windows Server Update Services

8. When the *Add Roles and Features Wizard* opens (see Figure 2-6), click Add Features.

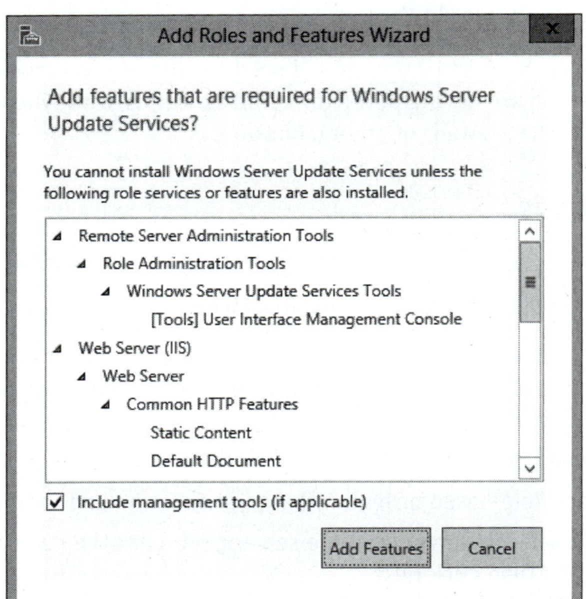

Figure 2-6

Adding features

9. Back on the *Select server roles* screen, click Next.
10. On the *Select features* page, click Next.
11. On the *Windows Server Update Services* page, click Next.
12. By default, the WID database and WSUS Services are selected (see Figure 2-7).

Figure 2-7

Selecting the database type

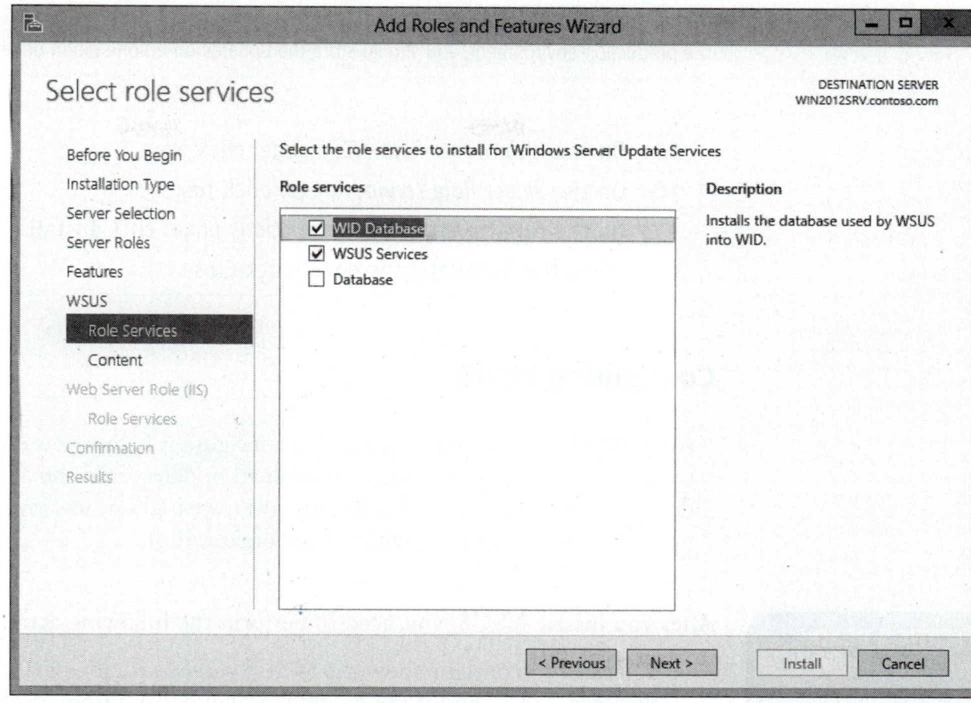

13. Click Next.

MORE INFORMATION

WID is short for Windows Internal Database. If you want to use a dedicated SQL server, deselect WID Database and select Database.

14. On the *Current Location* selection, type C:\Updates (see Figure 2-8), and then click Next.

Figure 2-8

Specifying the content location

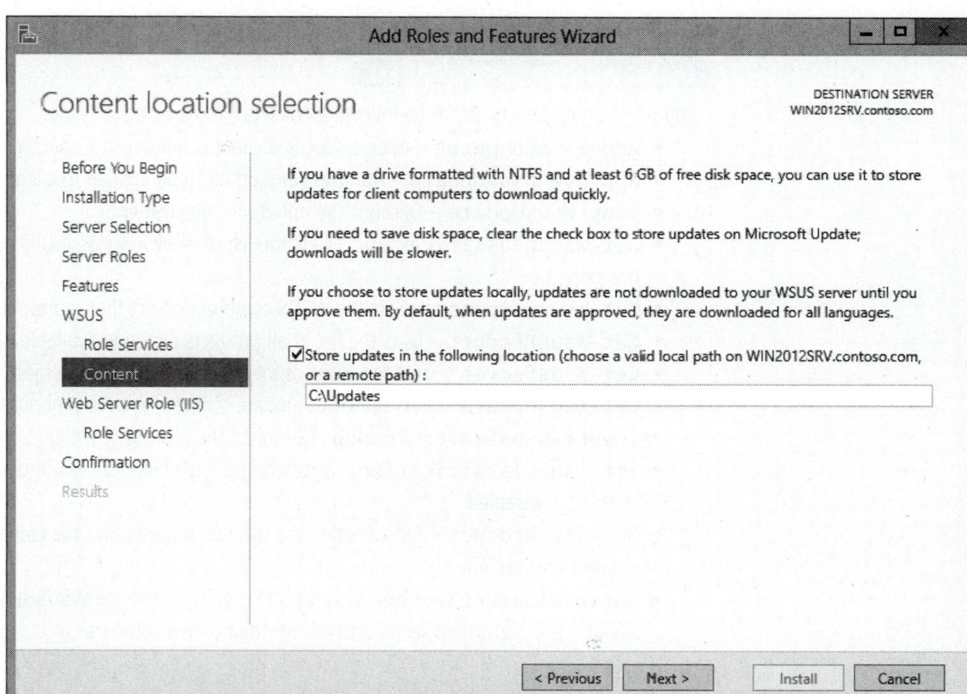

MORE INFORMATION
In a production environment, you should store the updates on a non-system drive.

15. On the *Web Server Role (IIS)* page, click Next.
16. On the *Select Role services* page, click Next.
17. On the *Confirm installation selections* page, click Install.
18. When the installation is done, click Close.

Configuring WSUS

After WSUS is installed, you need to configure it before you can use it. First, the WSUS server needs to be configured to download updates from the Microsoft Update site, download the updates, and configure groups based on how you want to deploy the updates to the computers within your organization.

CERTIFICATION READY
Install and configure the Windows Server Update Services (WSUS) role.
Objective 1.2

After you install WSUS, you need to perform the following actions:

- You need to configure how the WSUS server will download updates, what updates will be downloaded, and if the downloads will occur automatically or manually. You also must determine what updates need to be downloaded.
- You then need to organize the client computers into computers groups in a way that you deploy the updates into phases, starting with a test group and eventually deploying the updates to all of the computers.
- You need to configure the clients to use the WSUS using group policies.
- You need to approve the updates for deployment.
- You need to review the update status of the computers and generate reports as necessary.

The primary tool to manage WSUS is the Update Services console.

USING WINDOWS POWERSHELL

You can manage WSUS using the following cmdlets:

- `Add-WsusComputer` – Adds a specified client computer to a specified target group.
- `Approve-WsusUpdate` – Approves an update to be applied to clients.
- `Deny-WsusUpdate` – Declines the update for deployment.
- `Get-WsusClassification` – Gets the list of all WSUS classifications currently available in the system.
- `Get-WsusComputer` – Gets the WSUS computer object that represents the client computer.
- `Get-WsusProduct` – Gets the list of all products currently available on WSUS by category.
- `Get-WsusServer` – Gets the value of the WSUS update server object.
- `Get-WsusUpdate` – Gets the WSUS update object with details about the update.
- `Invoke-WsusServerCleanup` – Performs the process of cleanup on a specified WSUS server.
- `Set-WsusClassification` – Sets whether the classifications of updates that WSUS synchronizes are enabled or disabled.
- `Set-WsusProduct` – Sets whether the product representing the category of updates to synchronize is enabled or disabled.
- `Set-WsusServerSynchronization` – Sets whether the WSUS server synchronizes from Microsoft Update or an upstream server and the upstream server properties.

INITIAL CONFIGURATION OF WSUS USING THE UPDATE SERVICES CONSOLE

GET READY. To initially configure WSUS using the Update Services console, perform the following steps:

1. Open Server Manager.
2. At the top of *Server Manager*, click Tools > Windows Server Update Services.
3. When the *Complete WSUS Installation* dialog box opens (see Figure 2-9), click Run.

Figure 2-9

Running the WSUS installation

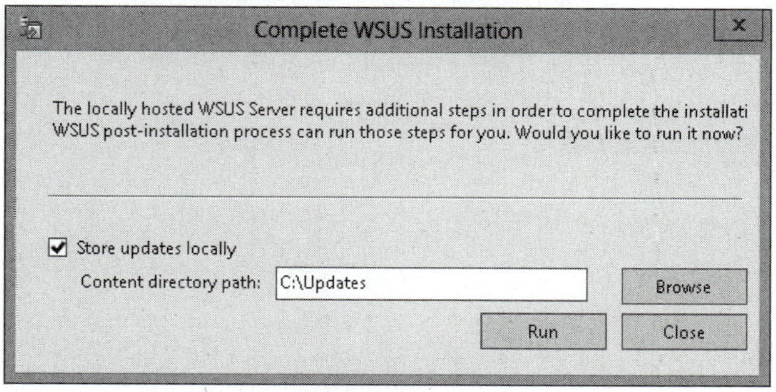

4. When the post-installation successfully is completed, click Close.
5. When the *Before You Begin* page opens, click Next.
6. On the *Join the Microsoft Update Improvement Program* page, click Next.
7. The *Choose Upstream Server* page appears. If you want to synchronize with another WSUS server, select the Synchronize from another Windows Server Update Services server option. Then specify the name of the server and the port (the default port is 8530). To synchronize the updates from Microsoft Update, leave the Synchronize from Microsoft Update option selected (see Figure 2-10), and then click Next.

Figure 2-10

Choosing an upstream server

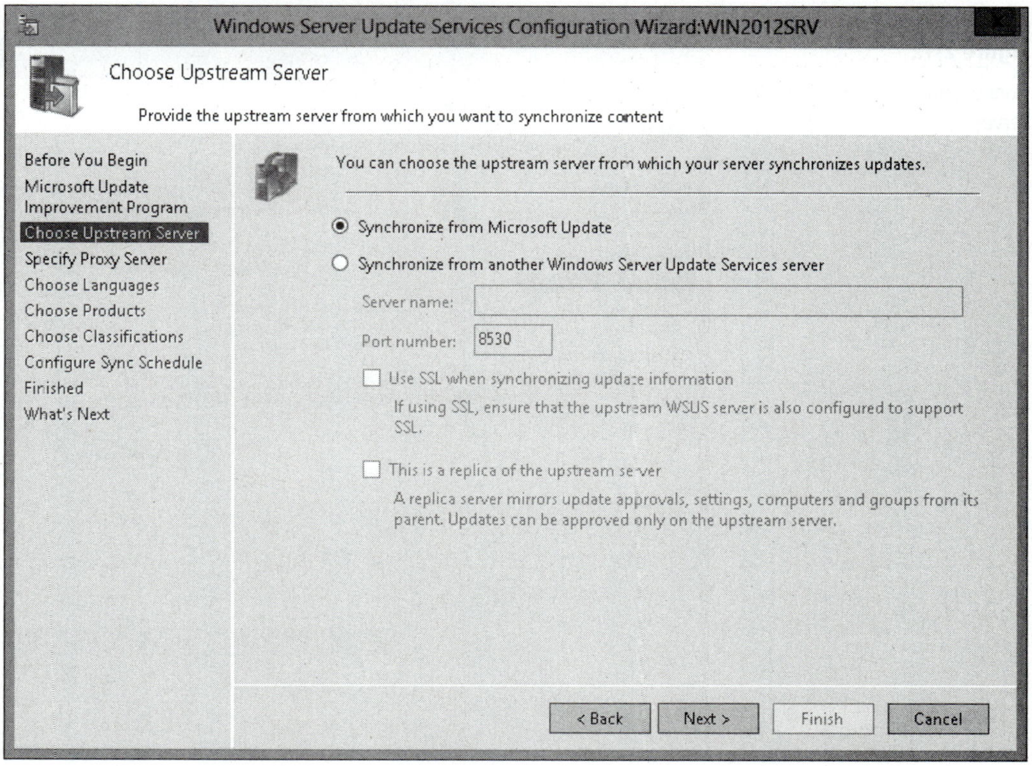

8. The *Specify Proxy Server* page appears (see Figure 2-11). If your organization is using a proxy server to access the Internet, select the Use a proxy server when synchronizing option. Then specify the Proxy server name, Port number, and the various credentials necessary to accessing the proxy server. Click Next.

Figure 2-11

Using the Specify Proxy Server page

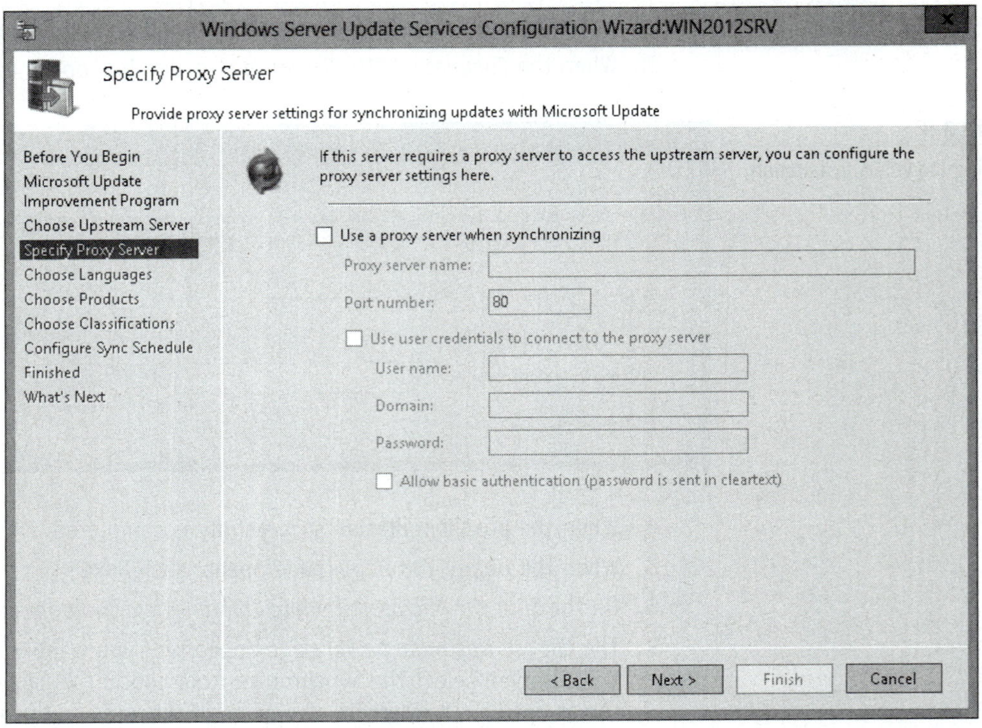

9. On the *Connect to Upstream Server* page (see Figure 2-12), click Start Connecting. This might take some time to complete.

Figure 2-12

Connecting to an upstream server

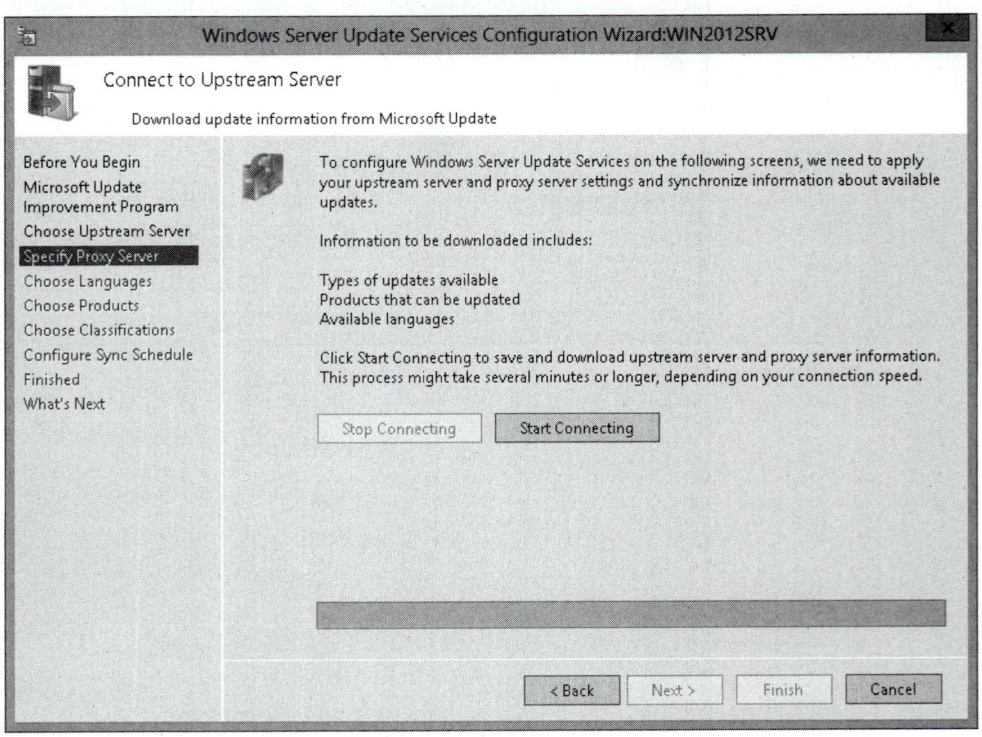

10. When the connection is complete, click Next.
11. On the *Choose Languages* page (see Figure 2-13), select the languages that you need to support, and then click Next.

Figure 2-13

Selecting languages

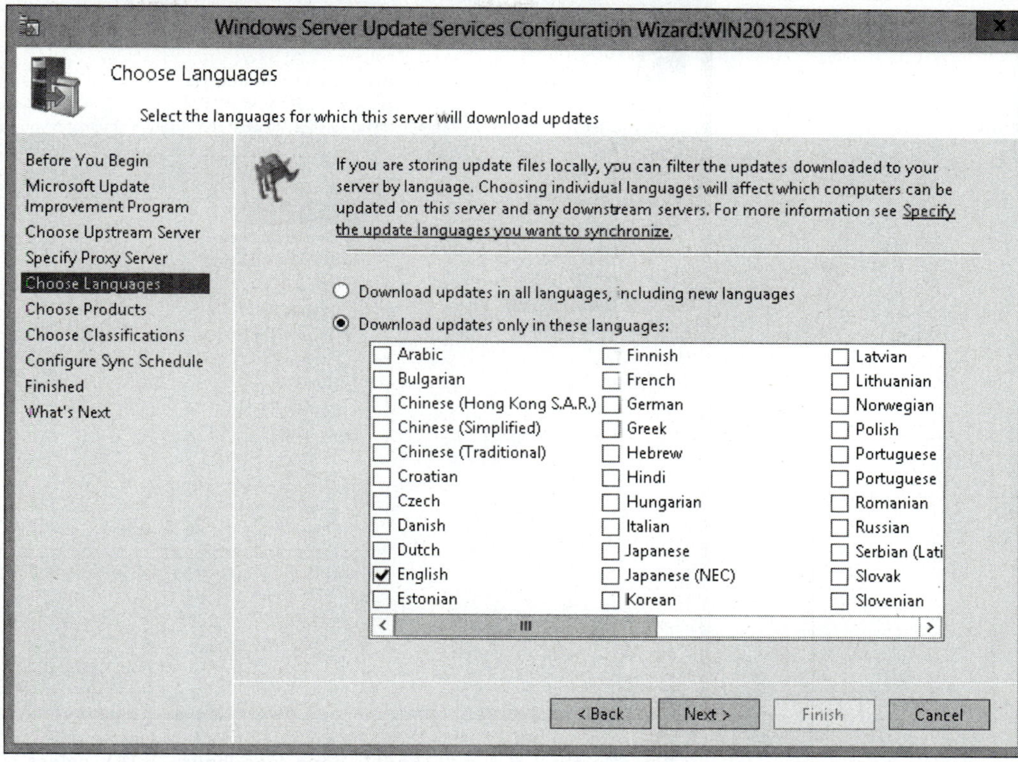

12. On the *Choose Products* page (see Figure 2-14), select the products that you want to download the updates for, and then click Next.

Figure 2-14

Selecting products

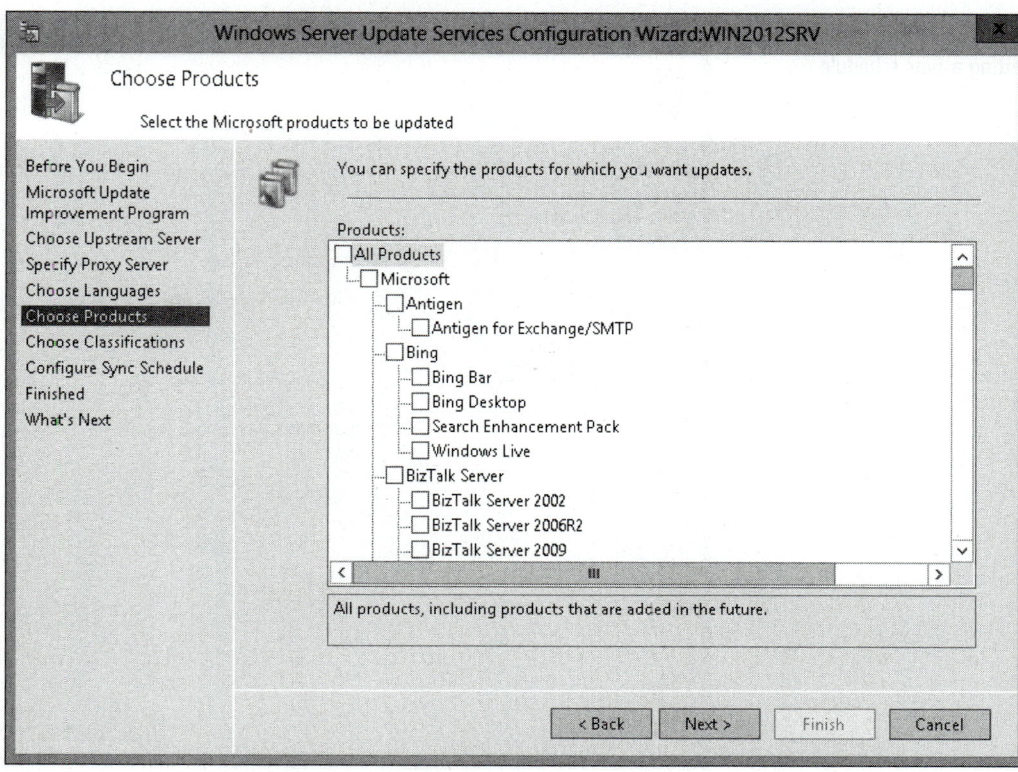

13. On the *Choose Classifications* page (see Figure 2-15), select the classifications that you want to download and then click **Next**.

Figure 2-15

Selecting classifications

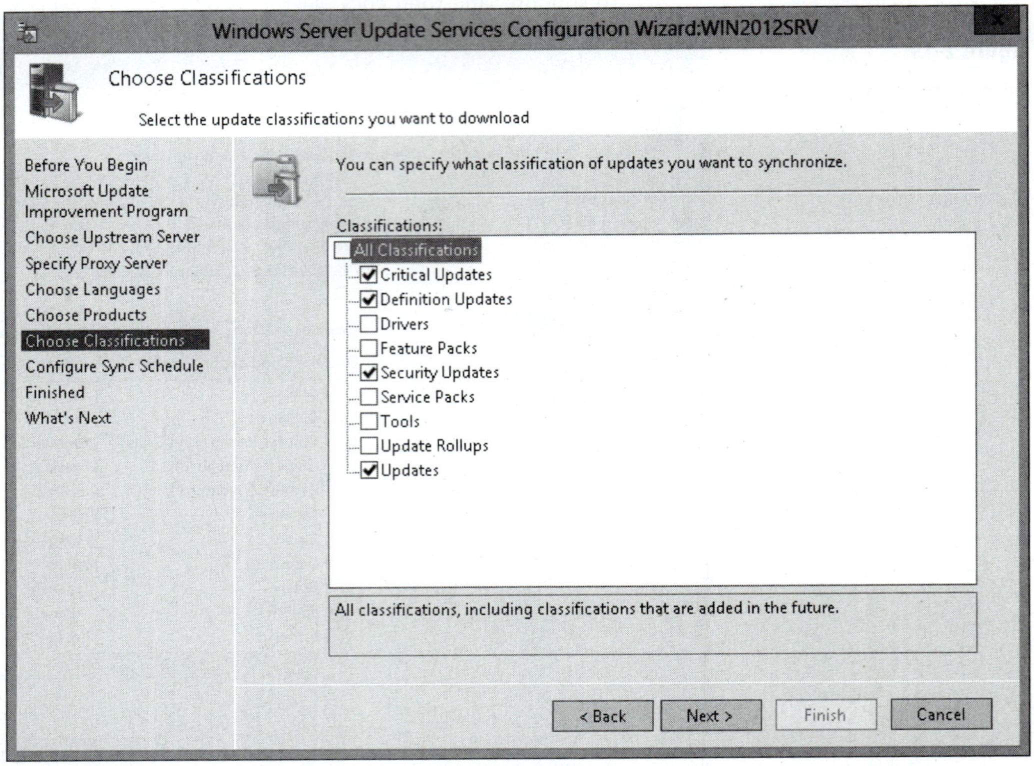

14. On the *Set Sync Schedule* page (see Figure 2-16), select either **Synchronize manually** or **Synchronize automatically**. If you choose to synchronize automatically, you must specify when the first synchronization occurs and how often to synchronize. Click **Next**.

Figure 2-16

Setting a sync schedule

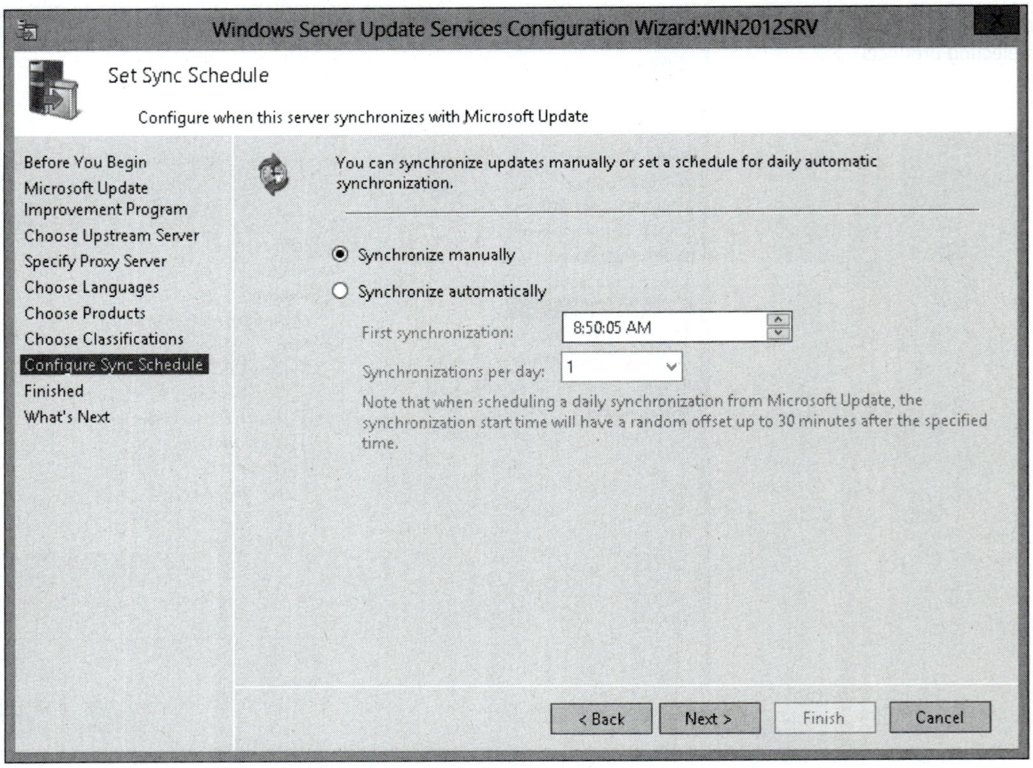

15. On the *Finish* page (see Figure 2-17), select Begin initial synchronization and then click Next.

Figure 2-17

Finishing the initial configuration

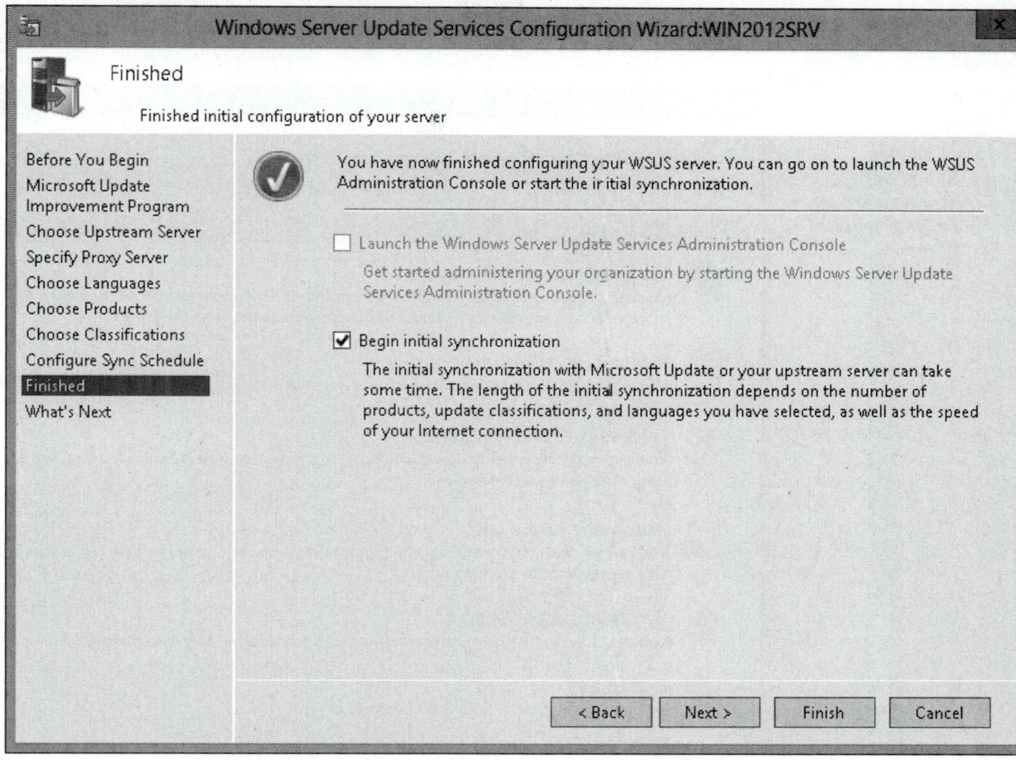

16. On the *What's Next* page, click Finish.

After you run the initial configuration, you can configure the most important options by selecting the Options node in the Update Services console (see Figure 2-18). These options include the following:

- **Update Source and Proxy Server:** Allows you to choose if the WSUS server gets updates from Microsoft Update or another WSUS Server. It also allows you to specify proxy settings if necessary.
- **Products and Classifications:** Allows you to specify which products you want to download updates for and what type of updates you want to download.
- **Update Files and Languages:** Allows you to specify where updates are stored and which languages to download for.
- **Automatic Approvals:** Specifies how to automatically approve installation of updates for selected groups and how to approve revisions to existing updates.
- **Synchronization Schedule:** Allows you to specify to synchronize updates manually or to set a schedule.
- **Computers:** Specifies how to assign computers to groups, which will be used in rolling out the updates.
- **Server Cleanup Wizard:** Used to remove old computers, updates, and update files from the server.

Figure 2-18
Update Services Options

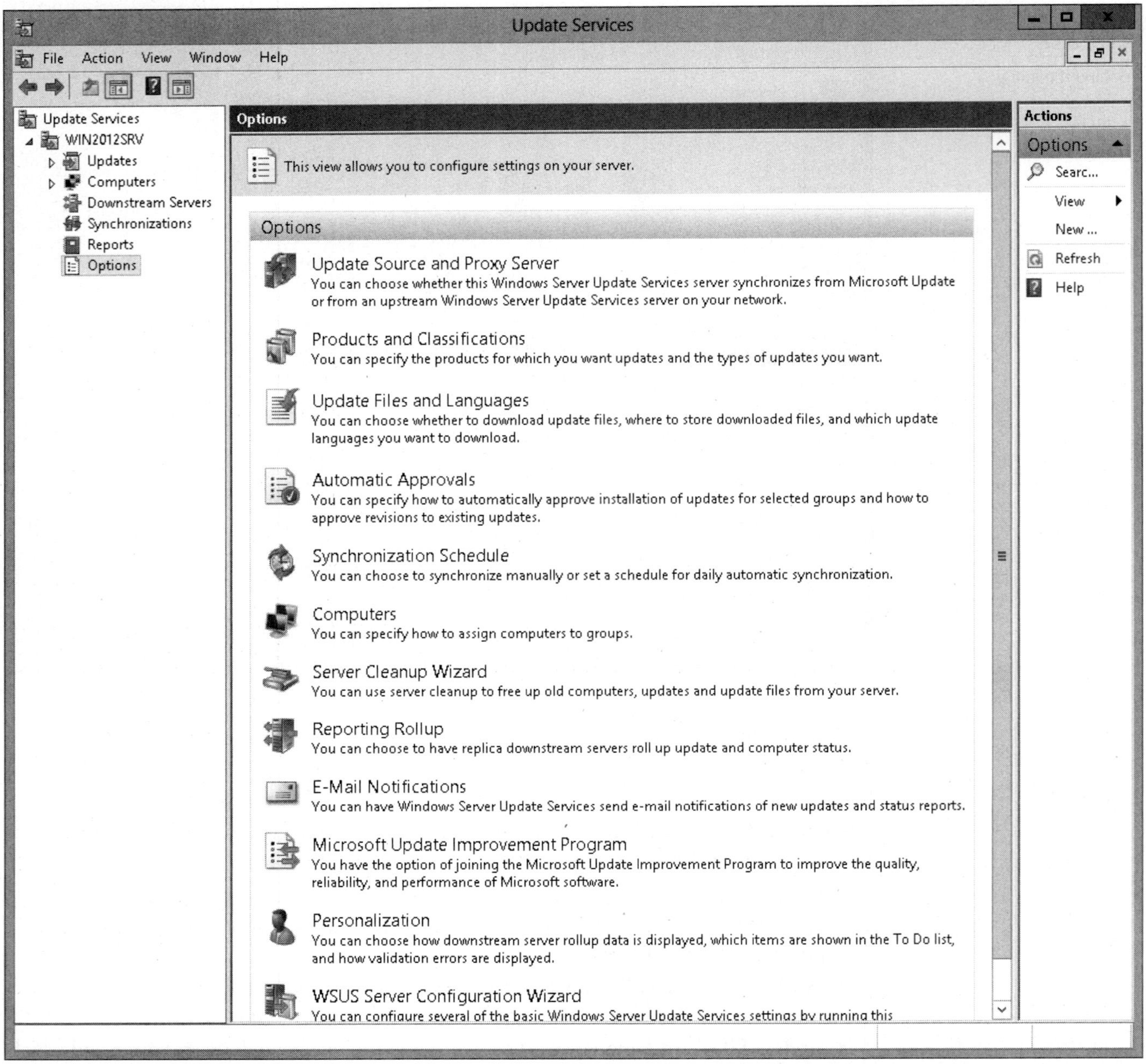

- **Reporting Rollup:** Allows you to specify how information is replicated to downstream servers.
- **E-Mail Notifications:** Allows you to configure e-mail notifications of new updates and of status reports.
- **Microsoft Update Improvement Program:** Specifies if you want to send information to Microsoft so that Microsoft can improve the quality of Microsoft products.
- **Personalization:** Allows you to specify how and what information is displayed in WSUS.
- **WSUS Server Configuration Wizard:** Allows you to run the same Wizard used during the initial configuration.

CONFIGURING WSUS SYNCHRONIZATION

CERTIFICATION READY
Configure WSUS synchronization.
Objective 1.2

To perform synchronization from Windows Update site or another WSUS server, you will need to perform the following:

- Configure the update source and proxy server.
- Specify what products and type of updates you want to download.
- Specify where to store the files.
- Specify what languages you want to support.
- Specify a synchronization schedule.

CONFIGURE THE UPDATE SOURCE AND PROXY SERVER

GET READY. To configure the update source and proxy server, perform the following steps:

1. Open Server Manager.
2. At the top of *Server Manager*, click Tools > Windows Server Update Services.
3. In the left pane, expand the nodes under the server and then click Options.
4. In the *Options* pane, click Update Source and Proxy Server. The *Update Source and Proxy Server* dialog box appears (see Figure 2-19).

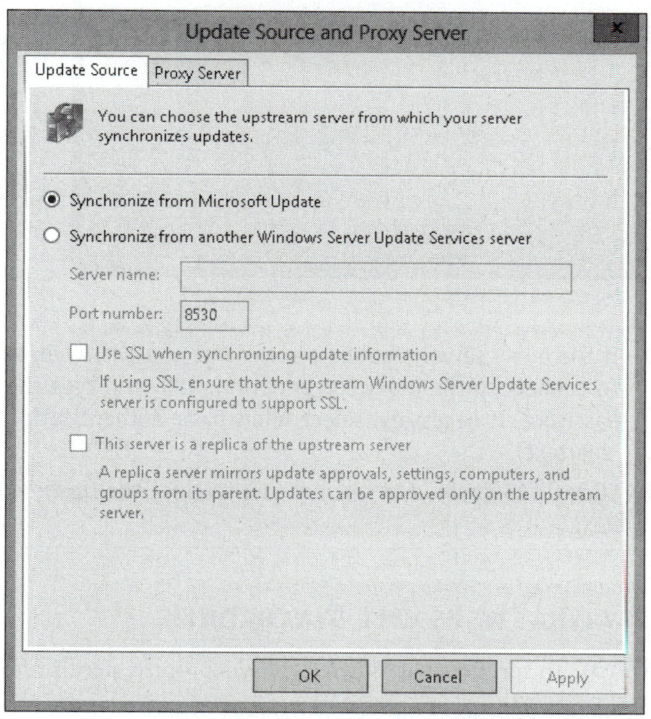

Figure 2-19
Configuring the Update Source settings

5. On the *Update Source* tab, the *Synchronize from Microsoft Update* option is selected by default. If you need to synchronize with another WSUS server, select the Synchronize from another Windows Server Update Services server option. Then specify the Server name and Port number (the default port is *8530*).
6. If the upstream WSUS server requires SSL, select the Use SSL when synchronizing update information option.

7. If you want to replicate update approvals, settings, computers, and groups from the upstream server, select This server is a replica of the upstream server.
8. If your server requires a proxy server to download from Microsoft Update, click the Proxy Server tab.
9. Select the Use a Proxy server when synchronizing option, and then type the Server name of the proxy server and the Port number (see Figure 2-20).

Figure 2-20

Configuring the Proxy Server settings

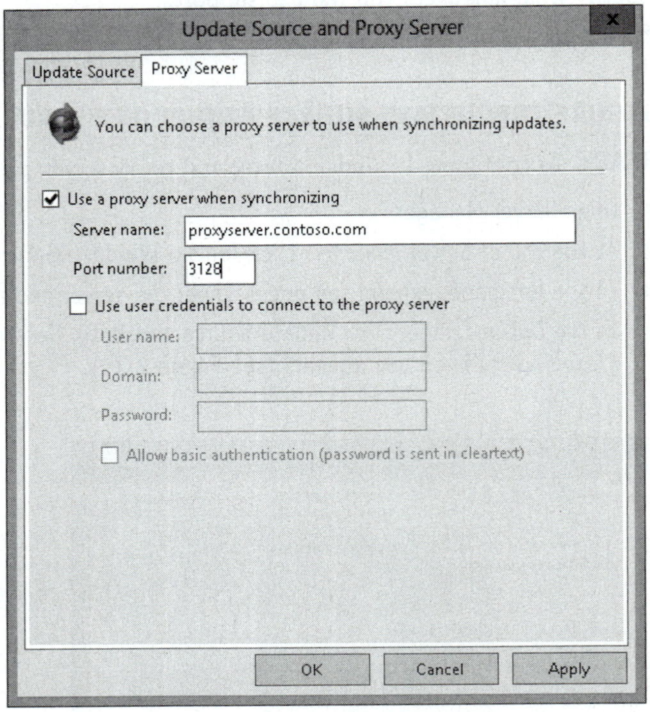

10. If the proxy server requires a user name and password, select the Use user credentials to connect to the proxy server option, and then type the user name, domain, and password. If necessary, select Allow basic authentication (password is sent in cleartext).
11. Click OK to apply your settings and to close the *Update Source and Proxy Server* dialog box.

SPECIFY WHAT WSUS WILL SYNCHRONIZE

GET READY. To specify what WSUS will synchronize, perform the following steps:

1. Open Server Manager.
2. At the top of *Server Manager*, click Tools > Windows Server Update Services.
3. In the left pane, expand the nodes under the server, and then click Options.
4. In the *Options* pane, click Products and Classifications. The *Products and Classifications* dialog box appears.
5. On the *Products* tab (see Figure 2-21), select any of the products that you want to synchronize and deselect any products that you do not want to synchronize.

Figure 2-21

Selecting and deselecting products

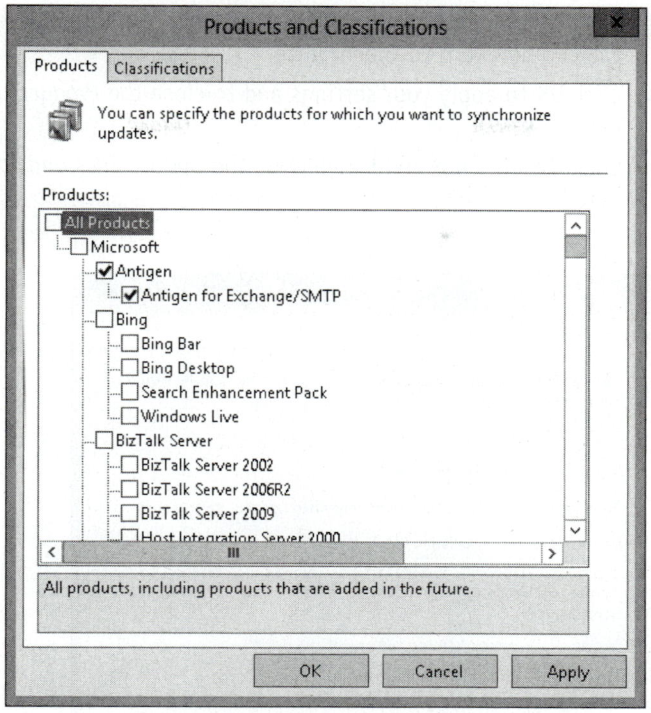

Take Note*

As Microsoft releases new products as well as new versions and/or editions of a product, when synchronization does occur, the new products, editions, and versions are added to the available list.

6. Click the Classifications tab (see Figure 2-22).

Figure 2-22

Selecting and deselecting classifications

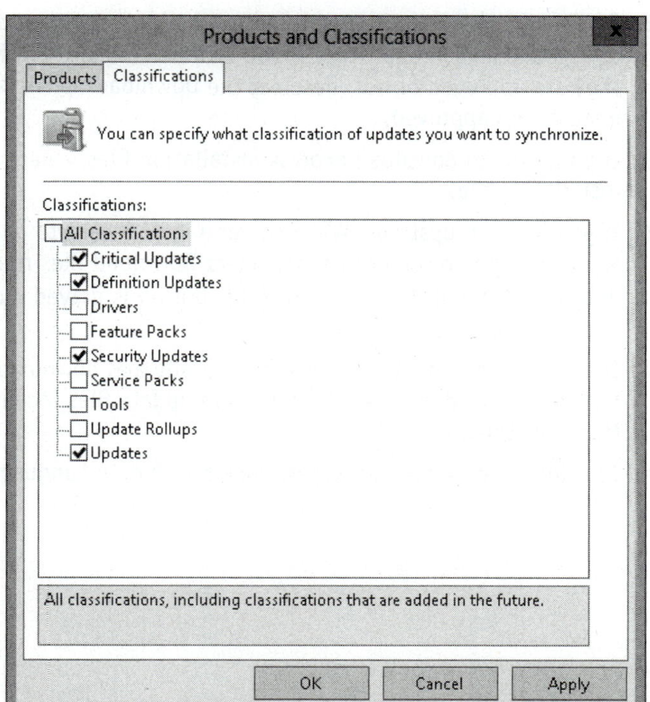

7. Select the updates that you want to synchronize and deselect the type of updates that do not want to synchronize.
8. Click OK to apply your settings and to close the *Products and Classifications* dialog box.
9. Click Update Files and Languages. The *Update Files and Languages* dialog box opens (see Figure 2-23).

Figure 2-23

Updating files

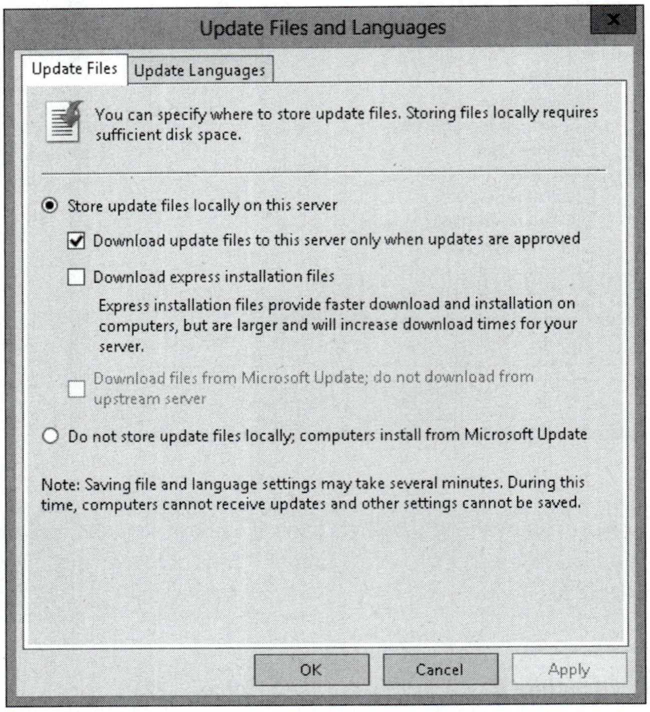

10. By default, the updates are stored on the local server and the files are only downloaded when approved. If you want the files to download regardless of whether they are approved or not, deselect the Download update files to this server only when updates are approved.
11. If you want to download express installation files, select Download express installation files.
12. If you have an upstream WSUS server and you want to download directly from the Microsoft update server instead, select Download files from Microsoft Update; do not download from upstream server. (This option is grayed out unless you have an upstream server.)
13. If you do not want to store the files locally and download the files from Microsoft Updates as needed, select Do not store update files locally; computers install from Microsoft Update.
14. To select or deselect languages, click the Update Languages tab (see Figure 2-24).

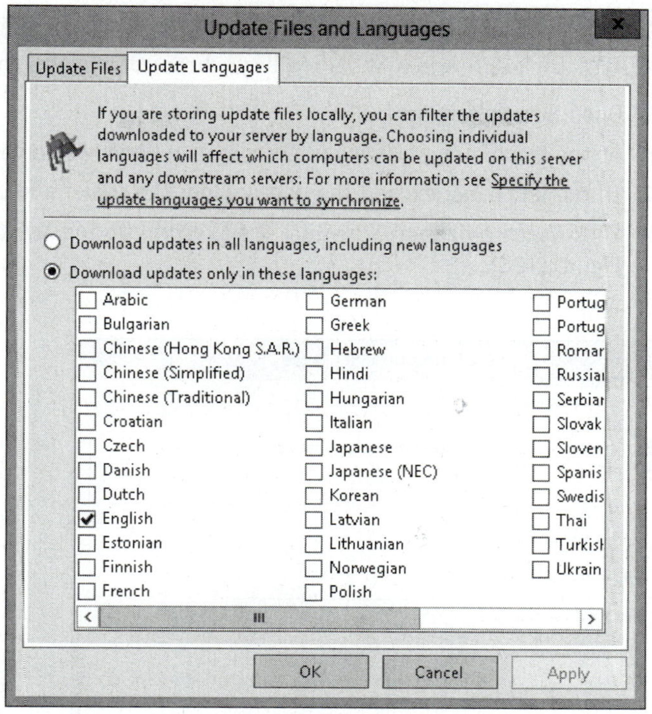

Figure 2-24

Updating languages

15. Select the languages that you want to download and deselect the languages that you don't want to download.
16. Click OK to apply your settings and to close the *Products and Classifications* dialog box.

You can manually synchronize the updates or you can schedule the updates. To manually synchronize, open the Update Services console and expand the nodes under the server in the left pane, click Synchronization > Synchronize Now (see Figure 2-25). To view if a synchronization succeeded or failed, view the center pane.

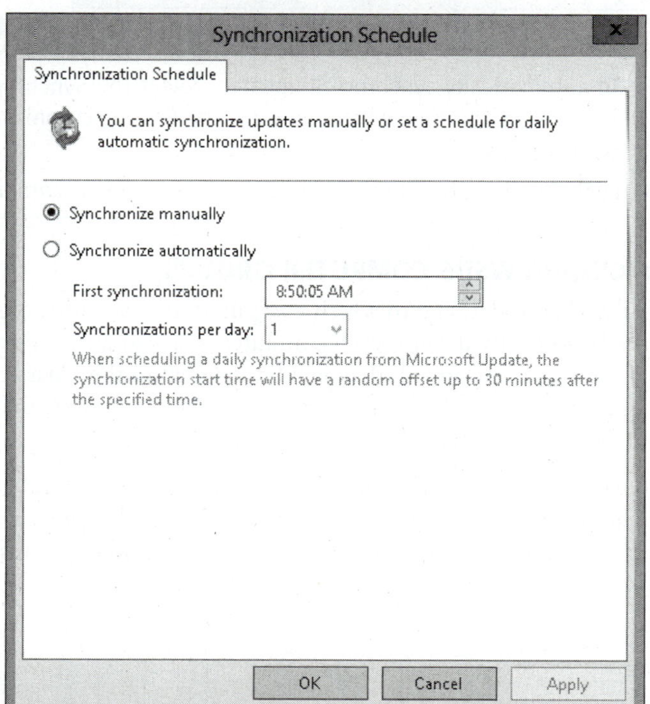

Figure 2-25

Performing a synchronization

SPECIFY A SYNCHRONIZATION SCHEDULE

GET READY. To specify when WSUS will synchronize, perform the following steps:

1. Open Server Manager.
2. At the top of *Server Manager*, click Tools > Windows Server Update Services.
3. In the left pane, expand the nodes under the server and click Options.
4. Click Synchronization Schedule. The *Synchronization Schedule* dialog box opens (see Figure 2-26).

Figure 2-26

Configuring a synchronization schedule

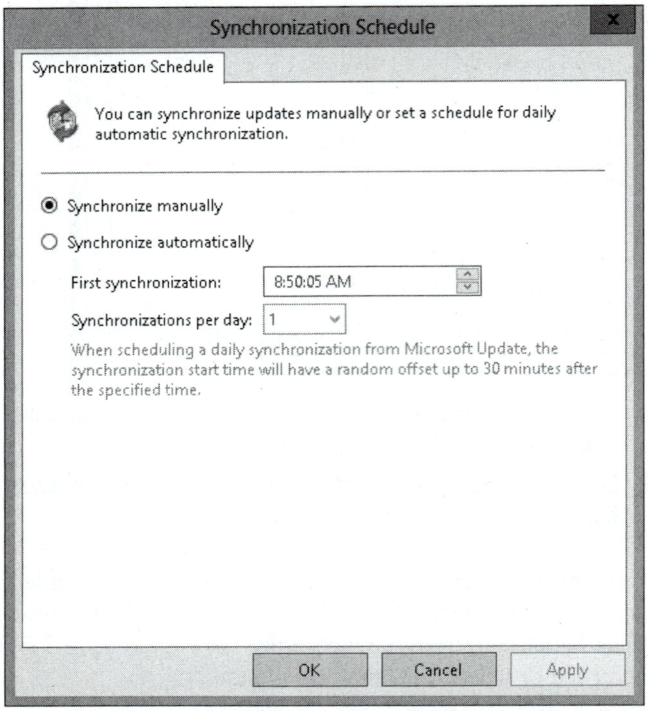

5. To automatically synchronize updates, select the Synchronize automatically option. Then select the time when you want the first synchronization to occur and how many times per day.
6. Click OK to apply your settings and to close the *Synchronization Schedule* dialog box.

CONFIGURING WSUS COMPUTER GROUPS

CERTIFICATION READY
Configure WSUS groups.
Objective 1.2

To specify what updates go to which computers at what time, organize your computers into ***computer groups***. By default, each computer is always assigned to the All Computers group. As new computers are added, they will be assigned to the Unassigned Computers group until you assign them to another group. Other than the computers that are members of the All Computers group, a computer can only be assigned to one other group.

When planning the computer groups, you should create several groups so that you can use a layered approach when pushing the updates. A layered approach allows you to push updates to a test group. You can then roll out the updates to other groups as needed.

CREATE A COMPUTER GROUP

GET READY. To create computer group, perform the following steps:

1. Open Server Manager.
2. At the top of *Server Manager*, click Tools > Windows Server Update Services.
3. In the left pane, expand Computers so that you can see *All Computers* (see Figure 2-27).

Figure 2-27

Viewing Computers node

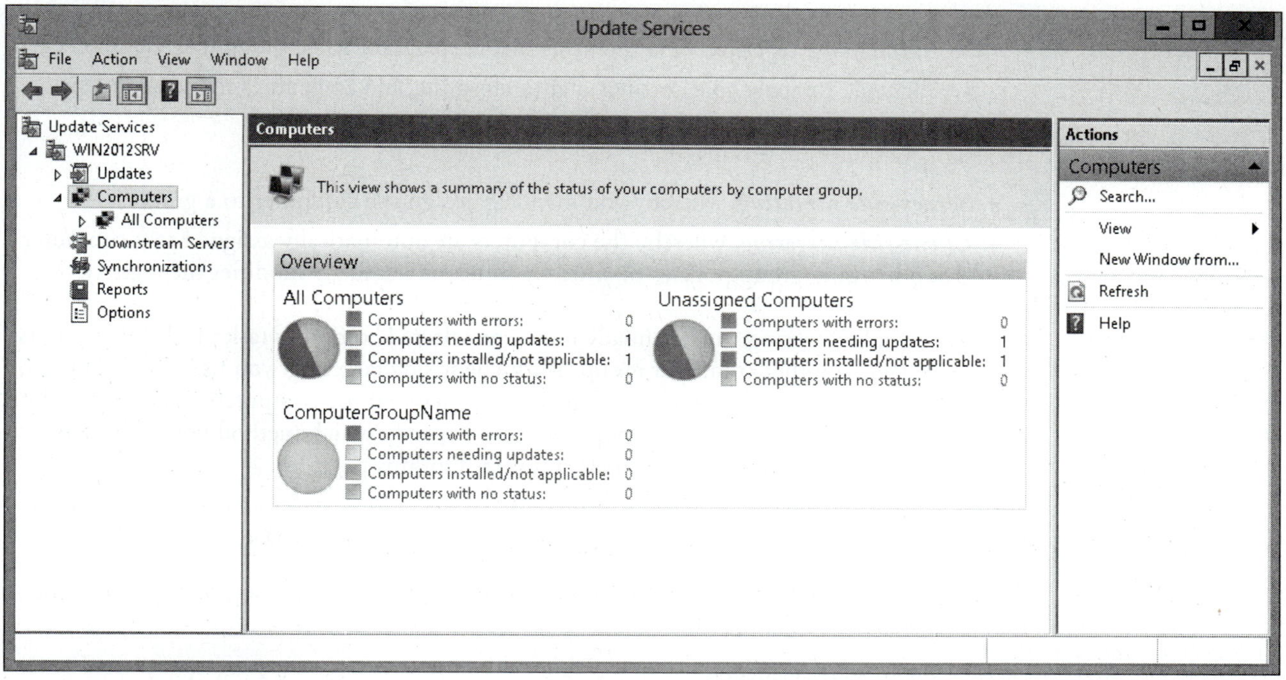

4. Right-click All Computers and choose Add Computer Group (see Figure 2-28). The *Add Computer Group* dialog box opens.

Figure 2-28

Adding a computer group

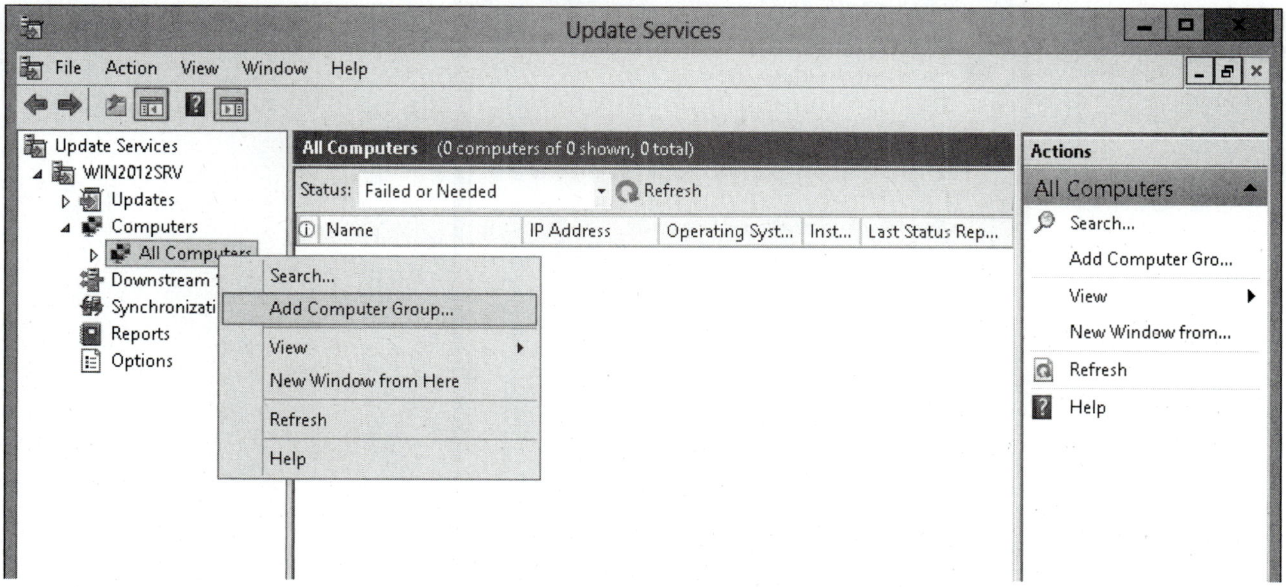

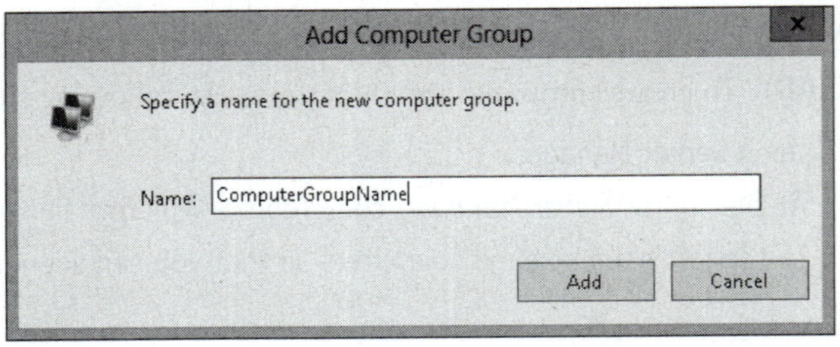

Figure 2-29
Typing a computer name group

5. In the *Name* text box, type the name of the computer name group (see Figure 2-29).
6. Click Add to apply your settings and to close the Add Computer Group dialog box.

To assign computers to groups, use:

- ***Server-side targeting***, whereby you manually assign the computer to a group.
- ***Client-side targeting***, whereby the computers are automatically assigned to a computer group by using group policies or whereby someone manually modifies the registry.

With server-side targeting, you manually move the selected computer task on the Computers page to move to another computer group. With client-side targeting, you use Group Policy or you edit the registry settings on client computers to enable those computers to automatically add themselves into the computer groups. You must specify which method you will use by selecting one of the two options on the Computers Options page.

SPECIFY THE METHOD OF ASSIGN COMPUTERS TO GROUPS

GET READY. To specify the method on how computers are assigned to a group, perform the following steps:

1. Open Server Manager.
2. At the top of *Server Manager*, click Tools > Windows Server Update Services.
3. In the left pane, expand the nodes under the server, and then click Options.
4. In the main pane, click Computers. The *Computers* dialog box opens (see Figure 2-30).

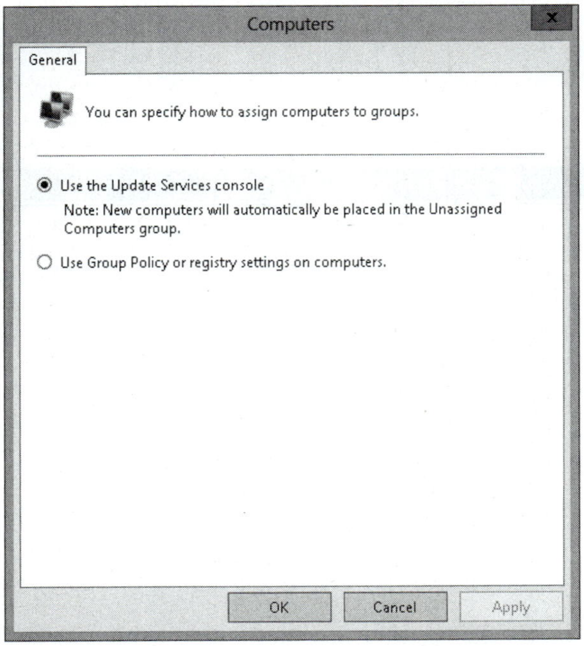

Figure 2-30
Specifying how computers are assigned to groups

5. To perform server-side targeting, select Use the Update Services console.
6. To perform client-side targeting, select Use Group Policy or registry settings on computers.
7. Click OK to apply your settings and to close the *Computers* dialog box.

MOVE A COMPUTER TO A DIFFERENT GROUP BY USING SERVER-SIDE TARGETING

GET READY. To move a computer to a different group by using Server-Side Targeting, perform the following steps:

1. Open Server Manager.
2. At the top of *Server Manager*, click Tools > Windows Server Update Services.
3. In the left pane, expand the nodes under the server. Expand the Computers node, and then click All Computers.
4. In the *All Computers* pane in the middle of the screen, right-click the computer you want to move, and then choose Change Membership (see Figure 2-31).

Figure 2-31

Moving a computer

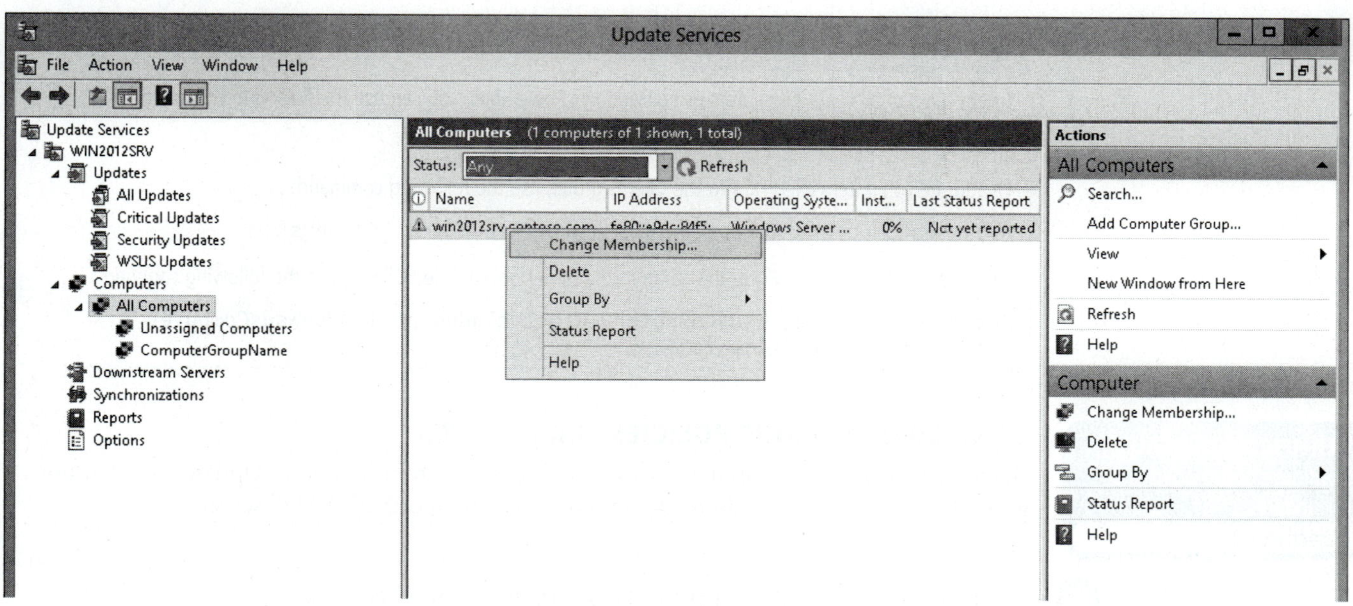

5. When the *Set Computer Group Membership* dialog box opens (see Figure 2-32), select the computer group you want to move the computer to, and then click OK.

Figure 2-32

Selecting a computer group

6. Click OK to apply your settings and to close the *Computers* dialog box.

USING WINDOWS POWERSHELL

To get a list of all client computers using Windows PowerShell, you can use the following command:

```
Get-WsusComputer -All
```

To add the computer called PC1 to the Clients group, use the following command:

```
Add-WsusComputer -Computer PC1 -TargetGroupName "Clients"
```

To add all computers with PC in the name to the target group called Clients, use the following command:

```
Get-WsusServer Get-WsusComputer -NameIncludes pc | Add-WsusComputer
-TargetGroupName "Clients"
```

CERTIFICATION READY
Configure group policies for updates.
Objective 1.2

CONFIGURING GROUP POLICIES FOR UPDATES

By default, Windows computers will get their updates from Windows Update. You can use group policies to have the domain computers use the specified WSUS server.

CONFIGURE A COMPUTER TO USE WSUS FOR UPDATES USING GROUP POLICIES

GET READY. To configure a computer to use WSUS for updates using group policies, perform the following steps on a domain controller or any computer that has Group Policy Management console:

1. Open Server Manager.
2. Click Tools > Group Policy Management.
3. Using the Group Management console, open Group Policy Object Editor for a group policy.

4. In *Group Policy Object Editor*, expand Computer Configuration, expand Policies, expand Administrative Templates, expand Windows Components, and then click Windows Update.
5. In the details pane, double-click Specify Intranet Microsoft update service location. The *Specify intranet Microsoft update service location* page appears (see Figure 2-33).

Figure 2-33

Specifying the intranet Microsoft update service location using group policies

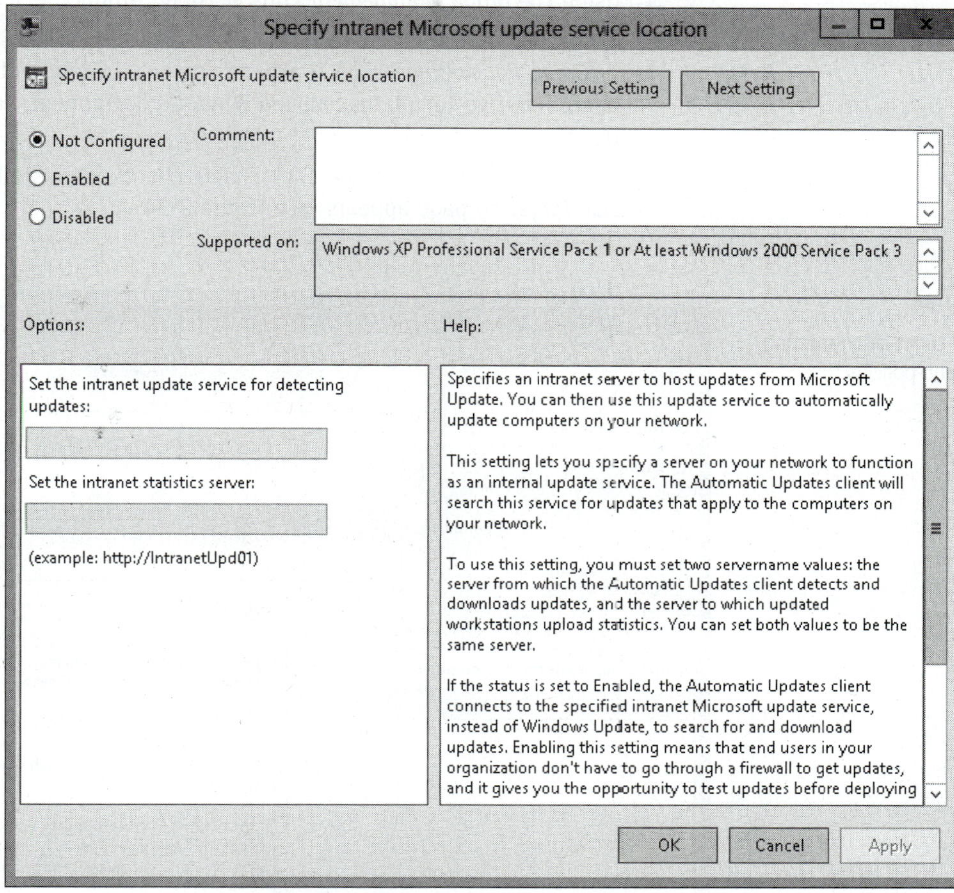

6. Select Enabled.
7. In the *Set the intranet update service for detecting updates* text box and in the *Set the intranet statistics server* text box, type the HTTP or the HTTPS URL of the WSUS server. The default URLs are http://<name of WSUS server>:8530 and https://<name of WSUS server>:8531.
8. Click OK to apply your settings and to close the *Specify intranet Microsoft update service location* page.

CERTIFICATION READY
Configure client-side targeting.
Objective 1.2

CONFIGURING CLIENT-SIDE TARGETING

If you have several computers, client-side targeting is an excellent option that automates the process of assigning computers to computer groups. For domain computers, you should use group policies.

ENABLE CLIENT-SIDE TARGETING USING GROUP POLICIES

GET READY. To enable client-side targeting using group policy, perform the following steps on a domain controller or any computer that has Group Policy Management console:

1. Open Server Manager.
2. Click Tools > Group Policy Management.
3. Using the *Group Management* console, open Group Policy Object Editor for a group policy.
4. In *Group Policy Object Editor*, expand Computer Configuration, expand Policies, expand Administrative Templates, expand Windows Components, and then click Windows Update.
5. In the details pane, double-click Enable client-side installations. The *Enable client-side targeting* page appears (see Figure 2-34).

Figure 2-34

Enabling client-side targeting using group policies

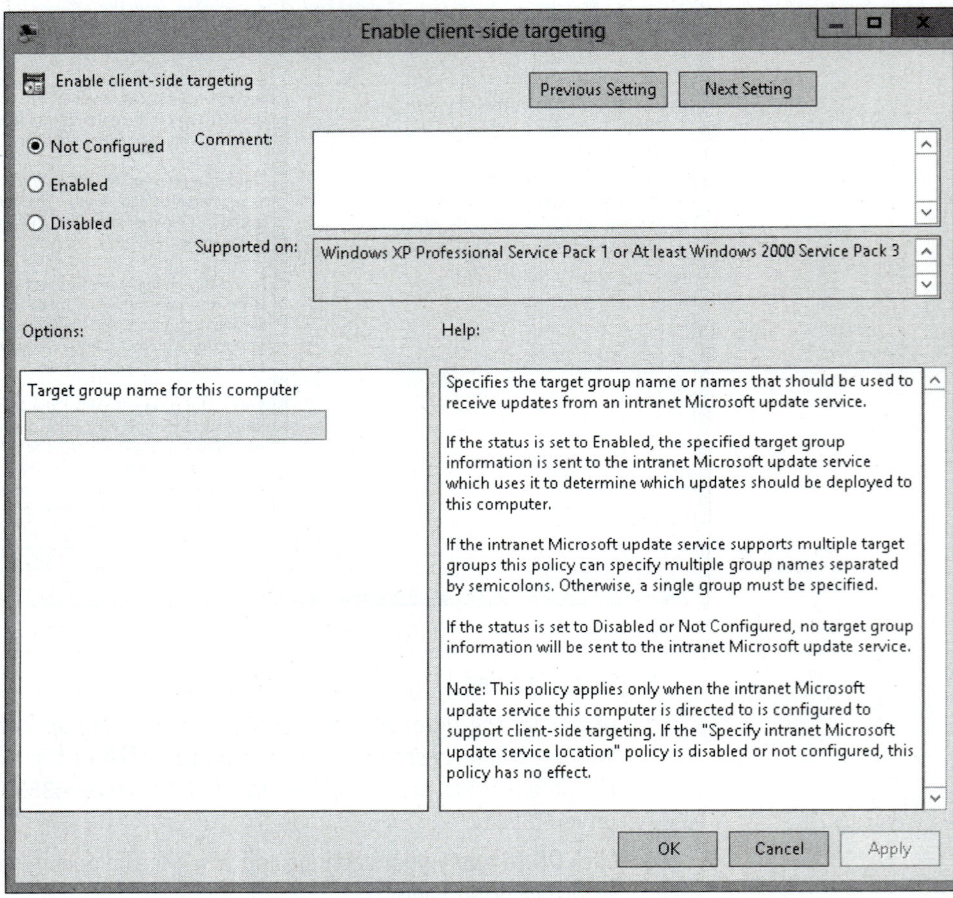

6. Select Enabled and in the *Target group name for this computer* box, type the name of the computer group name.
7. Click OK to apply your settings and to close the *Reschedule Automatic Updates scheduled installations* page.

For computers that are not part of the domain, you will have to modify the registry if you want to enable client-side targeting. The registry entries for the WSUS environment options are located in the following subkey:

`HKEY_LOCAL_MACHINE\Software\Policies\Microsoft\Windows\WindowsUpdate`

To enable client-side targeting, change the `TargetGroupEnabled (Reg_DWord)` value to a 1 and use the `TargetGroup (Reg_SZ)` value to specify the group that you want the computer to be a member of (see Figure 2-35). You also need the following subkey:

`HKEY_LOCAL_MACHINE\Software\Policies\Microsoft\Windows\WindowsUpdate\AU`

The `AU` key needs to have a `UseWUServer` value (`Reg_DWord`) set to `1`.

Figure 2-35

Modifying Windows Update Registry settings

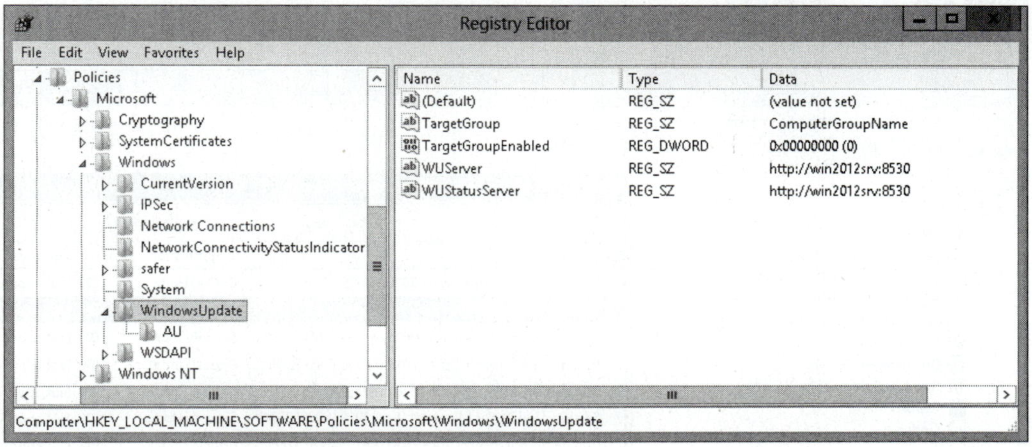

MORE INFORMATION

For more information on configuring automatic updates in a non-Active Directory environment, visit the TechNet site.

Approving Updates

One of the advantages of using WSUS is that you control which updates clients receive and when clients receive those updates. This gives you an opportunity to test the updates and then roll them out to the computer groups.

Although you can have updates automatically approve every update that is downloaded from Windows Update, you shouldn't do that until you've had an opportunity to test the updates. Updates are thoroughly tested by Microsoft, but every organization is different; a single update might cause unforeseen problems affecting hundreds of computers.

You can specify a deadline when you approve an update or set of updates on the WSUS server. Setting a deadline causes clients to install the update at a specific time. If the client contacts the server after the update deadline has passed, it tries to install the update as soon as possible. If you wish computers to install an update immediately, you can specify a deadline in the past. If an update has a deadline and requires a restart and the computer has not been restarted, the system reboots at the time of the deadline.

APPROVE UPDATES

GET READY. To approve updates in WSUS, perform the following steps:

1. Open Server Manager.
2. At the top of *Server Manager*, click Tools > Windows Server Update Services.
3. Expand the server and then expand Updates. Select one of the following options:
    - All Updates: Displays all updates (see Figure 2-36).
    - Critical Updates: Displays only critical updates, which are high-priority updates and are not security related.
    - Security Updates: Displays only updates that fix known security problems.
    - WSUS Updates: Displays updates related to the update process.

Figure 2-36

The All Updates option

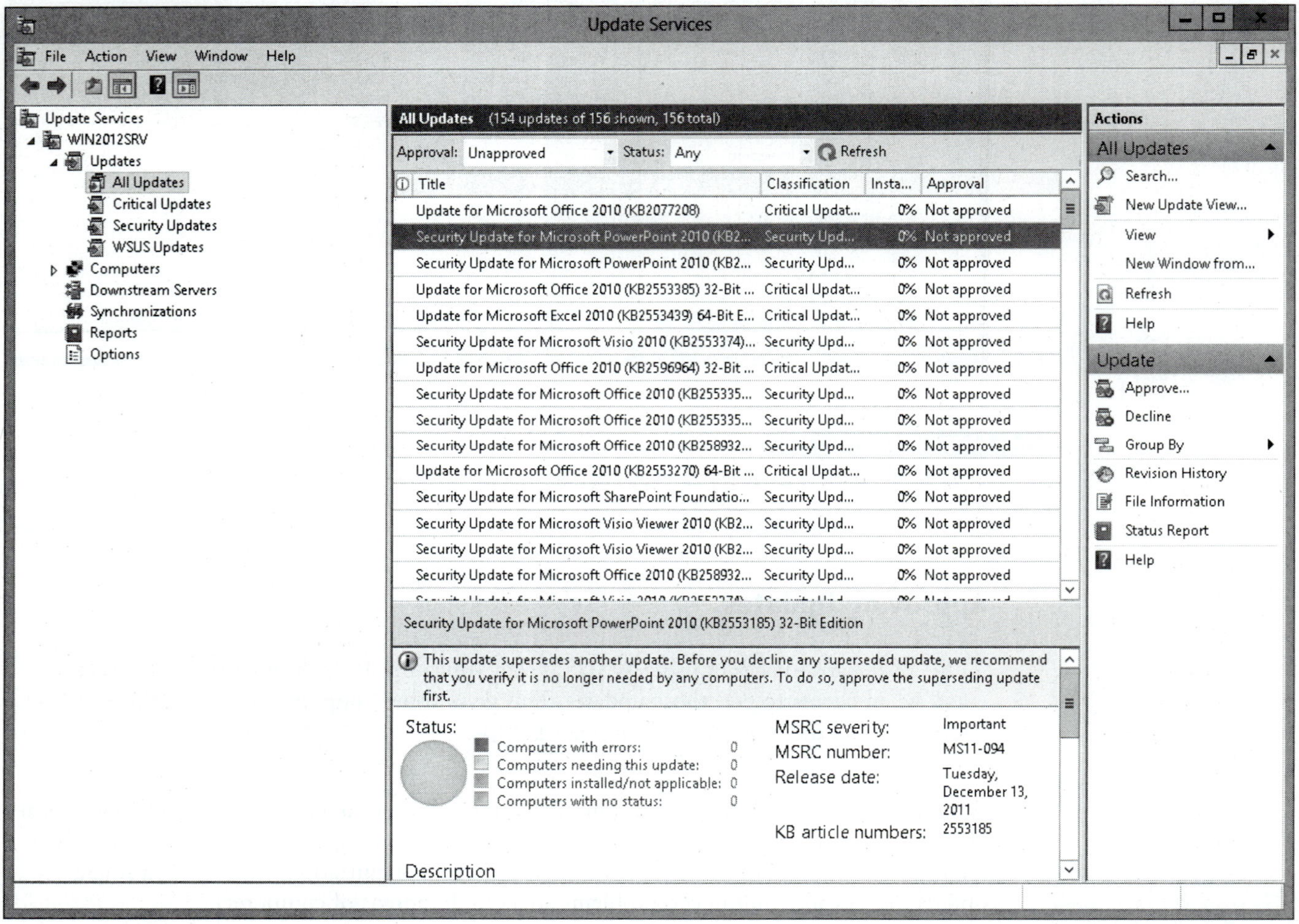

4. On the top of the screen, on the *Approval* drop-down, make sure Unapproved is selected.
5. On the top of the screen, on the *Status* drop-down menu, make sure Any is selected.
6. Click Refresh to display the updates.

7. To sort the updates so that the newest updates appear first, right-click any of the column headings and then select the Release Date option (see Figure 2-37). Then click the Release Date column header to sort by that date.

Figure 2-37

Choosing the Release Date option

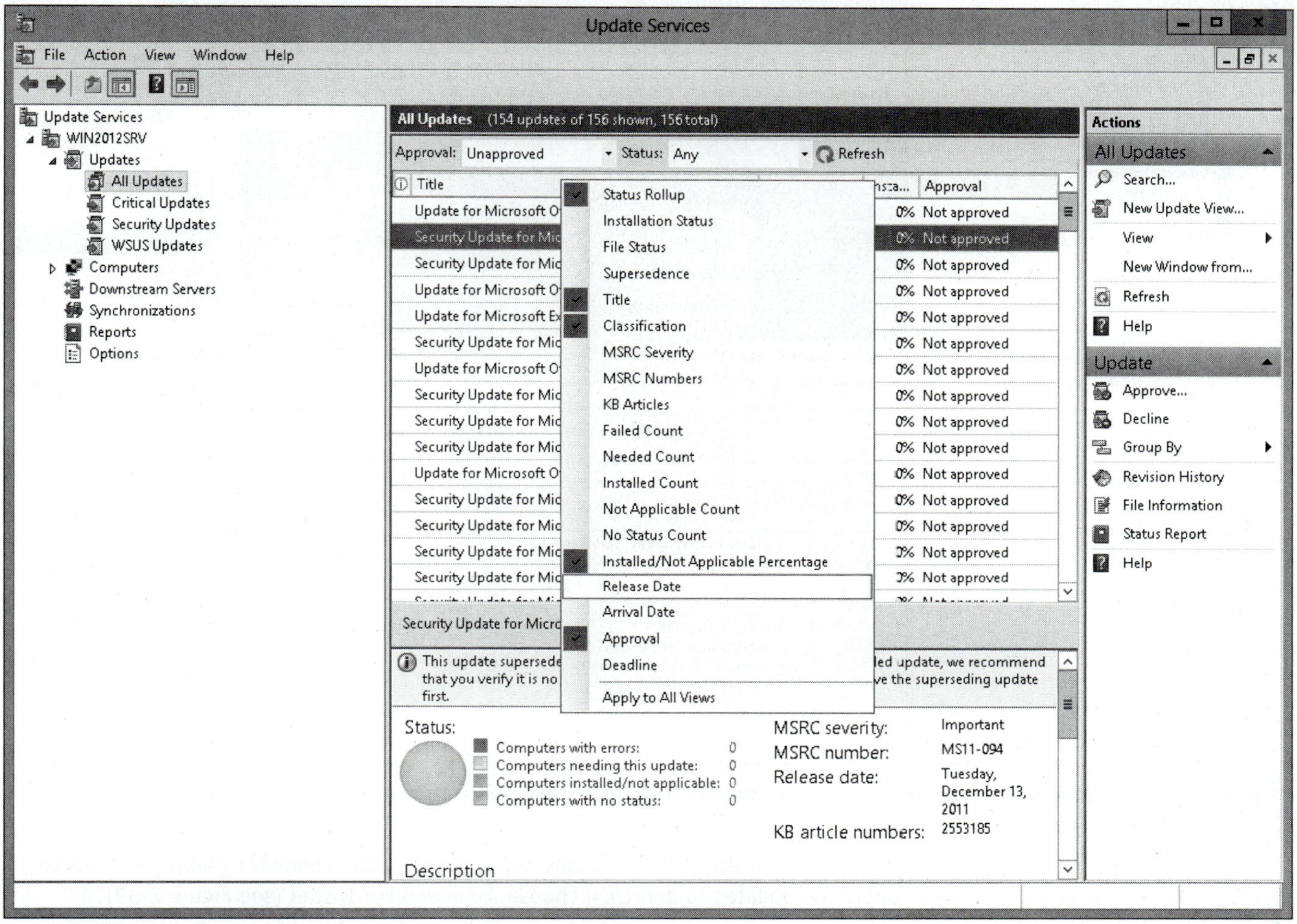

8. Select the updates that you want to approve. You can select multiple updates by pressing and holding the Ctrl key. When you're finished selecting your updates, release the Ctrl key.
9. Right-click the selected update and choose Approve (see Figure 2-38). Alternatively, select Decline if you want to prevent an update from being distributed.

Figure 2-38

Approving updates

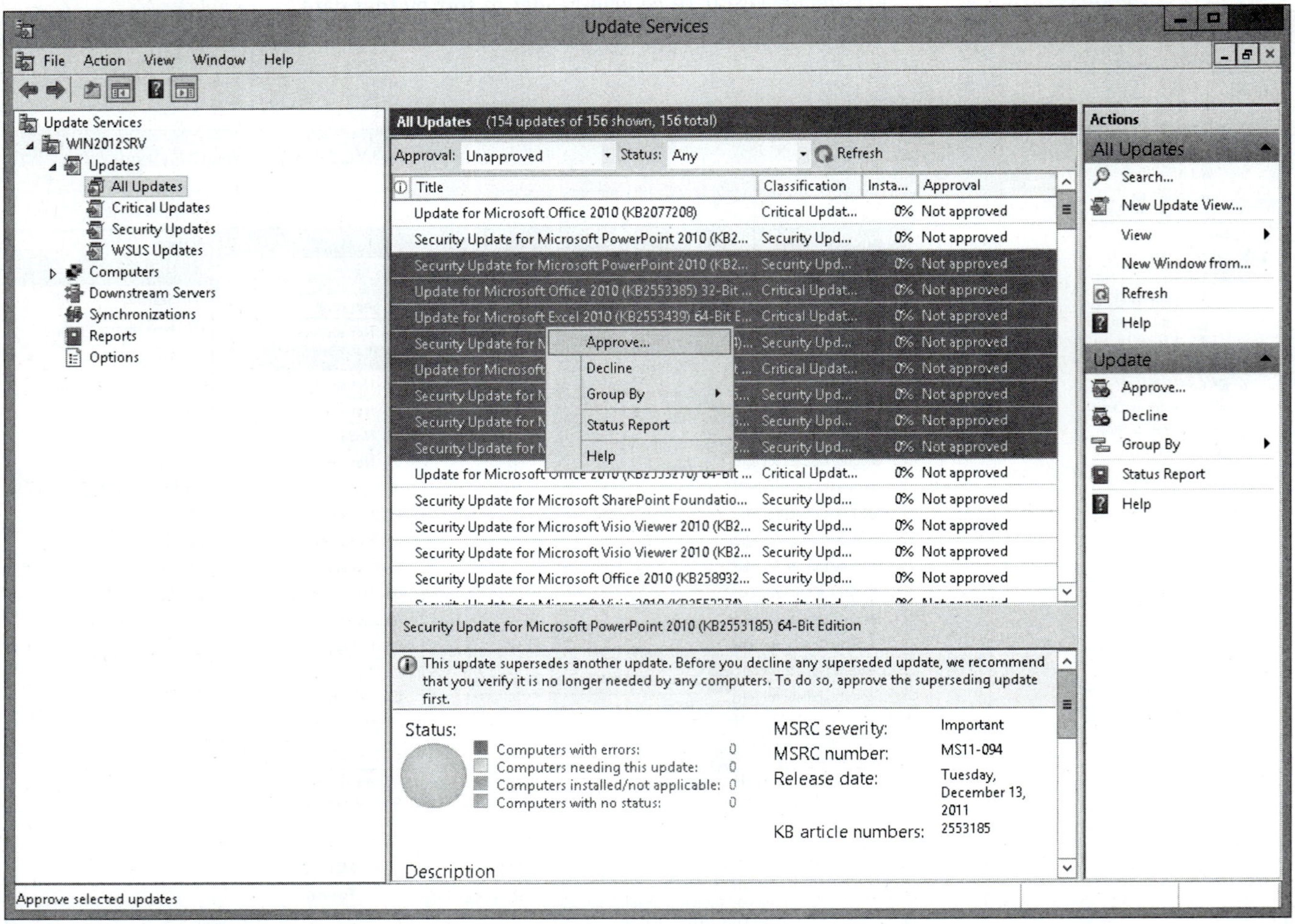

10. If the Approve Updates dialog box appears, select the computer group you want to apply the updates to and then choose Approved For Install (see Figure 2-39).

Figure 2-39

Approving updates for installation

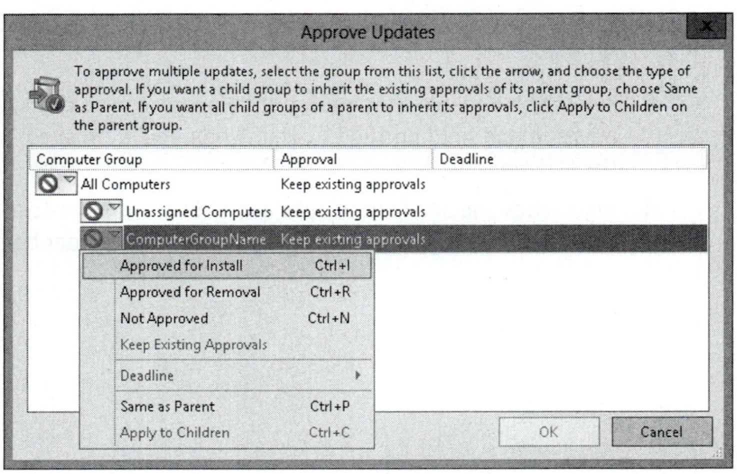

11. To force an update to be installed where a user cannot delay the installation, right-click the computer group, choose Deadline, and then select a deadline (see Figure 2-40).

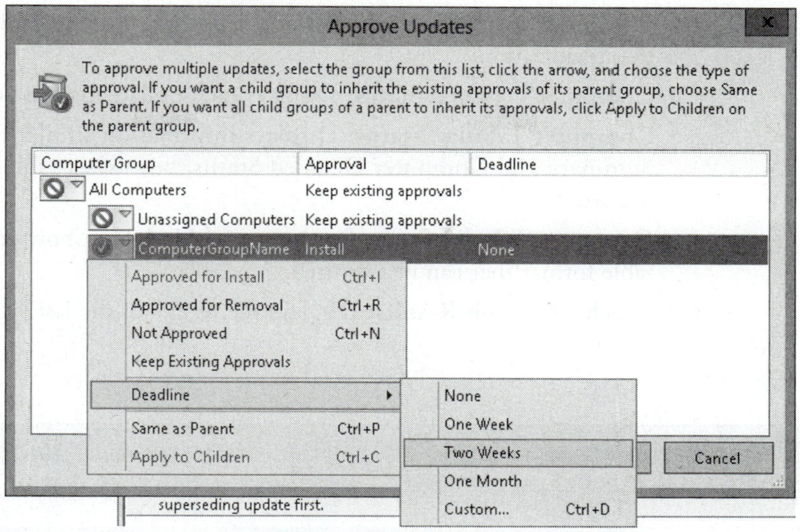

Figure 2-40

Selecting a deadline

12. Click OK.
13. If a license agreement appears, prompting you for an update, click I Accept.
14. Click Close.

USING WINDOWS POWERSHELL

To approve all unapproved updates with a status of failed or needed, use the following command:

```
Get-WsusUpdate -Classification All -Approval Unapproved -Status
FailedOrNeeded | Approve-WsusUpdate -Action Install -TargetGroupName "All
Computers"
```

To decline all unapproved updates with a status of failed or needed, use the following command:

```
Get-WsusUpdate -Classification All -Approval Unapproved -Status
FailedOrNeeded | Deny-WsusUpdate
```

Viewing Reports

To see detailed information about updates, computers, and synchronization, you can run the WSUS built-in reports.

WSUS includes the following reports (see Figure 2-41):

- **Update Status Summary:** Shows detailed information about every update that you choose to report on, the computer groups that an update has been approved for, and the number of computers the update was installed on.
- **Update Detailed Status:** Shows detailed information about every update that you choose to report on, the computer groups that an update has been approved for, and the number of computers the update was installed on. It also shows the update status for all computers.
- **Update Tabular Status:** Similar to the Update Status Summary report and the Update Detailed Status report, but uses a table format that can be exported.
- **Update Tabular Status for Approved Updates:** Shows all approved updates in a table format that can be exported.

- **Computer Status Summary:** Displays update information for every computer within the organization.
- **Computer Detailed Status:** Displays each update installed on each computer.
- **Computer Tabular Status:** Displays information similar to the Computer Status Summary and Computer Detailed Status, but uses a table format that can be exported.
- **Computer Tabular Status for Approved Updates:** Shows all approved updates in a table format that can be exported.
- **Synchronization Results:** Displays the results of the last synchronization.

Figure 2-41

Viewing Update Services reports

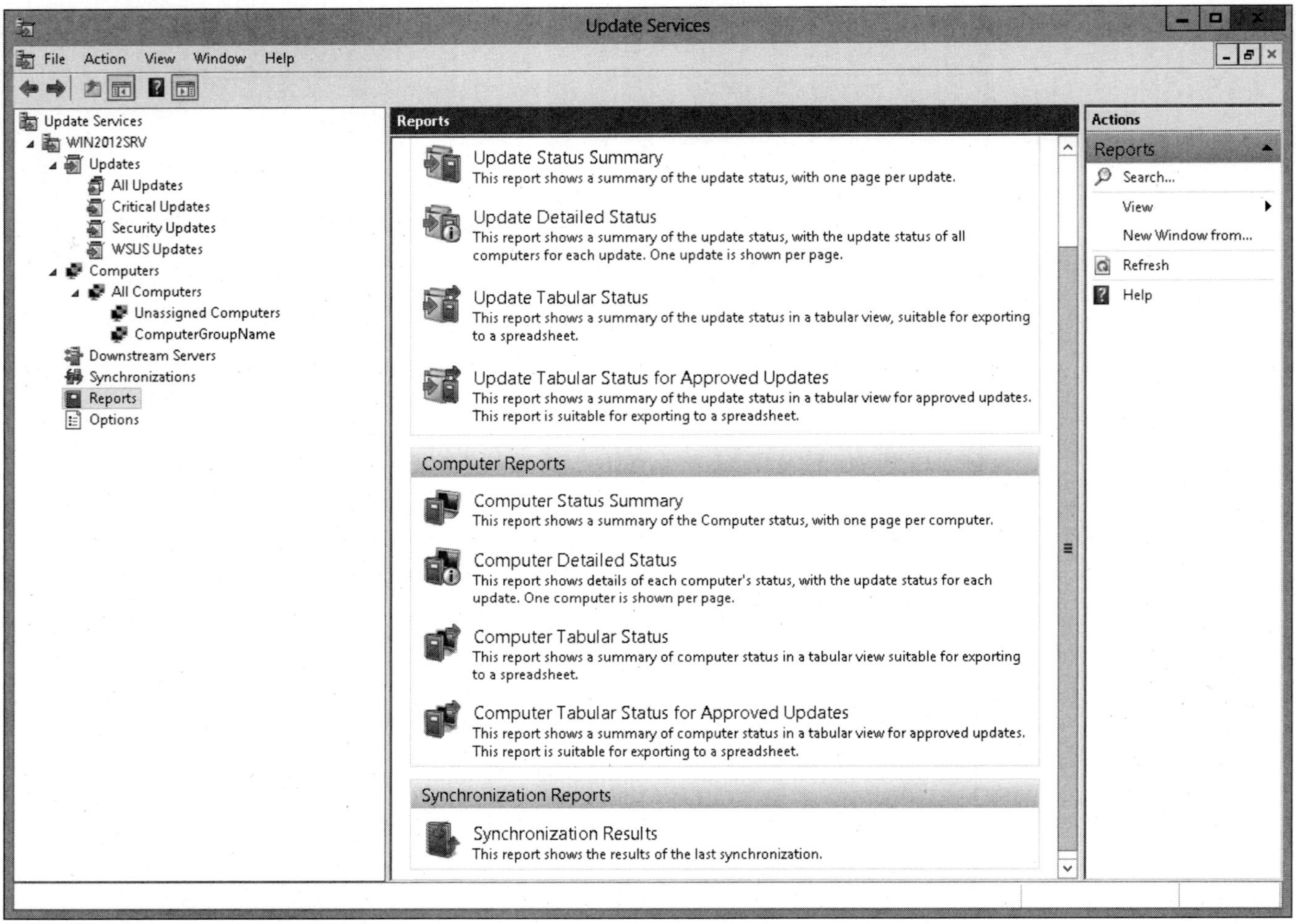

To view the reports, you must first install Microsoft .NET Framework 2.0 and then download and install Microsoft Report Viewer 2008 Redistributable on Microsoft's website.

Take Note*

If a message appears, alerting you to the fact that "Your current security settings do not allow this file to be downloaded," click *Tools > Internet Options*. Click the *Security* tab, and then click *Internet Zone > Custom Level*. In the Downloads section, select *Enable for File Download,* and then click *OK*.

INSTALL .NET FRAMEWORK 3.5 AND MICROSOFT REPORT VIEWER 2008 REDISTRIBUTABLE

GET READY. To install .NET Framework 3.5 (which includes .Net Framework 2.0) and Microsoft Report Viewer 2008 Redistributable, perform the following steps:

> **TAKE NOTE***
> The .NET Framework 3.5 includes .NET Framework 2.0 and 3.0.

1. Open Server Manager.
2. At the top of *Server Manager*, click Manage > Add Roles and Features.
3. When the *Before you begin* page opens, click Next.
4. On the *Select Installation Type* page, click Next.
5. On the *Select destination server* page, with the server selected, click Next.
6. On the *Select server roles* page, click Next.
7. Select NET Framework 3.5 (see Figure 2-42), and then click Next.

Figure 2-42

Installing .NET Framework 3.5

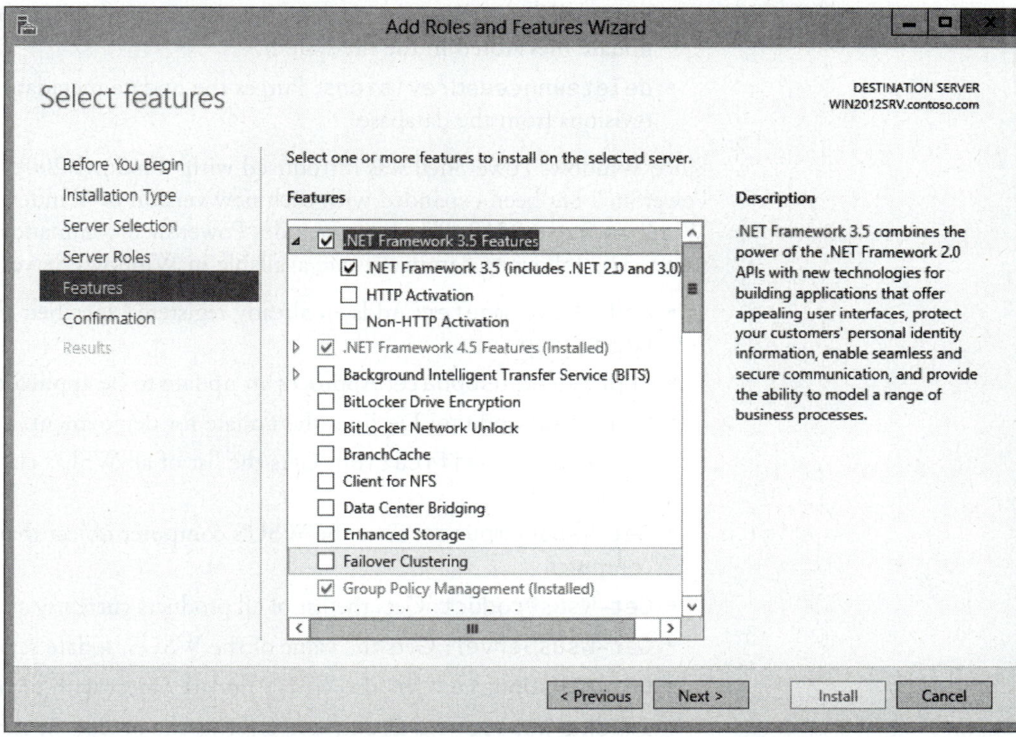

8. On the *Confirm installation selections* page, click Install.
9. When the installation is complete, click Close.
10. Double-click the ReportViewer.exe.
11. If the *Open File – Security Warning* dialog box opens, click Run.
12. On the *Welcome to Microsoft Report Viewer Redistributable 2008 Setup* page opens, click Next.
13. On the *License Terms* page, select I have read and accept the license terms. Then click Install.
14. When the installation is complete, click Finish.

Administrating WSUS with Commands

While commands can be incorporated into scripts, often commands can perform functions that you could not do otherwise. With WSUS with Windows Server 2012, you can use WSUSutil.exe and Windows PowerShell.

WSUSutil.exe (located in the %drive%\Program Files\Update Services\Tools folder on your WSUS server) allows you to manage the WSUS from the command line. Some of the options include:

- `export`: Exports the update metadata to an export package file.
- `import`: Imports the update metadata from an export package file.
- `movecontent`: Changes the file system location where the WSUS server stores update files and optionally copies any update files from the old location to the new location.
- `reset`: Checks that every update metadata row in the database has corresponding update files stored in the file system.
- `deleteunneededrevisions`: Purges the update metadata for unnecessary update revisions from the database.

Since Windows PowerShell was introduced with Windows 2008, the use of Windows PowerShell has been expanded with each new version of Windows Server. Starting with Windows Server 2012, Windows includes PowerShell commands to manage the WSUS server. The following commands are available in Windows Server 2012 PowerShell:

- `Add-WsusComputer`: Adds an already registered specified client computer to a specified target group.
- `Approve-WsusUpdate`: Approves an update to be applied to clients.
- `Deny-WsusUpdate`: Declines the update for deployment.
- `Get-WsusClassification`: Gets the list of all WSUS classifications currently available in the system.
- `Get-WsusComputer`: Gets the WSUS computer object that represents the client computer.
- `Get-WsusProduct`: Gets the list of all products currently available on WSUS by category.
- `Get-WsusServer`: Gets the value of the WSUS update server object.
- `Get-WsusUpdate`: Gets the WSUS update object with details about the update.
- `Invoke-WsusServerCleanup`: Performs the process of cleanup on a specified WSUS server.
- `Set-WsusClassification`: Sets whether the classifications of updates that WSUS synchronizes are enabled or disabled.
- `Set-WsusProduct`: Sets whether the product representing the category of updates to synchronize is enabled or disabled.
- `Set-WsusServerSynchronization`: Sets whether the WSUS server synchronizes from Microsoft Update or from an upstream server and uses the upstream server properties.

To list all the cmdlets that are available, use the `Get-Command *-Wsus*` cmdlet. To find more about the syntax, use the `Get-Help <cmdletname>` or search for the command on the TechNet website.

Troubleshooting Problems with Installing Updates

If you have problems with updates being installed with WSUS, there are several tools that can be used to troubleshoot the problem.

WSUS uses the following logs:

- **Application event log:** By opening the Application logs in the Event Viewer on the WSUS system, you can find errors related to synchronization, Update Services console errors, and WSUS database errors.
- **C:\Program Files\Update Services\LogFiles\Change.txt:** This log stores the record of every update installation, synchronization, and WSUS configuration change.
- **C:\Program Files\Update Services\LogFiles\softwareDistribution.txt:** This is a detailed log file usually used by Microsoft Support to debug a problem.

If WSUS is having problems synchronizing with Windows Update, open Windows Update on the server and see if you can download and install updates.

If you have a particular client having problems, verify that that client is connecting to the correct WSUS server. You can review the group policy results for the computer and you can review the C:\Windows\WindowsUpdate.log file. You can verify that a client can connect to the WSUS server by opening the following WSUS URL with Internet Explorer:

http://*WSUSServerName*/iuident.cab

If you are prompted to download the file, you are connecting the WSUS server, which would rule out connectivity problems and name-resolution problems. Lastly, look at the System logs and the Application logs in the client's event viewer.

If you make changes and you want to the changes to take effect immediately, you need to restart the Windows Update service. To restart this service, you can use the Services console, or you can use the following two commands:

```
Net stop wuauserv
Net start wuauserv
```

To make the Windows Update service query the WSUS server, you can run the following command:

```
Wuauclt /detectnow
```

Of course, after you start the services or start a query, you should then look at the client logs.

If you are using client-side targeting and change group membership, use the following command to check for updates and to update the WSUS update computer group membership:

```
Wuauclt /resetauthorization /detectnow
```

Lastly, to look at the installed updates that have been installed, you can use the Control Panel. Similarly, if an update is problematic, you can also use the Control Panel to remove the update.

Understanding System Center Configuration Manager (SCCM)

THE BOTTOM LINE

The WSUS is an excellent tool to push updates to the clients, but it is not the only tool available from Microsoft. The ***System Center Configuration Manager (SCCM)***, formerly known as System Management Server (SMS), is a more versatile system that can provide remote control, patch management, software distribution, operating system deployment, network access protection, hardware inventory, and software inventory. Of course, while WSUS is free, there is a cost in deploying SCCM.

To get the full capability of SCCM, SCCM uses an agent that must be installed on each computer. The agent can be pushed out from the SCCM console or can be pushed using group policies. If you have multiple sites, you can set up distribution points at the various sites so that updates, software packages, and operating system packages have to be pushed to the site only once and the local clients can receive the packages from the local distribution point.

When synchronizing updates with Windows Update, SCCM actually uses WSUS. However, while you install WSUS, it remains unconfigured, and SCCM is installed on top of WSUS.

MORE INFORMATION

For more information about SCCM, search for SCCM on the Microsoft website.

SKILL SUMMARY

IN THIS LESSON, YOU LEARNED:

- One way to keep Windows up to date is to use the Windows Update program, which scans your system to determine what updates and fixes your system needs.
- A service pack is a tested, cumulative set of hotfixes, security updates, critical updates, and updates, as well as additional fixes for problems found internally since the release of the product.
- Auto Update works in the background when you are connected to the Internet to identify when new updates are available and to download them to your computer.
- Windows Server Update Services (WSUS) is a program that is included with today's Microsoft Windows Servers that allows administrators to manage the distribution of updates and other patches to computers within an organization.
- With autonomous mode, an upstream WSUS server shares updates with its downstream server or servers during synchronization. However, the approval of updates is done separately on the WSUS servers.
- In replica mode, you have an upstream WSUS server shares updates and the approval of updates with its downstream server or servers.
- To install WSUS on Windows Server 2012, you install WSUS as a role.
- To specify what updates go to correct computers at the correct time, organize your computers into computer groups.
- By default, each computer is always assigned to the All Computers group. As new computers are added, they will be assigned to the Unassigned Computers group until you assign them to another group.

- With server-side targeting, you manually assign the computer to a group.
- With client-side targeting, you have the computers automatically assign computers to the computer groups using group policies or someone has to manually modify the registry.
- By default, Windows computers will get updates from Windows Update. You can use group policies to have the domain computers use the specified WSUS server.
- One of the advantages of using WSUS is that you control which updates clients receive and when clients receive those updates. This gives you an opportunity to test the updates and then roll them out to the computer groups.
- To see detailed information about updates, computers, and synchronization, you can run the WSUS built-in reports.

Knowledge Assessment

Multiple Choice

Select the correct answer for each of the following questions.

1. Which term best describes multiple hotfixes, security updates, and critical updates which are packaged together and thoroughly tested together?
   a. Cumulative patch
   b. Service pack
   c. Compiled update
   d. Out-of-band package
2. To specify which computers get which updates, into which of the following categories should you divide the computers?
   a. Packages
   b. Broadcast domains
   c. Computer groups
   d. Update definitions
3. Which of the following is the default port used for synchronization?
   a. 8080
   b. 3128
   c. 8530
   d. 23
4. Which of the following WSUS modes has upstream WSUS servers share updates and the approval of updates with WSUS downstream servers?
   a. Autonomous
   b. Replica
   c. Download
   d. Share
5. Which of the following is the process of downloading updates for a WSUS server?
   a. Transferal
   b. Replicating
   c. Targeting
   d. Synchronization

6. Which term best describes when computers are automatically assigned to a computer group using group policies or by modifying the registry?
   a. Replica targeting
   b. Server-side targeting
   c. Sync targeting
   d. Client-side targeting
7. Which of the following is required in order to view reports in WSUS?
   a. .Net Framework Viewer
   b. SQL Server Table Displayer
   c. Microsoft Report Viewer 2008 Redistributable
   d. Text Converter
8. Which of the following is the default database used by WSUS?
   a. PID
   b. FIX
   c. WID
   d. SID
9. Which of the following is the best strategy for getting all clients within an organization to use a WSUS server?
   a. Modify the registry of the client computers.
   b. Use a router that redirects to WSUS.
   c. Change the WSUS.TXT file in the C:\Windows folder.
   d. Use group policies.
10. If a client is not part of a domain, client-side targeting can be accomplished by doing which of the following?
    a. By using group policies
    b. By modifying the registry
    c. Modify the NTFS permissions
    d. Add the WSUS client role

Best Answer

Choose the letter that corresponds to the best answer. More than one answer choice may achieve the goal. Select the BEST answer.

1. You administer two servers (Server1 and Server2) with WSUS installed. If Server1 is part of the contoso.com domain and Server2 is a stand-alone server, which of the following options ensures that all updates that are approved on Server1 will automatically be approved on Server2?
   a. Update Source and Proxy Server
   b. Synchronization Schedule
   c. Automatic Approvals
   d. Computers
2. You have just added a new update to the WSUS server and you want to test the update to your test group. Which of the following commands is used so that you don't have to wait for the update to be deployed?
   a. `gpupdate /force`
   b. `wuauclt.exe /detectnow`
   c. `update /now`
   d. `wsusserver /startupdate`

3. You administer a server (Server1) with WSUS. You discover that certain updates listed in the WSUS administrative console are unavailable on Server1. Which of the following options ensures that all of the updates listed in the WSUS administrative console are available on the server?
   a. Running wsusutil.exe with the `/verify` option
   b. Running wuauclt.exe with the `/detectnow` option
   c. Running wuauclt.exe with the `/resetauthorization` option
   d. Running wsusutil.exe with the `reset` option

4. You administer a server (Server1) with WSUS. You use a group policy to configure all WSUS client computers to detect every update and install updates weekly. You just downloaded a critical update; which of the following actions should be taken to install the critical update during the next detection interval?
   a. Run the wuauclt.exe `/force` command.
   b. Configure the deadline settings for the update.
   c. Configure the Synchronization Schedule.
   d. Run the `gpupdate /force` command.

5. You administer a server (Server1) with WSUS. You want to deploy a new WSUS server (Server2) on a remote subnet and you want to replicate the metadata from Server1 to Server2. Which of the following actions should be taken with Server1 to start the process?
   a. Run the wbadmin.exe to start a backup WSUS.
   b. Run wbadmin.exe to start a backup of the System State.
   c. Run wsusutil.exe with the `export` option.
   d. Run wuauclt.exe with the `migrate` option.

Matching and Identification

1. Match the WSUSutil.exe option with the correct description or scenario.
   _______ a) `export`
   _______ b) `import`
   _______ c) `movecontent`
   _______ d) `reset`
   _______ e) `deleteunneededrevisions`
   1. Exports the update metadata to an export package file
   2. Used to move WSUS update files when a hard drive fills up
   3. Used after you restore a WSUS so that the update files match the WSUS database
   4. Imports the update metadata to an export package file
   5. Shrinks the database

2. Write the Windows PowerShell command for the specified function or scenario.
   ____________________ Gets a list of all WSUS classifications
   ____________________ Declines the update for deployment
   ____________________ Gets the list of all products currently available on WSUS by category
   ____________________ Sets whether the product representing the category of updates to synchronize is enabled or disabled
   ____________________ Approves an update to be applied to clients

Build a List

1. In order of first to last, specify the tasks to synchronize updates from Windows Update site or another WSUS server.
   _____ Specify where to store the files.
   _____ Specify a synchronization schedule.
   _____ Specify what products and type of updates you want to download.
   _____ Define the computer groups.
   _____ Specify what languages you want to support.
   _____ Configure the update source and proxy server.
   _____ Run Windows Update on the WSUS server.
2. You administer a server (Server1) with WSUS. Microsoft releases a widget program but this new widget program is not listed on the Products and Classifications list. Specify the correct order of the steps required to make sure that all of the updates of the widget program are available to all of the client computers. (Not all options will be used.)
   _____ Synchronize the WSUS server.
   _____ Run the Server reset wizard.
   _____ Add a computer group.
   _____ Move the computers to a new group.
   _____ Approve the updates.
   _____ Add the widget program in the Products and Classifications settings.
   _____ Modify the Products and Classification settings.
3. In order of first to last, specify the tasks that must be completed before you can deploy updates using WSUS. (Not all tasks will be required.)
   _____ Configure the clients to use WSUS using group policies.
   _____ Configure Internet Options in Internet Explorer to use the proxy server.
   _____ Create computer groups.
   _____ Select the type of updates to download and synchronize updates.
   _____ Approve the updates for deployment.
   _____ Add *Microsoft.com* to the Windows firewall to allow all packets.

Business Case Scenarios

Scenario 2-1: Updating Computers

You were just hired by the Contoso Company, which has more than 1,000 client computers at two office buildings located at two sites. You have determined that computers have not been patched in 18 months. What solution would you recommend, and how would you implement this solution?

Scenario 2-2: Creating Computer Groups in WSUS

You have the following departments within your organization:

Sales	150 computers
Marketing	75 computers
Management	50 computers
Manufacturing	200 computers
Information Technology	50 computers

How many groups should you create in WSUS? Why?

Monitoring Servers

LESSON 3

70-411 EXAM OBJECTIVE

Objective 1.3 – Monitor servers. This objective may include but is not limited to: configure Data Collector Sets (DCS); configure alerts; monitor real-time performance; monitor virtual machines (VMs); monitor events; configure event subscriptions; configure network monitoring.

LESSON HEADING	EXAM OBJECTIVE
Introducing the Microsoft Management Console (MMC)	
Using Server Manager	
Using Computer Management	
Using the Services Console	
Using Event Viewer	Monitor events
Understanding Logs and Events	
Filtering Events	
Adding a Task to an Event	
Configuring Event Subscriptions	Configure event subscriptions
Using Reliability Monitor	
Managing Performance	Monitor real-time performance
Using Task Manager	
Using Resource Monitor	
Using Performance Monitor	
Using Common Performance Counters	
Configuring Data Collector Sets (DCS)	Configure Data Collector Sets (DCS)
Configuring Performance Alerts	Configure alerts
Monitoring the Network	Configure network monitoring
Using the netstat Command	
Using Protocol Analyzers	
Monitoring Virtual Machines (VMs)	Monitor virtual machines (VMs)

KEY TERMS

Administrative Tools
Computer Management
Data Collector Sets (DCS)
event subscription
Event Viewer
Hyper-V Resource Metering
Microsoft Management Console (MMC)
netstat
Microsoft Network Monitor
performance
performance alert
Performance Monitor
process
Reliability Monitor
Resource Monitor
Server Manager
service
Services console
Task Manager

TAKE NOTE*

Now that you have installed and updated Windows server, you need to learn how to monitor the server. During this lesson, you will learn about common tools that are used in monitoring your servers and that are invaluable when troubleshooting a wide range of problems.

Introducing the Microsoft Management Console (MMC)

THE BOTTOM LINE

The ***Microsoft Management Console (MMC)*** is one of the primary administrative tools used to manage Windows and many of the network services provided by Windows. It provides a standard method to create, save, and open the various administrative tools provided by Windows. When you open Administrative Tools, most of these programs are MMC.

To start an empty MMC, go to the command prompt (or the Run box), type *mmc* or *mmc.exe*. To open the command prompt or the Run box in Windows Server 2012, move the mouse cursor to the exact lower-left corner until the desktop shortcuts menu opens (see Figure 3-1). Then choose *Run* or choose *Command Prompt (Admin)*.

Figure 3-1

Opening the Run command

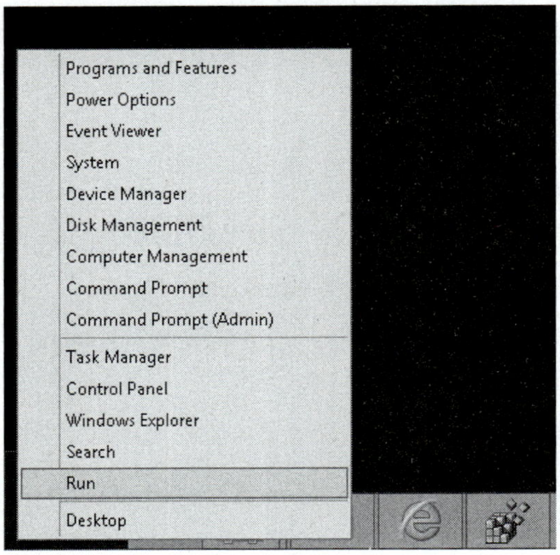

Every MMC has a console tree that displays the hierarchical organization of snap-ins (or pluggable modules) and extensions (a snap-in that requires a parent snap-in). By adding and deleting snap-ins and extensions, users can customize the console or access tools that are not located in Administrative Tools. You can add snap-ins to a MMC by clicking File > Add/Remove Snap-ins. Figure 3-2 shows the Add or Remove Snap-ins dialog box.

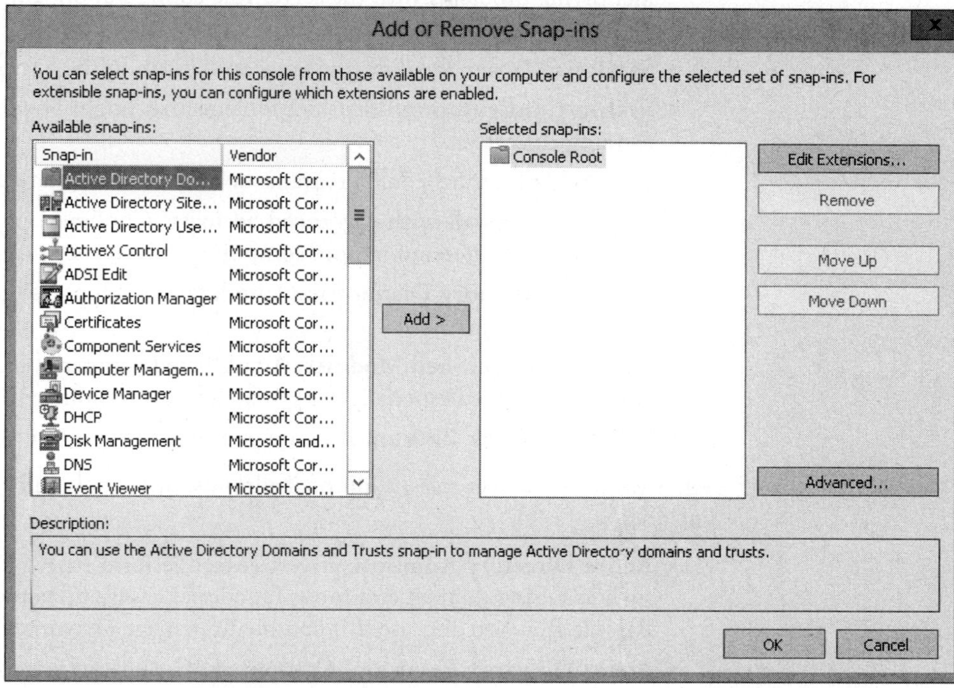

Figure 3-2

Adding snap-ins

Administrative Tools is a folder in the Control Panel that contains tools for system administrators and advanced users. To access Administrative Tools, open the Control Panel. If you are in Category view, click System and Security > Administrative Tools. If you are in Icon view, double-click Administrative Tools. The Administrative Tools are also available in the tools menu of Server Manager.

Some common administrative tools in this folder include:

- **Component Services:** Configure and administer Component Object Model (COM) components. Component Services is designed for use by developers and administrators.
- **Computer Management:** Manage local or remote computers by using a single, consolidated desktop tool. Using Computer Management, you can perform many tasks, such as monitoring system events, configuring hard disks, and managing system performance.
- **Data Sources (ODBC):** Use Open Database Connectivity (ODBC) to move data from one type of database (a data source) to another.
- **Event Viewer:** View information about significant events, such as programs starting or stopping or security errors that are recorded in event logs.
- **iSCSI Initiator:** Configure advanced connections between storage devices on a network.
- **Local Security Policy:** View and edit Group Policy security settings.
- **Performance Monitor:** View advanced system information about the processor, memory, hard disk, and network performance.
- **Print Management:** Manage printers and print servers on a network and perform other administrative tasks.

- **Resource Monitor:** View real-time information on CPU, memory, disk, and network utilization.
- **Security Configuration Wizard:** A Wizard that walks you through how to create a security policy that you can apply to any server on the network.
- **Server Manager:** A console that allows you to manage and secure multiple server roles, including managing the server's identity and system information; displaying server status; identifying problems with the server role configuration; and managing all roles installed on the server.
- **Services:** Manage the different services that run in the background on your computer.
- **System Configuration:** Identify problems that might be preventing Windows from running correctly.
- **Task Scheduler:** Schedule programs or other tasks to run automatically.
- **Windows Firewall with Advanced Security:** Configure advanced firewall settings on both this computer and remote computers on your network.
- **Windows Memory Diagnostics:** Check your computer's memory to see whether it is functioning properly.
- **Windows PowerShell Modules:** A task-based command-line shell and scripting language designed especially for system administration.
- **Windows Server Backup:** Back up and restore the server.

After you install server roles, additional administrative tools will be loaded. Some of these tools include:

- **Active Directory Administrative Center:** Perform Active Directory administrative tasks, such as raising domain and forest functional levels and enabling the Active Directory Recycle Bin. You also use this console to manage Dynamic Access Control.
- **Active Directory Users and Computers:** Create and manage Active Directory users, computers, and groups. You can also use this tool to create Organizational Units (OUs).
- **DNS Console:** Configure and manage the DNS Server role. This includes creating forward and reverse lookup zones and managing DNS records.
- **Group Policy Management:** Edit Group Policy Objects (GPOs) and manage their application in AD DS.
- **IIS Manager:** Manage websites.

You might assume these tools are used only to manage the local computer. However, many of them can be used to manage remote computers as well. For example, you can use the Computer Management tool or the Server Management console to connect to and manage other computers, assuming you have administrative rights to the computer.

Using Server Manager

Server Manager is a management console in Windows Server 2012 that helps you manage local and remote Windows Based servers. By managing servers as groups, you can perform the same administrative tasks quickly across multiple servers that have the same role or members of the same group.

You can use Server Manager to perform the following tasks on both local and remove servers:

- Add roles and features.
- Launch Windows PowerShell sessions.
- View events.

- Perform server configuration tasks.
- Add remote servers to a pool of servers that Server Manager can be used to manage.
- Install or uninstall roles, role services, and features on the local server or on remote servers that are running Windows Server 2012.
- View and make changes to server roles and features that are installed on local or remote servers.
- Perform management tasks (such as starting or stopping services or configuring network settings, users and groups, and Remote Desktop connections).
- Scanning roles for compliance with best practices.
- Running role-management tools.
- Determine server status, identify critical events, and analyze and troubleshoot configuration issues or failures.
- Restart servers.

Using Computer Management

The ***Computer Management*** console is one of the primary tools used to manage a computer running Windows 8 and can be very useful when managing a computer running Windows Server 2012. It includes the most commonly used MMC snap-ins.

The Computer Management console (see Figure 3-3) is available in Windows Server 2003, Windows Server 2008, Windows Server 2012, Windows XP, Windows Vista, Windows 7, and Windows 8. It includes multiple snap-ins, including Task Scheduler, Event Viewer, Shared Folders, Local Users and Groups, Performance, Device Management, Routing and Remote Access, Services, and WMI Control.

Figure 3-3

Viewing the Computer Management console

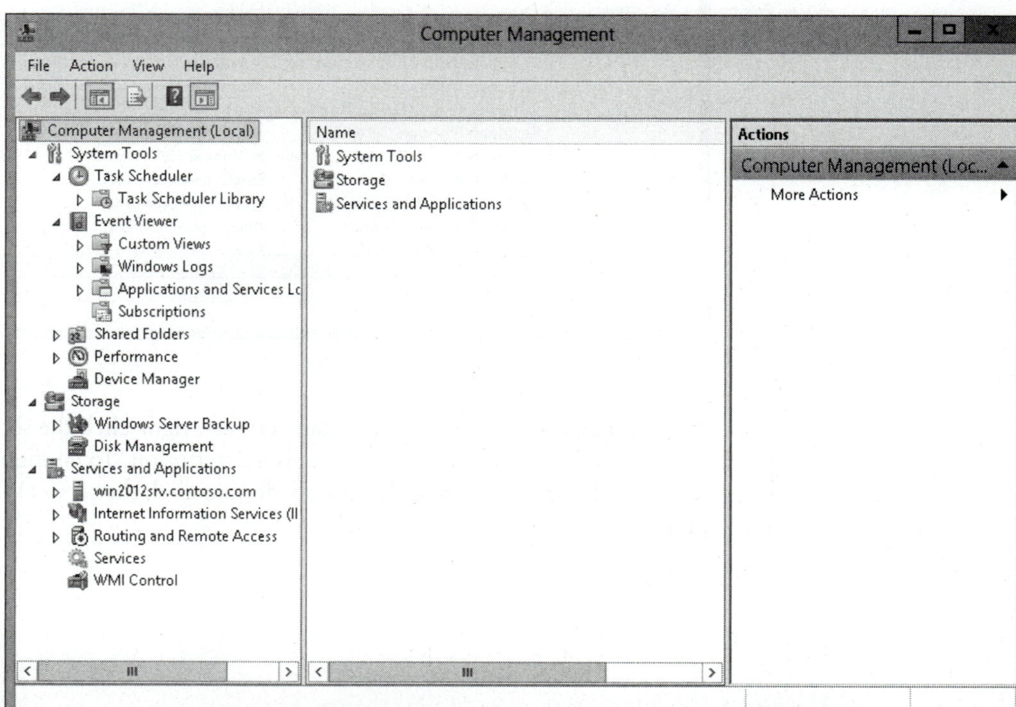

Using the Services Console

A ***service*** is a program, routine, or process that performs a specific system function to support other programs or to provide a network service. A service runs in the system background without a user interface. Some examples include World Wide Publishing services, Server services, Workstation services, and Windows Event Log services.

To manage services, use the ***Services console*** located on the Administrative Tools menu. The Services snap-in (see Figure 3-4) is also included in the Computer Management console and the Server Manager console. You can also execute `mmc services.mmc` from a command prompt or Run box.

Figure 3-4

Viewing the Services console

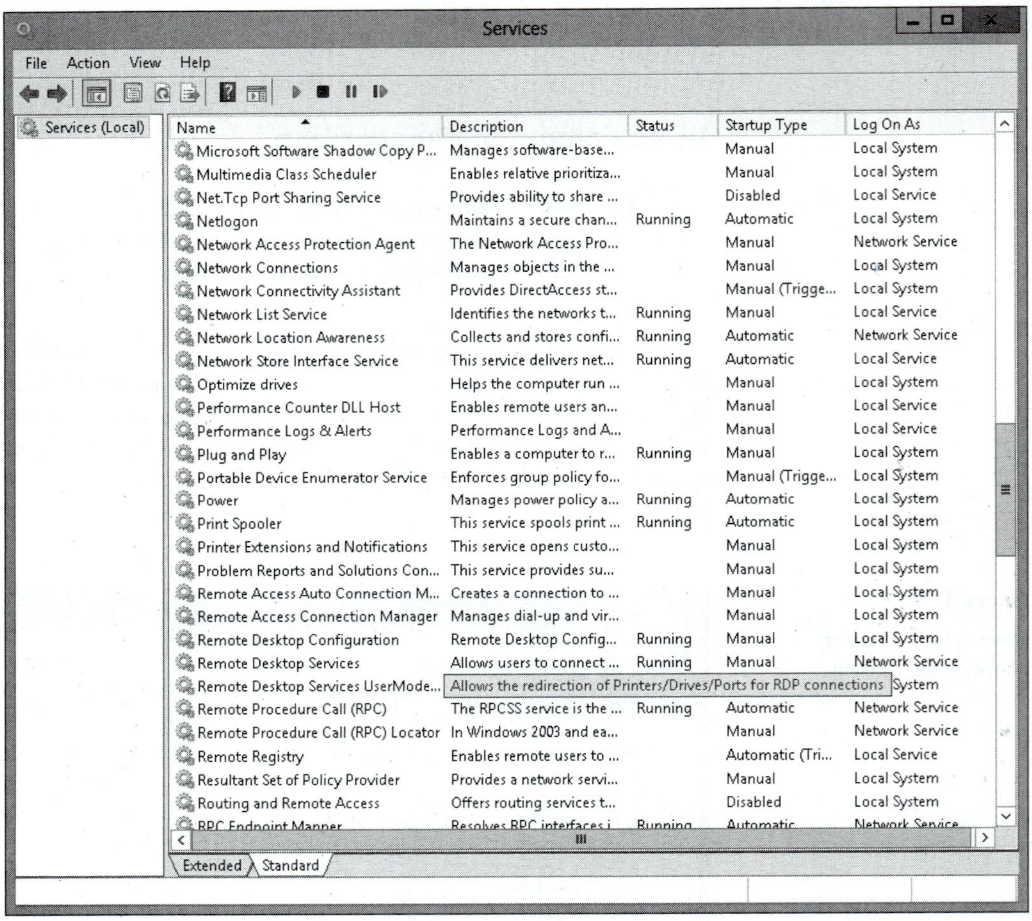

To start, stop, pause, resume, or restart services, right-click the service and choose the desired option. To the left of the service name is a description. To configure a service, right-click the service and choose *Properties* (or simply double-click the service). Figure 3-5 shows the Services properties.

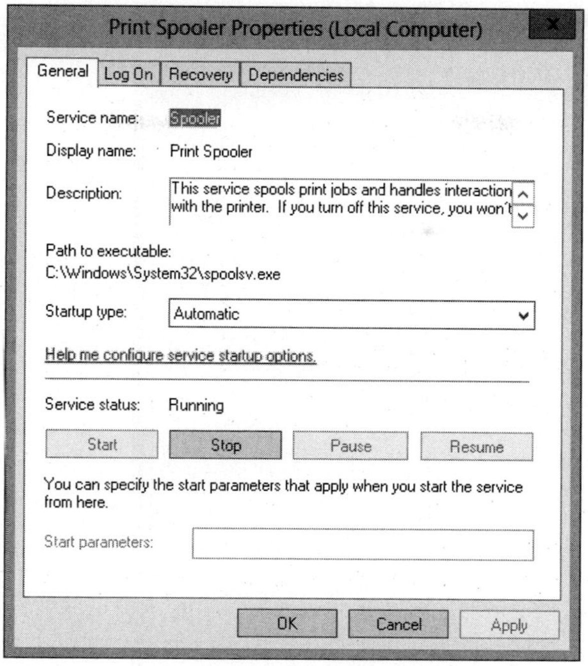

Figure 3-5
Configuring a service

On the General tab, click the *Start-up type* drop-down arrow and choose one of the following:

- **Automatic:** Specifies that the service should start automatically when the system starts.
- **Automatic (Delayed Start):** Specifies that the service should start automatically after the services marked as automatic have started (which is approximately two minutes).
- **Manual:** Specifies that a user or a dependent service can start the service. Services with manual start-up do not start automatically when the system starts.
- **Disable:** Prevents the service from being started by the system, a user, or any dependent service.

If you like doing things at the command prompt or you have a need use a script to start or stop a service, use the `sc` command to communicate with the Service Control Manager and services. The `sc config` command is used to modify a service entry in the registry and Service Database. You can also use the `net start` command to start services and the `net stop` command to stop services.

When you configure a service, you need to configure what account the service runs under. You can use the built-in accounts included with Windows, or you can use a service account that you create locally or on the domain. The built-in accounts include:

- **Local System:** Highly privileged account that can access most resources on the local computer.
- **NT Authority\LocalService:** Has the same privileges of the local Users group on the computer. When it accesses Network resources, it uses no credentials and a null session.
- **NT Authority\NetworkService:** Has the same level of access as the Users group on the local computer. When it accesses network resources, it does so under the context of the local computer account.

Figure 3-6 shows the *Log On* tab.

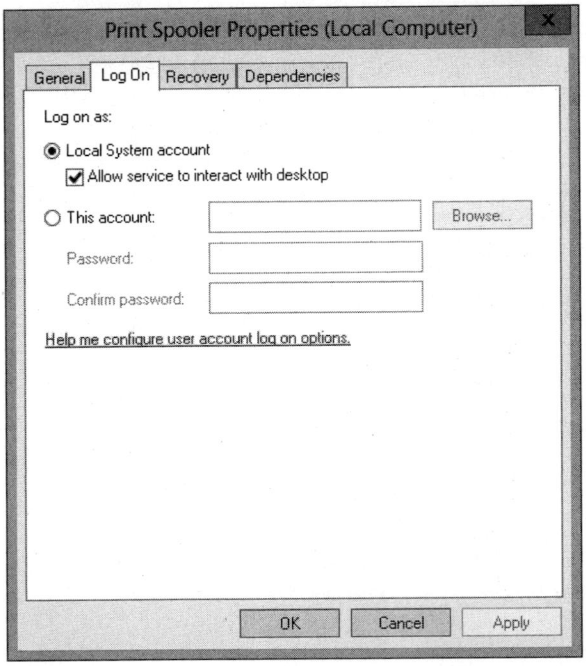

Figure 3-6
Viewing the Log On tab

You should always take care when changing the startup parameters for a service, including the *Startup type* and *Log on as* settings, because these changes might prevent key services from running correctly. In addition, Microsoft recommends that you do not change the *Allow service to interact with desktop* setting because this will allow the service to access any information displayed on the interactive user's desktop. A malicious user can then take control of the service or attack it from the interactive desktop. If you specify an account that does not have permission to log on as a service, the Services snap-in automatically grants the appropriate permissions to that account on the computer that you are managing. If you use a local or domain account, use a strong password and use a password that does not expire.

As a general rule, you should use the account with minimum rights and permissions for the service to operate. In addition, you should use different service accounts for different services. So if you install Exchange and SQL on a server, you should have a service account for Exchange and a different service account for SQL. SQL and Exchange should be on the same server only for small businesses that have only a handful of employees.

If you enable or disable a service and a problem occurs, you can try to start the service manually to see what happens. You can also check the Event Viewer for more information on some of the errors. If the system does not boot because of the enabled or disabled service, you should try to start the computer in Safe mode, which starts only the core services needed to operate, loads only the necessary drivers to operate, and loads in 640x480 screen resolution with the minimum number of colors. By using Safe mode, you should have an opportunity to fix the problem.

If you are new to Windows, particularly in administering and configuring Windows, you should click on each service and read the respective description for each service. You will learn that many service names are very descriptive. For now, let's cover two specific services:

- **Server:** Supports file, print, and named-piped sharing over the network. If the Services service is not started, you will not be able to access shared folders, including administrative shares such as C$ and IPC$.
- **Workstation:** Creates and maintains client network connections to remove servers using the SMB protocol. Without this service, you will not be able to access shared folders on other computers.

Using Event Viewer

THE BOTTOM LINE

One of the most useful troubleshooting tools is the Event Viewer, which is essentially a log viewer. Whenever you have problems, you should look in the Event Viewer to see any errors or warnings that might reveal what the problem is.

CERTIFICATION READY
Monitor events.
Objective 1.3

The ***Event Viewer*** is an MMC snap-in that enables you to browse and manage event logs. It is included in the Computer Management and is included in Administrative Tools as a stand-alone console. You can also execute the `eventvwr.msc` command.

Event Viewer enables you to perform the following tasks:

- View events from multiple event logs (see Figure 3-7).
- Save useful event filters as custom views that can be reused.
- Schedule a task to run in response to an event.
- Create and manage event subscriptions.

Figure 3-7

Event Viewer

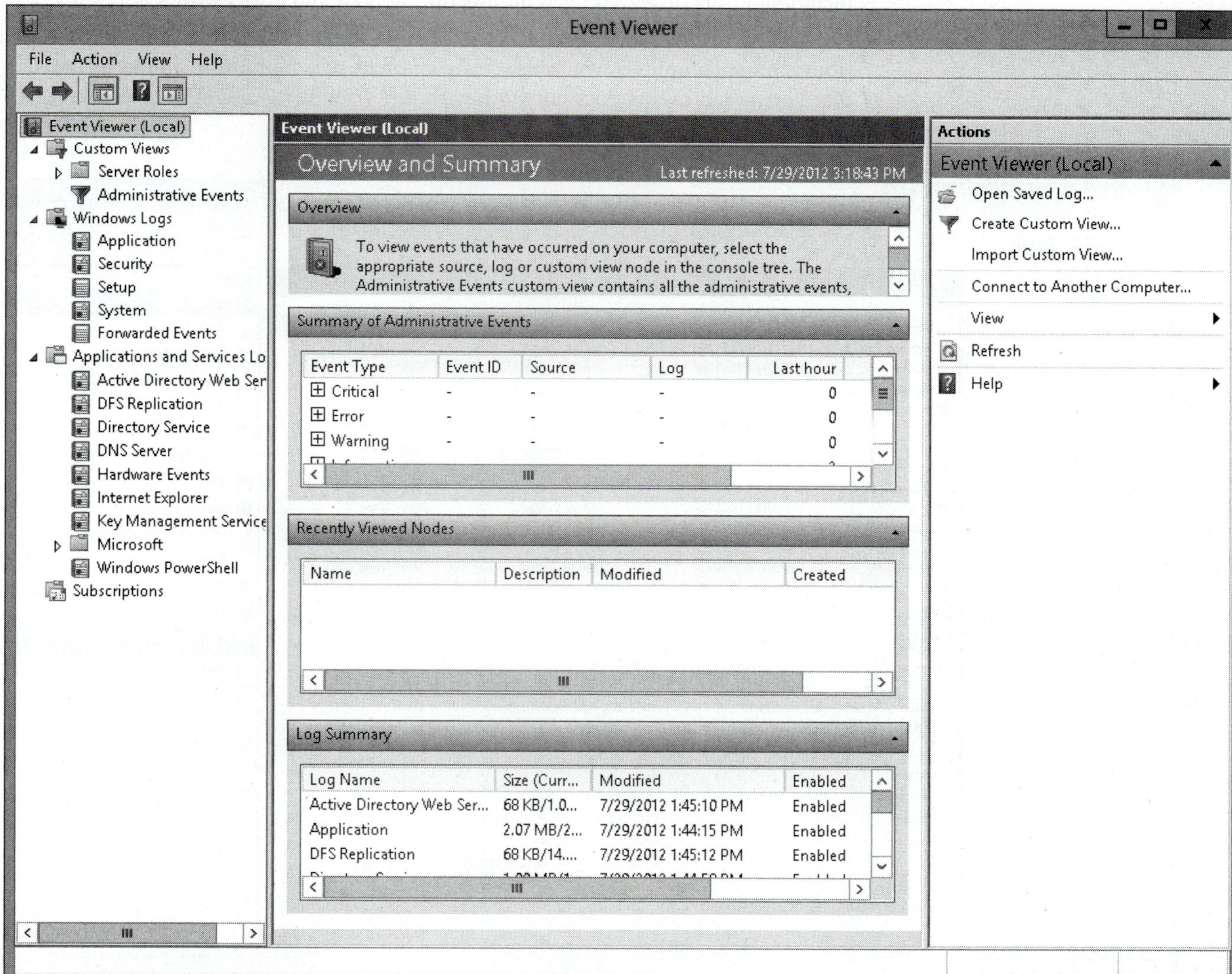

Understanding Logs and Events

> To get the best use of Windows logs, you need to understand how the logs are organized and how the events are categorized.

When you examine the Event Viewer more closely, you will see the following items:

- **Custom Views:** Allows you to create custom views of events. By default, it includes Administrative Events, which collects Critical, Error, and Warnings from all logs on the server. However, you can create your own customer view by right-clicking Custom Views and selecting Create Custom View.
- **Windows Logs:** Includes logs that were available in previous versions of Windows. They include:
  - **Application:** Contains events logged by applications or programs.
  - **Security:** Contains events such as valid and invalid logon attempts and access to designated objects such as files and folders, printers, and Active Directory objects. By default, the Security log is empty until you enable auditing.
  - **Setup:** Contains events related to application setup.
  - **System** (see Figure 3-8): Contains events logged by Windows system components, including errors displayed by Windows during boot and errors with services.
  - **Forwarded Events:** Stores events collected from remote computers. To collect events from remote computers, you must create an event subscription. It should be noted that Forwarded Events does not work with pre-Windows 7 and Windows Server 2008 operating systems.

Figure 3-8

Viewing System logs

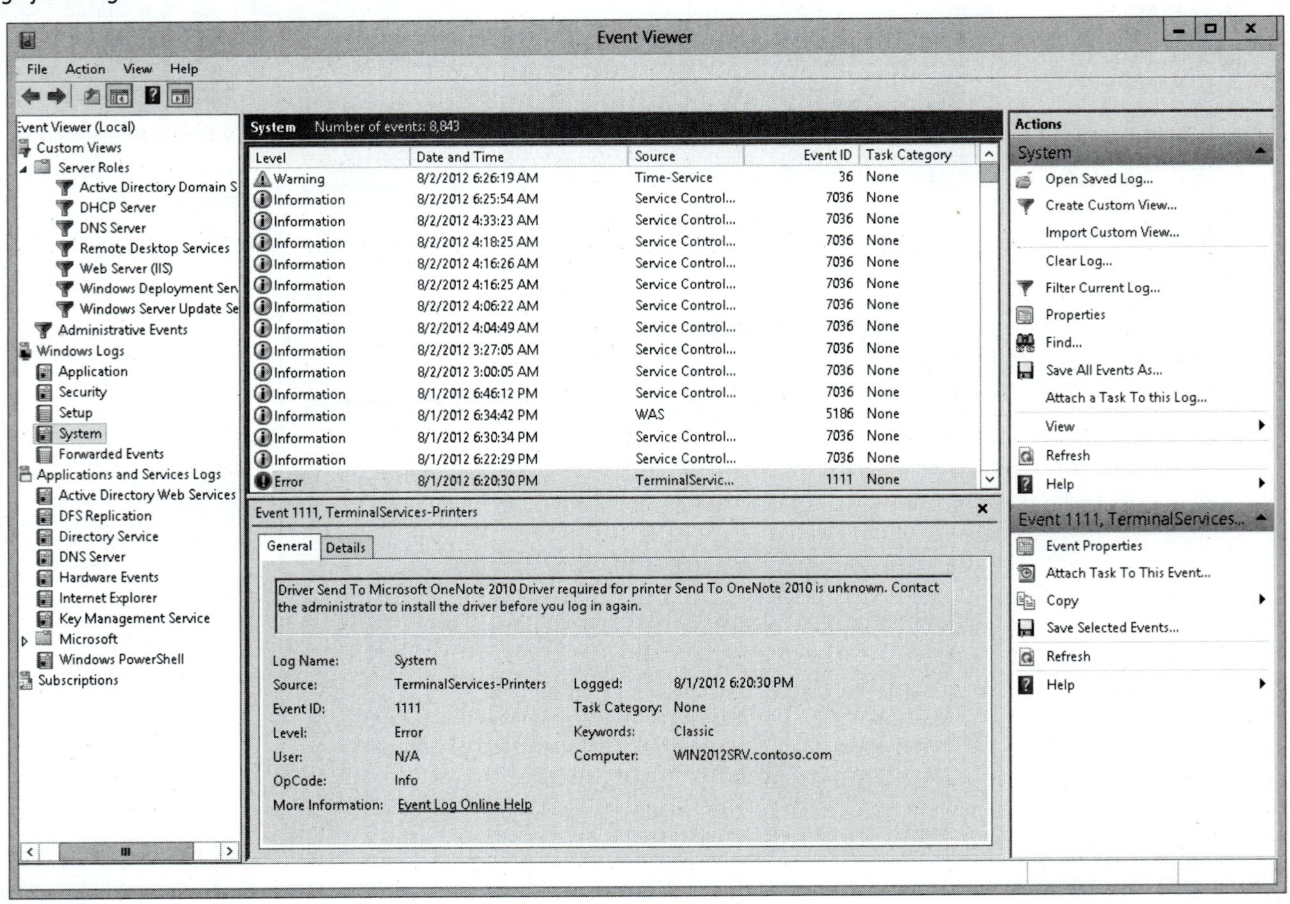

- **Applications and Services Logs:** Displays a set of events related to an application or service. Some examples include DHCP, DNS, and Active Directory.

When you open an event (see Figure 3-9), you will see the Log Name, Source, Event ID, Level, User (if applicable), Logged details (date and time), Computer, and other information.

Figure 3-9

Viewing an event

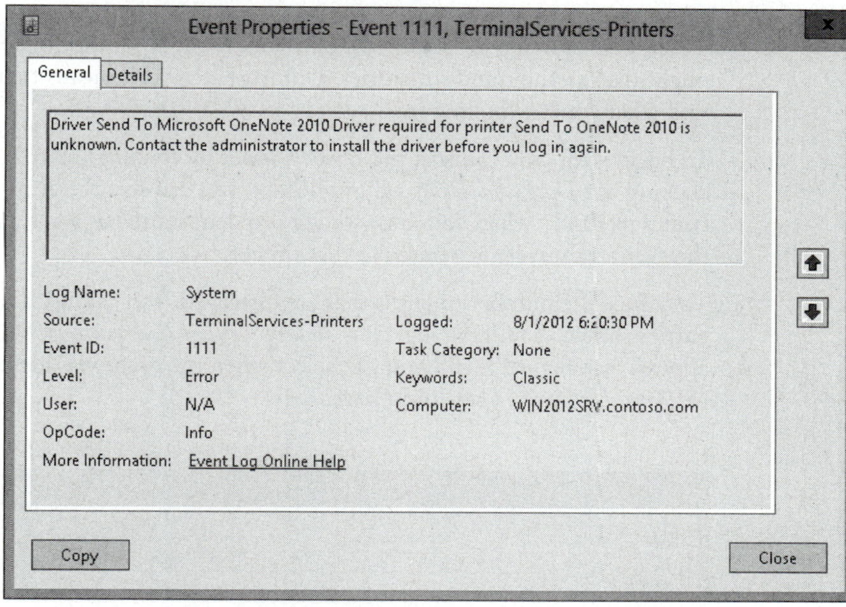

Table 3-1 shows the common fields displayed in the Event Viewer logs.

Table 3-1

Common Files Displayed in Event Viewer Logs

PROPERTY NAME	DESCRIPTION
`Source`	The software that logged the event, which can be a program name (such as "SQL Server") or a component of the system or of a large program (such as a driver name).
`Event ID`	A number identifying the particular event type.
`Level`	A classification of the event severity.
	Information: Indicates that a change in an application or component has occurred (such as an operation has successfully completed, a resource has been created, or a service started).
	Warning: Indicates that an issue has occurred that can impact service or result in a more serious problem if action is not taken.
	Error: Indicates that a problem has occurred that might impact functionality that is external to the application or component that triggered the event.
	Critical: Indicates that a failure has occurred from which the application or component that triggered the event cannot automatically recover.
	Success Audit: Shown in security logs to indicate that the exercise of a user right was successful.
	Failure Audit: Shown in security logs to indicate that the exercise of a user right has failed.

Filtering Events

When looking at the logs shown by Event Viewer, you can be overwhelmed by the number of events. Therefore, you need to know how to filter events so that you can focus on what you want to focus on.

When you open any of these logs, particularly the Application, Security, or System logs, they might display thousands of entries. Unfortunately, this means that it might take some time to find what you are looking for.

To begin with, you can sort the Event Viewer by clicking the column header. For example, by clicking the *Date and Time* column header, you can sort the events by date and time. This comes in handy when you know that a problem started at a certain time and you want to view the events that were generated at that time.

To reduce the number of items that are displayed, you can use a filter to reduce the number of entries shown. To filter a log, click *Action > Filter Current Log*. When the Filter Current Log appears (see Figure 3-10), you can select when the event was logged, the *Event level*, *Task category*, *Keywords*, *User*, and *Computer(s)*.

Figure 3-10

Filtering an event log

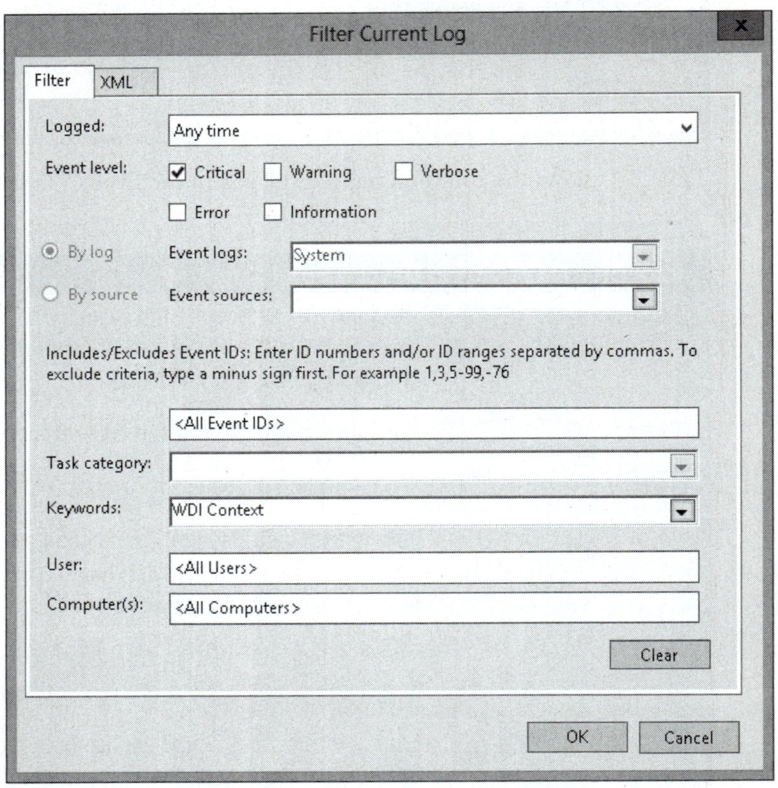

Adding a Task to an Event

When certain events occur, there are times you would like to execute a task. With the Event Viewer, you can attach a task to any event in the Event Viewer.

When you associate a task to an event, you create a scheduled task that can be found in Task Scheduler. Therefore, whenever the specified event appears, the task will be executed. If you need to modify the task after it has been created, you can open Task Scheduler to modify the task.

CREATE A BASIC TASK

GET READY. To create a basic task to an event, perform the following steps:

1. Open Server Manager by clicking the Server Manager button on the task bar. The *Server Manager* dashboard opens.
2. Click Tools > Event Viewer.
3. Right-click an event that you want to add a task to and choose Attach Task To This Event (see Figure 3-11).

Figure 3-11

Attaching a task to an event

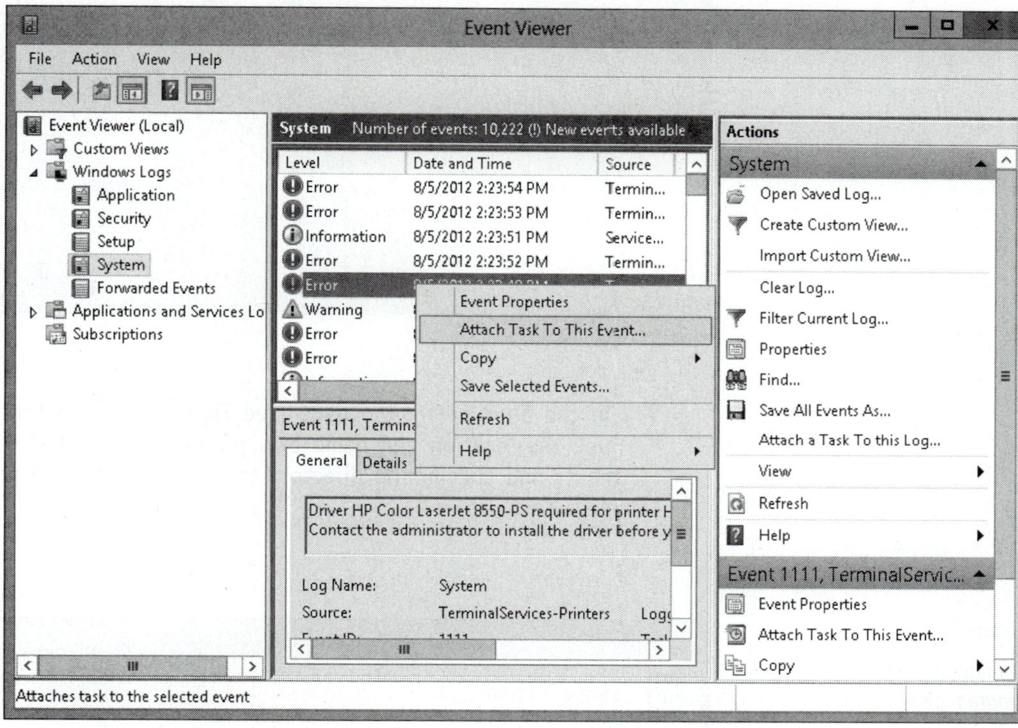

4. When the *Create Basic Task Wizard* starts, click Next.
5. When the *When a Specified Event Is Logged* page opens, click Next.
6. On the *Action* page (see Figure 3-12), choose one of the following options:

   Start a program

   Send an e-mail

   Display a message

   Since *Send an e-mail* and *Display a message* is being deprecated (which means that you should not use it unless you really need to and that it may not be available in the future), you should select Start a program and then click Next.

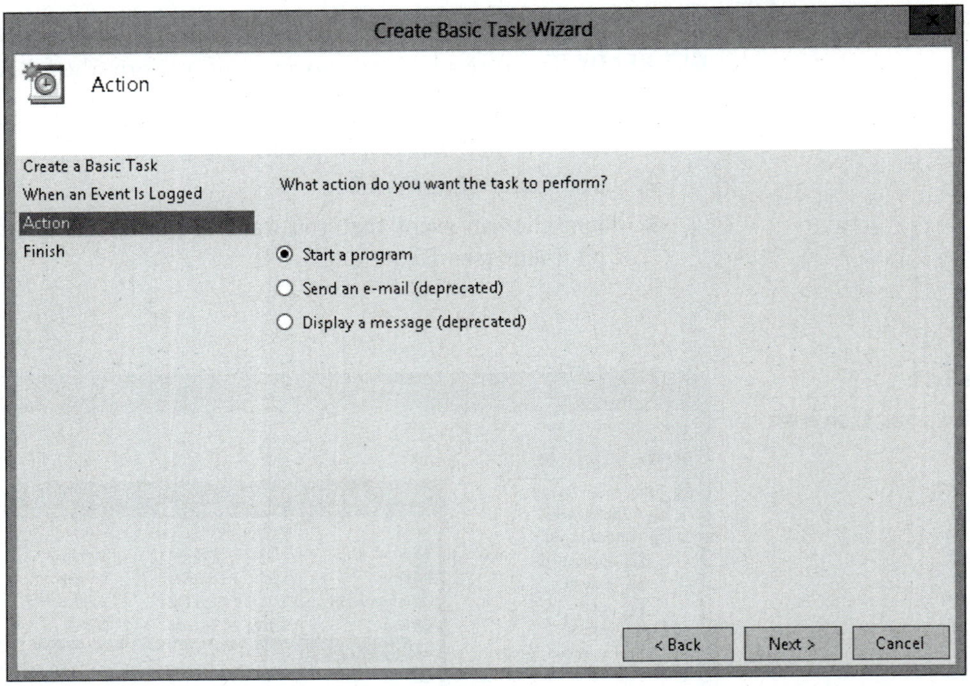

Figure 3-12

Choosing an action

7. On the *Start a Program* page (see Figure 3-13), in the *Program/script* text box, type the location and name of a program or script. If necessary, add any arguments and specify the directory to start in when the program or script is executed. Click **Next**.

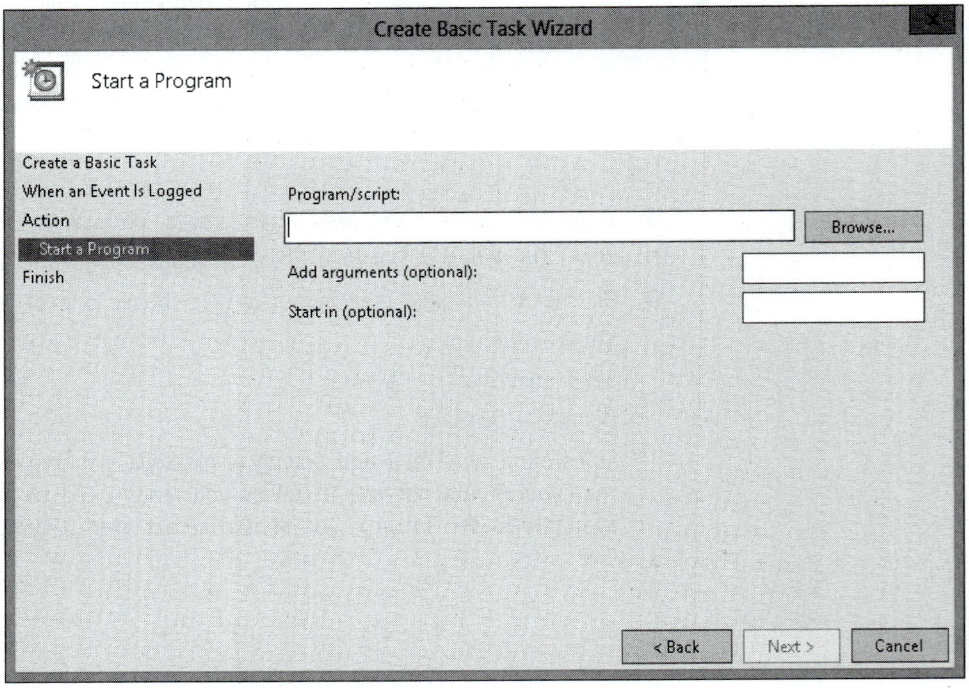

Figure 3-13

Configuring the *Start a Program* page

8. On the *Summary* page, click **Finish**.
9. When an *Event Viewer* dialog box appears, click **OK**.
10. Close the *Event Viewer*.

Configuring Event Subscriptions

Originally, the Event Viewer allowed you to view events on a single computer. However, troubleshooting an issue might require you to examine a set of events stored in multiple logs on multiple computers. Therefore, Microsoft enhanced Event Viewer to capture events from multiple computers so that you can view the events using one console.

CERTIFICATION READY
Configure event subscriptions.
Objective 1.3

Today's Event Viewer can be used to collect copies of events from multiple remote computers and store them locally. To specify which events to collect, you create an ***event subscription***. Among other details, the subscription specifies exactly which events will be collected and in which log they will be stored locally. Once a subscription is active and events are being collected, you can view and manipulate these forwarded events as you would any other locally stored events. Events are forwarded using Hypertext Transfer Protocol (HTTP) or Hypertext Transfer Protocol Secure (HTTPS).

To configure event subscriptions, perform the following steps:

1. Configure the forwarding computer.
2. Configure the Collecting Computer.
3. Create an Event Subscription.

CONFIGURE THE FORWARDING COMPUTER

GET READY. To configure a forwarding computer to forward events, perform the following steps:

1. Right-click **Start** and choose **Command Prompt (Admin)**.
2. At the command prompt, execute the following command:
   ```
   Winrm quickconfig
   ```
3. To add the collecting computer name to the Administrators group, execute the following command:
   ```
   Net localgroup "Administrators"
   <collecting_computer_name>$@<domain_name> /add
   ```
4. If a message appears, indicating that changes must be made, type ***Y*** and then press ***Enter***.
5. Close the *Command Prompt* window.

Executing the `winrm quickconfig` command on the forwarding computer accomplishes the following:

- It sets the Windows Remote Management (WS-Management) service to Automatic (Delayed Start) and starts the service.
- It configures the Windows Remote Management HTTP listener.
- It creates a Windows Firewall exception.

CONFIGURE THE COLLECTING COMPUTER

GET READY. To configure a collecting computer to forward events, perform the following steps:

1. Right-click Start and choose Command Prompt (Admin).
2. At the command prompt, execute the following command:
   `Wecutil qc`
3. Close the *Command Prompt* window.

By executing the `wecutil qc` command, you configure the receiving computer to receive events. The last step is to then specify the events you want to send to the receiving computer.

CREATE AN EVENT SUBSCRIPTION

GET READY. To create an event subscription on the collecting computer, perform the following steps:

1. Open Server Manager.
2. Click Tools > Event Viewer.
3. Right-click Subscriptions and choose Create Subscription (see Figure 3-14). The Subscription Properties dialog box opens.

Figure 3-14

Creating a subscription

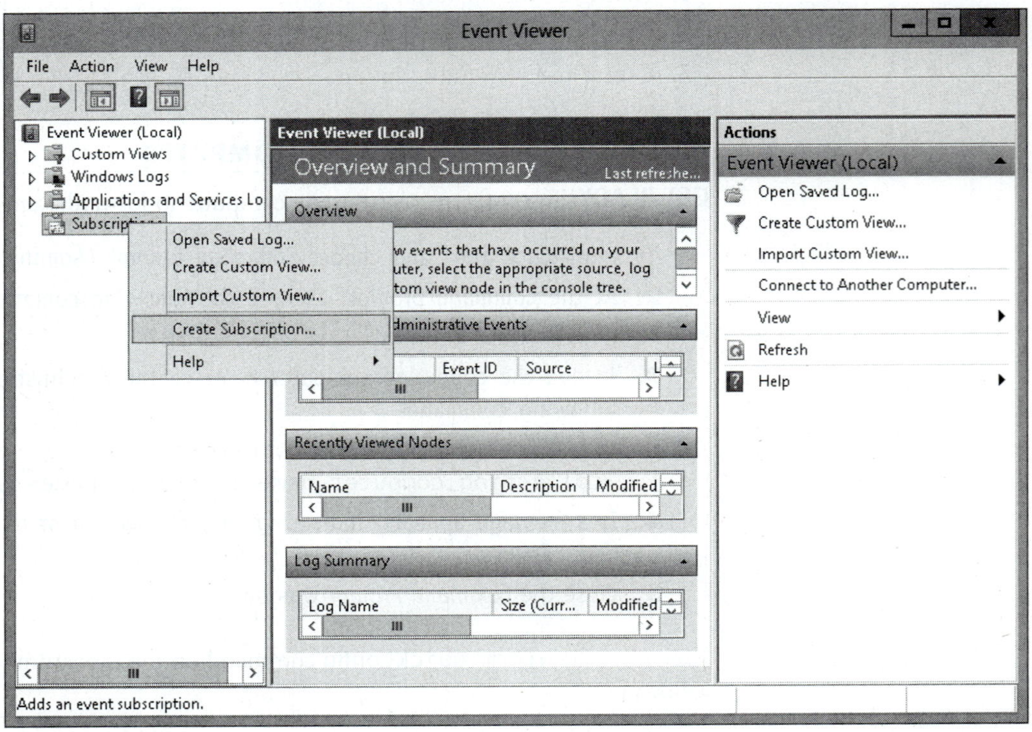

4. In the *Subscription name* text box, type the name for the subscription (see Figure 3-15).

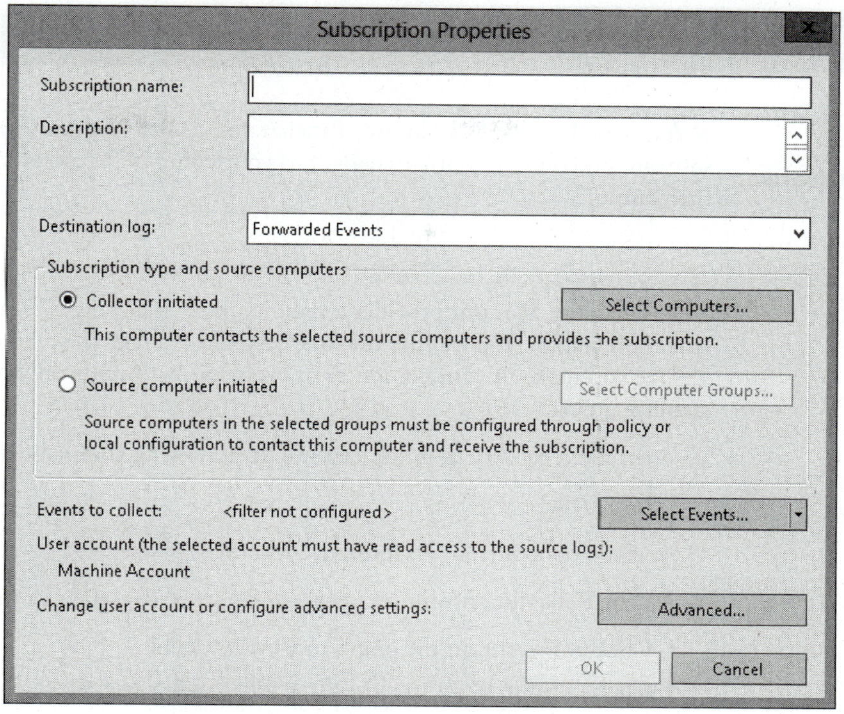

Figure 3-15

Configuring subscription properties

5. If necessary, in the *Description* text box, type a description.
6. In the *Subscription type and source computers* section, choose one of the following two options:
   - Collector initiated: The collecting computer polls the source computers to retrieve events. Then click the Select Computers button to select which computers to poll.
   - Source computer initiated: The forwarding computer contacts the collection computer. Then click the Select Computer Groups button to specify the forwarding computers.
7. Click Select Events. The *Query Filter* dialog box opens.
8. Specify the time range (by using the *Logged* drop-down box), event level (by selecting the appropriate check box), event logs (by using the *Event Logs* drop-down box), event sources (by using the *Event sources* drop-down box), keywords (by typing in the *Keywords* text box), or other parameters that specify which events you want forwarding.
9. Click OK to apply your settings and close the *Query Filter* dialog box.
10. Optionally, you can click the Advanced button to open the Advanced Subscription Settings dialog box and then configure the bandwidth used (Normal, Minimize Bandwidth, and Minimize Latency) and the protocol (HTTP or HTTPS). Click OK to close the Advanced Subscription Settings dialog box.
11. Close the *Event Viewer*.

Using Reliability Monitor

THE BOTTOM LINE

Reliability Monitor is a Control Panel/Action Panel tool that measures hardware and software problems and other changes to your computer that could affect the reliability of the computer.

The Reliability Monitor provides a stability index that ranges from 1 (the least stable) to 10 (the most stable). You can use the index to help evaluate the reliability of your computer. Any change you make to your computer or problem that occurs on your computer affects the stability index.

To open the reliability monitor, execute the following command at a command prompt:

```
perfmon /rel
```

Or you can open it from Performance Monitor.

When the Reliability Monitor opens (see Figure 3-16), you can then:

- Click any event on the graph to view its details.
- Click *Days* or *Weeks* to view the stability index over a specific period of time.

Figure 3-16

Viewing the Reliability Monitor information

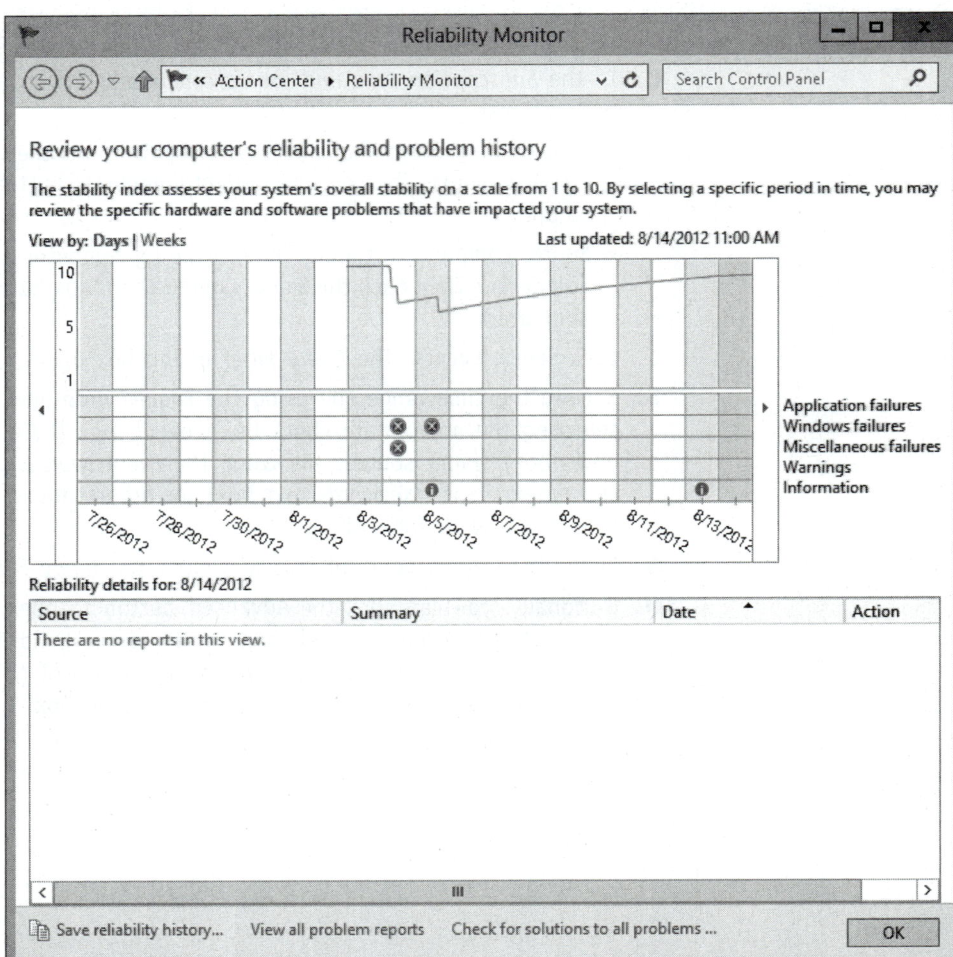

- Click items in the *Action* column to view more information about each event.
- At the bottom of the page, click *View all problem reports* to view only the problems that have occurred on your computer. This view doesn't include the other computer events that show up in Reliability Monitor, such as events about software installation.

If the Reliability Monitor is blank, you need to enable Reliability Monitor.

ENABLE RELIABILITY MONITOR

GET READY. To enable Reliability Monitor, perform the following steps:

1. Open Task Scheduler and enable and run the \Microsoft\Windows\RAC\RacTask in Task Scheduler.
2. Use the Registry Editor to change the HKEY_LOCAL_MACHINE\SOFTWARE\Microsoft\Reliability Analysis\WMI\WMIEnable value to 1.
3. Reboot the computer.

After you reboot the computer, it might take several hours for it to compile the data to be displayed in the Reliability Monitor.

Managing Performance

THE BOTTOM LINE

Performance is the overall effectiveness of how data moves through the system. Of course, it is important to select the proper hardware (processor, memory, disk system, and network) to satisfy the expected performance goals. Without the proper hardware, bottlenecks limit the effectiveness of software.

CERTIFICATION READY
Monitor real-time performance.
Objective 1.3

When a component limits overall performance, that component is known as a bottleneck. When you relieve one bottleneck, another bottleneck might be triggered. For example, one of the most common bottlenecks is the amount of memory the system has. By increasing the memory, you can often increase the overall performance of a system (up to a point). However, when you add more RAM, then RAM needs to be fed more data from the disk. Therefore, the disk becomes the bottleneck. So, although the system might become faster, if your performance is still lacking, you will have to look for new bottlenecks.

You usually cannot identify performance problems just by taking a quick look at performance. Instead, you need a baseline. You can get one by analyzing the performance when the system is running normally and within design specifications. Then when a problem occurs, compare the current performance to your baseline to see what is different. Because performance can also change gradually over time, it is highly recommended that you baseline your computer regularly so that you can chart your performance measures and identify trends. This will give you an idea about when the server needs to be upgraded or replaced or the workload of the server reduced.

There are several tools available with Windows for you to analyze performance. They include:

- Task Manager
- Performance Monitor
- Resource Monitor

Using Task Manager

Task Manager gives you a quick glance at performance and provides information about programs and processes running on your computer. A ***process*** is an instance of a program that is being executed.

Task Manager is one of the handiest programs you can use to take a quick glance at performance to see which programs are using the most system resources on your computer. You can see the status of running programs and programs that have stopped responding, and you can stop a program running in memory.

To start Task Manager, right-click the empty space on the taskbar and click *Task Manager* (or you can open the Security menu by pressing the *Ctrl+Alt+Del* keys and choosing *Start Task Manager*). When Task Manager starts, it displays only the running applications (see Figure 3-17).

Figure 3-17

Using Task Manager

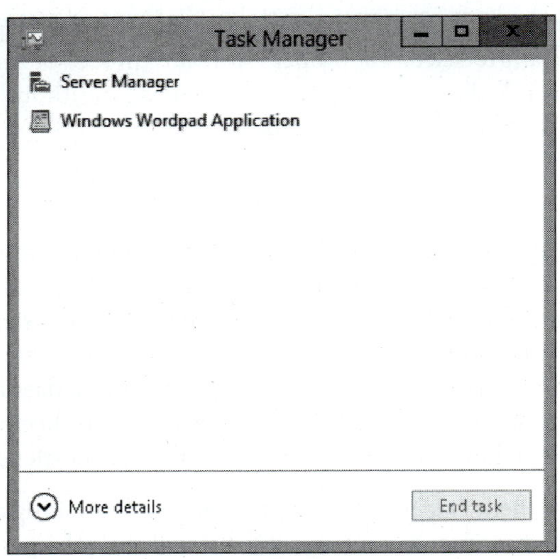

Click the *More Details* down-arrow to show all the available tabs (see Figure 3-18). When you first start the Performance Monitor on a computer running Windows Server 2012, five tabs are opened for Task Manager:

- Processes
- Performance
- Users
- Details
- Services

Figure 3-18

Viewing the Task Manager tabs

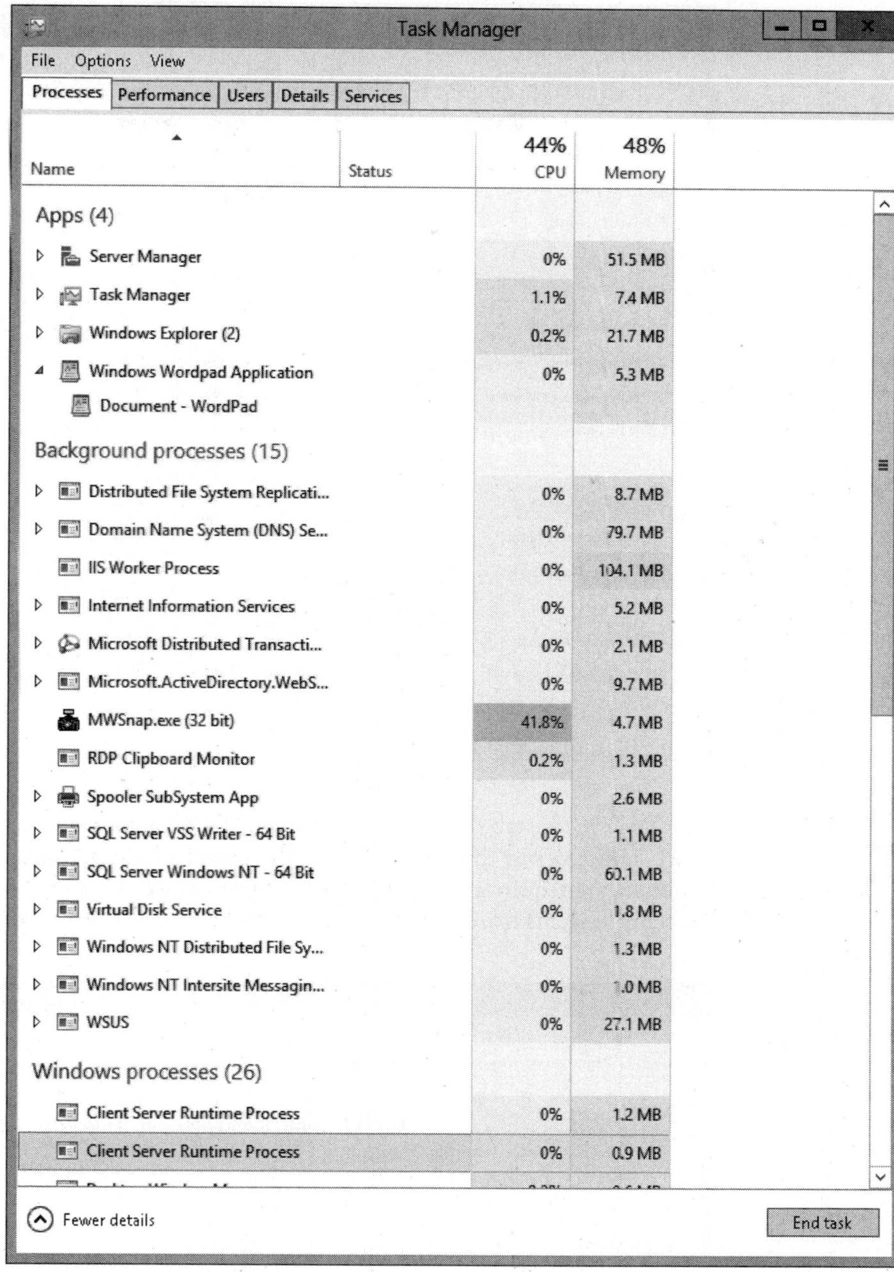

The Processes tab shows all processes running in memory and how much processing and memory each process uses. The processes will display applications (as designated by apps), background processes, and Windows Processes. On the Processes tab, you can perform the following tasks:

- To see the processes that use the most CPU utilization and memory, click the *CPU* column header.
- To stop a process, right-click the process and select *End task* (see Figure 3-19).
- To jump to the *Details* tab for a particular process, right-click the process and choose *Go to details*.
- If you want to see the executable that is running the processes, right-click the process and choose *Open file location*.

Figure 3-19

Ending a task

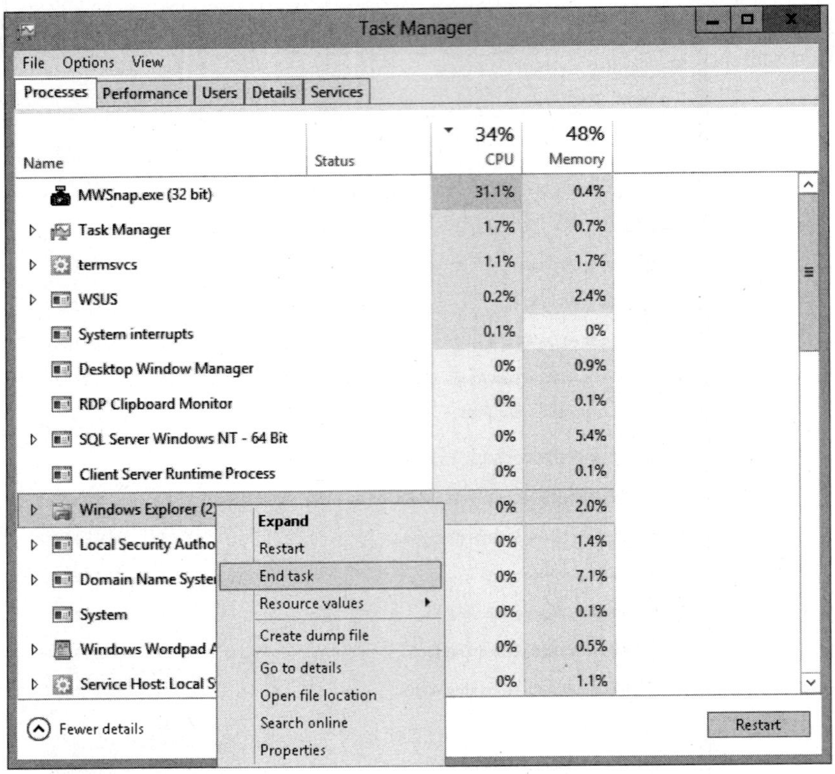

The *Performance* tab displays the amount of *CPU* usage (see Figure 3-20), physical *Memory* usage, and *Ethernet* throughput. For CPU usage, a high percentage indicates the programs or processes are requiring a lot of CPU resources, which can slow your computer. If the percentage seems frozen at or near 100%, then a program might not be responding.

Figure 3-20

Viewing CPU usage

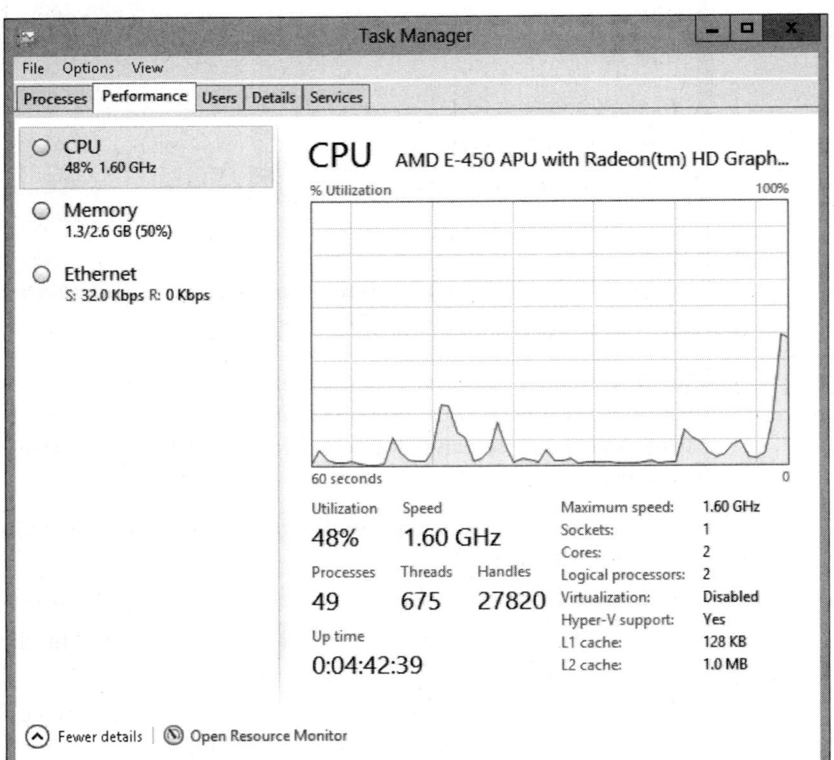

Click *Memory* (see Figure 3-21) to display how much of the paging file is being used (*In use* and *Available*), the amount of *Committed* and *Cached* memory, *Paged pool* and *Non-paged pool*. It also shows you the total amount of RAM, the *Speed* of the RAM, and the number of *Slots used* for memory on the motherboard.

Figure 3-21
Viewing Memory usage

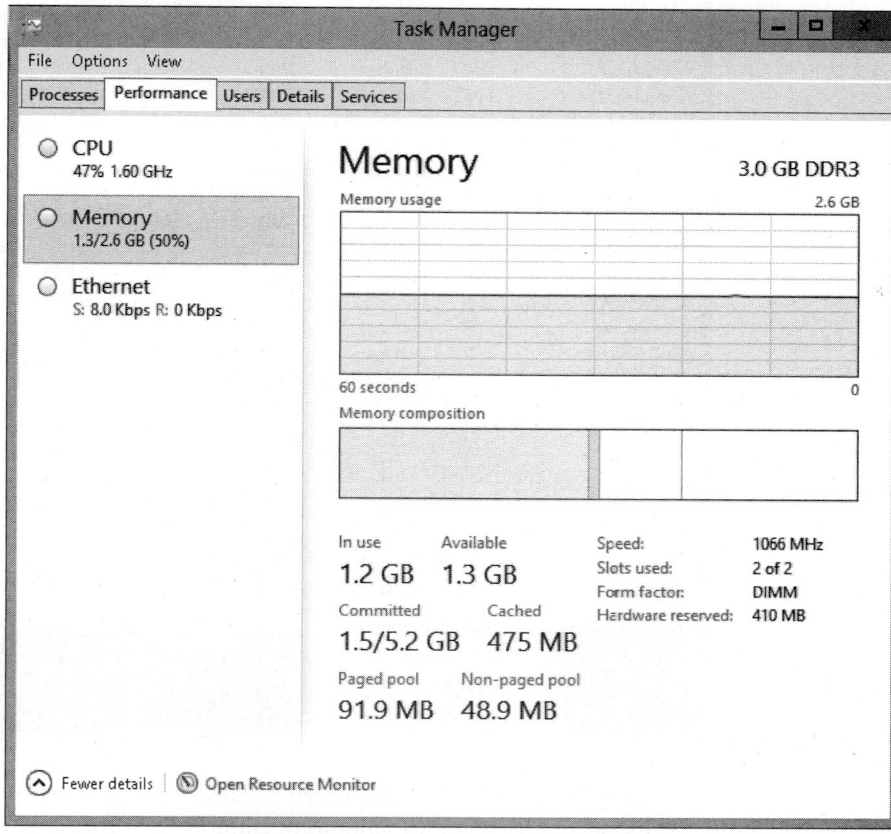

The *Users* tab displays the users who are currently logged in, the amount of CPU and memory usage that the each user is using, and the processes the user is running. It also gives you the ability to disconnect them.

The *Details* tab displays a more detailed look at the processes running on the computer, including the *Process Identification (PID)*. The PID is composed of unique numbers that identify a process while it is running. Similarly, you can stop the process and you can increase or decrease the process priority (see Figure 3-22).

If you are an advanced user, you might want to view other advanced memory values on the Processes tab. To do so, click View > Select Columns and then select or deselect values to be displayed or not displayed (see Figure 3-23). While there are nearly 40 columns to display, some of the more useful values include the following:

- **Working set (memory):** Shows the amount of memory in the private working set plus the amount of memory the process is using that can be shared by other processes.
- **Peak working set (memory):** Shows the maximum amount of working set memory used by the process.
- **Working set delta (memory):** Shows the amount of change in working set memory used by the process.

Figure 3-22

Setting a priority level

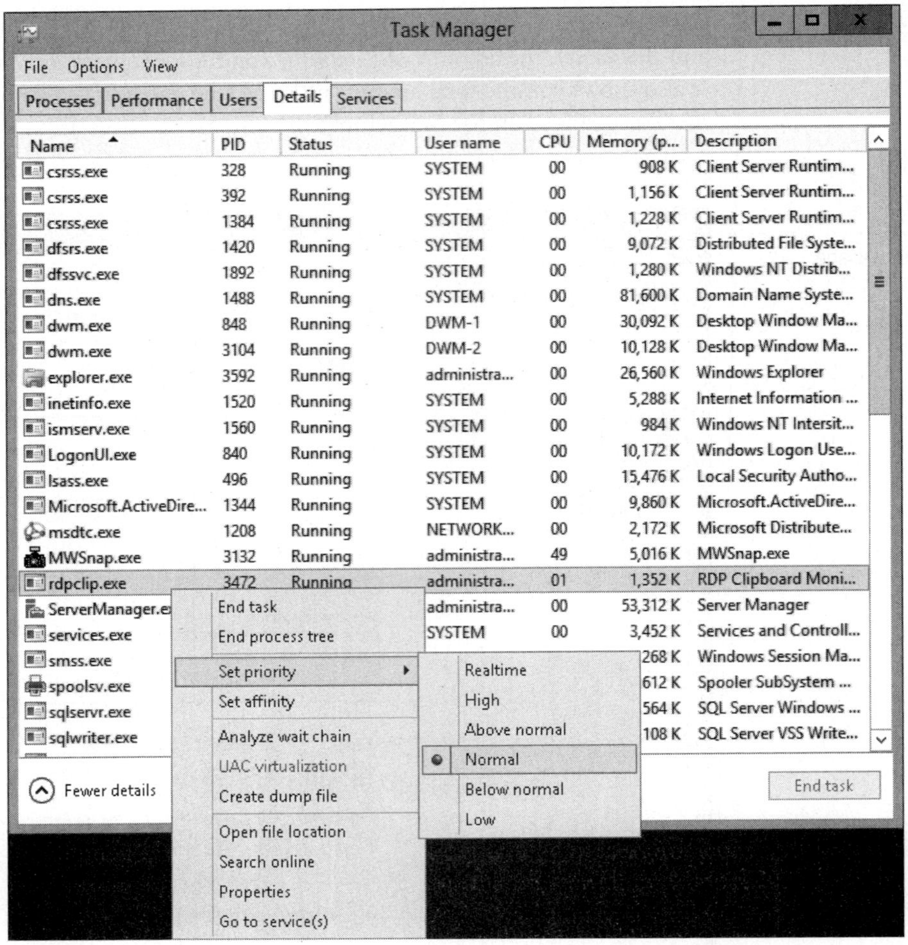

- **Commit Size:** Shows the amount of virtual memory that is reserved for use by a process.
- **Paged pool:** Shows the amount of committed virtual memory for a process that can be written to another storage medium, such as the hard disk.
- **NP pool:** NP is an abbreviation for Non-Paged. Shows the amount of committed virtual memory for a process that can't be written to another storage medium.

Figure 3-23

Adding columns to the Details tab

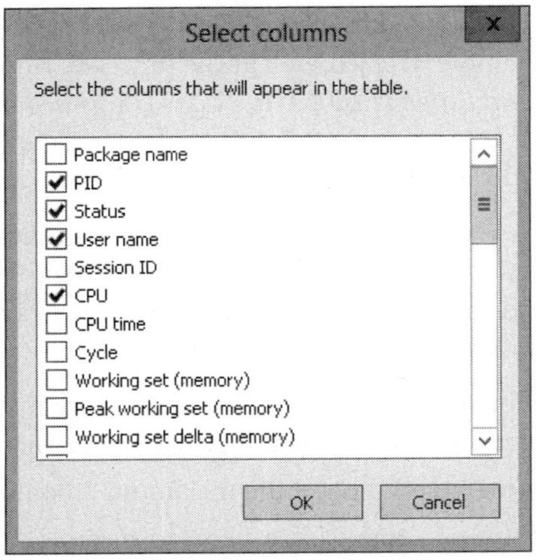

The Services tab displays all services on the computer that are running and not running. Similar to the Services console, you can start, stop, or restart services.

Using Resource Monitor

Resource Monitor is a system tool that allows you to view information about the use of hardware (CPU, memory, disk, and network) and software resources (file handlers and modules) in real time. You can filter the results according to specific processes or services that you want to monitor. In addition, you can use Resource Monitor to start, stop, suspend, and resume processes and services, and to troubleshoot when an application does not respond as expected.

Resource Monitor (see Figure 3-24) is a powerful tool for understanding how your system resources are used by processes and services. In addition to monitoring resource usage in real time, Resource Monitor can help you analyze unresponsive processes, identify which applications are using files, and control processes and services. To start Resource Monitor, start Server Manager and click *Tools* > *Resource Monitor*. Or, you can use Windows PowerShell and execute the `resmon.exe` command.

Figure 3-24

Viewing Resource Monitor

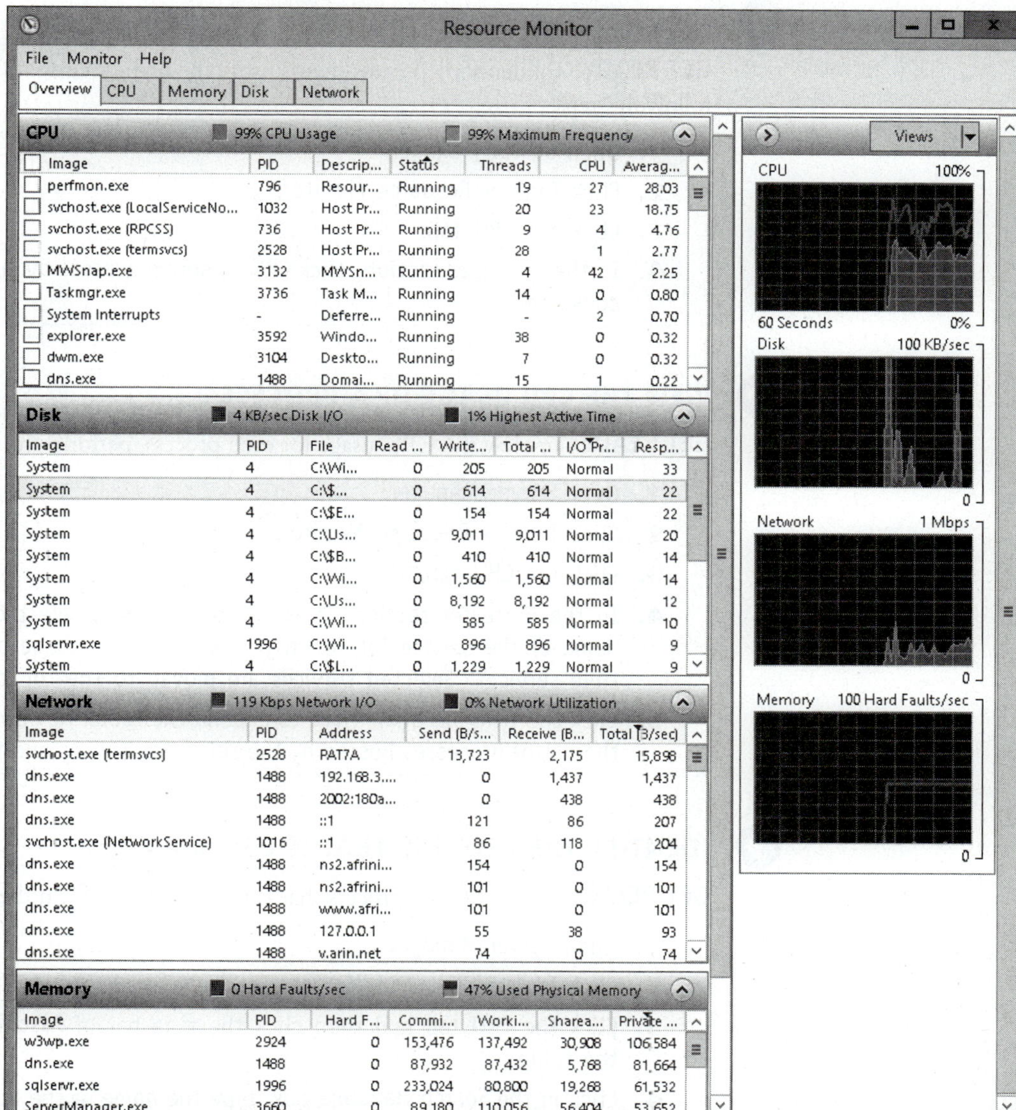

Resource Monitor includes five tabs:

- Overview
- CPU
- Memory
- Disk
- Network

The *Overview* tab displays basic system resource usage information; the other tabs display information about each specific resource. Each tab in Resource Monitor includes multiple tables that display detailed information about the resource featured on that respective tab.

The next four exercises cover common tasks for which to use the resource monitor. For example, if you want to find and determine the program (process) that is hogging the processor resources, you can use *Identify the highest current CPU usage*. If a file is locked and you cannot delete it because it is in use, you can use the *Identify the process that is using a file exercise* to see which process has the file open.

IDENTIFY THE HIGHEST CURRENT CPU USAGE

GET READY. To identify a process that is using the highest current CPU usage, perform the following steps:

1. Open Server Manager.
2. Click Tools > Resource Monitor.
3. Click the CPU tab.
4. In the *Processes* section, click CPU to sort processes by current CPU resource consumption.

VIEW THE CPU USAGE OF A PROCESS

GET READY. To view the CPU usage for each process, perform the following steps:

1. Open Server Manager.
2. Click Tools > Resource Monitor.
3. Click the CPU tab.
4. In the *Processes* section, in the *Image* column, select the check box next to the name of the service for which you want to see usage details. You can select multiple services. Selected services are moved to the top of the column.
5. Click the title bar of Services to expand the table. Review the data in Services to see the list of processes hosted by the selected services and to view their CPU usage.

IDENTIFY THE PROCESS THAT IS USING A FILE

GET READY. To identify the process that is using a file, perform the following steps:

1. Open Server Manager.
2. Click Tools > Resource Monitor.
3. Click the CPU tab and then click the title bar of Associated Handlers to expand the table.
4. Click in the Search Handlers box, type the name of the file you want to search for, and then click Search.

IDENTIFY THE NETWORK ADDRESS TO WHICH A PROCESS IS CONNECTED

GET READY. To identify the network address that a process is connected to, perform the following steps:

1. Open Server Manager.
2. Click Tools > Resource Monitor.
3. Click the Network tab and then click the title bar of TCP Connections to expand the table.
4. Locate the process whose network connection you want to identify. If there are a large number of entries in the table, you can click Image to sort by executable filename.
5. Review the *Remote Address* column and the *Remote Port* column to see which network address and port the process is connected to.

Using Performance Monitor

Performance Monitor is an MMC snap-in that provides tools for analyzing system performance. It is included in the Computer Management and it can be opened as a standalone console from Administrative Tools. It can also be started by executing the `perfmon` command. From a single console, you can monitor application and hardware performance in real time, specify which data you want to collect in logs, define thresholds for alerts and automatic actions, generate reports, and view past performance data in a variety of ways.

Performance Monitor (see Figure 3-25) provides a visual display of built-in Windows performance counters, either in real time or as a way to review historical data.

Figure 3-25

Viewing Performance Monitor

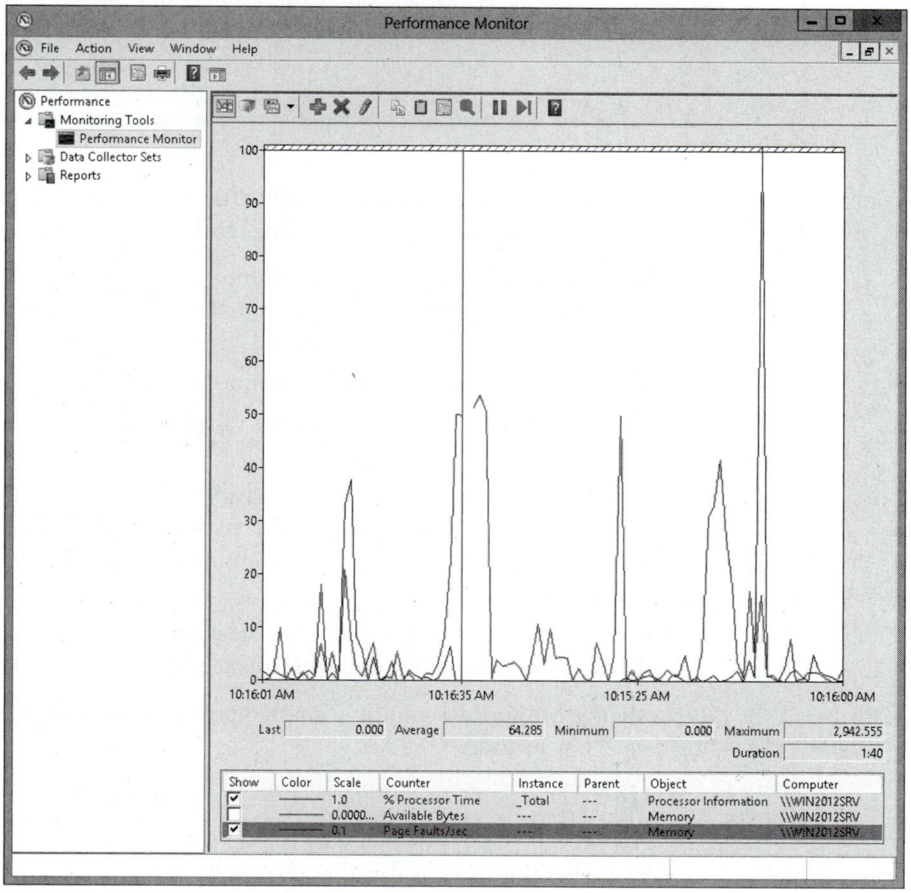

You can add performance counters to Performance Monitor by right-clicking the main pane and choosing Add Counters. Another way to add performance counters is to create and use custom Data Collector Sets. (Data Collector Sets will be explained later in this lesson.) Figure 3-26 shows the Add Counters dialog box. You can create custom views that can be exported as Data Collector Sets for use with performance and logging features.

Figure 3-26

Adding counters to Performance Monitor

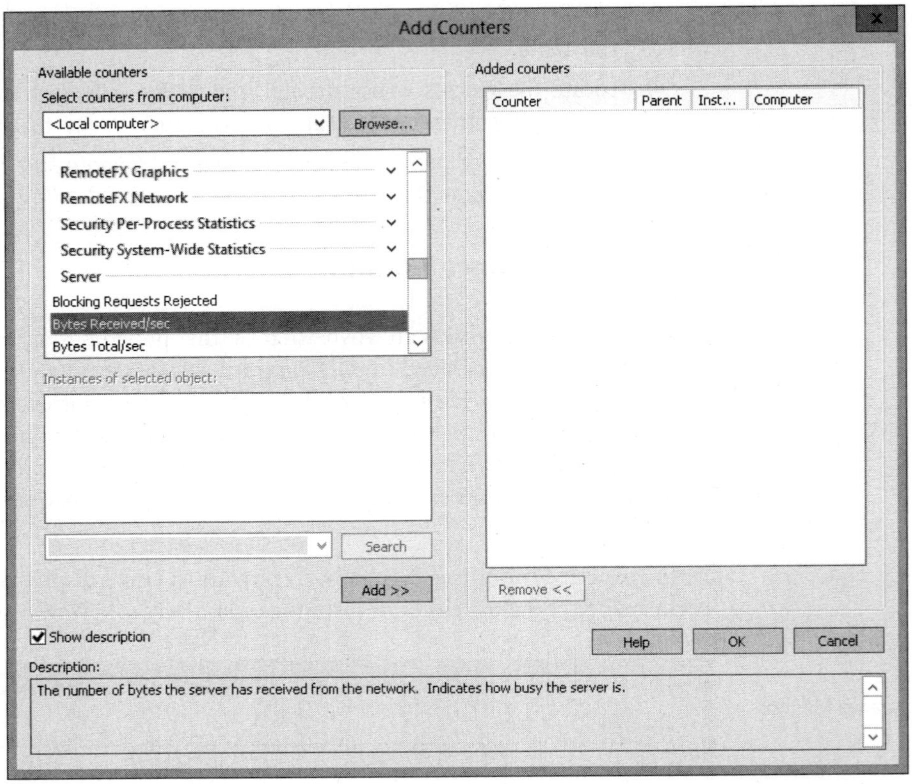

To control how and what is displayed, right-click Performance Monitor and choose Properties. The Performance Monitor Properties dialog box (see Figure 3-27) displays the following five tabs:

- **General:** Allows you to adjust the samples, such as how often samples are taken and how much data is displayed on the graph before the graph is redrawn. You can also choose to display the legend, the value bar, and the toolbar.
- **Source:** Allows you to display real-time data or to open a log file that you have saved.
- **Data:** Allows you to choose counters to appear as well as the color and scale of those counters.
- **Graph:** Allows you to configure the available views and if the view starts over or you can scroll to look at previous displayed data. It allows you to display or not display the vertical grid, horizontal grid, vertical scale numbers, time axis labels, as well as determine the maximum scale.
- **Appearance:** Allows you to display the color and fonts used by various components so that you can distinguish one Performance Monitor window from another.

Performance Monitor has multiple graph types that enable you to visually review performance log data. They include:

- **Line:** The default graph type; connects points of data with lines
- **Histogram Bar:** A bar graph showing data.
- **Report:** Values are displayed as text.

Figure 3-27

Configuring Performance Monitor properties

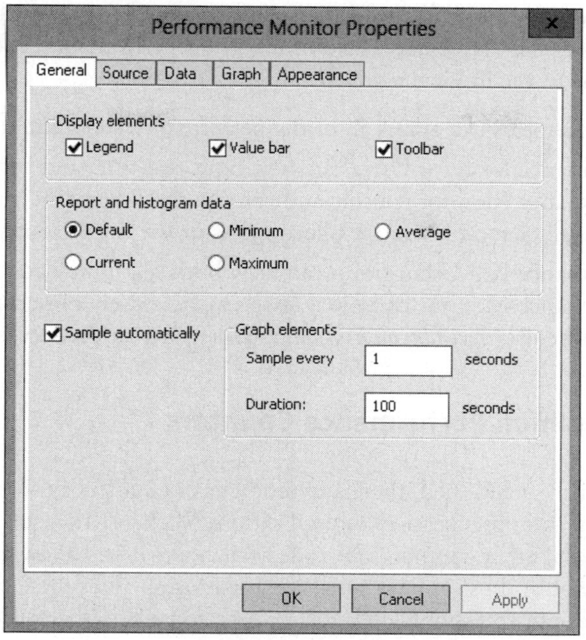

Figure 3-28 shows the Histogram Bar and Report Graph types.

Figure 3-28

Graph Types (Histogram Bar and Report)

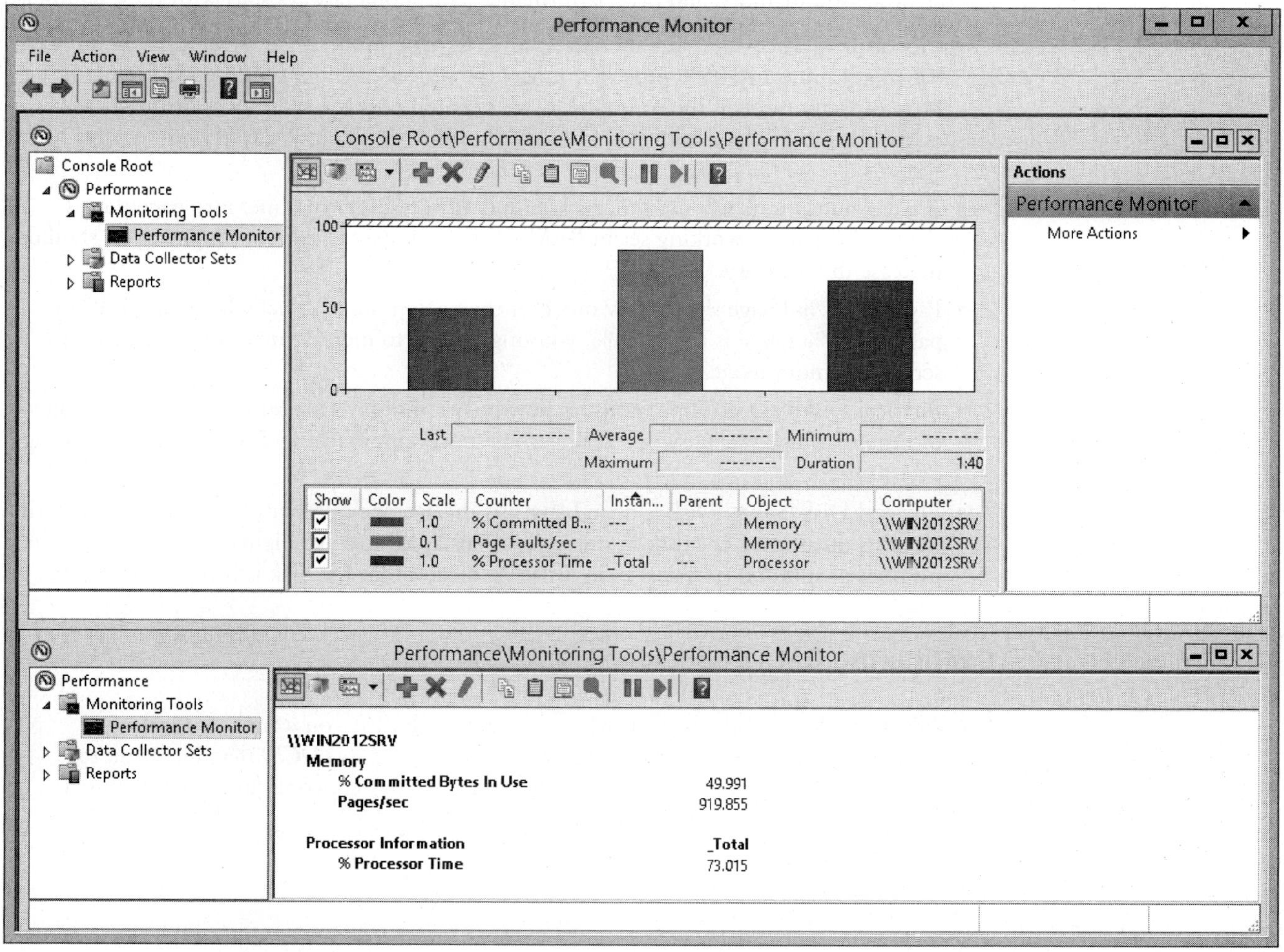

Performance programs and performance information is not available to everyone. Therefore, if a user needs to use Performance Monitor to view performance information, the user can be added to one of the following groups:

- Administrators can access all of the performance tools and data.
- Performance Monitor Users can view both real-time and historical data within the Performance Monitor console and can use the Reliability Monitor. However, they cannot create or modify Data Collector Sets or use the Resource View.
- Performance Log Users group can view both real-time data and historical data within the Performance Monitor console. However, these users can create or modify Data Collector Sets if the user has *Log on as a batch user* rights on the server.

Using Common Performance Counters

As previously mentioned, there are hundreds of counters available in Performance Monitor and as you add other services or applications (such as Microsoft Exchange or Microsoft SQL Server), other counters are made available that will allow you to monitor the performance of those applications. Although using all of these counters might take some heavy research, you should always start with some basic performance counters to get a glimpse on how your system is running.

A computer is composed of four primary systems: a processor, memory, disk, and a network. For the processor, memory, and disk performance, you should always start with these counters:

- Processor:%Processor Time measures how busy the processor is. Although the processor might jump to 100% processor usage, the processor should not be working at 80% capacity most of the time. If it is, you should upgrade the processor (using a faster processor or add additional processors) or move some of the services to other systems.
- A page fault occurs when a process attempts to access a virtual memory page that is not available in its working set in RAM. If the pages/sec is 1,000 or higher, you should increase the memory.
- Paging File:% Usage shows how much of the paging file is actually being used. If the paging file % usage is above 75%, you might need to increase memory or reduce the server's memory usage.
- Physical Disk:%Disk Time indicates how busy a disk is as measured by the percentage of time that disk was busy. If a disk is consistently approaching 100%, the disk is being over utilized.
- Physical Disk:%Avg. Disk Queue Length is the average number of read requests or write requests queued for the disk in question. A sustained average higher than two times the number of spindles (physical hard drives) indicates that the disk is being over utilized.

Configuring Data Collector Sets (DCS)

Rather than add individual performance counters each time you want to view the performance of a system, you can create ***Data Collector Sets (DCS)*** that allow you to organize a set of performance counts, event traces, and system configuration data into a single object that can be reused as needed.

CERTIFICATION READY
Configure Data Collector Sets (DCS).
Objective 1.3

Windows Performance Monitor uses performance counters, event trace data, and configuration information, which can be combined into Data Collector Sets as follows:

- Performance counters are measurements of system state or activity. They can be included in the operating system or can be part of individual applications. Windows Performance Monitor requests the current value of performance counters at specified time intervals.
- Event trace data is collected from trace providers, which are components of the operating system or of individual applications that report actions or events. Output from multiple trace providers can be combined into a trace session.
- Configuration information is collected from key values in the Windows registry.

Windows Performance Monitor can record the value of a registry key at a specified time or interval as part of a file.

CREATE A DATA COLLECTOR SET

GET READY. To create a DCS, perform the following steps:

1. Open **Server Manager**.
2. Click **Tools > Performance Monitor**.
3. In the left pane, expand **Data Collector Sets**.
4. Right-click the **User Defined** folder and choose **New > Data Collector Set** (see Figure 3-29).

Figure 3-29

Starting the *Creating a new Data Collector Set Wizard*

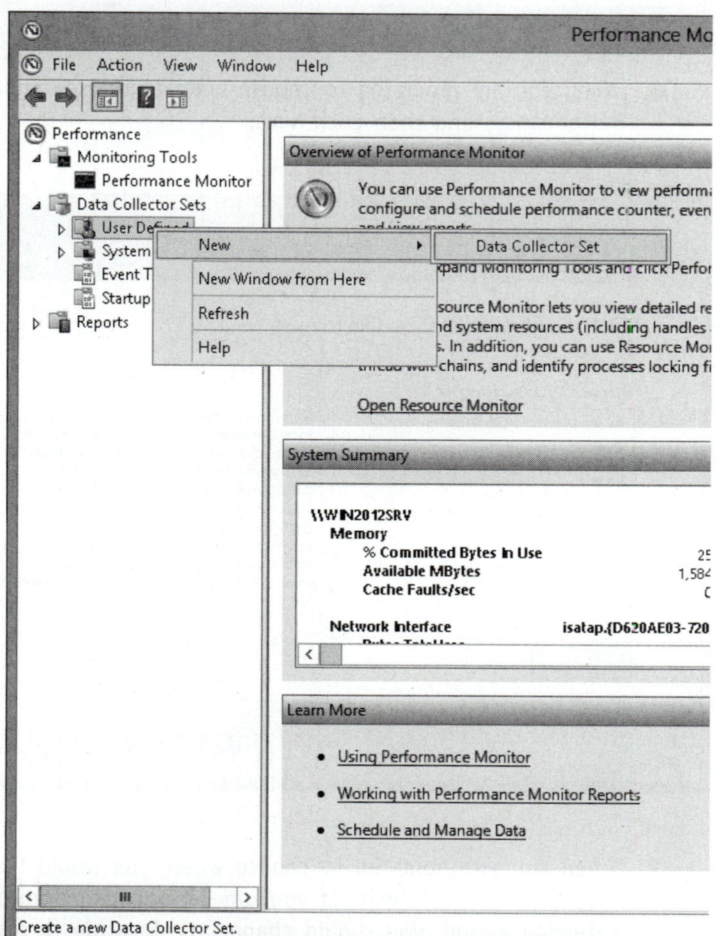

5. On the *Create new Data Collector Set* page (see Figure 3-30), when you are prompted to create a new data collector set, type a name in the Name text box. Ensure that the Create from a template (Recommended) option is selected and then click Next.

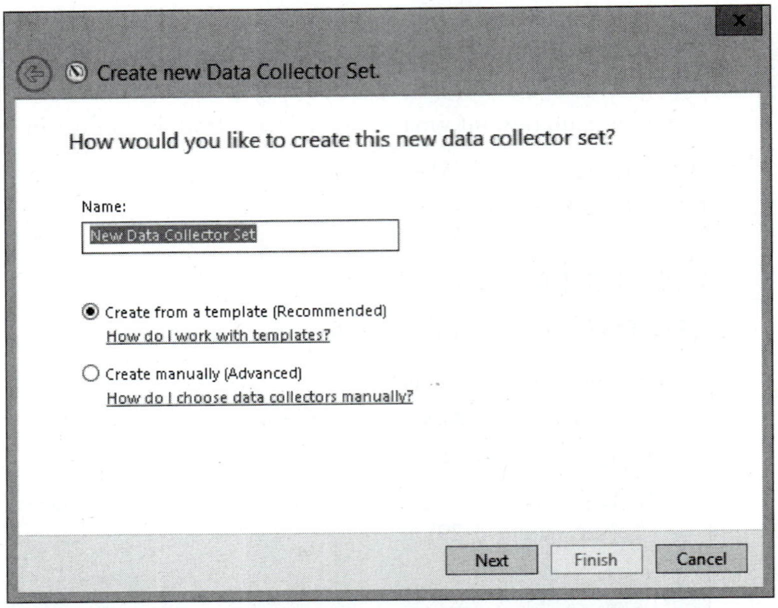

Figure 3-30

Creating a new Data Collector Set

6. When you are prompted to choose a template (see Figure 3-31), click System Performance, and then click Next.

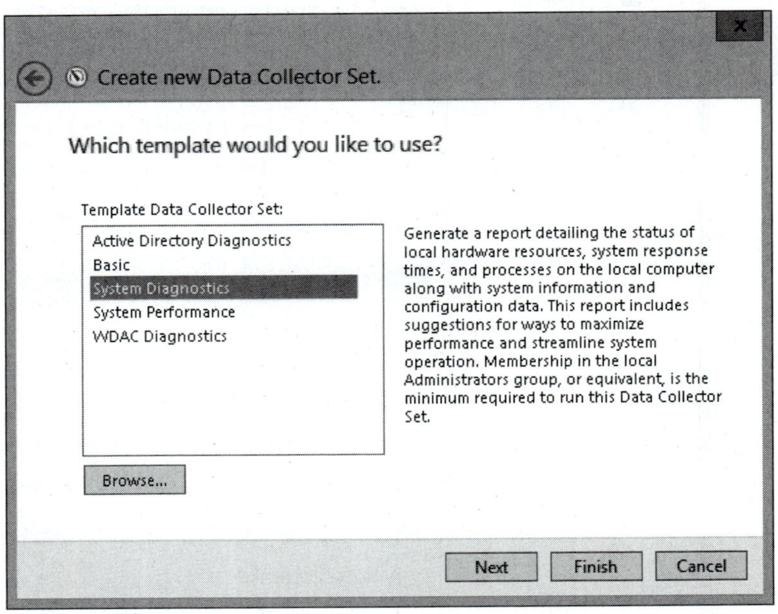

Figure 3-31

Selecting a template

7. When you are prompted to choose where you would like the data to be saved (see Figure 3-32), click Next. If you run Performance Monitor to collect data over an extended period, you should change the location to a nonsystem data drive.

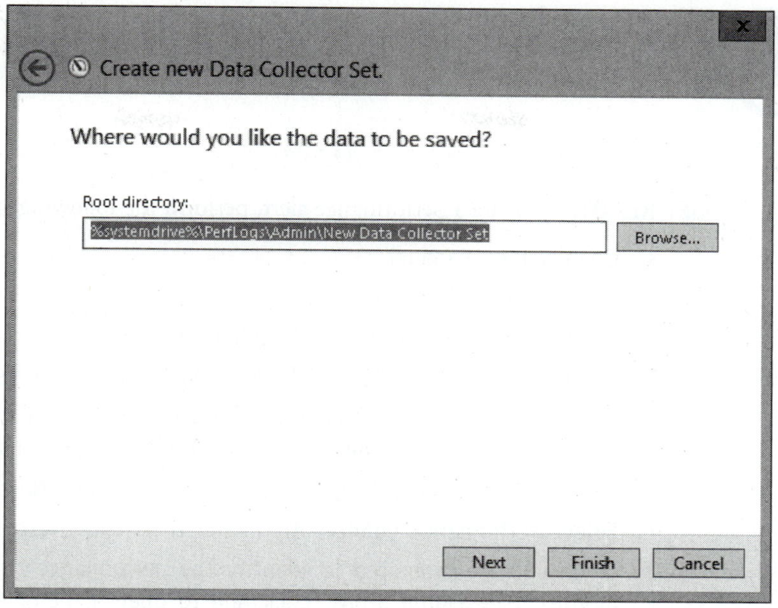

Figure 3-32

Choosing a location to save the data

8. When you are prompted to create the data collector set, with the Save and close option selected, click Finish.
9. To start the Data Collector Set, right-click the DCS and choose Start (see Figure 3-33).

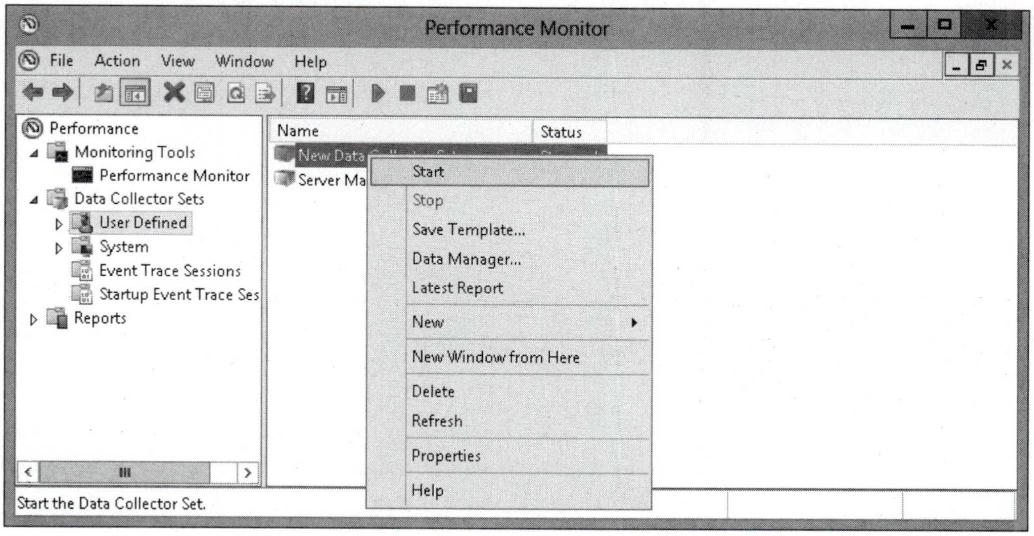

Figure 3-33

Starting the Data Collector Set

10. Close *Performance Monitor*.

Configuring Performance Alerts

In Performance Monitor, a ***performance alert*** is a notification or task that is executed when a performance value is reached. Performance Monitor can also be used to start certain tasks when certain counters reach a particular value. For example, if the processor reaches 90%, you can have Performance Monitor run a command to stop a service or perform some other action in an effort to reduce burden on the processor.

CERTIFICATION READY
Configure alerts.
Objective 1.3

When you configure performance alerts, you can perform almost any action that you can think. You can send a network message or log events into the application event log. You can configure alerts to start applications and performance logs.

CREATE A PERFORMANCE ALERT

GET READY. To create a performance alert, perform the following steps:

1. Open Server Manager.
2. Click Tools > Performance Monitor.
3. In the left pane, expand Data Collector Sets.
4. Right-click the User Defined folder, and then choose New > Data Collector Set.
5. On the *Create new Data Collector Set* page (refer to Figure 3-30), when you are prompted to create a new data collector set, type a name in the Name text box.
6. Select Create manually (Advanced), and then click Next.
7. Select Performance Counter Alert, and then click Next.
8. When you are prompted to identify the performance counter you would like to monitor (see Figure 3-34), click Add to open a dialog box, in which to select the desired counter. When you have added the counter, click OK.

Figure 3-34

Choosing performance counters

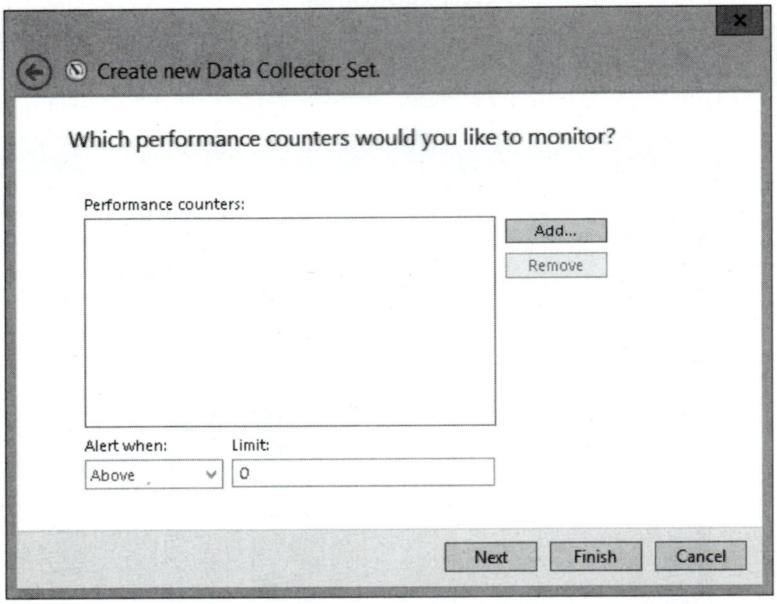

9. The limit will define when a performance alert is triggered. For the *Alert when* option, select either Above or Below and then in the Limit box, type the value. Click Next.
10. When you are prompted to create the data collector set, select Open properties for this data collector set. Click Finish.
11. When the Properties dialog box opens, click the Task tab.
12. In the Run this scheduled task when the data collector set stops text box, type the path of a script or command that you want to execute when the condition is met. If necessary, specify any task arguments in the Task Arguments text box.
13. To specify when the Data Collector Set will run, click the Schedule tab (see Figure 3-35).

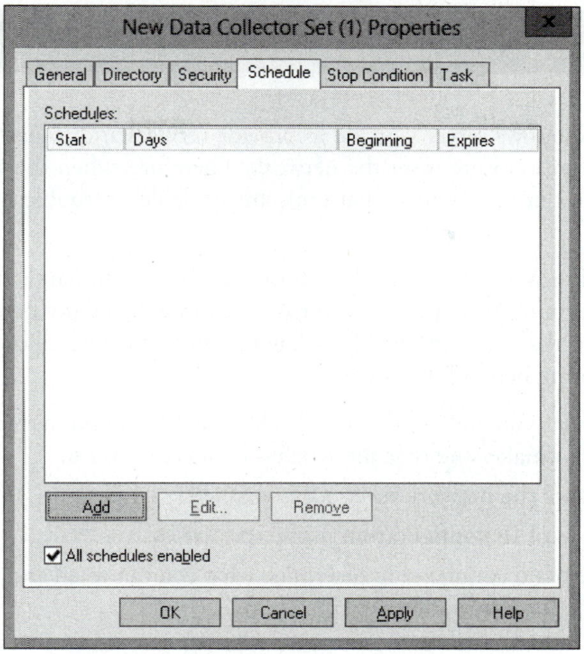

Figure 3-35
Viewing the Schedule tab

14. Click Add. In the *Folder Action* dialog box, specify the Beginning date that the task will run, the Expiration date for the task, and the Launch time (see Figure 3-36).

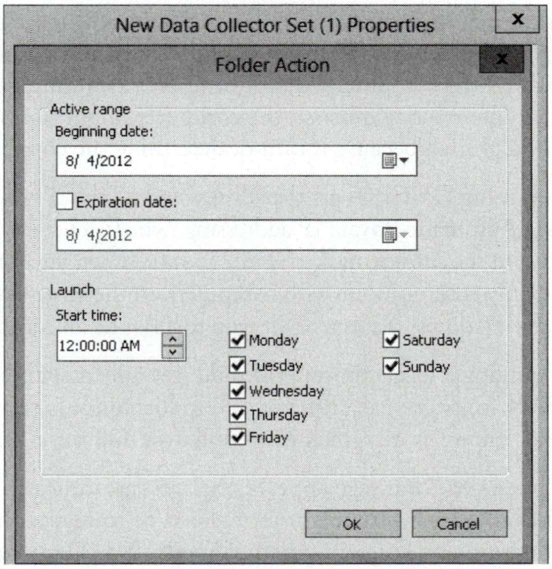

Figure 3-36
Configuring a schedule

15. Click OK to apply your settings and then click OK again to close the *Properties* dialog box.
16. Close *Performance Monitor*.

Monitoring the Network

THE BOTTOM LINE

Because a Windows server is made to provide services and to use services, it is essential that the server communicates over the network. Therefore, when the server is having network problems, you need to know what tools are available to troubleshoot those problems.

CERTIFICATION READY
Configure network monitoring.
Objective 1.3

When looking at any problem, don't forget the basic commands that are available to any computer running Windows. Of course, when looking at any problem, you must be systematic so that you can quickly isolate the problem. The following steps are typical of troubleshooting networking issues:

1. Make sure you are connected. Check to make sure the network cable is properly connected or make sure that the wireless connection is on.
2. Make sure the network interface is enabled.
3. Check local IP configuration using `ipconfig`.
4. Use the `ping` command to determine what you can reach and what you cannot reach:
   Ping the loopback address (127.0.0.1).
   Ping a local IP address.
   Ping a remote gateway.
   Ping a remote computer.
5. Identify each hop (router) between two systems using the `tracert` command.
6. Verify DNS configuration using the `nslookup` command. DNS will be discussed in detail Lessons 8 and 9.

Using `ipconfig` with the `/all` switch will show you the IP configuration of the computer. If the subnet mask is incorrect, the computer will not be able to calculate the correct network ID, which might cause packets to be sent to the wrong destination. If the default gateway is incorrect or missing, the computer will not be able to communicate with remote subnets. If the DNS server is incorrect or missing, the computer might not be able to resolve names and communication might fail because it cannot determine the correct IP address.

If the computer is using DHCP to get the address and a DHCP server does not respond, the computer will use Automatic Private IP addressing, which generates an IP address in the form of 169.254.xxx.xxx and the subnet mask of 255.255.0.0. When you have an Automatic Private IP address, you can only communicate with computers on the same network/subnet that have an Automatic Private IP address. So as a result, you will not be able to communicate with other hosts.

The process of pinging a local computer should last only a couple hundred milliseconds (ms) at most. For WAN connections, a time of 200 milliseconds is considered very good and a time between 200 and 500 ms is marginal. Anything over 500 ms is unacceptable.

If a "Request Timed Out" message appears, the message indicates that there is a known route to the destination computer but one or more hosts or routers along the path, including the source and destination, are not configured correctly. If a "Destination Host Unreachable" message appears, the message indicates that the system cannot find a route to the destination system and therefore does not know where to send the packet on the next hop.

If you can successfully ping the IP address but not the name, name resolution is the problem. Therefore, you need to check if you are pointing to a valid DNS server and ensure that the DNS server can properly resolve the name you are trying to reach. In addition, if you are using a HOSTS file, you should make sure there is no corresponding entry that could cause the system from not resolving the name using DNS.

Besides the basic troubleshooting tools just discussed, don't forget to check the Event Viewer for potential events that could cause network problems. If you suspect that an individual computer is sending or receiving too much data, you can use the Event Viewer or Performance Monitor. Lastly, you should check any firewalls to ensure that no packets are being blocked by the Windows Firewall or any other firewall on the network.

Using the netstat Command

The **netstat** command is used to view the TCP/IP connections, both inbound and outbound, on your computer. You can also use to view the packet statistics, such as how many packets have been sent and received and the number of errors.

When netstat is used without any options, netstat shows all the outbound TCP/IP connections (see Figure 3-37). If you use -n addresses, the addresses are converted to names.

Figure 3-37

Using the netstat command

You can also use the following options with netstat:

- netstat -a displays all connections
- netstat -r displays the route table plus active connections
- netstat -e displays Ethernet statistics
- netstat -s displays per-protocol statistics

You might also place a number after the netstat to have netstat update the list every few seconds. For example, when you perform the following command:

```
netstat -e 15
```

the command executes, waits the number of seconds specified by the number (in this example, 15), and then repeats until you press Ctrl+C.

Using Protocol Analyzers

For more complicated problems, you might need to dig deeper. One of the most powerful tools is a protocol analyzer/network analyzer, which allows you to view the actual packets on the network. Two popular software protocol analyzers are WireShark and ***Microsoft Network Monitor***.

A protocol analyzer grabs every packet on a network interface, puts a timestamp on the packet, and stores the packets in a storage area. You would use a filter to specify the packets that will be displayed. Then open each packet to look at the various TCP/IP layers to see what is happening. The packets can be saved to a file so that they can be analyzed later.

When you first capture packets on an interface, you will soon see that there are hundreds of packets. Usually, most of these packets can be ignored because they will have nothing to do with the problem you are trying to analyze. In these cases, you will need to use a filter to show only the packets that you are concerned with.

To install Microsoft Network Monitor, you must first download Network Monitor 3.4 from the Microsoft website. Then double-click the msi file and step through the Wizard.

CAPTURE PACKETS

GET READY. To capture packets, perform the following steps:

1. Double-click Microsoft Network Monitor 3.4. Microsoft Network Monitor opens (see Figure 3-38).

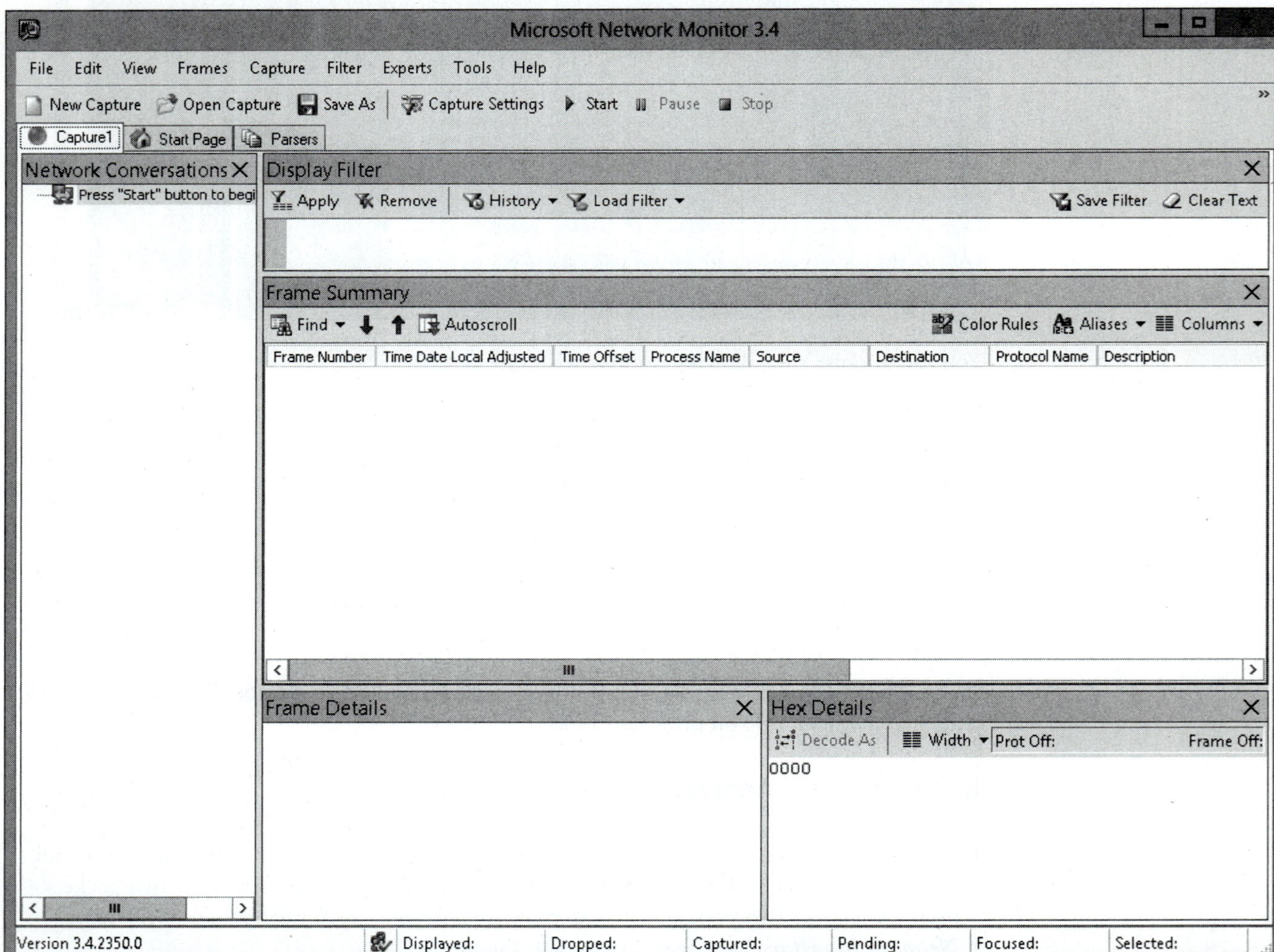

Figure 3-38

Using the Microsoft Network Monitor

2. Click File > New > Capture. A new capture tab opens.
3. To select the interface, click Capture Settings. The *Capture Settings* dialog box opens (see Figure 3-39). Select the interface that you want to capture packets from and make sure the other interfaces are deselected. Click Close.

Figure 3-39

Configuring capture settings

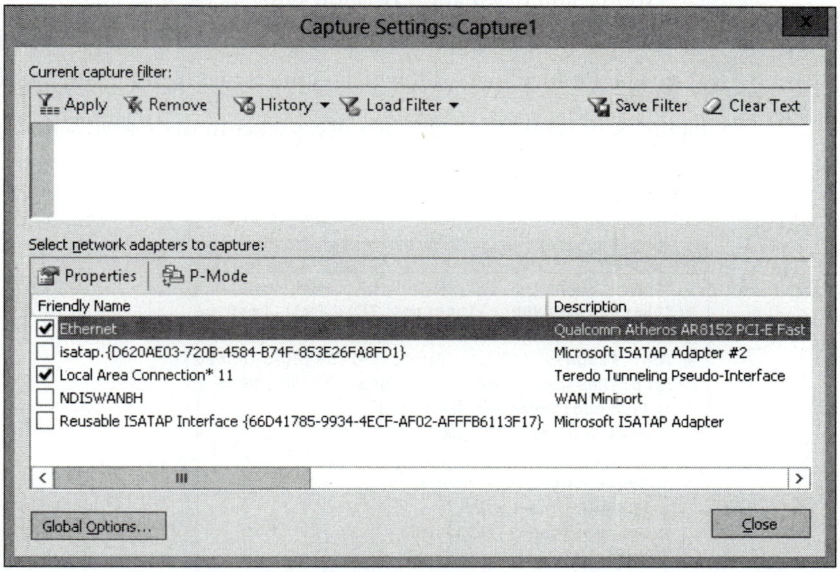

4. To begin capturing packets, click Start.
5. When you are done capturing packets, click Stop.
6. If you want to save the captures, click the Save As button. Specify the location and the name the capture file and then click Save.
7. Close *Network Monitor*.

Network Monitor also has a command-line utility called NMCap.exe, which can be used in scripts and when you want to minimize the effect on system resources.

To learn about NMCap.exe, use one of the following commands:

- `nmcap /?` displays the options available with `nmcap`.
- `nmcap /example` displays several examples on how to use `nmcap`.

If you want to capture all traffic on all network adapters, execute the following command:

```
nmcap /network * /capture /file d:\test.cap
```

You can stop the capturing of packets using NMCap.exe by pressing Ctrl+C or Ctrl+Break on the keyboard. If you are scripting, use the */TimeAfter xx minutes* option to specify the number of minutes that NMCap.exe will run.

If you use a .cap filename extension, the default limit size of the capture file is 20 Megs. To change the default size, add a colon and the size after the file. For example, if you want the maximum size to be 50 MB, use the */File t.cap:50M* option. Alternatively, you can use .chn extensions to create a chain of files—for example, to create a chain of chain.chn files (chain(1).chn, chain(2).chn, chain(3).chn, chain(4).chn, and so on).

Most packets will be using the TCP/IP mode, which is a simplified OSI model that will have up to four parts:

- The Ethernet (data link layer) header includes the destination and source MAC addresses.
- The IP header (network layer) shows the packet as an IPv4 or IPv6 packet and the source and destination IP addresses.
- The TCP header or UDP header (transport layer) includes the source and destination ports.
- The Protocol payload, which is the actual data for the specified protocol.

Figure 3-40 shows the four parts of a packet in the *Frame Details* pane.

Figure 3-40

Viewing the frame details

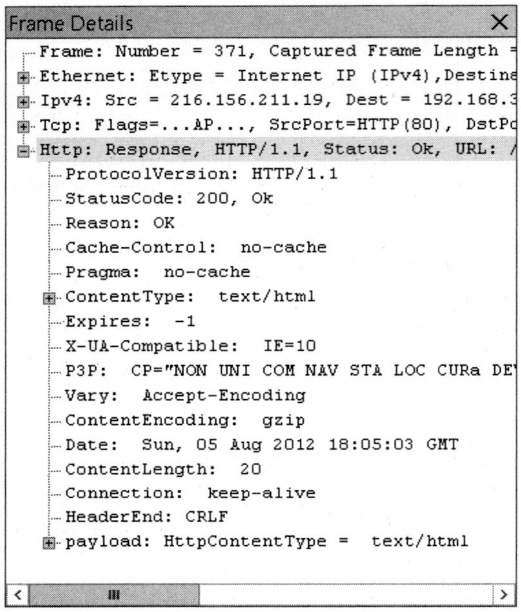

Using filters, you can capture or display only those frames that meet the criteria you specify. You can filter on any protocol, protocol element, or property. For example, you can only capture frames that originate from a particular IP address.

Typically, when you are trying to figure out a problem and you choose to use a protocol analyzer, you should already know what you are looking for. For example, if you are trying to figure out why a client is not getting an IP address from a DHCP server, you want to look for the four-part handshake that occurs when a computer gets an IP address. Therefore, you will need to use a filter that shows only the DHCP packets.

There are several pre-made filters that can help you isolate common problems. To access them, click *Filter* > *Display Filter* > *Load Filter* > *Standard Filters* (see Figure 3-41).

Figure 3-41

Choosing a standard filter

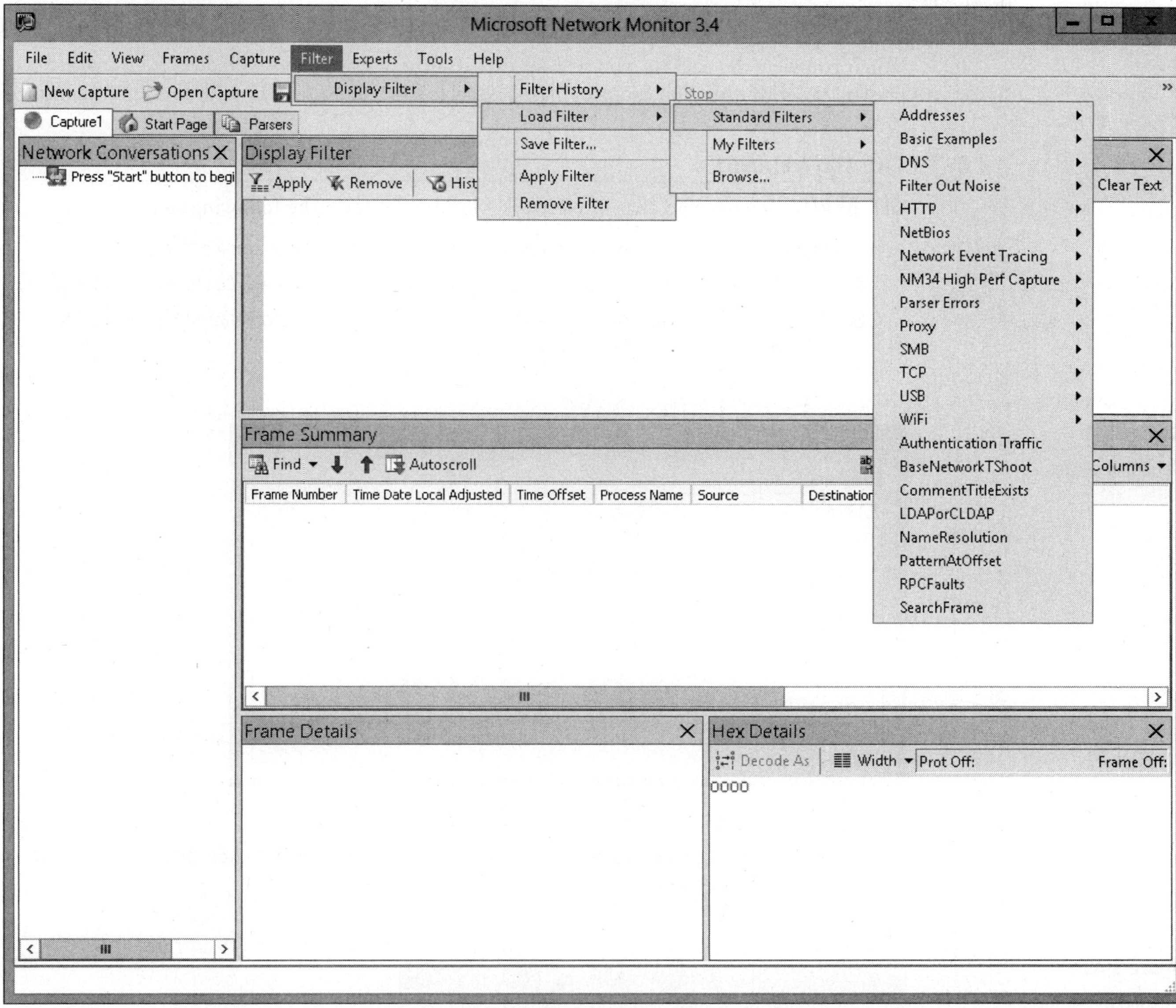

NMCap.exe also supports filtering. If you want to display remote desktop packets (TCP port 3389), execute the following command:

```
nmcap /network * /capture "tcp.port == 3389"
/file d:\test.cap
```

If you want to show all packets except for the packets using TCP port 3389, execute the following command:

```
nmcap /network * /capture "!(tcp.port == 3389)"
/file d:\test.cap
```

You can also use the same protocol names that are available in the graphical interface version of Network Monitor. For example, to capture all LDAP packets, execute the following command:

```
nmcap /network * /capture LDAP /file
d:\test.cap
```

To capture all packets that go to 10.0.01, execute the following command:

```
nmcap /network * /capture Ipv4.address ==
10.0.01 /file d:\test.cap
```

When you view the packets, you will see the IP addresses of the hosts. However, to make the packets easier to read, you can use Aliases, which allow you to turn IP addresses into names.

CREATE ALIASES

GET READY. To create an alias in Network Monitor, perform the following steps:

1. Open Network Monitor by clicking **Start > Microsoft Network Monitor**.
2. In the *Recent Captures* pane, click **New capture tab**. A new *Capture* tab opens.
3. In the Frame Summary pane, click **Aliases** and then select **Manage Aliases**. The *Aliases* dialog box opens (see Figure 3-42).

Figure 3-42

Managing aliases

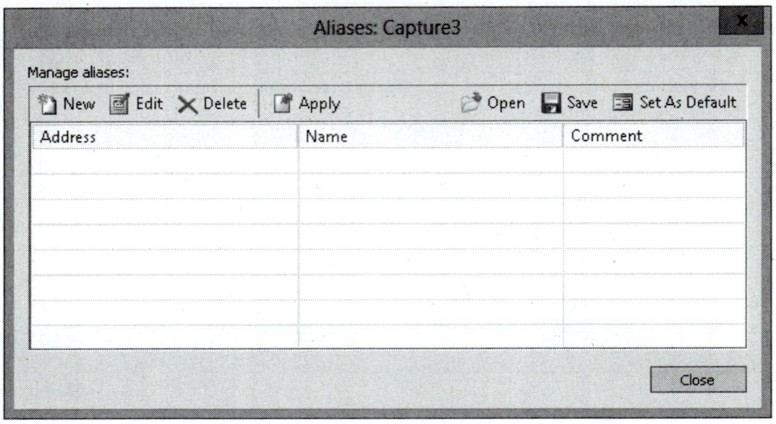

4. In the *Manage aliases* window, click **New**. The *Create New Alias* dialog box opens (see Figure 3-43).

Figure 3-43

Creating a new alias

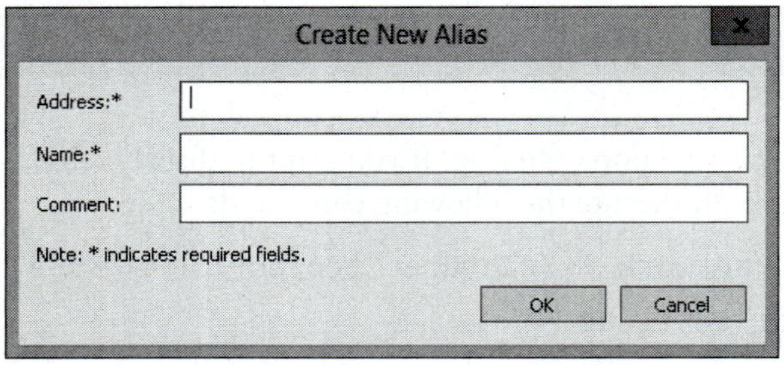

5. In the *Address* text box and the *Name* text box, type the address and name.
6. Click **OK** to accept your settings and close the *Create New Alias* dialog box.
7. Click **Close** to close the *Aliases* dialog box.
8. Close *Network Monitor*.

Monitoring Virtual Machines (VMs)

THE BOTTOM LINE

Just as you need to monitor physical computers, you also need to monitor virtual machines (VMs). Everything you have learned in this lesson applies to VMs. To monitor a virtual machine running Windows, you can still use Server Manager, Computer Management, Event Viewer, Performance Monitor, and all of the other tools. Since a single host can have many virtual servers, you need to make sure that one virtual computer does not use all of the resources that would take away from the other machines.

CERTIFICATION READY
Monitor virtual machines (VMs).
Objective 1.3

Hyper-V Resource Metering is a tool that allows you to view the resource usage of a host and individual VMs. In Windows Server 2012, it is activated and viewed with Windows PowerShell. Hyper-V Resource metering includes the following cmdlets:

- `Enable-VMResourceMetering` starts collecting data per virtual machine.
- `Disable-VMResourceMetering` disables resource metering per virtual machine.
- `Reset-VMResourceMetering` resets virtual machine resource-metering counters.
- `Measure-VM` displays resource-metering statistics for a specific virtual machine.

USING WINDOWS POWERSHELL

To enable Hyper-V resource metering on a Hyper-V host, execute the following Windows PowerShell commands:

```
Get-VM -ComputerName <HostName> | Enable-
VMResourceMetering
```

By default, the collection interval for Hyper-V metering data is one hour. To change the interval to one minute, execute the following command:

```
Set-vmhost -computername <HostName>
-ResourceMeteringSaveInterval 00:01:00
```

To get all VMs metering data for a host, execute the following command:

```
Get-VM -ComputerName <HostName> | Measure-VM
```

Figure 3-44 shows the enabling of Resource Metering and the data collected.

Figure 3-44
Enabling Resource Metering

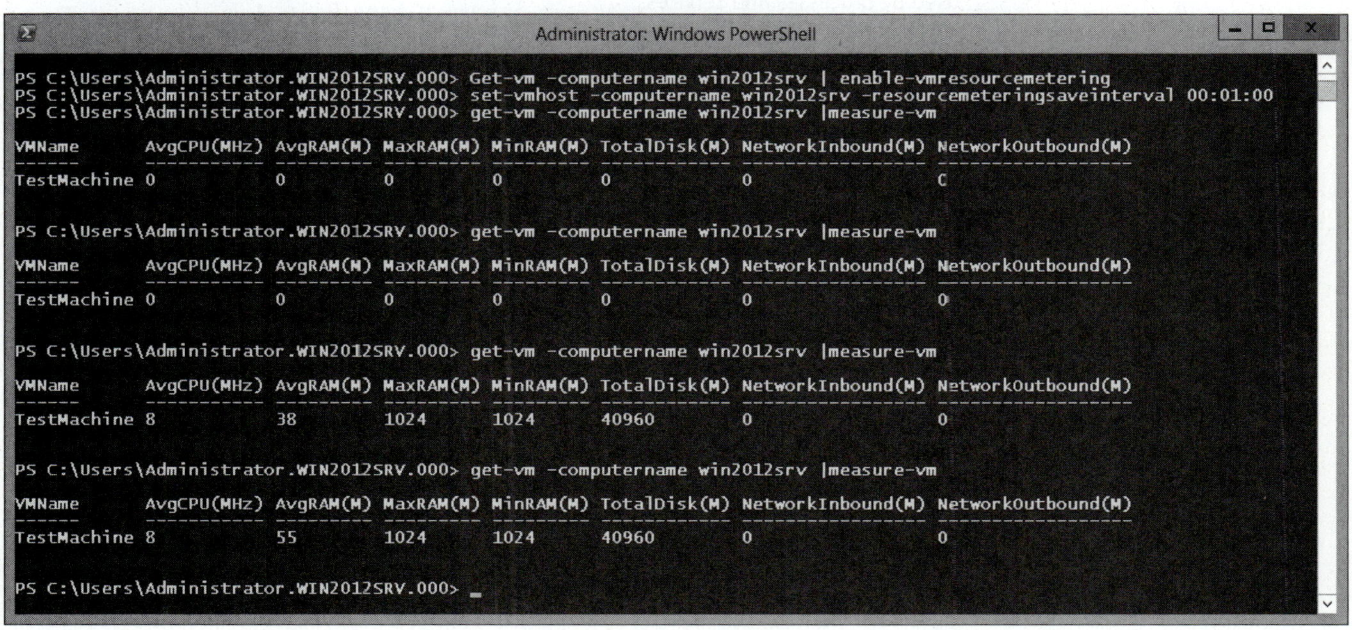

To retrieve metering data for a particular VM, execute the following command:

```
Get-VM -ComputerName <HostName> -Name
"<VMName>" | Measure-VM
```

SKILL SUMMARY

IN THIS LESSON, YOU LEARNED:

- The Microsoft Management Console (MMC) is one of the primary administrative tools used to manage Windows and many of the network services provided by Windows.
- Administrative Tools is a folder in the Control Panel that contains tools for system administrators and advanced users.
- Server Manager is a management console in Windows Server 2012 that helps you manage local and remote Windows-based servers. By managing servers as groups, you can perform the same administrative tasks quickly across multiple servers that have the same role or members of the same group.
- The Event Viewer enables you to browse and manage event logs.
- When looking at the logs shown by Event Viewer, you can be overwhelmed by the number of events. Therefore, you need to know how to filter events so that you can focus on what you want to focus on.
- Microsoft enhanced Event Viewer to capture events from multiple computers so that you can view the events using one console.
- The Reliability Monitor provides a stability index that ranges from 1 (the least stable) to 10 (the most stable). You can use the index to help evaluate the reliability of your computer.
- Performance is the overall effectiveness of how data moves through the system.
- Task Manager gives you a quick glance at performance and provides information about programs and processes running on your computer.
- Resource Monitor is a powerful tool for understanding how your system resources are used by processes and services.
- Performance Monitor provides tools for analyzing system performance.
- Rather than add individual performance counters each time you want to view the performance of a system, you can create Data Collector Sets (DCS), which allow you to organize a set of performance counts, event traces, and system configuration data into a single object that can be reused as needed.
- The `netstat` command is used to view the TCP/IP connections, both inbound and outbound, on your computer. You can also use `netstat` to view the packet statistics, such as how many packets have been sent and received and the number of errors.
- Hyper-V Resource Metering is a tool that allows you to view the resource usage of a host and individual VMs.

Knowledge Assessment

Multiple Choice

Select the correct answer for each of the following questions.

1. Which of the following is the primary tool to add or remove server roles?
   a. Computer Management
   b. Server Manager
   c. Add/Remove Programs
   d. Programs
2. Which of the following is used to view the Windows logs?
   a. Performance Monitor
   b. Reliability Monitor
   c. System Viewer
   d. Event Viewer
3. When you are troubleshooting a problem and decide to use the Event Viewer, which of the following should be used to help you focus on a reduced set of events?
   a. permissions
   b. rights
   c. views
   d. filters
4. Which of the following is used to modify a task after you add a basic task to an Event Viewer?
   a. Server Manager
   b. Event Viewer
   c. Reliability Monitor
   d. Task Scheduler
5. Which of the following allows you to view events from multiple computers using the Event Viewer?
   a. subscriptions
   b. Web services
   c. filters
   d. Remote Viewer
6. Which command is used to configure a collecting computer to receive an event subscription?
   a. `perfmon /rel`
   b. `wecutil qc`
   c. `winrm quickconfig`
   d. `winrm subscr`
7. Which program allows you to stop a running process?
   a. Performance Monitor
   b. Reliability Monitor
   c. Task Manager
   d. Event Viewer
8. Which program is used to determine what process is using a file?
   a. Performance Monitor
   b. Reliability Monitor
   c. Task Manager
   d. Resource Monitor

9. Which of the following is used to group multiple performance counters so that they can be used over and over in Performance Monitor?
   a. Replay Monitor
   b. Event Viewer
   c. Data Collector Sets
   d. Task Manager
10. Which program allows you to determine what processes are using which network connections?
   a. `netstat`
   b. `nbtstat`
   c. `ping`
   d. Task Manager

Best Answer

Choose the letter that corresponds to the best answer. More than one answer choice may achieve the goal. Select the BEST answer.

1. You want to capture all LDAP traffic to and from a server between 10:00 p.m. and 11:00 a.m. Which of the following actions should you perform?
   a. Run the Network Monitor and open the scheduling menu.
   b. Run the Network Monitor and open the capture menu.
   c. Create a scheduled task that runs the Netsh.exe command.
   d. Create a scheduled task that runs the NMCap.exe command.
2. Which of the following filters is used with Network Monitor when you want to capture all DHCP packets that pass between a client computer called PC1 (MAC address 00-20-C4-15-22-C1) and a DHCP server called Server1 (MAC address 00-18-31-C3-23-CD and IP address of 192.168.1.1)?
   a. IPv4.Address == 169.254.1.1 && DHCP
   b. IPv4 Address == 192.168.1.1 && DHCP
   c. Ethernet.Address == 001831C323CD && DHCP
   d. Ethernet.Address == 0020C41522C1 && DHCP
3. You just opened a capture file with Network Monitor. You want to show mnemonic host names instead of IP addresses. Which of the following actions should you perform?
   a. Create a new display filter and apply the filter to the capture display.
   b. Populate the Aliases table and apply the aliases to the capture.
   c. Click the Convert button.
   d. Click Options > Show Names.
4. You have installed a new server (Server1), which is a file and print server. You have received several calls from users who are complaining of slow performance when opening files from the server. Which two tasks determine which application is using the most processing? (Choose two answers.)
   a. Open the Event Viewer and review the Performance logs.
   b. Open the Task Manager and view the Processes tab.
   c. Open the Resource Monitor and use the Resource View to see the percentage of processor capacity by each application.
   d. Open Performance Monitor and view the appropriate performance counter.
5. You created a Data Collector Set. Which of the following actions prevents the DCS from logging data when the server has less than 1 GB of available disk space?
   a. Modify the Data Manager settings of the DCS.
   b. Create a passive file screen.
   c. Modify the DCS Actions Properties.
   d. Modify the Disk Redirect option.

6. When forwarding events, which group on the forwarding computer do you need to add the collection computer name to?
   a. Performance Users
   b. Domain Admins
   c. Administrators
   d. System Logon

Matching and Identification

1. Match each Windows Log to the appropriate description or usage.
   _______ a) Shows boot errors
   _______ b) Shows events collected from remote computers
   _______ c) Shows events generated by applications
   _______ d) Contains events related to the installation of applications
   _______ e) Shows invalid logins and access to audited files
   1. Application log
   2. Security log
   3. Setup log
   4. System log
   5. Forwarded Events

2. Identify the maximum value of the following performance counters.
   _____ %Processor Time
   _____ Pages/sec
   _____ Paging File:% Usage
   _____ % Avg. Disk Queue Length

Build a List

1. You need to configure Server2 to forward errors found in the System logs to Server1. Specify the correct order of the steps that are needed to configure Server1 and Server2.

   _____ Run `Winrm quickconfig` on Server1.
   _____ Run `Winrm quickconfig` on Server2.
   _____ Create a subscription on Server1.
   _____ Create a subscription on Server2.
   _____ Run `wecutil qc` on Server1.
   _____ Run `wecutil qc` on Server2.

2. Specify the order (from first to last) of the steps necessary to troubleshooting a network problem.

   _____ Ping a local IP address.
   _____ Ping a remote computer.
   _____ Verify DNS configuration using `nslookup`.
   _____ Run `ipconfig`.
   _____ Ping a remote gateway.
   _____ Make sure the network interface is enabled and the cable is connected.

Business Case Scenarios

Scenario 3-1: Troubleshooting a Performance Problem

You have several file servers. Several times during the day, the file server performance degrades significantly. What steps should you perform to determine the cause of the problem?

Scenario 3-2: Monitoring the Event Viewer of Multiple Computers

You have 40 essential servers that must be running as best as they can at all times. What is the most efficient way to review key events on all 40 servers each day?

Configuring Distributed File System (DFS)

LESSON 4

70-411 EXAM OBJECTIVE

Objective 2.1 – Configure Distributed File System (DFS). This objective may include but is not limited to: install and configure DFS namespaces; configure DFS replication targets; configure replication scheduling; configure remote differential compression settings; configure staging; configure fault tolerance.

LESSON HEADING	EXAM OBJECTIVE
Using Distributed File System	Configure Distributed File System (DFS)
Installing and Configuring DFS Namespace	Install and configure DFS namespaces
Installing and Configuring DFS Replication	Configure DFS replication targets
Scheduling Replication	Configure replication scheduling
Configuring Remote Differential Compression	Configure remote differential compression settings
Configuring Staging	Configure staging
Configuring Fault Tolerance Using DFS	Configure fault tolerance

KEY TERMS

Conflict and Deleted folder
DFS Namespace
DFS Replication
Distributed File System (DFS)
domain-based namespace
full mesh topology
hub/spoke topology
referral
remote differential compression (RDC)
replication group
staging folder

Using Distributed File System

THE BOTTOM LINE

Distributed File System improves on the use of the shared folders by enabling you to organize your shared folders and enabling you to distribute shares on multiple servers.

CERTIFICATION READY
Configure Distributed File System (DFS).
Objective 2.1

Distributed File System (DFS) is a set of technologies that enable a Windows server to organize multiple distributed SMB file shares into a distributed file system. Although the shares can be on different servers, the location is transparent to the users. Finally, DFS can provide redundancy to improve data availability while minimizing the amount of traffic passing over the WAN links. The two technologies in DFS include:

- DFS Namespaces
- DFS Replication

Installing and Configuring DFS Namespace

If you have a site with many file servers and many shared folders, some users will have difficulty finding the files that they need as they have to remember the server name and shared folder name that make up the UNC. ***DFS Namespace*** enables you to group shared folders into a single logical structure. In other words, a DFS Namespace is a shared folder of shared folders (which can be on multiple servers).

CERTIFICATION READY
Install and configure DFS namespaces.
Objective 2.1

DFS is a virtual namespace technology that enables you to create a single directory tree that lists other shared folders. Creating a DFS Namespace allows users to locate their files more easily. See Figure 4-1.

Figure 4-1

Linking to shared folders with DFS Namespace

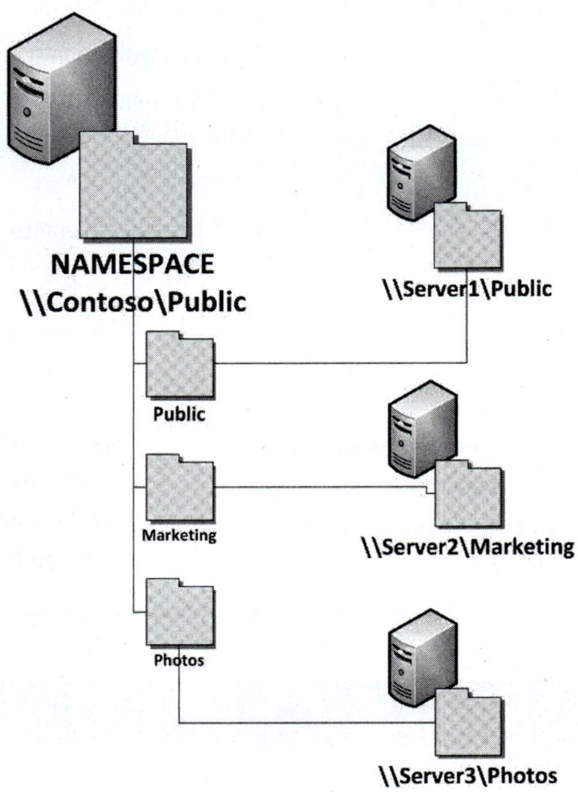

The actual shared folders are referred to as the targets of the virtual folders in the namespace. DFS can be combined with DFS Replication, which increases availability and automatically connects users to shared folders in the same Active Directory site, when available, instead of connecting to another folder connected over a slower WAN link.

INSTALLING DFS NAMESPACE

Installing DFS Namespace is a simple process of adding the appropriate role using Server Manager. However, you should also install the File Server service so that you can create file shares. The DFS Management Tools installs the DFS Management snap-in, the DFS Namespace module for Windows PowerShell, and command-line tools.

INSTALL DFS NAMESPACE

GET READY. To install DFS Namespace, perform the following steps:

1. Click the Server Manager button on the task bar to open *Server Manager*.
2. At the top of Server Manager, select Manage and click Add Roles and Features. The *Add Roles and Feature Wizard* opens.
3. On the *Before you begin* page, click Next.
4. Select Role-based or feature-based installation and then click Next.
5. Click Select a server from the server pool, click the name of the server to install DFS to, and then click Next.
6. Scroll down and expand File and Storage Services and then expand File and iSCSI Services. Select File Server and DFS Namespace (see Figure 4-2).

Figure 4-2
Selecting File Server and DFS Namespace

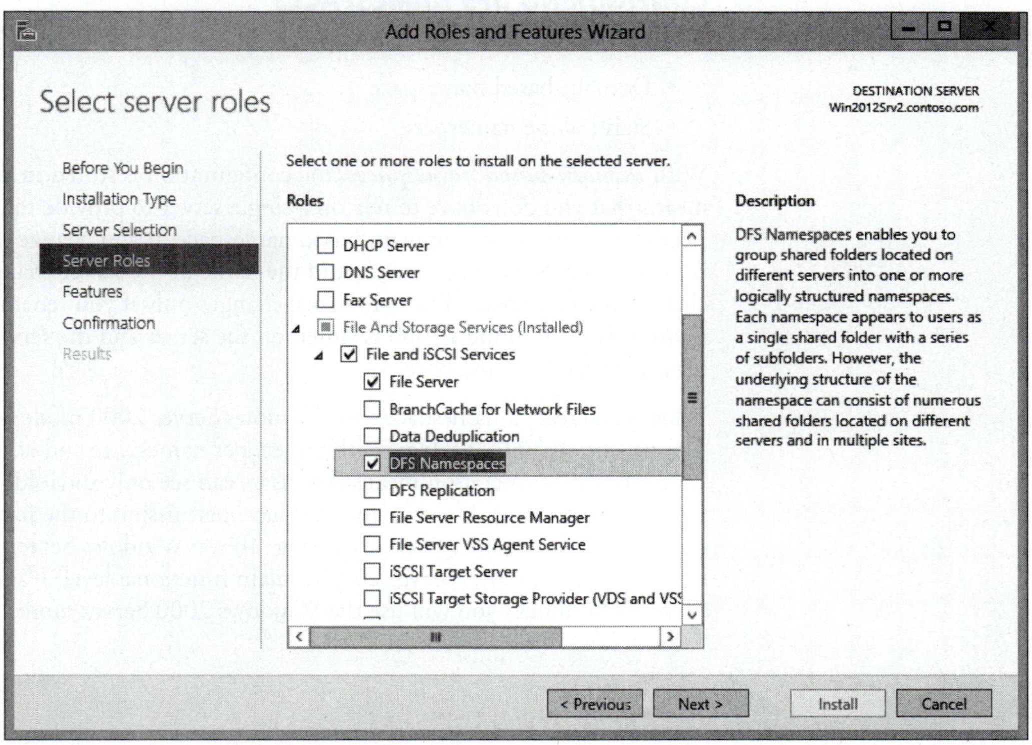

7. When asked to add features to DFS Namespace, as shown in Figure 4-3, click Add Features.

Figure 4-3

Adding DFS-related features

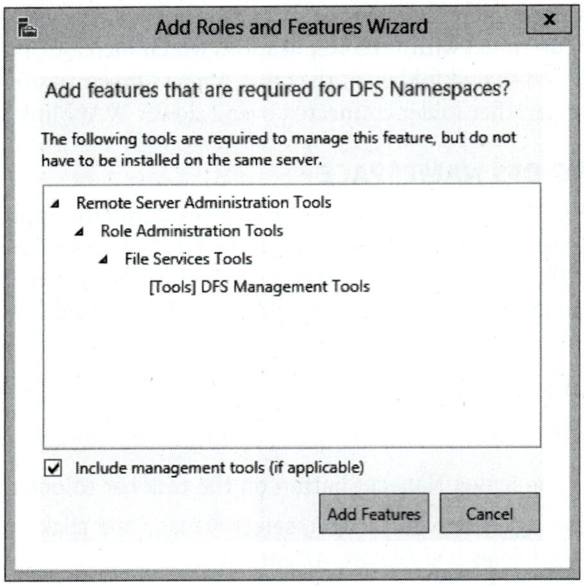

8. When you are back on the *Select server roles* page, click Next.
9. On the *Select features* page, click Next.
10. On the *Confirm installation selections*, click Install.
11. When the installation is complete, click the Close button.

CONFIGURING DFS NAMESPACES

There are two types of DFS namespaces:

- Domain-based namespace
- Stand-alone namespace

With ***domain-based namespaces***, the configuration is stored in Active Directory, which means that you don't have to rely on a single server to provide the namespace information to your clients. By using a domain-based namespace, if you change the name of the server that runs the DFS Namespace service and the name of the server changes, you will not have to change the namespace. The namespace changes only if you rename the domain. With a ***stand-alone DFS***, the configuration is stored on the server and the server name becomes part of the main path to the namespace.

When you create a namespace, the Windows Server 2008 mode is selected by default, which supports up to 50,000 folders with targets per namespace and access-based enumeration. Access-based enumeration means that users can see only the folders and files that they have permission to access. If a user does not have permission to the folder or file, the folder or file does not even show in a directory listing. To use Windows Server 2008 mode, Active Directory must use the Windows Server 2008 domain functional level. If you deselect the Windows Server 2008 mode, you will use the Windows 2000 Server mode, which supports only up to 5,000 folders.

CREATE A DFS NAMESPACE

GET READY. To create a DFS Namespace, perform the following steps:

1. Open Server Manager.
2. Click Tools > DFS Management to open the *DFS Management console* (see Figure 4-4).

Figure 4-4

Using the DFS Management console

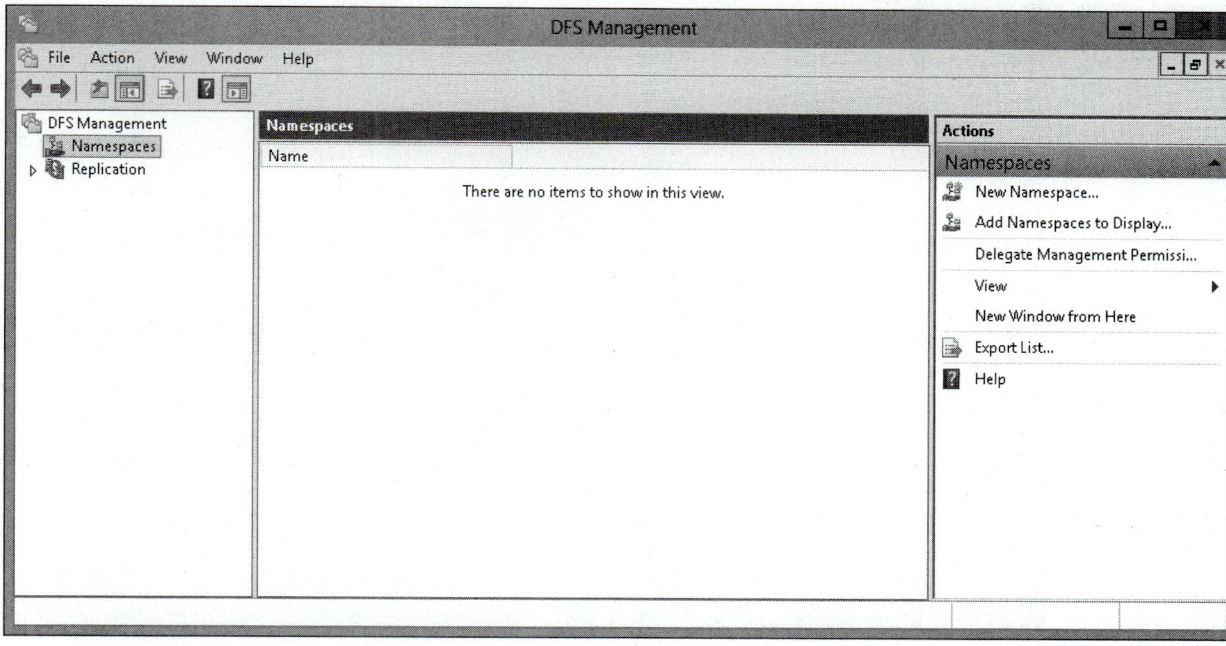

3. In the left-pane, right-click Namespaces and select New Namespace. The *New Namespace Wizard* starts.
4. On the *Namespace Server* page (see Figure 4-5), type in the name of the server that hosts the DFS Namespace in the *Server* text box. Click Next.

Figure 4-5

Entering the name of the server on the Namespace Server page

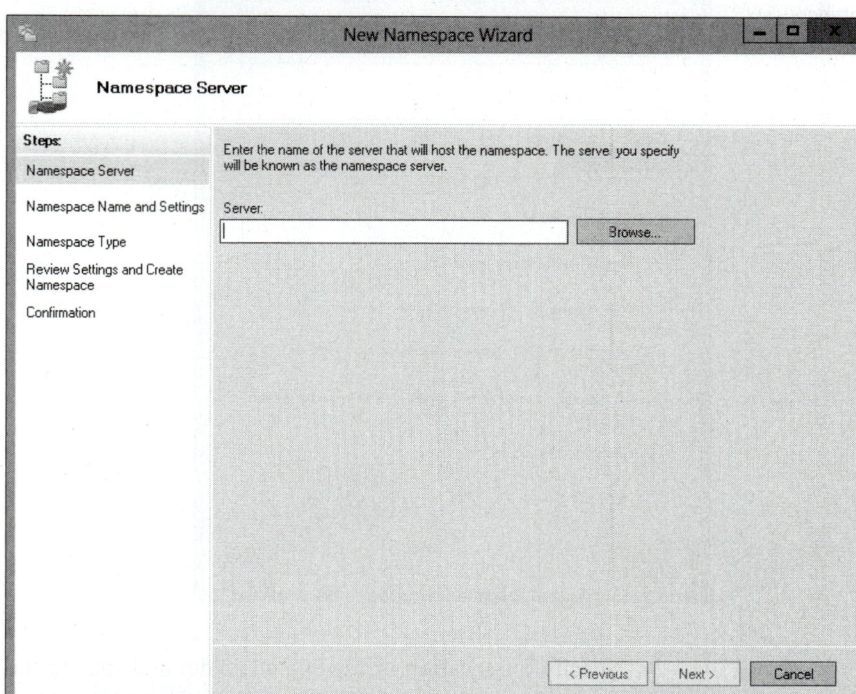

5. On the *Namespace Name and Settings* page, type the name of the namespace in the *Name* text box, as shown in Figure 4-6. The name appears after the server (stand-alone namespace) or domain name (domain-based namespace). Click Next.

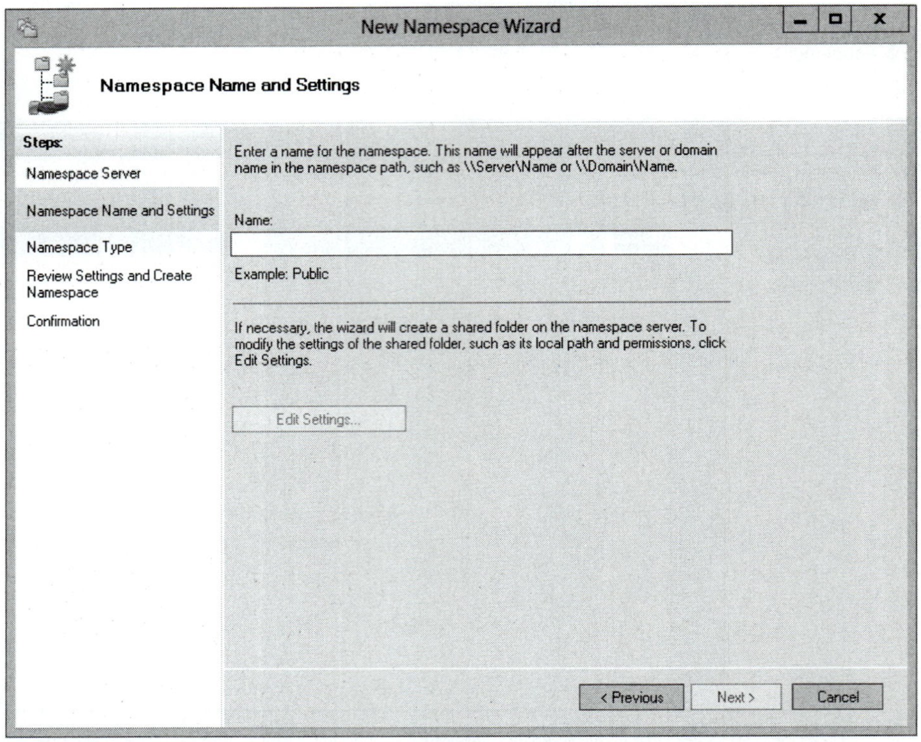

Figure 4-6

Entering the name of the namespace on the Namespace Name and Settings page

6. To change the location of the shared folder on the server and the shared permissions, click Edit Settings. The *Edit Settings* dialog box opens (see Figure 4-7).

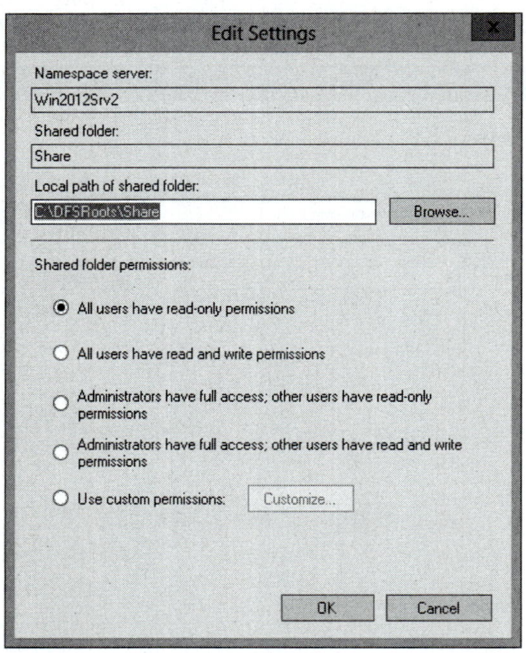

Figure 4-7

Opening the Edit Settings dialog box

7. Specify the location of the Shared Folder and specify the Shared folder permissions. Click OK to close the *Edit Settings* dialog box.
8. On the *Namespace Name and Settings* page, click Next.
9. On the *Namespace Type* page (see Figure 4-8), select either Domain-based namespace or Stand-alone namespace.

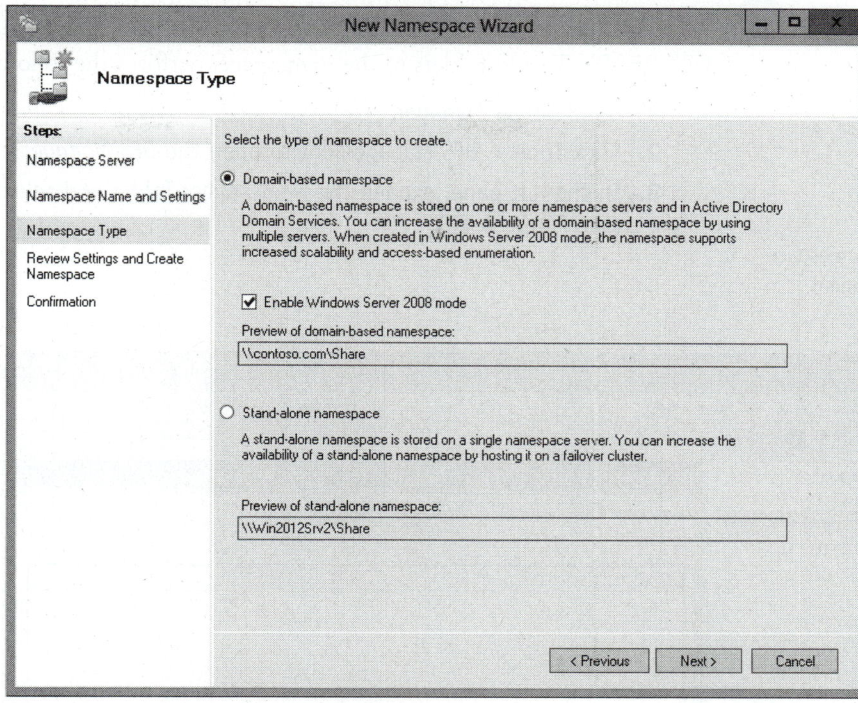

Figure 4-8

Selecting the namespace on the Namespace Type page

10. Leave the Enable Windows Server 2008 mode enabled. Notice the entire path of the domain-based namespace. Click Next.
11. On the *Review Settings and Create Namespace* page (see Figure 4-9), click Create.

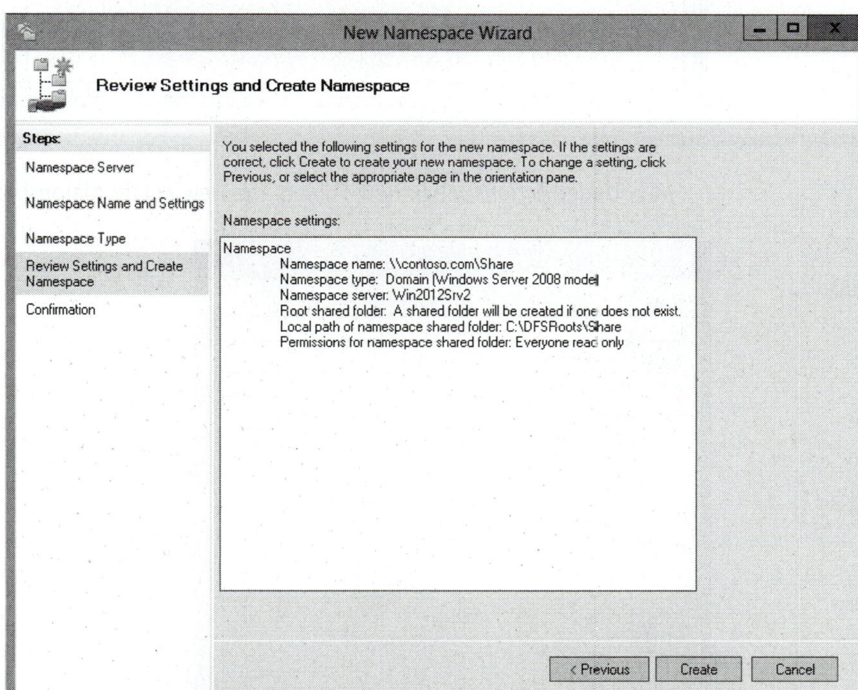

Figure 4-9

Reviewing the selected settings on the *Review Settings and Create Namespace* page

12. When the installation is complete, click the Close button.

After you create the namespace, you need to add folders to it that point to the share folders on your network. If you have a DFS replicated folder, you add each replicated folder to the target. By using the DFS replicated folder with the DFS namespace, you provide fault tolerance and better.

ADD FOLDERS TO THE NAMESPACE

GET READY. To add folders to the namespace, perform the following steps:

1. Open Server Manager.
2. Click Tools > DFS Management to open the *DFS Management console*.
3. In the left pane, expand the Namespaces folder and select the desired namespace (see Figure 4-10).

Figure 4-10

Opening the DFS Namespace in the DFS Management console

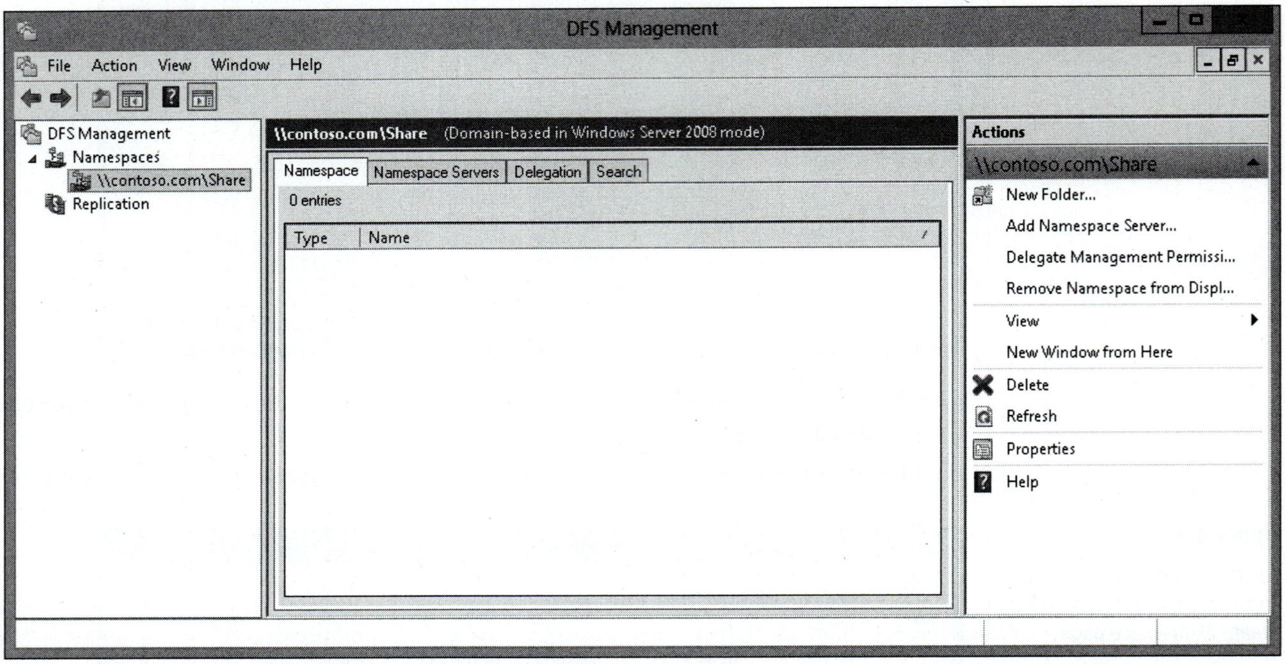

4. Under *Actions*, click New Folder. The *New Folder* dialog box opens (see Figure 4-11).

Figure 4-11

Adding a folder to the namespace

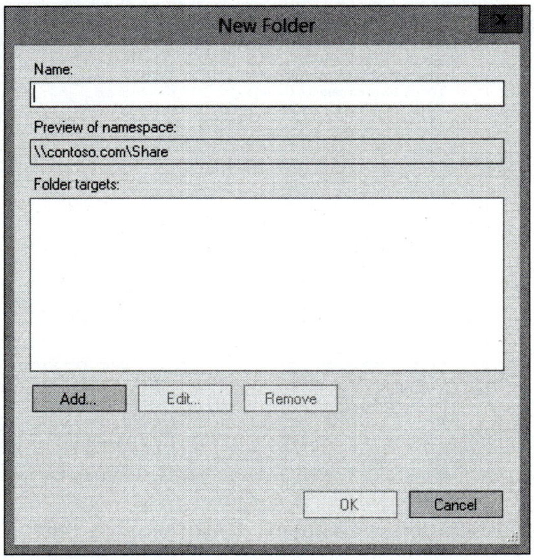

5. Type the name of the shared folder in the *Name* text box. The name should be a descriptive name, but does not have to be the same name as the shared folder that you will be referencing.

6. To specify the shared folder, click Add.
7. In the *Add Folder Target* dialog box (see Figure 4-12), type in the UNC to the desired shared folder. Click OK.

Figure 4-12

Adding a Folder Target to the namespace

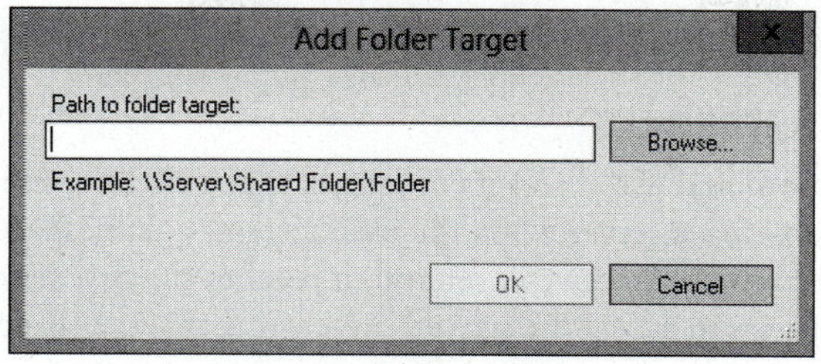

8. If you have DFS replicated folder for your target, add the replicated paths of the folder.
9. Click OK to close the *New Folder* dialog box.

USING WINDOWS POWERSHELL

You can manage DFS namespace using the following Windows PowerShell cmdlets:

- `Get-DfsnRoot` – Retrieves the configuration settings for the specified namespaces.
- `New-DfsnRoot` – Creates a new DFS namespace with the specified configuration settings.
- `Set-DfsnRoot` – Modifies the configuration settings for the specified existing DFS namespace.
- `Get-DfsnRootTarget` – Retrieves all the configured root targets for the specified namespace root, including the configuration settings of each root target.
- `New-DfsnRootTarget` – Adds a new root target with the specified configuration settings to an existing DFS namespace.
- `Set-DfsnRootTarget` – Sets configuration settings to specified values for a namespace root target of an existing DFS namespace.
- `Remove-DfsnRootTarget` – Deletes an existing namespace root target of a DFS namespace.
- `Get-DfsnServerConfiguration` – Retrieves the configuration settings of the specified DFS namespace server.
- `Set-DfsnServerConfiguration` – Modifies configuration settings for the specified server hosting DFS namespace(s).
- `New-DfsnFolder` – Creates a new folder in an existing DFS namespace with the specified configuration settings.
- `Get-DfsnFolder` – Retrieves configuration settings for the specified existing DFS namespace folder.
- `Set-DfsnFolder` – Modifies settings for the specified existing DFS namespace folder with folder targets.
- `Move-DfsnFolder` – Moves an existing DFS namespace folder to an alternate specified location in the same DFS namespace.
- `Grant-DfsnAccess` – Grants access rights to the specified user/group account for the specified DFS namespace folder with folder targets.
- `Get-DfsnAccess` – Retrieves the currently configured access rights for the specified DFS namespace folder with folder targets.
- `Revoke-DfsnAccess` – Revokes the right to access a DFS namespace folder with folder targets or enumerate its contents from the specified user or group account.
- `Remove-DfsnAccess` – Removes the specified user/group account from access control list (ACL) of the DFS namespace folder with folder targets.
- `Remove-DfsnFolder` – Deletes an existing DFS namespace folder with a folder target.
- `New-DfsnFolderTarget` – Adds a new folder target with the specified configuration settings to an existing DFS namespace folder.
- `Get-DfsnFolderTarget` – Retrieves configuration settings of folder target(s) of an existing DFS namespace folder.
- `Set-DfsnFolderTarget` – Modifies settings for the folder target of an existing DFS namespace folder.
- `Remove-DfsnFolderTarget` – Deletes a folder target of an existing DFS namespace folder.

To manage DFS Namespace, you can use the following commands:

- `DfsUtil` – Manages DFS namespaces, server, and client computers.
- `DfsCmd` – Configures DFS folders and folder targets in a DFS namespace.
- `DfsDiag` – Performs diagnostics tests of DFS Namespaces.

MANAGING REFERRALS

A ***referral*** is an ordered list of servers or targets that a client computer receives from a domain controller or namespace server when the user accesses a namespace root or a DFS folder with targets. After a computer receives a referral, it reaches the first server on the list. If the server is not available, it tries to access the second server. If that server is not available, it goes to the next server.

If you right-click the namespace and select Properties, you can help choose which server the client uses when you have multiple folders for a shared folder. Figure 4-13 shows the *Namespace Properties* dialog box. No matter what ordering method is selected, if a client is on the same site as the target, it always chooses the target. Then, by default, it chooses the closest server (lowest cost). You can also select *Random order*, which performs a load balancing for the targets at the other sites. Lastly, you can select the *Exclude targets outside of the client's side* option, which prevents the clients from accessing targets at other sites.

Figure 4-13

Configuring the referrals for a namespace

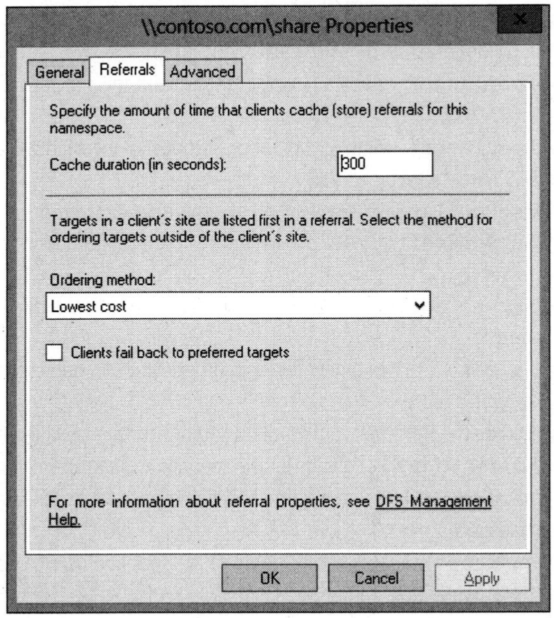

If a server becomes unavailable, you can have a client fall back to targets that were previously unavailable if the server becomes available again and at lower cost than the target the client uses. This is done by selecting the *Clients fail back to preferred targets* option.

In the Advanced tab (see figure 4-14), you can optimize polling. To maintain a consistent domain-based namespace across namespace servers, the namespace servers periodically poll Active Directory Domain Services (AD DS) to obtain the most current namespace data.

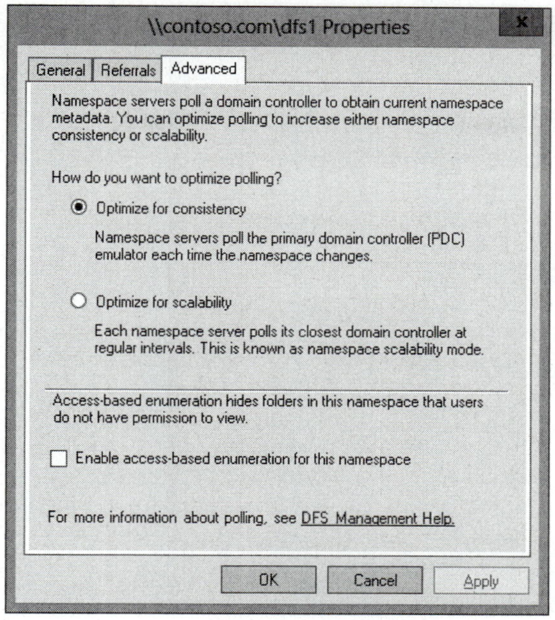

Figure 4-14

Optimizing namespace servers polling options

By default, the *Optimize for consistency* option is selected. It causes the namespace servers to poll the PDC emulator each time the namespace changes. If you have more than 16 namespace servers, you should choose the *Optimize for scalability* to reduce the load on the PDC Emulator. Unfortunately, this option increases the time it requires for changes to the namespace to replicate to all namespace servers, which may cause users to see inconsistent view of the namespace while namespace changes are replicated to all servers.

To control how targets are ordered, you can set priority on individual targets. For example, if you want one server to always be first or always be last, you can use the following procedure:

SET TARGET PRIORITY ON A ROOT TARGET FOR A DOMAIN-BASED NAMESPACE

GET READY. To set the target priority on a root target for a domain-based namespace, perform the following steps:

1. Open Server Manager.
2. Click Tools > DFS Management to open the *DFS Management console*.
3. In the left pane, expand the Namespaces folder and select the desired namespace.
4. In the center pane, click Namespace Servers tab.
5. Right-click the root target with the priority that you want to change, and then click Properties. The *Properties* dialog box opens as shown in Figure 4-15.

Figure 4-15

Opening the DFS namespace properties

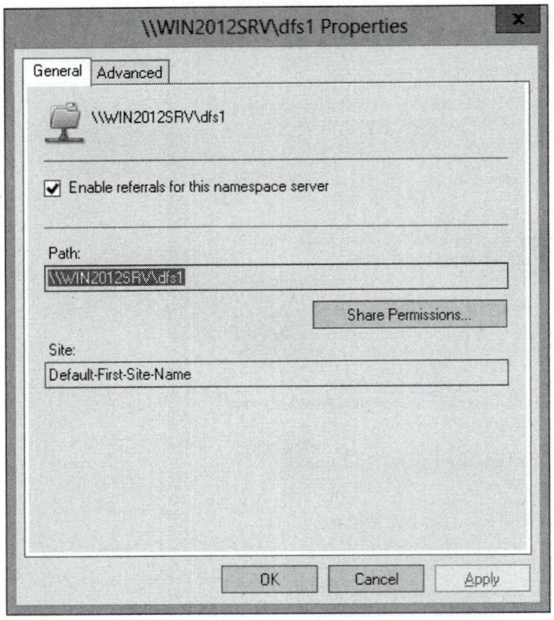

6. Click the Advanced tab. The *Advanced* tab is shown in Figure 4-16.

Figure 4-16

Optimizing namespace servers polling options

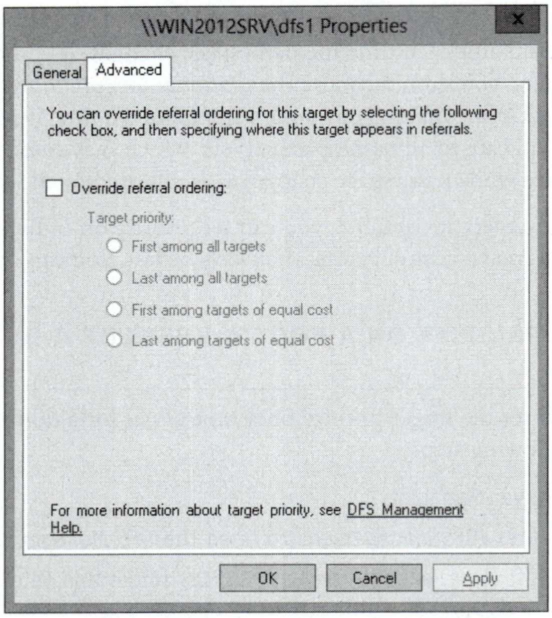

7. Click Override referral ordering, and then click the priority that you want.
   - First among all targets: Specifies that users should always be referred to this target if the target is available.
   - Last among all targets: Specifies that users should never be referred to this target unless all other targets are unavailable.
   - First among targets of equal cost: Specifies that users should be referred to this target before other targets of equal cost (which usually means other targets in the same site).
   - Last among targets of equal cost: Specifies that users should never be referred to this target if there are other targets of equal cost available (which usually means other targets in the same site).

8. Click OK to close the *Properties* dialog box.
9. Close the DFS Management console.

MANAGING DFS SECURITY

Because DFS Namespace is a specialized shared folder of shared folders, you still secure these folders with share permissions and NTFS permissions. It is recommended that you first configure the share and NTFS permissions on folders that host namespace roots and folder targets before configuring DFS. If you have multiple namespace root servers or folder target servers will be utilized, you need to manually synchronize permissions between the servers to avoid access problems.

Access-based enumeration hides files and folders that users do not have permission to access. To control access-based enumeration of files and folders in folder targets, you must enable access-based enumeration on each shared folder by using the following procedure.

ENABLE ACCESS-BASED ENUMERATION FOR A NAMESPACE

GET READY. To enable access-based enumeration for a namespace, perform the following steps:

1. Open Server Manager.
2. Click Tools > DFS Management to open the *DFS Management console*.
3. In the left pane, right-click the namespace and click Properties.
4. Click the Advanced tab.
5. Select the Enable access-based enumeration for this namespace.
6. Click OK to close the *Properties* dialog box.
7. Close the *DFS Management console*.

Installing and Configuring DFS Replication

The other part of DFS is DFS Replication. ***DFS Replication*** enables you to replicate folders between multiple servers. To allow efficient use of the network, it propagates only the changes, uses compression, and uses scheduling to replicate the data between the servers.

CERTIFICATION READY
Configure DFS replication targets.
Objective 2.1

To enable replication between multiple targets, you first create a replication group. The ***replication group*** is a collection of servers, known as servers, each of which holds a target of a DFS folder. You need a minimum of two targets to perform DFS Replication.

When you create a DFS replication group, you designate one server as the primary member of the replication group. Files then copy from the primary member to the other target servers. If any of the files in the target folders are different, DFS Replication overwrites the other files.

The primary disadvantage of using DFS Replication is that you need to have sufficient storage space available on each server that hosts the server and you need extra space so that DFS Replication can process the replication.

When using DFS Replication, you should keep in mind the following limitations:

- A replication group can have up to 256 members with 256 replicated folders.
- Each server can be a member of up to 256 replication groups, with as many as 256 connections (128 incoming and 128 outgoing).
- A member server can support up to 1 TB of replicated files.
- You can have up to 8 million replicated files per volume.

WARNING DFS Replication is not a replacement for backups. If a file gets deleted, changed, or corrupted on one target server, it will most likely be deleted, changed, or corrupted on the other target servers. Therefore, you still need to use backups to provide data protection and recovery.

The best method to recover from a disaster is to use backups. DFS Replication can also be used in conjunction with backups to provide a WAN backup solution. For example, if you have multiple sites, it becomes more difficult to perform backups, particular over the slower WAN links. One solution for this is to set up DFS Replication between the site servers to a central server or servers at the corporate office. Replication occurs when the WAN links are utilized the least such as in the evenings and during the weekends. You then back up the central computers located at the corporate office.

INSTALLING DFS REPLICATION

DFS Replication is another server role, similar to DFS Namespace. Therefore, you would use Server Manager to install DFS Namespace.

INSTALL DFS REPLICATION

GET READY. To install DFS Replication, perform the following steps:

1. Open Server Manager.
2. At the top of *Server Manager*, select Manage and click Add Roles and Features. The *Add Roles and Feature Wizard* opens.
3. On the *Before you begin* page, click Next.
4. Select Role-based or feature-based installation and then click Next.
5. Click Select a server from the server pool, click the name of the server to install DFS to, and then click Next.
6. Scroll down and expand File and Storage Services and expand file and iSCSI Services. Select DFS Replication, as shown in Figure 4-17. If *File Server* is not already installed, select it.

Figure 4-17

Selecting DFS Replication

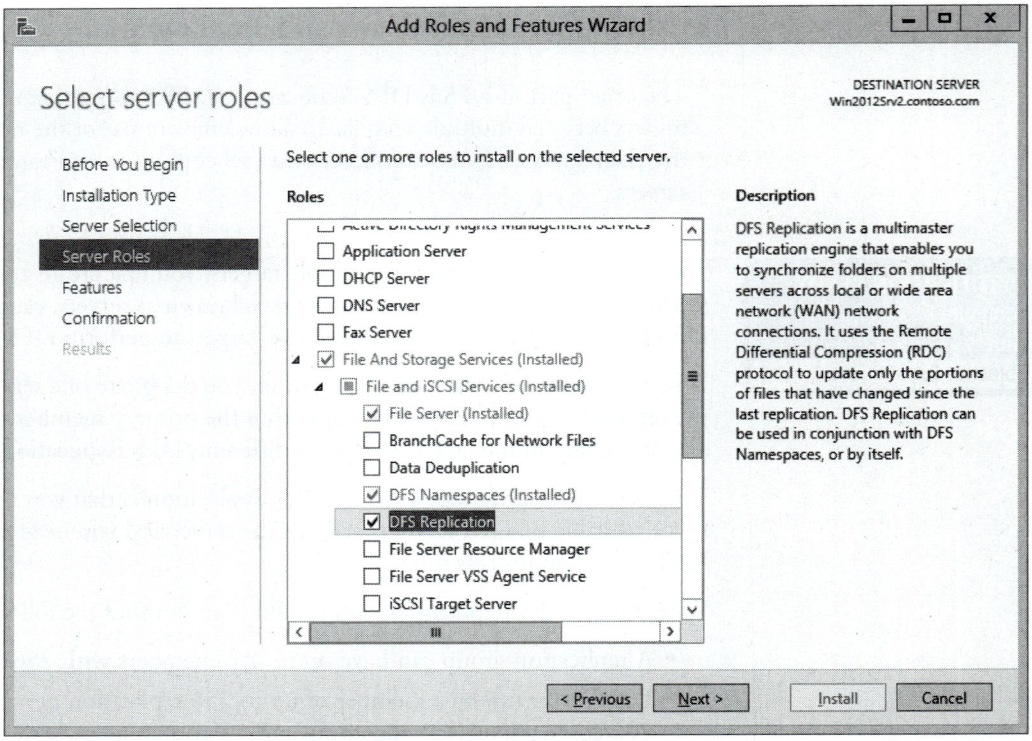

7. If you are asked to add features to DFS Namespace, click Add Features.
8. When you are back on the *Select server roles* page, click Next.
9. On the *Select features* page, click Next.
10. On the *Confirm installation selections* page, click Install.
11. When the installation is complete, click the Close button.

CONFIGURING DFS REPLICATION TARGETS

When you replicate folders using DFS, you are replicating local folders on a server to another local folder on another server. The folder is most likely shared so that users can access the folder, but this is not necessary.

By default, replication groups use a ***full mesh topology***, which means that all members replicate to all other members. If you have a simple DFS implementation consisting of two servers, there is some replication traffic between the two servers. However, by adding multiple servers to a replication group, replication traffic increases even more. Therefore, instead of using a full mesh topology, you can use a ***hub/spoke topology***, were as one server is used to replicate to the other members, which limit the replication traffic to specific pairs of members.

When you configure DFS Replication, you can configure the following settings:

- Bidirectional or unidirectional
- Percentage of available bandwidth
- Schedule when replication will occur

By default, DFS replication between two members is bidirectional. Bidirectional connections occur in both directions and include two one-way connections. If you desire only a one-way connection, you can disable one of the connections or use share permissions to prevent the replication process from updating files on certain member servers.

Because DFS Replication often occurs over a WAN link, you have to be aware of how much traffic DFS uses and how you can configure it when replication occurs to best utilize the WAN links. Therefore, you can schedule replication to occur only during the night when the WAN links are not used as much or you can specify the bandwidth used by DFS Replication.

CREATE A DFS REPLICATION GROUP

GET READY. To create a DFS replication group, perform the following steps:

1. Open Server Manager.
2. Click Tools > DFS Management. The *DFS Management console* opens.
3. Right-click Replication and select New Replication Group.
4. On the *Replication Group Type* page (see Figure 4-18), select Multipurpose replication group, and then click Next.

Figure 4-18

Selecting the replication group type

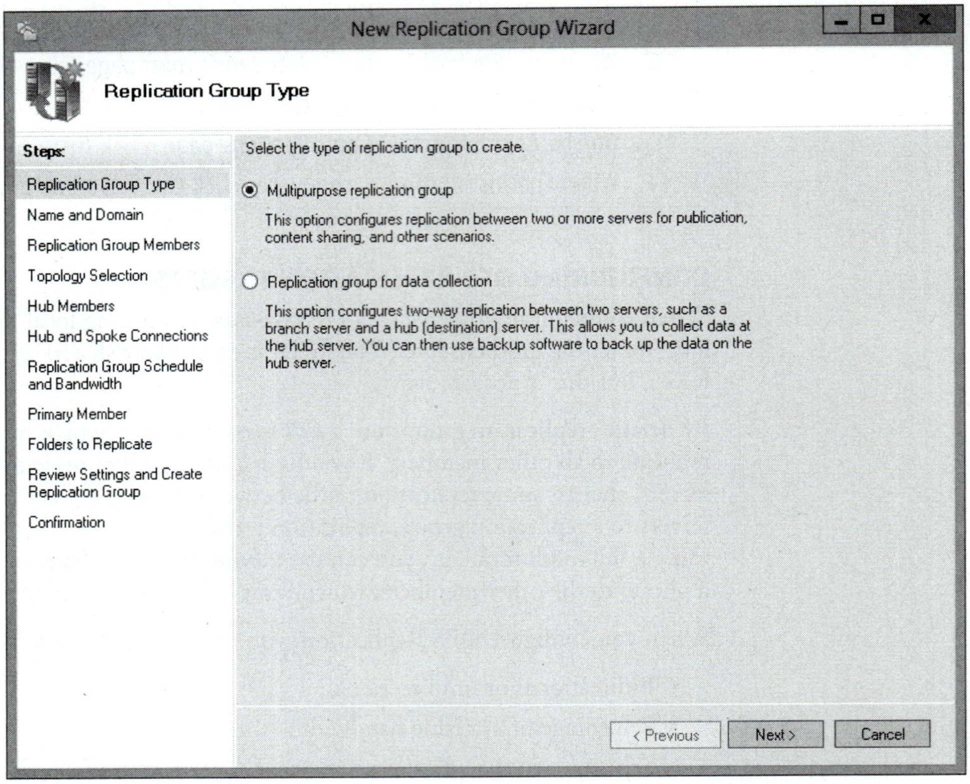

5. On the *Name and Domain* page (see Figure 4-19), type a descriptive name for the replication group in the Name of replication group text box. Click the Next button.

Figure 4-19

Specifying a name and domain used in DFS Replication

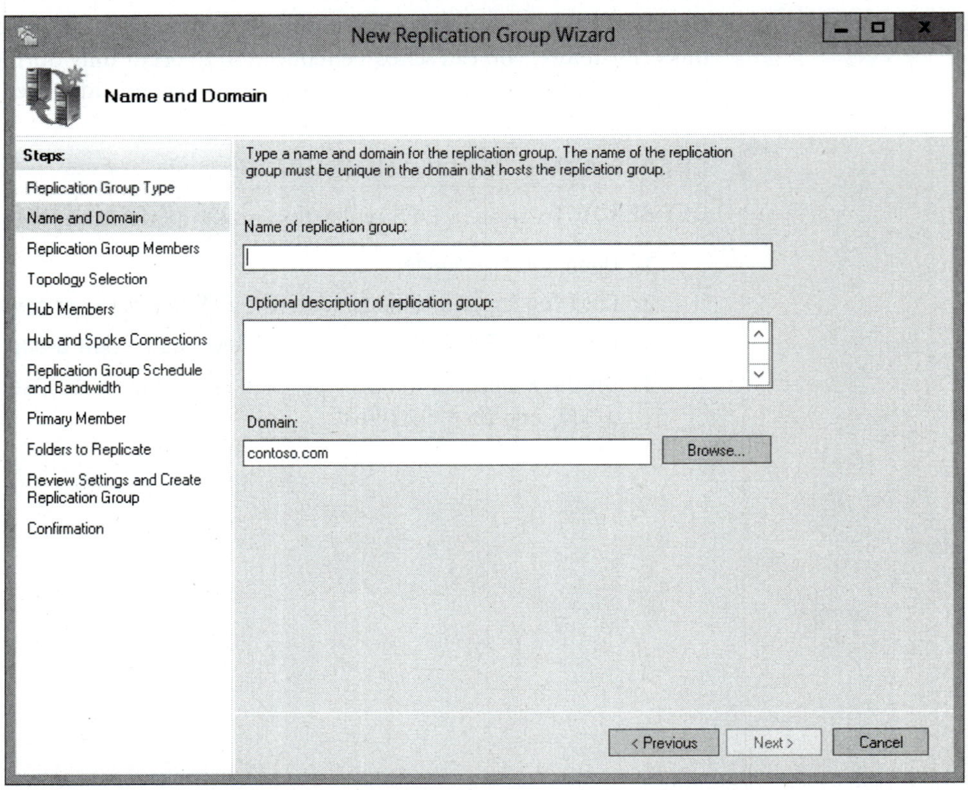

6. On the *Replication Group Members* page (see Figure 4-20), click the Add button.

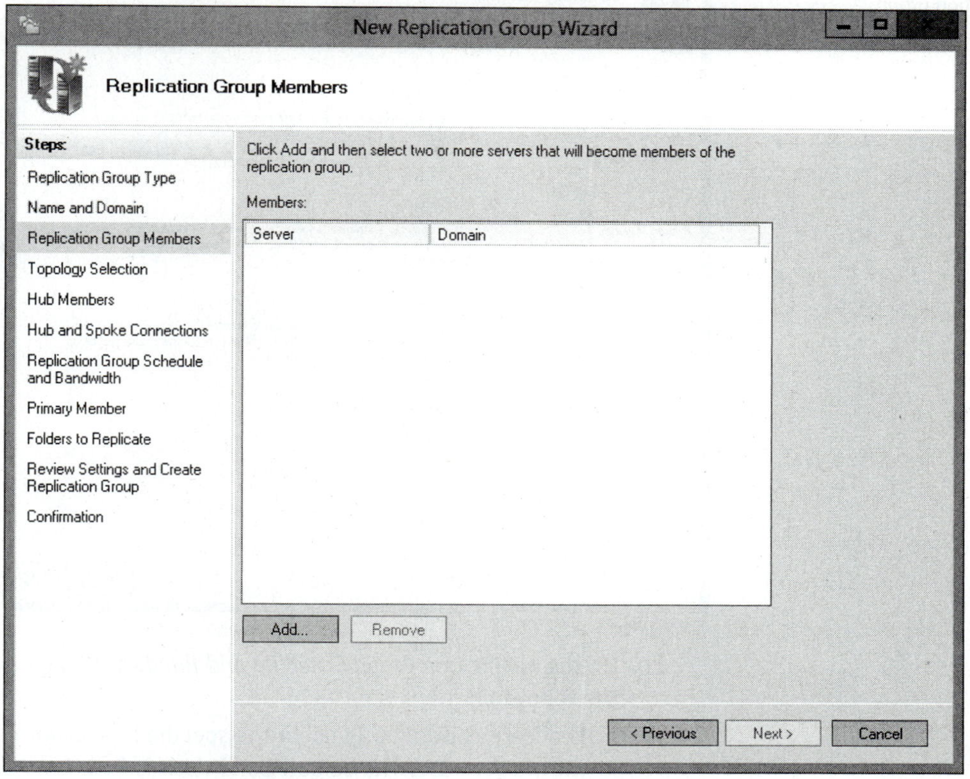

Figure 4-20

Defining replication group members

7. When the *Select Computers* dialog box opens (see Figure 4-21), type the name of the first server of the group and click OK.

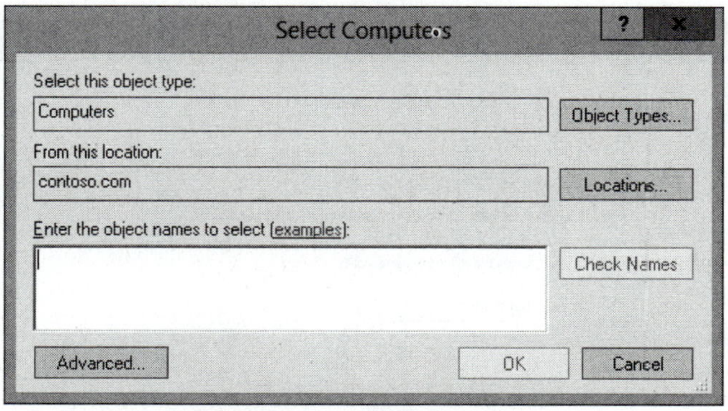

Figure 4-21

Select computers used in replication

8. Repeat step 7 until all of the target servers are added to the group.
9. On the *Replication Group Members* page, click Next.
10. On the *Topology Selection* page (see Figure 4-22), select Full Mesh, and then click Next.

Figure 4-22

Selecting a topology for the replication group

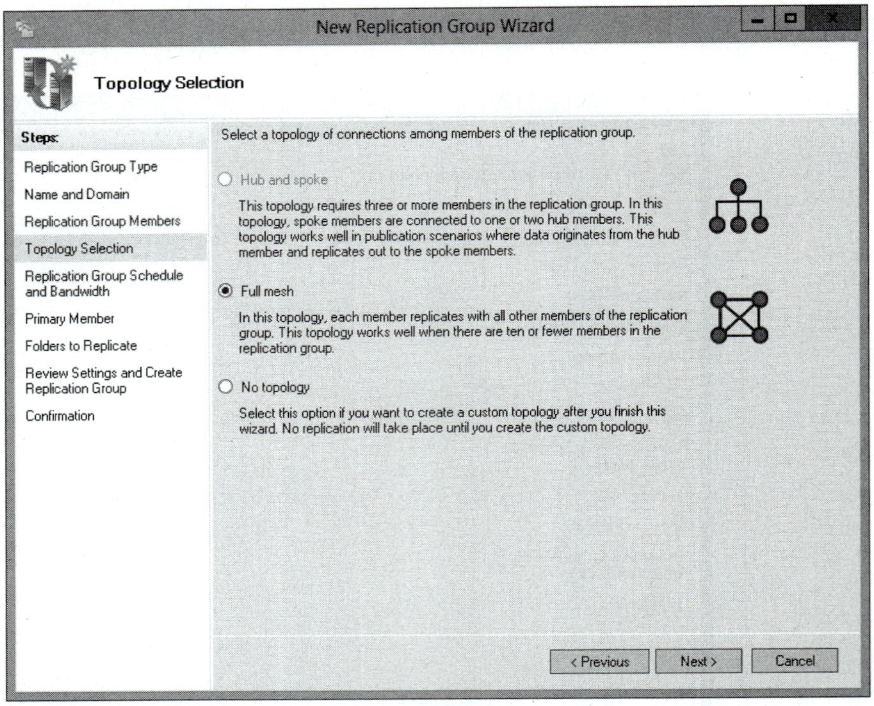

11. On the *Replication Group Schedule and Bandwidth* page (see Figure 4-23), click one of the following:
    a. Replicate continuously using the specified bandwidth. Specify the bandwidth that you want to use. The default bandwidth is Full.
    b. Replicate during the specified days and times. Then click Edit Schedule to specify which days and time you can replicate and the bandwidth used during those days and time.

    Click Next.

Figure 4-23

Specifying the bandwidth and schedule

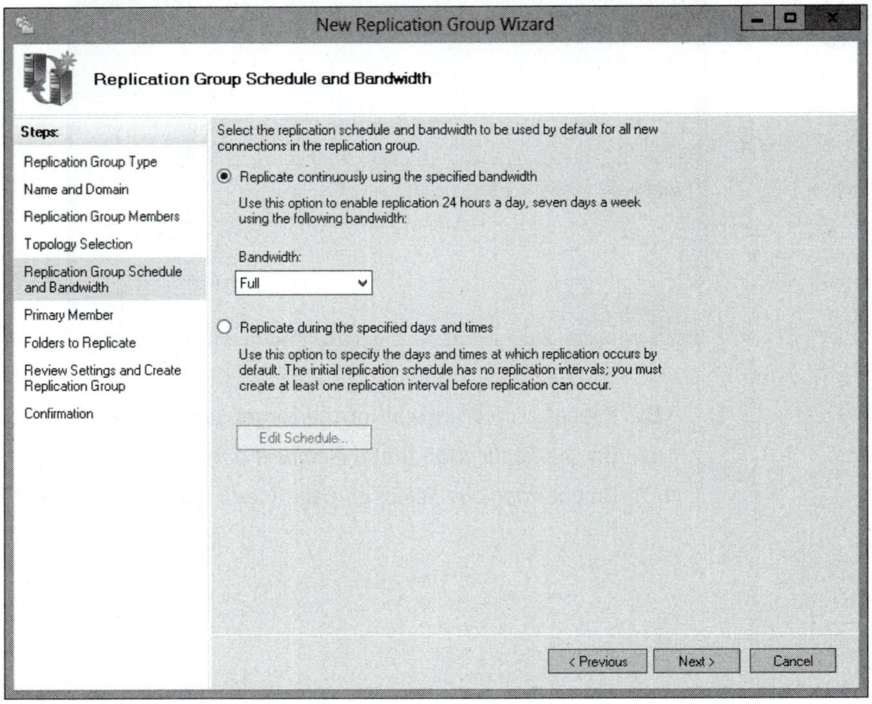

12. On the *Primary Member* page (see Figure 4-24), specify which server acts as the Primary member. Click Next.

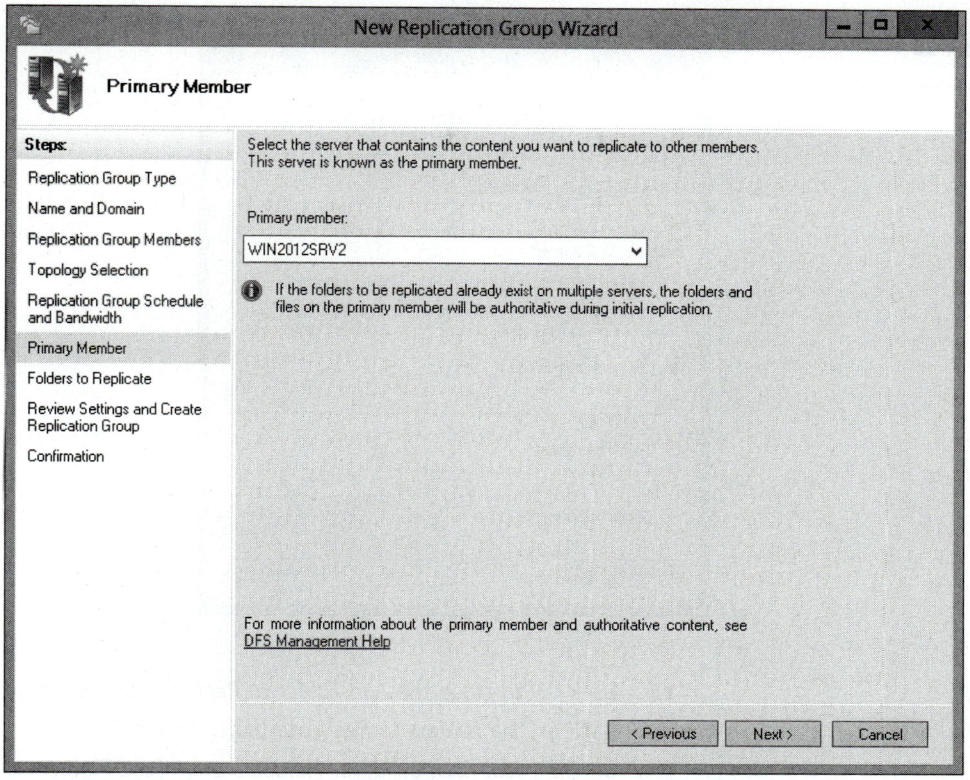

Figure 4-24
Specifying the primary member server

13. On the *Folders to Replicate* page (see Figure 4-25), click Add.

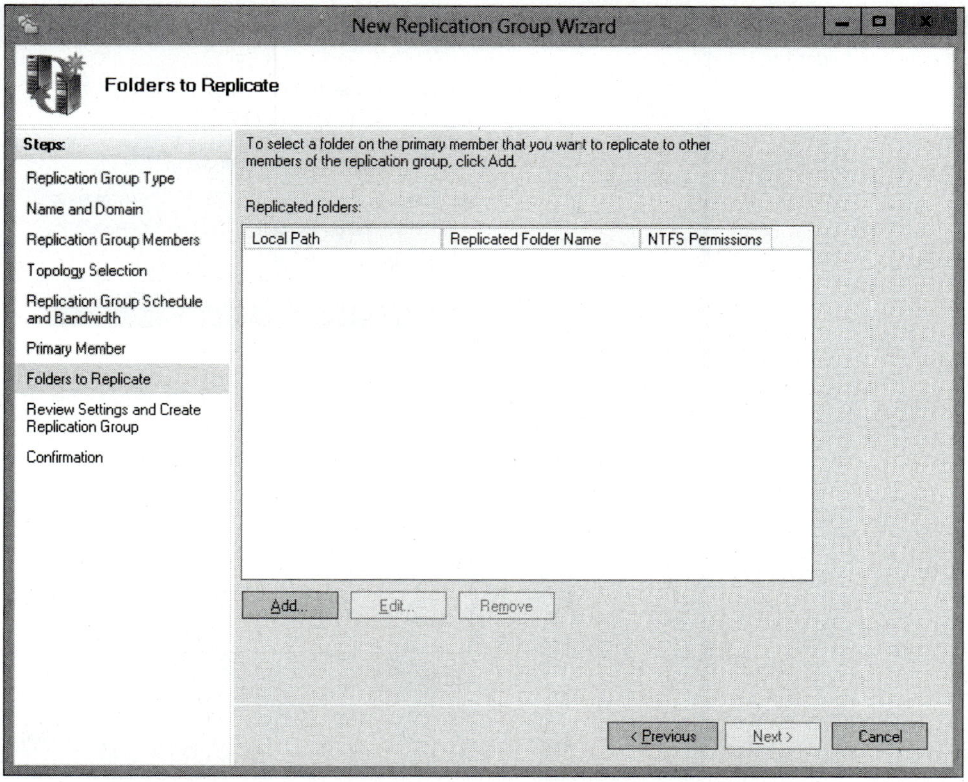

Figure 4-25
Adding folders to replicate

14. When the *Add Folder to Replicate* dialog box opens (see Figure 4-26), specify the local path name of the folder that you want to replicate. Do not type the UNC name.

Figure 4-26

Specifying the local folders to replicate

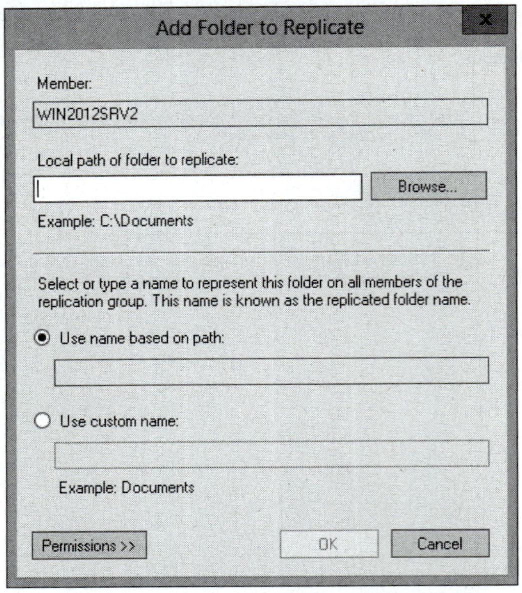

15. Click OK to close the *Add Folder to Replicate* dialog box.
16. Back on the *Folders to Replicate* page, click Next.
17. On the *Local Path on Other Members* page (see Figure 4-27), select each member server listed and click Edit.

Figure 4-27

Adding the remote folder to replicate

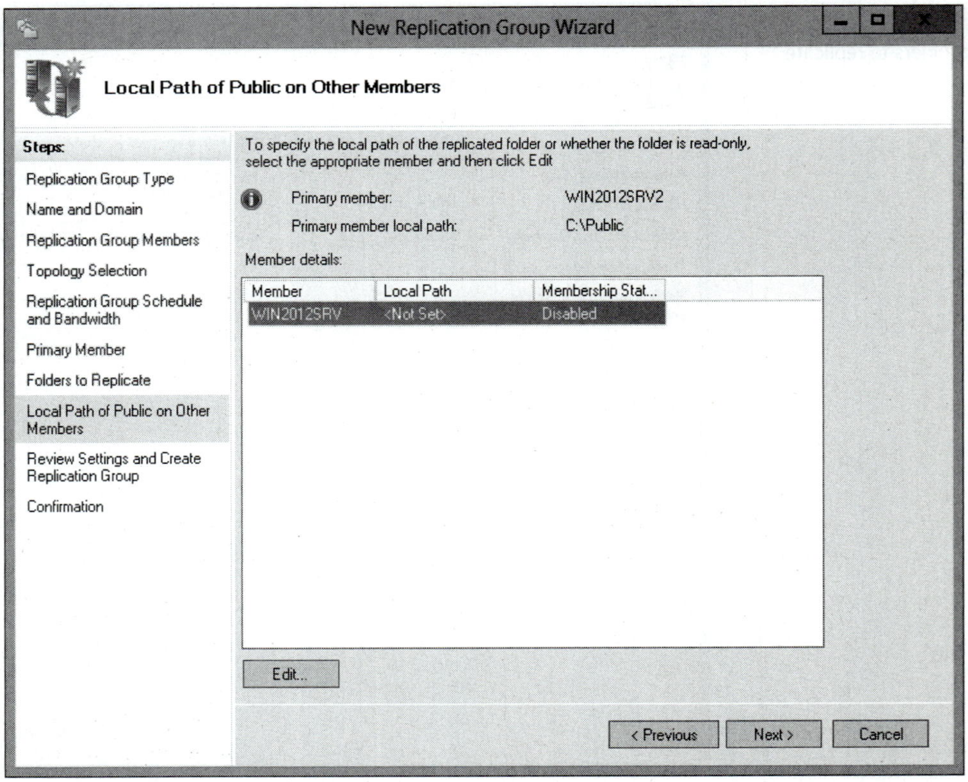

18. When the *Edit* dialog box opens (see Figure 4-28), select Enabled and type the local path on the member server. Click OK to close the *Edit* dialog box.

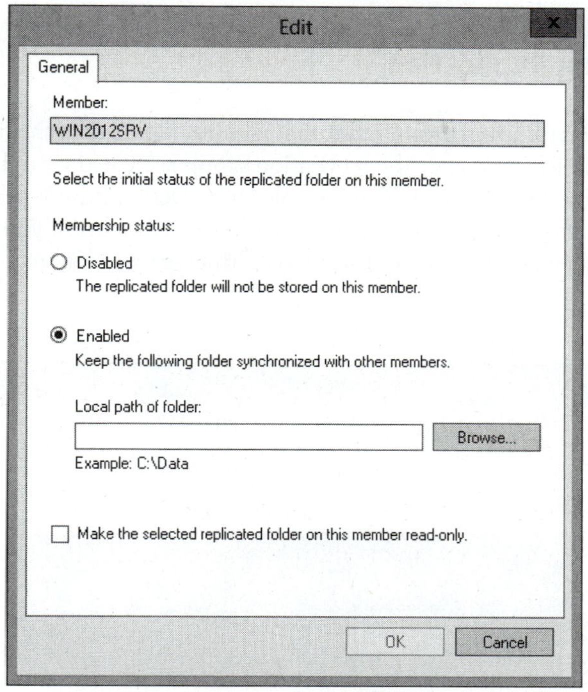

Figure 4-28
Configuring the membership status

19. Back on the *Local Path of Public on Other Members* page, click Next.
20. On the *Review Settings and Create Replication Group* page (see Figure 4-29), click Create.

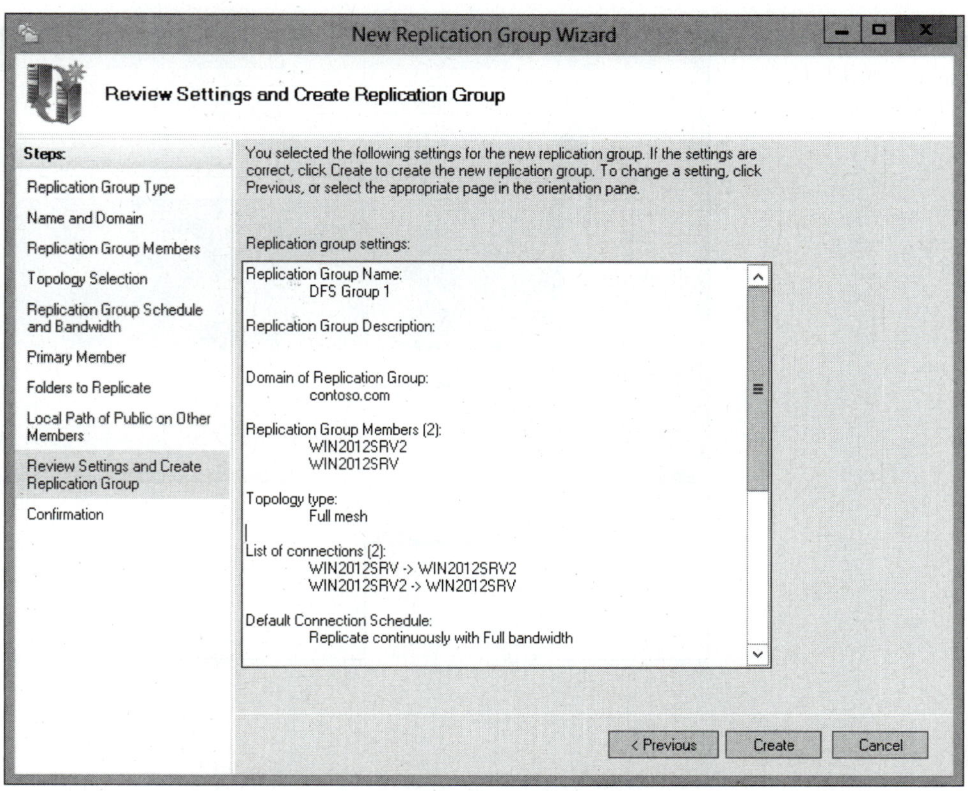

Figure 4-29
Reviewing the selected settings

21. When the replication group has been created, click Close.
22. If you get a Replication Delay message, click OK.

Scheduling Replication

CERTIFICATION READY
Configure replication scheduling.
Objective 2.1

When the replication group is created, you can define the scheduled group. You can also modify the schedule after the replication group is created by right-clicking the replication group in the DFS Management console and selecting Edit Replication Group Schedule. When the *Edit Schedule* dialog box opens (see Figure 4-30), you can select and deselect a range of time and then select the bandwidth usage (see Figure 4-31).

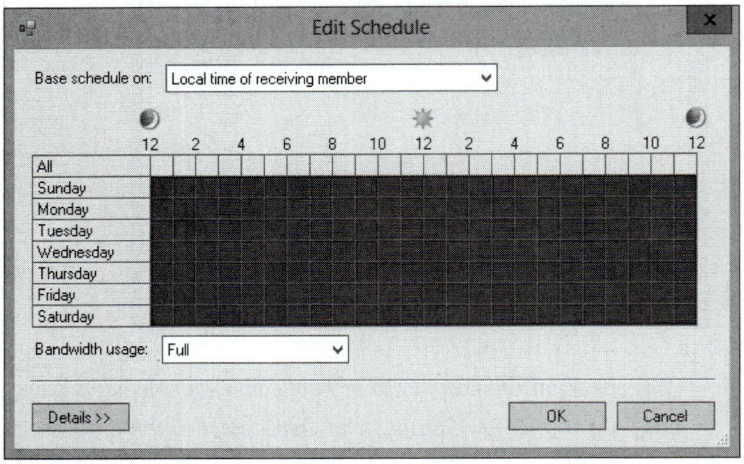

Figure 4-30
Editing a replication schedule

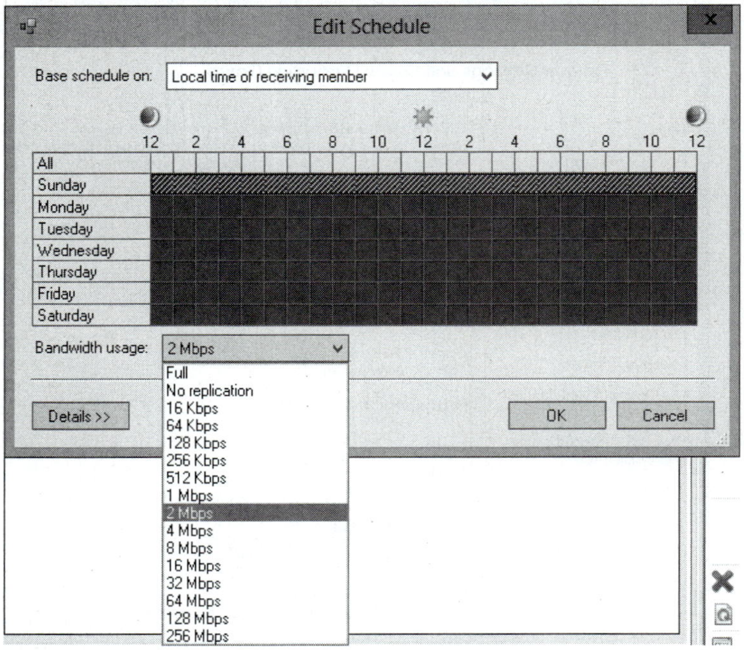

Figure 4-31
Specifying the scheduled bandwidth for replication

Configuring Remote Differential Compression

DFS Replication is an efficient, multiple-master replication engine that synchronizes DFS folders and replicates Active Directory Domain Services (AD DS) SYSVOL folder on domain controllers. It replaced the File Replication Service (FRS), which has been depreciated in Windows Server 2012.

CERTIFICATION READY
Configure remote differential compression settings.
Objective 2.1

DFS Replication uses a compression algorithm known as ***remote differential compression (RDC)***, which detects changes to the data in a file and replicates only those file blocks that changed instead of the entire file. As a result, not as much data needs to be transferred. If you disable RDC, you can conserve processor and disk input/output (I/O). Of course, you will consume much more bandwidth.

DISABLE REMOTE DIFFERENTIAL COMPRESSION

GET READY. By default, RDC is enabled. To disable RDC, perform the following steps:

1. Open Server Manager.
2. Click Tools > DFS Management to open the *DFS Management console*.
3. In the left pane, expand Replication, and select the replication group that you want to modify. Figure 4-32 shows the *DFS Replication* Group tabs.

Figure 4-32

Showing a created DFS Replication Group

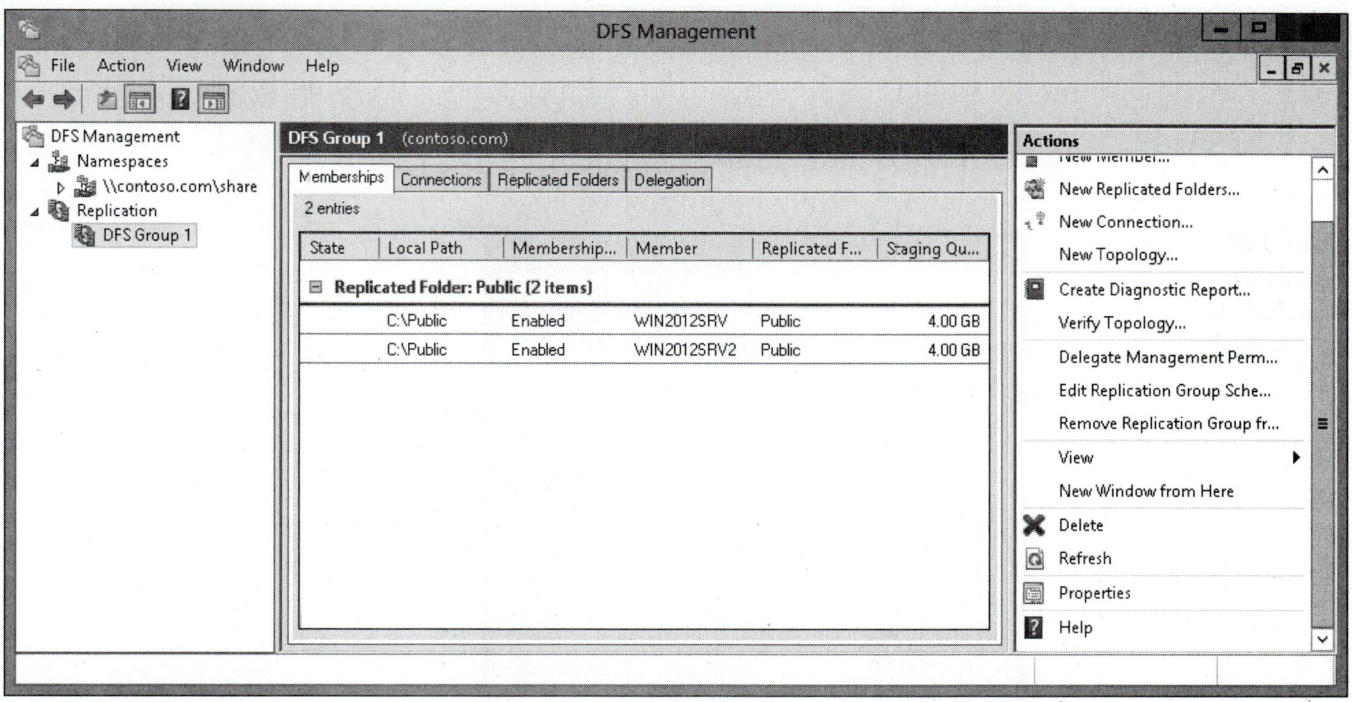

4. Select the Connections tab (see Figure 4-33).

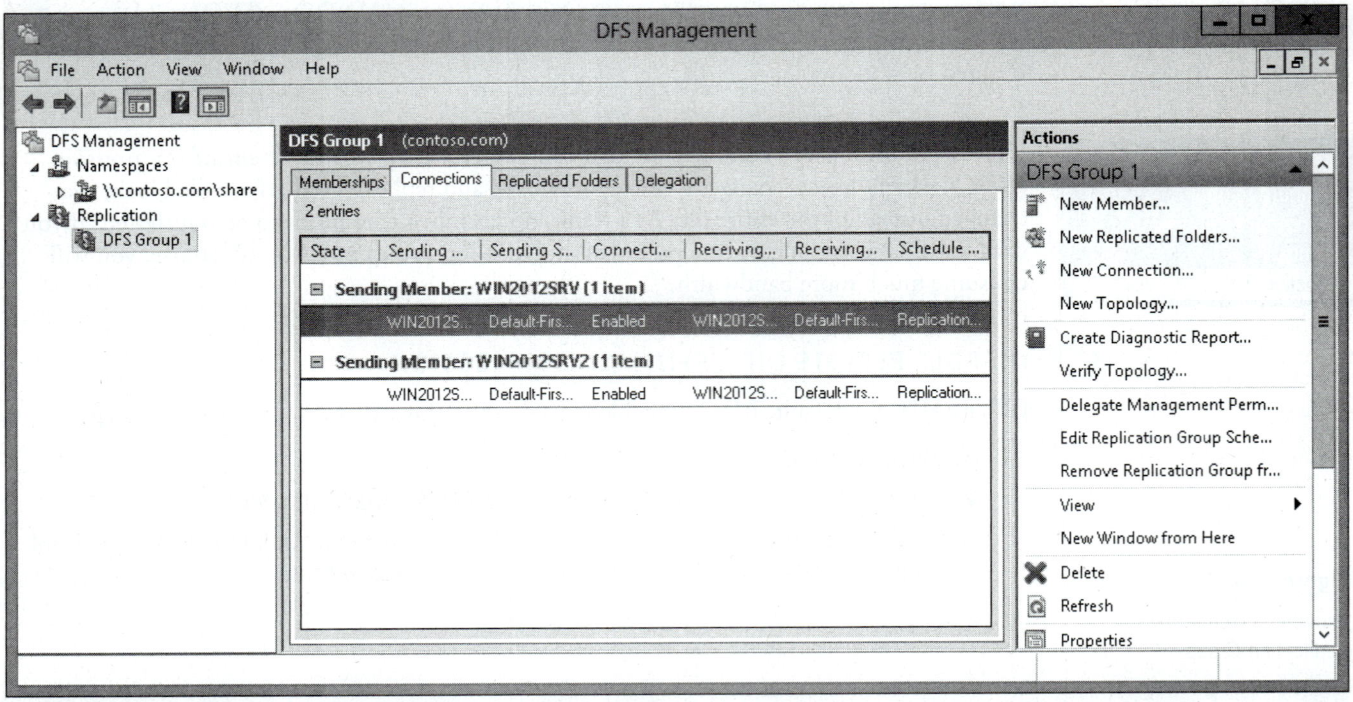

Figure 4-33

Showing the connections used in DFS Replication.

5. Right-click a connection and select Properties to display the *Properties* dialog box (see Figure 4-34).

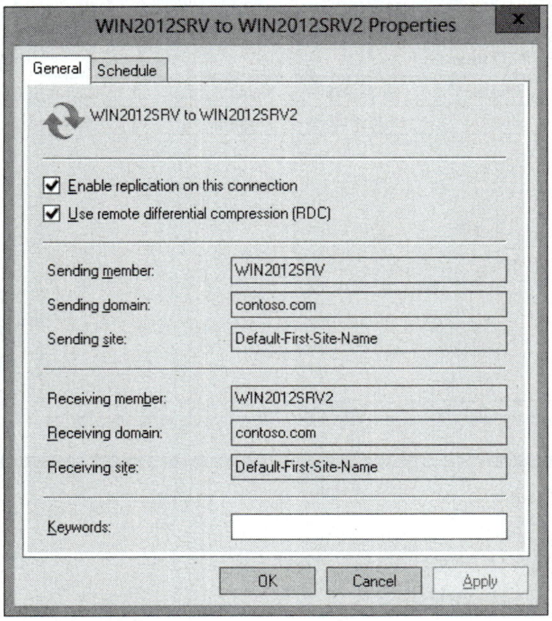

Figure 4-34

Enabling replication and remote differential compression (RDC)

6. Deselect the Use remote differential compression (RDC) option.
7. Click OK to close the *Properties* dialog box.

Configuring Staging

To figure what needs to be replicated, DFS uses staging folders. The ***staging folder*** acts as a cache for new and changed files that need to be replicated. It also is used to compress files that need to be sent. When received on the other end, it is used to decompress the file and install the file into the replicated folder.

CERTIFICATION READY
Configure staging.
Objective 2.1

Each replicated folder has its own staging folder, which, by default, is located under the local path of the replicated folder in the DfsrPrivate\Staging folder. The default size of each staging folder is 4,096 MB, which is determined by a quota. When the staging folder reaches 90%, it purges the oldest staged file until it reaches 60%.

It should also be noted that the staging folder quota does not determine the largest file that can be replicated. If a large file is still in the process of being replicated, any cleaning that occurs is retried later after the file has been replicated. You should increase the quota size only if you have multiple large files that change frequently. To keep processor and disk utilization to a minimum, the quota should be configured to the size of the combined nine largest files in the replicated folder.

On occasion, when the same file gets changed at approximately the same time on two different targets, a conflict occurs. DFS Replication uses a last-writer wins model, which determines which file it should keep and replicate. The losing file is renamed and stored in the Conflict and Deleted folder on the member that resolves the conflict.

Each replicated folder has its own ***Conflict and Deleted folder***, which is located under the local path of the replicated folder in the DfsrPrivate\ConflictandDeleted folder. By default, the quota size of the Conflict and Deleted folder is 660 MB. While the access control lists (ACLs) on the conflicted files are preserved, only members of the local Administrators group can access the files. You can view a log of conflict files and their original file names by viewing the ConflictandDeletedManifest.xml file in the DfsrPrivate folder.

MANAGE THE STAGING FOLDER AND CONFLICT AND DELETED FOLDER

GET READY. To edit the quota size or location of the staging folder and Conflict and Deleted folder, perform the following steps:

1. Open Server Manager.
2. Click Tools > DFS Management. The *DFS Management console* opens.
3. In the left pane, expand Replication.
4. In the left pane, click the replication group that contains the replicated folder with the quotas that you want to edit.
5. On the *Memberships* tab, right-click the replicated folder on the member with the quota that you want to edit, and then click Properties. The *Properties* dialog box opens (see Figure 4-35).

Figure 4-35

Viewing the properties of a DFS replicated folder

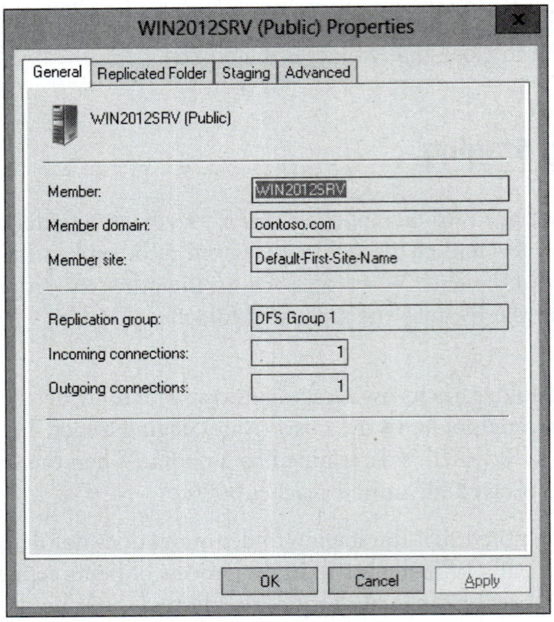

6. Select the Staging tab. Figure 4-36 shows the *Staging* tab.

Figure 4-36

Specifying the staging path and quota

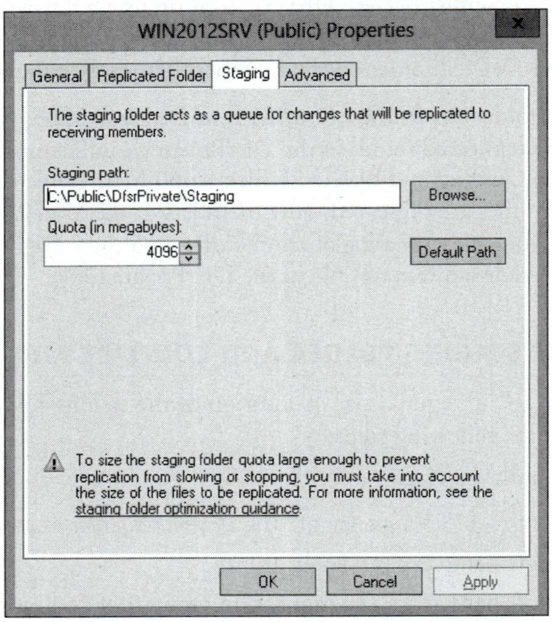

7. Change the Staging path and the quotas as needed and adjust the staging folder quota and path as necessary.
8. Select the Advanced tab. Figure 4-37 shows the *Advanced* tab.

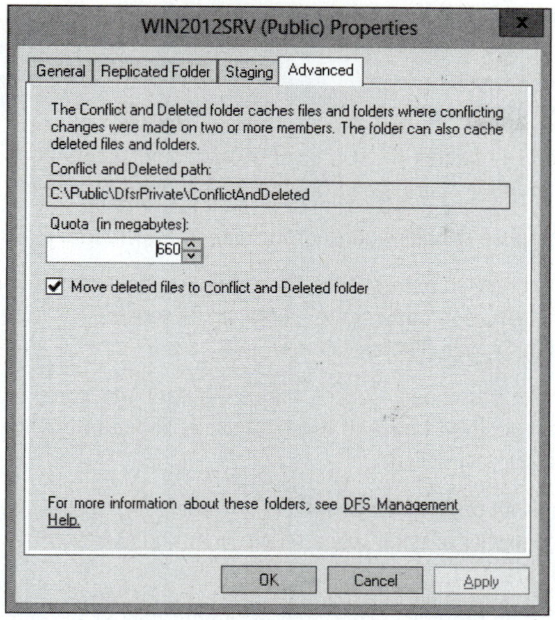

Figure 4-37

Specifying the Conflict and Deleted path and quota

9. Adjust the Conflict and Deleted folder quota as necessary.
10. Click OK to close the *Properties* dialog box.

Windows Server 2012 includes several tools to help monitor and troubleshoot DFS Replication. To generate a diagnostic report, you can right-click a replication group in the DFS Management console and click *Diagnostic Report*. You can also use the DfrsAdmin.exe in a script and schedule the script to run with task scheduler. Finally, you can use DfsrDiag.exe to perform diagnostic tests of DFS Replication.

Configuring Fault Tolerance Using DFS

To make shared files fault tolerant, you need to use both DFS Namespace and DFS Replication.

CERTIFICATION READY
Configure fault tolerance.
Objective 2.1

Each technology used in DFS has some impressive capabilities. DFS Namespace offers ease of use when trying to locate a shared folder and DFS Replication replicates files from one server to another. However, when they are combined, they can offer fault tolerance on the network.

1. Create the same folder on multiple servers. While the folders don't have to have the same name, it makes management easier and cuts down on confusion.
2. Share the folders.
3. Configure DFS Replication between the folders on the various servers.
4. Create a DFS Namespace that includes targets of all target folders for a replication group.

DFS Replication ensures the files are replicated between the servers, providing multiple copies of the files. The DFS namespace makes the access of the replicated folders transparent to the users when accessing the replicated folder. As far as the users are concerned, they access the DFS namespace/shared folder, and then they go to one of the replicated folders. If one of the replicated folders is not available, it is rerouted to another replicated folder.

SKILL SUMMARY

IN THIS LESSON, YOU LEARNED:

- Distributed File System (DFS) is a set of technologies that enable a Windows server to organize multiple distributed SMB file shares into a distributed file system.
- DFS Namespace enables you to group shared folders into a single logical structure.
- With domain-based namespaces, the configuration is stored in Active Directory, which means that you don't have to rely on a single server to provide the namespace information to your clients.
- With domain-based namespaces, the configuration is stored in Active Directory, which means that you don't have to rely on a single server to provide the namespace information to your clients.
- A referral is an ordered list of servers or targets that a client computer receives from a domain controller or namespace server when the user accesses a namespace root or a DFS folder with targets.
- The replication group is a collection of servers, known as servers, each of which holds a target of a DFS folder. You need to have a minimum of two targets to perform DFS Replication.
- By default, replication groups use a full mesh topology, which means that all members replicate to all other members.
- Instead of using a full mesh topology, you can use a hub/spoke topology, where one server is used to replicate to the other members, limiting the replication traffic to specific pairs of members.
- You can schedule DFS Replication to occur only during the night when the WAN links are not used as much or you can specify the bandwidth used by DFS Replication.
- DFS Replication uses a compression algorithm known as remote differential compression (RDC), which detects changes to the data in a file and replicates only those file blocks that changed instead of the entire file.
- The staging folder acts as a cache for new and changed files that need to be replicated. It is also used to compress files that need to be sent, and when received on the other end, it is used to decompress the file and install the file into the replicated folder.
- To make shared files fault-tolerant, you need to use DFS Namespace and DFS Replication.

■ Knowledge Assessment

Multiple Choice

Select the correct answer for each of the following questions.

1. What are the two types of DFS Namespace? (Select two answers.)
   a. Domain-based namespace
   b. Replicated named space
   c. Stand-alone namespace
   d. Server-based namespace

2. How many target folders can you have for each namespace in Windows Server 2008 mode?
   a. 1,000
   b. 5,000
   c. 25,000
   d. 50,000

3. What is an ordered list of servers and targets that a client computer receives from a domain controller or namespace server when a user accesses a namespace root or a DFS folder with targets?
   a. Replication list
   b. Referrals
   c. Target priority list
   d. SID control list

4. What is the default topology used in DFS Replication?
   a. Site-based topology
   b. Namespace topology
   c. Hub/spoke topology
   d. Full mesh topology

5. Which of the following is the compression algorithm used in DFS Replication found with Windows Server 2012?
   a. Remote differential compression
   b. EFS
   c. BitLocker
   d. FRS

6. Which is the default size of a staging folder?
   a. 1 GB
   b. 2 GB
   c. 4 GB
   d. 8 GB

7. Which is the collection of servers that hold targets of a DFS folder?
   a. Replication group
   b. Replication list
   c. Target list
   d. Referral list

8. Which of the following is a shared folder of shared folders? A
   a. DFS Namespace
   b. DFS Linkage
   c. DFS Replication
   d. FRS Replication

9. Which of the following replaced File Replication Services (FRS)?
   a. EFS Replication
   b. Remote differential compression
   c. NTFS Replication
   d. AD Dynamic Replication

10. What is the default quota size of the Conflict and Deleted folder?
    a. 660 MB
    b. 1.2 GB
    c. 2 TB
    d. 4 GB

Best Answer

Choose the letter that corresponds to the best answer. More than one answer choice may achieve the goal. Select the BEST answer.

1. What should you use to create a centralized backup environment of multiple sites?
   a. DFS Namespace
   b. DFS Linkage
   c. DFS Replication
   d. FRS Replication
2. Which of the following is used to prevent oversaturating of a WAN link?
   a. Namespace topology
   b. Referrals
   c. Quotas
   d. Scheduling
3. You find out that two people changed the same file from two different locations that are using DFS replication causing a conflict. What happened to the loosing file?
   a. In the ConflictandDeleted folder
   b. In the Staging folder
   c. In the Recycle Bin
   d. In the C:\Temp folder
4. You have an Active Directory domain named contoso.com. You have two servers, server1 and server2, which are namespace servers for the \\contoso\.com\DFS1 namespace. What should you do to configure the \\contoso.com\DFS1 namespace so that you only connect to Server2 when Server1 is unavailable?
   a. On the \\contoso.com\DFS1 namespace, modify the referrals settings.
   b. On the \\contosol.com\DFS1 namespace, modify the advanced settings.
   c. From the properties of the \\Server1\DFS1 namespace servers entry, modify the advanced settings.
   d. From the properties of the \\Server2\DFS1 namespace servers entry, modify the advanced settings.
5. You have a domain-based namespace called DFS, running Windows Server 2008 Server mode. How do you ensure users can only see files and folders in which the users have permission to access?
   a. Modify the discretionary access control list.
   b. Enable access-based enumeration.
   c. Modify the view permissions.
   d. Disable referrals.

Matching and Identification

1. Match the following terms with the related description or usage.
   _______ a) Domain-based namespace
   _______ b) Full mesh
   _______ c) Windows Server 2008 mode
   _______ d) Windows Server 2000 Server mode
   _______ e) Remote differential compression
   _______ f) Hub/spoke
   _______ g) DFS Replication
   _______ h) Full mesh
   _______ i) Stand-alone DFS
   _______ J) Referral

1. Detects changes to the data in a file and replicate only those changes.
2. Supports up to 5,000 folders.
3. Ordered list of servers or targets that a client computer that a user accesses a namespace root or a DFS folder with targets.
4. A single sever replicates to the other members.
5. Information is stored in Active Directory.
6. Supports up to 256 connections.
7. Supports up to 5,000 folders per namespace.
8. Supports access-based enumeration.
9. All members replicate to all other members.
10. Information stored on a member server.

Build a List

1. Identify the four basic steps in order when using DFS to create a Fault Tolerance shared folder. Not all steps will be used.

_____ Share the folders.
_____ Use robocopy to sync the folders.
_____ Configure DFS Replication between folders on the various servers.
_____ Run the prime utility.
_____ Create the same folder on multiple servers.
_____ Create a DFS namespace that includes targets of all target folder.
_____ Take ownership of all files and folders and reset permissions.

2. Identify the basic steps, in order, for creating a DFS Namespace. Not all steps will be used.

_____ Type the name of the server.
_____ Select stage now.
_____ Specify the location of the shared folder and shared permissions.
_____ Click Create.
_____ Type the name of the namespace.
_____ Select either Windows Server 2000 mode or Windows Server 2008 mode.
_____ Specify either domain-based namespace or stand-alone namespace.
_____ Start the New Namespace wizard.

3. Identify the basics steps for creating a DFS replication group. Not all steps will be used.

_____ Select the type of replication group.
_____ Configure the schedule and bandwidth used.
_____ Configure the mode.
_____ Select New Replication Group.
_____ Specify the folders to replicate.
_____ Type a descriptive name.
_____ Add the server.
_____ Configure the permissions.

Choose an Option

1. Identify the option that allows a user only to see a files that he or she has access to.

Figure 4-38

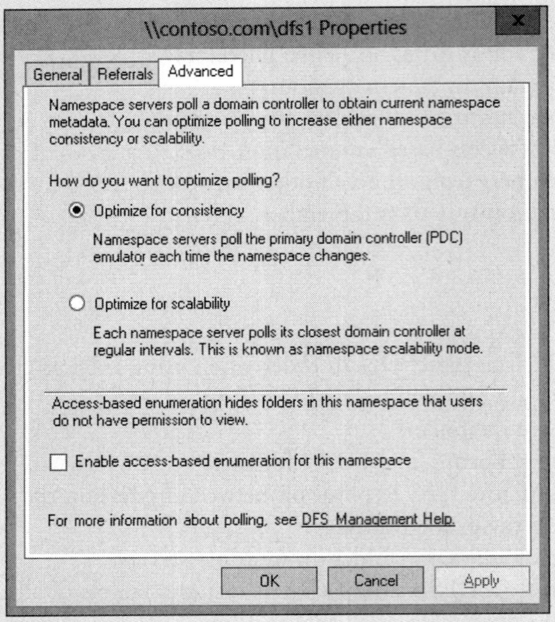

■ Business Case Scenarios

Scenario 4-1: Backing up Remote File Servers

You have 10 file site servers located with 2048 Mb/s WAN links. You tried to run backups over the WAN links and the backups took too long to execute. What can you do to alleviate this problem?

Scenario 4-2: Protecting Essential File Servers

You have a Project server that has key files that must be accessed from people in multiple sites throughout the country. These files must be accessible 24/7 while keeping performance as high as possible. What solution would you provide?

Configuring File Server Resource Manager (FSRM)

LESSON 5

70-411 EXAM OBJECTIVE

Objective 2.2 – Configure File Server Resource Manager (FSRM). This objective may include but is not limited to: install the FSRM role; configure quotas; configure file screens; configure reports.

LESSON HEADING	EXAM OBJECTIVE
Using File Server Resource Manager	Configure File Server Resource Manager (FSRM)
Installing File Server Resource Manager	Install the FRSRM role
Using Quotas	Configure quotas
Managing Files with File Screening	Configure file screens
Using Storage Reports	Configure reports
Enabling SMTP	

KEY TERMS

active screening
file group
file screen exception
file screen template
file screening
File Server Resource Manager (FSRM)
hard quota
passive screening
quota template
quotas
soft quota
storage reports

■ Using File Server Resource Manager

THE BOTTOM LINE

File Server Resource Manager (FSRM) is a suite of tools that enables you to control and manage the quantity and type of data stored on a file server. It enables you to define how much data a person can store, define what type of files that a user can store on a file server, and generate reports about the file server being used.

CERTIFICATION READY
Configure File Server Resource Manager (FSRM).
Objective 2.2

Using File Server Resource Manager enables you to perform the following tasks:

- Create quotas for a volume or folder tree, including generating e-mails when the quota limits are approached or exceeded.
- Create file screens to control the type of files that users can save.
- Send notifications when users try to save a blocked file.

- Schedule periodic storage reports or manually generate a storage report that helps you to identify trends in disk usage.
- Classify files based on defined properties and apply policies based on the classification. You can restrict access to files, encrypt files, and have files expire. File classification is discussed in more detail in the 70-412 course.

Installing File Server Resource Manager

Installing FSRM is a simple process because it is a Windows server role.

CERTIFICATION READY
Install the FRSRM role.
Objective 2.2

Similar to the previous Windows server roles, the FSRM is installed with Server Manager as a server role.

INSTALL FILE SERVER RESOURCE MANAGER

GET READY. To install FSRM, perform the following steps:

1. Open Server Manager.
2. At the top of *Server Manager*, select Manage and click Add Roles and Features to open the *Add Roles and Feature Wizard*.
3. On the *Before you begin* page, click Next.
4. Select Role-based or feature-based installation and then click Next.
5. Click Select a server from the server pool, click the name of the server to install FSRM to, and then click Next.
6. Scroll down and expand File and Storage Services and expand file and iSCSI Services. Select File Server Resource Manager (see Figure 5-1).

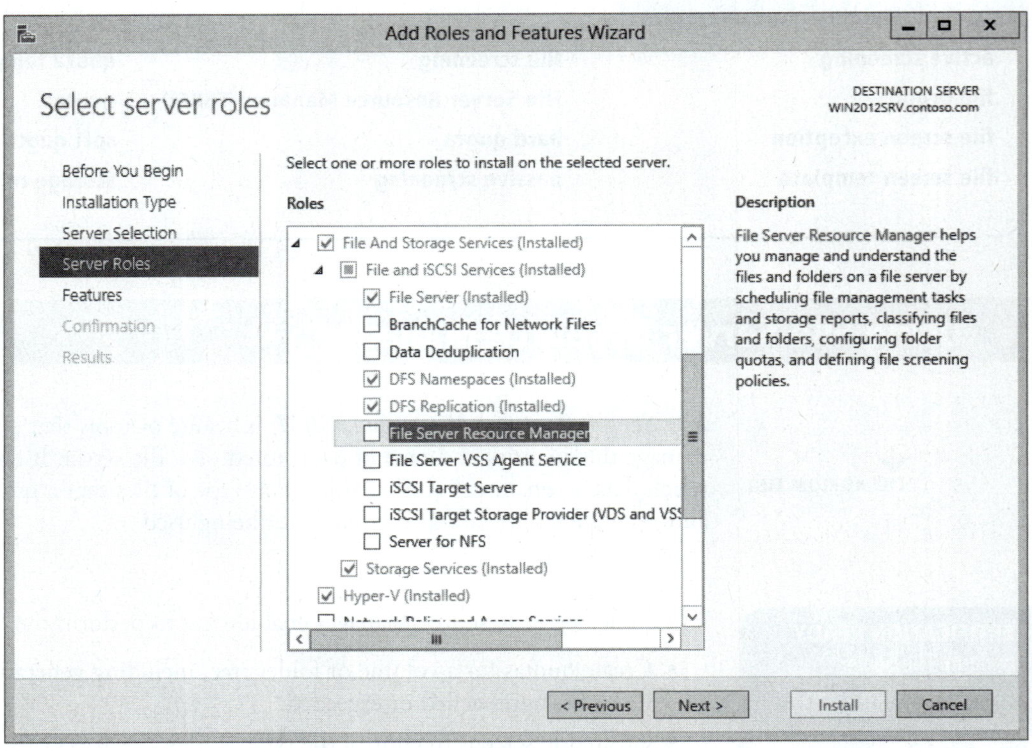

Figure 5-1
Selecting File Server Resource Manager

7. When you are asked to add additional features, click Add Features (see Figure 5-2).

Figure 5-2

Adding the FSRM tools

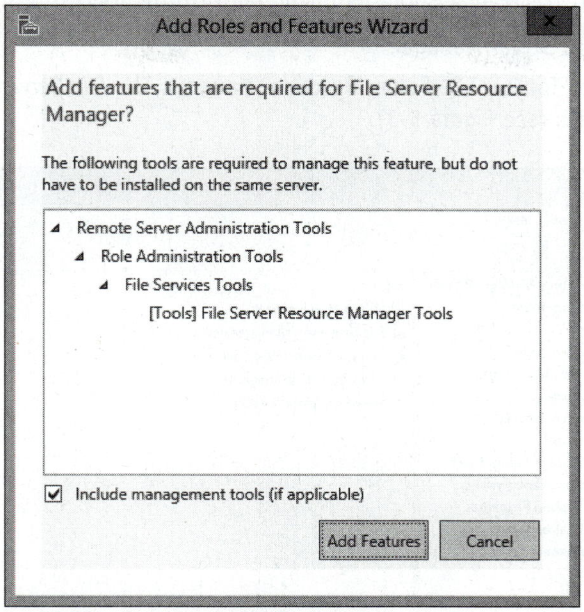

8. On the *Select server roles* page, click Next.
9. On the *Select features* page, click Next.
10. On the *Confirm installation selections*, click Install.
11. When the installation is complete, click the Close button.

Using Quotas

In the 70-410 course, you studied NTFS file quotas that defined how much data a user can store on a volume. ***Quotas*** defined with FSRM limit how much space a folder or volume can use.

CERTIFICATION READY
Configure quotas.
Objective 2.2

By using FSRM to create a quota, you limit the amount of disk space allocated to a volume or folder. The quota limit applies to the entire folder's subtree.

When you define the quotas, you can define either a hard quota or a soft quota:

- A ***hard quota*** prevents users from saving files after the space limit is reached and generates notifications when the volume of data reaches the configured threshold.
- A ***soft quota*** does not enforce the quota limit but generates a notification when the configured threshold is met.

NTFS quotas can create FSRM, can use e-mail, log an event, run a command or script, or generate a storage report for notification.

CREATING QUOTAS

You can create a quota on a volume or a folder using a ***quota template*** or by using custom properties. It is recommended that you use quota templates because quota templates can be applied to other volumes and folders in the future. In addition, if you modify the template, you have the option to change any quotas that used the quota template in the past.

CREATE A QUOTA TEMPLATE

GET READY. To create a quota template, perform the following steps:

1. Open Server Manager.
2. Click Tools > File Server Resource Manager. The *File Server Resource Manager console* opens (see Figure 5-3).

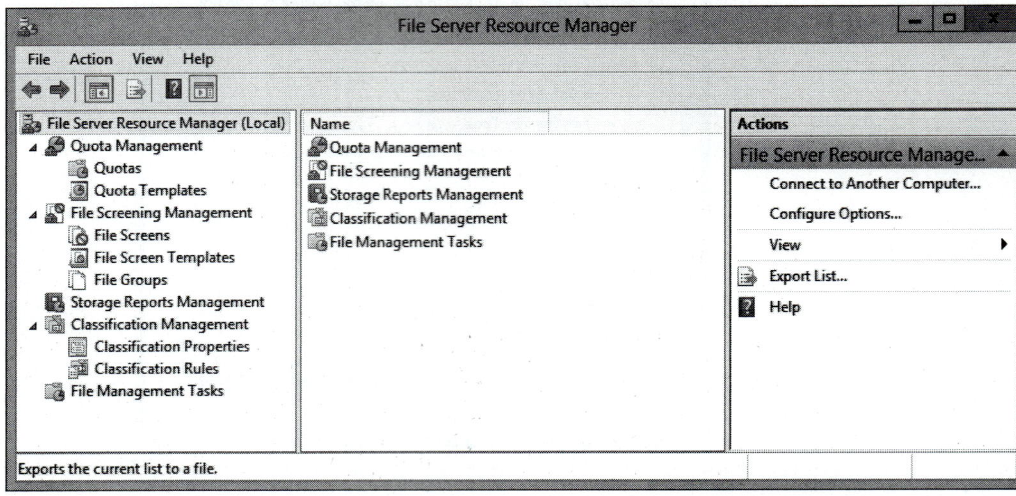

Figure 5-3

Viewing the File Server Resource Manager console

3. Under *Quota Management*, right-click Quota Templates and select Create Quota Template. The *Create Quota Template* dialog box opens (see Figure 5-4).

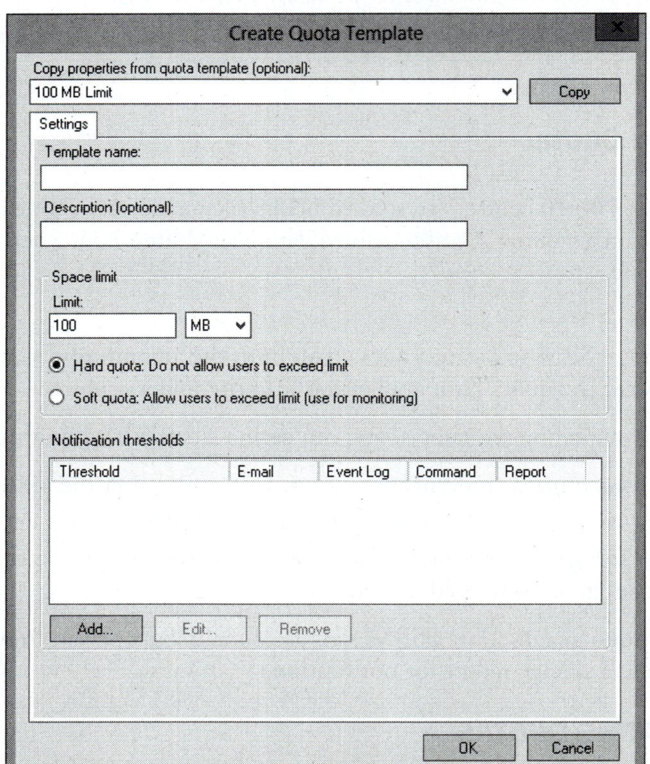

Figure 5-4

Opening the Create Quota Template dialog box

4. If you want to copy the properties of an existing template, you can select a template from the Copy properties from quota template drop-down list. Then click Copy.
5. In the *Template name* text box, type a name.

6. In the *Description (optional)* text box, type a description of the quota.
7. In the *Space limit* section, in the *Limit* text box, type a number and specify the unit (KB, MB, GB, or TB).
8. Select Hard quota or Soft quota.
9. To add a notification, click the Add button. The *Add Threshold* dialog box opens (see Figure 5-5).

Figure 5-5

Displaying the Add Threshold dialog box

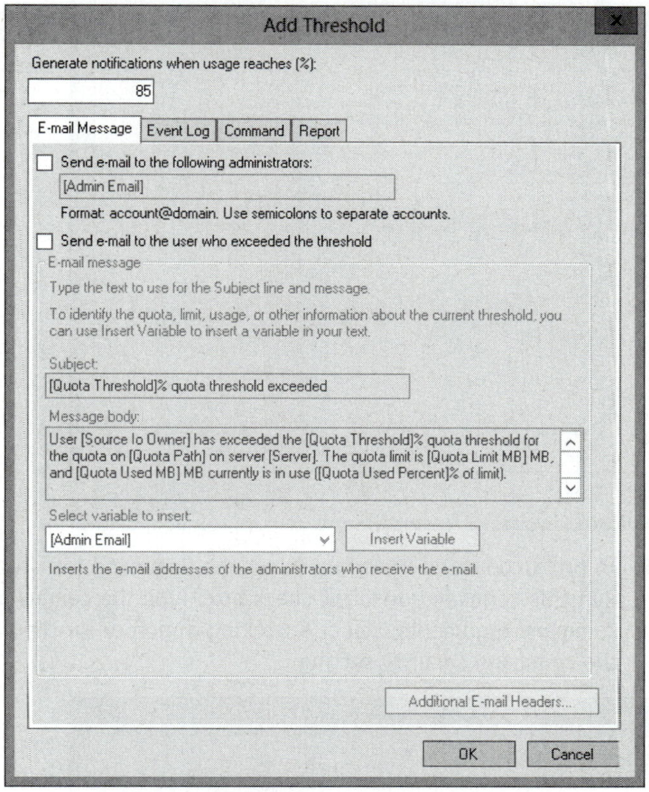

10. To set a quota limit percentage that generates a notification, type a number in the *Generate notifications when usage reaches (%)* text box. The default is 85%.
11. To configure e-mail notifications, on the *E-mail Message* tab, set the following options:
    - Select the Send e-mail to the following administrators check box, and then enter the names of the administrative accounts that receive the notifications using the account@domain format. Use semicolons to separate multiple accounts.
    - To send e-mail to the person who saved the file that reached the quota threshold, select the Send e-mail to the user who exceeded the threshold check box.
    - To configure the message, edit the default subject line and message body that are provided. Brackets indicate variable information. For example, [Source Io Owner] variable inserts the name of the user who saved the file that reached the quota threshold.
    - To configure additional headers (including From, Cc, Bcc, and Reply-to), click Additional E-mail Headers.
12. To log an event, select the Event Log tab (see Figure 5-6). Then select the Send warning to event log check box and edit the default log entry.

Figure 5-6

Logging an event on the Event Log tab

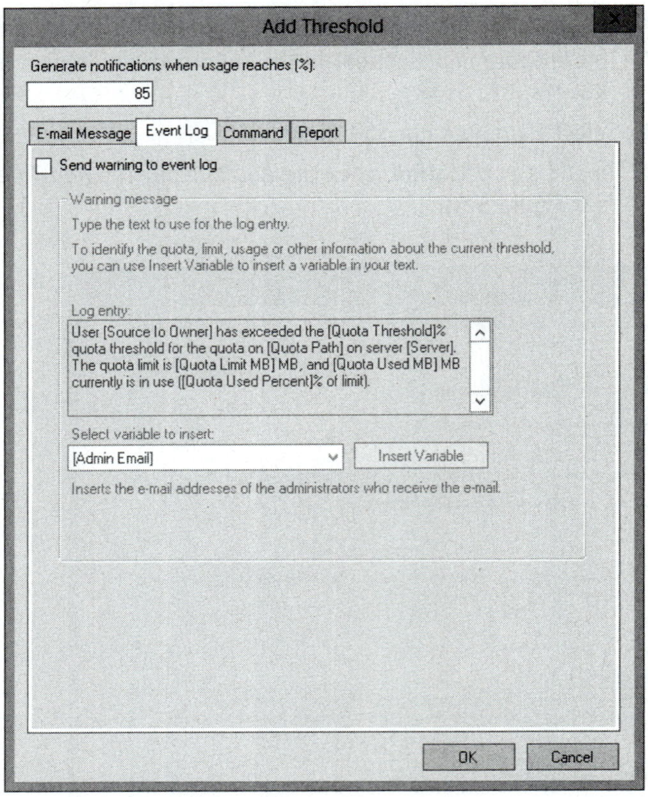

13. To run a command or script, select the Command tab (see Figure 5-7). Then select the Run this command or script check box. Type the command. You can also enter command arguments, select a working directory for the command or script, or modify the command security setting.

Figure 5-7

Running a command or script on the Command tab

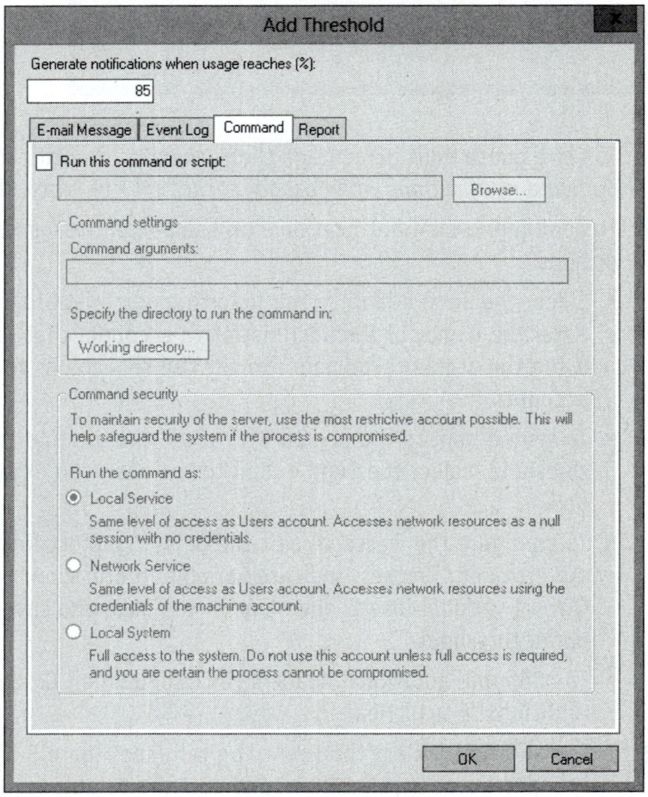

14. To generate one or more storage reports, select the Report tab (see Figure 5-8). Select the Generate reports check box, and then select which reports to generate. Optionally, you can enter one or more administrative e-mail recipients for the report or e-mail the report to the user who reached the threshold.

Figure 5-8

Generating storage reports on the Report tab

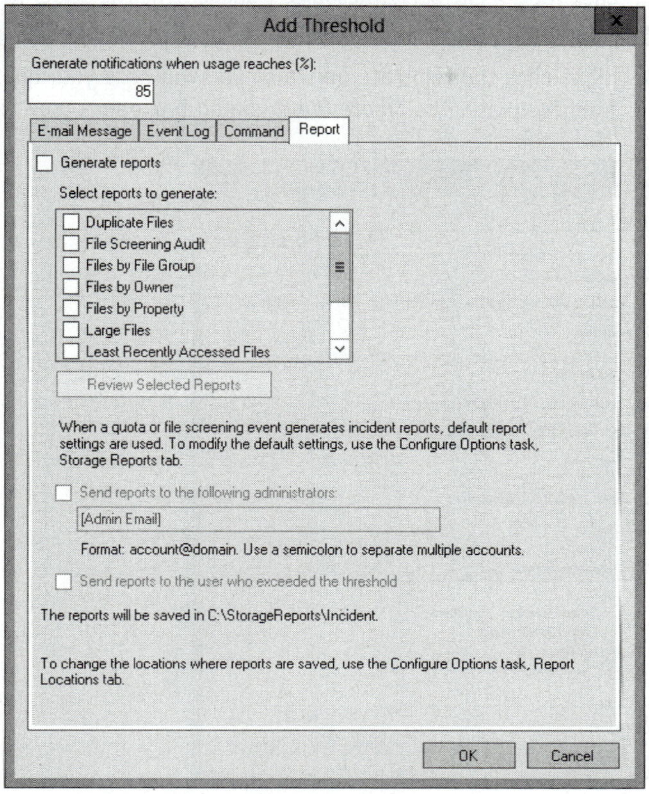

15. Click OK to save your notification threshold and close the *Add Threshold* dialog box.

16. Click OK to close the *Create Quota Template* dialog box. The quota template will be listed as shown in Figure 5-9.

Figure 5-9

Viewing the quota template

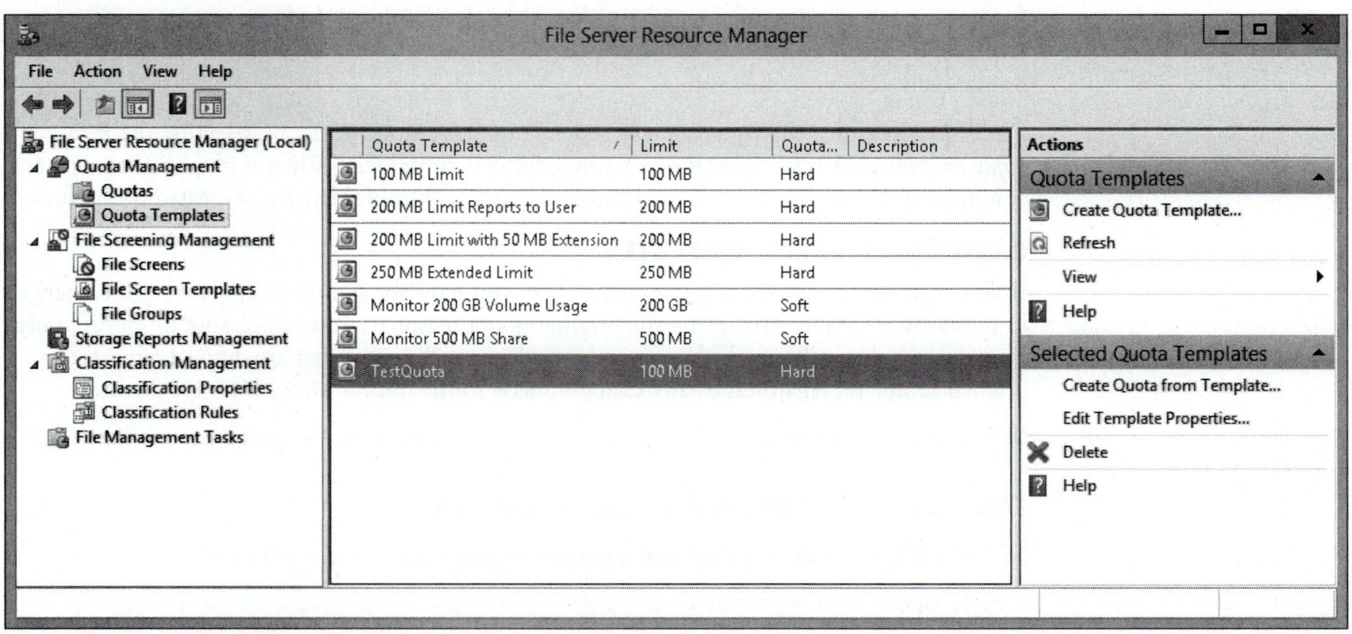

CREATE A QUOTA FROM A QUOTA TEMPLATE

GET READY. To create a quota from a Quota template, perform the following steps:

1. Open Server Manager.
2. Click Tools > File Server Resource Manager. The *File Server Resource Manager console* opens.
3. Under the *Quota Management* node, click the Quota Templates node.
4. Right-click the template on which you will base your quota and click Create Quota from Template. The *Create Quota* dialog box opens (see Figure 5-10).

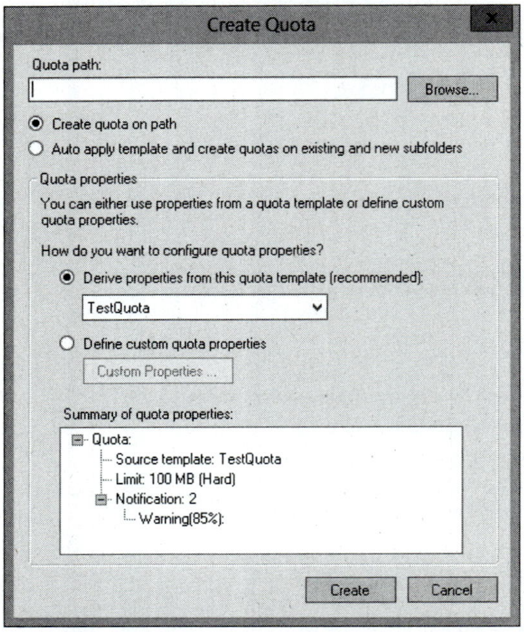

Figure 5-10

Creating a quota using a template

5. Type the volume or folder that the quota applies to in the *Quota path* text box.
6. Select the Create quota on path option.
7. Click Create.

If you want to create a quota without using a template, right-click *Quotas* and select *Create Quota* to open the *Create Quota* dialog box. You can then pull values from a quota template or manually configure the settings.

File Server Resource Manager can also generate quotas automatically by selecting the *Auto apply template* and create quotas on existing and new subfolders. When it is applied to a parent volume or folder, it is applied to each subfolder and each subfolder that is created in the future.

CHANGING QUOTAS TEMPLATES

If you need make changes to a quota template, you have the option of applying those changes to quotas that were created using the original quota template. You can choose to modify only those quotas that still match the original template or all quotas that are derived from the original template, regardless of any changes made to the quotas since they were created.

When you reapply the template, the properties of the quotas are overwritten.

CREATE A QUOTA FROM A QUOTA TEMPLATE

GET READY. To create a quota from a quota template, perform the following steps:

1. Open Server Manager.
2. Click Tools > File Server Resource Manager. The *File Server Resource Manager console* opens.

3. Click Quota Templates and select the quota template that you want to modify.
4. Right-click the quota template, and select Edit Template Properties. The *Quota Template Properties* dialog box opens.
5. Modify the quota template properties as needed.
6. Click OK. The *Update Quotas Derived from Template* dialog box opens (see Figure 5-11).

Figure 5-11

Updating quotas in the *Update Quotas Derived from Template* dialog box

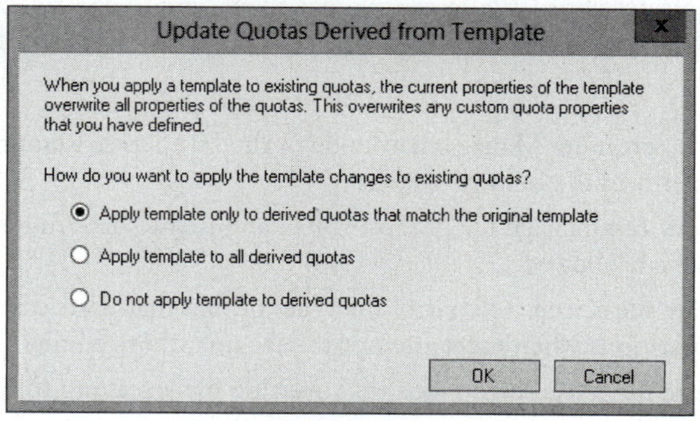

7. Select one of the following options:

   Apply template only to derived quotas that match the original template

   Apply template to all derived quotas

   Do not apply template to derived quotas
8. Click OK to close the *Update Quotas Derived from Template* dialog box.

MONITORING QUOTA USE

In addition to notifications that you set up, you can also view quota usage using one of the following methods with FSRM.

- To view the quota information, click *Quota Management*, and then click *Quotas*. In the Results pane, you can view the quota limit, the percentage of the limit that is used, the type of quota, and the source template. Figure 5-12 shows the quota usage.
- Running a Quota Usage report is discussed later in this lesson when Storage reports are discussed.

Figure 5-12

Using FSRM to show quota usage

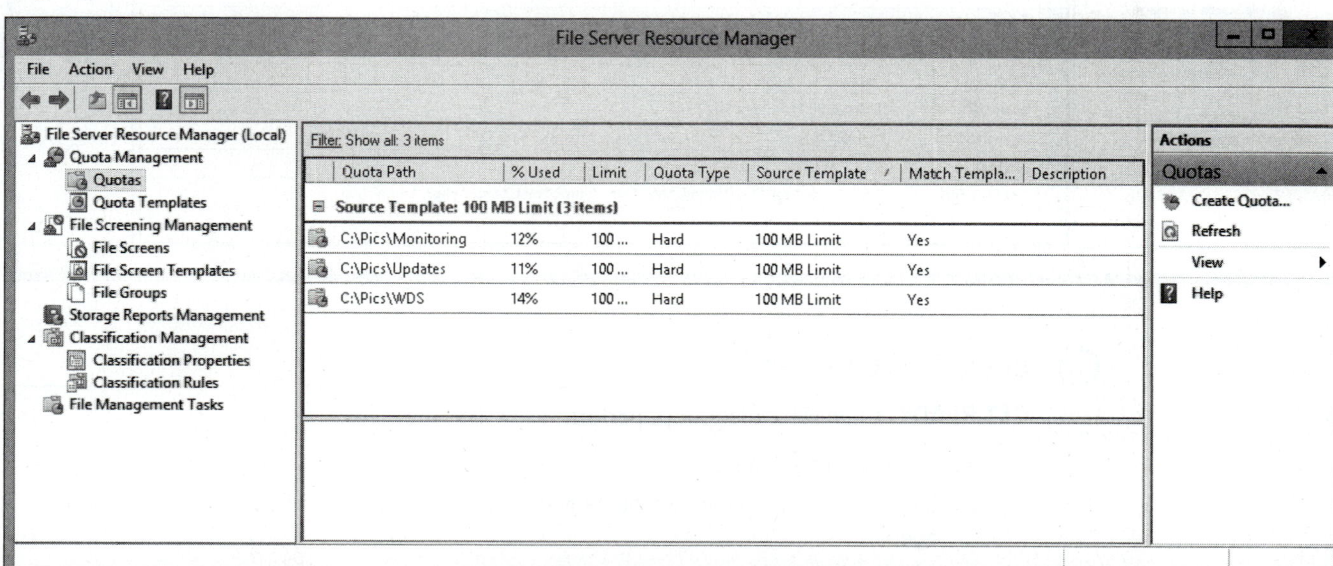

Managing Files with File Screening

Often on a corporate network, users try to save files such as movies, music, and games on the corporate server. Unfortunately, although much of this can cause legal problems associated with copyright, it also takes up disk space that can be used for something else, it costs money to provide the storage space, and it makes the backup sets larger. Therefore, Microsoft developed ***file screening*** that allows you to control the type of files that users can save and send notifications when users try to save a blocked file.

CERTIFICATION READY
Configure file screens.
Objective 2.2

In the File Screening Management node of the File Server Resource Manager MMC snap-in, you can perform the following tasks:

- Create and manage file groups, which are used to determine which files are blocked and which are allowed.
- Create file screens to control the types of files that users can save and generate notifications when users attempt to save unauthorized files.
- Create file screen exceptions that override file-screening rules.
- Define file-screening templates to simplify file-screening management.

CREATING FILE GROUPS

A ***file group*** is used to define a namespace for a file screen, file screen exception, or Files by File Group storage report. It consists of a set of file name patterns, which are grouped by the following:

- Files to include
- Files to exclude

FSRM already includes pre-built file groups (see Figure 5-13).

Figure 5-13
Displaying file groups

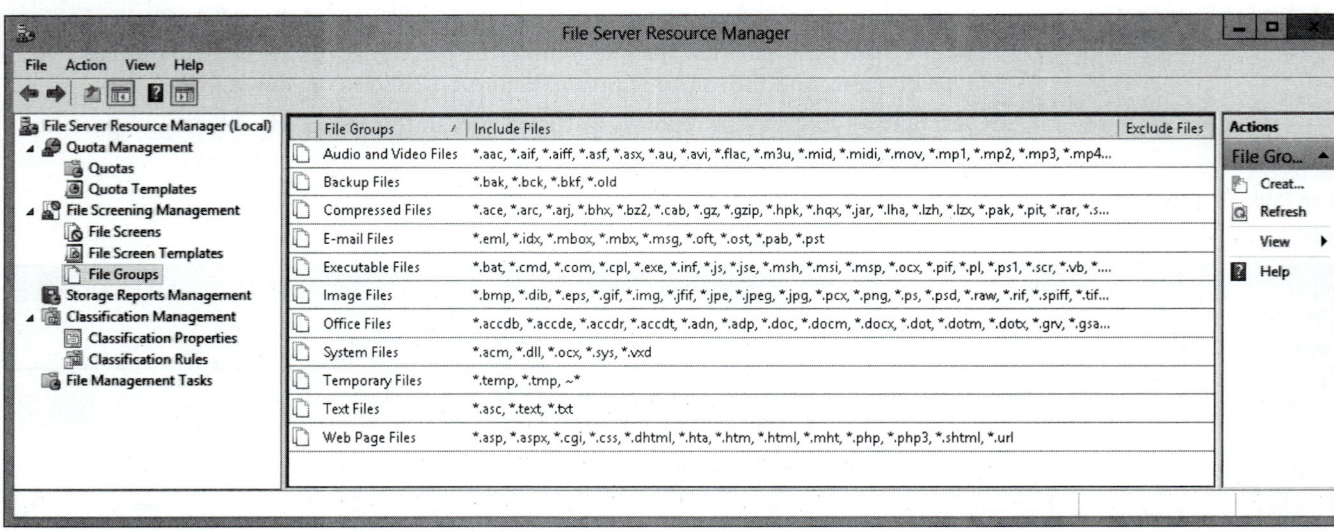

CREATE FILE GROUPS

GET READY. To create a file group, perform the following steps:

1. Open Server Manager.
2. Click Tools > File Server Resource Manager. The *File Server Resource Manager console* opens.

3. In *File Screening Management*, click the File Groups node.
4. Right-click File Groups and select Create File Group. The *Create File Group Properties* dialog box opens (see Figure 5-14).

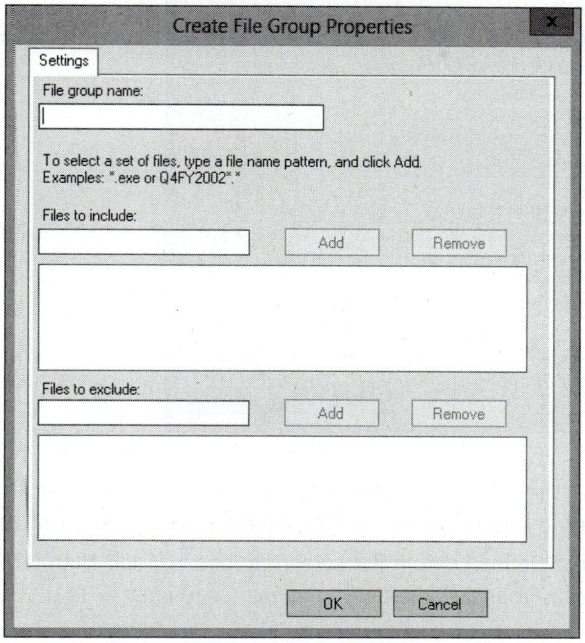

Figure 5-14

Creating a file group with the Create File Group Properties dialog box

5. In the *File group name* text box, type a name of the file group.
6. To add files to include, type a filename or filename pattern using the * wildcard character in the *Files to include* text box, and then click Add.
7. To add files to exclude, type a filename or filename pattern using the * wildcard character in the Files to exclude text box and click Add.
8. Click OK to close the *Create File Group Properties* dialog box.

CREATING A FILE SCREEN

When you create a file screen, there are two screening types:

- ***Active screening***: Prevents users from saving the defined unauthorized files.
- ***Passive screening***: Allows users to save a file, but allows the monitoring and notification when a user saves an unauthorized file.

CREATE A FILE SCREEN

GET READY. To create a file screen, perform the following steps:

1. Open Server Manager.
2. Click Tools > File Server Resource Manager. The *File Server Resource Manager console* opens.
3. Under *File Screening Management*, click the File Screens node.
4. Right-click File Screens, and then click Create File Screen. The *Create File Screen* dialog box opens (see Figure 5-15).

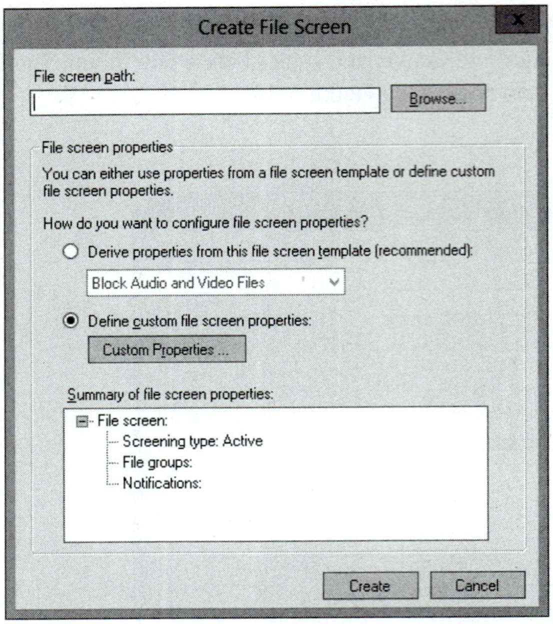

Figure 5-15

Creating a file screen with the Create File Screen dialog box

5. Type the path to a folder to be used by the file screen in the *File screen path* text box. The file screen applies to the selected folder and all of its subfolders.
6. Select Define custom file screen properties, and then click Custom Properties. The *File Screen Properties* dialog box opens (see Figure 5-16).

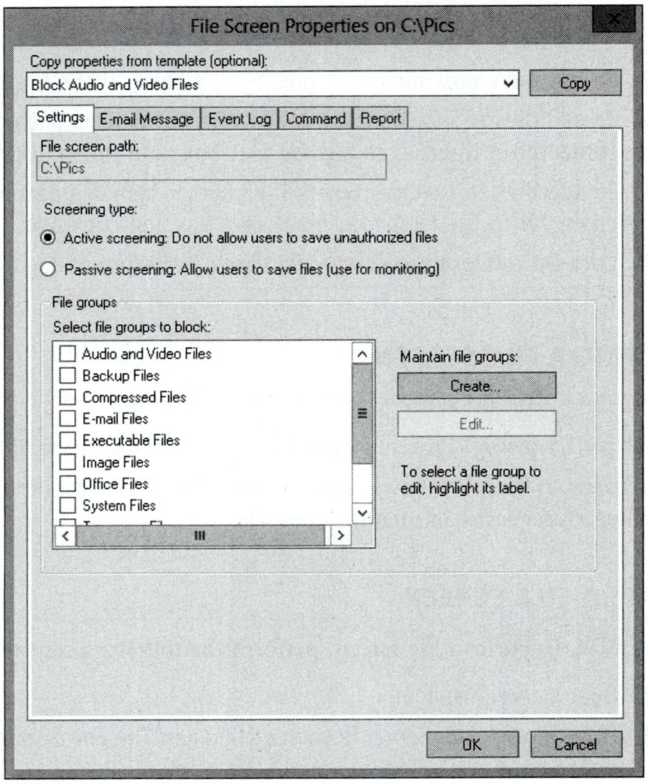

Figure 5-16

Opening the File Screen Properties dialog box

7. If you want to copy the properties of an existing template to use as a base for your file screen, select a template from the *Copy properties from template* drop-down list. Then click Copy.

8. Under *Screening* type, click the Active screening or Passive screening option.
9. Under *File groups*, select each file group that you want to include in your file screen.
10. To configure e-mail notifications, click the E-mail Message tab, and then set the following options:
    - Select the Send e-mail to the following administrators check box, and then enter the names of the administrative accounts that will receive the notifications using the account@domain format. Use semicolons to separate multiple accounts.
    - To send e-mail to the person who saved the file that reached the quota threshold, select the Send e-mail to the user who exceeded the threshold check box.
    - To configure the message, edit the default subject line and message body that are provided. Brackets indicate variable information. For example, the [Source Io Owner] variable inserts the name of the user who saved the file that reached the quota threshold.
    - To configure additional headers (including From, Cc, Bcc, and Reply-to), click Additional E-mail Headers.
11. To log an event, select the Event Log tab. Then select the Send warning to event log check box, and edit the default log entry.
12. To run a command or script, select the Command tab. Then select the Run this command or script check box. Type the command. You can also enter command arguments, select a working directory for the command or script, or modify the command security setting.
13. To generate one or more storage reports, select the Reports tab. Then select the Generate reports check box, and then select which reports to generate. Optionally, you can enter one or more administrative e-mail recipients for the report or e-mail the report to the user who reached the threshold.
14. Click OK to close the *File Screen Properties* dialog box.
15. In the *Create File Screen* dialog box, click Create to save the file screen. The *Save Custom Properties as a Template* dialog box opens (see Figure 5-17).

Figure 5-17

Saving the file screen settings as a template

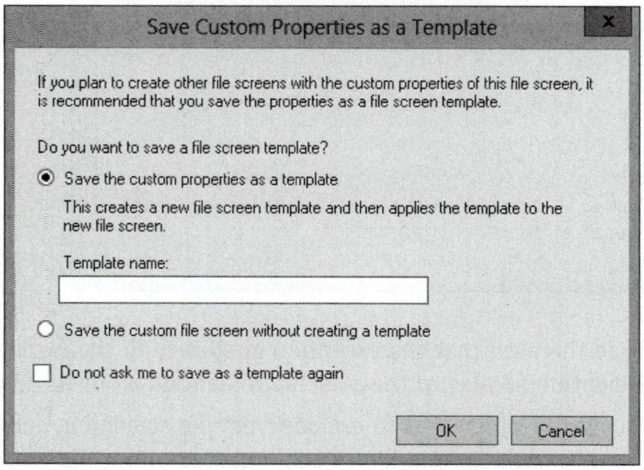

16. To save a template that is based on these customized properties (recommended) and apply the settings, select Save the custom properties as a template and enter a name for the template.
17. If you do not want to save a template when you save the file screen, select Save the custom file screen without creating a template.
18. Click OK to close the *Save Custom Properties as a Template* dialog box. The new file screen appears under *File Screens*.

CREATING A FILE SCREEN EXCEPTION

Sometimes, after you have made a file screening, you need to allow exceptions. For example, you might create a file screen that prevents users from saving videos. But now the marketing office needs to save a video of its latest commercial. To allow files that other file screens are blocking, create a ***file screen exception***, which is a special type of file screen that overrides any file screening that would otherwise apply to a folder and all its subfolders in a designated exception path.

CREATE A FILE SCREEN EXCEPTION

GET READY. To create a file screen exception, perform the following steps:

1. Open Server Manager.
2. Click Tools > File Server Resource Manager. The *File Server Resource Manager console* opens.
3. Under *File Screening Management*, click the File Screens node.
4. Right-click File Screens, and click Create File Screen Exception. The *Create File Screen Exception* dialog box opens (see Figure 5-18).

Figure 5-18

Creating a file screen exception

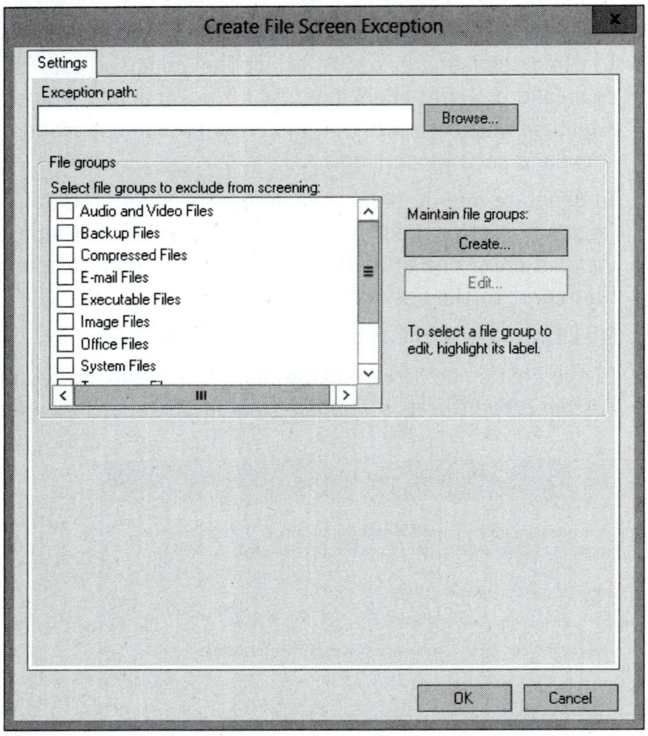

5. Type the path that the exception applies to in the *Exception path* text box. The exception applies to the selected folder and all of its subfolders.
6. To specify which files to exclude from file screening, select each file group that you want to exclude from file screening listed under *File groups*.
7. Click OK to close the *Create File Screen Exceptions* dialog box.

CREATING A FILE SCREEN TEMPLATE

A ***file screen template*** defines a set of file groups to screen, the type of screening to perform (active or passive), and (optionally) a set of notifications that are generated automatically when a user saves, or attempts to save, an unauthorized file. Similar to quota templates, you can simplify the management of file screens by updating the templates, which update all of the file screens that use the template.

CREATE A FILE SCREEN TEMPLATE

GET READY. To create a file screen template, perform the following steps:

1. Open Server Manager.
2. Click Tools > File Server Resource Manager. The *File Server Resource Manager console* opens.
3. In *File Screening Management*, click the File Screen Templates node.
4. Right-click File Screen Templates, and then click Create File Screen Template. The *Create File Screen Template* dialog box opens.
5. If you want to copy the properties of an existing template to use as a base for your new template, select a template from the *Copy properties from template* drop-down list. Then, click Copy.
6. Modify values on the *Settings* tab, including the template name, screening type, and selected file groups to block.
7. Click OK to close the *Create File Screen Template* dialog box.

When you change a file screen template, and click *OK* to save the changes, you have the following options:

- Apply template only to derived file screens that match the original template
- Apply template to all derived file screens
- Do not apply template to derived file screens

Using Storage Reports

To help you manage storage, you can use FSRM to generate ***storage reports*** that show the state of file server volumes and anyone who exceeds the quota or uses files that aren't allowed.

CERTIFICATION READY
Configure reports.
Objective 2.2

The reports that FSRM can create are as follows:

- **Duplicate Files:** Shows a list of files that are the same size and have the same last modified date.
- **File Screening Audit:** Creates a list of the audit events generated by file-screening violations for specific users during a specific time period.
- **Files by File Group:** Creates a list of files sorted by selected file groups defined with FSRM.
- **Files by Owner:** Creates a list of files sorted by selected users that own them.
- **Large Files:** Creates a list of files that are larger than a specified size.
- **Least Recently Accessed Files:** Creates a list of files that have not been accessed for a specified number of days.
- **Most Recently Accessed Files:** Creates a list of files that have been accessed within a specified number of days.
- **Quota Usage:** Creates a list of quotas that exceed a specified percentage of the storage limit.

When reports are generated, they are automatically saved in the C:\StorageReports\Scheduled folder. You can also have reports e-mailed to administrators.

SCHEDULE A STORAGE REPORT

GET READY. To schedule a storage report, perform the following steps:

1. Open Server Manager.
2. Click Tools > File Server Resource Manager. The *File Server Resource Manager console* opens.

3. Right-click Storage Reports Management, and select Schedule a new report task. The *Storage Reports Task Properties* dialog box opens (see Figure 5-19).

Figure 5-19

Creating a storage report

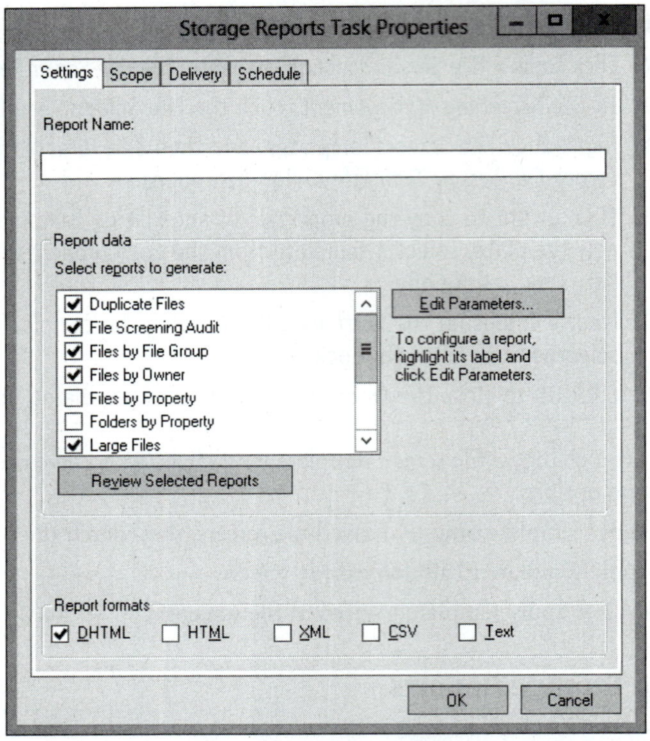

4. In the *Report Name* text box, type the name of the report.
5. In the *Report data* section, select the report that you want to generate and deselect the reports that you don't want to generate.
6. Click the Scope tab to display it (see Figure 5-20).

Figure 5-20

Defining the scope

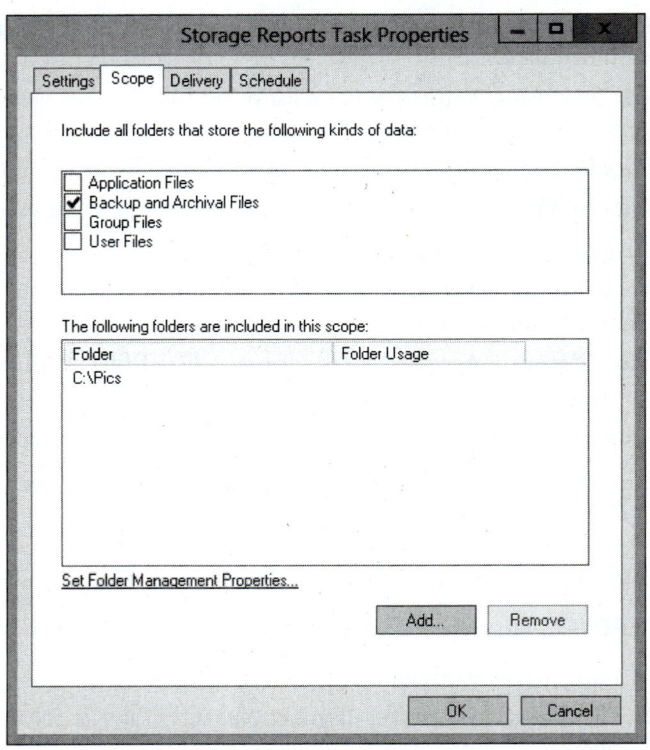

7. Select the file groups that you want to include in the report.
8. Click Add and browse to the volume or folder that you want to report on, and click OK.
9. Click the Delivery tab to display it (see Figure 5-21).

Figure 5-21

Specifying who gets the reports

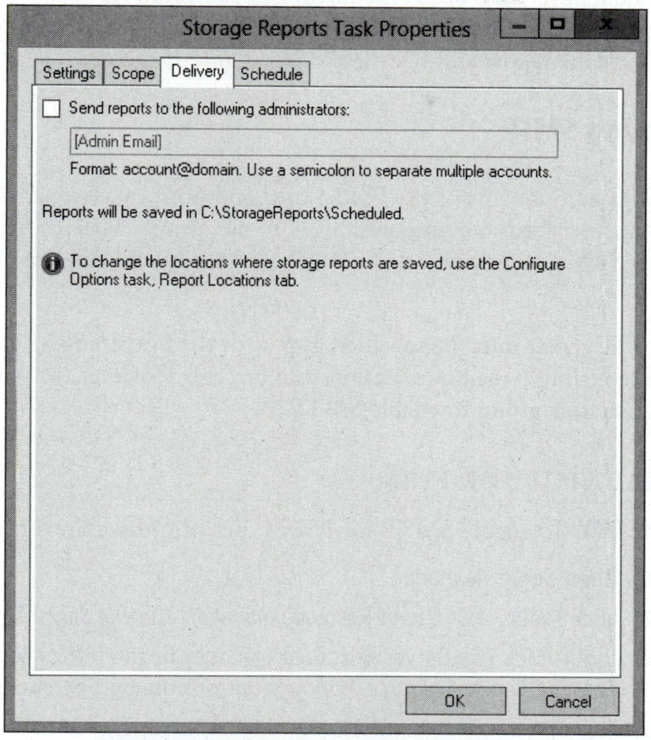

10. If you want the reports e-mailed to a user, select the Send reports to the following administrators and specify the e-mail address. If you need to send to multiple users, separate the e-mail addresses with semicolons (;).
11. Click the Schedule tab to display it (see Figure 5-22).

Figure 5-22

Scheduling the storage reports

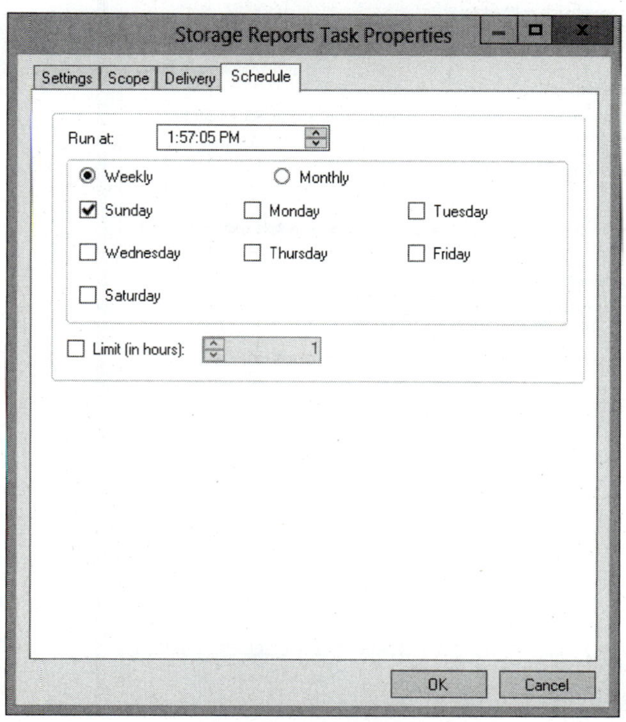

12. Specify the time and select the days that you want the report to be generated.
13. Click OK to close the *Storage Reports Task Properties* dialog box.

After the reports have been scheduled, you can run a report at any time by right-clicking the storage report and selecting *Run Report Task Now*. If you need to change a scheduled report, right-click the report and select *Edit Report Task Properties*.

Enabling SMTP

Various components of the FSRM can send notifications via e-mail. However, to send e-mail, you need to configure FSRM to use Simple Mail Transfer Protocol (SMTP) so that FSRM knows where to forward the e-mail to be delivered.

An SMTP server must be specified as part of the initial FSRM configuration so that quota or file screening e-mail notifications can be sent. However, you must be a member of the Administrators group to enable SMTP.

ENABLE SMTP FOR FSRM

GET READY. To enable SMTP for FSRM, perform the following steps:

1. Open Server Manager.
2. Click Tools > File Server Resource Manager. The *File Server Resource Manager console* opens.
3. Right-click File Server Resource Manager in the left pane and select Configure Options. The *File Server Resource Manager Options* dialog box opens (see Figure 5-23).

Figure 5-23

Specifying the SMTP server

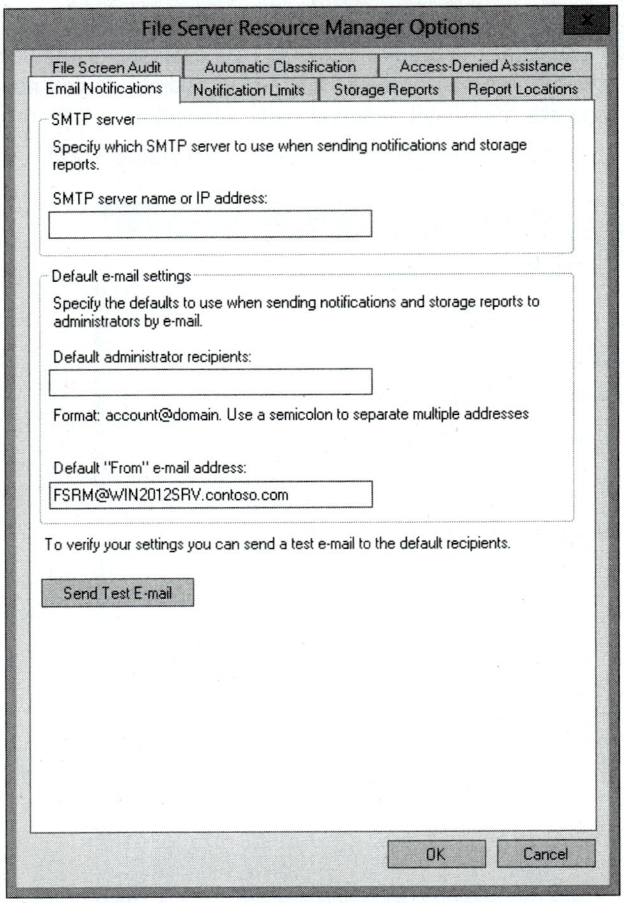

4. On the E-mail Notifications tab, type the computer name or the IP address of the SMTP server in the *SMTP server name or IP address* text box.
5. If you have not already specified an e-mail account to which the e-mail notifications will be sent, type the e-mail address under *Default administrator recipients*.
6. Click OK to save the new e-mail notification settings.

SKILL SUMMARY

IN THIS LESSON, YOU LEARNED:

- File Server Resource Manager (FSRM) is a suite of tools that enables you to control and manage the quantity and type of data stored on a file server.
- The FSRM is installed with Server Manager as a server role.
- Quotas defined with FSRM limit how much space a folder or volume can use.
- A hard quota prevents users from saving files after the space limit is reached and generates notifications when the volume of data reaches the configured threshold.
- A soft quota does not enforce the quota limit, but it generates a notification when the configured threshold is met.
- You can create a quota on a volume or a folder using a quota template or using custom properties.
- It is recommended that you use quota templates when creating quotas because quota templates can be applied to other volumes and folders in the future. In addition, if you modify the template, you have the option to change to any quotas that used the quota template in the past.
- File screening enables you to control the type of files that users can save and send notifications when users try to save a blocked file.
- A file group is used to define a namespace for a file screen, file screen exception, or a Files by File Group storage report.
- Active screening prevents uses from saving the defined unauthorized files.
- Passive screening allows users to save files, and it allows the monitoring and notification when a user does save an unauthorized file.
- To allow files that other file screens block, create a file screen exception, which is a special type of file screen that overrides any file screening that would otherwise apply to a folder and all its subfolders in a designated exception path.
- A file screen template defines a set of file groups to screen, the type of screening to perform (active or passive), and (optionally) a set of notifications that are generated automatically when a user saves or attempts to save an unauthorized file.
- To help you manage storage, you can use FSRM to generate storage reports that show the state of their file server volumes and anyone who exceeds the quota or uses disallowed files.
- A Simple Mail Transfer Protocol (SMTP) server must be specified as part of the initial FSRM configuration so that quota or file screening e-mail notifications can be sent.

Knowledge Assessment

Multiple Choice

Select the correct answer for each of the following questions.

1. Which type of quota used with FSRM prevents users from saving files when the quota is exceeded?
   a. Hard quota
   b. Soft quota
   c. Passive quota
   d. Active quota
2. Which of the following is supported when you define quotas using FSRM? (Choose all that apply.)
   a. Compress a drive.
   b. Place an event in the Windows logs.
   c. Send an e-mail.
   d. Run a command or script.
3. Which of the following do you perform when you change a quota template? (Choose all that apply.)
   a. Apply template only to derived quotas that match the original template.
   b. Reset all quota templates on the system to the default quota template.
   c. Apply template to all derived quotas.
   d. Remove all quota templates.
4. Which of the following is used to control the type of files that users can save to a file server?
   a. Control Panel
   b. Windows Explorer
   c. EFS
   d. FSRM
5. Which type of screening prevents users from saving the defined unauthorized files?
   a. Hard screening
   b. Soft screening
   c. Passive screening
   d. Active screening
6. Which tool is used to manage file servers, including configuring quotas and blocking certain files?
   a. Quota Management
   b. File Screening
   c. File Server Resource Manager
   d. File Management
7. Which type of quota used by FSRM will send notifications only when the quota is exceeded?
   a. Hard quota
   b. Soft quota
   c. Screen quota
   d. Warning quota

8. Which of the following enables users to use certain files but notifies an administrator via an e-mail when the user saves those types of files?
   a. File scanning
   b. Hard screening
   c. Soft screening
   d. Passive screening
9. Which of the following do you set up when you want to allow a file that is blocked with file screening?
   a. Allow rule
   b. Hard exception
   c. Passive exception
   d. Screen exception
10. Which of the following do you use to simplify the management of file screens?
    a. Template groups
    b. File screen template
    c. Management groups
    d. File definitions

Best Answer

Choose the letter that corresponds to the best answer. More than one answer choice may achieve the goal. Select the BEST answer

1. Which option do you use if you want a quota template to be applied to the parent folder, each subfolder, and each subfolder created in the future?
   a. Inherent
   b. Drill-down
   c. Auto apply
   d. Overwrite
2. Which of the following can you use to see whether a FSRM quota is exceeded on a folder? (Choose two answers.)
   a. Open FSRM and select Quotas under Quota Management.
   b. Enable SMTP.
   c. Set up alarms.
   d. Run a Quota Usage Report.
3. When you configure screening, what should you use to apply the screening to a bunch of files?
   a. File group
   b. File list
   c. Screen group
   d. Screen policy
4. Which of the following can you use to show a list of duplicate files on a volume?
   a. Quotas
   b. File screening
   c. File comparison
   d. Storage reports
5. How do you enable SMTP for FSRM?
   a. Open the View menu and select Forwarder.
   b. Select Configure Options.
   c. Install SMTP server role.
   d. Install MS Exchange.

Matching and Identification

1. Identify the tasks you can perform with FSRM.
   _______ a) Control the type of files that users can save.
   _______ b) Control the print queue.
   _______ c) Control who can own a file or folder.
   _______ d) Create quotas for a volume or folder.
   _______ e) Restrict access based on defined properties.
   _______ f) Enforce encryption of a folder.
   _______ g) Schedule storage reports.
   _______ h) Limit the depth of a folder.

2. Identify the tasks you can perform with FSRM file screening?
   _______ a) Specify who can own a file.
   _______ b) Control the types of files users can save.
   _______ c) Filter what files can be displayed in a list based on permissions.
   _______ d) Create file screen exceptions.
   _______ e) Define file-screening templates.
   _______ f) Create and manage file groups.

3. Identify the tasks that storage reports provided by FSRM.
   _______ a) Quota Usage
   _______ b) File Screening Audit
   _______ c) Files Used by Group
   _______ d) Large Files
   _______ e) Duplicate Files
   _______ f) Files that are System Files
   _______ g) Files by Owner

4. Identify the file-screening templates provided in FSRM.
   _______ a) Block Executable Files
   _______ b) Block Audio and Video Files
   _______ c) Block Executable Files
   _______ d) Block E-mail Files
   _______ e) Block Batch Files and Scripts
   _______ f) Block Image Files
   _______ g) Block Image Files

Build a List

1. Identify the steps, in order, to create a file screen. Not all steps will be used.
   _____ Select Active screening or Passive screening.
   _____ Define quotas.
   _____ Right-click File Screens and click Create File Screen.
   _____ Type the path to a folder.
   _____ Define the reports.
   _____ Open FSRM.
   _____ Select Define custom file screen properties and then click Custom Properties.
   _____ Configure notifications, event logging, or commands.

Business Case Scenarios

Scenario 5-1: Blocking Audio and Video Files

You were just hired as an administrator for Contoso Corporate. You looked for a file server and discovered that several users have been using the file server as a personal repository for audio and video files that have been downloaded using the corporate network. How should you stop users form saving these files?

Scenario 5-2: Managing Disk Space

You have a file server that is used to store files used by the various projects throughout your organization. After a while, you realize that you are quickly running out of disk space. When you look at the usage, you determine that the reason the system is filling up is that older projects are never removed or archived. What solution would you propose to deal with this?

6 LESSON

Configuring File Services and Disk Encryption

70-411 EXAM OBJECTIVE

Objective 2.3 – Configure file and disk encryption. This objective may include but is not limited to: configure BitLocker encryption; configure the Network Unlock feature; configure BitLocker policies; configure the EFS recovery agent; manage EFS and BitLocker certificates including backup and restore

Lesson Heading	Exam Objective
Securing Files	Configure file and disk encryption
Encrypting Files with EFS	Configure the EFS recovery agent
Managing EFS Certificates	Manage EFS and BitLocker certificates including backup and restore
Encrypting Files with BitLocker	Configure BitLocker encryption Configure BitLocker policies
Managing BitLocker Certificates	Manage EFS and BitLocker certificates including backup and restore
Configuring the Network Unlock Feature	Configure the Network Unlock feature

KEY TERMS

BitLocker Drive Encryption (BDE)
BitLocker To Go
data recovery agent (DRA)
decryption
Encrypting File System (EFS)
encryption
Network Unlock
pre-provisioning
Trusted Platform Module (TPM)

■ Securing Files

THE BOTTOM LINE

Encryption is the process of converting data into a format that cannot be read by another user. Once a user has encrypted a file, it automatically remains encrypted when the file is stored on disk. ***Decryption*** is the process of converting data from encrypted format back to its original format.

CERTIFICATION READY
Configure file and disk encryption.
Objective 2.3

Encryption algorithms can be divided into three classes:

- Symmetric
- Asymmetric
- Hash function

Symmetric encryption uses a single key to encrypt and decrypt data. Therefore, it is also referred to as secret-key, single-key, shared-key, and private-key encryption. To use symmetric key algorithms, you need to initially send or provide the secret key to both the sender and the receiver.

Asymmetric key, also known as public-key cryptography, uses two mathematically related keys. One key is used to encrypt the data and the second key is used to decrypt the data. Unlike symmetric key algorithms, it does not require a secure initial exchange of one or more secret keys to both sender and receiver. Instead, you can make the public key known to anyone and use the other key to encrypt or decrypt the data. The public key can be sent to someone or it can be published within a digital certificate via a Certificate Authority (CA). Secure Socket Layer (SSL)/Transport Layer Security (TLS) and Pretty Good Privacy (PGP) use asymmetric keys.

For example, say you want a partner to send you data. Therefore, you send the partner the public key. The partner then encrypts the data with the key and sends you the encrypted message. You then use the private key to decrypt the message. If the public key falls into someone else's hands, that person still cannot decrypt the message.

The last type of encryption is the hash function. Different from the symmetric and asymmetric algorithms, a hash function is meant as one-way encryption. That means that after the data has been encrypted, it cannot be decrypted. One example of its use is to use the hash function to encrypt a password that is stored on disk. Anytime a password is entered and it needs to be verified that it is the correct password, the same hash calculation is performed on the entered password and compared to the hash value of the password stored on disk. If the two match, the user must have typed in the password. This avoids storing the passwords in a readable format that a hacker might try to access.

No matter what encryption algorithm you choose, they all use keys to encrypt data. The key must be long enough so that an attacker cannot try all possible combinations to figure out what the key is. Therefore, a key length of 80 bits is generally considered the minimum for strong security with symmetric encryption algorithms. 128-bit keys are commonly used and considered strong.

Today, newer versions of Windows offer two file encrypting technologies: Encrypting File System (EFS) and BitLocker Drive Encryption. EFS protects individual files or folders, whereas BitLocker protects entire volumes.

Encrypting Files with EFS

In addition to protecting data files on a stolen system or drive, encryption can protect files.

Encrypting File System (EFS) can encrypt files on an NTFS volume that cannot be used unless the user has access to the keys required to decrypt the information. By default, when you encrypt a file with EFS, the file or folder turns green to show that the file is encrypted.

After a file has been encrypted, you do not have to manually decrypt an encrypted file before you can use it. Instead, you work with the file or folder just like any other file that is not encrypted. When you open a file that is encrypted with EFS, the file is automatically decrypted as needed. When you save the file, it is automatically decrypted. However, if another user tries to access the same file, he cannot open it because he does not have the proper key to open the file.

EFS uses an encryption key to encrypt your data, which is stored in a digital certificate. The first time a user encrypts a file or folder, an encryption certificate and key are created and bound to the user account. The user who creates the file is the only person who can read it. As the user works, EFS encrypts the files using a key generated from the user's public key. Data encrypted with this key can be decrypted only by the user's personal encryption certificate, which is generated using a private key.

CONFIGURING EFS

To encrypt or decrypt a folder or file, enable or disable the encryption attribute just as you set any other attribute, such as read-only, compressed, or hidden. If you encrypt a folder, all files and subfolders created in the encrypted folder are automatically encrypted. Microsoft recommends that you encrypt at the folder level. You can also encrypt or decrypt a file or folder using the `Cipher` command.

ENCRYPT A FOLDER OR FILE USING EFS

GET READY. To encrypt a folder or file, perform the following steps:

1. Right-click the folder or file you want to encrypt, and then click Properties. The *Properties* dialog box opens.
2. Click the General tab, and then click Advanced. The *Advanced Attributes* dialog box appears (see Figure 6-1).

Figure 6-1

Displaying the Advanced Attributes dialog box

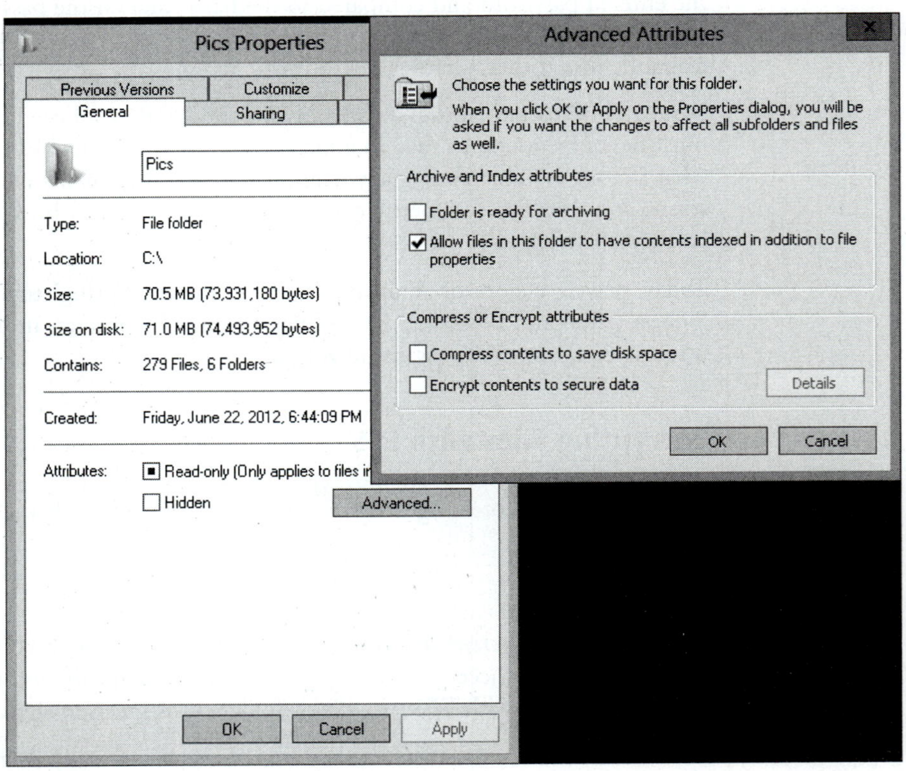

3. Select the Encrypt contents to secure data checkbox.
4. Click OK to close the *Advanced Attributes* dialog box.
5. Click OK to close the *Properties* dialog box.
6. If you encrypt a file in an unencrypted folder, it gives you a warning (see Figure 6-2). If you want to encrypt only the file, select Encrypt the file only and click OK. If you want to encrypt the folder and all content in the folder, select the Encrypt the file and its parent folder (recommended) option. Click OK.

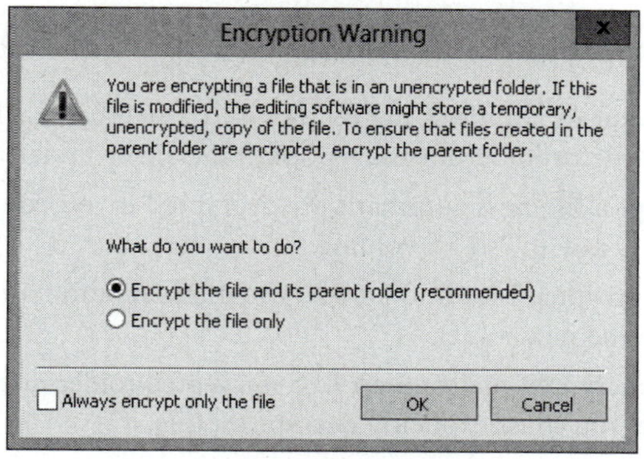

Figure 6-2
Encrypting a file in an unencrypted folder

7. If you encrypt a folder, it asks you to confirm the changes (see Figure 6-3). If you want to encrypt only the folder, select Apply changes to this folder only. If you want to apply to all folders, select Apply changes to this folder, subfolders and files. Click OK to close the Confirm Attribute Changes dialog box.

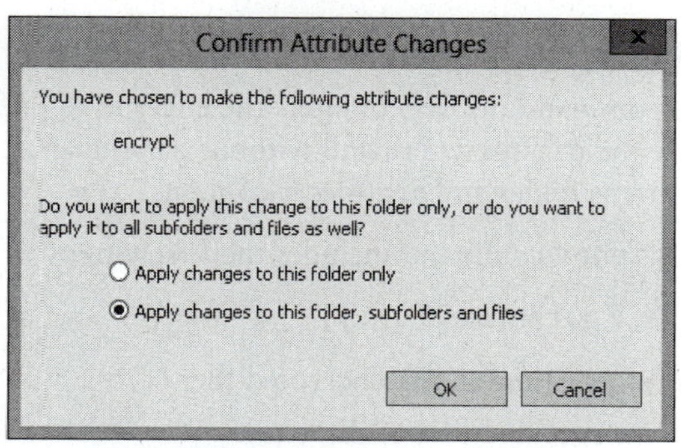

Figure 6-3
Confirming attribute changes

DECRYPT A FOLDER OR FILE

GET READY. To decrypt a folder or file, perform the following steps:

1. Right-click the folder or file you want to decrypt, and then click Properties. The *Properties* dialog box opens.

2. Click the General tab, and then click Advanced. The *Advanced Attributes* dialog box opens.
3. Clear the Encrypt contents to secure data checkbox.
4. Click OK to close the *Advanced Attributes* dialog box.
5. Click OK to close the *Properties* dialog box.
6. When it asks you to confirm the changes. If you want to decrypt only the folders, select Apply changes to this folder only. If you want to apply to all folders, select Apply changes to this folder, subfolders and files. Click OK.

When working with EFS, keep the following in mind:

- You can encrypt or compress NTFS files only when using EFS; you can't do both. If the user marks a file or folder for encryption, that file or folder is uncompressed.
- If you encrypt a file, it is automatically decrypted if you copy or move the file to a volume that is not an NTFS volume.
- Moving unencrypted files into an encrypted folder automatically causes those files to be encrypted in the new folder.
- Moving an encrypted file from an EFS-encrypted folder does not automatically decrypt files. Instead, you must explicitly decrypt the file.
- Files marked with the System attribute or that are in the root directory cannot be encrypted.
- Remember that an encrypted folder or file does not protect against the deletion of the file, listing the files or directories. To prevent deletion or listing of files, use NTFS permissions.
- Although you can use EFS on remote systems, data that is transmitted over the network is not encrypted. If encryption is needed over the network, use SSL/TLS (Secure Sockets Layer/Transport Layer Security) or IPsec.

USING THE CIPHER COMMAND

The `cipher.exe` command displays or alters the encryption of folders and files on NTFS volumes. If you use the `cipher` command without parameters, `cipher` displays the encryption state of the current folder and any files it contains.

The syntax of the `cipher` command includes the following:

```
CIPHER /options [pathname [...]]
```

- `/C`: Displays information on the encrypted file.
- `/D`: Decrypts the specified files or directories.
- `/E`: Encrypts the specified files or directories. Directories are marked so that files added afterward will be encrypted. The encrypted file can become decrypted when it is modified if the parent directory is not encrypted. It is recommended that you encrypt the file and the parent directory.
- `/H`: Displays files with the hidden or system attributes. These files are omitted by default.
- `/K`: Creates a new certificate and key for use with EFS. If this option is chosen, all the other options are ignored.

- /N: This option works only with /U. This prevents keys from being updated. It is used to find the encrypted files on the local drives.
- /R: Generates an EFS recovery key and certificate, and then writes them to a .PFX file (containing certificate and private key) and a .CER file (containing only the certificate).
- /S: Performs the specified operation on the given directory and all files and subdirectories in it.
- /U: Tries to touch all the encrypted files on local drives. This updates the user's file encryption key or recovery keys to the current ones if they are changed. This option does not work with other options except /N.
- /W: Removes data from available unused disk space on the entire volume. If this option is chosen, all other options are ignored. The directory specified can be anywhere in a local volume. If it is a mount point or points to a directory in another volume, the data on that volume is removed.
- /X: Backs up the EFS certificate and keys to the specified filename that follows the /X:. If EFS file is provided, the current user's certificate(s) used to encrypt the file is backed up. Otherwise, the user's current EFS certificate and keys are backed up.
- /ADDUSER: Adds a user to the specified encrypted file(s).
- /REKEY: Updates the specified encrypted file(s) to use the configured EFS current key.
- /REMOVEUSER /certhash: <Hash>: Removes a user from the specified file(s). CERTHASH must be the SHA1 hash of the certificate to remove.

For example, to use cipher to encrypt a subfolder named c:\Data\Reports, and then execute the following command:

```
cipher /e c:\Data\Reports
```

To decrypt the folder, execute the following command:

```
cipher /d c:\Data\Reports
```

SHARING FILES PROTECTED WITH EFS WITH OTHERS

When EFS was originally created, an EFS file could be accessed by only the one person who encrypted the file. In later versions of NTFS, if you need to share an EFS-protected file with other users, you add an encryption certificate to the file.

SHARE A FILE PROTECTED WITH EFS WITH OTHERS

GET READY. To share a file protected with EFS with others, perform the following steps:

1. Right-click the encrypted file and select Properties.
2. On the *General* tab, click Advanced. The *Advanced Attributes* dialog box opens.
3. Click Details. The *User Access* dialog box opens (see Figure 6-4).

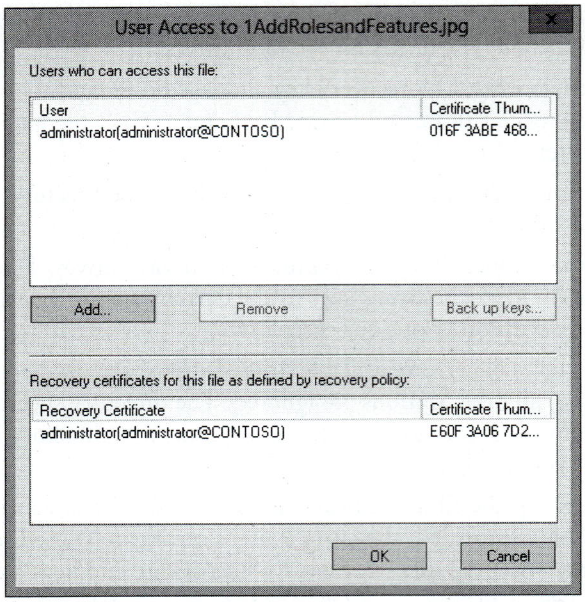

Figure 6-4

Opening the User Access dialog box

4. Click the Add button. The *Encrypting File System* dialog box opens (see Figure 6-5).

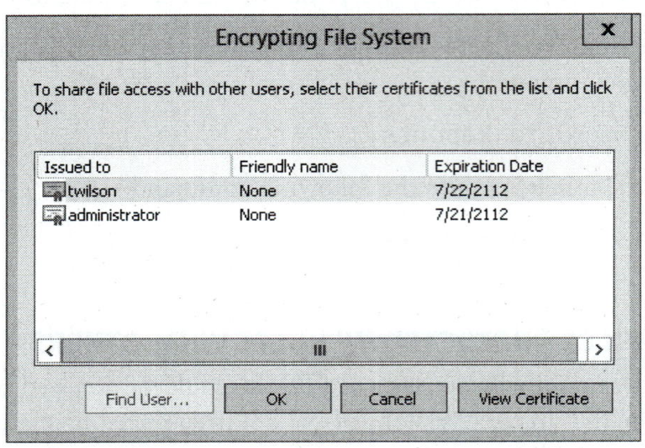

Figure 6-5

Opening the Encrypting File System dialog box

5. Select the user you want to grant access to and click OK to close the *Encrypting File System* dialog box.
6. Click OK to close the *User Access* dialog box.
7. Click OK to close the *Advanced Attributes* dialog box.
8. Click OK to close the *Properties* dialog box.

TAKE NOTE*

If the user that you want to add cannot be found, the user has not encrypted a file with EFS and therefore, he does not have an EFS certificate. However, EFS certificates can be generated with group policies and a Microsoft Certificate Authority (CA).

CONFIGURING EFS WITH GROUP POLICIES

To help you manage the use of EFS, you can use group policies to meet your organization's security needs. To establish an EFS policy, right-click *Computer Configuration\Policies\Windows Settings\Security Settings\Public Key Policies\Encrypting File System* and select *Properties* (see Figure 6-6).

Figure 6-6

Selecting Encrypting File System properties

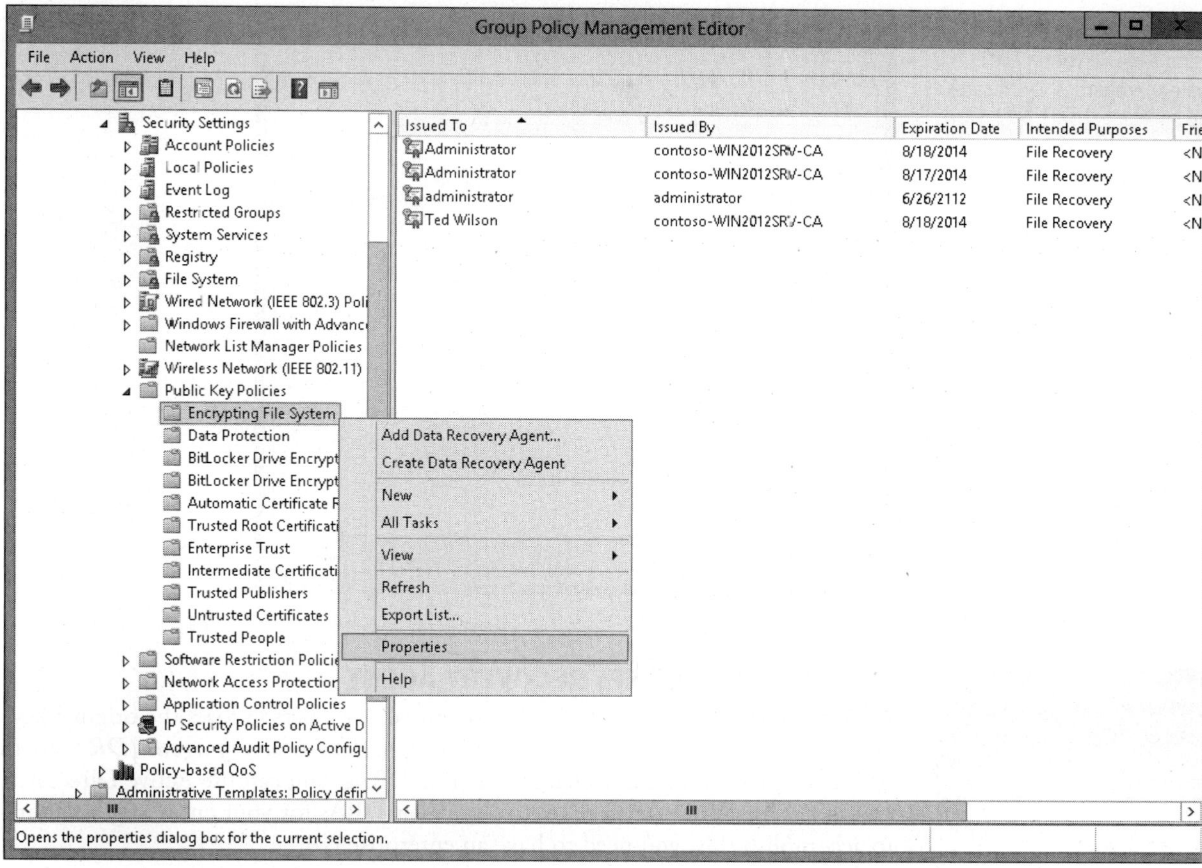

Under the *General* tab (see Figure 6-7), you can choose to allow or disallow the use of EFS. If you do not configure any policy settings for EFS, it is allowed. If you choose to use EFS, you can automatically encrypt a user's Documents folder, require a smart card for use with EFS, or notify users to make backup copies of their encryption keys. In addition, you can require strong encryption and you can use Elliptic Curve Cryptography (ECC) encryption.

Figure 6-7

Using the Encrypting File System Properties General tab

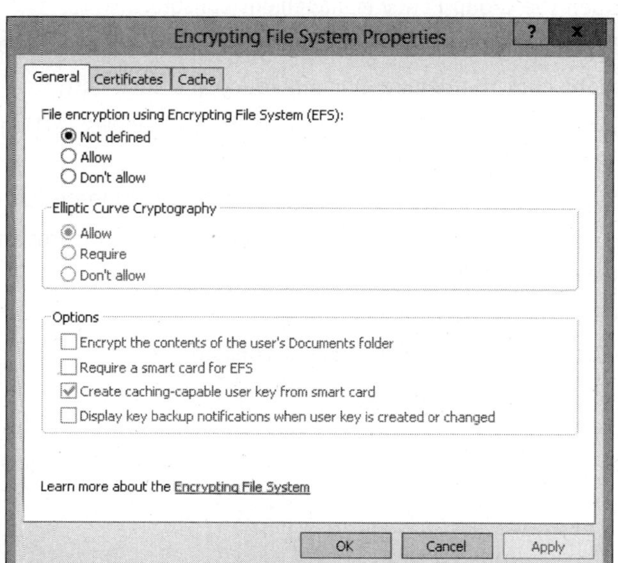

By clicking the *Certificates* tab (see Figure 6-8), you can specify the key size for the certificates and allow EFS to generate self-signed certificates when a CA is not available.

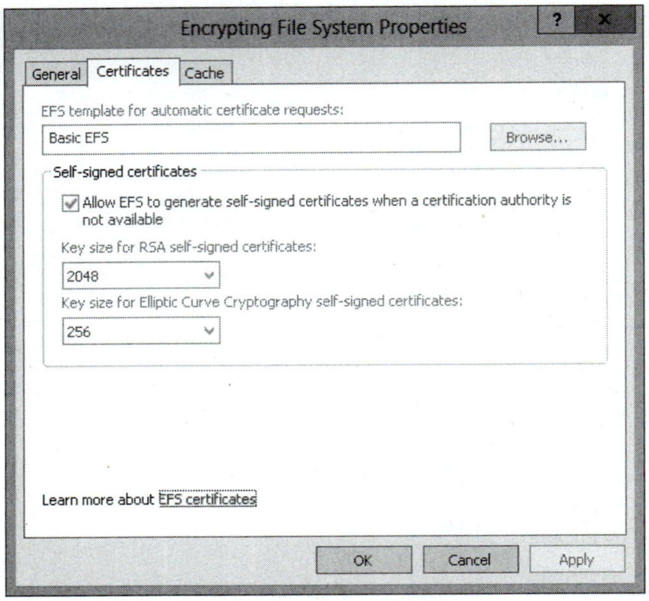

Figure 6-8
Using the Encrypting File System Properties Certificates tab

CERTIFICATION READY
Configure the EFS recovery agent.
Objective 2.3

CONFIGURING THE EFS RECOVERY AGENT

If for some reason, a person leaves the company or a person loses the original key and the encrypted files cannot be read, you can set up a ***data recovery agent (DRA)*** that can recover EFS-encrypted files for a domain. To define DRAs, you can use Active Directory group policies to configure one or more user accounts as DRAs for your entire organization. However, to accomplish this, you need to have an enterprise CA.

ADD RECOVERY AGENTS FOR EFS

GET READY. To add new users as recovery agents, assign the EFS recovery certificates issued by the enterprise CA to the user account, and then perform the following steps:

1. Log in as the DRA account.
2. Open the Group Policy Management console.
3. Expand Forest, Domains, and then the name of your domain.
4. Right-click the Default Domain Policy and click Edit.
5. Expand Computer Configuration\Policies\Windows Settings\Security Settings\Public Key Policies\.
6. Right-click Encrypting File System, and select Create Data Recovery Agent.
7. Click Encrypting File System and notice the certificates that are displayed (see Figure 6-9).
8. Close the Group Policy Editor.
9. Close Group Policy Management console.

Figure 6-9

Viewing the Encrypting File System certificates

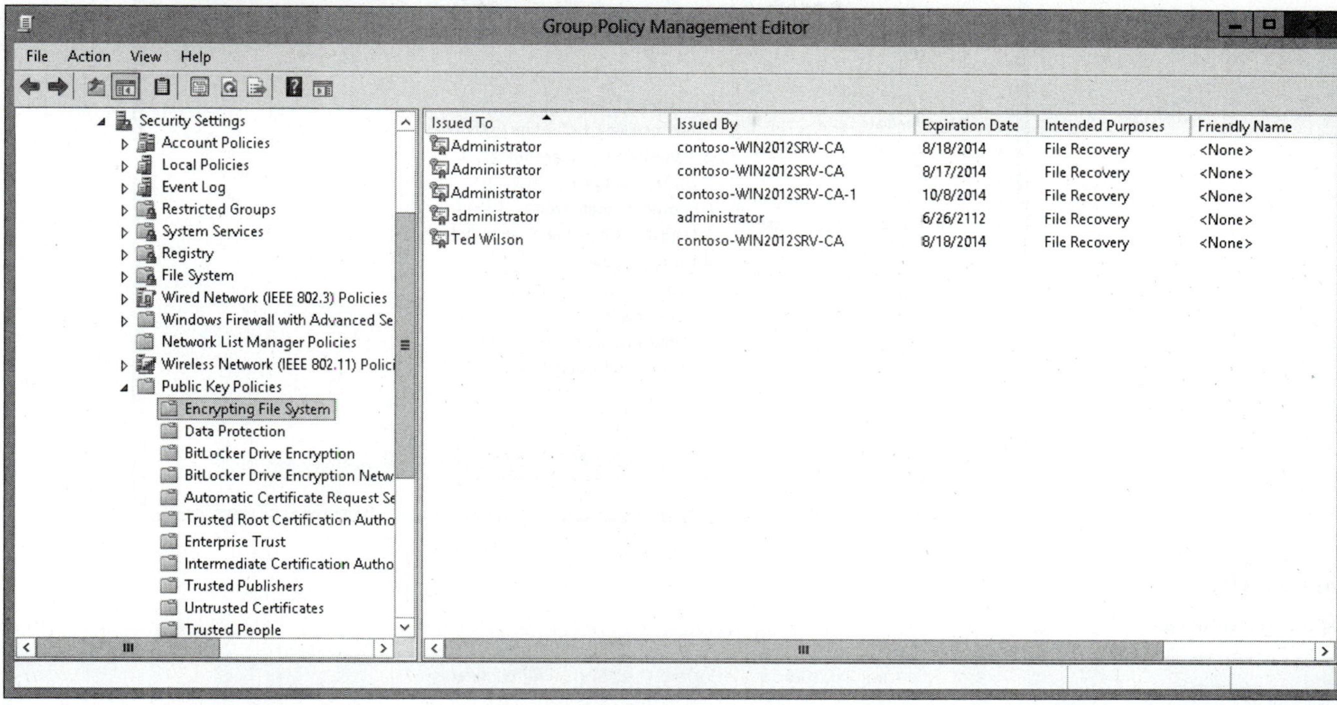

Managing EFS Certificates

CERTIFICATION READY
Manage EFS and BitLocker certificates including backup and restore.
Objective 2.3

The first time you encrypt a folder or file, an encryption certificate is automatically created. If your certificate and key are lost or damaged and you don't have a backup, you won't be able to use the files that you have encrypted. Therefore, you should back up your encryption certificate.

BACK UP AN EFS CERTIFICATE

GET READY. To back up your EFS certificate, perform the following steps:

1. Open a command prompt.
2. Execute the `certmgr.msc` command. If you are prompted for an administrator password or confirmation, type the password or provide confirmation. The certmgr console opens (see Figure 6-10).
3. In the left pane, double-click Personal, and then click Certificates.
4. In the main pane, right-click the certificate that lists *Encrypting File System under Intended Purposes*. Select All Tasks, and then click Export (see Figure 6-11). If there is more than one EFS certificate, you should back up all of them one by one.

Figure 6-10

Opening the certmgr console

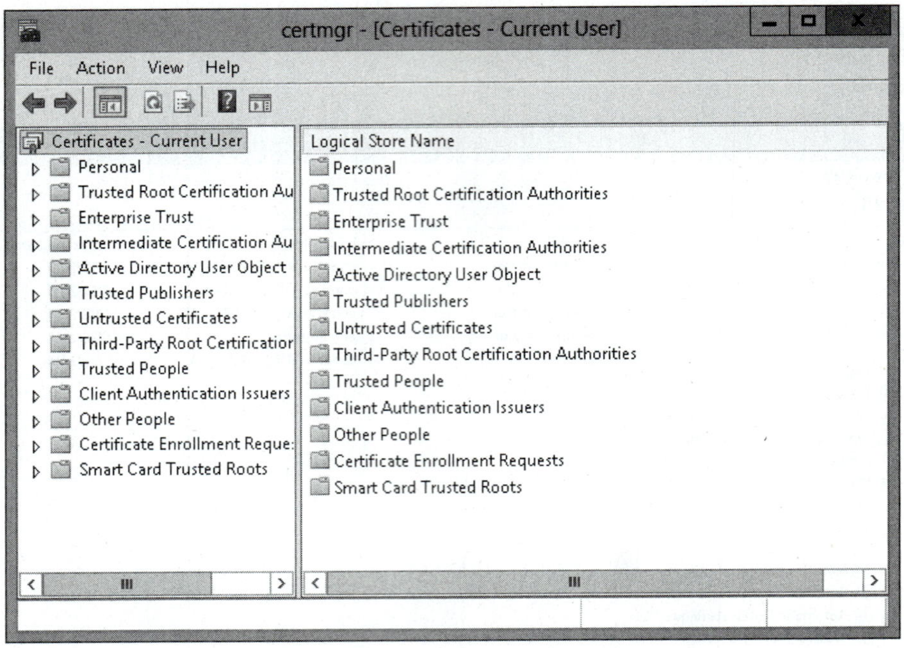

Figure 6-11

Exporting a certificate

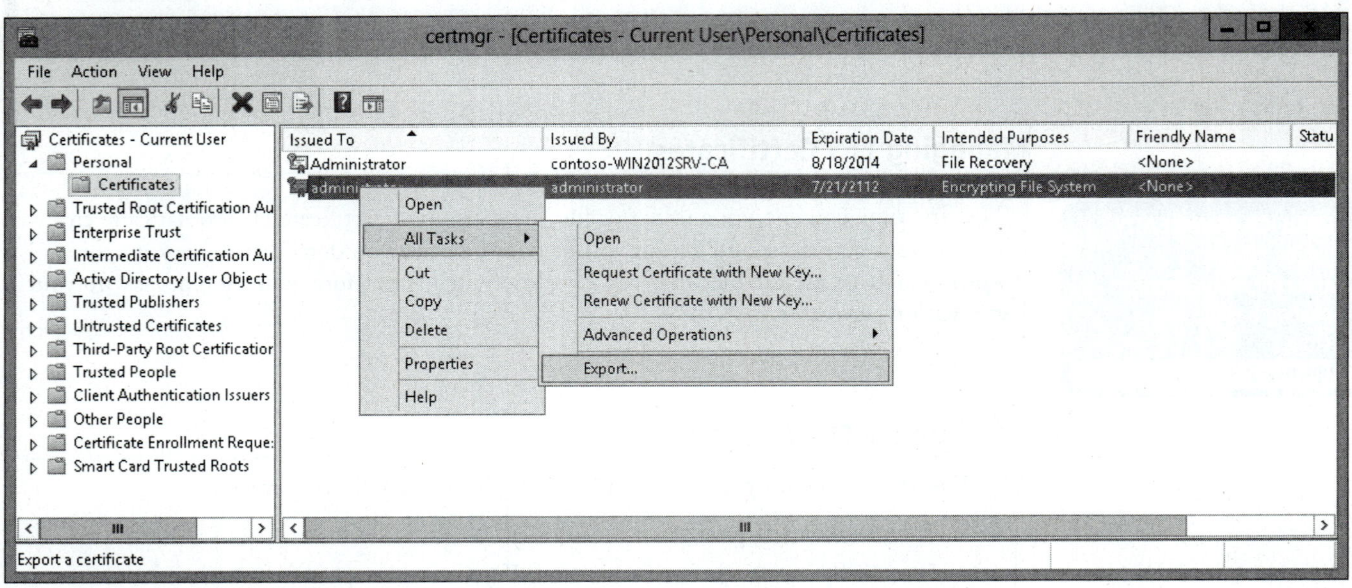

5. When the *Certificate Export Wizard* starts, click Next.
6. On the *Export Private Key* page, click Yes, export the private key (see Figure 6-12), and then click Next.

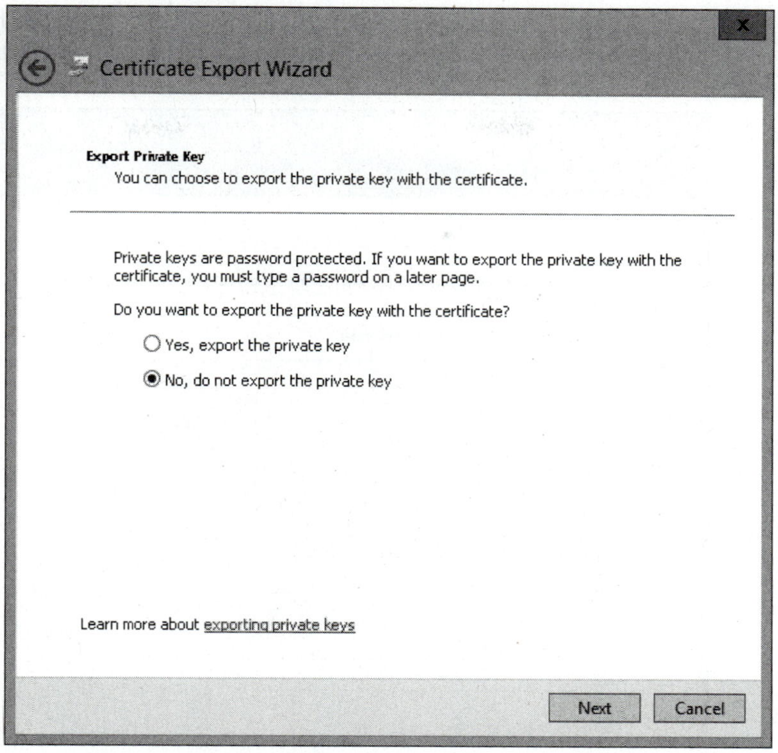

Figure 6-12

Exporting the private key on the Export Private Key page

7. On the *Export File Format* page (see Figure 6-13), click Personal Information Exchange—PKCS #12 (.PFX), and then click Next.

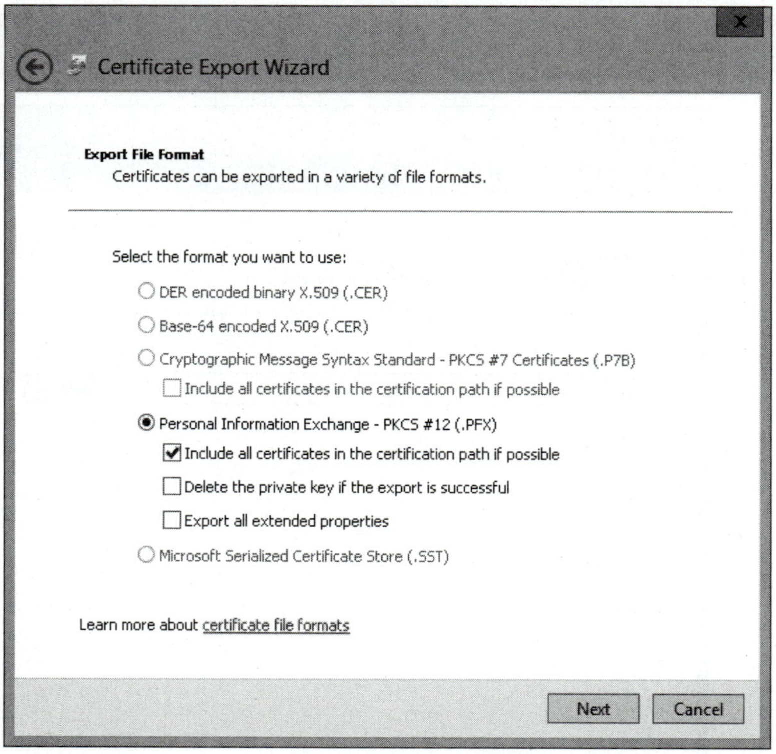

Figure 6-13

Selecting the Personal Information Exchange on the Export File Format page

8. On the *Security* page, select the Password checkbox (see Figure 6-14), and type in the password in the *Password* and *Confirm password* text boxes. Click Next.

Figure 6-14

Selecting Password on the Security page

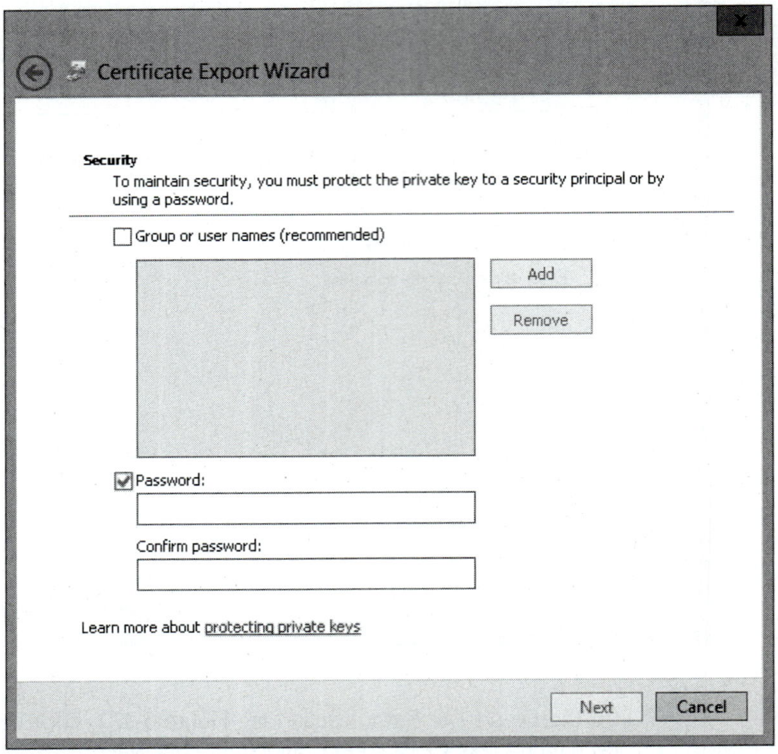

9. On the *File to Export* page (see Figure 6-15), type a name for the file and the location (include the whole path) or click Browse, navigate to a location, type a filename, and then click Next.

Figure 6-15

Specifying the filename (and its location) to export

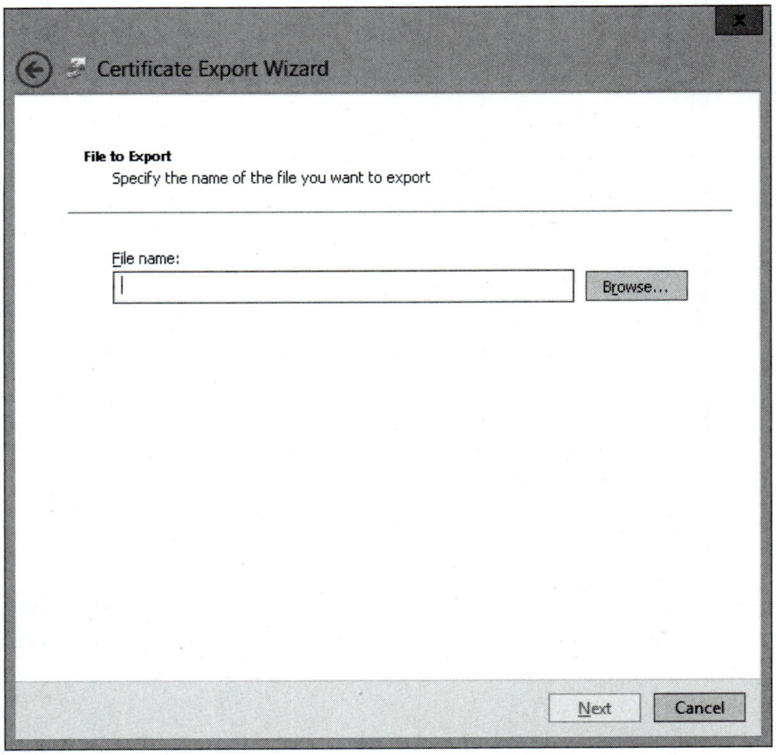

10. Click Next, and then click Finish.
11. When the export is successful, click OK.

You should then place the certificate in a safe place.

RESTORE AN EFS CERTIFICATE

GET READY. To restore your EFS certificate, perform the following steps:

1. Open a command prompt.
2. Execute the `certmgr.msc` command. If you are prompted for an administrator password or confirmation, type the password or provide confirmation.
3. In the left pane, double-click Personal, and then click Certificates.
4. Right-click Certificates, select All Tasks, and then select Import.
5. When the *Certificate Import Wizard* starts, click Next.
6. On the *File to Import* page, specify the path and name of the certificate, and click then Next.
7. If it asks for a password, provide the password and click Next.
8. On the *Certificate Store* page, click Next.
9. On the *Completing the Certificate Import Wizard* page, click Finish.
10. When the import is successful, click OK.

Encrypting Files with BitLocker

Unlike EFS, BitLocker allows you to encrypt the entire volume. Therefore, if a drive or laptop is stolen, the data is still encrypted even if the thief installs it in another system for which he is an administrator.

CERTIFICATION READY
Configure BitLocker encryption.
Objective 2.3

BitLocker Drive Encryption (BDE) is the feature in Windows Vista, Windows 7, Windows Server 2008, Windows Server 2008 R2, and Windows Server 2012 that can use a computer's ***Trusted Platform Module (TPM)***, which is a microchip that is built into a computer. It is used to store cryptographic information, such as encryption keys. Information stored on the TPM can be more secure from external software attacks and physical theft. BitLocker Drive Encryption can use a TPM to validate the integrity of a computer's boot manager and boot files at startup, and to guarantee that a computer's hard disk has not been tampered with while the operating system was offline. BitLocker Drive Encryption also stores measurements of core operating system files in the TPM.

TAKE NOTE*
For workstations, BitLocker is a feature of Windows 7 Enterprise, Windows 7 Ultimate, Windows 8 Pro, and Windows 8 Enterprise. It is not supported on other editions of Windows.

The system requirements of BitLocker are:

- Because BitLocker stores its own encryption and decryption key in a hardware device that is separate from your hard disk, you must have one of the following:
    - A computer with TPM. If your computer was manufactured with TPM version 1.2 or higher, BitLocker stores its key in the TPM.
    - A removable USB memory device, such as a USB flash drive. If your computer doesn't have TPM version 1.2 or higher, BitLocker stores its key on the flash drive.
- Have at least two partitions: a system partition (contains the files needed to start your computer and must be at least 350 MB for computers running Windows 8) and an operating system partition (contains Windows). The operating system partition is

encrypted, and the system partition remains unencrypted so that your computer can start. If your computer doesn't have two partitions, BitLocker creates them for you. Both partitions must be formatted with the NTFS file system.

- Your computer must have a BIOS that is compatible with TPM and supports USB devices during computer startup. If this is not the case, you need to update the BIOS before using BitLocker.

TAKE NOTE*

BitLocker is not commonly used on servers, but may become more common in the future as BitLocker has been improved to work on failover cluster volumes and SANs. Instead, most organizations use physical security for servers (such as locked server room and/or server rack that can be accessed only by a handful of people) to prevent the computer and drives from being stolen.

Instead, Bitlocker is more commonly used with mobile computers and to a lesser extent, Desktop computers. However, it takes a domain infrastructure with Windows servers to get the most benefits from BitLocker and the management of systems running BitLocker.

BitLocker supports NTFS, FAT16, FAT32 and ExFAT on USB, Firewire, SATA, SAS, ATA, IDE, and SCSI drives. It does not support CD File System, iSCSI, Fiber Channel, eSATA, and Bluetooth. BitLocker also does not support dynamic volumes; it supports only basic volumes.

BitLocker has five operational modes for OS drives, which define the steps involved in the system boot process. These modes, in a descending order from the most to least secure, are as follows:

- **TPM + startup PIN + startup key**: The system stores the BitLocker volume encryption key on the TPM chip, but an administrator must supply a personal identification number (PIN) and insert a USB flash drive containing a startup key before the system can unlock the BitLocker volume and complete the system boot sequence.
- **TPM + startup key**: The system stores the BitLocker volume encryption key on the TPM chip, but an administrator must insert a USB flash drive containing a startup key before the system can unlock the BitLocker volume and complete the system boot sequence.
- **TPM + startup PIN**: The system stores the BitLocker volume encryption key on the TPM chip, but an administrator must supply a PIN before the system can unlock the BitLocker volume and complete the system boot sequence.
- **Startup key only**: The BitLocker configuration process stores a startup key on a USB flash drive, which the administrator must insert each time the system boots. This mode does not require the server to have a TPM chip, but it must have a system BIOS that supports access to the USB flash drive before the operating system loads.
- **TPM only**: The system stores the BitLocker volume encryption key on the TPM chip, and accesses it automatically when the chip has determined that the boot environment is unmodified. This unlocks the protected volume and the computer continues to boot. No administrative interaction is required during the system boot sequence.

When you use BitLocker on fixed and removable data drives that are not the OS volume, you can use one of the following:

- Password
- Smart card
- Automatic Unlock

When you enable BitLocker using the BitLocker Drive Encryption control panel, you can select the *TPM + startup key*, *TPM + startup PIN*, or *TPM only* option. To use the

TPM + startup PIN + startup key option, you must first configure the *Require additional authentication at startup* Group Policy setting, found in the Computer Configuration\Policies\Administrative Templates\Windows Components\BitLocker Drive Encryption\Operating System Drives container.

CONFIGURING BITLOCKER ENCRYPTION

Before you can use BitLocker on a server running Windows Server 2012, you must first install Bit Locker using Server Manager. You can then determine whether you have TPM and turn on BitLocker.

INSTALL BITLOCKER

GET READY. To install BitLocker on a computer running Windows Server 2012, perform the following steps:

1. Click the Server Manager button on the task bar to open Server Manager.
2. At the top of Server Manager, select Manage and click Add Roles and Features. The *Add Roles and Feature Wizard* opens.
3. On the *Before you begin* page, click Next.
4. Select Role-based or feature-based installation and then click Next.
5. Click Select a server from the server pool, click the name of the server to install BitLocker to, and then click Next.
6. On the *Select server roles* page, click Next.
7. On the *Select features page*, select BitLocker Drive Encryption (see Figure 6-16).

Figure 6-16
Using the Select Features page

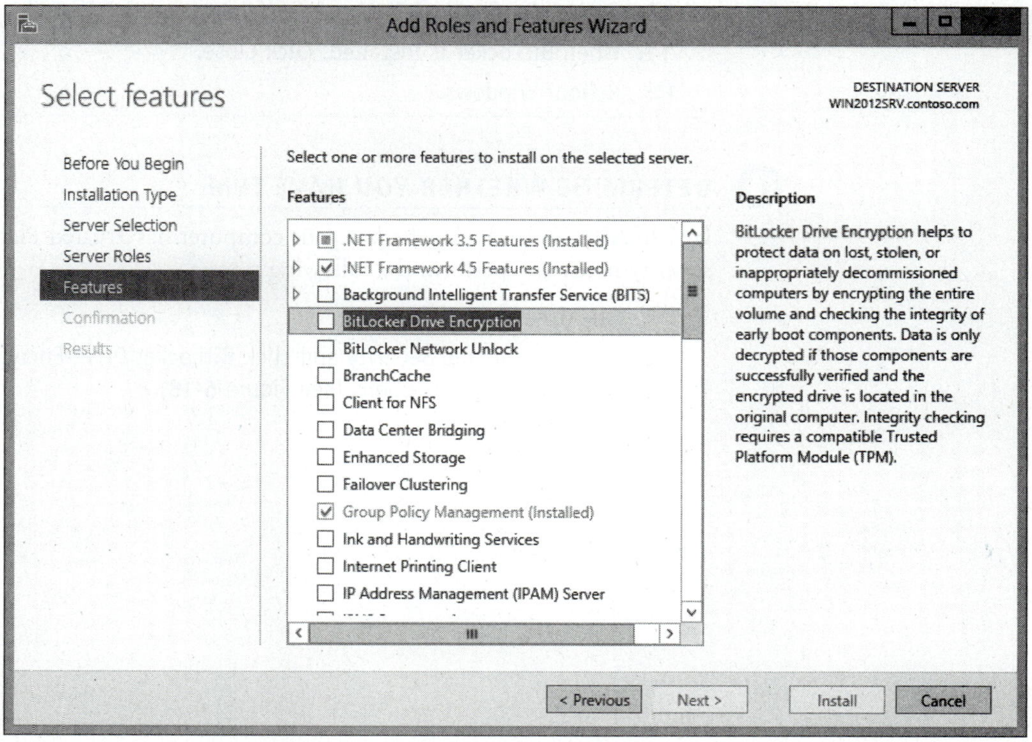

8. When the *Add Roles and Features Wizard* dialog box appears (see Figure 6-17), click Add Features.

Figure 6-17

Opening the Add Roles and Features Wizard

9. On the *Select Features* page, click Next.
10. On the *Confirm installation selections* page, click Install.
11. When BitLocker is installed, click Close.
12. Reboot Windows.

DETERMINE WHETHER YOU HAVE TPM

GET READY. To find out whether your computer has Trusted Platform Module (TPM) security hardware, perform the following steps:

1. Open the Control Panel.
2. Click System and Security and click BitLocker Drive Encryption. The *BitLocker Drive Encryption* window opens (see Figure 6-18).

Figure 6-18

Displaying the BitLocker Drive Encryption window

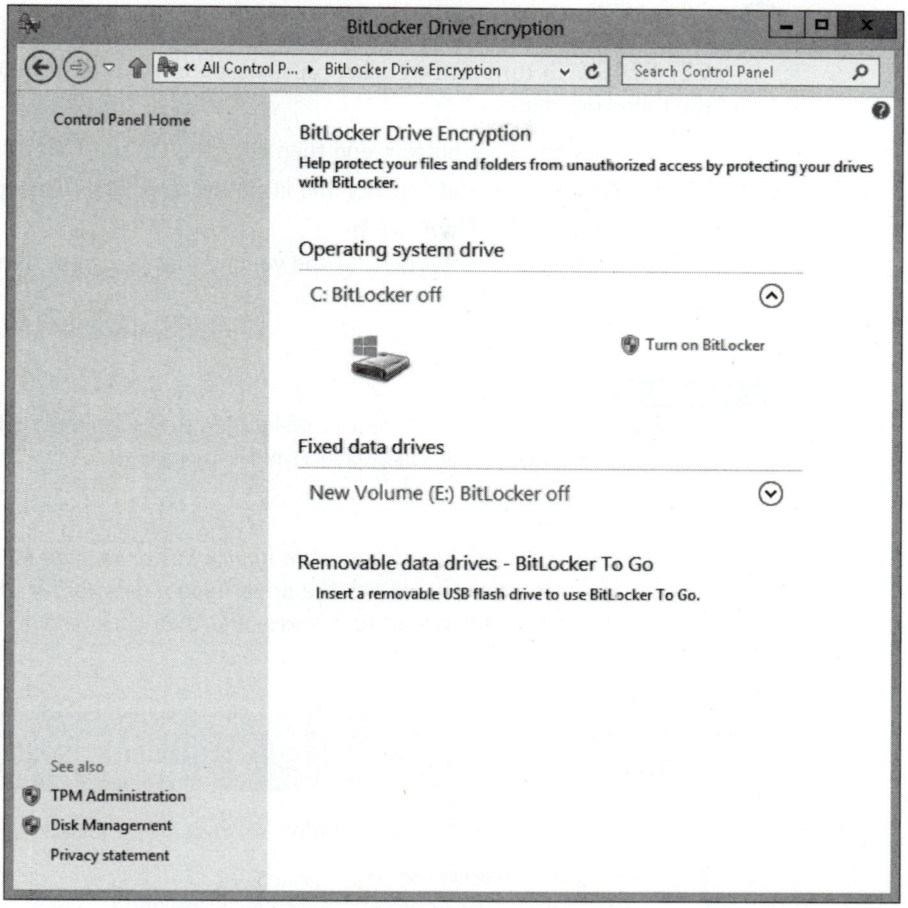

3. In the left pane, click TPM Administration. If you are prompted for an administrator password or confirmation, type the password or provide confirmation.

The TPM Management on Local Computer snap-in tells you whether your computer has the TPM security hardware (see Figure 6-19). If your computer doesn't have it, you'll need a removable USB memory device to turn on BitLocker and store the BitLocker startup key that you need whenever you start your computer.

Figure 6-19

Showing that the system does not have Compatible Trusted Platform Module (TPM)

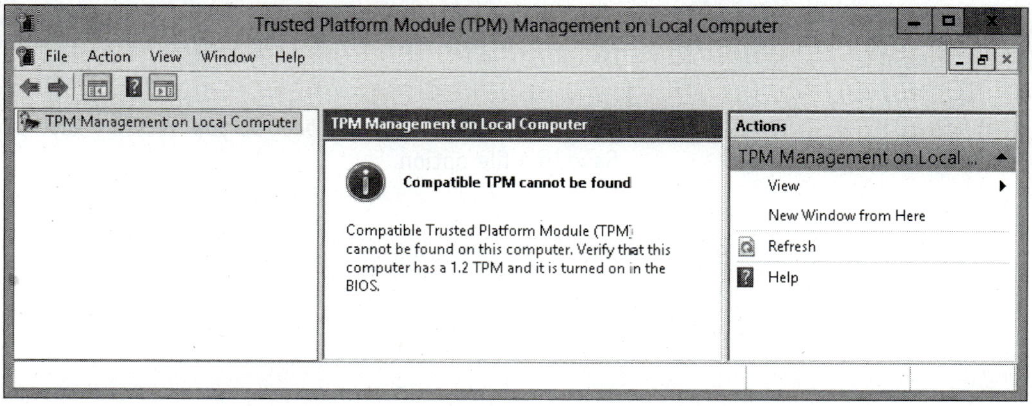

TURN ON BITLOCKER

GET READY. To turn on BitLocker on a computer running Windows Server 2012, perform the following steps:

1. Click the **Start** button, and then click the **Control Panel**.
2. Click **System and Security** and click **BitLocker Drive Encryption**. The *BitLocker Drive Encryption* window opens.
3. Click **Turn on BitLocker** for the volume that you want to encrypt. A *BitLocker Drive Encryption (X:)* window opens.

MORE INFORMATION

If your computer has a TPM chip, Windows provides a Trusted Platform Module (TPM) Management console that you can use to change the chip's password and modify its properties.

4. On the *Choose how you want to unlock this drive* page (see Figure 6-20), select the **Use a password to unlock the drive**. Type a password in the *Enter your password* and *Reenter your password* text boxes, and then click **Next**.

Figure 6-20

Using the *Choose how you want to unlock this drive* page

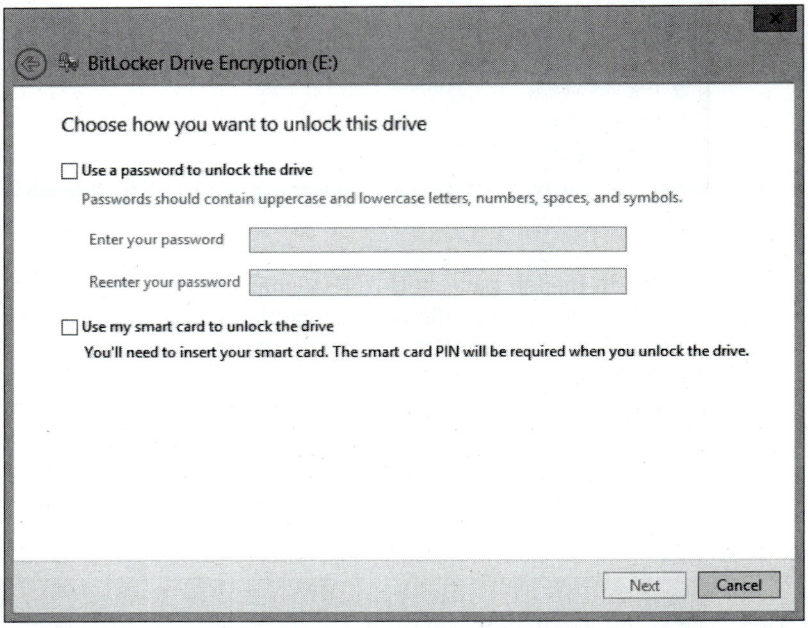

5. On the *How do you want to back up your recovery key?* page (see Figure 6-21), click **Save to a file** option.

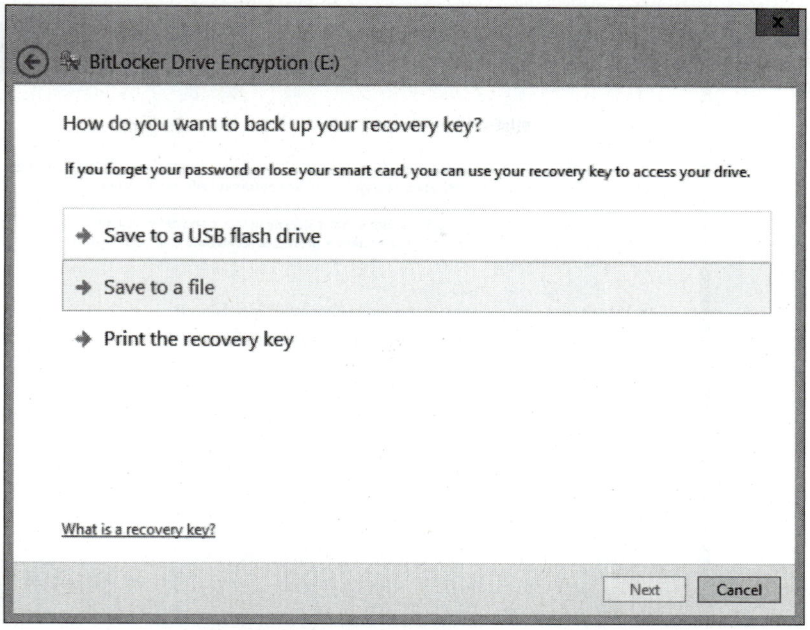

Figure 6-21

Using the *How do you want to back up your recovery key?* page

6. When the *Save BitLocker recovery key as* dialog box appears (see Figure 6-22), click Save.

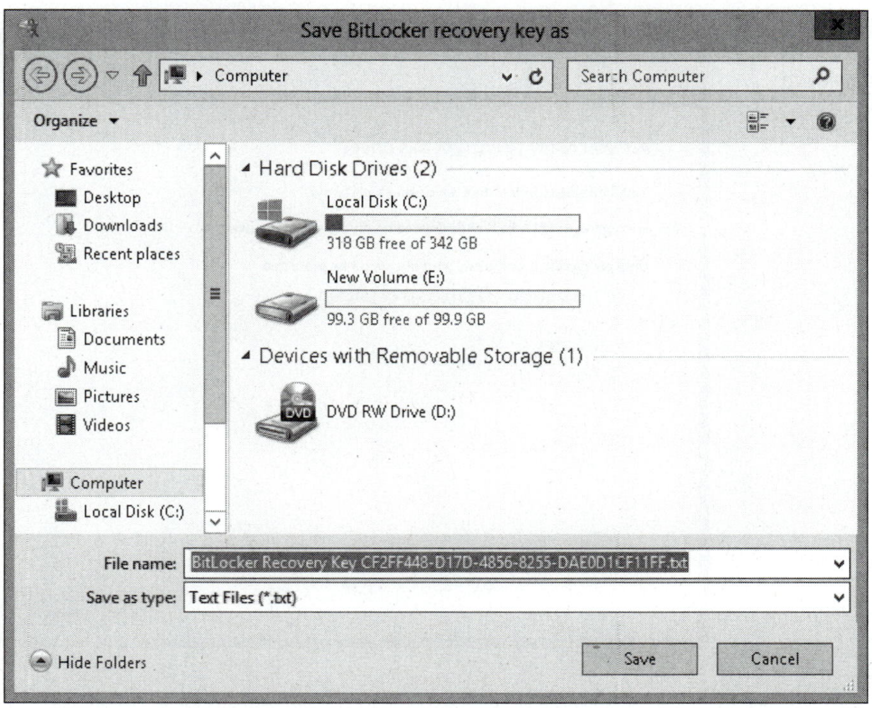

Figure 6-22

Using the *Save BitLocker recovery key as* dialog box

7. After the file is saved, make sure the key is stored in a safe place. Then click Next.
8. On the *Choose how much of your drive to encrypt* page (see Figure 6-23), select either Encrypt used disk space only or the Encrypt entire drive option, and then click Next.

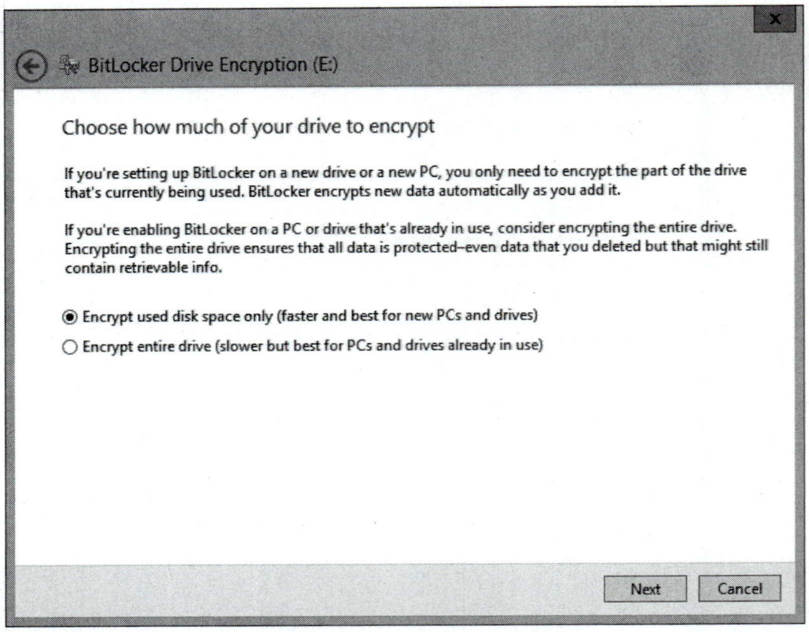

Figure 6-23

Using the *Choose how much of your drive to encrypt* page

9. On the *Are you ready to encrypt this drive?* page (see Figure 6-24), click Start encrypting.

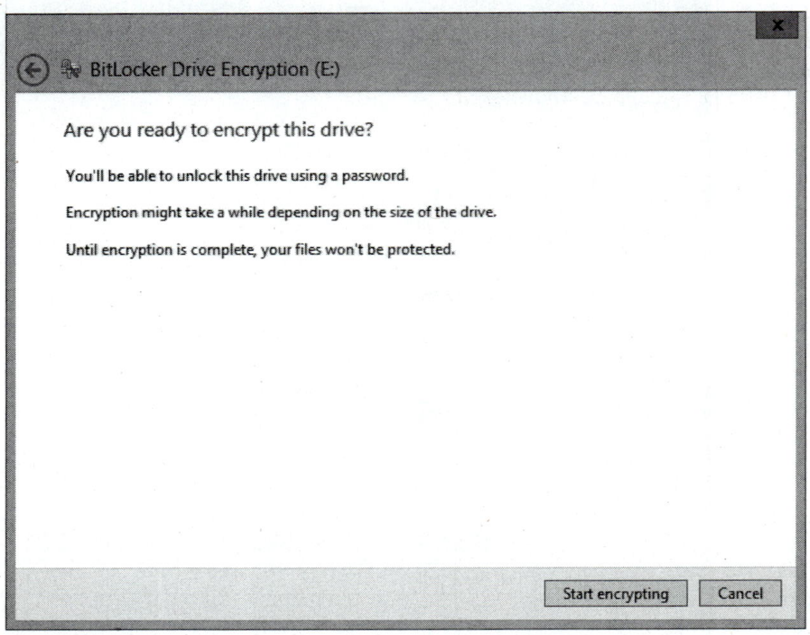

Figure 6-24

Using the *Are you ready to encrypt this drive?* page

10. When the drive is encrypted, click Close.

When the encryption process is complete, you can open the BitLocker Drive Encryption Control Panel to ensure that the volume is encrypted, or turn off BitLocker, such as when performing a BIOS upgrade or other system maintenance.

The BitLocker Control Panel applet enables you to recover the encryption key and recovery password at will. Figure 6-25 shows the following options available after you use BitLocker to encrypt a drive:

- Back up recovery key
- Change password
- Add smart card
- Turn off Bit Locker

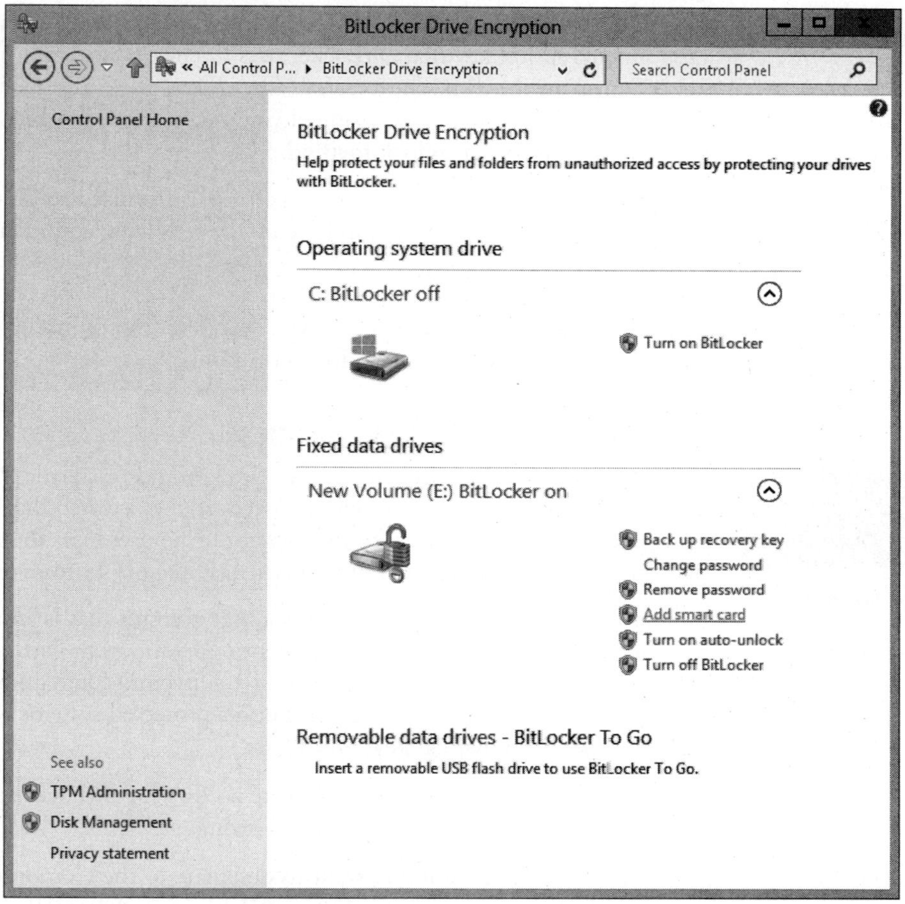

Figure 6-25

Showing the BitLocker applet options for a BitLocker-encrypted volume

You should consider carefully how to store this information, because it allows access to the encrypted data. It is also possible to escrow this information into Active Directory.

Standard users can change the password or PIN if they know the current PIN or password. By default, a user has five attempts to type in the current PIN or password. When this happens, the administrator has to reset the volume PIN or password, or the system needs to be rebooted. To make sure that password or pin is not too easy to guess, you can define how complex the password is using a group policy. To define the complexity, enable and configure the Configure use of passwords for fixed data drives settings found in Computer Configuration\Policies\Administrative Templates\Windows Components\BitLocker Drive Encryption\.

CONFIGURING BITLOCKER TO GO

BitLocker To Go is a new feature in Windows 7 and Windows Server 2008 R2 that enables users to encrypt removable USB devices, such as flash drives and external hard disks. While BitLocker has always supported the encryption of removable drives, BitLocker To Go enables you to use the encrypted device on other computers without having to perform an involved recovery process. Because the system is not using the removable drive as a boot device, a TPM chip is not required.

To use BitLocker To Go, insert the removable drive and open the BitLocker Drive Encryption Control Panel. The device appears in the interface with a *Turn on BitLocker* link just like that of the computer's hard disk drive.

BITLOCKER PRE-PROVISIONING

Starting with Windows 8, BitLocker supports ***pre-provisioning***, which allows BitLocker to be enabled before the operating is installed. During pre-provisioning, Windows generates a random encryption key that BitLocker uses to encrypt the volume. The random encryption key is stored on the disk, unprotected. After Windows is installed, users can fully protect the encryption key for the pre-provisioned volume by activating BitLocker on the volume and selecting the BitLocker unlock method.

To enable BitLocker pre-provisioning, you use customized a Windows Preinstallation Environment (WinPE) image and execute the following command:

```
Manage-bde -on x:
```

You need to protect the drive letter (x). After Windows is installed, the BitLocker status for the volume is BitLocker Waiting for Activation.

CONFIGURING BITLOCKER POLICIES

CERTIFICATION READY
Configure BitLocker policies.
Objective 2.3

If for some reason, the user loses the startup key and/or startup PIN needed to boot a system with BitLocker, the user can supply the recovery key created during the BitLocker configuration process and regain access to the system. If the user loses the recovery key, you can use a data recovery agent designated within Active Directory to recover the data on the drive.

Similar to EFS, a data recovery agent is a user account that is an administrator who is authorized to recover BitLocker drives for an entire organization with a digital certificate on a smart card. In most cases, administrators of Active Directory Domain Services (AD DS) networks use DRAs to ensure access to their BitLocker-protected systems while avoiding maintaining a large number of individual keys and PINs.

It is a little bit more complicated to create a DRA for BitLocker than it is for EFS. To create a DRA for BitLocker, you must do the following:

- Add the user account you want to designate to the Computer Configuration\Policies\Windows Settings\Security Settings\Public Key Policies\BitLocker Drive Encryption container in a GPO or to the system's Local Security Policy.
- Configure the Provide the unique identifiers for your organization policy setting in the Computer Configuration\Policies\Administrative Templates\Windows Components\BitLocker Drive Encryption container with unique identification fields for your BitLocker drives (see Figure 6-26).
- Enable DRA recovery for each type of BitLocker resource you want to recover (see Figure 6-27):
    - Choose how BitLocker-protected operating system drives can be recovered.
    - Choose how BitLocker-protected fixed drives can be recovered.
    - Choose how BitLocker-protected removable drives can be recovered.

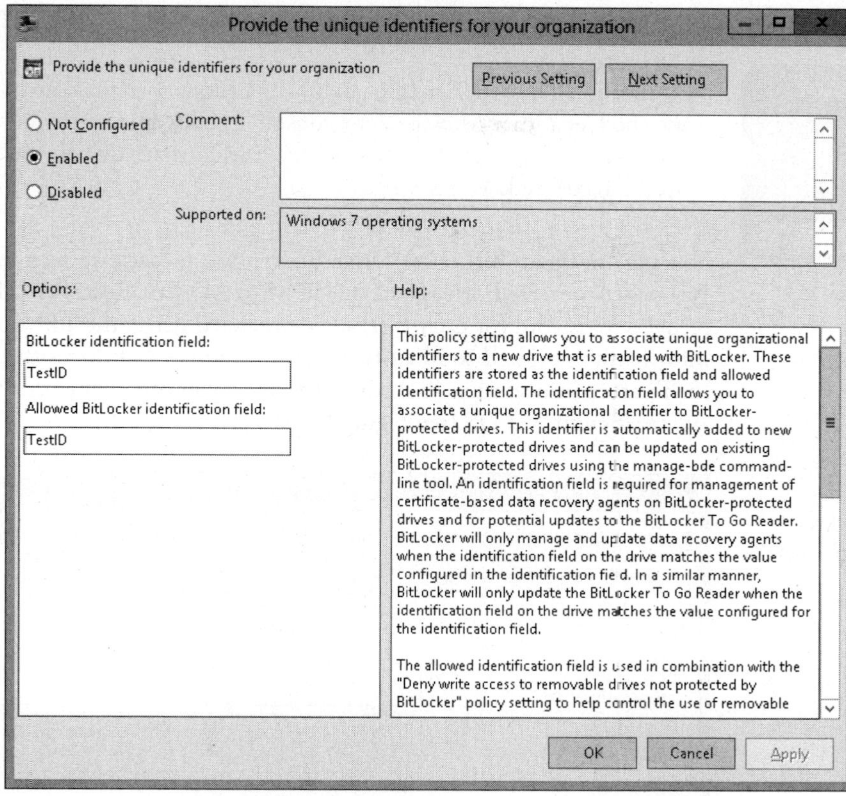

Figure 6-26

Configuring the *Provide the unique identifiers for your organization* policy setting

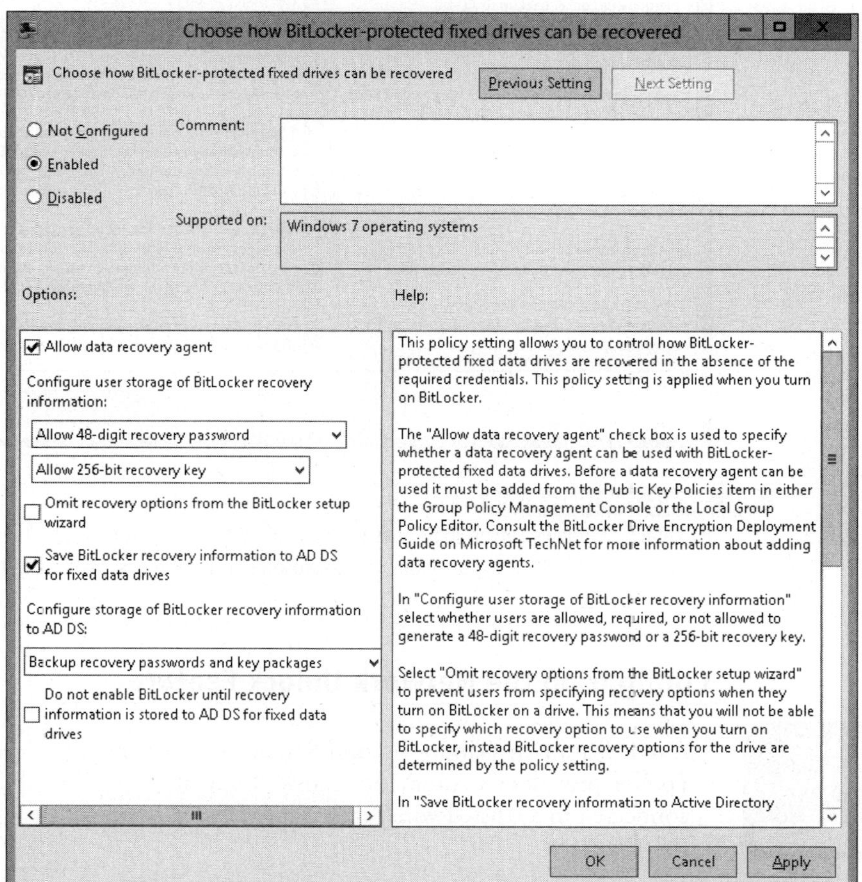

Figure 6-27

Configuring how BitLocker-protected fixed drives can be recovered

Managing BitLocker Certificates

CERTIFICATION READY
Manage EFS and BitLocker certificates including backup and restore.
Objective 2.3

Similar to EFS, you should back up the necessary digital certificates and keys. You can use the Certificate Management console to back up any digital certificates, such as DRA certificates. It has also been mentioned earlier that you can use the Control Panel to back up the recovery key.

You can configure BitLocker Drive Encryption to back up recovery information for BitLocker-protected drives and the TPM to AD DS. Recovery information includes the recovery password for each BitLocker-protected drive, the TPM owner password, and the information required to identify which computers and drives the recovery information applies to. To store information in Active Directory, you can enable the *Store BitLocker Recovery Information* in AD DS (see Figure 6-28).

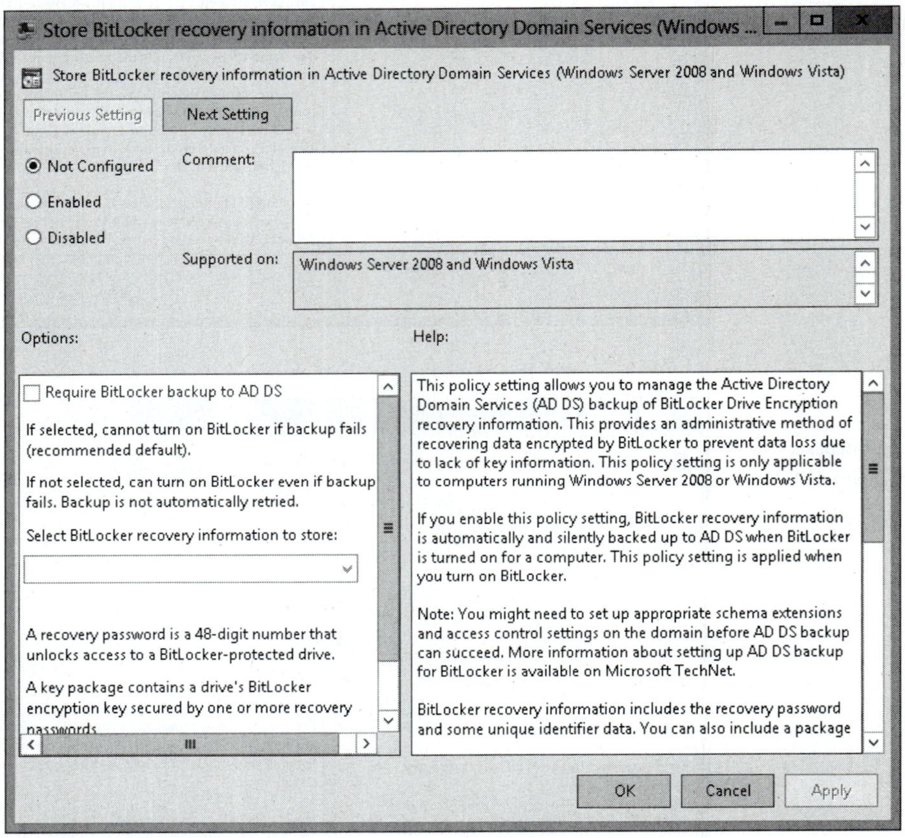

Figure 6-28
Enabling Store BitLocker Recovery Information in AD DS

MORE INFORMATION
By default, Windows Server 2012 does not have the BitLocker DRA template. Therefore, if you need information on creating the BitLocker DRA template, visit Microsoft's TechNet Blogs. Managing the CA is discussed in the MOAC 70-412 course.

Configuring the Network Unlock Feature

CERTIFICATION READY
Configure the Network Unlock feature.
Objective 2.3

A new feature in Windows 8 and Windows Server 2012 is Network Unlock. ***Network Unlock*** provides an automatic unlock of operating system volumes at system reboot when connected to a trusted wired corporate network.

The hardware and software requirements for Network Unlock include:

- Windows 8 installation on UEFI firmware with UEFI DHCP drivers
- BitLocker Network Unlock feature using Server Manager
- Windows Server 2012 Windows Deployment Services (WDS) role
- DHCP server, separate from the WDS server and the Domain Controller
- A Network Unlock certificate
- Network Unlock Group Policy settings configured (see Figure 6-29)

Figure 6-29

Configuring Network Unlock Group Policy settings

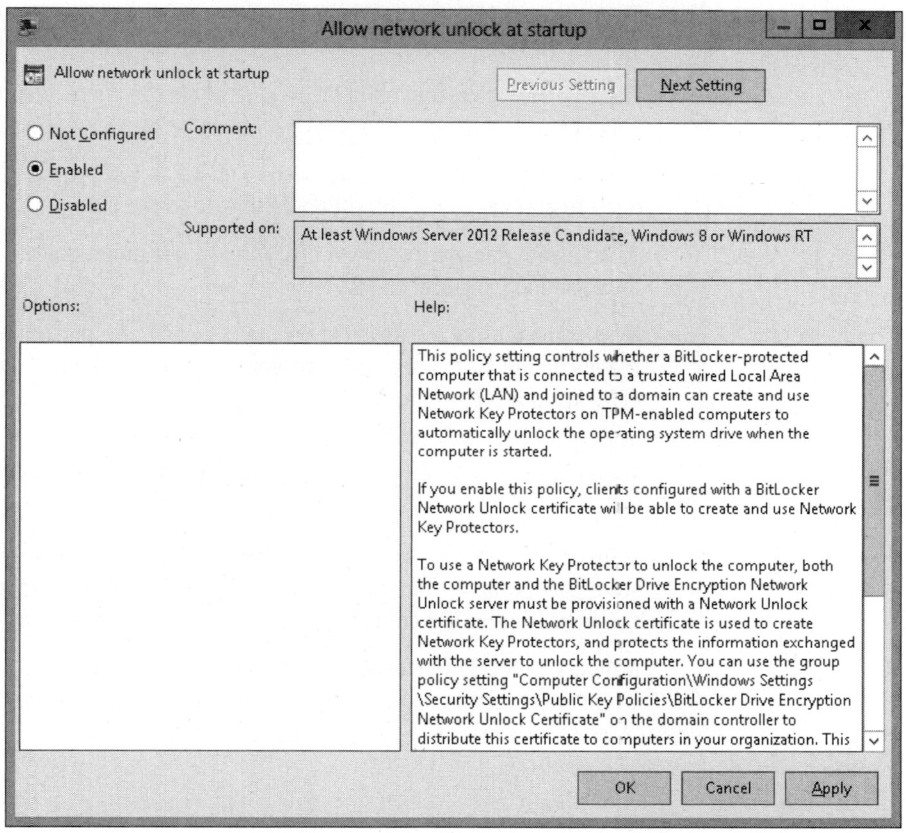

Network Unlock works similarly to the TPM plus startup key, but instead of reading a startup key from a USB device, Network Unlock uses an unlock key. The key is composed of a key that is stored on the machine's local TPM and a key that Network Unlock receives from Windows Deployment Services. If the WDS server is unavailable such as when you are not connected directly to the organization's network, BitLocker cannot communicate with a WDS server and instead displays the startup key unlock screen.

The client requires a DHCP driver implemented in the Unified Extensible Firmware interface. As the server boots, it gets the key from the WDS server using DHCP. BitLocker Network Unlock is installed on the server with WDS server role installed. To protect the keys being transferred over the network, the WDS server needs a special X.509 certificate that must be installed on all that clients that use Network Unlock.

SKILL SUMMARY

IN THIS LESSON, YOU LEARNED:

- Encryption is the process of converting data into a format that cannot be read by another user. Once a user has encrypted a file, it automatically remains encrypted when the file is stored on disk. Decryption is the process of converting data from encrypted format back to its original format.
- Encrypting File System (EFS) can encrypt files on an NTFS volume that cannot be used unless the user has access to the keys required to decrypt the information.
- To encrypt or decrypt a folder or file, you enable or disable the encryption attribute just as you set any other attribute, such as read-only, compressed, or hidden.
- The `cipher.exe` command displays or alters the encryption of folders and files on NTFS volumes.
- In later versions of NTFS, if you need to share an EFS-protected file with other users, you need to add the user's encryption certificate to the file.
- To help you manage the use of EFS, you can use group policies and to meet your organization's security needs.
- If for some reason, a person leaves the company or a person loses the original key, so that the encrypted files cannot be read, you can set up a data recovery agent (DRA) to recover EFS-encrypted files for a domain.
- BitLocker Drive Encryption (BDE) is the feature in Windows Vista, Windows 7, Windows Server 2008, Windows Server 2008 R2, and Windows Server 2012 that uses a computer's TPM.
- A Trusted Platform Module (TPM) is a microchip that is built into a computer. It is used to store cryptographic information, such as encryption keys. Information stored on the TPM can be more secure from external software attacks and physical theft.
- Network Unlock provides an automatic unlock of operating system volumes at system reboot when connected to a trusted wired corporate network.

Knowledge Assessment

Multiple Choice

Select the correct answer for each of the following questions.

1. Which encryption technology would you use to protect individual files on a computer running Windows Server 2012?
   a. EFS
   b. BitLocker
   c. IPSec
   d. SSL
2. When using EFS, the encryption key is stored in which of the following?
   a. Text file
   b. Passkey
   c. Digital certificate
   d. Token

3. What happens when you move an EFS-encrypted file to a FAT32 volume?
   a. It remains encrypted.
   b. It is re-encrypted.
   c. It is decrypted.
   d. You have the option to decrypt or encrypt.
4. Which encryption algorithm uses a single key to encrypt and decrypt data?
   a. Symmetric
   b. Asymmetric
   c. Hash function
   d. Antimetric
5. How do you define the DRAs?
   a. Registry
   b. Active Directory Users and Computers
   c. GPOs
   d. Active Directory Sites and Services
6. How do you decrypt an EFS-encrypted file for a person who has left an organization?
   a. Create the master certificate to encrypt the certificate, and then decrypt the certificate.
   b. Use a USB with the username and username password in a text file.
   c. Remove the computer with the files from the domain.
   d. Use a DRA.
7. If you don't have a TPM on your computer, what can you use to store the key to use BitLocker?
   a. A text file on a CD or DVD
   b. A second hard drive
   c. The BIOS Setup program
   d. USB memory device
8. Which Windows technology is used to encrypt a USB disk device?
   a. BitLocker
   b. BitLocker To Go
   c. EFS
   d. SSL
9. Which command do you use to encrypt a folder with EFS?
   a. Use the `EFS` command.
   b. Use the `Cipher` command.
   c. Use the `Encrypt` command
   d. Use the `EFSConfig` command
10. How do you configure Windows to automatically encrypt a user's Documents folder?
    a. Use the Control Panel.
    b. Use the `Cipher` command.
    c. Use group policies.
    d. Use the Security tab in Windows Explorer.

Best Answer

Choose the letter that corresponds to the best answer. More than one answer choice may achieve the goal. Select the BEST answer.

1. Which of the following should you use to protect a drive and all of its files if it is stolen?
   a. EFS
   b. BitLocker
   c. IPSec
   d. SSL

2. How can you control the key size used in EFS?
   a. Use the `cipher` command.
   b. Use a GPO.
   c. Use a certificate.
   d. Use a DRA.

3. To automatically unlock a drive protected by BitLocker, which server would the client get a key from?
   a. WDS server
   b. DHCP server
   c. BitLocker Web server
   d. Any server with a BitLocker encrypted drive

4. What happens if you have an EFS-encrypted file and you copy the file to a folder that is not encrypted and on an NTFS volume?
   a. File automatically becomes decrypted.
   b. File remains encrypted.
   c. File remains encrypted if it is locked.
   d. File becomes decrypted if it has the System attribute turned on.

5. Which server do you install the BitLocker Network Unlock feature on?
   a. WDS Server
   b. DHCP server
   c. BitLocker Web server
   d. DNS Server

Matching and Identification

1. Identify the requirements to use Network Unlock.
   _____ DHCP Server, separate from WDS and DC
   _____ BitLocker Network Unlock feature
   _____ DNS Server with Unlock Service resource record
   _____ Network Unlock certificates
   _____ Windows Server 2012 WDS role
   _____ Windows 8 Network Unlock Agent

2. Identify the encryption method (symmetric, asymmetric, and hash function) for the following.
   _____ a) Uses one key to encrypt and another key to decrypt
   _____ b) SSL
   _____ c) A one-way encryption that cannot be decrypted
   _____ d) Uses a single key to encrypt and decrypt
   _____ e) EFS

Build a List

1. Identify the steps, in order, to encrypt a file using EFS. Not all of the steps will be used.
   _____ Open the File menu and select Encryption.
   _____ Click OK.
   _____ Right-click the files and click Properties.
   _____ Select Encrypts contents to secure data.
   _____ Select Encrypt using EFS.
   _____ Click the Advanced tab.
   _____ Click the Protect tab.

2. Identify the steps, in order, to back up the EFS certificates. Not all of the steps will be used.
   _____ Expand Personal and click Certificates.
   _____ Expand Certificates, and expand EFS.
   _____ Open certmgr.msc.
   _____ Right-click the EFS certificate and click Export.
   _____ Right-click the EFS certificate and click Backup.
   _____ Specify the cer format.
   _____ Specify the pfx format.
   _____ Select to export the private key.
   _____ Specify the location.
   _____ Specify the password.

3. Identify the steps, in order, to protect a drive with BitLocker. Not all of the steps will be used.
   _____ Save recovery key to USB device.
   _____ Click System and Security.
   _____ Click Turn on BitLocker.
   _____ Click Encryption.
   _____ Specify a password.
   _____ Open Control Panel.
   _____ Encrypt the drive.
   _____ Test the drive.
   _____ Click BitLocker Drive Encryption.

Business Case Scenarios

Scenario 6-1: Protecting the Laptop Computer

You have just purchased 75 new laptops that will be given to the sales team and 50 new laptops that will be given to the engineering team. Last year, a person from the marketing department left her computer at the hotel, which had details about upcoming products. This information was leaked to the Internet. What can you do to make sure that if this happens again, the information is still safe?

Scenario 6-2: Accessing EFS-Encrypted Files

You have a user who encrypts many of his data files with EFS. So his manager tries to open the files but cannot read the files because the user does not have the correct key. What can you do to unlock these files?

7 LESSON

Configuring Advanced Audit Policies

70-411 EXAM OBJECTIVE

Objective 2.4 – Configure advanced audit policies. This objective may include but is not limited to: implement auditing using Group Policy and AuditPol.exe; create expression-based audit policies; create removable device audit policies.

LESSON HEADING	EXAM OBJECTIVE
Enabling and Configuring Auditing	
Implementing Auditing Using Group Policies	Implement auditing using Group Policy and AuditPol.exe
Implementing Advanced Audit Policy Settings	Configure advanced audit policies
Implementing Auditing Using AuditPol.exe	Implement auditing using Group Policy and AuditPol.exe
Viewing Audit Events	
Creating Expression-Based Audit Policies	Create expression-based audit policies
Creating Removable Device Audit Policies	Create removable device audit policies

KEY TERMS

auditing
advanced audit policy settings
AuditPol.exe
Global Object Access Auditing
Removable Storage Access policy

■ Enabling and Configuring Auditing

THE BOTTOM LINE

Security can be divided into three areas. Authentication is used to prove the identity of a user. Authorization gives access to the user who was authenticated. To complete the security picture, you need to enable ***auditing*** so that you can have a record of the users who have logged in, what the users accessed or tried to access, and what action the users performed such as rebooting, shutting down a computer, or accessing a file.

It is important that you protect your information and service resources from people who should not have access to them, and at the same time, it's important you make those resources available to authorized users. Along with authentication and authorization, you need to enable auditing so that you can have a record of the following:

- Who has successfully logged in
- Who has attempted to log in but failed
- Who has made changes to accounts in Active Directory
- Who has accessed or changed certain files
- Who has used a certain printer
- Who restarted a system
- Who has made system changes

Using auditing logs enables you to determine whether any security breaches have occurred and to what extent.

Implementing Auditing Using Group Policies

CERTIFICATION READY
Implement auditing using Group Policy and AuditPol.exe.
Objective 2.4

To enable auditing, you specify what types of system events to audit using Group Policy or the local security policy (Computer Settings\Policies\Security Settings\Local Policies\Audit Policy).

Table 7-1 shows the basic events to audit that are available in Windows Server 2008, Windows Server 2008 R2, and Windows Server 2012. After you enable logging, you then open the Event Viewer security logs to view the security events. As you can see, most major Active Directory events are already audited, although there is not a group policy that includes these settings.

Table 7-1
Audit Events

Event	Explanation	Default Settings Defined for Domain Controllers
Account logon	Determines whether the operating system (OS) audits each time the computer validates an account's credentials, such as account logon. Account logon events are generated when a domain user account is authenticated on a domain controller.	Successful account logons
Account management	Determines whether to audit each event of account management on a computer, including changing passwords and creating or deleting user accounts.	Successful account management activities
Directory service access	Determines whether the OS audits user attempts to access Active Directory objects, the previous change value, and the new assigned value.	
Logon	Determines where the OS audits each instance of a user attempting to log on to or log off his or her computer. Logon events are generated when a domain user interactively logs on to a domain controller or a network logon to a domain controller is performed to retrieve logon scripts and policies.	Successful logons
Object access	Determines whether the OS audits user attempts to access non-Active Directory objects including NT File System (NTFS) files, folders, and printers.	

(continued)

Table 7-1
(continued)

Event	Explanation	Default Settings Defined for Domain Controllers
Policy change	Determines whether the OS audits each instance of an attempt to change user rights assignments, auditing policies, account policies, or trust policies.	Successful policy changes
Privilege use	Determines whether to audit each instance of a user exercising a user right.	
Process tracking	Determines whether the OS audits process-related events, such as process creation, process termination, handle duplication, and indirect object access. This is usually used for troubleshooting, because enabling the auditing of process tracking can affect performance.	
System	Determines whether the OS audits if the system time is changed, if the system is started or shut down, if there is an attempt to load extensible authentication components, if there is a loss of auditing events due to auditing system failure, and if the security log exceeds a configurable warning threshold level.	Successful system events

Although it is easy to enable auditing for everything, it is usually not a good idea. Any time that you enable auditing, you need to select only what you need because of the following reasons:

- High levels of auditing can affect the performance of the computer that you audit.
- When you search through the security logs, you will find far too many events, which can make it more difficult for you to find the potential problems you need to find.
- The logs quickly fill up, replacing older events with newer events.

Most audit settings require you to enable only specific audit settings. However, object auditing is a little bit more complex. After you enable object access auditing, you have to enable auditing on the specific object that you want to enable. These objects include registry objects, files, folders, and printers.

When you enable object auditing, you generate many other events that also get recorded including Audit Filtering Platform Connection and Audit Filtering Platform Packet Drop, which shows packets that get connected or dropped at the Transmission Control Protocol (TCP) and User Datagram Protocol (UDP) level. To cut these packets, you can use the advanced audit policy Configuration for Object Access or the `AuditPol.exe` command not to record these events. Advanced audit policy configuration and `AuditPol` are discussed in the following section.

IMPLEMENTING AN AUDIT POLICY

AUDIT ACCOUNT LOGON

GET READY. To audit account logon successes and failures, perform the following steps:

1. Open Server Manager.
2. Click Tools > Group Policy Management to open the *Group Policy Management console*.
3. Expand the Domain Controllers to show the *Default Domain Controllers Policy*. Then right-click the Default Domain Control Default Policy and click Edit. *Group Policy Management Editor* appears.

4. Expand Computer Configuration, Windows Settings, Security Settings, Local Policies, and select Audit Policy (see Figure 7-1).

Figure 7-1

Enabling auditing using group policies

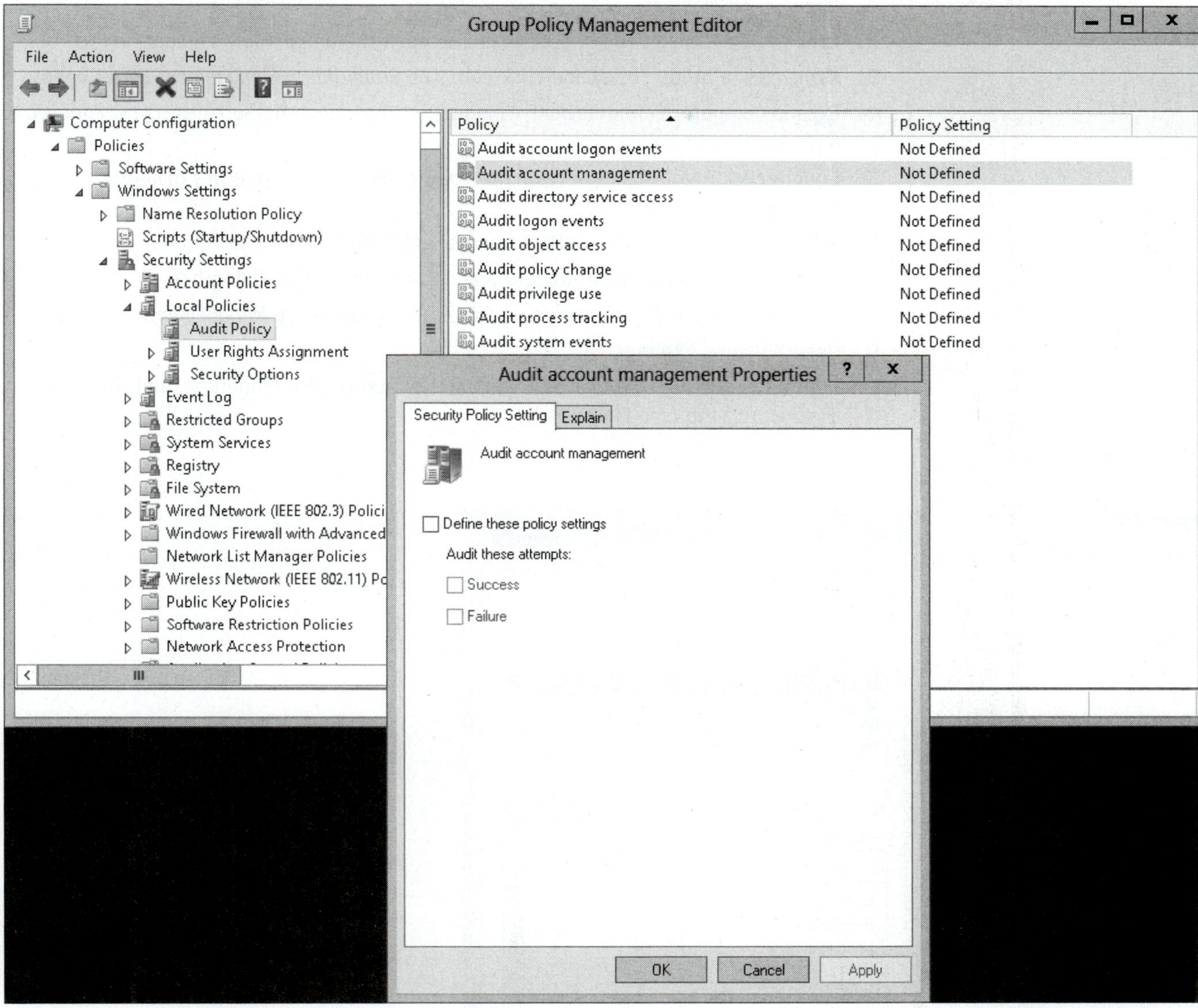

5. Double-click Audit account logon events. The *Audit account logon events Properties* dialog box opens.
6. Select Define these policy settings and select both Success and Failure.
7. Click OK to close the *Audit account logon events Properties* dialog box.

IMPLEMENTING OBJECT ACCESS AUDITING USING GROUP POLICIES

Auditing NTFS files, NTFS folders, and printers is a two-step process. You must first enable object access using Group Policy. Then you must specify which objects you want to audit.

TAKE NOTE*

You should not audit every file and folder on a computer. Auditing every file and folder can dramatically affect the performance of the computer.

AUDIT FILES AND FOLDERS

GET READY. To audit files and folders, perform the following steps:

1. Open Server Manager.
2. Click Tools > Group Policy Management to open the *Group Policy Management console*.
3. Right-click a group policy and click Edit. The *Group Policy Management Editor* opens.
4. Expand Computer Configuration, Windows Settings, Security Settings, Local Policies, and select Audit Policy.
5. Double-click Audit object access. The *Audit object access Properties* dialog box appears.
6. Select Define these policy settings and select both Success and Failure.
7. Click OK to close the *Audit account logon events Properties* dialog box.
8. Close the *Group Policy Management Editor* and *Group Policy Management*.
9. Open Windows Explorer.
10. Right-click the file or folder that you want to audit, click Properties, and then click the Security tab (see Figure 7-2).

Figure 7-2

Viewing the Security tab

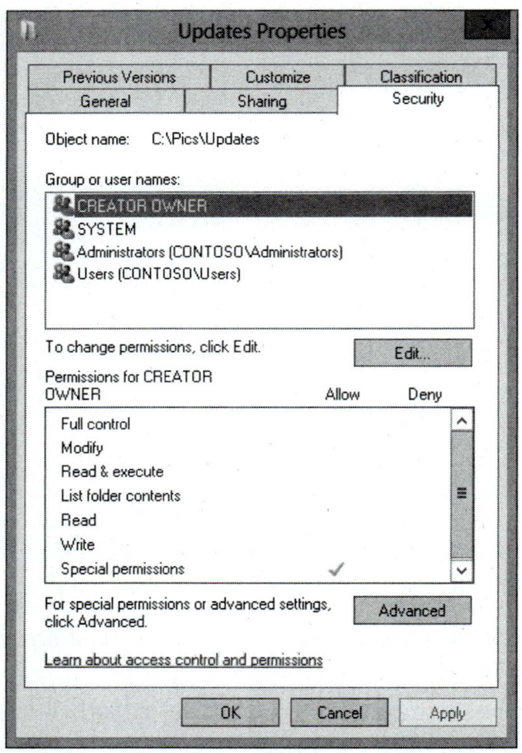

11. Click the Advanced button. The *Advanced Security Settings for Updates* dialog box opens (see Figure 7-3).

Figure 7-3

Opening the *Advanced Security Settings for Updates* dialog box

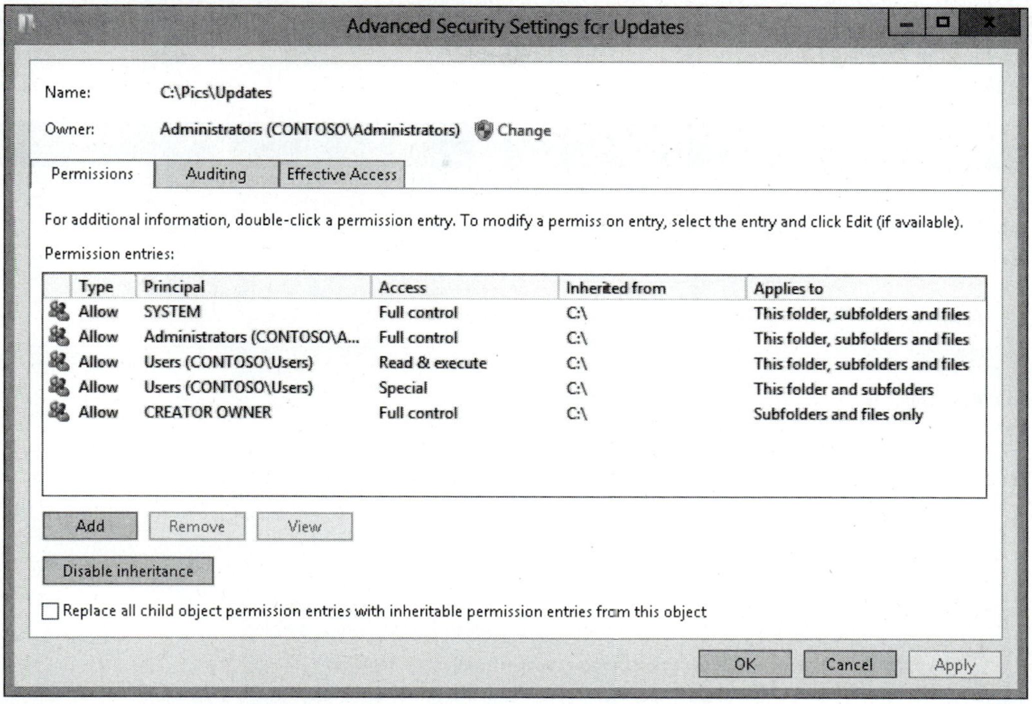

12. In the *Advanced Security Settings for Updates* dialog box, click the Auditing tab (see Figure 7-4).

Figure 7-4

Using the Auditing tab

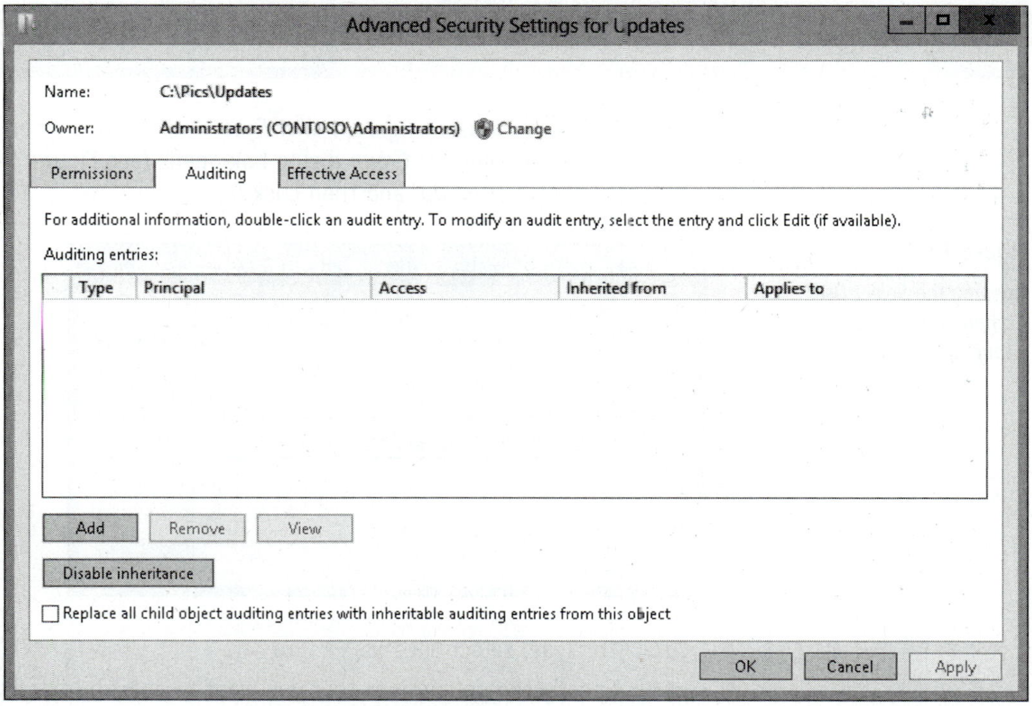

13. To add an auditing entry, click Add. The *Auditing Entry for Updates* dialog box opens (see Figure 7-5).

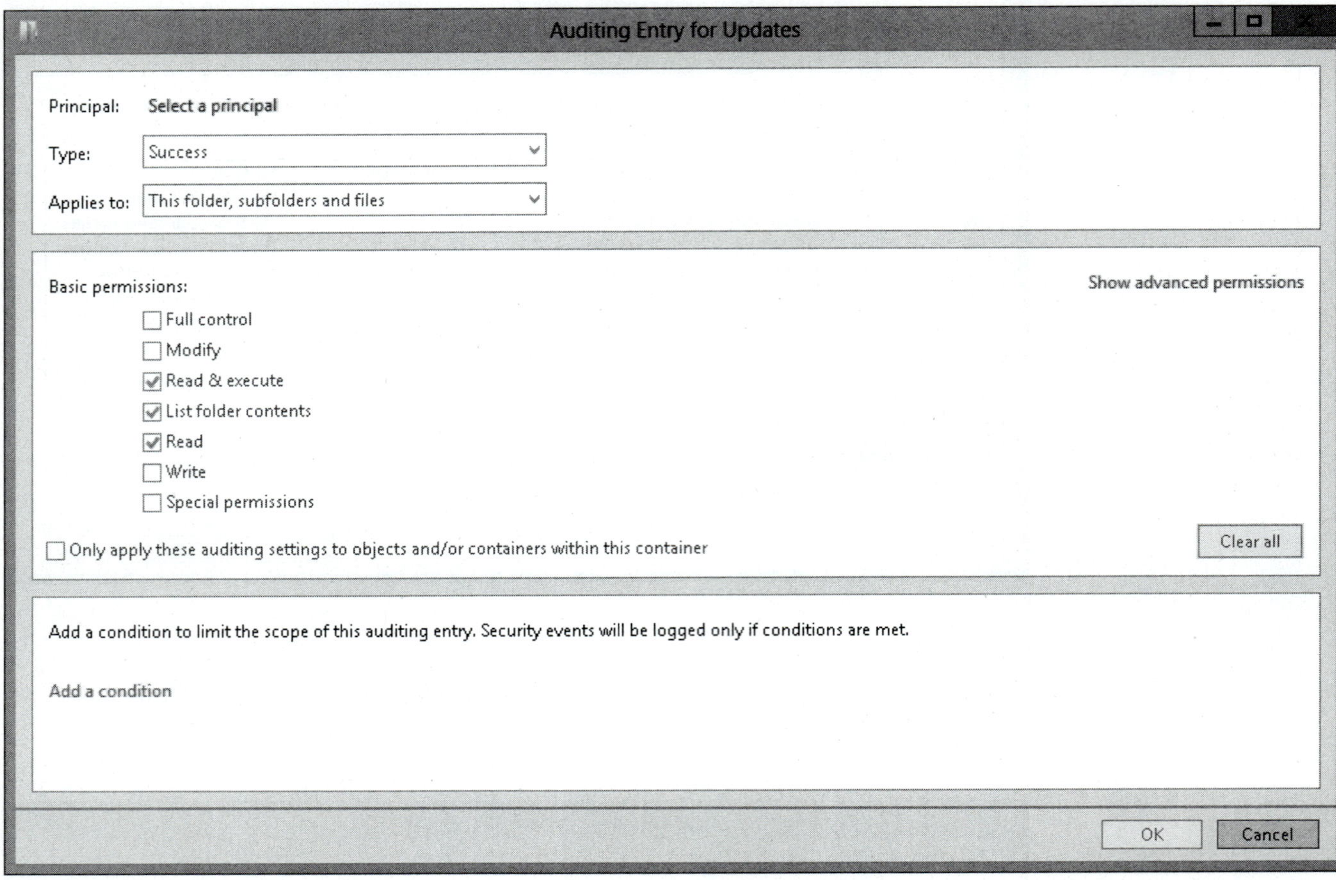

Figure 7-5

Opening the *Auditing Entry for Updates* dialog box

14. To specify a user or group, click Select a principal. When the *Select User, Computer, Service Account, or Group* dialog box opens (see Figure 7-6), type a name for a *username* or *group*, and then click OK.

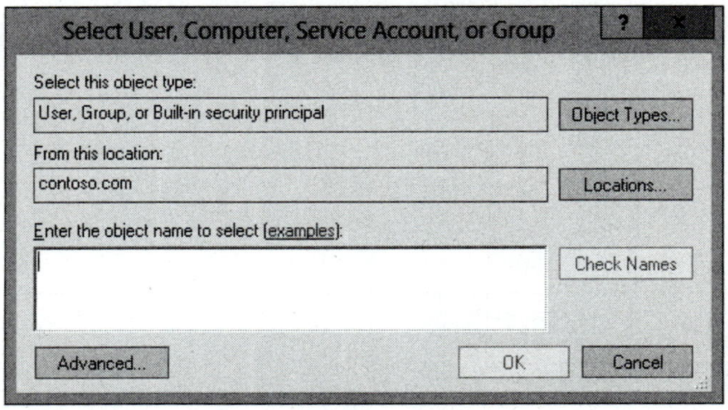

Figure 7-6

Opening the *Select User, Computer, Service Account, or Group* dialog box

15. For *Type*, select Success, Fail, or All.
16. Specify the permissions that you want to audit by selecting or deselecting the appropriate permission.
17. Click OK to close the *Auditing Entry for Updates* dialog box.
18. Click OK to close the *Advanced Security Settings for Updates* dialog box.
19. Click OK to close the *Properties* dialog box.

AUDIT PRINTER EVENTS

GET READY. To audit printer events, make sure the audit object access is enabled. Then, perform the following steps:

1. Open the Control Panel and click View devices and printers.
2. Right-click a printer and select Printer properties.
3. Select the Security tab (see Figure 7-7).

Figure 7-7

Selecting the Security tab in the Printer Properties dialog box

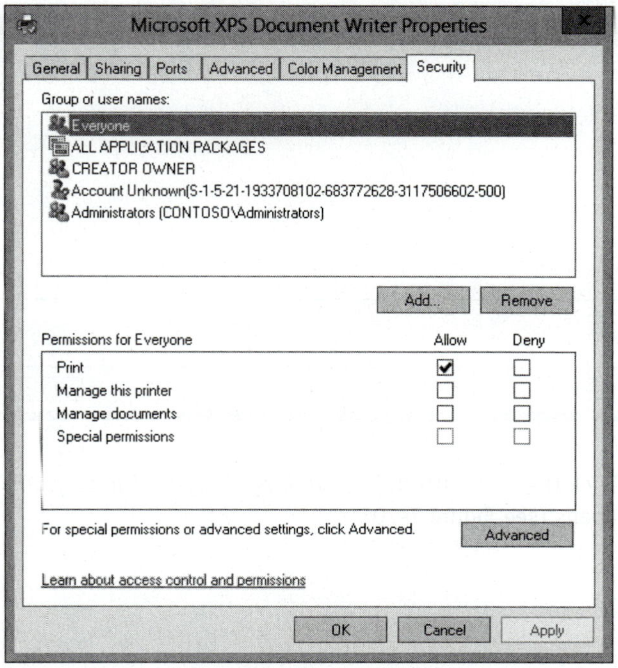

4. On the *Security* tab, click Advanced. The *Advanced Security Settings for Microsoft XPS Document Writer* dialog box opens (see Figure 7-8).

Figure 7-8

Opening the Advanced Security Settings for Microsoft XPS Document Writer dialog box

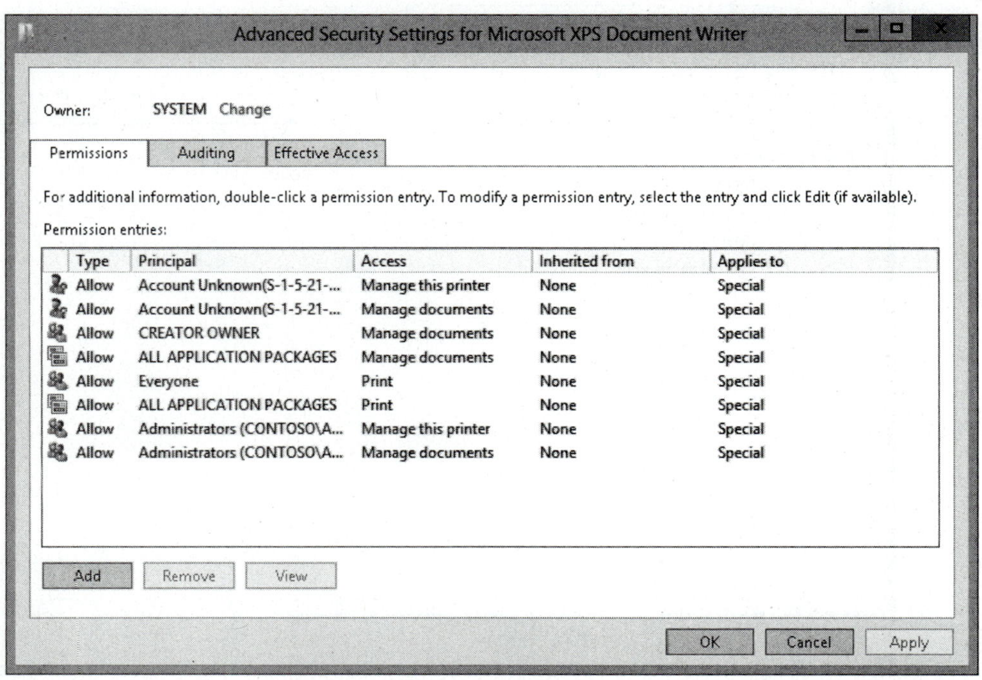

5. Select the Auditing tab (see Figure 7-9).

Figure 7-9

Selecting the Auditing tab

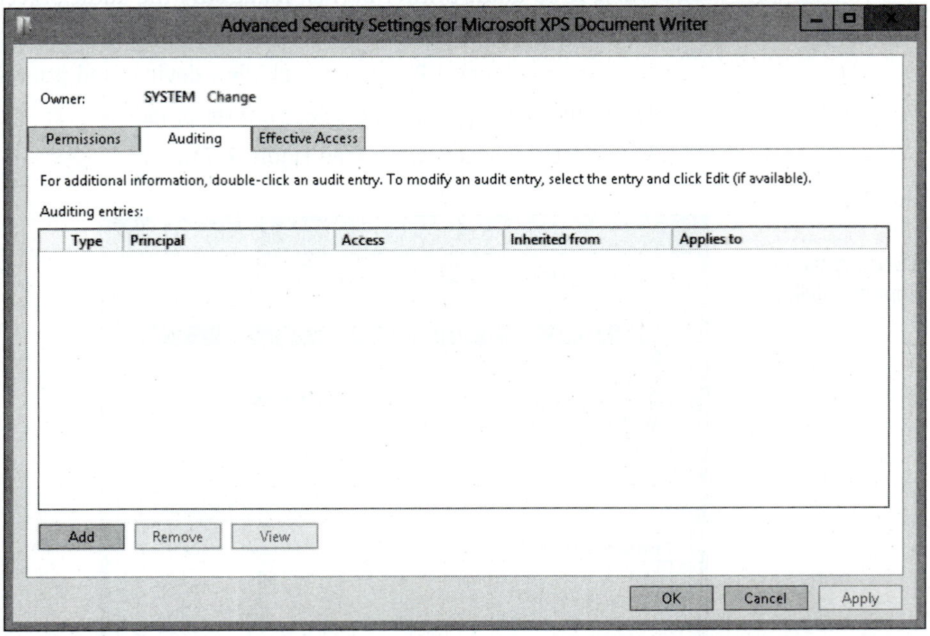

6. Click the Add button. The *Auditing Entry for Microsoft XPS Document Writer* dialog box opens (see Figure 7-10).

Figure 7-10

Opening the Auditing Entry for Microsoft XPS Document Writer dialog box

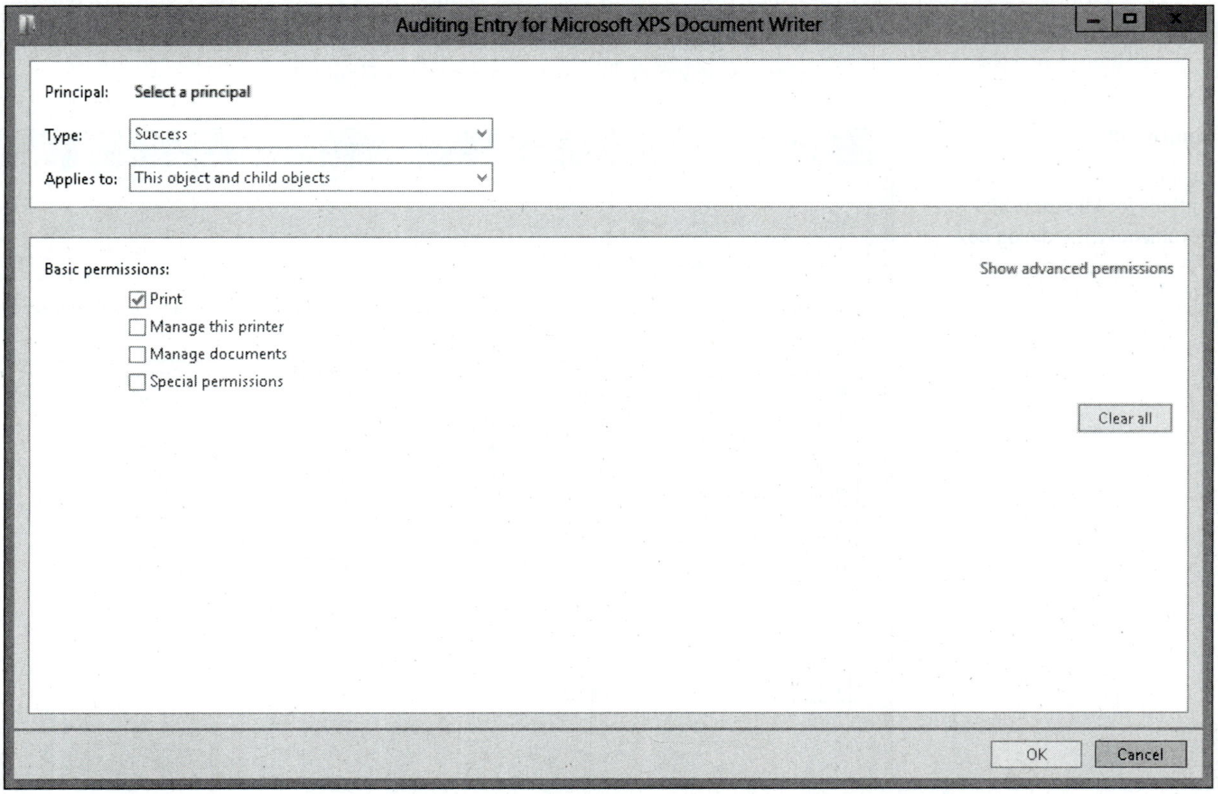

7. To specify a user or group, click Select a principal. When the *Select User, Computer, Service Account, or Group* dialog box opens, type a name for a *username* or *group*, and then click OK.
8. For Type, select Success, Fail, or All.
9. Specify the permissions that you want to audit by selecting or deselecting the appropriate permission.
10. Click OK to close the *Auditing Entry for Microsoft XPS Document Writer* dialog box.
11. Click OK to close the *Advanced Security Settings for Microsoft XPS Document Writer* dialog box.
12. Click OK to close the *Properties* dialog box.

By default, when a group policy is applied to an Active Directory domain or OU, the group policy is inherited by all OUs at the lower levels. However, inherited policy can be overridden by a Group Policy Object (GPO) that is linked at a lower level.

Implementing Advanced Audit Policy Settings

Starting with Windows Server 2008 R2, Windows introduced ***advanced audit policy settings***, which enable you to have more control over what events get recorded by using multiple subsettings instead of the traditional nine basic audit settings. Windows Server 2008 R2 introduced 53 subsettings. Windows Server 2012 has 56 subsettings. As result of using advanced audit policy settings, you cut down the number of log entries, so that you can focus on what is important to you.

CERTIFICATION READY
Configure advanced audit policies.
Objective 2.4

IMPLEMENTING ADVANCED AUDIT POLICY SETTINGS USING GROUP POLICIES

To access a new policy, open Group Policy Editor for a group policy and go to Configuration\Policies\Windows Settings\Security Settings\Advanced Audit Policy Configuration (see Figure 7-11). Tables 7-2 through 7-10 show the nine primary groups with the subsettings and common events generated by the subsettings.

Figure 7-11

Accessing Advanced Audit Policy

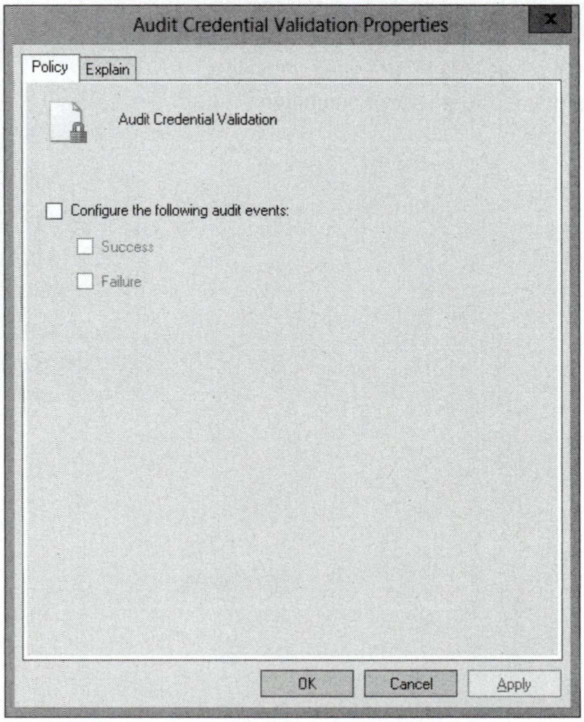

Table 7-2

Account Logon

SETTING	DESCRIPTION	COMMON EVENTS:
Audit Credential Validation	Generates audit events on credentials submitted for a user account logon request. Events show on the domain controller for domain accounts and on the local computer for local accounts. Note: Event volume: High on domain controllers	4774: An account was mapped for logon. 4775: An account could not be mapped for logon. 4776: The domain controller attempted to validate the credentials for an account. 4777: The domain controller failed to validate the credentials for an account.
Audit Kerberos Authentication Service	Generates audit events for Kerberos authentication ticket-granting ticket (TGT) requests. Note: Event volume: High on Kerberos Key Distribution Center (KDC) servers	4768: A Kerberos authentication ticket (TGT) was requested. 4771: Kerberos pre-authentication failed. 4772: A Kerberos authentication ticket request failed.
Audit Kerberos Service Ticket Operations	Generates security audit events for Kerberos service ticket requests. Note: Event volume: High on a domain controller that is a Key Distribution Center	4769: A Kerberos service ticket was requested. 4770: A Kerberos service ticket was renewed.
Audit Other Account Logon Events	Generated by responses to credential requests submitted for a user account logon that are not credential validation or Kerberos tickets when working with Remote Desktop session, locking and unlocking a workstation, working with a screen saver, and accessing a wireless network granted to a user or computer account.	4649: A replay attack was detected. 4778: A session was reconnected to a Window station. 4779: A session was disconnected from a Window Station. 4800: The workstation was locked. 4801: The workstation was unlocked. 4802: The screen saver was invoked. 4803: The screen saver was dismissed. 5632: A request was made to authenticate to a wireless network. 5633: A request was made to authenticate to a wired network.

Table 7-3

Account Management

SETTING	DESCRIPTION	COMMON EVENTS:
Audit Application Group Management	Generates audit events when application group management tasks are performed, such as when an application group is created, changed, or deleted, or a member is added to or removed from an application group.	4783: A basic application group was created. 4784: A basic application group was changed. 4790: An LDAP query group was created.
Audit Computer Account Management	Generates audit events when a domain computer account is created, changed, or deleted.	4741: A computer account was created. 4742: A computer account was changed. 4743: A computer account was deleted.
Audit Distribution Group Management	Generates audit events when a distribution group is created, changed, deleted, or when a member is added to or removed from a distribution group.	4744: A local distribution group was created. 4746: A member was added to a local distribution group. 4747: A member was removed from a local distribution group. 4748: A local distribution group was deleted. 4749: A global distribution group was created. 4750: A global distribution group was changed. 4751: A member was added to a global distribution group. 4752: A member was removed from a global distribution group. 4753: A global distribution group was deleted. 4759: A universal distribution group was created. 4760: A security-disabled universal group was changed. 4761: A member was added to a universal distribution group. 4762: A member was removed from a universal distribution group.
Audit Other Account Management Events	Generates user account management audit events when the password hash of an account is accessed, when the Password Policy Checking application programming interface (API) is called or when changes are made to the domain password policy or domain account lockout policy.	4782: The password hash for an account was accessed. 4793: The Password Policy Checking API was called.

(continued)

Table 7-3

(continued)

Setting	Description	Common Events:
Audit Security Group Management	Generates audit events when a security group is created, changed, or deleted, a member is added to or removed from a security group, or a group's type is changed.	4727: A global security group was created. 4728: A member was added to a global security group. 4729: A member was removed from a global security group. 4730: A global security group was deleted. 4731: A local security group was created. 4732: A member was added to a local security group. 4733: A member was removed from a local security group. 4734: A local security group was deleted. 4735: A local security group was changed. 4737: A global security group was changed. 4754: A universal security group was created. 4755: A universal security group was changed. 4756: A member was added to a security-enabled universal group. 4757: A member was removed from a universal security group. 4758: A security-enabled universal group was deleted. 4764: A group's type was changed.
Audit User Account Management	Generates audit events when the following user account management tasks are performed: A user account is created, changed, deleted, renamed, disabled, enabled, locked out, or unlocked. A user account password is set or changed. Security identifier (SID) history is added to a user account. The Directory Services Restore Mode password is set. Permissions on accounts that are members of Administrators groups are changed. Credential Manager credentials are backed up or restored.	4720: A user account was created. 4722: A user account was enabled. 4723: An attempt was made to change an account's password. 4725: A user account was disabled. 4726: A user account was deleted. 4738: A user account was changed. 4740: A user account was locked out. 4767: A user account was unlocked. 4780: The ACL was set on accounts that are members of Administrators groups. 4781: The name of an account was changed.

Table 7-4

Detailed Tracking

SETTING	DESCRIPTION	COMMON EVENTS:
Audit DPAPI Activity	Generates audit events when encryption or decryption calls are made into the data protection application interface (DPAPI), which is used to protect secret information such as stored passwords and key information.	4692: Backup of data protection master key was attempted. 4693: Recovery of data protection master key was attempted. 4694: Protection of auditable protected data was attempted. 4695: Unprotection of auditable protected data was attempted.
Audit Process Creation	Generates audit events when a process is created (starts) and the name of the program or user that created it.	4688: A new process has been created. 4696: A primary token was assigned to a process.
Audit Process Termination	Generates audit events when an attempt is made to end a process.	4689: A process has exited.
Audit RPC Events	Generates audit events when inbound remote procedure call (RPC) connections are made.	5712: A remote procedure call (RPC) was attempted.

Table 7-5

DS Access

SETTING	DESCRIPTION	COMMON EVENTS:
Audit Detailed Directory Service Replication	Generates security audit events with detailed tracking information about the data that is replicated between domain controllers. Note: Event volume: These events can create a very high volume of event data.	4928: An Active Directory replica source naming context was established. 4929: An Active Directory replica source naming context was removed. 4934: Attributes of an Active Directory object were replicated. 4935: Replication failure begins. 4937: A lingering object was removed from a replica.
Audit Directory Service Access	Generates events when an Active Directory Domain Services (AD DS) object is accessed for those objects that have configured system access control lists (SACLs) in the method specified. Note: Audit events are generated only on objects with configured SACLs and only when they are accessed in a manner that matches the SACL settings.	4662: An operation was performed on an object.

(continued)

Table 7-5

(continued)

Setting	Description	Common Events:
Audit Directory Service Changes	Generates audit events when changes are made to objects in Active Directory Domain Services (AD DS) including when objects are created, deleted, modified, moved, or undeleted. Note: Directory Service Changes auditing, where appropriate, indicates the old and new values of the changed properties of the objects that were changed.	5136: A directory service object was modified. 5137: A directory service object was created. 5138: A directory service object was undeleted. 5139: A directory service object was moved. 5141: A directory service object was deleted.
Audit Directory Service Replication	Generates audit events when replication between two domain controllers begins and ends.	4932: Synchronization of a replica of an Active Directory naming context has begun. 4933: Synchronization of a replica of an Active Directory naming context has ended.

Table 7-6

Logon/Logoff

Setting	Description	Common Events:
Audit Account Lockout	Generated by a failed attempt to log on to an account that is locked out.	4625: An account failed to log on.
Audit User/Device Claims	Allows you to audit user and device claims information in the user's logon tokens. This setting is introduced with Windows Server 2012.	
Audit IPsec Extended Mode	Generates audit events for the results of the Internet Key Exchange (IKE) protocol and Authenticated Internet Protocol (AuthIP) during Extended Mode negotiations.	4978: During Extended Mode negotiation, IPsec received an invalid negotiation packet. 4979: IPsec Main Mode and Extended Mode security associations were established. 4980: IPsec Main Mode and Extended Mode security associations were established. 4984: An IPsec Extended Mode negotiation failed.

(continued)

Table 7-6

(continued)

Setting	Description	Common Events:
Audit IPsec Main Mode	Generates events for the results of the IKE protocol and AuthIP during Main Mode negotiations.	4650: An IPsec Main Mode security association was established. 4651: An IPsec Main Mode security association was established. 4652: An IPsec Main Mode negotiation failed. 5049: An IPsec Security Association was deleted. 5453: An IPsec negotiation with a remote computer failed because the IKE and AuthIP IPsec Keying Modules (IKEEXT) service is not started.
Audit IPsec Quick Mode	Generates audit events for the results of the IKE protocol and AuthIP during Quick Mode negotiations.	4977: During Quick Mode negotiation, IPsec received an invalid negotiation packet. 5451: An IPsec Quick Mode security association was established.
Audit Logoff	Generates audit events when logon sessions are terminated.	4634: An account was logged off. 4647: User initiated logoff.
Audit Logon	Generates audit events when a user attempts to log on to a computer including logon success and failure, logon attempts by using explicit credentials, and security identifiers (SIDs) are filtered.	4624: An account successfully logged on. 4625: An account failed to log on. 4648: A logon was attempted using explicit credentials.
Audit Network Policy Server	Generates audit events for RADIUS (IAS) and Network Access Protection (NAP) activity on user access requests (Grant, Deny, Discard, Quarantine, Lock, and Unlock).	6272: Network Policy Server granted access to a user. 6273: Network Policy Server denied access to a user. 6276: Network Policy Server quarantined a user. 6278: Network Policy Server granted full access to a user because the host met the defined health policy.

(continued)

Table 7-6

(continued)

Setting	Description	Common Events:
Audit Other Logon/Logoff Events	Generates audit events for other logon or logoff events, such as the following: • A Remote Desktop session disconnects or connects. • A workstation is locked or unlocked. • A screen saver is invoked or dismissed. • A replay attack is detected. This event indicates that a Kerberos request was received twice with identical information. • A user or computer is granted access to a wireless network. • A user or computer is granted access to a wired 802.1x network.	4649: A replay attack was detected. 4778: A session was reconnected to a Window Station. 4779: A session was disconnected from a Window Station. 4800: The workstation was locked. 4801: The workstation was unlocked. 4802: The screen saver was invoked. 4803: The screen saver was dismissed. 5632: A request was made to authenticate to a wireless network. 5633: A request was made to authenticate to a wired network.
Audit Special Logon	Generates audit events when a special logon is used or a member of a special group logs on.	4964: Special groups have been assigned to a new logon.

Table 7-7

Object Access

Setting	Description	Common Events:
Audit Application Generated	Generates audit events when applications attempt to use the Windows Auditing APIs.	4665: An attempt was made to create an application client context. 4666: An application attempted an operation: 4667: An application client context was deleted. 4668: An application was initialized.
Audit Certification Services	Generates events when Active Directory Certificate Services (AD CS) operations are performed, such as the following: • AD CS starts. • AD CS shuts down. • AD CS is backed up or is restored. • Certificate revocation list (CRL)-related tasks are performed. • Certificates are requested, issued, or revoked. • AD CS templates are modified.	4868: The Certificate Manager denied a pending certificate request. 4870: Certificate Services revoked a certificate. 4886: Certificate Services received a certificate request. 4887: Certificate Services approved a certificate request and issued a certificate. 4888: Certificate Services denied a certificate request. 4889: Certificate Services set the status of a certificate request to pending.

(continued)

Table 7-7

(continued)

Setting	Description	Common Events:
		4895: Certificate Services published the CA certificate to AD DS. 4896: One or more rows have been deleted from the certificate database. 4898: Certificate Services loaded a template.
Audit Detailed File Share	Records attempts to access files and folders on a shared folder. It logs an event every time a file or folder is accessed. Note: Event volume: High on a file server or domain controller because of SYSVOL network access required by Group Policy.	5145: A network share object was checked to see whether the client can be granted desired access.
Audit File Share	Records events when a file share is accessed. Note: Event volume: High on a file server or domain controller because of SYSVOL network access required by Group Policy.	5140: A network share object was accessed. 5142: A network share object was added. 5143: A network share object was modified. 5144: A network share object was deleted.
Audit File System	Records user attempts to access file system objects as specified by the configured SACLs, and only if the type of access requested (such as Write, Read, or Modify) and the account making the request match the settings in the SACL.	4664: An attempt was made to create a hard link. 4985: The state of a transaction has changed. 5051: A file was virtualized.
Audit Filtering Platform Connection	Generates audit events when connections are allowed or blocked by the Windows Filtering Platform, such as the following: • The Windows Firewall service blocks an application from accepting incoming connections on the network. • The Windows Filtering Platform allows or blocks a connection. • The Windows Filtering Platform permits or blocks a bind to a local port. • The Windows Filtering Platform permits or blocks the listening of an application or service on a port for incoming connections. Note: Event volume: High	5031: The Windows Firewall Service blocked an application from accepting incoming connections on the network. 5150: The Windows Filtering Platform blocked a packet. 5151: A more restrictive Windows Filtering Platform filter has blocked a packet. 5154: The Windows Filtering Platform has permitted an application or service to listen on a port for incoming connections. 5155: The Windows Filtering Platform has blocked an application or service from listening on a port for incoming connections. 5156: The Windows Filtering Platform has allowed a connection. 5157: The Windows Filtering Platform has blocked a connection. 5158: The Windows Filtering Platform has permitted a bind to a local port. 5159: The Windows Filtering Platform has blocked a bind to a local port.

(continued)

Table 7-7

(continued)

Setting	Description	Common Events:
Audit Filtering Platform Packet Drop	Records packets that are dropped by the Windows Filtering Platform.	5152: The Windows Filtering Platform blocked a packet. 5153: A more restrictive Windows Filtering Platform filter has blocked a packet.
Audit Handle Manipulation	Generates audit events when a handle to an object is opened or closed. Note: Event volume: High, depending on how SACLs are configured.	4656: A handle to an object was requested. 4658: The handle to an object was closed. 4690: An attempt was made to duplicate a handle to an object.
Audit Kernel Object	Records attempts to access the system kernel, which includes mutexes and semaphores. Only kernel objects with a matching SACL generate security audit events.	4659: A handle to an object was requested with intent to delete. 4660: An object was deleted. 4661: A handle to an object was requested. 4663: An attempt was made to access an object.
Audit Other Object Access Events	Generates audit events for the management of Task Scheduler jobs or COM+ objects.	4698: A scheduled task was created. 4699: A scheduled task was deleted. 4700: A scheduled task was enabled. 4701: A scheduled task was disabled. 4702: A scheduled task was updated. 5148: The Windows Filtering Platform has detected a Denial of Service (DoS) attack and entered a defensive mode; packets associated with this attack will be discarded. 5149: The DoS attack has subsided and normal processing is being resumed. 5888: An object in the COM+ Catalog was modified. 5889: An object was deleted from the COM+ Catalog. 5890: An object was added to the COM+ Catalog.
Audit Registry	Records user attempts to access registry objects based on the SACLs.	4657: A registry value was modified. 5039: A registry key was virtualized.
Audit Removable Storage	Records user attempts to access file system objects on a removable storage device. This setting is introduced with Windows Server 2012.	4663: Successful attempts to access a removal storage device. 4656: Failed attempts to access removal storage device.

(continued)

Table 7-7

(continued)

Setting	Description	Common Events:
Audit SAM	Generated by attempts to access Security Accounts Manager (SAM) objects.	4659: A handle to an object was requested with intent to delete. 4660: An object was deleted. 4661: A handle to an object was requested. 4663: An attempt was made to access an object.
Audit Central Access Policy Staging	Records access requests where the permission granted or denied by a proposed policy differs from the current central access policy on an object. This setting is introduced with Windows Server 2012.	

Table 7-8

Policy Change

Setting	Description	Common Events:
Audit Audit Policy Change	Generates audit events when changes are made to audit policy.	4715: The audit policy (SACL) on an object was changed. 4719: The system audit policy was changed. 4817: Auditing settings on an object were changed. 4907: Auditing settings on an object were changed.
Audit Authentication Policy Change	Generates audit events when changes are made to authentication policy.	4713: Kerberos policy was changed. 4739: Domain Policy was changed. 4865: A trusted forest information entry was added. 4866: A trusted forest information entry was removed. 4867: A trusted forest information entry was modified.
Audit Authorization Policy Change	Generates audit events when the following changes are made to the authorization policy.	4704: A user right was assigned. 4705: A user right was removed.
Audit Filtering Platform Policy Change	Generates audit events for IPsec services status, changes to IPsec settings, status and changes to the Windows Filtering Platform engine and providers, and changes to the IPsec Policy Agent service activities.	4709: IPsec Services was started. 4710: IPsec Services was disabled.

(continued)

Table 7-8

(continued)

SETTING	DESCRIPTION	COMMON EVENTS:
Audit MPSSVC Rule-Level Policy Change	Generates audit events when changes are made to policy rules for the Microsoft Protection Service (MPSSVC.exe), which is used by Windows Firewall.	4946: A change has been made to Windows Firewall exception list. A rule was added. 4947: A change has been made to Windows Firewall exception list. A rule was modified. 4948: A change has been made to Windows Firewall exception list. A rule was deleted. 4950: A Windows Firewall setting has changed. 4954: Windows Firewall Group Policy settings have changed. The new settings have been applied. 4956: Windows Firewall has changed the active profile. 4957: Windows Firewall did not apply the specified rule.
Audit Other Policy Change Events	Generates events for security policy changes that are not otherwise audited in the Policy Change category, such as Trusted Platform Module (TPM) configuration changes, Kernel-mode cryptographic self tests, Cryptographic provider operations, and Cryptographic context operations or modifications.	4670: Permissions on an object were changed. 4909: The local policy settings for the TPM Base Services (TBS) were changed. TPM is short for Trusted Platform Module. 4910: The group policy settings for the TBS were changed. 5447: A Windows Filtering Platform filter has been changed. 6144: Security policy in the group policy objects has been applied successfully. 6145: One or more errors occurred while processing the security policy in the group policy objects.

Table 7-9

Privilege Use

SETTING	DESCRIPTION	COMMON EVENTS:
Audit Non-Sensitive Privilege Use	Generated when sensitive privileges (user rights) such as the following are used: • Act as part of the operating system • Back up files and directories • Create a token object • Debug programs	4672: Special privileges assigned to new logon. 4673: A privileged service was called. 4674: An operation was attempted on a privileged object.

(continued)

Table 7-9

(continued)

SETTING	DESCRIPTION	COMMON EVENTS:
	• Enable computer and user accounts to be trusted for delegation • Generate security audits • Impersonate a client after authentication • Load and unload device drivers • Manage auditing and security log • Modify firmware environment values • Replace a process-level token • Restore files and directories • Take ownership of files or other objects	
Audit Sensitive Privilege Use	Generated by the use of non-sensitive privileges (user rights), such as access this computer from the network, add workstation to domain, allow logon locally, change the system time, create a page file, and shut down the system.	4672: Special privileges assigned to new logon. 4673: A privileged service was called. 4674: An operation was attempted on a privileged object.

Table 7-10

System

SETTING	DESCRIPTION	EVENTS:
Audit IPsec Driver	Audits the activities of the IPsec driver, including the startup and shutdown of IPsec services, packets dropped due to integrity check failure, and packets dropped due to replay check failure.	4960: IPsec dropped an inbound packet that failed an integrity check. 4961: IPsec dropped an inbound packet that failed a replay check. 4962: IPsec dropped an inbound packet that failed a replay check. 4963: IPsec dropped an inbound clear text packet that should have been secured. 5478: IPsec Services has started successfully. 5479: IPsec Services has been shut down successfully.

(continued)

Table 7-10
(continued)

Setting	Description	Events:
Audit Other System Events	Records the events of startup and shutdown of the Windows Firewall service and driver, security policy processing by the Windows Firewall service, cryptography key file operations, and migration operations.	5024: The Windows Firewall Service has started successfully. 5025: The Windows Firewall Service has been stopped. 5030: The Windows Firewall Service failed to start. 5032: Windows Firewall was unable to notify the user that it blocked an application from accepting incoming connections on the network. 5033: The Windows Firewall Driver has started successfully. 5034: The Windows Firewall Driver has been stopped. 5035: The Windows Firewall Driver failed to start.
Audit Security State Change	Audits changes in the security state of a system, including system startup and shutdown, change of system time, and system recovery from CrashOnAuditFail.	4608: Windows is starting up. 4609: Windows is shutting down. 4616: The system time was changed. 4621: Administrator recovered system from CrashOnAuditFail.
Audit Security System Extension	Audits events related to security system extensions, including when a security extension code is loaded (such as an authentication, notification, or security package) or a service is installed.	4610: An authentication package has been loaded by the Local Security Authority. 4697: A service was installed in the system.
Audit System Integrity	Audit events that violate the integrity of the security subsystem include the following: • Auditing events are lost due to a failure of the auditing system. • A process uses an invalid local procedure call (LPC) port in an attempt to impersonate a client, and a remote procedure call (RPC) integrity violation is detected. • A code integrity violation with an invalid hash value of an executable file is detected. • Cryptographic tasks are performed.	4612: Internal resources allocated for the queuing of audit messages have been exhausted, leading to the loss of some audits. 4615: Invalid use of LPC port. 5056: A cryptographic self-test was performed. 5060: Verification operation failed.

REMOVING ADVANCED AUDIT POLICY CONFIGURATION

It is not recommended you use both basic audit policy settings and advanced audit policy settings because they may cause conflicts or erratic behavior. By default, when you apply Advanced Audit Configuration Policy, the basic audit policies are ignored.

If you need to go back to the basic audit settings after enabling Advanced Audit Policy Configuration, you need to perform the following:

1. Set all *Advanced Audit Policy* subcategories to `Not configured`.
2. Delete the `%systemroot%\security\audit\audit.csv` on the domain controllers for group policies and on the local computer for local policies.
3. Reconfigure and apply the *basic audit policy settings*.

Implementing Auditing Using AuditPol.exe

CERTIFICATION READY
Implement auditing using Group Policy and AuditPol.exe.
Objective 2.4

To manage auditing at the command prompt or by creating scripts, you use the ***AuditPol.exe*** command, which displays information about and performs functions to manipulate audit policies.

The syntax for `AuditPol.exe` includes the following commands:

- `/get`: Displays the current audit policy.
- `/set`: Sets the audit policy.
- `/list`: Displays selectable policy elements.
- `/backup`: Saves the audit policy to a file.
- `/restore`: Restores the audit policy from a file that was previously created by using `auditpol /backup`.
- `/clear`: Clears the audit policy.
- `/remove`: Removes all per-user audit policy settings and disables all system audit policy settings.
- `/resourceSACL`: Configures global resource SACLs.
- `/?`: Displays help at the command prompt.

`Auditpol.exe` also includes the following subcommands:

- `/user:<username>`: Specifies the security principal for a per-user audit. Specify the username by security identifier (SID) or by name. Requires either the `/category` or `/subcategory` subcommand when used with the `/set` command.
- `/category:<name>`: Specifies one or more auditing categories separated by a pipe (|) and specified by a name or Globally Unique Identifier (GUID).
- `/subcategory:<name>`: Specifies one or more auditing subcategories separated by a pipe (|) and specified by a name or GUID.
- `/success:enable`: Enables success auditing when using the `/set` command.

- `/success:disable`: Disables success auditing when using the `/set` command.
- `/failure:enable`: Enables failure auditing when using the `/set` command.
- `/failure:disable`: Disables failure auditing when using the `/set` command.
- `/file`: Specifies the file to which an audit policy is to be backed up or from which an audit policy is to be restored.

For example, to configure auditing for user account management for success and failed attempts, execute the following command:

```
auditpol.exe /set /subcategory:"user account management" /
success:enable /failure:enable
```

To disable the Filtering Platform Connection successful events, use the following command:

```
auditpol.exe /set /subcategory:"Filtering
Platform  Connection" /success:disable
```

To delete the per-user audit policy for all users, reset, or disable the system audit policy for all subcategories, and you want to set the audit policies settings to disable, execute the following command:

```
auditpol.exe /clear
```

If you want to delete the per-user audit policy for all users, reset, or disable the system audit policy for all subcategories, and you want to set all the audit policies settings to disable without a confirmation prompt, execute the following command:

```
auditpol.exe /clear /y
```

To remove the per-user audit policy for the jsmith account, perform the following command:

```
auditpol.exe /remove /user:jsmith
```

To remove the per-user audit policy for all users, perform the following command:

```
auditpol.exe /remove /allusers
```

To see all possible categories and subcategories, execute the following command:

```
auditpol.exe /list /subcategory:*
```

If you want to get an authoritative report on what audit settings are being applied, use the following command:

```
auditpol.exe /get /category:*
```

To back up the audit policy for all users into a .CSV text file called auditpolicy.csv, execute the following command:

```
auditpol.exe /backup /file:C\auditpolicy.csv
```

To restore system audit policy settings from the auditpolicy.csv file, execute the following command:

```
auditpol.exe /restore /file:c:\auditpolicy.csv
```

Viewing Audit Events

As you know from the 70-410 exam and Lesson 3, the audit events can be viewed by opening the Security logs in the Event Viewer (see Figure 7-12).

Figure 7-12

Opening security logs in the Event Viewer

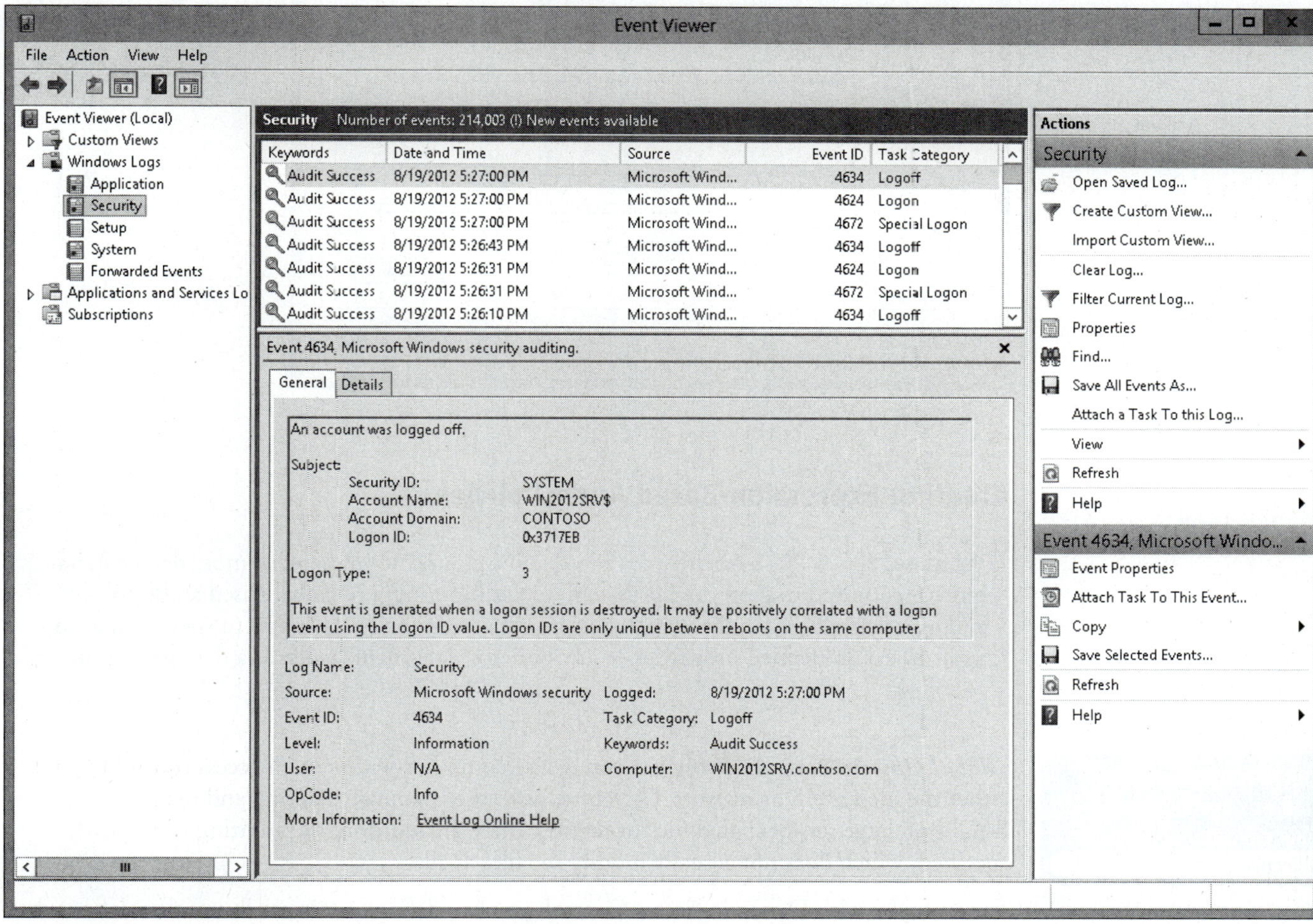

Much like the other logs found in the Event Viewer, you usually want to grab certain events. For example, you can use a filter (see Figure 7-13) and specify the Event ID range (for example, 4774 shows an account that was mapped for logon) that you seek and a date/time range.

Figure 7-13

Filtering security events

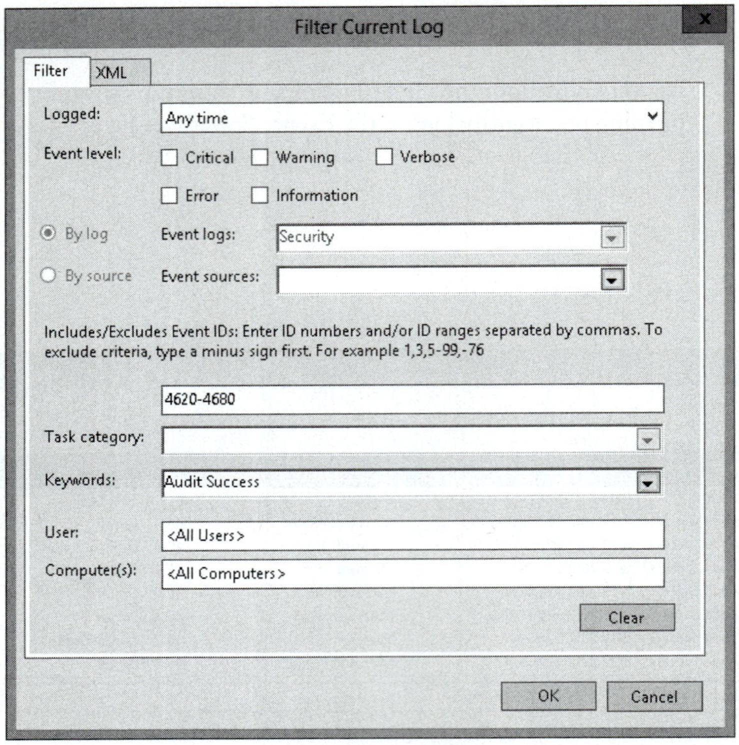

Creating Expression-Based Audit Policies

Windows Server 2012 has new advanced audit policies to implement more detailed and more precise auditing on the file system, including configure global based audit policies and expression-based audit. Expression-based audit policies allow you to specify what to audit based on defined properties or attribute for documents (such as a department or country).

CERTIFICATION READY
Create expression-based audit policies.
Objective 2.4

Global Object Access Auditing lets you define computer-wide system access control lists for either the file system or registry. Therefore, instead of manually altering and maintaining SACLs on large sets of shared files or registry entry. In addition, the auditing is implicitly specified, which does not actually modify the files at all.

For example, with Dynamic Access Control, you can define certain attributes that define what a department a file belongs to, such as the Finance department, which is assigned to a large set of files. You would then specify auditing based on the attribute. Dynamic Access Control is discussed in the 70-412 course.

DEFINE GLOBAL OBJECT ACCESS AUDITING

GET READY. To define Global Object Access Auditing, perform the following steps:

1. Open Server Manager.
2. Click Tools > Group Policy Management to open the *Group Policy Management console*.
3. Right-click a group policy and click Edit. *Group Policy Management Editor* opens.

4. Expand Computer Configuration\Policies\Windows Settings\Security Settings\Advanced Audit policy\Audit Policies and click Global Object Access Auditing to display the *Global Object Access Auditing* settings (see Figure 7-14).

Figure 7-14

Displaying the Global Object Access Auditing settings

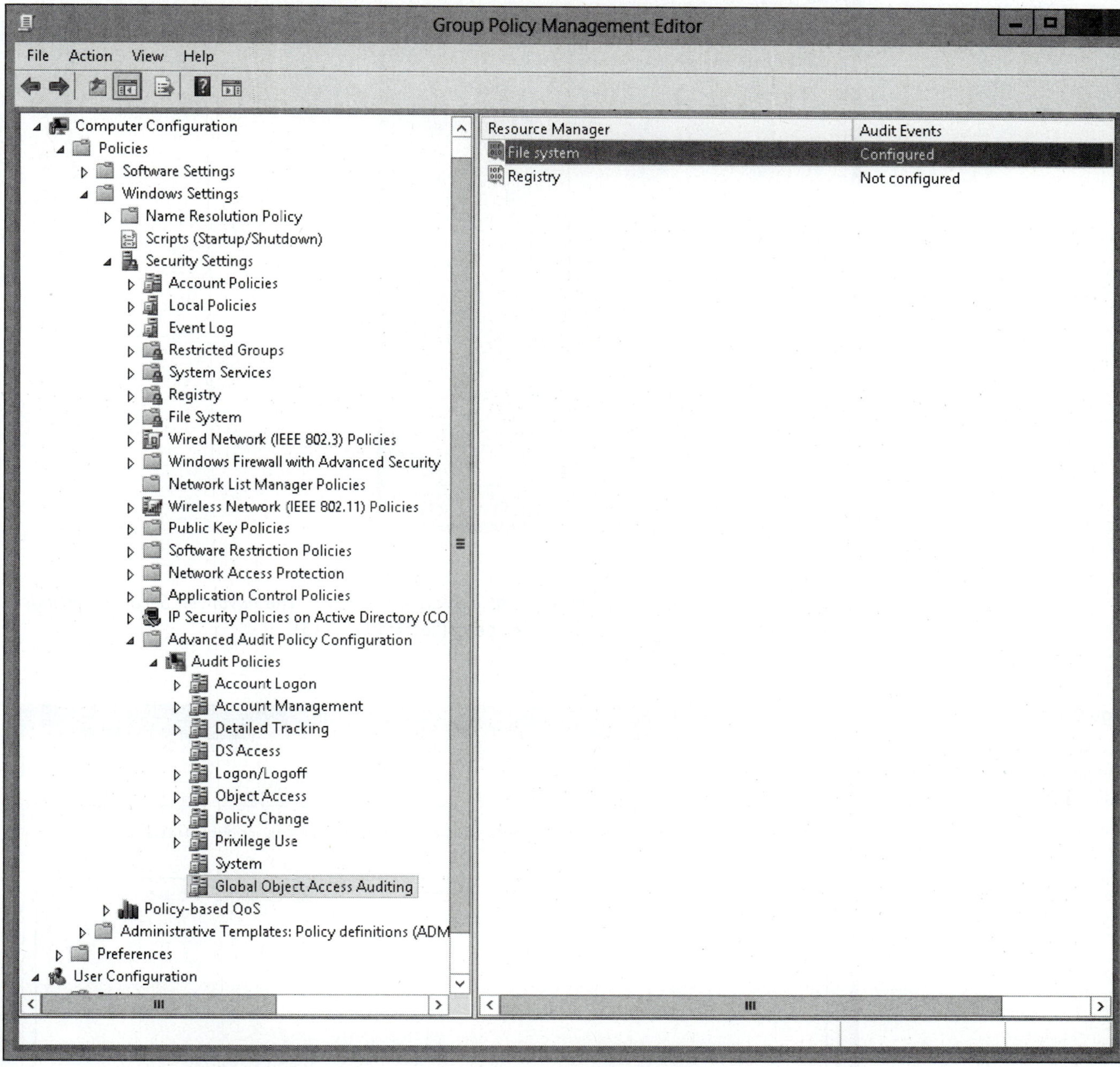

5. Under *Resource Manager*, double-click File System to display the *File system Properties* dialog box (see Figure 7-15).

Figure 7-15

Opening the File system Properties dialog box

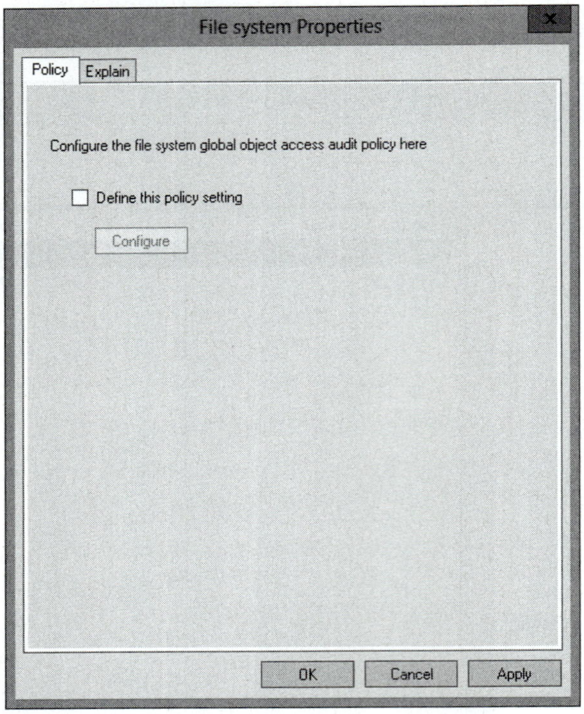

6. Select Define this policy settings and click Configure. The *Advanced Security Settings for Global File SACL* dialog box opens (see Figure 7-16).

Figure 7-16

Opening the *Advanced Security Settings for Global File SACL* dialog box

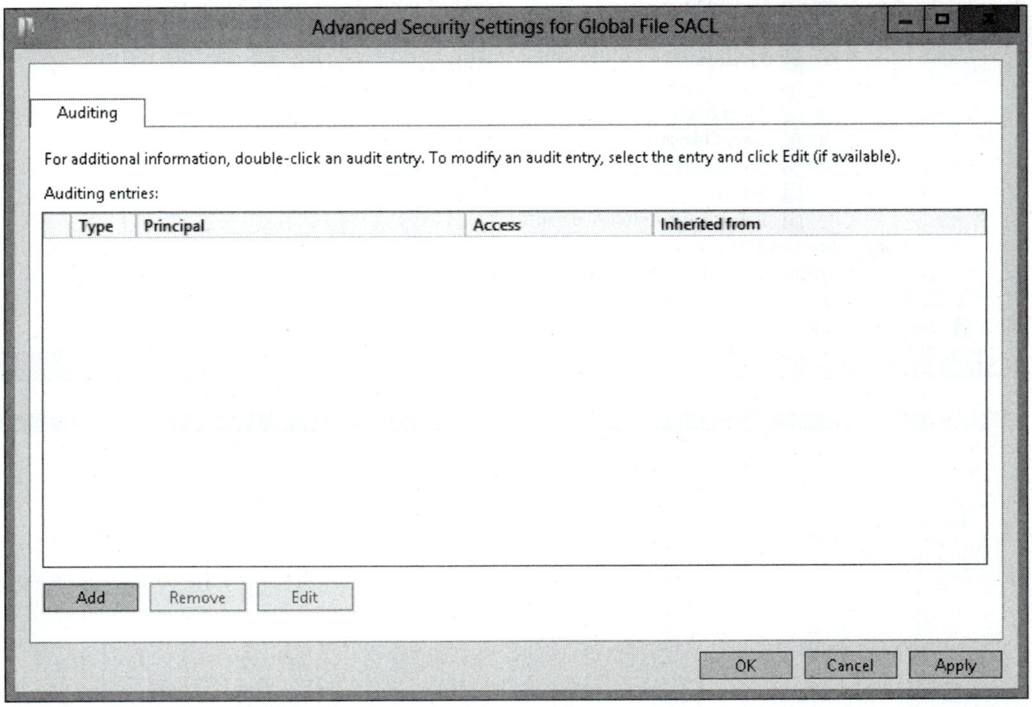

7. In the *Advanced Security Settings for Global File SACL* dialog box, click Add. The *Auditing Entry for Global File SACL* dialog box opens (see Figure 7-17).

Figure 7-17

Opening the *Auditing Entry for Global File SACL* dialog box

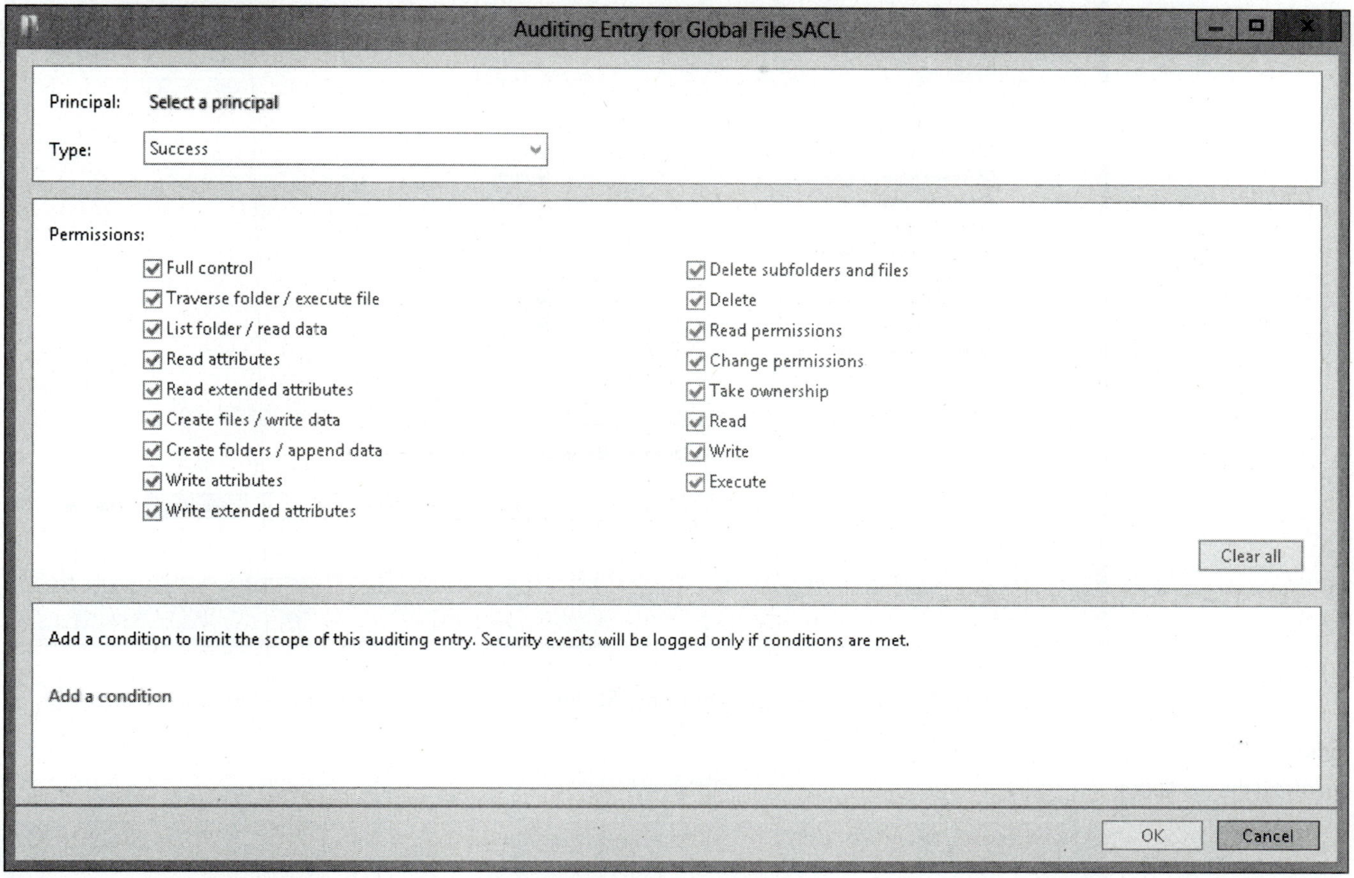

8. Click Select a principal. The *Select User, Computer, Service Account, or Group* dialog box opens. Type a name of a user or group in the *Enter the object name to select* box and click OK.
9. For the Type, select Success, Fail, or All.
10. Select the permissions that you want and deselect the permissions that you don't want.
11. Click Add a condition. A condition is added (see Figure 7-18).

Figure 7-18

Adding a condition

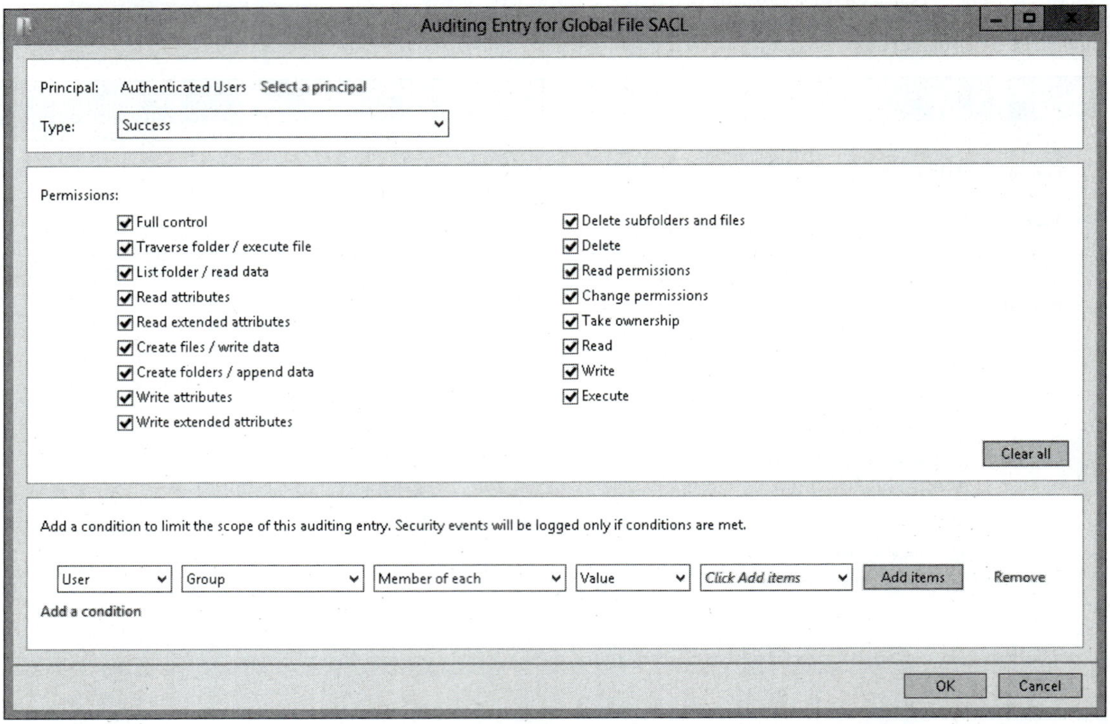

12. Select the following options: Resource, Department, Any of, Value, and Finance (see Figure 7-19).

Figure 7-19

Specifying the conditions

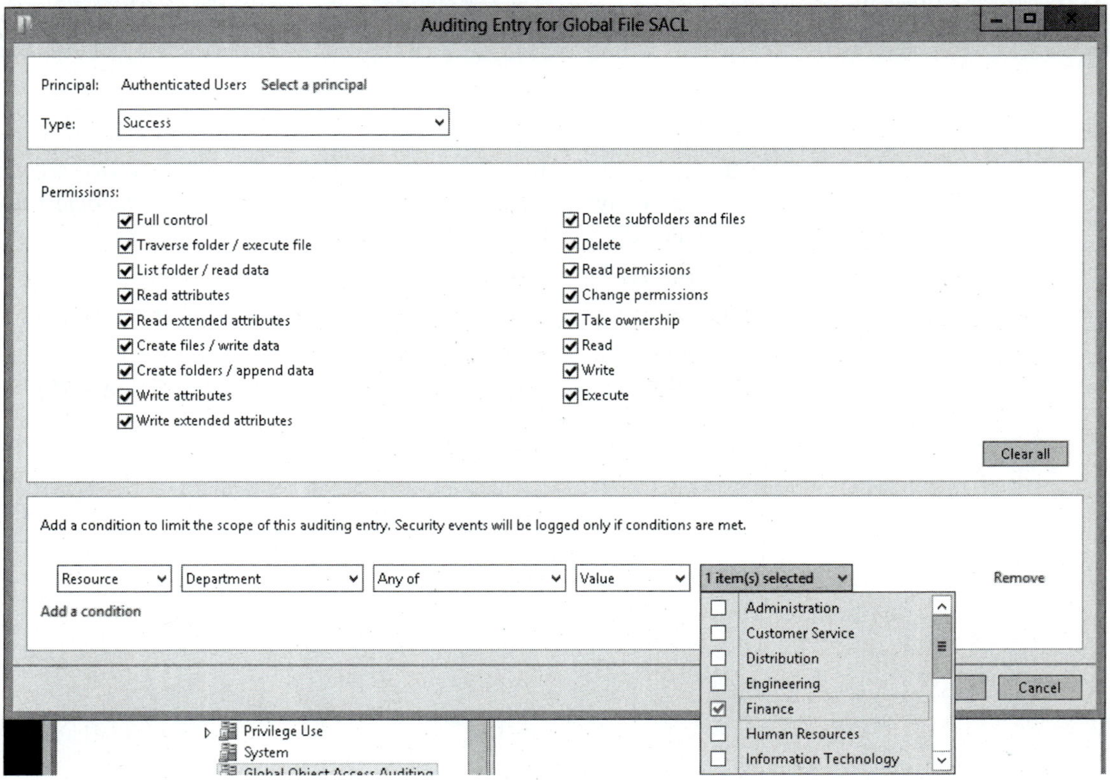

13. Click OK to close the *Auditing Entry for Global File SACL* dialog box.
14. Click OK to close the Advanced Security Settings for Global File SACL dialog box.
15. Click OK to close the *File system Properties* dialog box.
16. Close the *Group Policy Management Editor* and *Group Policy Management*.

Creating Removable Device Audit Policies

In previous versions of Windows, it was difficult to determine whether a user connects a removal storage device such as a USB thumb drive to the computer. Because the USB devices can be used to copy confidential information and might introduce malware to the organization, the organization might want to keep track of who uses removable storage devices.

CERTIFICATION READY
Create removable device audit policies.
Objective 2.4

Organizations can limit or deny users the ability to use removable storage devices by using the ***Removable Storage Access policy***. However, in earlier versions of the Windows and Windows Server operating systems, administrators could not track the use of removable storage devices.

CONFIGURE THE MONITORING OF REMOVABLE STORAGE DEVICES

GET READY. To configure the monitoring of removal storage devices such as USB drives, perform the following steps:

1. Open Server Manager.
2. Click Tools > Group Policy Management to open the *Group Policy Management console*.
3. In the console tree, right-click a group policy object, and then click Edit.
4. Double-click Computer Configuration, double-click Security Settings, double-click Advanced Audit Policy Configuration, and double-click Object Access.
5. Double-click Audit Removable Storage. The *Audit Removal Storage Properties* dialog box opens (see Figure 7-20).

Figure 7-20
Opening the Audit Removal Storage Properties dialog box

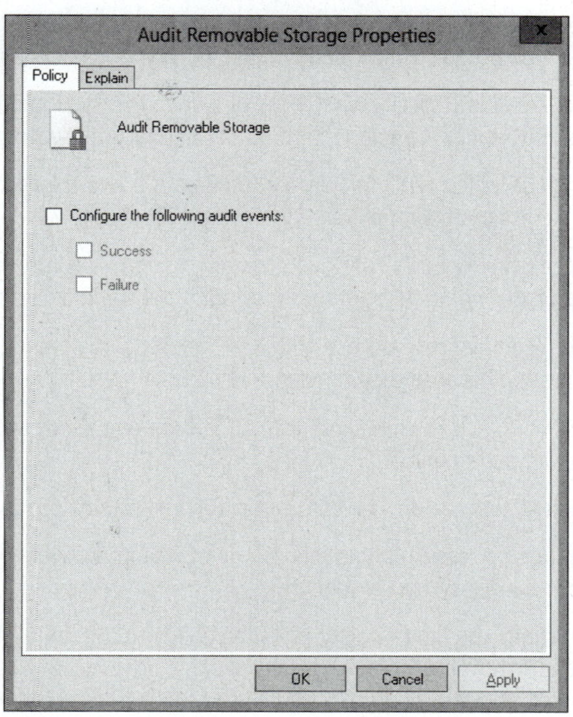

6. Select the Configure the following audit events check box, select the Success check box, and then click OK.
7. Click OK to close the *Group Policy Management Editor*.

If you open the Event Viewer, you should look for event 4663 (see Figure 7-21) for successful attempts to access a removal storage device and 4656 for failed attempts.

Figure 7-21

Displaying a 4663 Event

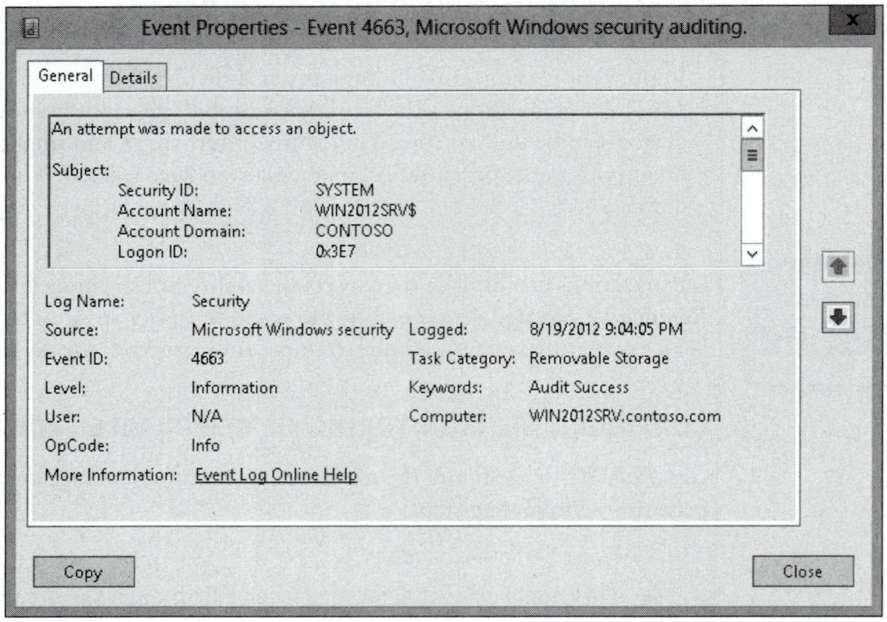

SKILL SUMMARY

IN THIS LESSON, YOU LEARNED:

- You need to enable auditing so that you can have a record of the users who have logged in, a record of what the user accessed or tried to access, and a record of what action a user has performed such as rebooting or shutting down a computer or accessing a file.
- To enable auditing, specify what types of system events to audit using Group Policy or the local security policy (Computer Settings\Policies\Security Settings\Local Policies\Audit Policy).
- Auditing NTFS files, NTFS folders, and printers is a two-step process. You must first enable Object Access using Group Policy. Then you must specify which objects you want to audit.
- Advanced Security Audit Policy Settings give you more control over what events get recorded by using 56 new settings instead of the traditional nine basic audit settings.
- It is not recommended you use both basic audit policy settings and Advanced Audit Policy Configuration because they can cause unexpected results.
- The `AuditPol.exe` command displays information about and performs functions to manipulate audit policies.
- The audit events can be viewed by opening the security logs in the Event Viewer.
- Global Object Access Auditing lets you define computer-wide system access control lists for either the file system or registry.
- Organizations can limit or deny users the ability to use removable storage devices by using the Removable Storage Access policy.

Knowledge Assessment

Multiple Choice

Select the correct answer for each of the following questions.

1. Where do you view the security events collected by auditing with group policies?
   a. Log viewer
   b. SysInfo
   c. Event Viewer
   d. Sys Viewer

2. To audit who accessed a file, which of the following must you first enable?
   a. System auditing
   b. Process tracking
   c. Object access auditing
   d. Directory service access

3. To audit who modified a group policy, which of the following should you change?
   a. Privilege Use
   b. Policy change
   c. System
   d. Directory service access

4. In which audit group do you find the Audit Filtering Platform Connection and Audit Filtering Platform Packet Drop?
   a. System auditing
   b. Process tracking
   c. Object access auditing
   d. Directory service access

5. Which of the following do you need to perform when you want to remove Advanced Auditing Policies?
   a. Delete the group policy
   b. Use basic audit policies with the *Enforce* option.
   c. Use basic audit policies with the *No Override* option.
   d. Delete the Audit.csv file from the %systemroot%\security\audit\ folder.

6. Which command should you use to show the current audit policies on a machine?
   a. `auditpol.exe /get /subcategory:*`
   b. `auditpol.exe /list /category:*`
   c. `auditpol.exe /set /subcategory:*`
   d. `auditpol.exe /backup /file *`

7. How many audit policy subsettings are found in the Advanced Audit Policy Settings?
   a. 21
   b. 53
   c. 56
   d. 61

8. Which command clears the audit policy on a computer?
   a. `auditpol /clear`
   b. `auditpol /remove`
   c. `auditpol /disable`
   d. `auditpol /undone`

9. Which of the following should you use to give you more control on what events to audit?
   a. Granular Control Audit Policy
   b. Pick and Choose Audit Policy
   c. Advanced Audit Policy Settings
   d. User-Defined Audit Policy Settings

10. Which of the following do you define when you configure auditing files and printers?
   a. System Access Control Lists
   b. Global Object Control Lists
   c. Discretionary Access Control Lists
   d. Programmed Access Control Lists

Best Answer

Choose the letter that corresponds to the best answer. More than one answer choice may achieve the goal. Select the BEST answer.

1. Which type of audit policy do you use to specify what to audit based on defined properties or attributes for a document?
   a. Attribute detection audit policies
   b. Variable audit policies
   c. Flexible audit policies
   d. Expression-based audit policies

2. Which is used to record who has connected a USB storage device on a computer?
   a. Removable device audit policy
   b. USB device audit policy
   c. Pluggable device audit policy
   d. Plug and play audit policy

3. Which command should you use to get the current audit policy?
   a. `audit /display`
   b. `auditpol /get`
   c. `get-auditpol`
   d. `showaudit`

4. What category is used to audit the registry?
   a. Key auditing
   b. Hive auditing
   c. Object auditing
   d. System auditing

5. Which of the following are reasons not to enable auditing for everything? (Choose all that apply.)
   a. Logs quickly fill up
   b. Makes it difficult to find relevant events
   c. Makes it impossible to secure computer
   d. Affects performance of computer

6. What audit setting do you use to record changes to the local users and groups on a computer?
   a. Object access
   b. Logon
   c. Account management
   d. Directory service access

Matching and Identification

1. Match the Audit Event category that you would use for the following events. Not all items will be used and items can be used more than once.
   _______ a) Modify an Active Directory account
   _______ b) Operating System logins
   _______ c) Changing the time
   _______ d) Reboot a server
   _______ e) Log on to the computer
   _______ f) Auditing a file
   _______ g) Auditing a printer
   _______ h) Changing user rights
   _______ i) Filtering Platform Connection
   _______ j) Removable devices
   1. Account logon
   2. Account management
   3. Directory service access
   4. Logon
   5. Object access
   6. Policy change
   7. Privilege use
   8. Process tracking
   9. System

Build a List

1. Identify the steps in order to audit a printer. Not all of the steps will be used.
   _____ Click Advanced.
   _____ Specify what you are auditing, such as Success, Fail, or both.
   _____ Open Printer Properties.
   _____ Open Properties.
   _____ Select Security.
   _____ Select Auditing.
   _____ Open View devices and printers.
   _____ Open Device Manager.
   _____ Click the Add button and add the user or group.
2. Identify the steps to audit the registry settings.
   _____ Enable object auditing using the registry.
   _____ Enable object auditing using group policies.
   _____ Use Group Policy to specify what you want to audit.
   _____ Open the key or setting that you want to audit and specify what you want to audit.
   _____ Enable Advanced Audit Policy Settings.
3. Identify the steps in order to remove Advanced Auditing Configuration. Not all of the steps will be used.
   _____ Delete the HKEY_LOCAL_MACHINE\SOFTEWARE\POLICIES\ADVANCED SECURITY key in the registry.
   _____ Configure all Advanced Audit Policies subcategories to Not configured.
   _____ Reconfigure and apply the basic audit policy settings.
   _____ Delete the Audit folder in the SYSVOL volume.
   _____ Delete the `%systemroot%\security\audit\audit.csv`.

■ Business Case Scenarios

Scenario 7-1: Establishing an Audit Policy

You just established an audit policy that enables account logon, logon, object access, and account management. However, when you look at the logs, you see a large number of Audit Filtering Platform Connection and Audit Filtering Platform Packet Drop events that consume most of the security logs. What can you do to alleviate this problem?

Scenario 7-2: Monitor the Use of Mobile Storage Devices

Your manager assigns you the task of seeing how many users use mobile storage devices such as USB thumb drives. What would you use to accomplish this?

Configuring DNS Zones

LESSON 8

70-411 EXAM OBJECTIVE

Objective 3.1 – Configure DNS zones. This objective may include but is not limited to: configure primary and secondary zones; configure stub zones; configure conditional forwards; configure zone and conditional forward storage in Active Directory; configure zone delegation; configure zone transfer settings; configure notify settings.

LESSON HEADING	EXAM OBJECTIVE
Understanding DNS	
Understanding DNS Names and Zones	
Understanding the Address Resolution Mechanism	
Configuring and Managing DNS Zones	
Installing DNS	
Configuring Primary and Secondary Zones	Configure primary and secondary zones
Configuring Active Directory-Integrated Zones	Configure zone and conditional forward storage in Active Directory
Configuring Zone Delegation	Configure zone delegation
Configuring Stub Zones	Configure stub zones
Configuring Caching-Only Servers	
Configuring Forwarding and Conditional Forwarding	Configure conditional forwards
Configuring Zone Transfers	Configure zone transfer settings Configure notify settings
Using the Dnscmd Command to Manage Zones	

KEY TERMS

- **Active Directory-integrated zone**
- **caching-only server**
- **conditional forwarding**
- **DNS Notify**
- **dnscmd.exe**
- **Domain Name System (DNS)**
- **forward lookup zone**
- **forwarder**
- **full zone transfer (AXFR)**
- **fully qualified domain names (FQDNs)**
- **host**
- **incremental zone transfer (IXFR)**
- **iterative query**
- **name server**
- **primary name server**
- **primary zone**
- **resource record (RR)**
- **second-level domains**
- **secondary zone**
- **stub zone**
- **subdomain**
- **top-level domains**
- **zone transfer**

Understanding DNS

THE BOTTOM LINE

Domain Name System (DNS) is a naming service that is used by TCP/IP network and is an essential service used by the Internet. Every time a user accesses a web page, the user must type a URL. Before the client communicates with the web server, the client computer needs to use DNS to retrieve the IP address of the web server, similarly to someone using a phone book to find a phone number. When an enterprise client needs to communicate with a corporate server, the enterprise client also uses DNS to find the IP address of the corporate service. The DNS servers are often referred to as ***name servers***.

The Transmission Control Protocol/Internet Protocol (TCP/IP) is the most popular networking protocol suite used in the world and is the same protocol used with the Internet. Of course, the Internet is a worldwide network that links billions of computers. For a client computer or host to communicate on a TCP/IP network, a client must have an IP address.

Traditional IP addresses based on IPv4 were based on a four-byte address written in a four-octet format. Each octet ranges from 0 to 255. An example of an IP address is 24.64.251.189 or 192.168.1.53. Most users would have difficulty remembering hundreds of telephone numbers and hundreds of IP addresses. Naming resolution enables an administrator to assign logical names to a server or network resource by IP address and translates a logical name to an IP address.

With early TCP/IP networks, name resolution was done with hosts files, which were stored locally on each computer. The hosts files were simple text files with a host name and IP addresses on each line (see Figure 8-1). In Windows, the hosts file is located in the C:\Windows\System32\Drivers\etc folder. The disadvantage of using hosts files is that every time you need to add a new entry, you need to add or modify the hosts file on every computer in your organization, which is not a practical way to provide up-to-date name resolution.

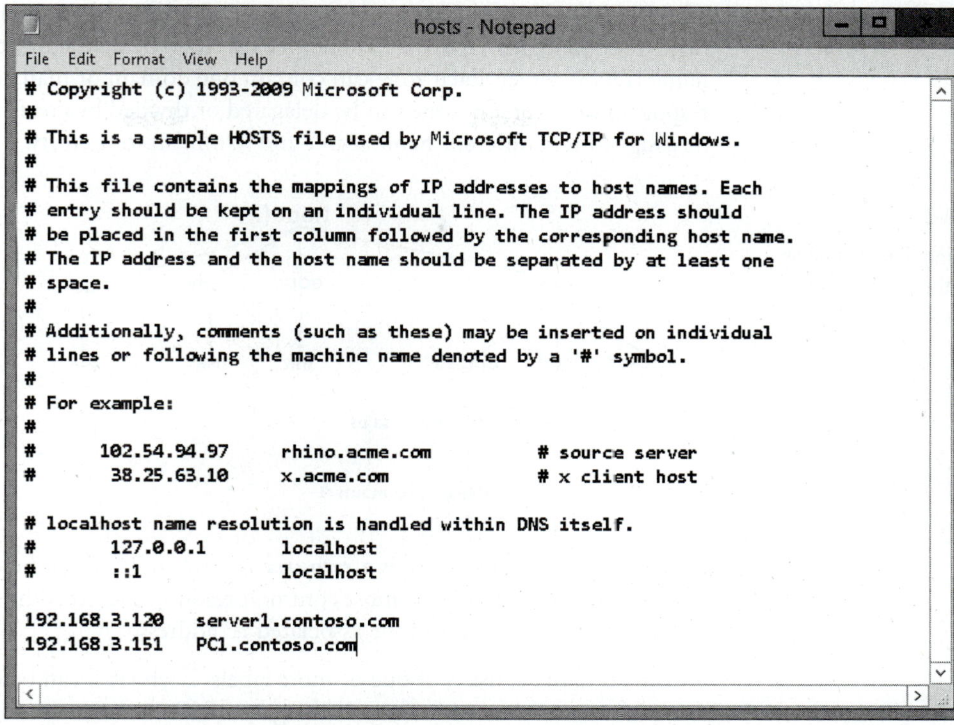

hosts - Notepad

File Edit Format View Help

```
# Copyright (c) 1993-2009 Microsoft Corp.
#
# This is a sample HOSTS file used by Microsoft TCP/IP for Windows.
#
# This file contains the mappings of IP addresses to host names. Each
# entry should be kept on an individual line. The IP address should
# be placed in the first column followed by the corresponding host name.
# The IP address and the host name should be separated by at least one
# space.
#
# Additionally, comments (such as these) may be inserted on individual
# lines or following the machine name denoted by a '#' symbol.
#
# For example:
#
#      102.54.94.97     rhino.acme.com          # source server
#       38.25.63.10     x.acme.com              # x client host

# localhost name resolution is handled within DNS itself.
#       127.0.0.1       localhost
#       ::1             localhost

192.168.3.120   server1.contoso.com
192.168.3.151   PC1.contoso.com
```

Figure 8-1

Using a Hosts file

DNS was developed as a system and a protocol to provide up-to-date name resolution. The benefits of DNS include the following:

- Ease of use and simplicity: Allows users to access computers and network resources with easy-to-remember names.
- Scalability: Allows the workload of name resolution to be distributed across multiple servers and databases.
- Consistency: Allows the IP addresses to be changed while keeping the host names consistent, making network resources easier to locate.

A DNS resolver is a service that uses the DNS protocol to query for information about DNS servers using UDP and TCP port 53.

Understanding DNS Names and Zones

DNS uses ***fully qualified domain names (FQDNs)*** to map a host name to an IP address. An FQDN describes the exact relationship between a host and its DNS domain. For example, computer1.sales.microsoft.com represents an FQDN; the computer1 host is located in the sales domain, which is located in the Microsoft second-level domain, which is located in the .com top-level domain.

DNS is a hierarchical distributed naming system used to locate computers and services on a TCP/IP network. DNS clients send queries to a DNS server and the Domain Name Service receives and resolves queries such as translating a host or domain name to an IP address. Because it is so closely tied to the Internet and TCP/IP network, it is an essential service that enables the Internet and network to function and it is required by many network services, including Active Directory.

DNS is known as a distributed naming system because the information stored with DNS is not found on a single DNS server. Instead, the information is distributed among multiple DNS servers, all of which are linked into a hierarchical structure.

The DNS is a hierarchical system consisting of a tree of domain names. At the top of the tree is the root zone (see Figure 8-2). The tree can then be divided into zones, each served by a name (DNS) server. Each zone can contain one domain or many domains. The administrative responsibility over any zone can be delegated or divided by creating a subdomain, which can be assigned to a different name server and administrative entity.

Figure 8-2

Distributing domain names through the DNS hierarchy system

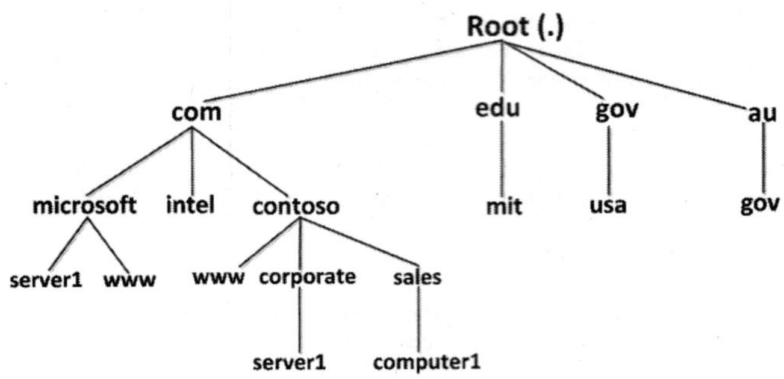

Each node or leaf in the tree is a ***resource record (RR)***, which holds information associated with the domain name. The most common resource record is the host address (A or AAA), which lists a host name and the associated IP address.

A domain name consists of one or more labels. Each label can be up to 63 characters. The full domain name cannot exceed a total length of 253 characters.

The right-most label designates the top-level domain. For example, *microsoft.com* consists of two labels. The top-level domain is com. The hierarchy of domains descends from right to left. Each label to the left specifies a subdomain of the domain or label on the right. Therefore, in our example, *microsoft* is a subdomain of the *com* domain.

Traditionally, ***top-level domains*** consist of generic top-level domains and internationally country codes (such as *us* for United States, *uk* for United Kingdom, *de* for Germany, and *jp* for Japan). Traditional generic top-level domains include the following:

.com	Commercial
.org	Organization (originally intended for nonprofit organizations)
.edu	Educational
.gov	U.S. governmental entities
.net	Network (originally intended for the portal to a set of smaller websites)

Over the years, many other generic domains have been added, such as aero, biz, coop, info, int, jobs, name, and pro. More recently, organizations can purchase their own top-level domains.

Second-level domains are registered to individuals or organizations. Examples include:

microsoft.com	Microsoft Corporation domain
mit.edu	Massachusetts Institute of Technology
gov.au	Australian government.

Second-level DNS domains can have many subdomains, and any domain can have hosts.

A ***host*** is a specific computer or other network device in a domain. For example, *computer1.sales.contoso.com* is the host called *computer1* in the sales subdomain of the *contoso.com* domain. A host has at least one IP address associated with it. For example, www.microsoft.com represents a particular address.

If you have *server1.corporate.contoso.com*, *com* is the top domain. *contoso* is a subdomain of com, and corporate is a subdomain of *contoso*. In the *corporate* domain, you find one or more addresses assigned to *server1*, which as 192.168.1.53. So as a result, when you type *server1.corporate.contoso.com* into your browser, the client sends a query to a DNS server asking what the IP address is for *server1.corporate.contoso.com*. The DNS server responds back with the 192.168.1.53 address. The client then communicates with the server with the address of 192.168.1.53.

Understanding the Address Resolution Mechanism

Every time a user accesses a network resource by a domain or host name, and the name has to be resolved to an IP address, the name and IP address are added to a cache so that you don't have to constantly contact the DNS server to resolve the IP address. If the name is not in the cache, the client contacts the first DNS server specified in the system's IP configuration. If the DNS server is available and it cannot determine the address, the client does not ask another DNS server. However, because the DNS is distributed hierarchical system, the local DNS server might need to contact other DNS servers to resolve the IP address.

The DNS client is known as the DNS resolver. Because a client computer or server depends on a DNS server to resolve IP addresses and identify certain network services, a client computer and servers alike can be DNS clients.

When a DNS client queries a DNS server, it performs a recursive query, whereas the host asks the DNS server to respond with the requested data or it responds that the domain does not exist. The DNS server can perform a recursive query with another DNS server if it is configured to forward requests to another DNS server because it does not know the answer (see Figure 8-3).

Figure 8-3

Using recursive query which performs DNS forwarding when needed

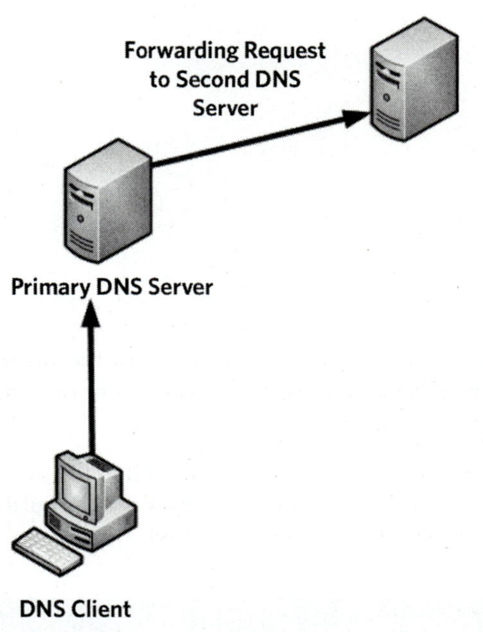

When the DNS server receives the response, it first checks its own cache. It then checks to see whether it is the authority for the requested domain. If it knows the answer, it responds with the answer.

If the client DNS server does not know the answer and it is not configured to forward requests to another DNS server, the client DNS server uses the DNS hierarchy to determine the correct answer. Instead of performing a recursive query, the client DNS server performs an ***iterative query***, which gives the best current answer back if it does not know the exact answer. For example, when a user types www.contoso.com in his or her browser, and the client DNS server does not know the answer, the client DNS server contacts one of the root DNS servers to determine the addresses of a *com* name server. The client DNS server then contacts the *com* name server to get the name server for *contoso.com*. The DNS server contacts the *contoso.com* name server to get the IP address of *www.contoso.com*. The client DNS server responds to the client with the resolved IP address. In addition, it adds the address to its cache for future queries. Figure 8-4 shows an iterative query.

Figure 8-4

Performing an iterative query

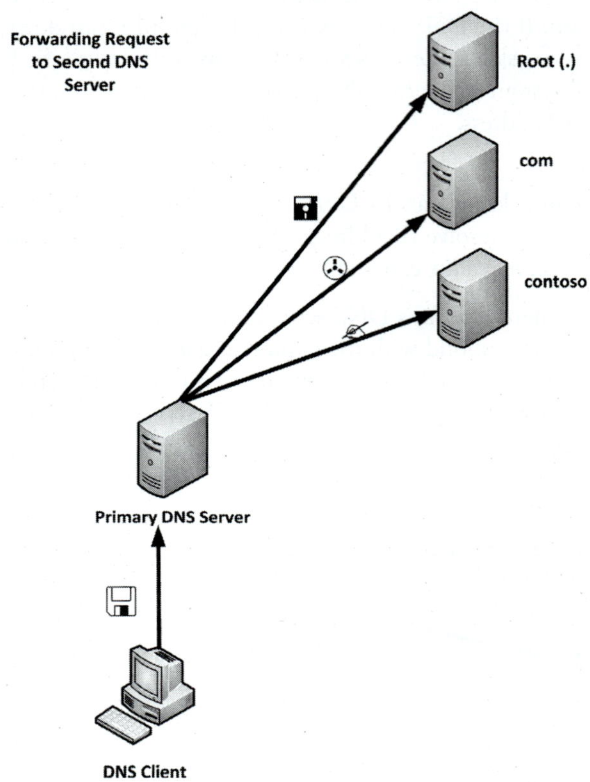

In some instances, the client DNS server does not know the answer and it cannot determine the answer, so the client DNS server responds to the client that the answer cannot be found or the query is a nonexistent domain.

Most DNS clients are configured with two or more DNS servers. The second DNS server is contacted for DNS queries only when the first server is not available. If the first server cannot answer the query, the second DNS server is not used.

■ Configuring and Managing DNS Zones

THE BOTTOM LINE

To provide DNS services, you first need to deploy DNS. Then after you have DNS servers, you have to create each zone and then add resource records to each zone. Because DNS is an essential service for a network, you should give some thought to it and plan before you deploy DNS.

The steps in deploying DNS include the following:

1. Install DNS on one or more servers.
2. Configure the DNS server, if necessary.
3. Create forward and reverse lookup zones.
4. Add resource records to the forward and reverse lookup zones.
5. Configure the clients to use the DNS servers.

Installing DNS

Before you can start using DNS, you have to install DNS. As you do with other Windows server roles, use Server Manager to deploy DNS.

As with any server role, before you deploy DNS, you need to plan your infrastructure. Some of the considerations involve how busy the servers are, what kind of fault-tolerance is needed, what kind of performance is required, and what kind of security is needed.

INSTALL DNS

GET READY. To install DNS on Windows Server 2012, perform the following steps:

1. Open *Server Manager* by clicking the Server Manager button on the task bar.
2. At the top of Server Manager, select Manage and click Add Roles and Features.
3. On the *Before you begin* page, click Next.
4. Select Role-based or feature-based installation, and then click Next.
5. Click Select a server from the server pool, click the name of the server to install DNS to, and then click Next.
6. Click DNS Server (see Figure 8-5).

Figure 8-5

Selecting DNS Server to install

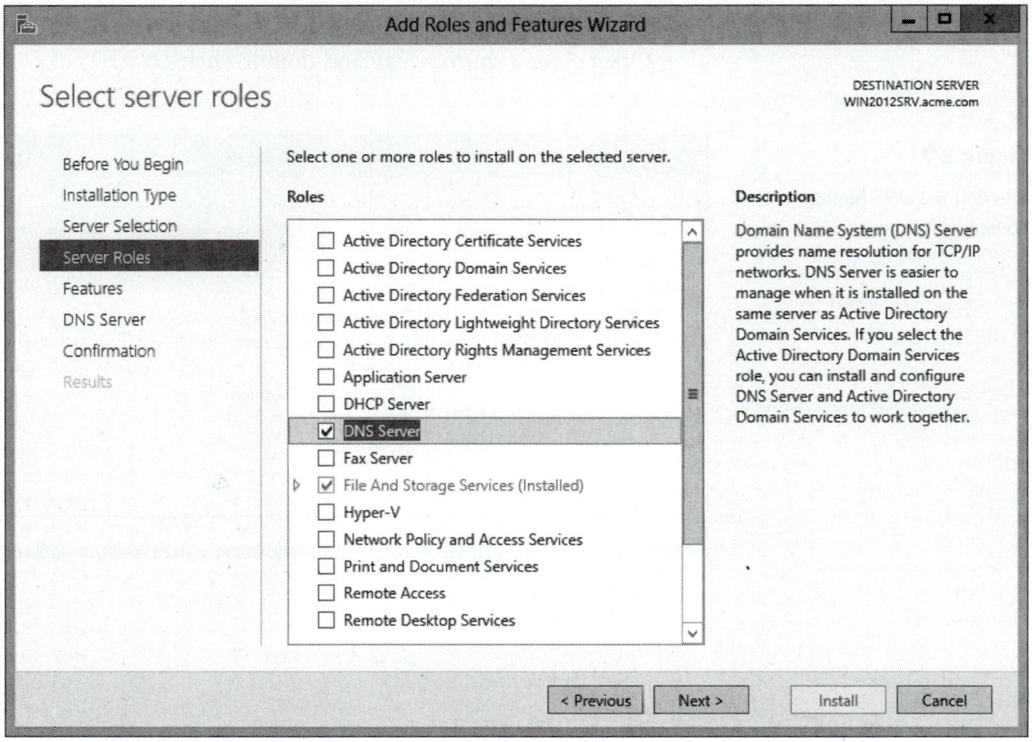

7. When the *Add Roles and Features Wizard* dialog box appears, select Add Features, and then click Next (see Figure 8-6).

Figure 8-6

Adding roles and features

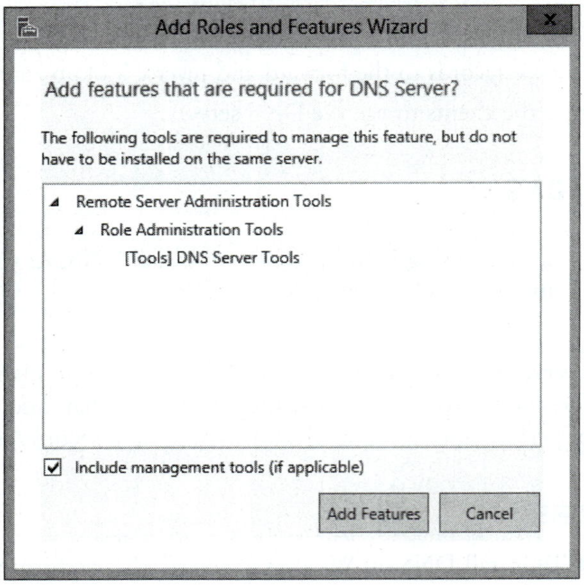

8. When the *Select features* page opens, click Next.
9. On the *DNS Server* page, click Next.
10. On the *Confirm installation selections* page, click the Install button.
11. When the installation is done, click the Close button.

When DNS is installed, you use the DNS console (see Figure 8-7). To open the DNS console, perform one of the following:

- Open *Server Manager*, open the *Tools* menu, and then select *DNS*.
- Open *Administrative Tools* and double-click *DNS*.

Figure 8-7

Viewing the DNS Manager console

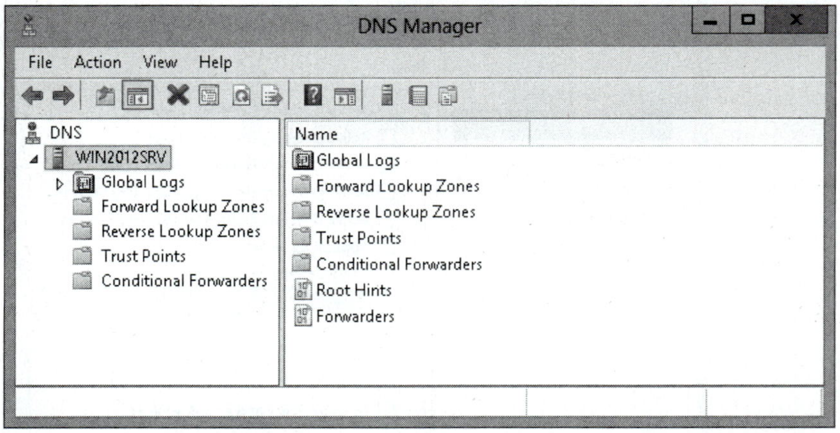

Configuring Primary and Secondary Zones

On DNS original implementation, the DNS server would host either a primary or secondary zone or both. The ***primary zone*** provides an authoritative, read-write copy of the zone, while the ***secondary zone*** provides an authoritative, read-only copy of the primary zone.

CERTIFICATION READY
Configure primary and secondary zones
Objective 3.1

When you need to make changes to the DNS zone, make the changes on the primary zone and the changes are replicated to the secondary zone. The secondary DNS zone enables the administrator to offload DNS query traffic and provide redundancy for name resolution queries. You then have to configure replication between the primary servers and the secondary servers.

Originally, the DNS was stored on a local file. By default, the primary zone file is named *zone_name.dns*, which is located in the *%systemroot%*\System32\DNS folder. By default, the *%systemroot%* is in the C:\Windows folder.

A server can host all primary zones, all secondary zones, or a mix of primary and secondary zones. Sometimes, servers that host primary zones are referred to as ***primary name servers*** and servers that host secondary zones are referred to as ***secondary name servers***.

When creating zones, there are two types of lookup zones to create:

- Forward lookup zone
- Reverse lookup zone

A ***forward lookup zone*** contains most of the resource records for a domain. Of course, as the name indicates, a forward lookup zone is used primarily to resolve host names to IP addresses. A ***reverse lookup zone*** is used to resolve IP addresses to host names. In the next two exercises, you create a standard primary zone for the contoso.com and a secondary zone for the contoso.com.

CREATE A STANDARD FORWARD LOOKUP PRIMARY ZONE

GET READY. To create a standard forward lookup primary zone, perform the following steps:

1. Open Server Manager.
2. Click Tools > DNS to open the DNS Manager console.
3. If necessary, expand the DNS console to a full-screen view.
4. Expand the server so that you can see the *Forward Lookup Zones* and *Reverse Lookup Zones* folders.
5. Right-click Forward Lookup Zones, and then click New Zone (see Figure 8-8).

Figure 8-8
Creating a new forward lookup zone

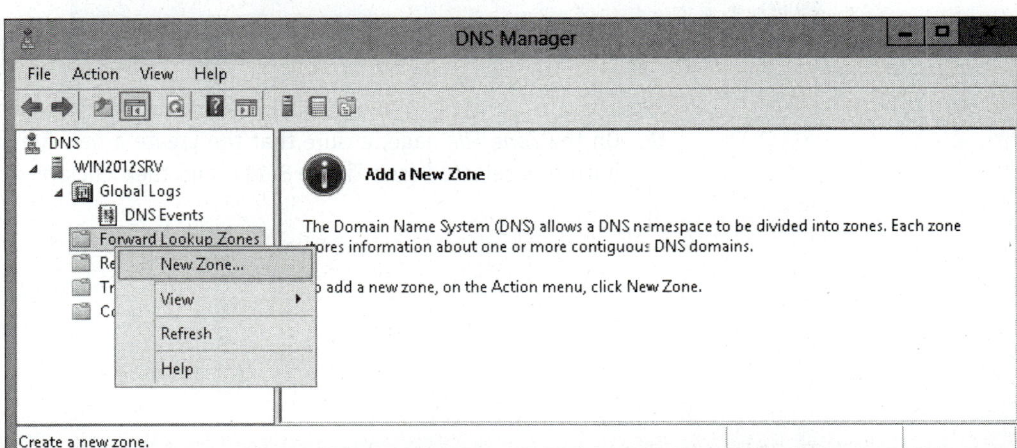

6. When the *Welcome to the New Zone Wizard* page opens, click Next.
7. On the *Zone Type* page, select the Primary zone radio button (see Figure 8-9), and then click Next.

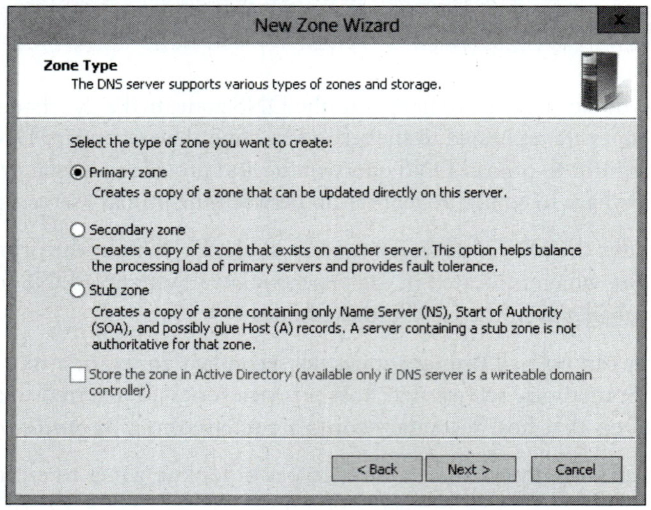

Figure 8-9

Selecting the zone type

8. The *Zone Name* page opens. In the Zone name text box, enter the name of the domain, such as contoso.com (see Figure 8-10), and then click Next.

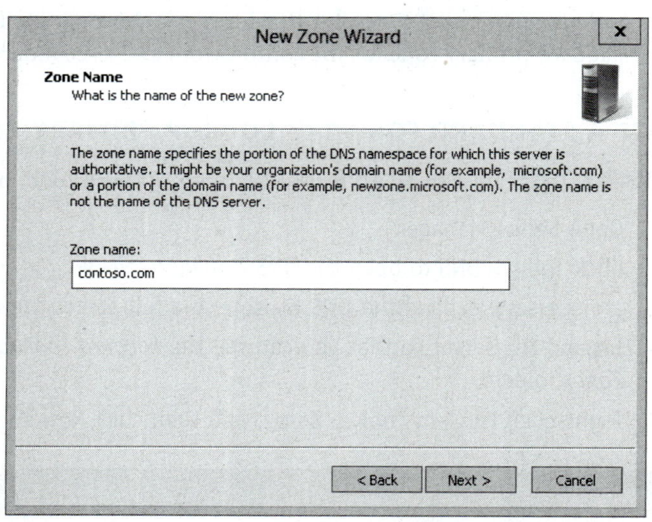

Figure 8-10

Specifying the zone name

9. On the *Zone File* page, ensure that the Create a new file with this file name radio button is selected (see Figure 8-11), and then click Next.

Figure 8-11

Creating a zone file

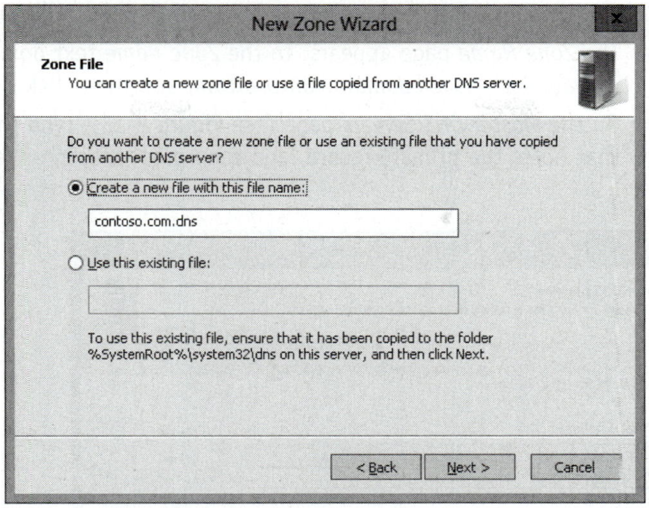

10. On the *Dynamic Update* page, ensure that the Do not allow dynamic updates radio button is selected (see Figure 8-12), and then click Next.

Figure 8-12

Specifying Dynamic Update settings

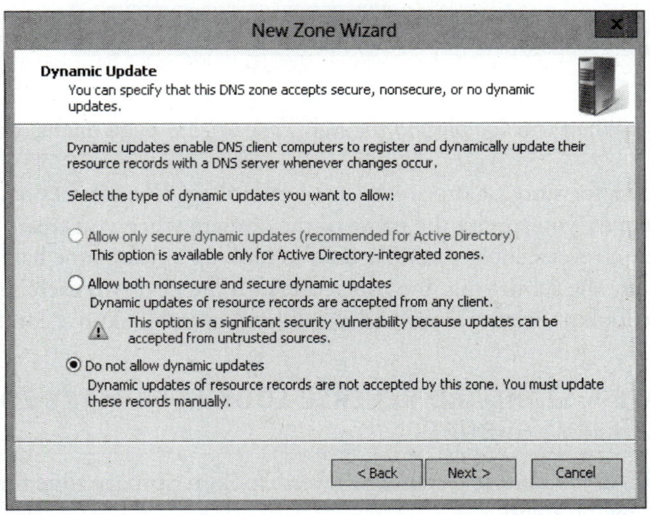

11. When the *Completing the New Zone Wizard* page appears, click Finish.

CREATE A STANDARD FORWARD LOOKUP SECONDARY ZONE

GET READY. To create a standard forward lookup secondary zone, perform the following steps:

1. Open Server Manager.
2. Click Tools > DNS to open *DNS Manager console*.
3. If necessary, expand the DNS console to a full-screen view.
4. Expand the server so that you can see the *Forward Lookup Zones* and *Reverse Lookup Zones* folders.
5. Right-click Forward Lookup Zones, and then click New Zone.
6. When the *Welcome to the New Zone Wizard* page opens, click Next.

7. On the *Zone Type* page, select the Secondary zone radio button and click Next.
8. The *Zone Name* page appears. In the *Zone name* text box, enter the name of the domain such as *subdomain.contoso.com*, and then click Next.
9. On the *Master DNS Servers* page (see Figure 8-13), type the IP address of the server that hosts the primary record, and then press the Enter key. Click Next.

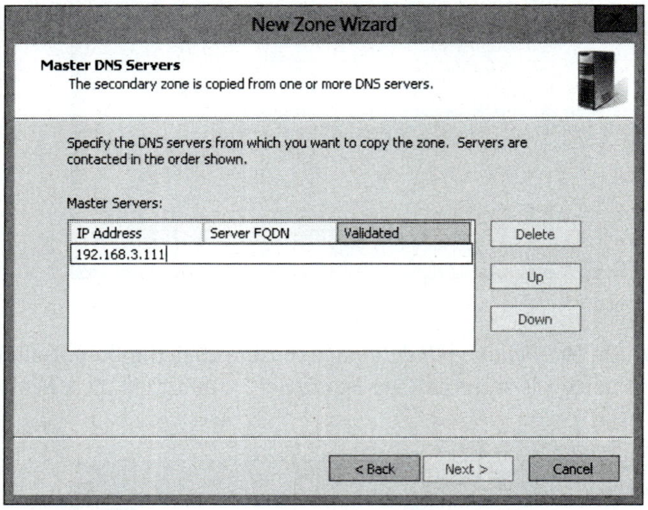

Figure 8-13

Entering the IP address on the Master DNS Servers page

10. When the *Completing the New Zone Wizard* page opens, click Finish.

Because a forward lookup zone is used to look up IP addresses based on domain name and host names, you specify the name of the domain when you create the forward lookup zone. Because a reverse lookup zone is used to look up a host name based on an IP address, you have to specify the subnet that the zone covers. In the next two exercises, you create a standard reverse lookup primary zone and a standard reverse lookup secondary zone.

CREATE A STANDARD REVERSE LOOKUP PRIMARY ZONE FOR AN IPV4 SUBNET

GET READY. To create a standard reverse lookup primary zone for an IPv4 subnet, perform the following steps:

1. Open Server Manager.
2. Click Tools > DNS to open the DNS Manager console.
3. If necessary, expand the DNS console to a full-screen view.
4. Expand the server so that you can see the *Forward Lookup Zones* and *Reverse Lookup Zones* folders.
5. Right-click Reverse Lookup Zones and click New Zone.
6. When the *Welcome to the New Zone Wizard* page appears, click Next.
7. On the *Zone Type* page, select the Primary zone radio button and click Next.
8. When the *Reverse Lookup Zone Name* page opens, select IPv4 Reverse Lookup Zone (see Figure 8-14).

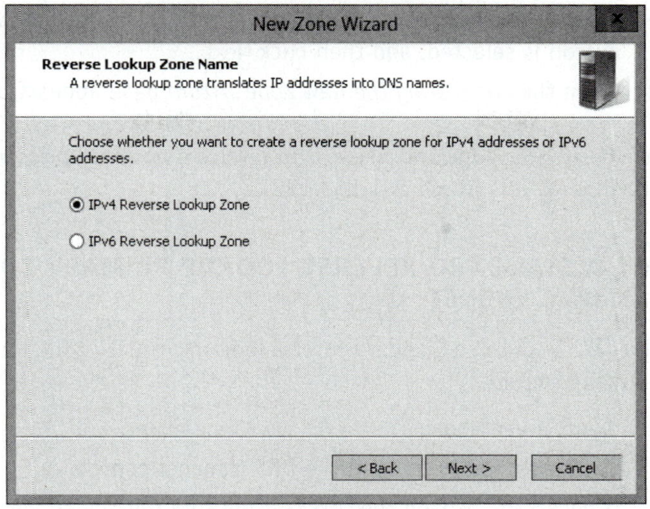

Figure 8-14

Selecting the IPv4 reverse lookup zone type

9. Type in the subnet prefix. For example, if you have a subnet of 192.168.1.0 (with a subnet mask of 255.255.255.0), you type 192.168.1 (see Figure 8-15). Click Next.

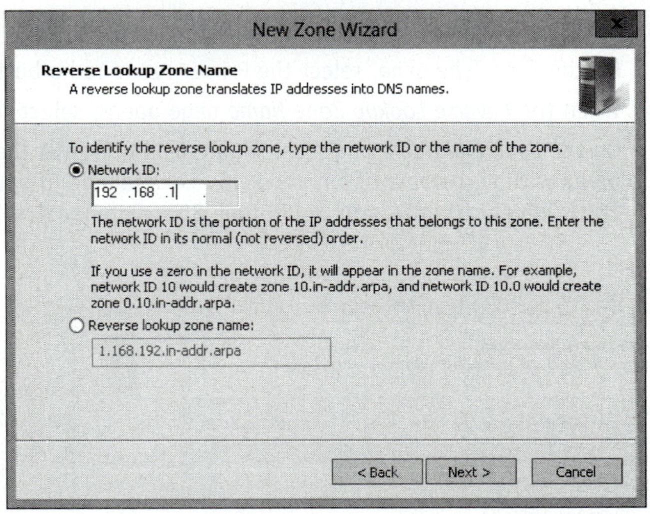

Figure 8-15

Entering the reverse lookup zone name

10. On the *Zone File* page (see Figure 8-16), keep the default value, and then click Next.

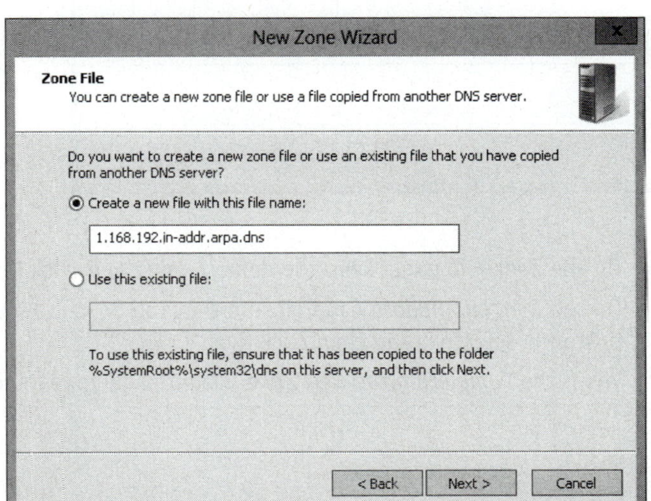

Figure 8-16

Specifying the Zone File page

11. On the *Dynamic Update* page, ensure that the Do not allow dynamic updates radio button is selected, and then click Next.
12. When the *Completing the New Zone Wizard* page appears, click Finish.

When it creates the zone and file, it is in reverse notation. For example, if you create the 192.168.1 zone, it is stored as 1.168.192.

CREATE A STANDARD REVERSE LOOKUP PRIMARY ZONE FOR AN IPV6 SUBNET

GET READY. To create a standard reverse lookup primary zone for an IPv6 subnet, perform the following steps:

1. Open Server Manager.
2. Click Tools > DNS to open the DNS Manager console.
3. If necessary, expand the DNS console to a full-screen view.
4. Expand the server so that you can see the *Forward Lookup Zones* and *Reverse Lookup Zones* folders.
5. Right-click Reverse Lookup Zones and click New Zone.
6. When the *Welcome to the New Zone Wizard* page appears, click Next.
7. On the *Zone Type* page, select the Primary zone radio button and click Next.
8. When the *Reverse Lookup Zone Name* page opens, select IPv6 Reverse Lookup Zone.
9. On the *Zone File Name* page (see Figure 8-17), type in the subnet prefix. End the prefix with::/*<number of bits masked>*. For example, if you have a 64-bit prefix of 2001:0db8:ac10:fe01, you would type 2001:0db8:ac10:fe01::/64. Click Next.

Figure 8-17

Specifying the reverse lookup zone name for IPv6

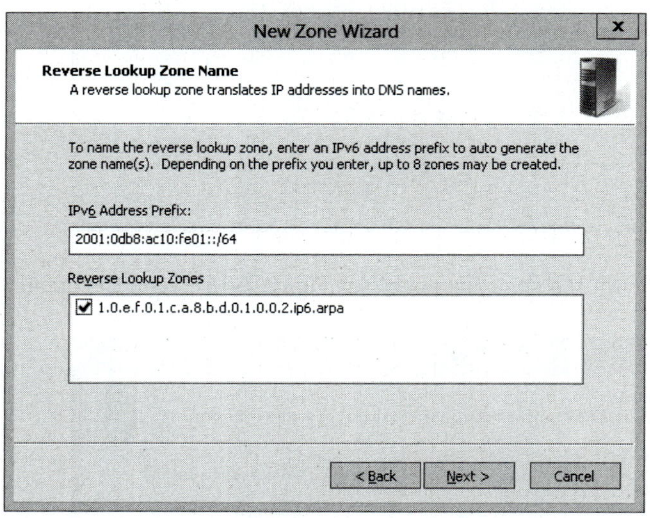

10. On the *Zone File* page, keep the default value and click Next.
11. On the *Dynamic Update* page, ensure that the Do not allow dynamic updates radio button is selected, and then click Next.
12. When the *Completing the New Zone Wizard* page appears, click Finish.

Configuring Active Directory-Integrated Zones

Today, DNS can instead be stored in and replicated with Active Directory, as an ***Active Directory-integrated zone***. By using Active Directory-integrated zones, DNS follows a multi-master model, whereas each server enables all DNS servers to have authoritative read-write copies of the DNS zone. When a change is made on one DNS server, it is replicated to the other DNS servers.

CERTIFICATION READY
Configure zone and conditional forward storage in Active Directory.
Objective 3.1

Microsoft recommends using Active Directory to store DNS and for good reason. The benefits include:

- Fault tolerance: Because each server is an authoritative read-write copy of DNS, you have the DNS information stored on multiple servers. In addition, you can update the DNS records from any DNS server.
- Security: Zone transfers are securely replicated as part of Active Directory. In addition, similar to Active Directory objects, you can manage who can access which records by using discretionary access control lists (DACL). Finally, you can configure secure dynamic updates, which allow records to be updated only by the client that first registered the record.
- Efficient replication: Zone transfers are replicated more efficiently when using Active Directory, especially if the information has to be replicated over slow WAN links.

There are three different replication scopes available for Active Directory-integrated zones. They include:

- To all domain controllers in the domain (the only replication scope available in Windows 2000)
- To all domain controllers that are DNS servers in the local domain (default), which is known as the DomainDNSZones application partition
- To all domain controllers that are also DNS servers in the entire forest, which is known as the ForestDNSZones application

In the following exercise, you create an Active Directory-integrated zone.

CREATE AN ACTIVE DIRECTORY-INTEGRATED STANDARD FORWARD LOOKUP PRIMARY ZONE

GET READY. To create a standard forward lookup primary zone, perform the following steps:

1. Open Server Manager.
2. Click Tools > DNS to open the *DNS Manager console*.
3. If necessary, expand the DNS console to a full-screen view.
4. Expand the server so that you can see the *Forward Lookup Zones* and *Reverse Lookup Zones* folders.
5. Right-click Forward Lookup Zones and click New Zone.
6. When the *Welcome to the New Zone Wizard* page opens, click Next.
7. On the *Zone Type* page, select the Primary zone radio button.
8. Make sure the Store the zone in Active Directory option is selected (see Figure 8-18) and click Next.

Figure 8-18

Selecting the zone type

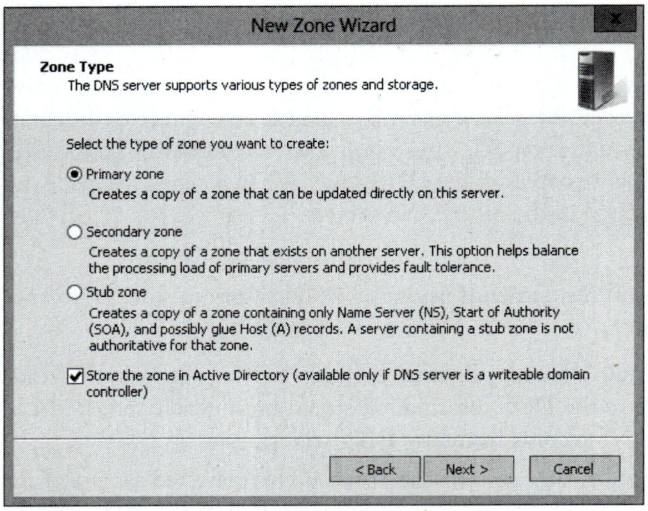

9. On the *Active Directory Zone Replication Scope* page, make sure that To all DNS servers running on domain controllers in this domain option is selected (see Figure 8-19) and click Next.

Figure 8-19

Specifying the Active Directory zone replication scope

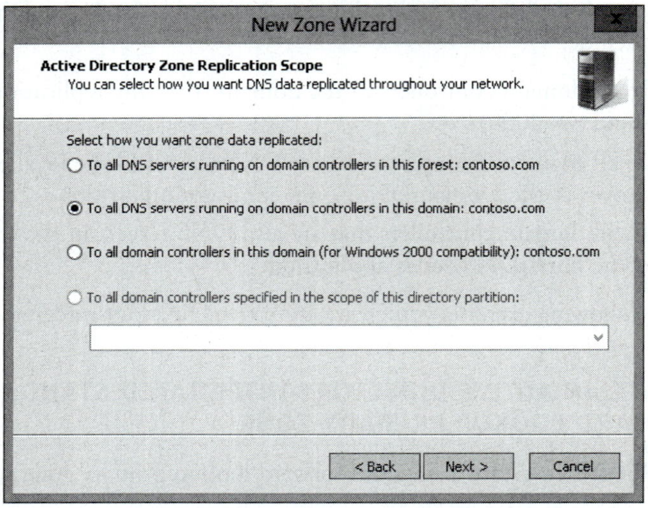

10. The *Zone Name* page appears. In the *Zone name* text box, enter the name of the domain, such as contoso.com, and then click Next.
11. On the *Zone File* page, ensure that the Create a new file with this file name radio button is selected, and then click Next.
12. On the *Dynamic Update* page, ensure that the Do not allow dynamic updates radio button is selected, and then click Next.
13. When the *Completing the New Zone Wizard* page appears, click Finish.

Configuring Zone Delegation

A DNS ***subdomain*** is a child domain that is part of a parent domain and has the same domain suffix as the parent domain. Subdomains allow you to assign unique names to be used by a particular department, subsidiary, function, or service within the organization. However, you can create a different zone for the subdomain, which can be stored on another server. As a result, you can increase performance for the DNS zones as the traffic is delegated to multiple servers.

CERTIFICATION READY
Configure zone delegation.
Objective 3.1

Subdomains allow you to break up larger domains into smaller, more manageable domains. For example, if you have *contoso.com*, you can create a *sales* subdomain and a *support* subdomain. When done, you will have the parent domain *contoso.com* and two subdomains: *sales.contoso.com* and *support.contoso.com*.

In the following exercise, you create a subdomain.

CREATE A SUBDOMAIN

GET READY. To create a subdomain, perform the following steps:

1. Open **Server Manager**.
2. Click **Tools > DNS** to open the *DNS Manager console*.
3. If necessary, expand the **DNS console** to a full-screen view.
4. Expand the server so that you can see the *Forward Lookup Zones* and *Reverse Lookup Zones* folders.
5. Right-click **Forward Lookup Zones** and click **New Domain** (see Figure 8-20). The *New DNS Domain* dialog box appears.

Figure 8-20

Creating a new subdomain

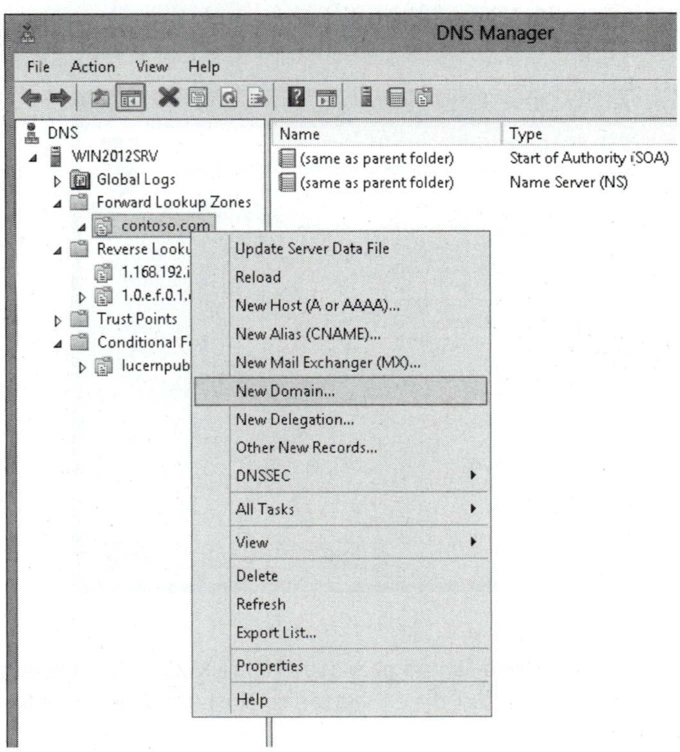

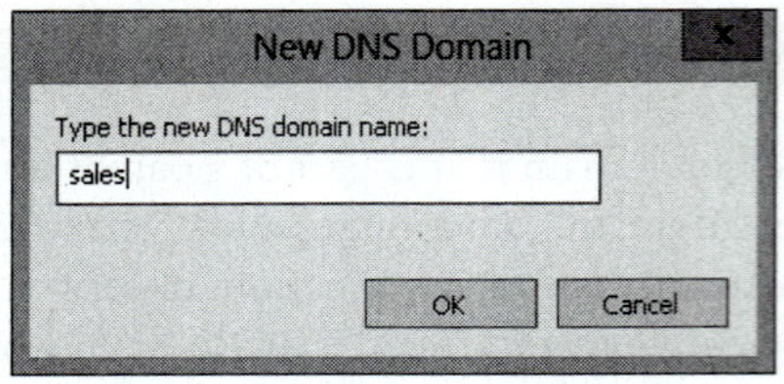

Figure 8-21

Specifying the subdomain name

6. Type the name of the subdomain in the text box (see Figure 8-21), and then click the OK button to close the *New DNS Domain* dialog box.

When you delegate a DNS zone, you add subdomains within a domain, except the subdomain is stored in another zone. If the subdomain is placed on another server, you can distribute the DNS traffic among multiple servers, allowing for better performance.

DELEGATE A DNS DOMAIN

GET READY. To delegate a DNS domain on Windows Server 2012, perform the following steps:

1. Open Server Manager.
2. Click Tools > DNS to open the *DNS Manager console*.
3. If necessary, expand the DNS console to a full-screen view.
4. Expand the server so that you can see the *Forward Lookup Zones* and *Reverse Lookup Zones* folders.
5. Right-click a forward lookup zone and click New Delegation.
6. When the *Welcome to the New Delegation Wizard* starts, click Next.
7. Type the name of the delegated subdomain in the delegated domain text box (see Figure 8-22), and then click Next.

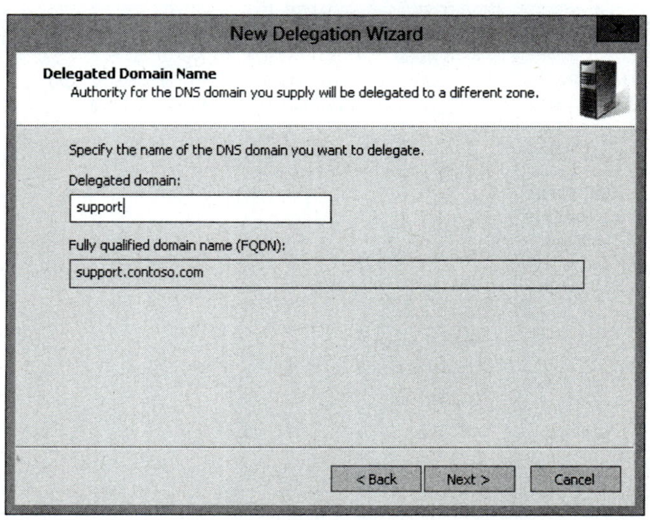

Figure 8-22

Entering the name of the delegated subdomain

8. On the *Name Servers* page (see Figure 8-23), click the Add button and enter the IP addresses. Click the OK button to close the *New Name Server* record. Click Next.

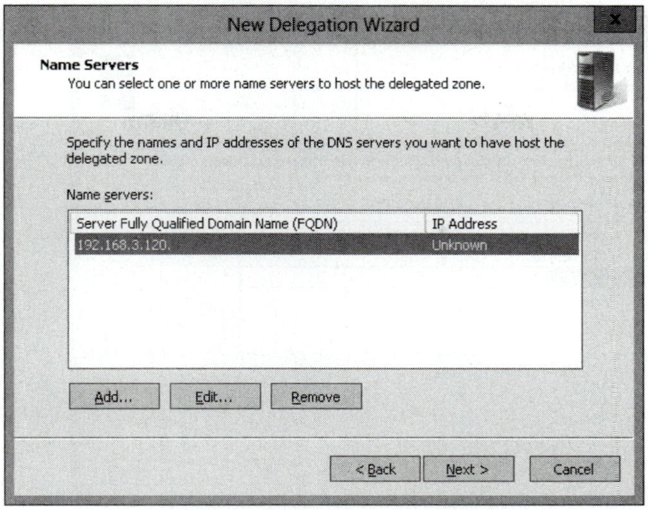

Figure 8-23

Specifying name servers for the delegated zone

9. When the wizard is complete, click the Finish button.

Configuring Stub Zones

CERTIFICATION READY
Configure stub zones.
Objective 3.1

A ***stub zone*** is a copy of a zone that contains only necessary resource records (Start of Authority (SOA), Name Server (NS), and Address/Host (A) record) in the master zone and acts as a pointer to the authoritative name server. The stub zone allows the server to forward queries to the name server that is authoritative for the master zone without going up to the root name servers and working its way down to the server. While a stub zone can improve performance, it does not provide redundancy or load sharing.

In the following exercise, you create a stub zone.

CREATE A STUB ZONE

GET READY. To create a stub zone, perform the following steps:

1. Open Server Manager.
2. Click Tools > DNS to open the *DNS Manager console*.
3. If necessary, expand the DNS console to a full-screen view.
4. Expand the server so that you can see the *Forward Lookup Zones* and *Reverse Lookup Zones* folders.
5. Right-click Forward Lookup Zones and click New Zone.
6. When the *Welcome to the New Zone Wizard* page opens, click Next.
7. When the *Zone Type* page opens, select the Stub zone radio button and click Next.
8. When the *Zone Name* page opens, enter the domain name such as contoso.com in the *Zone name* text box, and then click Next.
9. On the *Zone File* page, click Next.
10. On the *Master DNS Servers* page (see Figure 8-24), type the IP address of the server that hosts the primary record and press the Enter key. Click Next.

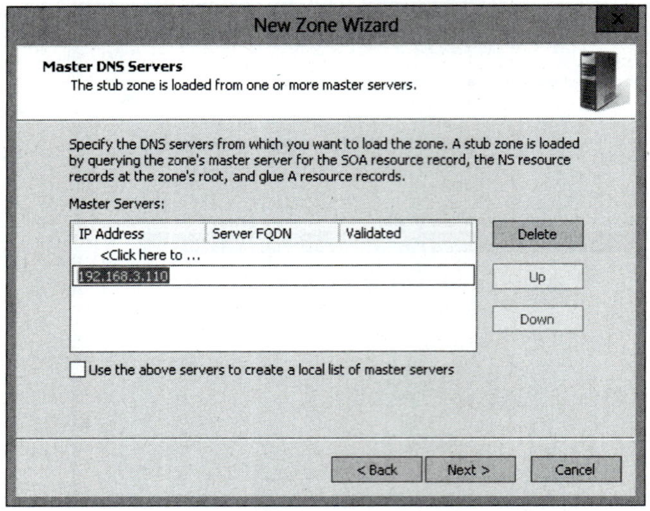

Figure 8-24

Specifying the master DNS server for a stub zone

11. When the *Completing the New Zone Wizard* appears, click Finish.

Configuring Caching-Only Servers

Another type of server is the ***caching-only server***. A caching-only server does not host any zones and is not authoritative for any domain. Instead, it receives client requests, and as the DNS servers fulfill DNS queries, the server adds the information to its cache. When answering subsequent client queries asking for the same information, the DNS server already has the information. Typically, you use caching-only DNS servers when DNS is needed locally, but you do not want to create a separate domain or zone.

To install a caching-only DNS server, first install a DNS server on the server computer. Because a caching-only server is configured to cache only, you do not configure the DNS server, including loading and creating zones. You should also verify the server root hints are configured and updated correctly. When a DNS entry is cached, the cache record remains on the server until the TTL value of the resource record is exceeded.

Configuring Forwarding and Conditional Forwarding

By default, when a client contacts a DNS server and the DNS server does not know the answer, it performs an iterative query to find the answer, which means it first contacts the root domain and additional DNS servers until it finds the authoritative DNS server for the zone. However, DNS servers can be configured to be forwarded to another DNS server or a conditional forwarder based on the domain name queried.

CERTIFICATION READY
Configure conditional forwards.
Objective 3.1

Many organizations have multiple levels of DNS servers. For example, an organization can have multiple DNS servers for its internal users and multiple DNS servers for Internet access, which provide addresses for external websites and other network services. Another example is an organization that has one level of DNS servers for internal users and an Internet Service Provider (ISP) that DNS services. In either of these two cases, you can configure the internal

DNS servers to forward the DNS queries to the external DNS servers or the ISP servers. As a result, clients and the internal DNS servers perform recursive queries, and the external or ISP DNS performs iterative queries.

By using a ***forwarder***, you control name resolution queries and traffic, which can improve the efficiency of name resolution for the computers in your network. You can manage the DNS traffic between the organization's network and the Internet by allowing only internal DNS servers to communicate over the Internet, allowing for a more secure environment because DNS information can be used to hack into a network. In addition, by having all DNS traffic going through single DNS servers, a single server can build a larger cache of DNS data. As a result, Internet traffic is decreased and clients receive faster response times.

CONFIGURE FORWARDERS

GET READY. To configure a DNS server to forward DNS queries to another DNS server, perform the following steps:

1. Open Server Manager.
2. Click Tools > DNS to open the *DNS Manager console*.
3. If necessary, expand the DNS console to a full-screen view.
4. Right-click the DNS server and select Properties. The *Server Properties* dialog box opens.
5. Select the Forwarders tab (see Figure 8-25).

Figure 8-25

Selecting the Forwarders tab

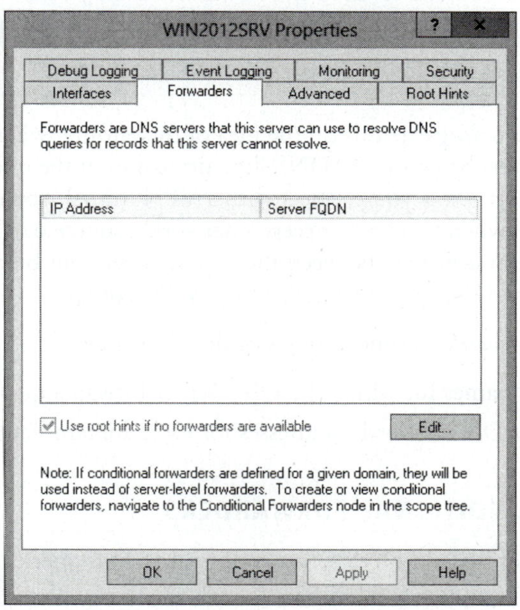

6. Click the Edit button. The *Edit Forwarders* dialog box opens (see Figure 8-26).

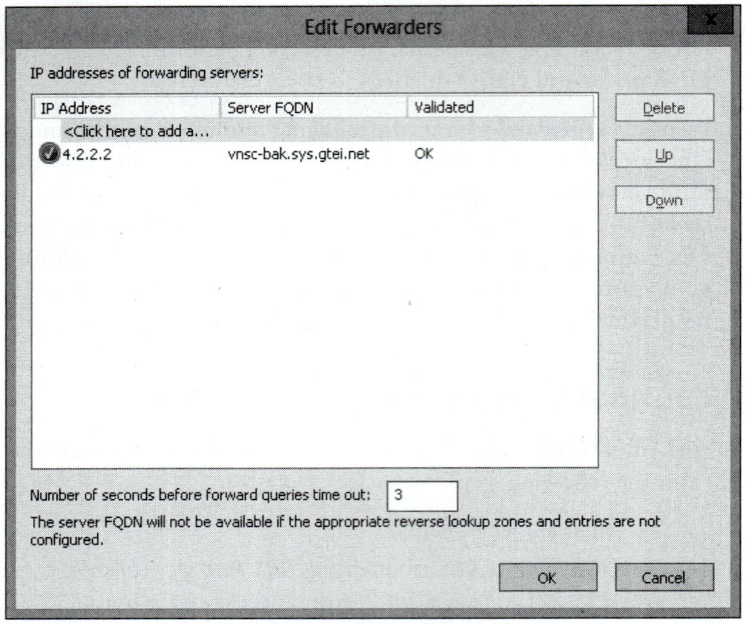

Figure 8-26

Modifying the Forwarders list

7. In the *IP address column*, type the IP address of the DNS server that you want to forward DNS queries to and press the Enter key.
8. Click the OK button to close the *Forwarders* dialog box.
9. Click the OK button to close the server Properties dialog box.
10. When the installation is done, click the Close button.

Conditional forwarding expands on the idea of forwarding, where you forward those queries to other DNS servers based on the DNS domain names in the query. Therefore, if you have a partner organization where you connect with a VPN tunnel, you can forward those request to the partner's DNS when you try to access a network resource on the partner network. Of course, coordination is needed between the two organizations because firewalls have to be configured to allow DNS traffic to traverse the VPN tunnel.

The *conditional forwarder* setting consists of the following:

- The domain names for which the DNS server forwards queries
- One or more DNS server IP addresses for each domain name specified

CONFIGURE CONDITIONAL FORWARDERS

GET READY. To configure a DNS server to forward DNS queries to another DNS server, perform the following steps:

1. Open Server Manager.
2. Click Tools > DNS to open the *DNS Manager console*.
3. If necessary, expand the DNS console to a full-screen view.
4. Expand the server so that you can see the *Conditional Forwarders* folder.
5. Right-click Conditional Forwarders Zones and click New Conditional Forwarder (see Figure 8-27). The New Conditional Forwarder dialog box appears.

Figure 8-27

Creating a conditional forwarder

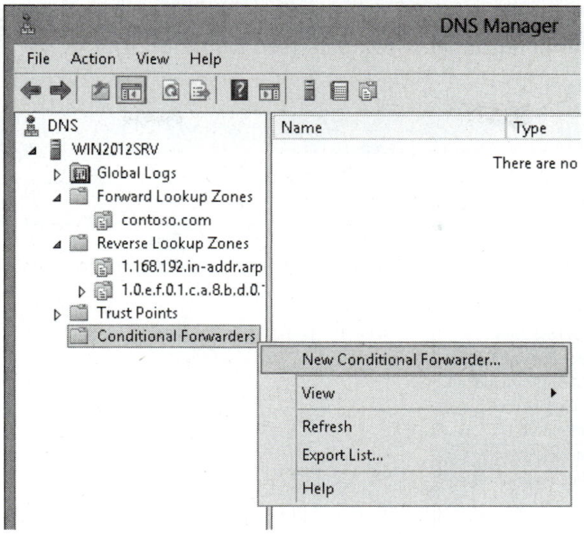

6. Type the name of the DNS domain included in DNS queries that you want to forward in the *DNS Domain* text box (see Figure 8-28).

Figure 8-28

Identifying the name and IP address of a conditional forwarder

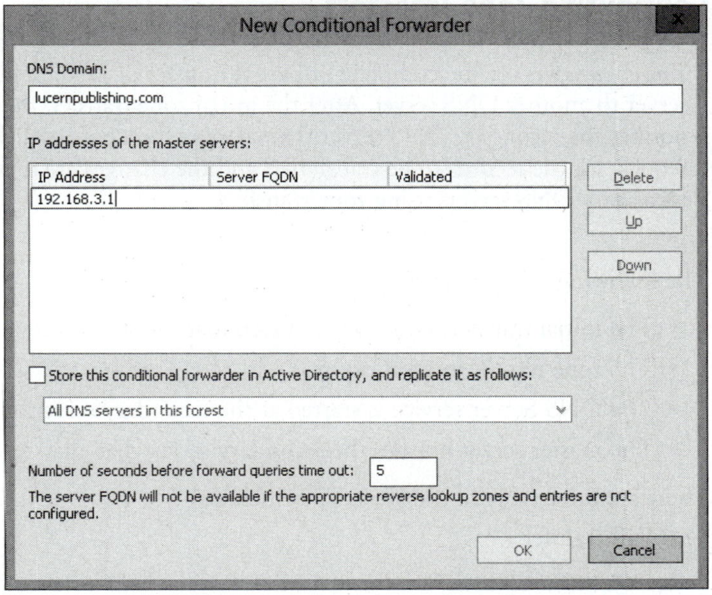

7. In the *IP Address* column, type the IP address of the DNS server that you want to forward to, and then press the Enter key.

8. Click the OK to close the *New Conditional Forwarder* dialog box. The zone appears under Conditional Forwarders (see Figure 8-29).

Figure 8-29

Viewing the conditional forwarders

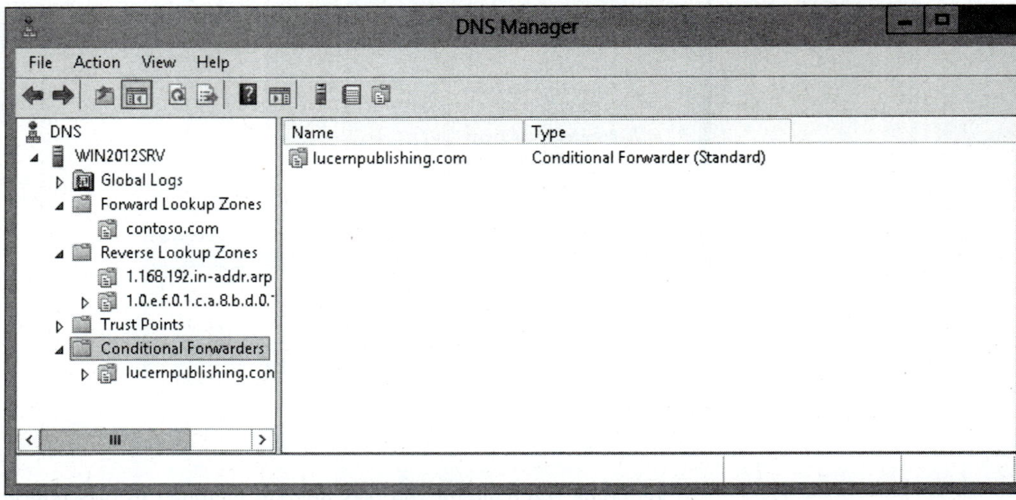

Configuring Zone Transfers

Zone transfers are the complete or partial transfer of DNS data from a zone on a DNS server to another DNS server. After the initial zone transfer, the primary DNS server notifies the secondary DNS server that changes have occurred. The secondary servers then request for the records to be transferred and the changes are then replicated to all the secondary DNS servers using zone transfers.

CERTIFICATION READY
Configure zone transfer settings.
Objective 3.1

The following events trigger a zone transfer:

- The initial transfer occurs when a secondary zone is created.
- The zone refresh interval expires.
- The DNS Server service is started at the secondary server.
- The master server notifies the secondary server that changes have been made to a zone.

There are three types of transfers. They include:

- Full transfer
- Incremental transfer
- DNS Notify

UNDERSTANDING FULL AND INCREMENTAL TRANSFERS

A ***full zone transfer (AXFR)***, which copies the entire zone, is used when you first add a new DNS secondary server for an existing zone. With large zones, AXFRs can be time-consuming and resource-intensive.

An ***incremental zone transfer (IXFR)*** retrieves only resource records that have changed within a zone. To determine whether a zone transfer is needed, the serial number on the secondary server is compared with the serial number of the primary server. If the primary server database is higher, than a transfer of resource records is needed. Because the IXFR does only a partial zone transfer, it uses less bandwidth.

CONFIGURING NOTIFY SETTINGS

CERTIFICATION READY
Configure notify settings.
Objective 3.1

Instead of the secondary zone servers polling the primary server for serial numbers, the ***DNS Notify*** method allows the primary DNS server to use a "push" mechanism to notify secondary servers that it has been updated and that the resource records need to be transferred. The DNS is not a mechanism for transferring data. Instead, it is used with AXFR and IXFR to notify a secondary server that new records are available for transfer.

By default, zone transfers are disabled. When you enable them, you can choose one of the following:

- To any server: Allows a data transfer to any server that asks for a zone transfer (least secure).
- Only to servers listed on the Name Servers tab: Restricts zone transfers to secondary DNS servers as defined with NS resource records.
- Only to the following servers: Restricts zone transfers to those servers specified in the accompanied list.

In the following exercise, you enable and configure a zone transfer.

CONFIGURE ZONE TRANSFER SETTINGS

GET READY. To deploy DNS on Windows Server 2012, perform the following steps:

1. Open Server Manager.
2. Click Tools > DNS to open the *DNS Manager console*.
3. If necessary, expand the DNS console to a full-screen view.
4. Expand the server so that you can see the *Forward Lookup Zones* and *Reverse Lookup Zones* folders.
5. Right-click the forward or reverse lookup zone that you want to configure and click Properties. The *Properties* dialog box opens.
6. Click the Zone Transfers tab (see Figure 8-30).

Figure 8-30
Viewing the Zone Transfers tab

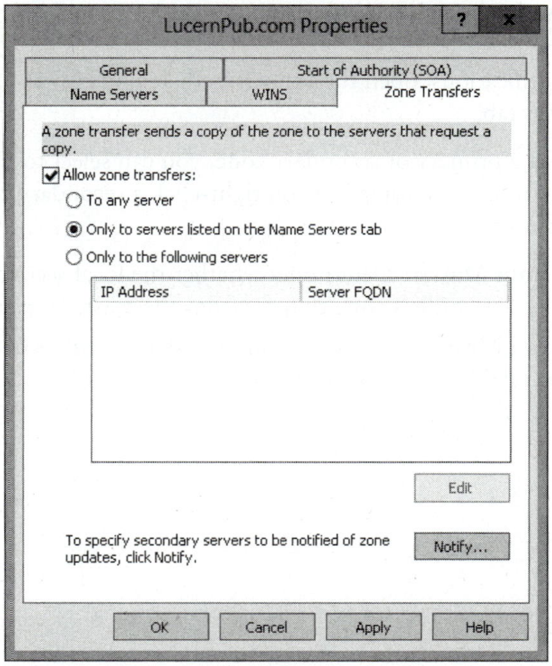

7. Select the Allow zone transfers option.
8. Select the type of zone transfer:
   - To any server
   - Only to servers listed on the Name Servers
   - Only to the following servers

   If you select Only to the following servers, click the Edit button to specify the addresses that you want to perform zone transfers.
9. To configure the Notify options, click the Notify button to display the *Notify* dialog box (see Figure 8-31). Then select the Servers listed on the Name Servers tab option or select The following servers option and specify which servers you want to notify. Click the OK button to close the *Notify* dialog box.

Figure 8-31

Configuring Notify options in the Notify dialog box

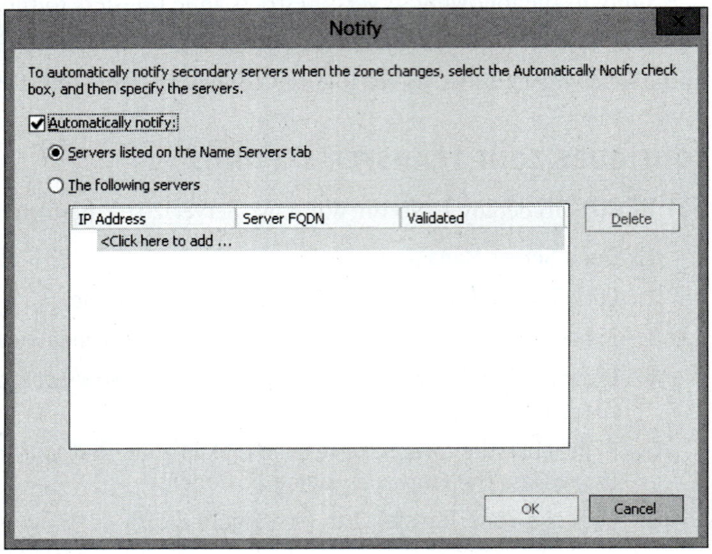

10. Click OK to close the *Properties* dialog box.

To configure notifications, open the Properties dialog box for the zone and click the *Notify in the Zone Transfers* tab.

If you right-click a primary or secondary zone, you can select to *Reload*, which reloads the secondary zone from local storage. If you right-click a secondary zone, you can also select one of following options:

- **Transfer from Master:** Determines whether the local secondary zone serial number has expired and then pulls a zone transfer from the master server.
- **Reload from Master:** Performs a zone transfer regardless of the serial number in the secondary zone's SOA resource records.

Using the Dnscmd Command to Manage Zones

THE BOTTOM LINE

The ***dnscmd.exe*** command allows an administrator to display and change properties of the DNS servers, zones, and resource records. Because `dnscmd.exe` can be executed at the command prompt, it can also be used in script batch files to help automate the management and updates of existing DNS server configurations.

The `dnscmd.exe` command was introduced with Windows Server 2008. With it, you can perform the following:

- Create, delete, and view zones and records
- Reset server and zone properties
- Perform zone maintenance operations, such as updating the zone, reloading the zone, refreshing the zone, writing the zone back to a file or to Active Directory, and pausing or resuming the zone
- Clear the cache
- Stop and start the DNS service
- View statistics

For example, to view the zones on a DNS server called `server1.contoso.com`, execute the following command:

```
dnscmd server1.contoso.com /enumzones
```

To add an Active Directory-integrated primary zone called `support.contoso.com on server1.contoso.com,` execute the following command:

```
dnscmd server1.contoso.com /zoneadd support.contoso.com /dsprimary
```

To create a secondary zone called `support.contoso.com on server1.contoso.com,` perform the following command from the primary zone located at 10.0.0.2:

```
dnscmd server1.contoso.com /zoneadd support.contoso.com /secondary
10.0.0.2
```

To delete the secondary zone called `support.contoso.com,` perform the following command:

```
dnscmd server1.contoso.com /zonedelete support.contoso.com
```

To create an Active Directory conditional forwarder called `lucernpublishing.com` to the server2.lucernpublishing.com server while setting the replication scope to All DNS servers in this forest, perform the following command:

```
dnscmd server1.contoso.com /zoneadd lucernpublishing.com /
dsforwarder server2.lucernpublishing.com /forest
```

To force a secondary DNS zone for `support.contoso.com` to update from the master zone, perform the following command:

```
dnscmd server1.contoso.com /zonerefresh support.contoso.com
```

SKILL SUMMARY

IN THIS LESSON, YOU LEARNED:

- Domain Name System (DNS) is a naming service that is used by TCP/IP network and is essential service used by the Internet. The DNS servers are often referred to as name server.
- Each node or leaf in the tree is a resource record (RR), which holds information associated with the domain name.
- The primary zone provides an authoritative, read-write copy of the zone, while the secondary zone provides an authoritative, read-only copy of the primary zone.
- A forward lookup zone contains most of the resource records for a domain. Of course, as the name indicates, forward lookup zones are primarily used to resolve host names to IP addresses.
- A reverse lookup zone is used to resolve IP addresses to host names.
- Today, DNS can be stored in and replicated with Active Directory as an Active Directory-integrated zone.
- By using Active Directory-integrated zones, DNS follows a multi-master model, whereas each server allows all DNS servers to have authoritative read-write copies of the DNS zone. When a change is made on one DNS server, it is replicated to the other DNS servers.
- A stub zone is a copy of a zone that contains only necessary resource records (SOA, NS, and an A record) in the master zone and acts as a pointer to authoritative name server.
- The stub zone allows the server to forward queries to the name server that is authoritative for the master zone without going up to the root name servers and working its way down to the server.
- By using a forwarder, you control name resolution queries and traffic, which can improve the efficiency of name resolution for the computers in your network.
- Conditional forwarding expands on the idea of forwarding, where you forward those queries to other DNS servers based on the DNS domain names in the query.
- Zone transfers are the complete or partial transfer of DNS data from a zone on a DNS server to another DNS server.
- A full zone transfer (AXFR), which copies the entire zone, is used when you first bring a new DNS secondary server for an existing zone. With large zones, full transfers can be very time-consuming and resource extensive.
- An incremental zone transfer (IXFR) retrieves only resource records that have changed within a zone.
- Instead of the secondary zone servers polling the primary server for serial numbers, the DNS Notify method allows the primary DNS server to use a "push" mechanism to notify secondary servers that it has been updated and that the resource records need to be transferred.
- The `dnscmd.exe` command allows an administrator to display and change properties of the DNS servers, zones, and resource records.

Knowledge Assessment

Multiple Choice

Select the correct answer for each of the following questions.

1. How many primary zones can a zone have?
   a. 1
   b. 2
   c. 3
   d. Unlimited
2. Which are often known as name servers?
   a. DNS servers
   b. Active Directory servers
   c. Domain controllers
   d. Translation servers
3. Which zone is used to translate host names to IP addresses.
   a. Forward lookup zone
   b. Reverse lookup zone
   c. Primary zone
   d. Secondary zone
4. Which would you use when you create a reverse lookup zone for the 172.25.0.0 subnet (subnet mask of 255.255.0.0)?
   a. 172.25
   b. 172.25.0.0
   c. 25.172
   d. 0.0.25.172
5. Which is each node or leaf in the DNS tree referred to as?
   a. Setting
   b. Resource record
   c. Property
   d. Row
6. Which is used to automatically create and update the host's primary DNS server?
   a. Master client
   b. Dynamic updates
   c. Secondary zone
   d. Active Directory client
7. Which zone contains only the necessary resource records that act as an authoritative name server?
   a. Forwarding zone
   b. Conditional forwarding zone
   c. Secondary zone
   d. Stub zone
8. Which forwards queries to other DNS servers based on the DNS domain name in the query?
   a. Stub forwarding
   b. Dynamic forwarding
   c. conditional forwarding
   d. Intelligent forwarding

9. Which sends DNS information from a zone on a DNS server to another DNS server?
   a. Zone lookup
   b. Dynamic transfer
   c. Resource record synchronization
   d. Zone transfer

10. Which command do you use to create a zone to a DNS on a DNS server?
   a. `dnscmd /create`
   b. `dnscmd /zoneadd`
   c. `dnscmd /zonerefresh`
   d. `dnscmd /start`

Best Answer

Choose the letter that corresponds to the best answer. More than one answer choice may achieve the goal. Select the BEST answer.

1. Which would you use to send name resolution queries to another DNS server?
   a. Primary zone
   b. Forwarding zone
   c. Conditional zone
   d. Secondary zone

2. Which type of transfer copies the entire zone to another DNS server?
   a. Full transfer
   b. Incremental transfer
   c. Standard transfer
   d. Notify transfer

3. Which setting enables you to notify secondary name servers when a zone has been updated and the resource records that need to be transferred are listed?
   a. `forward` command
   b. Primary transfer
   c. Secondary transfer
   d. DNS Notify

4. Which would you use if you wanted several DNS servers to each act as a master for a zone? C
   a. Primary zone
   b. Secondary zone
   c. Active Directory-integrated zone
   d. Replicating zone

5. Which type of server stores DNS requests for future use but is not authoritative for any zone? D
   a. Primary name server
   b. Conditional forwarding server
   c. Stub server
   d. Caching-only server

Matching and Identification

1. Identify which of the following is a benefit of DNS.
   _____ Durability
   _____ Scalability
   _____ Strong fault tolerance
   _____ Fast modifications
   _____ Ease of use
   _____ Consistency

2. Identify the benefits of using Active Directory-integrated zones. (Not all answers will be used.)
   _____ Security
   _____ Self-healing
   _____ Customized selected replication
   _____ Fault tolerance
   _____ Efficient replication

3. Identify the types of zone transfers? (Not all answers will be used.)
   _____ Incremental transfer
   _____ Registered transfer
   _____ Full transfer
   _____ Hidden transfer
   _____ Dynamic transfer
   _____ DNS Notify

4. Which of the following triggers a zone transfer? (Not all answers will be used.)
   _____ The zone refresh interval expires.
   _____ Initial transfer occurs when a secondary zone is created.
   _____ The fail safe mechanism has been triggered.
   _____ DNS Server service is started at the secondary server.
   _____ WINS has an update for DNS.
   _____ The master server notifies the second server that changes have been made to the zone.
   _____ The Jet database service is restarted.

Build a List

1. Identify the four basic steps, in order, of deploying DNS. Not all steps will be used.
   _____ Configure the DNS Server.
   _____ Configure the clients to use DNS servers.
   _____ Add resource records to the forward and lookup zones.
   _____ Migrate resource records from a database.
   _____ Install DNS on one or more servers.
   _____ Configure sequence numbers.
   _____ Create forward and reverse lookup zones.

Business Case Scenarios

Scenario 8-1: Implementing DNS

You have three large sites in your organization: the corporate office, the engineering site, and the manufacturing site. You want to make sure that you install DNS so that all of the zones have fault tolerance while still allowing changes on any DNS server and for the best performance possible. What do you recommend, and why do you recommend this particular solution?

Scenario 8-2: Controlling DNS Updates

You have an organization that often has visitors connect to the organization's network. You are worried that someone might modify a DNS record so to hijack a computer name. What can you use to prevent this, and how do you implement it?

9 LESSON

Configuring DNS Records

70-411 EXAM OBJECTIVE

Objective 3.2 – Configure DNS records. This objective may include but is not limited to: create and configure DNS Resource Records (RR), including A, AAAA, PTR, SOA, NS, SRV, CNAME, and MX records; configure zone scavenging; configure record options, including Time To Live (TTL) and weight; configure round robin; configure secure dynamic updates.

LESSON HEADING	EXAM OBJECTIVE
Configuring DNS Record Types	Create and configure DNS Resource Records (RR), including A, AAAA, PTR, SOA, NS, SRV, CNAME, and MX records
Creating and Configuring DNS Resource Records	
Configuring Record Options	Configure record options, including Time To Live (TTL) and weight
Configuring Round Robin	Configure round robin
Configuring Secure Dynamic Updates	Configure secure dynamic updates
Configuring Zone Scavenging	Configure zone scavenging
Using the DNSCMD Command to Manage Resource Records	
Troubleshooting DNS Problems	

KEY TERMS

aging
Canonical Name (CNAME) record
DNS zone database
dynamic updates
Host (A and AAAA) record
Mail Exchanger (MX) record
Name Server (NS) record
Pointer (PTR) record
resource record (RR)
round robin
scavenging
secure dynamic updates
Service Location (SRV) record
Start of Authority (SOA) record

Configuring DNS Record Types

THE BOTTOM LINE

A ***DNS zone database*** is made up of a collection of resource records, which are used to answer DNS queries. Each ***resource record*** (RR) specifies information about a particular object. Each record has a type, an expiration time limit, and some type-specific data.

CERTIFICATION READY
Create and configure DNS Resource Records (RR), including A, AAAA, PTR, SOA, NS, SRV, CNAME, and MX records.
Objective 3.2

On an organization's network, many of the resource records are automatically created. For example, the clients or the DHCP servers create the host and Pointer (PTR) records. When you install a DNS server, NS records are usually created. When you install domain controllers, Service Location (SRV) records are created.

Creating and Configuring DNS Resource Records

When you create a user account, certain properties define the user account, such as first name, last name, and login name. When you define a printer in Active Directory, you define a name of the printer and a location. A printer does not have a first name or a last name. Just as you have different types of objects in Active Directory, you also have different types of resource records in DNS, with different fields.

When you create a new zone, two types of records are automatically created:

- ***Start of Authority (SOA) record:*** Specifies authoritative information about a DNS zone, including the primary name server, the e-mail of the domain administrator, the domain serial number, and the expiration and reload timers of the zone.
- ***Name Server (NS) record:*** Specifies an authoritative name server for the host.

You have to add additional resource records as needed. Figure 9-1 shows a zone with common resource records. The most common resource records are as follows:

- ***Host (A and AAAA) record:*** Maps a domain/host name to an IP address.
- ***Canonical Name (CNAME) record:*** Sometimes referred to as an Alias, maps an alias DNS domain name to another primary or canonical name.
- ***Pointer (PTR) record:*** Maps an IP address to a domain/host name.
- ***Mail Exchanger (MX) record:*** Maps a DNS domain name to the name of a computer that exchanges or forwards e-mail for the domain.
- ***Service Location (SRV) record:*** Maps a DNS domain name to a specified list of host computers that offer a specific type of service, such as Active Directory domain controllers.

Figure 9-1

Viewing the zone with common resource records

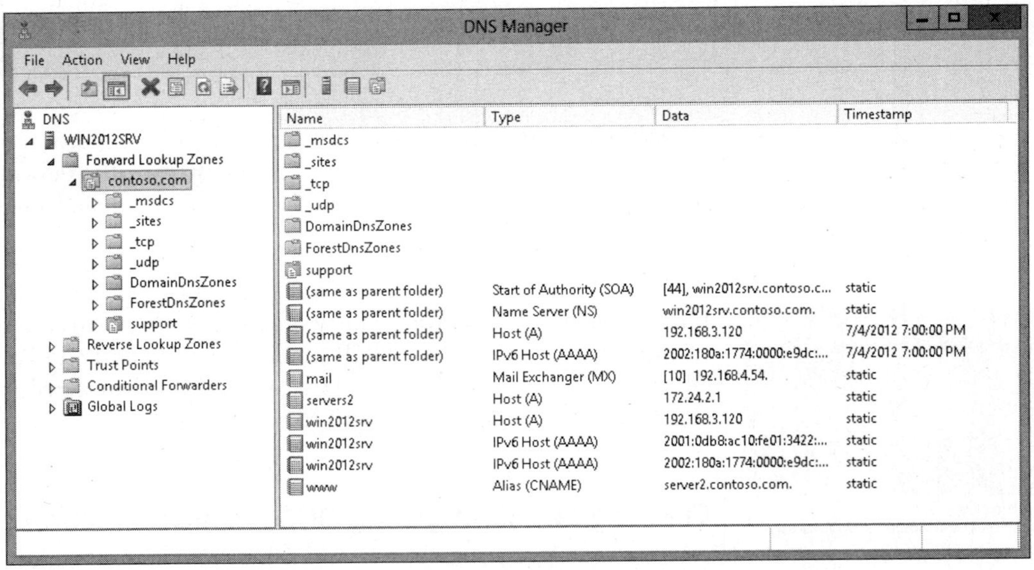

The PTR records in the reverse lookup zone and all of the other record types are in the forward lookup zone.

START OF AUTHORITY (SOA) RECORDS

The SOA record specifies authoritative information about the zone. Therefore, there is only one SOA record for a zone. It includes the following fields:

- **Authoritative server:** Contains the name of the primary DNS server authoritative for the zone.
- **Responsible person:** Shows the e-mail address of the administrator who is responsible for the zone. Instead of using the at (@) symbol, it uses a period (.).
- **Serial number:** Shows the version or how many times the zone has been updated. As explained previously, it is used to determine whether the zone's secondary server needs to initiate a zone transfer with the master server. If the serial number of the master server is higher, the secondary server initiates a zone transfer.
- **Refresh shows:** Determines how often the secondary server for the zone checks to see whether the zone data is changed.
- **Retry:** After sending a zone transfer request, the Retry value determines how long (in seconds) the zone's secondary server waits before sending another request.
- **Expire:** After a zone transfer, Expire determines how long (in seconds) the zone's secondary server continues to respond to zone queries before discarding its own zone as invalid.
- **Minimum TTL:** Specifies a default Time to Live (TTL) value, which defines the default time. A resource record remains in a DNS cache after a DNS query has retrieved a record. If a resource record has its own TTL value, the TTL value of the resource record is used instead of the TTL defined in the SOA record.

Figure 9-2 shows the SOA resource record.

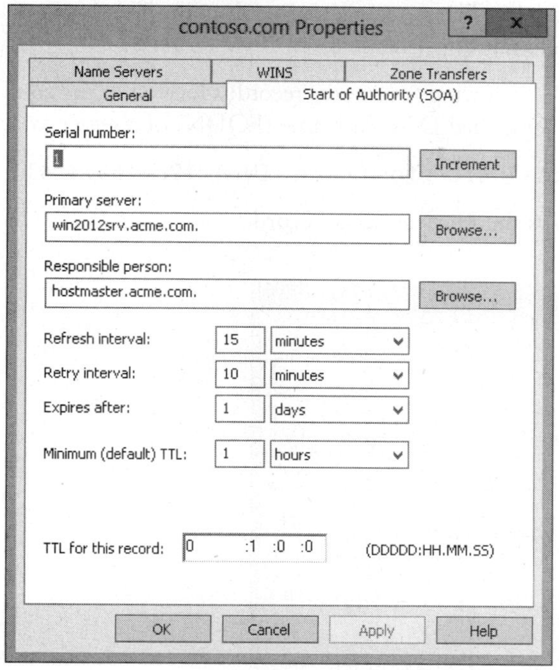

Figure 9-2

Viewing the SOA resource record

NAME SERVER (NS) RECORDS

The Name Server (NS) resource record identifies a DNS server that is authoritative for a zone, including the primary and secondary copies of the DNS zone. Because a zone can be hosted on multiple servers, there is a single record for each DNS server hosting the zone. The Windows Server DNS Server service automatically creates the first NS record for a zone when the zone is created. Figure 9-3 shows the NS resource record.

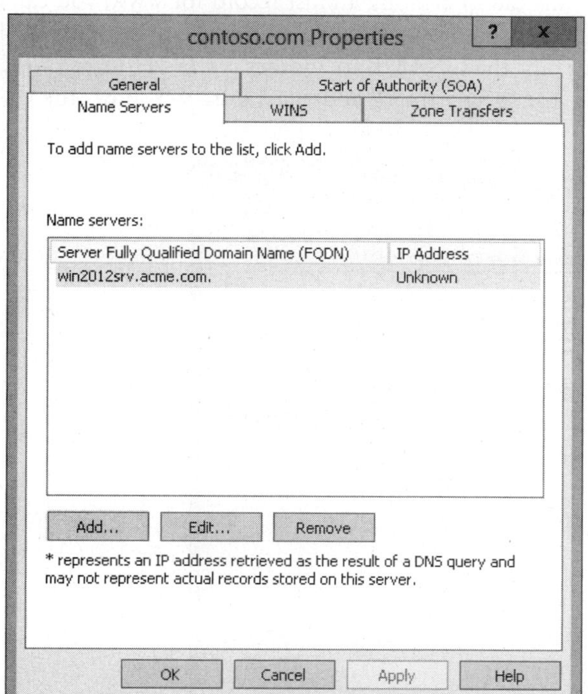

Figure 9-3

Viewing the NS resource record

HOST (A AND AAAA) RECORDS

The most common resource records found in DNS are the Host (A and AAAA) records. The A stands for address. The A record maps a domain/host name to an IPv4 address; the AAAA record maps a domain/host name to an IPv6 address.

For example, the following A resource record is located in the zone *server1.sales.contoso.com* and maps the Fully Qualified Domain Name (FQDN) of a server to an IP address of 192.168.3.41:

```
Server1.sales.contoso.com. IN A 192.168.3.41
```

Figure 9-4 shows the Host resource record.

Figure 9-4

Viewing the Host resource record

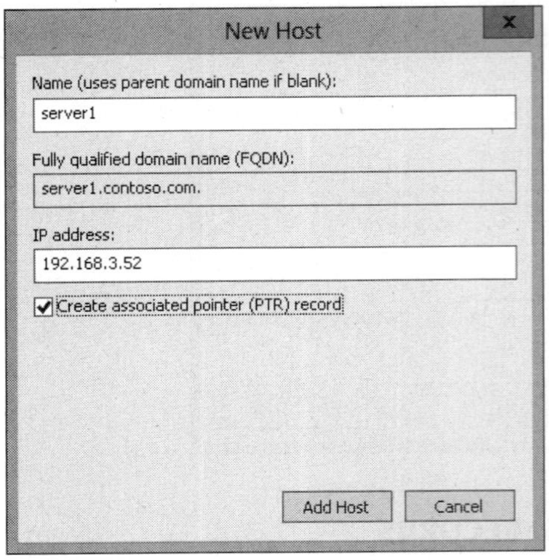

CANONICAL NAME (CNAME) RECORDS

The Canonical Name (CNAME) resource record is an alias for a host name. It is used to hide the implementation details of your network from the clients that connect to it, particularly if you need to make changes in the future.

For example, instead of creating a Host record for www, you can create a CNAME that specifies the web server that hosts the www websites for the domain. If you need to change servers, you just point the CNAME to another server's Host record. Of course, you need to have Host records that specify the IP address. Figure 9-5 shows the CNAME resource record.

Figure 9-5

Viewing the CNAME resource record

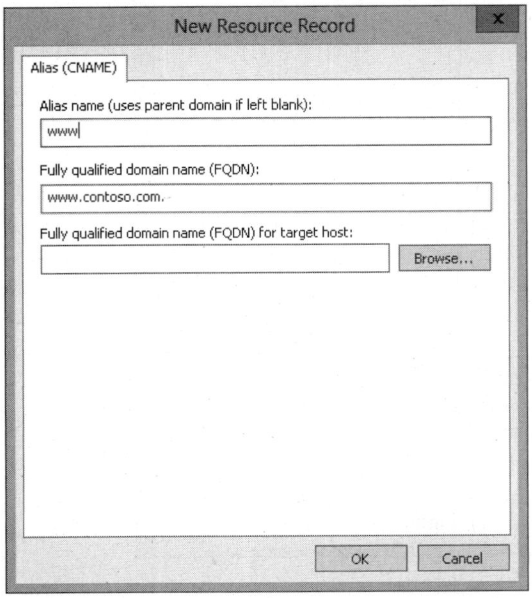

POINTER (PTR) RECORDS

The Pointer records (PTR) are used for the opposite reason of the Host records. They resolve host names from an IP address. Different from the Host record, the IP address is written in reverse. For example, the IP address 192.168.3.41 that points to `server1.sales.contoso` is:

```
41.3.168.192.in-addr.arpa. IN PTR
server1.sales.contoso.com.
```

Figure 9-6 shows the PTR resource record.

Figure 9-6

Viewing the PTR resource record

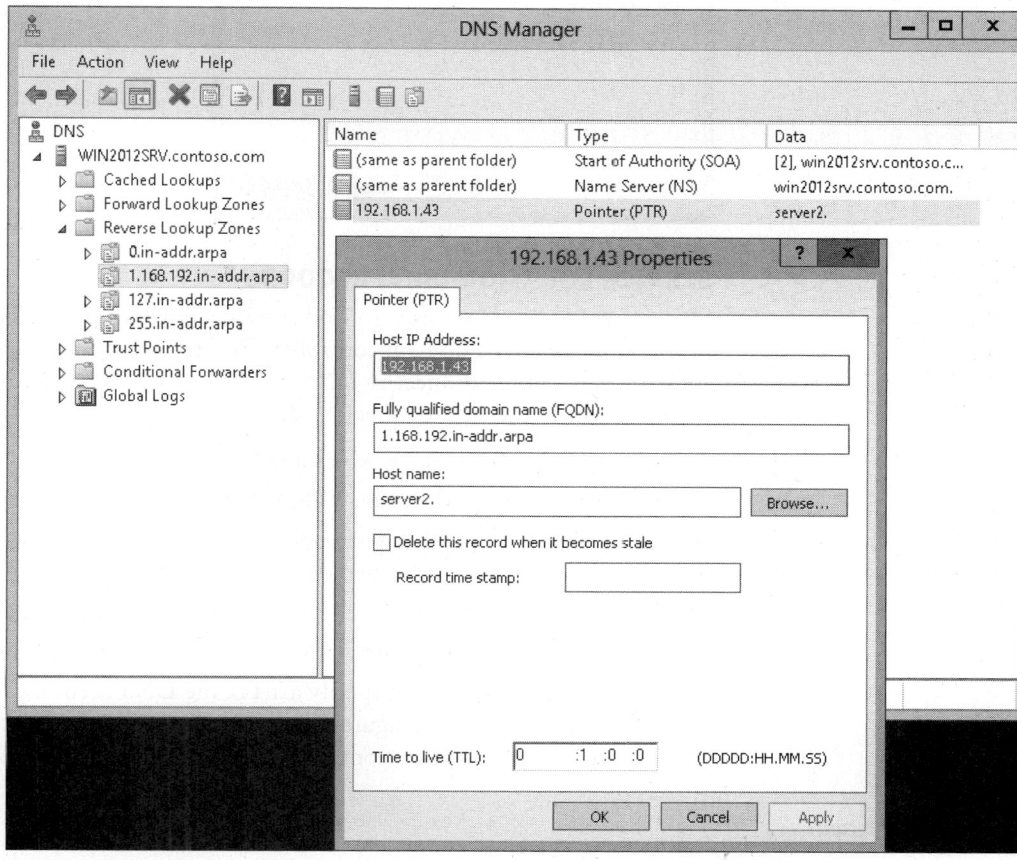

MAIL EXCHANGER (MX) RECORDS

The Mail Exchanger (MX) resource record specifies an organization's mail server, service, or device that receives mail via Simple Mail Transfer Protocol (SMTP). For fault tolerance, you can designate a second mail server. Therefore, if the primary mail server is not available, the e-mail can be sent to the secondary server. Although each mail external mail server requires an MX record, the primary server is designed with a lower priority number.

For example, if you have three mail servers that can receive e-mail over the Internet, you would have three MX records for the `contoso.com` domain:

```
@ IN MX 5 mailserver1.contoso.com.

@ IN MX 10 mailserver2.contoso.com.

@ IN MX 20 mailserver3.contoso.com.
```

The primary mail server is the first one because it has a lower priority number. Figure 9-7 shows the MX resource record.

Figure 9-7

Viewing the MX resource record

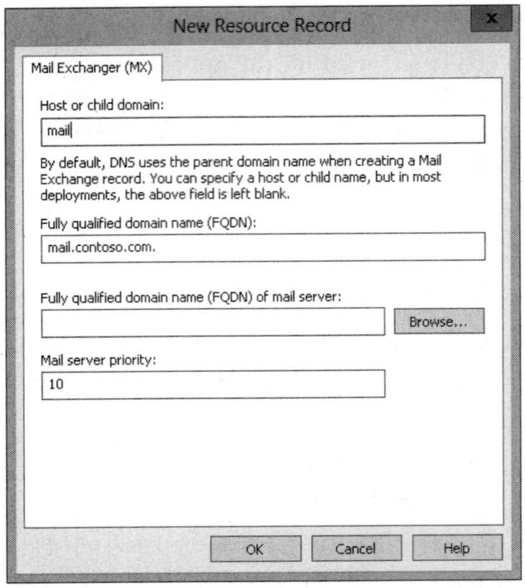

SERVICE LOCATION (SRV) RECORDS

SRV resource records are used to find specific network services. For example, when you install Active Directory via a domain controller, SRV records are automatically added to the DNS zone. If users cannot connect to DNS services or the SRV records are not in the zone, users cannot log in to the Active Directory domain.

The format for an SRV record is as follows:

```
Service_Protocol.Name [TTL] Class SRV Priority Weight Port Target
```

For example, to log in with Lightweight Directory Access Protocol (LDAP), you could have the following SRV records for two domain controllers:

```
ldap._tcp.contoso.com. IN SRV 0 0 389 dc1.contoso.com.
ldap._tcp.contoso.com. IN SRV 10 0 389 dc2.contoso.com.
```

Because these examples do not specify a TTL, the DNS client uses the minimum TTL specified in the SOA resource record. Figure 9-8 shows the SRV resource record, and Figure 9-9 shows the SRV records for a domain controller, specifically to find the LDAP and Kerberos servers.

Figure 9-8

Viewing the SRV record

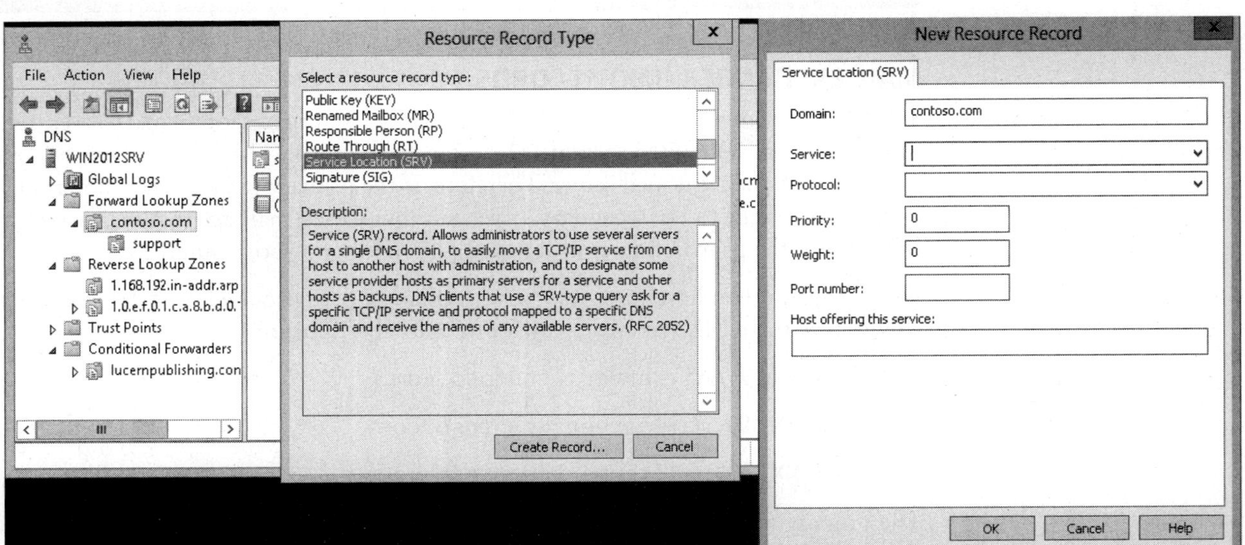

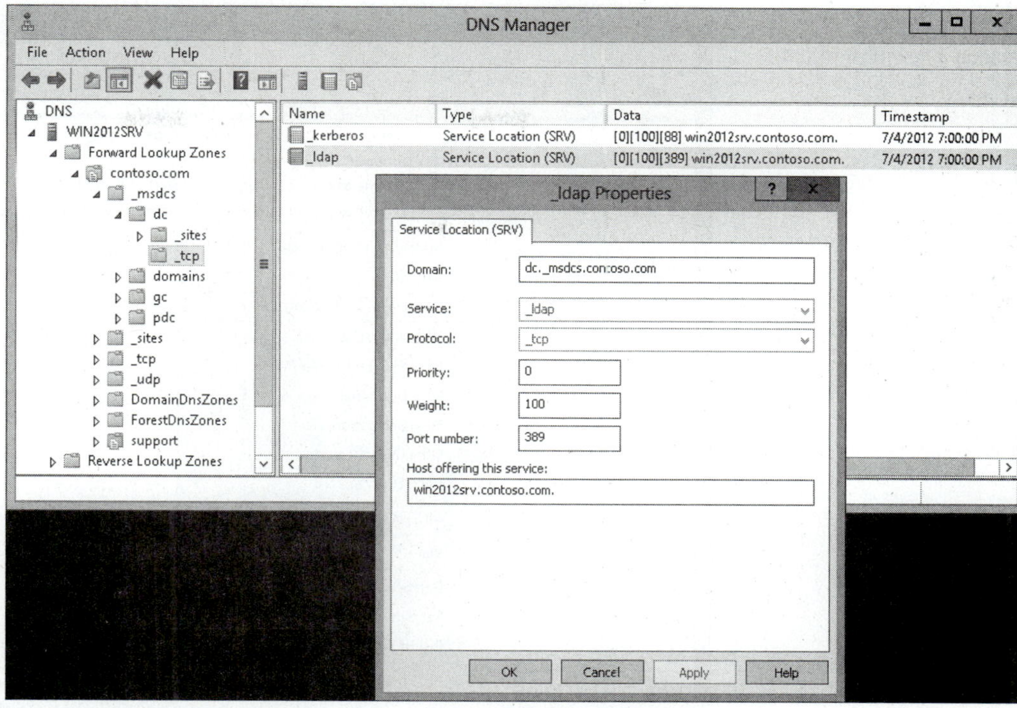

Figure 9-9
Viewing the SRV resource record for a domain

TAKE NOTE*

With SRV records, for the domain to be added to a DNS zone, the zone must allow dynamic updates.

CERTIFICATION READY
Configure record options, including Time To Live (TTL) and weight
Objective 3.2

Configuring Record Options

Managing resources is easy with Windows servers because the DNS console provides a GUI interface.

Before you can create resource records, you need to first create the appropriate forward lookup zones and reverse lookup zones.

CREATE A HOST RECORD

GET READY. To create a Host record, perform the following steps:

1. Open Server Manager by clicking the Server Manager button on the task bar.
2. Click Tools > DNS to open the *DNS Manager console*.
3. If necessary, expand the DNS console to a full-screen view.
4. Expand the server to display the *Forward Lookup Zones* and *Reverse Lookup Zones* folders.
5. Right-click the zone that you want to create a Host resource record for and select New Host (A or AAAA) (see Figure 9-10). The *New Host* dialog box appears.

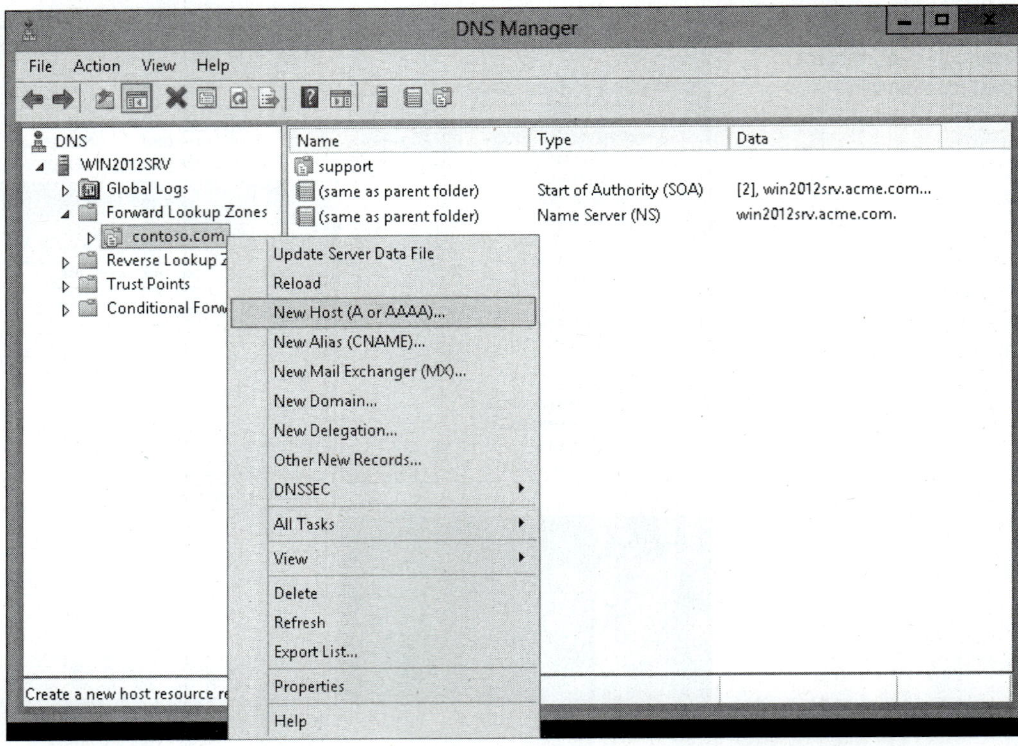

Figure 9-10
Creating a new Host record

6. In the *Name* text box, type the name of the host.
7. In the *IP address* text field, type the IP address (IPv4 or IPv6).
8. If you want to also create a PTR record, select the Create associated pointer (PTR) record option.
9. Click Add Host.
10. If you need to create additional Host records, add the appropriate host names and IP addresses. If you do not want to create more, click the Done button.

If the reverse lookup zone does not exist to store the PTR record, a warning that the associated pointer (PTR) record cannot be created.

To change a resource record, you just double-click the resource record to display the Properties dialog box, and then you make the appropriate changes. Of course, when you create resource records or change resource records, it takes time to replicate the resource records to the other DNS servers for the domain.

By opening the View menu and selecting the Advanced option in the DNS console, administrators can see additional options when managing and configuring the resource records, including the TTL for the resource record.

To view the TTL settings for individual resource records, you need to use the DNS Manager console in Advanced mode. Figure 9-11 shows the same resource record in Normal view and in Advanced view.

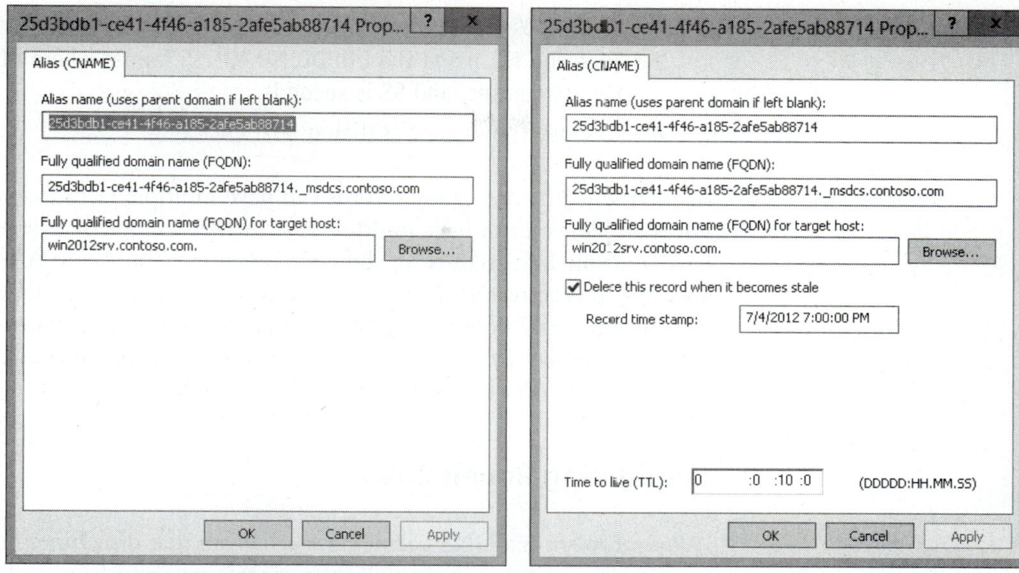

Figure 9-11

Viewing the Normal view and Advanced view for a resource record

MODIFY THE TTL VALUE FOR A RESOURCE RECORD

GET READY. To modify the Time to Live (TTL) value for a resource record, perform the following steps:

1. Open Server Manager by clicking the Server Manager button on the task bar.
2. Click Tools > DNS to open the *DNS Manager console*.
3. If necessary, expand the DNS console to a full-screen view.
4. Expand the server to display the *Forward Lookup Zones* and *Reverse Lookup Zones* folders.
5. To view additional options, click View > Advancec (see Figure 9-12).

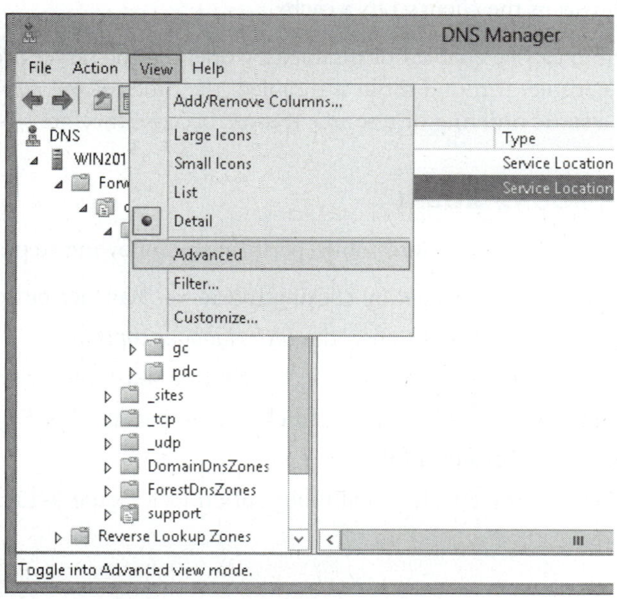

Figure 9-12

Selecting the Advanced option

6. To modify a record, double-click a resource record. The *Properties* dialog box opens.
7. Type the TTL using the DDDDD:HH.MM.SS format where DDDDD is days, HH is hours, MM is minutes, and SS is seconds.
8. To close the *Properties* dialog box, click OK.

As mentioned before, many records can have multiple records assigned with the same name. For example, you can have multiple A or AAAA records that have the same name or you have multiple MX records for the same domain. With A and AAAA records, you don't define a weight to each record. Instead, each record is equal. With MX records, you must define a weight or priority (lowest number takes priority), so that it knows which SMTP server an e-mail should be sent to first. If that one is not available, it tries the second SMTP server listed with the next lowest priority.

Configuring Round Robin

Round robin is a DNS balancing mechanism that distributes network load among multiple servers by rotating resource records retrieved from a DNS server.

CERTIFICATION READY
Configure round robin.
Objective 3.2

By default, DNS uses round robin to rotate the resource records returned in a DNS query where multiple resource records of the same type exist for a query's DNS host name.

For example, you can create the following Host records for webserver.contoso.com:

192.168.3.151	webserver.contoso.com
192.168.3.152	webserver.contoso.com
192.168.3.153	webserver.contoso.com

When the first client queries for webserver.contoso.com, the client gets back 192.168.3.151. When the second client queries for webserver.contoso.com, the client gets back 192.168.3.152. The third client gets back 192.168.3.153. When the fourth client accesses the webserver, the client gets 192.168.3.151. If one of these clients tries to access the webserver a second time before the TTL time expires, the client goes back to the same address because that address is in the client's DNS cache.

Round robin can be enabled or disabled by opening the server properties within the DNS Manager console. If round robin is disabled, the order of the response for these queries is based on a static ordering of resource records because they are stored in the zone.

DISABLE ROUND ROBIN

GET READY. To disable round robin, perform the following steps:

1. Open Server Manager by clicking the Server Manager button on the task bar.
2. Click Tools > DNS to open the *DNS Manager console*.
3. If necessary, expand the DNS console to a full-screen view.
4. Right-click the DNS server and choose Properties. The *Properties* dialog box opens.
5. Click the Advanced tab.
6. Deselect the Enable round robin option (see Figure 9-13).

Figure 9-13
Disabling round robin

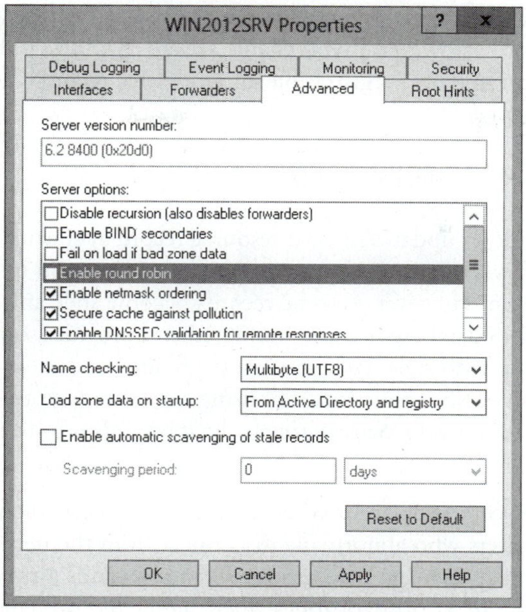

7. Click the OK button to close the *Properties* dialog box.

Configuring Secure Dynamic Updates

DNS supports ***dynamic updates***, where resource records for the clients are automatically created and updated at the host's primary DNS server. For Active Directory-integrated zones, these records are automatically replicated to the other DNS servers. However, because standard dynamic updates are insecure, Microsoft added secure dynamic updates.

CERTIFICATION READY
Configure secure dynamic updates.
Objective 3.2

For years, Windows DNS has supported dynamic updates, whereas a DNS client host registers and dynamically updates the resource records with a DNS server. If a host's IP address changes, the resource record (particularly the A record) for the host is automatically updated, while the host utilizes the DHCP server to dynamically update its Pointer (PTR) resource record. Therefore, when a user or service needs to contact a client PC, it can look up the IP address of the host. With larger organizations, this becomes an essential feature, especially for clients that frequently move or change locations and use DHCP to automatically obtain an IP address. For dynamic DNS updates to succeed, the zone must be configured to accept dynamic updates, as shown in Figure 9-14.

Figure 9-14
Enabling secure dynamic updates

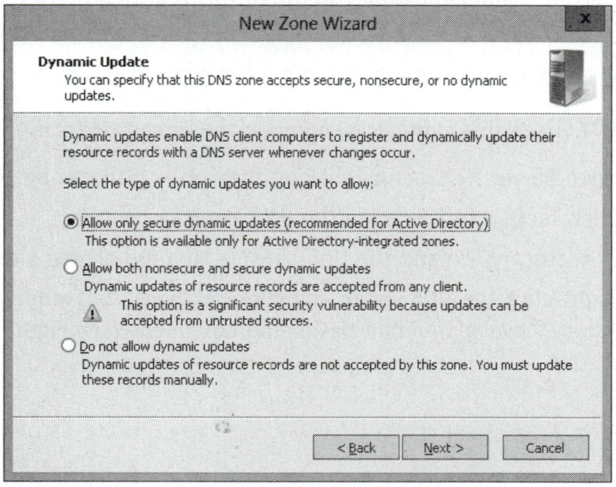

Unfortunately, standard dynamic updates are not secure because any one can update a standard resource record. However, if you enable ***secure dynamic updates***, only updates from the same computer can update a registration for a resource record.

Configuring Zone Scavenging

By default, Windows updates its own resource record at startup time and every 24 hours after startup. This is to ensure the records are up-to-date and to help guard against accidental deletion. However, as some records become stale and are not removed or updated, the DNS database becomes outdated and provides some inaccurate information to clients. To help with stale data, you can configure zone scavenging to clean up the stale records. ***Aging*** in DNS is the process of using timestamps to track the age of dynamically registered resource records. ***Scavenging*** is the mechanism to remove stale resource records.

CERTIFICATION READY
Configure zone scavenging.
Objective 3.2

Typically, stale DNS records occur when a computer is permanently removed from the network. Mobile users who abnormally disconnect from the network can also cause stale DNS records. To help manage stale records, Windows adds a time stamp to dynamically added resource records in primary zones where aging and scavenging are enabled. Manually added records are time stamped with a value of 0, and they are automatically excluded from the aging and scavenging process.

TAKE NOTE*
Scavenging and aging must be enabled at the DNS server and on the zone.

To enable aging and scavenging, you must do the following:

- Resource records must be either dynamically added to zones or manually modified to be used in aging and scavenging operations.
- Scavenging and aging must be enabled both at the DNS server and on the zone.

Scavenging is disabled by default.

DNS scavenging depends on the following two settings:

WARNING Be careful when enabling scavenging because it can accidently remove records that you want to keep. As a result, users cannot resolve certain DNS queries, making some network services unavailable.

- **No-refresh interval:** The time between the most recent refresh of a record time stamp and the moment when the time stamp can be refreshed again. When scavenging is enabled, this is set to *7 days* by default.
- **Refresh interval:** The time between the earliest moment when a record time stamp can be refreshed and the earliest moment when the record can be scavenged. The refresh interval must be longer than the maximum record refresh period. When scavenging is enabled, this is set to *7 days* by default.

A DNS record becomes eligible for scavenging after both the no-refresh and refresh intervals have elapsed. If the default values are used, this is a total of 14 days.

ENABLE AGING/SCAVENGING AT THE SERVER

GET READY. To enable aging/scavenging at the server, perform the following steps:

1. Open Server Manager by clicking the Server Manager button on the task bar.
2. Click Tools > DNS to open the *DNS Manager console*.
3. If necessary, expand the DNS console to a full-screen view.
4. Right-click the DNS server and click Set Aging/Scavenging for all Zones. The *Server Aging/Scavenging Properties* dialog box opens (see Figure 9-15).

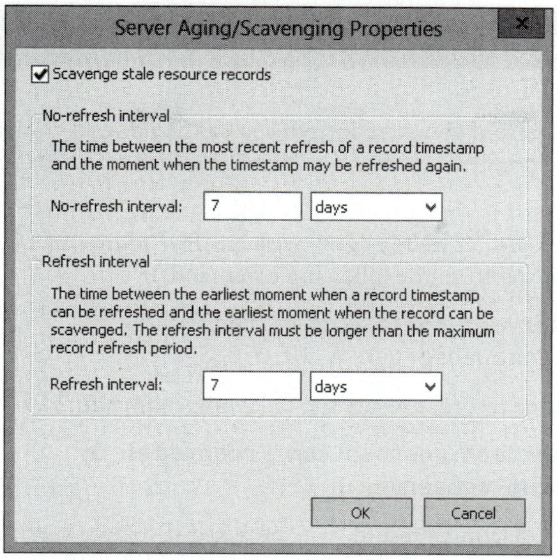

Figure 9-15

Opening the Server Aging/Scavenging Properties dialog box

5. Click the Scavenge stale resource records option.
6. Modify the no-refresh interval and refresh interval as needed.
7. Click the OK button to close the *Server Aging/Scavenging Properties* dialog box.
8. If you want the aging/scavenging settings to apply to all existing Active Directory-integrated zones, select the Apply these settings to the existing Active Directory-integrated zones option. Click OK to close the Server Aging/Scavenging Confirmation dialog box.

TAKE NOTE* It is best that you enable scavenging on only one DNS server. This gives you better control of the aging/scavenging settings and more control when scavenging occurs and how often.

ENABLE AGING/SCAVENGING AT THE ZONE

GET READY. To enable aging/scavenging at the zone, perform the following steps:

1. Open Server Manager by clicking the Server Manager button on the task bar.
2. Click Tools > DNS to open the *DNS Manager console*.
3. If necessary, expand the DNS console to a full-screen view.
4. Expand the server so that you can display the *Forward Lookup Zones* and *Reverse Lookup Zones* folders.
5. Right-click the zone and click Properties.
6. On the *General* tab, click the Aging button. The *Zone Aging/Scavenging Properties* dialog box opens.
7. Click the Scavenge stale resource records option.
8. Modify the no-refresh interval and refresh interval as needed.
9. Click the OK button to close the *Server Aging/Scavenging Properties* dialog box.
10. When you are prompted to apply aging/scavenging settings to the Standard Primary zone, click Yes.
11. Click the OK button to close the *Properties* dialog box.

Using the DNSCMD Command to Manage Resource Records

THE BOTTOM LINE

In the previous lesson, you were introduced to the `dnscmd` command to create zones. You can also use the `dnscmd` command to manage resource records.

To add a host record for `webserver` with an IPv4 address of `10.0.0.5` on `server1.contoso.com`, perform the following command:

```
dnscmd server1.contoso.com /recordadd
contoso.com webserver A 10.0.0.5
```

To delete the same record, execute the following command:

```
dnscmd server1.contoso.com /recorddelete
contoso.com webserver a
```

Because you are deleting a record, you are asked if you are sure that you want to delete the record. If you do not want to be asked, you can add the `/f` parameter:

```
dnscmd server1.contoso.com /recorddelete
contoso.com webserver a /f
```

MORE INFORMATION

For more information about the `dnscmd` command, perform the `dnscmd.exe /?` to show the available options. In addition, you can perform a search for `dnscmd` from Microsoft's TechNet website.

Troubleshooting DNS Problems

THE BOTTOM LINE

Because DNS is an essential service that can bring any network down when it is not available, you need to know how to troubleshoot it. Microsoft provides several tools to help you troubleshoot DNS problems, including the `IPConfig` command, the `NSLookup` command, and the DNS console.

When a client cannot access a resource, the problem is with the client or the server. As with any problem, you should quickly determine the scope of the problem. Does the problem affect only one computer or does it affect multiple computers? If it affects just one user, the problem most likely resides on the client's computer or it is user error. If the problem affects multiple users, the problem is most likely with the server hosting the network resource or service, a network connectivity problem, or a DNS issue.

If you suspect a DNS issue, you can use the `ipconfig` command to verify the IP configuration of the client. Used without parameters, `ipconfig` displays the IP address, subnet mask, and default gateway for all adapters. When you execute `ipconfig /all` (see Figure 9-16), it displays the full TCP/IP configuration for all adapters, including host name, DNS servers, and the physical address (or MAC address).

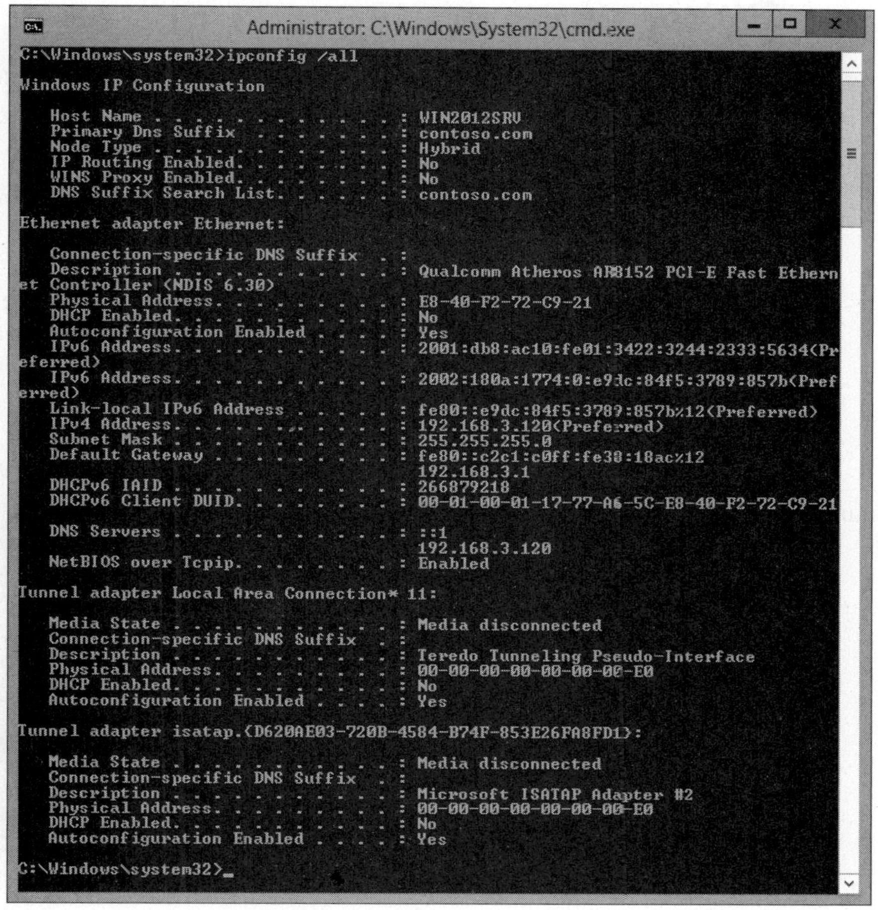

Figure 9-16

Showing the IP configuration

If you find problems with the DNS, the `ipconfig` command can be used in certain situations:

- `ipconfig /flushdns`: Flushes and resets the contents of the DNS client resolver cache.
- `ipconfig /displaydns`: Displays the contents of the DNS client resolver cache, which includes both entries preloaded from the local hosts file and any recently obtained resource records for name queries resolved by the computer.
- `ipconfig /registerdns`: Initiates manual dynamic registration for the DNS names and IP addresses that are configured at a computer. You can use this parameter to troubleshoot a failed DNS name registration or resolve a dynamic update problem between a client and the DNS server without rebooting the client computer.

If you used the `nslookup` command to test DNS resolution and found a problem with name resolution, you can fix the problem at the DNS server. Unfortunately, previous DNS results that your system processes, such as when you access a web page using a browser, are cached in your memory. Therefore, if you correct the problem, you may need to flush your DNS cache using the `ipconfig /flushdns` command so that it can query and obtain the corrected values.

If you determine that old information is cached on the local DNS server, you can wait until the DNS data expires or you can clear the cache on the local DNS server. The following steps show you how to clear the cache from a DNS server.

CLEAR THE DNS CACHE

GET READY. To clear the DNS cache on a DNS server, perform the following steps:

1. Open Server Manager by clicking the Server Manager button.
2. Click Tools > DNS to open the *DNS Manager console*.
3. If necessary, expand the DNS console to a full-screen view.
4. Right-click the server and click Clear Cache.

`Nslookup.exe` is a command-line administrative tool for testing and troubleshooting DNS name resolution. Entering *hostname* in `nslookup` provides a forward lookup of the host name to IP address. Entering *IP_Address* in `nslookup` performs a reverse lookup of IP address to host name (see Figure 9-17).

Figure 9-17

Using the `Nslookup` command

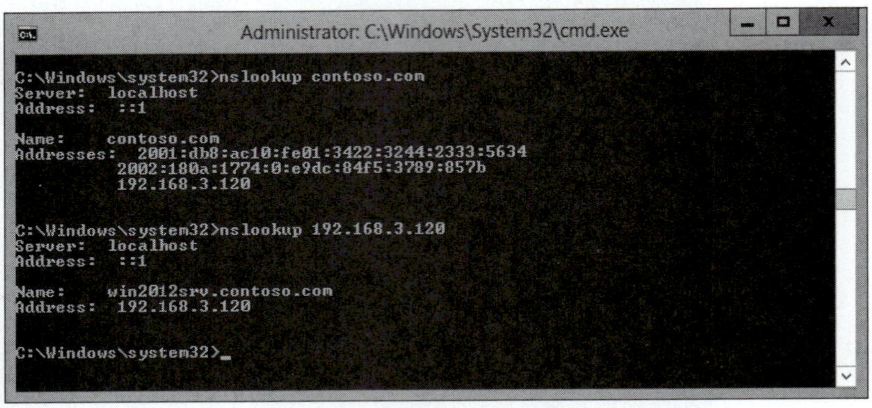

If you type `nslookup` without any parameters, you start `nslookup.exe` in interactive mode. You can use the `help` or `?` to generate a list of available commands (see Figure 9-18). To exit `nslookup` interactive mode, use the `quit` command.

Figure 9-18

Using `Nslookup help`

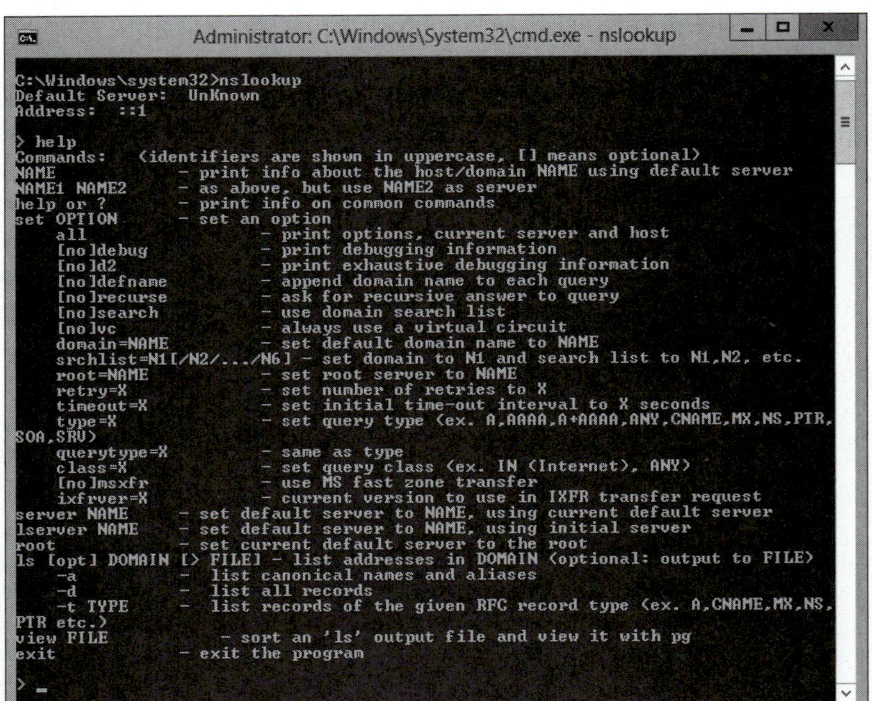

While in interactive mode, by default, if you type a host name, the `nslookup` command displays the IP address. If you type an IP address, you get back the host name.

To look at the different data types in the domain name space, use the `set type` command. For example, to look at MX records for a domain, you need to use the `set type=mx` command, and then you can perform your query for MX records (see Figure 9-19).

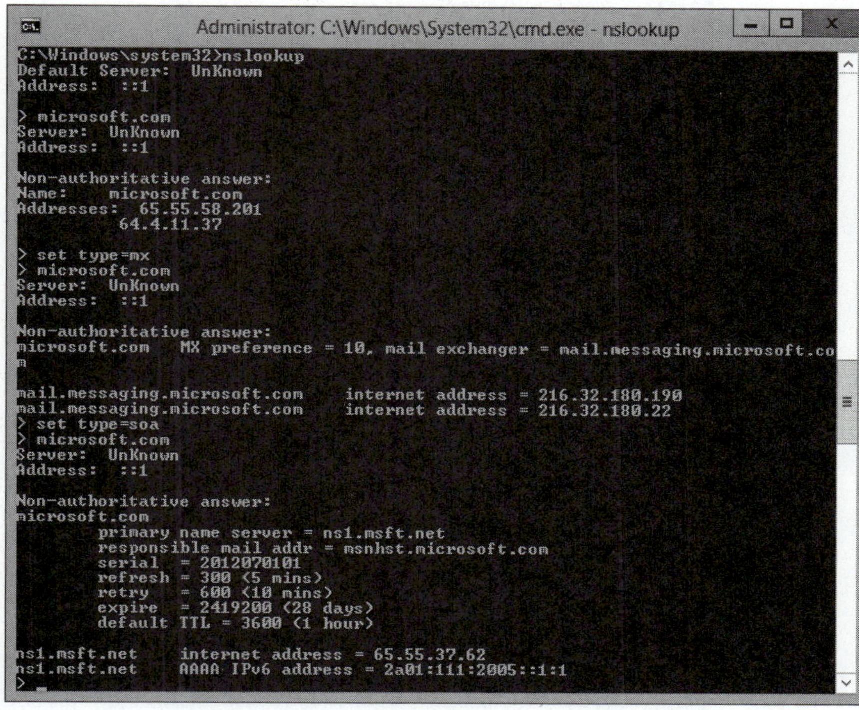

Figure 9-19

Showing MX records in `Nslookup` interactive mode

By default, when you use the `nslookup` command in interactive mode, it queries the client's DNS server. If you need to check the name resolution of another server, you can use the `server` command. For example, if you want to jump to another DNS server (such as one that has an IP address of 4.2.2.2), type the following command:

```
server 4.2.2.2
```

If you cannot connect to a remote server, you need to check any firewalls between the client and the remote DNS server, specifically over UDP and TCP port 53.

Finally, you can use the DNS console to help troubleshoot DNS problems, specifically if the server can perform a simple query against the DNS server or a recursive query to other DNS servers.

TEST A DNS SERVER

GET READY. To test a DNS server, perform the following steps:

1. Open Server Manager, and then click Tools > DNS to open the *DNS Manager console*. If necessary, expand the *DNS console* to a full-screen view.
2. Right-click the server and click Properties. The *Properties* dialog box opens.
3. Click the Monitor tab.
4. Select the A simple query against this DNS server and A recursive query to other DNS servers options (see Figure 9-20).

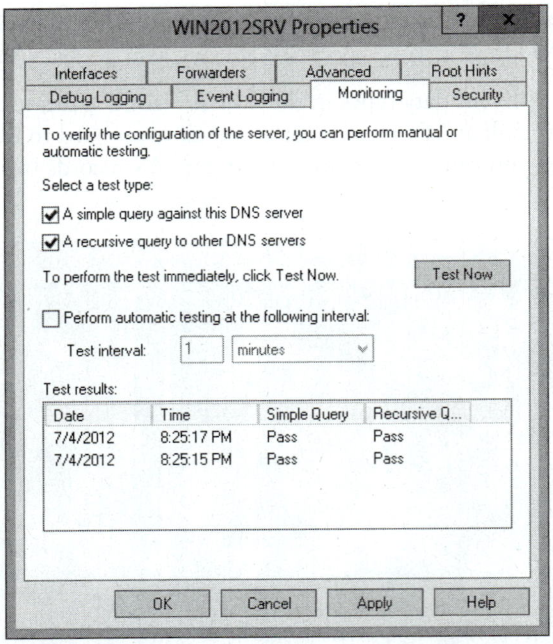

Figure 9-20

Testing simple and recursive queries for a DNS server

5. Click the Test Now button.
6. When you are done, click the OK button.

SKILL SUMMARY

IN THIS LESSON, YOU LEARNED:

- A DNS zone database is made up of a collection of resource records, which are used to answer DNS queries.
- Each resource record specifies information about a particular object. Each record has a type, an expiration time limit, and some type-specific data.
- Start of Authority (SOA) records specify authoritative information about a DNS zone, including the primary name server, the e-mail of the domain administrator, the domain serial number, and the expiration and reload timers of the zone.
- Name Server (NS) records specify an authoritative name server for the host.
- Host A and Host AAAA records map a domain or host name to an IP address.
- Alias (CNAME) records map an alias DNS domain name to another primary or canonical name.
- Pointer (PTR) records map an IP address to a domain or host name.
- Mail exchanger (MX) records map a DNS domain name to the name of a computer that exchanges or forwards mail for the domain.
- Service location (SRV) records map a DNS domain name to a specified list of host computers that offer a specific type of service, such as Active Directory domain controllers.
- Minimum TTL specifies a default Time to Live (TTL) value, which defines the default time a resource record remains in a DNS cache after a DNS query has retrieved a record.

- If a resource record has its own TTL value, the TTL value of the resource record is used instead of the TTL defined in the SOA record.
- While each external mail server requires an MX record, the primary server is designed with a lower priority number.
- If users cannot connect to DNS services or the SRV records are not in the zone, users cannot log in to the Active Directory domain.
- DNS supports dynamic updates, whereas resource records for the clients are automatically created and updated at the host's primary DNS server.
- If you enable secure dynamic updates, only updates from the same computer can update a registration for a resource record.
- Round robin is a DNS balancing mechanism that distributes network load among multiple servers by rotating resource records retrieved from a DNS server.
- Aging in DNS is the process of using timestamps to track the age of dynamically registered resource records.
- Scavenging is the mechanism to remove stale resource records.
- Microsoft provides several tools to help you troubleshoot DNS problems, including the IPConfig command, the NSLookup command, and the DNS console.

Knowledge Assessment

Multiple Choice

Select the correct answer for each of the following questions.

1. Which records are automatically created when you create a zone? (Choose all that apply.)
   a. SOA
   b. SRV
   c. NA
   d. MX

2. Which DNS resource record is used to map a host name to an IP address?
   a. A record
   b. PTR record
   c. MX record
   d. SRV record

3. Which DNS resource record specifies the authoritative information about a zone?
   a. A record
   b. PTR record
   c. SOA record
   d. SRV record

4. Which resource record defines an alias for a host name?
   a. AAAA record
   b. PTR record
   c. CNAME record
   d. SRV record

5. Which type of zone do you find a PTR record in?
   a. Forward lookup zone
   b. Reverse lookup zone
   c. Primary zone
   d. Secondary zone
6. Which record do you use to specify an organization's mail server.
   a. A record
   b. PTR record
   c. SRV record
   d. MX record
7. Which of the following do you use to ensure the only computer that can update its own resource record is used?
   a. Round robin
   b. Scavenging
   c. Aging
   d. Secure dynamic updates
8. To scavenge DNS records, where must you enable scavenging and aging? (Choose two answers.)
   a. DHCP server
   b. DNS server
   c. Each resource record
   d. Zone
9. Which command do you use to clear a computer's DNS cache?
   a. `ipconfig /registerdns`
   b. `ipconfig /flushdns`
   c. `nslookup /clearcache`
   d. `clearcache`
10. When is the TTL that is defined by the SOA overwritten?
    a. When the DNS request is made in quick mode
    b. When round robin is enabled
    c. When scavenging is enabled
    d. When a resource record has its own TTL

Best Answer

Choose the letter that corresponds to the best answer. More than one answer choice may achieve the goal. Select the BEST answer.

1. Where do you define the default time for that address resource records that will stay in DNS cache?
   a. SOA
   b. SRV
   c. PTR
   d. CNAME
2. You have a new server called Server1 that you just assigned an IPv6 address. You need to ensure that clients can find the server's address. Which resource record should you use?
   a. A
   b. AAAA
   c. CNAME
   d. SRV

3. You have a server, called Server1 running Microsoft Exchange 2010. You want to add a second server (Server2) to be used with your e-mail. How can you ensure that the incoming e-mails will be directed to the two servers with the Server2 having the higher priority?
   a. Set the priority of Server1 to 5 and set the priority of Server2 to 20.
   b. Set the priority of Server1 to 20 and set the priority of Server2 to 5.
   c. Create an SRV record for Server1.
   d. Create an SRV record for Server2

4. You have a custom application that uses DNS records to define the host, protocol, and port number used by the application. Which DNS record would you create?
   a. A
   b. AAAA
   c. SRV
   d. PTR

5. You have a server called Server1 that is running Windows Server 2012. What command would you use to delete the PTR record for 10.1.1.127?
   a. `dnscmd /recorddelete 10.1.1.127`
   b. `dnscmd  /zondelete 127.in-addr.arpa`
   c. `dnsmcd /recordelete 10.in-addr.arpa 127.1.1 PTR`
   d. `dnscmd /RRDelete 10.1.1.127`

Matching and Identification

1. Identify the type of resource record (A, AAAA, PTR, SOA, NS, MX, and SRV) in the description or scenario given. Resource records may be repeated.
   _______ 1) Defines the e-mail address of the administrator for a zone
   _______ 2) Used to convert a host name to an IPv4 address
   _______ 3) Used to convert an IPv6 address to a host name
   _______ 4) Defines the incoming e-mail servers
   _______ 5) Used to identify the DNS servers for a zone
   _______ 6) Used to convert a host name to an IPv6 address
   _______ 7) Used to convert an IPv4 address to a host name.
   _______ 8) Defines the default TTL for a zone
   _______ 9) Used to identify the domain controllers
   _______ 10) Shows the number of times a DNS zone has been updated

2. Identify whether the resource record should be placed in the forward lookup zone or reverse lookup zone.
   ________________ A
   ________________ AAAA
   ________________ PTR
   ________________ SOA
   ________________ NS
   ________________ MX
   ________________ SRV

Build a List

1. You have three web servers (Server1, Server2 and Server3) that will be used to handle requests for your companies websites. Specify in order the tasks that need to be done to enable round robin between the three web servers. Not all tasks will be used.
   _______ Verify that robin is enabled in the DNS server properties.
   _______ Specify a priority of 10 for Server1
   _______ Specify a priority of 10 for Server2
   _______ Specify a priority of 10 for Server3
   _______ Create A record for Server1
   _______ Create A record for Server2
   _______ Create A record for Server3
2. Specify in order the tasks that need to be done to enable zone scavenging for the contoso.com zone. Not all tasks will be used.
   _______ Enable Round-Robin.
   _______ Enable the Scavenging agent.
   _______ Enable dynamic update or secure dynamic update for the contoso.com zone.
   _______ Change the refresh interval to 0 for each resource record.
   _______ Enable scavenging and aging on the DNS server.
   _______ Enable scavenging and aging on the contoso.com zone.
3. You need to install two frontend e-mail servers (Server1 and Server2) used to receive incoming e-mail. The e-mail servers will provide fault tolerance to each other. What steps in order do you need to enable both of these servers to receive e-mails with the same priorities? Not all tasks will be used.
   _______ Enable round robin.
   _______ Create an SRV record for Server1.
   _______ Create an SRV record for Server2.
   _______ Create an A record for Server1.
   _______ Create an A record for Server2.
   _______ Create an MX record for Server1 and assign it a priority of 10.
   _______ Create an MX record for Server2 and assign it a priority of 10.
   _______ Create an MX record for Server2 and assign it a priority of 5.

■ Business Case Scenarios

Scenario 9-1: Distributing Traffic Web Servers

You just installed three web servers, which are used to serve your company's web page on the Internet. You want to ensure that web requests are evenly distributed to the three web servers. What do you need to do, and what are the steps you need to perform to accomplish this?

Scenario 9-2: Configuring DNS Time To Live (TTL)

Where is the default Time To Live (TTL) information defined at, and how do you override the default TTL for individual records?

Configuring VPN and Routing

LESSON 10

70-411 EXAM OBJECTIVE

Objective 3.3 – Configure VPN and routing. This objective may include but is not limited to: install and configure the Remote Access role; implement Network Address Translation (NAT); configure VPN settings; configure remote dial-in settings for users; configure routing.

LESSON HEADING	EXAM OBJECTIVE
The Remote Access Role	
Installing and Configuring the Remote Access Role	Install and configure the Remote Access role
Configuring VPN Settings	Configure VPN settings
Configuring Remote Dial-In Settings for Users	Configure remote dial-in settings for users
Troubleshooting Remote Access Problems	
Implementing NAT	Implement Network Address Translation (NAT)
Disabling Routing and Remote Access	
Configuring Routing	Configure routing

KEY TERMS

Challenge Handshake Authentication Protocol (CHAP)
demand-dial routing
Extensible Authentication Protocol (EAP-MS-CHAPv2)
IKEv2
layer 2 switches
Layer 2 Tunneling Protocol (L2TP)
layer 3 switches
Microsoft CHAP version 2 (MS-CHAP v2)
network address translation (NAT)
Password Authentication Protocol (PAP)
Point-to-Point Tunneling Protocol (PPTP)
remote access server (RAS)
routers
routing
Routing and Remote Access (RRAS)
Routing Information Protocol (RIP)
routing table
Secure Socket Tunneling Protocol (SSTP)
split tunnel
static routes
virtual private networks (VPNs)

The Remote Access Role

THE BOTTOM LINE

Today, it is common for an organization to use a ***remote access server (RAS)***. A RAS enables users to connect remotely to a network using various protocols and connection types. By connecting to the RAS over the Internet, users can connect to their organization's network so that they can access data files, read e-mail, and access other applications just as if they were sitting at work.

To provide RAS, Microsoft includes ***Routing and Remote Access (RRAS)***, which provides the following functionality:

- A virtual private network (VPN) gateway where clients can connect to an organization's private network using the Internet.
- Connect two private networks using a VPN connection using the Internet.
- A dial-up remote access server, which enables users to connect to a private network using a modem.
- Network address translation (NAT), which enables multiple users to share a single public network address.
- Provide routing functionality, which can connect subnets and control where packets are forwarded based on the destination address.
- Provide basic firewall functionality and allow or disallow packets based on addresses of source and/or destination and protocols.

An early method to connect to an organization's network is over an analog phone line or ISDN line using a modem. Because the modem creates a dedicated connection to the server, the connection does not typically need to be encrypted. However, by today's networking standards and bandwidth requirements, the phone and ISDN system do not have the bandwidth needed. Therefore, this method typically is not used today.

Installing and Configuring the Remote Access Role

CERTIFICATION READY
Install and configure the Remote Access role.
Objective 3.3

Before you can use RRAS, you need to first add the Remote Access Role. Then, you need to initially configure RRAS so that you can specify which options are available with it.

INSTALLING ROUTING AND REMOTE ACCESS

To install the Remote Access Role, you use the Server Manager to install the proper role. Because the remote access computer is used to connect an organization's internal private network with the Internet, the server should have two network cards.

INSTALL THE REMOTE ACCESS ROLE

GET READY. To install the Remote Access Role, perform the following steps:

1. Click the Server Manager button on the task bar to open the *Server Manager*.
2. At the top of *Server Manager*, click Manage and click Add Roles and Features. The *Add Roles and Feature Wizard* opens.
3. On the *Before you begin* page, click Next.
4. Select Role-based or feature-based installation and then click Next.

5. Click Select a server from the server pool, click the name of the server to install Remote Access Role to, and then click Next.
6. Scroll down and select Remote Access (see Figure 10-1). If you need Routing Information Protocol (RIP), expand Remote Access and select Routing.

Figure 10-1

Selecting the Remote Access role

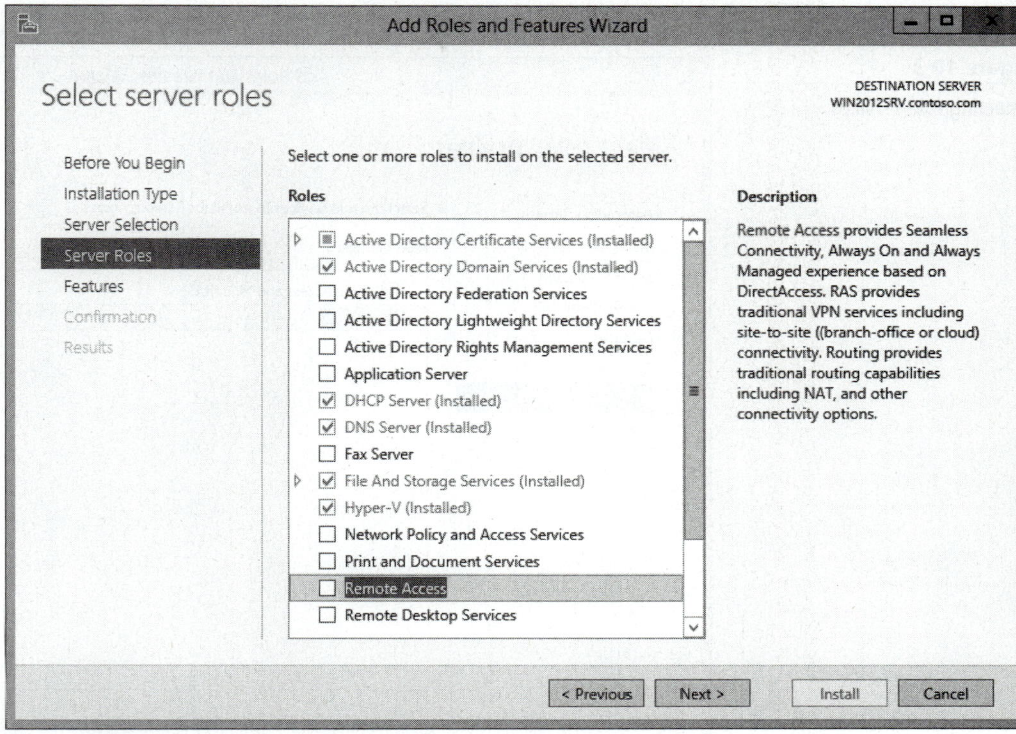

7. When the *Add Roles and Features Wizard* dialog box opens, select Add Features, and then click Next (see Figure 10-2).

Figure 10-2

Adding additional features for the Remote Access role

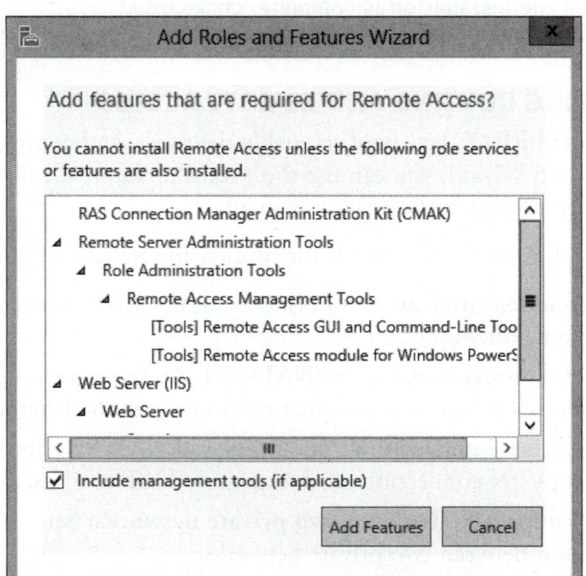

8. On the *Select server roles* page, click **Next**.
9. On the *Select features* page, click **Next**.
10. On the *Remote Access* page, click **Next**.
11. On the *Select role services* page, keep **DirectAccess and VPN (RAS)** selected and select **Routing** (see Figure 10-3). Click **Next**.

Figure 10-3
Selecting role services

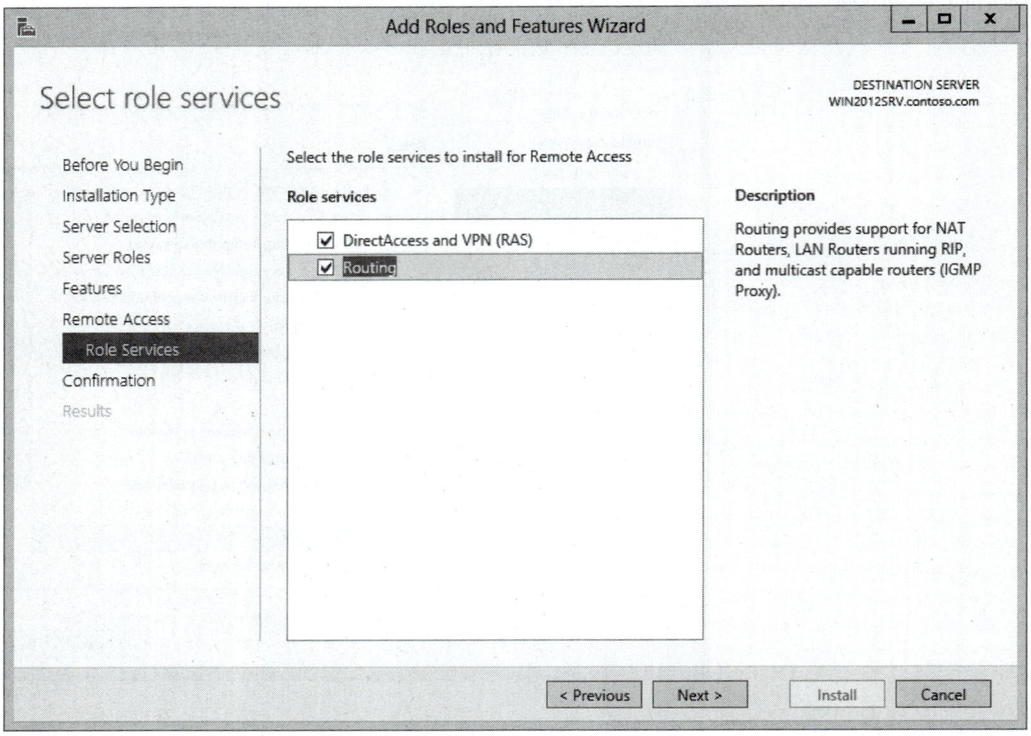

12. On the *Confirm installation selections* page, click **Install**.
13. When the installation is complete, click **Close**.

CONFIGURING ROUTING AND REMOTE ACCESS

After you install RRAS, you need to enable the server and configure RRAS. When you start the RRAS Setup Wizard, you can use the wizard to automatically configure RRAS for specific applications or configure the service manually.

The wizard offers five basic options for configuring RRAS:

- **Remote access (dial-up or VPN):** Sets up the server to accept incoming remote access connections (dial-up or VPN).
- **Network address translation (NAT):** Sets up the server to provide NAT services to clients on the private network that need to access the Internet.
- **Virtual private network (VPN) access and NAT:** Sets up the server to support incoming VPN connections and to provide NAT services.
- **Secure connection between two private networks:** Sets up a demand-dial or persistent connection between two private networks.
- **Custom configuration:** Enables you to choose individual services, including NAT, LAN routing, and VPN access (see Figure 10-4).

TAKE NOTE*

You cannot have Windows Firewall service running while enabling and configuring RRAS.

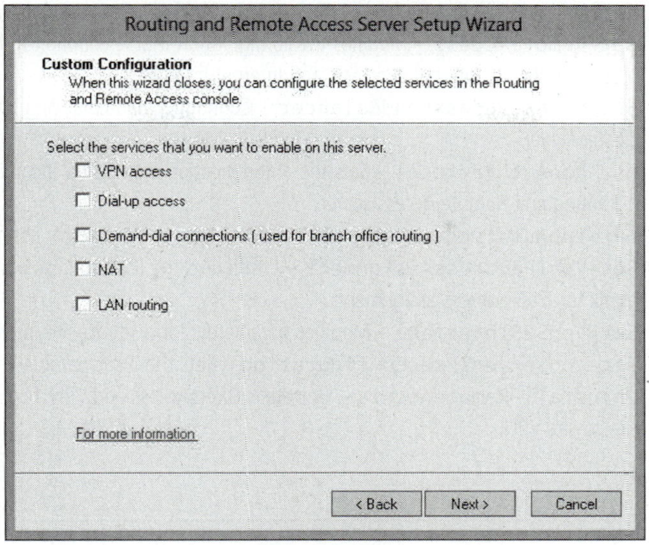

Figure 10-4

Selecting services on the Custom Configuration page

USING WINDOWS POWERSHELL

You can manage remote access services by using the following Windows PowerShell cmdlets:

- `Add-RemoteAccessLoadBalancerNode` – Adds a server to the load balancing cluster.
- `Add-VpnIPAddressRange` – Adds a new IPv4 address range from which IPv4 addresses can be assigned to VPN clients.
- `Add-VpnS2SInterface` – Creates a site-to-site interface with the specified parameters.
- `Clear-VpnS2SInterfaceStatistics` – Clears statistics for a site-to-site interface.
- `Connect-VpnS2SInterface` – Connects a site-to-site interface that is currently not connected.
- `Disconnect-VpnS2SInterface` – Disconnects a site-to-site interface that is currently connected.
- `Disconnect-VpnUser` – Disconnects a VPN connection originated by a specific user or originating from a specific client computer.
- `Get-RemoteAccess` – Displays the configuration of DirectAccess and VPN (both Remote Access VPN and site-to-site VPN).
- `Get-RemoteAccessConnectionStatistics` – Displays the statistics of real-time, currently active DirectAccess and VPN connections and the statistics of DirectAccess and VPN historical connections for a specified time duration.
- `Get-RemoteAccessConnectionStatisticsSummary` – Displays the summary statistics of real-time, currently active DirectAccess and VPN connections and the summary statistics of DirectAccess and VPN historical connections for a specified time duration.
- `Get-RemoteAccessHealth` – Obtains the current health of a Remote Access deployment.
- `Get-RemoteAccessLoadBalancer` – Displays load balanced cluster settings.
- `Get-RemoteAccessUserActivity` – Displays the resources accessed over the active DirectAccess and VPN connections and the resources accessed over historical DirectAccess and VPN connections.
- `Get-VpnAuthProtocol` – Retrieves authentication parameters configured on a VPN server.
- `Get-VpnS2SInterface` – Retrieves configuration details for a site-to-site interface.
- `Get-VpnS2SInterfaceStatistics` – Retrieves statistics of a site-to-site interface.
- `Get-VpnServerIPsecConfiguration` – Gets IPsec parameters configured on the VPN server.
- `Install-RemoteAccess` – Performs prerequisite checks for DirectAccess to ensure that it can be installed, installs DirectAcccess for remote access (includes management of remote clients) or for management of remote clients only, and installs VPN (both Remote Access VPN and site-to-site VPN).
- `Remove-RemoteAccessLoadBalancerNode` – Removes a server from the network load balancing (NLB) cluster.
- `Remove-VpnIPAddressRange` – Removes an existing IPv4 address range from the pool for IP address assignment.

(continued)

- `Remove-VpnS2SInterface` – Removes a specified site-to-site interface.
- `Set-RemoteAccess` – Modifies the configuration that is common to both DirectAccess and VPN, such as SSL certificate, Internal interface, and Internet interface.
- `Set-RemoteAccessLoadBalancer` – Configures load balancing on the Remote Access server or the cluster server.
- `Set-VpnAuthProtocol` – Sets the authentication method for incoming site-to-site VPN interfaces on a Routing and Remote Access server.
- `Set-VpnAuthType` – Sets the authentication type to be used for connecting to a VPN.
- `Set-VpnIPAddressAssignment` – Configures the IPv4 address assignment method or the IPv6 prefix for IPv6 address assignment.
- `Set-VpnS2SInterface` – Modifies parameters for a site-to-site interface.
- `Set-VpnServerIPsecConfiguration` – Sets the IPsec parameters for a site-to-site server.
- `Uninstall-RemoteAccess` – Uninstalls DirectAccess and VPN, both remote access VPN and site-to-site VPN.

CONFIGURING RRAS FOR DIAL-UP REMOTE ACCESS

Dial-up remote access enables remote computers that have a modem to connect to the organization's network as if the remote computers were connected locally. Because it uses the public phone system or ISDN phone lines, it is at much slower transfer speeds when compared to DSL, cable technology, and other forms of networking found at home. For this reason, dial-up remote access is becoming less common. To support multiple dial-users that connect simultaneously, you must have a modem bank that supports multiple modem connections over the phone lines.

CONFIGURE DIAL-UP REMOTE ACCESS

GET READY. To configure dial-up remote, perform the following steps:

1. Open Server Manager.
2. Click Tools > Routing and Remote Access. The *Routing and Remote Access console* opens (see Figure 10-5).

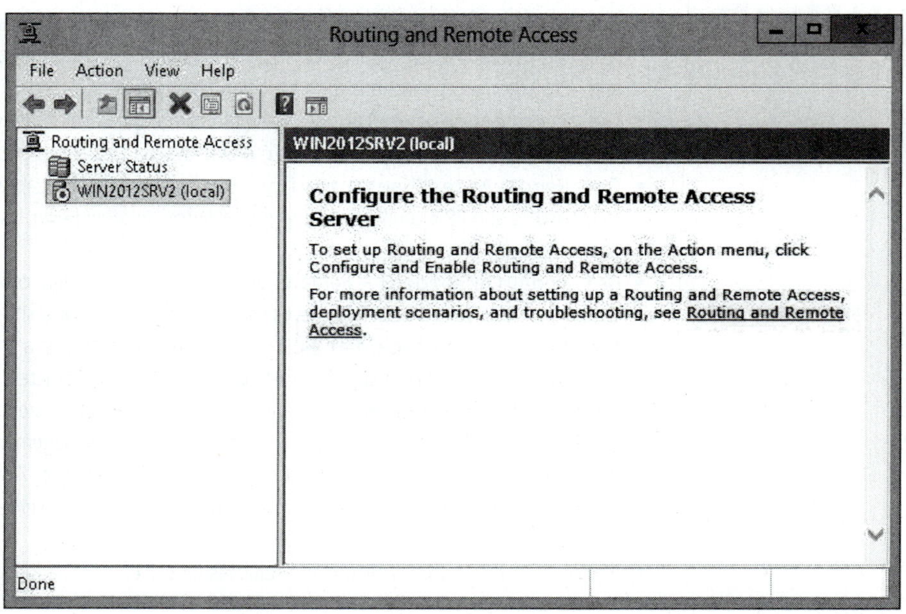

Figure 10-5
Opening the Routing and Remote Access console

3. Right-click the server and select Configure and Enable Routing and Remote Access (see Figure 10-6). The *Routing and Remote Access Server Setup Wizard* opens.

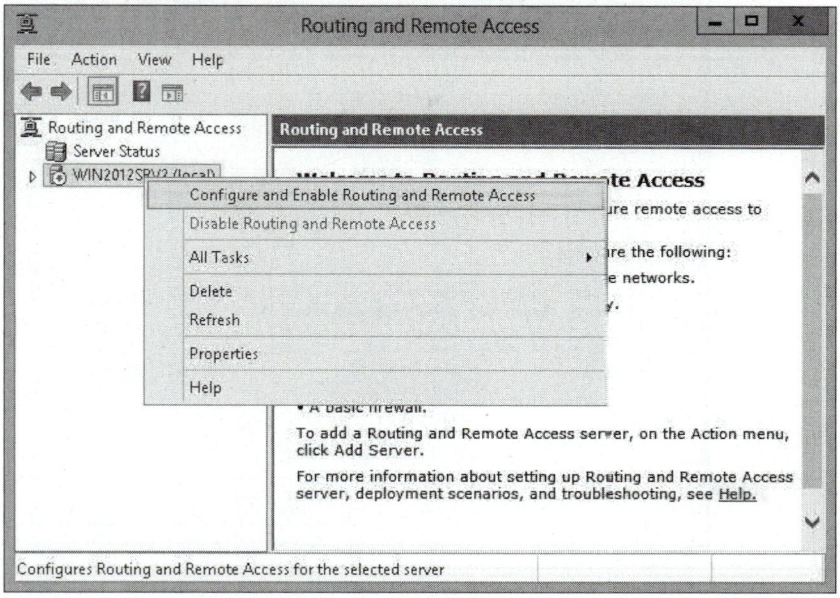

Figure 10-6

Configuring and enabling RRAS

4. On the *Welcome* page, click Next.
5. On the *Configuration* page (see Figure 10-7), select Remote access (dial-up or VPN) and then click Next.

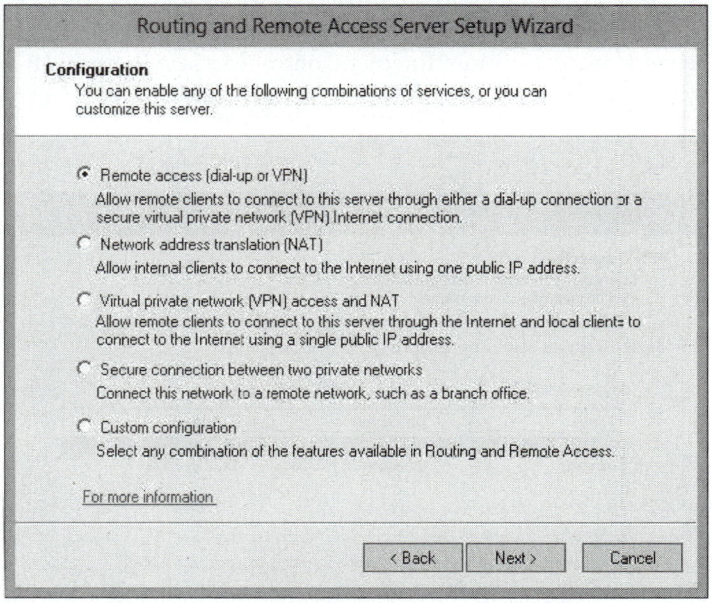

Figure 10-7

Specifying the RRAS services on the Configuration page

6. On the *Remote Access* page (see Figure 10-8), select Dial-Up and click Next.

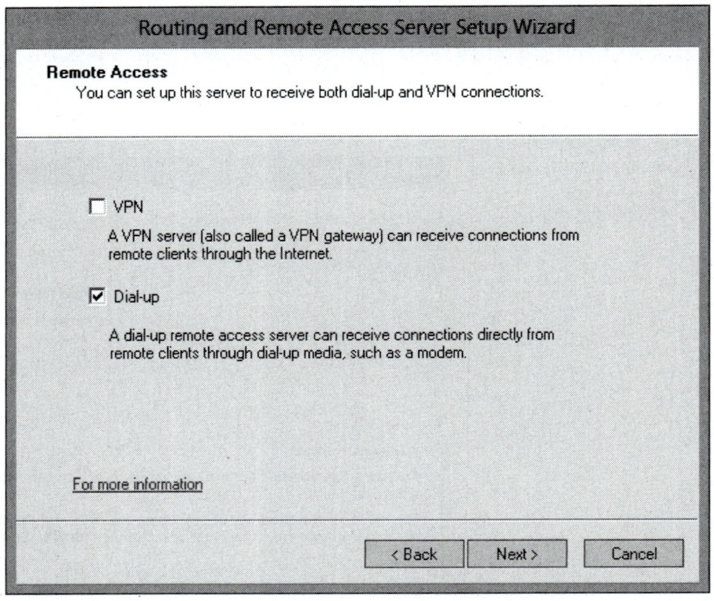

Figure 10-8
Using the Remote Access page

7. If your server has more than one network interface, the *Network Selection* page will appear (see Figure 10-9). Click the interface to which you wish to assign remote clients, and then click Next.

TAKE NOTE*

If you intend to protect your RRAS server by using a firewall instead, do not enable the *Enable security on the selected interface by setting up static packet filters* option. In addition, if you enable this option, by default, you will not be able to ping the IP address of the public network adapter because Internet Control Message Protocol (ICMP) packets are blocked by the packet filters.

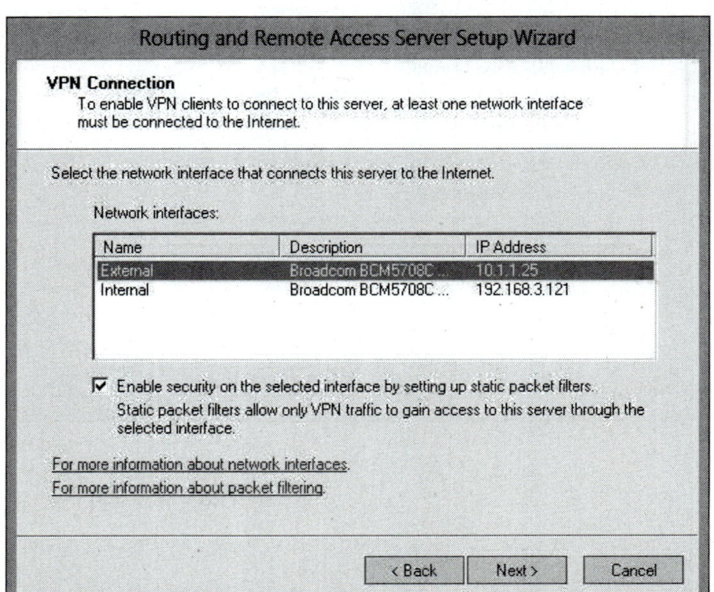

Figure 10-9
Selecting the VPN interface

8. On the *IP Address Assignment* page (see Figure 10-10), you can select either Automatically (to use a DHCP server to assign addresses) or From a specified range of addresses (addresses are supplied by the routing and remote access server). Select From a specified range of addresses and then click Next.

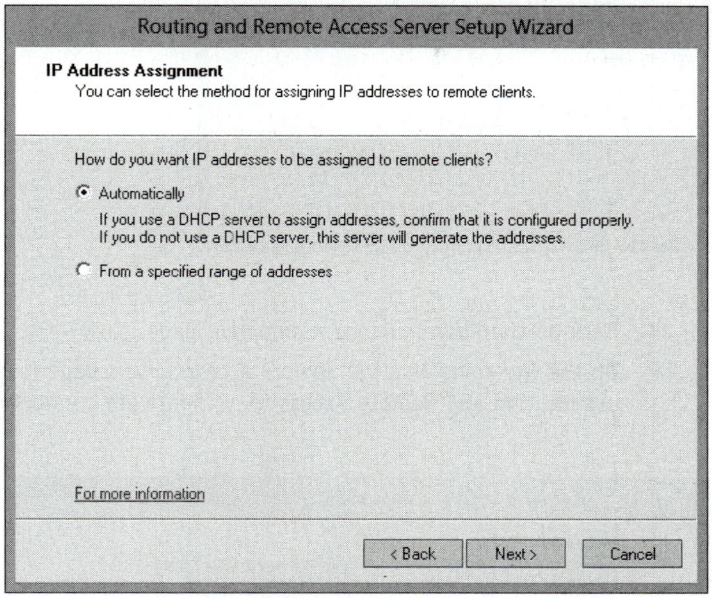

Figure 10-10

Specifying the method of IP address assignment

9. On the *Address Range Assignment* page (see Figure 10-11), click New.

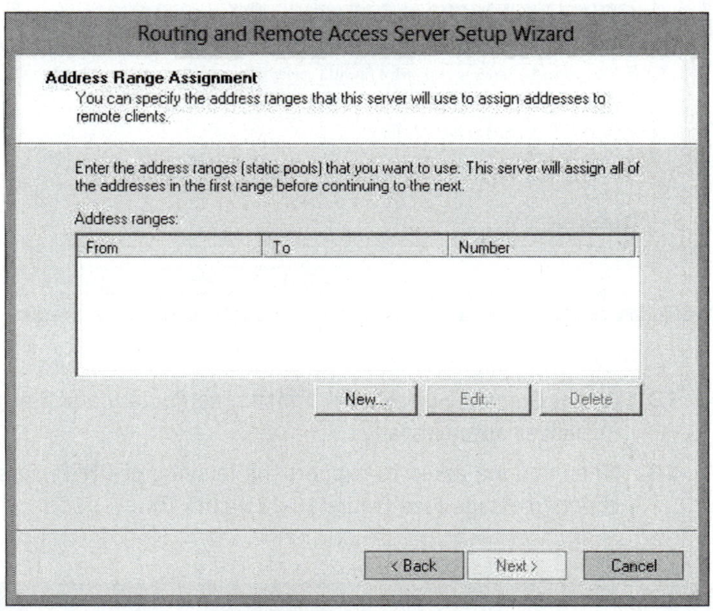

Figure 10-11

Using the Address Range Assignment page

10. When the *New IPv4 Address Range* dialog box opens, fill in start IP address and End IP address (see Figure 10-12). Click OK.

Figure 10-12

Using the New IPv4 Address Range dialog box

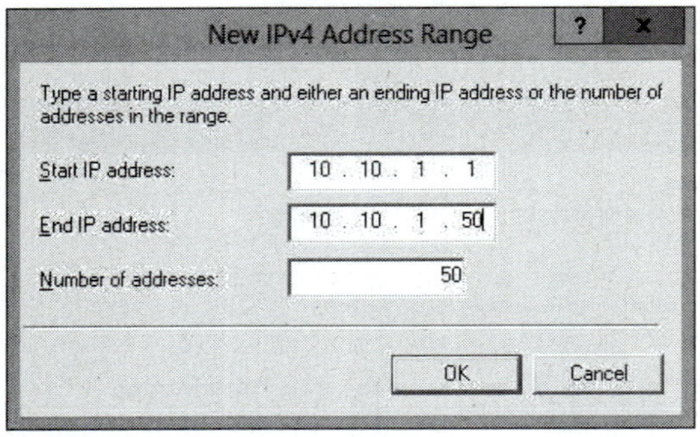

11. Back on the *Address Range Assignment* page, click Next.
12. On the *Managing Multiple Remote Access Servers* page (see Figure 10-13), select No, use Routing and Remote Access to authenticate connection requests. Click Next.

Figure 10-13

Managing Multiple Remote Access Servers page

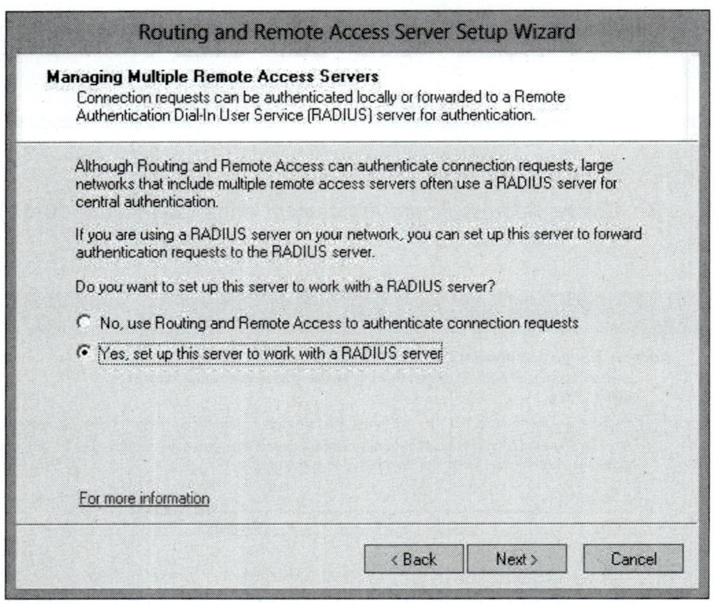

13. On the *Summary* page, click Finish. The *Routing and Remote Access service* starts and initializes automatically.
14. When you are asked to support the relaying of DHCP messages from remote access clients message (see Figure 10-14), click OK.

Figure 10-14

Relaying of DHCP messages warning

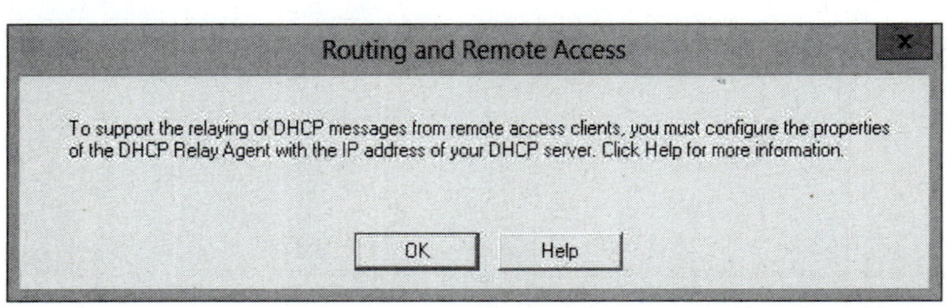

15. When the configuration is complete, the console looks similar to Figure 10-15.

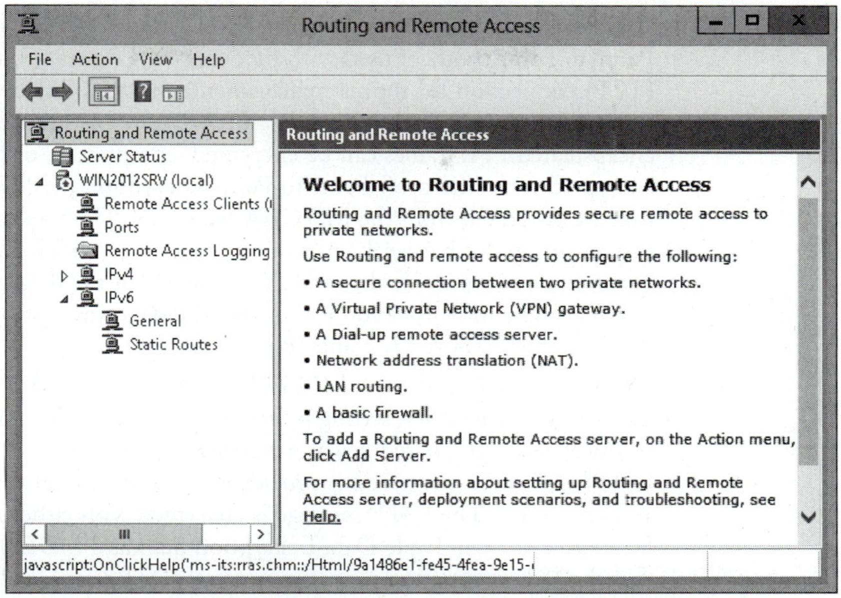

Figure 10-15

Viewing the configured *Routing and Remote Access* console

Configuring VPN Settings

Virtual private networks (VPNs) link two computers or network devices through a wide-area network (WAN) such as the Internet. Because the Internet is a public network and is considered insecure, the data sent between the two computers or devices is encapsulated and encrypted.

CERTIFICATION READY
Configure VPN settings.
Objective 3.3

VPN connections provide the following:

- **Encapsulation:** Private data is encapsulated or placed in a packet with a header containing routing information that allows the data to traverse the transit network such as the Internet.
- **Authentication:** Proves the identity of the user or computer that tries to connection.
- **Data encryption:** Ensures confidentiality is maintained by the sender encrypting the data before it is sent so that unauthorized people cannot read the private data. When it is received, the intended recipient decrypts it. Of course, the encryption and decryption depend on the sender and receiver. Both must have a common or related encryption key; larger keys offers better security.
- **Data integrity:** Verifies that the data sent over the VPN connection has not been modified in transit. This is usually done with a cryptographic checksum that is based on an encryption key that is known only to the sender and receiver. When the data is received, the same checksum calculation is done and the value is compared to the one that was calculated before the data was sent. If the values match, the data has not been tampered with.

The VPN can be used in the following scenarios:

- A client connects to the RAS server to access internal resources from off-site.
- Two remote sites together by creating a VPN tunnel between a RAS server located at each site.
- Two different organizations create a VPN tunnel so that users from one organization can access the resources in the other organization.

The three types of tunneling protocols used with a VPN/RAS server running on Windows Server 2012 include:

- ***Point-to-Point Tunneling Protocol (PPTP):*** A VPN protocol based on the legacy Point-to-Point protocol used with modems. PPTP uses a Transmission Control Protocol (TCP) connection for tunnel management, and a modified version of Generic Route Encapsulation (GRE) to encapsulate PPP frames for tunneled data. Payloads of the encapsulated PPP frames can be encrypted, compressed, or both. The PPP frame is encrypted with Microsoft Point-to-Point Encryption (MPPE) by using encryption keys that are generated from the MS-CHAPv2 or EAP-TLS authentication process. PPTP is easy to set up but has weak encryption technology. PPTP-based VPN connections, however, do not provide data integrity (proof that the data was not modified in transit) or data origin authentication (proof that the data was sent by the authorized user). PPTP uses TCP port 1723 and IP protocol ID 47.
- ***Layer 2 Tunneling Protocol (L2TP):*** Used with IPsec to provide security. L2TP is the industry standard when setting up secure tunnels. L2TP supports either computer certificates or a preshared key as the authentication method for IPsec. By using IPsec, L2TP/IPsec VPN connections provide data confidentiality, data integrity, and data authentication. The L2TP message is encrypted with either Advanced Encryption Standard (AES) or Triple Data Encryption Standard (3DES) by using encryption keys that the IKE negotiation process generates. L2TP uses UDP Port 500, UDP Port 1701, UDP Port 4500, and IP Protocol ID 50.
- ***IKEv2:*** IKE is short for Internet Key Exchange, which is a tunneling protocol that uses IPsec Tunnel Mode protocol over UDP port 500. IKEv2 encapsulates datagrams by using IPsec ESP or AH for transmission over the network. The message is encrypted with one of the following protocols by using encryption keys that are generated from the IKEv2 negotiation process: AES 256, AES 192, AES 128, and 3DES encryption algorithms. It supports mobility (MOBIKE), whereas the VPN connection is more resilient when moving from one wireless hotspot to another or switching from wireless to a wired connection. It also supports VPN Reconnect. IKEv2 is supported only on Windows 7, Windows 8, Windows Server 2008 R2, and Windows Server 2012.
- ***Secure Socket Tunneling Protocol (SSTP):*** Introduced with Windows Server 2008, which uses the HTTPS protocol over TCP port 443 to pass traffic through firewalls and web proxies that might block PPTP and L2TP/IPsec. By using SSL, SSTP VPN connections provide data confidentiality, data integrity, and data authentication.

TAKE NOTE*

If you need to use a VPN connection behind a firewall that only allows https, you have to use SSTP.

Authentication for VPN connections takes one of the following forms:

- User-level authentication by using Point-to-Point Protocol (PPP) authentication. User-level authentication is usually username and password. With a VPN connection, if the VPN server authenticates, the VPN client attempts the connection using a PPP user-level authentication method and verifies that the VPN client has the appropriate authorization. If the method uses mutual authentication, the VPN client also authenticates the VPN server. By using mutual authentication, clients are ensured that the client does not communicate with a rogue server masquerading as a VPN server.
- Computer-level authentication that uses IKE to exchange either computer certificates or a pre-shared key. Microsoft recommends using computer-certificate authentication because it is a much stronger authentication method. Computer-level authentication is performed only for L2TP/IPsec connections.

When using VPNs, Windows 8 and Windows Server 2012 support the following forms of authentication:

- ***Password Authentication Protocol (PAP):*** Uses plain text (unencrypted passwords). PAP is the least secure authentication and is not recommended.

- ***Challenge Handshake Authentication Protocol (CHAP):*** A challenge-response authentication that uses the industry standard md5 hashing scheme to encrypt the response. CHAP was an industry standard for years and is still quite popular.
- ***Microsoft CHAP version 2 (MS-CHAP v2):*** Provides two-way authentication (mutual authentication). MS-CHAP v2 provides stronger security than CHAP. Finally, MS-CHAP v2 is the only authentication protocol that Windows Server 2012 provides that allows you to change an expired password during the connection process.
- ***Extensible Authentication Protocol (EAP-MS-CHAPv2):*** A universal authentication framework that allows third-party vendors to develop custom authentication schemes, including retinal scans, voice recognition, fingerprint identifications, smart cards, Kerberos, and digital certificates. It also provides a mutual authentication method that supports password-based user or computer authentication.

TAKE NOTE*

If you wish to use smart cards for remote connections, you need to use Extensible Authentication Protocol (EAP)

If you have multiple remote access servers, you can choose to use a RADIUS server. A RADIUS server provides authentication, authorization, and accounting for the remote access clients. RADIUS servers are discussed in detail in Lesson 12.

CONFIGURING THE VPN CONNECTION ON THE SERVER

To configure the Windows server to accept VPN connection, you first need to run the Routing and Remote Access Server Setup wizard, so that it knows which network adapters will be used to accept VPN connections and how the IP addresses will be assigned. You can also configure a RADIUS server during this time to handle authentication request.

CONFIGURE AND ENABLE VPN REMOTE ACCESS

GET READY. To configure and enable VPN Remote Access, perform the following steps:

1. Open Server Manager.
2. Click Tools > Routing and Remote Access. The *Routing and Remote Access console* opens.
3. Right-click the server and select Configure and Enable Routing and Remote Access. The *Routing and Remote Access Server Setup Wizard* opens.
4. On the *Welcome* page, click Next.
5. On the *Configuration* page, select Remote access (dial-up or VPN) and click Next.
6. On the *Remote Access* page, select VPN and click Next.
7. On the *VPN Connection* page (see Figure 10-16), select the external network card that is connected to the Internet.

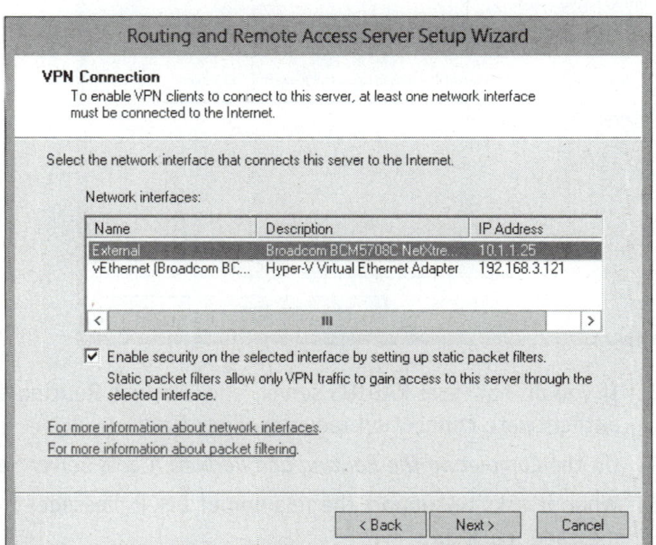

Figure 10-16

Configuring and enabling routing and remote access

8. On the *IP Address Assignment* page, click from a specified range of addresses and click Next.
9. On the *Address Range Assignment* page, click New.
10. When the *New IPv4 Address Range* dialog box opens, fill in the Start IP address and End IP address. Click OK.
11. Back on the *Address Range Assignment* page, click Next. On the *Managing Multiple Remote Access Servers* page (as shown in Figure 10-17), if you have a RADIUS server, click Yes, set up this server to work with a RADIUS server and then click Next.

Figure 10-17

Managing Multiple Remote Access Servers page

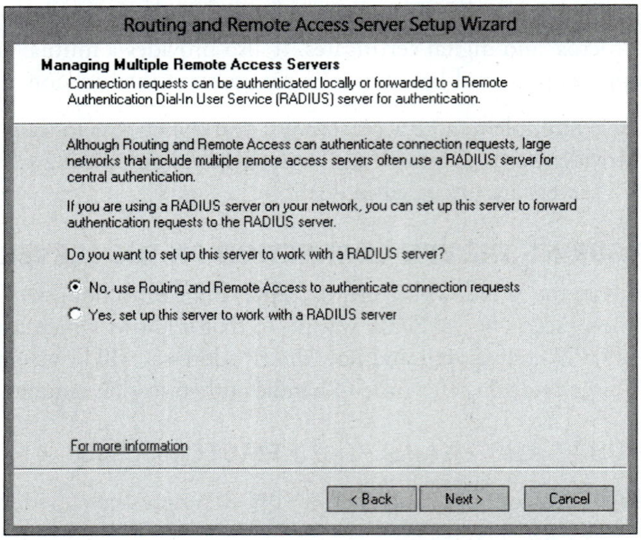

12. On the *RADIUS Server Selection* page (see Figure 10-18), enter the Primary RADIUS server and Alternate RADIUS server. Then, in the *Shared secret* text box, type in the shared secret password. Click Next.

Figure 10-18

Specifying the RADIUS Servers on the RADIUS Server Selection page

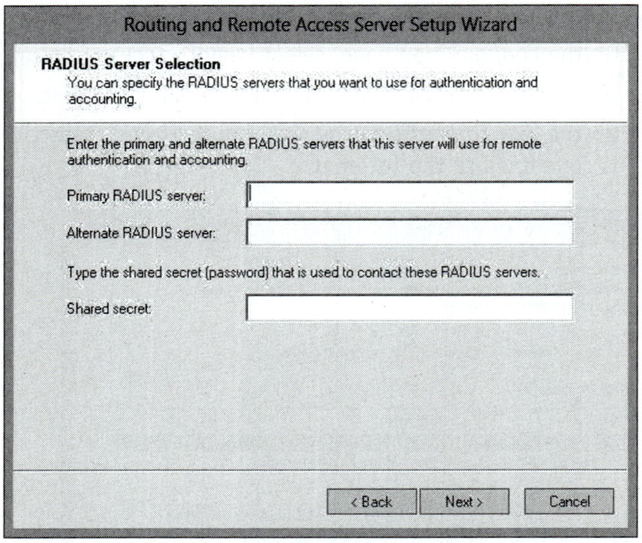

13. If you do not have RADIUS server, click No, use Routing and Remote Access to authenticate connection requests. Click Next.
14. On the *Completing the Routing and Remote Access Server Setup Wizard* page, click Finish.
15. When it asks to support the relaying of DHCP messages from remote access clients message, click OK.

After the VPN server is configured using the Configure and Enable Routing and Remote Access Wizard, you can further configure the VPN server by right-clicking the server in RRAS and selecting *Properties*. The General tab (see Figure 10-19) allows you to enable routing and remote access without using the wizard.

Figure 10-19

Enabling routing and remote access with the General tab

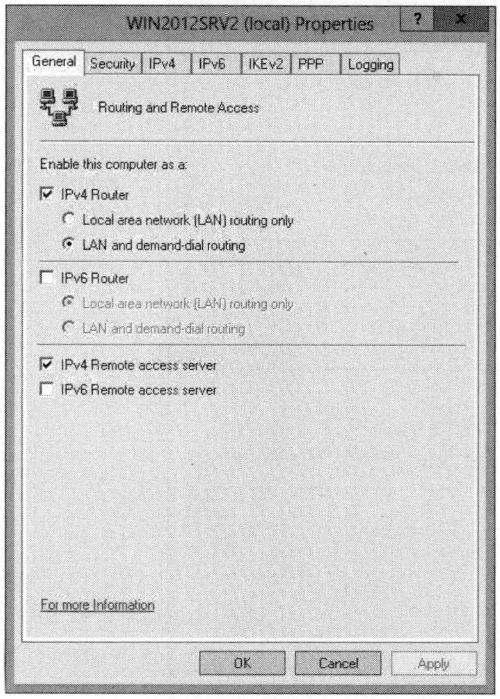

From the *Security* tab (see Figure 10-20), you can configure authentication methods, specify the Preshared key for IPsec and L2TP/IKv2 connections, and specify the SSL certificate that is used by SSTP.

Figure 10-20

Using the Security tab

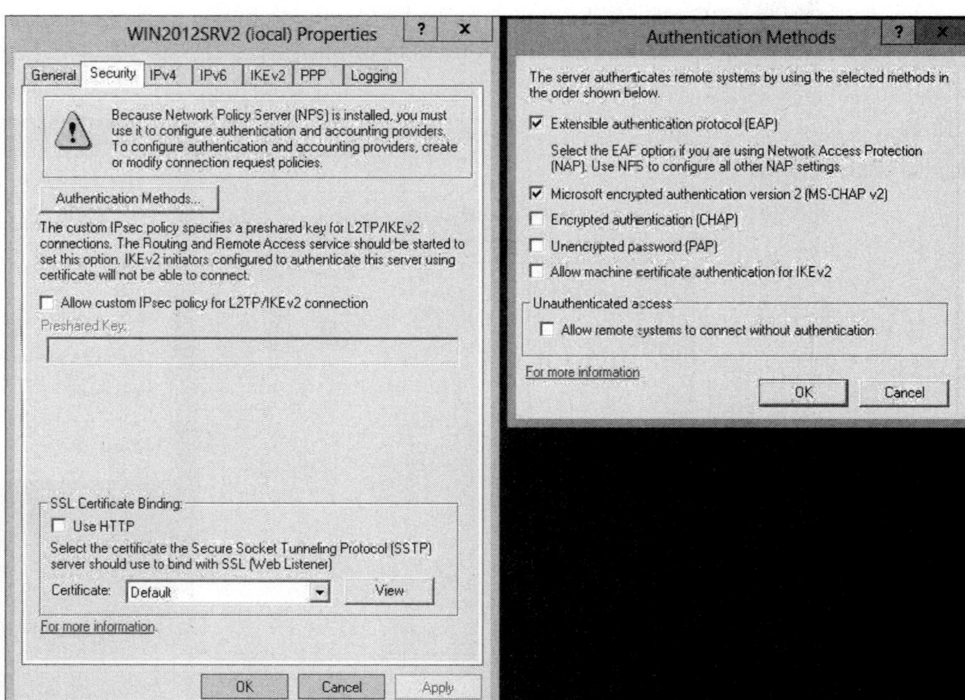

The IPv4 tab allows you to configure the IPv4 address assignments (see Figure 10-21), whereas the IPv6 allows you to specify the IPv6 prefix assignment. The IKEv2 allows you configure IKEv2 parameters, such as idle-timeout and network outage time.

Figure 10-21

Using the IPv4 tab

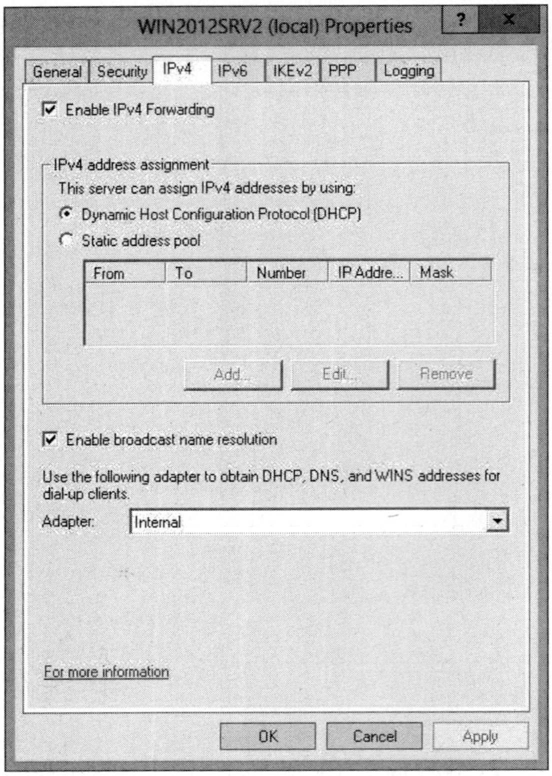

By default, RRAS allows up to 128 ports for each of the VPN protocol types. If you want to change the number of ports, right-click *Ports* and select *Properties*. You can then click the Configure button to open the Configure Device – WAN miniport dialog box so that you can specify the maximum number of ports (see Figure 10-22).

Figure 10-22

Specifying the number of ports

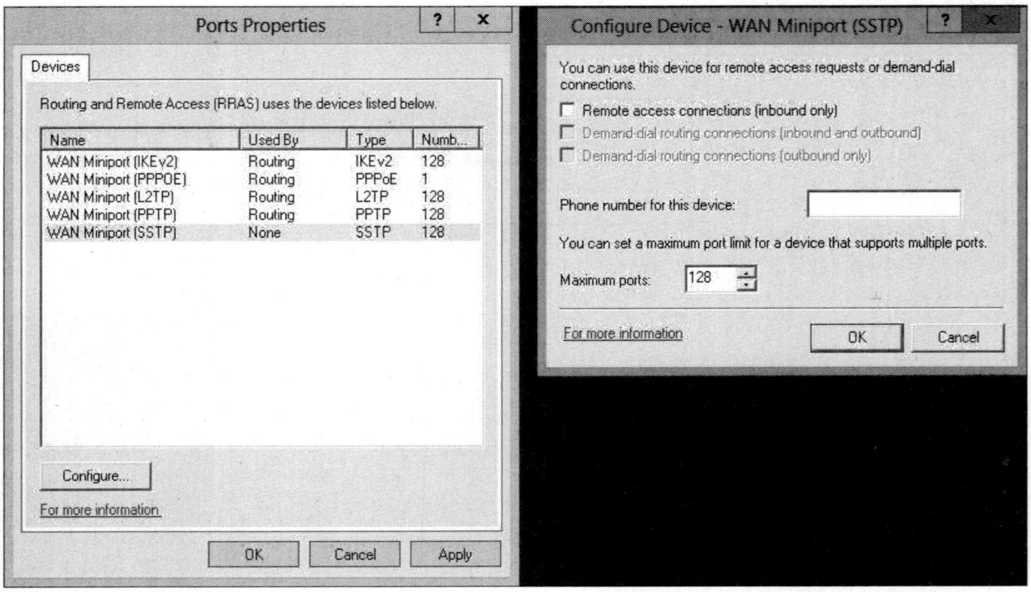

CREATING A VPN CONNECTION ON A CLIENT

If you want to configure a client so that it can connect to a VPN server, you will use the Network and Sharing Center to start the wizard to set up a new connection or network. When you run the wizard, you will define the name or IP address that will be used when connecting to the remote network.

CREATE A VPN TUNNEL

GET READY. To create a VPN connection on Windows Server 2012, perform the following steps:

1. From the Control Panel, select Network and Internet to access the *Network and Sharing Center*.
2. From the *Network and Sharing Center* (see Figure 10-23), choose Set up a new connection or network.

Figure 10-23

Opening the Network and Sharing Center

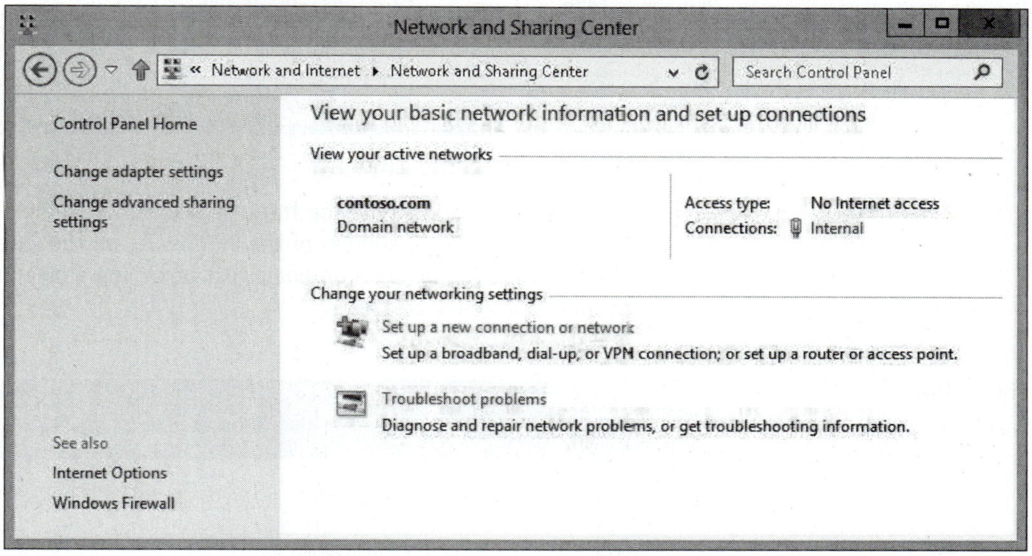

3. On the Set Up a Connection or Network page (as shown in Figure 10-24), choose Connect to a workplace. Click Next.

Figure 10-24

Connecting to a workplace with the *Set Up a Connection or Network* page

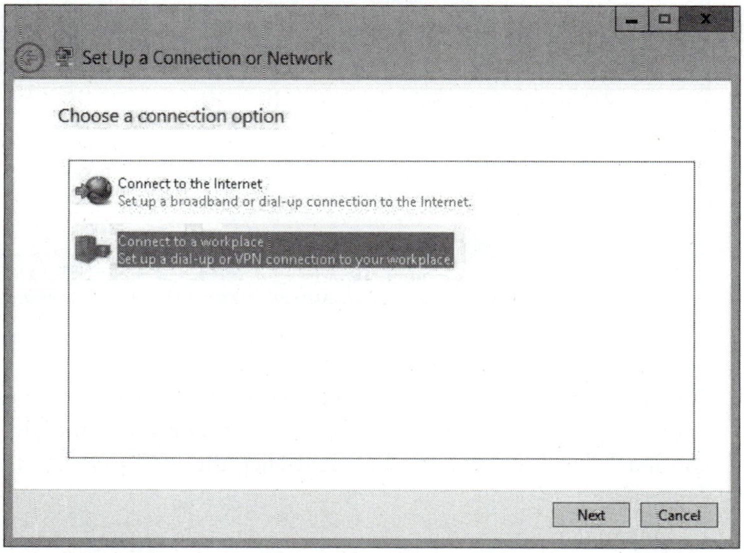

4. On the *Connect to a Workplace* page, (see Figure 10-25), answer the question, "How do you want to connect?" Choose Use my Internet connection or Dial directly.

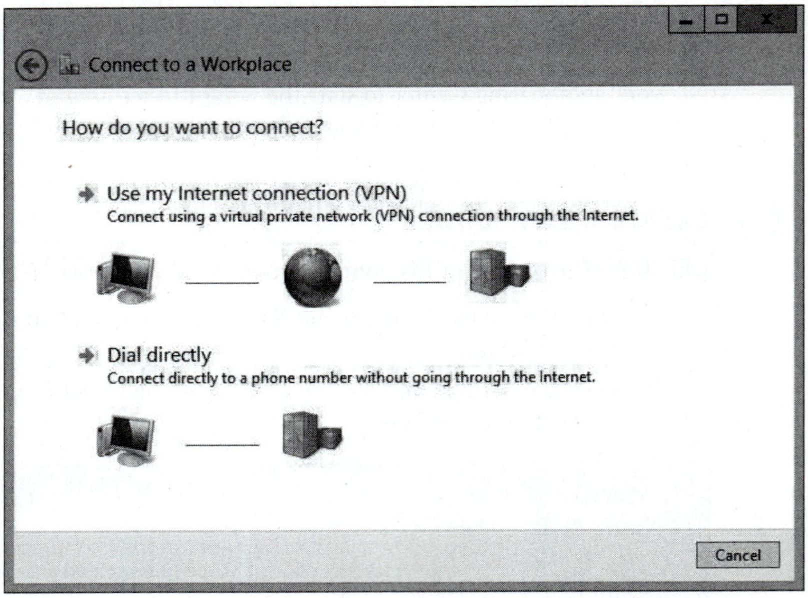

Figure 10-25

Connecting to a workplace

5. When it asks you to type the Internet address to connect to (see Figure 10-26), type the DNS name or IP address of the VPN server on the Internet in the *Internet address* text box. In the *Destination name* text box, type a meaningful name for the VPN connection. Click Create.

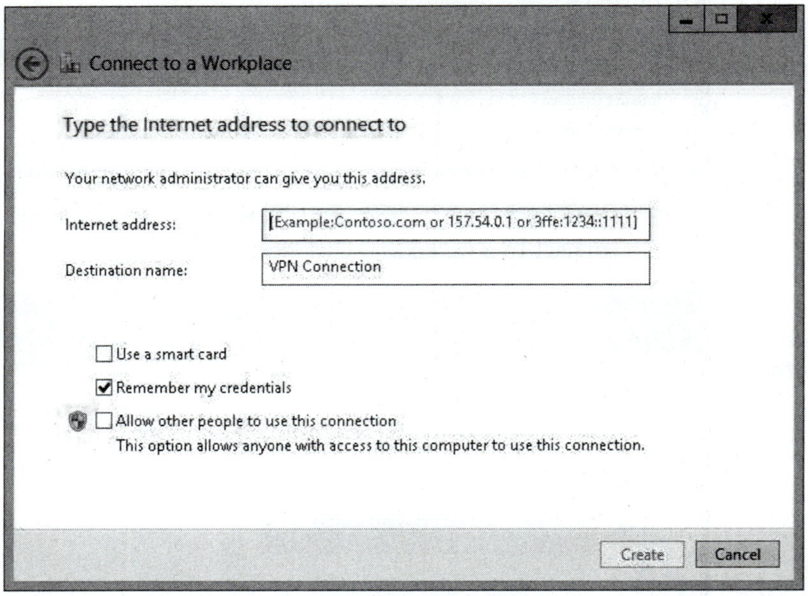

Figure 10-26

Entering the Internet address and destination name

When the connection is created, it shows under Network Connections (see Figure 10-27 and Figure 10-28). To use the VPN client, you still need to configure the VPN connection. To configure the client, you need to right-click the *VPN connection* you just created and click *Properties*.

Figure 10-27

Connecting to a network connections after the connections are created

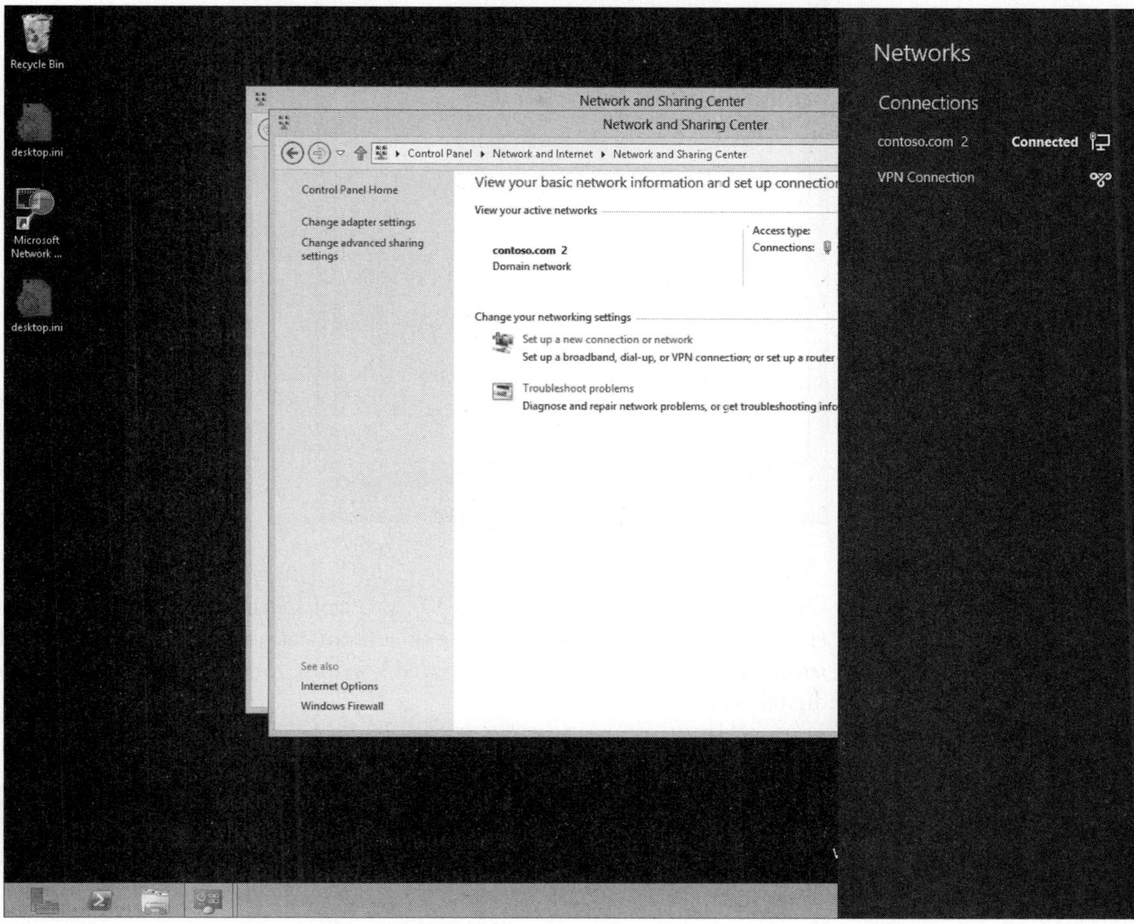

Figure 10-28

Viewing network connections in the Network and Sharing Center

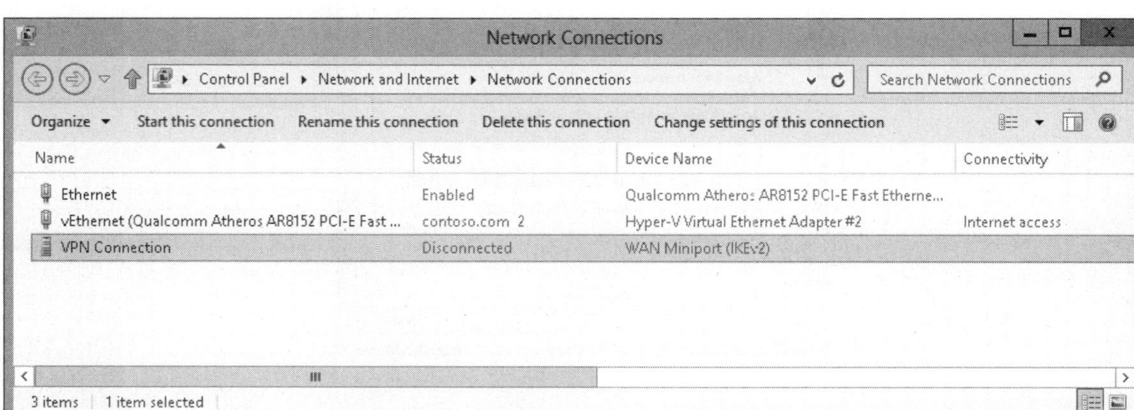

On the *General* tab, you can change the host name or IP address of the VPN server, as shown in Figure 10-29. The *Options* tab allows you to specify if the VPN connection remembers your credentials or not and how much idle time it waits before the VPN connection hangs up (disconnects).

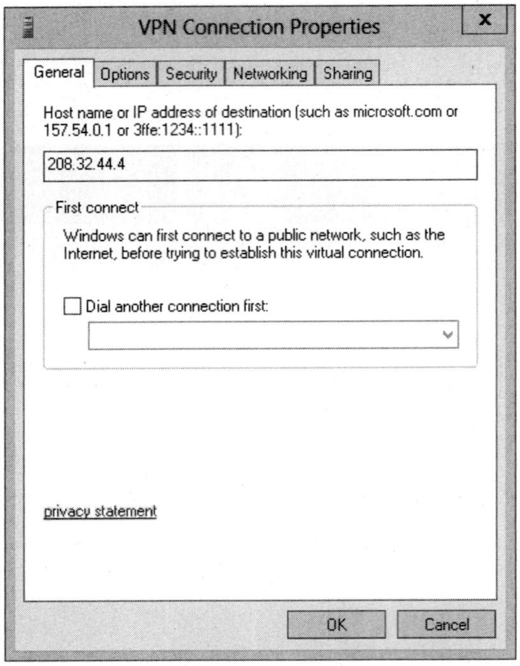

Figure 10-29

Specifying the hostname or IP address of the VPN server on the General tab

On the *Security* tab (see Figure 10-30), you can specify the type of VPN, whether data encryption is required, and the type of authentication. If you use L2TP, click the *Advanced settings* button to specify the pre-shared key used for authentication or if you are to use a digital certificate.

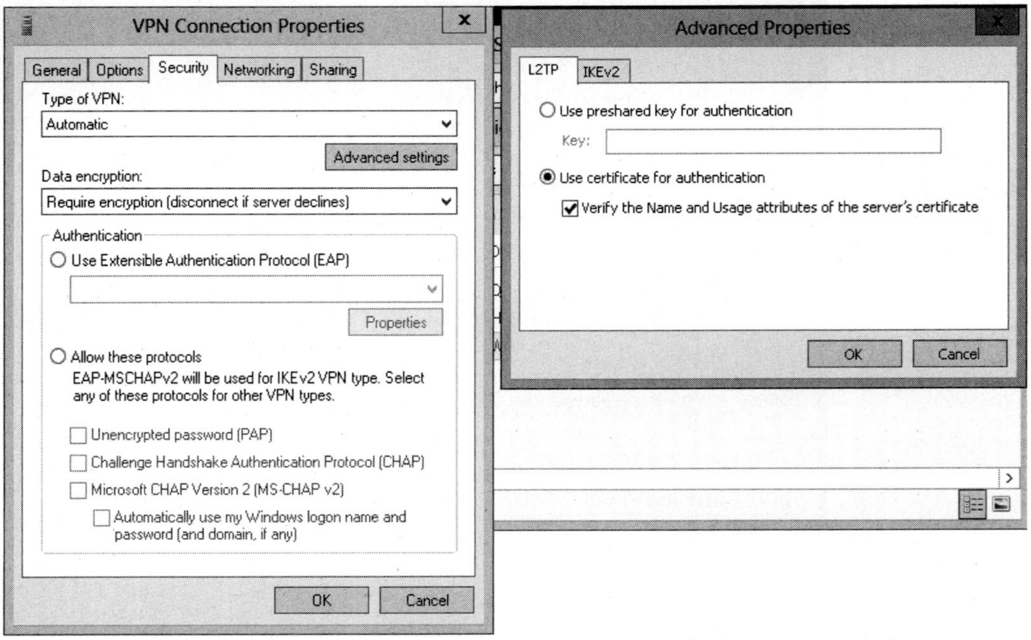

Figure 10-30

Security tab

To connect using the VPN once the VPN connection is created and configured, open the Network and Sharing Center and click *Change adapter settings*. Then, right-click your VPN connection and click the *Connect/Disconnect* (see Figure 10-31).

Figure 10-31

Connecting to a VPN server

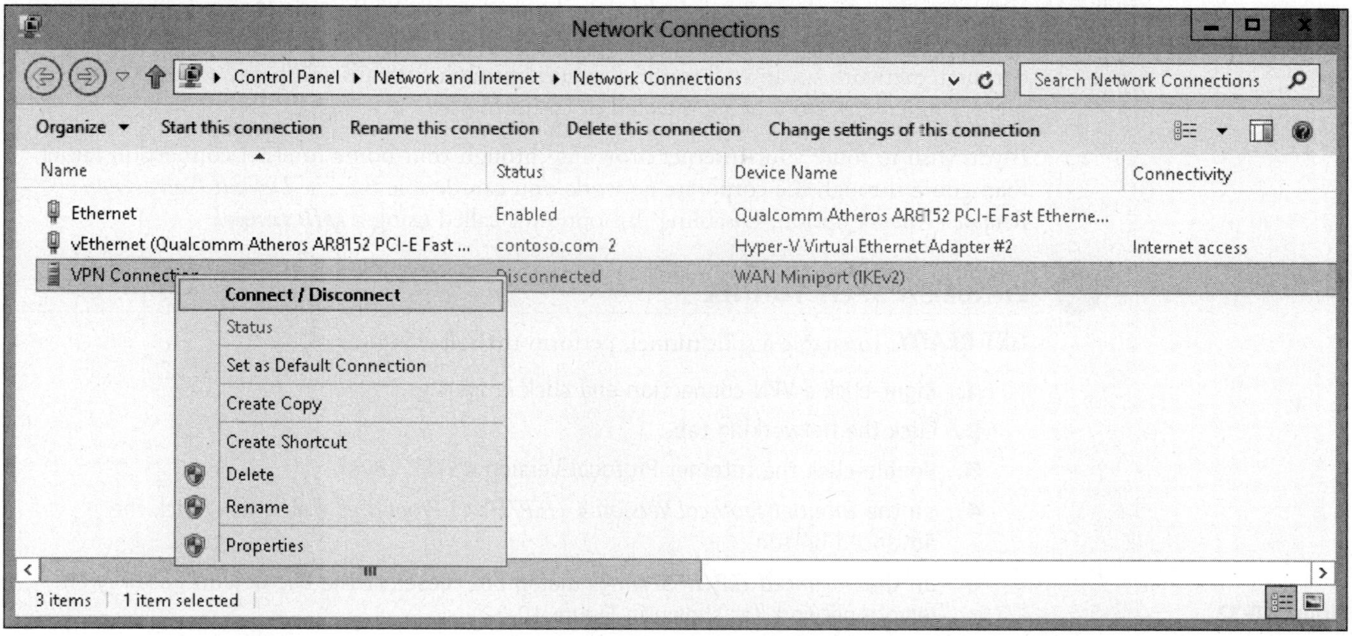

VPN RECONNECT

To provide constant connectivity, you use Internet Key Exchange version 2 (IKEv2), which automatically establishes a VPN connection when Internet connectivity is available. Only Windows 7, Windows 8, Windows Server 2008 R2, and Windows Server 2012 support VPN Reconnect.

On the server, you must do the following:

1. Create a user account with remote access permission.
2. Install a certificate with Server Authentication and IP security IKE intermediate extended key usage on the VPN server.
3. Install Routing and Remote Access and configure it as a VPN server.
4. Configure the Network Policy Server (NPS) to grant access for Extensible Authentication Protocol-Microsoft Challenge-Handshake Authentication Protocol version 2 (EAP-MSCHAPv2) authentication. NPS is discussed in Lessons 12 and 13.

On the client, you would do the following:

1. Specify the VPN server address or host name when configuring the VPN connection properties.
2. When you specify the VPN tunnel type, in the *Type of VPN* list, select *IKEv2* and select an encryption and authentication. VPN Reconnect supports two types of Authentication: *Extensible Authentication Protocol (EAP)* and *X.509 Machine Certificates.*
3. By default, the *Mobility* check box is enabled for *VPN Reconnect in Advanced properties.* If the check box is clear, the client cannot switch its local tunnel endpoint.
4. On the *Networking* tab, you can select *IPv4, IPv6,* or both protocols.
5. After the VPN connection is established, you can view the connection status on the *Details* tab of the *connection status* page.

CONFIGURING SPLIT TUNNELING

By default, when you connect to a VPN using the previous configuration, all web browsing and network traffic goes through the default gateway on the Remote Network unless you are communicating with local home computers. Having this option enabled helps protect the corporate network because all traffic also goes through firewalls and proxy servers, which prevent a network from being infected or compromised.

If you wish to route your Internet browsing through your home Internet connection rather than going through the corporate network, you can disable the *Use Default Gateway on Remote Network* option. Disabling this option is called using a ***split tunnel***.

ENABLE A SPLIT TUNNEL

GET READY. To enable a split tunnel, perform the following steps:

1. Right-click a VPN connection and click **Properties**.
2. Click the **Networking** tab.
3. Double-click the **Internet Protocol Version 4 (TCP/IPv4)**.
4. On the *Internet Protocol Version 4 (TCP/IPv4) Properties* dialog box, click the **Advanced** button.
5. On the *Advanced TCP/IP Settings* dialog box, deselect the **Use default gateway on remote network** (as shown in Figure 10-32).

Figure 10-32

Enabling split tunneling by enabling the *Use Default Gateway on Remote Network* option

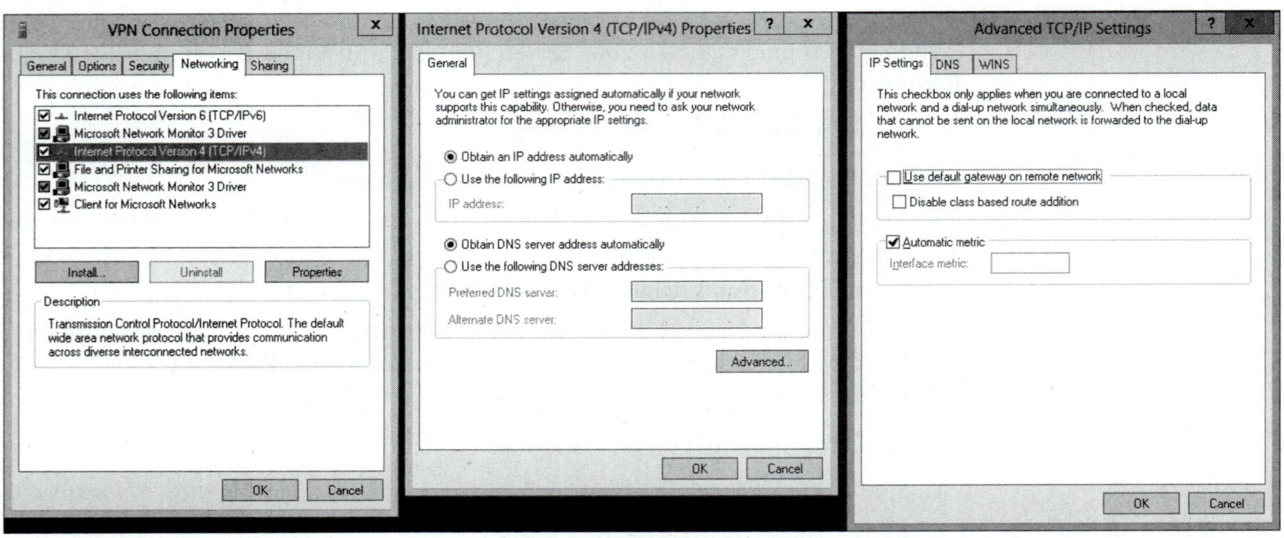

6. Click **OK** to close the *Advanced TCP/IP Settings* dialog box.
7. Click **OK** to close the *Internet Protocol Version 4 (TCP/IPv4) Properties* dialog box.
8. Click **OK** to close the *VPN Connection Properties* dialog box.

If you have to configure multiple clients to connect to a remote server, it can be a lot of work and it can be easy to make an error. To help simplify the administration of the VPN client into an easy-to-install executable, you can use the RAS Connection Manager Administration Kit (CMAK), which can also be installed as a feature in Windows Server 2012. After an executable file is created that includes all of the VPN settings, the executable file is deployed on the client computers.

Configuring Remote Dial-In Settings for Users

When you connect through a dial-in connection or a VPN connection, the remote access connection must be authorized by the server running Network Policy Server (NPS) RRAS role service or another third-party RADIUS server.

CERTIFICATION READY
Configure remote dial-in settings for users.
Objective 3.3

Besides making sure that the username and password are valid, the remote access server verifies the dial-in properties of the user account and verifies if any NPS Network Policies have been applied, which specify which users can connect through the RRAS server and which users cannot connect.

For domain users, the dial-in properties are configured in the user account Properties dialog box, specifically the Dial-in tab, which is accessed in the Active Directory Users and Computers console, as shown in Figure 10-33. If you are dialing into a standalone server, you would open the user account in Local Users and Groups console in Computer Management.

Figure 10-33
Configuring Dial-in Properties

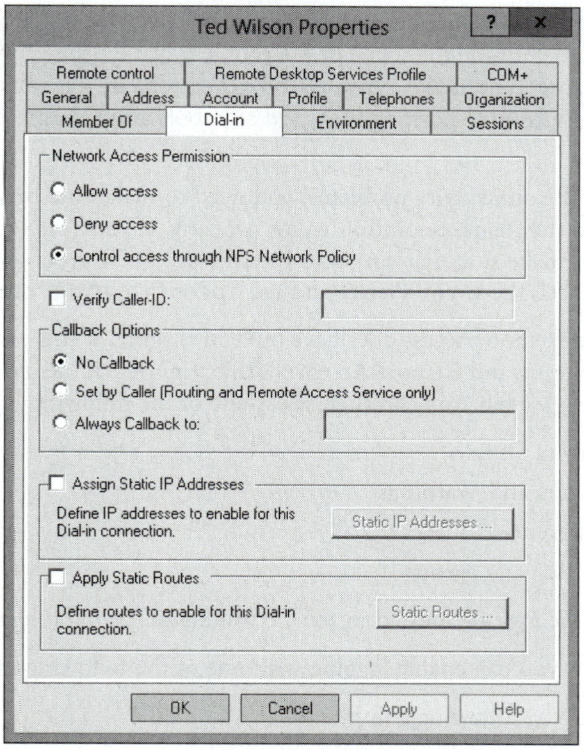

In Windows Server 2012, by default, the Control access through NPS Network Policy is selected. By selecting the Control access through the NPS Network Policy, access permissions are determined by first matching the NPS Network Policy applied to the connection. NPS is discussed in more detail in Lessons 12 and 13.

If the Deny Access option is selected, the user will be blocked and will not be able to connect to the RRAS server. If the Allow Access option is selected, the use is automatically granted. It should be noted that NPS Network Policy can also perform some restrictions such as time restrictions.

If the Verify Caller ID check box is selected, the server verifies the caller's phone number. If the phone number does not match the configured phone number, the connection attempt is denied, assuming the caller, the phone system between the caller and the server, and the remote access server all support caller ID. If you configure a caller ID phone number for a user and one of the components do not support caller ID, the connection attempt is denied.

By default, the Callback Options setting is No Callback. If the Set By Caller option is selected, the server calls the caller back at a number specified by the caller. This option is used to avoid phone charges for the client.

If the Always Callback To: option is selected, an administrator must specify a number that the server always uses during the callback process. This option helps to make sure that only users from a certain number can call in. If the username and password have been compromised for a user, the user can still call in only from a specified number.

Finally, you can configure a static IP address or addresses and static routes that should apply to this user whenever he or she connects to a Remote Access server. These options make sure that the same IP address is assigned to a client and to make sure the user has the desired routes to resources.

Troubleshooting Remote Access Problems

When troubleshooting remote access problems, follow basic troubleshooting techniques where you determine the scope of the problem, gather symptoms, come up with a list of possible causes, and make a plan to solve the problem. Then use the normal Windows and network troubleshooting tools and any tools available specifically for remote access.

With network connectivity problems, you need to make sure that you are connected to the network and that name resolution works properly. If your VPN connection is to operate over the Internet, make sure that you have Internet access. To troubleshoot network connectivity problems, check the Event Viewer and use `ipconfig`, `ping`, `tracert`, and `nslookup`.

Routing and Remote Access does have built-in logging, if it is enabled. To enable logging, open the Routing and Remote Access console, right-click the *server*, select *Properties*, and select the *Logging* tab. You can then select one of the following logging levels:

- Log Errors Only
- Log Errors and Warnings
- Log all events
- Do not log any events

By default, the logs are located in the C:\Windows\Tracing folder/.

Alternatively, you can enable logging with one of the following methods:

- Execute the following command:

```
Netsh ras set tracing * enabled
```

- Set the following registry value:

  HKEY_LOCAL_MACHINE\SOFTWARE\Microsoft\Tracing\ EnableFileTracing=1

WARNING Because logging uses system resources, you should disable logging when you have solved the problem.

When troubleshooting VPN problems, you should perform the following:

- Use the `ping` or `nslookup` command to verify that the correct IP address is being returned for the host name. Don't always expect to have a successful ping because many firewalls on the Internet can block Internet Control Message Protocol (ICMP) packets.
- Verify that the user is using the correct username, password, and domain name.
- Verify that the user account is not locked, expired, or disabled.

- Verify that the user is not affected by logon hour restrictions.
- Verify that the correct VPN protocol and authentication are selected.
- If used, verify that you have the correct and valid digital certificate. The certificate must be issued with a valid date, is trusted, and is not revoked. The certificate must also have a valid digital certificate.
- Some certificates need to be checked to see whether they have been revoked or not. Therefore, make sure that the Certificate Revocation List (CRL) list is available over the Internet.
- Verify that the Routing and Remote Access service runs on the VPN server.
- Verify that the VPN server is enabled for remote access from the VPN Server Properties dialog box's General tab.
- Verify the appropriate ports (PPTP, L2TP, SSTP, and IKEv2) are enabled and available on the VPN server.
- Verify that the user in Active Directory Users and Computers is allowed to connect. If the connection is based on network policies, verify that the user is allowed to connect. Again, network policies are covered in Lessons 12 and 13.
- Verify that the connection's parameters have permission through network policies.
- Make sure that a firewall is not blocking any necessary packets or protocols, such as IKE. Also remember that RRAS static packet filters will block ICMP packets that are used by `ping` and `tracert`.
- If you have NAT in between the client and the VPN server, you need to configure Windows client supports IPsec NAT traversal (NAT-T). NAT is discussed later in this lesson.

If you receive an error message, the error message might give you some indication of where to look for the cause of the error. Common errors are listed in Table 10-1.

Table 10-1

Common VPN Errors

ERROR	DESCRIPTION
Error 800: VPN Server is unreachable	For whatever reason the PPTP, L2TP, SSTP, or IKEv2 packets cannot get to the VPN server. Verify that the appropriate ports are open on all relevant firewalls, including host firewalls (on the client and server).
Error 721: Remote Computer is Not Responding	For whatever reason, GRE traffic (part of PPTP) is not getting to the VPN. Therefore, check the standard ports are open on all relevant firewalls, including host firewalls (on the client and server) for PPTP.
Error 741 or 742: Encryption Mismatch Error	These errors occur if the VPN client requests an invalid encryption level or the VPN server does not support an encryption type that the client requests. On the client, check the VPN connection properties (Security tab) to verify that the proper encryption is selected. If you are using NPS, check the encryption level in the network policy in the NPS console or check the policies on other RADIUS servers. Finally, check the server to verify that the correct encryption level is enabled.
0x80092013: The revocation function was unable to check revocation because the revocation server was offline	Client is failing the certificate revocation check. Ensure the CRL check servers on the server side are exposed on the Internet.

Implementing NAT

Although CIDR helped use the IPv4 addresses more efficiently, additional steps had to prevent the exhaustion of IPv4 addresses. ***Network address translation (NAT)*** is used with masquerading to hide an entire address space behind a single IP address. In other words, it allows multiple computers on a network to connect to the Internet through a single IP address.

CERTIFICATION READY
Implement Network Address Translation (NAT).
Objective 3.3

NAT enables a local-area network (LAN) to use one set of IP addresses for internal traffic and a second set of addresses for external traffic. The NAT computer or device is usually a router (including routers made for home and small-office Internet connections) or a proxy server. As a result, you can do the following:

- Provide a type of firewall by hiding internal IP addresses.
- Enable multiple internal computers to share a single external public IP address.

The private addresses are reserved addresses not allocated to any specific organization. Because these private addresses cannot be assigned to global addresses used on the Internet and are not routable on the Internet, you must use a NAT gateway or proxy server to convert between private and public addresses. The private network addresses are expressed in RFC 1918:

- 10.0.0.0–10.255.255.255
- 172.16.0.0–172.31.255.255
- 192.168.0.0–192.168.255.255

NAT obscures an internal network's structure by making all traffic appear originated from the NAT device or proxy server. To accomplish this, the NAT device or proxy server uses stateful translation tables to map the "hidden" addresses into a single address and then rewrites the outgoing Internet Protocol (IP) packets on exit so that they appear to originate from the router. As data packets are returned from the Internet, the responding data packets are mapped back to the originating IP address using the entries stored in the translation tables.

When NAT is used to connect a private network to a public network, the following process occurs:

1. The client on the internal private network creates an IP packet, which is forwarded to the computer or device running NAT.
2. The computer or device running NAT changes the outgoing packet header to indicate the packet originated from the NAT computer or device's external address. It then sends the remapped packet over the public network such as the Internet to its intended destination. During this process, it will store the source address and the remapped NAT information in a table so that it can keep track of all source computers.
3. When the destination computer responds with packets, the destination computer sends packets back to the computer or device running NAT.
4. When the computer or device receives the packets back from the destination computer, the computer or device running NAT changes the packet header to the private address of the destination client. It then sends the packet to the client computer.

TAKE NOTE*

If you have an IPsec VPN server behind a NAT device, you need to configure the Windows clients to use Traversal NAT (NAT-T). For more information, visit Microsoft's Support website.

Enabling NAT is a simple process, which can be selected using the Routing and Remote Access Server Setup Wizard. To support NAT, you must have a server that has two network interfaces, one for the private network and one for the public network.

Disabling Routing and Remote Access

There may be times when you will need to disable and remove the settings used in Routing and Remote Access.

DISABLE ROUTING AND REMOTE ACCESS

GET READY. To disable Routing and Remote Access, perform the following steps:

1. Open Server Manager.
2. Click Tools > Routing and Remote Access.
3. Right-click the server, and select Disable Routing and Remote Access (see Figure 10-34).

Figure 10-34

Disabling Routing and Remote Access

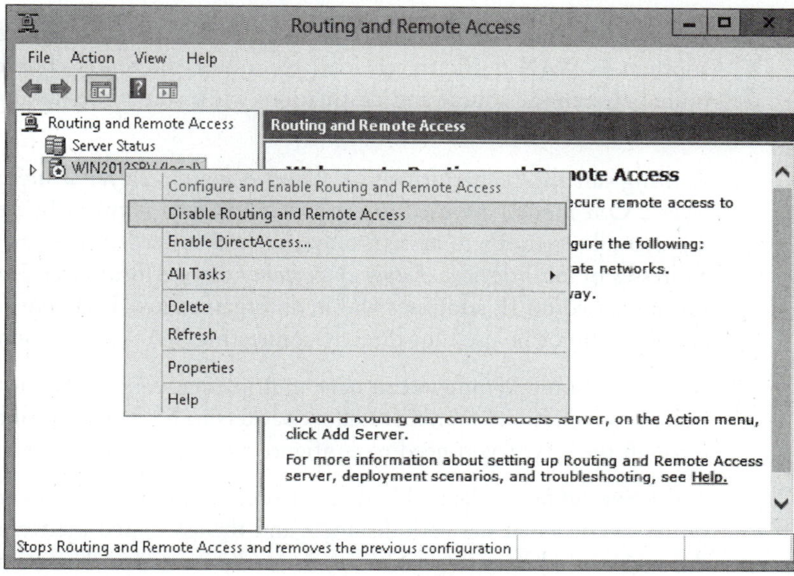

4. When you are asked if you want to continue, click Yes.
5. When the configuration is complete, the console will look similar to Figure 10-35.

Figure 10-35

Showing that the Routing and Remote Access is Disabled

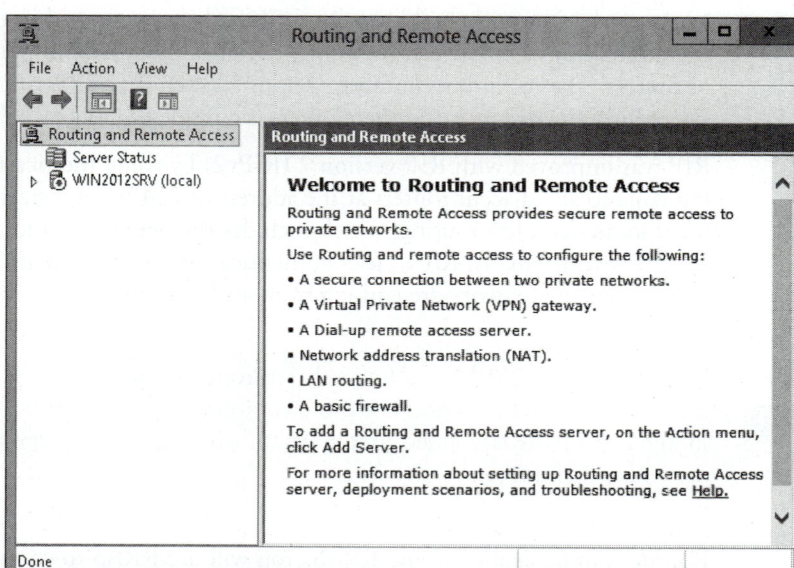

Configuring Routing

Routing is the process of selecting paths in a network where data will be sent. Routing is required to send traffic from one subnet to another within an organization, and it is required to send traffic from one organization to another. A computer running Windows can act as a router and include its own routing table, so that you can specify which direction data is sent toward its final destination.

CERTIFICATION READY
Configure routing.
Objective 3.3

Routers operate at the OSI Reference Model Layer 3, Network layer. Therefore, they are sometimes referred to as Layer 3 devices. Routers join subnets together to form larger networks and join networks together over extended distances or WANs. They can also connect dissimilar LANs, such as Ethernet LAN to a Fiber Distributed Data Interface (FDDI) backbone.

As larger networks are formed, there may be multiple pathways to get from one place to another. As WAN traffic travels multiple routes, the router chooses the fastest or cheapest route between the source and destination, while sometimes taking consideration of the current load.

Routing can also be performed by a layer 3 switch. ***Layer 2 switches*** (which operate at the layer 2 OSI model) are used to connect a host to a network by performing packet switching that allows traffic to be sent only to where it needs to be sent based on mapping MAC addresses of local devices. ***Layer 3 switches*** can perform layer 2 switching, but also perform routing based on IP addresses within an organization. Different from a router, layer 3 switches cannot be used for directly connecting WAN connections.

A server running Windows can have multiple network cards, each network card can be connected to a different subnet. To allow packets to be sent from one subnet to another subnet through the server, you need to configure routing on the server.

A ***routing table*** is a data table that is stored in a router or networked computer that lists the routes of particular network distances and the associated metrics or distances associated with those routes. The routing tables are manually created with ***static routes***, or are dynamically created with routing protocols such as ***Routing Information Protocol (RIP)***, based on the current routing topology.

Microsoft Windows supports the Routing Information Protocol through RRAS. RIP has been a popular distance-vector routing protocol for small organizations. RIP uses broadcasts where the entire routing table is sent to the other routers within the network. To determine the distance or cost between networks, RIP uses the metric of hop count, which is the count of routers. The maximum number of hops allowed for RIP is 15. The hop count of 16 is considered infinite distance and therefore, it is considered nonreachable.

RIP was improved with RIP version 2 (RIPv2) by using multicasts to send the entire routing table to all adjacent routers at the address of 224.0.0.9 instead of using broadcast. It also incorporates classless routing, which includes the network mask to allow classless routing advertisement. Finally, RIPv2 uses authentication to ensure that routes being distributed throughout the network are coming from authorized sources.

TAKE NOTE* Windows Server 2012 is a software-based router that can be used for lightly trafficked subnets on a small network. For more complex network with heavy network traffic, you should use a hardware-based router, which would give you more reliability and improved network performance.

Routing can be enabled using RRAS. You will use RRAS to configure RIP or define static routes. You can also define static routes using the `Route` command.

CONFIGURE ROUTING

GET READY. To configure routing on Windows Server 2012, perform the following steps:

1. Open Server Manager.
2. Click Tools > Routing and Remote Access.
3. Right-click the server and select Configure and Enable Routing and Remote Access.
4. When the *Routing and Remote Access Server Setup Wizard* opens, click Next.
5. On the *Configuration* page, select Custom configuration and click Next.
6. On the *Custom Configuration* page, select LAN routing and click Next.
7. On the *Completing the Routing and Remote Access Server Setup Wizard* page, click Finish.
8. When the Routing and Remote Access service is ready to use, click the Start service button.

MANAGING STATIC ROUTES

Static-routed IP networks are best suited for small, single-paths that don't change much. To view the IP routing table using RRAS, expand the server node, expand the IPv4 or IPv6 nodes, right-click the static routes node, and then click *Show IP Routing Table* (see Figure 10-36).

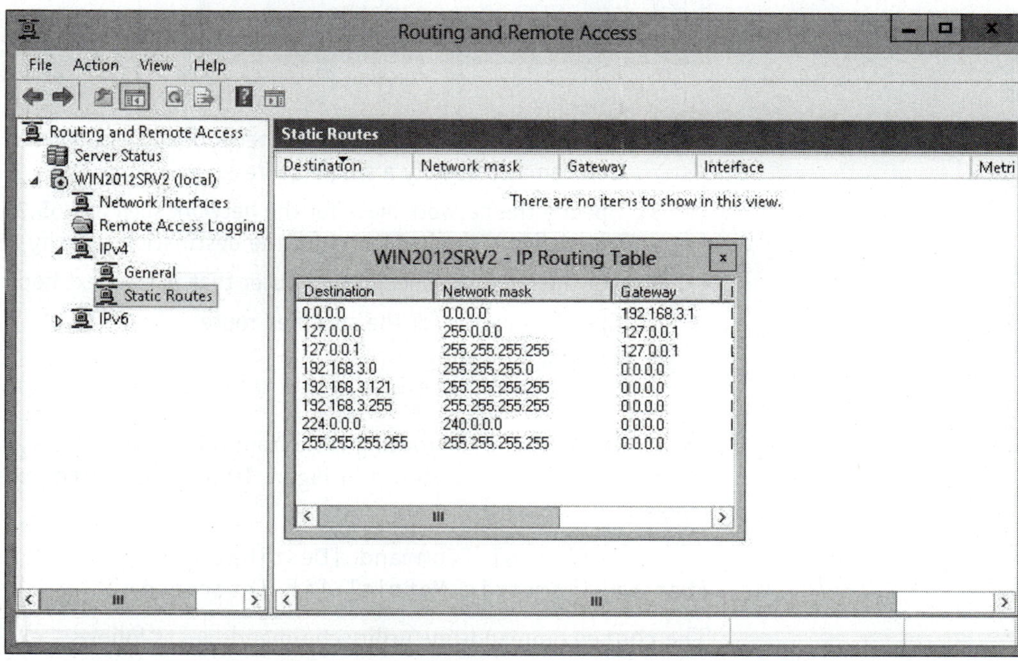

Figure 10-36

Displaying static routes using RRAS

When you define routes, you specify the network address of the destination, the network mask, and the local router or next hop to get to its destination. When the packet reaches the local router, the router will then use its routing table to determine what the next hop that the packet needs to be sent to. The process will continue until the packet reaches the destination network, where the packets are then sent to the destination host.

CREATE A NEW STATIC ROUTE USING RRAS

GET READY. To create a new static route using RRAS, perform the following steps:

1. Open **Server Manager**.
2. Click the **Tools > Routing and Remote Access**.
3. Expand **server note** and expand the **IPv4** node.
4. Right-click **Static Routes** node and select **New Static Route**.
5. When the *IPv4 Static Route* dialog box opens (see Figure 10-37), specify the interface that you want to assign the static route.

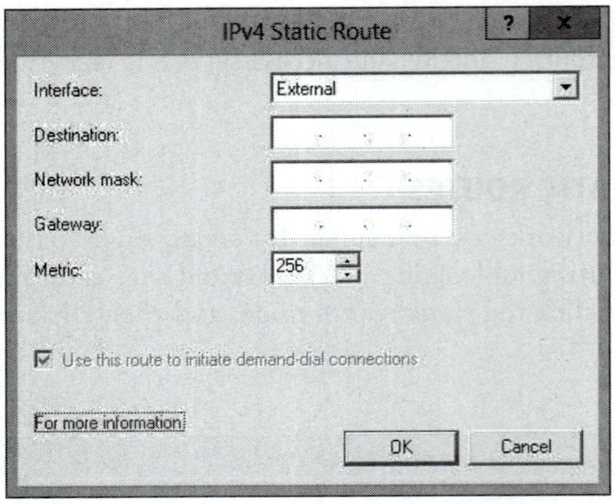

Figure 10-37

Defining an IPv4 static route

6. For the destination, type in the network address, such as 172.24.0.0 or 192.168.5.0. You can also specify a single address.
7. Specify the network mask for the network such as 255.255.00 or 255.255.255.0. If you define a single address for the destination, specify 255.255.255.255.
8. For the *Gateway*, specify the router that is the next hop toward the final destination.
9. Specify a metric for the specified route.
10. Click **OK**.

To view or configure the routing table from the command line, use the `route.exe` command-line utility, as shown in Figure 10-38. The `route.exe` utility syntax is as follows:

```
route [-f] [-p] [Command [Destination] [mask Netmask]
[Gateway] [metric Metric] [if Interface]
```

The `route` command-line utility commands are as follows:

- `print`: Displays the routing table.
- `add`: Adds a route to the routing table. To make routes persistent, which will be available after the server is rebooted, you must also use the –p switch.
- `change`: Modifies an existing route.
- `delete`: Deletes an existing route.

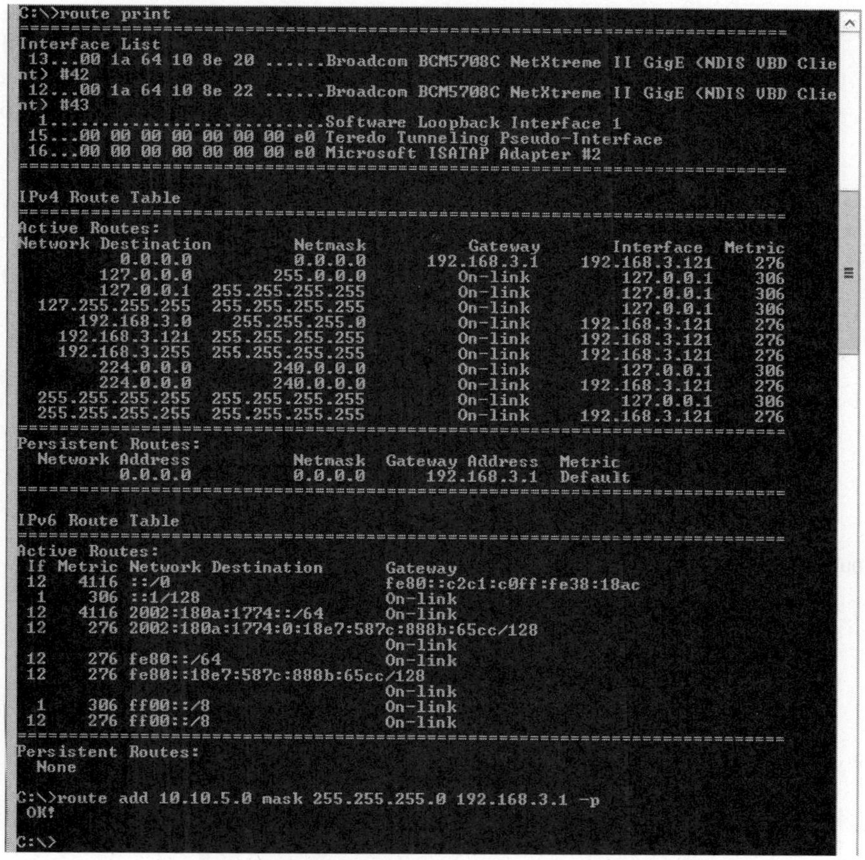

Figure 10-38

Route command

To display the routing table, execute the following command:

```
route print
```

To add a route to 10.10.5.0 network, which will be sent to the 192.168.1.20 router, execute the following command:

```
route add 10.10.5.0 mask 255.255.255.0 192.168.1.20
```

To add a route to 10.10.5.0 network, which will be sent to the 192.168.1.20 router and make the route persistent, execute the following command:

```
route add 10.10.5.0 mask 255.255.255.0 192.168.1.20
-p
```

To change the 10.10.5.0 route to use the 192.168.1.21 router, use the following command:

```
route change 10.10.5.0 mask 255.255.255.0
192.168.1.21
```

To delete the 10.10.5.0 route, use the following command:

```
route delete 10.10.5.0
```

CONFIGURING RIP

Microsoft Windows supports the Routing Information Protocol through RRAS. RIP has been a popular distance-vector routing protocol for small organizations. RIP uses broadcasts where the entire routing table is sent to the other routers within the network. To determine the distance or cost between networks, RIP uses the metric of hop count, which is the count of routers. The maximum number of hops allowed for RIP is 15. The hop count of 16 is considered infinite distance and therefore, it is considered nonreachable.

RIP was improved with RIP version 2 (RIPv2) by using multicasts to send the entire routing table to all adjacent routers at the address of 224.0.0.9, instead of using broadcasts. It also incorporates classless routing, which includes the network mask to allow classless routing advertisement. Lastly, RIPv2 uses authentication to ensure that routes being distributed throughout the network are coming from authorized sources.

CONFIGURE ROUTING

GET READY. To configure RIP on Windows Server 2012, perform the following steps:

1. Open Server Manager.
2. Click Tools > Routing and Remote Access.
3. Expand the server node, and expand IPv4.
4. Right-click the General tab and select New Routing Protocol. The *New Routing Protocol* dialog box opens (see Figure 10-39).

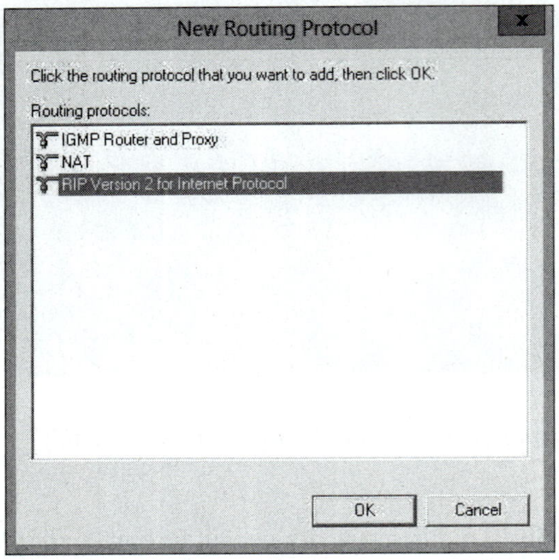

Figure 10-39
Specifying a new routing protocol

5. Select RIP Version 2 for Internet Protocol.
6. Click OK to close the *New Routing Protocol* dialog box. A RIP node will appear under IPv4.
7. Right-click RIP and select New Interface. The *New Interface for RIP Version 2 for Internet Protocol* dialog box opens (see Figure 10-40).

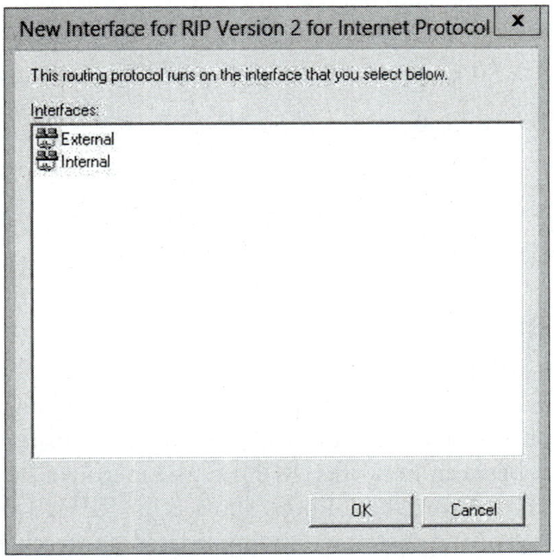

Figure 10-40
Specifying the new interface for RIP Version 2 for Internet Protocol

8. Select the interface on which you want to use RIP.
9. Click OK to close the *New Interface for RIP Version 2 for Internet Protocol* dialog box. The *RIP Properties* dialog box opens (see Figure 10-41).

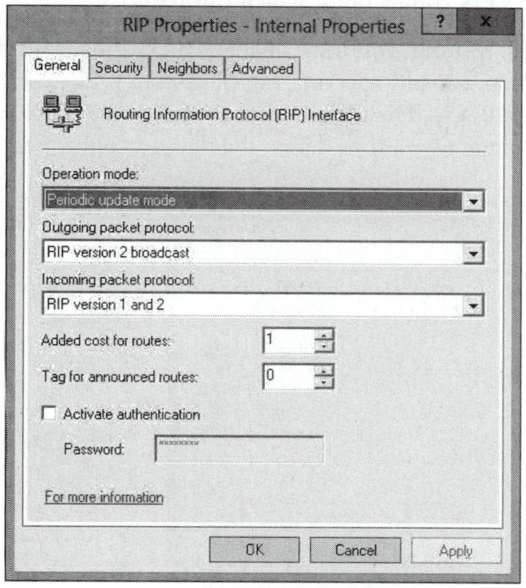

Figure 10-41

Configuring the RIP Properties

10. Click OK to close the *RIP Properties* dialog box.

If you need to configure RIP, right-click the *RIP node* and select *Properties*. For example, if you want to specify which routes to accept, select the *Security* tab; if you want to specify the neighbors that the RRAS router interfaces with, select the *Neighbors* tab (see Figure 10-42).

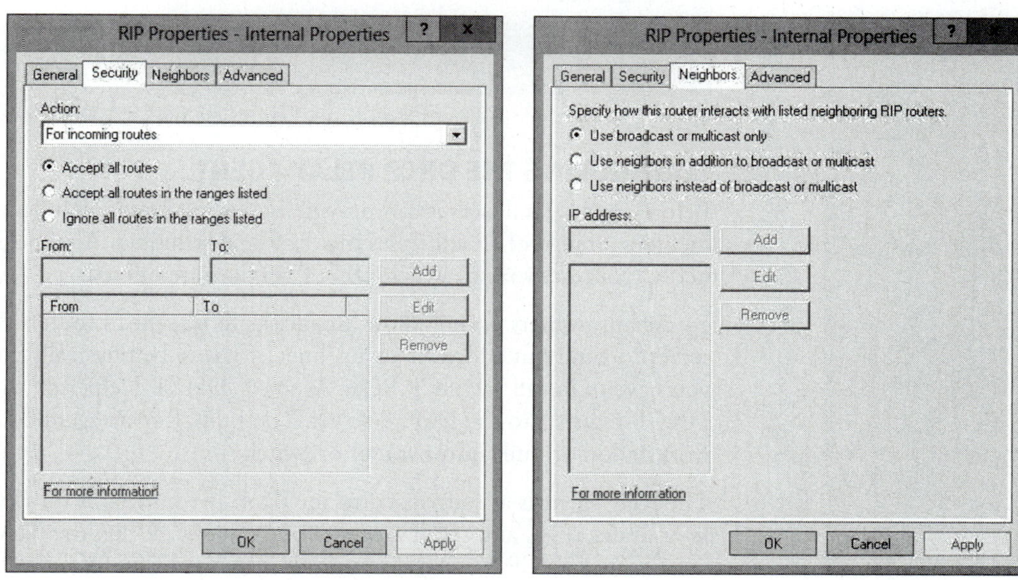

Figure 10-42

Configuring the RIP Security and Neighbors tabs

CONFIGURING DEMAND-DIAL ROUTING

Routing and Remote Access also supports ***demand-dial routing***, which is a connection to a remote site that is activated when data is sent to the remote site. When there is not more data to be sent, the link is disconnected. The use of demand-dial routing can be used with dial-up telephone lines or VPN connections, which can reduce connection costs.

To use demand-dial routing, you must enable demand-dial routing by right-clicking the server, selecting *Properties* and selecting the *General* tab. Then select *LAN and demand-dial routing* (see Figure 10-43). Then, right-click *Network Interfaces*, select *New Demand-dial Interface* to go through a wizard to define the dial-up connection or VPN connection.

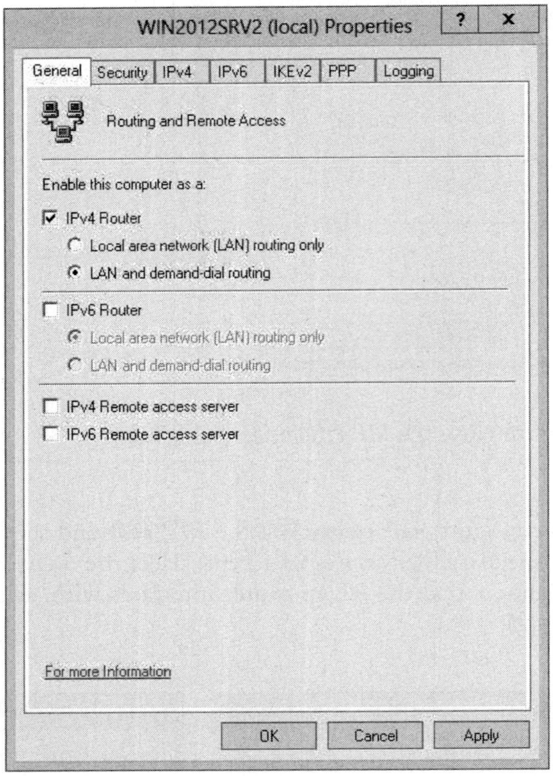

Figure 10-43

Enabling demand-dial routing

CONFIGURING THE DHCP RELAY AGENT

Before your DHCP server can provide IP address leases, you have to define a scope that includes a range of IP addresses that can be distributed. A scope defines a single physical subnet on your network to which DHCP services are offered.

By default, routers do not allow broadcasts to be sent to routers. Therefore, for the DHCP server to hand out addresses to a subnet, it has to be physically connected to the subnet, or you have to install a DHCP Relay Agent or DHCP Helper on the subnet that relays the DHCP requests to the DHCP server. The DHCP relay agent could be a Windows server or workstation or built into a router or switch.

The relay agent is already installed for IPv4. If you need it for IPv6, right-click the *General node* under IPv6, and select *New Routing Protocol*. When the New Routing Protocol dialog box opens, DHCP v6 relay Agent is already highlighted. Click *OK*.

CONFIGURE THE DHCP RELAY AGENT

GET READY. To configure the DHCP Relay Agent, perform the following steps:

1. Open Server Manager.
2. Click Tools > Routing and Remote Access.
3. Expand the server node and the IPv4 node.
4. Right-click DHCP Relay Agent and select Properties. The *DHCP Relay Agent Properties* dialog box opens (see Figure 10-44).

Figure 10-44

Specifying the DHCP Server that the DHCP Relay Agent Relays To

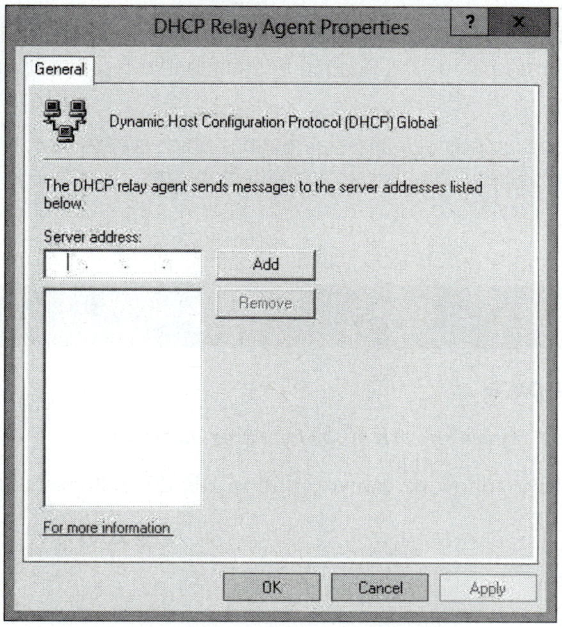

5. In the *Server* address box, type in the address of the DHCP server and click Add.
6. Click OK to close the *DHCP Relay Agent Properties* dialog box.

SKILL SUMMARY

IN THIS LESSON, YOU LEARNED:

- Remote access server (RAS) enables users to connect remotely to a network using various protocols and connection types.
- To provide remote access server, Microsoft includes Routing and Remote Access (RRAS), which provides a Virtual Private Network (VPN), a dial-up remote access server, and Network Address Translation (NAT). It also provides routing functionality and basic firewall functionality.
- After you install RRAS, you need to enable the server and configure RRAS.
- Virtual private networks (VPNs) link two computers or network devices through a wide-area network (WAN) such as the Internet.
- To provide constant connectivity, use Internet Key Exchange version 2 (IKEv2), which automatically establishes a VPN connection when Internet connectivity is available.
- Split tunneling is when you route your Internet browsing through your home Internet connection rather than going through the corporate network when using a VPN connection.

(continued)

- When you connect through a dial-in connection or a VPN connection, the remote access connection must be authorized by the server running Network Policy Server (NPS), RRAS role service, or other third-party RADIUS server.
- Network address translation (NAT) is used with masquerading to hide an entire address space behind a single IP address. In other words, it allows multiple computers on a network to connect to the Internet through a single IP address.
- Routing is the process of selecting paths in a network where data will be sent.
- Microsoft Windows supports the Routing Information Protocol (RIP) through RRAS.
- The routing tables are manually created with static routes or are dynamically created with routing protocols such as Routing Information Protocol (RIP), based on the current routing topology.
- RRAS also supports demand-dial routing, which is when a connection to a remote site is activated because data is sent to the remote site.

Knowledge Assessment

Multiple Choice

Select the correct answer for each of the following questions.

1. Which of the following can you find in RRAS? (Choose all that apply.)
   a. Routing
   b. OSPF
   c. RIP
   d. NAT
2. If you want to use VPN Reconnect, which VPN protocol should you use?
   a. PPTP
   b. L2TP
   c. IKEv2
   d. SSTP
3. You want to make a server running Windows Server 2012 into a VPN server. However, the networking team allows only HTTPS through the firewall. Which VPN protocol should you use?
   a. PPTP
   b. L2TP
   c. IKEv2
   d. SSTP
4. You want to start using smartcards with the VPN. What authentication protocol should you use?
   a. PAP
   b. CHAP
   c. MS-CHAPv2
   d. EAP
5. Which authentication protocol should you not use because it is the least secure?
   a. PAP
   b. CHAP
   c. MS-CHAPv2
   d. EAP

6. How do you allow split tunneling?
   a. Open Advanced TCP/IP Settings and select Use default gateway on remote network.
   b. Open Advanced TCP/IP Settings and deselect Use default gateway on remote network.
   c. Open Advanced TCP/IP Settings and select Don't use default gateway on remote network.
   d. Open Advanced TCP/IP Settings and deselect Don't use default gateway on remote network.
7. What is the easiest way to set up a VPN client on a computer for a user that is not technical?
   a. Use PAP.
   b. Type up step-by-step instructions with screenshots to give to the user.
   c. Use a Group Policy to configure the settings.
   d. Use CMAK to create an executable to install.
8. Which option would you use to make sure that a user can dial in using only his or her home phone?
   a. Verify Caller ID
   b. Always Callback To
   c. No Callback
   d. Set By Caller
9. Which tab in the RIP properties would you use to prevent routes being received from a router located on 10.10.10.10?
   a. General
   b. Security
   c. Neighbors
   d. RIP Nodes
10. Which option should you use with the `Route` command when creating a static route that will ensure the route is still available if the computer is rebooted?
    a. `/consistent`
    b. `/save`
    c. `-p`
    d. `-s`

Best Answer

Choose the letter that corresponds to the best answer. More than one answer choice may achieve the goal. Select the BEST answer.

1. You have a main office and 12 branch offices. The users and computers are within a single domain. All servers are Windows Server 2008 R2 and Windows Server 2012. You must make sure that all data is encrypted by using end-to-end encryption. In addition, instead of using usernames and passwords, you need to use computer-level authentication. What should you do?
   a. Configure a PPTP connection and MS-CHAPv2.
   b. Configure L2TP with IPsec and EAP-TSL authentication.
   c. Configure L2TP with IPsec and MS-CHAPv2.
   d. Configure SSTP with IPsec and PAP.
2. When establishing a VPN connection, which of the following verifies that data has not been modified while in transit?
   a. Encapsulation
   b. Authentication
   c. Data encryption
   d. Data integrity

3. You have a single DHCP server that services the corporate office and 25 remote sites. How do you install a DHCP relay agent on a remote site so that you can forward DHCP requests to the DHCP server?
   a. Configure DNS with Dynamic Update.
   b. Install RRAS and enable routing.
   c. Install RRAS and enable NAT.
   d. Install NAP.

4. Which of the following would you use to enable NAT?
   a. Services for Network File System (NFS)
   b. Wireless LAN Service
   c. Network Load Balancing (NLB)
   d. Routing and Remote Access service (RRAS)
   e. Health Registration Authority (HRA)
   f. Simple TCP/IP Services
   g. Connection Manager Administration Kit (CMAK)
   h. Network Policy Server (NPS)
   i. Windows System Resource Manager (WSRM)

5. You just enabled SSTP on a server called Server1. When a user tries to log in, he receives an error: Error 0x80092013: The revocation function is unable to check revocation because the revocation server was offline. You look at your certificate and it looks fine. What would you do to overcome this problem?
   a. Renew the certificate.
   b. Publish the CRL distribution point to a site that is available over the Internet.
   c. Add the RRAS server to the client personal store.
   d. Upgrade the certificate to V3.

Matching and Identification

1. Identify the correct VPN protocol (PPTP, L2TP, SSTP, or IKEv2) for the following items.
   _______ a) Uses MPPE for encryption
   _______ b) Requires UDP port 500, UDP Port 1701, and UDP port 4500
   _______ c) Supports VPN Reconnect
   _______ d) Requires only UDP port 500
   _______ e) Requires port 1723
   _______ f) Uses a certificate or preshared key and is combined with IPsec for encryption
   _______ g) Uses port 443

2. Identify the correct authentication protocol (PAP, CHAP, MS-CHAPv2, and EAP-MS-CHAPv2) for the following items.
   _______ a) Used in older network devices and uses a challenge-response method with md5 hashing
   _______ b) Allows you to change an expired password during the connection process
   _______ c) Required when using smartcards
   _______ d) Username and password are sent in plaintext
   _______ e) Default authentication used when performing a VPN connection with Windows 8

3. Identify the routing protocols supported by Windows Server 2012.
   _______ a) RIP v2 for Internet Protocol
   _______ b) IGMP Router and Proxy
   _______ c) OSPF
   _______ d) BGP
   _______ e) NAT

Build a List

1. Specify the steps, in order, that are used to configure a VPN server. Not all steps will be used.
   _____ Run the Configure and Enable Routing Remote Access Wizard.
   _____ Configure VPN parameters using server properties in RRAS.
   _____ Create a VPN connection on the client.
   _____ Enable VPN Service.
   _____ Install RRAS.
   _____ Install VPN console.
   _____ Install VPN Service.

Choose an Option

1. In the figure, circle the option that you would use to enable split tunneling.

Figure 10-45

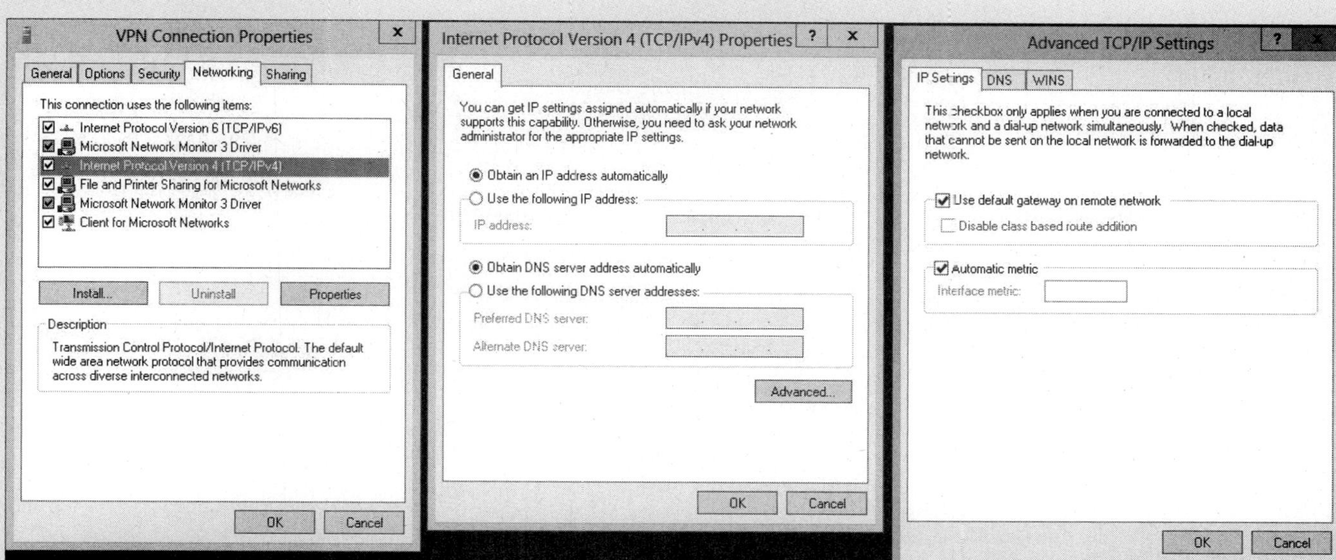

Business Case Scenarios

Scenario 10-1: Installing a VPN Server

Your manager comes up to you and says that you need to install a VPN server so that users can work while they are doing sales calls with customers. Your manager wants you to make it as secure as possible with the VPN technologies that appear in this lesson. How would you configure the server?

Scenario 10-2: Configuring Routing

You have a corporate office with 12 remote sites. Each remote site has a site server that also acts as a router. When you look at each of the servers, you realize that the previous administrator used the route command to specify static routes. However, as you have had to do maintenance and move some of the network connections, you find it difficult to modify all of the servers to reflect the changes. In addition, you will be adding four more sites over the next six months. What do you recommend to your manager so that you don't have to buy any more network equipment?

11 LESSON

Configuring Direct Access

70-411 EXAM OBJECTIVE

Objective 3.4 – Configure DirectAccess. This objective may include but is not limited to: implement server requirements; implement client configuration; configure DNS for DirectAccess; configure certificates for DirectAccess.

LESSON HEADING	EXAM OBJECTIVE
Understanding DirectAccess	Configure DirectAccess
Looking at the DirectAccess Connection Process	
Understanding DirectAccess Requirements	Implement server requirements
Running the DirectAccess Getting Started Wizard	
Running the Remote Access Setup Wizard	Implement client configuration
Preparing for DirectAccess Deployment	Configure DNS for DirectAccess Configure certificates for DirectAccess
Troubleshooting DirectAccess	

KEY TERMS

DirectAccess

DirectAccess Connectivity Assistant (DCA)

Name Resolution Policy Table (NRPT)

Network Connectivity Assistant (NCA)

network location server (NLS)

■ Understanding DirectAccess

THE BOTTOM LINE

DirectAccess is a new feature introduced with Windows 7 and Windows Server 2008 R2 that provides seamless intranet connectivity to DirectAccess client computers when they are connected to the Internet. Different from the traditional virtual private network (VPN) connections, DirectAccess connections are automatically established and they provide always-on seamless connectivity.

CERTIFICATION READY
Configure DirectAccess.
Objective 3.4

DirectAccess overcomes the limitations of VPNs by automatically establishing a bi-directional connection from client computers to the organization's network using IPsec and Internet Protocol version 6 (IPv6). For organizations that have not deployed IPv6, you can use transition mechanisms such as 6to4 and Teredo IPv6 transition technologies for connectivity across the IPv4 Internet and the Intra-Site Automatic Tunnel Addressing (ISATAP)IPv6 transition technology, so that DirectAccess clients can access IPv6-capable resources across your IPv4-only intranet. As a result, remote client computers are automatically connected to the organization's network so that they can be easily managed and kept up-to-date with critical updates and configuration changes.

Looking at the DirectAccess Connection Process

A DirectAccess connection to a target intranet resource is initiated when the DirectAccess client connects to the DirectAccess server through IPv6. IPsec is then negotiated between the client and server. Finally, the connection is established between the DirectAccess client and the target resource.

This general process can be broken down into the following specific steps:

1. The DirectAccess client computer running Windows 8, Windows 7 Enterprise, or Windows 7 Ultimate detects that it is connected to a network.
2. The DirectAccess client computer determines whether it is connected to the intranet. If the client is connected to the intranet, it does not use DirectAccess.
3. The DirectAccess client connects to the DirectAccess server by using IPv6 and IPsec.
4. If the client is not using IPv6, it will try to use 6to4 or Teredo tunneling to send IPv4-encapsulated IPv6 traffic.
5. If the client cannot reach the DirectAccess server using 6to4 or Teredo tunneling, the client tries to connect using the Internet Protocol over Hypertext Transfer Protocol Secure (IP-HTTPS) protocol. IP-HTTPS uses a Secure Sockets Layer (SSL) connection to encapsulate IPv6 traffic.
6. As part of establishing the IPsec session for the tunnel to reach the intranet DNS server and domain controller, the DirectAccess client and server authenticate each other using computer certificates for authentication.
7. If Network Access Protection (NAP) is enabled and configured for health validation, the Network Policy Server (NPS) determines whether the client is compliant with system health requirements. If it is compliant, the client receives a health certificate, which is submitted to the DirectAccess server for authentication.
8. When the user logs on, the DirectAccess client establishes a second IPsec tunnel to access the resources of the intranet. The DirectAccess client and server authenticate each other using a combination of computer and user credentials.
9. The DirectAccess server forwards traffic between the DirectAccess client and the intranet resources to which the user has been granted access.

The ***Name Resolution Policy Table (NRPT)*** is used to determine the behavior of the DNS clients when issuing queries and processing so that internal resources are not exposed to the public via the Internet and to separate traffic that isn't DirectAccess Internet traffic from DirectAccess Internet traffic. By using the NRPT, the DirectAccess clients use the intranet DNS servers for internal resources and Internet DNS for name resolution of other resources. The NRPT is managed using group policies, specifically, Computer Configuration\Policies\Windows Settings\Name Resolution Policy.

Understanding DirectAccess Requirements

Compared to other forms of remote access, DirectAccess is more complex, which has more required components. Of course, with the complexity, you get much more functionality that you did with other remote access technologies.

CERTIFICATION READY
Implement server requirements.
Objective 3.4

Besides installing DirectAccess on the VPN server, you need to make sure that you prepare the network, the server, and the clients. A little planning also goes a long way when implementing DirectAccess.

UNDERSTANDING DIRECTACCESS SERVER REQUIREMENTS

To use DirectAccess, the DirectAccess server requires the following:

- The server must be part of an Active Directory domain.
- The server must be running Windows Server 2008 R2 or Windows Server 2012.
- If the DirectAccess server is connected to the intranet and published over Microsoft Forefront Threat Management Gateway (TMG) or Microsoft Forefront Unified Access Gateway 2010 (UAG), a single network adapter is required. If the DirectAccess server is connected as an edge server, it will need two network adapters (one for the Internet and one for the intranet).
- Implementation of DirectAccess in Windows Server 2012 does not require two consecutive static, public IPv4 addresses as was required with Windows Server 2008 R2. However, to achieve two-factor authentication with a smart card or Operational Data Provider (OTP) deployment, DirectAccess server still needs two public IP addresses.
- You can deploy Windows Server 2012 DirectAccess behind a NAT support, which avoids the need for additional public addresses. However, only IP over HTTPS (IP-HTTPS) is deployed, allowing a secure IP tunnel to be established using a secure HTTP connection.
- With Windows Server 2012, you can use Network Load Balancing (up to eight nodes) to achieve high availability and scalability for both DirectAccess and RRAS.

In addition, you need the following in your network infrastructure:

- An Active Directory domain that runs a minimum of Windows Server 2008 R2 domain functional level.
- Group policy for central administration and deployment of DirectAccess client settings.
- One domain controller running Windows Server 2008 SP2, Windows Server 2008 R2, or Windows Server 2012.
- Public Key Infrastructure (PKI) to issue computer certificates for authentication and health certificates when NAP is deployed and computer certificates for authentication. The SSL certificates installed on the DirectAccess server must have a Certificate Revocation List (CRL) distribution point that is reached from the Internet. Finally, the certificate Subject filed must contain the Fully Qualified Domain Name (FQDN)that can be resolved to a public IPv4 address assigned to the DirectAccess server by using the DNS on the Internet.

- When using Intra-Site Automatic Tunnel Addressing Protocol (ISATAP), DNS must run on at least Windows Server 2008 R2, Windows Server 2008 with the Q958194 hotfix, Windows Server 2008 SP2 or later, or a third-party DNS server that supports DNS message exchanges over the ISATAP.
- IPsec policies. DirectAccess utilizes IPsec policies that are configured and administered with Windows Firewall with Advanced Security.
- Internet Control Message Protocol Version 6 (ICMPv6) Echo Request traffic. You must create separate inbound and outbound rules that allow ICMPv6 Echo Request messages. DirectAccess clients that use Teredo for IPv6 connectivity to the intranet use the ICMPv6 message when establishing communication.
- IPv6 and transition technologies such as ISATAP, Teredo, and 6to4 must be available for use on the DirectAccess server. For each DNS server running Windows Server 2008 or higher, you need to remove the ISATAP name from the global query block list.
- Network Access Protection (NAP) is an optional component of the DirectAccess solution that allows you to provide compliance checking and enforce security policy for DirectAccess clients over the Internet. Unlike Windows Server 2008 R2, Windows Server 2012 DirectAccess provides the capability to configure NAP health checks directly from the setup user interface.

UNDERSTANDING DIRECTACCESS CLIENT REQUIREMENTS

To use DirectAccess, the clients must be Windows 7 Enterprise Edition, Windows 7 Ultimate Edition, Windows 8, Windows Server 2008 R2, or Windows Server 2012. You will not be able to deploy DirectAccess for Windows Vista or earlier or Windows Server 2008 or earlier. Finally, the client must be joined to an Active Directory domain.

Running the DirectAccess Getting Started Wizard

To configure DirectAccess itself, you use the newly created Remote Access Management console. By using the Remote Access Management console, you can configure DirectAccess by using one of two available wizards: the Getting Started Wizard or the Remote Access Setup Wizard.

The Getting Started Wizard allows you to quickly configure DirectAccess with the default recommended settings. While this wizard allows for the quickest setup, it does not allow you much control on the available options.

RUN THE DIRECTACCESS GETTING STARTED WIZARD

GET READY. To perform the quick configuration of DirectAccess, using the Getting Started Wizard, perform the following steps:

1. Start Server Manager.
2. Click Tools > Remote Access Management. The Remote Access Management console opens (see Figure 11-1).

Figure 11-1

Opening the Remote Access Management console

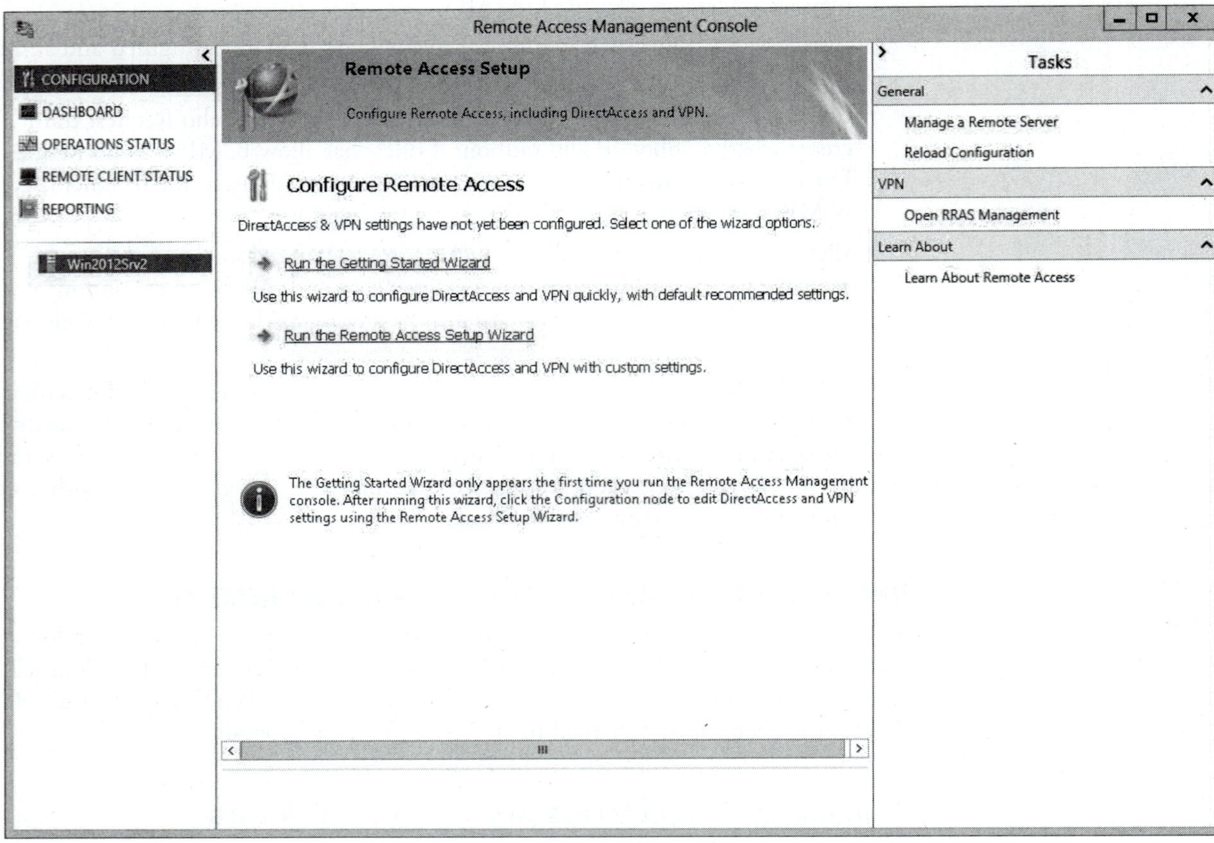

3. Click Run the Getting Started Wizard link.
4. When the *Getting Started Wizard* starts (see Figure 11-2), click Deploy DirectAccess only.

Figure 11-2

Starting the Configure Remote Access Wizard

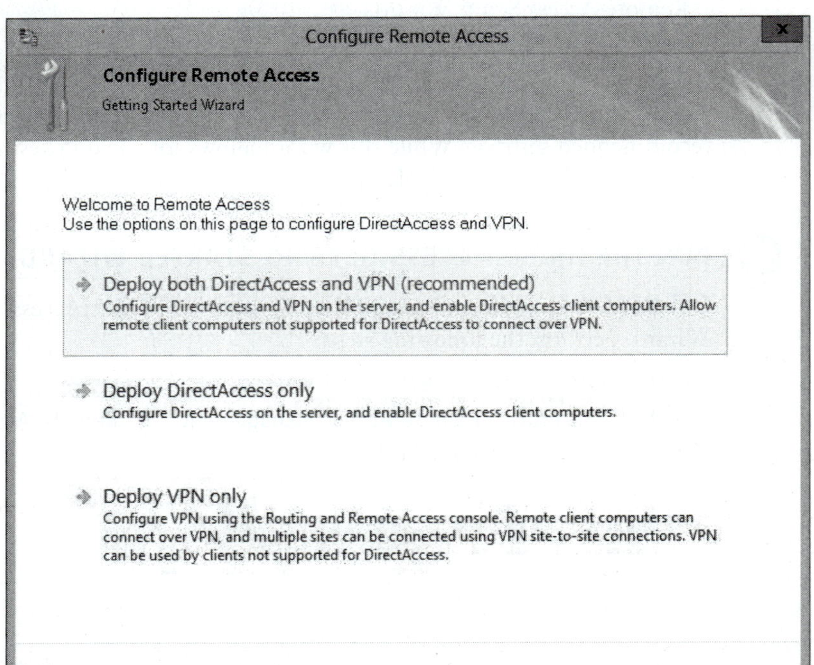

5. On the *Configure DirectAccess and VPN settings* page (see Figure 11-3), select the appropriate topology.

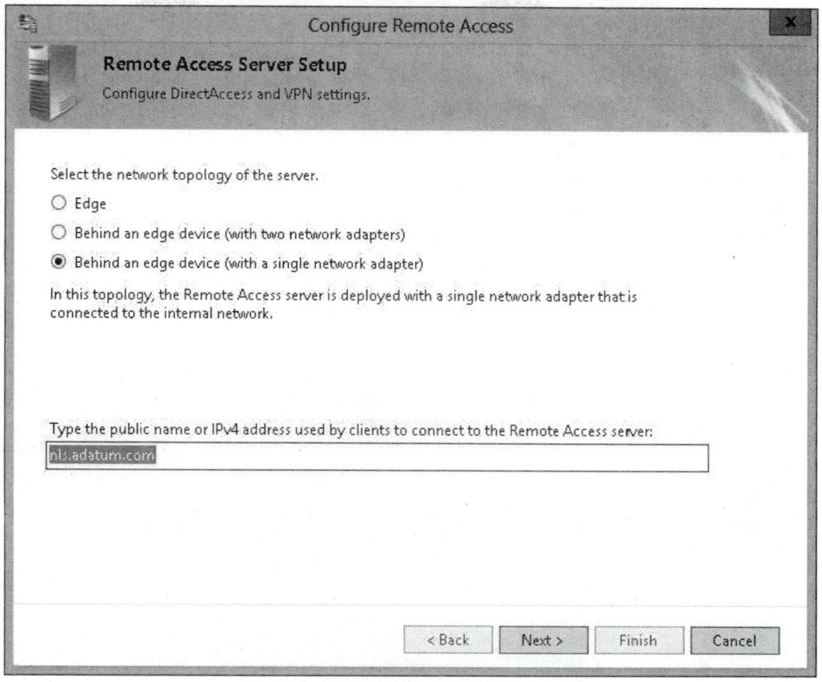

Figure 11-3

Selecting a topology on the *Configure DirectAccess and VPN Settings* page

6. Specify the public name or IPv4 address that the clients will use to connect to the Remote Access server in the appropriate text box. Click Next.
7. The Configure Remote Access page should display a message that says the Remote Access settings will be applied (see Figure 11-4). Click the here link to show the settings that have been modified (see Figure 11-5).

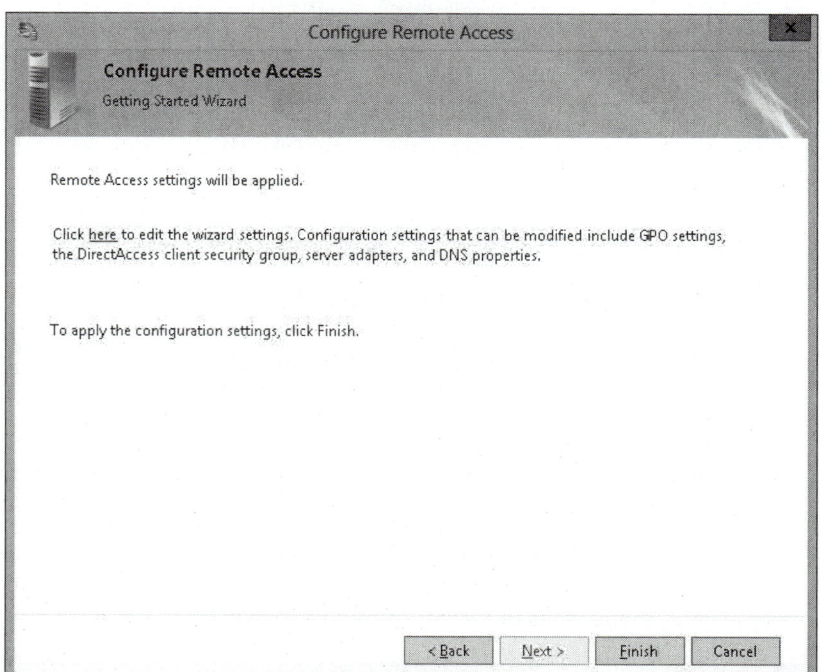

Figure 11-4

Finishing the Getting Started Wizard

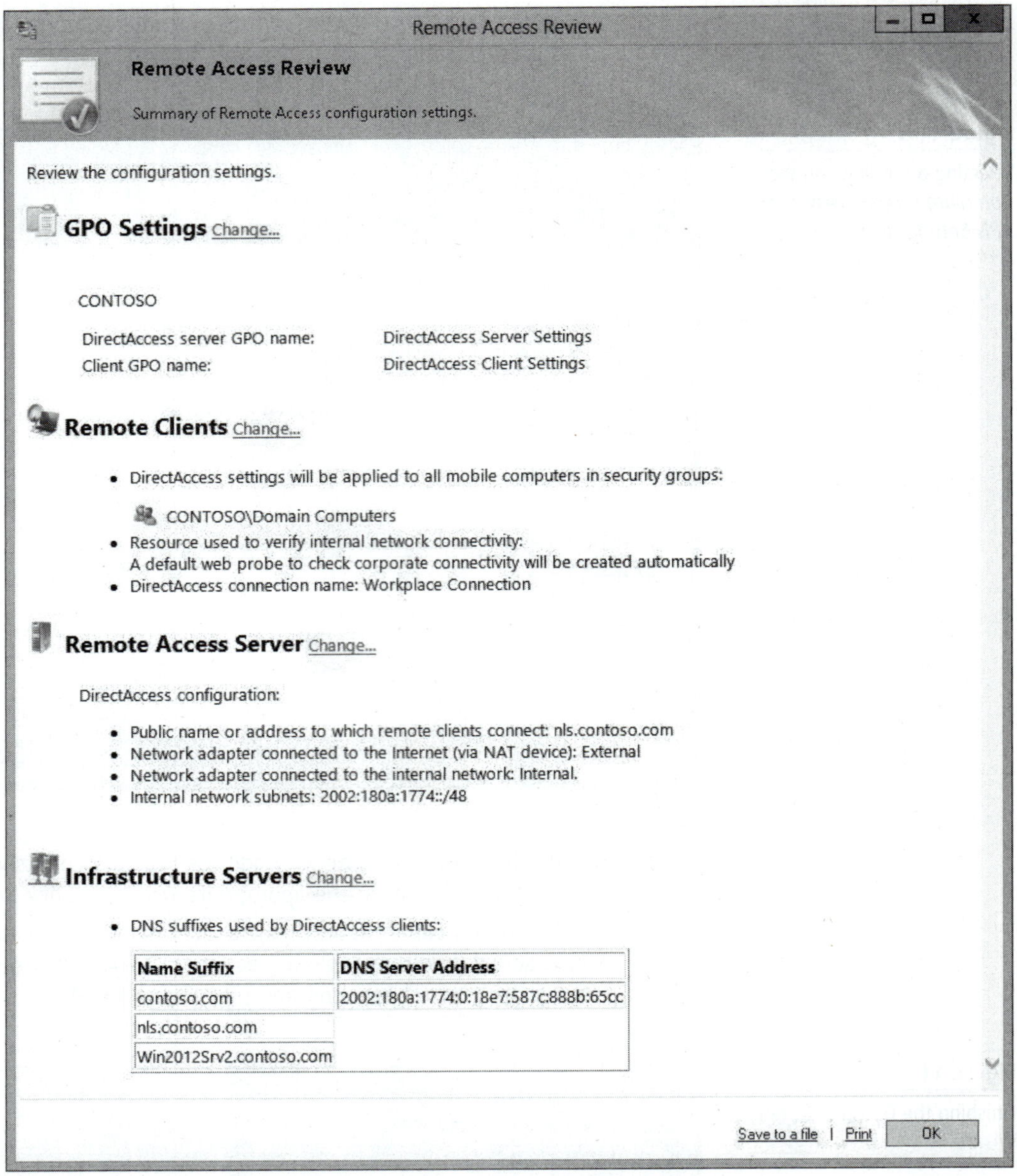

Figure 11-5

Viewing the settings applied using the Getting Started Wizard

8. Click Finish.

Running the Remote Access Setup Wizard

For more control, you can run the Remote Access Setup Wizard instead.

The Remote Access Setup Wizard breaks the installation to the following steps, as shown in Figure 11-6:

Step 1: Remote Clients: Allows you to specify which clients within your organization can use DirectAccess. You specify the computer groups that you want to include and specify if you want to include Windows 7 clients.

Figure 11-6

Using the Access Setup Wizard

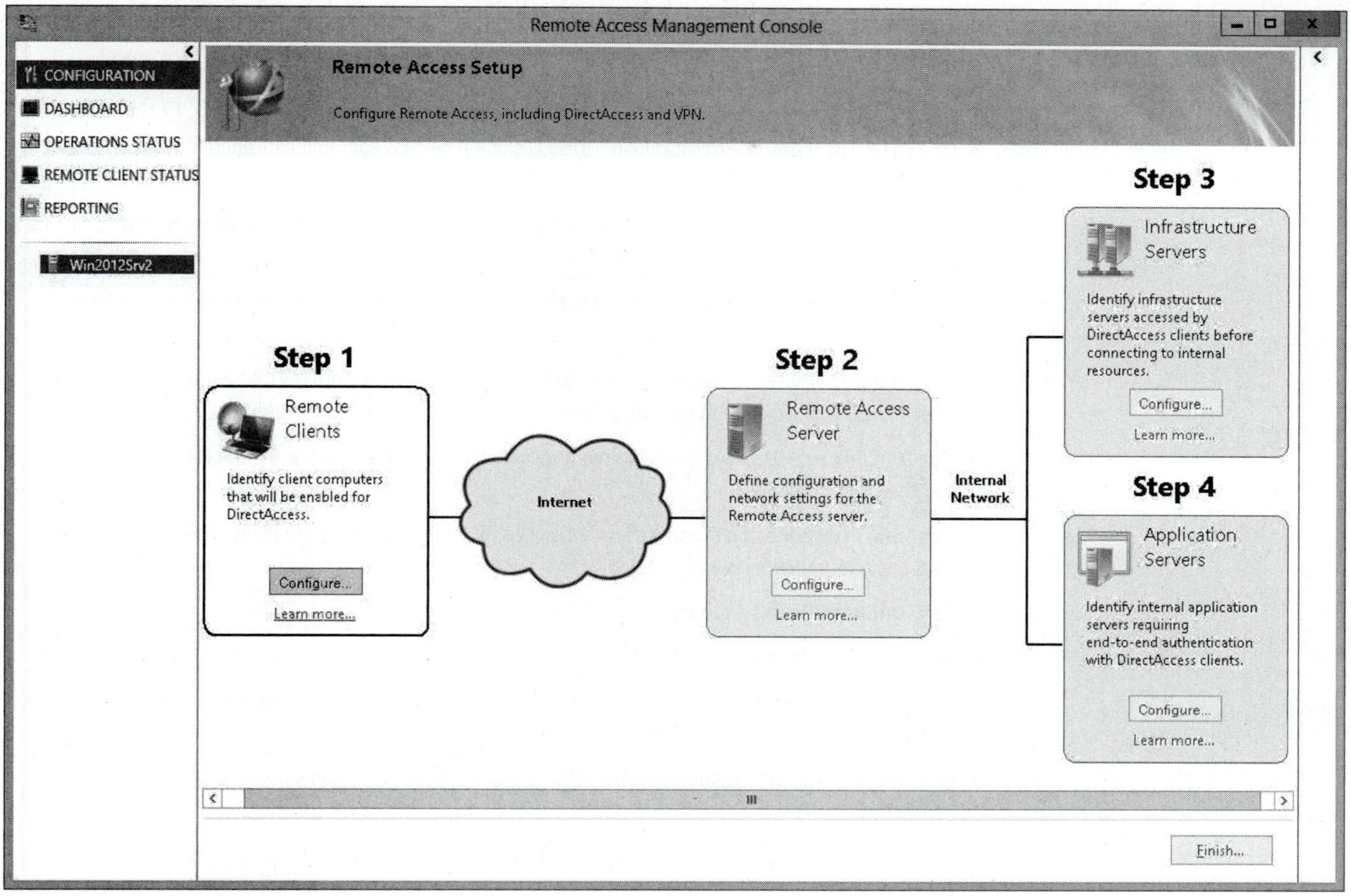

Step 2: Remote Access Server: Allows you to configure the network connections based on one or two network cards and which adapters are internal and which adapters are external. You can also specify the use of smartcards and specify the certificate authority (CA) to use for DirectAccess to provide secure communications.

Step 3: Infrastructure Servers: Allows you to configure how the clients access the core infrastructure services, such as Active Directory domain controllers and DNS servers. You also specify an internal web server that can provide location services for infrastructure components to your DirectAccess clients.

Step 4: Application Servers: Allows you to configure your end-to-end authentication and security for the DirectAccess components. It also allows you to provide secure connections with individual servers that you want to establish secure connections with.

USING WINDOWS POWERSHELL

You can manage services using Windows PowerShell by using the following cmdlets:

- `Add-DAAppServer` – Adds a new application server security group to the DirectAccess (DA) deployment, adds an application server to an application server security group that is already part of the DirectAccess deployment, and adds or updates application server Group Policy Object (GPO) in a domain.
- `Add-DAClient` – Adds one or more client computer security groups (SGs) to the DirectAccess (DA) deployment, adds one or more DA client Group Policy objects (GPOs) in one or more domains, adds one or more SGs of down-level clients to the DA deployment in a multi-site deployment, or adds one or more down-level DA client GPOs in one or more domains in a multi-site deployment.

(Continued)

- `Add-DAClientDnsConfiguration` – Adds the specified DNS suffix, DNS server addresses, or proxy server set to the Name Resolution Policy Table.
- `Add-DAEntryPoint` – Adds an entry point to a multi-site deployment.
- `Add-DAMgmtServer` – Adds the specified Management servers to the DirectAccess deployment.
- `Disable-DAMultiSite` – Disables a multi-site deployment that contains a single entry point.
- `Disable-DAOtpAuthentication` – Disables one-time password authentication for DirectAccess users.
- `Enable-DAMultiSite` – Enables and configures a multi-site deployment, and adds the first entry point.
- `Enable-DAOtpAuthentication` – Enables and configures one-time password authentication for DirectAccess users.
- `Get-DAAppServer` – Displays the list of application server security groups that are part of the DirectAccess deployment and the properties of the connections made to the groups.
- `Get-DAClient` – Displays the list of client security groups that are part of the DirectAccess deployment and the client properties.
- `Get-DAClientDnsConfiguration` – Displays all the Name Resolution Policy Table entries and the local name resolution property.
- `Get-DAEntryPoint` – Displays the settings for an entry point.
- `Get-DAEntryPointDC` – Retrieves a list of entry points and the associated domain controllers.
- `Get-DAMgmtServer` – Displays the configured Management servers. *Management server* here refers to update servers, Domain Controllers, and other servers.
- `Get-DAMultiSite` – Retrieves global settings applied to all entry points in a multi-site deployment.
- `Get-DANetworkLocationServer` – Displays the detailed Network Location Server configuration.
- `Get-DAOtpAuthentication` – Displays one-time password authentication settings for DirectAccess.
- `Get-DAServer` – Displays the properties of the DirectAccess Server.
- `Remove-DAAppServer` – Removes the specified lit of application server security groups (SGs) from the DirectAccess (DA) deployment, removes the specified application servers from the specified DA application server SG, and removes the application server Group Policy objects in the specified domains.
- `Remove-DAClient` – Removes one or more client computer security groups (SGs) from the DirectAccess (DA) deployment, removes one or more DA client Group Policy objects (GPOs) from domains, removes one or more SGs of down-level clients (down-level clients can connect only to the specified site) from the DA deployment in a multi-site deployment, and removes one or more down-level DA client GPOs from domains in a multi-site deployment.
- `Remove-DAClientDnsConfiguration` – Removes the Name Resolution Policy Table (NRPT) entry corresponding to the specified DNS suffix from the NRPT.
- `Remove-DAEntryPoint` – Removes an entry point from a multi-site deployment.
- `Remove-DAMgmtServer` – Removes the specified management servers from the DirectAccess deployment.

- `Set-DAClient` – Configures the properties related to a DirectAccess client.
- `Set-DAClientDnsConfiguration` – Configures the DNS server and proxy server addresses of a Name Resolution Policy Table entry and configures the local name resolution property.
- `Set-DAEntryPoint` – Configures settings for the entry point.
- `Set-DAEntryPointDC` – Modifies domain controller settings for the entry point.
- `Set-DAMultiSite` – Configures global settings for all entry points in a multi-site deployment.
- `Set-DANetworkLocationServer` – Configures the Network Location Server.
- `Set-DAOtpAuthentication` – Configures one-time password authentication settings for DirectAccess.
- `Set-DAServer` – Sets the properties specific to the DirectAccess server.
- `Update-DAMgmtServer` – Updates the list of Management servers of the DirectAccess deployment.

IMPLEMENTING CLIENT CONFIGURATION

CERTIFICATION READY
Implement client configuration.
Objective 3.4

With Window 7 and Windows Server 2008 R2, DirectAccess used the ***DirectAccess Connectivity Assistant (DCA)***, which is a free Solution Accelerator that is installed on the DirectAccess clients and adds an icon to the notification area of the desktop. The DCA provides tools to help users reconnect if a problem occurs. It also helps with diagnostics used by the help desk. It is also used to detect whether one-time passwords (OTP) are required, and it helps your system determine whether it is connected to the intranet or the Internet.

In Windows 8, the DCA was replaced by the ***Network Connectivity Assistant (NCA)***. Although the DCA has to be downloaded from Microsoft, the NCA is included in the Windows 8 operating system, and installation and deployment are not required.

CONFIGURE REMOTE CLIENTS

GET READY. To configure the Direct Access Server, perform the following steps:

1. Start Server Manager.
2. Click Tools > Remote Access Management. The *Remote Access Management console* opens.
3. Click the Run the Remote Access Setup Wizard link.
4. When the *Configure Remote Access Wizard* starts, click Deploy DirectAccess only.
5. Under *Step 1, Remote Clients*, click Configure. The *DirectAccess Client Setup Wizard* opens.
6. On the *Deployment Scenario* page (see Figure 11-7), select Deploy full DirectAccess for client access and remote management. Click Next.

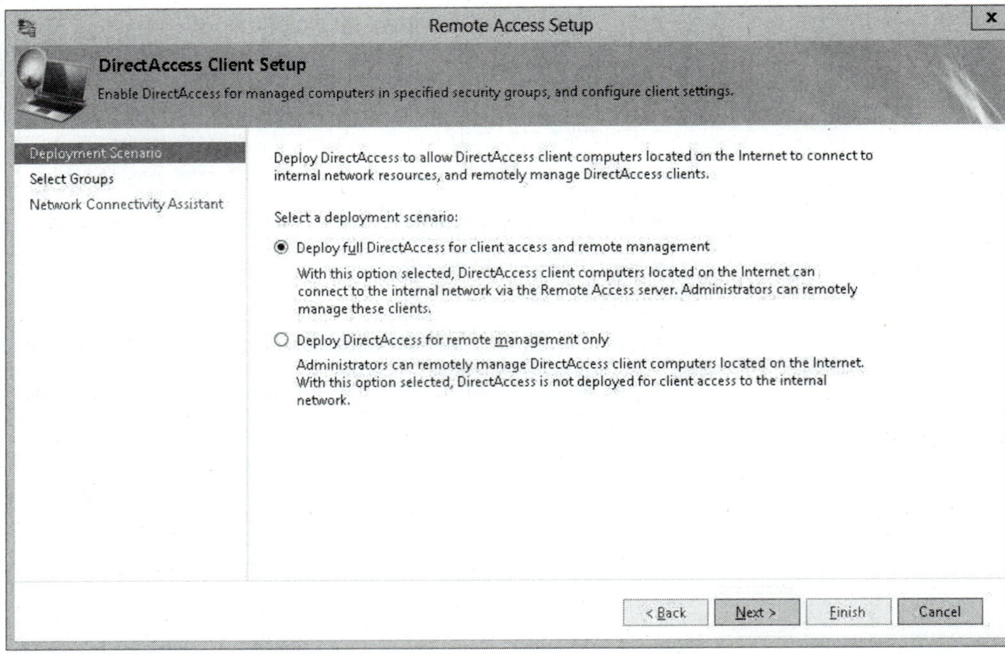

Figure 11-7

Specifying the deployment scenario

7. On the *Select Groups* page (as shown in Figure 11-8), select Add. Type the name of the group of computers that you want to include as DirectAccess clients and click OK.

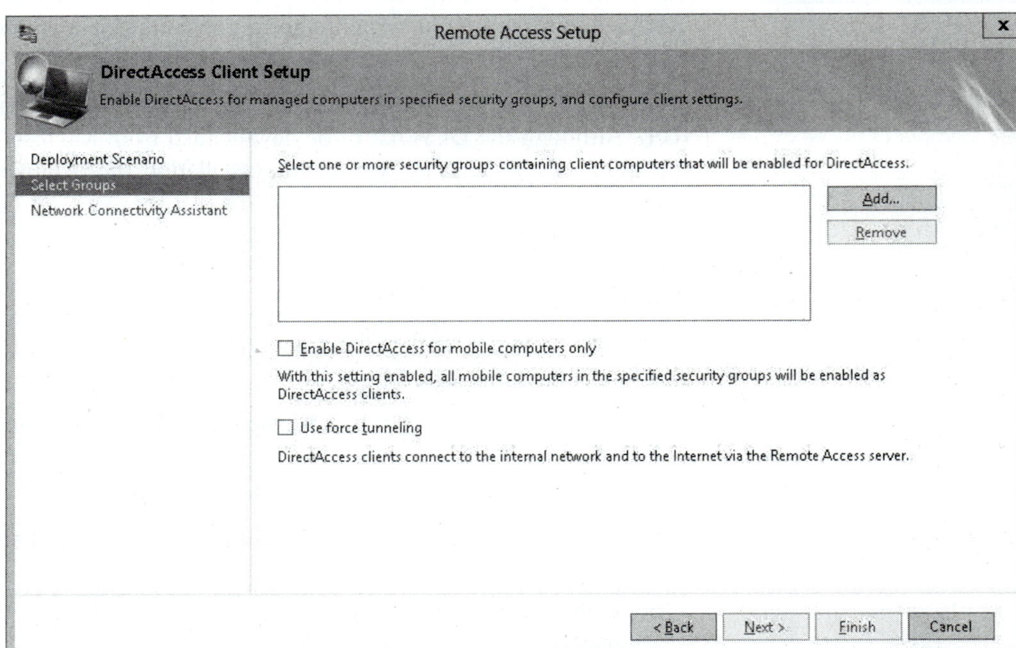

Figure 11-8

Selecting client groups

8. Back on the *Select Groups* page, if Forefront UAG is configured to use force tunneling for DirectAccess clients, select Use force tunneling. Click Next.
9. On the *Network Connectivity Assistant* page (see Figure 11-9), double-click a blank resource space.

Figure 11-9

Configuring the Network Connectivity Assistant

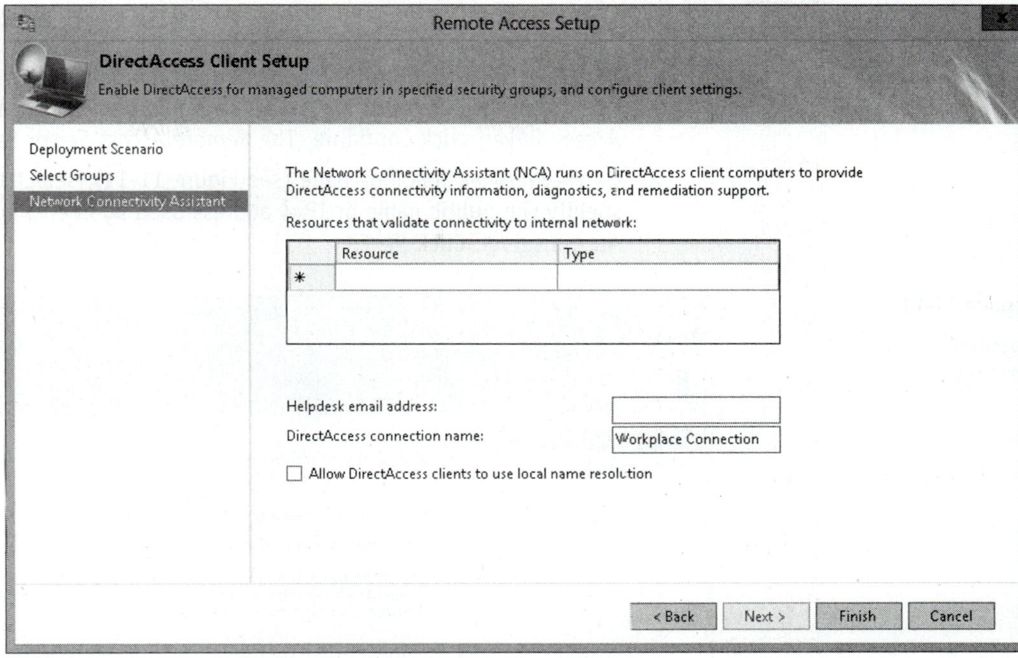

10. When the Configure Corporate Resources for NCA dialog box opens (see Figure 10-10), specify HTTP or ping and specify an URL or FQDN in the text box. Click Add.

Figure 11-10

Configuring corporate resources for NCA

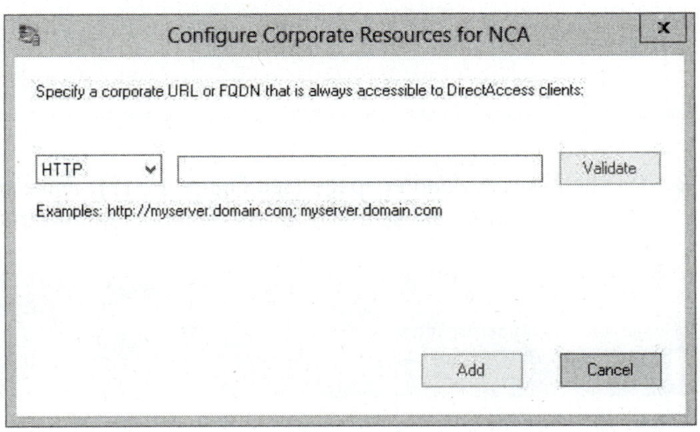

11. In the *Helpdesk email address* text box, specify an address to the organization's help desk.
12. By default, the DirectAccess connection name is *Workplace Connection*. If you wish to change it, do so.
13. If you want DirectAccess clients to use local DNS servers for name resolution, select the Allow DirectAccess clients to use local name resolution.
14. Click Finish.

IMPLEMENTING DIRECTACCESS SERVER

Using the Remote Access Server Setup Wizard, you can configure the DirectAccess server. It also allows you to specify what method of authentication to use.

CONFIGURE THE DIRECTACCESS REMOTE ACCESS SERVER

GET READY. To configure the DirectAccess server, perform the following steps:

1. Continuing with the *Remote Access Setup Configuration* page, under *Step 2, Remote Access Server*, click Configure. The *Remote Access Server Setup Wizard* starts.
2. On the *Network Topology* page (see Figure 11-11), select the appropriate topology and specify the public name or IPv4 address used by clients to connect to the Remote Access server. Click Next.

Figure 11-11

Specifying the network topology

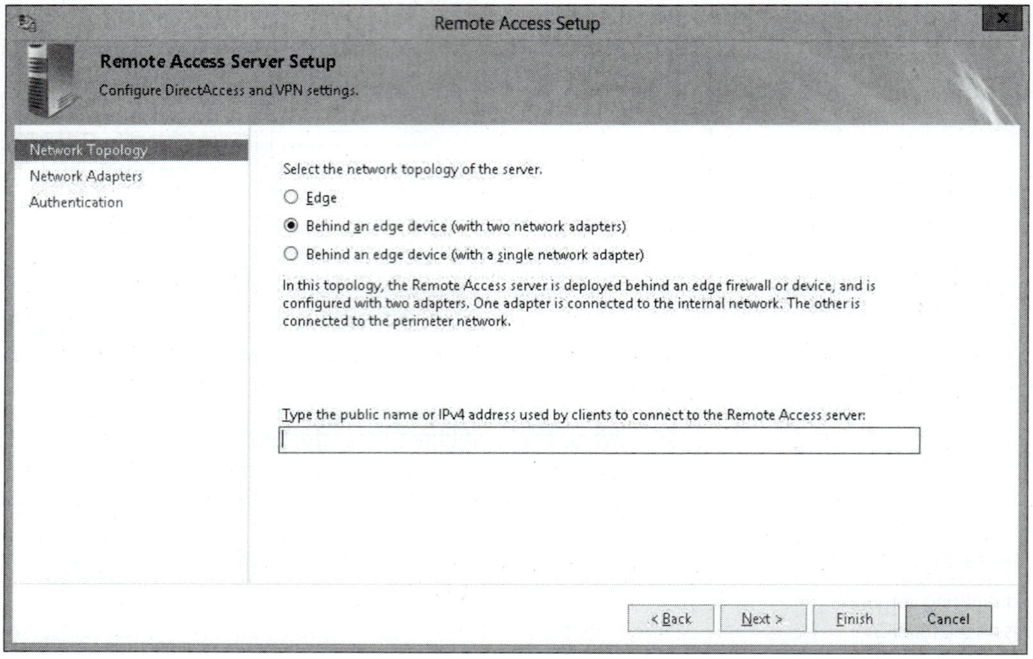

3. On the *Network Adapters* page (see Figure 11-12), make sure that the appropriate network adapters are selected for the external and internal networks.

Figure 11-12

Configuring the network adapters

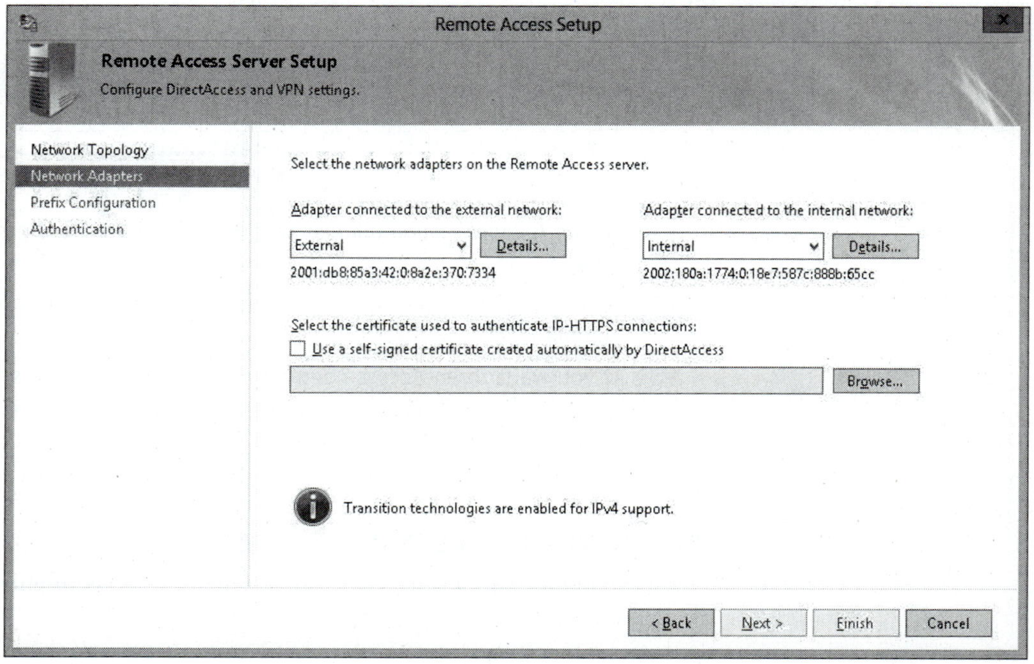

4. Specify the digital certificate that you want to use for-HTTPS connections or select the Use a self-signed certificate created automatically by DirectAccess. Click Next.
5. On the *Prefix Configuration* page (see Figure 11-13), specify the internal network IPv6 and IPv6 prefix assigned to DirectAccess client computers. Click Next.

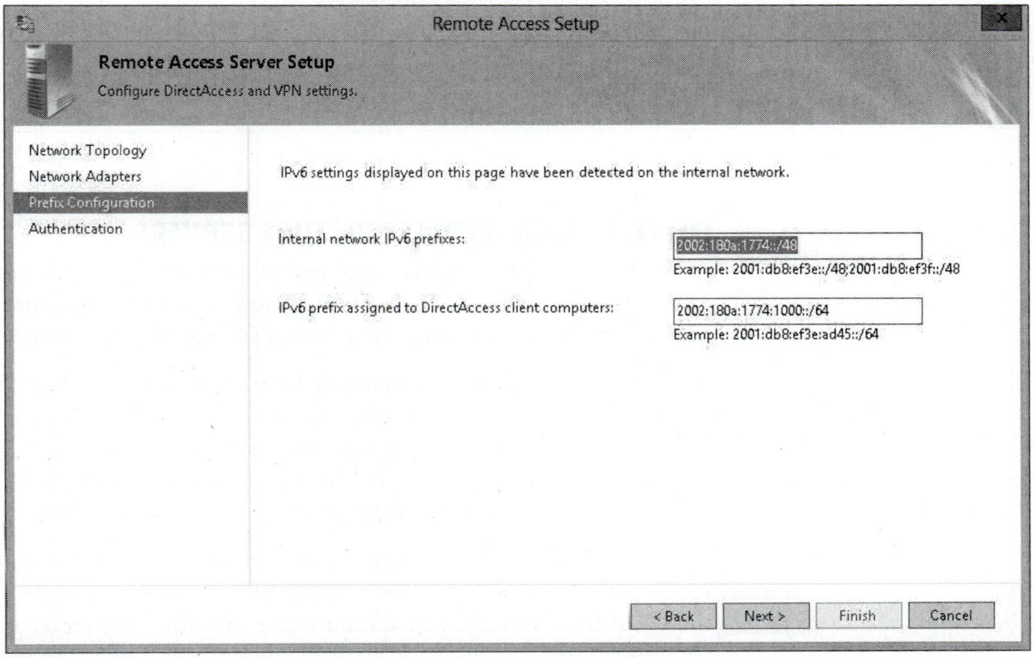

Figure 11-13
Specifying the IPv6 prefixes

6. On the *Authentication* page (see Figure 11-14), specify whether you want to use Active Directory credentials (username/password) or Two-factor authentication. If you choose *Two-factor authentication*, you can select Use OTP.

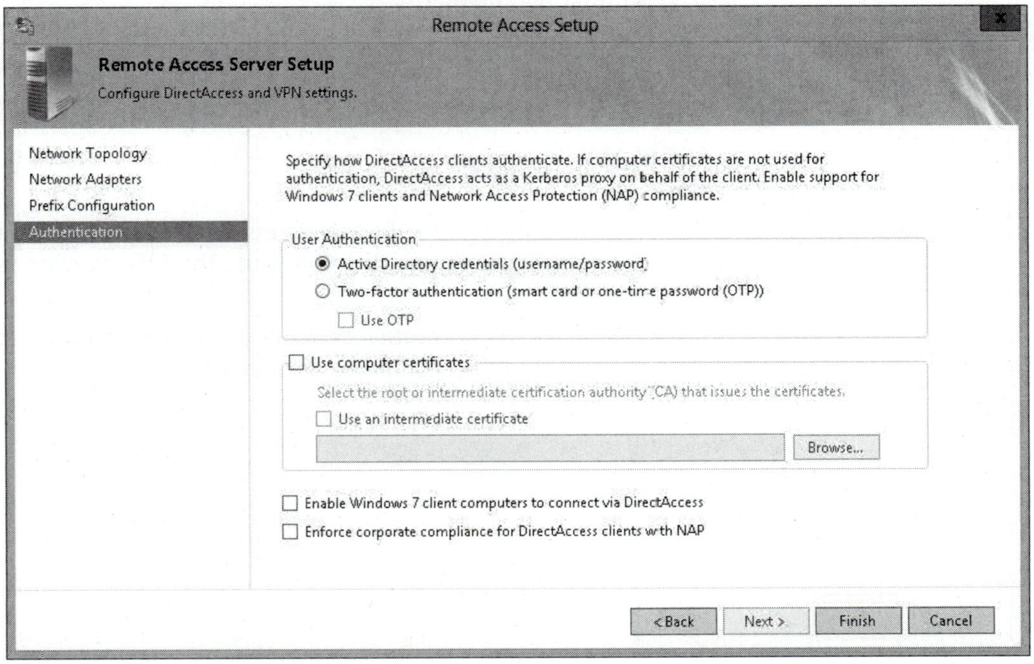

Figure 11-14
Specifying authentication

7. If desired, you can use computer certificates. If you select the Use computer certificates, you have to choose the *root* or *intermediate certification authority (CA)*. If you decide to use *intermediate certification authority*, you need to select the *Use an intermediate certificate*.
8. If you wish to allow Windows 7 clients, enable the *Enable Windows 7 client computers* to connect via DirectAccess.
9. If you want to use Network Access Protection (NAP), select the Enforce corporate compliance for DirectAccess clients with NAP.
10. Click Finish.

IMPLEMENTING INFRASTRUCTURE SERVERS

After the DirectAccess server is configured, you need to configure the infrastructure servers to support DirectAccess. For example, you will need to configure the DNS servers, and you need to specify your management servers such as WSUS servers.

DirectAccess clients use the ***network location server (NLS)*** to determine their locations. The network location server is an internal web server. If the client computer can connect with HTTPS to the URL specified, the client computer assumes it is on the intranet and disables DirectAccess components. If the client cannot reach the NLS, it assumes it is on the Internet. The URL for the NLS is distributed using a GPO.

To configure a network location server, install IIS on a Windows server. Then for a website, bind a name such as nsl.contoso.com and associate a NLS DNS name to the IP address. Finally, you should make sure that this server is highly available. So use technology such as Network Load Balancing and make sure you have redundant hardware.

To ensure that DirectAccess clients can correctly detect when they are on the Internet, you can configure IIS server to deny connections from Internet-based clients with the IP and Domain Restrictions Web server (IIS) role service. Alternatively, you can ensure that the CRL distribution point location in the certificate being used for network location cannot be accessed from the Internet.

CONFIGURE THE DIRECTACCESS INFRASTRUCTURE SERVERS

GET READY. To configure the DirectAccess Infrastructure servers, perform the following steps:

1. Continuing with the *Remote Access Setup Configuration* page, under *Step 3, Infrastructure Server*, click Configure. The *Infrastructure Server Setup Wizard* starts.
2. On the *Network Location Server* page (see Figure 11-15), type the URL of the network location in the appropriate box. Click Next.

Figure 11-15

Specifying the Network Location server

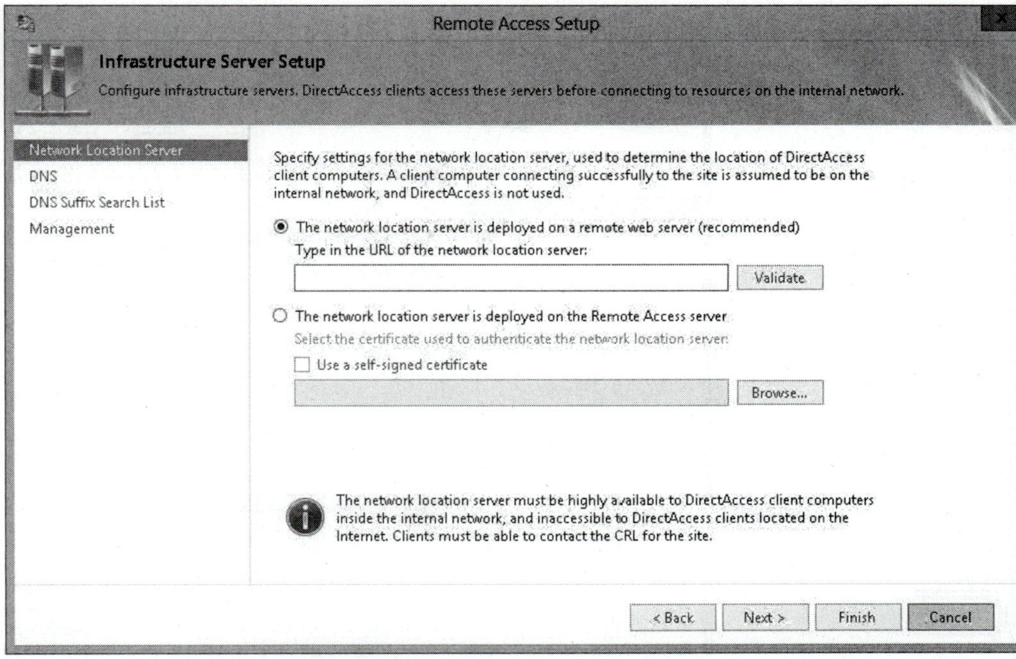

3. On the *DNS* page (see Figure 11-16), verify the DNS suffixes and internal DNS servers. Then, click Next.

Figure 11-16

Specifying the DNS servers

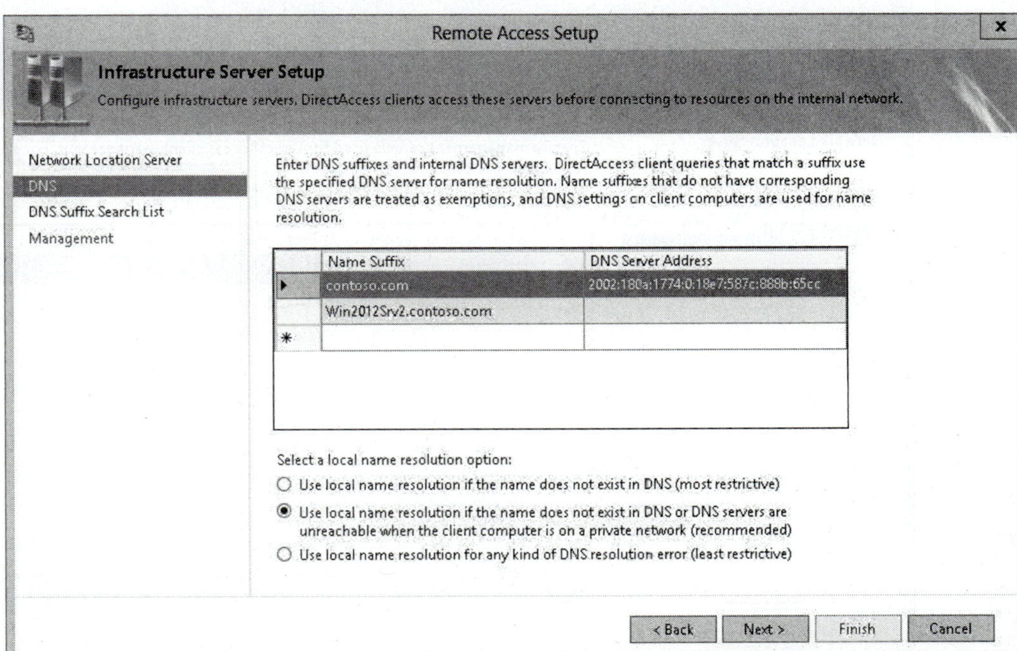

4. On the *DNS Suffix Search List* page (see Figure 11-17), verify the domain suffixes and click Next.

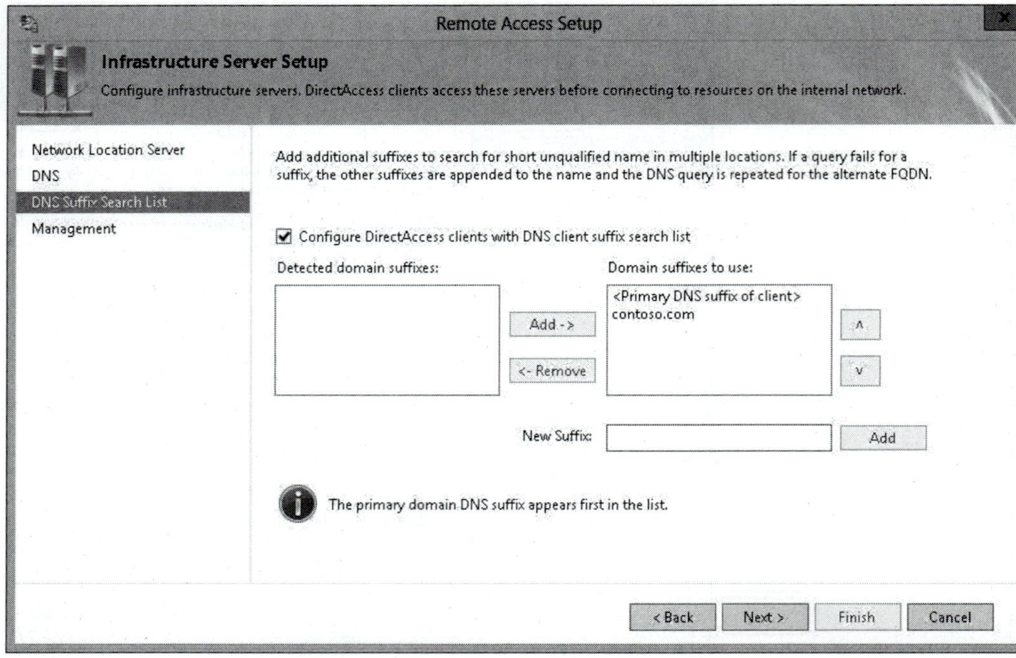

Figure 11-17

Specifying the DNS Suffix Search List

5. On the *Management* page (see Figure 11-18), double-click the first line of the *Management Servers* box.

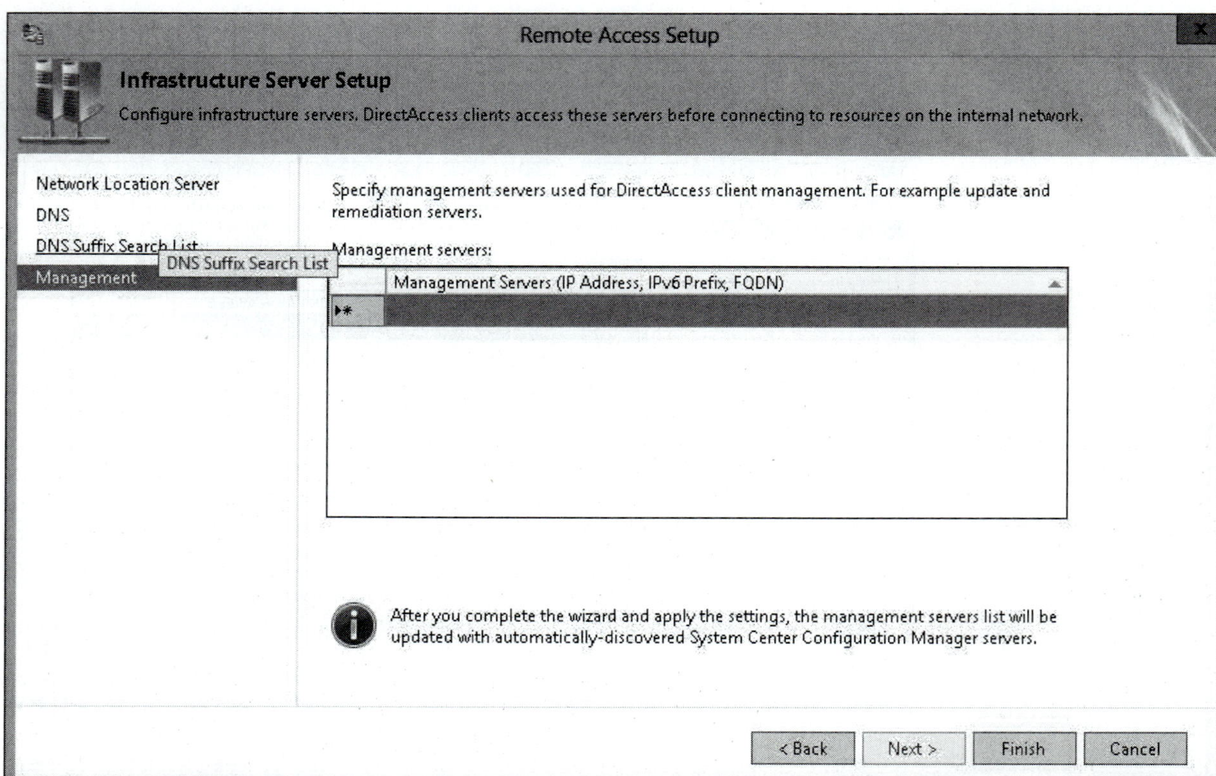

Figure 11-18

Specifying the management servers

6. When the *Add a Management Server* dialog box opens (see Figure 11-19), add the names of your management servers, such as your Windows Update Server. Click OK.
7. Click Finish.

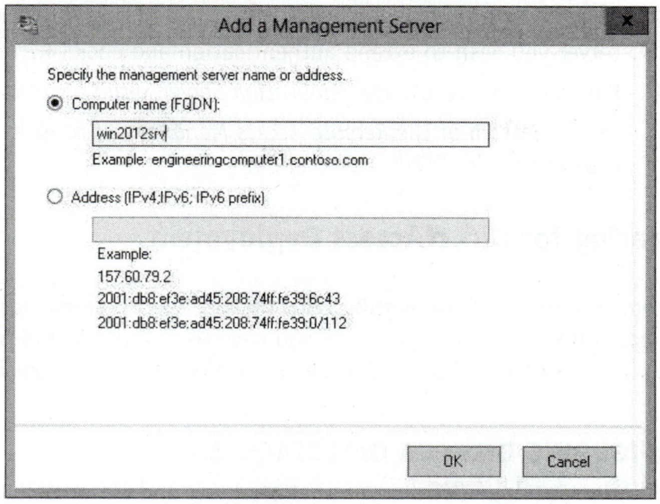

Figure 11-19

Adding a management server

CONFIGURING THE APPLICATION SERVERS

As mentioned earlier, you can add an extra level of authentication and encryption to those servers that you must protect at all costs. Using the DirectAccess Application Server Setup Wizard, you select those servers.

CONFIGURE APPLICATION SERVERS FOR DIRECTACCESS

GET READY. To configure the application servers for DirectAccess, perform the following steps:

1. Continuing with the *Remote Access Setup Configuration* page, under *Step 4, Application Servers*, click Configure. The *DirectAccess Application Server Setup Wizard* starts.
2. On the *DirectAccess Application Server Setup* page (see Figure 11-20), if you wish to add an additional layer of authentication and encryption between the Direct Access clients and selected internal application servers, select the Extend authentication to selected application servers option.

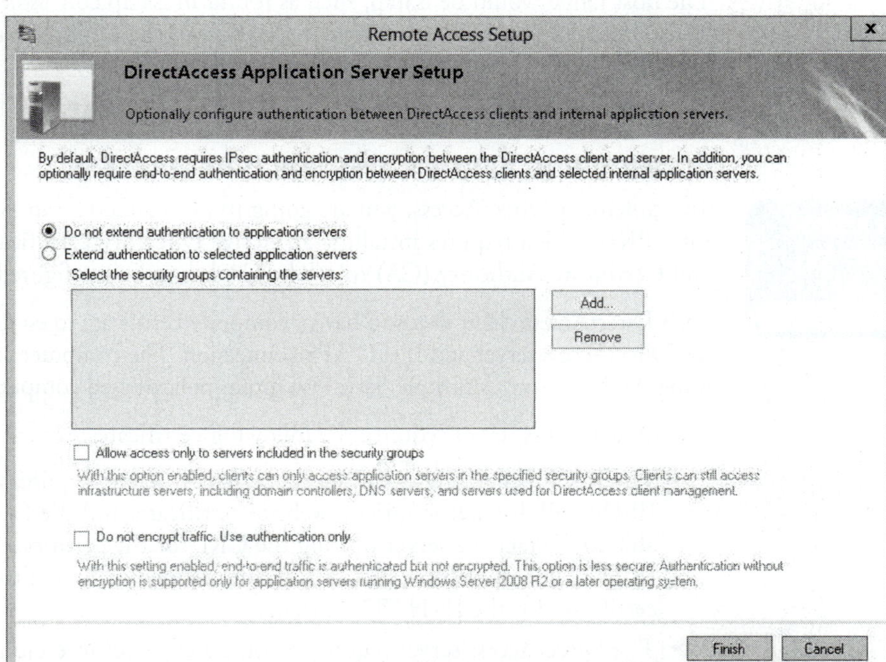

Figure 11-20

Specifying the DirectAccess application servers

3. If you selected to extend authentication, click Add. Then type in the name of the server you wish to extend authentication and click OK.
4. Back on the *DirectAccess Application Server Setup* page, click Finish.
5. At the bottom of the *Remote Access Management console*, click Finish to apply all of the changes for Steps 1 through 4.

Preparing for DirectAccess Deployment

Before installing and configuring DirectAccess, there is some work that needs to be completed. You need to make sure that you have IPv6 and any transitional IPv6 technologies in place. You need a certificate server, and you need to have external and internal DNS entries.

CONFIGURING DNS FOR DIRECTACCESS

CERTIFICATION READY
Configure DNS for DirectAccess.
Objective 3.4

As a VPN technology that has internal resources and external clients, DirectAccess requires internal and external DNS. DirectAccess requires two external DNS A records, both of which point to the first of your two consecutive IP addresses that you specified for the DirectAccess server. These are:

- DirectAccess server, such as directaccess.contoso.com
- Certificate Revocation List (CRL), such as crl.contoso.com

Internally, DNS needs the DNS records for the NLS server and one for the CRL.

The dynamic update feature of DNS makes it possible for a DNS client computer to register and dynamically update the resource records with a DNS server whenever a client changes its networks address or host name. However, it also allows any authorized client to register any unused host name, including those special or reserved names, such as Web Proxy Automatic Discovery Protocol (WPAD) and the Intra-site Automatic Tunnel Addressing Protocol (ISATAP).

ISATAP provides a transition between networks that are based on IPv4 to IPv6, which is used to encapsulate IPv6 packets with an IPv4 header, making it possible for the IPv6 packets to be transmitted through an ISATAP router. Because ISATAP does not support automatic router discovery, ISATAP hosts a potential list (PRL) to discover available ISATAP routers. The host name would be isatap, such as found in isatap.contoso.com. Therefore, if you need to use ISATAP, you need to remove ISATAP from the DNS global query block list by executing the following command at a command prompt:

```
dnscmd /config /globalqueryblocklist isatap
```

CONFIGURING CERTIFICATES FOR DIRECTACCESS

CERTIFICATION READY
Configure certificates for DirectAccess.
Objective 3.4

To implement DirectAccess, you are going to need a Certificate Services public key infrastructure (PKI), which requires installing an Active Directory Certificate Services (AD CS) role and Certificate Authority (CA) role. The CA has to be configured as an Enterprise Root CA.

Each DirectAccess client needs to have a computer certificate to establish the IPsec connection to the DirectAccess server and IP-HTTPS connection. The computer certificates are usually assigned using the Microsoft Certificate Server via group policy-based computer certificate auto-enrollment.

The DirectAccess server requires the following certificates:

- The IP-HTTPS listener on the DirectAccess server requires a website certificate. The IP-HTTPS listener requires a website certificate, and the DirectAccess client must be able to contact the server hosting the CRL for the certificate. If the CRL check fails, the IP-HTTPS connection fails. It is recommended you use a third-party commercial certificate for the IP-HTTPS listener.
- The DirectAccess server requires a computer server to establish the IPsec connections with the DirectAccess clients.

CONFIGURE CERTIFICATE REQUIREMENTS

GET READY. To configure the certificate requirements on the domain controller with the CA (Enterprise CA), perform the following steps:

1. If necessary, open Server Manager.
2. Click Tools > Certificate Authority. The *Certification Authority console* opens.
3. Right-click the server and select Properties.
4. When the *Properties* dialog box opens (see Figure 11-21), select the Extensions tab.

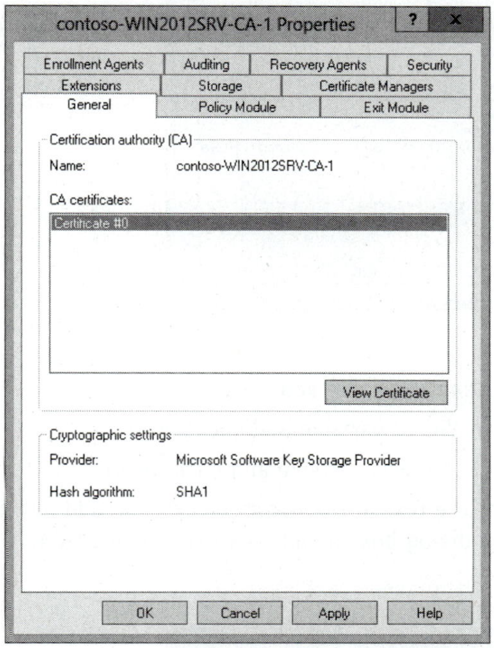

Figure 11-21
Displaying the CA certificates

5. On the *Extensions* tab (see Figure 11-22), click Add.

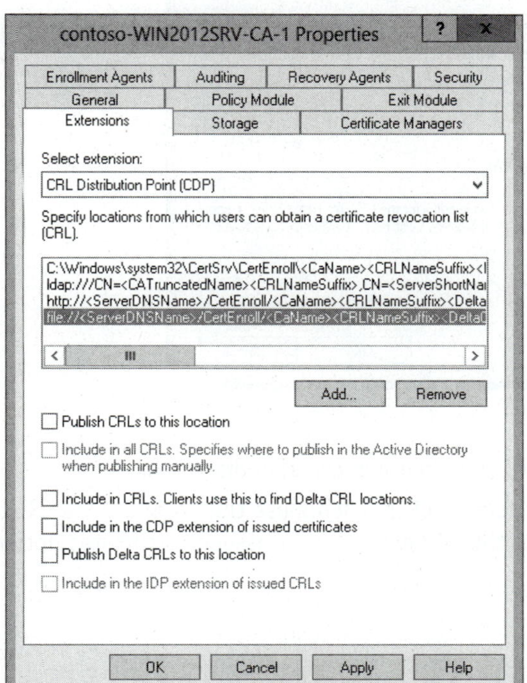

Figure 11-22
Specifying certificate extensions

6. On the *Add Location* dialog box (as shown in Figure 11-23), type http://crl.contoso.com/crld/ in the *Location* text box.

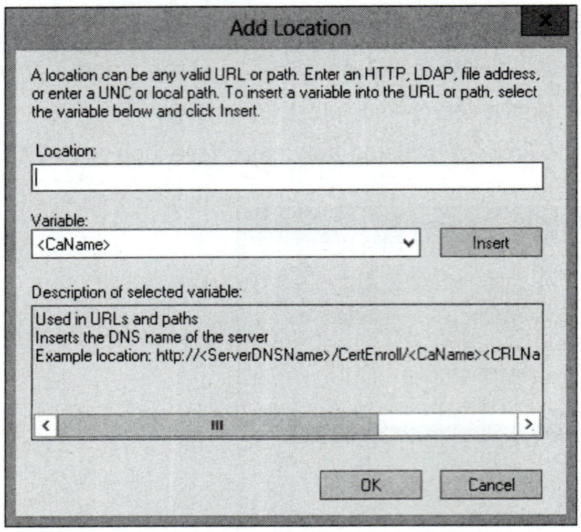

Figure 11-23

Adding a location for CRL

7. Select the CAName variable and click Insert.
8. Select CRLNameSuffix variable and click Insert.
9. Select DeltaCRLAllowed variable and click Insert.
11. At the end of the text in the *Location* text box, add .crl. When you are finished, the Add Location dialog box should look like Figure 11-24.

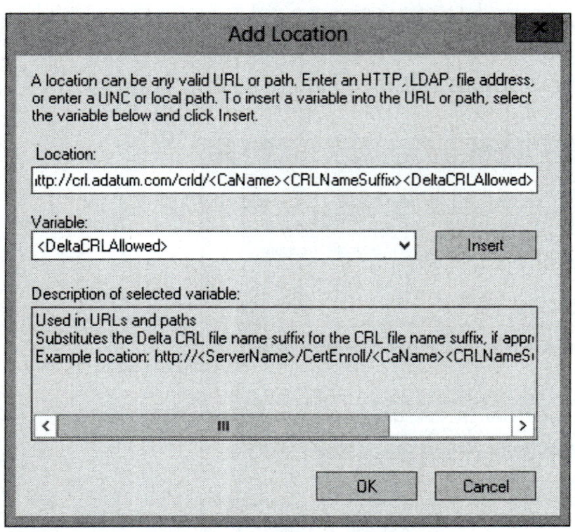

Figure 11-24

An example location for CRL

12. Click OK to close the *Add Location* dialog box.
13. Select Include in CRLs. Clients use this to find Delta CRL locations. option and the Include in the CDP extensions of issued certificates option.

14. On the *Add Location* dialog box, type \\win2012srv\crldist$\ in the *Location* text box.
15. Select the CAName variable and click Insert.
16. Select CRLNameSuffix variable and click Insert.
17. Select DeltaCRLAllowed variable and click Insert.
18. After you insert DeltaCRLAllowed, at the end of the text in the *Location* text box, add .crl.
19. Click OK to close the *Add Location* dialog box.
20. Click OK to close the *Properties* dialog box.
21. When it asks you to restart Active Directory Certificate Services, click Yes.
22. On the *Certificate Authority console*, right-click Certificate Templates and click Manage. The *Certificate Templates console* opens.
23. Right-click the Web Server template, and select Duplicate Template.
24. When the *Properties of New Template* dialog box opens (as shown in Figure 11-25), select the General tab.

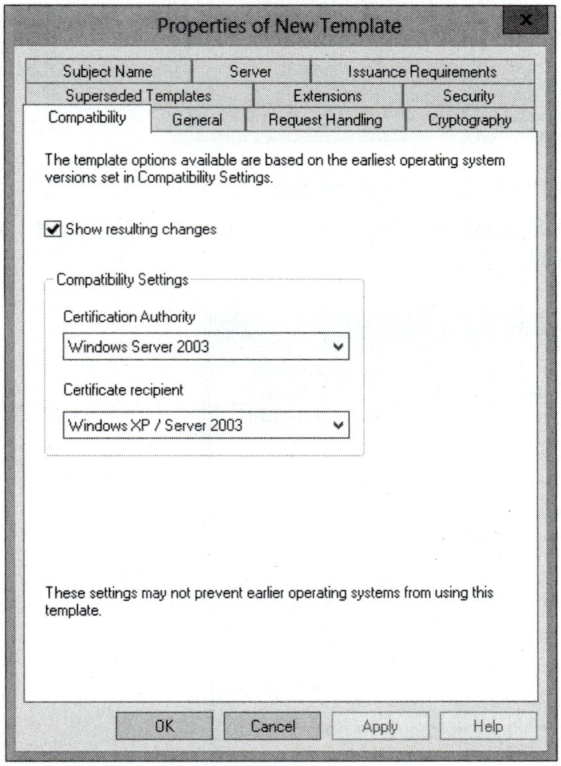

Figure 11-25

Opening the properties of a certificate templates

25. On the *General* tab (see Figure 11-26), type Contoso Web Server Certificate in the *Template display name* text box.

Figure 11-26

Defining the template display name and template name

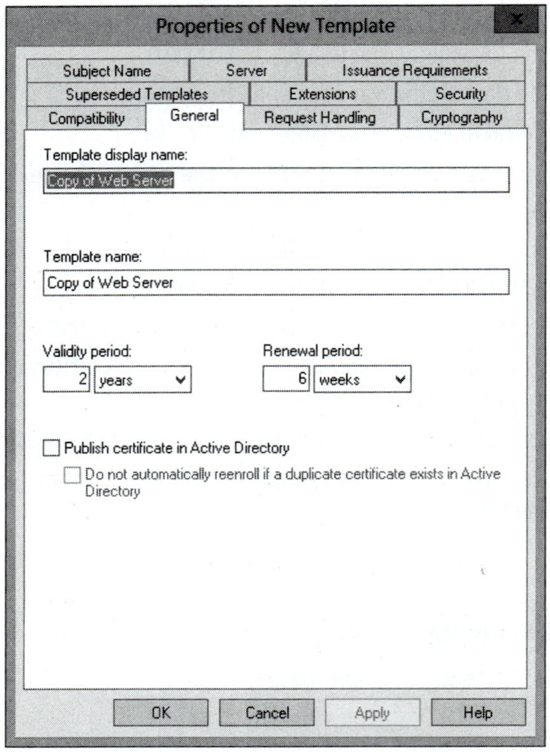

26. Select the Request Handling tab.
27. In the *Request Handling* tab (see Figure 11-27), select the Allow private key to be exported.

Figure 11-27

Specifying the purpose of the certificate

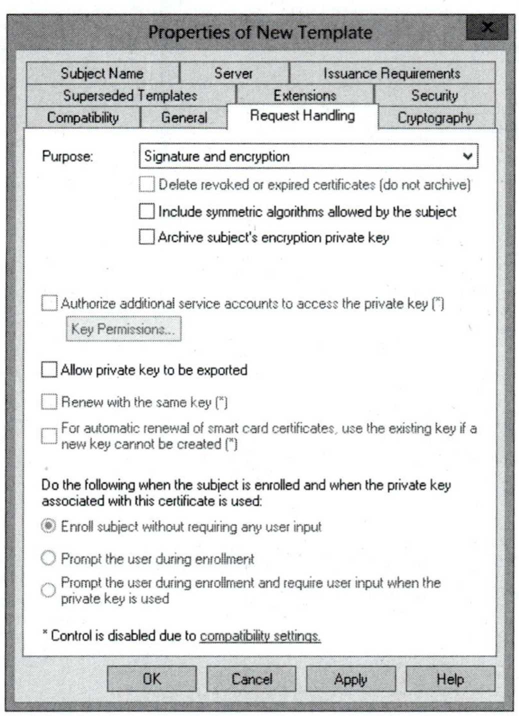

28. Select the Security tab.
29. On the *Security* tab (see Figure 11-28), make sure Authenticated Users is selected. Then click Enroll under the *Allow* column.

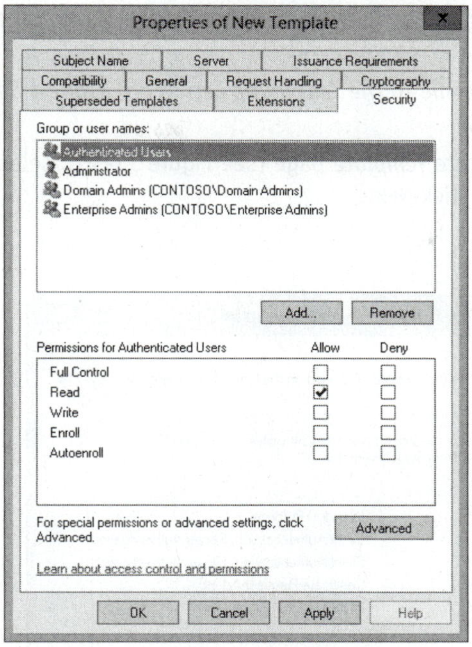

Figure 11-28

Specifying the permissions assigned to the certificate template

30. Click OK to close the *Properties of New Template* dialog box.
31. Close the *Certificate Template console*.
32. In the *Certification Authority console*, right-click Certificate Templates, select New, and select the Certificate Template to Issue.
33. Select the Contoso Web Server Certificate and click OK.
34. Close the *Certification Authority console*.
35. In *Server Manager*, click Tools > click Group Management.
36. In the *Group Management console*, right-click Default Domain Policy and select Edit.
37. On the *Group Policy Management Editor*, navigate to Computer Configuration\Policies\Windows Settings\Security Settings\Public Key Policies, as shown in Figure 11-29.

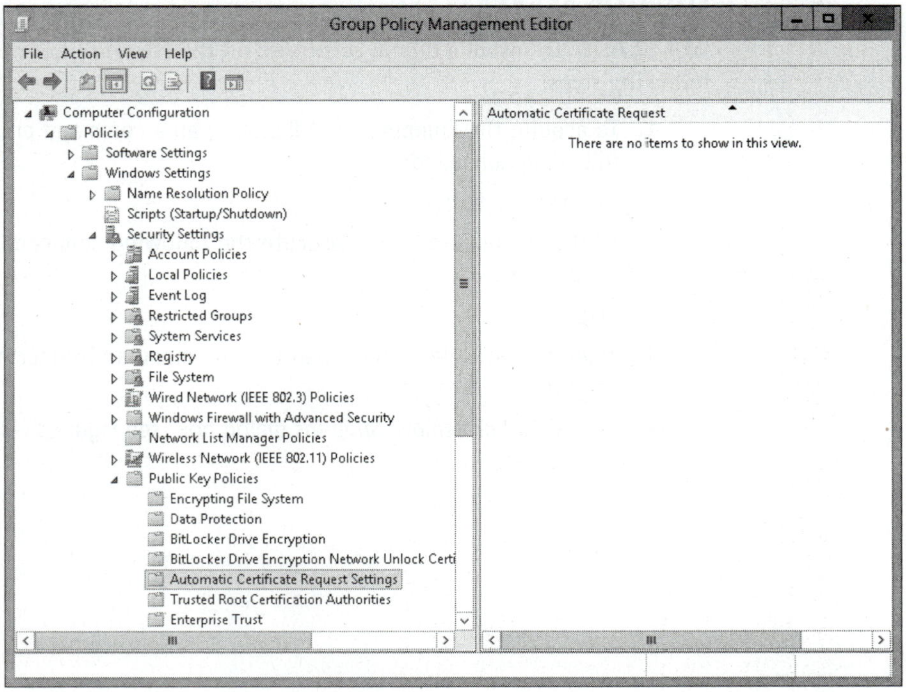

Figure 11-29

Viewing the Public Key policies

38. Right-click Automatic Certificate Request, select New, and select Automatic Certificate Request.
39. When the *Welcome to the Automatic Certificate Request Setup Wizard* starts, click Next.
40. On the *Certificate Template* page (see Figure 11-30), select the Computer certificate template and click Next.

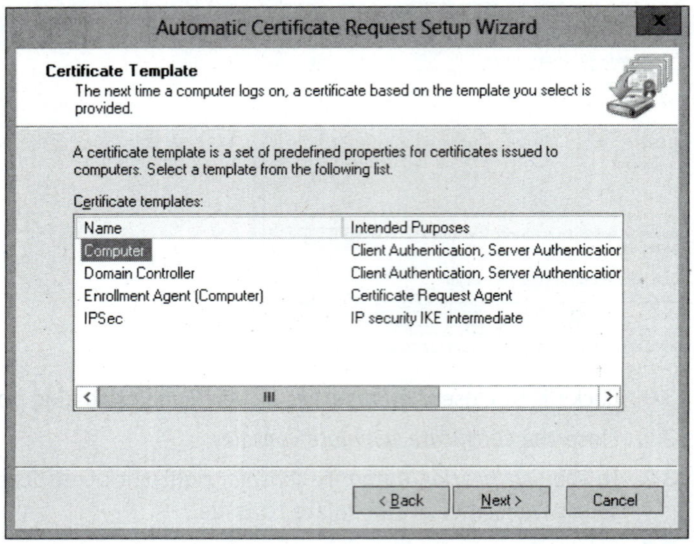

Figure 11-30
Specifying which certificates are automatically requested

41. When the wizard is complete, click Finish.

INSTALL A DIGITAL CERTIFICATE ON THE NETWORK LOCATOR SERVER

GET READY. To install a digital certificate on the Network Locator Server, perform the following steps:

1. To acquire the Computer certificate, open a command prompt and execute the following command:

   ```
   gpudate /force
   ```

2. At the command prompt, execute the following command, and then press Enter:

   ```
   mmc
   ```

3. When the console opens, open the File menu and select Add/Remove Snap-in.
4. On the *Add or Remove Snap-ins* dialog box (see Figure 11-31), double-click Certificates.

Figure 11-31

Opening the Add or Remove Snap-ins dialog box

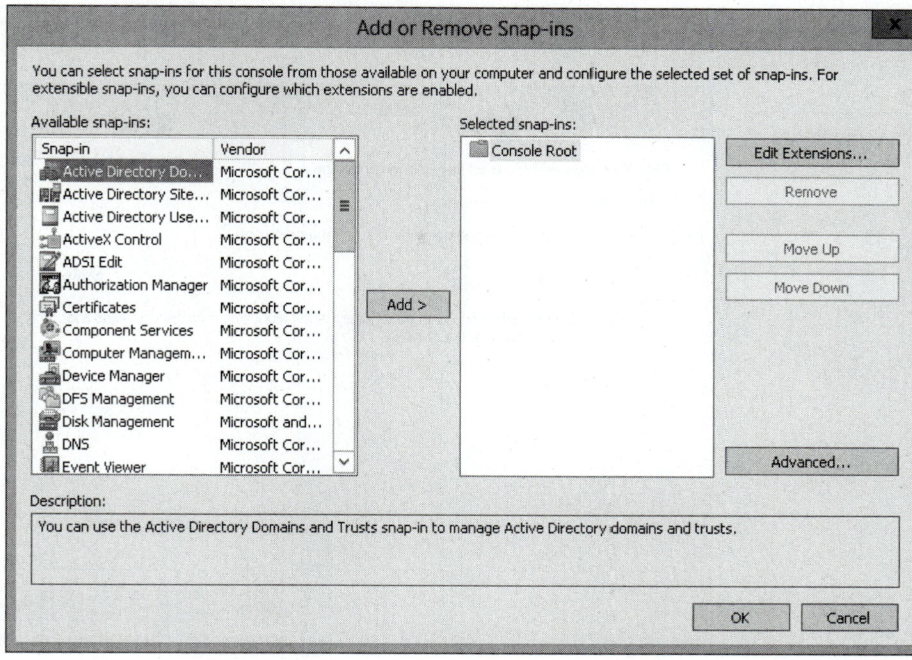

5. When the *Certificates Snap-in* dialog box opens (see Figure 11-32), select Computer account, and click Finish.

Figure 11-32

Specifying which certificates to manage

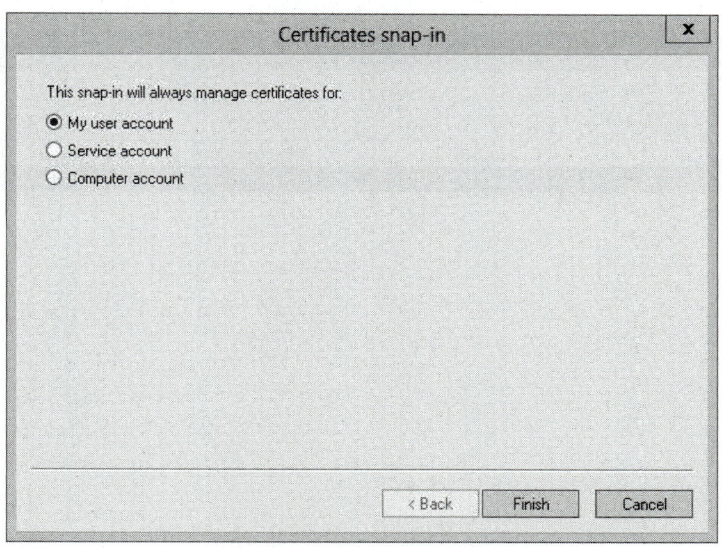

6. When the *Select Computer* dialog box opens (see Figure 11-33), click Finish.

Figure 11-33

Selecting which computer to connect to

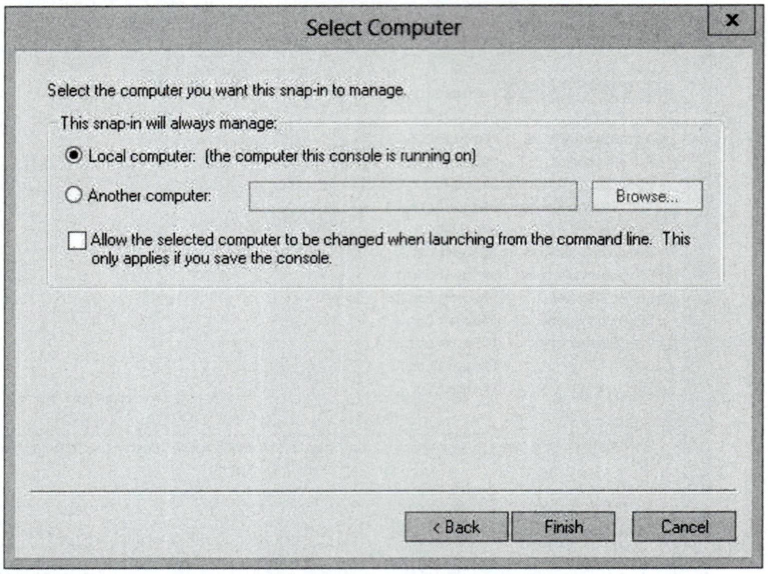

7. Click OK to close the *Add or Remove Snap-ins* dialog box.
8. In the console, navigate to \Personal\Certificates. You should see the Computer certificate, as shown in Figure 11-34.

Figure 11-34

Viewing the computer certificate

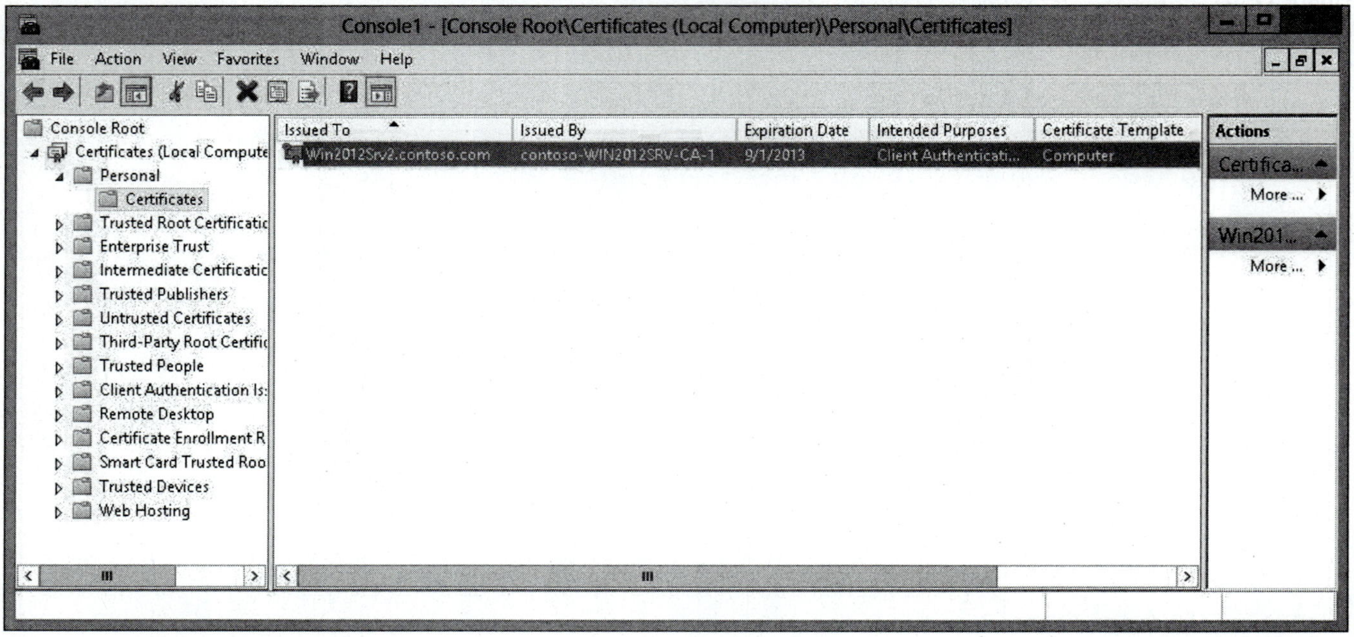

9. Right-click Certificates, select All Tasks, and then select Request New Certificate.
10. When the *Certificate Enrollment Wizard* opens, click Next.
11. On the *Select Certificate Enrollment Policy* page, click Next.
12. On the *Request Certificates* page (see Figure 11-35), select Contoso Web Server Certificate.

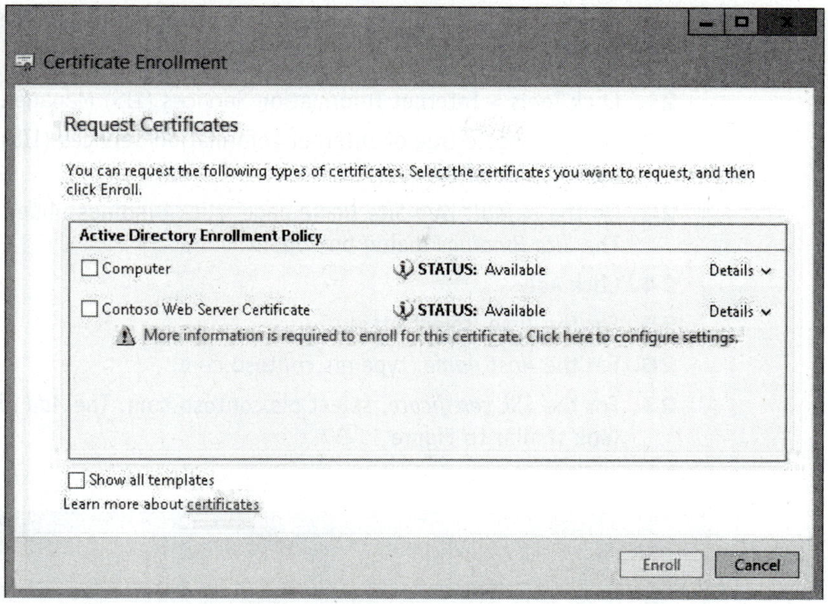

Figure 11-35

Requesting a certificate

13. Click More information is required to enroll for this certificate. Click here to configure settings.
14. When the *Certificate Properties* dialog box opens (see Figure 11-36), select Common name for the *Subject name Type*.

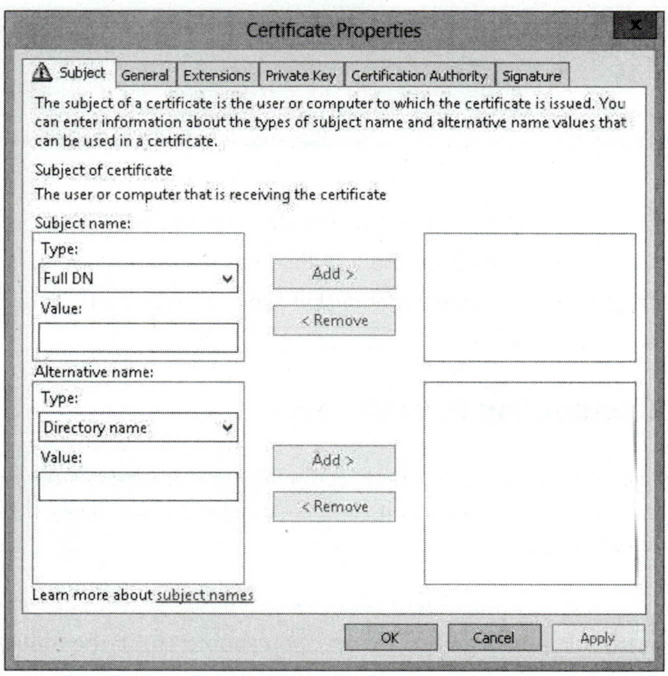

Figure 11-36

Specifying the subject of a certificate

15. In the *Value* text box, type nls.contoso.com. Click the top Add button. The CN=nls.contoso.com value should appear on the right side of the dialog box.
16. Click OK to close the *Certificate Properties* dialog box.
17. Back on the *Request Certificates* page, click Enroll.
18. When the certificate installation succeeds, click Finish. The certificate appears in the *Personal\Certificates* folder.

19. Close the console window. If you are prompted to save settings, click No.
20. Open Server Manager.
21. Click Tools > Internet Information Services (IIS) Manager.
22. In the console tree of Internet Information Services (IIS), navigate to and click Default Web site.
23. On the *Default Web Site Home* page, click Bindings under *Edit Site in the Actions pane*. The *Site Bindings* dialog box opens.
24. Click Add.
25. For the *Type*, select https.
26. For the *Host name*, type nls.contoso.com.
27. For the *SSL certificate*, select nls.contoso.com. The *Add Site Binding* dialog box should look similar to Figure 11-37.

Figure 11-37

Configuring an IIS site binding

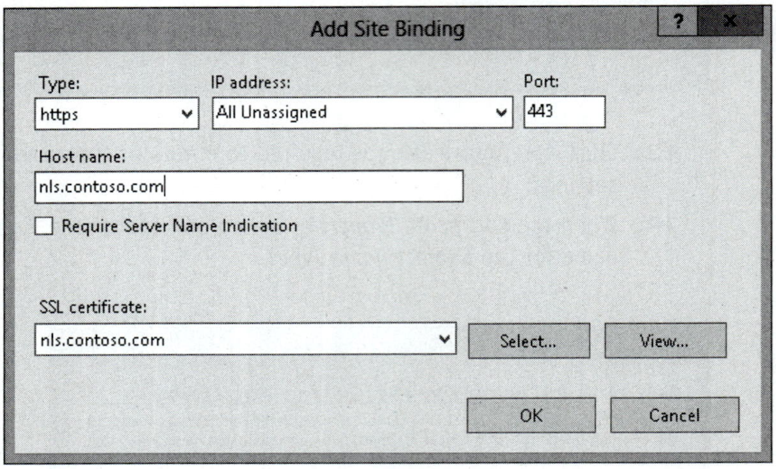

28. Click OK to close the *Add Site Bindings* button.
29. Click Close to close the *Site Bindings* dialog box.
30. Close the *Internet Information Services (IIS) Manager console*.

Troubleshooting DirectAccess

Because DirectAccess is a new technology and it depends on several components, it is easy to have problems with it. Of course, you should first verify that you have met the system requirements.

When troubleshooting DirectAccess, you should check the following:

- The DirectAccess client computer must run Windows 8, Windows 7 Ultimate, or Windows 7 Enterprise edition.
- The DirectAccess client computer must be a member of an Active Directory Domain Services (AD DS) domain, and its computer account must be a member of one of the security groups configured with the DirectAccess Setup Wizard.

- The DirectAccess client computer must have received computer configuration Group Policy settings for DirectAccess.
- The DirectAccess client must have a global IPv6 address, which should begin with a 2 or 3.
- The DirectAccess client must be able to reach the IPv6 addresses of the DirectAccess server.
- The DirectAccess client on the Internet must correctly determine that it is not on the intranet. You can type the `netsh dnsclient show state` command to view the network location displayed in the Machine Location field (outside corporate network or inside corporate network).
- Use the `netsh namespace show policy` command to show the NRPT rules as configured on the group policy.
- Use the `netsh namespace show effectivepolicy` command to determine the results of network location detection and the IPv6 addresses of the intranet DNS servers.
- The DirectAccess client must not be assigned the domain firewall profile.
- The DirectAccess client must be able to reach the organization's intranet DNS servers using IPv6. You can use Ping to attempt to reach the IPv6 addresses of intranet servers.
- The DirectAccess client must be able to communicate with intranet servers using application layer protocols. If File and Printer Sharing is enabled on the intranet server, test application layer protocol access by typing net view \\IntranetFQDN.
- Use the DirectAccess Connectivity Assistant on computers running Windows 7 and Network Connectivity Assistant on computers running Windows 8 to determine the intranet connectivity status and to provide diagnostic information.

SKILL SUMMARY

IN THIS LESSON, YOU LEARNED:

- DirectAccess provides seamless intranet connectivity to DirectAccess client computers when they are connected to the Internet, whereas connections are automatically established and they provide always-on seamless connectivity.
- The Name Resolution Policy Table (NRPT) is used to determine the behavior of the DNS clients when issuing queries and processing so that internal resources are not exposed to the public via the Internet, and to separate traffic that is not DirectAccess Internet traffic from traffic that is.
- To use DirectAccess, clients must be Windows 7 Enterprise Edition, Windows 7 Ultimate Edition, Windows 8, Windows Server 2008 R2, or Windows Server 2012.
- In Windows 8, the DCA was replaced by the Network Connectivity Assistant (NCA).
- The DirectAccess Connectivity Assistant (DCA) provides tools to help users reconnect if a problem occurs and helps with diagnostics used by the help desk. It is also used to detect whether one-time passwords (OTP) are required and helps your system determine whether it is connected to the intranet or the Internet.
- DirectAccess clients use the network location server (NLS) to determine their location. NLS is an internal web server.
- Before deploying DirectAccess, you need to make sure that you have IPv6 and any transitional IPv6 technologies in place, a certificate server, and external and internal DNS entries.

Knowledge Assessment

Multiple Choice

Select the correct answer for each of the following questions.

1. You have the following servers for DirectAccess:
   - Domain Controller/DNS server running Windows Server 2008 operating at Windows Server 2003 domain functional level
   - Certificate Authority running Windows Server 2012
   - File server running Windows Server 2008 R2
   - DirectAccess Server running Windows Server 2012

   Which of the following servers do you need to modify?
   a. Upgrade the domain controller to Windows Server 2008 R2.
   b. Run the Certificate Authority in Windows Server 2008 R2 compatibility mode.
   c. Upgrade the file server to Windows Server 2012.
   d. Install the IIS 6.0 compatibility tools on the DirectAccess server.

2. You are to configure the network location server (NLS). Which web server (IIS) role service should you install on the NLS server?
   a. Request Filtering
   b. URL authorization
   c. IP and domain restrictions
   d. Certificate mapper

3. You have installed and configured a DirectAccess server. You created a group called DAClients. However, when users log on to their computers, the computers are not configured to use DirectAccess. What do you need to do to configure the clients to use DirectAccess?
   a. Make sure that the DirectAccess administrator account has administrative access to the client.
   b. Enable the DirectAccess service on the client.
   c. Install NCA on the client.
   d. Make sure that the client computer is added to the DAClients group.

4. You are configuring DirectAccess on Server1. Which step do you need to perform to ensure that Server1 can initiate connections to DirectAccess client computers?
   a. Remote clients
   b. DirectAccess server
   c. Infrastructure servers
   d. Application servers

5. How can you identify the URL of the network location server that a client is using?
   a. Run the `show namespace nsl` command.
   b. Run the `show nsl` command.
   c. Run the `netsh namespace show effective policy` command.
   d. Run the `ipconfig /all` command.

6. What two steps do you need to perform on the DNS server so that it can support DirectAccess?
   a. Remove the WPAD from the DNS global query block.
   b. Remove the ISATAP from the DNS global query block.
   c. Add a record for the NSL server.
   d. Add the SRV record for the DirectAccess server.

7. You have a client that is configured for DirectAccess. The client is connected to the Internet from home. How can you verify whether the client can resolve the DirectAccess server called server1.contosol.com?
   a. Run the `netsh.exe dnsclient show state.`
   b. Run the `ipconfig /all` command.
   c. Run the `netsh connect` command.
   d. Run the `ping server1.contoso.com` command.

8. You have configured a server called Server1 as a DirectAccess server. How do you need to configure the Windows Firewall on the server to support DirectAccess?
   a. Allow ICMPv6 Echo Request.
   b. Allow ICMP v6 Redirect.
   c. Allow IPv6-Route.
   d. Allow IGMPv6.

9. Which table is used to determine the behavior of the DNS clients when determining the address of internal resources?
   a. NAP
   b. NPS
   c. NRTP
   d. NCA

10. Which of the following clients can connect to a DirectAccess server? (Choose all that apply.)
    a. Windows 7 Professional
    b. Windows 8 Enterprise
    c. Windows 7 Ultimate
    d. Windows 8 Professional

Best Answer

Choose the letter that corresponds to the best answer. More than one answer choice may achieve the goal. Select the BEST answer.

1. When setting up DirectAccess, which step would you use to specify the certificate authority?
   a. Remote clients
   b. Remote Access Server
   c. Infrastructure servers
   d. Application servers

2. When setting up DirectAccess, which step would you use to specify the Network Location Server?
   a. Remote clients
   b. Remote Access Server
   c. Infrastructure servers
   d. Application servers

3. Which tool is available in Windows 8 that enables you to diagnose DirectAccess connections?
   a. DirectAccess Connectivity Assistant (DCA)
   b. Network Connectivity Assistant (NCA)
   c. DirectAccess Troubleshooter
   d. TestDA

4. Which server is used to determine whether the server is connected to the intranet or the Internet?
   a. DNS Validator
   b. DirectAccess Detector
   c. DirectAccess Broadcaster
   d. Network Location Server

5. Why does the DirectAccess need certificates? (Choose all that apply.)
   a. To support IPsec
   b. To support PPTP
   c. To support SSTP
   d. To support DNS lookup

Matching and Identification

1. Configuring DirectAccess is divided into four primary steps. Identify the DirectAccess step for the specific task.
   _______ a) Identify the DirectAccess server.
   _______ b) Define the NLS.
   _______ c) Define the type of authentication used by the clients.
   _______ d) Define the internal servers available externally.
   _______ e) Specify the group for DirectAccess clients.

Build a List

1. Identify the four basic steps in order when configuring DirectAccess by placing the number of the step in the appropriate space. Not all steps will be used.
   _______ Infrastructure servers
   _______ NLS setup
   _______ Remote clients
   _______ RRAS setup
   _______ Remote Access Server
   _______ Application servers
   _______ DirectAccess Diagnostics

2. Identify the steps used when a DirectAccess client connects to a DirectAccess server by placing a number of the step in the appropriate space.
   _______ Connect to the server using IPv6 and IPsec or an IPv6 transitional technology.
   _______ Try to connect with IP-HTTPS to encapsulate IPv6 traffic.
   _______ Determine whether the client passes health validation.
   _______ Client determines whether it is connected to the Internet or the intranet.
   _______ Try to contact the intranet DNS server and domain controllers for authentication.
   _______ Establish an IPsec tunnel to resources on the intranet.

Choose an Option

1. Circle which tab you would use to define the CRL location when configuring the Certificate Authority.

Figure 11-38

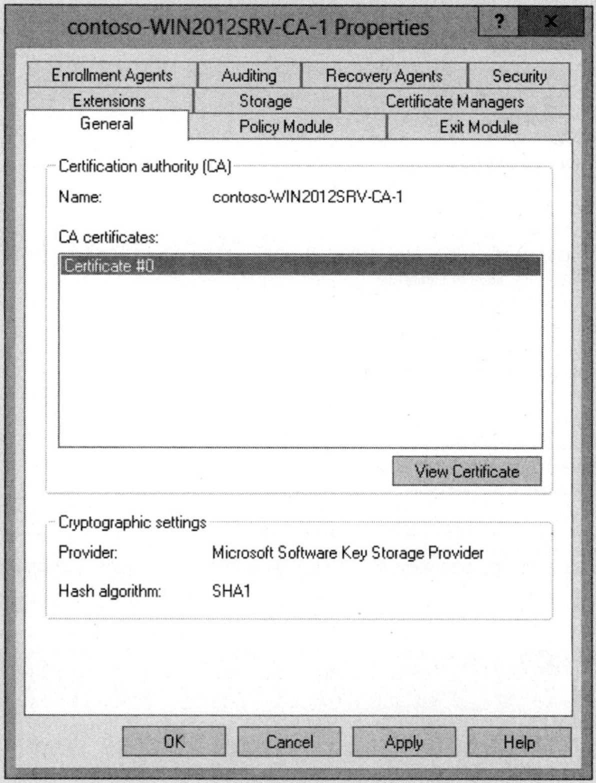

2. You need to install a digital certificate on the NLS. Circle the template that you want to use.

Figure 11-39

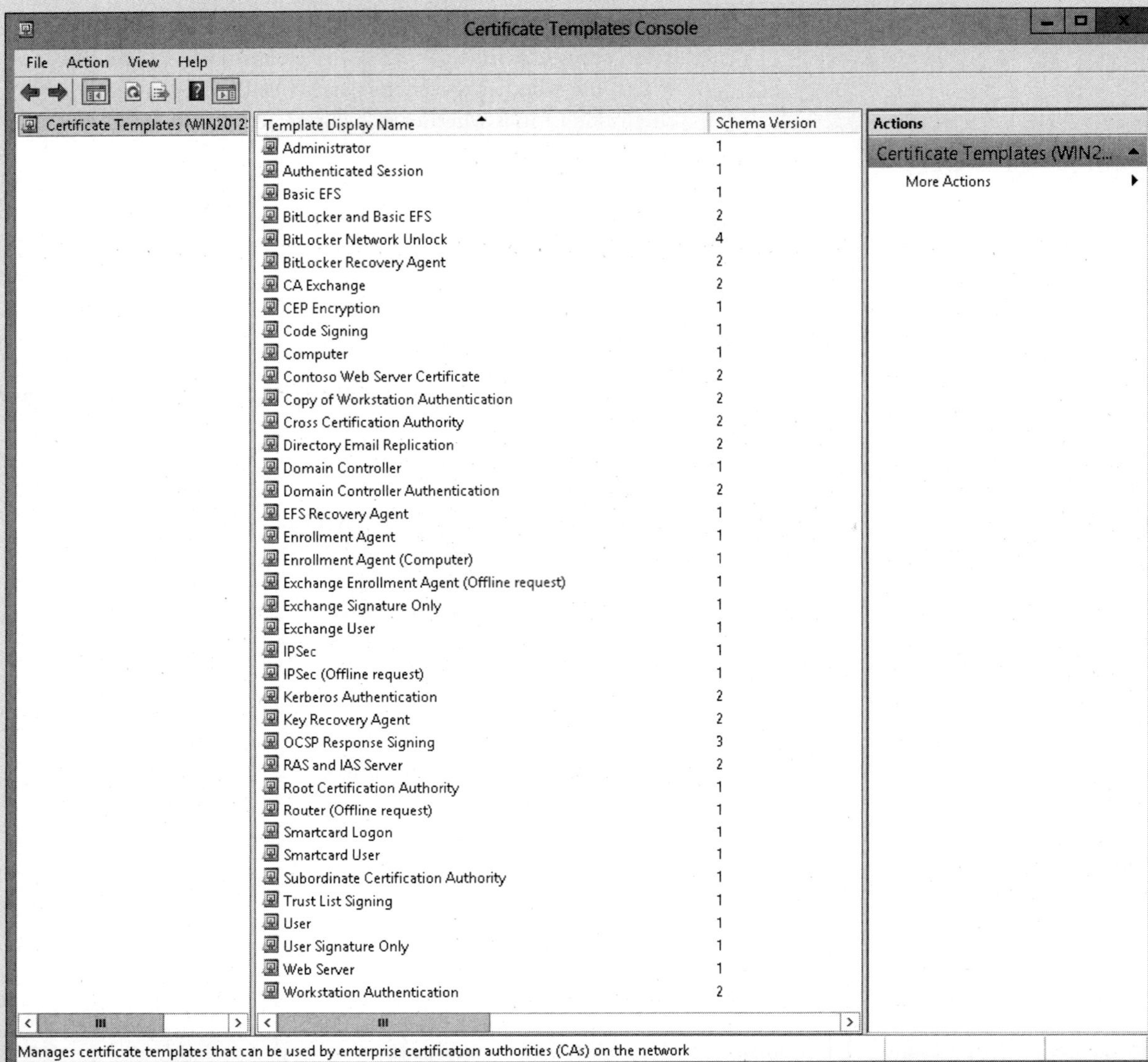

Business Case Scenarios

Scenario 11-1: Understanding DirectAccess

You are an administrator with the Contoso Corporation. The Contoso Corporation has about 1,100 users. Among those 1,100 users, there are 200 users who use VPN to connect to the organization network when they are not in the office. However, you realize that you are having trouble keeping the clients updated and performing other maintenance tasks as needed because these clients are often not connected to the network. What should you do?

Scenario 11-2: Installing DirectAccess

You are installing DirectAccess on an internal server. However, you need to configure the network location server (NLS). Your manager wants to know what the NLS is and what is required. What do you tell your manager?

Configuring a Network Policy Server

LESSON 12

70-411 EXAM OBJECTIVE

Objective 4.1 – Configure Network Policy Server (NPS). This objective may include but is not limited to: configure multiple RADIUS server infrastructures; configure RADIUS clients; manage RADIUS templates, configure RADIUS accounting; configure certificates.

LESSON HEADING	EXAM OBJECTIVE
Configuring a Network Policy Server Infrastructure	Configure Network Policy Server (NPS)
Installing and Configuring Network Policy Server	
Configuring Multiple RADIUS Server Infrastructures	Configure multiple RADIUS server infrastructures
Configuring RADIUS Clients	Configure RADIUS clients
Managing RADIUS Templates	Manage RADIUS templates
Configuring RADIUS Accounting	Configure RADIUS accounting
Understanding NPS Authentication Methods	Configure certificates

KEY TERMS

access client

authentication, authorization, and accounting (AAA)

authorization

Network Policy Server (NPS)

RADIUS clients

RADIUS proxy

RADIUS templates

Remote Authentication Dial-In User Service (RADIUS)

■ Configuring a Network Policy Server Infrastructure

THE BOTTOM LINE

Remote Authentication Dial-In User Service (RADIUS) is a networking and client/server protocol that provides centralized ***authentication, authorization, and accounting (AAA)*** management for computers that connect and use a network service. It can be used in wireless and remote access connection technologies, 802.1x switches, and Remote Desktop Services Gateway.

CERTIFICATION READY
Configure Network Policy Server (NPS).
Objective 4.1

RADIUS is defined in the Internet Engineering Task Force (IETF) RFCs 2865 and 2866. Microsoft's RADIUS server is ***Network Policy Server (NPS)***. By installing and configuring RADIUS, you can create and enforce wide network access policies for client health, connection request authentication, and connection request authorization.

As mentioned before, RADIUS is used for authentication, authorization, and accounting. ***Authorization*** is the process that determines what a user is permitted to do on a computer system or network. After a client or device is authenticated, the client or device must be authorized to access any type of network resource. The authorization controls what resources an authenticated user can and cannot access. Finally, accounting keeps track of what resources a user has accessed or attempted to access.

When you implement RADIUS, Windows Server 2012 computers running Routing and Remote Access and/or wireless access points can forward access requests to a single RADIUS server (see Figure 12-1). The RADIUS server then queries the domain controller for authentication and applies NPS Network Policies to the connection requests. NPS Network Policies are discussed in the next two lessons.

Figure 12-1
Looking at RADIUS servers and clients

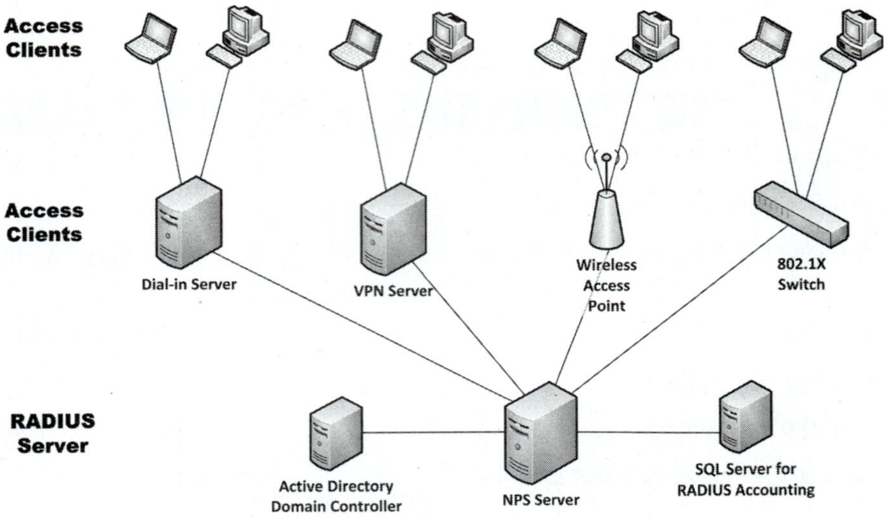

TAKE NOTE*

RADIUS clients (also referred to as access servers) are servers (such as servers running RRAS) and devices (such as wireless access points and 802.1X switch) that forward RADIUS requests to a RADIUS server. An ***access client*** is a computer or device that contacts or connects to a RADIUS client, which requires authentication and authorization to connect.

When NPS is used as a RADIUS server, authentication, authorization, and accounting follow these steps:

1. When an access client accesses a VPN server or wireless access point, a connection request is created that is sent to the NPS server.
2. The NPS server evaluates the Access-Request message.
3. If required, the NPS server sends an Access-Challenge message to the access server. The access server processes the challenge and sends an updated Access-Request to the NPS server.
4. The user credentials are checked and the dial-in properties of the user account are obtained by using a secure connection to a domain controller.
5. When the connection attempt is authorized with both the dial-in properties of the user account and network policies, the NPS server sends an Access-Accept message to the access server. If the connection attempt is either not authenticated or not authorized, the NPS server sends an Access-Reject message to the access server.

6. The access server completes the connection process with the access client and sends an Accounting-Request message to the NPS server, where the message is logged.
7. The NPS server sends an Accounting-Response to the access server.

RADIUS has been officially assigned UDP ports 1812 for RADIUS Authentication and 1813 for RADIUS Accounting by the Internet Assigned Numbers Authority (IANA). However, before IANA officially allocated ports 1812 and 1813, ports 1645 and 1646 were used for authentication and accounting. Although Microsoft RADIUS servers default to port 1812 and 1813, others can still use 1645 an 1646. Therefore, if the RADIUS server is separated by a firewall, you should open all four ports.

Installing and Configuring Network Policy Server

Installing NPS is a simple process, which is done with Server Manager. After NPS is installed, you then use the Network Policy Server console to configure NPS.

INSTALL NETWORK POLICY SERVER

GET READY. To install NPS, follow these steps:

1. Click the Server Manager button on the task bar to open *Server Manager*.
2. At the top of Server Manager, select Manage and click Add Roles and Features. The *Add Roles and Feature Wizard* opens.
3. On the *Before you begin* page, click Next.
4. Select Role-based or feature-based installation, and then click Next.
5. Click Select a server from the server pool, click the name of the server to install Network Policy and Access Services to, and then click Next.
6. On the *Server Roles* page (see Figure 12-2), select Network Policy and Access Services.

Figure 12-2

Installing Network Policy and Access Services

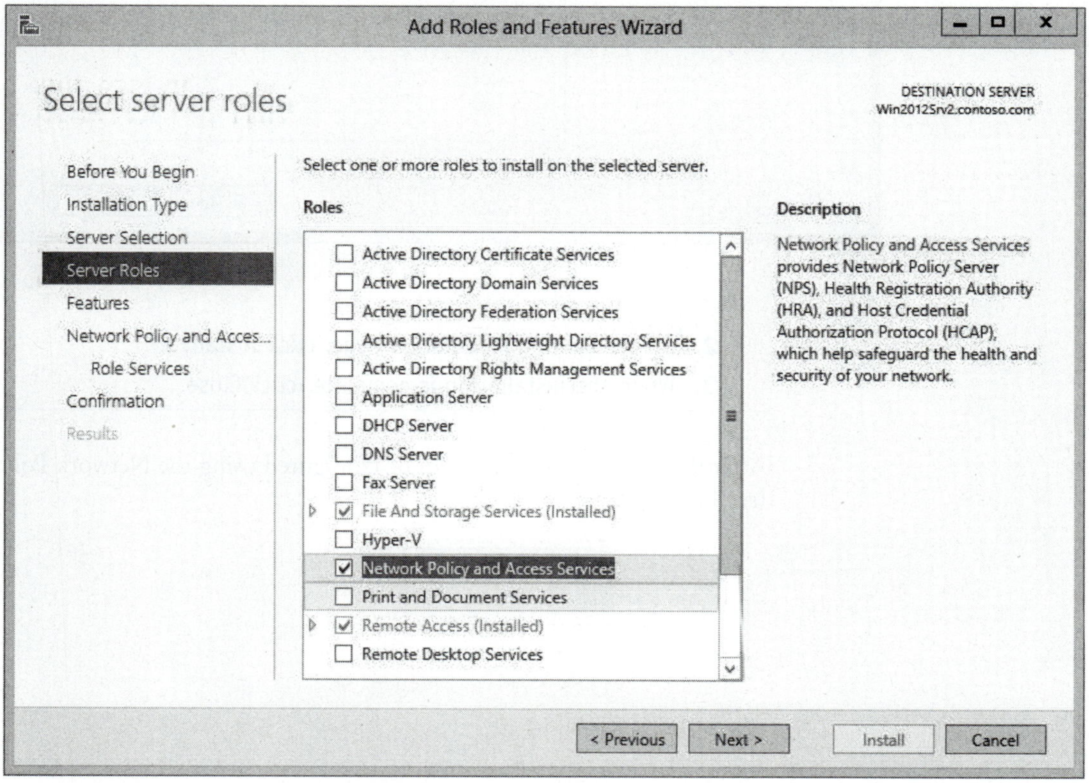

7. When it asks you to add features that are required for Network Policy and Access Services, click Add Features.
8. Back on the *Select server roles* page, click Next.
9. On the *Select features* page, click Next.
10. On the *Network Policy and Access Services* page, click Next.
11. On the *Select role services* page (see Figure 12-3), with the NPS selected, click Next.

Figure 12-3

Selecting Network Policy and Access Service Role Services

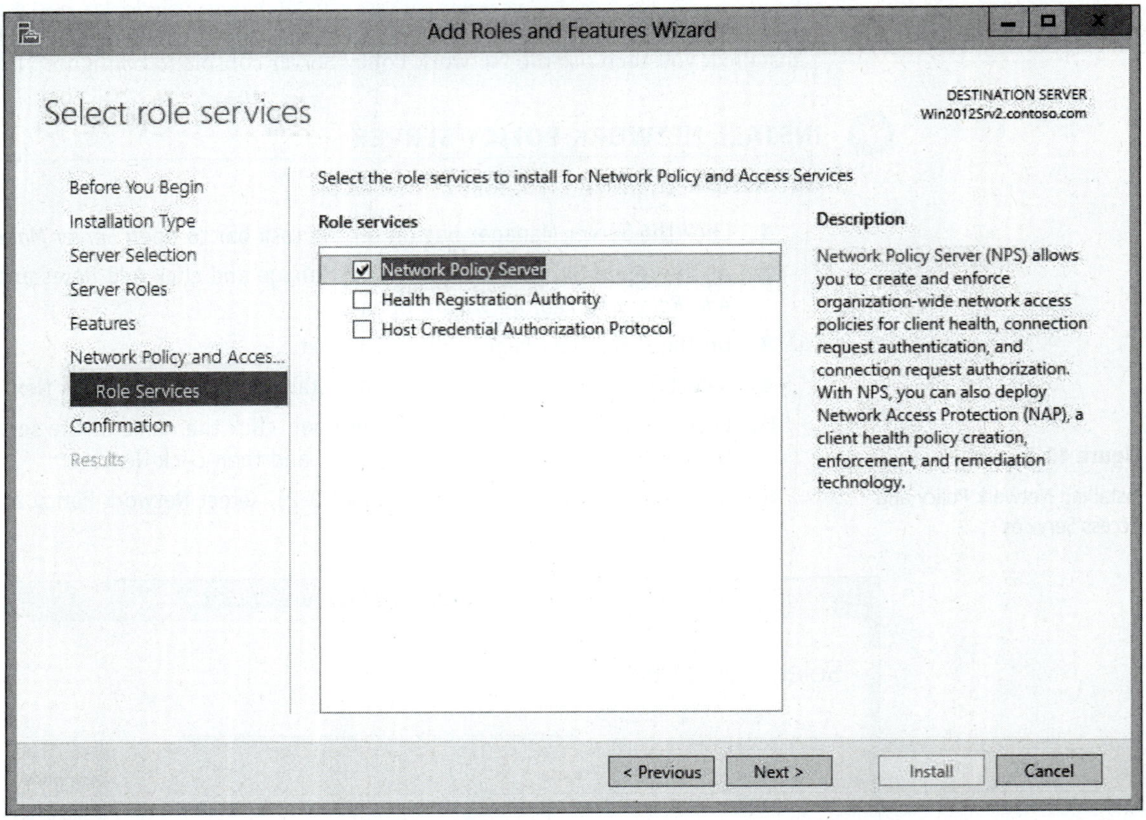

12. On the *Confirm installation* page, click Install.
13. When the installation is complete, click Close.

After the NPS is installed, it can be configured using the Network Policy Server console (see Figure 12-4).

Figure 12-4

Opening the Network Policy Server console

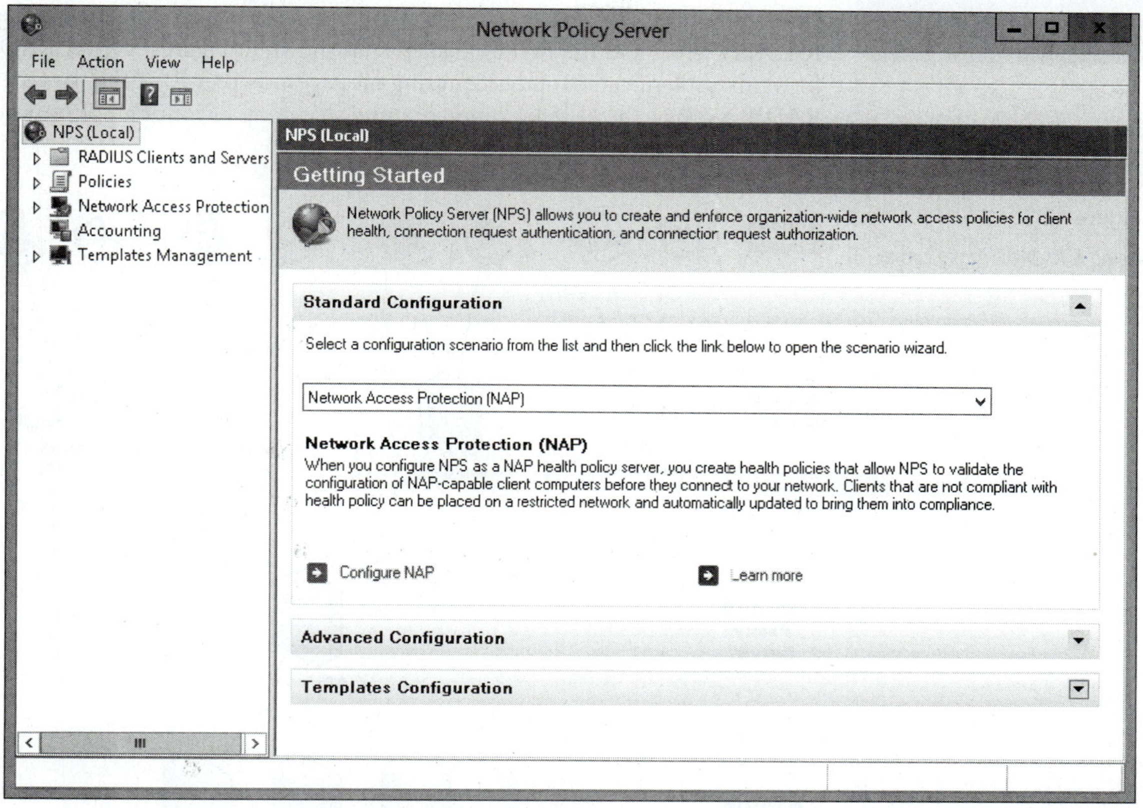

USING WINDOWS POWERSHELL

You can manage RADIUS settings using the following Windows PowerShell cmdlets:

- `Add-RemoteAccessRadius` – Adds a new external RADIUS server for VPN authentication, accounting for DirectAccess and VPN, or one-time password authentication for DirectAccess.
- `Get-RemoteAccessAccounting` – Displays the accounting configuration for Remote Access, such as the different types of accounting that are enabled and the respective configuration.
- `Get-RemoteAccessRadius` – Displays the list of RADIUS servers, including RADIUS for VPN authentication, RADIUS for DirectAccess and VPN Accounting, and RADIUS for one-time password authentication for DirectAccess.
- `Remove-RemoteAccessRadius` – Removes an external RADIUS server from being used for VPN authentication, accounting for both DirectAccess and VPN, or one-time password authentication for DirectAccess.
- `Set-RemoteAccessAccounting` – Sets the enabled state for inbox and RADIUS accounting for both external RADIUS and Windows accounting, and configures the settings when enabled.
- `Set-RemoteAccessRadius` – Edits the properties associated with an external RADIUS server being used for VPN authentication, accounting for DirectAccess and VPN, and one-time password authentication for DirectAccess.

Configuring Multiple RADIUS Server Infrastructures

So far, only a simple installation of NPS has been discussed. However, for larger and more complex organizations, you will most likely have multiple RADIUS servers so that you can provide enhanced performance and redundancy.

CERTIFICATION READY
Configure multiple RADIUS server infrastructures.
Objective 4.1

If you have multiple RADIUS servers, you can configure RADIUS clients to use a primary RADIUS server and alternate RADIUS servers. If the primary RADIUS server becomes unavailable, the request is sent to the Alternate RADIUS server.

Another multiple RADIUS server infrastructure is to place a ***RADIUS proxy*** between the RADIUS server and the RADIUS clients (as shown in Figure 12-5). A RADIUS proxy forwards authentication and accounting messages to other RADIUS servers. When NPS is a RADIUS proxy, the NPS becomes a central switching or routing point through which RADIUS access and account messages flow.

Figure 12-5
Using a RADIUS proxy server

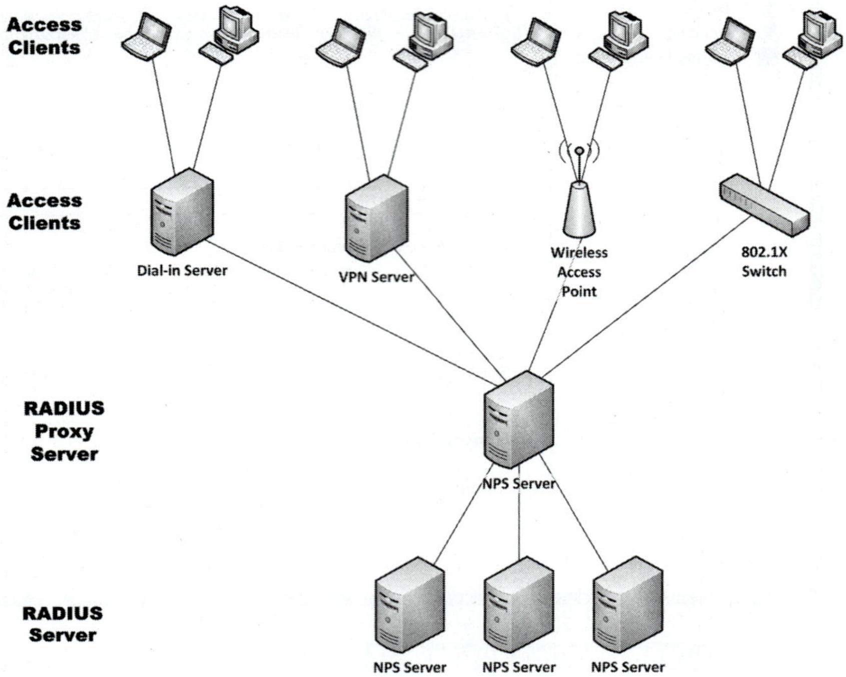

When you configure NPS as a RADIUS proxy, you create a new connection request policy that NPS uses to determine which connection requests to forward to other RADIUS servers. In addition, the connection request policy is configured by specifying a remote RADIUS server group that contains one or more RADIUS servers, which tell NPS where to send the connection requests that match the connection request policy.

To configure load balancing, you must have more than one RADIUS server per remote RADIUS server group. Based on load and resources, you can configure the following:

- **Priority:** Priority specifies the order of importance of the RADIUS server to the NPS proxy server. The lower the number, the higher priority the NPS proxy gives to the RADIUS server. If a RADIUS server is assigned the highest priority of 1, the NPS proxy sends connection requests to the RADIUS server first. If the server is not available, it then sends connection requests to RADIUS servers with priority 2, and so on. You can assign the same priority to multiple RADIUS servers, and then use the Weight setting to load balance between them.
- **Weight:** NPS uses this Weight setting to determine how many connection requests to send to each group member when the group members have the same priority level. Weight setting must be assigned a value between 1 and 100, and the value represents a percentage of 100%. If two servers are assigned the same priority and weight, the connection requests are distributed evenly between the two servers.
- **Advanced settings:** If the remote RADIUS server is unavailable, you can start sending connection requests to other group members. The Advanced settings determine when it considers the server is not available and sends the requests to the next RADIUS server.

ADD A REMOTE RADIUS SERVER GROUP

GET READY. To add a remote RADIUS group, perform the following steps:

1. Open the Server Manager.
2. Click Tools > Network Policy Server. The *Network Policy Server console* opens.
3. In the console tree, double-click RADIUS Clients and Servers, right-click Remote RADIUS Server Groups, and then click New. The *New Remote RADIUS Server Group* dialog box opens (see Figure 12-6).

Figure 12-6

Creating a new RADIUS server group

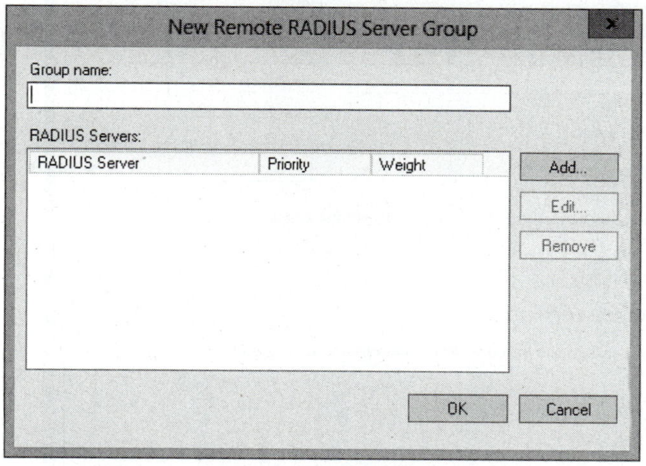

4. In *Group name*, type a name for the remote RADIUS server group in Group name.
5. Click Add. The *Add RADIUS Servers* dialog box opens (see Figure 12-7).

Figure 12-7

Adding a RADIUS server to the RADIUS server group

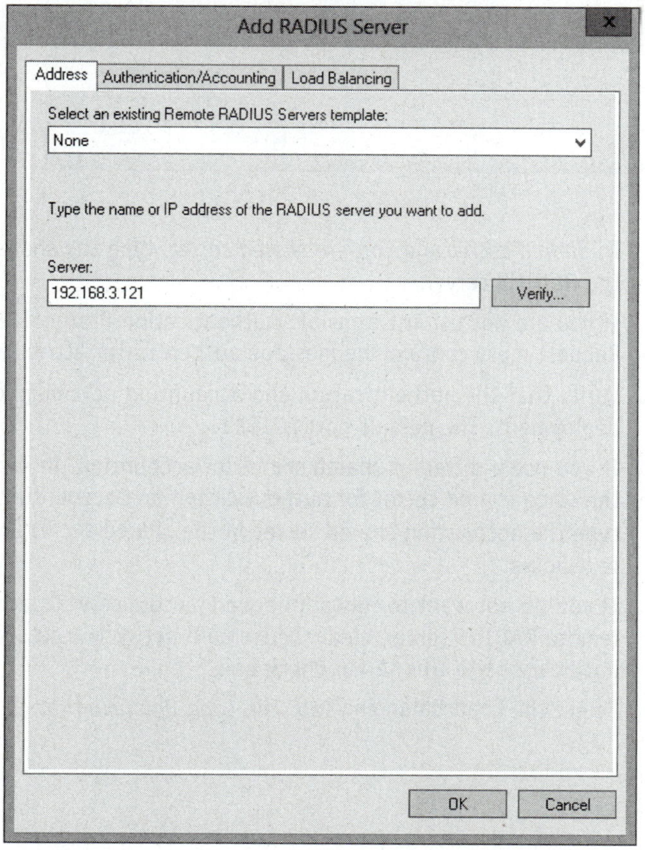

6. Type the IP address of the RADIUS server that you want to add to the group or type the Fully Qualified Domain Name (FQDN) of the RADIUS server.
7. Select the Authentication/Accounting tab. The *Authentication/Accounting* tab is shown in Figure 12-8.

Figure 12-8

Configuring Authentication and Accounting RADIUS

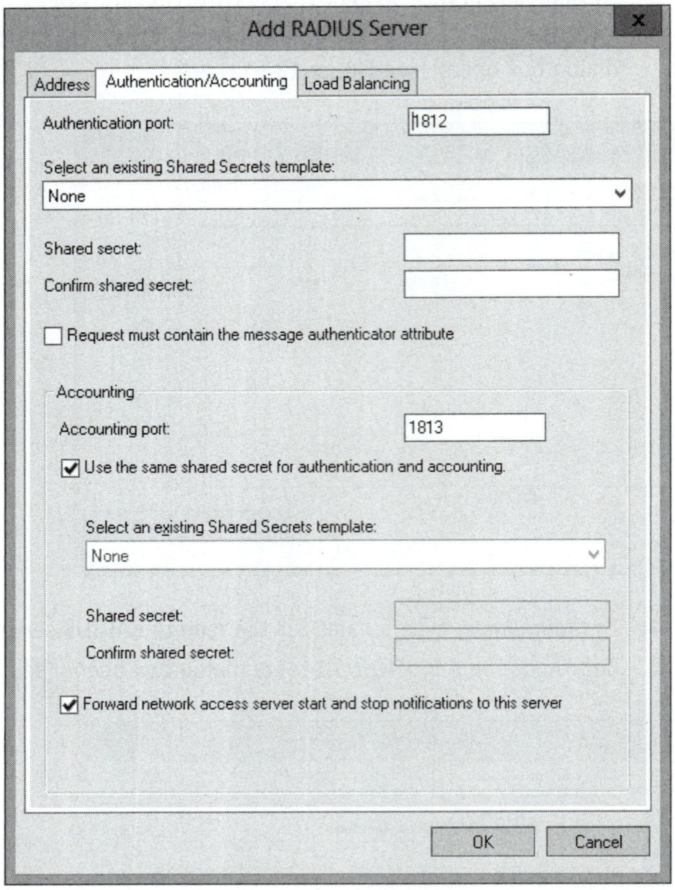

8. In *Shared secret* and *Confirm shared secret*, type the shared secret that you used for the RADIUS server.
9. If you are not using Extensible Authentication Protocol (EAP) for authentication, click Request must contain the message authenticator attribute.
10. Verify that the authentication and accounting port numbers are correct for your deployment. The default port is 1813.
11. If you use a different shared secret for accounting, in Accounting, clear the Use the same shared secret for authentication and accounting check box, and then type the accounting shared secret in the Shared secret and Confirm shared secret text boxes.
12. If you do not want to forward network access server start and stop messages to the remote RADIUS server, clear the Forward network access server start and stop notifications to this server check box.
13. Select the Load Balancing tab. The *Load Balancing* tab is shown in Figure 12-9.

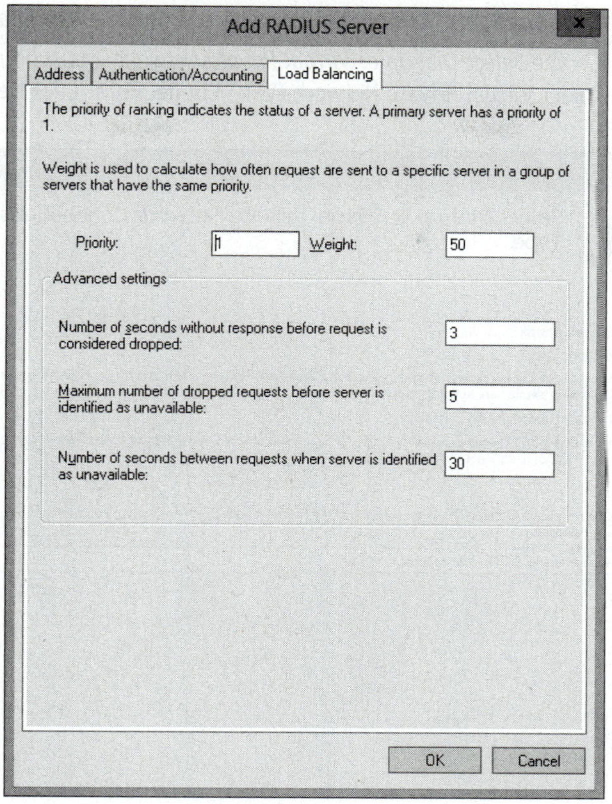

Figure 12-9
Configuring RADIUS load balancing

14. When you want to perform load balancing, you can specify how often requests are sent to a specific server in a group by specifying the weight assigned to the server.
15. Click OK to close the *Add RADIUS Server* dialog box.
16. Click OK to close the *New Remote RADIUS Server* group.

Configuring RADIUS Clients

To configure NPS as a RADIUS server, you can use either standard configuration or advanced configuration in the NPS console or in Server Manager.

CERTIFICATION READY
Configure RADIUS clients.
Objective 4.1

The standard configuration includes:

- RADIUS server for dial-up or VPN connections
- RADIUS server for 802.1X wireless or wired connections
- NAP policy server (The NAP policy server is discussed in Lesson 14)

When you configure NPS as a RADIUS server for dial-up or VPN connections, you create a network policy.

CONFIGURE NPS FOR RADIUS SERVER FOR VPN CONNECTIONS

GET READY. To configure NPS for RADIUS server for VPN connections, perform the following steps:

1. Open the Server Manager.
2. Click Tools > Network Policy Server. The *Network Policy Server console* opens.
3. In the main pane, select RADIUS server for Dial-Up or VPN Connections under the *Standard Configuration*.

4. Click Configure VPN or Dial-Up. The *Configure VPN or Dial-Up Wizard* opens.
5. On the *Select Dial-up or Virtual Private Network Connections Type* page (see Figure 12-10), select Virtual Private Network (VPN) Connections. Click Next.

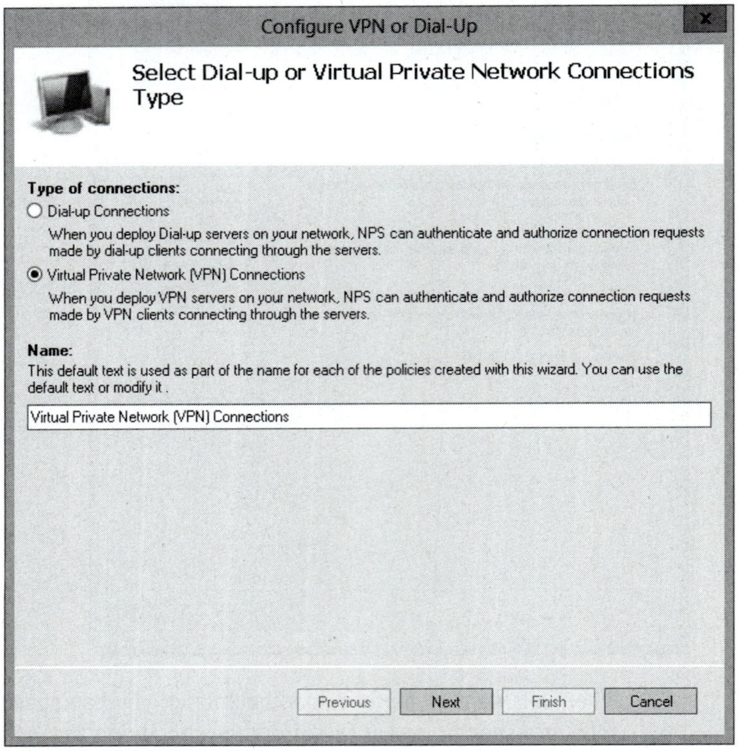

Figure 12-10

Specifying connections on the *Dial-up or Virtual Private Network Connections Type* page

6. On the *Specify Dial-Up or VPN Server* page (see Figure 12-11), click Add.

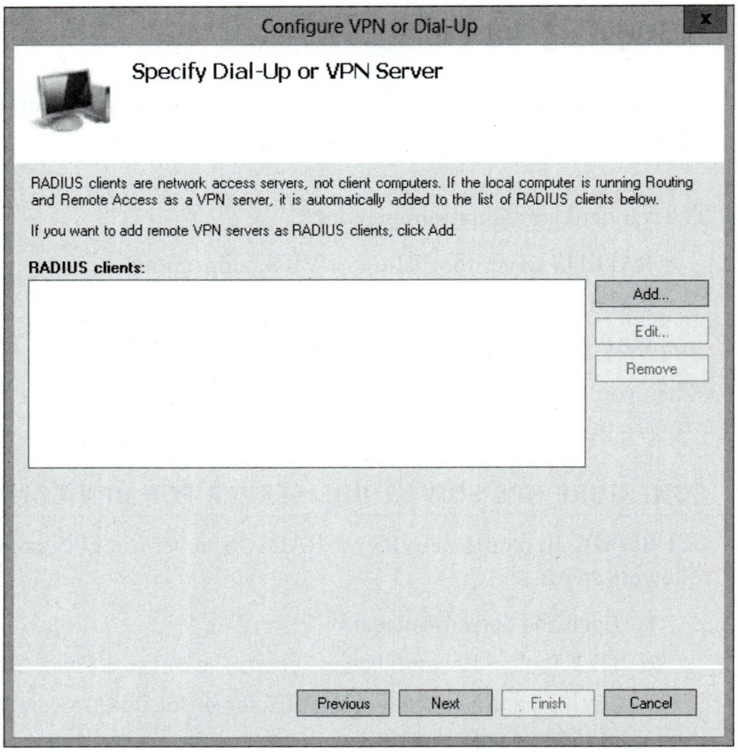

Figure 12-11

Showing the RADIUS clients page

7. When the *New RADIUS Client* dialog box opens (see Figure 12-12), type a friendly name for the RADIUS client in the *Friendly name* text box.

Figure 12-12

Adding RADIUS clients

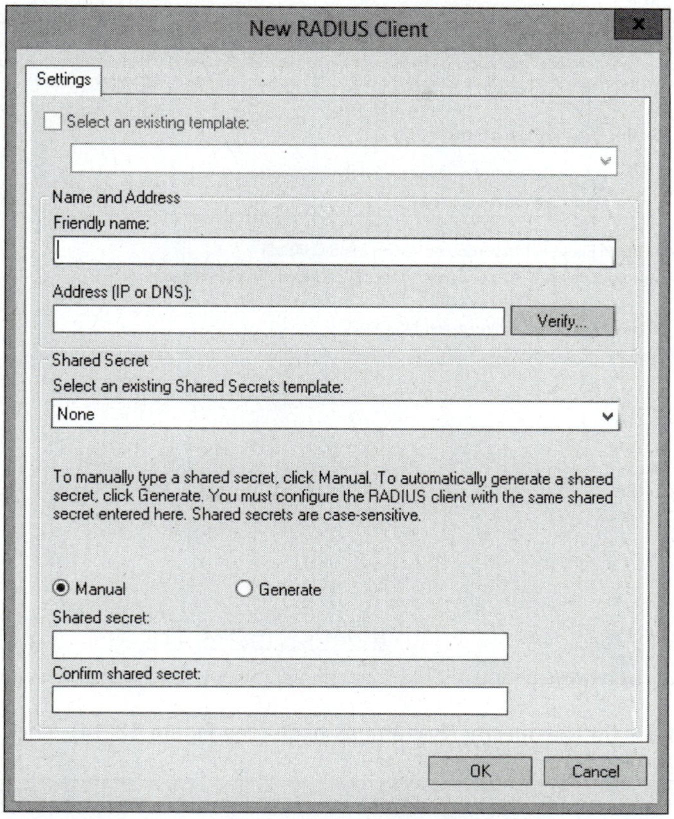

8. In the *Address (IP or DNS)* text box, type the address of the remote access server.
9. At the bottom of the dialog box, type in a shared secret password to be used for RADIUS setup.
10. Click OK to close the *Remote Access Properties* dialog box.
11. Back on the *Specify Dial-Up or VPN Server* page, click Next.
12. On the *Configure Authentication Methods* page (see Figure 12-13), select an authentication method and click Next.

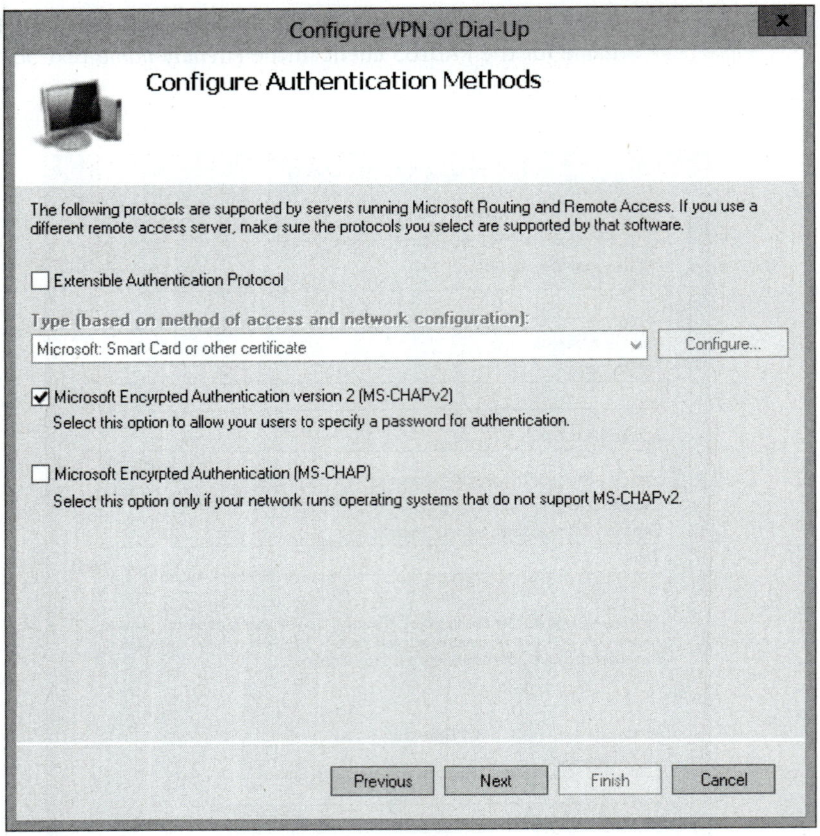

Figure 12-13

Specifying authentication methods

13. On the *Specify User Groups* page (see Figure 12-14), click Add.

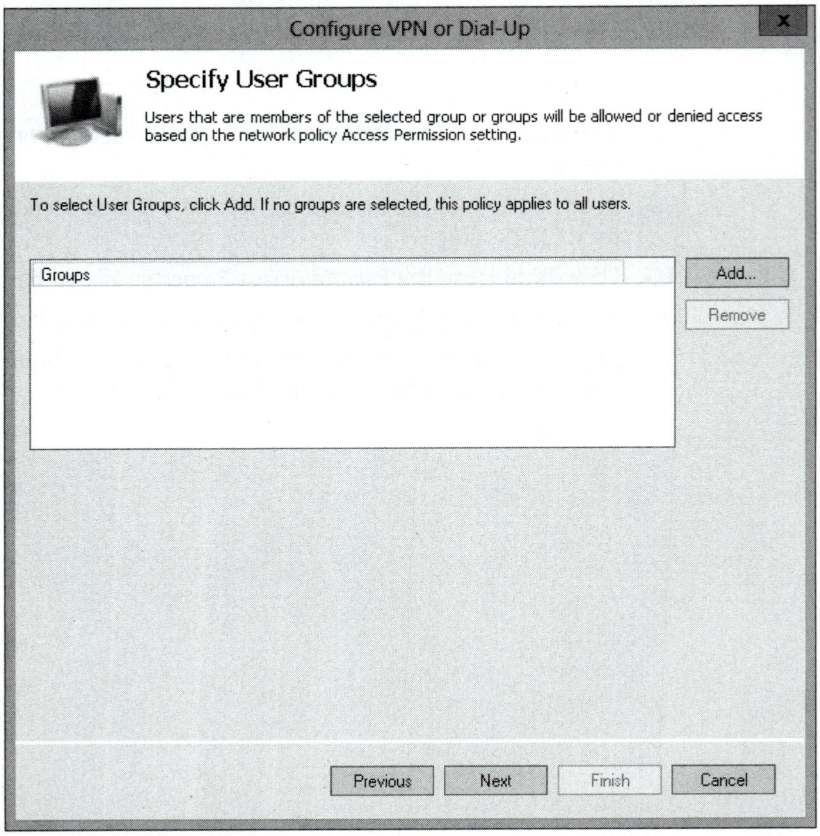

Figure 12-14

Specifying user groups

14. When the *Select Group* dialog box opens, type a name of the group in the *Enter the object name to select* text box and click OK.
15. Back at the Specify User Groups, click Next.
16. An IP filter enables you to specify what addresses or protocols are allowed or not allowed through the remote servers. If you have an IP Filter template, you can select it on the *Specify IP Filters* page (see Figure 12-15).

Figure 12-15

Specifying IP filters

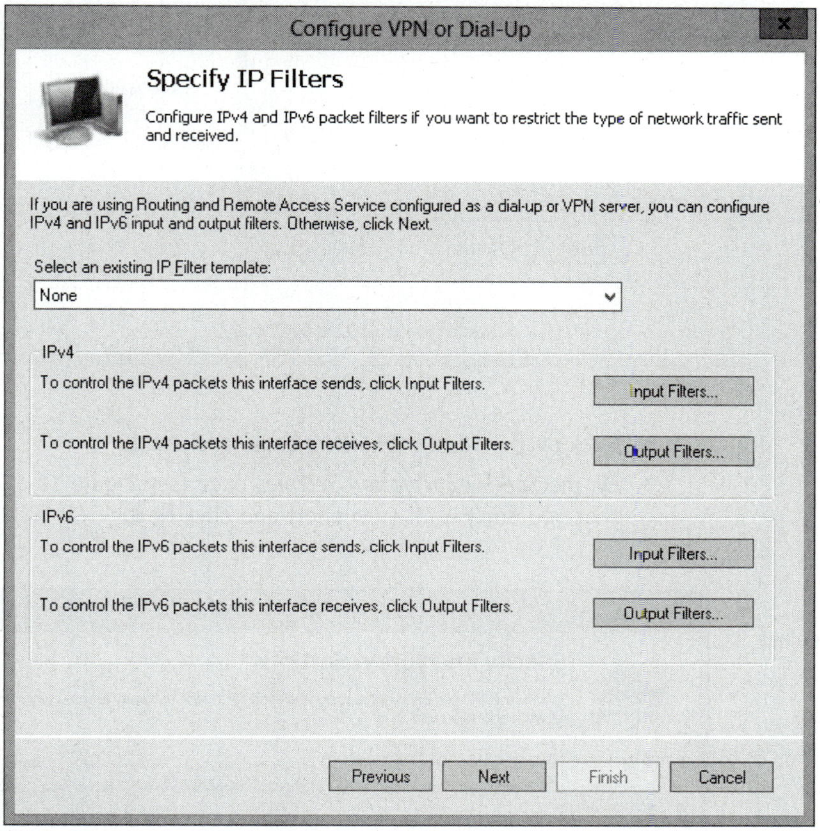

17. If you do not have an IP filter to choose, you can manually specify what filters you want by clicking the Input Filters or Output Filters for IPv4 or IPv6, which opens the *Inbound or Outbound Filters* dialog box. You then click the Add button to open the *Add IP Filter* dialog box (see Figure 12-16). Then specify the source network, destination network, and protocol. Click OK to close the *Add IP Filter* and click OK to close the *Inbound or Outbound Filters* dialog box.

Figure 12-16

Configuring inbound filters

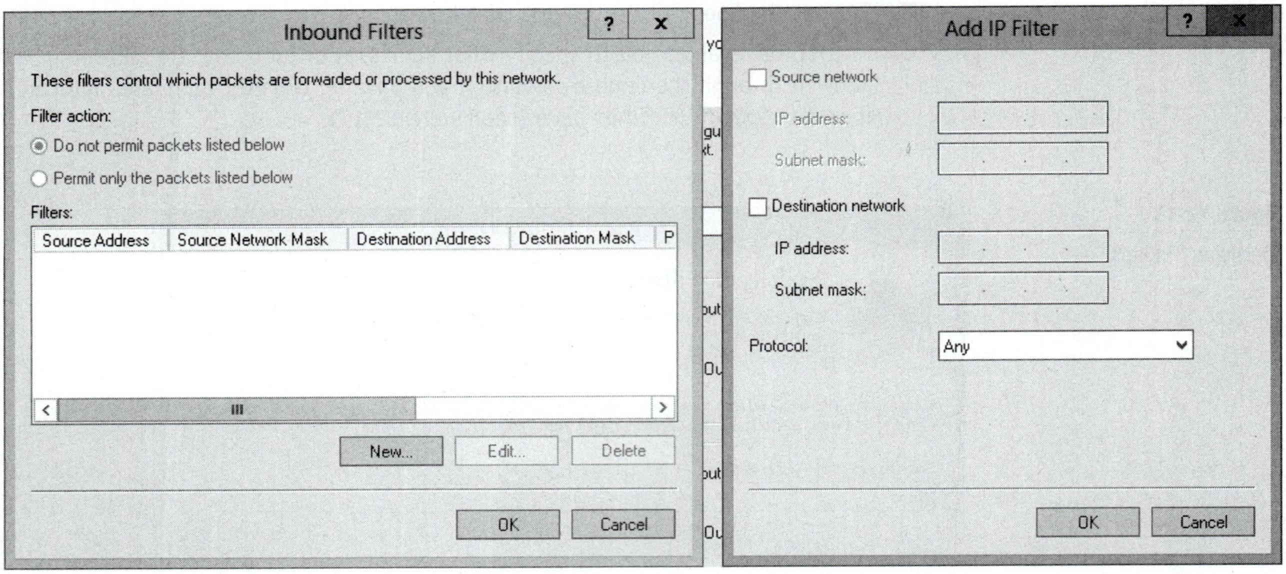

18. Back on the *Specify IP Filters* page, click Next.
19. On the *Specify Encryption Settings* page (see Figure 12-17), deselect the encryption that you don't want to support and click Next.

Figure 12-17

Specifying encryption settings

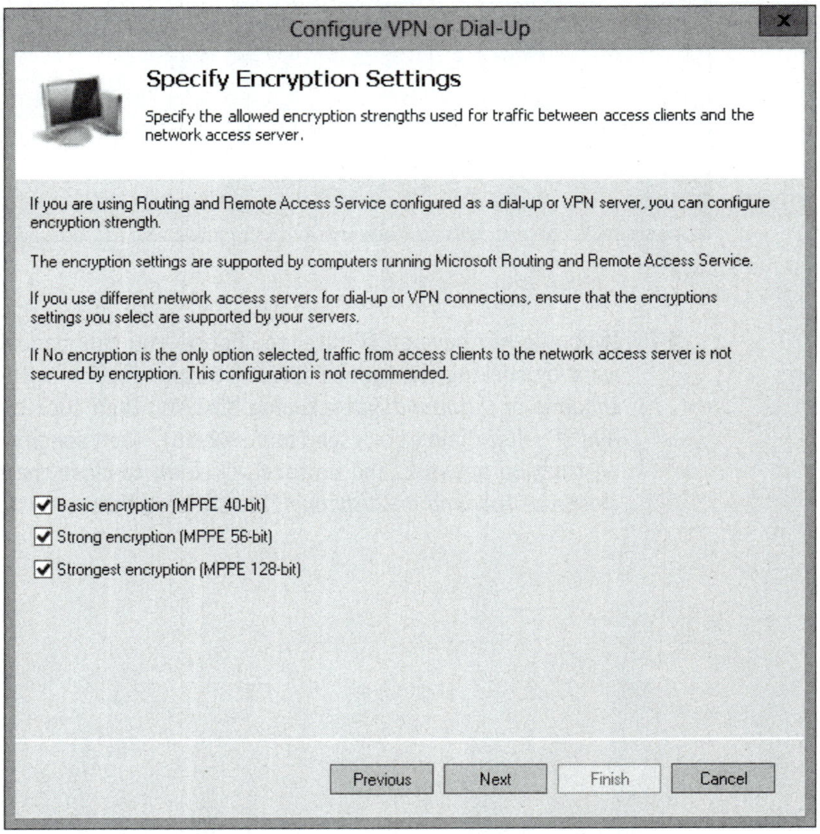

20. The *Specify a Realm Name* page appears as shown in Figure 12-18. If you need to specify a realm (a user account location such as a domain name or server name), specify the realm name in the appropriate text box. Click Next.

Figure 12-18

Specifying a realm name

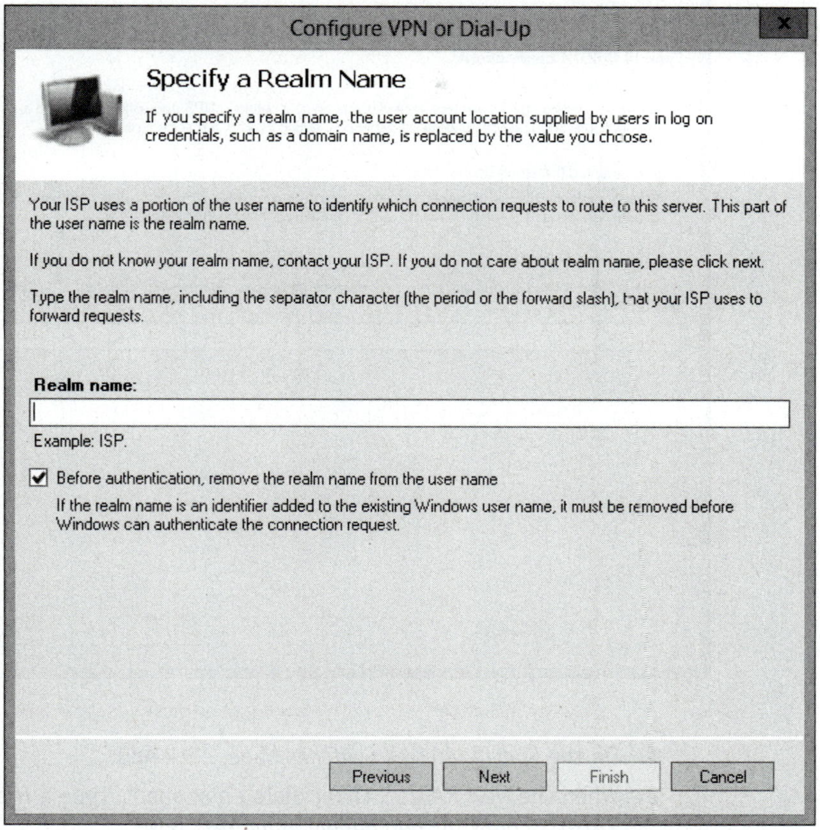

21. When the wizard is complete, click Finish.

CONFIGURE NPS FOR 802.1X WIRELESS CONNECTIONS

GET READY. To configure NPS for 802.1X wireless or wired connections, perform the following steps:

1. Open the Server Manager.
2. Click Tools > Network Policy Server. The *Network Policy Server console* opens.
3. In the main pane, under *Standard Configuration*, select RADIUS server for 802.1X Wireless or Wired Connections.
4. Click Configure 802.1X. The *802.1X Wizard* opens.
5. On the *Select 802.1X Connections Type* page (see Figure 12-19), select 802.1X Secure Wireless Connections. Click Next.

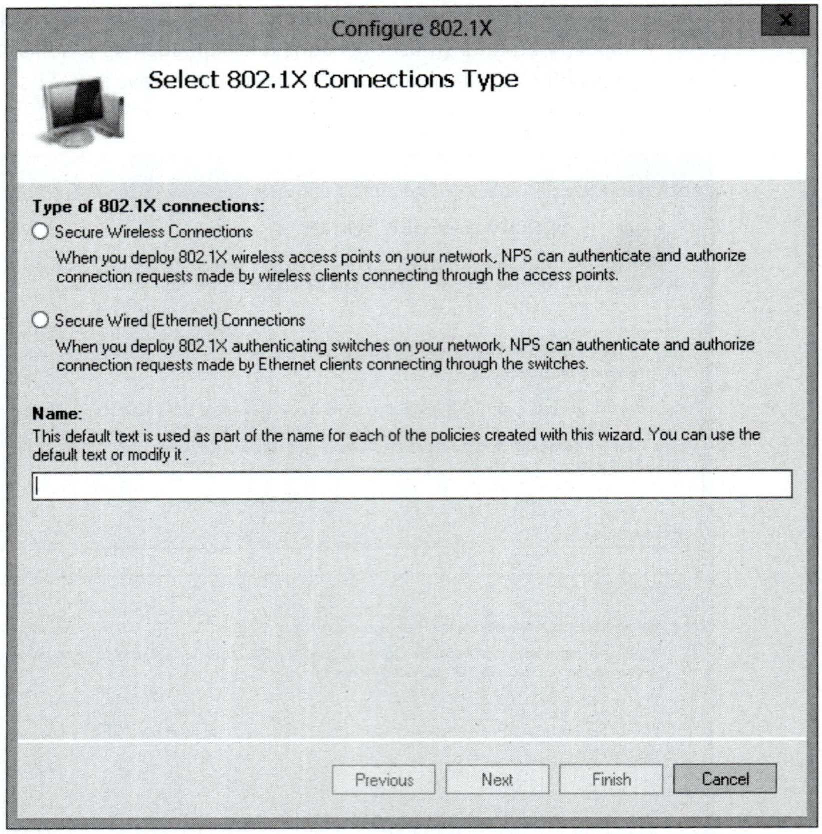

Figure 12-19

Selecting the 802.1X connections type

6. On the *Specify 802.1X Switches* page, click **Add**.
7. When the *New RADIUS Client* dialog box opens, type a friendly name for the RADIUS client in the *Friendly name* text box.
8. Type the address of the remote access server in the *Address (IP or DNS)* text box.
9. At the bottom of the dialog box, type in a shared secret password to be used for RADIUS setup.
10. Click **OK** to close the *New RADIUS Client* dialog box.
11. Back on the *Specify 802.1X Switches* page, click **Next**.
12. On the *Configure Authentication Methods* page, choose the appropriate authentication method (see Figure 12-20), select an authentication method, and click **Next**.
13. On the *Specify User Groups* page, click **Add**.
14. When the *Select Group* dialog box opens, type a name of the group in the *Enter the object name to select* text box and click **OK**.
15. Back at the Specify User Groups page, click **Next**.

Figure 12-20

Configuring authentication methods for 802.1X

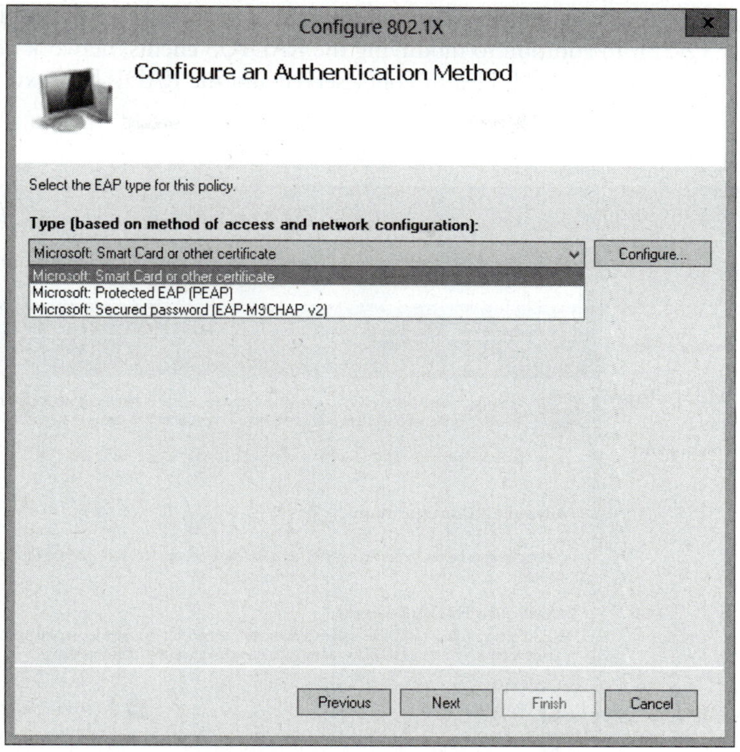

16. On the *Configure Traffic Controls* page (see Figure 12-21), you can specify traffic control attributes, which are sent to the RADIUS server with authentication and authorization requests by clicking the **Configure** button. When you are done, click **Next**.

Figure 12-21

Configuring traffic controls

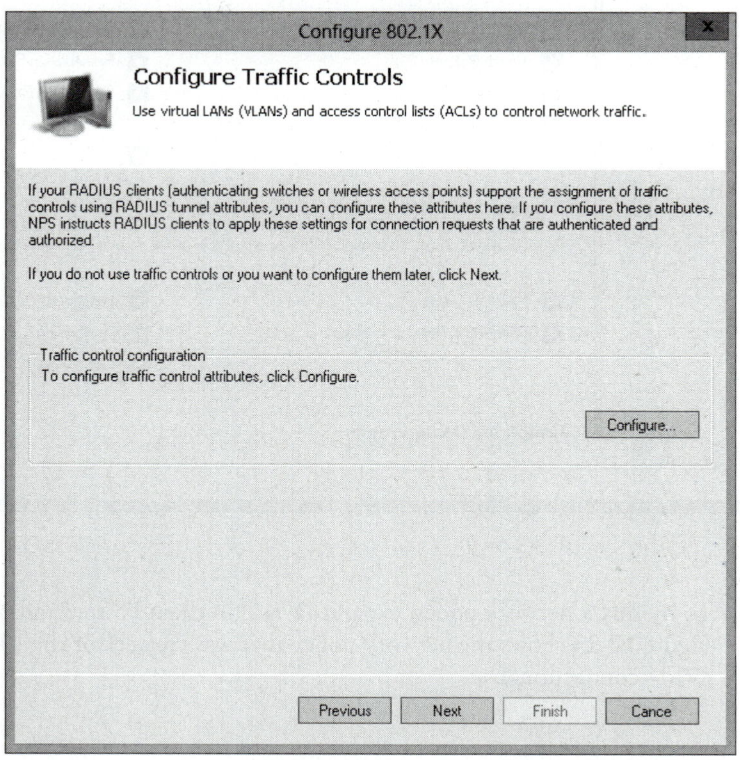

17. When the wizard is complete, click **Finish**.

If you want more control in the configuration, use NPS Advanced Configuration (see Figure 12-22). In addition to modifying the RADIUS clients, network policies, and accounting, you can configure NAP Health Policy server, and the RADIUS proxy.

Figure 12-22

Looking at NPS Advanced Configuration

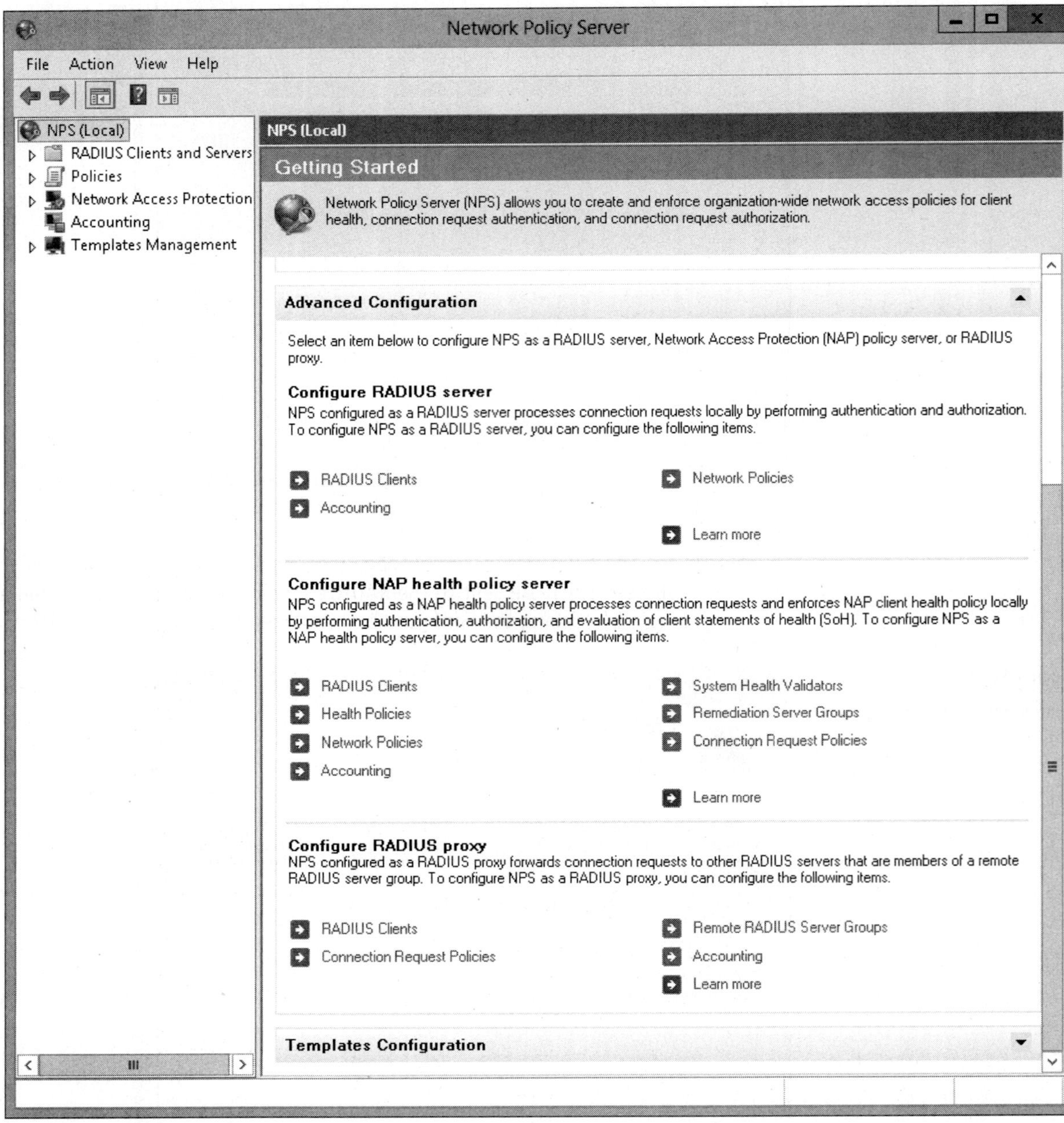

To modify a network policy, expand *Policies* in the NPS tree and click *Network Policies*. Figure 12-23 shows the network policy that was created for the Virtual Private Network (VPN connections).

Figure 12-23

Looking at network policies

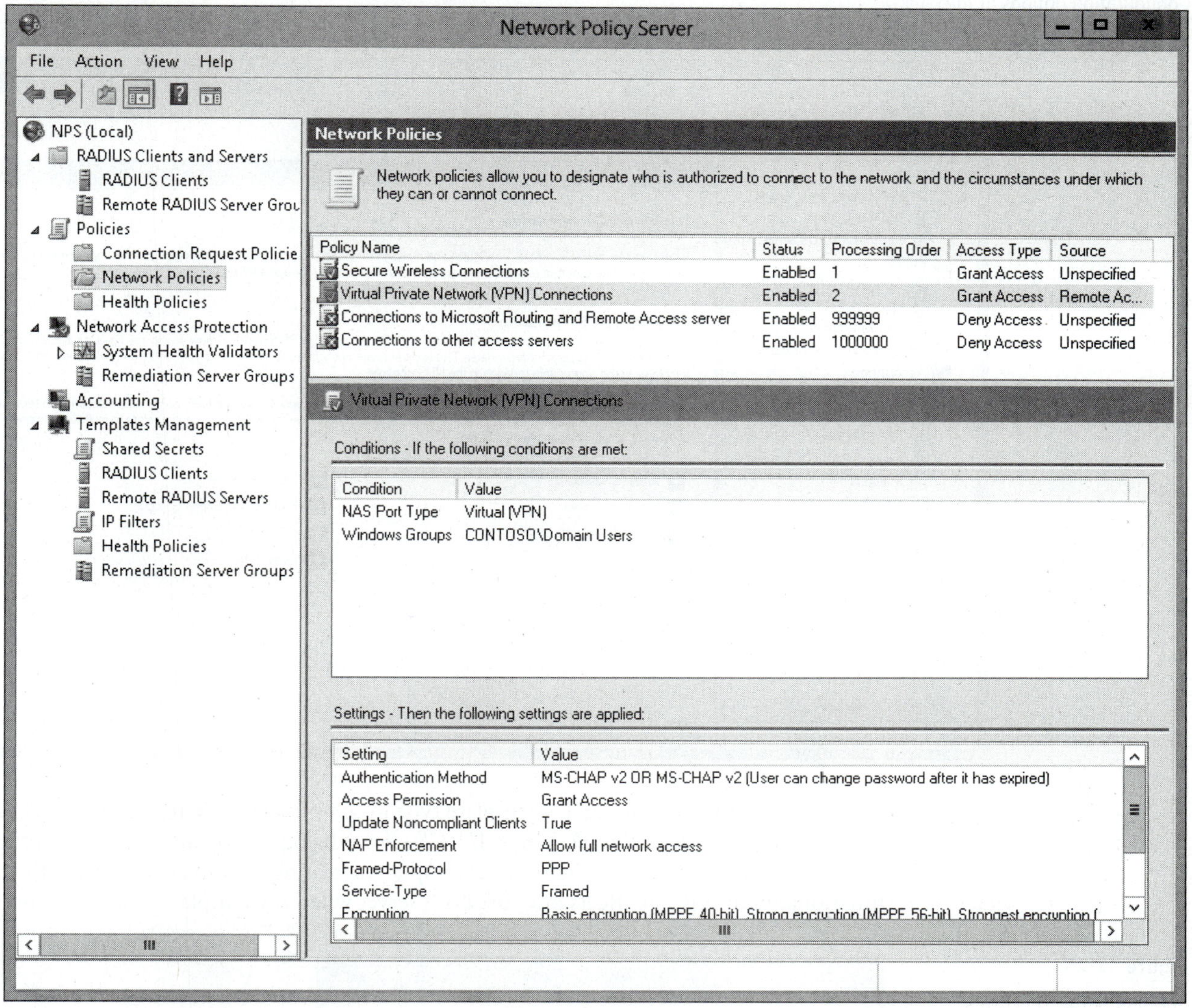

Managing RADIUS Templates

> ***RADIUS templates*** enable you to create RADIUS configuration elements that can be reused on local NPS servers and can be exported to other NPS servers.

CERTIFICATION READY
Manage RADIUS templates.
Objective 4.1

Much like the use of other templates, RADIUS templates (especially RADIUS clients and Remote RADIUS servers) are designed to reduce the amount of time and cost that it takes to configure RADIUS on one or more servers. Creating a RADIUS template does not affect the functionality of NPS. It affects only the NPS server when the template is selected and applied when configuring RADIUS. The RADIUS templates are available (see Figure 12-24) for configuration in Templates Management.

Figure 12-24

Looking at Template Configuration options in the NPS console

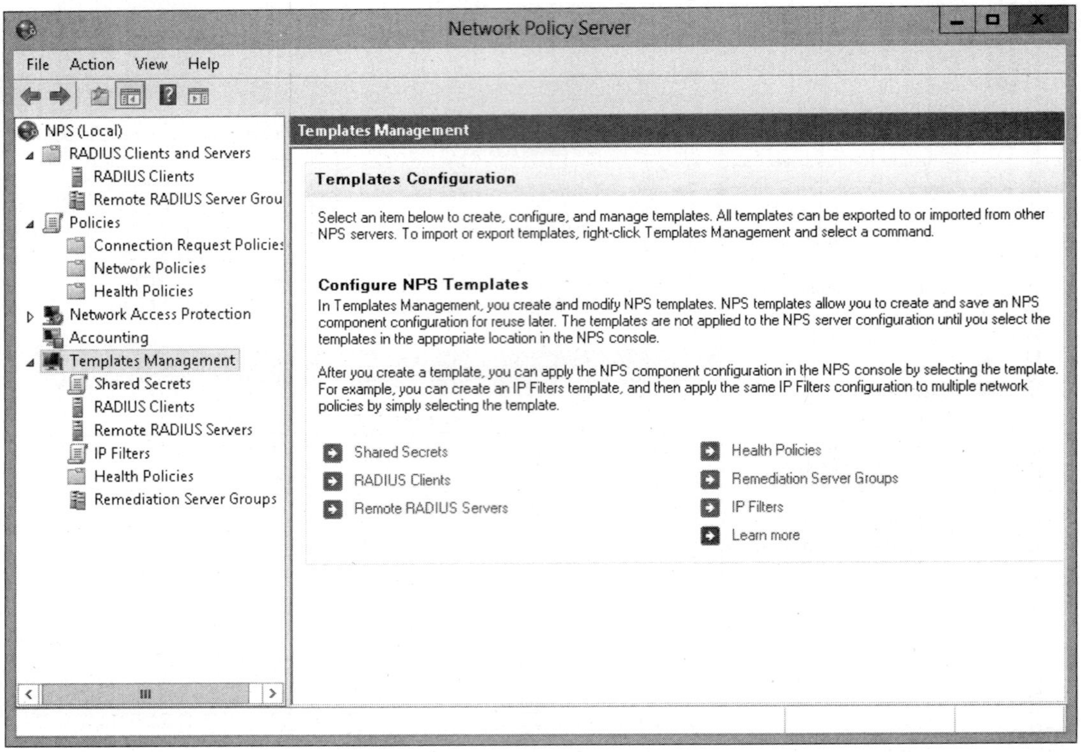

To create a template, right-click a template type in the NPS console tree, such as *RADIUS Clients*, and then select *New*. A *New RADIUS Client* dialog box opens (as shown in Figure 12-25) that allows you to configure your template. Creating a template does not affect the functionality of NPS. It affects only the NPS server when the template is selected and applied

Figure 12-25

Creating a RADIUS clients template

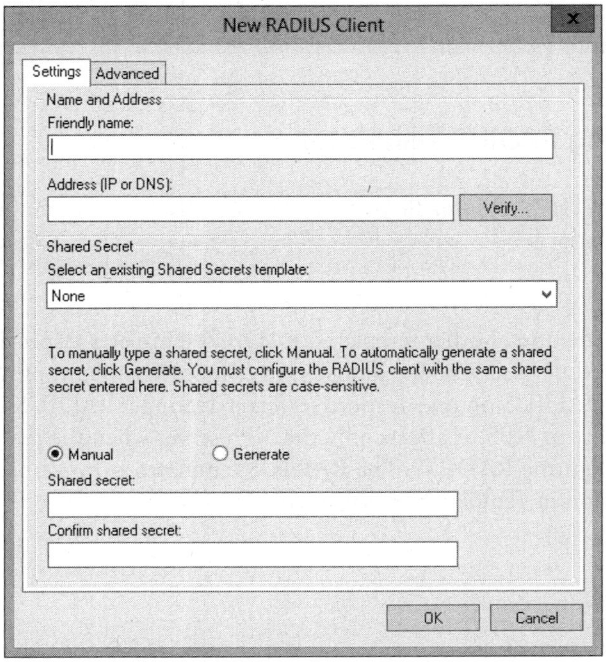

when configuring RADIUS. For example, if you right-click *RADIUS Clients* in the *RADIUS Clients and Servers* group and select *Properties*, you can apply the RADIUS template that was previously created, as shown in Figure 12-26.

Figure 12-26

Using the RADIUS clients template

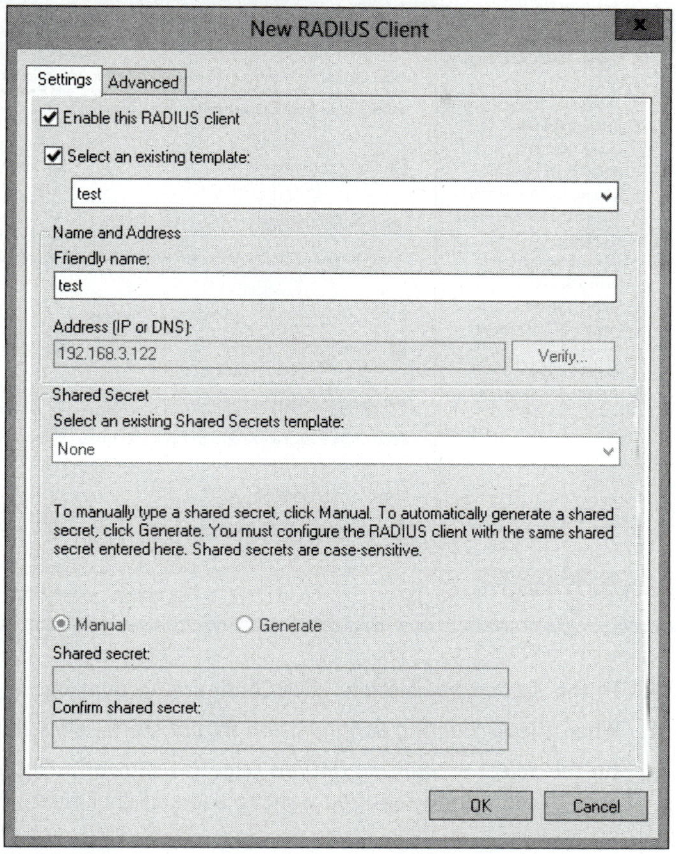

Configuring RADIUS Accounting

> NPS supports ***RADIUS accounting***, which you can use to track network usage for auditing and billing purposes.

CERTIFICATION READY
Configure RADIUS accounting.
Objective 4.1

When configured for accounting, NPS can log accounting data to a text log file and/or a SQL Server database. When accounting is enabled, at the start of the service delivery, the NPS server generates an Accounting-Start message describing the type of service being delivered and the user it is being delivered to, which is sent to the RADIUS Accounting server. The RADIUS Accounting server sends back an acknowledgment to the RADIUS client. At the end of service delivery, the client generates an Accounting-Stop message that describes the type of service that was delivered, and optional statistics, such as elapsed time, input and output octets, or input and output packets. It then sends that data to the RADIUS Accounting server, which sends back an acknowledgment to the RADIUS client.

ENABLE AND CONFIGURE ACCOUNTING IN NPS

GET READY. To enable and configure accounting on NPS, perform the following steps:

1. Open the Server Manager.
2. Click Tools > Network Policy Server. The Network Policy Server console opens.
3. On the NPS tree, click Accounting. The *Accounting* pane is shown in Figure 12-27.

Figure 12-27

Looking at the Accounting configuring options

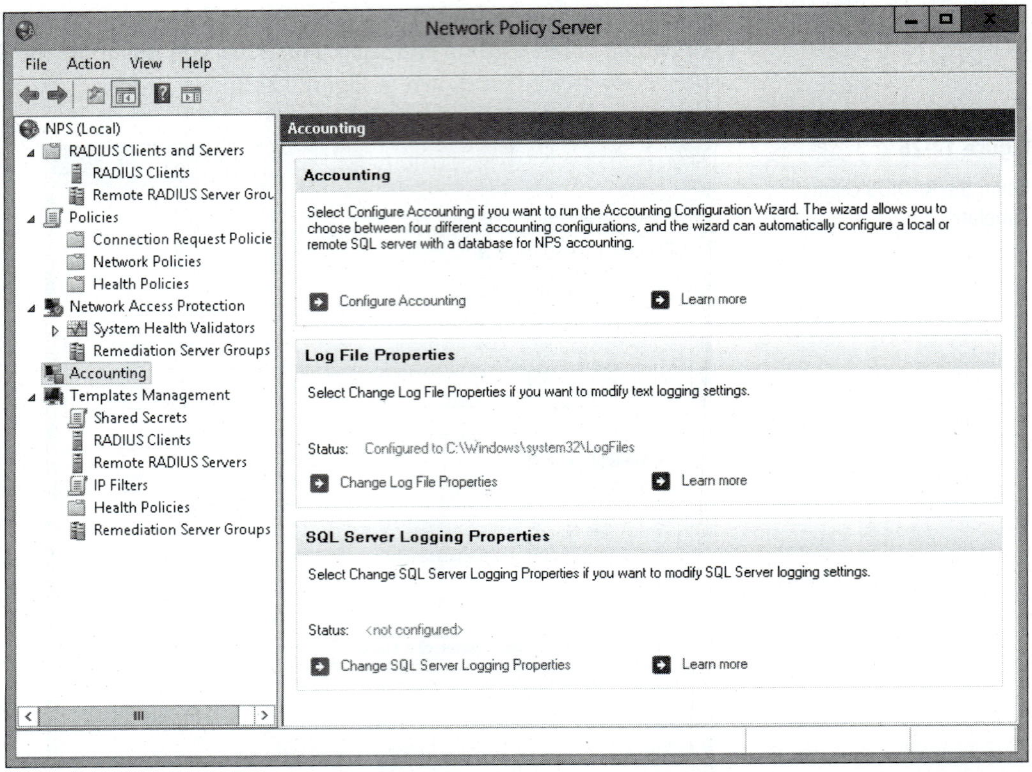

4. In the *Accounting* section, click Configure Accounting.
5. When the *Accounting Configuration Wizard* starts, click Next.
6. On the *Select Accounting Options* page (as shown in Figure 12-28), select the accounting option that you want to use and click Next.

Figure 12-28

Selecting Accounting options

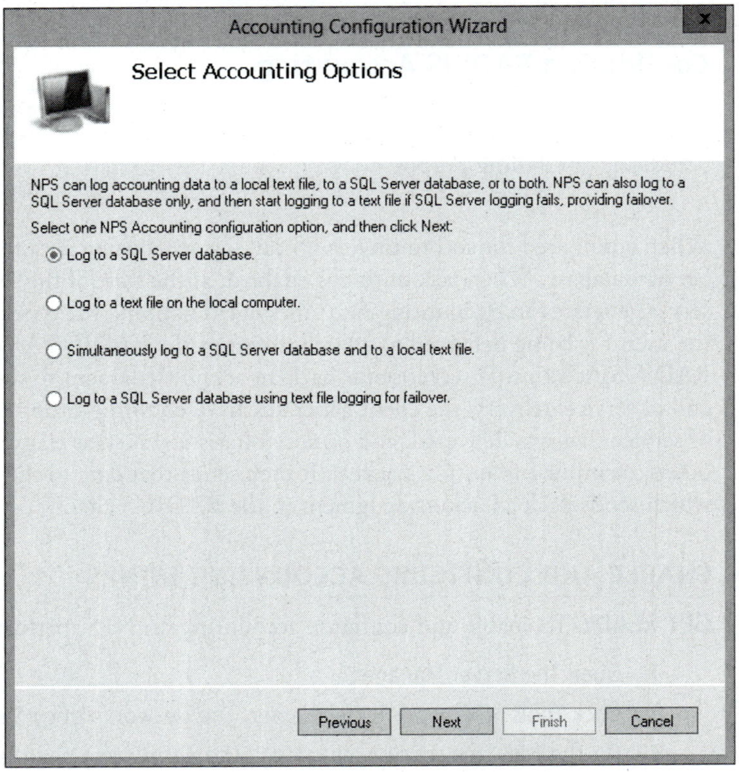

7. If you choose to use the SQL server, the *Configure SQL Server Logging* page appears (see Figure 12-29). To configure the SQL connection, click Configure.

Figure 12-29

Configuring SQL Server logging

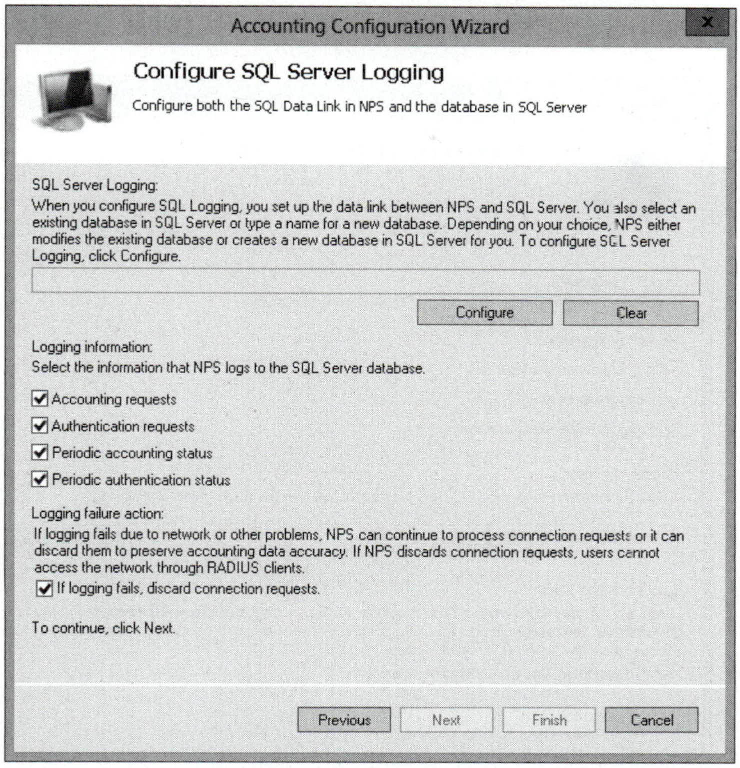

8. When the *Data Link Properties* dialog box opens (see Figure 12-30), specify the name of the SQL server in the *Select or enter a server name* text box and click Refresh. Then specify the user name and password that has access to the SQL server database that you want to log to. Select the database using the *Select the database on the server* pull-down menu. To verify the SQL connection, click Test Connection. Click OK to close the *Data Link Properties* dialog box.

Figure 12-30

Configuring the Data Link properties

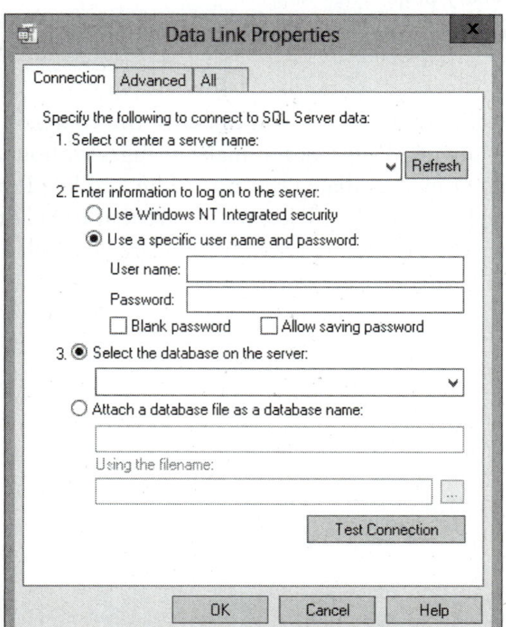

9. If you select to save the data into a local text file, the *Configure Local File Logging* page appears (see Figure 12-31). Notice the path of the log file is C:\Windows\System32\LogFiles. Click **Next**.

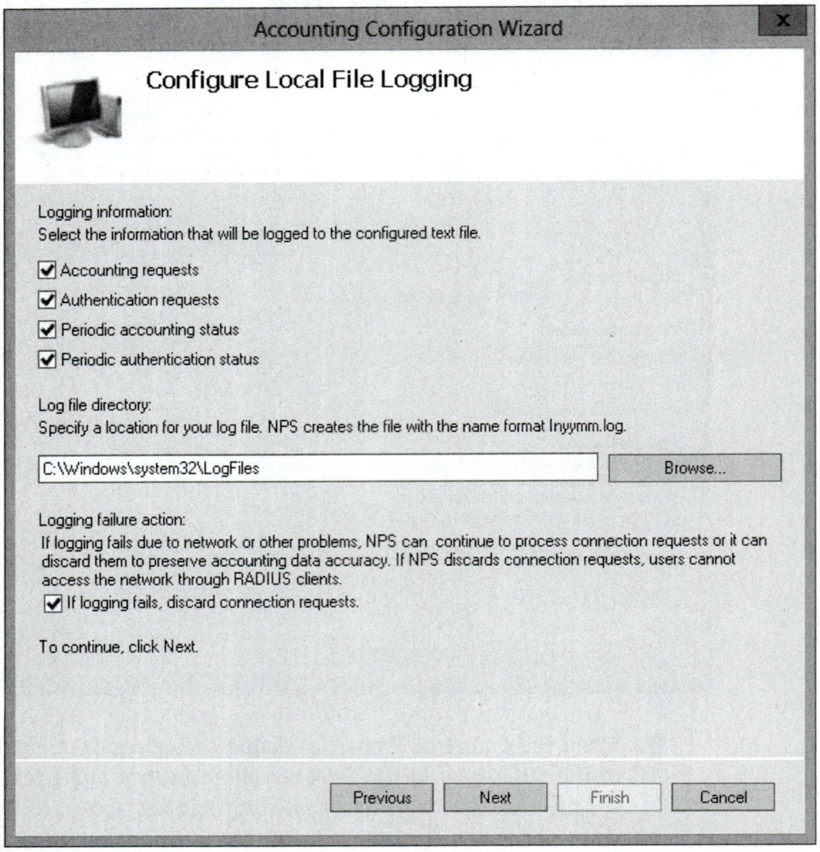

Figure 12-31
Configuring local file logging

10. On the *Summary* page, click **Next**.
11. On the *Conclusion* page, click **Close**.

After you run the Accounting Wizard, you can click the Change Log File Properties or the Change SQL Server Logging Properties to make changes without rerunning the wizard. The Change Log File Properties dialog box opens the Log File Properties, as shown in Figure 12-32. If you choose the Log Files, make sure that the C drive is large enough to hold the logs or move the log files to a drive that is large enough.

Figure 12-32

Configuring Log File properties

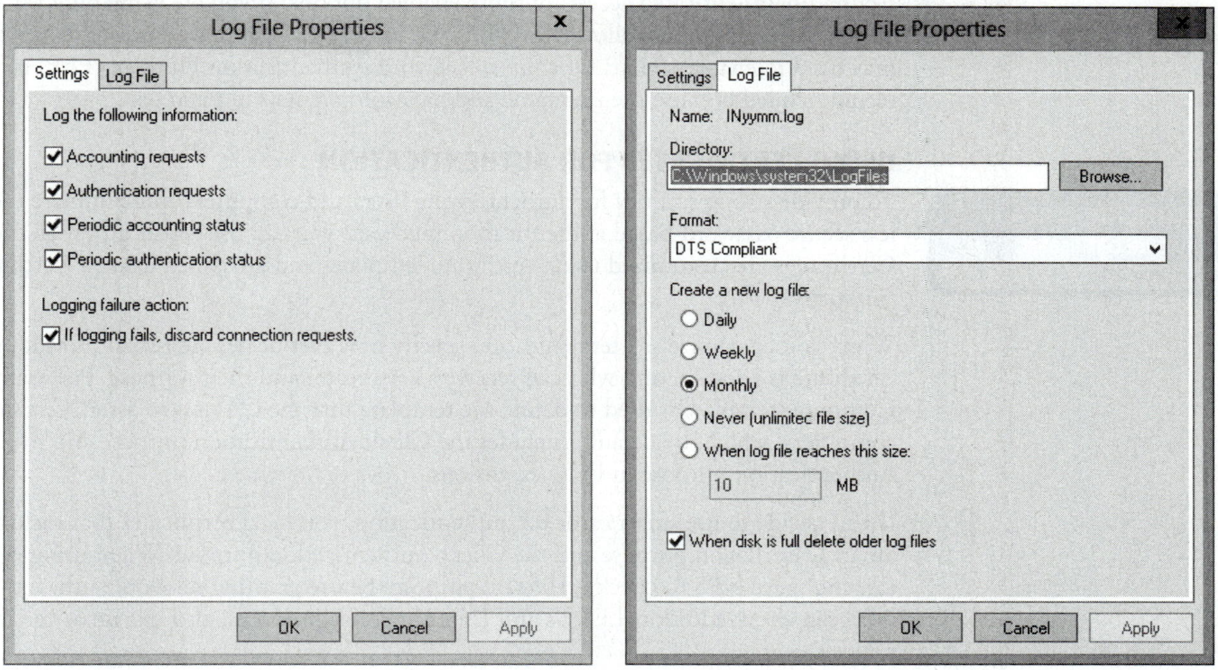

When selecting which RADIUS attributes to record, you should include the RADIUS Class attribute, which will be used to track usage and simplify the identification of which department or user to charge the usage. It should be noted that if a request is lost, a duplicate request may be sent. Therefore, to accurately track usage, you will need to delete duplicate requests.

Understanding NPS Authentication Methods

As already stated throughout the lesson, NPS authenticates and authorizes a connection request before allowing or denying access when a user attempts to connect to a network through a network access server such as a VPN server. NPS must receive proof of the identity of the user or computer.

Authentication is usually broken down into the following categories:

- Password-based credentials
- Certificate-based credentials

When you deploy NPS, you can specify the required type of authentication method for access to your network.

USING PASSWORD-BASED AUTHENTICATION

When a user uses password-based credentials, the network access server passes the username and password to the NPS server, which verifies the credentials against the user account database, either a domain database or a local server database. Unfortunately, password-based authentication is not considered strong security. As a result, certificate authentication or multi-factor authentication is recommended.

However, if you do use password-based authentication, it is processed from the most secure (Microsoft Challenge-Handshake Authentication Protocol v2 or MS-CHAPv2) to the least secure (unauthenticated access) of those enabled options. If you are using only Microsoft clients, you should only allow MS-CHAPv2. However, if you have some non-MS clients, you may need to enable CHAP. Of course, Password Authentication Protocol (PAP) is never recommended because the username and password are sent in plain text.

USING CERTIFICATES FOR AUTHENTICATION

CERTIFICATION READY
Configure certificates.
Objective 4.1

To provide strong security for authenticating users and computers and eliminate the need for less secure password-based authentication methods, you can use certificates with the NPS. Certificates are customized using certificate templates and are issued using a Certificate Authority.

When you customize the template, you specify how certificates are issued (how long a certificate is good for and who can receive a certificate) and their purpose. For example, the Computer template is used to define the template that the CA uses to assign certificates to computers, which, by default, includes the Client Authentication purpose and the Server Authentication purpose in EKU extensions.

If you decide to use smart cards for authentication, you need certificates that include the Smart Card Logon purpose and the Client Authentication purpose. When using NPS, you can configure NPS to check certificate purposes before granting network authorization. NPS can check additional EKUs and Issuance Policy purposes, also known as certificate policies.

If you decide to use Protected Extensible Authentication Protocol Microsoft Challenge-Handshake Authentication Protocol v2 (PEAP-MS-CHAP v2), Protected Extensible Authentication Protocol Transport Layer Security (PEAP-TLS), or Extensible Authentication Protocol Transport Layer Security (EAP-TLS) as the authentication method, the computers need a digital certificate installed, and the NPS server must use a server certificate that meets the minimum server certificate requirements.

AUTOMATICALLY ADD WORKSTATION AUTHENTICATION CERTIFICATES TO ALL WORKSTATIONS

GET READY. To automatically add workstation certificates to all workstations, perform the following steps:

1. On the server that has the Certificate Authority, open the Server Manager.
2. Click Tools > Certificate Authority. The Certificate Authority opens.
3. Expand the server. Then right-click Certificate Templates and select Manage. The *Certificate Templates console* opens.
4. Right-click the Workstation Authentication template and select Duplicate Template. The *Properties of New Template* dialog box opens.
5. Select the General tab.
6. Type a new name for the certificate template in the *Template display name* text box.
7. Select the Security tab.
8. In *Group or user names*, click Domain Computers (see Figure 12-33).

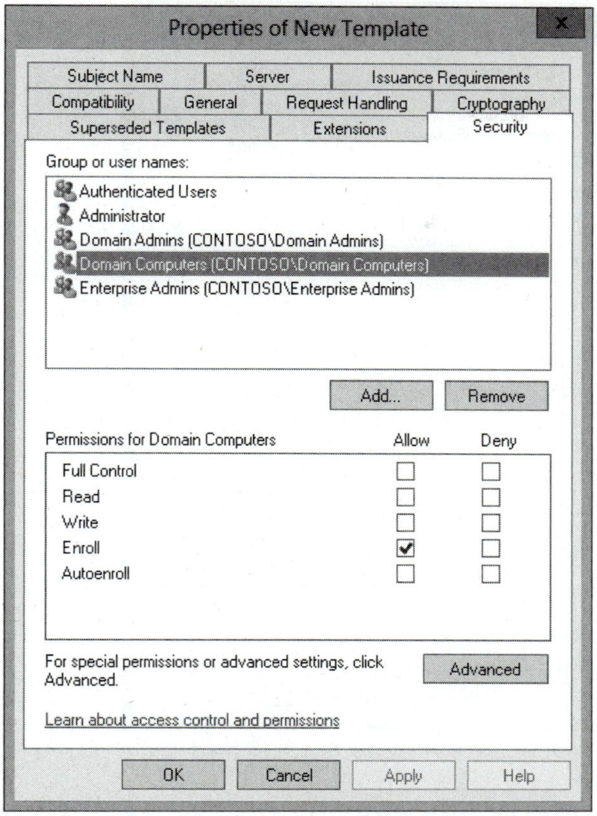

Figure 12-33

Configuring security for a template

9. Under *Allow*, select the Enroll and Autoenroll permission check boxes.
10. Click OK to close the *Properties of New Template* dialog box.
11. Close the *Certificate Templates console*.
12. On the *Certificate Authority console*, right-click Certificate Templates, select New, and select Certificate Template to Issue. The *Enable Certificate Templates* dialog box opens.
13. Click the name of the certificate template you just configured, and then click OK.
14. Close the *Certificate Authority console*.
15. From the Server Manager, click Tools > Group Policy Management console. The *Group Policy Management console* opens.
16. Right-click the Default Domain Policy and select Edit. The *Group Policy Management Editor* opens.
17. Open *Computer Configuration\Policies\Windows Settings\Security Settings\Public Key Policies*.
18. Double-click Certificate Services Client – Auto-Enrollment. The *Certificate Services Client – Auto-Enrollment* dialog box opens (see Figure 12-34).
19. Select Enabled for the Configuration Model.
20. Select the Renew expired certificates, update pending certificates, and remove revoked certificates check box.
21. Select the Update certificates that use certificate templates check box.
22. Click OK to close the *Certificate Services Client – Auto-Enrollment* dialog box.

Figure 12-34

Configuring user and computer certificate—Auto-Enrollment

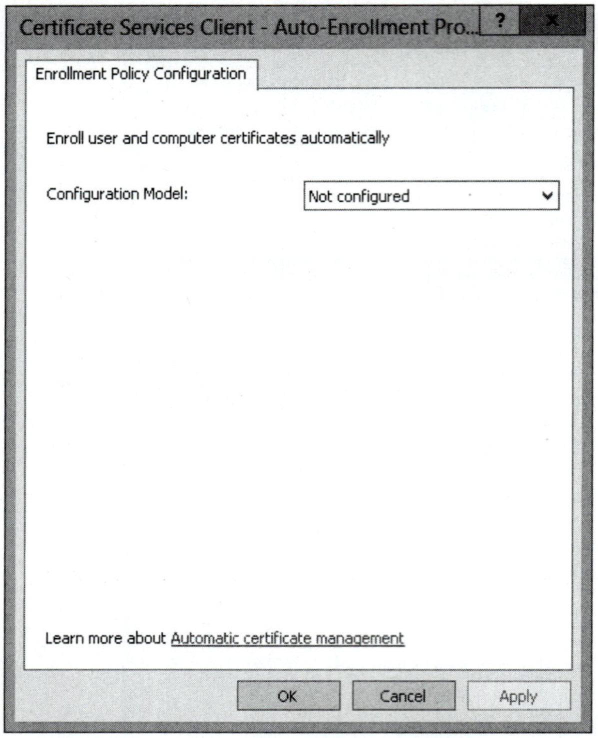

AUTOMATICALLY ADD RAS AND IAS SERVER CERTIFICATES TO ALL WORKSTATIONS

GET READY. To automatically add workstation certificates to all workstations, perform the following steps:

1. On the server that has the Certificate Authority, open the Server Manager.
2. Click Tools > Certificate Authority. The *Certificate Authority* opens.
3. Expand the server, right-click Certificate Templates, and then select Manage. The *Certificate Templates console* opens.
4. Right-click the RAS and IAS template and select Duplicate Template. The *Properties of New Template* dialog box opens.
5. Select the General tab.
6. Type a new name for the certificate template in the *Template display name* text box.
7. Select the Security tab.
8. In *Group or user names*, click RAS and IAS Servers.
9. Under *Allow*, select the Enroll and Autoenroll permission check boxes.
10. Click OK to close the *Properties of New Template* dialog box.
11. Close the *Certificate Templates console*.
12. Back on the *Certificate Authority console*, right-click Certificate Templates, select New, and select Certificate Template to Issue. The *Enable Certificate Templates* dialog box opens.
13. Click the name of the certificate template you just configured, and then click OK.
14. Close the *Certificate Authority console*.

SKILL SUMMARY

IN THIS LESSON, YOU LEARNED:

- Microsoft's RADIUS server is Network Policy Server (NPS).
- By installing and configuring RADIUS, you can create and enforce wide network access policies for client health, connection request authentication, and connection request authorization.
- When you implement RADIUS, Windows Server 2012 computers running Routing and Remote Access and/or wireless access points can forward access requests to a single RADIUS server.
- Installing NPS is a simple process, which is done with Server Manager. After NPS is installed, you use the Network Policy Server console to configure NPS.
- If you have multiple RADIUS servers, you can configure RADIUS clients to use a primary RADIUS server and alternate RADIUS servers. If the primary RADIUS server becomes unavailable, the request is sent to the alternate RADIUS server.
- Much like the use of other templates, RADIUS templates are designed to reduce the amount of time and cost that it takes to configure RADIUS on one or more servers.
- Creating a RADIUS template does not affect the functionality of NPS. It affects the RADIUS server only when the template is selected and applied when configuring NPS.
- NPS supports RADIUS accounting, which you can use to track network usage for auditing and billing purposes.
- To provide strong security for authenticating users and computers and eliminate the need for less secure password-based authentication methods, you can use certificates with the NPS.

Knowledge Assessment

Multiple Choice

Select the correct answer for each of the following questions.

1. Which ports does NPS use for authentication and accounting? (Choose four answers.)
   a. 389
   b. 1812
   c. 1813
   d. 80
   e. 1645
   f. 1646

2. You have several VPN servers configured using RRAS. What is the best way to collect information on when and how long someone is connected through the VPN?
   a. Health policies
   b. RADIUS Accounting
   c. System health validators (SHVs)
   d. Connection request policy
   e. Windows Accounting provider

3. Which do you use to provide central authentication of VPN and wireless connections on the network?
   a. Use an NPS server.
   b. Use a HRA.
   c. Use CMAK.
   d. Use RRAS.

4. Which of the following are access clients? (Choose all that apply.)
   a. Domain controller
   b. VPN server
   c. Dial-up server
   d. 802.1X server

5. Which of the following is used to save a configuration so that it can be reused on other NPS servers?
   a. filter
   b. shared secrets
   c. templates
   d. health policy

6. Which two locations can NPS log to? (Choose two answers.)
   a. Oracle database
   b. SQL server
   c. Text file
   d. XML repository

7. To use EAP-TSL, each client must have which of the following?
   a. Digital certificate
   b. Workstation token
   c. Health policy
   d. Workstation template

8. Which of the following are used with NPS templates? (Choose all that apply.)
   a. Remote RADIUS servers
   b. RADIUS passwords
   c. RADIUS proxy
   d. RADIUS clients

9. Microsoft's RADIUS server is known as which of the following?
   a. Network Policy Server
   b. Routing and Remote Access Server
   c. Network Access Policy Server
   d. AAA Server

10. Which of the following tracks network usage for auditing and billing purposes?
    a. RADIUS Authorization
    b. RADIUS Access
    c. RADIUS Accounting
    d. RADIUS Auditing

11. Which of the following is the default location for the log files if you use text files for RADIUS accounting?
    a. C:\Temp
    b. C:\Windows\System32\LogFiles
    c. C:\Logs
    d. C:\RADIUS\Logs

Best Answer

Choose the letter that corresponds to the best answer. More than one answer choice may achieve the goal. Select the BEST answer.

1. You have a server called Server1 that runs Network Policy Server. You install a second server called Server2 that sends all request to server1. What should you do?
   a. Modify health policies.
   b. Modify the RADIUS clients.
   c. Modify the remote RADIUS server groups.
   d. Modify the network policies.
2. You have a server called Server1 that runs Network Policy Server. Server1 is configured to use SQL logging. You install Server2, which also runs Network Policy Server. You want to make sure that the two servers are configured the same. Therefore, you export the NPS settings from Server1 and import the settings into Server2. What should you do next?
   a. Create an ODBC data course to Server1.
   b. Create an ODBC data source to a SQL server.
   c. Manually configure the SQL logging settings.
   d. Restart the Server2.
3. When using a RADIUS proxy, which policy is used to determine what connection requests are forwarded to another RADIUS server?
   a. RADIUS proxy policy
   b. Dynamic policy
   c. Proxy forward policy
   d. Connection request policy
4. Which of the following are reasons that to use multiple RADIUS servers? (Choose two answers.)
   a. To enable auditing
   b. To provide multiple RADIUS services
   c. To break up the workload when performing authentication
   d. To provide fault-tolerance
5. When a computer or device accesses a VPN server and uses RADIUS for authentication, what is the computer or device referred to as?
   a. RADIUS client
   b. Access server
   c. Access client
   d. RADIUS proxy

Matching and Identification

1. Match the term with the definition.
   _______ a) RADIUS clients
   _______ b) Access client
   _______ c) RADIUS
   _______ d) RADIUS proxy

   1. A networking and client/server protocol that provides AAA management for computers and network devices.
   2. Servers that use AAA services for central authentication.
   3. A workstation that connects to a network through a remote server and requires authentication to connect to the network.
   4. A server that provides central switching for RADIUS access and account messages.

2. Identify which of the following are password-based authentication and which are certificate-based authentication.
   _______ a) MS-CHAPv2
   _______ b) PEAP-MS-CHAPv2
   _______ c) CHAP
   _______ d) PAP
   _______ e) EAP-TLS

Build a List

1. Identify the three As, in order, for AAA management. Not all of the answers will be used.
   _____ Accounting
   _____ Authentication
   _____ Allowed access
   _____ Attribute
   _____ Authorization
   _____ Application
   _____ Access control

2. Specify the correct steps, in order, to use RADIUS authentication.
   _____ The connection attempt is authorized.
   _____ The NPS server sends an Accounting-Response to the access server.
   _____ The request is forward to a NPS server, which evaluates the connection request.
   _____ User credentials are checked and the dial-in properties are obtained.
   _____ The access server sends an Accounting-Request message to the NPS server.
   _____ A client computer accesses a VPN server, and a connection request is generated.

Business Case Scenarios

Scenario 12-1: Supporting Multiple VPN Servers

You have two VPN servers. One is located on the main corporate office and the second is located at the backup site. You want to provide centralized authentication and logging. What should you do?

Scenario 12-2: Securing VPN Connections

Your manager approaches you to discuss implementing VPN for the corporate users. However, he is concerned about security. What do you recommend to maintain the best security?

Configuring NPS Policies

LESSON 13

70-411 EXAM OBJECTIVE

Objective 4.2 – Configure NPS policies. This objective may include but is not limited to: configure connection request policies; configure network policies for VPN clients (multilink and bandwidth allocation, IP filters, encryption, IP addressing); manage NPS templates; import and export NPS policies.

Lesson Heading	Exam Objective
Managing NPS Policies	Configure NPS policies
Configuring Connection Request Policies	Configure connection request policies
Configuring Network Policies	Configure network policies for VPN clients (multilink and bandwidth allocation, IP filters, encryption, IP addressing)
Managing NPS Templates	Manage NPS templates Import and export NPS policies

KEY TERMS

connection request policies
health policies
network policies
Network Policy Server templates
NPS policy

■ Managing NPS Policies

THE BOTTOM LINE

An ***NPS policy*** is a set of permissions or restrictions that are used by remote access authenticating servers that determine who, when, and how a client can connect to a network. With the remote access policies, connections can be authorized or denied based on user attributes, group membership, time of day, type of connection, and many other variables.

CERTIFICATION READY
Configure NPS policies.
Objective 4.2

Network Policy Server (NPS) provides three types of policies:

- ***Connection request policies:*** A policy that establishes sets of conditions and settings that specify which RADIUS servers perform the authentication, authorization, and accounting of connection requests received by the NPS server from RADIUS clients. It can also be used to designate which RADIUS servers are used for RADIUS accounting.
- ***Network policies:*** A policy that establishes sets of conditions, constraints, and settings that specify who is authorized to connect to the network and the circumstances under which they can or cannot connect.
- ***Health policies:*** A policy that establishes one or more system health validators (SHVs) and other settings that enable you to define client computer configuration requirements for the Network Access Policy (NAP)-capable computers that attempt to connect to your network. Health policies are used only with NAP. NAP is discussed in Lesson 14.

Figure 13-1 shows the Policies pane in NPS.

Figure 13-1
Looking at NPS policies

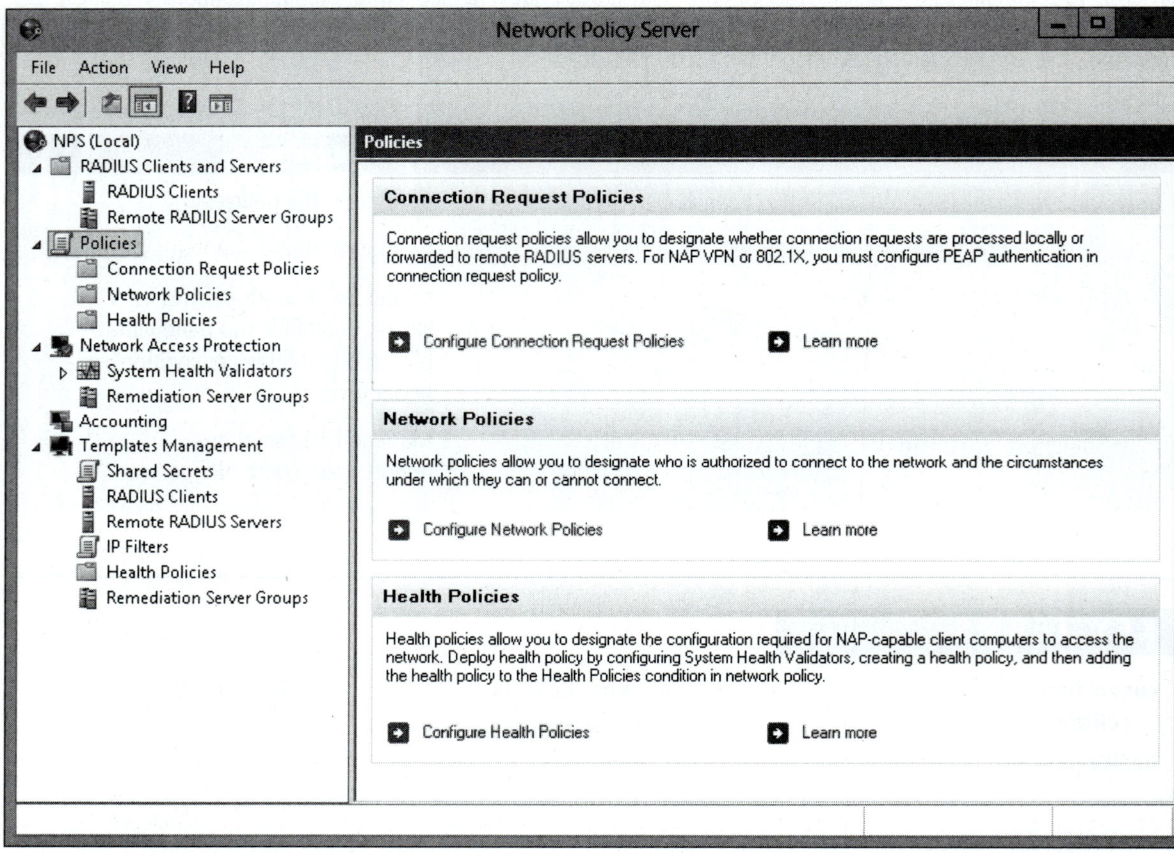

Configuring Connection Request Policies

Connection request policies determine which RADIUS servers will perform the authentication and authorization of connection requests of RADIUS clients for servers running NPS. It can also be used to specify RADIUS accounting.

CERTIFICATION READY
Configure connection request policies.
Objective 4.2

Connection request polices are applied to NPS as a RADIUS server or as a RADIUS proxy. The policies are based on a range of factors such as the following:

- The time of day and day of the week
- The realm name in the connection request

- The type of connection requested
- The IP address of the RADIUS client

When you create a connection request policy, you define the following parameters:

- Type of network access server such as Remote Access server (VPN dial-up)
- Condition that species who or what can connect to the network based on one or more RADIUS attributes
- Settings that are applied to an incoming RADIUS message, such as authentication, accounting, and attribute manipulation

RADIUS Access-Request messages are processed or forwarded by NPS only if the settings of the incoming message match at least one of the connection request policies configured on the NPS server. If the policy settings match and the policy requires that the NPS server processes the message, NPS acts as a RADIUS server, authenticating and authorizing the connection request.

Connection request policy conditions are one or more RADIUS attributes that are compared to the attributes of the incoming RADIUS Access-Request message (see table 13-1). If there are multiple conditions, then all the conditions in the connection request message and in the connection request policy must match in order for the policy to be enforced by NPS.

Table 13-1

Conditions Used in Connection Request Policies

Group	Attribute	Description
Username	User Name	Designates the user name (including the realm/domain name and a user account name) that is used by the access client in the RADIUS message.
Connection Properties	Access Client IPv4 Address	Designates the Internet Protocol version 4 (IPv4) address of the Access client that requests access from the RADIUS client.
	Access Client IPv6 Address	Designates the Internet Protocol version 6 (IPv6) address of the Access client that requests access from the RADIUS client.
	Framed Protocol	Designates the type of framing for incoming packets, such as Point-to-Point Protocol (PPP), Serial Line Internet Protocol (SLIP), Frame Relay, and X.25.
	Service Type	Designates the type of service requested, such as framed (for example, PPP connections) and login (for example, Telnet connections).
	Tunnel Type	Designates the type of tunnel that is created by the requesting client, such as Point-to-Point Tunneling Protocol (PPTP) and Layer Two Tunneling Protocol (L2TP).
Day and Time Restriction	Day and Time Restriction	Designates the day of the week and the time of day a connection can be made.
Identity Type	Identity Type	Used to restrict the policy to only clients that can be identified through the special mechanism, such as NAP statement of health (SoH).

(continued)

Table 13-1
(continued)

Group	Attribute	Description
RADIUS Client Properties	Calling Station ID	Designates the phone number used by the caller (the access client). This attribute is a character string. You can use pattern-matching syntax to specify area codes.
	Client Friendly Name	Designates the name of the RADIUS client computer that requests authentication.
	Client IPv4 Address	Specifies the IPv4 address of the RADIUS client that forwarded the connection request to NPS.
	Client IPv6 Address	Specifies the IPv6 address of the RADIUS client that forwarded the connection request to NPS.
	Client Vendor	Specifies the name of the vendor of the RADIUS client that sends reconnection requests to NPS.
Gateway	Called Station ID	Specifies a character string that is the telephone number of the network access server (NAS).
	NAS Identifier	Specifies a character string that is the name of the NAS.
	NAS IPv4 Address	Designates the IPv4 address of the network access server (the RADIUS client).
	NAS IPv6 Address	Designates the IPv6 address of the network access server (the RADIUS client).
	NAS Port Type	NAS Port Type condition specifies the type of media used by the access client, such as analog phone lines, Integrated Services Digital Network (ISDN) tunnels, VPN connection, IEEE 802.11 wireless, and Ethernet switches.

The default connection request policy uses NPS as a RADIUS server and processes all authentication requests locally. If you do not want the NPS server to act as a RADIUS server and process connection requests locally, you can delete the default connection request policy.

To configure a server running NPS to act as a RADIUS proxy and forward connection requests to other NPS or RADIUS servers, you must configure a remote RADIUS server group in addition to adding a new connection request policy that specifies conditions and settings that the connection requests must match.

CREATE A CONNECTION REQUEST POLICY

GET READY. To create a connection request policy, perform the following steps:

1. Open Server Manager.
2. Click Tools > Network Policy Server. The *Network Policy Server console* opens.
3. Double-click Policies in the NPS tree.
4. Right-click Connection Request Policies, and then click New. The *New Connection Request Policy Wizard* appears (see Figure 13-2).

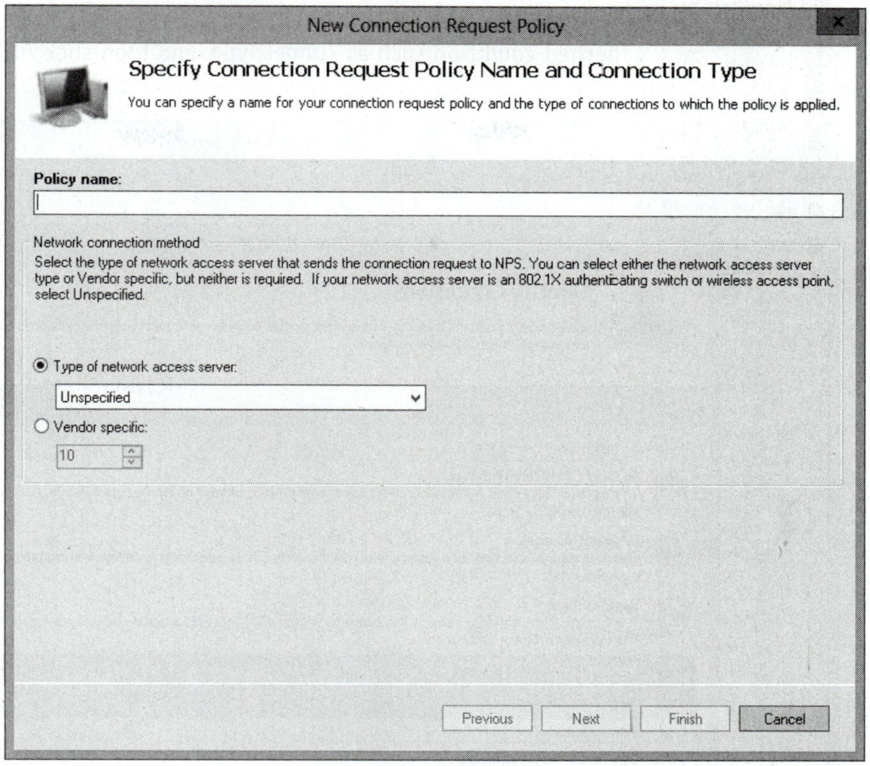

Figure 13-2

Defining the policy name

5. In the *Policy name* text box, type a meaningful name to identify the policy.
6. If desired, select the type of network access server, such as Remote Desktop Gateway, Remote Access Server (VPN-Dial up), DHCP Sever, Health Registration Authority, or Host Credential Authorization Protocol (HCAP) Server. Click Next.
7. On the *Specify Conditions* page (see Figure 13-3), click Add.

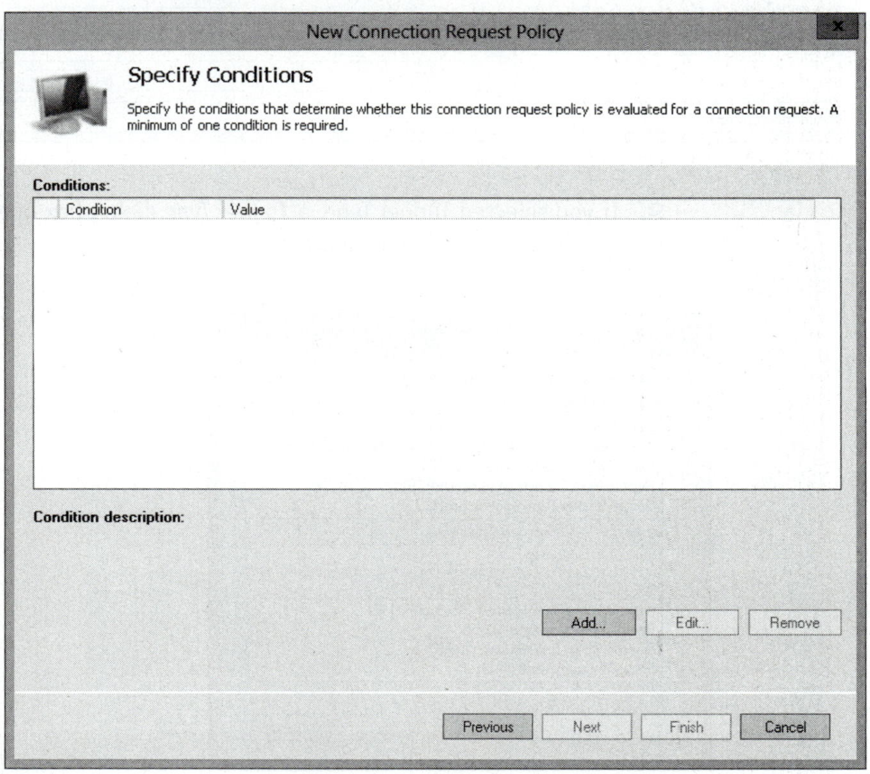

Figure 13-3

Specifying conditions

8. When the *Select condition* dialog box opens (as shown in Figure 13-4), select the desired condition such as Tunnel Type, and then click Add.

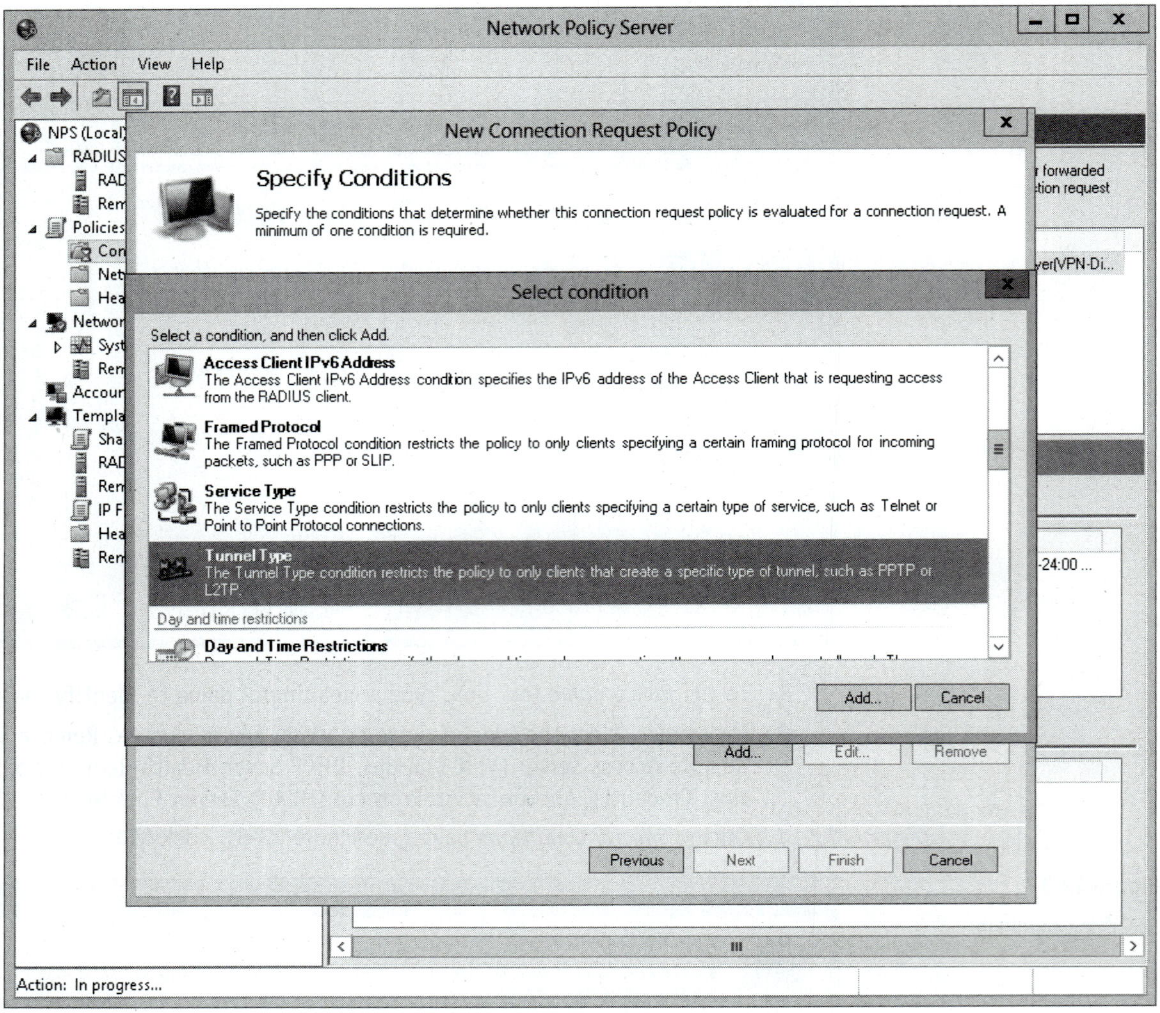

Figure 13-4
Selecting a condition

9. If you selected Tunnel Type, a *Tunnel Type* dialog box opens (see Figure 13-5). Select the desired tunnel type and click OK.

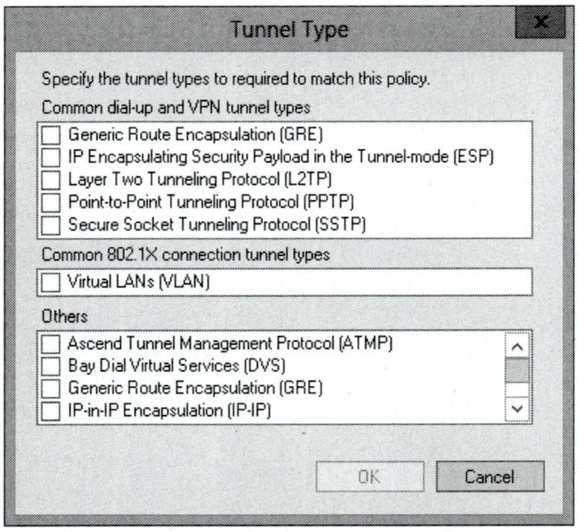

Figure 13-5
Selecting a tunnel type

10. Repeat the process of adding conditions as desired. After the conditions have been added, click Next.

11. On the *Specify Connection Request Forwarding* page (see Figure 13-6), select Authenticate requests on this server, or Accept users without validation credentials. If you have a remote RADIUS server group, you can select the Forward requests to the following remote RADIUS server group for authentication and specify the group. Click Next.

Figure 13-6

Specifying Connection Request Forwarding page

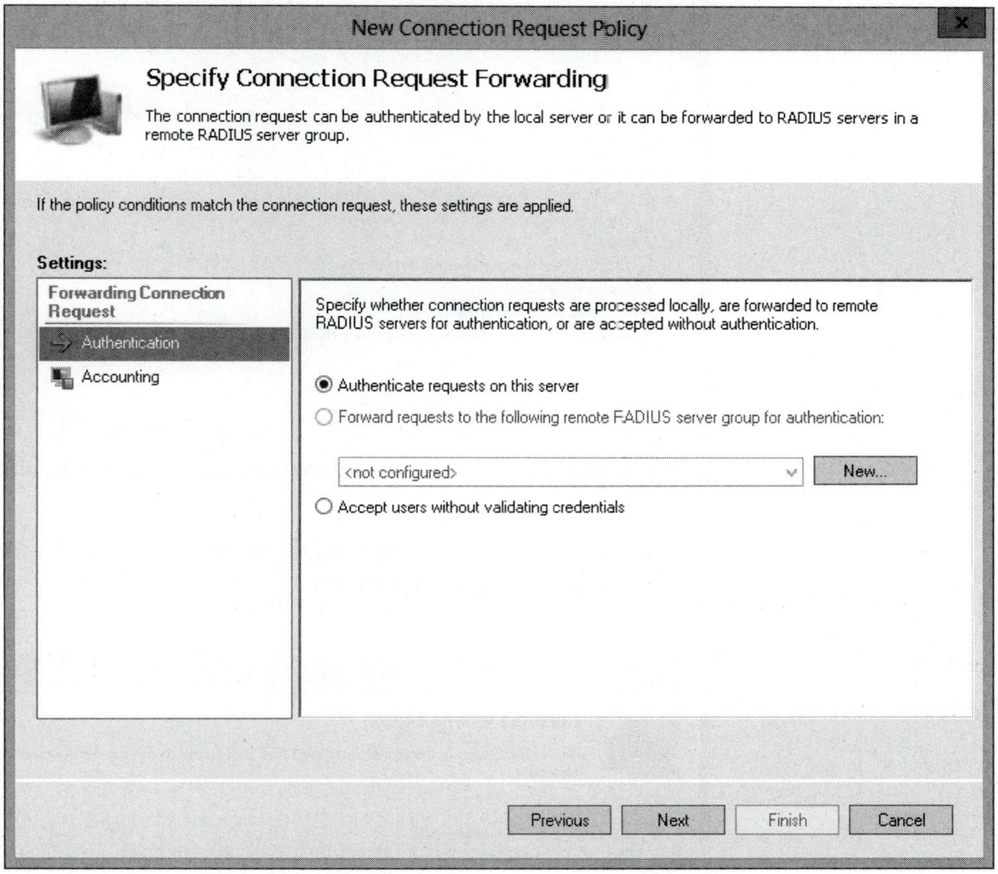

12. On the *Specify Authentication* page (see Figure 13-7), if you want to override the network policy authentication settings, select the Override network policy authentication settings and select or deselect the authentication methods as desired. Click Next.

Figure 13-7

Specifying Authentication page

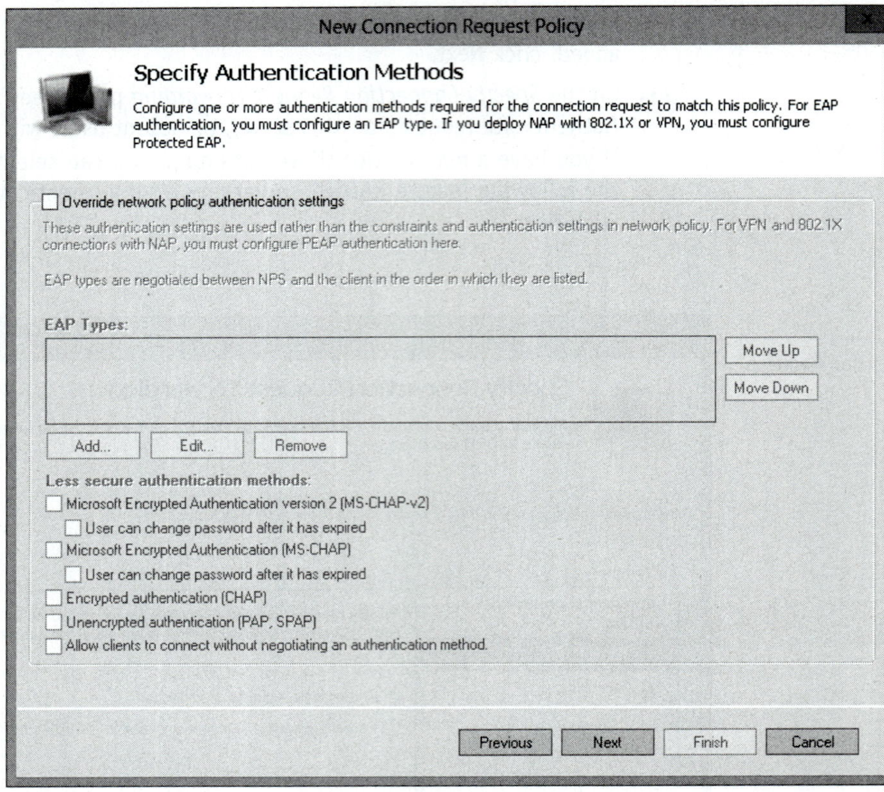

13. On the *Configure Settings* page (as shown in Figure 13-8), specify the Realm name or RADIUS attribute. Click Next.

Figure 13-8

Configuring Settings page

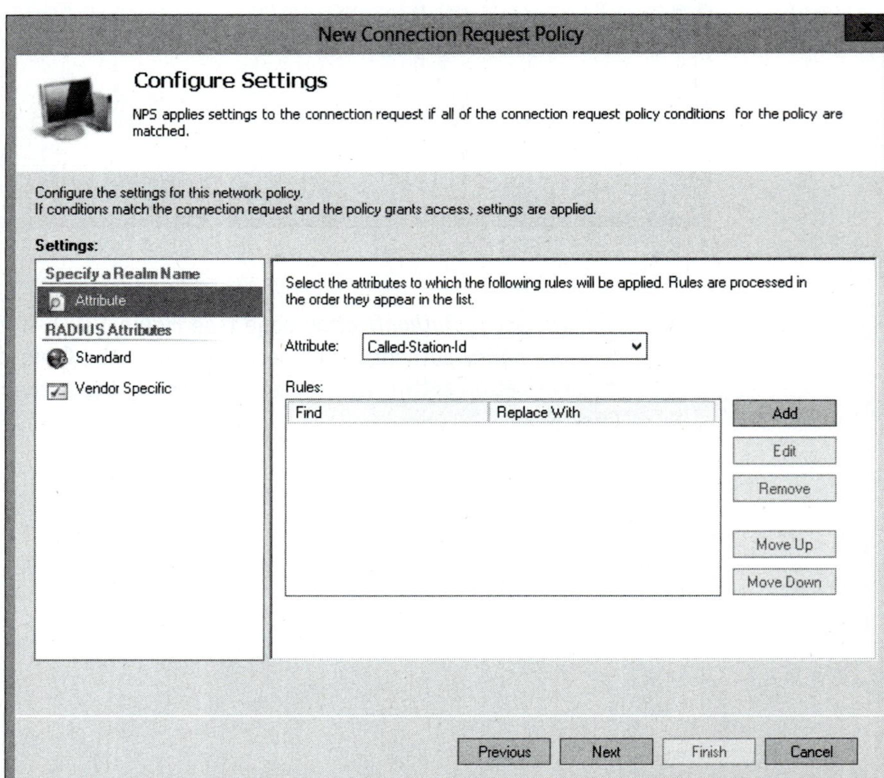

14. On the Completing Connection Request Policy Wizard page (see Figure 13-9), click Finish. When created, the Network Policy is listed in the *Network Policies* pane.

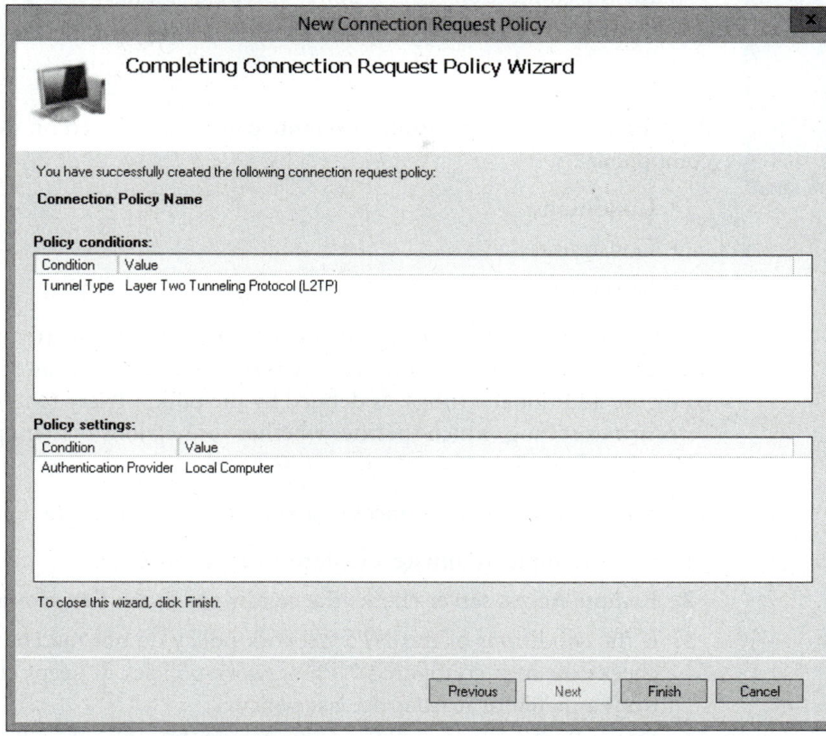

Figure 13-9
Completing the Connection Request Policy Wizard

After a connection request policy has been created, you can modify the policy by right-clicking the policy and selecting *Properties*. When the Properties dialog box opens, you then select the *Overview* tab (as shown in Figure 13-10), *Conditions* tab, or the *Settings* tab.

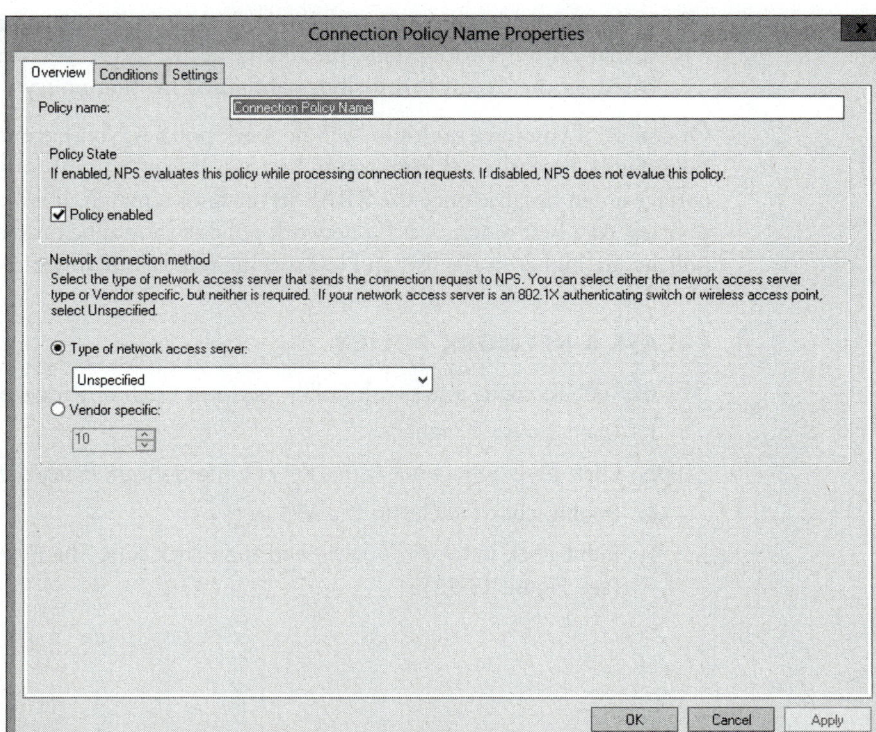

Figure 13-10
Configuring Connection Request Policy properties

Configuring Network Policies

CERTIFICATION READY
Configure network policies for VPN clients (multilink and bandwidth allocation, IP filters, encryption, IP addressing).
Objective 4.2

While the connection request policy specified settings for the RADIUS server, the network policy will allow or disallow the remote access.

An NPS network policy evaluates remote connections based on the following three components:

- Conditions
- Constraints
- Settings

If the conditions and constraints defined by the connection attempt match those configured in the network policy, the remote access server will either allow or deny the connection and configure additional settings, as defined by the policy. Every remote access policy has an Access Permissions setting, which specifies whether connections matching the policy should be allowed or denied.

When a user attempts to connect to a remote access server, the following process takes place:

1. User attempts to initiate a remote access connection.
2. Remote Access server checks the conditions in the first configured NPS network policy.
3. If the conditions of this NPS network policy do not match, the Remote Access server checks the next configured NPS network policies. It keeps checking each policy until it finds a match or reaches the last policy.
4. Once the Remote Access Server finds an NPS network policy with conditions that match the incoming connection attempt, the Remote Access server checks any constraints (such as time of day or minimum encryption level) that have been configured for the policy.
5. If the connection attempt does not match any configured constraints, the Remote Access Server denies the connection.
6. If the connection attempt matches both the conditions and the constraints of a particular NPS network policy, the remote access server will allow or deny the connection, based on the Access Permissions configured for that policy.

Of course, if you have multiple NPS network policies, you have to specify the order in which the policies are evaluated from top to bottom. It is important to place these policies in the correct order, because once the RRAS server finds a match, it will stop processing additional policies. As a best practice, NPS network policies should be ordered so that more specific policies are higher in the list, and less specific policies are lower in the list.

CREATE A NETWORK POLICY

GET READY. To create a network policy, perform the following steps:

1. Open Server Manager.
2. Click Tools > Network Policy Server. The *Network Policy Server console* opens.
3. Double-click Policies in the *NPS tree*.
4. Right-click Network Policies, and then click New. The *New Network Policy Wizard* opens (see Figure 13-11).

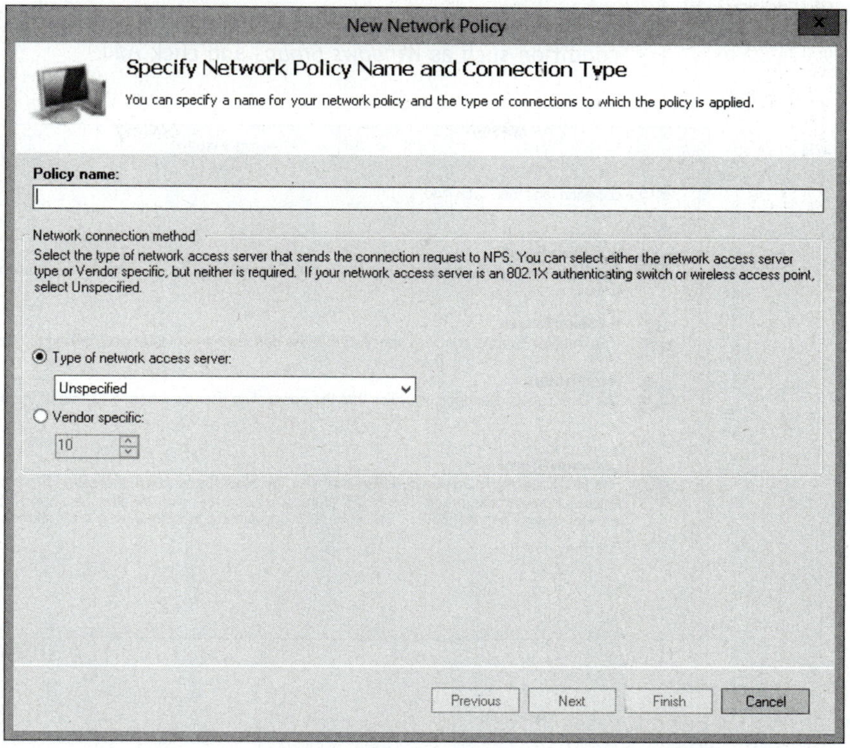

Figure 13-11

Starting the New Network Policy Wizard

5. In the *Policy name* text box, type a meaningful name to identify the policy.
6. If desired, select the type of network access server, such as Remote Desktop Gateway, Remote Access Server (VPN-Dial up), DHCP Sever, Health Registration Authority, or HCAP Server. Click Next.
7. On the *Specify Conditions* page (see Figure 13-12), click Add.

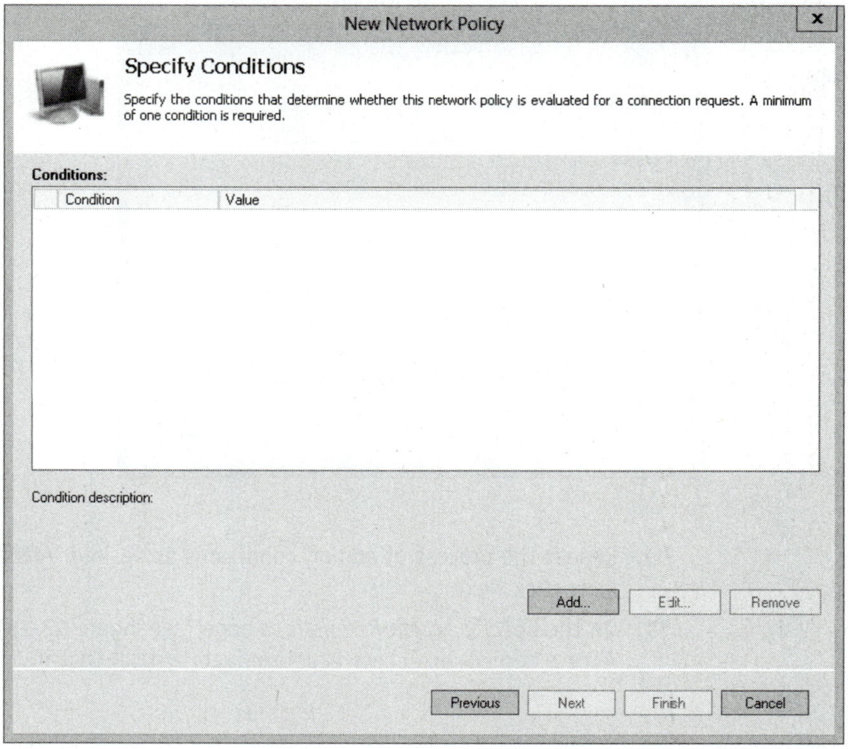

Figure 13-12

Specifying conditions

8. When the *Select condition* dialog box opens (see Figure 13-13), select the desired condition such as *Windows Groups* and click Add.

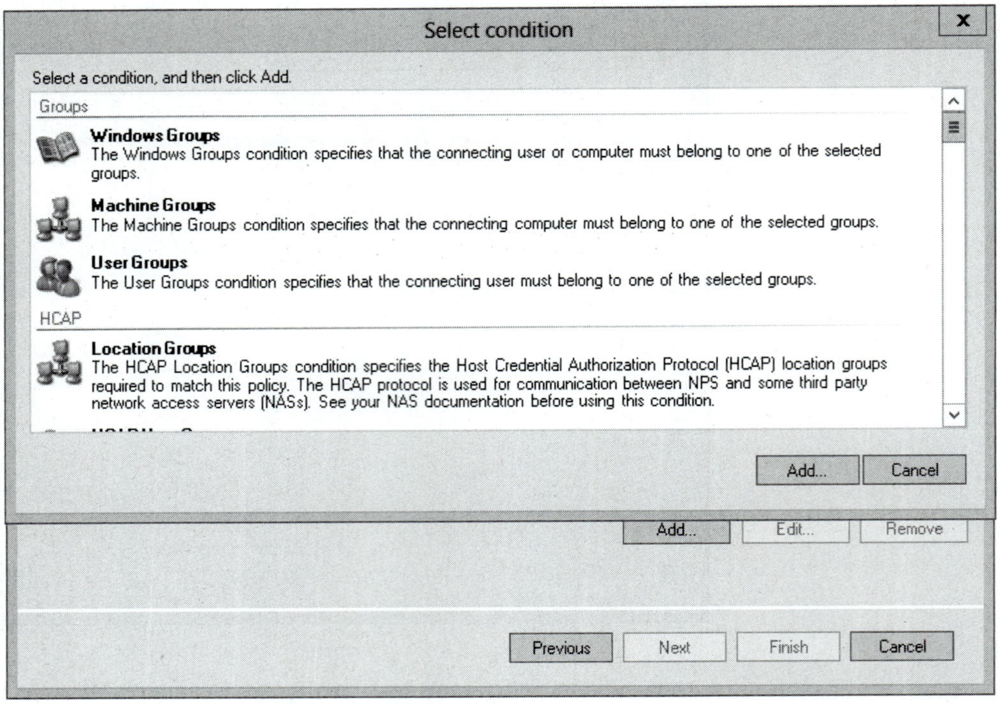

Figure 13-13

Selecting conditions

9. If you selected *Windows Groups*, a *Windows Groups* dialog box opens (see Figure 13-14). Click Add Groups. When the *Select Group* dialog box opens, type the name of the desired group and click OK.

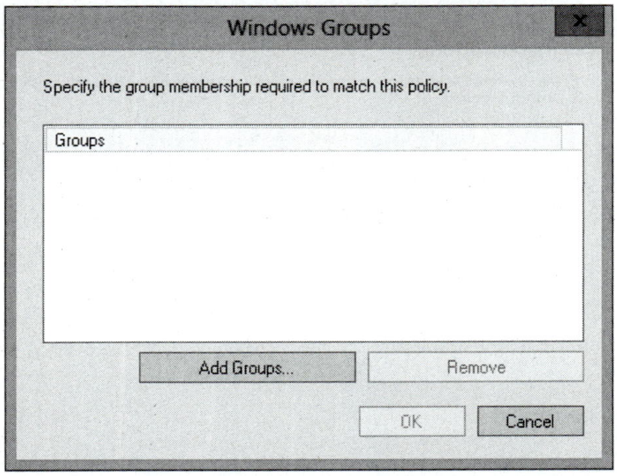

Figure 13-14

Adding Windows groups

10. Repeat the process of adding conditions as desired. After the conditions have been met, click Next.

11. On the *Specify Access Permissions* page (see Figure 13-15), select Access granted, Access denied, or Access is determined by User Dial-in Properties.

Figure 13-15

Specifying access permissions

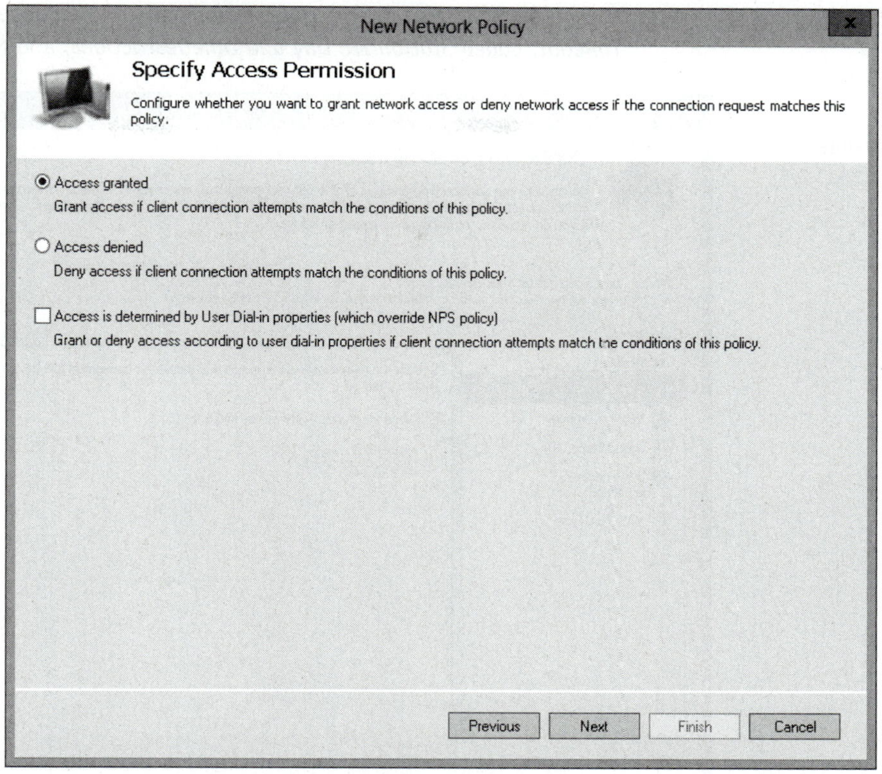

12. On the *Configure Authentication Methods* page (see Figure 13-16), select or deselect the authentication methods. If you need to add an EAP type, click Add to specify Microsoft: Smart Card or other certificate, Microsoft: Protected EAP (PEAP), or Microsoft: Secured password (EAP-MSCHAP v2). Click Next.

Figure 13-16

Configuring authentication methods

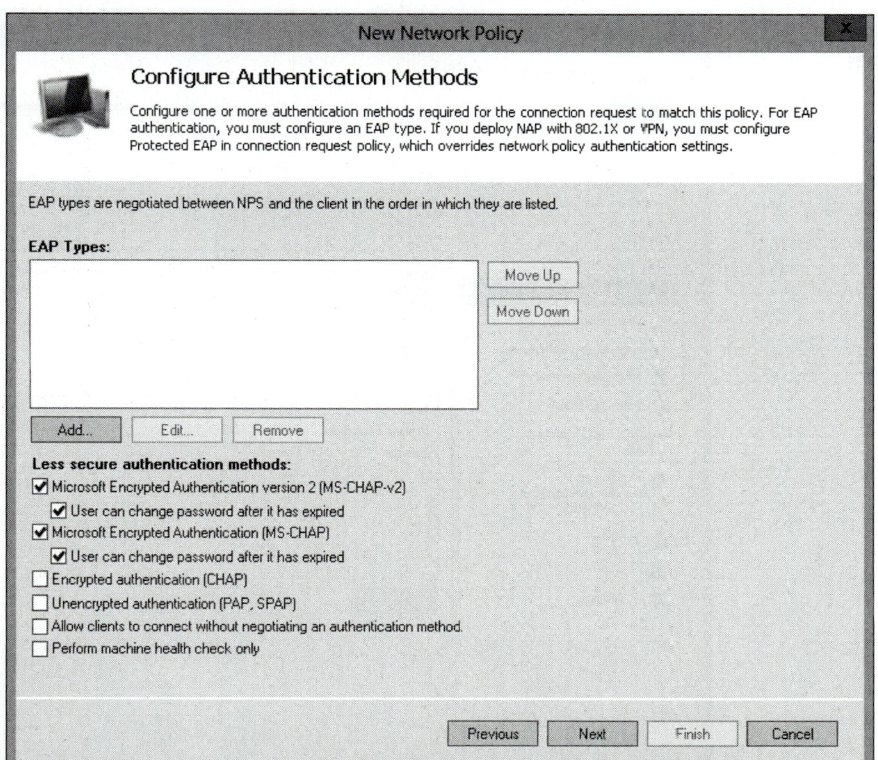

13. On the *Configure Constraints* page (see Figure 13-17), specify the *Idle Timeout, Session Timeout, Called Station ID, Day and time restrictions*, and *NAS Port Type*. Click Next.

Figure 13-17
Configuring constraints

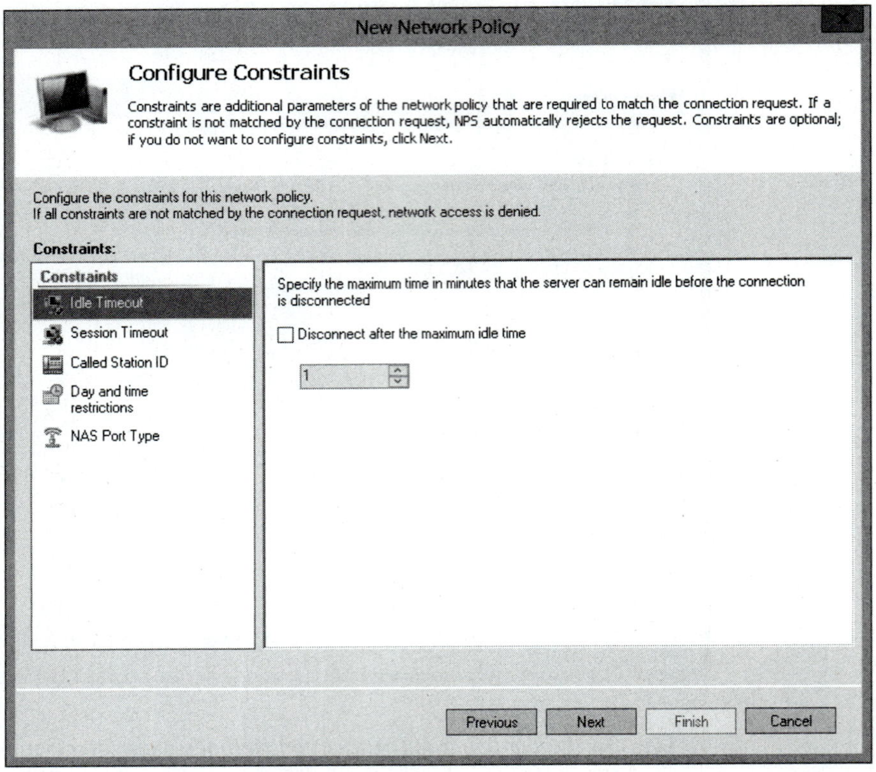

14. On the *Configure Settings* page (see Figure 13-18), specify *RADIUS attributes, Network Access Protection* settings, and *Routing and Remote Access* settings. Click Next.

Figure 13-18
Configuring settings

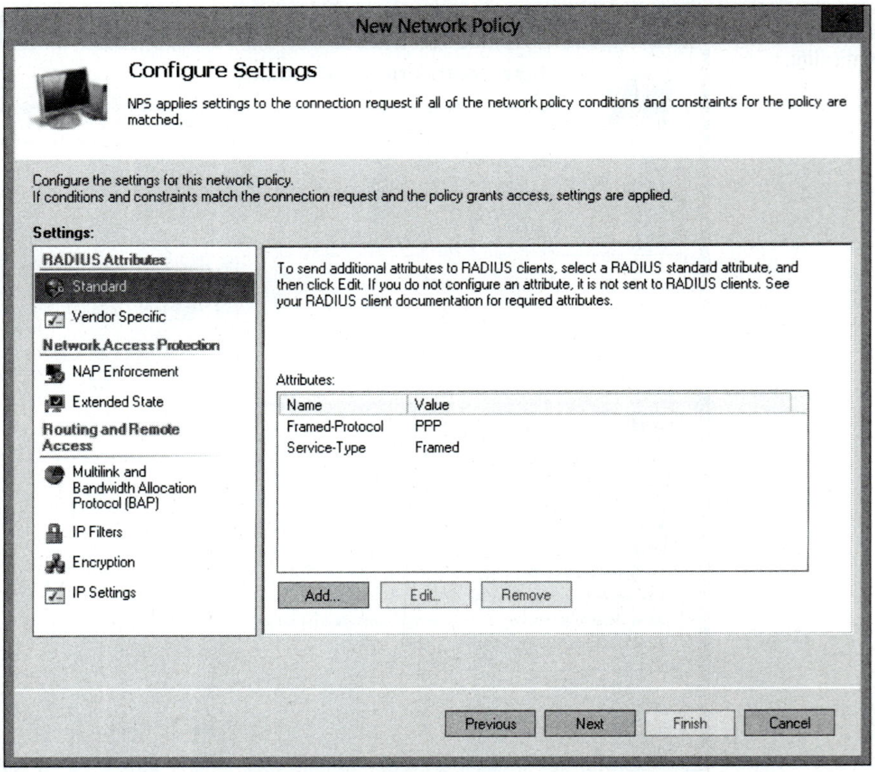

15. On the *Completing New Network Policy* page (see Figure 13-19), click Finish. When created, the network policy is listed in the *Network Policies* pane.

Figure 13-19

Completing new network policies

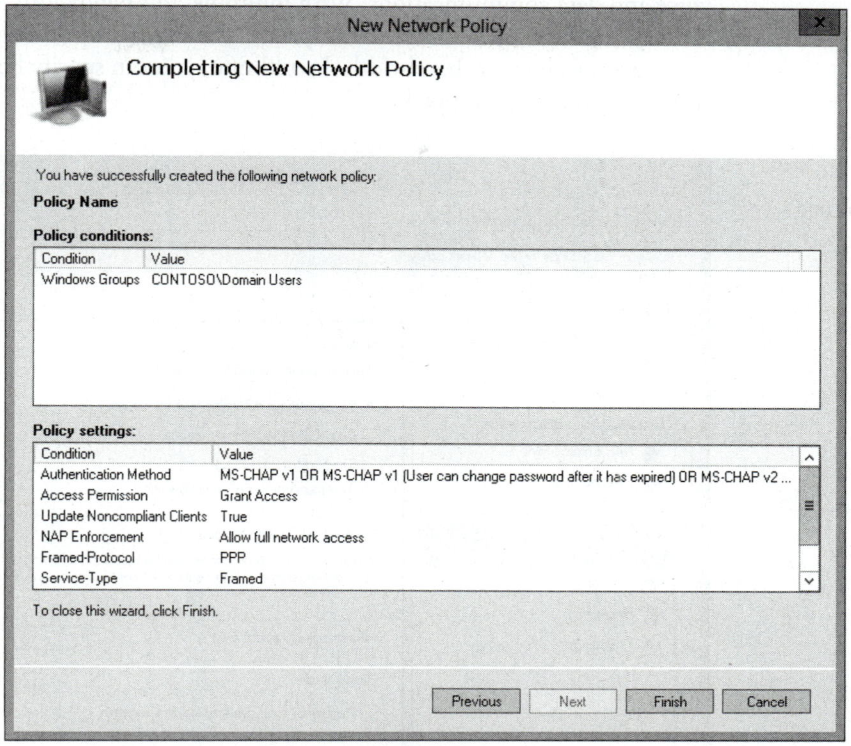

After the network policy has been created, you can modify the network policy by right-clicking the network policy and selecting *Properties*. When the Properties dialog box opens (see Figure 13-20), you can then select the *Overview* tab, *Condition* tab, *Constraints* tab, and *Settings* tab.

Figure 13-20

Configuring Network Policy properties

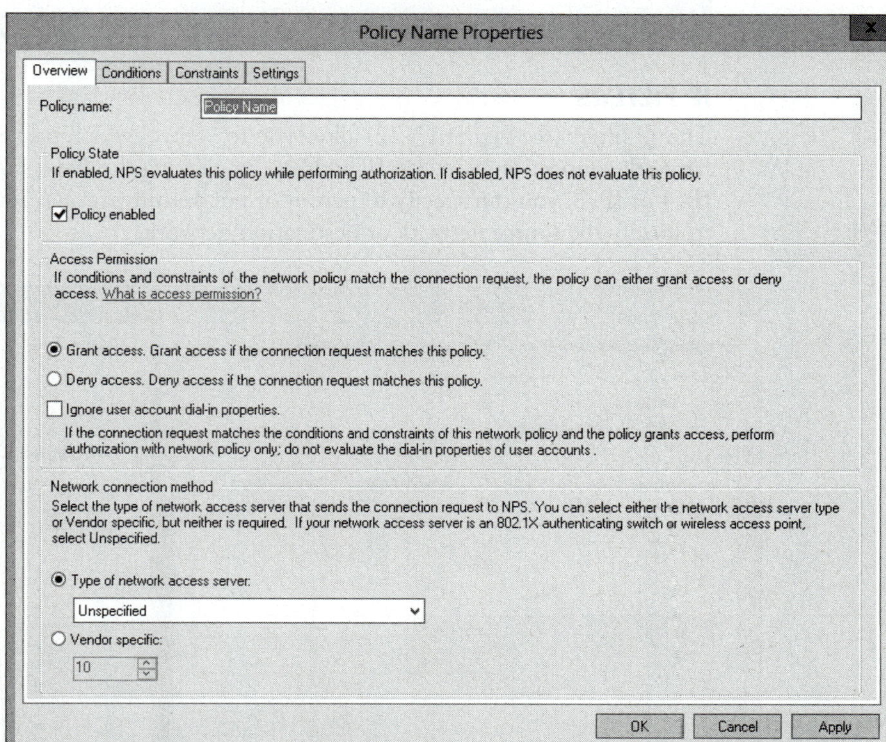

MULTILINK AND BANDWIDTH ALLOCATION

When ISDN was introduced, ISDN included multiple channels, which allow simultaneous voice and data communications. With multilink and Bandwidth Allocation Protocol (BAP) settings (see Figure 13-21), you can specify whether multiple connections form a single connection to increase bandwidth. In addition, you can specify how BAP determines when these extra lines are dropped.

Figure 13-21

Configuring Multilink and BAP settings

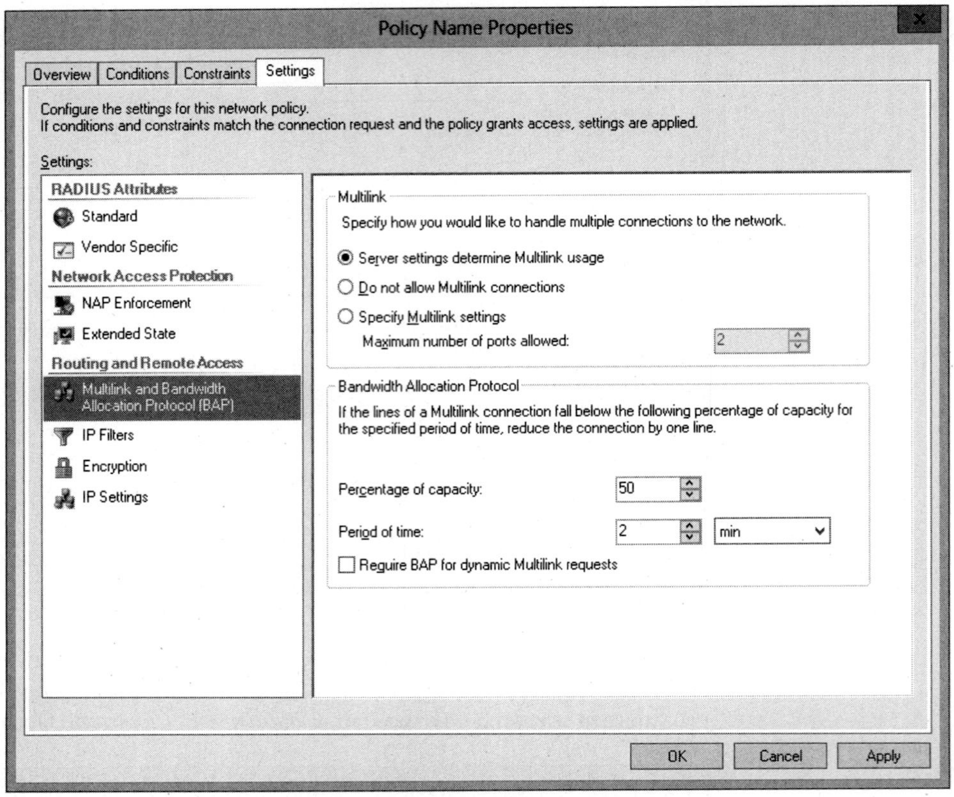

IP FILTERS

The IP filters (see Figure 13-22) allow you to control which packets are allowed through the network connection based on IP address. By clicking the *Input Filters* or *Output Filters* for IPv4 or IPv6, you can specify to permit or not permit packets. You then use the New button to specify the source network or destination network.

Figure 13-22

Configuring an IPv4 Inbound filter

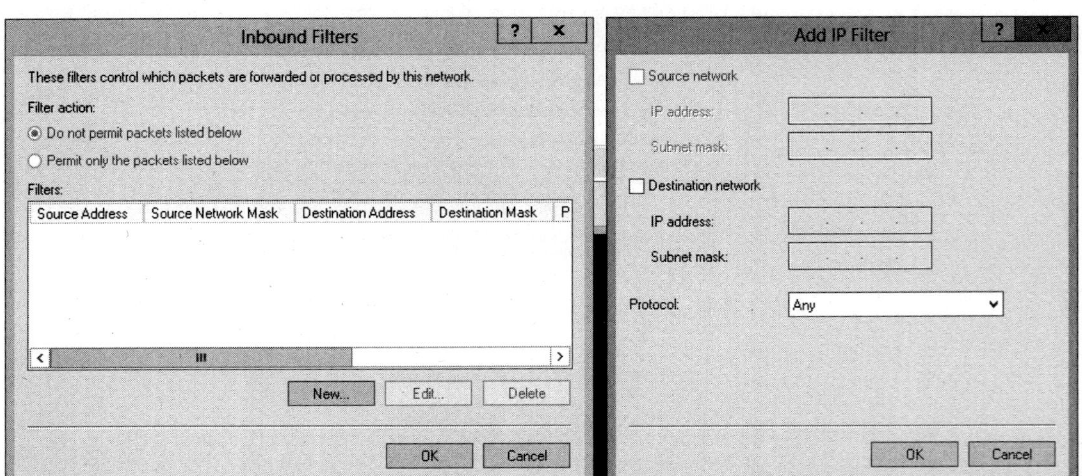

ENCRYPTION

The Encryption settings (as shown in Figure 13-23) enable you to specify the supported encryption used with network connections. The available encryption options include the following:

- **Basic Encryption (MPPE 40-Bit):** For dial-up and PPTP-based VPN connections, MPPE is used with a 40-bit key. For L2TP/IPsec VPN connections, 56-bit DES encryption is used.
- **Strong Encryption (MPPE 56-Bit):** For dial-up and PPTP VPN connections, MPPE is used with a 56-bit key. For L2TP/IPsec VPN connections, 56-bit DES encryption is used.
- **Strongest Encryption (MPPE 128-Bit):** For dial-up and PPTP VPN connections, MPPE is used with a 128-bit key. For L2TP/IPsec VPN connections, 168-bit Triple DES encryption is used.
- **No Encryption:** This option allows unencrypted connections that match the remote access policy conditions. Clear this option to require encryption.

Figure 13-23

Configuring encryption settings

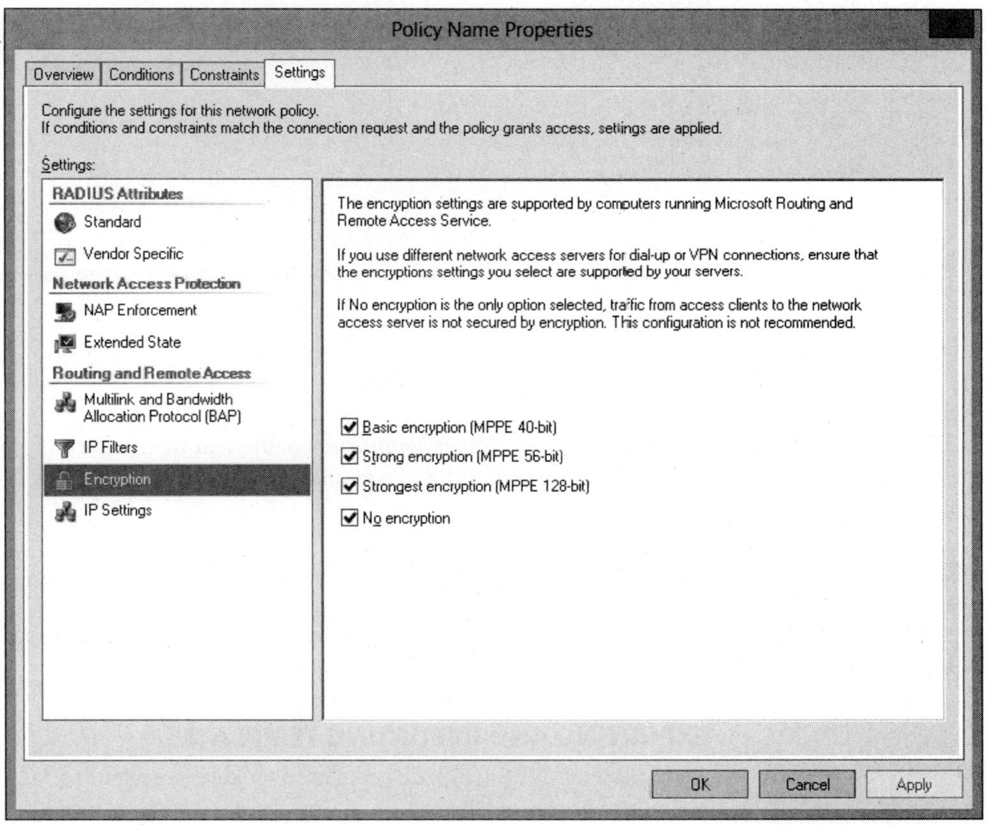

IP ADDRESSING

The last setting in the Routing and Remote Access is IP settings (see Figure 13-24), which specify how IP addresses are assigned. IP settings include the following options:

- Server Must Supply An IP Address.
- Client May Request An IP Address.
- Server Settings Determine IP Address Assignment (the default setting).
- Assign A Static IP Address.

The assigned IP address is typically used to accommodate vendor-specific attributes for IP addresses.

Figure 13-24

Configuring IP assignment settings

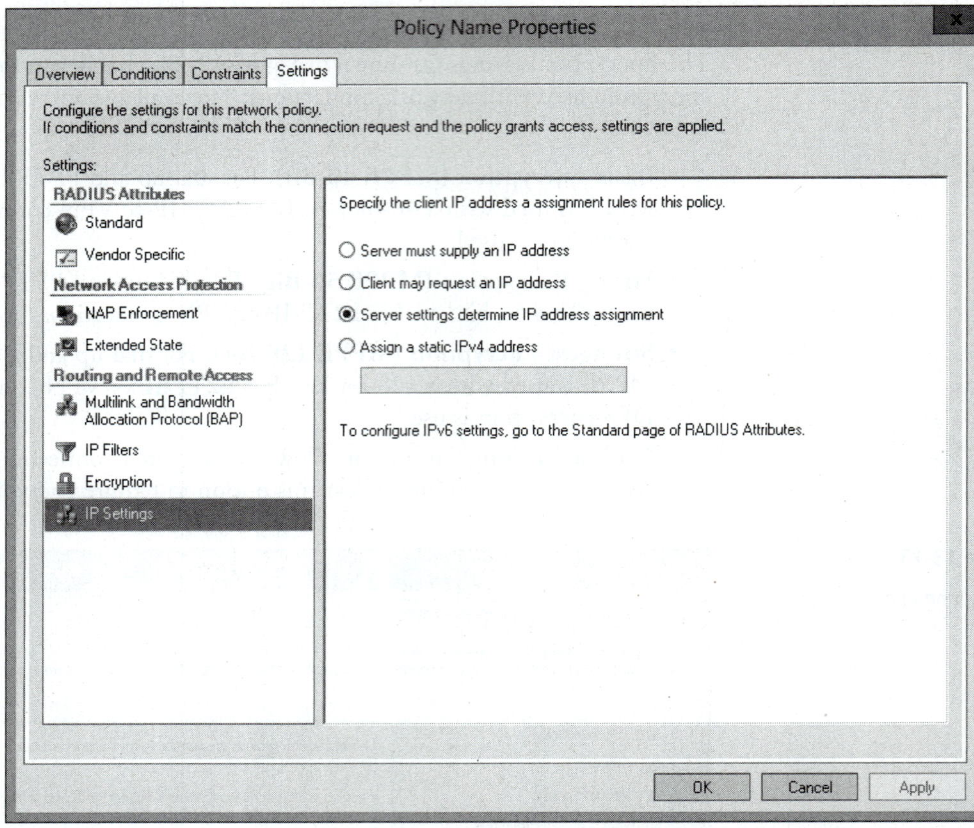

Managing NPS Templates

Network Policy Server templates enable you to create configuration elements that can be reused on the local NPS server and can be exported to other NPS servers.

CERTIFICATION READY
Manage NPS templates.
Objective 4.2

Much like the use of other templates, NPS templates are designed to reduce the amount of time and cost that it takes to configure NPS on one or more servers. Creating a template does not affect the functionality of NPS. It affects only the NPS server when the template is selected and applied when configuring NPS.

CERTIFICATION READY
Import and export NPS policies.
Objective 4.2

EXPORTING AND IMPORTING TEMPLATES

The following NPS template types are available (see Figure 13-25) for configuration in Templates Management:

- Shared Secrets
- RADIUS Clients
- Remote RADIUS Servers
- IP Filters
- Health Policies
- Remediation Server Groups

Figure 13-25

Configuring templates in NPS

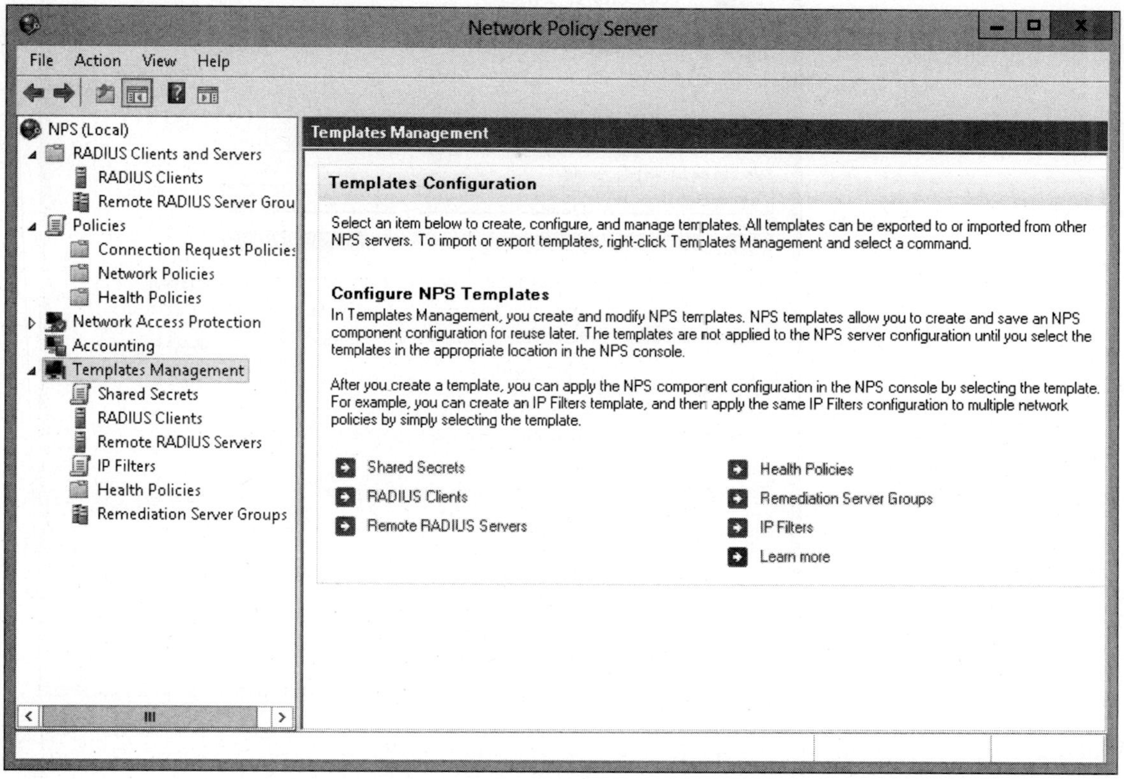

To create a template, right-click a template type in the NPS console tree, such as *IP Filters*, and then select *New*. A new IP Filters Template dialog box opens (as shown in Figure 13-26) that enables you to configure your template. Creating a template does not affect the functionality of NPS. It affects only the NPS server when the template is selected and applied when configuring NPS, as shown in Figure 13-27.

Figure 13-26

Creating a new IP filter template

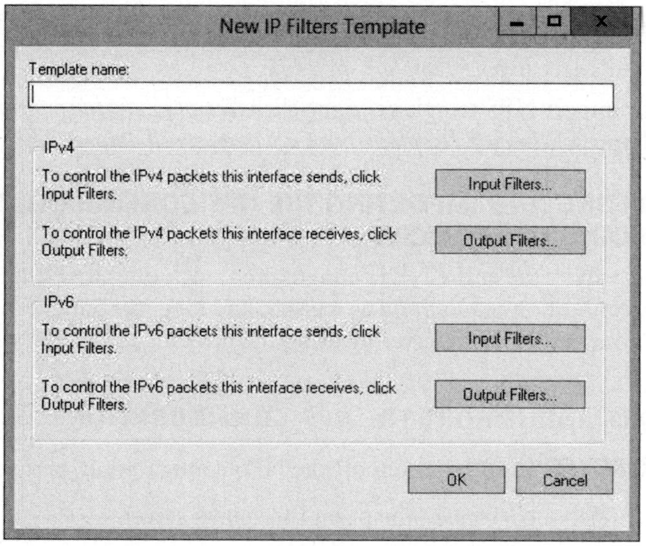

Figure 13-27

Applying the template

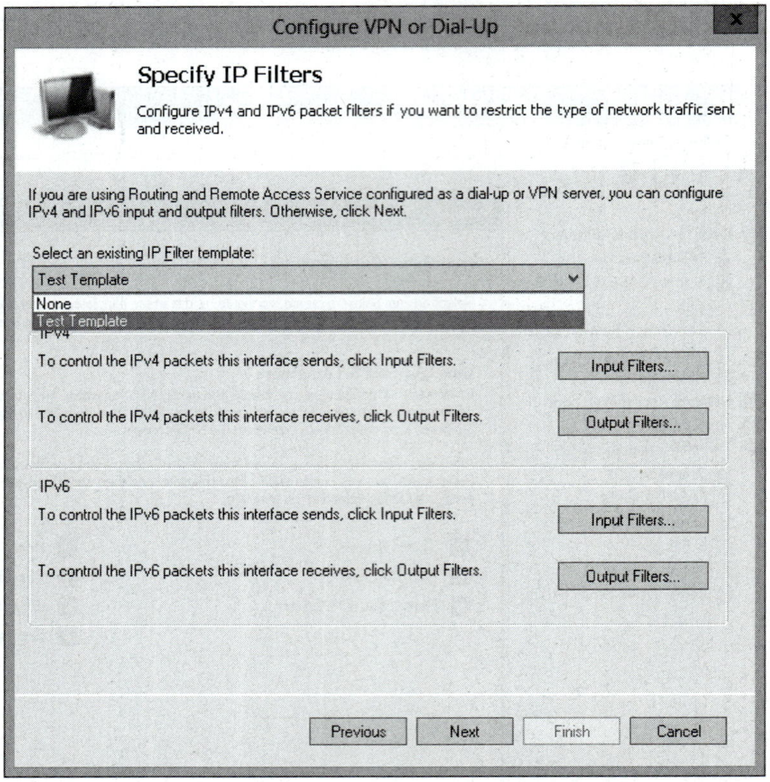

You can use a template that you've created in Templates Management by navigating to a location in the NPS console where the template can be applied. For example, if you create a new Shared Secrets template that you want to apply to a RADIUS client configuration, expand NPS, expand RADIUS Clients and Servers, and select *RADIUS Clients*. Then right-click the RADIUS client and select *Properties*. To apply the template, select an existing Shared Secrets template, and then select the template you created from the list of templates.

To export and import templates so that they can be used on other NPS servers, perform the following steps:

1. To export NPS templates, right-click *Templates Management* in the NPS console, and then select *Export Templates to a File*.
2. To import NPS templates, right-click *Templates Management* in the NPS console, and then click *Import Templates from a Computer* or *Import Templates from a File*.

EXPORTING AND IMPORTING THE NPS CONFIGURATION INCLUDING NPS POLICIES

You can export the entire NPS configuration, including RADIUS clients and servers, network policy, connection request policy, registry, and logging configuration, from one NPS server for import on another NPS server by using the `netsh` command.

EXPORT AND IMPORT THE NPS CONFIGURATION

GET READY. To export and import the NPS configuration, perform the following steps:

1. Open a command prompt on the source server.
2. Type **netsh**, and then press **Enter**.
3. At the *netsh prompt*, type **nps**, and then press **Enter**.

WARNING Do not use this procedure if the source NPS database has a higher version number than the version number of the destination NPS database. You can view the version number of the NPS database from the display of the `netsh nps show config` command.

4. At the *netsh nps prompt*, type export filename="path\file.xml"exportPSK=YES, where path is the folder location where you want to save the NPS server configuration file, and file is the name of the XML file that you want to save. Press Enter.
5. When the export is complete, close the command prompt.
6. Copy the XML file to the destination NPS server.
7. Open a command prompt on the target server.
8. At a command prompt on the destination NPS server, type netsh nps import filename="path\file.xml", and then press Enter. A message appears indicating whether the import from the XML file was successful.
9. When the import is complete, close the command prompt.

SKILL SUMMARY

IN THIS LESSON, YOU LEARNED:

- An NPS policy is a set of permissions or restrictions that are used by remote access authenticating servers that determine who, when, and how a client can connect to a network.
- With the remote access policies, connections can be authorized or denied based on user attributes, group membership, time of day, type of connection, and many other variables.
- Connection request policies are policies that establish sets of conditions and settings that specify which RADIUS servers perform the authentication, authorization, and accounting of connection requests received by the NPS server from RADIUS clients.
- Network policies are policies that establish sets of conditions, constraints, and settings that specify who is authorized to connect to the network and the circumstances under which they can or cannot connect.
- With multilink and Bandwidth Allocation Protocol (BAP) settings, you can specify whether multiple connections form a single connection to increase bandwidth. In addition, you can specify how BAP determines when these extra lines are dropped.
- The IP filters allow you to control which packets are allowed through the network connection based on IP address.
- The Encryption settings enable you to specify the supported encryption used with network connections.
- The last setting in the Routing and Remote Access is IP settings, which specify how IP addresses are assigned.
- Network Policy Server templates enable you to create configuration elements that can be reused on local NPS server and can be exported to other NPS servers.
- You can export the entire NPS configuration, including RADIUS clients and servers, network policy, connection request policy, registry, and logging configuration from one NPS server for import on another NPS server by using the `netsh` command.

Knowledge Assessment

Multiple Choice

Select the correct answer for each of the following questions.

1. Which three types of policies are available on the Network Policy Server (NPS)? (Choose all that apply.)
   a. Health policies
   b. Network policies
   c. Connection request policies
   d. Accounting policies
2. Which policy is used to establish sets of conditions and settings that specify which RADIUS servers perform the authentication, authorization, and accounting of connection requests received by the NPS server from RADIUS clients?
   a. Health policies
   b. Network policies
   c. Connection request policies
   d. Accounting policies
3. Which policy establishes sets of conditions, constraints, and settings that specify who is authorized to connect to the network?
   a. Health policies
   b. Network policies
   c. Connection request policies
   d. Accounting policies
4. Which policy would you use if you want to limit when a user can log in through the VPN?
   a. Health policies
   b. Network policies
   c. Connection request policies
   d. Accounting policies
5. How do you specify which RADIUS server handles authentication for a VPN server?
   a. Health policies
   b. Network policies
   c. Connection request policies
   d. Accounting policies
6. How can you stop an NPS server to stop acting as a RADIUS server and to stop process connections requests locally?
   a. Stop the RADIUS Server service.
   b. Stop the RADIUS Client service.
   c. Delete the default network policy.
   d. Delete the default connection request policy.
7. Which of the following are remote connections based on when creating network policies? (Choose all that apply.)
   a. Parameters
   b. Constraints
   c. Conditions
   d. Settings

8. Which of the following are remote connections based on when creating a connection request policy? (Choose all that apply.)
   a. Parameters
   b. Constraints
   c. Conditions
   d. Settings
9. What technology allows you to decrease allocated bandwidth when using multilink?
   a. NAT
   b. PAT
   c. TAP
   d. BAP
10. If you use an ISDN line, which of the following allows you to use multiple connections to allow for higher bandwidth?
    a. Shared links
    b. Multilink connections
    c. BAP
    d. Dynamic links
11. How many bits does Basic Encryption support?
    a. 40-bit
    b. 56-bit
    c. 128-bit
    d. 168-bit

Best Answer

Choose the letter that corresponds to the best answer. More than one answer choice may achieve the goal. Select the BEST answer.

1. You have three NPS servers known as Server1, Server2, and Server3. On Server1, you have a Remote RADIUS Server Group that contains Server2 and Server3. Server2 and Server 3 are configured to authentication remote users. What do you need to do to configure Server1 to forward RADIUS authentication requests to Server2 and Server3?
   a. Create a network policy.
   b. Create a remediation server group.
   c. Create a connection request policy.
   d. Create a health policy.
2. When you right-click a network policy and select Properties to open the policy Properties dialog box, which tab should you use to configure encryption?
   a. Overview
   b. Conditions
   c. Constraints
   d. Settings
3. What do you need to do to configure a NPS server as a RADIUS proxy? (Choose two answers.)
   a. Define a network policy.
   b. Define a connection request policy.
   c. Configure a RADIUS server group.
   d. Add the computer to the RADIUS proxy group.

4. You are an administrator for the Contoso Corporation where you have a single Active Directory domain and an enterprise root certificate authority. You decide to use NAP to protect the VPN connections. You build the following two servers:
Server1NPS, Remediation server, and SHVS.
Server2VPN server and RADIUS Server

What do you need to do to make sure that all client computers that attempt a VPN connection have the system health policy applied to?
a. Configure the clients as RADIUS clients.
b. Add the NAP role to the domain controller
c. Reconfigure Server1 as a RADIUS client.
d. Reconfigure Server2 as a RADIUS client.

5. You have a server running Windows Server 2012 that is configured as a RRAS server and NAP server. You want only members of the global Group named Sales to connect using a VPN connection.
a. Add the Sales group to the RAS and IAS Servers group
b. Create a new network policy and define a group-based condition for the Sales group. Set the access permission of the policy to Access Granted. Set the processing order of the policy to 1.
c. Create a new Connection Request policy and define a group-based condition for the Sales group. Set the access permission of the policy to Access Granted. Set the processing order of the policy to 1.
d. Create a new network policy and define a group-based condition for the Sales group. Set the access permission of the policy to Access Granted. Set the processing order of the policy to Default.

Matching and Identification

1. Identify which encryption level you would use with the following specifications:
_______ a) PPTP with 40-bit encryption keys
_______ b) L2TP/IPsec with 168-bit Triple DES encryption keys
_______ c) PPTP with 128-bit keys
_______ d) PPTP with 56-bit keys
_______ e) L2TP/IPsec with 56-bit DES encryption keys

2. Match the condition with the appropriate description.
_______ a) Calling Station ID
_______ b) NAS Identifier
_______ c) Tunnel type
_______ d) Called Station ID
_______ e) Service Type
_______ f) NAS Port Type
1. The telephone of the network access server
2. If it is a framed connection or login connection.
3. The type of VPN protocol used
4. Designates the phone number used by the caller
5. The name of the network access server
6. Type of media used

3. Identify the policies that you can create with the Network Policy Server.
   _______ a) authorization policies
   _______ b) authentication policies
   _______ c) Network policies
   _______ d) Health policies
   _______ e) User policies
   _______ f) computer policies
   _______ g) Network Connection policies
   _______ h) auditing policies

Build a List

1. Specify the correct order of steps for using network policies.
   _____ Checks each NPS policy for matching conditions.
   _____ If all matches, the connection is allowed. If not, the connection is denied.
   _____ User tries to make a remote access connection.
   _____ Checks each NPS policy for constraints.

Business Case Scenarios

Scenario 13-1: Defining Policies

You have two VPN servers. One is located on the main corporate office and the second is located at the backup site. You want to create policies that forward authentication and authorization requests to an NPS server and have the users approved if they are members of the Help Desk, Management, or Sales group. What should you do?

Scenario 13-2: Duplicating Servers

You are an administrator for the Contoso Corporation. You recently had a server failure where the RADIUS server was down for an extended period of time. You need to create a second NPS server for your organization to provide fault tolerance in the DR site. However, the server will only be used when the first server is not available. Describe the easiest way to duplicate all of the settings of the first NPS server on to the second NPS server and how to further configure the server to provide the specified functionality.

14 LESSON

Configuring Network Access Protection (NAP)

70-411 EXAM OBJECTIVE

Objective 4.3 – Configure Network Access Protection (NAP). This objective may include but is not limited to: configure System Health Validators (SHVs); configure health policies; configure NAP enforcement using DHCP and VPN; configure isolation and remediation of non-compliant computers using DHCP and VPN; configure NAP client settings.

Lesson Heading	Exam Objective
Using Network Access Protection (NAP)	Configure Network Access Protection (NAP)
Installing Network Access Protection	
Configuring NAP Enforcement	Configure NAP enforcement using DHCP and VPN
Configuring System Health Validators	Configure System Health Validators (SHVs)
Configuring Health Policies	Configure health policies
Configuring Isolation and Remediation	Configure isolation and remediation of non-compliant computers using DHCP and VPN
Configuring NAP Client Settings	Configure NAP client settings

KEY TERMS

802.1X enforcement
DHCP enforcement
Health Registration Authority (HRA)
Internet Protocol Security (IPsec) enforcement
NAP Agent
NAP health policy server
Network Access Protection (NAP)
remediation servers
Remote Desktop Gateway (RD Gateway) enforcement
Statement of Health (SoH)
System Health Agents (SHAs)
System Health Validators (SHVs)
VPN enforcement

Using Network Access Protection (NAP)

THE BOTTOM LINE

You have probably heard the phrase "a chain is as strong as its weakest link." With networking, this can be applied where a network is only as secure as the least-secure computer attached to it. If a computer is not secure and it goes out to web server, the web server can infect the computer. That computer can then be used to attack the network, bypass security, infect other computers, capture and forward confidential information, and so on. As a result, many tools help secure a computer. Ensuring a computer has up-to-date security patches and a reputable anti-virus/anti-malware software package installed is important. Although a corporate desktop computer that is constantly connected to the network is easy to manage and although it is easy to ensure that the computer has an up-to-date security patches and an up-to-date antivirus package, laptops that are rarely on the network or unmanaged computers that are not part of the domain, so they are much more difficult to control. To help solve this problem, Microsoft developed Network Access Protection (NAP) to ensure that all computers connected to your network have the most up-to-date security patches and an up-to-date anti-virus/malware package.

CERTIFICATION READY
Configure Network Access Protection (NAP).
Objective 4.3

Network Access Protection (NAP) is Microsoft's software for controlling network access for computers based on the health of the host such as if it is the newest security patches and a current anti-virus/anti-malware software package. As a computer connects to the network, the health status of the computer is evaluated to determine whether it should be allowed to connect to the network based on health policies. If a computer is not compliant with the system health requirements, the computer can be denied access to the network or given restricted access to the network. In some situations, automatic remediation can occur, which brings the computer into compliance.

NAP can be used on any computer that runs Windows and supports NAP. The different types of computers that connect to an organization's network include the following:

- **Desktop computers:** These Windows computers don't typically move much and are part of the domain. Because they are part of the domain, they are easier to manage with group policies, managed anti-virus/anti-malware systems, and administrative control.
- **Roaming laptops:** These Windows computers move often and might not be connected to the organization's network office. Because they are typically part of the domain, they can be managed but might not get the newest updates because they are not always connected to the network.
- **Unmanaged home computers:** These Windows computers are not usually connected directly to the network but connect through a VPN connection. Because they are usually personal computers, they are not part of the domain. Therefore, they usually do not get security updates and might not have an up-to-date anti-virus/anti-malware software package.
- **Visiting laptops:** These Windows computers are unmanaged computers often used by consultants or vendors who need to connect to your organization's network. Because they are unmanaged, they might not have the newest up-to-date security patches and an up-to-date anti-virus/anti-malware software package.

NAP includes a number of built-in enforcement methods that define the mechanisms that NAP can use:

- ***DHCP enforcement*:** This enforcement method uses DHCP configuration information to ensure that NAP clients remain in compliance. If a computer is out of compliance, NAP provides a Dynamic Host Configuration Protocol (DHCP) configuration that limits a person's access to the network until the computer is compliant. DHCP enforcement is considered the weakest form of NAP enforcement because it can be bypassed with the client computer using static IP addresses.

- ***Internet Protocol Security (IPsec) enforcement*:** This enforcement method uses IPsec that has been secured by specially configured PKI certificates known as health certificates, which are issued to clients that meet defined compliance standards. If clients cannot provide the necessary health certificate, they cannot participate in IPsec-secured traffic. IPsec enforcement is considered the strongest form of NAP enforcement. DirectAccess uses the Internet Protocol Security enforcement.
- ***VPN enforcement*:** This enforcement method restricts the level of network access that a remote access clients can obtain, based on the health information that the client computers present when the VPN connection is made.
- ***802.1x enforcement*:** This enforcement method uses 802.1x-aware network access points, such as network switches or wireless access points, to restrict network access of noncompliant resources.
- ***Remote Desktop Gateway (RD Gateway) enforcement*:** This enforcement method allows authorized remote users to connect to resources on an organization network, from any Internet-connected device. NAP can restrict connection attempts by RD Gateway clients just as with other enforcement methods.

Each of these NAP enforcement methods has its strengths and weaknesses. Although combining enforcement methods enables you to eliminate most of the weaknesses of your NAP deployment, using multiple NAP implementations makes the implementation complex to initiate and manage.

The overall architecture of NAP involves the following components:

- **NAP client-side components:** Windows Server 8, Windows 7, Windows Vista, Windows XP with SP3, Windows Server 2012, Windows Server 2008 R2, and Windows Server 2008. Microsoft also provides third-party vendors that can use NAP API to write additional clients for additional operating systems, such as Macintosh and Linux computers.
- **NAP enforcement points:** A server or device that enforces compliance. Depending on the enforcement method in use, a NAP enforcement point can take a number of different forms, such as an 802.1X-capable Wireless Access Point (WAP) for 802.1X enforcement, a Windows Server 2008 DHCP server for the DHCP enforcement method, or a Health Registration Authority (HRA) that can obtain health certificates from client computers when the IPsec enforcement method is used.
- ***NAP health policy server*:** A server running the Network Policy Server (NPS) server role that receives information from NAP enforcement points. The health policy server stores NAP health requirement policies and provides health state validation for NAP clients.
- ***System Health Agents (SHAs)*:** A component that maintains information and reporting on one or more elements of the health of a NAP client. Newer versions of Windows have a built-in Windows SHA that monitors the settings configured in the Windows Security Center. Third-party vendors can use the NAP API to write additional SHAs to plug into third-party products.
- ***Statement of Health (SoH)*:** Each SHA creates an SoH that transmits to the NAP Agent. Each SHA generates a new SoH whenever the status is updated, such as when an update to the anti-virus package is released but has not been installed on the client.
- ***NAP Agent*:** This maintains information about the health of the NAP client computer and transmits information between the NAP enforcement clients and the SHAs. The NAP Agent combines the SoH from each SHA into a single System Statement of Health (SSOH), which it then passes to the enforcement clients. The enforcement clients then use this SSOH to request network access by passing the SSOH information on to the NAP server components.

- ***Health Registration Authority (HRA)*:** A computer that runs Windows Server 2012 and Internet Information Services (IIS) and that obtains health certificates from a certification authority (CA) for compliant computers.
- **Health requirements server:** A server that provides the current health state information to NPS health policy server. Examples of health requirements include an anti-virus software management server, or a Windows Server Update Services (WSUS) or System Center Configuration Manager (SCCM) server that sends updates to client computers.
- ***Remediation servers*:** An optional component that can be deployed to allow noncompliant client computers to achieve network compliance and gain network access. Examples include anti-virus software or a WSUS server.

The following describes the NAP connection process:

1. When the NAP client connects to a network that requires NAP, each SHA on the NAP client validates its system health and generates an SoH.
2. The NAP client combines the SoHs from multiple SHAs into a SSoH, and sends the information to a NAP health policy server that is defined with the NAP enforcement point.
3. The NAP health policy server uses its installed SHVs and the health requirements policies to determine whether the NAP client meets health requirements.
4. The NAP health policy server combines the SoHRs from the multiple SHVs into a System Statement of Health Response (SSoHR) and sends the SSoHR back to the NAP client through the NAP enforcement point.
5. If the client is compliant, the enforcement point allows the connection. If the client is noncompliant, the computer can be connected to a remediation network.
6. If the computer is noncompliant, the noncompliant computer can attempt to come into compliance.
7. If the status of the computer changes, the entire process starts over.

Installing Network Access Protection

NAP is provided by NPS. Therefore, to install NAP, you install NPS.

Because NAP is offered through NPS, the installation is similar to installing NPS, as discussed in Lesson 12. However, you want to add HRA, which is used to issue health certificates to NAP client computers that are compliant with network health requirements. For HRA to function, you need to have a CA available.

INSTALL NETWORK POLICY SERVER

GET READY. To install Network Policy Server, perform the following steps:

1. Open Server Manager.
2. At the top of Server Manager, select Manage and click Add Roles and Features. The *Add Roles and Feature Wizard* opens.
3. On the *Before you begin* page, click Next.
4. Select Role-based or feature-based installation, and then click Next.
5. Click Select a server from the server pool, click the name of the server to install Network Policy and Access Services to, and then click Next.

6. On the *Server Roles* page, select the Network Policy and Access Services and click Next.
7. When you are asked to add features that are required for Network Policy and Access Services, click Add Features.
8. On the *Select server roles* page, click Next.
9. On the *Select features* page, click Next.
10. On the *Network Policy and Access Services* page, click Next.
11. On the *Select role services* page (see Figure 14-1), with the Network Policy Server selected, select Health Registration Authority so that there is a checkmark in the checkbox. Click Next.

Figure 14-1

Selecting the role services

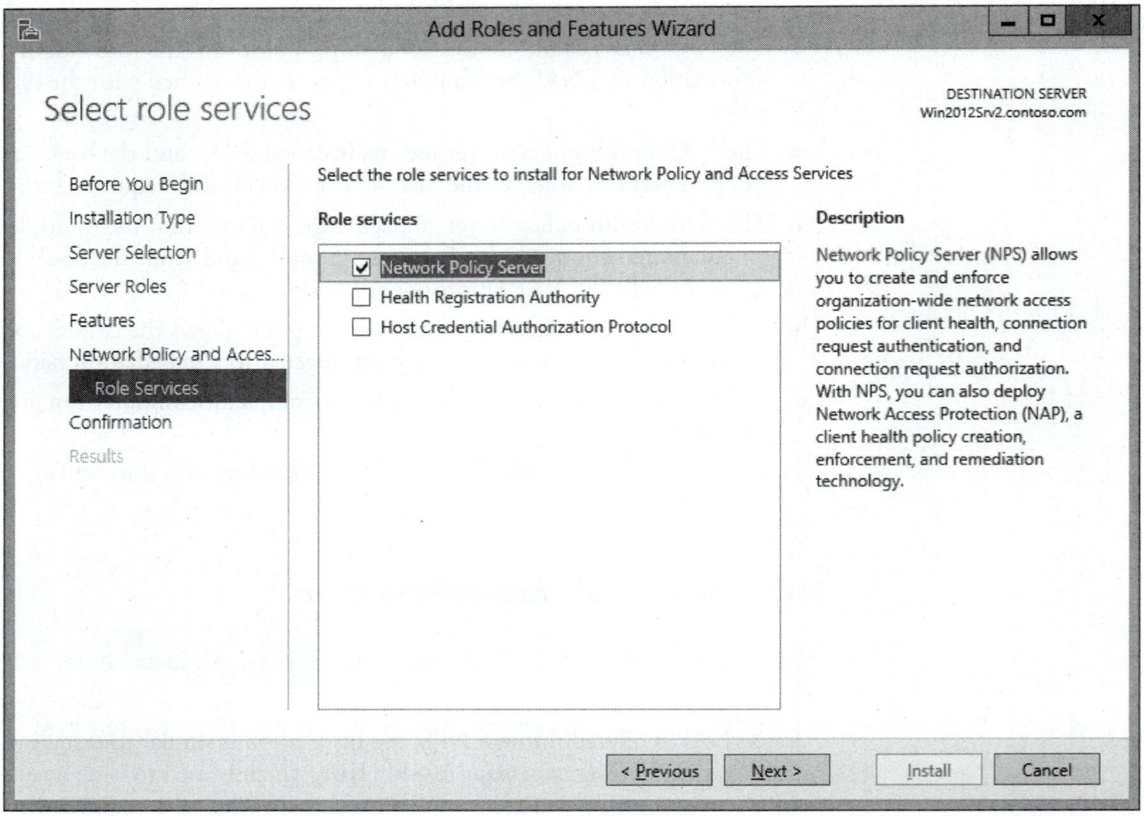

12. When the *Add Roles and Features Wizard* dialog box opens, click Add Features.
13. On the *Select role services* page, click Next. The *Certification Authority* page appears, as shown in Figure 14-2.
14. If the CA is located on the current sever, select Use the local CA to issue health certificates for this HRA server. If the CA is on another server, select Use an existing remote CA and then specify the name of the server. Click Next.

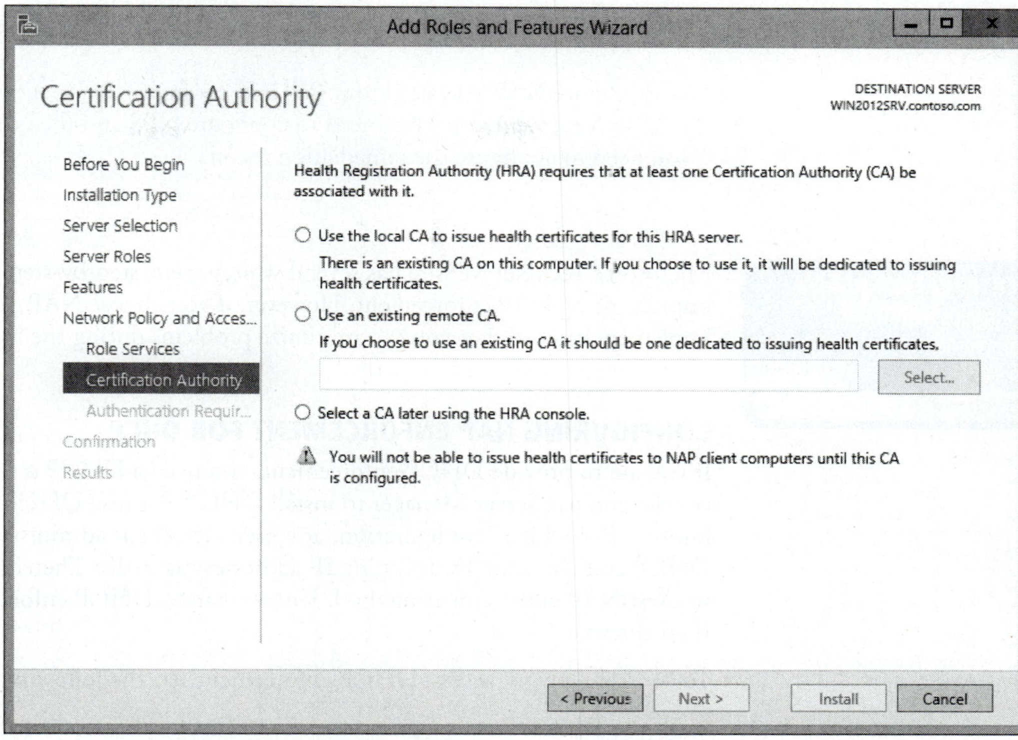

Figure 14-2

Specifying the Certificate Authority

15. On the *Authentication Requirements* page (see Figure 14-3), select the Yes, required requestors to be authenticated as members of a domain (recommended). Click Next.

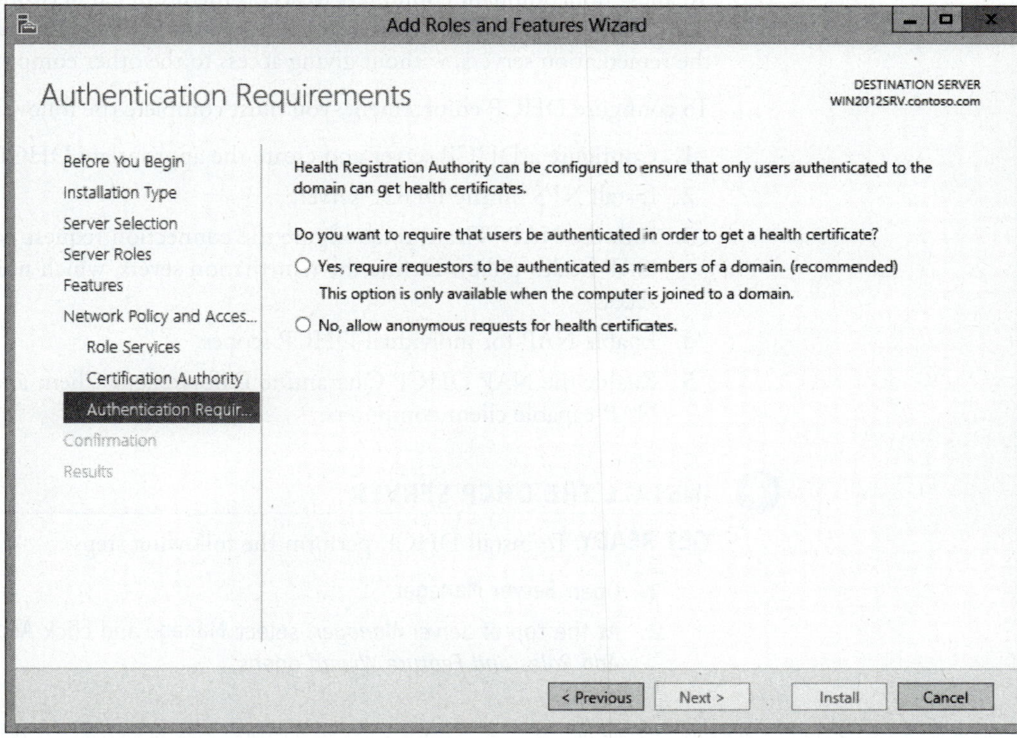

Figure 14-3

Configuring the authentication requirements

16. On the *Confirm installation selection* page, click Install.
17. When the installation is complete, click Close.

Configuring NAP Enforcement

To configure NAP, you need to install and configure the server on which you will apply NAP enforcement. You then need to configure NPS and the NAP-related policies. Finally, you need to configure the remediation servers.

CERTIFICATION READY
Configure NAP enforcement using DHCP and VPN.
Objective 4.3

Microsoft's TechNet website has several whitepapers, step-by-step guides, and checklists when implementing NAP enforcement. However, if you choose NAP, you need to plan the implementation so that you can minimize problems during the initial implementation until everything is configured properly.

CONFIGURING NAP ENFORCEMENT FOR DHCP

If you are to provide DHCP enforcement, you need a DHCP server. As shown in the 70-410 course, you use Server Manager to install DHCP. Because DHCP enforcement relies on a limited IPv4 address configuration, any user with client administrator access can override the DHCP configuration by assigning IP addresses manually. Therefore, DHCP is considered the weakest NAP enforcement method. Unfortunately, DHCP enforcement is not possible for IPv6 clients.

To control network access, DHCP enforcement sets the following:

- The DHCP Router option is set to 0.0.0.0 so that noncompliant computers do not have a configured default gateway.
- The subnet mask is set to 255.255.255.255 so that there are no routes to the attached subnet.

To allow noncompliant computers to access the restricted network's remediation servers, the DHCP server assigns the Classless Static Routes DHCP option, which contains host routes to the remediation servers, without giving access to the other computers.

To configure DHCP enforcement, you must complete the following:

1. Configure a DHCP server and create the appropriate DHCP scopes.
2. Install NPS on the DHCP server.
3. Run the NAP Wizard to configure the connection request policy, network policy, and NAP health policy. Define the remediation severs, which noncompliant clients can access.
4. Enable NAP for individual DHCP scopes.
5. Enable the NAP DHCP Quarantine Enforcement Client and start the NAP service on NAP-capable client computers.

INSTALL THE DHCP SERVER

GET READY. To install DHCP, perform the following steps:

1. Open Server Manager.
2. At the top of *Server Manager,* select Manage and click Add Roles and Features. The *Add Roles and Feature Wizard* opens.

3. On the *Before you begin* page, click Next.
4. Select Role-based or feature-based installation, and then click Next.
5. Click Select a server from the server pool, click the name of the server to install DHCP Server to, and then click Next.
6. On the *Server Roles* page, select the DHCP Server and click Next.
7. When you are asked to add features that are required for Network Policy and Access Services, click Add Features.
8. Back on the *Select server roles* page, click Next.
9. On the *Select features* page, click Next.
10. On the *DHCP* page, click Next.
11. On the *Confirm installation selection* page, click Install.
12. When the installation is complete, click Close.

CONFIGURE THE DHCP SERVER

GET READY. To configure the DHCP, perform the following steps:

1. Open Server Manager.
2. Click Tools > DHCP. The *DHCP console* opens.
3. Expand the server node, and expand the IPv4 node (see Figure 14-4).

Figure 14-4

Opening the DHCP console

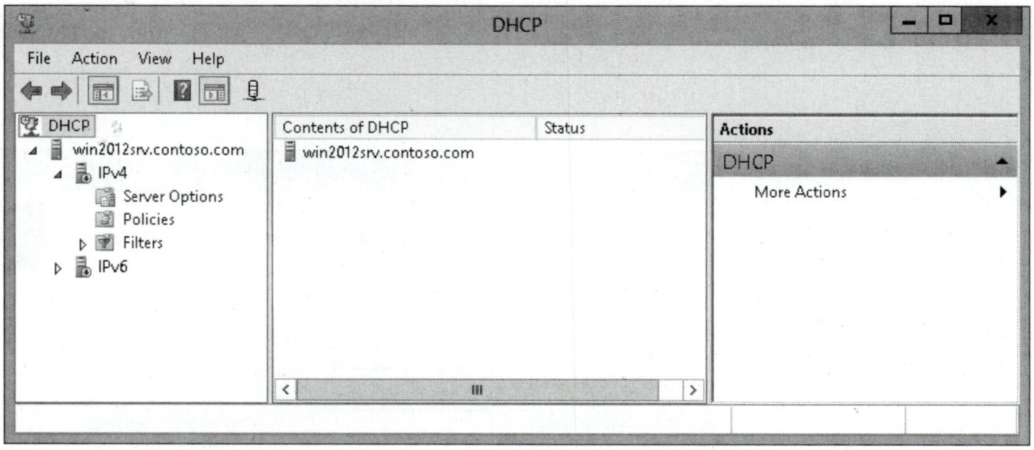

4. Right-click IPv4 node and click New Scope.
5. When the *New Scope Wizard* starts, click Next.
6. On the *Scope Name* page (see Figure 14-5), in the *Name and Description* text box, type a descriptive name and description of the scope.

Figure 14-5
Defining the scope name

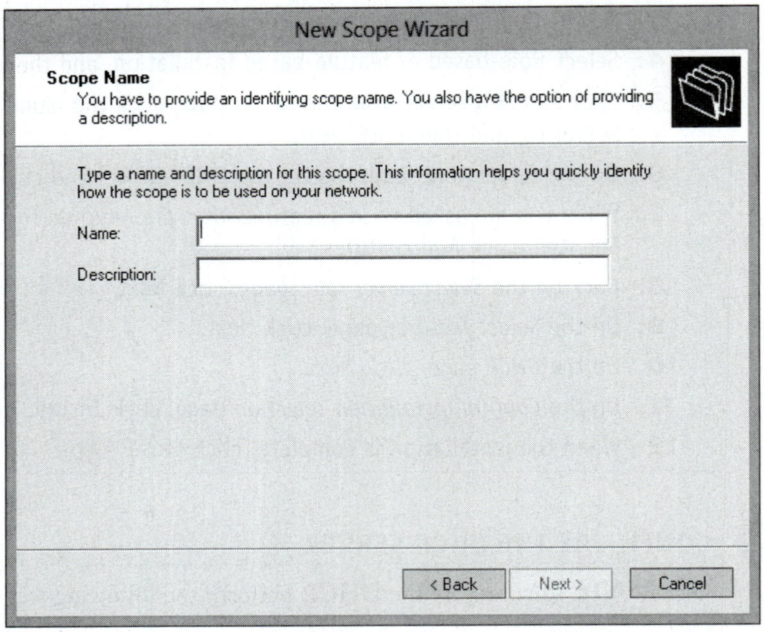

7. On the *IP Address Range* page (as shown in Figure 14-6), enter the following information:

    Start IP address: 192.168.1.201

    End IP address: 192.168.1.250

    Click Next.

Figure 14-6
Specifying the IP address range

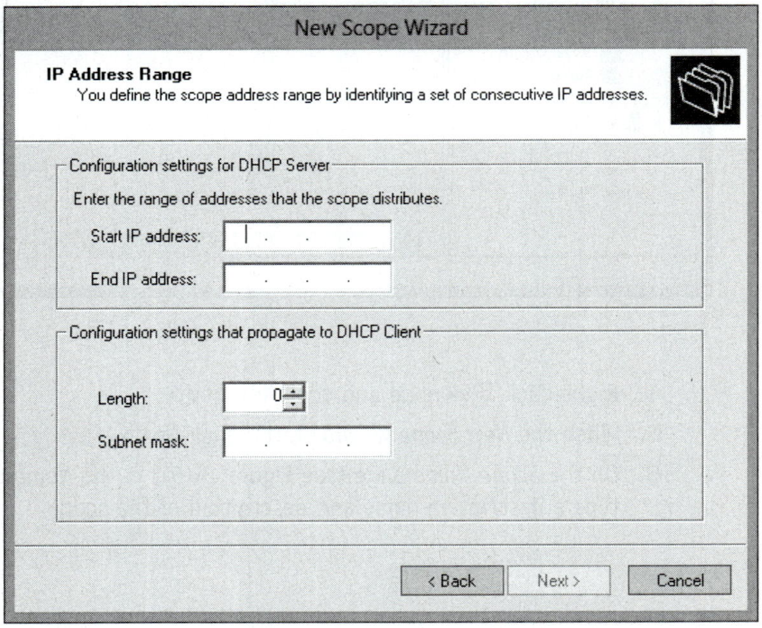

8. On the *Add Exclusions and Delay* page, click Next.
9. On the *Lease Duration* page, click the lease time to 8 hours (see Figure 14-7). Click Next.

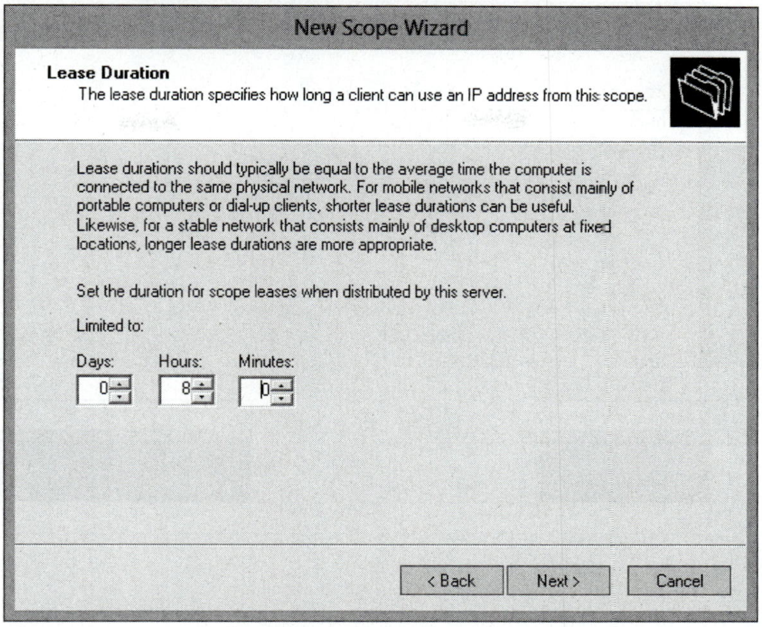

Figure 14-7

Specifying the lease duration

10. On the *Configure DHCP Options* page, click Next.
11. For the *Router (Default Gateway)* page (see Figure 14-8), type 192.168.1.1 for the IP address and click the Add button. Click Next.

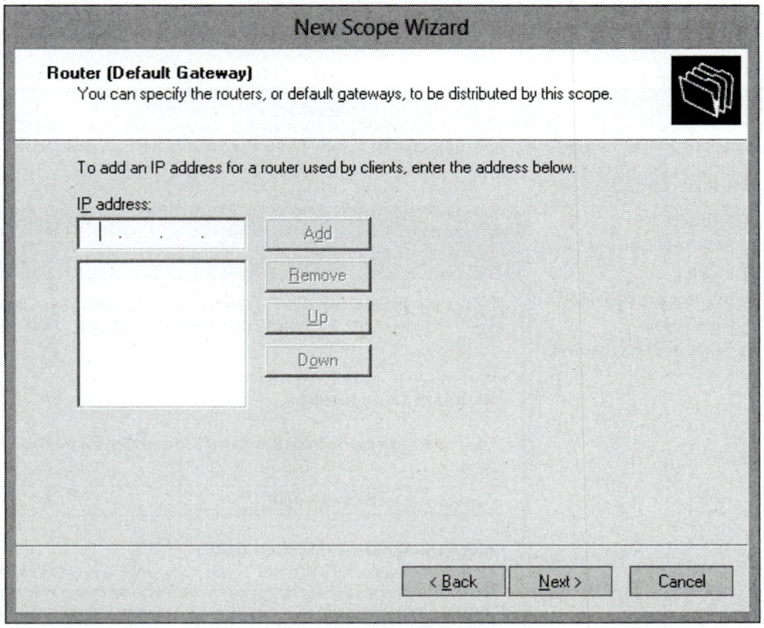

Figure 14-8

Defining the default gateway

12. On the *Domain Name and DNS Servers* page, click Next.
13. On the *WINS Servers* page, click Next.
14. On the *Activate Scope* page, with the *Yes, I want to activate the scope now option* already selected, click Next.
15. When the *Completing the New Scope Wizard* page appears, click Finish.
16. At the top of the tree, right-click the server and click Authorize (see Figure 14-9).

Figure 14-9

Authorizing the DHCP server

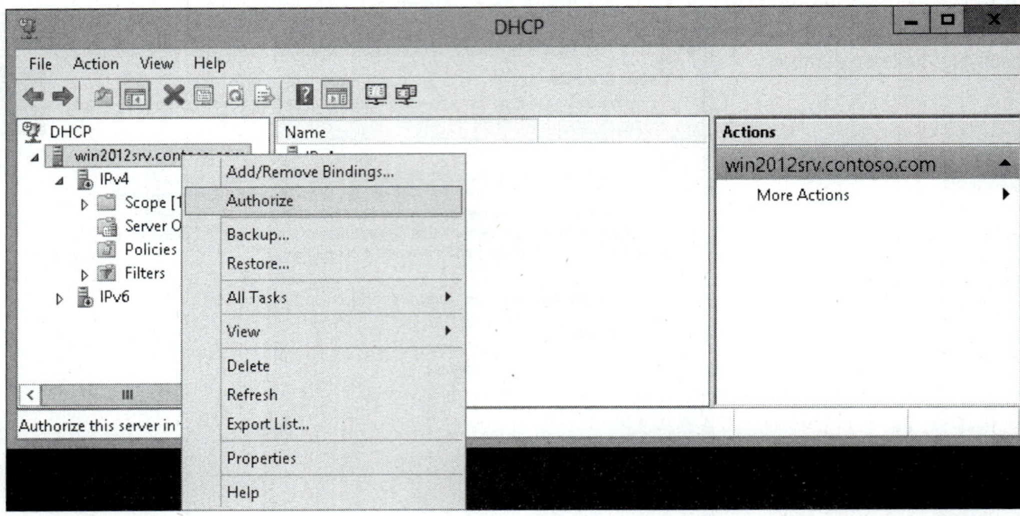

CONFIGURE NAP FOR DHCP SERVER

GET READY. To configure NAP for DHCP servers, perform the following steps:

1. Open Server Manager.
2. Click Tools > Network Policy Server. The *Network Policy Server console* opens (see Figure 14-10).

Figure 14-10

Starting the Network Policy Server console

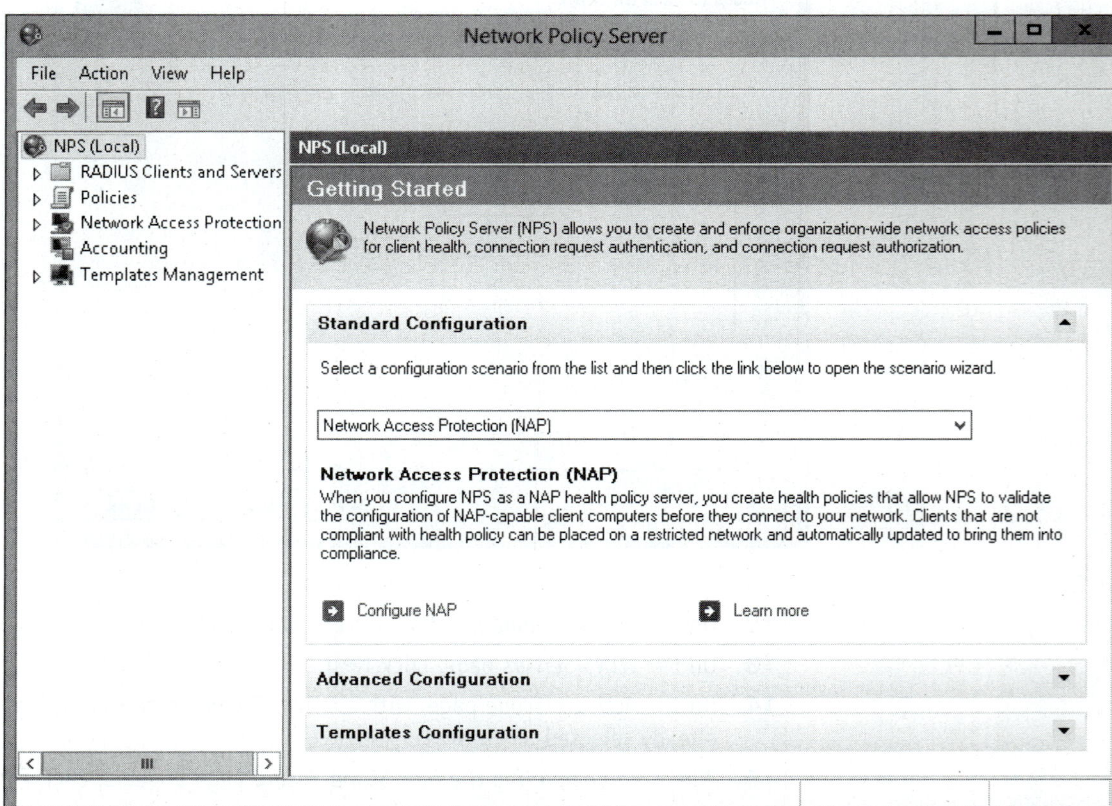

3. In the main pane, click Configure NAP to start the *Configure NAP Wizard*.
4. When the *Select Network Connection Method For Use with NAP Wizard* opens, select the Dynamic Host Configuration Protocol (DHCP) for the network connection method (see Figure 14-11). Click Next.

Figure 14-11

Selecting the network connection method

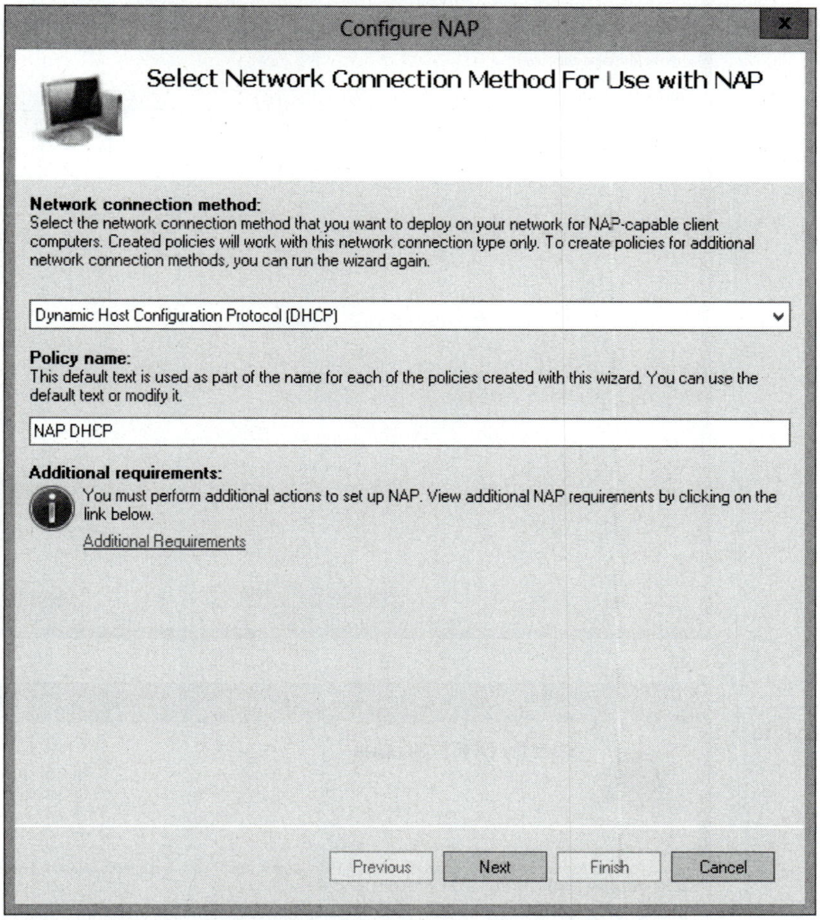

5. If the server is not running DHCP and is providing NAP for RADIUS clients, you can add the RADIUS clients on the *Specify NAP Enforcement Servers Running DHCP Server* page (see Figure 14-12). Because this server is already running DHCP, click Next.
6. On the *Specify DHCP Scopes* page (see Figure 14-13), click the Add button to open the *MS-Server Class* page. Type NAP DHCP in the text box and click OK. On the *Specify DHCP Scopes* page, click Next.

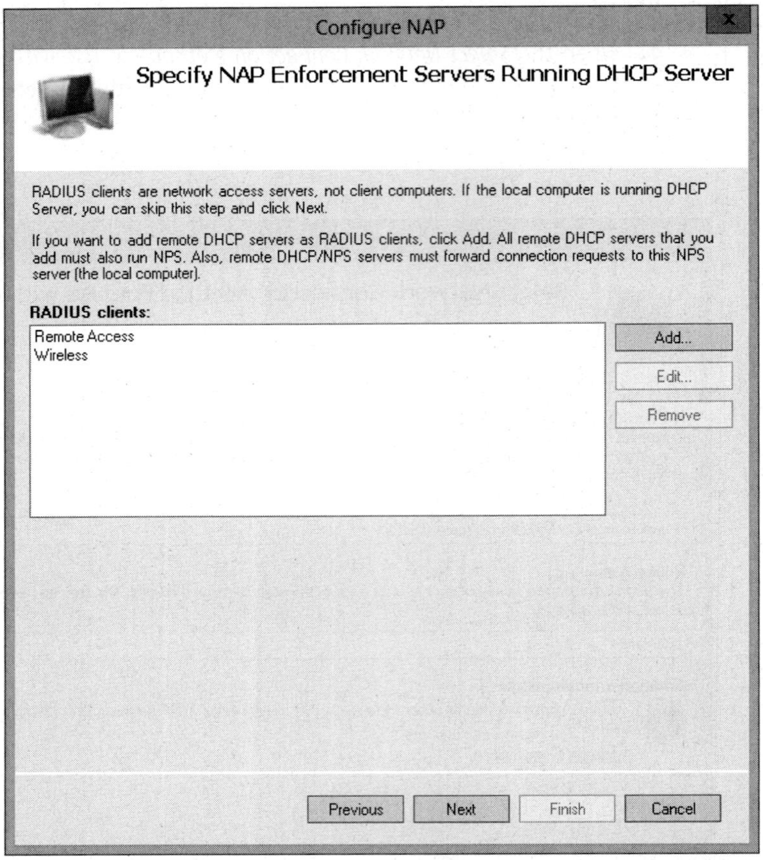

Figure 14-12

Specifying NAP enforcement servers running DHCP server

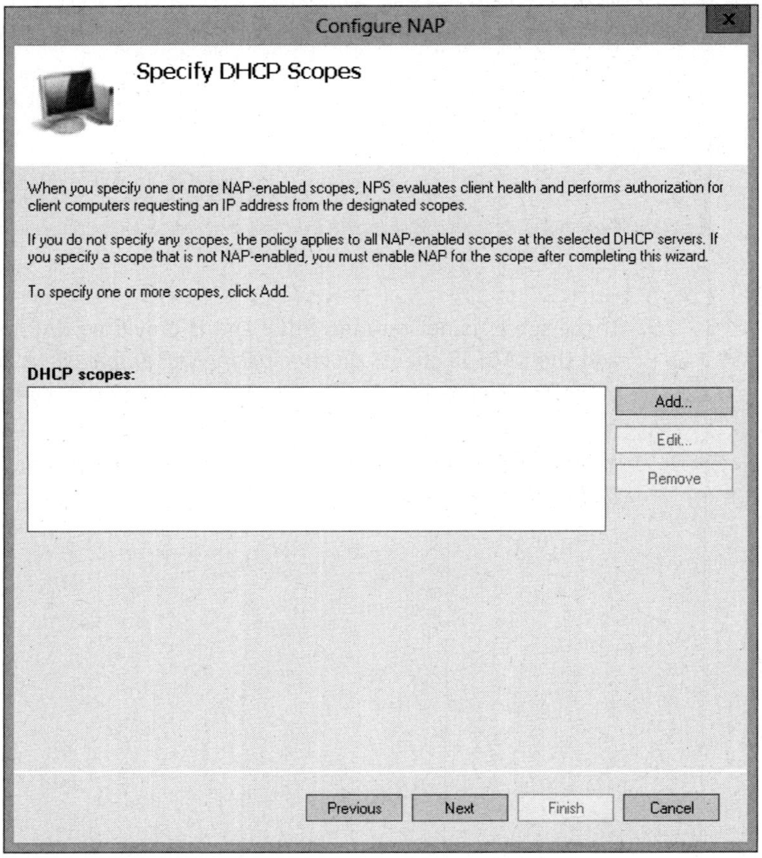

Figure 14-13

Specifying the DHCP scopes to apply to NAP

7. On the *Configure Machine Groups* page (see Figure 14-14), click the Add button to open the *Select Group* dialog box. Type the name of the computer group and click OK. If no computer groups are added, the policy is added to all computers that connect using DHCP. Back at the *Configure Machine Groups* page, click Next.

Figure 14-14

Specifying the computer groups that NAP will apply to

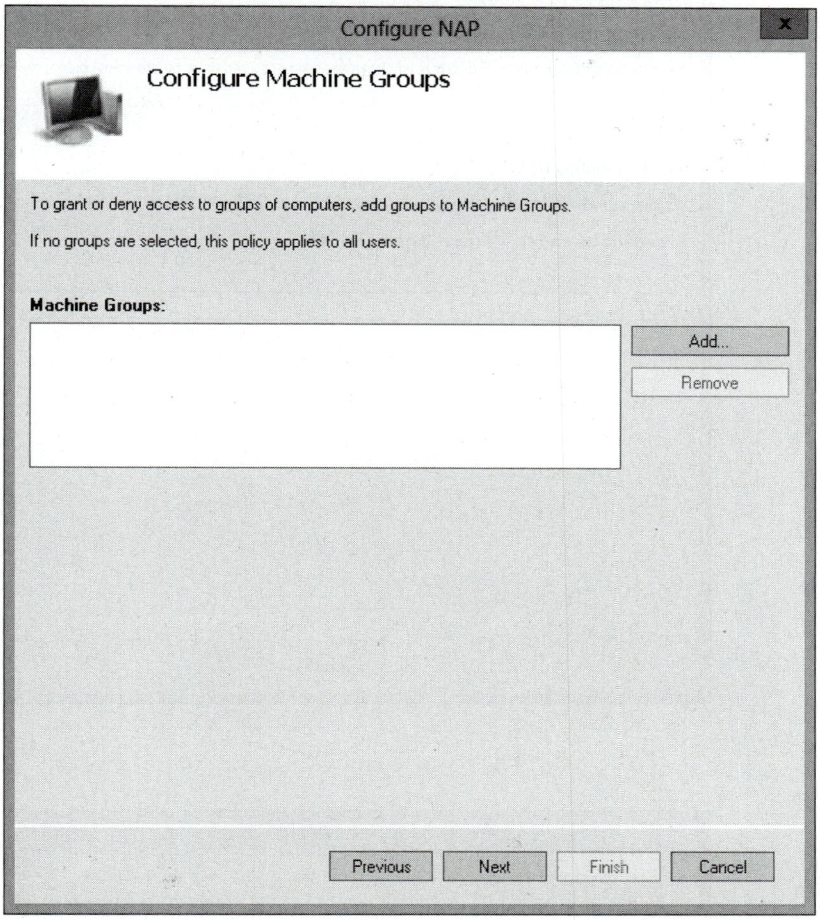

8. On the *Specify a NAP Remediation Server Group and URL* page (see Figure 14-15), you specify each computer that can be used for remediation, including WSUS, anti-virus management severs, and so on. To add a computer, click the New Group to open the *New Remediation Server Group* dialog box (see Figure 14-16). In the *Group Name* text box, provide a group name, and then click Add to open the *Add New Server* dialog box. Type the name of the server and IP address and click OK to close the *Add New Server* dialog box and click OK to close the *New Remediation Server Group* dialog box.

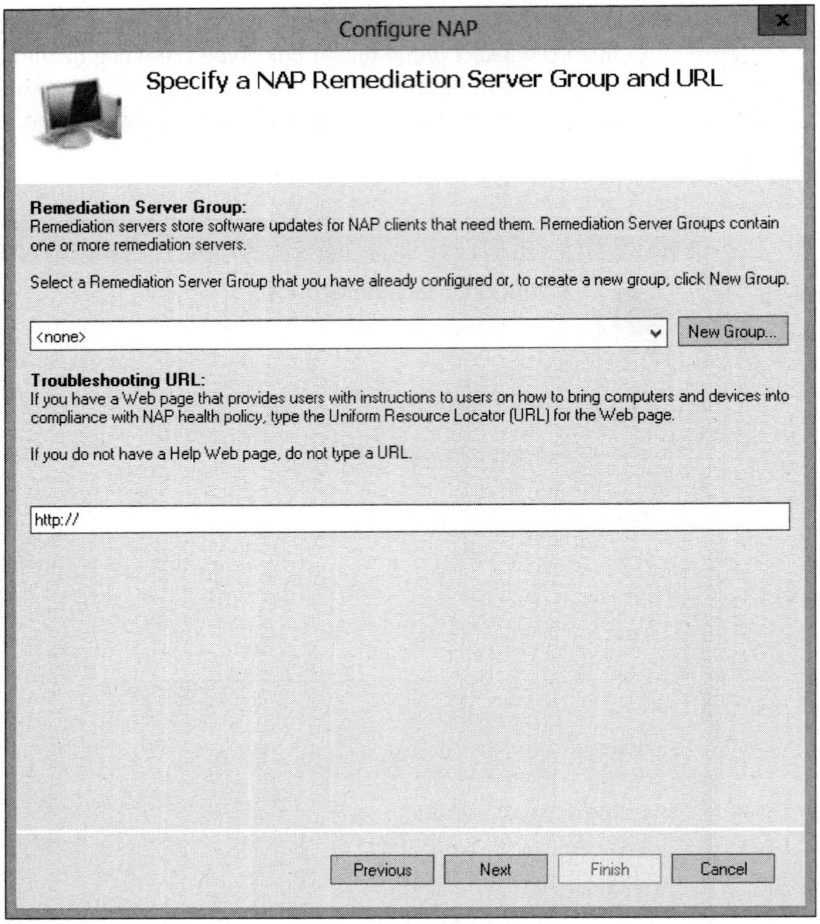

Figure 14-15

Specifying the NAP Remediation Server group and URL

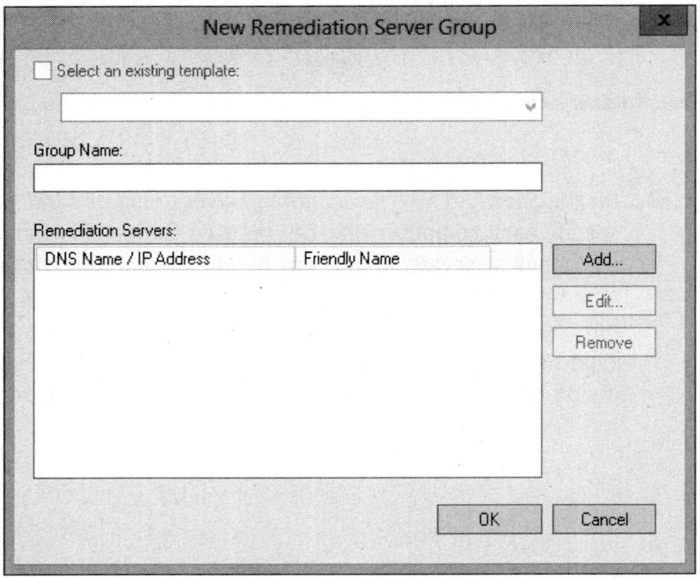

Figure 14-16

Adding computers to the Remediation Server group

9. You can also specify the URL in the *Help Web* page dialog box that provides instructions to the user to get his or her computer to be compliant. Click Next.
10. On the *Define NAP Health Policy* page (see Figure 14-17), you can define if a computer is to auto-remediate (if possible) and you can specify if you want to deny or allow access if the computer is not compliant. Click Next.

Figure 14-17
Defining NAP Health Policy

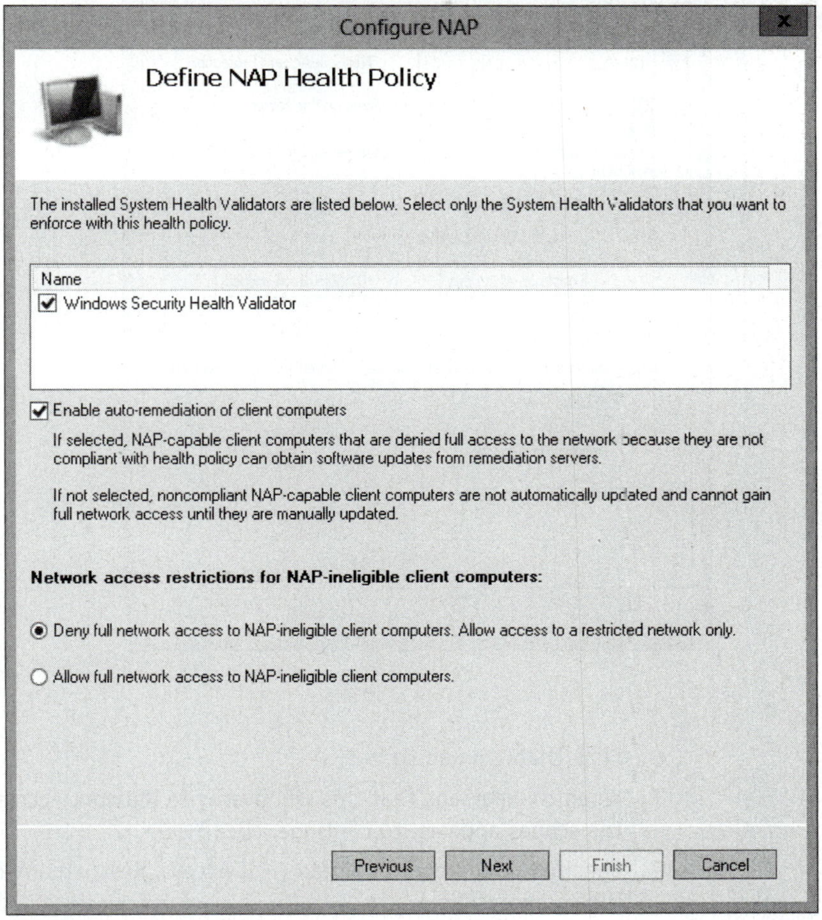

11. On the *Completing NAP Enforcement Policy and RADIUS Client Configuration* page, click Finish.

When you enable NAP for the individual DHCP scopes, you can enable for all of the DHCP scopes at once or individual scopes. When you are first implement NAP, you should specify individual scopes until you get everything working just right.

ENABLE NAP ON ALL DHCP SCOPES

GET READY. To enable NAP on all DHCP scopes, perform steps:

1. Open Server Manager.
2. Click Tools > DHCP. The *DHCP console* opens.

3. Expand the server node.
4. Right-click the IPv4 node and click Properties. The *IPv4 Properties* dialog box opens.
5. Click the Network Access Protection tab (see Figure 14-18).

Figure 14-18

Enabling NAP for all DHCP scopes

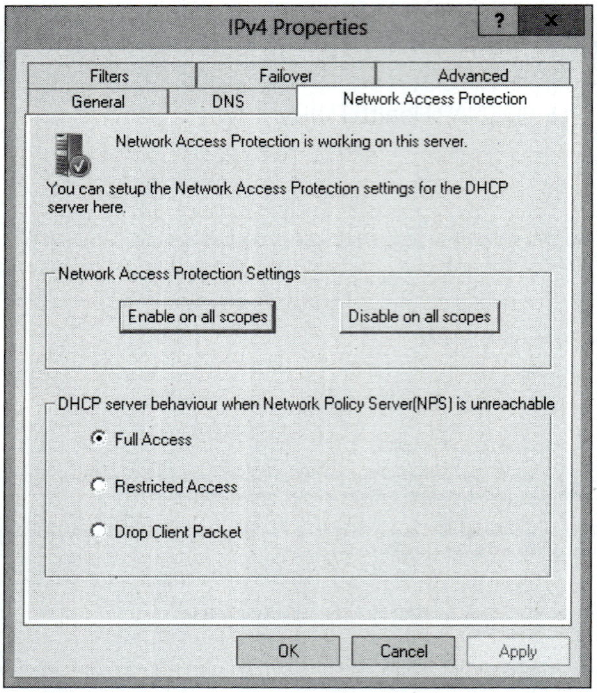

6. Click Enable on all scopes.
7. When the message that this will overwrite Network Access Protection settings of all the scopes appears, to continue, click Yes.
8. Specify the appropriate action (Full Access, Restricted Access, Drop Client Packet) if NPS is unreachable.
9. Click OK to close *IPv4 Properties* dialog box.

ENABLE NAP ON AN INDIVIDUAL DHCP SCOPE

GET READY. To enable NAP on a single DHCP scope, perform the following steps:

1. Open Server Manager.
2. Click Tools > DHCP. The *DHCP console* opens.
3. Expand the server node and expand the IPv4 node.
4. Right-click an IPv4 scope and click Properties. A *Scope Properties* dialog box opens.

5. Click the Network Access Protection tab (see Figure 14-19).

Figure 14-19

Enabling NAP for individual DHCP scopes

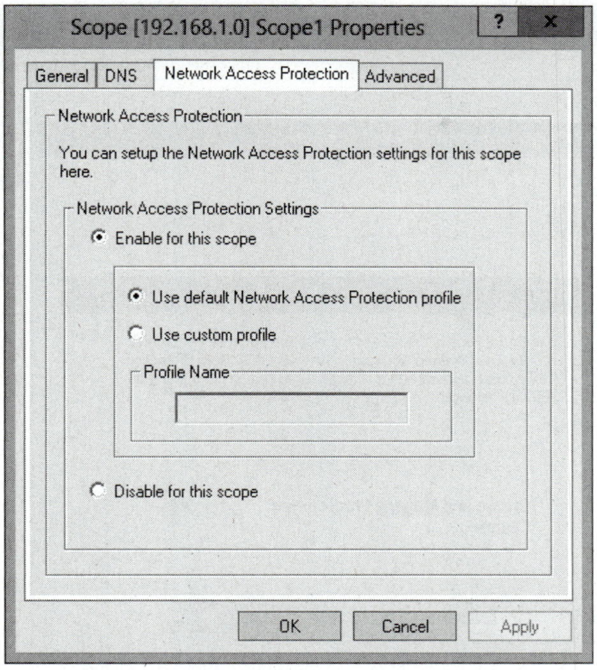

6. Click Enable for this scope.
7. Click OK to close *Scope Properties* dialog box.

ENABLE THE NAP DHCP QUARANTINE ENFORCEMENT CLIENT AND START NAP SERVICE ON A DHCP SERVER

GET READY. To enable the NAP DHCP Quarantine Enforcement Client and start the NAP service on a DHCP server, perform the following steps:

1. Click the Start button, right-click the Start button, and select Command Prompt (Admin).
2. At the command prompt, execute the `napclcfg.msc` command. The *NAP Client Configuration console* opens (see Figure 14-20).

Figure 14-20

Opening the NAP Client Configuration console

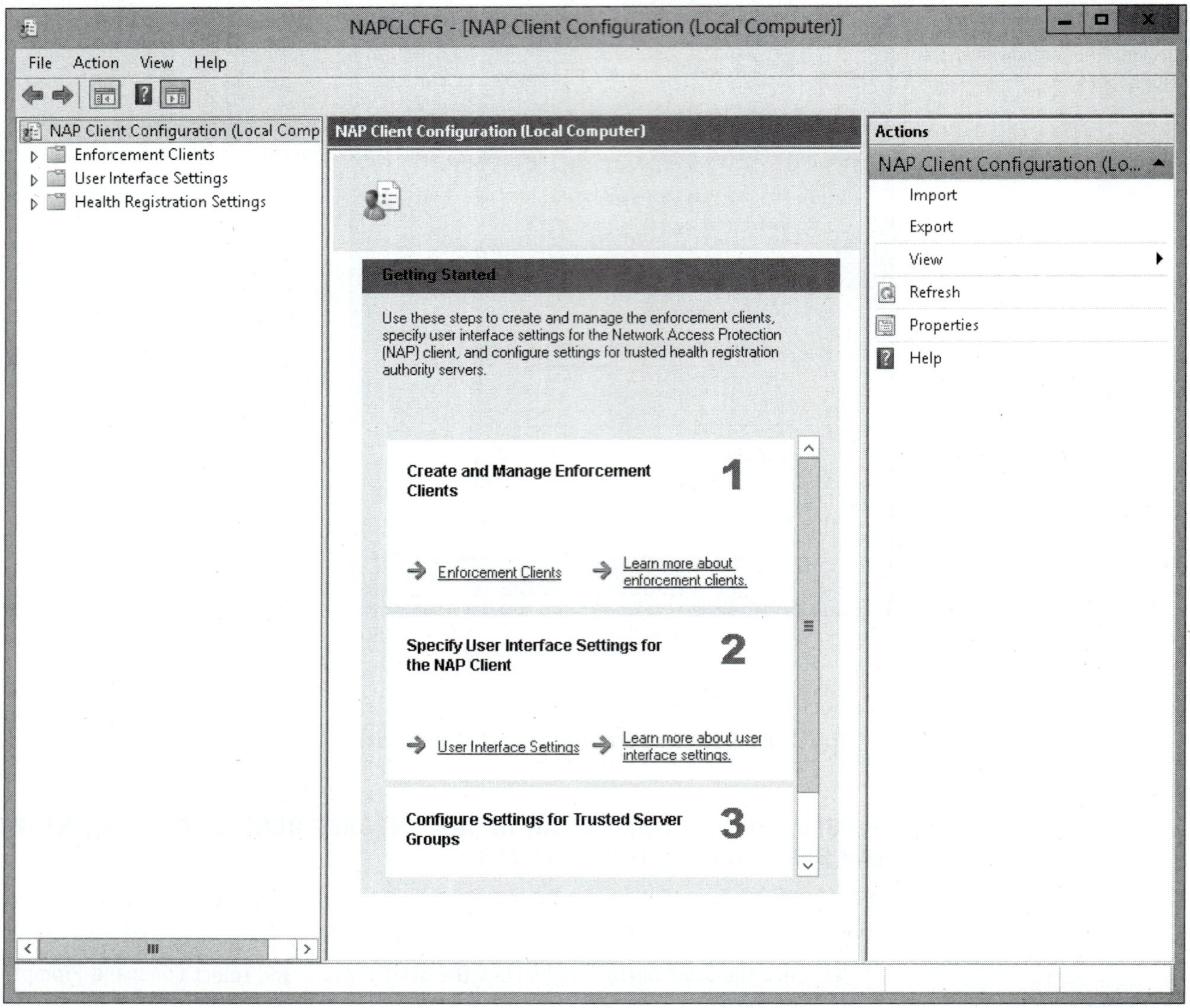

3. In the left pane, click Enforcement Clients. Figure 14-21 shows the enforcement clients.
4. In the center pane, double-click DHCP Quarantine Enforcement Client to open the *DHCP Quarantine Enforcement Client Properties* dialog box (see Figure 14-22).

Figure 14-21

Configuring the enforcement clients

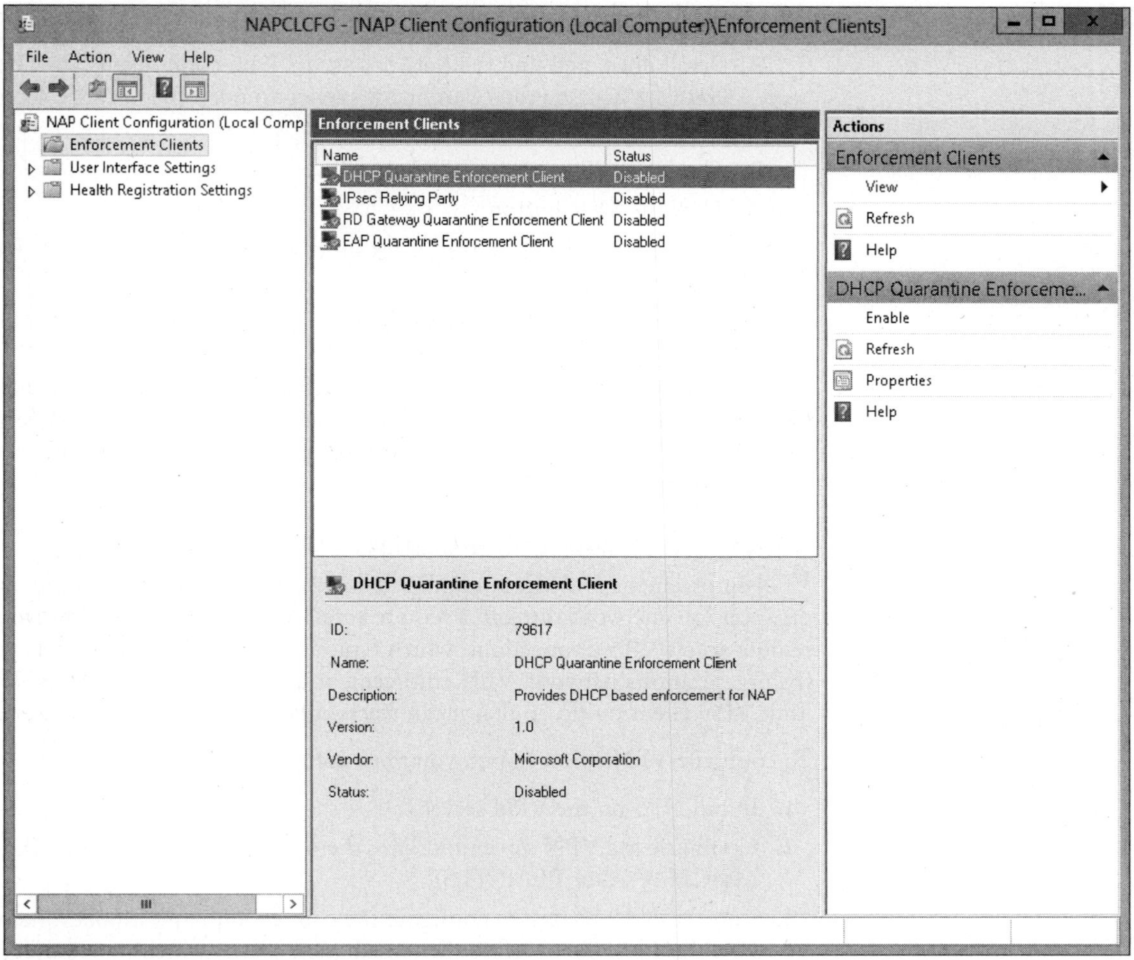

Figure 14-22

Enabling enforcement client for DHCP

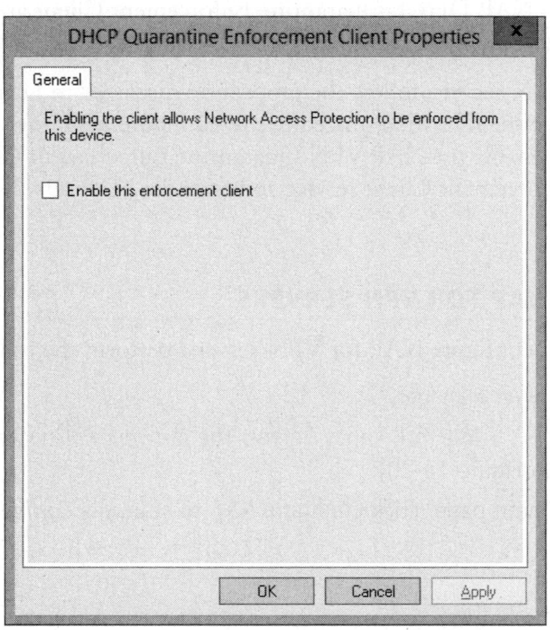

5. Select the Enable this enforcement client option. Click OK to close the *DHCP Quarantine Enforcement Client Properties* dialog box.
6. Close the *NAP Client Configuration Client console*.
7. At the command prompt, execute the `services.msc` command.
8. Scroll down and find the Network Access Protection Agent. Then double-click the Network Access Protection Agent service to open the *Network Access Protection Agent Properties* dialog box.
9. Change the Startup type to Automatic.
10. Click the Start button.
11. After the service is started, click OK to close the *Network Access Protection Agent Properties* dialog box.
12. Close the *Services console* and close the command prompt.

Alternatively, you can configure a GPO to enable NAP enforcement clients. Navigate to Computer Configuration\Policies\Windows Settings\Security Settings\Network Access Protection\NAP Client Configuration\Enforcement Clients and enable the DHCP Quarantine Enforcement Client.

CONFIGURING NAP ENFORCEMENT FOR VPN

VPN enforcement provides strong limited network access for all computers that connect to the organization's network through a remote access VPN connection. However, it applies only to remote access VPN connections, which typically do not affect computers connected directly to the organization's network. VPN enforcement uses a set of remote-access IP packet filters to limit VPN client traffic, so that it can reach only the resources on the restricted network.

To configure VPN enforcement, you must complete the following:

1. Install NPS on the VPN server.
2. Configure the VPN server and have them use PEAP-based authentication (either PEAP-MS-CHAP v2 or PEAP-TLS).
3. Run the *NAP Wizard* to configure the connection request policy, network policy, and NAP health policy. Define the remediation severs, which noncompliant clients can access.
4. Enable the NAP DHCP Quarantine Enforcement Client and start the NAP service on NAP-capable client computers.

To configure VPN servers, follow the procedures discussed in Lesson 10 to install a VPN server. Then, use the following procedures to configure NAP for VPN servers. Finally, follow similar steps to enable the NAP VPN Quarantine Enforcement Client as the NAP DHCP Quarantine Enforcement Client service and start the NAP service as you did for the DHCP server.

CONFIGURE NAP FOR VPN SERVERS

GET READY. To configure NAP for VPN servers, perform the following steps:

1. Open Server Manager.
2. Click Tools > Network Policy Server. The *Network Policy Server console* opens (refer to Figure 14-10).
3. In the main pane, click Configure NAP to start the *Configure NAP Wizard*.

4. When the *Select Network Connection Method For Use with NAP* wizard opens, select the Virtual Private network (VPN) for the network connection method (see Figure 14-23). Click Next.

Figure 14-23

Selecting the Virtual Private Network (VPN) for the Network Connection

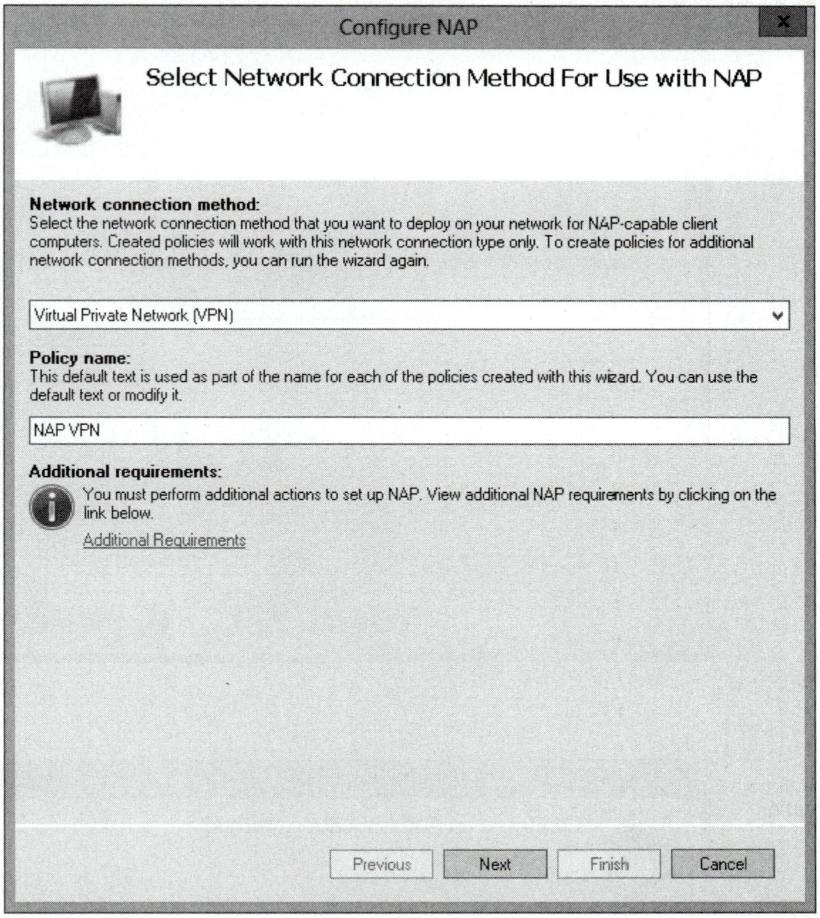

5. By default, NPS already supports Remote Access and Wireless RADIUS clients. If you want to add additional RADIUS clients on the *Specify NAP Enforcement Servers Running DHCP Server* page, click the Add button. For now, click Next.
6. On the *Configure User and Machine Groups* page (see Figure 14-24), you can specify who gets access based on the machine group or the user group, by clicking the appropriate Add button. When the *Select Group* dialog box opens, type the name of the group and click OK. If no computer groups are added, the policy is added to all computers that connect using VPN. On the *Configure User Groups and Machine Groups* page, click Next.
7. On the *Configure an Authentication Method* page (see Figure 14-25), *Secure Password (PEAP-MS-CHAP v2)* is already selected. If you support smart-cards, select Smart Card or other certificate (EAP-TLS). Click Next.

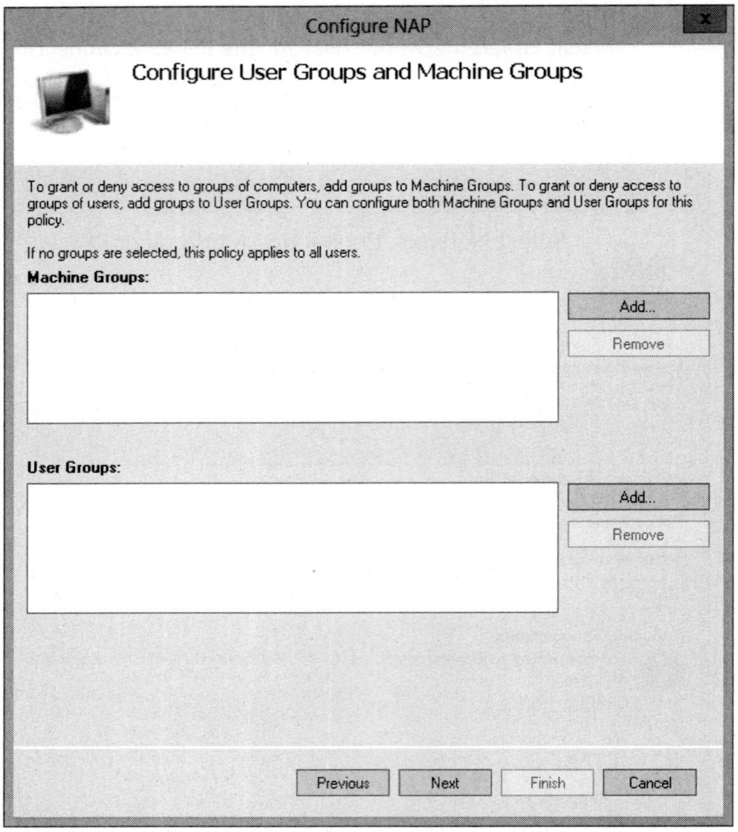

Figure 14-24
Specifying user and machine groups for NAP

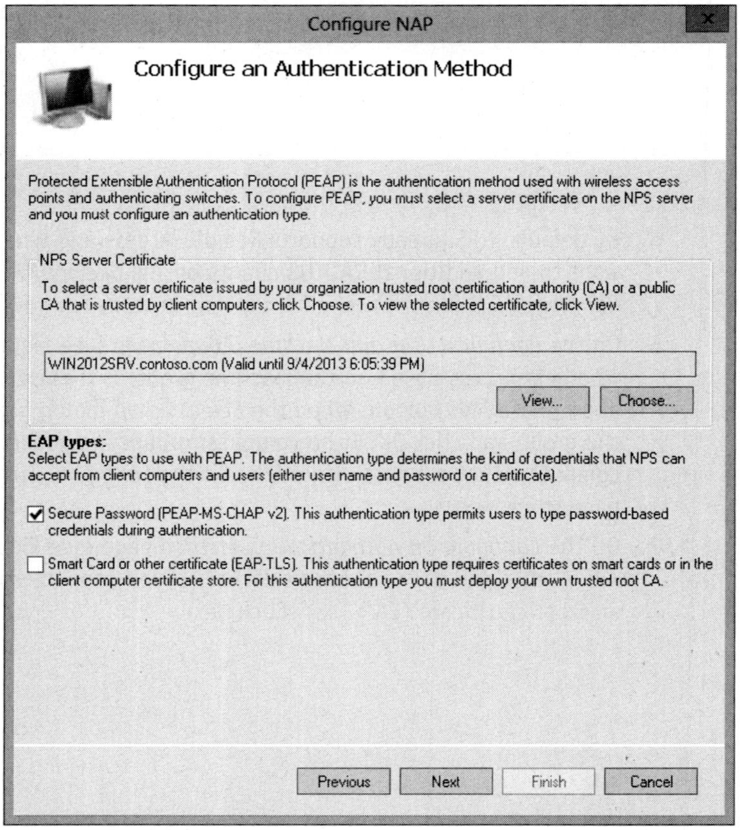

Figure 14-25
Configuring an authentication method for NAP

8. On the *Specify a NAP Remediation Server Group and URL* page, specify each computer that can be used for remediation, including WSUS, anti-virus management severs, and so on. To add a computer, click the New Group to open the *New Remediation Server Group* dialog box. In the *Group Name* text box. provide a group name and click Add to open the *Add New Server* dialog box. Type the name of the server and IP address and click OK to close the *Add New Server* dialog box. Click OK to close the *New Remediation Server Group* dialog box.
9. You can also specify the URL in the *Help Web* page dialog box that would provide instructions to the user to get his computer to be compliant. Click Next.
10. On the *Define NAP Health Policy* page, you can define a computer to auto-remediate (if possible) and you can specify if you want to deny or allow access if the computer is not compliant. Click Next.
11. On the *Completing NAP Enforcement Policy and RADIUS Client Configuration* page, click Finish.

Configuring System Health Validators

As mentioned before, the System Health Agents (SHAs) and System Health Validators (SHVs) provide health-state status and validation. Windows 8 includes a Windows Security Health Validator SHA that monitors the Windows Security Center settings. Windows Server 2012 includes a corresponding Windows Security Health Validator SHV.

CERTIFICATION READY
Configure System Health Validators (SHVs).
Objective 4.3

System Health Validators (SHVs) settings define the requirements for client computers that connect to your network. They are configured using the Network Policy Server console, as shown in Figure 14-26.

Figure 14-26
Managing the Windows SHV

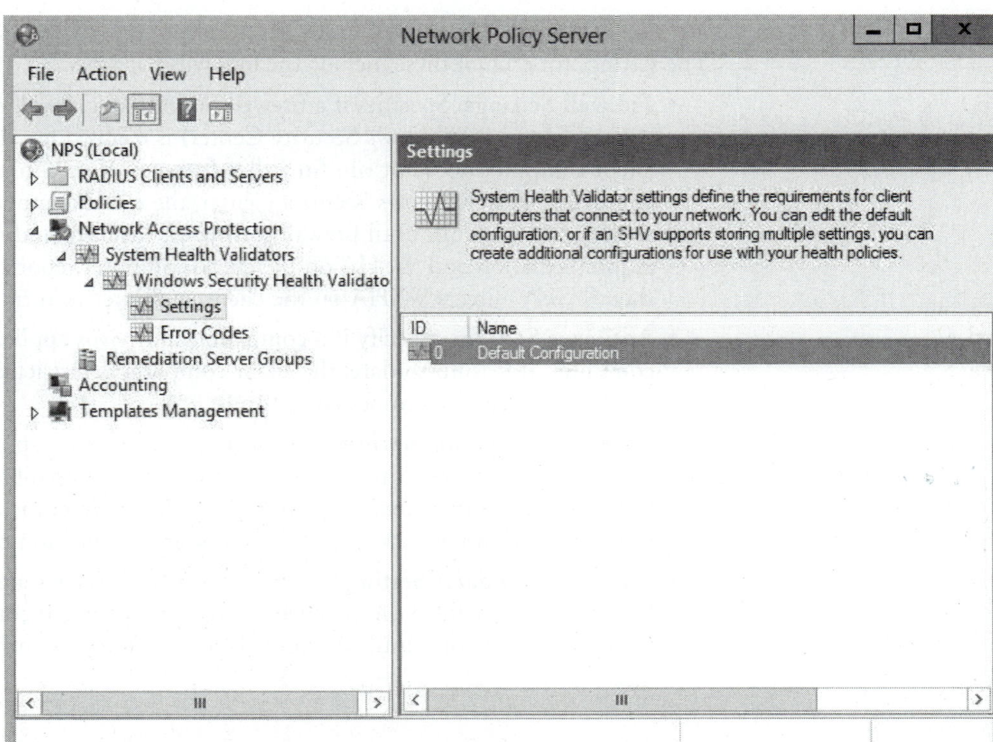

If you double-click a *SHV*, you open the Windows Security Health Validator box (see Figure 14-27). When you configure SHV, there are two sets of configurations:

- Windows 8, Windows 7, Windows Vista
- Windows XP

Figure 14-27

Configuring Windows SHV

The settings for each of these include the following options:

- **Firewall Settings:** Specifies if a firewall (Windows Firewall or firewall software that is compatible with Windows Security Center) is enabled for all network connections. If the client computer does not run firewall software or does run a firewall that is not compliant with Windows Security Center, the client computer is restricted to a remediation network until firewall software is installed and running. If you enable NAP autoremediation and WSHA on the client computer reports that no firewall is enabled, then WSHV directs WSHA on the client computer to turn on Windows Firewall.
- **Antivirus Settings:** Specify if a compatible anti-virus application runs on the client computer. If it is up-to-date, the client computer is restricted to a remediation network until the computer becomes compliant.
- **Spyware Protection Settings:** Specify if an antispyware application (Windows Defender or some other spyware protection software that is compatible with the Windows Security Center) runs on the client computer. If it is up-to-date, the client computer is restricted to a remediation network until the computer becomes compliant.
- **Automatic Updates Settings:** When Automatic Updates are on and Microsoft Update Services is not enabled on the client computer, the client computer is restricted to a remediation network until Microsoft Update Services is enabled.

- **Security Updates Settings:** If you select Restrict access for clients that do not have all available security updates installed, the client computer is restricted to a remediation network. However, this option should not be selected unless the computers that have the Windows Update Agent running are registered with a server running Windows Server Update Service (WSUS) or similar server. You can specify the minimum severity of the updates (Critical Only, Important and above, Moderate and above, and Low and above), and the number of hours allowed since the client has checked for security updates (maximum of 72 hours). Figure 14-28 shows the Security Updates Settings.

Figure 14-28

Configuring Security Updates settings

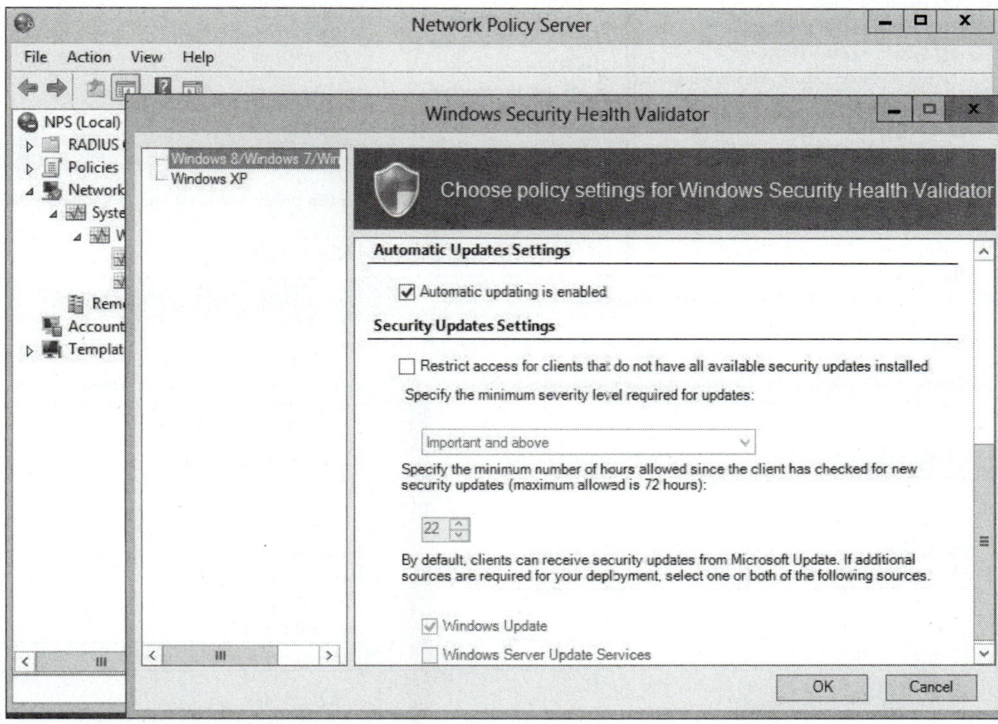

Configuring Health Policies

Health policies consist of one or more system health validators and other settings that enable you to define client computer configuration requirements for the NAP-capable computers that attempt to connect to your network.

CERTIFICATION READY
Configure health policies.
Objective 4.3

Typically, the health policies are in pairs, one for NAP-compliant and the other for NAP-noncompliant, as shown in Figure 14-29. To use the NAP-compliant policy, the client must pass all SHV checks, and to use the NAP-noncompliant policy, the client just has to fail one or more of the SHV checks.

Figure 14-29

Viewing the health policies

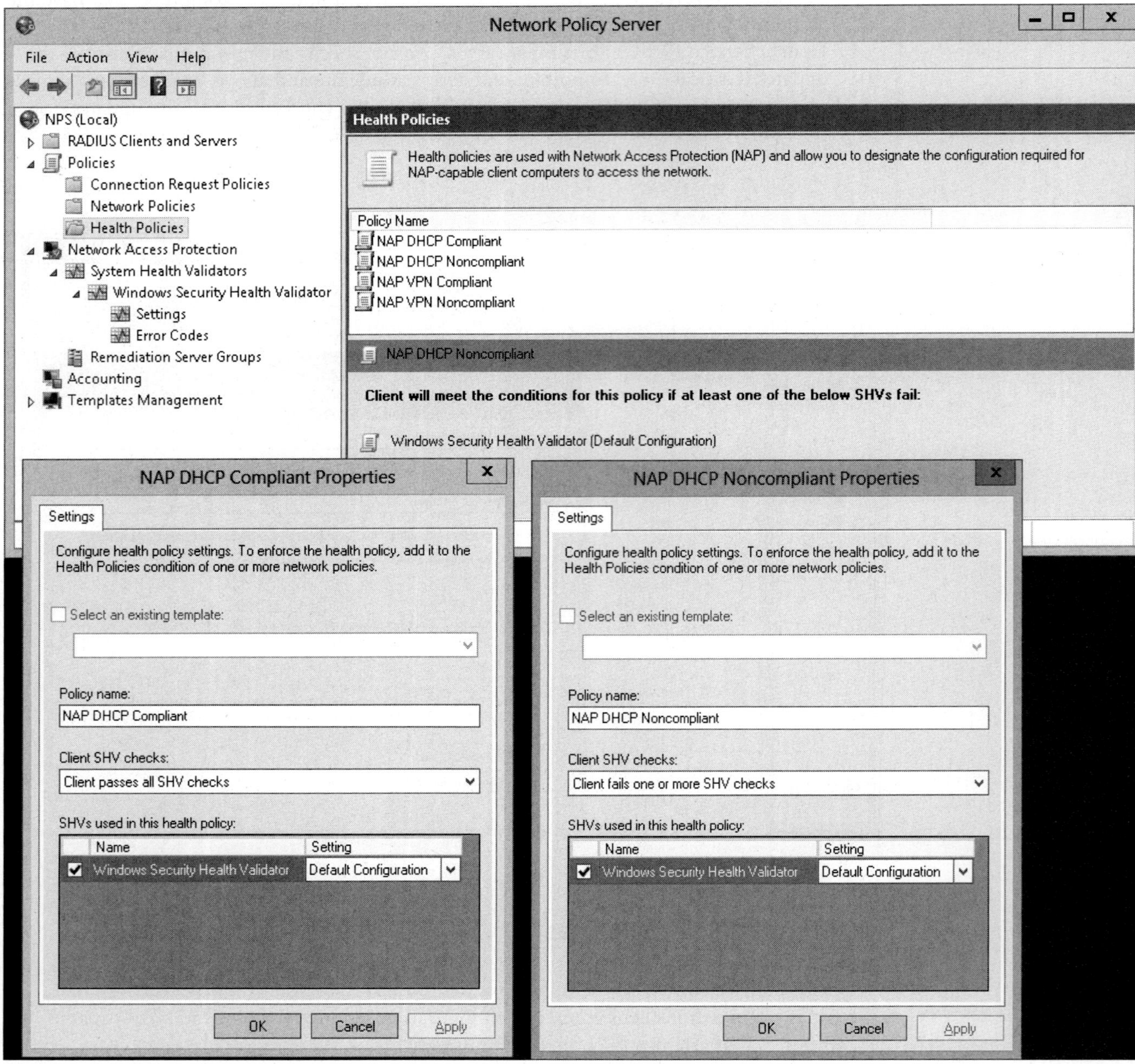

The health policies are connected directly to the network policies and connection Request Policies. As you open the network policies, the Condition tab specifies the health policy that it is connected to, as shown in Figure 14-30.

As you can see in Figure 14-31, for NAP DHCP health policies, the network policies include NAP DHCP-compliant, NAP DHCP-noncompliant, and NAP DHCP nonNAP-capable policies. If you open each policy, you find the following NAP enforcement settings:

- **NAP DHCP-compliant**: Allow full network access.
- **NAP DHCP-noncompliant**: Allow limited access, as shown in Figure 14-32.
- **NAP DHCP nonNAPcapable properties**: Allow full network access.

Figure 14-30

Displaying the conditions of a health policy

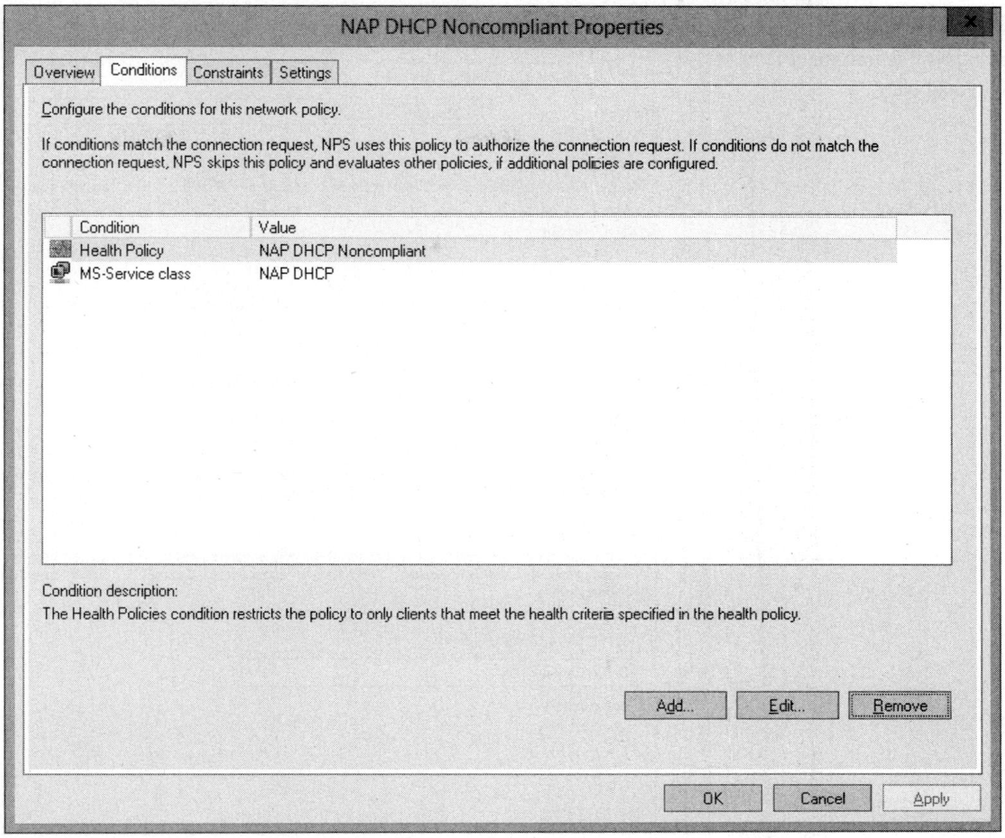

Figure 14-31

Displaying the network policies

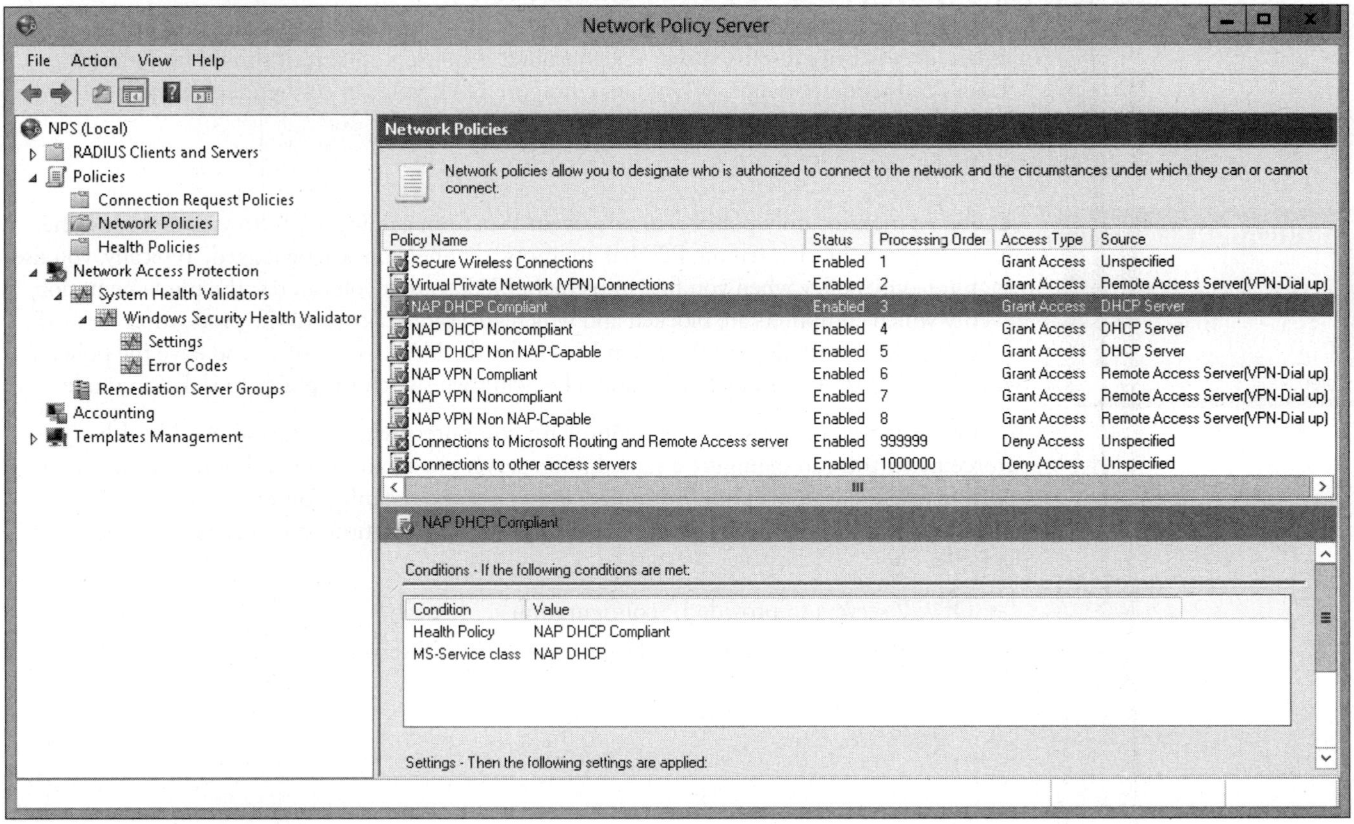

Figure 14-32

Viewing NAP Enforcement for a network policy

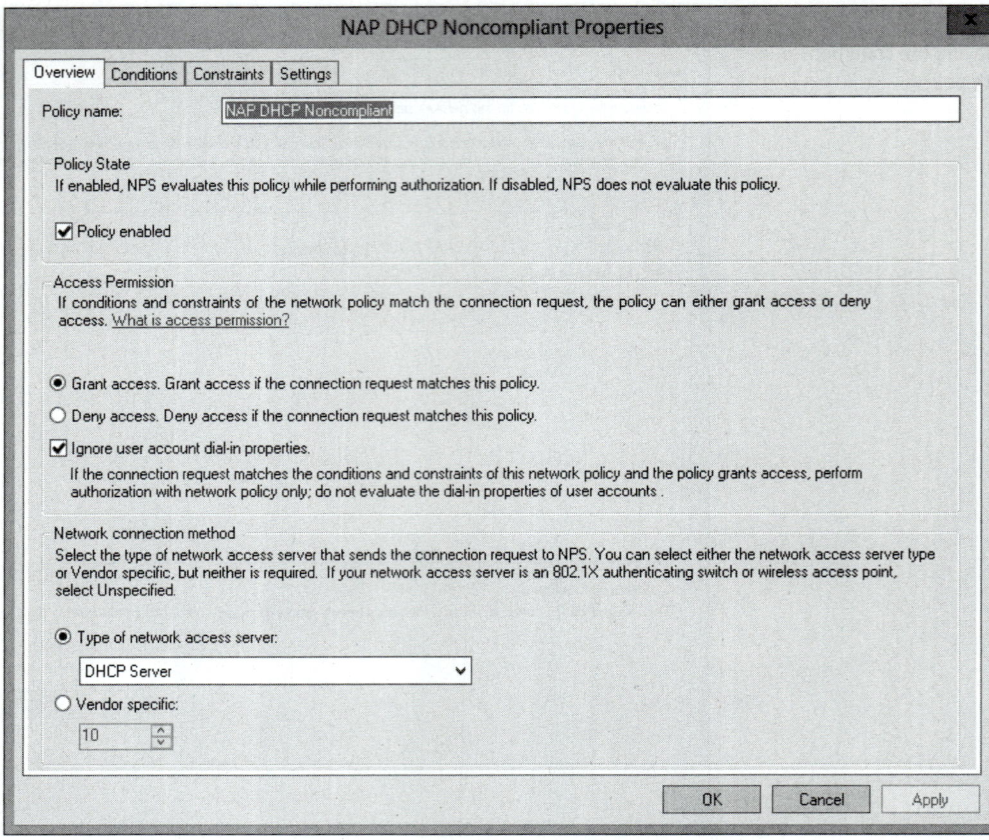

Configuring Isolation and Remediation

It has already been discussed that if a computer is non-compliant, it should be isolated from production network. When you configure NAP, you can configure either a monitor-only policy or an isolation policy.

CERTIFICATION READY
Configure isolation and remediation of non-compliant computers using DHCP and VPN.
Objective 4.3

Although a monitor-only policy cannot prevent PCs from gaining access to your network, the compliance state of each remote PC that attempts a connection will be logged. Typically, you use a monitor-only policy when you first implement NAP so that you can test the implementation to verify which computers are blocked and which are granted access to the production network by viewing the security logs in the Event Viewer on the NAP server. After you have the policies tweaked and NAP is working like it should be, you then switch the policy to isolation mode.

To provide assistance to users of noncompliant computers when requiring NAP health enforcement, you can configure a remediation server group and troubleshooting URL that is available to users if they fail the compliance check. Each organization has its own remediation server depending on the requirements of the SHVs. Remediation servers typically consists of the following:

- DHCP servers to provide IP configuration
- Naming servers, including DNS servers and WINS servers

- Active Directory domain controllers (read-only domain controllers are recommended to minimize security risks)
- Internet proxy servers so that noncompliant NAP clients can access the Internet
- HRAs so that noncompliant NAP clients can obtain a health certificate for the IPsec enforcement method
- Web server that contains the troubleshooting URL server, so users can access information on compliance
- Anti-virus/anti-malware servers to retrieve updated anti-virus/anti-malware updates
- Software update servers so that clients can get Windows updates

CONFIGURE ISOLATION MODE OR THE LIST OF REMEDIATION SERVERS

GET READY. To configure the isolation mode or the list of remediation servers, perform the following steps:

1. Open Server Manager.
2. Click Tools > Network Policy Server. The *Network Policy Server console* opens.
3. Under *Policies*, click Network Policies.
4. In the right pane, double-click the appropriate network policy.
5. Click the Settings tab.
6. To modify the NAP Enforcement, including whether the policy has full network access or limited access, click NAP Enforcement.
7. To change the Remediation Servers Group and Troubleshooting URL, click Configure.

Configuring NAP Client Settings

For clients to use NAP, they must have the Security Center enabled and have the NAP Agent service running.

CERTIFICATION READY
Configure NAP client settings.
Objective 4.3

You can use the Enable Security Center in the Group Policy procedure to enable Security Center on NAP-capable clients using Group Policy. Some NAP deployments that use Windows Security Health Validator require Security Center. In addition, you need to open the Services console to start and set the startup type to Automatic the Network Access Protection Agent service.

ENABLE THE SECURITY CENTER AND START THE NETWORK ACCESS PROTECTION AGENT SERVICE

GET READY. To enable the Security Center and start the NAP Agent service using Group Policy, perform the following steps:

1. Open Server Manager.
2. Click Tools > Group Policy Management. The *Group Policy Management console* opens.
3. Navigate to a GPO, right-click the GPO, and then click Edit. The *Group Policy Management Editor* opens.
4. In the console tree, navigate to Computer Configuration\Administrative Templates\Windows Components\Security Center.

5. Double-click Turn on Security Center (Domain PCs only), click Enabled, and then click OK.
6. Navigate to Computer Configuration\Policies\Windows Settings\Security Settings\System Services.
7. Double-click the Network Access Protection Agent service. The *Network Access Protection Agent Properties* dialog box.
8. Select Automatic and click OK to close the *Network Access Protection Agent Properties* dialog box.
9. Close the *Group Policy Management Editor* and close the *Group Policy Management console*.

To verify a client's configuration, you can run the following command:

```
netsh nap client show state
```

Figure 14-33 shows the `netsh nap client show state` command.

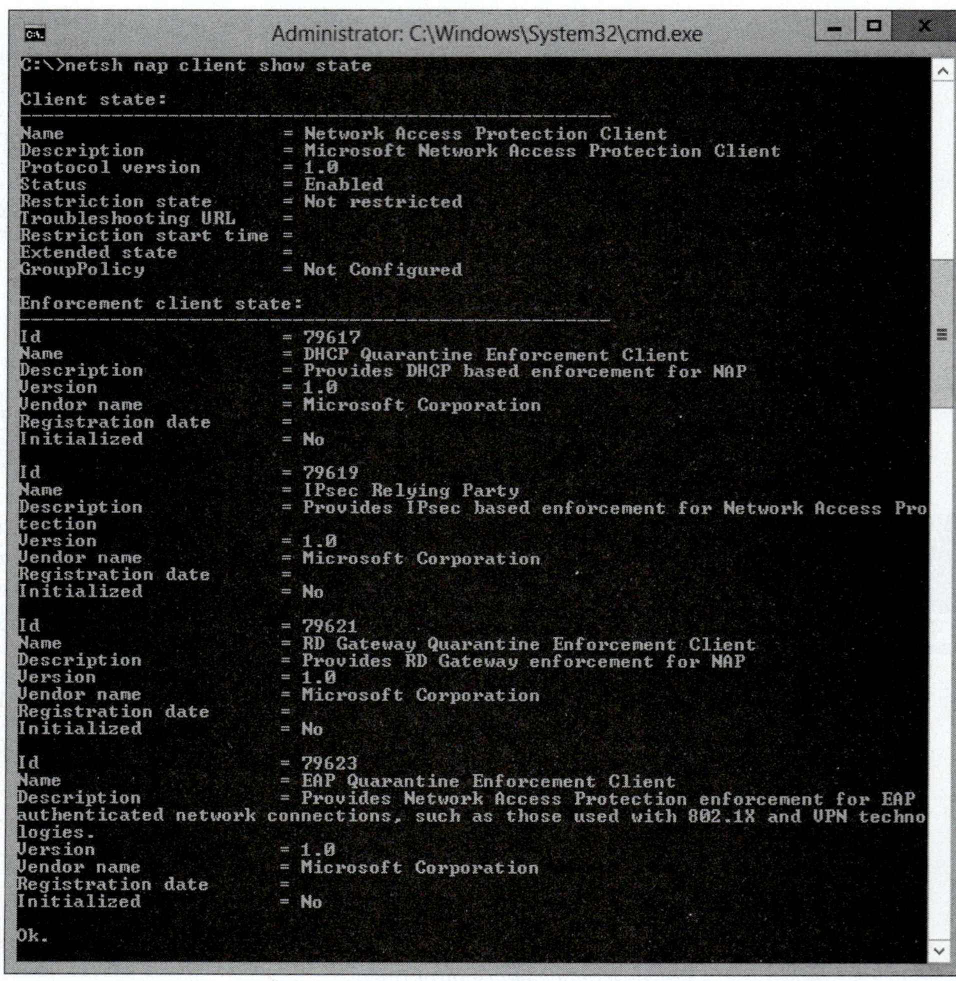

Figure 14-33

Using the `netsh nap client show state` command

SKILL SUMMARY

IN THIS LESSON, YOU LEARNED:

- Network Access Protection (NAP) is Microsoft's software for controlling networks for computers based on the health of the host, such as whether it has the newest security patches and a current anti-virus/anti-malware software package.
- NAP includes built-in enforcement methods that define the mechanisms that NAP can use, including DHCP, Internet Protocol Security (IPsec), VPN, 802.1, and Remote Desktop Gateway (RD Gateway).
- System Health Agents (SHAs) are components that maintain information and reporting on one or more elements of the health of a NAP client.
- Each SHA creates a Statement of Health (SoH) that transmits to the NAP Agent. Each SHA generates a new Statement of Health whenever the status is updated, such as when an update to the anti-virus package was released but has not been installed on the client.
- NAP Agent maintains information about the health of the NAP client computer and transmits information between the NAP enforcement clients and the SHAs.
- A remediation server is an optional component that can be deployed to allow noncompliant client computers to achieve network compliance and gain network access.
- System Health Validators (SHVs) settings define the requirements for client computers that connect to your computer.
- Health policies consist of one or more system health validators and other settings that enable you to define client computer configuration requirements for the Network Access Protection (NAP)-capable computers that attempt to connect to your network.
- Although a monitor-only policy cannot prevent PCs from gaining access to your network, the compliance state of each remote PC attempting a connection will be logged.
- Typically, you use a monitor-only policy when you first implement NAP to test the implementation so that you can verify which computers are blocked and which are granted access to the production network by viewing the security logs in the Event Viewer on the NAP server.
- To provide assistance to users of noncompliant computers when requiring NAP health enforcement, you can configure a remediation server group and troubleshooting URL that will be available to users if they fail the compliance check.
- For clients to use NAP, they must have the Security Center enabled and have the NAP Agent service running.

Knowledge Assessment

Multiple Choice

Select the correct answer for each of the following questions.

1. Which of the following NAP enforcement mechanisms is considered the weakest?
   a. DHCP
   b. IPsec
   c. VPN
   d. 802.1
   e. RD Gateway

2. Which of the following NAP enforcement mechanisms is considered the strongest?
   a. DHCP
   b. IPsec
   c. VPN
   d. 802.1
   e. RD Gateway
3. Which component used with NAP maintains information and reports on the health of a NAP client?
   a. Statement of Health
   b. Health Registration Authority
   c. NAP Agent
   d. System Health Agent
4. Which is the most common System Health Agent used in Windows?
   a. Windows NAP Agent
   b. Windows Security Center
   c. NPS service
   d. HRA service
5. Which is used to make a computer compliant when you have quarantined computers that are not compliant when using NAP?
   a. Reload Windows.
   b. Reset the computer account in the domain.
   c. Reboot the computer.
   d. Use remediation servers.
6. With NAP, what defines the requirements for client computers to connect to a network that is connected?
   a. SHA
   b. RHA
   c. SoH
   d. SHV
7. Which of the following is typically a remediation server when using NAP? (Choose all that apply.)
   a. Anti-virus management server
   b. File server
   c. DHCP server
   d. DNS server
   e. Print server
   f. Domain controller
   g. WSUS server
8. You just implemented NAP. How can you ensure that domain computers are up-to-date?
   a. WSUS
   b. WDS
   c. SCOM
   d. SVH
9. Which server is used as the NAP health policy server?
   a. NAT
   b. DNS
   c. PMO
   d. NPS

10. Which of the following is used as a Windows Security Health Validator? (Choose all that apply.)
    a. Strong password
    b. Anti-virus program
    c. Spyware
    d. A locked down computer

Best Answer

Choose the letter that corresponds to the best answer. More than one answer choice may achieve the goal. Select the BEST answer.

1. You want to enable NAP so that all portal computers using wireless connections have an active firewall. Which type of enforcement policy should you implement?
   a. IPsec enforcement
   b. 802.1x enforcement
   c. EAP enforcement
   d. DHCP enforcement
2. Which command would you use to check whether a client is compliant with a health policy that you define to be used with NAP?
   a. `ipconfig /nap`
   b. `netsh nap client show config`
   c. `netsh nap client show state`
   d. `netstat /nap`
3. How can you ensure that the health of all clients can be monitored and reported when using NAP?
   a. Create a GPO that enables Security Center on the client computers.
   b. Create a GPO that enables Security Center on the domain controllers.
   c. Create a GPO that installs the NAP authorization package.
   d. Create a GPO that enforces EAP authentication
4. You decide to implement NAP. You have created a group policy to enable NAP on the client computers and for the client computers to get updates from WSUS. How can you ensure that client computers that do not have critical security updates cannot access data production servers?
   a. Enable automatic updates on each client.
   b. Remote the computer from the domain.
   c. Quarantine clients that do not have the critical updates.
   d. Remote network access using user rights.
5. You have users who connect to the corporate network using their laptops. Because these computers often access confidential data, you need to be sure that users access network resources only from computers that comply with the company policy of having an anti-virus, anti-spyware and have the newest Windows updates. You decide to use NAP. Which type of enforcement policy should you implement?
   a. IPsec enforcement
   b. 802.1x enforcement
   c. EAP enforcement
   d. DHCP enforcement

Matching and Identification

1. Match the term with the correct definition with the correct description or scenario?
    _____ a) NAP health policy server
    _____ b) System Health Agents
    _____ c) Statement of Health
    _____ d) NAP Agent
    _____ e) Health Registration Authority
    _____ f) Health requirements server
    _____ g) Remediation servers
    _____ h) System Health Validators
    1. Server that provides the current health state information to NPS server
    2. Maintains information and reporting on one or more elements of the health of a NAP client
    3. Optional servers used to make a noncompliant computer compliant
    4. An electronic statement that shows the health of a client
    5. Used to deliver health certificates from a CA
    6. Defines the requirements for client computers that connect to the network
    7. The component that transmits the information between the NAP enforcement clients and the System Health Agents.
    8. Server running NPS

Build a List

1. Specify, in order, the NAP connection process steps. Not all steps will be used.
    _____ The NAP health policy server determines whether the NAP client meets health requirements.
    _____ The SHA locks down the computer.
    _____ The NAP health policy sends a System Statement of Health Response.
    _____ Each SHA on the NAP client validates its system health and generates an SoH.
    _____ The SHA uses UAC to determine whether the computer can connect to the network.
    _____ If the client is compliant, the connection is made.
    _____ Combine SoHs from multiple SHAs into an SSoH.

2. Identify which steps need to be completed when you configure NAP DHCP enforcement.
    _____ Install NPS on a dedicated NPS server.
    _____ Run the NAP Wizard to configure the policies and define the remediation servers.
    _____ Enable NAP for the DHCP scopes.
    _____ Configure a DHCP server and create the appropriate DHCP scopes.
    _____ Link the DHCP server to the NPS server.
    _____ Configure the clients to support NAP.
    _____ Install NPS on the DHCP server.

3. Identify which steps need to be completed when you configure NAP VPN enforcement.
    _____ Configure the VPN servers and the VPN protocols.
    _____ Run the NAP Wizard to configure the policies.
    _____ Install NAP role on the server.
    _____ Enable the DHCP.
    _____ Configure the clients to support NAP.
    _____ Install the NPS on the VPN server.

Identify the Option

1. You have deployed NAP. However, noncompliant computers cannot access the remediation network. Which option do you need to change?

Figure 14-34

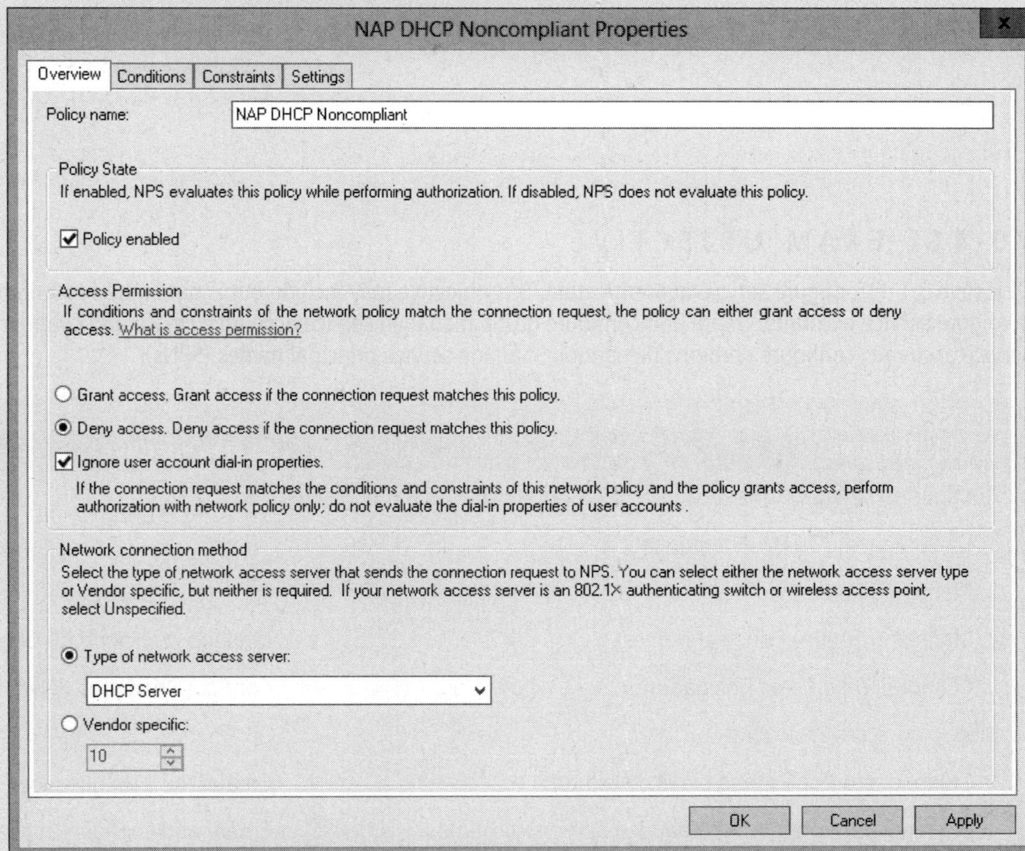

Business Case Scenarios

Scenario 14-1: Implementing NAP

You have a network with around 1,000 clients that connect to it. In addition, you have an additional 50 consultants and vendors that connect to your network each week directly and through the VPN. How can you ensure that all computers connecting to your network have an updated antivirus software package, an updated anti-spyware package, and the newest security patches, and if they don't, how can they get an updated antivirus software package, an updated anti-spyware package, and the newest security patches?

Scenario 14-2: Configuring Remediation Servers

You have implemented NAP with DHCP enforcement so that you make sure you have an updated antivirus software package, an updated anti-spyware package, and the newest security patches. Which servers do you need to set up as remediation servers and why?

15 LESSON

Configuring Service Authentication

70-411 EXAM OBJECTIVE

Objective 5.1 – Configure service authentication. This objective may include but is not limited to: create and configure service accounts; create and configure group managed service accounts; create and configure managed service accounts; configure Kerberos delegation; manage service principal names (SPNs).

Lesson Heading	Exam Objective
Configuring Service Authentication	
Understanding NTLM Authentication	
Managing Kerberos	
Managing Service Principal Names	Manage service principal names (SPNs)
Configuring Kerberos Delegation	Configure Kerberos delegation
Managing Service Accounts	
Creating and Configuring Service Accounts	Create and configure service accounts
Creating and Configuring Managed Service Accounts	Create and configure managed service accounts
Creating and Configuring Group Managed Service Accounts	Create and configure group managed service accounts

KEY TERMS

authentication
constrained delegation
group managed service accounts
Kerberos
Kerberos delegation
managed service accounts (MSAs)
NT LAN Manager (NTLM)
service account
service principal name (SPN)

Configuring Service Authentication

THE BOTTOM LINE

Authentication is the act of confirming the identity of a user or system and is an essential part used in authorization when the user or system tries to access a server or network resource. Because authentication is such a key component in security, you need to choose the appropriate authentication method. Two types of authentication that Windows supports are NT LAN Manager (NTLM) and Kerberos.

Although Kerberos is the default authentication protocol for today's domain computers, NTLM is the default authentication protocol for Windows NT, standalone computers that are not part of a domain, and situations in which you authenticate to a server using an IP address. NTLM also acts as a fallback authentication protocol if Kerberos authentication cannot be completed, such as when it is blocked by a firewall.

Understanding NTLM Authentication

NT LAN Manager (NTLM) is a suite of Microsoft security protocols that provides authentication, integrity, and confidentiality to users. NTLM is an integrated single sign-on mechanism, which is probably best recognized as part of Integrated Windows Authentication for HTTP authentication. It provides maximum compatibility with different versions of Windows and compared to Kerberos, it is the easiest to implement.

NTLM uses a challenge-response mechanism for authentication in which clients are able to prove their identities without sending a password to the server. After a random 8-byte challenge message is sent to the client from the server, the client uses the user's password as a key to generate a response back to the server using an MD4/MD5 hashing algorithm (one-way mathematical calculation) and DES encryption (a commonly used encryption algorithm that encrypted and decrypted data with the same key).

Managing Kerberos

Kerberos is a computer network authentication protocol, which allows hosts to prove their identity over a non-secure network in a secure manner. It can also provide mutual authentication so that both the user and server verify each other's identity. For security reasons, Kerberos protocol messages are protected against eavesdropping and replay attacks.

The Kerberos protocol is a secure protocol that supports ticketing authentication. With Kerberos, security and authentication are based on secret key technology, and every host on the network has its own secret key. The Key Distribution Center maintains a database of these secret keys. Although Kerberos is more secure than NTLM, it is more complicated than NTLM, which requires additional configuration (such as requiring a service principal name (SPN) for the domain account).

When a user logs in to a network resource using Kerberos, the client transmits the username to the authentication server, along with the identity of the service the user wants to connect to (for example, a file server or a SharePoint server). The authentication server constructs a ticket, which contains a randomly generated session key, which is encrypted with the file server's secret key. The ticket is then sent to the client as part of its credentials, which includes the session key encrypted with the client's key/password. If the user types the right password, the client can decrypt the session key, present the ticket to the file or SharePoint server, and give the user the shared secret session key to communicate between them. Tickets are time stamped and typically expire after only a few hours.

For all of this to work and to ensure security, the domain controllers and clients must have the same time. Windows operating systems include the Time Service tool (W32Time service). Kerberos authentication will work if the time interval between the relevant computers is within the maximum enabled time parameters. The default is five minutes. You can also turn off the Time Service tool and install a third-party time service. Of course, if you have problems authenticating, you should make sure that the time is correct for the domain controllers and the client that is experiencing the problem.

Kerberos offers several benefits. When the client connects to a server or service, Kerberos uses the current client ticket proving that the client is authenticated. As a result, the service does not have to perform authentication to a domain controller. In addition, Kerberos can perform a double-hop authentication, which forwards Kerberos tickets from one service to a supporting service. Both of these Kerberos benefits improve authentication performance.

To secure the double-hop authentication, you can configure Kerberos constrained delegation. ***Constrained delegation*** restricts which services are allowed to delegate user credentials by specifying, for each application pool or service, the services to which a Kerberos ticket can be forwarded.

Kerberos settings are configured with Group Policies, specifically *\Computer Configuration\Policies\Windows\Settings\Security Settings\Account Policies\Kerberos Policy* (see Figure 15-1). It contains the following GPO entries:

- **Enforce user logon restrictions:** Enforces the Key Distribution Center (KDC) to check the validity of a user account every time a ticket request is submitted. If a user does not have the right to log on locally or if his or her account has been disabled, he or she will not get a ticket. By default, the setting is on.
- **Maximum lifetime for service ticket:** Defines the maximum lifetime of a service ticket (Kerberos ticket). The default lifetime is 10 hours.
- **Maximum lifetime for user ticket:** Defines the maximum lifetime ticket for a Kerberos TGT ticket (user ticket). The default lifetime is 10 hours.

Figure 15-1

Configuring Kerberos settings

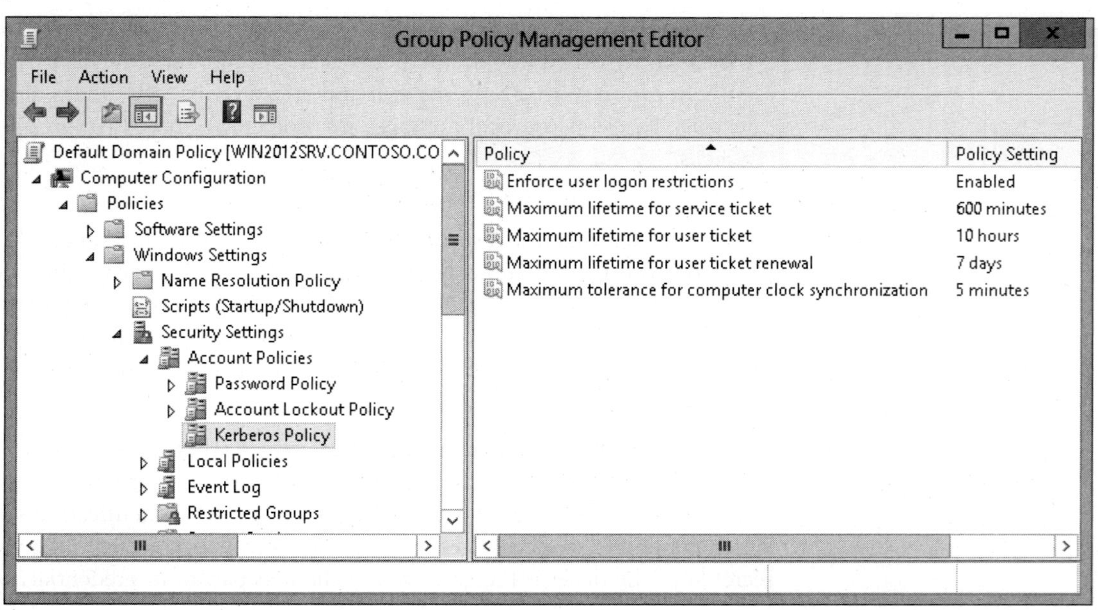

- **Maximum lifetime for user ticket renewal:** Defines how long a service or user ticket can be renewed. By default, it can be renewed up to 7 days.
- **Maximum tolerance for computer clock synchronization:** Defines the maximum time skew that can be tolerated between a ticket's timestamp and the current time at the KDC. Kerberos uses a timestamp to protect against replay attacks. The default setting is 5 minutes.

Managing Service Principal Names

A service or application that is secured by Kerberos must have an identity (a user account or computer account) within the realm (in this case, the domain) that the system exists on. Although Active Directory can identify an account using a simple username, the Kerberos standard includes information such as the service class, host name, and port that the account can use.

CERTIFICATION READY
Manage service principal names (SPNs).
Objective 5.1

A ***service principal name (SPN)*** is the name by which a client uniquely identifies an instance of a service. The client locates the service based on the SPN, which consists of three components:

1. The service class, such as HTTP (which includes both the HTTP and HTTPS protocols) or SQLService
2. The host name
3. The port (if port 80 is not being used)

To establish an SPN for https://portal.contoso.com on port 443, you use HTTP/portal.contoso.com:443. Kerberos authentication service then uses the SPN to authenticate a service.

When a domain controller's KDC receives the service ticket request from a client, it looks up the requested SPN. The KDC then creates a session key for the service and encrypts the session key with the password of the account with which the SPN is associated. The KDC issues a service ticket, containing the session key, to the client. The client presents the service ticket to the service. The service, which knows its own password, decrypts the session key and authentication is complete.

If a client submits a service ticket request for an SPN that does not exist in the identity store, no service ticket can be established and the client throws an access denied error. For this reason, each component of a SharePoint infrastructure that uses Kerberos authentication requires at least one SPN. For example, the intranet web application app pool account must have an SPN of HTTP/intranet.contoso.com.

The SPN is associated with the application pool, not the server. In addition, for each web application, you should assign two SPNs, one with the fully qualified domain name for the service and one with the NetBIOS name of the service.

You can use ADSI Edit to add SPNs to an account. To configure an SPN for a service or application pool account, you must have domain administrative permissions or a delegation to modify the `ServicePrincipalName` property. In addition, you must run ADSI Edit from a domain controller or load the Windows Server 2012 Remote Server Administration Tools feature.

CONFIGURE AN SPN FOR A SERVICE OR APPLICATION POOL ACCOUNT

GET READY. To configure an SPN for a Service or Application Pool Account, perform the following steps:

1. Open Server Manager.
2. Click Tools > ADSI Edit. The *ADSI Edit console* opens.

3. Right-click ADSI Edit in the console tree, and then click Connect To (see Figure 15-2).

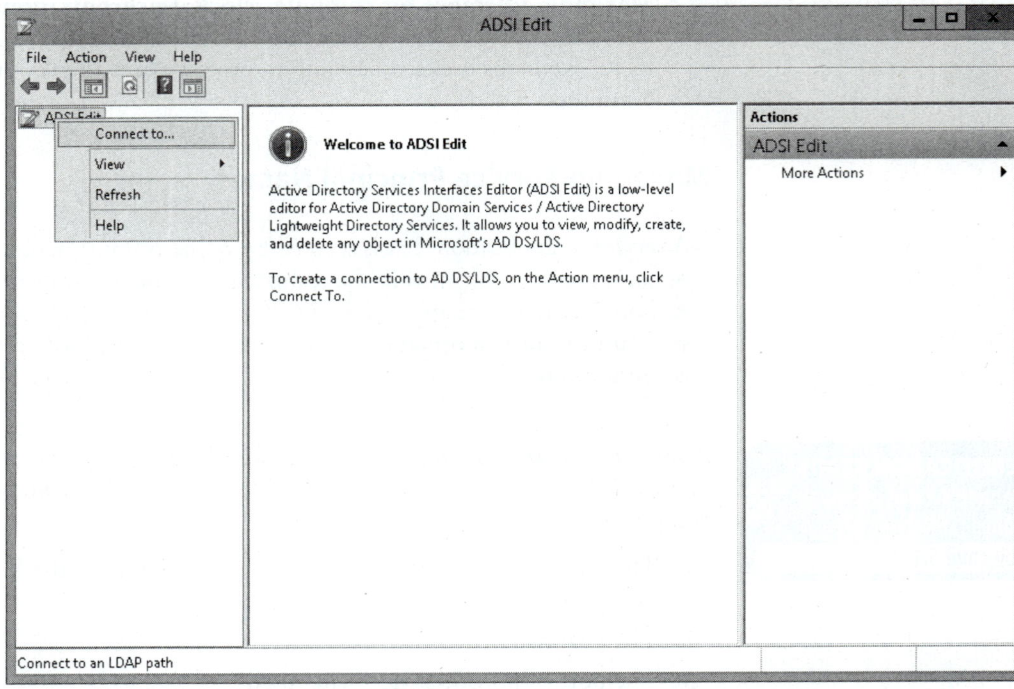

Figure 15-2

Connecting ADSI Edit to a domain controller

4. When the *Connection Settings* dialog appears, click OK (see Figure 15-3).

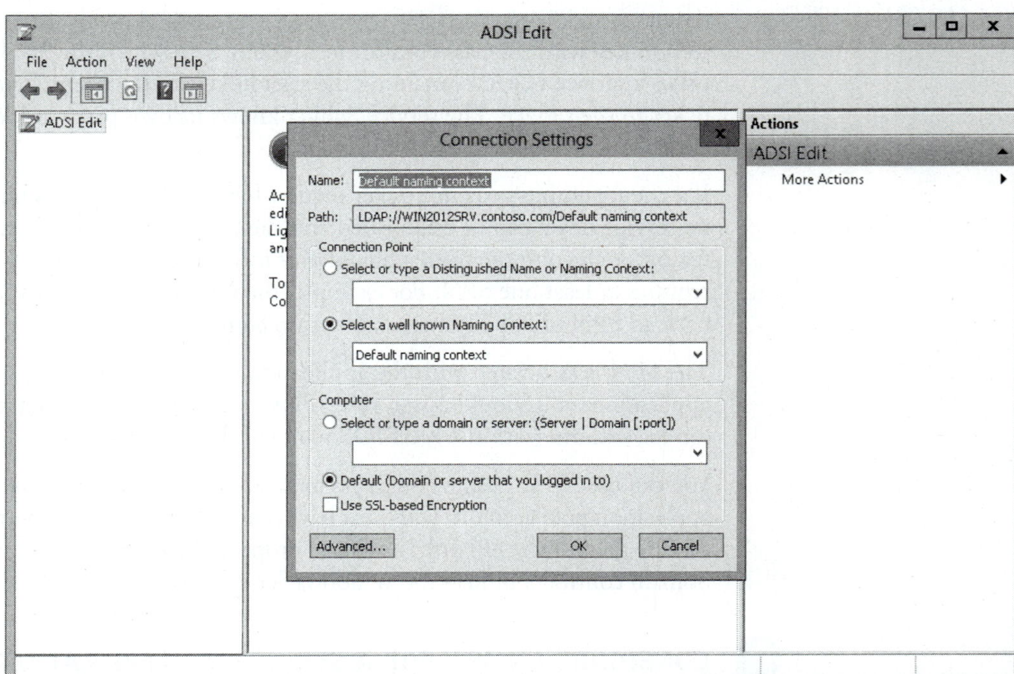

Figure 15-3

Specifying the connection settings

5. Expand Default Naming Context in the console tree, expand the domain, and then expand the nodes representing the OUs in which the account exists. Click the OU in which the account exists.

6. In the *Details* pane, right-click the service account and then click Properties (see Figure 15-4).

Figure 15-4

Opening the properties of an account

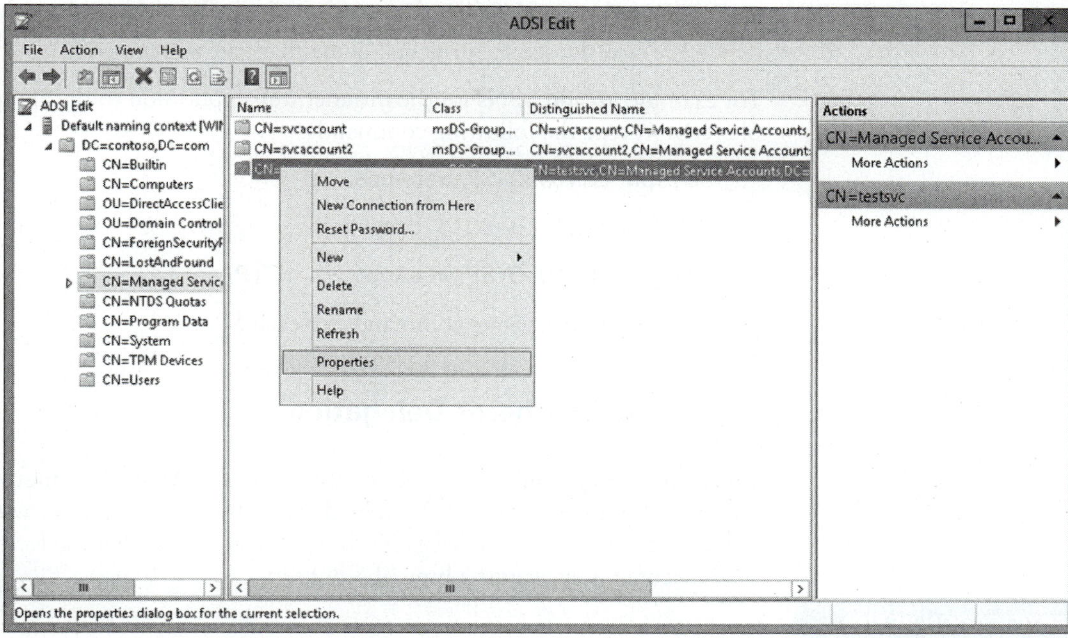

7. In the *Attributes* list, double-click servicePrincipalName to display the *Multi-valued String Editor* dialog box (see Figure 15-5).

Figure 15-5

Managing the SPNs for an object

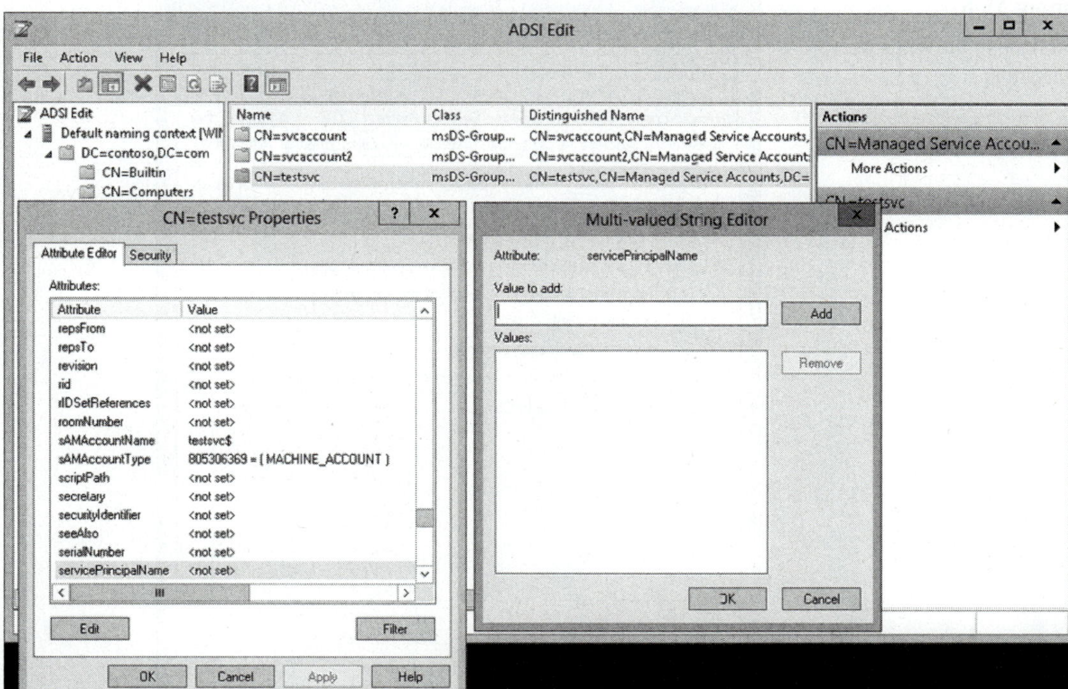

8. In the *Value to add* field, type the SPN and then click Add.
9. Click OK twice.

Alternatively, you can use the setspn.exe to add SPNs to an account. The syntax is as follows:

```
setspn <domain\user> -s <SPN>
```

whereby:

- *<domain\user>* identifies the security principal to which you want to add an SPN.
- *<SPN>* is the service principal name that you want to add.

For example, to add SPNs for the intranet web application to the app pool account used in SharePoint, type the following commands:

```
setspn CONTOSO\SP_WebApps -s
HTTP/portal.contoso.com
setspn CONTOSO\SP_WebApps -s HTTP/portal
```

You must perform separate commands for each SPN.

Configuring Kerberos Delegation

Kerberos delegation allows a Kerberos ticket to be created for another service on the originating user's behalf. This can be done with full delegation or with constrained delegation. Constrained delegation is when you specify that the Kerberos delegation can be executed only against a limited set of services.

CERTIFICATION READY
Configure Kerberos delegation.
Objective 5.1

To configure Kerberos delegation, you simply open *Active Directory Users and Computers*, go to the account that has an SPN, open the account's properties, and click *Delegation*. Figure 15-6 shows the Delegation tab.

Figure 15-6
Configuring the Kerberos delegation

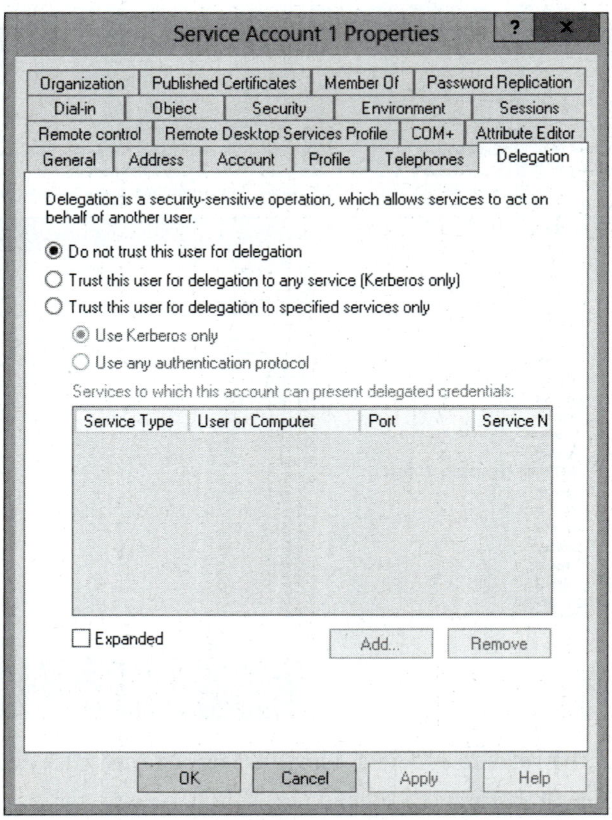

To allow full delegation, select the *Trust this user for delegation to any service (Kerberos only)*. To allow for constrained delegation, select the *Trust this user for delegation to specified services only*. You can then select to use only for Kerberos, or you can specify *Use any authentication protocol*, and then click the *Add* button, to specify which services to be delegated for a user or computer and specify the user or computer.

Managing Service Accounts

THE BOTTOM LINE

A ***service account*** is an account under which an operating system, process, or service runs. A service account can allow the application or service specific rights and permissions to function properly while minimizing the permissions required for the users using the application server. Service accounts are used to run Microsoft Exchange Microsoft SQL Server, Internet Information Services (IIS), and SharePoint.

On a local computer, you can configure an application run the Local Service, Network Service, or Local System (as discussed in Lesson 3, "Monitoring Servers"). Although these service accounts are simple to configure and use, they are typically shared among multiple applications and services, and they cannot be managed on a domain level. In addition, often you need to use accounts that have domain administrative rights and/or permissions. Besides the traditional service account, Microsoft has introduced managed service accounts and group managed service accounts.

Creating and Configuring Service Accounts

The traditional service account is a standard user account. Therefore, it is created with the Active Directory Users and Computers console.

CERTIFICATION READY
Create and configure service accounts.
Objective 5.1

Typically with user accounts, you specify how often a password gets changed. When a user logs on and a password is due to be changed, the user will be prompted to change the password. With service accounts, there is no interactive login. Therefore, you will configure the password not to expire. Unfortunately, anytime you have an account that does not expire, the password is more vulnerable because more time is available for cracking a password.

To reduce the risk of using service accounts, you should follow these guidelines:

- Require a unique account to run the service on each server.
- If possible, set up the account as a local account rather than a global domain account.
- Use a strong password for the service account.
- Make sure that the password changes often. Of course, when you change the password for the account, you will have to change the password for the services or applications that use the service account simultaneously.
- Give the account the least amount of access (user rights, NTFS permissions, and share permissions) it needs to perform its necessary tasks.
- Do not share the password, and store the password in a safe location.

CREATE A SERVICE ACCOUNT

GET READY. To configure a forwarding computer to forward events, perform the following steps:

1. Open Server Manager.
2. Click Tools > Active Directory Users and Computers.
3. In the console tree, double-click the Domain node to expand the node.
4. In the *Details* pane, right-click the organizational unit where you want to add the service account, click New, and then click User. The *New Object – User Wizard* starts (see Figure 15-7).

Figure 15-7

Creating a new user

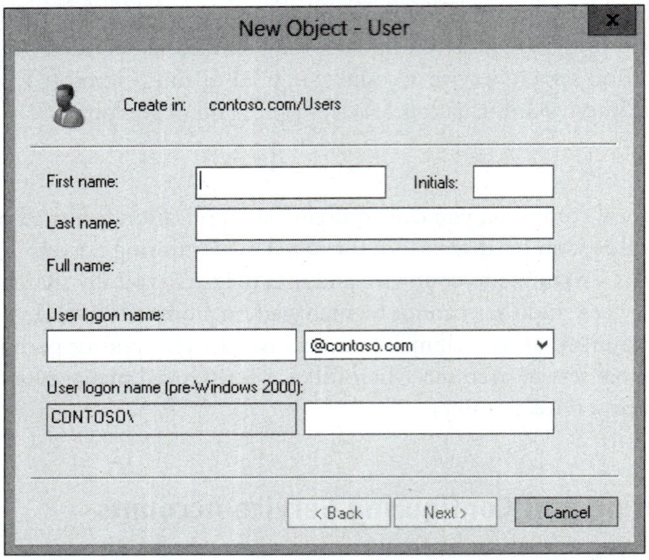

5. In the *First name* text box, type a first name for the service account.
6. In the *Last name* text box, type a last name for the service account.
7. Modify *Full name* as desired.
8. In the *User logon name* text box, type the name in which the service account will log on. Click Next. The password options appear (see Figure 15-8).

Figure 15-8

Specifying the password options

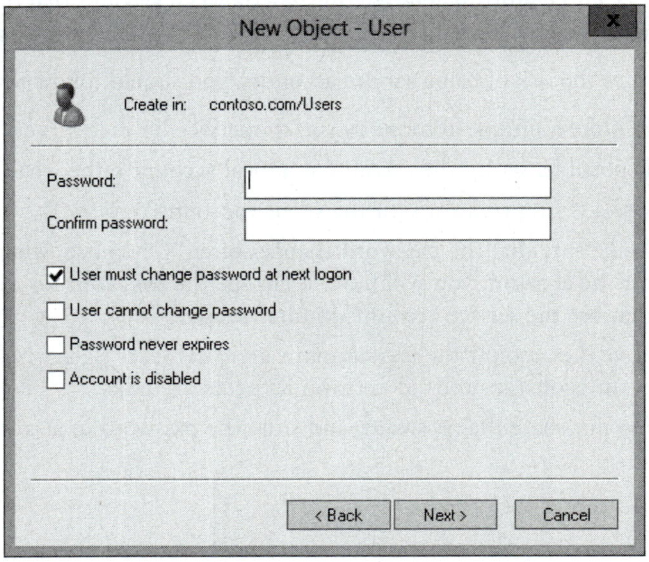

9. In the *Password* and *Confirm password* dialog boxes, type a password for the service account.
10. If you don't want the password to expire, select the Password never expires option. When a dialog box opens saying that the password should never expire and that the user will not be required to change the password at next logon, click OK.
11. Click Next.
12. Click Finish to complete creating a service account.

After the service account is created, you can double-click the service account in Active Directory Users and Computers console to open the account properties. You can then add the account to groups, using the Member Of tab (see Figure 15-9).

Figure 15-9

Configuring service accounts

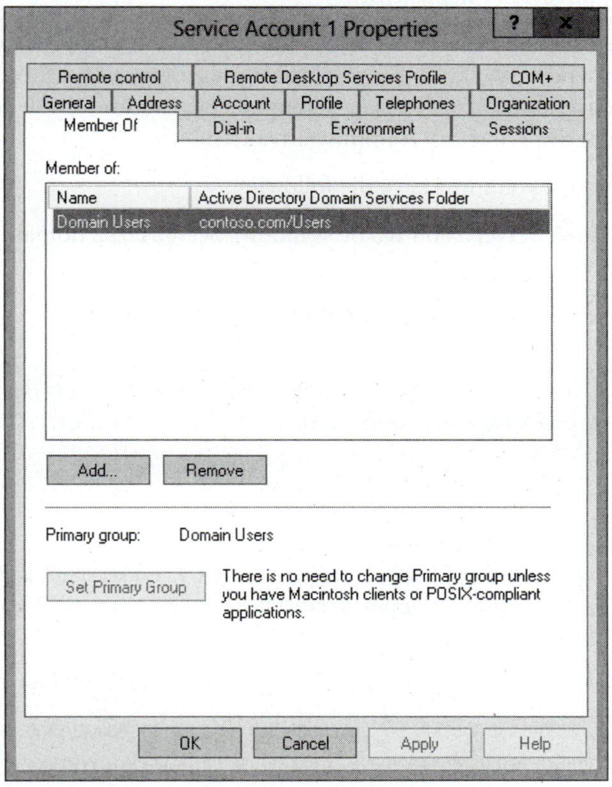

Creating and Configuring Managed Service Accounts

Managed service accounts (MSAs), introduced with Windows Server 2008 R2, are used to improve the use of the traditional service account in Windows. They are an Active Directory `msDS-ManagedServiceAccount` object class that enables automatic password management and SPN management for service accounts.

CERTIFICATION READY
Create and configure managed service accounts.
Objective 5.1

Rather than manually changing the account password and the password for the service or application, you use the MSA where the password will automatically change on a regular basis.

As mentioned previously, MSAs are stored in Active Directory Directory Services (AD DS) as `msDS-ManagedServiceAccount` objects in Windows Server 2008 and `MSDS-GroupManagedServiceAccount` on Windows Server 2012. This class inherits structural aspects from the Computer class (which inherits from the User class). This enables an MSA to fulfill user-like functions such as providing authentication and security context for a running service, while it uses the same automatic password update mechanism used by Computer objects in AD DS. However, a standard MSA cannot be shared between multiple computers or be used in server clusters where the service is replicated between nodes.

Similar to computer accounts, a managed service account establishes a complex, cryptographically random, 240-character password and changes that password when the computer changes its password. By default, this occurs every 30 days. An MSA cannot be locked out and cannot perform interactive logons.

MSAs provide the following benefits to simplify administration:

- Automatic password management
- Simplified SPN management

MSAs are stored in the `CN=Managed Service Accounts, DC=<domain>, DC=<com>` container, which can be used if you enable the Advanced Features option in the View menu within Active Directory Users and Computers. In addition, you can also see the container using the Active Directory Administrative Center.

To have MSAs, you must have the following:

- Windows Server 2008 R2 or Windows Server 2012 domain controller
- .NET Framework 3.5.x
- Active Directory module for Windows PowerShell

TAKE NOTE* For Windows Server 2012, the Windows PowerShell cmdlets default to managing the group managed service accounts (covered in the next section) rather than the original standalone MSAs.

USING WINDOWS POWERSHELL

Before you can create an MSA object type, you need to create a key distribution services root key for the domain. To create the root key, run the following cmdlet from the Active Directory PowerShell module for Windows PowerShell:

```
Add-KDSRootKey -EffectiveTime ((Get-Date).AddHours(-10))
```

You specify 10 hours so that AD DS replication has a chance to replicate the changes to other domain controllers in the domain. For testing environments, you can use the `add-kdsrootkey -EffectiveImmediately instead.`

USING WINDOWS POWERSHELL

To create and associate an MSA, perform the following steps:

1. Create an Active Directory AD service account with the following command:

```
New-ADServiceAccount -Name <MSA_Name>
-DNSHostname <DNS name of Domain_Controller>
```

2. `Add-ADComputerServiceAccount` associates the MSA with a computer account in the AD DS domain:

```
Add-ADComputerServiceAccount -identity <Host_Computer_Name>
-ServiceAccount <MSA_Name>
```

3. `Install-ADServiceAccount` installs the MSA on a host computer in the domain, and makes the MSA available for use by services on the host computer:

```
Install-ADServiceAccount -Identity <MSA_Name>
```

When you create a managed service account, you must specify a short account name of fewer than 15 characters. The dollar sign suffix lengthens the name; the resulting SAM Account Name must be 15 characters or less. Although you can create a managed service account with a longer name in Active Directory, you will be unable to install or use the managed account on a computer.

For example, to create the testsvc account on the domain controller, perform the following command at the Active Directory Module for Windows PowerShell:

1. `new-adserviceaccount -name testsvc -dnshostname win2012srv.contoso.com`
2. `add-adcomputerserviceaccount -identity win2012srv -serviceaccount testsvc`

Then go to the win2012srv and execute the following command using Windows PowerShell:

```
Install-ADServiceAccount -Identity testsvc
```

After you install the managed service account, you can configure a service to use the account as its logon identity. When you specify the logon account, be sure that the name includes the dollar sign ($).

USE THE MSA WITH A SERVICE

GET READY. To configure a forwarding computer to forward events, perform the following steps:

1. Open Server Manager.
2. Click Tools > Services. The *Services console* opens.
3. Double-click the desired service. The services *Properties* dialog box opens.
4. Click the Log On tab.
5. Select This account option and type the name of the service account in the *This account* text box (see Figure 15-10).

Figure 15-10
Using the MSA

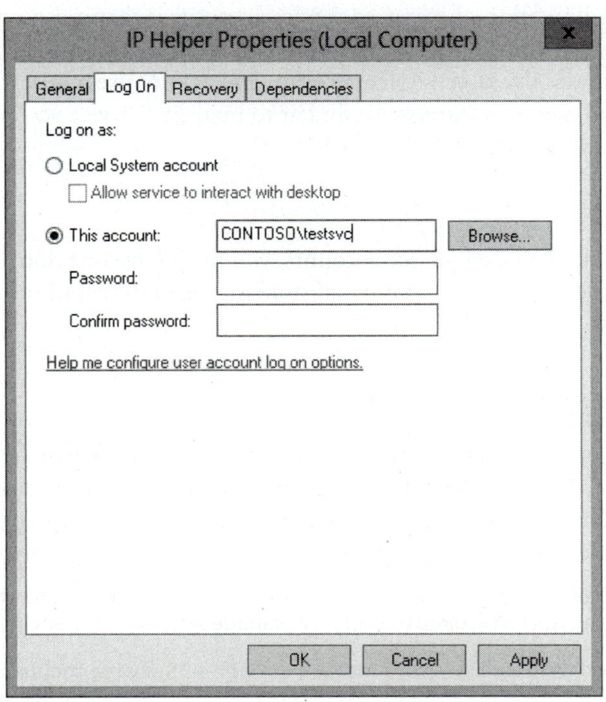

6. Clear the password in the *Password and Confirm password* text boxes.
7. Click OK.
8. When it says that the account has been granted the Log On As Service, click OK.
9. When it states that the new logon name will not take effect until you stop and restart the service, click OK.

After you install the managed service account, you can configure a service to use the account as its logon identity. In the Services console, open the properties of a service and click the *Log On* tab. Select *This Account*, and then click *Browse*. Type the name of the managed service account, and then click *OK*. On the Log On tab, confirm that the name appears with a dollar sign ($). The account will be given the Log On As Service right.

If you move a service to another computer and you want to use the same managed service account on the target system, you must first use the Uninstall-`ADServiceAccount` cmdlet to remove the managed service account from the current computer and then use the `Install-ADServiceAccount` cmdlet on the new computer.

If necessary, when you create the new MSA, you can also specify the SPN by using the `-ServicePrincipalNames <SPN_string>.`

```
New-ADServiceAccount -Name svcaccount

-DNSHostname win2012srv.contoso.com

-ServicePrincipalNames

HTTP/portal.contoso.com,HTTP://portal
```

To change the parameter for a service account, you use `Set-ADServiceAccount.` To delete a group service account using a Windows PowerShell command, you use the `Remove-ADServiceAccount.` To display a list of the service accounts, use the `Get-ADServiceAccount.`

Creating and Configuring Group Managed Service Accounts

CERTIFICATION READY
Create and configure group managed service accounts.
Objective 5.1

The one limitation of managed service accounts is that it can only be used on one server. Therefore, if you have a cluster or farm where you need to run the system or application service under the same service account, you cannot use managed service accounts. ***Group managed service accounts*** are similar to managed service accounts, but they can be used on multiple servers at the same time.

To use group managed service accounts, you must have one domain controller that is running Windows Server 2012, so that it can store managed password information. Similar to MSAs, you have to create a KDS root key.

USING WINDOWS POWERSHELL

To create a group managed service account, by using use the `New-ADServiceAccount` with the `-PrincipalsAllowedtoRetrieveManagedPassword` option to define one or more comma-separated computer accounts or AD DS groups. For example, to create the group *Managed Service Account* called groupsvc that will be used on server1, server2, and server3, use the following command:

```
new-adserviceaccount -name groupsvc -dnshostname win2012srv.contoso.com
-PrincipalsAllowedToRetrieveManagedPassword server1, server2, server3
```

You can then go to each server and use the `Install-ADServiceAccount command.`

SKILL SUMMARY

IN THIS LESSON, YOU LEARNED:

- Authentication is the act of confirming the identity of a user or system and is an essential part used in authorization when the user or system tries to access a server or network resource.
- NT LAN Manager (NTLM) is a suite of Microsoft security protocols that provides authentication, integrity, and confidentiality to users. It provides maximum compatibility with different versions of Windows, and compared to Kerberos it is the easiest to implement.
- Kerberos is a computer network authentication protocol, which allows hosts to prove their identity over a non-secure network in a secure manner. It can also provide mutual authentication so that both the user and server verify each other's identity.
- Kerberos settings are configured with Group Policies, specifically\Computer Configuration\Policies\Windows\Settings\Security Settings\Account Policies\Kerberos Policy.
- You can use ADSI Edit or use the setspn command to add SPNs to an account.
- Kerberos delegation allows a Kerberos ticket to be created for another service on the originating user's behalf. This can be done with full delegation or with constrained delegation.
- Constrained delegation is when you specify that the Kerberos delegation can be executed only against a limited set of services.
- A service account is an account under which an operating system, process, or service runs. A service account can allow the application or service specific rights and permissions to function properly while minimizing the permissions required for the users using the application server.
- Managed service accounts (MSAs), introduced with Windows Server 2008 R2, are used to improve the use of the traditional service account in Windows. They are an Active Directory msDS-ManagedServiceAccount object class that enables automatic password management and SPN management for service accounts.
- Group managed service accounts are similar to managed service accounts, but they can be used on multiple servers at the same time.

Knowledge Assessment

Multiple Choice

Select the correct answer for each of the following questions.

1. Which act confirms the identity of a user or system?
   a. Authentication
   b. Authorization
   c. Auditing
   d. Accounting

2. Which fallback authentication is used when Kerberos does not work?
   a. SSL
   b. SSH
   c. MS-CHAPv2
   d. NTLM

3. By default, what is the maximum amount time that a clock can be off in order for Kerberos to work?
   a. 60 seconds
   b. 90 seconds
   c. 300 seconds
   d. 600 seconds

4. Which authentication protocol uses the Key Distribution Center that maintains a database of secret keys and is more secure than NTLM?
   a. SSL
   b. Kerberos
   c. MS-CHAPv2
   d. NTLM

5. Which of the following is the format for Kerberos?
   a. SQLService/service1:1433
   b. service1:1433
   c. service1:1433:SQLService
   d. SQLService:1433/service1

6. Which name uniquely identifies an instance of a service for a client?
   a. TGT
   b. KDC
   c. ADSI
   d. SPN

7. Which command do you use to configure an SPN for a user account?
   a. `addspn`
   b. `configspn`
   c. `setspn`
   d. `getspn`

8. What allows a Kerberos ticket to be created for another service on the originating user's behalf?
   a. Kerberos delegation
   b. SPM
   c. Managed service accounts
   d. Group managed service accounts

9. By default, how often do passwords change for managed service accounts?
   a. 1 day
   b. 10 days
   c. 30 days
   d. 60 days

10. Which account runs a service on multiple computers that belong to a cluster and that automatically have the password changed on a regular basis?
    a. User account
    b. Managed service account
    c. Group managed service account
    d. Computer account

Best Answer

Choose the letter that corresponds to the best answer. More than one answer choice may achieve the goal. Select the BEST answer.

1. Which is a managed service account most similar to?
  a. A user account
  b. A computer account
  c. A security group
  d. A distribution group

2. Which is best for a service account that needs to run a service?
  a. User accounts
  b. Computer accounts
  c. Managed service accounts
  d. Group managed service accounts

3. What should you do when you create a service account?
  a. Change the password only if it becomes compromised.
  b. Configure the password not to expire.
  c. Use a domain-based account.
  d. Use an easy-to-remember password.

4. Which of the following is required to create managed service accounts? (Choose all that apply.)
  a. Active Directory module for Windows PowerShell
  b. Windows Server 2008 R2 or higher domain controller
  c. Password Sync tool
  d. .Net Framework 2.0 or higher

5. Which command would you use to create the root key?
  a. `Set-KDSRootKey_EFFECTIVETIME ((GET-DATE).NOW())`
  b. `GenerateRootKey_EFFECTIVETIME()`
  c. `Set-KDSRootKey.CurrentDate()`
  d. `Add-KDSRootKey _EFFECTIVETIME ((GET-DATE).AddHours(-10))`

Matching and Identification

1. Match the default values for the Kerberos values as defined in Group Policies. Not all answers will be used.
  _______ a) Enforce user logon restrictions
  _______ b) Maximum lifetime for service ticket
  _______ c) Maximum lifetime for user ticket
  _______ d) Maximum lifetime for user ticket renewal
  _______ e) Maximum tolerance for computer clock synchronization

1. 5 minutes
2. 15 minutes
3. 4 hours
4. 8 hours
5. 10 hours
6. On
7. Off
8. 1 day
9. 2 days
10. 3 days
11. 7 days
12. 10 days

Build a List

1. Identify the three basic commands in order when creating a Managed Service Account. Not all answers will be used.
   _____ `Add-ADComputerServiceAccount`
   _____ `Install-ADServiceAccount`
   _____ `Set-ADServiceAccount`
   _____ `Create-ADServiceAcount`
   _____ `New-ADServiceAccount`
   _____ `Link-ADServiceAccount`

2. Identify the basic commands in order when creating a group Managed Service Account. Not all answers will be used.
   _____ `Add-ADComputerServiceAccount`
   _____ `Install-ADServiceAccount`
   _____ `Set-ADServiceAccount`
   _____ `Create-ADServiceAcount`
   _____ `New-ADServiceAccount`
   _____ `Link-ADServiceAccount`

Choose an Option

1. You are creating a service account. In Figure 15-11, which option should you select when creating the account?

Figure 15-11

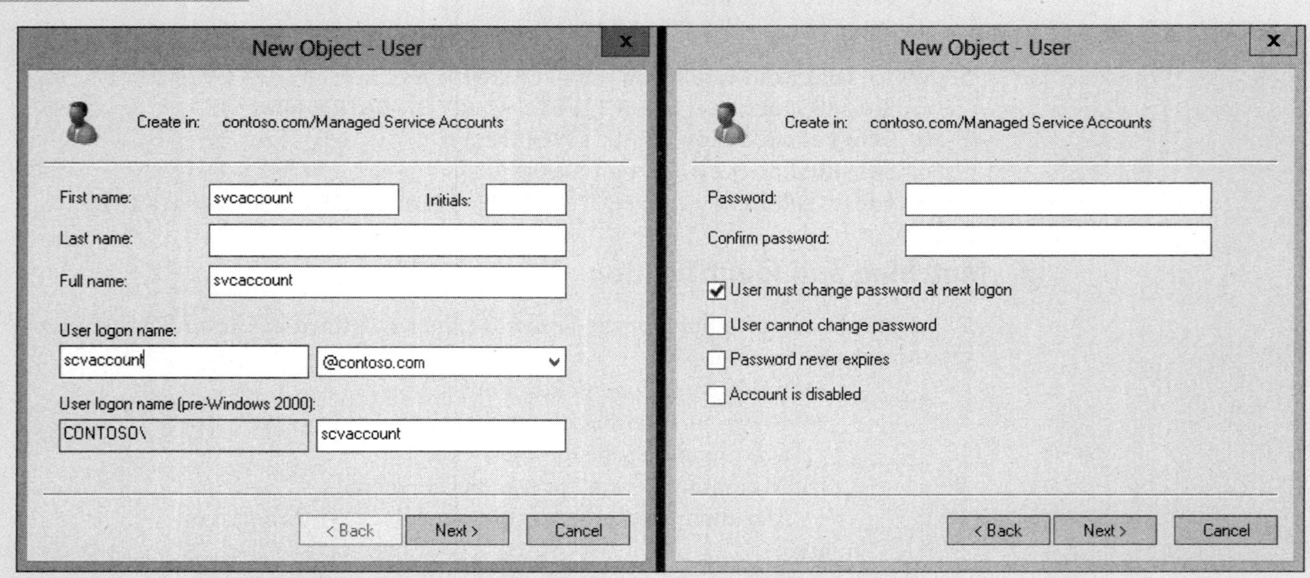

2. You have a junior administrator who is configuring a service to use a Managed Service Account. The junior administrator wants you to review the screen to make sure he is doing it correctly. Identify the problem in Figure 15-12.

Figure 15-12

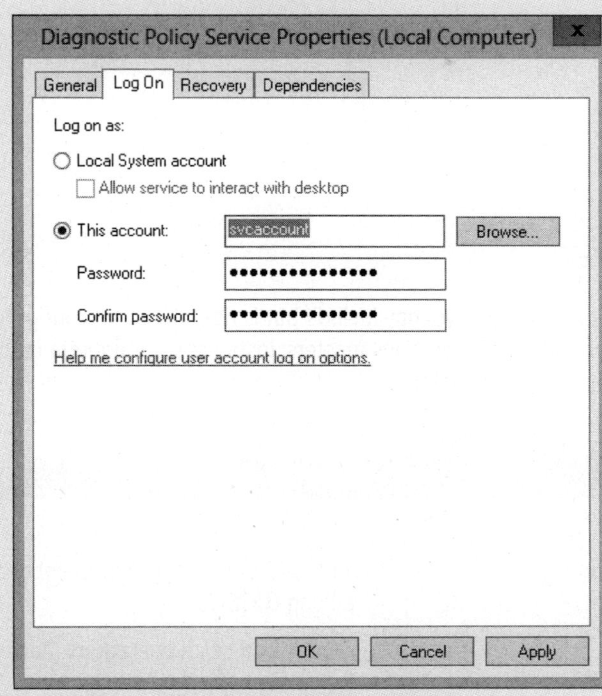

Business Case Scenarios

Scenario 15-1: Creating and Using a Service Account

You are an administrator of the Contoso Corporation. You installed a cluster of computers that need to use the same service account for the Widget application/services. What solution would you use?

Scenario 15-2: Using Kerberos

You have a client application/service placed on Server1. When a user accesses the application/service, you want the server to send a Kerberos request on behalf of the user who is running the application.

16 LESSON Configuring Domain Controllers

70-411 EXAM OBJECTIVE

Objective 5.2 – Configure Domain Controllers. This objective may include but is not limited to: configure universal group membership caching (UGMC); transfer and seize operations masters; install and configure a read-only domain controller (RODC); configure domain controller cloning.

Lesson Heading	Exam Objective
Understanding Domain Controllers	
Managing Global Catalogs and Configuring Universal Group Membership Caching	Configure universal group membership caching (UGMC)
Managing Operations Masters	Transfer and seize operations masters
Installing and Configuring an RODC	Install and configure a read-only domain controller (RODC)
Cloning a Domain Controller	Configure domain controller cloning

KEY TERMS

domain controllers
Domain Naming Master
domains
global catalog
Infrastructure Master
ntdsutil.exe
operations masters
Primary Domain Controller (PDC) Emulator
read-only domain controller (RODC)
Relative Identifier (RID) Master
Schema Master
universal group membership caching (UGMC)

■ Understanding Domain Controllers

THE BOTTOM LINE

The domain controllers are the servers that store and run the Active Directory database. Active Directory is a major component in authentication, authorization, and auditing. Therefore, you need to know how the different types of domain controllers and how they are used to create the Active Directory environment.

You can look at Active Directory from two sides: logical and physical. First, when you hear Active Directory, you most likely focus on the logical components that make up Active Directory. The logical components (which administrators create, organize, and manage) include:

- **Organization units:** Containers in a domain that allow you to organize and group resources for easier administration, including providing delegating administrative rights.
- ***Domains*:** An administrative boundary for users and computers, which are stored in a common directory database. A single domain can span multiple physical locations or sites and can contain millions of objects.
- **Domain trees:** Collection of domains that are grouped together in hierarchical structures and that share a common root domain. A domain tree can have a single domain or many domains. A domain (known as the parent domain) can have a child domain. A child domain can have its own child domain. Because the child domain is combined with the parent domain name to form its own unique Domain Name System (DNS) name, the domains with a tree have a contiguous namespace.
- **Forests:** A collection of domain trees that share a common Active Directory Domain Services (AD DS). A forest can contain one or more domain trees or domains, all of which share a common logical structure, global catalog, directory schema, and directory configuration, as well as automatic two-way transitive trust relationships. A forest can be a single domain tree or even a single domain. The first domain in the forest is called the *forest root domain*. For multiple domain trees, each domain tree consists of a unique namespace.

The physical components that make up Active Directory include the following:

- ***Domain controllers*:** The servers that contain the Active Directory databases. A domain partition stores only the information about objects located in that domain. All domain controllers in a domain receive changes and replicate those changes to the domain partition stored on all other domain controllers in the domain. As a result, all domain controllers are peers in the domain and manage replication as a unit.
- **Global catalog servers:** A domain controller that stores a full copy of all Active Directory objects in the directory for its host domain and a partial copy of all objects for all other domains in the forest. Applications and clients can query the global catalog to locate any object in a forest. A global catalog is created automatically on the first domain controller in the forest. Optionally, other domain controllers can be configured to serve as global catalogs.
- **Operations Masters:** Specialized domain controllers that perform certain tasks so that multi-master domain controllers can operate and synchronize properly.
- **Read-only domain controllers:** Specialized domain controllers that are intended for use in branch offices and servers in a low physical security environment that holds only a non-writable copy of Active Directory.

When a user logs on, Active Directory clients locate an Active Directory server (using the DNS SRV resource records) known as a domain controller in the same site as the computer.

Each domain has its own set of domain controllers to provide access to the domain resources, such as users and computers. For fault tolerance, a site should have two or more domain controllers. That way, if one domain controller fails, the other domain controller can still service the clients. Note that whenever an object (such as a username or password) is modified, it is automatically replicated to the other domain controllers within a domain.

A domain controller is a Windows server that stores a replica of the account and security information for the domain and defines the domain boundaries. To make a computer running Windows Server 2012 a domain controller, you must install the AD DS and execute dcpromo from Server Manager.

Managing Global Catalogs and Configuring Universal Group Membership Caching

Although the global catalog is not one of the five operation masters, global catalogs provide a critical functionality for Active Directory. As mentioned previously, as a domain controller, a ***global catalog*** stores a full copy of all objects in the domain. In addition, as a global catalog, it also has a partial copy of all objects for all other domains in the forest. The partial copy of all objects is used for logon, object searches, and universal group membership. A global catalog is created automatically on the first domain controller in the forest. Optionally, other domain controllers can be configured to serve as global catalogs.

CERTIFICATION READY
Configure universal group membership caching (UGMC).
Objective 5.2

One of the primary functions of a global catalog is to provide search capability of any object in the forest. When a user or an application performs a search in Active Directory, a search request is sent to the global catalog over TCP port 3268, which is used by Active Directory to direct these requests to a global catalog server. The global catalogs are identified by the global catalog SRV records (_gc).

Another function of global catalog is to resolve User Principal Names (UPNs). All users log on with the domain username (*domain_name\username*) or the UPN, which uses an e-mail address format (such as username@domainname.ext). The global catalog is used to resolve the UPN name to a username. The global catalog server stores enough information about the user to permit or deny the logon request, such as time restrictions.

As you recall from the 70-410 course, there are three types of groups: domain local groups, global groups, and universal groups. Universal groups can include any object from any trusted domain, and universal groups can be utilized to apply permissions to any resource in the domain.

Membership of universal groups is stored only in the global catalog and is replicated across the forest. When universal groups were initially introduced, having a lot of universal of groups would affect network traffic because information was replicated every time it was changed. Since Windows Server 2003, incremental universal group membership replication was introduced, which significantly decreased the amount of replication traffic of universal groups.

When a user logs on, the domain controller must be able to view the membership of the universal groups, so that it can be determined whether a user is allowed or denied logon based on the membership of the universal group. If the membership of the universal groups cannot be determined, a user's logon request denies the request, and the user cannot log on. The only exception to this is that the Administrator account can always log on. Therefore, for all other users to log on, there must be at least one domain controller acting as a global catalog available or you need Universal Group Membership Caching enabled.

Naturally, if a global catalog is available locally, the domain controller will contact the local global catalog. If not, the domain controller will have to communicate with a remote global catalog, which might have to be accessed over a WAN link. When files or other network resources need to be accessed over a WAN link, performance is slower.

If the global catalog is in a remote site, the authentication must traverse the WAN link to access the required information. Initially, it was recommended to have global catalogs at every site. Nonetheless, every organization should have at least two global catalogs for fault tolerance.

ENABLE GLOBAL CATALOGS

GET READY. To make a domain controller into a global catalog, perform the following steps:

1. Open Server Manager.
2. Click Tools > Active Directory Sites and Services. The *Active Directory Sites and Services console* opens.
3. Expand Sites, expand the site, expand Servers, and expand the specific domain controller that you want to make into a global catalog (see Figure 16-1).

Figure 16-1

Navigating to domain controllers

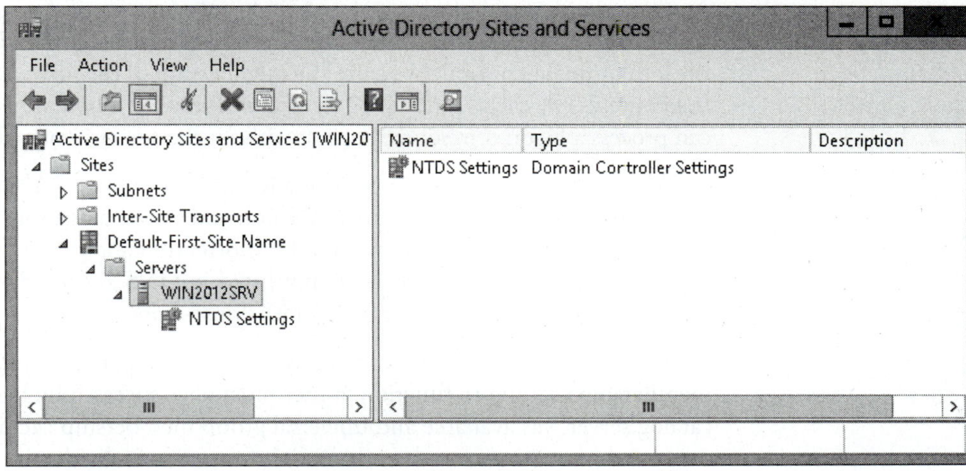

4. Right-click NTDS Settings and click Properties. *The NTDS Settings Properties* dialog box opens (see Figure 16-2).

Figure 16-2

Opening the NTDS Settings Properties dialog box

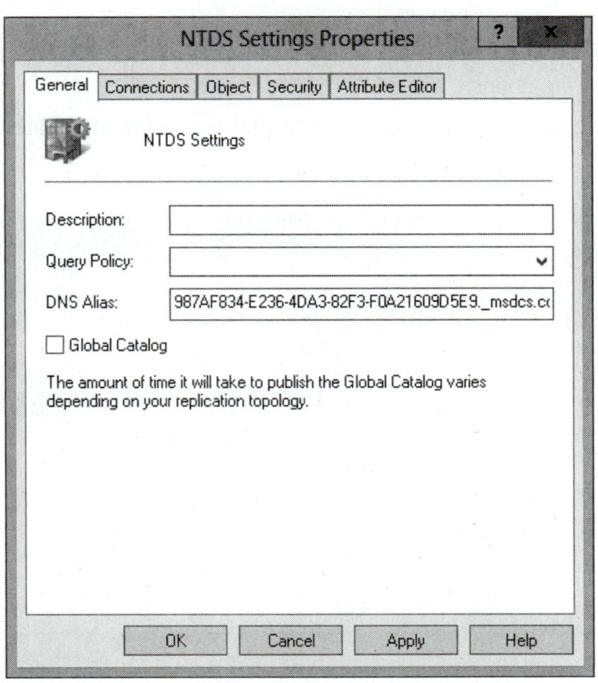

5. Select the Global Catalog option.
6. Click OK to close the *NTDS Settings Properties* dialog box.

USING WINDOWS POWERSHELL

To enable or disable a global catalog, use the Windows PowerShell `Set-ADObject` command. For example, to turn Server01 to a global catalog, use the following:

```
Set-ADObject "CN=NTDS Settings,CN=Server01,CN=Servers,CN=Default-First-Site-Name,CN=Sites,CN=Configuration,DC=Contoso,DC=COM"
-Replace@{options='1'}
```

To disable a global catalog, use `options='0'`.

Another way to avoid placing a global catalog at every site and to avoid going over a WAN link for login information is to use ***universal group membership caching (UGMC)***. UGMC allows the local domain controller to store the membership of the universal groups in its local cache indefinitely. The cache is refreshed by default every eight hours. As a result, domain controllers can process a logon or resource request without the presence of a global catalog server.

UGMC provides better logon performance and minimizes WAN usage. When a user logs on, requests do not have to go over a WAN link and WAN usage for replication traffic because the domain controller does not have to hold information about forest-wide objects. In addition, these remote domain controllers are not listed in DNS as providers of global catalog services for the forest, further reducing bandwidth constraints.

Universal group membership caching is enabled on a per-site basis. For universal group membership caching to function, a user must have successfully logged on when a global catalog server was available and universal group membership caching was enabled. Universal membership caching records each user's information individually.

ENABLE UNIVERSAL GROUP MEMBERSHIP CACHING

GET READY. To enable universal group membership caching, perform the following steps:

1. Open Server Manager.
2. Click Tools > Active Directory Sites and Services. The *Active Directory Sites and Services console* opens.
3. Expand Sites, and click the site that you want to enable universal group membership caching (see Figure 16-3).

Figure 16-3
Navigating to a site

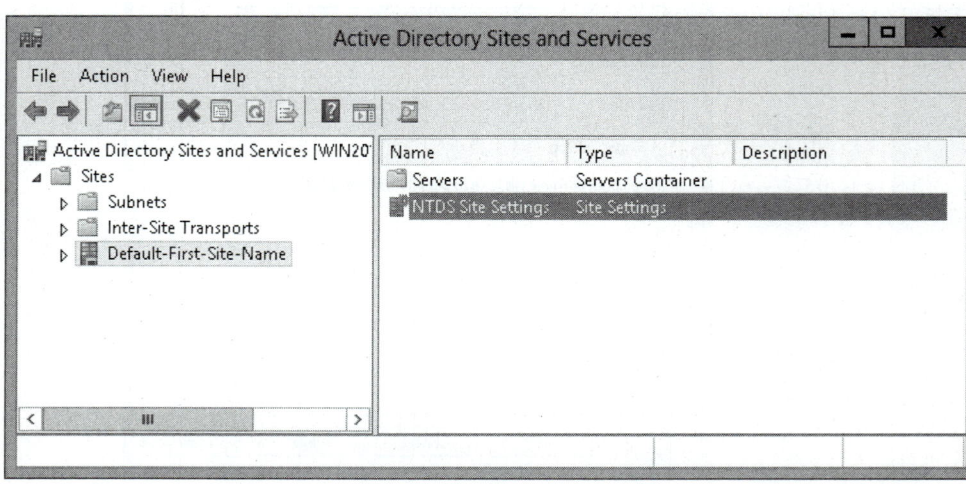

4. Right-click NTDS Settings and click Properties. The *NTDS Site Settings Properties* dialog box opens (see Figure 16-4).

Figure 16-4

Opening the NTDS Site Settings Properties dialog box

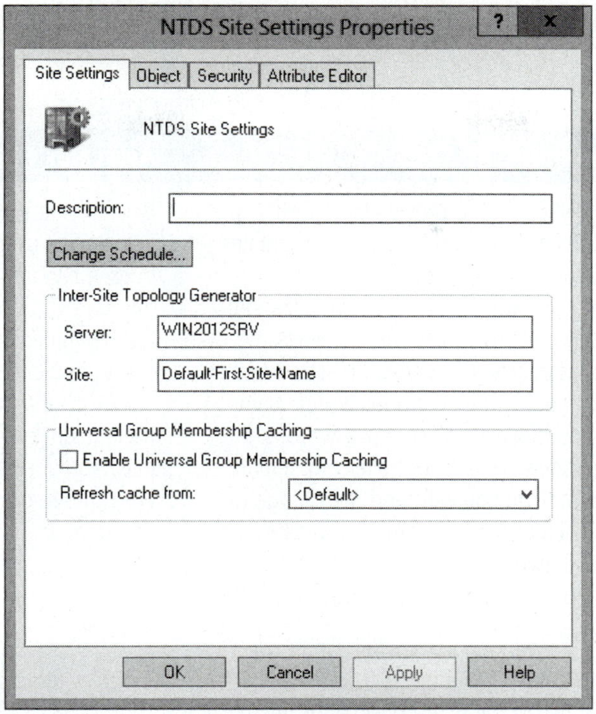

5. Select the Enable Universal Group Membership Caching option.
6. Click OK to close the *NTDS Settings Properties* dialog box.

Managing Operations Masters

CERTIFICATION READY
Transfer and seize operations masters.
Objective 5.2

Operations masters, sometimes referred to as *Flexible Single Master Operations (FMSO)*, are specialized domain controllers that perform certain tasks that can be handled only by a single domain controller in a multi-master environment.

TAKE NOTE*
As of 2005, the term *FSMO* has been deprecated in favor of *operations masters*.

With Active Directory, domain controllers follow a multi-master replication model that ensures copies of all domain objects are found on each domain controller within a domain so that they can be quickly and easily accessed and to provide fault tolerance. To help resolve conflicts and such, all transactions use version IDs and timestamps. However, some critical functions need to have the assurance of little or no risk of error.

For example, when you add attributes to an Active Directory object, you change the schema of the domain database. Although it is relatively easy to make those changes, it is considered a big deal when you modify the schema because it affects all objects for that object type you are about to change and it can corrupt the database. Luckily, making changes in a controlled way provides a virtually 100% success rate. However, if two administrators attempt to make similar changes at the same time from two different locations (and two different domain controllers), the chances of problems significantly rise. Therefore, to prevent this type of problem, there is only one specific domain controller that can handle this type of function. In this particular case, it is the Schema Master, which is discussed next.

The five operations master roles are shown in Table 16-1. When you install a domain, the first domain controller installed for a domain has the Primary Domain Controller, RID Master, and Infrastructure Master. Similarly, the first domain controller in the root domain has the Domain Naming and Schema Master roles.

Table 16-1

Operations Master Roles

Operations Master Roles	Description	Affect of Failure
Primary Domain Controller (PDC) Emulator (*one per domain*)	Originally created to provide backward compatibility with Windows NT 4.0 domains. It also coordinates password changes, account lockouts, and time synchronization; manages edits to Group Policy Objects (GPOs); and acts as a domain master browser (provides a list of workgroups and domains when you browse). When a password is changed, the domain controller that initiates a password change will send the change to the PDC Emulator, which in turn updates the global catalog server and provides immediate replication to other domain controllers in the domain.	Because the PDC emulator is the most heavily one used, and by the tasks that it does, it can affect users when it is down. For example, if a password is changed, it might not be immediately replicated, which can cause problems when a user tries to access resources. If the system clocks drift too much, users might not be able to log on as Kerberos fails. Account lockout will not work and you will not be able to raise the functional level of a domain.
Infrastructure Master (*one per domain*)	Used to track which objects belong to which domain because it is responsible for reference updates from its domain objects to other domains. When you rename or move a member of a group (and the members that reside in different domain from the group), the infrastructure master is responsible for updating the group so that it knows the new name or location of the member.	Typically, the loss of the infrastructure master will not be visible to users. However, it might be seen if you recently moved or renamed a large number of accounts.
Relative Identifier (RID) Master (*one per domain*)	When a domain controller creates a user, group, or computer object, it assigns the object a unique security ID (SID). The SID consists of a domain security ID that identifies the domain to which the object belongs and a relative ID that identifies the object within the domain. The RID master is responsible for assigning relative identifiers to domain controllers in the domain. The RID master assigns a block of 500 identifiers to each domain controller. When 50% of the supply of RIDs is used, it contacts the RID to request a new supply.	Although the loss of the RID master will not be seen by users, it can be seen when administrators are creating objects and the domain runs out of relative IDs to assign. In addition, you will not be able to move objects between domains.
Schema Master (*one per forest*)	Controls all the updates and modifications to the schema. To update the schema of a forest, you must have access to the Schema Master.	Although the loss of the Schema Master will not affect the users, you cannot modify the schema or install any applications, such as Microsoft Exchange, that would modify the schema. You will also not be able to raise the functional level of the forest.
Domain Naming Master (*one per forest*)	Holds the Domain Naming Master role that controls the addition or removal of domains in the forest.	Although the loss of the Domain Naming Master will not affect users, you will not be able to add or remove domains from the forests.

According to Microsoft, when you place the Operations Master roles, you should follow these guidelines:

- Place the domain-level roles on high-performance domain controllers.
- Do not place the infrastructure master on a global catalog server unless you have only one domain or all the domain controllers in your forest are also global catalogs.
- The Schema Master and Domain Naming Master should be on domain controllers in the forest-root domain.
- If the Primary Domain Controller (PDC) Emulator becomes overworked, you should offload non-AD DS roles to other servers, upgrade the PDC Emulator, or move the PDC Emulator to a more powerful computer.

VIEWING THE OPERATIONS MASTERS ROLE HOLDERS

The easiest way to view the holders of all Operations Masters at once, you can execute the following command at a command prompt (see Figure 16-5):

```
netdom query fsmo
```

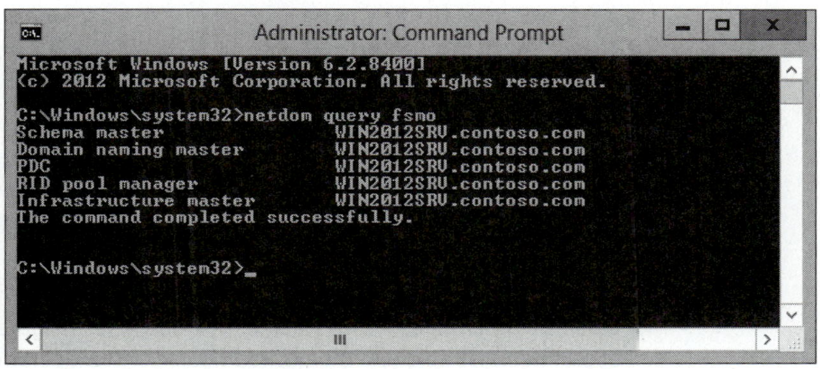

Figure 16-5

Viewing the holders of the Operations Masters roles at the command prompt

To view the RID Masters, PDC Emulators, or Infrastructure Master, you use the Active Directory Users and Computers console. To view the holder of the Domain Naming Master role, you use the Active Directory Domains and Trusts console. To view the holder of the Schema Master role, you use the Active Directory Schema. The next three exercises show how to view the holders of the roles. To complete these tasks, you need to be a member of the domain administrator. In addition, to view the holder of the Schema Master, you need to be a member of the Schema Admins.

VIEW THE HOLDERS OF RID MASTER, PDC EMULATOR, OR INFRASTRUCTURE MASTER

GET READY. To view the holders of RID Master, PDC Emulator, and Infrastructure Master, perform the following steps:

1. Open Server Manager.
2. Click Tools > Active Directory Users and Computers. The *Active Directory Users and Computers* console opens.
3. Right-click the domain and click Operations Masters (see Figure 16-6).

Figure 16-6

Selecting Operations Masters

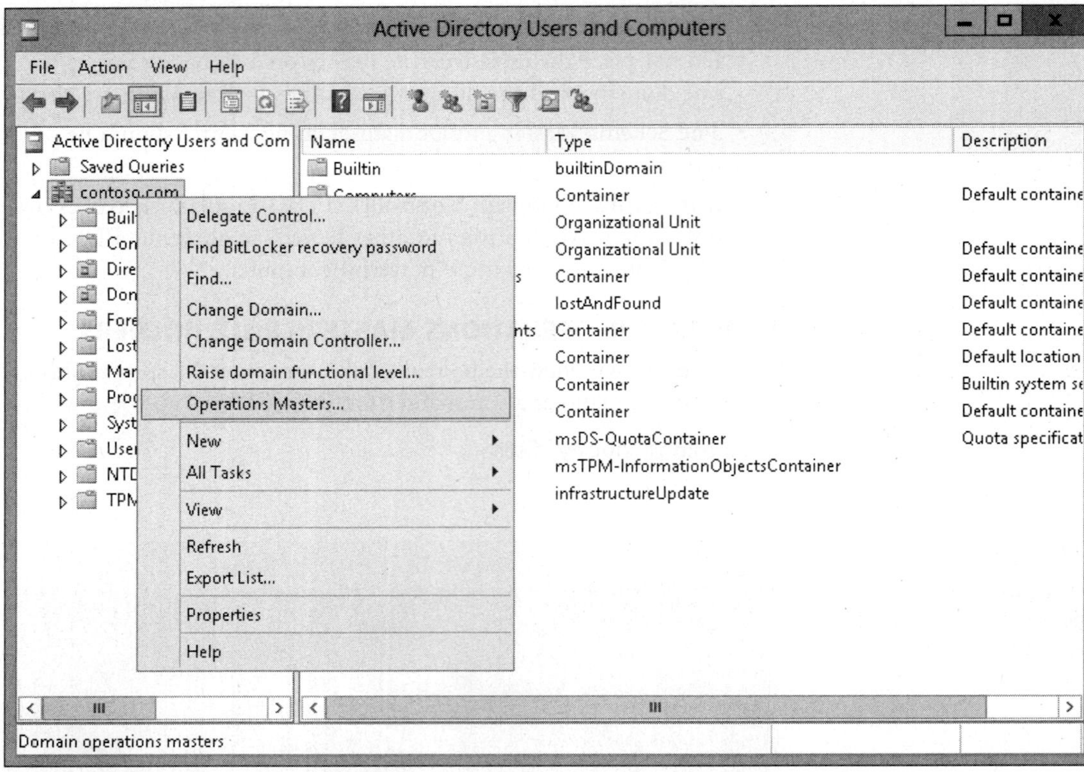

4. When the *Operations Masters* dialog box opens (see Figure 16-7), select the appropriate tab to show the desired holder of the Operations Masters.

Figure 16-7

Using the Active Directory Users and Computers console to view the holders of the domain-based Operation Masters roles

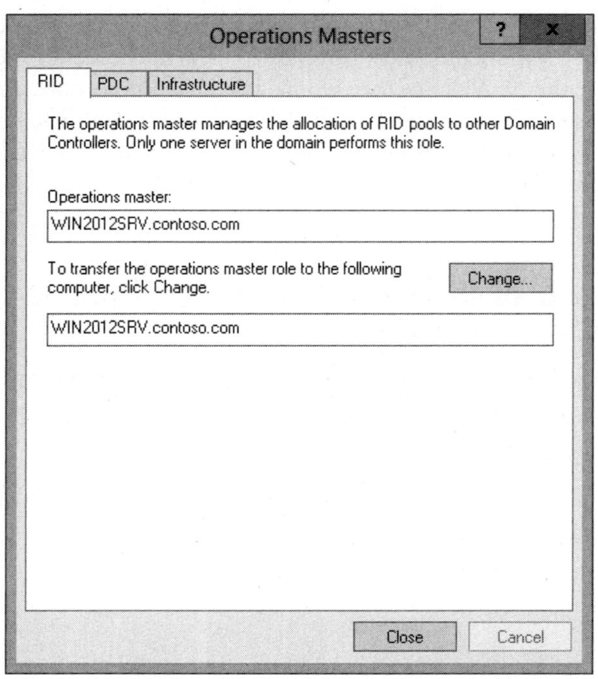

5. When you are done, click Close to close the *Operations Masters* dialog box.
6. Close the *Active Directory Users and Computers console*.

VIEW THE DOMAIN NAMING OPERATIONS MASTER ROLE HOLDER

GET READY. To view the holder of the Domain Naming Operations Master role holder, perform the following steps:

1. Open Server Manager.
2. Click Tools > Active Directory Domains and Trusts. The *Active Domains and Trusts console* opens.
3. Right-click Active Directory Domains and Trusts and select Operations Master. The *Operations Master* dialog box showing current Domain Naming Operations Master opens (see Figure 16-8).

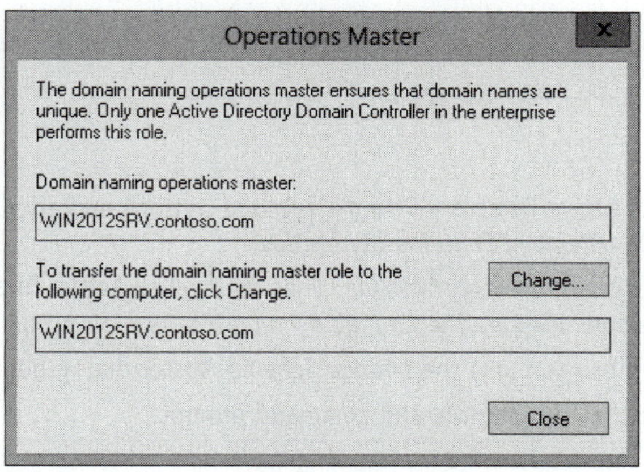

Figure 16-8

Using the Active Directory Domains and Trusts console to view the holders of the Domain Naming Operations Master

4. Click Close to close the *Operations Master* dialog box.
5. Close the *Active Directory Domains and Trusts console*.

VIEW THE SCHEMA MASTER OPERATIONS MASTER ROLE HOLDER

GET READY. To view the holder of the Schema Master Operations Master role holder, perform the following steps:

1. Right-click the start button and select Command Prompt (Admin). The command prompt opens.
2. Execute the mmc command. The *MMC console* opens.
3. Open the File menu and select Add/Remove Snap-in. The *Add or Remove Snap-ins* dialog box opens (see Figure 16-9).

Figure 16-9

Opening the Add or Remove Snap-in dialog box

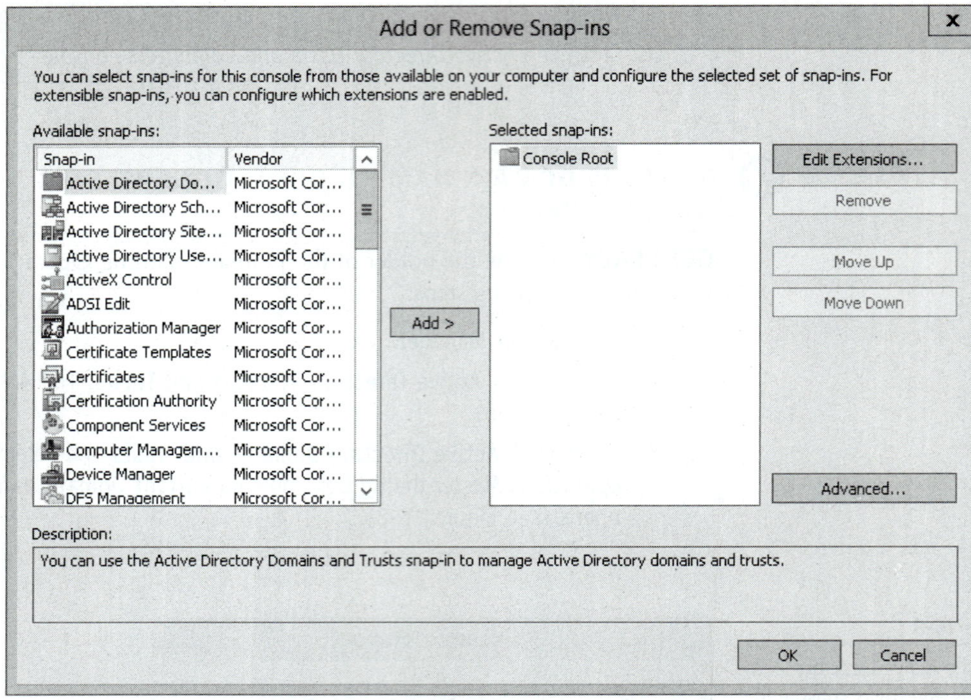

4. Select Active Directory Schema (second option) and click Add. Then click OK to close the *Add/Remove Snap-ins* dialog box.
5. Click Active Directory Schema. Then right-click Active Directory Schema and select Operations Master. The *Change Schema Master* dialog box opens.
6. Click Close to close the *Change Schema Master* dialog box.
7. Close the *MMC console* and command prompt.

TAKE NOTE*

To activate the necessary DLL files for Active Directory Schema, you need to register the schmmgmt.dll DLL file using the following syntax: `regsvr32 schmmgmt.dll`.

TRANSFERRING THE OPERATIONS MASTERS ROLE

From time to time, you might need to move the operation master roles to other domain controllers. If you are planning to do maintenance where a domain controller that holds the Operations Master will be down for an extended period of time, you are going to retire a domain controller that holds a role of Operations Master or you need to move the role to a domain controller with more resources, you will need to transfer the Operations Master. Transferring a FSMO role requires that the source domain controller and the target domain controller be online. These are the same tools that are used to view the current role holders in the previously listed procedures.

TRANSFER THE HOLDERS OF RID MASTER, PDC EMULATOR, OR INFRASTRUCTURE MASTER

GET READY. To transfer the holders of RID Master, PDC Emulator, and Infrastructure Master, perform the following steps:

1. Open Server Manager.
2. Click Tools > Active Directory Users and Computers. The *Active Directory Users and Computers* console opens.
3. In the console tree, right-click the Active Directory Users and Computers node and select Change Domain Controller (see Figure 16-10).

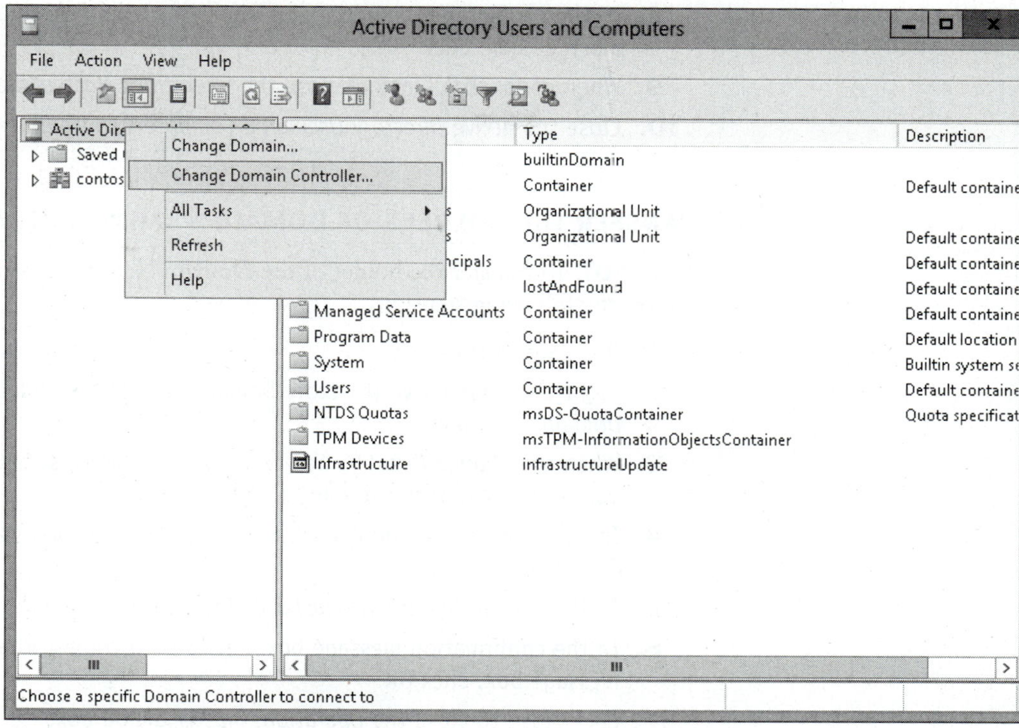

Figure 16-10

Selecting the Change Domain Controller option

4. When the *Change Directory Server* dialog box opens (see Figure 16-11), select the domain controller that you want to transfer the role to and click OK.

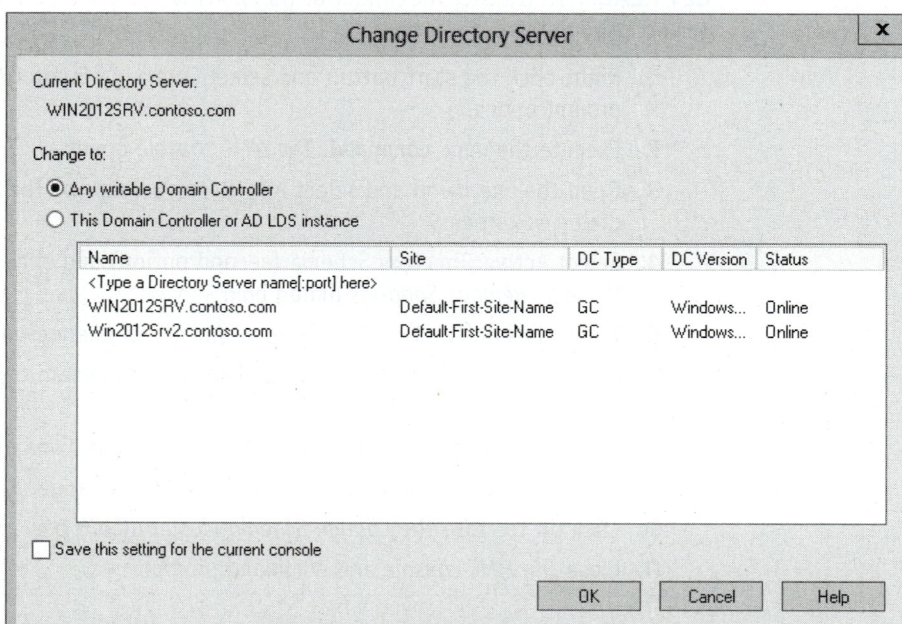

Figure 16-11

Selecting a domain controller to transfer the role to

5. Right-click the domain, and select Operations Masters.
6. Select the tab that reflects the role you are transferring.
7. Click Change.

8. In the *confirmation message* box, click Yes to confirm the change in roles. In the next message box, click OK.
9. When done, click Close to close the *Operations Masters* dialog box.
10. Close the *Active Directory Users and Computers console*.

TRANSFER THE HOLDERS OF DOMAIN NAMING OPERATIONS MASTER ROLE

GET READY. To transfer the holder of the Domain Naming Operations Master role holder, perform the following steps:

1. Open Server Manager.
2. Right-click the Active Directory Domains and Trusts node and select Connect To Domain Controller.
3. When the *Change Directory Server* dialog box opens, select the domain controller that you want to transfer the role to and click OK.
4. In the console tree, right-click Active Directory Domains and Trusts and select Operations Master.
5. In the *Change Operations Master* dialog box, click Change.
6. In the confirmation message box, click Yes to confirm the change in roles. In the next message box, click OK.
7. Click Close to close the *Operations Master* dialog box.
8. Close the *Active Directory Domains and Trusts console*.

TRANSFER THE HOLDERS OF SCHEMA MASTER OPERATIONS MASTER ROLE

GET READY. To transfer the holder of the Schema Master Operations Master role holder, perform the following steps:

1. Right-click the start button and select Command Prompt (Admin). The command prompt opens.
2. Execute the mmc command. The *MMC console* opens.
3. Open the File menu and select Add/Remove Snap-in. The *Add or Remove Snap-ins* dialog box opens.
4. Select Active Directory Schema (second option) and click Add. Then click OK to close the *Add/Remove Snap-ins* dialog box.
5. Right-click Active Directory Schema and select Change Domain Controller.
6. Select the Specify Name option and select the domain controller that you want to switch to. Click OK.
7. In the console tree, right-click Active Directory Schema and select Operations Master.
8. In the *Change Schema Master* dialog box, click Change.
9. Click OK to close the *Change Schema Master* dialog box.
10. Close the *MMC console* and command prompt.

SEIZING THE OPERATIONS MASTERS ROLE

If a domain controller that holds an Operations Master role has an unrecoverable failure, you cannot transfer roles because the current domain controller is not online. Therefore, you need to size the role. Seizing a FSMO role is a drastic measure that should be performed only in the event of a permanent role holder failure.

To seize a role of an Operations Master, you use the ***ntdsutil.exe*** utility. The ntdsutil.exe is a command-line tool that allows you to manage Active Directory including performing maintenance on the Active Directory database, manage and control single master operations, and remove metadata left behind by domain controllers that were removed from the network without being properly uninstalled.

SEIZE THE ROLE OF AN OPERATIONS MASTER HOLDER

GET READY. To seize the holder of the Schema Master Operations Master role holder, perform the following steps:

1. Right-click the start button and select Command Prompt (Admin). The command prompt opens.
2. From the command prompt, execute the ntdsutil command.
3. At the ntdsutil prompt, execute the roles command.
4. At the fsmo maintenance prompt, execute the connections command.
5. At the server connections prompt, execute the following command:

   connect to server <FQDN_of_desired_role_holder>

   An example of this would be:

   connect to server server1.contoso.com
6. At the server connections prompt, execute the quit command.
7. At the fsmo maintenance prompt, type one of the following commands:

   seize schema master

   seize naming master

   seize RID master

   seize PDC

   seize infrastructure master

Figure 16-12 shows the commands to seize the PDC Emulator role.

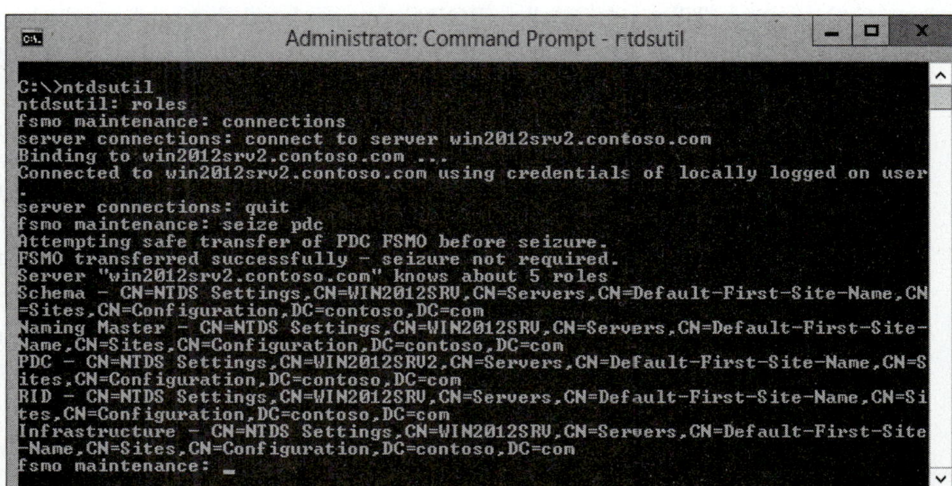

Figure 16-12
Seizing the PDC Emulator role

8. If an *"Are you sure?"* dialog box appears, click Yes to continue.
9. At the fsmo maintenance prompt, execute the quit command.
10. At the ntdsutil prompt, execute the quit command.
11. Close the command prompt.

USING WINDOWS POWERSHELL

To enable or disable a global catalog, you would use the Windows PowerShell `Move-ADDirectoryServerOperationMasterRole` command. For example, to seize the operations master roles, use the following command:

```
Move-ADDirectoryServerOperationMasterRole -Identity Server01
-OperationMasterRole RIDMaster,InfrastructureMaster,DomainNamingMaster
-Force
```

Installing and Configuring an RODC

THE BOTTOM LINE

Windows Server 2008 introduced the ***read-only domain controller (RODC)***, which contains a full replication of the domain database. It was created to be used in places where a domain controller is needed but the physical security of the domain controller could not be guaranteed. For example, it might be placed in a remote site that is not very secure and that has a slower WAN link. Because it has a slow WAN link, a local domain controller would benefit the users at that site.

CERTIFICATION READY
Install and configure a read-only domain controller (RODC).
Objective 5.2

An RODC does not perform any outbound replication and accepts only inbound replication connections from writable domain controllers. Because the RODC has only a read-only copy of the Active Directory database, the administrator needs to connect to a writable domain controller to make changes to Active Directory.

To deploy an RODC, you need the following:

- Ensure that the forest functional level is Windows Server 2003 or higher.
- Deploy at least one writable domain controller running Windows Server 2008 or higher.

If any domain controllers run Windows Server 2003, you need to configure permissions on DNS application directory partitions to allow them to replicate to RODCs by running the `ADPrep /RODCPrep` command. The `adprep.exe` command is located on the \support\adprep folder on the Windows Server 2012 installation disk.

When you install an RODC, you need to define a delegated administrator that has local administrative permission to the RODC, even though the account is not a member of the Domain Admin or domain built-in Administrators group.

Because RODCs need to be as secure as possible, you can configure each RODC to have its own Password Replication Policy (PRP). On writable domain controllers, Active Directory passwords are stored locally within the ntds.dit file. Because the RODC is put in a place where the security cannot be guaranteed, you can specify a particular list of user or group accounts whose password information should be stored (or cached) on a particular RODC.

For example, if you have a Site1 branch, you can configure the RODC to cache only passwords for those users who are members of the Site1 security group. In addition, you can configure specific users or groups whose password information should not be cached on an RODC such as administrative accounts.

To allow enterprise-wide configuration of the RODC Password Replication Policy, Windows Server 2012 creates the following security groups:

- **Denied RODC Password Replication Group:** Members of this group are placed in the Deny list of the Password Replication Policies of all RODCs by default. Some of the groups include Administrators, Server Operators, Backup Operators, Account Operators, and Denied RODC Password Replication Group.
- **Allowed RODC Password Replication Group:** Members of this group are placed in the Allow list of the Password Replication Policies of all RODCs by default. This group has no members when Windows Server 2012 is first installed.

INSTALL A READ-ONLY DOMAIN CONTROLLER

GET READY. To install a Read-only domain controller, perform the following steps:

1. Open Server Manager.
2. On the left pane, click AD DS. On the right-pane, click More in the yellow bar (see Figure 16-13).

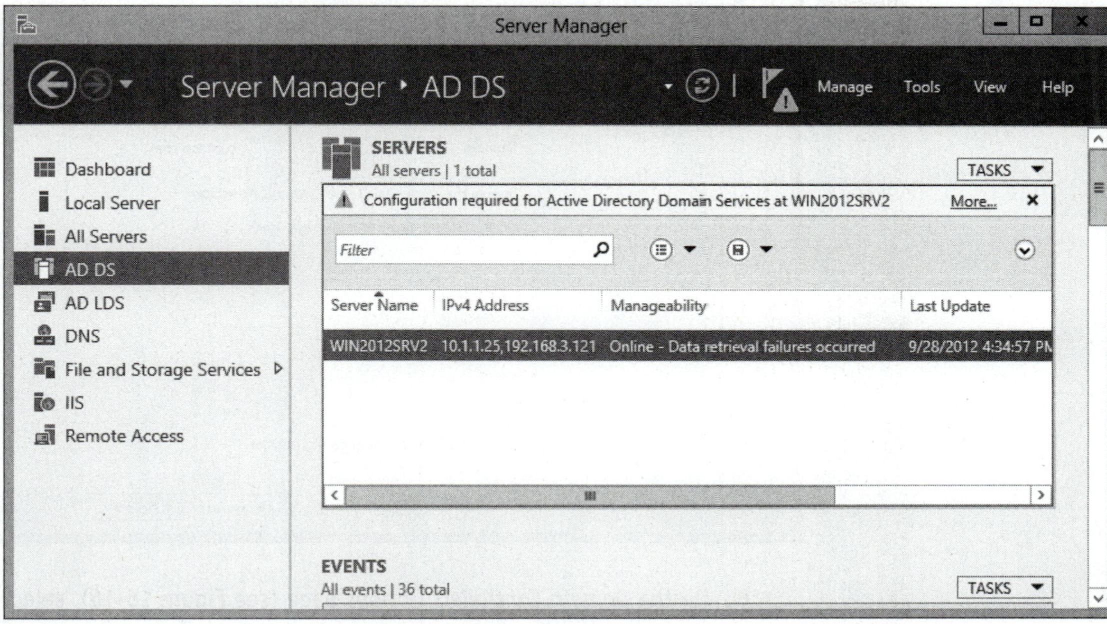

Figure 16-13

Installing AD DS on a new computer

3. When the *All Servers Task Details* window opens (see Figure 16-14), click Promote this server to a domain controller. The *Active Directory Domain Services Configuration Wizard* starts.

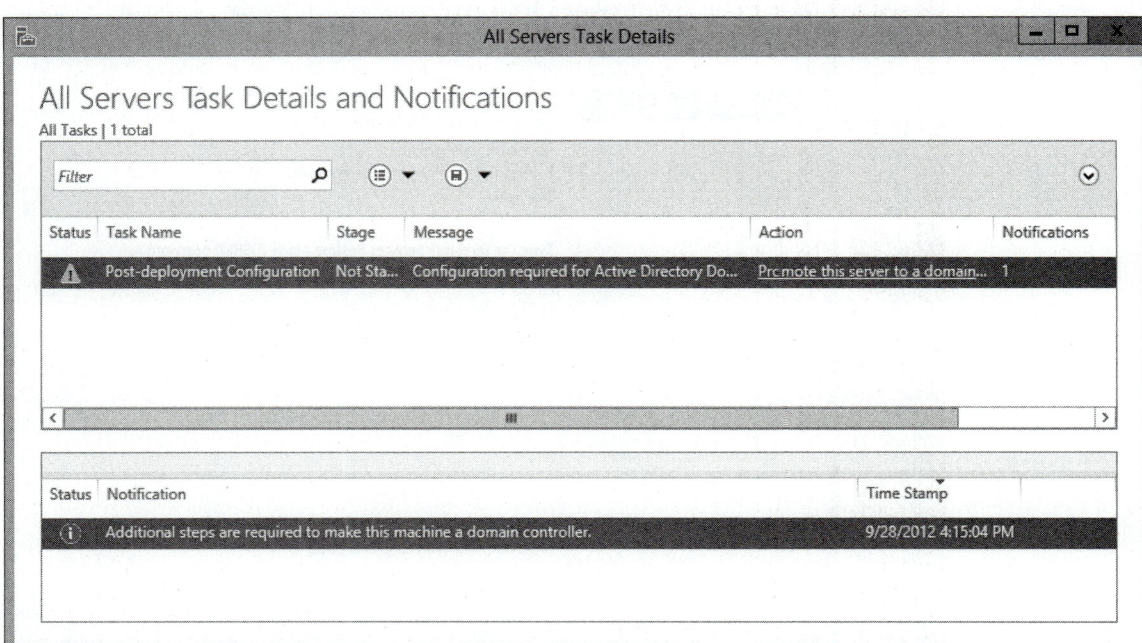

Figure 16-14

Promoting the server to a domain controller

4. On the *Deployment Configuration* page (see Figure 16-15), with the Add a domain controller to an existing domain already selected, click Next.

Figure 16-15

Adding a domain controller to an existing domain

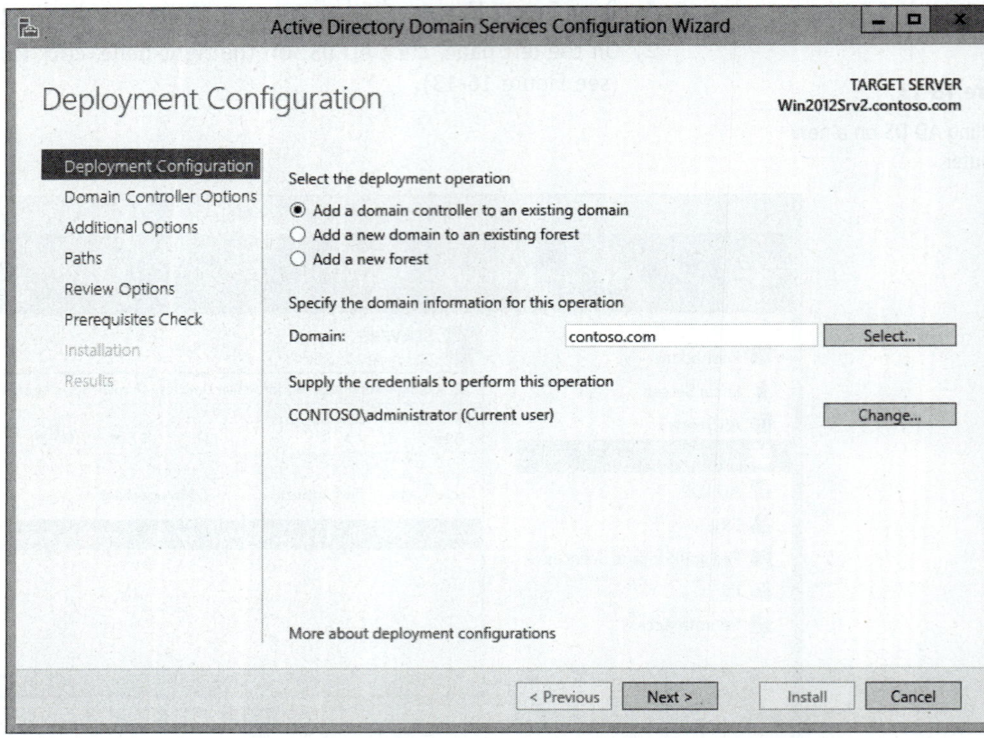

5. On the *Domain Controllers Options* page (see Figure 16-16), select Read only domain controller (RODC). Select the correct site name. Type a Directory Service Restore Mode (DSRM) password in the *Password and Confirm password* text boxes. Click Next.

Figure 16-16

Selecting an RODC

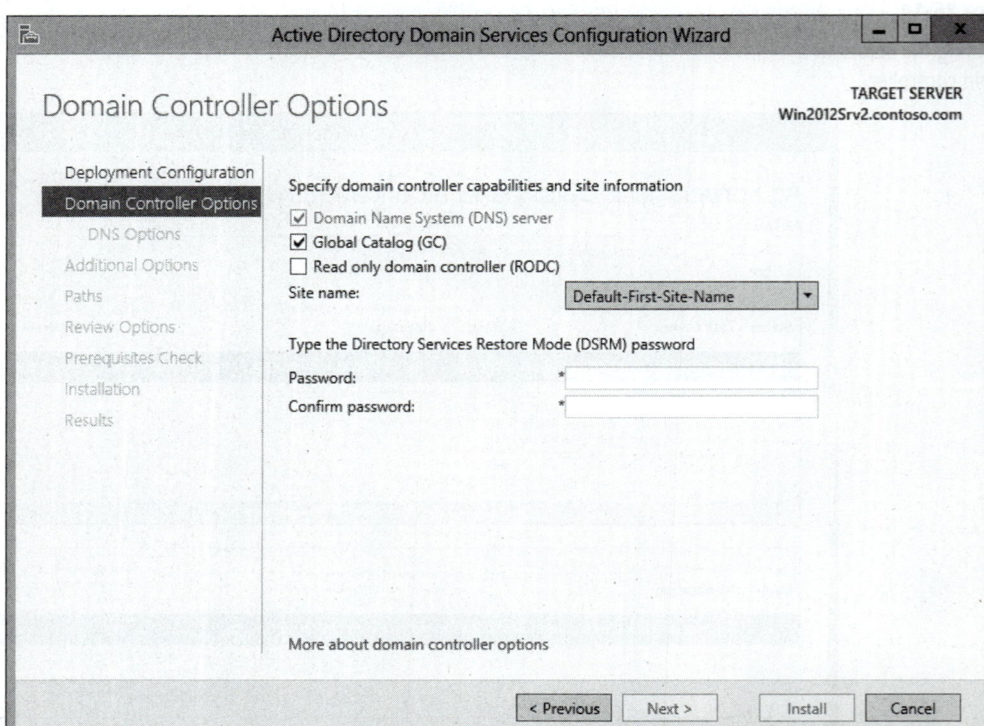

6. On the *RODC Options* page (see Figure 16-17), click Select in the *Delegated administrator account* section. When the *Select User or Group* dialog box opens, type the name of the account to be used as a delegated administrator in the *Enter the object names to select* text box and click OK. Click Next.

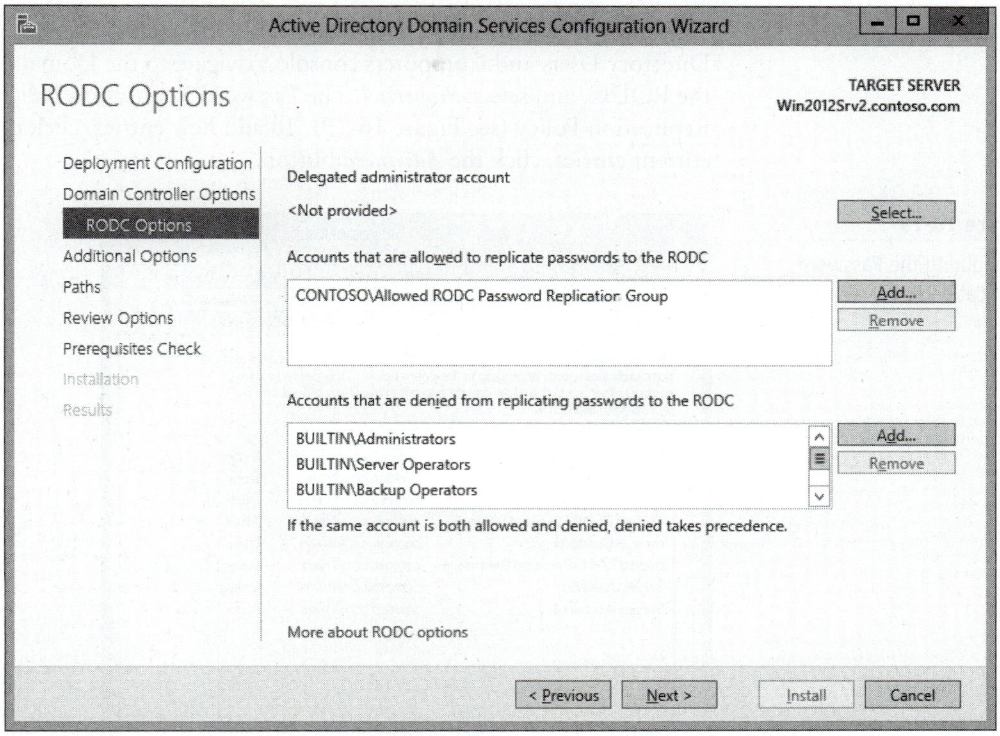

Figure 16-17
Specifying the delegated administrator

7. On the *Additional Options* page (see Figure 16-18), click Next.

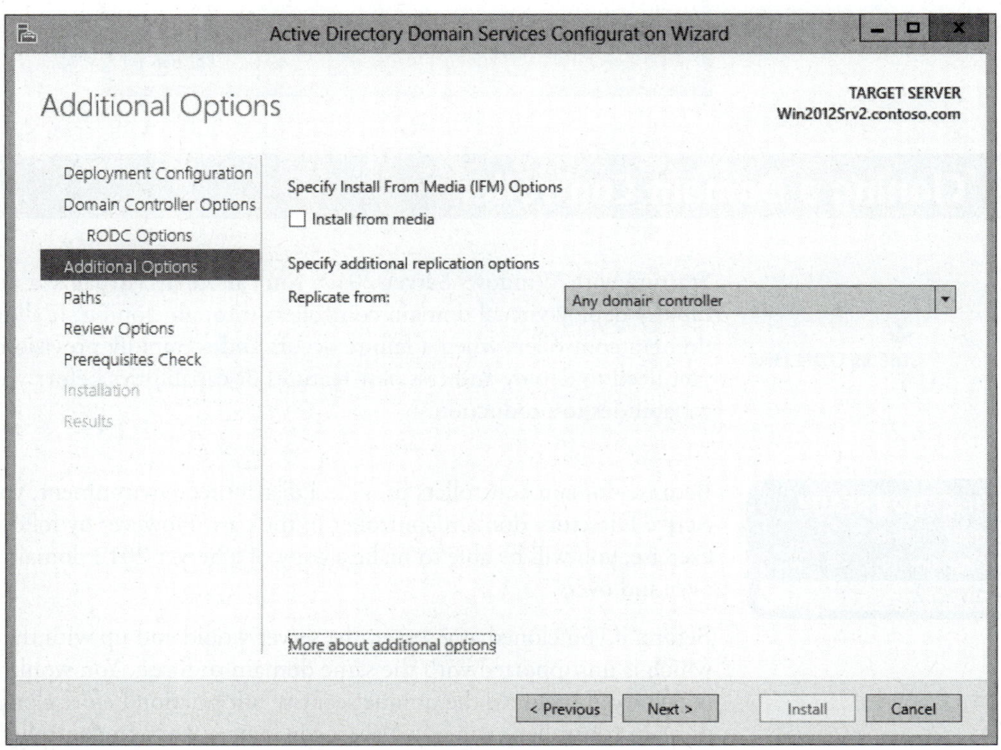

Figure 16-18
Selecting additional options

8. On the *Paths* page, click Next.
9. On the *Review Options* page, click Next.
10. On the *Prerequisites Check* page, click Install.
11. When the installation is complete, restart the domain controller.

To modify the Password Replication Policy, after the RODC was installed, just open the Active Directory Users and Computers console, navigate to the Domain Controllers OU, right-click the RODC, and select *Properties*. The Password Replication Policy is shown in the Password Replication Policy (see Figure 16-19). To add new entries, click the *Add* button. To modify the current entries, click the *Advanced* button.

Figure 16-19

Configuring the Password Replication Policy

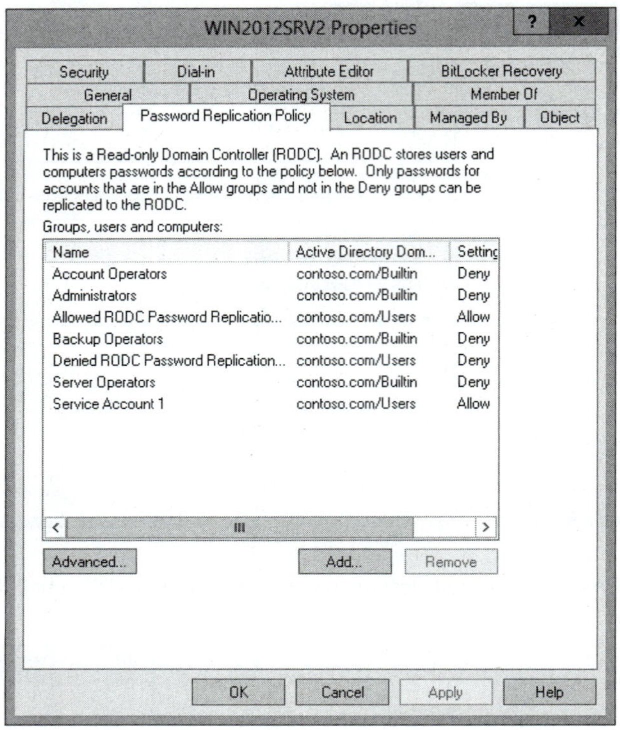

Cloning a Domain Controller

THE BOTTOM LINE

Starting with Windows Server 2012, you can safely virtualize a domain controller and rapidly deploy virtual domain controllers through cloning. It allows you to quickly restore domain controllers when a failure occurs and to rapidly provision a test environment when you need to deploy and test new features or capabilities before you apply the features or capabilities to production.

CERTIFICATION READY
Configure domain controller cloning.
Objective 5.2

Because domain controllers provide a distributed environment, you could not safely clone an Active Directory domain controller in the past. However by following the steps in the next exercise, you will be able to make a copy of a Server 2012 domain controller that can be used over and over.

Before, if you cloned any server, the server would end up with the same domain or forest, which is unsupported with the same domain or forest. You would then have to run sysprep, which would remove the unique security information before cloning and then promote a domain controller manually. When you clone a domain controller, you perform safe cloning, which a cloned domain controller automatically runs a subset of the sysprep process and promotes the server to a domain controller automatically.

The four primary steps to deploy a cloned virtualized domain controller are as follows:

1. Grant the source virtualized domain controller the permission to be cloned by adding the source virtualized domain controller to the Cloneable Domain Controllers group.
2. Run `Get-ADDCCloningExcludedApplicationList` cmdlet in Windows PowerShell to determine which services and applications on the domain controller are not compatible with the cloning.
3. Run `New-ADDCCloneConfigFile` to create the clone configuration file, which is stored in the C:\Windows\NTDS.
4. In Hyper-V, export and then import the virtual machine of the source domain controller.

DEPLOY A CLONED VIRTUALIZED DOMAIN CONTROLLER

GET READY. To deploy a cloned virtualized domain controller, perform the following steps:

1. Open Server Manager.
2. Click Tools > Active Directory Users and Computers. The *Active Directory Users and Computers console* opens.
3. Navigate to and click the Domain Controllers OU.
4. Right-click the source virtualized domain controller and select Properties. The domain controller *Properties* dialog box opens.
5. Click the Member Of tab.
6. Click Add. When the *Select Groups* dialog box opens, type Cloneable Domain Controllers in the *Enter the object names to select* text box and click OK.
7. Close the *Active Directory Users and Computers console*.
8. To display the list of services and programs installed that are not compatible with cloning of the AD server on the source virtualized domain controller, run the following command from Windows PowerShell:

   ```
   Get-ADDCCloningExcludedApplicationList
   ```

9. Review the list and remove any services and applications that you believe are not safe to clone. The others need to be tested or verified from the vendor.
10. After the list has been cleaned up and you still have items that you want to be included in the cloning, create a CustomDCCloneAllowList.xml file by running the following command:

    ```
    Get-ADDCCloningExcludedApplicationList
    -GenerateXml
    ```

11. Click the Windows PowerShell icon on the task bar. The *Windows PowerShell* command prompt opens.
12. Run the `New-ADDCCloneConfigFile` cmdlet on the source virtual DC while specifying the configuration settings for the clone domain controller, such as the name, the IP address, and DNS resolver. For example:

    ```
    New-ADDCCloneConfigFile –Static -IPv4Address
    "192.168.3.125" -IPv4DNSResolver "192.168.3.120"
    -IPv4SubnetMask "255.255.255.0" -CloneComputerName
    "VServer2" -IPv4DefaultGateway "192.168.3.1"
    -SiteName "Site1"
    ```

    Make sure the site exists. A DCCloneConfig.xml file is created in the C:\Windows\NTDS folder.

13. Go back to the *Server Manager Dashboard*.

14. Click Tools > Hyper-V Manager. The *Hyper-V Manager console* opens (see Figure 16-20).

Figure 16-20

Opening the Hyper-V Manager

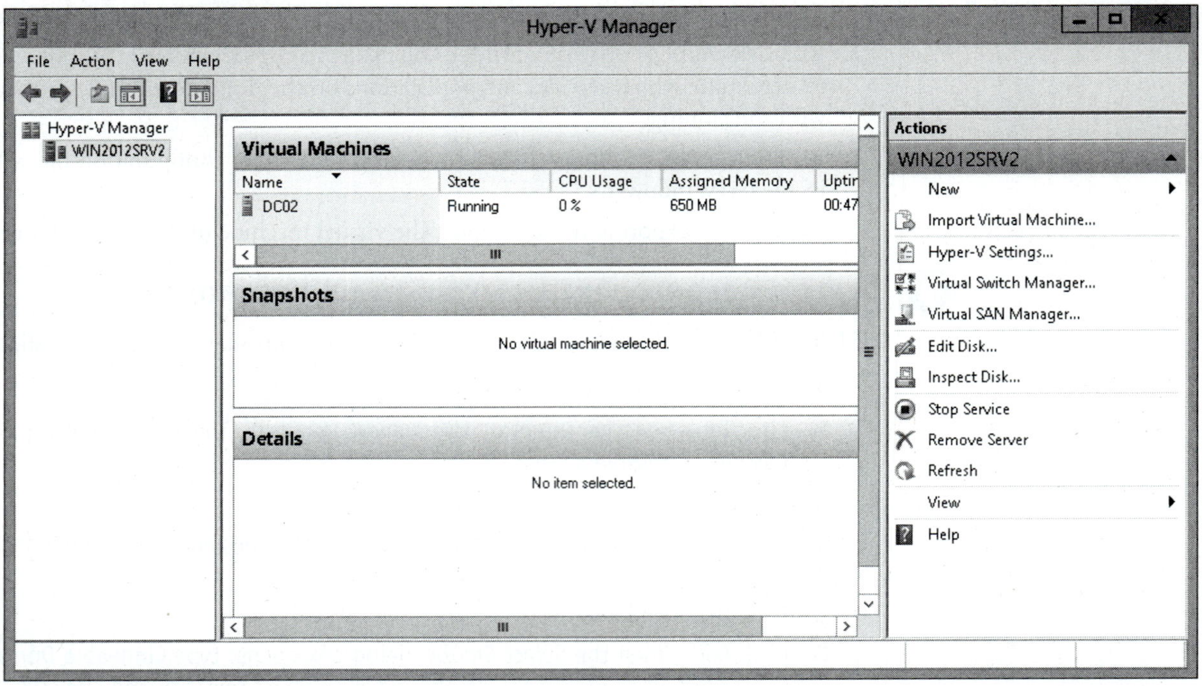

15. Right-click the source virtual domain controller and click Turn Off (see Figure 16-21). If you asked if you are sure, click Turn Off.

Figure 16-21

Turning off a virtual machine

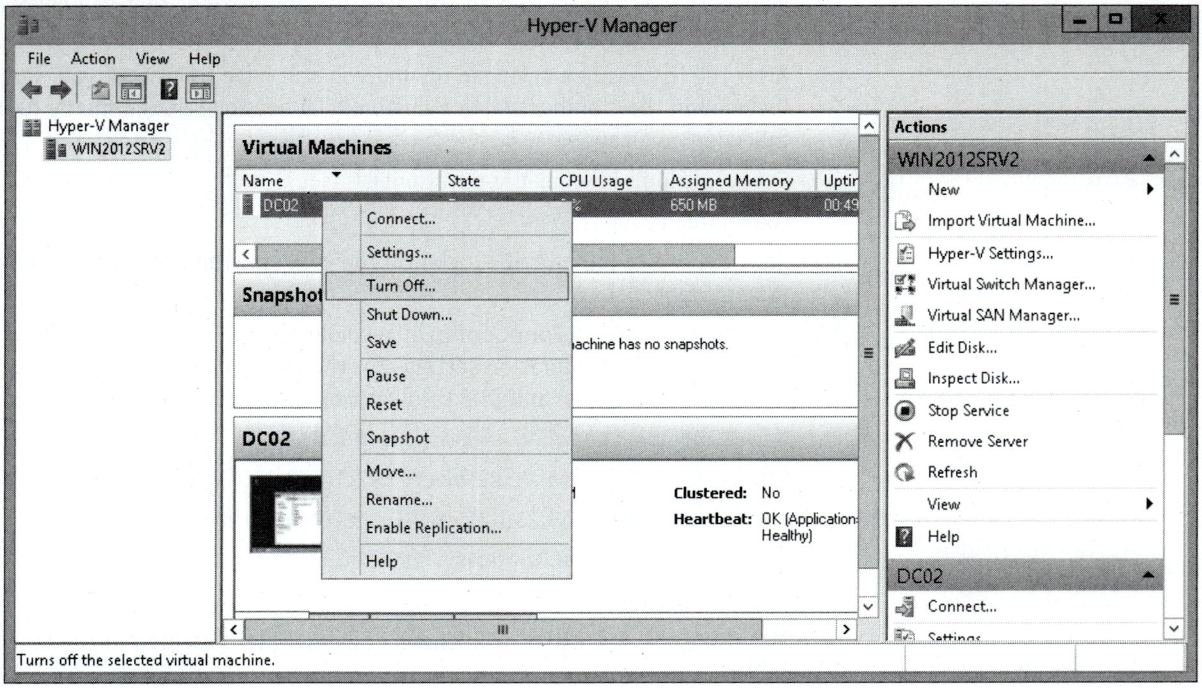

16. Right-click the source virtual domain controller in Hyper-V Manager and select Export. Specify the folder where you want to export to in the *Location* text box (such as d:\clone) and click Export. Exporting the image will take several minutes.
17. Right-click the source virtual domain controller and click Start.
18. In Hyper-V, open the Action menu and click Import Virtual Machine.
19. When the *Import Virtual Machine Wizard* starts, click Next.
20. On the *Locate Folder* (see Figure 16-22), specify the exported folder (such as D:\Clone\DC02) in the *Folder* text box and click Next.

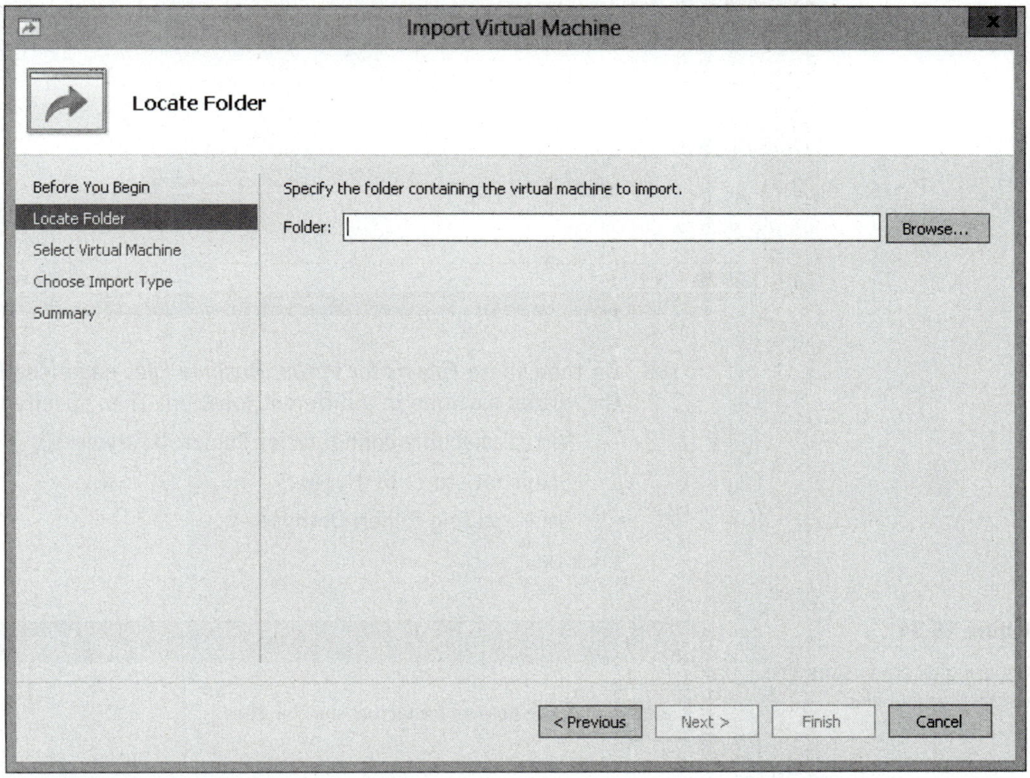

Figure 16-22
Specifying the virtual machine to import

21. On the *Select Virtual Machine* page, click Next.
22. On the *Choose Import Type* page (see Figure 16-23), select copy the virtual machine (create a new unique ID) and click Next.

Figure 16-23

Choosing the import type

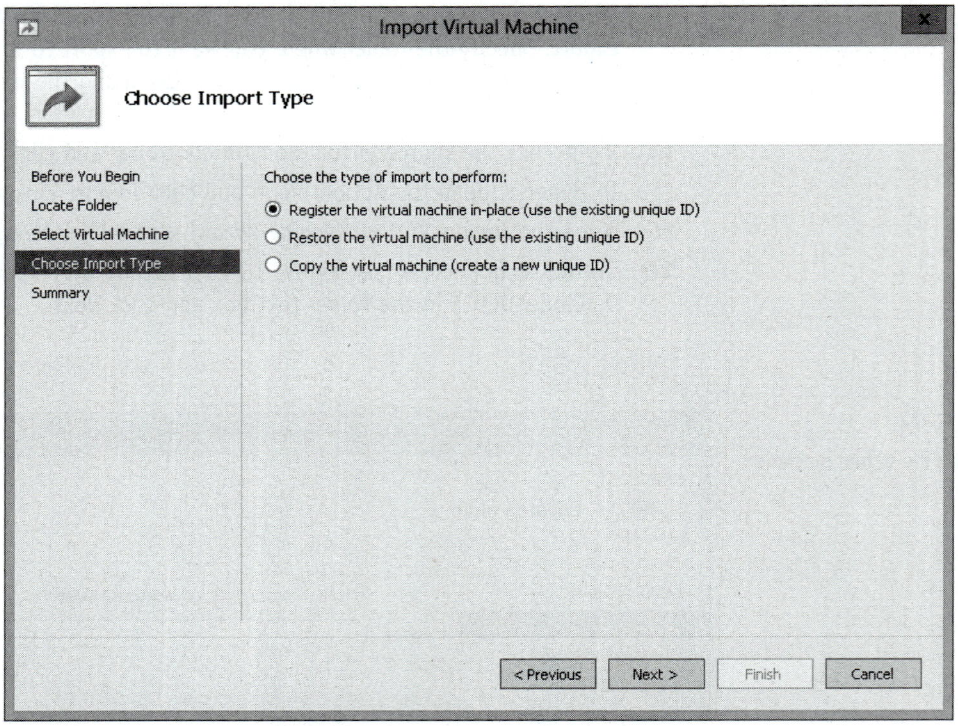

23. On the *Choose Folders for Virtual Machine Files* page (see Figure 16-24), select Store the virtual machine in a different location. Then specify the following locations:

    Virtual machine configuration folder: D:\Hyper-V\

    Snapshot store: D:\Hyper-V

    Smart paging folder: D:\Hyper-V

    Click Next.

Figure 16-24

Choosing where to store the virtual machine files

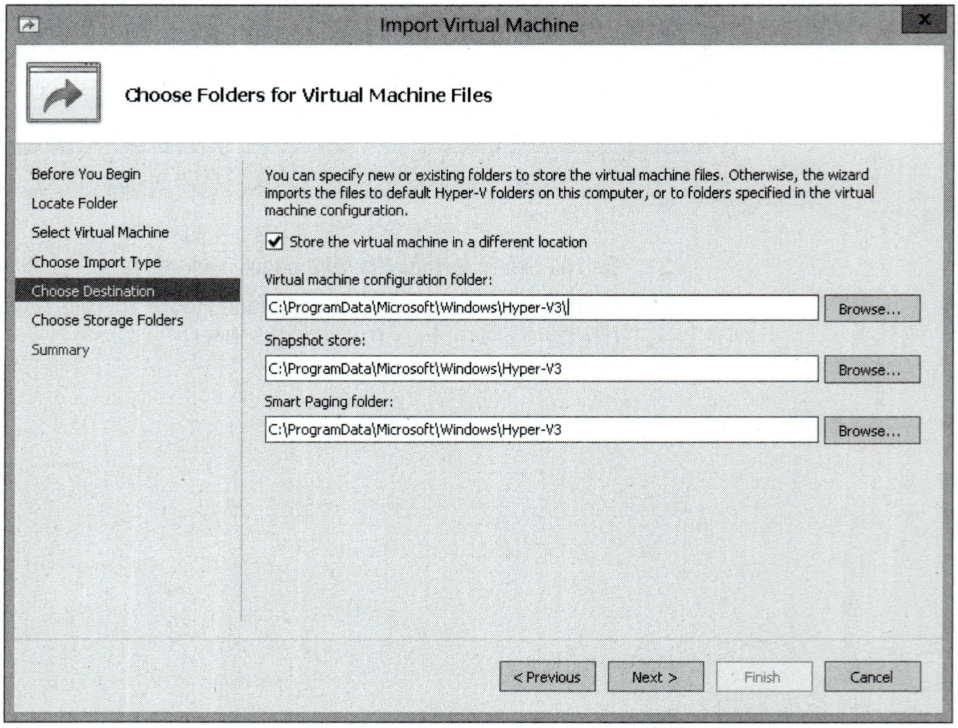

24. On the *Choose Folders to Store Virtual Hard Disks* page (see Figure 16-25), type D:\Hyper-V in the *Location* text box. Click Next.

Figure 16-25

Choosing where to store the virtual hard disks.

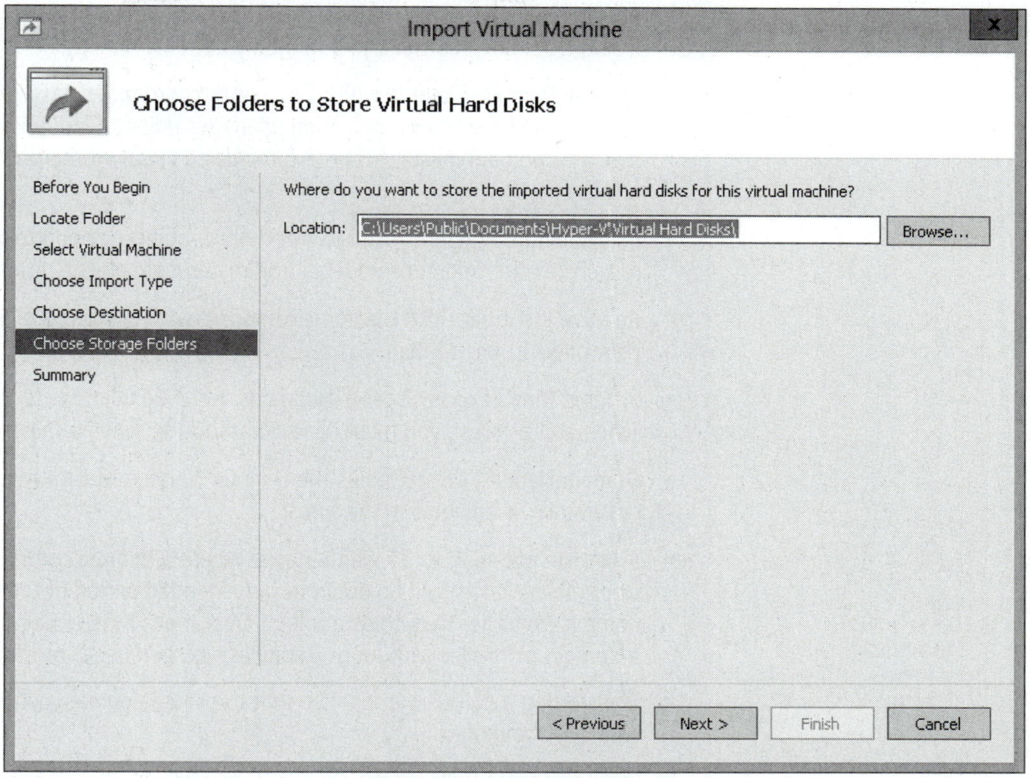

25. On the *Completing Import Wizard* page, click Finish. Importing will take several minutes.
26. When the import is complete, right-click the new server and click Start.

SKILL SUMMARY

IN THIS LESSON, YOU LEARNED:

- A domain is an administrative boundary for users and computers that are stored in a common directory database. A single domain can span multiple physical locations or sites and can contain millions of objects.
- Domain controllers are servers that contain the Active Directory databases. A domain partition stores only the information about objects located in that domain. All domain controllers in a domain receive changes and replicate those changes to the domain partition stored on all other domain controllers in the domain.
- A global catalog stores a full copy of all objects in the domain. In addition, as a global catalog, it also has a partial copy of all objects for all other domains in the forest. The partial copy of all objects is used for logon, object searches, and universal group membership.

(continued)

- Another way to avoid placing a global catalog at every site and to avoid going over a WAN link for login information is to use universal group membership caching (UGMC).
- Operations masters, sometimes referred to as *Flexible Single Master Operations (FMSO)*, are specialized domain controllers that perform certain tasks that can be handled only by a single domain controller in a multi-master environment.
- Primary Domain Controller (PDC) Emulator coordinates password changes, account lockouts, and time synchronization; manages edits to Group Policy Objects (GPOs); and acts as a domain master browser (provides a list of workgroups and domains when you browse).
- Infrastructure Master is used to track which objects belong to which domain because it is responsible for reference updates from its domain objects to other domains.
- Relative Identifier (RID) Master is responsible for assigning relative identifiers to domain controllers in the domain.
- Schema Master controls all the updates and modifications to the schema. To update the schema of a forest, you must have access to the schema master.
- Domain Naming Master holds the Domain Naming Master role that controls the addition or removal of domains in the forest.
- If you are planning to do maintenance where a domain controller that holds the Operations Master will be down for an extended period of time, you are going to retire a domain controller that holds a role of Operations Master or you need to move the role to a domain controller with more resources, you will need transfer the Operations Master.
- Transferring a FSMO role requires that the source domain controller and the target domain controller be online.
- If a domain controller that holds an Operations Master role has an unrecoverable failure, you cannot transfer roles because the current domain controller is not online. Therefore, you will need to size the role.
- The Read-only domain controller (RODC), which contains a full replication of the domain database, cannot be modified directly. It was created to be used in places where a domain controller is needed but the physical security of the domain controller could not be guaranteed.
- Starting with Windows Server 2012, you can safely virtualize a domain controller and rapidly deploy virtual domain controllers through cloning.

■ Knowledge Assessment

Multiple Choice

Select the correct answer for each of the following questions.

1. Which of the following is found on a domain controller? (Choose all that apply.)
   - **a.** Service Master
   - **b.** global catalog
   - **c.** RID Master
   - **d.** PDC Emulator

2. Which of the following is not an Operation's Master?
   a. global catalog
   b. PDC Emulator
   c. Schema Master
   d. RID Master

3. What is the cause of the problem if account lockout is not working?
   a. The PDC Emulator is down.
   b. The Infrastructure Master is down.
   c. The RID Master is down.
   d. The Schema Master is down.

4. What do you use to transfer the holder of the RID Master?
   a. Active Directory Users and Computers
   b. Active Directory Sites and Services
   c. Active Directory Domains and Trusts
   d. ADSI Edit

5. What do you use to transfer the holder of the Schema Master?
   a. Active Directory Users and Computers
   b. Active Directory Sites and Services
   c. Active Directory Domains and Trusts
   d. Active Directory Schema

6. What do you use to seize the role of the Domain Naming Operations Master?
   a. Active Directory Domains and Trusts
   b. ADSI Edit
   c. Active Directory Sites and Services
   d. ntdsutil.exe

7. You are creating a self-served kiosk console at a local mall. At the mall, the Kiosk will need to access a domain controller. What should you use?
   a. global catalog
   b. PDF Emulator
   c. RODC
   d. RID Master

8. What are you cloning when you use the New-ADDCCloneConfigFile?
   a. Physical domain controller
   b. Virtual domain controller
   c. A server located within a ZIP file
   d. A mounted domain controller

9. What is the minimum forest functional level for RODC?
   a. Windows Server 2003
   b. Windows Server 2008
   c. Windows Server 2008 R2
   d. Windows Server 2012

10. You deployed a Read-only domain controller (RODC) running Windows Server 2008 to a branch office. You need to ensure that users at the branch office are able to log on to the domain by using the RODC. What should you do?
   a. Configure a bridgehead server in the main office that points to the read-only domain.
   b. Configure a Password Replication Policy on the RDOC.
   c. Enable the Password Authentication using RODC option for each user.
   d. Add the users to the RODC Users Group.

Best Answer

Choose the letter that corresponds to the best answer. More than one answer choice may achieve the goal. Select the BEST answer.

1. Where is the membership of universal groups stored?
  a. domain controller
  b. global catalog
  c. PDC Emulator
  d. Schema Master

2. You are trying to log on and you cannot reach a global catalog. What will happen?
  a. You cannot log in.
  b. You can still log in if you access another domain controller.
  c. You can still log in if you can access the PDF Emulator.
  d. You can still log in if UGMC is enabled.

3. The domain controller that has the PDC Emulator will be down for a few hours when the site is shut down for maintenance. What should you do?
  a. Go to another server and transfer the PDC Emulator role.
  b. Go to another server and seize the PDC Emulator role.
  c. Physically move the server to another site.
  d. Do nothing.

4. Which of the following roles affects the users the most if it is down?
  a. PDC Emulator
  b. Infrastructure Master
  c. RID Master
  d. Schema Master

5. How many PDC Emulators can a forest have?
  a. 1
  b. 2
  c. Unlimited
  d. Depends on how many domains you have

Matching and Identification

1. Identify the scope for the Operations Masters.

Domain_____	a) Infrastructure Master
Domain_____	b) RID Master
Forest_____	c) Domain Naming Master
Forest_____	d) Schema Master
Domain_____	e) PDC Emulator

2. Identify the Operations Master

RID Master_____	a) Assigns a Security ID to an object.
PDC Emulator_____	b) Initiates password changes.
Schema Master_____	c) Control the updates and modifications to the schema.
Infrastructure Master_____	d) Used to determine which objects belong to which domains.
PDC Emulator_____	e) Master time server.
PDC Emulator_____	f) Manages edits to GPOs.
Domain Naming Master_____	g) Used to add and remove domains.
PDC Emulator_____	h) Provides a list of workgroups and domains.

Build a List

1. Identify the steps in order to clone a virtualized domain controller. Not all steps will be used.
   _____ Export the virtual machine.
   _____ Run `New-ADDCCloneConfigFil`.
   _____ Run `sysprep` on the system.
   _____ Run the `Get-ADDCCloningExcludedApplicationList`.
   _____ Run the `Autoconfig` command.
   _____ Import the virtual machine.
   _____ Add the source VM DC to the Cloneable Domain Controllers Group.

2. Identify the steps in order to clone an RODC domain controller. Not all steps will be used.
   _____ Run the `ADPrep /RODCPrep` command.
   _____ Change the ntid.dit file to read-only.
   _____ Install the domain controller.
   _____ Assign the Read permission to all files on the server.
   _____ Run the `ADPrep /sysprep` command.
   _____ Create a Password Replication Policy.
   _____ Open the System Properties and select Read-Only.

3. Identify the steps in order to seize the role of the Schema Master. Not all steps will be used.
   _____ Run the `connect to server` command.
   _____ Run the `ntdsutil` command.
   _____ Run the `roles` command.
   _____ Run the `fsmo` command.
   _____ Run the `seize` command.
   _____ Open a command prompt.
   _____ Run the `transfer` command.
   _____ Run the `connections` command.

■ Business Case Scenarios

Scenario 16-1: Planning Domain Controllers and Global Catalog

You work for the Contoso Corporation. You have the main corporate office (1,200 users), 2 other large sites (up to 500 users each), and 10 small sites (no more than 10 users). How would you deploy the domain controllers, Operations Master roles, and global catalogs?

Scenario 16-2: Establishing a Help Station in an Information Lobby

You work for the Contoso Corporation. At a car show, you need to establish a Sales station that needs to record information for potential users to a system that requires access to a domain controller. However, you want only the sales people to be able to log in to the application and domain controller. What should you do?

17 LESSON

Maintaining Active Directory

70-411 EXAM OBJECTIVE

Objective 5.3 – Maintain Active Directory. This objective may include but is not limited to: back up Active Directory and SYSVOL; manage Active Directory offline; optimize an Active Directory database; clean up metadata; configure Active Directory snapshots; perform object- and container-level recovery; perform Active Directory restore.

Lesson Heading	Exam Objective
Automating User Account Management	
Backing Up and Restoring Active Directory	
Understanding the Active Directory Database, SYSVOL, and System State	
Using Windows Backup	Back up Active Directory and SYSVOL Perform Active Directory restore
Configuring Active Directory Snapshots	Configure Active Directory snapshots
Performing Object- and Container-Level Recovery	Perform object- and container-level recovery
Managing Active Directory Offline	Manage Active Directory offline
Optimizing an Active Directory Database	Optimize an Active Directory database
Cleaning up Metadata	Clean up metadata

KEY TERMS

Active Directory database mounting tool
Active Directory Recycle Bin
Active Directory snapshot
authoritative restore
backup
Directory Services Restore Mode (DSRM)
Extensible Storage Engine (ESE)
metadata
Microsoft Windows Backup
nonauthoritative restore
Restartable Active Directory Domain Services
system state
SYSVOL

Automating User Account Management

THE BOTTOM LINE

Active Directory Users and Computers and the Active Directory Administrative Center provide graphical user interfaces (GUIs) for creating one or more user accounts. However, sometimes you have many accounts that you want to import from a list that was generated by a database, or you want to export a list from Active Directory so that you import the list into another system, or you want a list in a spreadsheet to manipulate as needed. Microsoft includes several tools, including CSVDE.exe and LDIFDE.exe.

CSVDE is a command-line tool that exports or imports Active Directory Domain Services (AD DS) objects to or from a comma-delimited text file (also known as a comma-separated value text file or .csv file). You can open the comma-delimited file with any text editor such as Notepad, and with Microsoft Excel. When you use Microsoft Excel, the data is displayed in the proper row and columns so that you can manipulate the data with the available Excel tools.

The simplest form of using the CSVDE command is:

```
csvde -f filename
```

This exports all objects in your Active Directory domain. Typically, you want to list just the users or computers or you want to list only users with a certain attribute.

The available parameters for the CSVDE command are:

-i: Turn on Import mode (The default is Export.)

-f *filename*: Input or Output filename.

-s *servername*: The server to bind to. (The default is aDC of computer's domain.)

-t *portnum*: Port Number. (The default is 389.)

The following options are available only when using the CSVDE to export information:

-l list: List of attributes (comma-separated) to look for in an LDAP search.

-o list: List of attributes (comma separated) to omit from input.

-k: The import goes on ignoring, Constraint Violation and Object Already Exists errors.

For example, to export a list of user accounts, you can use the following example:

```
csvde -s server1 -f c:\ADUsers.csv -r "(&(objectClass=user)
(objectCategory=person)
(!userAccountControl=514)" -d
"OU= DC=corporate,dc=contoso,dc=com" -l
cn,SamAccountName,Distinguishname,department,
description,physicalDeliveryOfficeName,title,
manager,telephoneNumber,mobile,ipPhone,mail
```

The -s option specifies to pull a list from the domain controller called *server1*. The -f option specifies to save the list to the C:\ADUsers.csv. The `"(&(objectClass=user)(objectCategory=person)` option specifies only users. The `(!userAccountControl=514)`specifies only active accounts. The –l specifies which attributes you want to include such as the common name, SAMAccountName, distinguished name, department, and so on.

To import, from a .csv file, use something such as the following example:

```
csvde -i -f filename -k
```

The -i parameter specifies Import mode. The -f parameter identifies the file name to import from or export to. The -k parameter is useful during import operations because it instructs CSVDE to ignore errors, including Object Already Exists.

You cannot use the CSVDE to import passwords. In addition, the account is initially disabled. After you reset the password, you can enable the object in AD DS.

The LDIFDE.exe is used to import or export Active Directory objects, including users. You can use this command to store information and perform batch operations against directories that conform to the LDAP standards.

Different from the `CSVDE` command, the `LDIFDE` command implements these batch operations by using LDIF files. The LDIF file format consists of a block of lines, which together constitute a single operation. Multiple operations in a single file are separated by a blank line.

The contents of the LDIF file look similar to the following example:

```
dn: CN=John Smith,OU=Sales,OU=User Accounts,DC=contoso,DC=com
changetype: add
objectClass: top
objectClass: person
objectClass: organizationalPerson
objectClass: user
cn: John Smith
sn: Smith
title: Sales Manager
description: Sales Team Managear
givenName: John
displayName: Smith, John
company: Contoso Corp
sAMAccountName: john.smith
userPrincipalName: john.smith@contoso.com
mail: john.smith@contoso.com
```

Although the LDIF file format is not as intuitive as the comma-separated file format, the LDIF format is a standard that is supported by many directory services and databases. Fortunately, the options of the `LDIFDE` command are similar to the `CSVDE` command.

For example, to import an LDIF file called *NewUsers.ldf*, you use the following command:

```
ldifde -i -f C:\NewUsers.ldf -k
```

USING WINDOWS POWERSHELL

You can also use Windows PowerShell to import and export .csv user files. They include:

- `Import-CSV - Creates objects from .csv files that can then be piped into other Windows PowerShell cmdlets.`
- `New-ADUser - Creates the objects that are imported from the Import-CSV cmdlet.`

You can also use Windows PowerShell to import and export .csv user files. They include the following:

- **Import-CSV:** Creates objects from .csv files that can then be piped into other Windows PowerShell cmdlets.
- **New-ADUser:** Creates the objects that are imported from the Import-CSV cmdlet.

MORE INFORMATION

For more information on using the `CSVDE` command, `LDIFDE` command, or the `Import-CSV/New-ADUser PowerShell` cmdlets, search for these commands at the Microsoft's TechNet website.

Backing Up and Restoring Active Directory

THE BOTTOM LINE

When working with servers, there is no good time for a failure. Active Directory is a complicated database that stores information about your users, computers, groups, and other objects. Just like any other database, it can become corrupt, or objects might be accidentally or maliciously deleted. No matter what happens, the best method to data recovery is using backup.

A ***backup*** or the process of backing up refers to making copies of data so that these additional copies can be used to restore the original after a data-loss event. They can be used to restore entire systems following a disaster or to restore small sets of files or objects that are accidentally deleted or corrupted.

Traditionally, magnetic tapes have been the most commonly used medium for bulk data storage, backup, and archiving. Tape is a sequential access medium, so even though access times might be poor, the rate of continuously writing or reading data can actually be fast.

For larger organizations, you might use multiple tape drives connected together with a tape library that can automatically swap and manage tapes. Recently because of increased capacity at lower cost, hard drives have become a viable option for backups. Hard disks can be included in the SAN, NAS, internal hard drives, and external hard drives. Some disk-based backup systems, such as virtual tape libraries, support data de-duplication, which can dramatically reduce the amount of disk storage capacity consumed by daily and weekly backup data.

Usually hard disks are used to provide backup of recent data, and the data is copied to tape and taken off site for longer term storage and archiving. If a failure occurs, you can quickly restore from the disks. If you need to recover or read data from the past, you will then have to retrieve the tapes from off site and read the tapes.

Another media that is becoming more popular for backups is to use recordable optical disks, such as CDs, DVDs, and even Blu-ray. Unfortunately, the newer formats tend to cost more, which might prohibit their use for backups. There is also some concern about the lifetime of a selected optical disk because some optical disks degrade and lose data within a couple of years.

More recently, cloud computing (sometimes just referred to as the *cloud*) can be used for backups. Cloud computing is the use of computing resource (hardware and software) that is delivered as a service over the network, such as the Internet. As far as the client of cloud computing is concerned, cloud computing looks like a "black box." The client does not need to know what makes the computer resources work. As far as they are concerned, it just works and the vendor of the cloud computing is concerned with providing the managing and maintenance of the computing resources.

Understanding the Active Directory Database, SYSVOL, and System State

The Active Directory database uses the ***Extensible Storage Engine (ESE)***, which is an indexed and sequential access method (ISAM) database. The ESE (Esent.dll) indexes the data in the database file and provides the mechanism to store and retrieve data. It supports up to a little over 2 billion objects and up to 16 TB in size. The maximum size of a database record is 8,110 bytes, based on an 8-kilobyte (KB) page size. The ntds.dit file is approximately 400 MB in size per 1,000 users.

The Active Directory database is stored in Active Directory database file (C:\Windows\NTDS\Ntds.dit) and its associated log and temporary files. It includes the following:

- **Ntds.dit:** The physical database file in which all directory data is stored. This file consists of three internal tables: the data table, link table, and security descriptor (SD) table. It contains the schema information, configuration information, and domain information.
- **Edb.log:** The log file into which directory transactions are written before being committed to the database file. Transaction log files used by ESE are 10 MB in size.
- **Edb.chk:** The file that is used to track the point up to which transactions in the log file have been committed.
- **Res1.log and Res2.log files:** Files that are used to reserve space for additional log files if edb.log becomes full.
- **Temp.edb:** A file that is used as a scratch pad to store information about in-progress large transactions and to hold pages pulled out of Ntds.dit during maintenance operations.

Figure 17-1 shows the Active Directory database files.

Figure 17-1

Looking at the Active Directory database

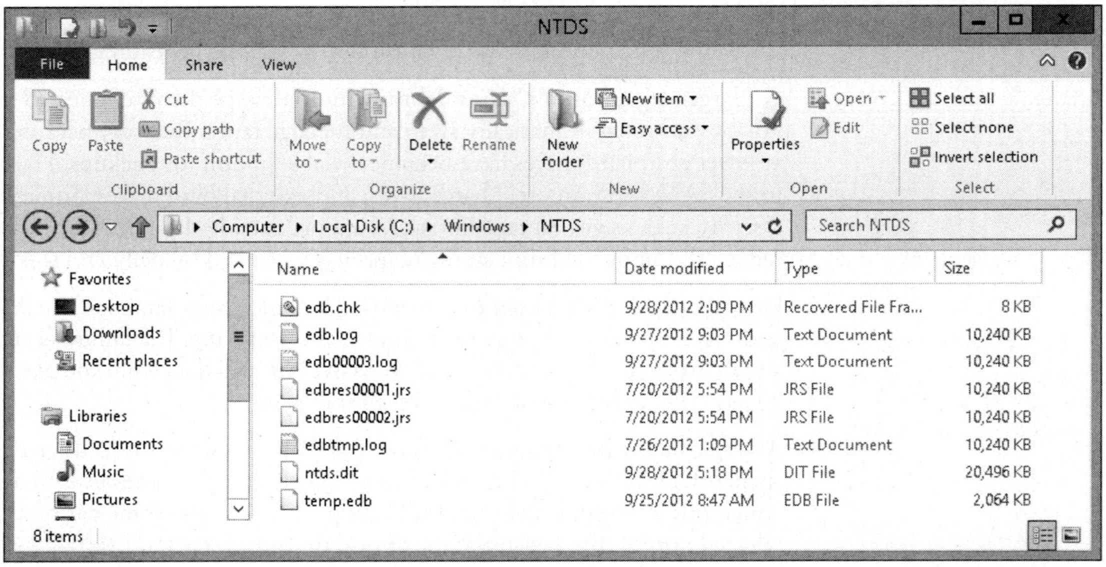

The Windows ***system state*** is a collection of system components that are not contained in a simple file but can be backed up easily. It includes the following:

- Boot files (such as bootmgr)
- DLL cache folder
- Registry (including COM settings)
- SYSVOL (Group Policy and logon scripts)
- Active Directory NTDS.DIT (domain controllers)
- Certificate Store (if the service is installed)
- User profiles
- COM+ and WMI information
- Cluster service information
- IIS metabase
- System files that are under Windows Resource Protection

Therefore, if you need to back up Active Directory, you need to back up the system state so that you can get all the Active Directory components.

Windows backup and most commercial backup software packages back up the Windows system state. To perform a complete restore of a system running Windows, you need to back up all files on the drive and the system state.

The ***SYSVOL*** is a shared directory that stores the server copy of the domain's public files that must be shared for common access and replication throughout a domain (see Figure 17-2). The SYSVOL folder on a domain controller contains the following items:

- **Login scripts:** Stores the logon scripts that are administrated from Active Directory Users and Computers and group policies.
- **Windows Group Policy:** Configuring settings that control the working environment of user and computer accounts and that provide the centralized management and configuration of operating systems, applications, and user settings in an Active Directory environment.
- **Distributed File System (DFS) staging folder and files:** Used to synchronize data and files between domain controllers.
- **File system junctions:** A physical location on a hard disk that points to data that is located elsewhere on your disk or other storage device to manage a single instance stored.

Figure 17-2

Looking at the SYSVOL folder

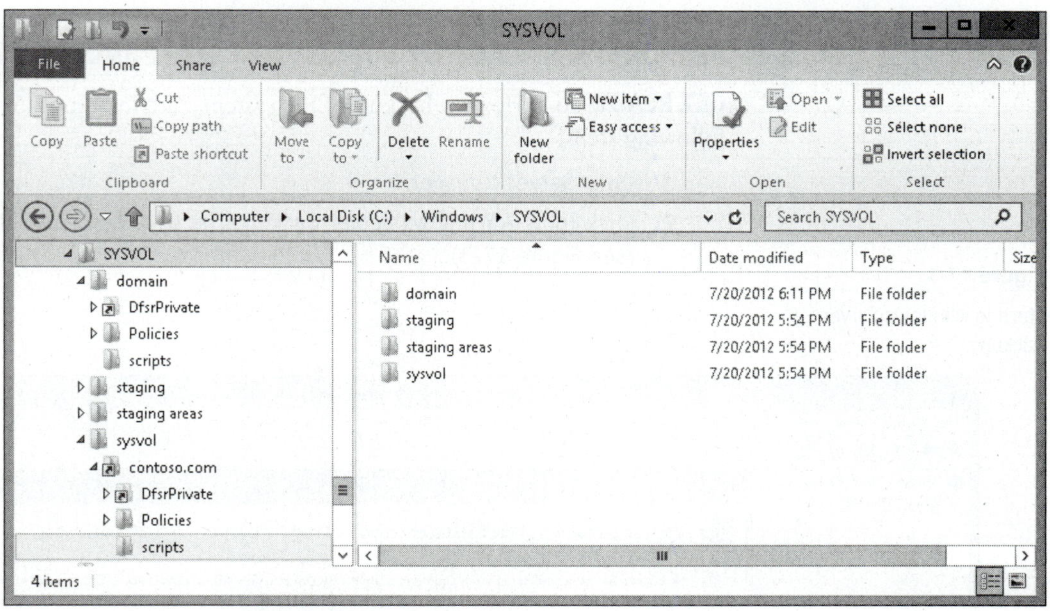

Using Windows Backup

Windows includes ***Microsoft Windows Backup***, which allows you to back up a system. However, third-party backup software packages usually offer more features and options.

To access the backup and recovery tools for Windows Server 2012, you must install the Windows Server Backup feature using the Add Roles and Features Wizard. To run the Windows Server Backup, you must be a member of the Backup Operators or Administrators group.

You can create a backup by using the Backup Schedule Wizard or by using the Backup Once option. You can back up to any local drive or to a shared folder on another server.

Finally, you perform a backup using wbadmin.exe, which is the Backup command-line tool. To find more information about the wbadmin.exe, you can use `wbadmin.exe /?` from a command prompt or search the Microsoft TechNet website.

CERTIFICATION READY
Back up Active Directory and SYSVOL
Objective 5.3

PERFORMING A BACKUP OF ACTIVE DIRECTORY AND SYSVOL

You can create a backup by using the Backup Schedule Wizard or by using the Backup Once option. You can back up to any removable local drive or to a shared folder on another server.

INSTALL WINDOWS SERVER BACKUP

GET READY. To install Windows Server Backup, perform the following steps:

1. Open Server Manager.
2. Click Manage and click Add Roles and Features.
3. When the *Add Roles and Features Wizard* starts, click Next.
4. On the *Select installation type* page, click Next.
5. On the *Select destination server pack*, click Next.
6. On the *Select server roles* page, click Next.
7. Click to select the Windows Server Backup and click Next.
8. On the *Confirm installation selections* page, click Install.
9. When the installation is complete, click Close.

PERFORM A BACKUP OF THE SYSTEM STATE INCLUDING ACTIVE DIRECTORY

GET READY. To perform a backup of the system state including Active Directory, perform the following steps:

1. Open Server Manager.
2. Click Tools > Windows Server Backup. The *Windows Server Backup console* opens (see Figure 17-3).

Figure 17-3

Starting Windows Server Backup

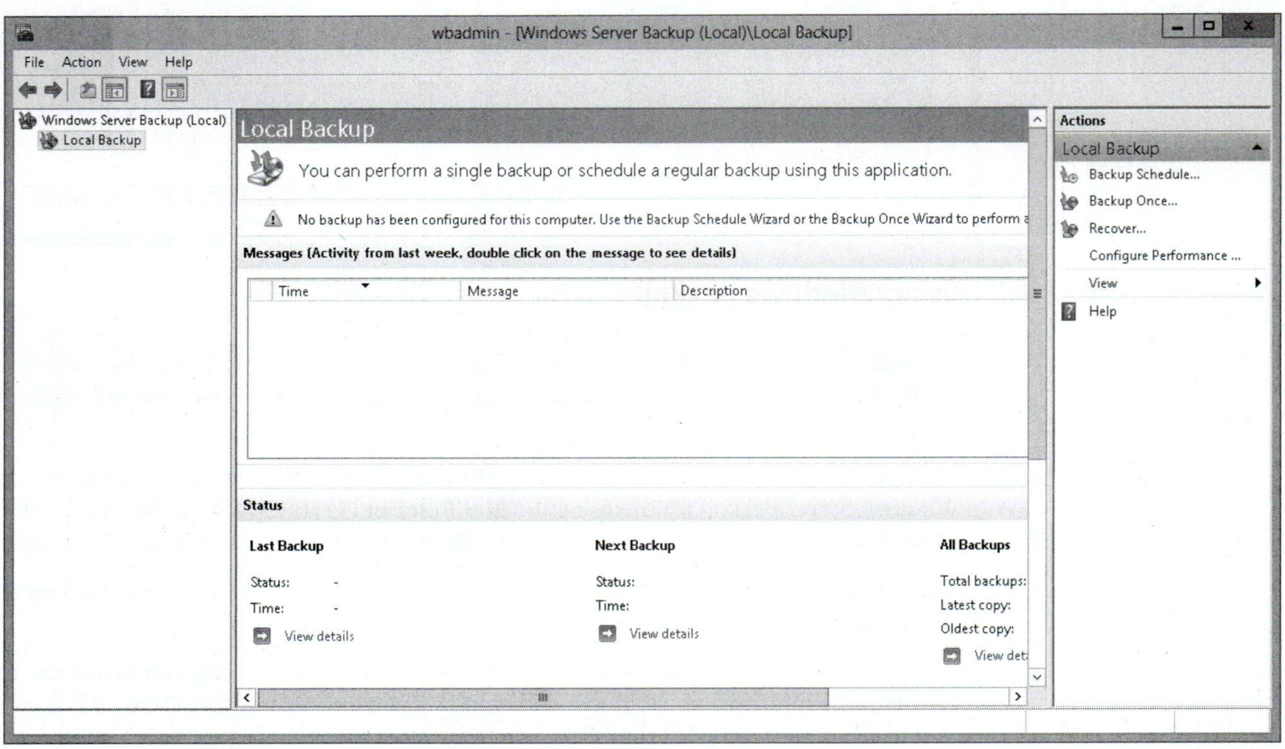

3. Under *Actions*, click Backup Once.
4. When the *Backup Once Wizard* starts, if this is the first time you have run the Backup Once Wizard, click Different Options (see Figure 17-4) and click Next.

Figure 17-4

Selecting different options

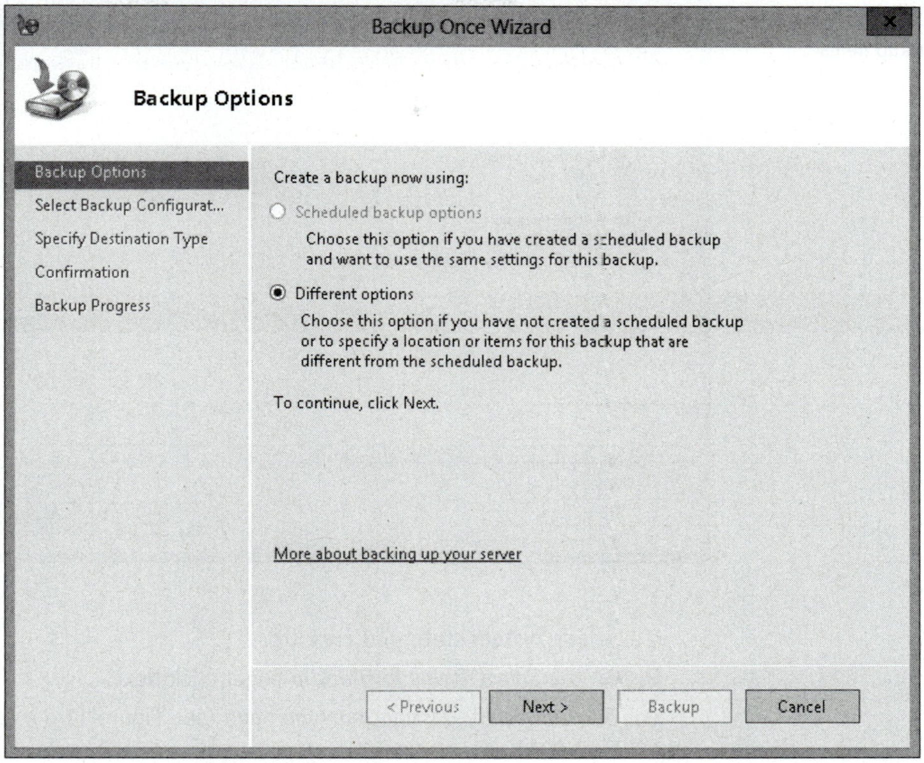

5. On the *Select Backup Configuration* page (see Figure 17-5), click Custom and click Next.

Figure 17-5

Selecting the backup configuration

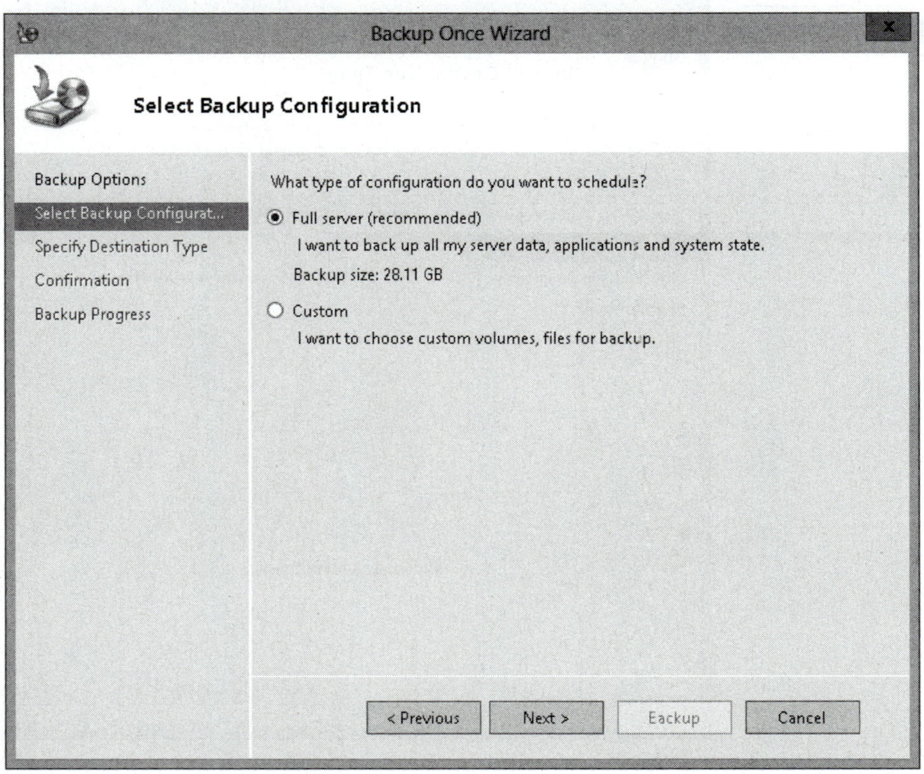

6. On the *Select Items for Backup* page, click **Add Items**. The *Select Items* dialog box opens (see Figure 17-6).

Figure 17-6
Selecting backup items

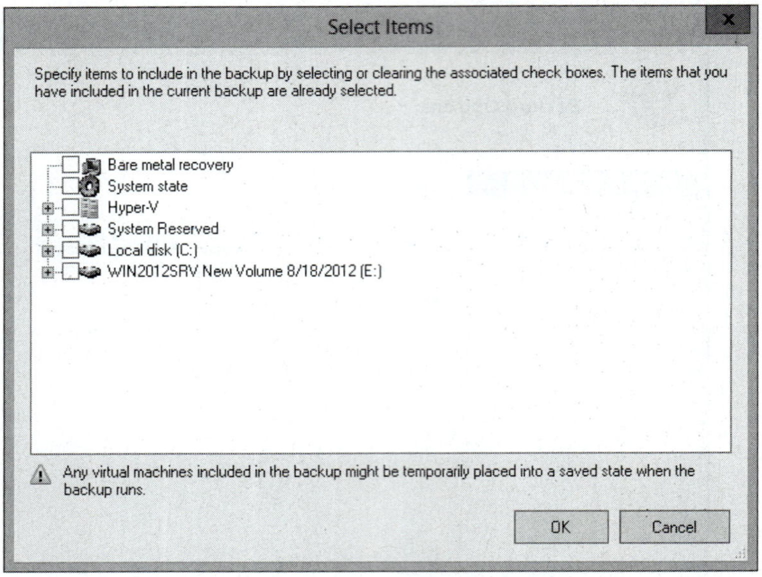

7. Select **System state** and click **OK**.
8. On the *Select Items for Backup* page, click **Next**.
9. On the *Specify Destination Type* page (see Figure 17-7), select **Remote shared** folder. Click **Next**.

Figure 17-7
Specifying destination type

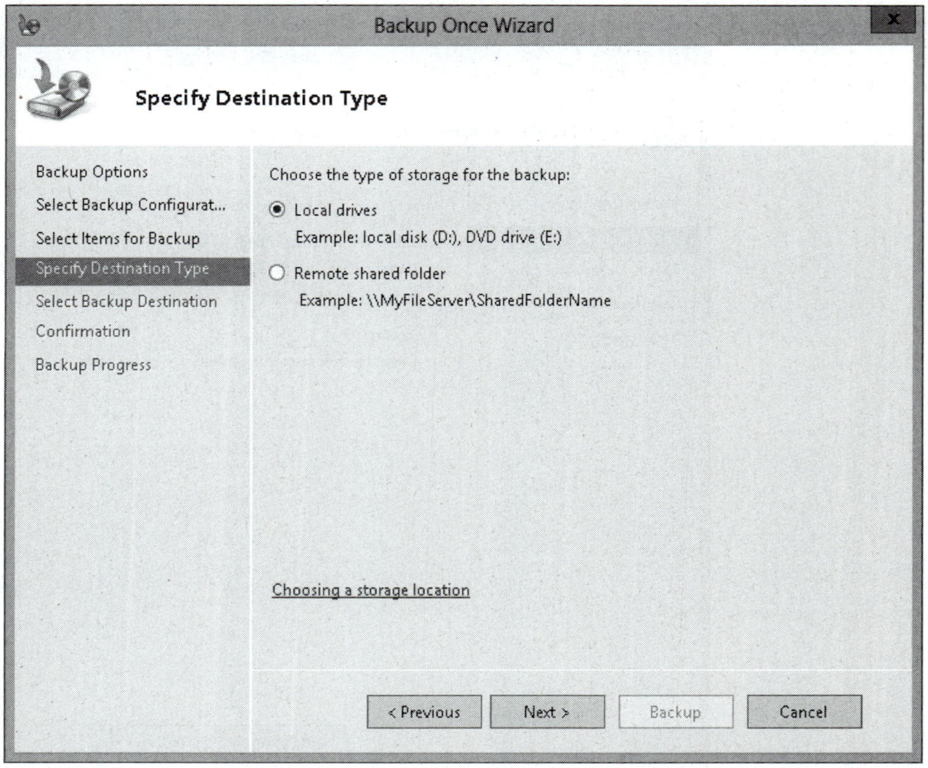

10. On the *Specify Remote Folder* page (see Figure 17-8), type the path of the remote folder (such as \\win2012srv2\backups) and click **Next**.

Figure 17-8

Specify remote folder

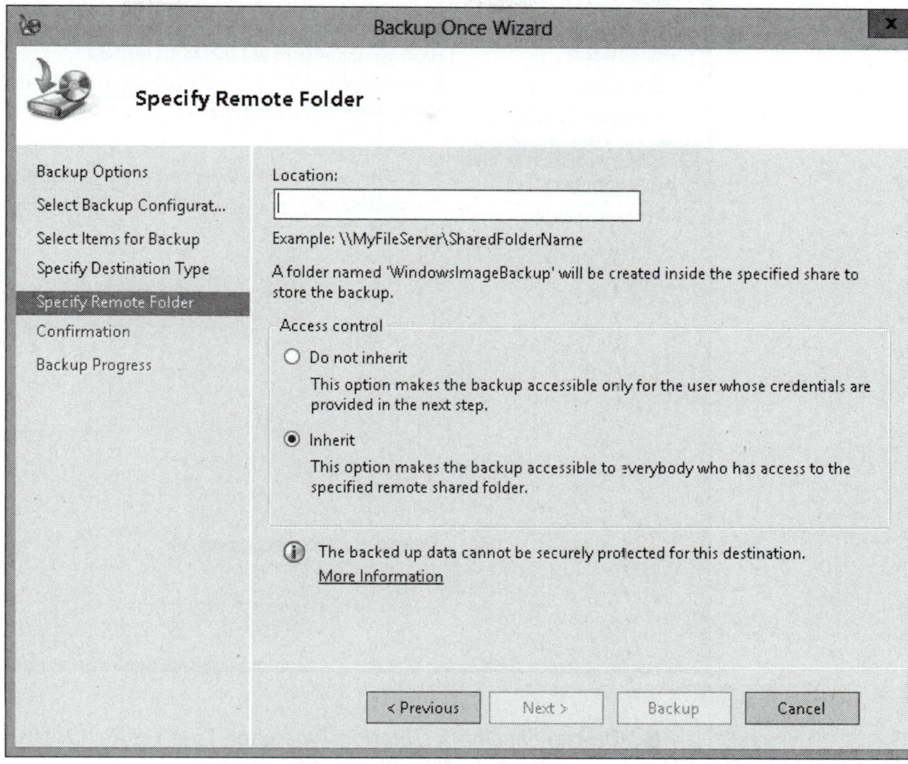

11. On the *Confirmation* page, click **Backup**. The backups will take a few minutes.
12. When the backup is completed, click **Close**.

Windows Server Backup stores the details about your backups in a file called a backup catalog. The catalog is stored in the same place that you store your backups. Because the catalog specifies what is within a backup, you need the backup catalog to use a Windows backup file.

SCHEDULE A BACKUP OF THE SYSTEM STATE INCLUDING ACTIVE DIRECTORY

GET READY. To schedule a backup of the system state including Active Directory, perform the following steps:

1. Under *Actions*, click **Backup Schedule**.
2. When the *Backup Schedule Wizard* starts, click **Next**.
3. On the *Select Backup Configuration* page, select **Custom** and click **Next**.
4. On the *Select Items for Backup* page, click **Add Items**. When the *Select Items* dialog box opens, select **System state** and click **OK**. Click **Next**.
5. On the *Specify Backup Time* page (see Figure 17-9), with the **Once a day** already selected, click **Next**.

Figure 17-9

Specifying when to perform a backup

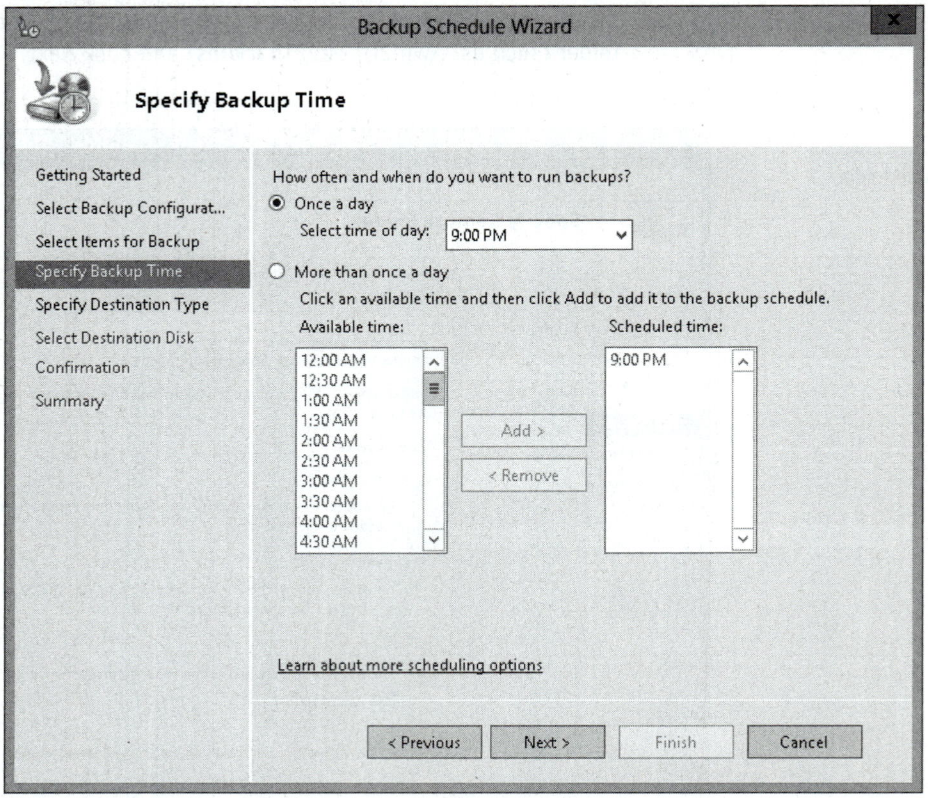

6. On the *Specify Destination Type* page (see Figure 17-10), select Back up to a shared network folder. Click Next.

Figure 17-10

Specifying the destination type

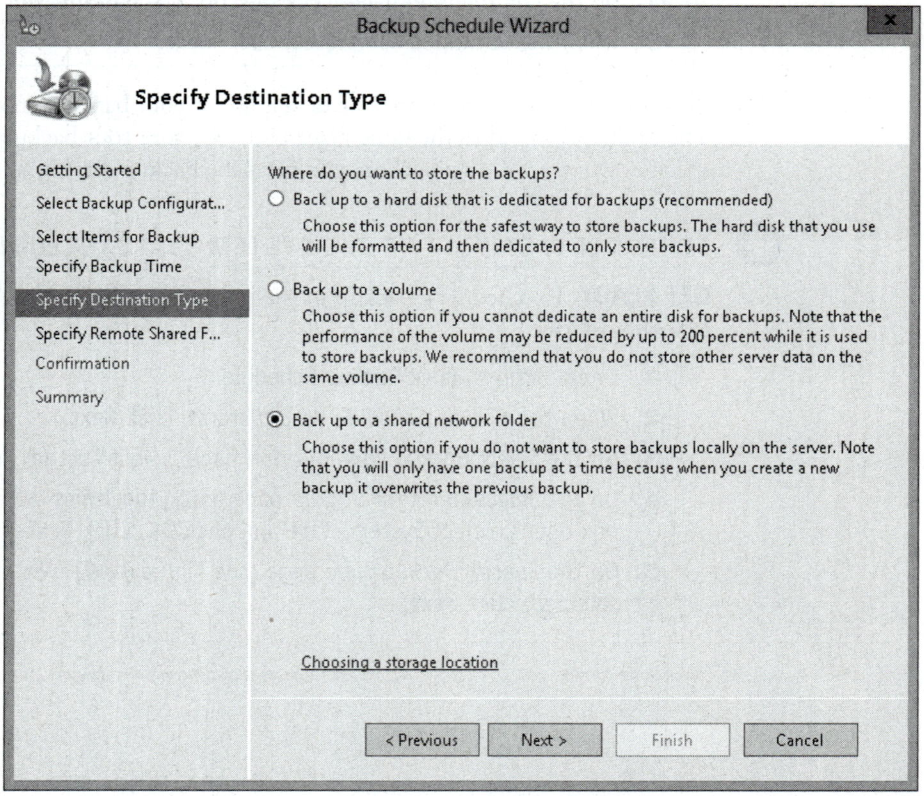

7. When a warning occurs saying that each backup will erase the previous backups, click OK.
8. On the *Specify Remote Folder* page, type the path of the remote folder (such as \\win2012srv2\backups) and click Next.
9. When the *Windows Security* dialog box opens (see Figure 17-11), specify a username and password that will used to perform the backups and click OK.

Figure 17-11

Specifying who the backups run under

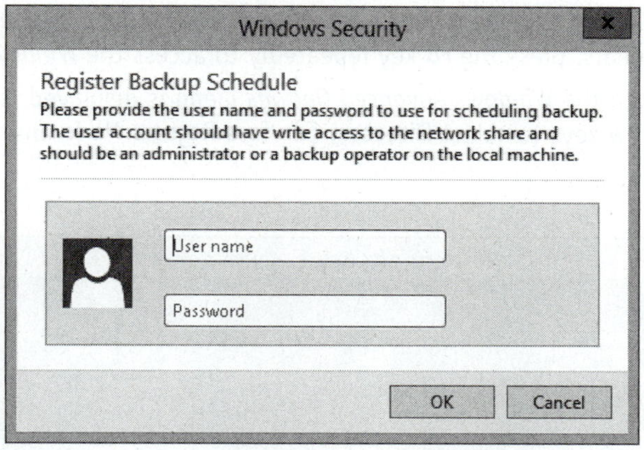

10. On the *Confirmation* page, click Finish.
11. When the backup is scheduled, click Close.
12. Close *Windows Server Backup*.

PERFORMING AN ACTIVE DIRECTORY RESTORE

CERTIFICATION READY
Perform Active Directory restore.
Objective 5.3

There are two types of restores that you can perform with Active Directory:

- A nonauthoritative restore
- An authoritative restore

TAKE NOTE*
Of course, if you perform a complete authoritative restore of Active Directory, any changes to Active Directory since the backup will be lost.

With a ***nonauthoritative restore***, you restore a backup of Active Directory as of the date of the backup. The AD DS restarts on the domain controller, and the domain controller contacts the other domain controllers to get updates since the backups were completed. The other domain controllers replicate the information to the restored domain controller so that they are the same. So if there are problems (such as corrupt data or missing objects) within the database that is stored in all of the domain controllers, the same information is sent to the restored domain controller and the same problem still exists. You use only a nonauthoritative restore if the problem has not spread to the other domain controllers (highly unlikely) or you want to restore the domain controller so that it is functional again.

An ***authoritative restore*** is an override type restore that the information on the restored domain controller will be replicated to the other domain controllers. To restore an object or container within Active Directory that has been inadvertently deleted, you need to perform an authoritative restore. To accomplish this, when an authoritative restore is performed, Windows increments the version number is higher than any version number used in the other domain controllers.

TAKE NOTE*
If an object is inadvertently deleted, you might consider using the Active Directory Recycle Bin before performing an authoritative restore. The Active Directory Recycle Bin is discussed later in the lesson.

To perform an authoritative restore, you need to reboot the computer into the ***Directory Services Restore Mode (DSRM)***, which is a mode of Windows that takes the Active Directory offline. You access this mode from the Advanced Boot menu, which is accessed before Windows completes booting by pressing the F8 key.

PERFORM A RESTORE OF THE SYSTEM STATE

GET READY. To perform a restore of the System State, perform the following steps:

1. Restart the domain controller. After the *BIOS POST* screen but before the Windows log appears, press the F8 key repeatedly to access the *Windows Advanced Options* menu.
2. When the *Windows Advanced Options* menu is displayed (see Figure 17-12), use the arrow keys to select Directory Services Restore Mode and press the Enter key.

Figure 17-12

Accessing the Advanced Options menu

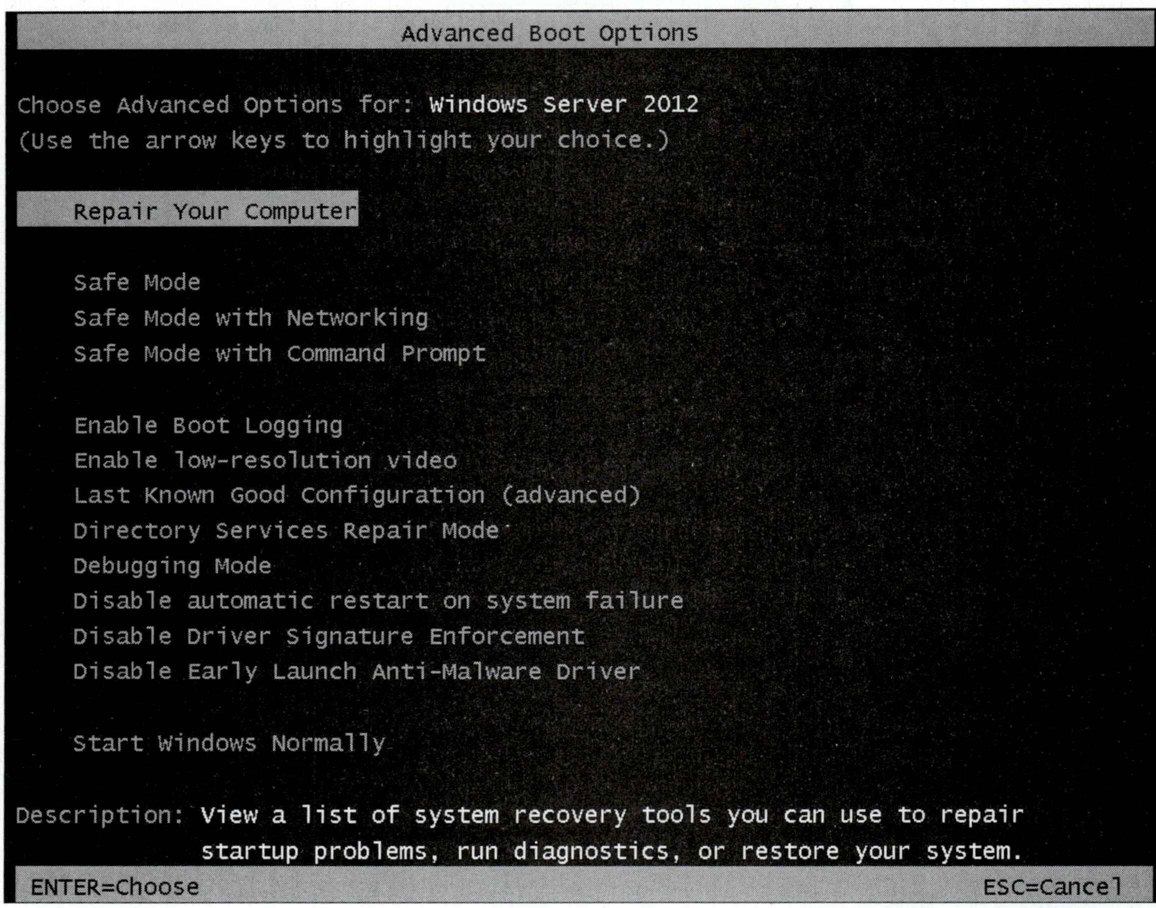

3. Log in as the local administrator (DSRM), not the domain administrator.
4. Open Server Manager.
5. Click Tools > Windows Server Backup. The *Windows Server Backup console* opens.
6. Under *Actions*, click Recover.
7. When the *Recovery Wizard* starts (see Figure 17-13), select A backup stored on another location and click Next.
8. On the *Specify Location type* page, click Remote shared folder and click Next.

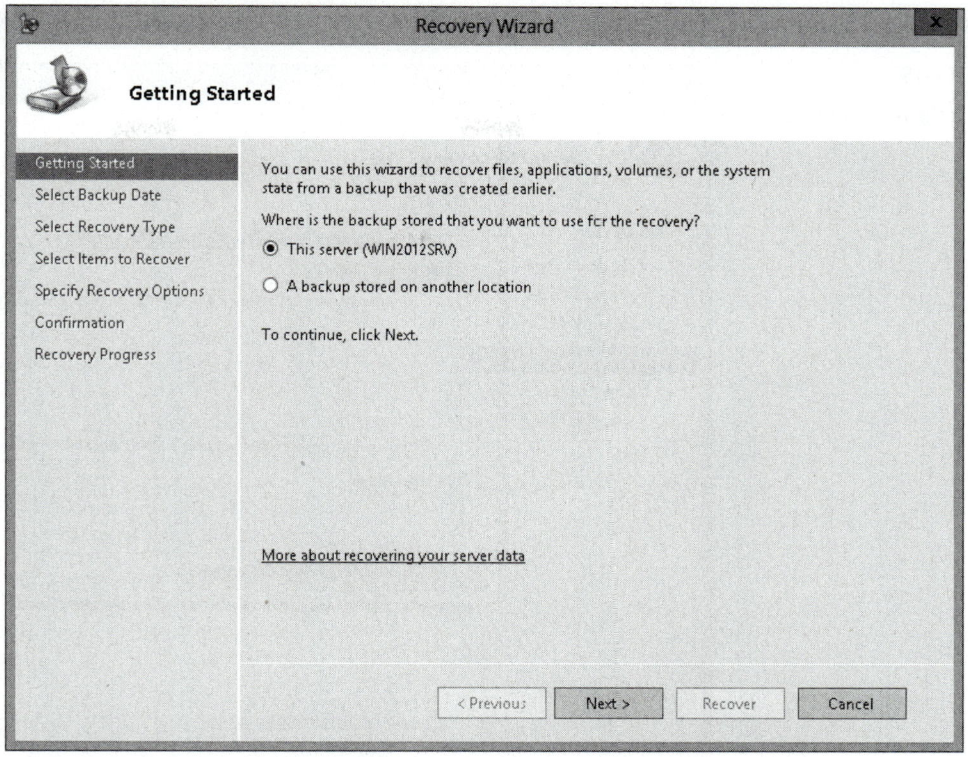

Figure 17-13

Specifying where the backup is located

9. On the *Specify Remote Folder* page, type the path (such as \\win2012srv2\backups) and click Next.
10. On the *Select Backup Date* page (see Figure 17-14), select the date of the backup that you want to restore from and click Next.

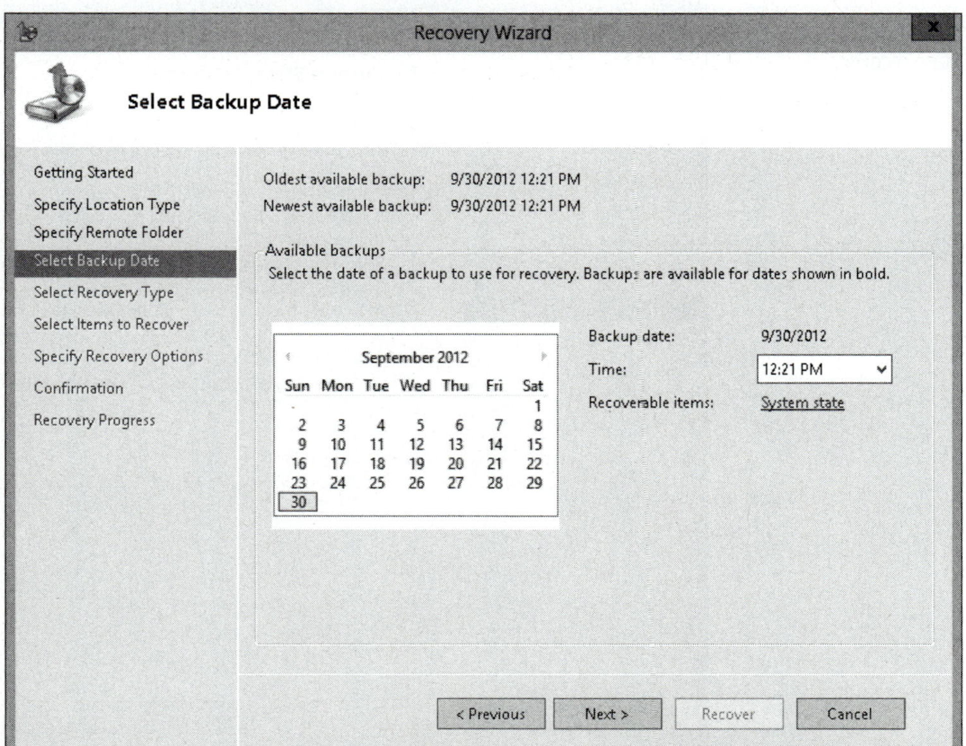

Figure 17-14

Selecting the backup date

11. On the *Select Recovery Type* page (see Figure 17-15), click **System state**. Click **Next**.

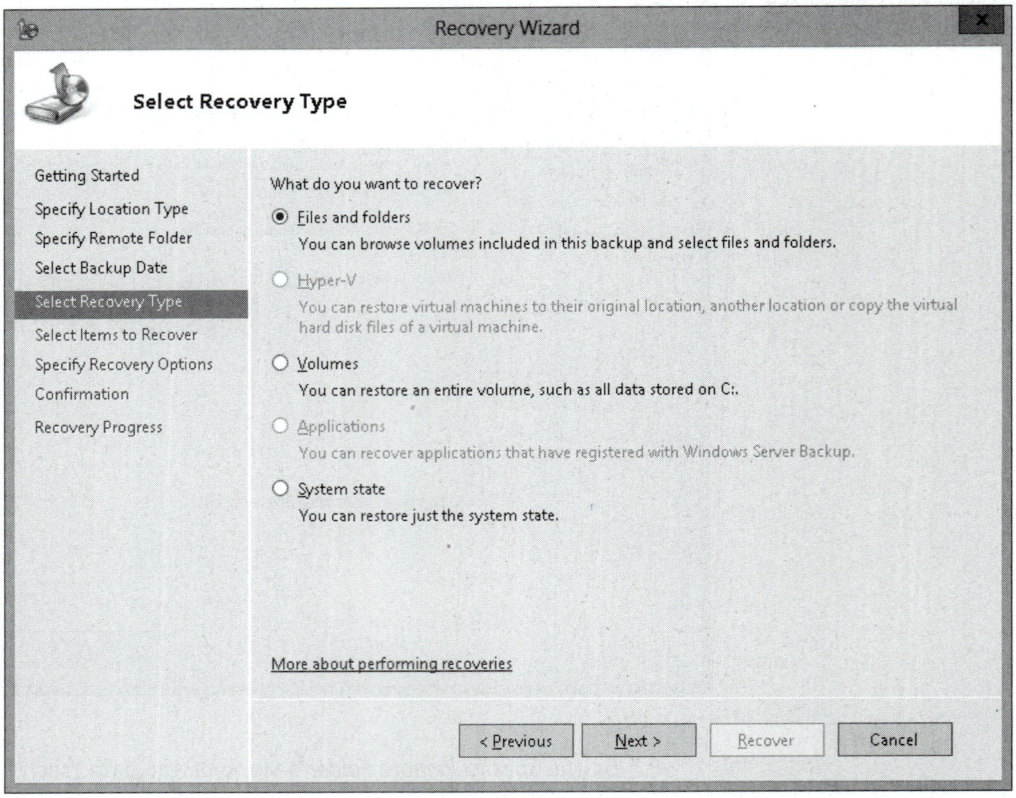

Figure 17-15
Selecting the recovery type

12. On the *Select Location for System State Recovery* page (see Figure 17-16), select **Perform an authoritative restore of Active Directory files** and click **Next**.

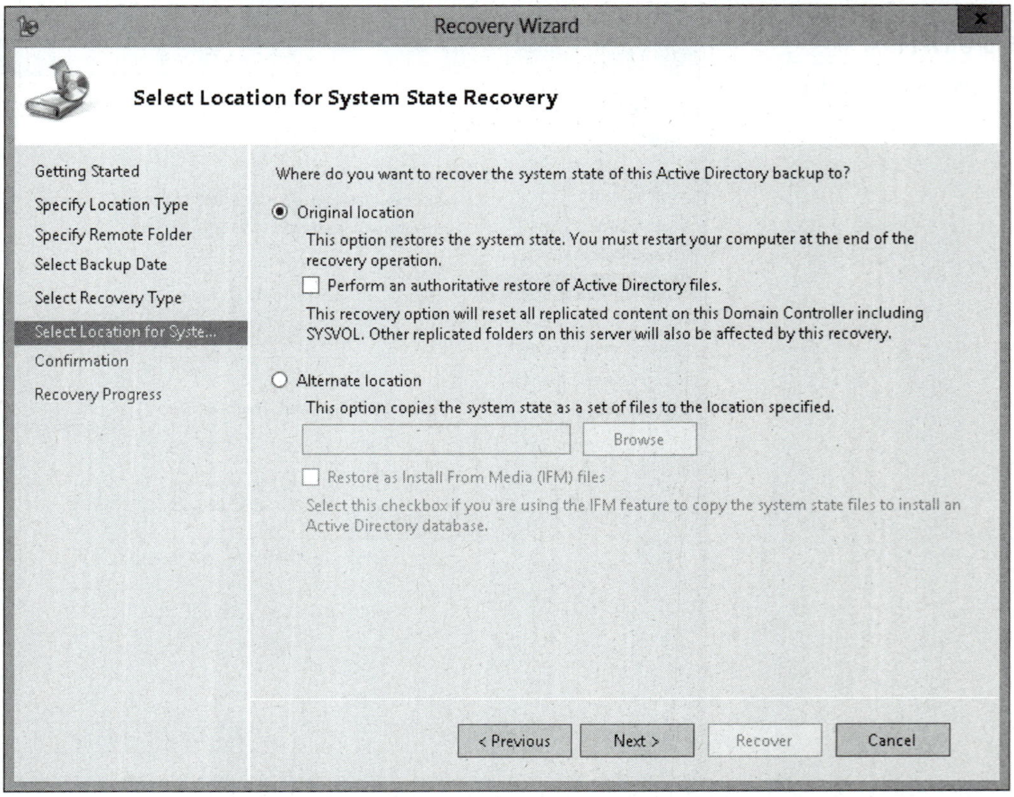

Figure 17-16
Selecting the location for system state recovery

13. When the warning appears that this recovery option will cause all replicated content on the local server to re-synchronize after recovery, click OK.
14. When it asks for you to continue, click OK.
15. Click the Confirmation page, and click Recover.
16. When it asks if you want to continue gain, click Yes.
17. When the backup is completed, click Restart.

To perform an authoritative restore of an object or subtree, you need to know the distinguished name of the object. For example, the user object for jsmith in the Sales OU of the contoso.com domain has a distinguished name of cn=jsmith,ou=Sales,dc=contoso,dc=com.

When you do an authoritative restore process, a back-links file is created. A back-link is a reference to an attribute within another object that also needs to be restored with the object. For example, if you have authoritatively restored a user object that was a member of five Active Directory groups, a backlink to each of those groups need to be restored so that the user is added again to each group appropriately. The authoritative restore process creates an LDIF file containing each back-link that needs to be restored; after the authoritative restore completes, you need to use the LDIFDE command-line utility to restore the back-links contained within that file. For more information about the LDIFDE, search the Microsoft TechNet website.

PERFORM AN AUTHORITATIVE RESTORE

GET READY. Before you reboot the computer, you need to mark items as an authoritative restore. To perform an authoritative restore, perform the following steps:

1. Open a command prompt window.
2. Execute the ntdsutil command.
3. From the *Ntdsutil* menu, execute the activate instance NTDS command.
4. Execute the authoritative restore command.
   a. To restore a single object, execute the restore object <ObjectDN> command.
   b. To restore a container and the objects it contains, execute the restore subtree <ContainerDN> command. The *Authoritative Restore Confirmation Dialog* window opens.
5. When the *Authoritative Restore Confirmation* dialog box opens, click Yes to perform the authoritative restore. When the record or records have been updated, the names of the back-link files are displayed.
6. Be sure to write down the name of the back-link files.
7. Execute the quit command.
8. Press the Enter key to return to the command prompt.
9. Restart the domain controller in normal mode.
10. If back-links need to be restored, right-click the Start button and execute the ldifde -i -f <LDIF file name> -s <FQDN of the local DC> command.
11. Close the command prompt window.
12. Reboot the domain controller.

Configuring Active Directory Snapshots

Another tool used in recovery of Active Directory is the ***Active Directory database mounting tool*** to create and view Active Directory snapshots. An ***Active Directory snapshot*** is a shadow copy, created by the Volume Shadow Copy Service (VSS), of the volumes that contain the Active Directory database and log files.

CERTIFICATION READY
Configure Active Directory snapshots.
Objective 5.3

To create and use snapshots, perform the following steps:

1. Create a snapshot with ntdsutil.exe.
2. Mount the snapshot with the Active Directory database mounting tool.
3. View the objects within the snapshot.
4. When done with the snapshot, dismount the snapshot.

By default, only members of the Domain Admins group and the Enterprise Admins group are allowed to view the snapshots.

CREATE AN ACTIVE DIRECTORY SNAPSHOT

GET READY. To create an Active Directory snapshot, perform the following steps:

1. Right-click the Start button and select Command Prompt (Admin). The command prompt window opens.
2. At the command prompt, execute the ntdsutil command.
3. At the ntdsutil prompt, execute the snapshot command.
4. At the snapshot prompt, execute the activate instance ntds command.
5. Execute the create command.
6. Execute the quit command twice.
7. Close the command prompt window.

MOUNT AN ACTIVE DIRECTORY SNAPSHOT

GET READY. To mount an Active Directory snapshot, perform the following steps:

1. Right-click the Start button and select Command Prompt (Admin). The command prompt window opens.
2. At the command prompt, execute the ntdsutil command.
3. At the ntdsutil prompt, execute the activate instance ntds command.
4. Execute the snapshot command.
5. To return a list of all snapshots, at the snapshot prompt, execute the list all command.
6. Execute the mount {GUID} command, where GUID is the GUID returned by the create snapshot command or displayed with the list all command.
7. Execute the quit command twice to exit ntdsutil.
8. To mount the snapshot, execute the dsamain -dbpath c:\$snap_datetime_volumec$\windows\ntds\ntds.dit -ldapport 50000. You need to specify the date-time as shown on the list. The port number, 50000, can be any open and unique TCP port number.
9. A message indicates that Active Directory Domain Services startup is complete. Do not close the command prompt window and leave the command you just ran, Dsamain.exe, running while you continue to the next step.

After the snapshot, you can view the snapshot using multiple tools, including Active Directory Users and Computers (as shown in the next procedure), LDP.exe, or ADSIEDIT.exe. You can also use LDIFDE and CSVDE to export the information from the snapshot and import the data into production. When you use the CSVDE or LDIFDE, you use the `-s <servername>` and `-t <port number>`.

Unfortunately, the snapshots are read-only and you cannot modify the contents of a snapshot. Moreover, there are no direct methods with which to move, copy, or restore objects or attributes from the snapshot to the production instance of Active Directory.

VIEW AN AD DS SNAPSHOT

GET READY. To view an AD DS Snapshot, perform the following steps:

1. Open Server Manager.
2. Click Tools > Active Directory Users and Computers. The *Active Directory Users and Computers console* opens.
3. Right-click the root node, and then click Change Domain Controller. The *Change Directory Server* dialog box appears.
4. Click <Type a Directory Server name[:port] here> (see Figure 17-17) and replace the <Type a Directory Server name[:port] here> text with the name of the domain controller and port number using the DCservername:port# format and press Enter.

Figure 17-17

Specifying the snapshot to view

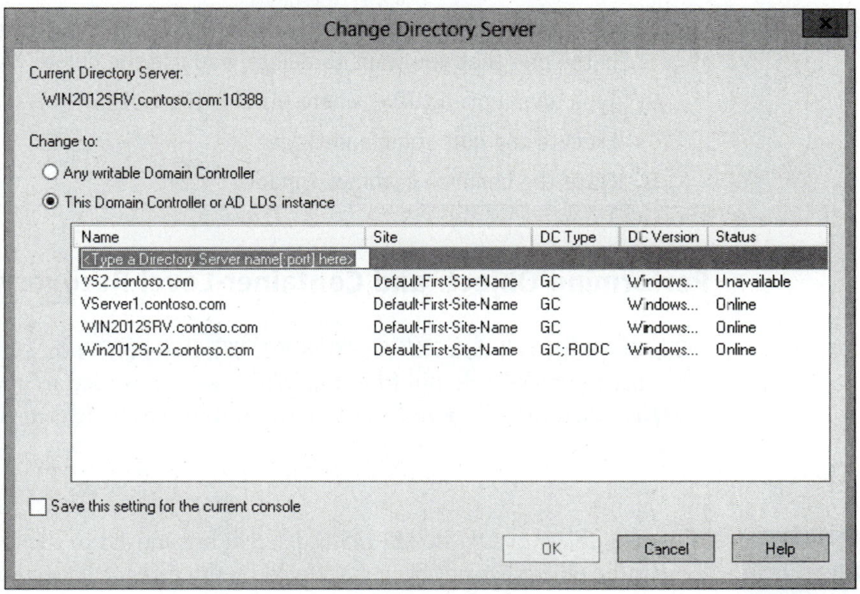

5. Click OK.

When you are done with the snapshot, you should unmount the snapshot. Of course, when you need to free up disk space or to do regular maintenance, you will want to delete the snapshot as well.

UNMOUNT AN AD DS SNAPSHOT

GET READY. To unmount an Active Directory Domain Service snapshot, perform the following steps:

1. Switch to the command prompt in which the snapshot is mounted.
2. Press Ctrl+C to stop DSAMain.exe.
3. Execute the ntdsutil command

4. Execute the activate instance ntds command.
5. Execute the snapshot command.
6. Type unmount <GUID>, where GUID is the GUID of the snapshot, and then press Enter.
7. Execute the quit command twice.
8. Close the command prompt window.

DELETE AN AD DS SNAPSHOT

GET READY. To delete an Active Directory Domain Service snapshot, perform the following steps:

1. Right-click the Start button and select Command Prompt (Admin). The command prompt window opens.
2. Execute the ntdsutil command
3. Execute the snapshot command.
4. Execute the list all command.
5. Execute the delete <number of snapshot> command. For example, if the second entry is the one that you want to delete, you use the delete 2 command.
6. Type unmount <GUID>, where GUID is the GUID of the snapshot, and then press Enter.
7. Execute the quit command twice
8. Close the command prompt window.

Performing Object- and Container-Level Recovery

Starting with Windows Server 2008 R2, Windows offers the Active Directory Recycle Bin. Similar to the Recycle Bin found in Windows that is used to undelete deleted files, the ***Active Directory Recycle Bin*** can be used to undelete deleted Active Directory containers and objects.

CERTIFICATION READY
Perform object- and container-level recovery.
Objective 5.3

When an object or OU in AD DS is deleted, it is moved to the Deleted Objects container. As long as the object has not been scavenged by the garbage collection process after reaching the end of the object tombstone lifetime, you can restore the deleted object. However, when the item is deleted, certain attributes are removed such as group membership. By default, the garbage collection occurs every 12 hours.

The LPD.exe tool, included with Windows Server 2012, allows users to perform operations against any LDAP-compatible directory, including Active Directory. LDP is used to view objects stored in Active Directory along with their metadata, such as security descriptors and replication metadata.

RESTORE A DELETED OBJECT WITHOUT USING THE RECYCLE BIN

GET READY. To restore a deleted object without using the Recycle Bin, perform the following steps:

1. Click the Start button, type ldp, and press Enter. LDP opens (see Figure 17-18).

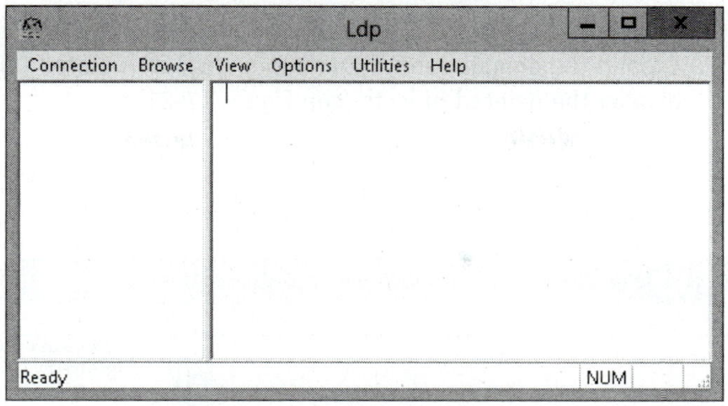

Figure 17-18

Starting the LDP program

2. Click Connection > Connect. When the *Connect* dialog box opens (see Figure 17-19), type the name of the domain controller in the *Server* text box, and click OK.

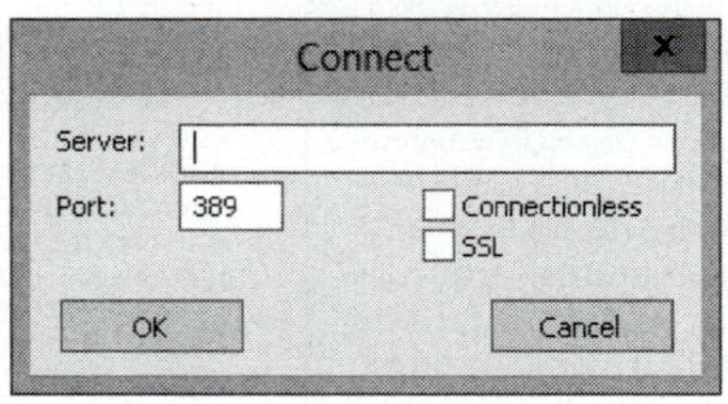

Figure 17-19

Specifying the server to connect to

3. Click Connection > Bind. When the *Bind* dialog box opens, click OK.
4. Click the Options > Controls. When the *Controls* dialog box opens, click Return Deleted Objects in the *Load Predefined* list (see Figure 17-20), and then click OK.

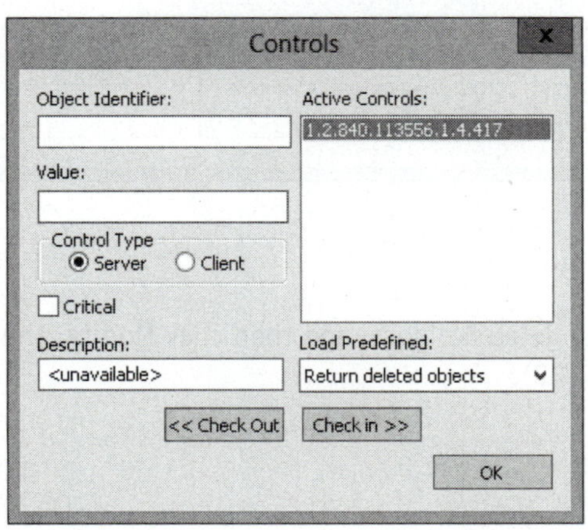

Figure 17-20

Selecting to return deleted objects

5. Click **View > Tree**, and then click **OK**.
6. Expand the domain, and then double-click **CN=Deleted Objects,DC=contoso,DC=com** to display the deleted objects (see Figure 17-21).

Figure 17-21
Showing deleted objects

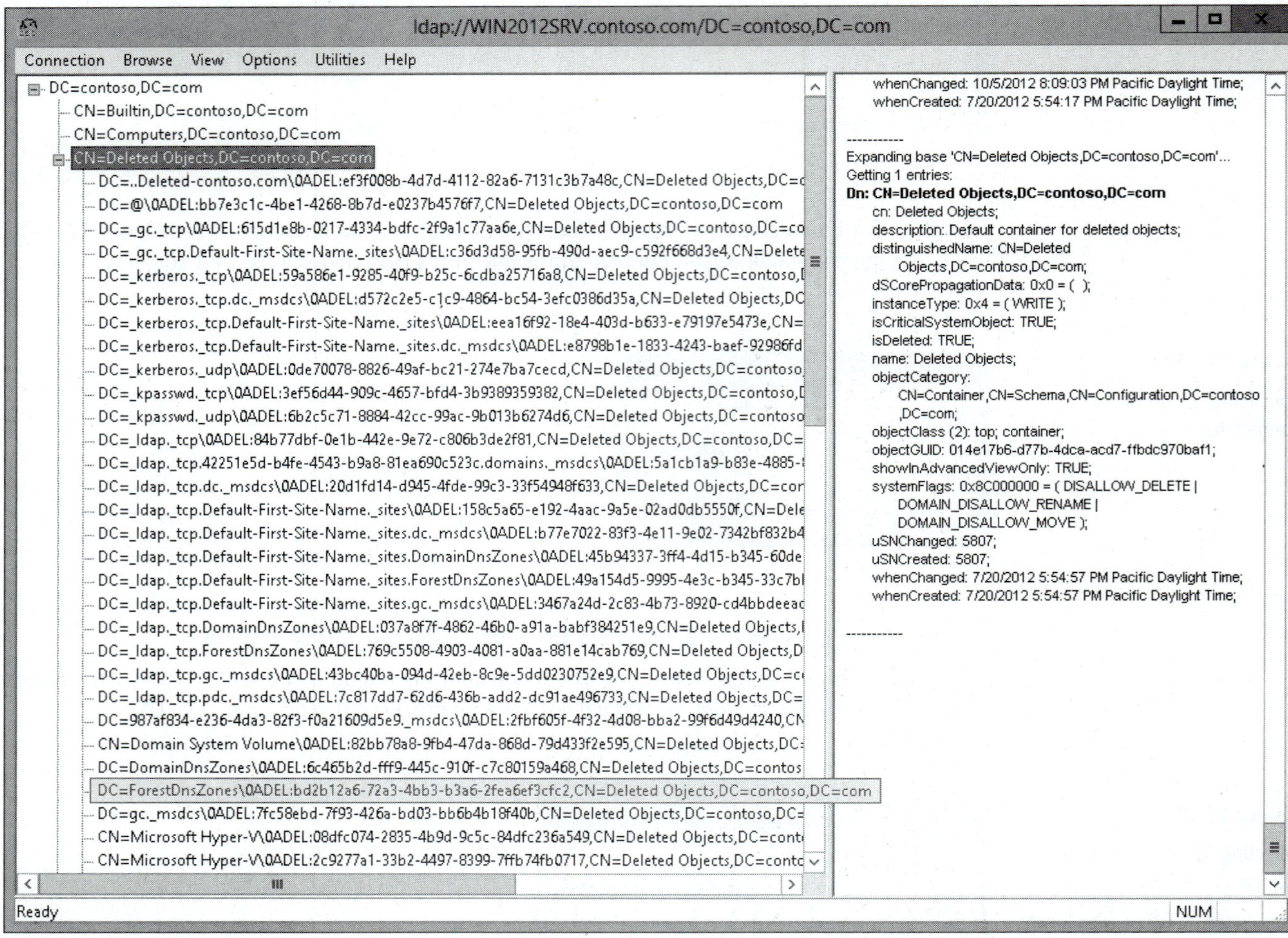

7. Right-click the deleted object, and then click **Modify**. The *Modify* dialog box opens (see Figure 17-22).

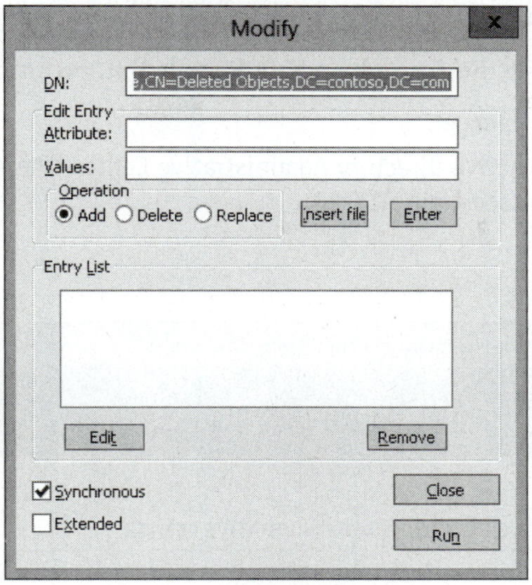

Figure 17-22

Modifying an object

8. In the *Attribute* box, type isDeleted. In the *Operation* section, click the Delete option, then click Enter.
9. In the *Attribute* box, type distinguishedName.
10. In the *Values* box, type the distinguished name of the object in the parent container or the organizational unit into which the object should be restored. For example, type the distinguished name of the object before it was deleted.
11. In the *Operation* section, click Replace. Click Enter.
12. Select the Extended checkbox.
13. Click Run.
14. Click Close to close the *Modify* dialog box.
15. Close LDP.

After the account has been undeleted, you need to reset the password (for a user object), and enable the object (if disabled). You then need to add the account to the appropriate groups.

Starting with Windows Server 2008 R2, Windows includes an Active Directory Recycle Bin that can be used to undelete an object. Different from the manual restore, all of the attributes are maintained including group membership. Starting with Windows Server 2012, you can use the Active Directory Administrative Center to recover objects from the Recycle Bin. By default, the deleted object stays in the Recycle Bin for 180 days.

Before you can use the Active Directory Recycle Bin, you need to have the forest functional level set to Windows Server 2008 R2 or higher. You also need to manually enable the Active Directory Recycle Bin. In Windows Server 2012, you can enable the Recycle Bin by performing one of the following actions:

- From the Active Directory module for Windows PowerShell prompt, use the `Enable-ADOptionalFeature` cmdlet.
- From Active Directory Administrative Center, select the domain, and then click *Enable Active Directory Recycle Bin* in the Tasks pane.

Only items deleted after the Active Directory Recycle Bin is turned on can be restored from the Active Directory Recycle Bin.

ENABLE THE ACTIVE DIRECTORY RECYCLE BIN

GET READY. To enable the Active Directory Recycle Bin, perform the following steps:

1. Open Server Manager.
2. Click Tools > Active Directory Administrative Center. The *Active Directory Administrative Center* opens (see Figure 17-23).

Figure 17-23

Opening Active Directory Administrative Center

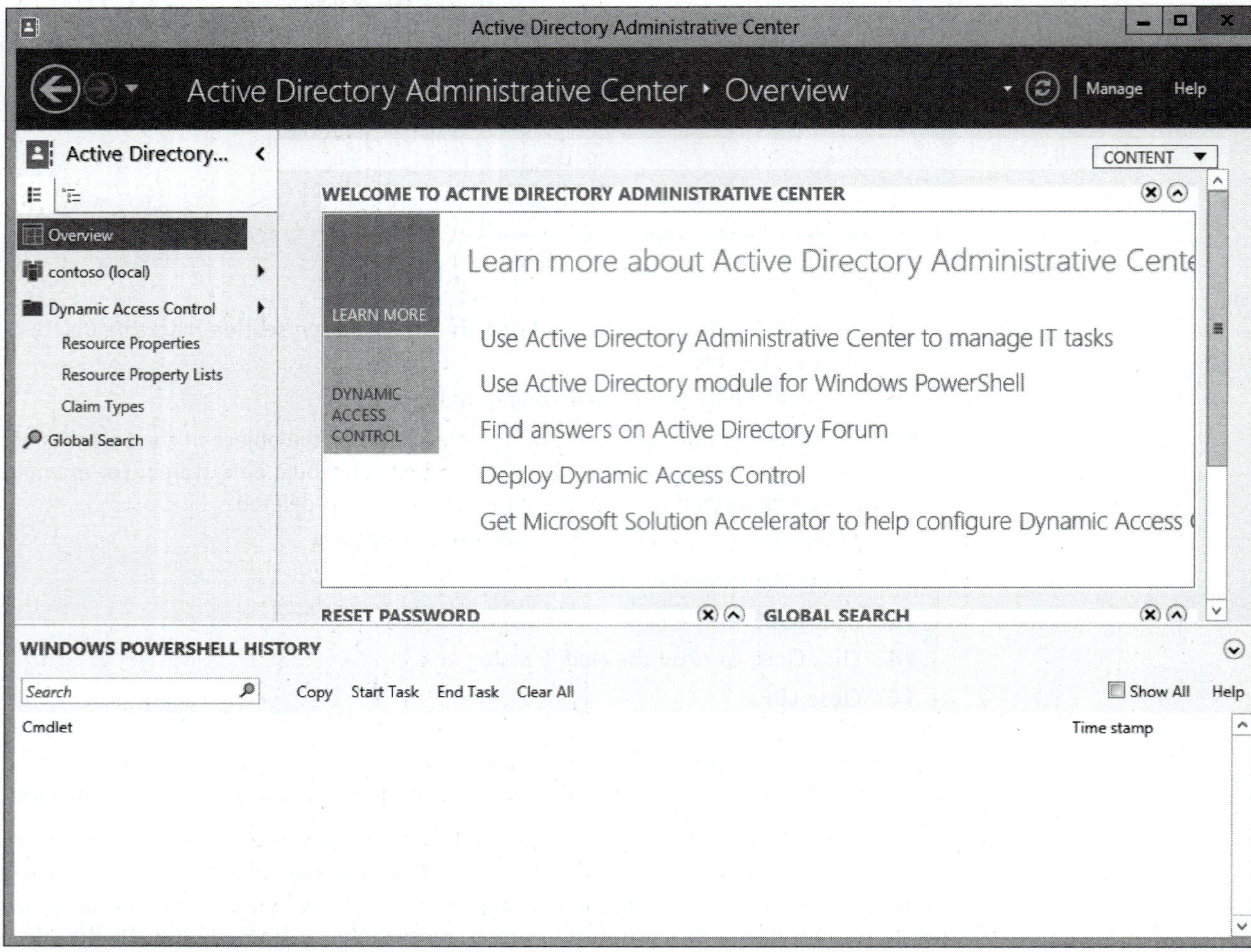

3. Click the domain. The domain options appear (see Figure 17-24).

Figure 17-24

Selecting the domain options

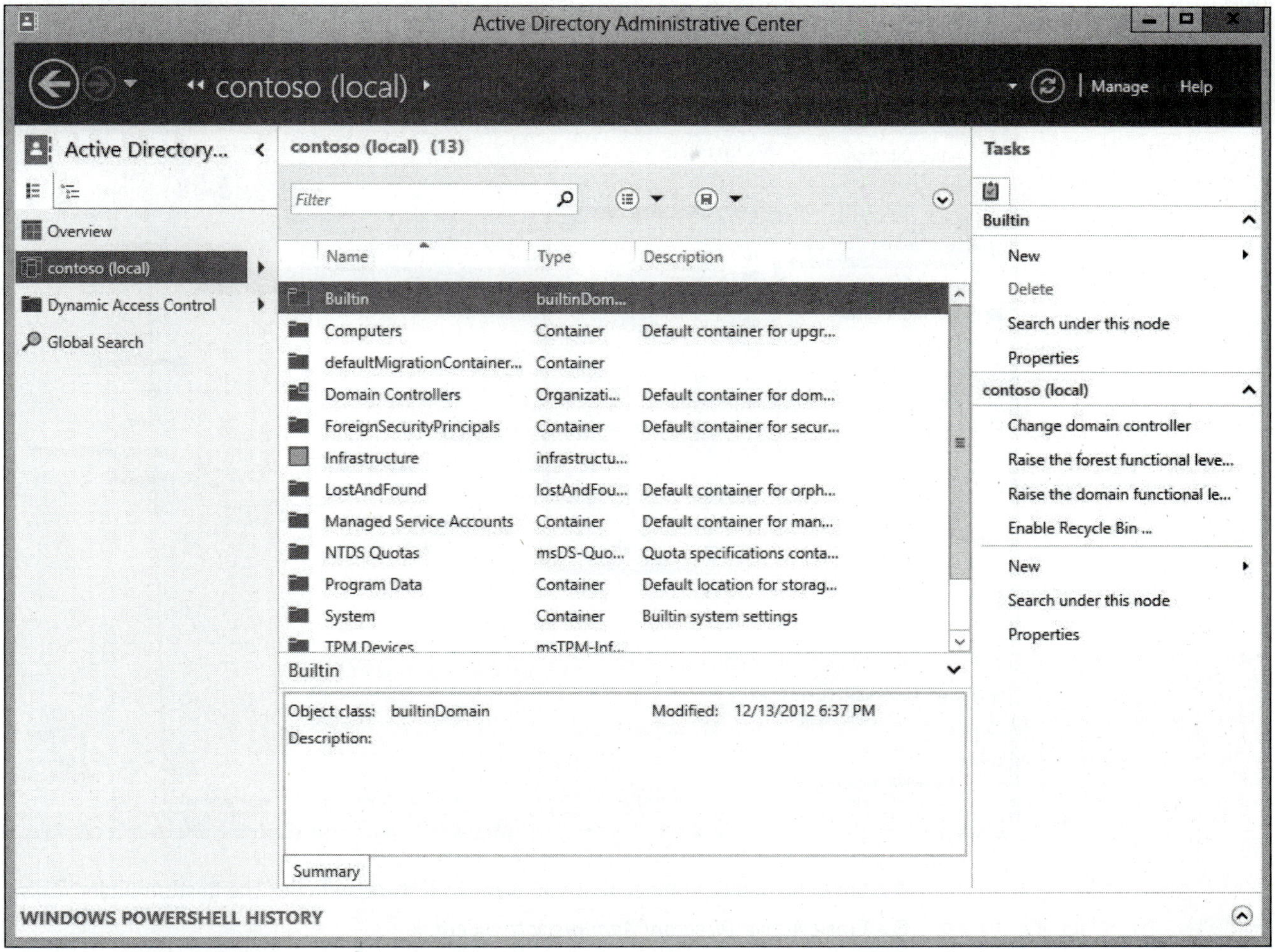

4. Click Enable Recycle Bin. When it says that once the Recycle Bin has been enabled, it cannot be disabled and asks if you want to continue, click OK.
5. When it says to refresh the AD Administrative Center now, click OK.
6. Press the F5 key on the keyboard to refresh the *Active Directory Administrative Center*.
7. Close *Active Directory Administrative Center*.

After the Active Directory Recycle Bin has been enabled, you can access the Deleted Objects container using the Active Directory Administrative Center. You can choose to restore the objects to their original location or to an alternate location within AD DS.

RESTORE AN OBJECT USING THE ACTIVE DIRECTORY RECYCLE BIN

GET READY. To restore an object using the Active Directory Recycle Bin, perform the following steps:

1. Open Server Manager.
2. Click Tools > Active Directory Administrative Center. The *Active Directory Administrative Center* opens.
3. Click the small arrow next to the domain and select Deleted Objects (see Figure 17-25).

Figure 17-25

Selecting the Deleted Objects folder

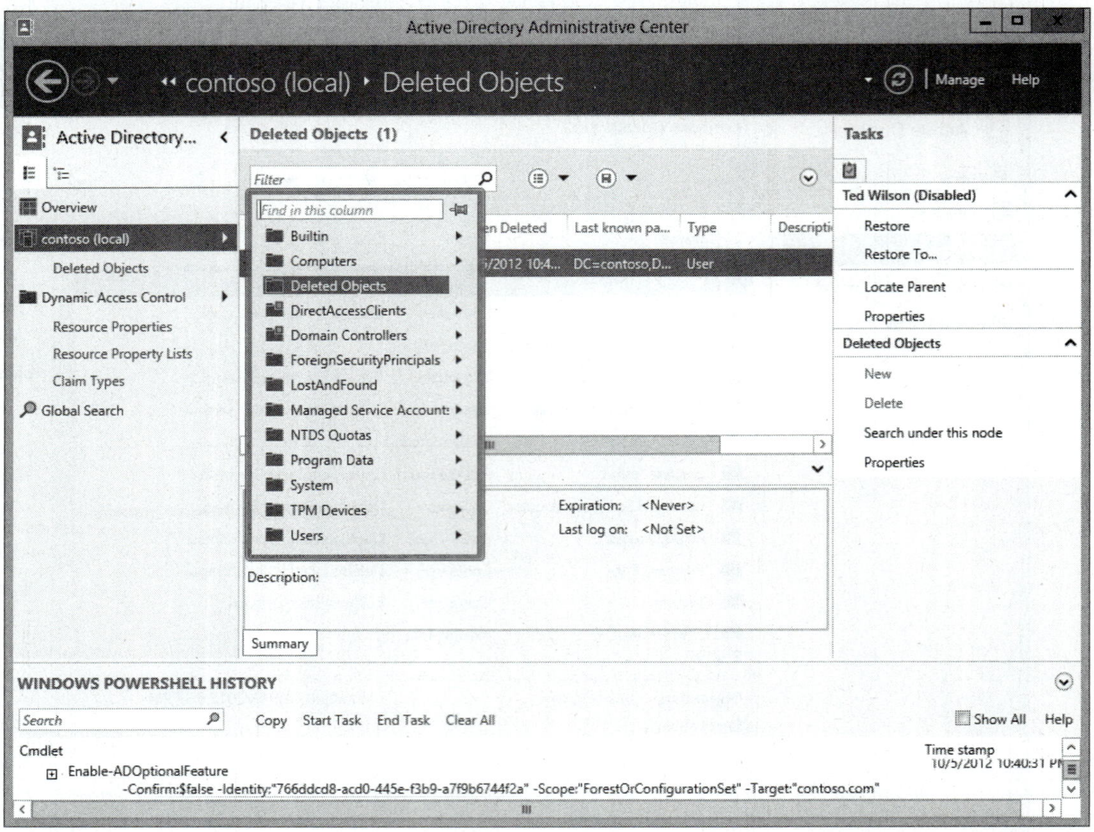

4. Click the deleted object that you want to restore and click the Restore under *Tasks*.
5. Close *Active Directory Administrative Center*.

Managing Active Directory Offline

THE BOTTOM LINE

In previous versions of Windows, to perform certain tasks such as defrag the Active Directory database, you need to reboot the domain controller in DSRM, so that the Active Directory Domain Services will not be running. Starting with Windows Server 2012, Windows servers include ***Restartable Active Directory Domain Services***, which allows you to stop and start AD DS without restarting the domain controller and stopping other services that might be on the server. As a result, you can perform these tasks quicker than you could before.

CERTIFICATION READY
Manage Active Directory offline.
Objective 5.3

Restartable AD DS is available by default on all domain controllers that run Windows Server 2012. There are no functional-level requirements or any other prerequisites for using this feature.

TAKE NOTE*

To perform state restore of a domain controller while AD DS is stopped, you must reboot the domain controller into DSRM. You can perform an authoritative restore of Active Directory objects while AD DS is stopped by using Ntdsutil.exe.

To start or stop the AD DS, you open the Services console to control the service (see Figure 17-26). There are three domain controller states:

- **AD DS Started:** In this state, AD DS is started.
- **AD DS Stopped:** This is a unique mode that combines the characteristics of both a domain controller in DSRM and a domain-joined member server.
- **DSRM:** This mode (or state) allows standard AD DS administrative tasks.

Figure 17-26

Selecting the Deleted Objects folder

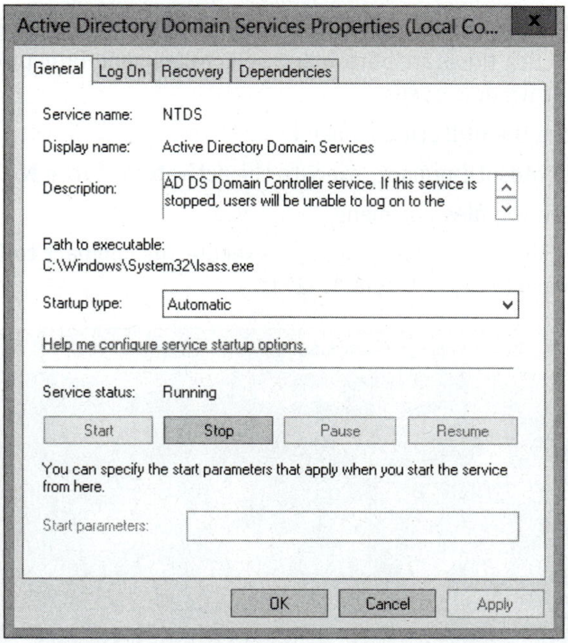

Optimizing an Active Directory Database

THE BOTTOM LINE

As mentioned previously, certain tasks that you must take the domain services offline first. One common task is to perform an offline defragmentation of the Active Directory database.

CERTIFICATION READY
Optimize an Active Directory database.
Objective 5.3

Similar to running the Optimize and defragment drive tool in Windows to defragment a hard drive, you can use `ntdsutil` to defragment the Active Directory database to free up disk space. To perform an offline defragmentation procedure, you create a new, compacted version of the database file in a different location. When the new defragmented database is created, the procedure copies the compacted ntds.dit file back to the original location.

TAKE NOTE*

Although the Active Directory is a multi-master replicating database, the size of the database on each domain controller can vary.

You can also use the `ntdsutil` command to look for errors in Active Directory. The `integrity` command is used to detect low level (binary level) database corruption, which reads every byte of the data file and makes sure that the correct headers exist in the database itself and that all of the tables are functioning and are consistent. You can also use the semantic checker to check the integrity of the contents of the Active Directory database.

DEFRAGMENT AND CHECK THE INTEGRITY OF THE ACTIVE DIRECTORY DATABASE

GET READY. To defragment and check the integrity of the Active Directory Database, perform the following steps:

1. Open **Server Manager**.
2. Click **Tools > Services**. The *Services console* opens.
3. Right-click the **Active Directory Domain Services** service and click **Stop**. When it asks if you want to stop other services, click **Yes**.
4. Right-click the **Start** button and select **Command Prompt (Admin)**. The command prompt window opens.
5. Execute the **ntdsutil** command.
6. At the ntdsutil prompt, execute the **activate instance NTDS** command.
7. Execute the **files** command.
8. At the file maintenance prompt, execute the **compact to C:** command. The database is compacted (see Figure 17-27).

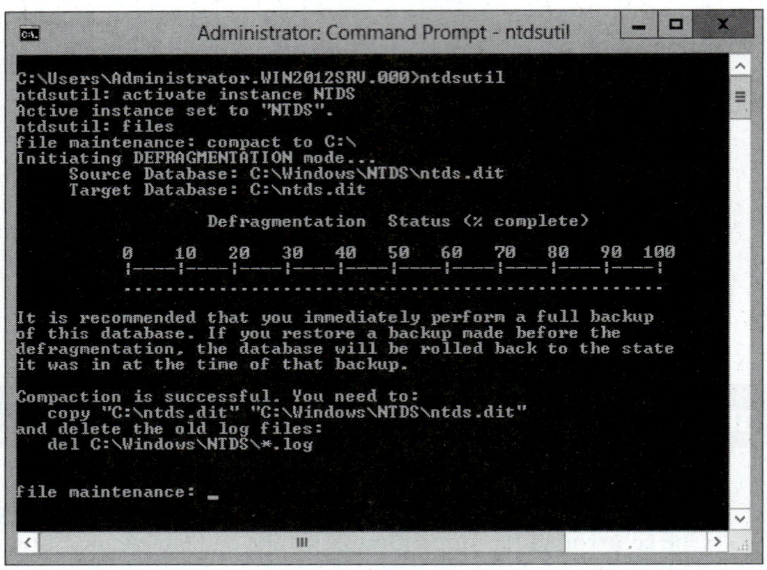

Figure 17-27
Defragmenting an Active Directory database

9. To check the integrity of the offline database, execute the **integrity** command.
10. At the file maintenance prompt, execute the **quit** command.
11. To perform a semantic database consistency check, execute the **semantic database analysis** command.
12. At the semantic checker prompt, execute the **go** command.
13. Execute the **quit** command twice.
14. Close the command prompt.
15. Go back to the *Service console*. Right-click the **Active Directory Domain Services** service and click **Start**.
16. Close the *Services console*.

If you have a domain controller that has a C drive, which is running low on disk space, you can move the database to a different drive. On a domain controller that is running Windows Server 2008, you do not need to restart the domain controller in DSRM to move database files. You can stop the AD DS service and then restart the service after you move the files to their permanent location. To perform the actual move, you use ntdsutil.exe.

MOVE THE ACTIVE DIRECTORY DATABASE

GET READY. Assuming that you have already stopped the AD DS service, to move the Active Directory database, perform the following steps:

1. Right-click the Start button and select Command Prompt (Admin). The command prompt window opens.
2. Execute the ntdsutil command.
3. At the ntdsutil prompt, execute the activate instance ntds command.
4. Execute the files command.
5. At the file maintenance: prompt, to move the Ntds.dit file, execute the move db to <drive>:\<directory> command (for example: move db to d:\ntds). If the directory path contains any spaces, the entire path must be surrounded by quotation marks. For example, to move the database to the *D:\Active Directory* folder, use the move db to "D:\Active Directory ".
6. To move the log files, execute the move logs to<drive>:\<directory> command.
7. Execute the quit command twice.
8. Close the command prompt.

After you move the database, you should check the integrity of the database. When everything checks out, you should restart the AD DS server.

Cleaning Up Metadata

THE BOTTOM LINE

To retire a domain controller, the proper method to demote a domain controller is to remove the Active Directory Domain Services. However, if the demotion fails or the server itself fails where you cannot recover the system, you need to clean up the metadata, which means you must manually remove the domain controller from Active Directory. The ***metadata*** is the data that identifies the domain controllers.

CERTIFICATION READY
Clean up metadata.
Objective 5.3

There are several ways to clean up the server metadata. Today, the most common method to remove the metadata is to use Active Directory Users and Computers and ntdsutil. Other methods include using the Active Directory Sites and Services and ADSIEdit. During the next procedure, the server metadata is removed using Active Directory Users and Computers.

CLEAN UP SERVER METADATA USING ACTIVE DIRECTORY USERS AND COMPUTERS

GET READY. To clean up server metadata using the Active Directory Users and Computers console, perform the following steps:

1. Open Server Manager.
2. Click Tools > Active Directory Users and Computers. The *Active Directory Users and Computers console* opens.
3. Expand the domain, and click Domain Controllers.
4. Right-click the computer object of the domain controller that you want to clean up and click Delete.
5. When asked if you are sure, click Yes.
6. In the *Deleting Domain Controller* dialog box, select This Domain Controller is permanently offline and can no longer be demoted using the *Active Directory Domain Services Installation Wizard (DCPROMO)*, and then click Delete.

Figure 17-28

Deleting the domain controller

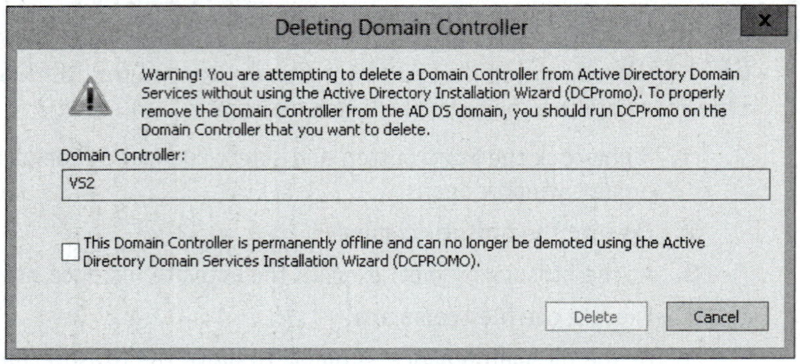

7. If the domain controller is a global catalog server, in the *Delete Domain Controller* dialog box, click Yes to continue with the deletion.
8. If the domain controller currently holds one or more operations master roles, click OK to move the role or roles to the domain controller that is shown.
9. Close the *Active Directory Users and Computers* console.

The following procedure shows how to use ntdsutil.exe to remove the server metadata from Active Directory. Compared to using the ntdsutil.exe on Windows Server 2003 or earlier, the process of removing server metadata is simplified.

CLEAN UP SERVER METADATA USING NTDSUTIL

GET READY. To clean up server metadata using `ntdsutil`, perform the following steps:

1. Right-click the Start button and select Command Prompt (Admin). The command prompt window opens.
2. Execute the ntdsutil command.
3. At the ntdsutil, execute the metadata cleanup command.
4. At the metadata cleanup prompt, execute the remove selected server <servername> command. When a warning appears, click Yes to remove the server object and metadata.
5. Execute the quit command twice.
6. Close the command prompt.

SKILL SUMMARY

IN THIS LESSON, YOU LEARNED:

- You might have many accounts that you want to import from a list that was generated by a database or you want to export a list from Active Directory so that you import the list into another system or you want a list in a spreadsheet to manipulate as needed. Microsoft includes several tools, including CSVDE.exe and LDIFDE.exe.
- A backup or the process of backing up refers to making copies of data so that these additional copies can be used to restore the original after a data-loss event.
- The Active Directory database uses the Extensible Storage Engine (ESE), which is an indexed and sequential access method (ISAM) database.
- The Active Directory database is stored in an Active Directory database file (C:\Windows\NTDS\Ntds.dit) and its associated log and temporary files.

- The Windows system state is a collection of system components that are not contained in a simple file but can be backed up easily.
- The SYSVOL is a shared directory that stores the server copy of the domain's public files that must be shared for common access and replication throughout a domain.
- Windows includes Microsoft Windows Backup, which allows you to back up a system. However, third-party backup software packages usually offer more features and options.
- With a nonauthoritative restore, you restore a backup of Active Directory as of the date of the backup.
- An authoritative restore is an override type restore that the information on the restored domain controller will be replicated to the other domain controllers.
- To perform an authoritative restore, you need to reboot the computer into the Directory Services Restore Mode (DSRM), which is a mode of Windows that takes the Active Directory offline.
- An Active Directory snapshot is a shadow copy, created by the Volume Shadow Copy Service (VSS), of the volumes that contain the Active Directory database and log files.
- The Active Directory Recycle Bin can be used to undelete deleted Active Directory containers and objects.
- Windows servers include Restartable Active Directory Domain Services, which allows you to stop and start AD DS without restarting the domain controller and stopping other services that might be on the server.
- You can use ntdsutil to defragment the Active Directory database to free up disk space.
- The metadata is the data that identifies the domain controllers.
- However, if the demotion failed of a domain controller or a domain controller fails where you cannot recover the system, you need to clean up the metadata, which means you manually remove the domain controller from Active Directory.

■ Knowledge Assessment

Multiple Choice

Select the correct answer for each of the following questions.

1. Which Windows PowerShell applet enables the Active Directory Recycle Bin?
   a. `Enable-ADOptionalFeature`
   b. `Set-ADRB`
   c. `Enable-ADRecycleBin`
   d. `Enable-RecycleBin`
2. Which of the following does the system state contain? (Choose all that apply.)
   a. boot files
   b. \Window folder
   c. \Windows\System32 folder
   d. User profiles
   e. Active Directory database
   f. IIS database
   g. registry

3. With the Windows Backup, how do you back up the Active Directory database?
   a. Back up the C:\Windows\NTDS folder.
   b. Back up the system state.
   c. Enable database backup even while locked.
   d. Use DFS.
4. Which of the following is included with the SYSVOL folder? (Choose all that apply.)
   a. Login scripts
   b. Encrypted passwords
   c. User accounts
   d. DFS staging folder and files
5. Which mode do you need to use when you perform an authoritative restore?
   a. Safe mode
   b. Directory Services Restore Mode (DSRM)
   c. Network mode
   d. Defrag mode
6. How do you create an Active Directory snapshot?
   a. Use Active Directory Users and Computers.
   b. Use Active Directory Domains and Trusts.
   c. Use Active Directory Sites and Services.
   d. Use ntdsutil.exe.
7. How can you determine the size of the Active Directory database?
   a. Run the Active Directory Sizer tool.
   b. Run the Performance Monitor.
   c. Use Windows Explorer to view the properties of the C:\Windows\ntds\ntds.dit file.
   d. Use Windows Explorer to view the properties of the SYSVOL folder.
8. How do you compress the size of an Active Directory database?
   a. Use the `defrag` command.
   b. Use the `ntdsutil` command with the Files options.
   c. Use the `ntdsutil` command with the Metadata cleanup options.
   d. Use the Active Directory Sites and Services console.
9. Which utility can you use to remove the server metadata? (Choose two answers.)
   a. Active Directory Recycle Bin
   b. Active Directory Users and computers
   c. Computer Management console
   d. ntdsutil.exe
10. You mount an Active Directory snapshot. What do you need to do so that you can query the snapshot by using LDAP?
    a. Active Directory Users and Computers
    b. Active Directory Domains and Trusts
    c. dsamain.exe
    d. ntdsutil.exe

Best Answer

Choose the letter that corresponds to the best answer. More than one answer choice may achieve the goal. Select the BEST answer.

1. Which is the most important method used to recover from a failover?
   a. Backup
   b. Redundant power supplies
   c. Redundant servers
   d. Redundant hard drives

2. A user account was deleted and you need to restore the user account. What type of restore do you need to perform?
   a. Full restore
   b. Nonauthoritative restore
   c. Authoritative restore
   d. OU restore

3. You have a domain with four domain controllers. Server1 is a domain controller, DHCP server, DNS server, and a database server. You need to move the database to another drive. The solution must minimize impact to the users. What should you do?
   a. Restart the computer in Save mode.
   b. Restart the computer in DSRM.
   c. Stop the AD DS service.
   d. Create an image of the server.

4. Which do you use to enable the Active Directory database?
   a. Active Directory Users and Computers
   b. Active Directory Domains and Trusts
   c. Active Directory Administrative Center
   d. ntdsutil.exe

5. Which do you use to restore a deleted account using the Active Directory Recycle Bin?
   a. Active Directory Users and Computers
   b. Active Directory Domains and Trusts
   c. Active Directory Administrative Center
   d. ntdsutil.exe

6. Which is the minimum forest functional level to use the Active Directory Recycle Bin?
   a. Windows Server 2003
   b. Windows Server 2008
   c. Windows Server 2008 R2
   d. Windows Server 2012

Matching and Identification

1. Identify which of the following are included in the Windows Server 2012 System State.
   _____ IIS metabase
   _____ COM+ and WMI information
   _____ INI storage folder
   _____ bootmgr
   _____ System32 folder
   _____ DLL cache folder
   _____ Certificate store
   _____ Active Directory database
   _____ Registry
   _____ login scripts
   _____ boot.ini
   _____ Software installation programs used by GPOs

Build a List

1. Identify the steps in order to perform an authoritative restore of a deleted user account. Not all steps will be used.
   _____ Perform the restore.
   _____ Reboot the computer in normal mode.
   _____ Log in as a domain administrator.
   _____ Log in as the local administrator.
   _____ Log in as a domain administrator.
   _____ Reboot the computer in DSRM.
   _____ Use ntdsutil to specify the object that is marked as an authoritative restore.
   _____ Reboot the computer in Safe mode.
2. Identify the steps in order to take and query a snapshot. Not all steps will be used.
   _____ Use Active Directory Users and Computers to access the snapshot.
   _____ Use ntdsutil to display the users in Active Directory.
   _____ Use the dsamain command.
   _____ Use the ntdsutil mount command.
   _____ Use Active Directory Sites and Services to create the snapshot.
   _____ Use Active Directory Users and Computers to create the snapshot.
   _____ Use ntdsutil to create the snapshot.
3. Identify the steps in order to compress an Active Directory database?
   _____ Start the ntdsutil.exe.
   _____ Use the compact to command.
   _____ Use the activate instance NTDS command.
   _____ Use the integrity command.
   _____ Execute the files command.
   _____ Quit ntdsutil.
   _____ Stop the AD DS.
   _____ Use the move command.

■ Business Case Scenarios

Scenario 17-1: Recovering Objects from Active Directory

You are an administrator at the Contoso Corporation. Just before you got hired, the company had an incident where a lot of information was removed from Active Directory and it could not be recovered. What would you do to make sure that you have the best chance to recover deleted accounts with minimal disruption.

Scenario 17-2: Recreating a Domain Controller

You are an administrator at the Contoso Corporation. You have three domain controllers for your organization. Unfortunately, one of the domain controllers suffered a catastrophic failure and you do not have a backup of the domain controller. What should you do to replace the domain controller?

Configuring Account Policies

LESSON 18

70-411 EXAM OBJECTIVE

Objective 5.4 – Configure account policies. This objective may include but is not limited to: configure domain user password policy; configure and apply Password Settings Objects (PSOs); delegate password settings management; configure local user password policy; configure account lockout settings.

LESSON HEADING	EXAM OBJECTIVE
Working with Account Policies	
Configuring Domain User Password Policy	Configure domain user password policy
Configuring Account Lockout Settings	Configure account lockout settings
Configuring and Applying Password Settings Objects	Configure and apply Password Settings Objects (PSOs)
Configuring Local User Password Policy	Configure local user password policy
Delegating Password Settings Management	Delegate password settings management

KEY TERMS

account lockout settings
account policies
fine-grained password policies
Group Policies
Group Policy Objects (GPOs)
password policy
Password Settings Object (PSO)

Working with Account Policies

THE BOTTOM LINE

Group Policies are one of the most powerful features of Active Directory that controls the working environment for user accounts and computer accounts. Group Policies provide centralized management and configuration of operating systems, applications, and user settings in an Active Directory environment. For example, you can use Group Policy to specify how often a user has to change his or her password, what the background image on a person's computer is, or whether spell checking is required before a user can send an e-mail.

Thousands of settings can be used to restrict certain actions, make a system more secure, or standardize a working environment. A setting can control a computer registry, NTFS security, audit and security policy, software installation, folder redirection, offline folders, or logon and logoff scripts. Group Policies is one of the most powerful features of Active Directory that controls the working environment for user accounts and computer accounts. Group Policy (see Figure 18-1) provides the centralized management and configuration of operating systems, applications, and user settings in an Active Directory environment. As each server version is released, Microsoft usually adds more parameters.

Group Policy Objects (GPOs) are collections of user and computer settings including the following:

- **System settings:** Application settings, desktop appearance, and behavior of system services.
- **Security settings:** Local computer, domain, and network security settings.
- **Software installation settings:** Management of software installation, updates, and removal.
- **Scripts settings:** Scripts for when a computer starts or shuts down and for when a user logs on and off.
- **Folder redirection settings:** Storage for users' folders on the network.

Account policies (Computer Configuration\Windows Settings\Security Settings\Account Policies as shown in Figure 18-1) are domain level policies that define the security-related attributes assigned to user objects. Account policies contain three subsets:

- **Password Policy:** Determine settings for passwords, such as enforcement and lifetimes.
- **Account Lockout Policy:** Determine the circumstances and length of time that an account is locked out of the system.
- **Kerberos Policy:** Determine Kerberos-related settings, such as ticket lifetimes and enforcement. Kerberos Policy settings do not exist in local computer policies.

X REF

Kerberos settings are discussed in lesson 15.

Figure 18-1

Accessing the account policies

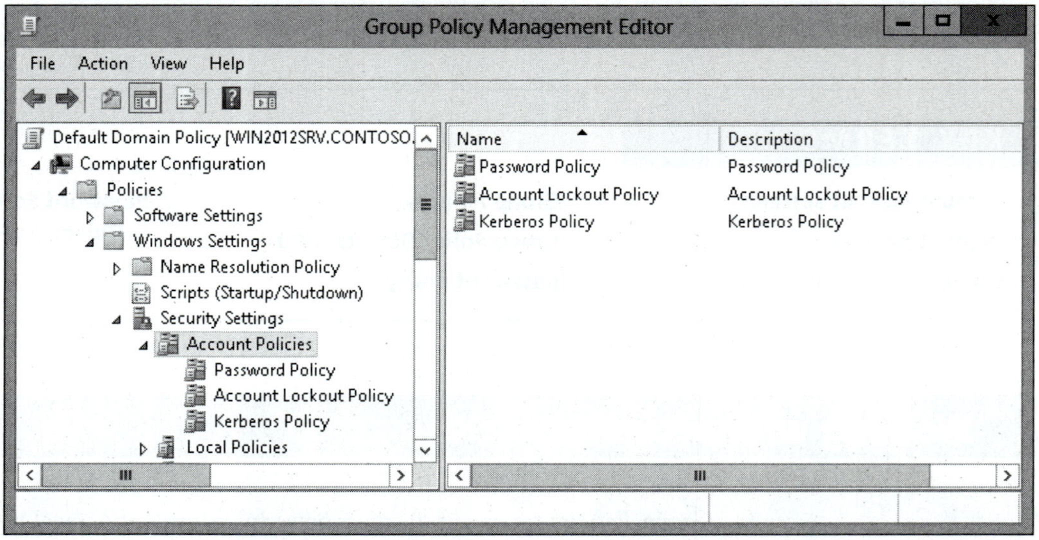

Unlike the other policies, there is only one account policy per domain, which is usually defined in the Default Domain Policy. If you do not want to use the Default Domain Policy, you can link a new policy to the root of the domain and give it precedence over the Default Domain Policy. The domain level account policies are enforced by the domain controllers.

Traditionally, if you needed to have different password policies for different people, you would have to create different domains for those people. However, starting with Windows Server 2008, fine-grained password policies were created that override the domain-wide policy.

Configuring Domain User Password Policy

As the name indicates, a ***password policy*** defines the password parameters that a user uses.

CERTIFICATION READY
Configure domain user password policy.
Objective 5.4

Much of today's data protection is based on the password. Think about your life. You use passwords to secure your voice mail, your ATM access, your e-mail account, your Facebook account, and a host of other things. To keep these accounts secure, you need to select strong passwords and you need to enforce users to choose strong passwords.

UNDERSTANDING STRONG PASSWORDS

One basic component of your information security program is ensuring that all employees select and use strong passwords, which is a password that is not easy to guess by humans or computer programs. The strength of a password can be determined by looking at the password's length, complexity, and randomness.

For example, a pin that you use with a credit card or to open a door might be a four-digit number. Each number can range from 0 to 9, which gives 10 possibilities for each digit. If you have 4 digits with 10 possibilities, you have the following:

10^4=10x10x10x10=10,000 possibilities

If you have a password that is two characters and you can use only lowercase characters (there are 26 available lowercase characters), you have the following:

26^2=26x26=676 possibilities

If you increase that to four characters, you have the following:

26^4=26x26x26x26=456,976 possibilities

If you increase that to eight characters, you have the following:

26^8=26x26x26x26x26x26x26x26=208,827,064,576 possibilities

If you use uppercase characters (26 characters), lowercase characters (26 characters, digits (10 characters), and special characters (!@#$%^&*()_-+={}[]|\:;"',.<>, giving another 28 characters), your total significantly increases to 90 characters.

90^8=90x90x90x90x90x90x90x90=4,304,672,100,000,000 possibilities

So the trick with strong passwords is how to create a strong password that you can remember. One way is to start with a phrase or sentence, remove the spaces between the words in a sentence, and then do some character substitution. For example, instead of using the "a" character, you substitute @. Lastly, you can add a couple of digits at the end.

For example, you can start with *I want a strong password*. Remove the spaces, and it becomes *Iwantastrongpassword*. Substitute @ for *a*, and you have *Iw@nt@strongp@ssword*. Lastly, add a four-digit number such as *Iw@nt@strongp@ssword9394*.

CONFIGURING PASSWORD POLICY SETTINGS

Password policies is the first folder under Account Policies (see Figure 18-2). The settings include:

- **Enforce password history:** Defines the number of unique, new passwords that must be associated with a user account before an old password can be reused. The default setting is 24 previous passwords (see Figure 18-3).
- **Maximum password age:** Defines the number of days that a password can be used before the user must change it. The default setting is 42 days.
- **Minimum password age:** Defines the number of days that a password must be used before the user can change it. The default value is one day, which is appropriate if you also enforce password history.
- **Minimum password length:** Defines the minimum number of characters that a user's password must contain. The default value is seven.
- **Complexity requirements:** Defines a default password filter that is enabled by default. A complex password defines the following characteristics:
  - Does not contain your name or your username.
  - Contains at least six characters.
  - Contains characters from three of the following four groups: uppercase letters [A...Z], lowercase letters [a...z], numerals [0...9], and special, non-alphanumeric characters (such as !@#)(*&^%).

Figure 18-2

Viewing the Password Policy settings

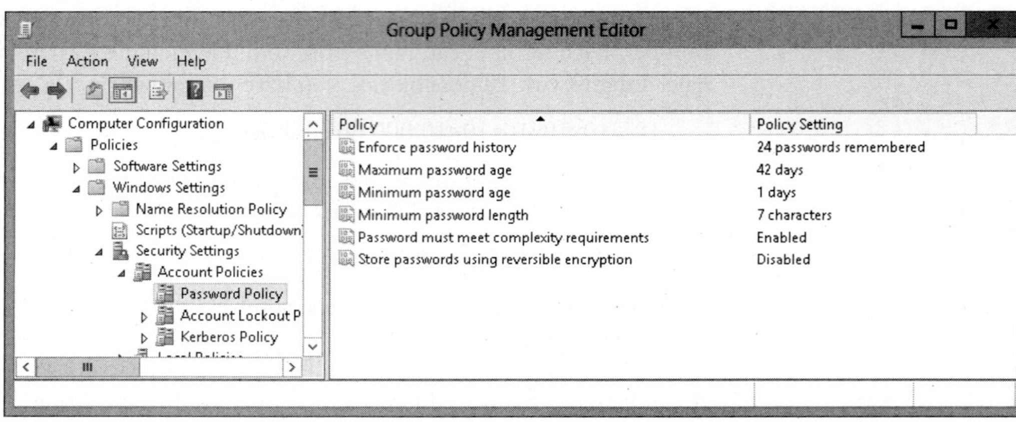

Figure 18-3

Viewing the Enforce password history

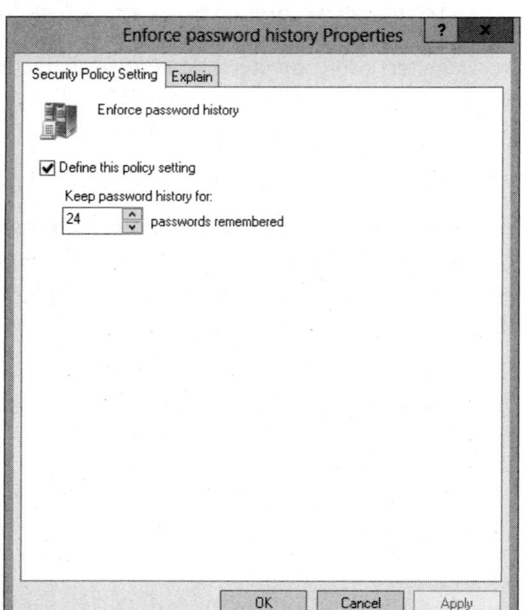

Figure 18-4 shows the option to enforce complex passwords.

Figure 18-4

Viewing the Complexity requirements

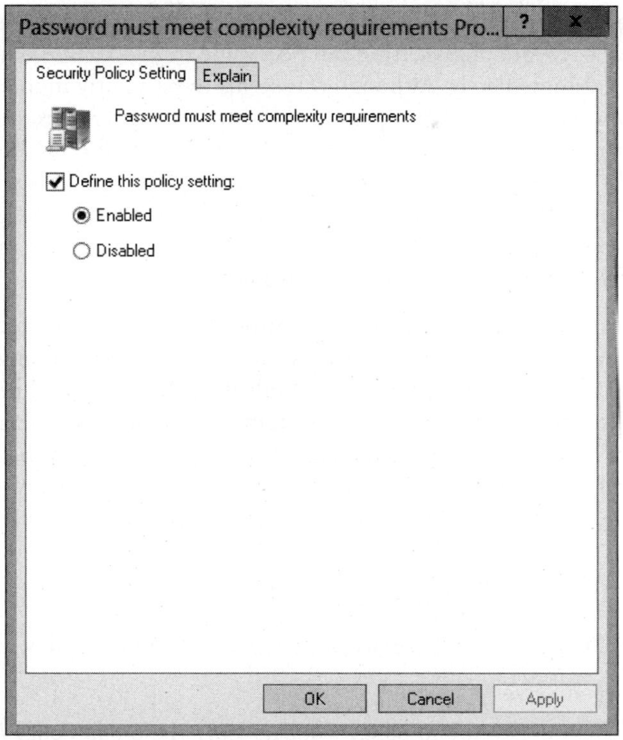

The length of a password is a key component of its strength. Password length is the number of characters used in a password. A password with two characters is considered highly insecure, because there is a limited set of unique passwords that can be made using two characters. Therefore, a two-character password is considered easy to guess.

On the other side of the spectrum is the 14-character password. Although a relative to a secure 2-character password, a 14-character password is difficult for most users to remember. When passwords become long, users often require writing down their passwords, which defeats any security benefits you might have from requiring a 14-character password in the first place.

As these scenarios illustrate, the trick to setting a minimum password length is balancing usability with security. Microsoft permits you to set a minimum password length ranging from 1 to 14 (a setting of 0 means no password is required, which is never appropriate in a production environment). The generally accepted minimum password length is eight characters.

The password history is the setting that determines the number of unique passwords that must be used before a password can be re-used. This setting prevents users from recycling the same passwords through a system. The longer the period of time a password is used, the greater the chances it can be compromised.

Microsoft allows you to set the password history value between 0 and 24. Ten is a fairly common setting in standard environments, although Windows Server 2012 defaults to 24 on domain controllers.

The minimum password age setting controls how many days users must wait before they can reset their password. This setting can be a value from 1 to 998 days. If set to 0, passwords can be changed immediately. Although this seems to be a fairly innocent setting, too low a value can allow users to defeat your password history settings. For example, if you set this value to 0 and your password history is set to 10, all users have to do is reset their password 10 times in a row, and then they can go back to their original password. This setting must be set to a lower value than the maximum password age, unless the maximum password age is set to 0, which means passwords never expire. Ten days or greater is usually a good setting, although this can vary widely depending on administrator preferences.

> **TAKE NOTE***
> If you select a password not to expire, the maximum password age will not apply.

The maximum password age setting controls the maximum period of time that can elapse before you are forced to reset your password. This setting can range from 1 to 999 days, or it can be set to 0 if you never want passwords to expire. A general rule for this setting is 90 days for user accounts; although for administrative accounts, it's generally a good idea to reset passwords more frequently. In high security areas, 30 days is not an uncommon setting. We discussed the different settings you can use to ensure the best password security for your environment. Now, let's look at how to review those settings on a Windows 7 workstation.

CONFIGURE PASSWORD POLICIES

GET READY. To configure password policies, perform the following steps:

1. Open Server Manager.
2. Click Tools > Group Policy Management. The *Group Policy Management console* opens.
3. Find and right-click Default Domain Policy and click Edit. The *Group Policy Management Editor* opens.
4. In the left window pane, expand the Computer Configuration node, expand the Policies node, and expand the Windows Settings folder. Then, expand the Security Settings node. In the *Security Settings* node, expand Account Policies and select Password Policy.
5. To modify a setting, double-click the setting in the right window pane to open the *Properties* dialog box for the setting. Then, make the desired value changes.
6. Click OK to close the setting's *Properties* dialog box.
7. Close the *Group Policy Management Editor* window for this policy.

Configuring Account Lockout Settings

To help prevent hacking, Windows uses ***account lockout settings*** that specify when an account is locked when there are too many incorrect logon attempts.

> **CERTIFICATION READY**
> Configure account lockout settings.
> Objective 5.4

If a hacker has enough time, he or she can crack any password. To help prevent the cracking of a password, you can limit how many times a hacker can guess a password before the account is locked. Account lockout refers to the number of incorrect logon attempts permitted before a system locks an account.

Each bad logon attempt is tracked and added to the bad logon counter. When the counter exceeds the account lockout threshold, the account is locked and no further logon attempts are permitted.

Group policies include the following account lockout settings:

- **Account lockout duration:** Determines the length of time a lockout will remain in place before another logon attempt can be made. This can be set from 0 to 99,999 minutes. If set to 0, an administrator will need to manually unlock the account.
- **Account lockout threshold:** Determines the number of failed logons permitted before account lockout occurs. This can be set from 0 (no account lockouts) to 999 attempts before lockout.
- **Reset account lockout counter after:** Determines the period of time, in minutes, that must elapse before the account lockout counter is reset to 0 bad logon attempts.

Figure 18-5 shows the account lockout settings.

Figure 18-5

Viewing account lockout policies

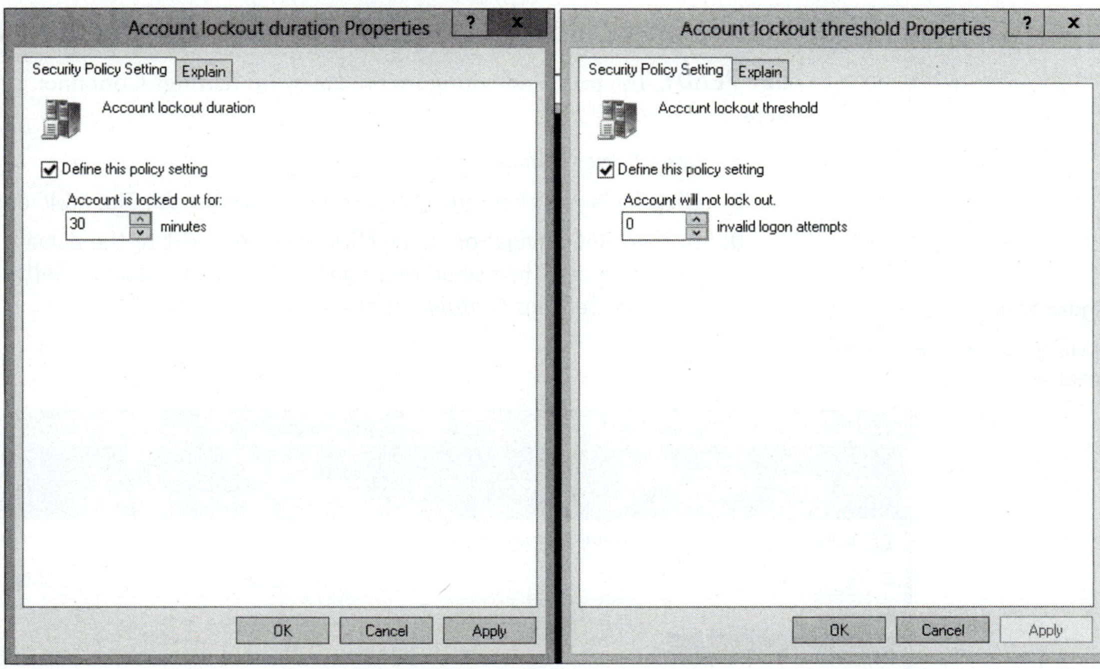

CONFIGURE ACCOUNT LOCKOUT SETTINGS

GET READY. To configure account lockout settings, follow these steps:

1. Open Server Manager.
2. Click Tools > Group Policy Management. The *Group Policy Management console* opens.
3. Find and right-click Default Domain Policy and click Edit. The *Group Policy Management Editor* opens.
4. In the left window pane, expand the Computer Configuration node, expand the Policies node, and expand the Windows Settings folder. Then, expand the Security Settings node. In the *Security Settings* node, expand Account Policies and select Account Lockout Policy.
5. To modify a setting, double-click the setting in the right window pane to open the *Properties* dialog box for the setting. Then, make the desired value changes.
6. Click OK to close the setting's *Properties* dialog box.
7. Close the *Group Policy Management Editor* window for this policy.

Configuring and Applying Password Settings Objects

If you need to use different password policies for different sets of users, you can use fine-grained password policies, which are applied to user objects or global security groups.

CERTIFICATION READY
Configure and apply Password Settings Objects (PSOs).
Objective 5.4

Fine-grained password policies allow you to specify multiple password policies within a single domain so that you can apply different restrictions for password and account lockout policies to different sets of users in a domain. To use a fine-grained password policy, your domain functional level must be at least Windows Server 2008. To enable fine-grained password policies, you first create a ***Password Settings Object (PSO)***. You then configure the same settings that you configure for the password and account lockout policies. You can create and apply PSOs in the Windows Server 2012 environment by using the Active Directory Administrative Center (ADAC) or Windows PowerShell.

CREATE AND CONFIGURE PASSWORD SETTINGS CONTAINER

GET READY. To create and configure the Password Settings Container, perform the following steps:

1. Open Server Manager.
2. Click Tools > Active Directory Administrative Center. The *ADAC* opens.
3. In the ADAC navigation pane, click the arrow next to the domain and select the System folder. Then scroll down and double-click Password Settings Container. The *Password Settings Container* is shown in Figure 18-6.

Figure 18-6

Opening the Password Settings Container

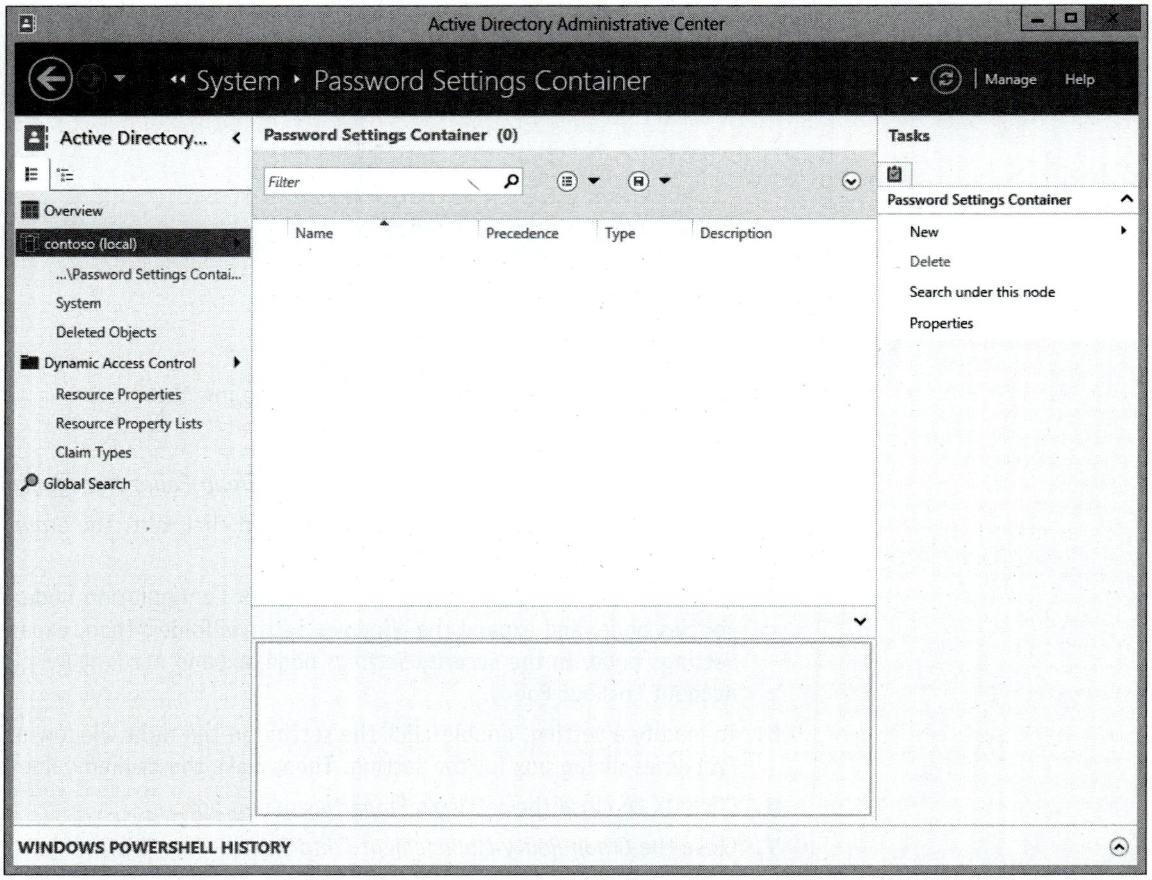

4. In the *Tasks* pane, click New, and then click Password Settings. The *Create Password Settings* window opens (see Figure 18-7).

Figure 18-7

Creating a New Password Settings Container

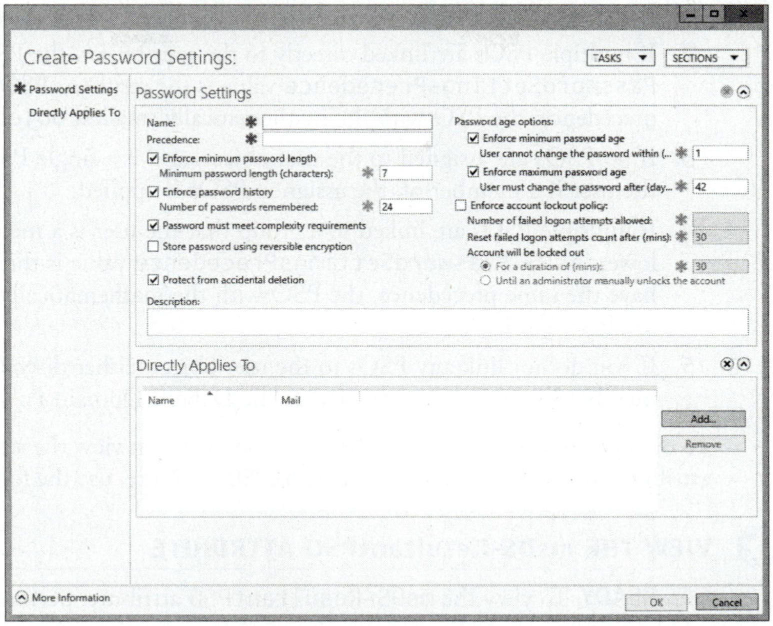

5. In the Name text box, type a name of the Password Settings Container.
6. In the *Precedence* text box, type a Precedence number. Passwords with a lower precedence number overwrite Password Settings Containers with a higher precedence number.
7. Fill in or edit the appropriate fields for the settings that you want to use.
8. Under *Directly Applies To*, click Add. When the *Select Users or Groups* dialog box, opens specify the name of the user or group that you want the Password Settings Container to effect and then click OK.
9. Click OK to submit the creation of the PSO.
10. Close the *ADAC*.

USING WINDOWS POWERSHELL

To create and manage PSOs in your domain using Windows PowerShell, use the following command:

```
New-ADFineGrainedPasswordPolicy
```

For example, to create a new PSO named TestPwd with specified settings, you would use:

```
New-ADFineGrainedPasswordPolicy TestPswd -ComplexityEnabled:$true
-LockoutDuration:"00:30:00" -LockoutObservationWindow:"00:30:00"
-LockoutThreshold:"3" -MaxPasswordAge:"42.00:00:00"
-MinPasswordAge:"1.00:00:00" -MinPasswordLength:"7"
-PasswordHistoryCount:"24" -Precedence:"1"
-ReversibleEncryptionEnabled:$false
-ProtectedFromAccidentalDeletion:$true
```

To modify an existing PSO, use the following command:

```
Set-ADFineGrainedPasswordPolicySubject
```

To link a user or group to an existing PSO, use the following command:

```
Add-ADFineGrainedPasswordPolicySubject
```

For example, to link the Sales group to the TestPswd PSO, use the following command:

```
Add-ADFineGrainedPasswordPolicySubject TestPwd -Subjects Sales
```

If you have multiple PSOs that are applied to a user or group that the user is a member of, the following process determines the resultant PSO.

1. If a single PSO is linked directly to a user object, the resultant PSO is the single PSO.
2. If multiple PSOs are linked directly to the user object, the PSO with the lowest `msDS-PasswordSettingsPrecedence` value is the resultant PSO. If two PSOs have the same precedence, the PSO with the mathematically smallest `objectGUID` is the resultant PSO.
3. If no PSOs are assigned to the user object, and if a single PSO is assigned to a group that the user is a member of, the assigned PSOs is applied.
4. If multiple PSOs are linked to a group that the user is a member of, the PSO with the lowest `msDS-PasswordSettingsPrecedence` value is the resultant PSO. If two PSOs have the same precedence, the PSO with the mathematically smallest `objectGUID` is the resultant PSO.
5. If you do not link any PSOs to the user object, either directly or through group membership, the policy defined in the Default Domain Policy is applied.

To determine which PSO is applied to a user, you can view the `msDS-ResultantPSO` attribute. To view the `msDS-ResultantPSO` attribute, use the following procedure.

VIEW THE msDS-ResultantPSO ATTRIBUTE

GET READY. To view the `msDS-ResultantPSO` attribute, perform the following steps:

1. Open Server Manager.
2. Open Tools > Active Directory Users and Computers. The *Active Directory Users and Computers console* opens.
3. Open the View menu and make sure that Advanced Features is checked. If it is not, click the Advanced Features option.
4. Navigate to the user, right-click the user, and click Properties. The user *Properties* dialog box opens.
5. Click the Attribute Editor tab. The *Attribute Editor* tab is shown in Figure 18-8.

Figure 18-8

Viewing user attributes

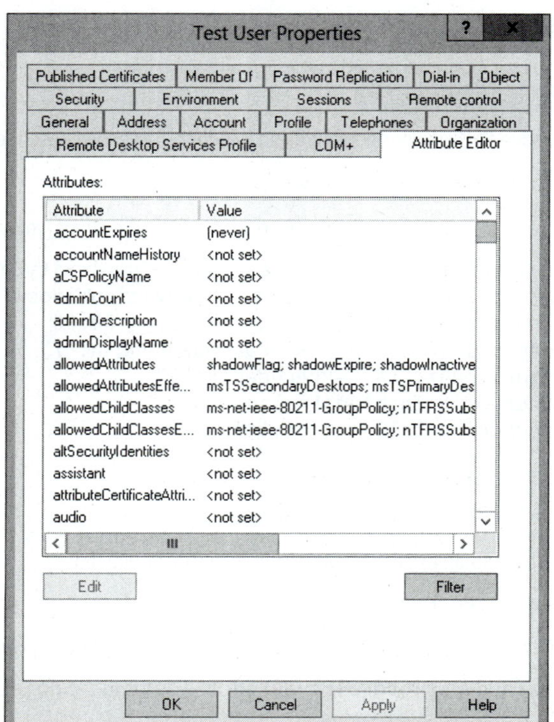

6. Click Filter, and click Constructed.
7. Scroll down and find the msDS-ResultantPSO attribute to see the current PSO being applied.
8. Clicked OK to close the *Properties* dialog box.
9. Close the *Active Directory Users and Computers console*.

Configuring Local User Password Policy

If you have a standalone computer that is not part of a domain, you can still configure password policies and/or account lockout policies using the local policies.

CERTIFICATION READY
Configure local user password policy.
Objective 5.4

The easiest method to access the account policies is to execute the secpol.msc from a command prompt, which opens the Local Security Policy (see Figure 18-9). The password-policy and account-policy settings can be located within the Local Security Policy console by expanding Security Settings, and then expanding Account Policies.

Figure 18-9

Opening the Local Security Policy

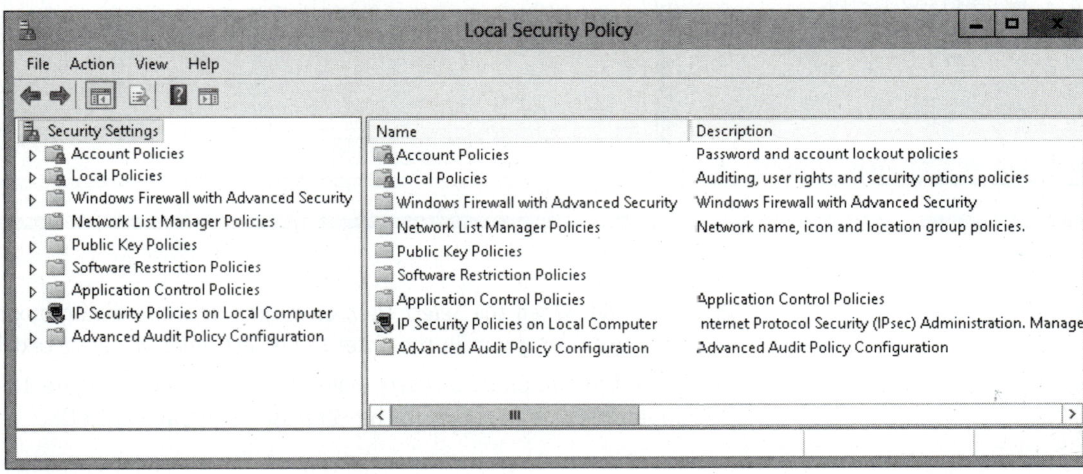

Delegating Password Settings Management

By default, only members of the Domain Admins group can set fine-grained password policies. However, you can also delegate the ability to set these policies to other users.

CERTIFICATION READY
Delegate password settings management.
Objective 5.4

By default, the Domain Admins group has Read and Write capabilities to the Default Domain Policy. If you want to give access to others to manage the Default Domain Policy, you need to add the user to the access list and assign the permissions as described in the next procedure.

MANAGE GPO PERMISSIONS

GET READY. To manage GPO permissions, perform the following steps:

1. Open Server Manager.
2. Open Tools > Group Policy Management. The *Group Policy Management console* opens.
3. Click Default Domain Policy. If you get a warning saying that you selected a link, click OK.

4. Click the Delegation tab. The groups and users that have access to manage the GPO are displayed (see Figure 18-10).

Figure 18-10

Displaying the Delegation tab

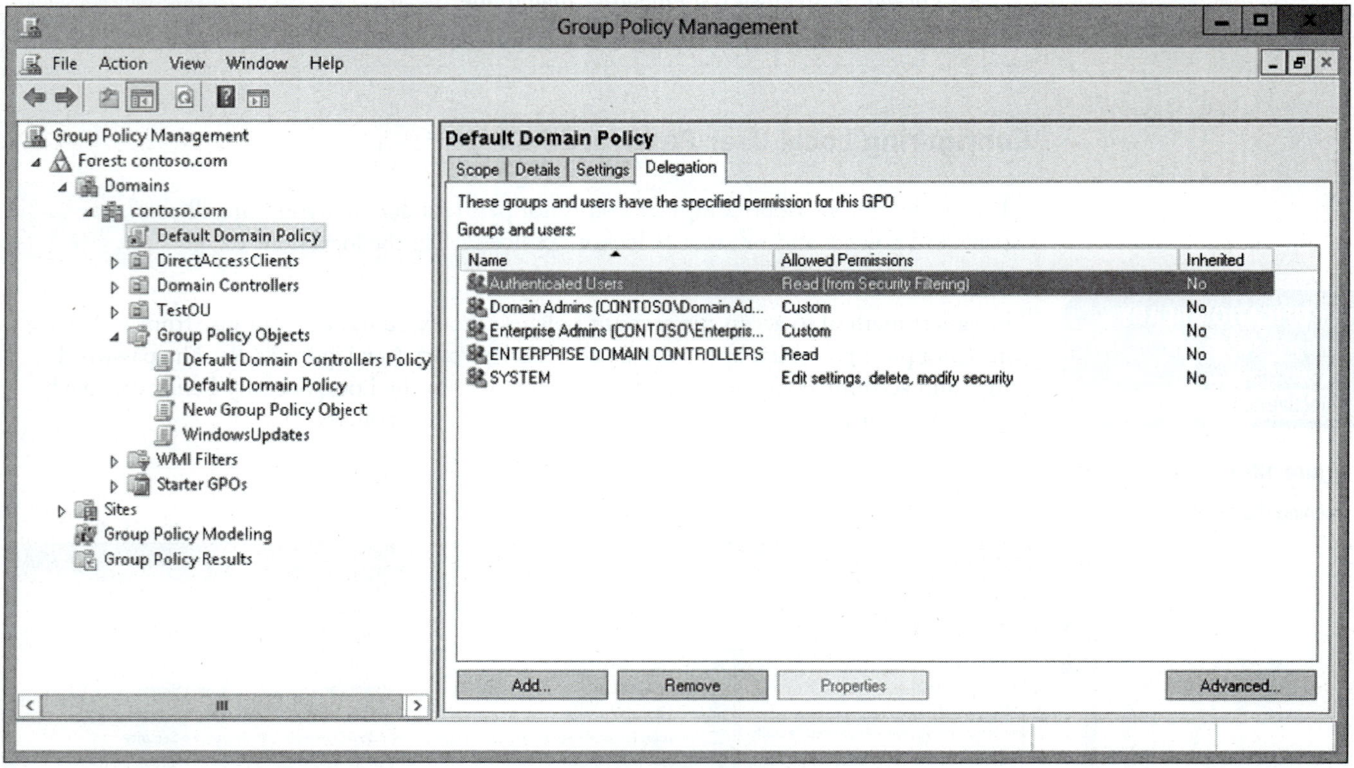

5. Click Add. When the *Select User, Computer, or Group* dialog box opens, type the name of the user or group in the *Enter the object name to select* text box and click OK.
6. When the *Add Group or Users* dialog box appears (see Figure 18-11), select the appropriate permissions in the *Permissions* list and click OK.

Figure 18-11

Assigning permissions to a GPO

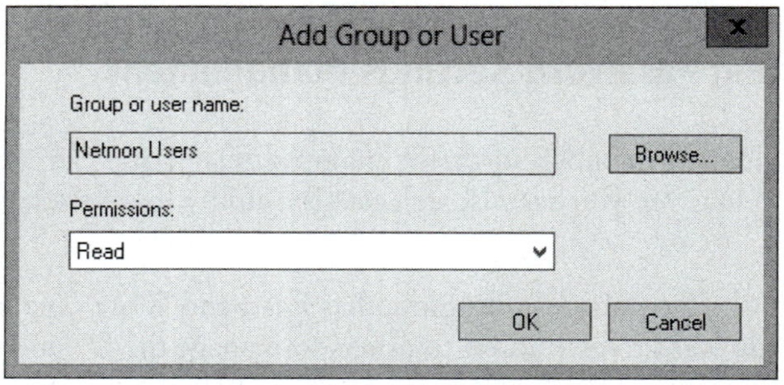

7. Click OK to submit the creation of the PSO.
8. Close the *Group Policy Management console*.

To assign a PSO to a user, it is best to assign the PSO to a global security group and then add the user to the global security group. If you need a support person to assign the PSO to a user, he or she needs to have the ability to add the user account to the group that the PSO is assigned to. To assign management permissions to the PSO, follow the next procedure.

MANAGE PASSWORD SETTINGS OBJECT PERMISSIONS

GET READY. To manage permissions to a PSO:

1. Open Server Manager.
2. Open Tools > Active Directory Administrative Center. The *ADAC* opens.
3. Navigate to the System\Password Settings Container.
4. Right-click the Password Settings Container and click Properties. The *Password Settings Object Settings* window opens.
5. Under the *Extensions* section (see Figure 18-12), click Add. When the *Select Users, Computers, Service Accounts, or Groups* dialog box opens, type the name of the user account or group and click OK.

Figure 18-12

Viewing the users and groups that have access to the PSO

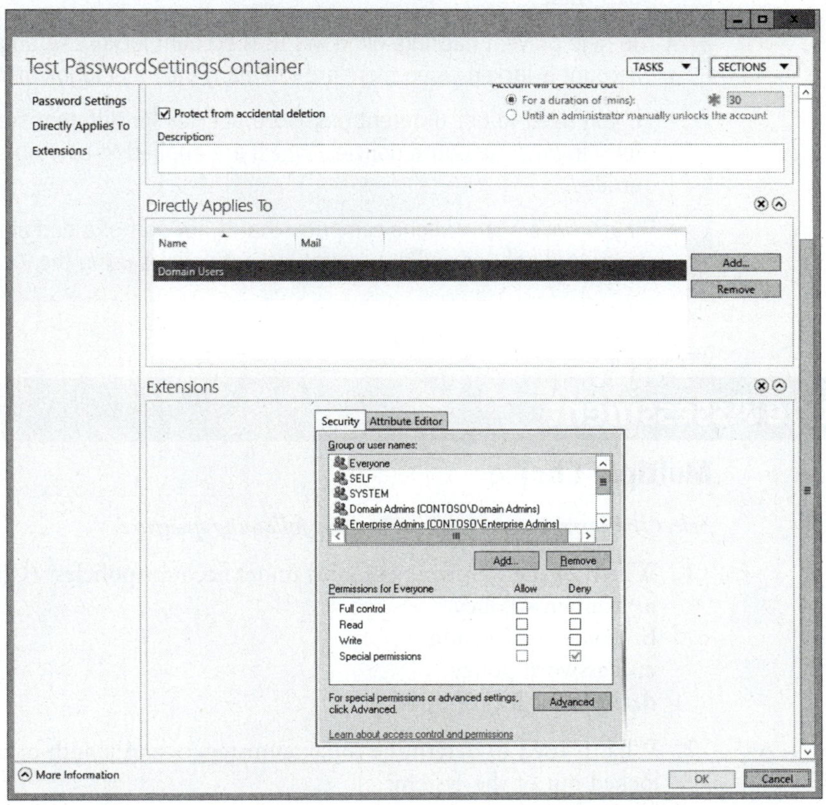

6. Click to assign the appropriate permissions under the Allow or Deny column.
7. Click OK.
8. Close the *ADAC*.

SKILL SUMMARY

IN THIS LESSON, YOU LEARNED:

- Group Policies provide centralized management and configuration of operating systems, applications, and user settings in an Active Directory environment.
- Group Policy Objects (GPOs) are collections of user and computer settings.
- Account policies are domain level policies that define the security-related attributes assigned to user objects.
- There is only one account policy per domain, which is usually defined in the Default Domain Policy.
- As the name indicates, a password policy defines the password parameters that a user uses.
- To help prevent hacking, Windows uses account lockout settings that specify when an account is locked when there are too many incorrect logon attempts.
- If you need to use different password policies for different sets of users, you can use fine-grained password policies, which are applied to user objects or global security groups.
- If you have a standalone computer that is not part of a domain, you can still configure password policies and/or account lockout policies using the local policies.

Knowledge Assessment

Multiple Choice

Select the correct answer for each of the following questions.

1. Which of the following is found under account policies? (Choose all that apply.)
   a. Kerberos Policy
   b. Folder redirection
   c. Password policy
   d. Account lockout policy

2. What is used to determine the circumstances and length of time that an account will be locked out of the system?
   a. Kerberos Policy
   b. Folder redirection
   c. Password policy
   d. Account lockout policy

3. What determines settings for passwords, including enforcement and lifetime?
   a. Kerberos Policy
   b. Folder redirection
   c. Password policy
   d. Account lockout policy

4. How many password policies can you define for each domain?
   a. 1
   b. 2
   c. 4
   d. unlimited

5. What is the default value for Enforce password history?
 a. 1
 b. 4
 c. 10
 d. 24

6. What value must you assign to the Account lockout duration to ensure that the administrator will have to manually unlock the account?
 a. 0
 b. 1
 c. 24
 d. 999

7. Which do you use if you want to assign different password policies to different sets of people?
 a. Exception password policies
 b. One-off password policies
 c. Fine-grained password policies
 d. User-defined password policies

8. Which do you use to configure a password policy a standalone computer running Windows?
 a. secpol.msc
 b. password.msc
 c. gpupdate.exe
 d. ntdsutil.exe

9. Which domain level does the forest have to be to use fine-grained password policies?
 a. Windows Server 2003
 b. Windows Server 2008
 c. Windows Server 2008 R2
 d. Windows Server 2012

10. Which policy do you normally find the password policy?
 a. Default Domain policy
 b. Domain Controller policy
 c. Default Password policy
 d. PSO Policy

Best Answer

Choose the letter that corresponds to the best answer. More than one answer choice may achieve the goal. Select the BEST answer.

1. What is a collection of users and computer settings that are assigned to a domain or organization unit?
 a. folder permissions
 b. group membership
 c. registry settings
 d. GPO

2. Which of the following is considered a complex password? (Choose all that apply.)
 a. 43test.w@ttle
 b. John.home.333
 c. Password01
 d. PWLetMeIn

3. What do you assign a password settings policy to?
   a. An OU
   b. A computer
   c. A domain controller
   d. A global security group

4. Which setting prevents users from resetting the password several times in a row so that he or she can reset the password back to the original password?
   a. Maximum password age
   b. Minimum password age
   c. Complexity requirements
   d. Minimum password length

5. Which Windows PowerShell command creates a Password Settings Object (PSO)?
   a. Get-ADFineGrainedPasswordPolicy
   b. Set-ADFineGrainedPasswordPolicy
   c. New-ADFineGrainedPasswordPolicy
   d. StartADFineGrainedPasswordPolicy

6. Which account can manage PSOs?
   a. Domain Admins
   b. Account Operators
   c. GPManagers
   d. Power Users

Matching and Identification

1. Identify the default values for account policies?
   _____ a) Enforce password history
   _____ b) Maximum password age
   _____ c) Minimum password age
   _____ d) Minimum password length
   _____ e) Complexity requirements

2. Match the definition of the term used with password policies.
   _____ a) Minimum password age
   _____ b) Complexity requirements
   _____ c) Maximum password age
   _____ d) Minimum password length
   _____ e) Enforce password history
   1. Defines the number of days that a password can be used before the user must change it.
   2. Defines the minimum number of characters that a user's password must contain.
   3. Defines the number of days that a password must be used before the user can change it.
   4. Defines the number of unique, new passwords that must be associated with a user account before an old password can be reused.
   5. Defines a default password filter.

3. Identify which of the following are used for the password complexity requirements?
   _____ a) Minimum of six characters
   _____ b) Minimum of seven characters
   _____ c) Minimum of eight characters
   _____ d) Does not contain your name
   _____ e) Has lowercase and uppercase
   _____ f) Contains three of the four groups (uppercase, lowercase, numbers, and special characters)
   _____ g) Contains each of the four (uppercase, lowercase, numbers, and special characters) types of characters

Build a List

4. Identify the order in which PSOs are processed? Not all will be used.
   _____ PSOs with higher precedents linked to group that the user is a member of
   _____ PSOs with lower precedents linked to group that the user is a member of
   _____ PSOs linked to a user object with lower precedents
   _____ PSOs linked to a user object with higher precedents
   _____ PSO that was created first

Business Case Scenarios

Scenario 18-1: Making Passwords Compliant

You are an administrator at the Contoso Corporation. You have the responsibility to make sure that the passwords for all users are at least eight characters and that are changed every 90 days. You must ensure that each password is a strong password. You also have users who are on the road. Because these users use laptops that contain confidential information, you must ensure that each password is 10 characters and that get changed every 30 days. What should you do?

Scenario 18-2: Preventing Intrusion

Recently, you have had a couple accounts where the password has been compromised. You need to take extra steps in preventing the intrusion. What are the steps you can take?

19 LESSON

Configuring Group Policy Processing

70-411 EXAM OBJECTIVE

Objective 6.1 – Configure Group Policy processing. This objective may include but is not limited to: configure processing order and precedence; configure blocking of inheritance; configure enforced policies; configure security filtering and WMI filtering; configure loopback processing; configure and manage slow-link processing; configure client-side extension (CSE) behavior.

LESSON HEADING	EXAM OBJECTIVE
Understanding Group Policy Processing	
Configuring Processing Order and Precedence	Configure processing order and precedence
Using Filtering with Group Policies	Configure blocking of inheritance Configure enforced policies
Configuring Security Filtering and WMI Filtering	Configure security filtering and WMI filtering
Configuring Loopback Processing	Configure loopback processing
Configuring Client-Side Extension Behavior	Configure client-side extension (CSE) behavior Configure and domain controller manage slow-link processing
Troubleshooting GPOs	

KEY TERMS

client-side extensions
Default Domain Controller Policy
Default Domain Policy
group policy objects (GPOs)
inheritance
loopback processing
Merge mode
Replace mode
Result Set of Policy (RSoP)
Security group filtering
Windows Management Instrumentation (WMI)
WMI filtering

■ Understanding Group Policy Processing

THE BOTTOM LINE

Group policies are defined using ***group policy objects (GPOs)***, which are the collection of configuration instructions that the computer processes. To assign a group policy, it is linked to an Active Directory container (site, domain, or organizational unit). However, you can take steps to control which group policy affects a computer or user.

You can use several mechanisms to scope a GPO, including:

- A GPO link to a site, domain, or organizational unit (OU)
- The GPO link enabled or disabled
- Enforce option of the GPO
- The Block Inheritance option of an OU
- Security group filtering
- WMI filtering
- Loopback policy processing
- Preferences targeting (discussed in Lesson 22, "Configuring Group Policy Preferences")

Configuring Processing Order and Precedence

To understand how group policies are applied, you must first look at the order in which group policies are applied.

CERTIFICATION READY
Configure processing order and precedence.
Objective 6.1

When configuring group policies, the settings are applied to the computer or the user. Computer configuration settings are processed when a computer starts, and user configuration settings are processed when a user logs on. Group policies are processed in the following way:

1. When a computer first starts up, it establishes a secure link between the computer and a domain controller.
2. The computer obtains a list of GPOs that are applied to the computer.
3. Computer configuration settings are applied synchronously (one by one) during computer startup before the Logon dialog box is presented to the user. If any startup scripts are configured through GPOs, the scripts are processed synchronously and have a default timeout of 600 seconds (10 minutes) to complete. Because the user has not logged on yet, the process is hidden.
4. When the computer configuration settings have been applied and the startup scripts have been applied, users have the Ctrl+Alt+Del option to log on.
5. A user is authenticated and the user profile is loaded.
6. The computer obtains a list of GPOs that are applied to the user. Again, GPO processing is hidden from the user.
7. After the user policies run, any logon scripts defined by GPOs run, which are executed asynchronously (multiple scripts to be processed at the same time).
8. The login script defined for the user in Active Directory user properties is executed.
9. The user's desktop is displayed.

UNDERSTANDING GROUP POLICY INHERITANCE

A computer and user can be affected by multiple GPOs. GPOs are processed in the following order:

1. Local group policy
2. Site
3. Domain
4. OU

Although the domain and OU are used to deploy GPOs based on the location of the user and computers within Active Directory hierarchy, the Site is used to define GPOs based on physical location.

By default, a Group Policy uses ***inheritance*** in which settings are inherited from the container above. In other words, group policy settings flow down into the lower containers and objects. Generally speaking, the settings are cumulative, unless there is a conflict with a setting defined in a previous GPO. By default, if there is a conflict between settings, the domain controller that is processed later overwrites the setting that was established previously.

If a site, domain, or OU has multiple GPOs, the group policies are processed in order as stated by its precedence. A GPO with higher precedence (lower number) prevails over a GPO with lower precedence (higher number).

When Active Directory is installed, two domain GPOs are created by default:

- ***Default Domain Policy:*** Linked to the domain. It affects all users and computers in the domain, including domain controllers. It specifies the password, account lockout, and Kerberos policies. These policies can be configured only at the domain level. To configure other settings at the domain level, you should create additional GPOs linked to the domain.
- ***Default Domain Controller Policy:*** Linked to the Domain Controllers organization unit, which then affects the domain controllers. It contains the default user rights assignments. You should also use it for auditing policies. It has a security filter to include only Authenticated Users.

Let's say that you have the contoso.com domain that has the Sales OU, which contains the West OU (see Figure 19-1). You create GPO1 and GPO2 GPOs and link them to the

Figure 19-1

Displaying GPOs for a domain

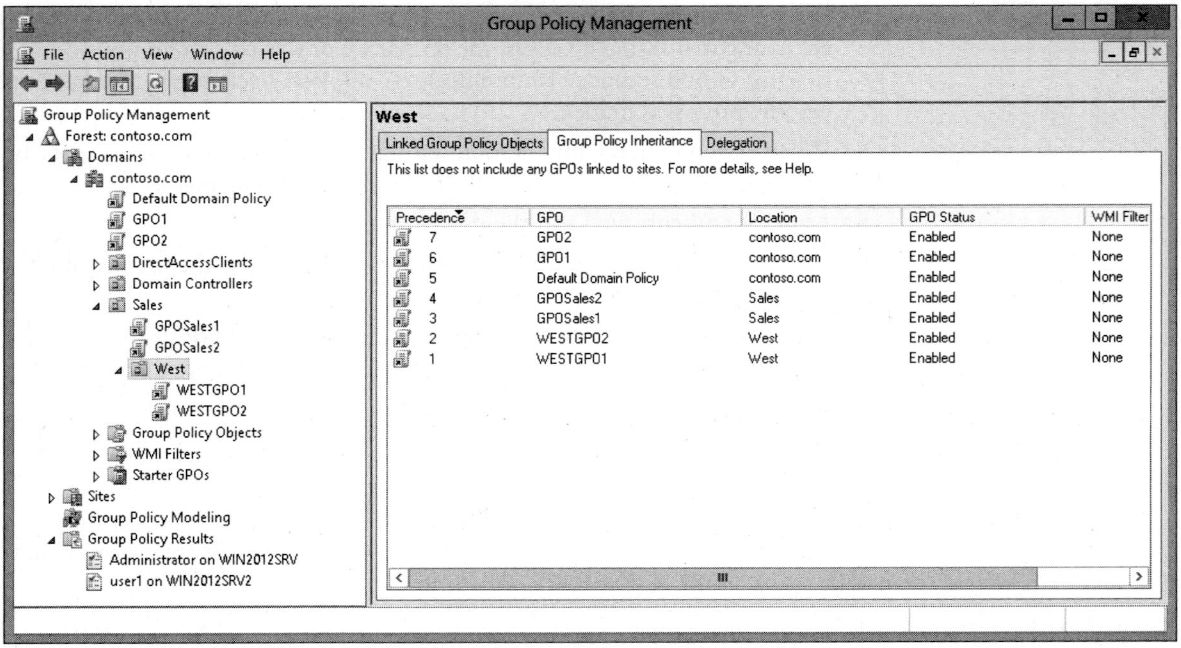

domain. You create GPOSales1 and GPOSales2 and link them to the Sales OU. You create WESTGPO1 and WESTGPO2 and link them to the WEST OU. The policies are processed in the following order:

1. Local group policy
2. GPO2
3. GPO1
4. Default Domain Policy
5. GPOSales2
6. GPOSales1
7. WESTGPO2
8. WESTGPO1

If all the GPOs configure the same setting, the setting defined with the GPO with the highest precedence (lowest number) will be used. Of course, if you configure settings defined in the password, account lockout, or Kerberos policy, only the Default Domain Policy would be used because these can be set only at the domain level. If you need to change the precedence, use the following procedure.

CHANGE THE PRECEDENCE OF A GPO

GET READY. To change the precedence of a GPO for a container, perform the following steps:

1. Open Server Manager.
2. Click Tools > Group Policy Management. The *Group Policy Management console* opens.
3. Navigate to and click the container (site, domain, or OU) that has GPOs that you want to modify.
4. Click the Linked Group Policy Objects tab.
5. Click the GPO that you want to modify. Then, use the arrow icons (Up, Down, Move To Top, and Move To Bottom) to move the GPO up or down on the list (see Figure 19-2).

Figure 19-2

Changing the precedence

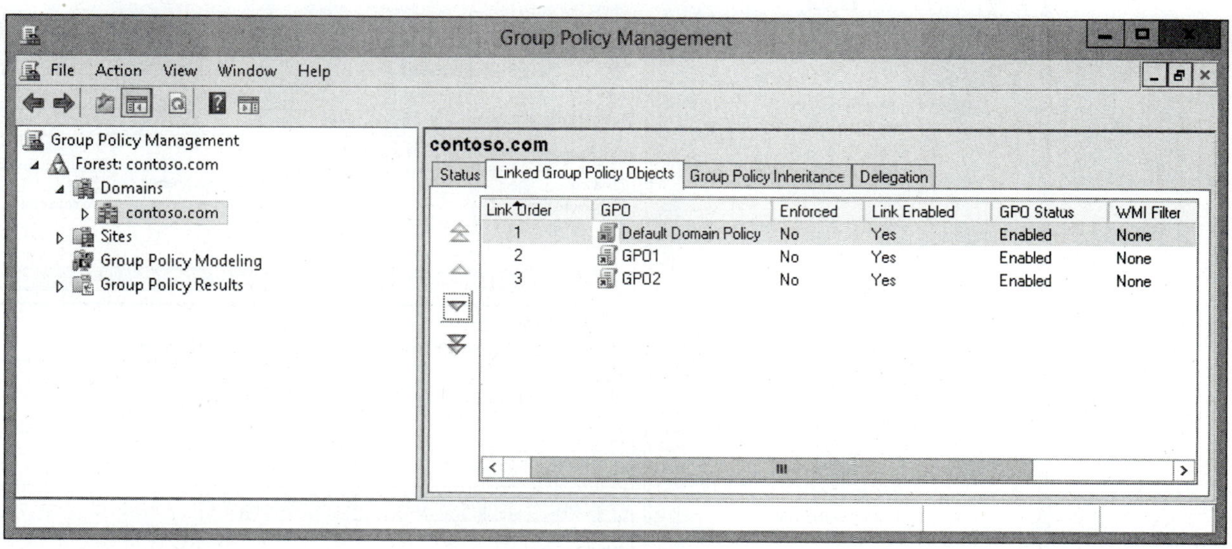

6. Close the *Group Policy Management console*.

MANAGING GROUP POLICY LINKS

To disable a group policy for a container, you right-click the GPO for the container and click the *Link Enabled* link. A checkmark shows that the link is enabled (see Figure 19-3) whereas no checkmark means that the link is disabled. Disabling the link for a container affects only the container and does not affect other containers that a GPO is linked to.

Figure 19-3

Showing a link is enabled for a GPO

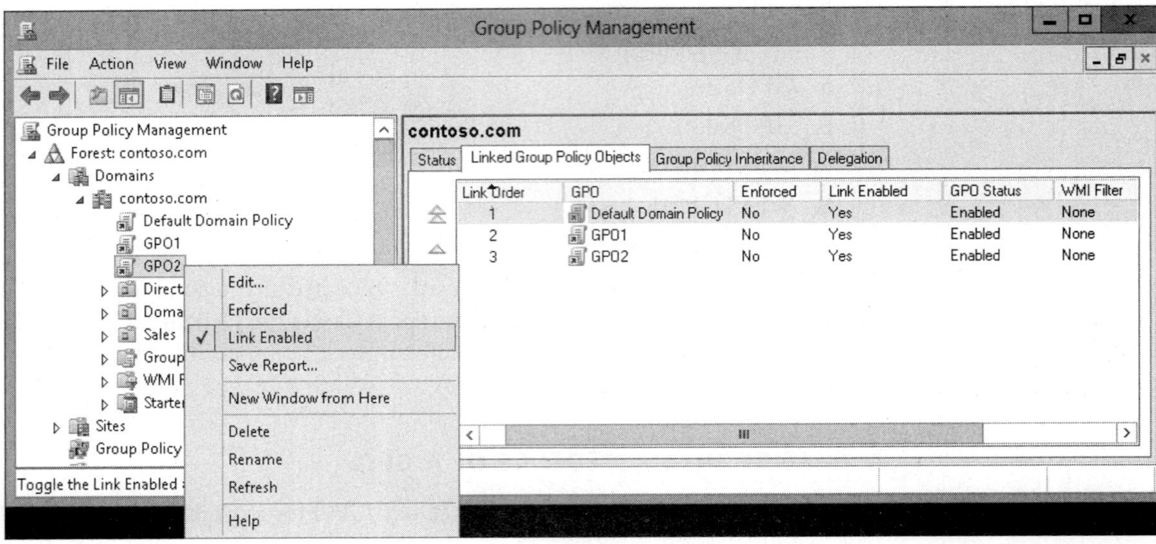

After a GPO is created, you can manage how the GPO is used by performing the following actions:

- To view the containers that a GPO is linked to, you click the GPO in Group Policy Management and view the Scope tab (see Figure 19-4).

Figure 19-4

Showing the containers a GPO is linked to

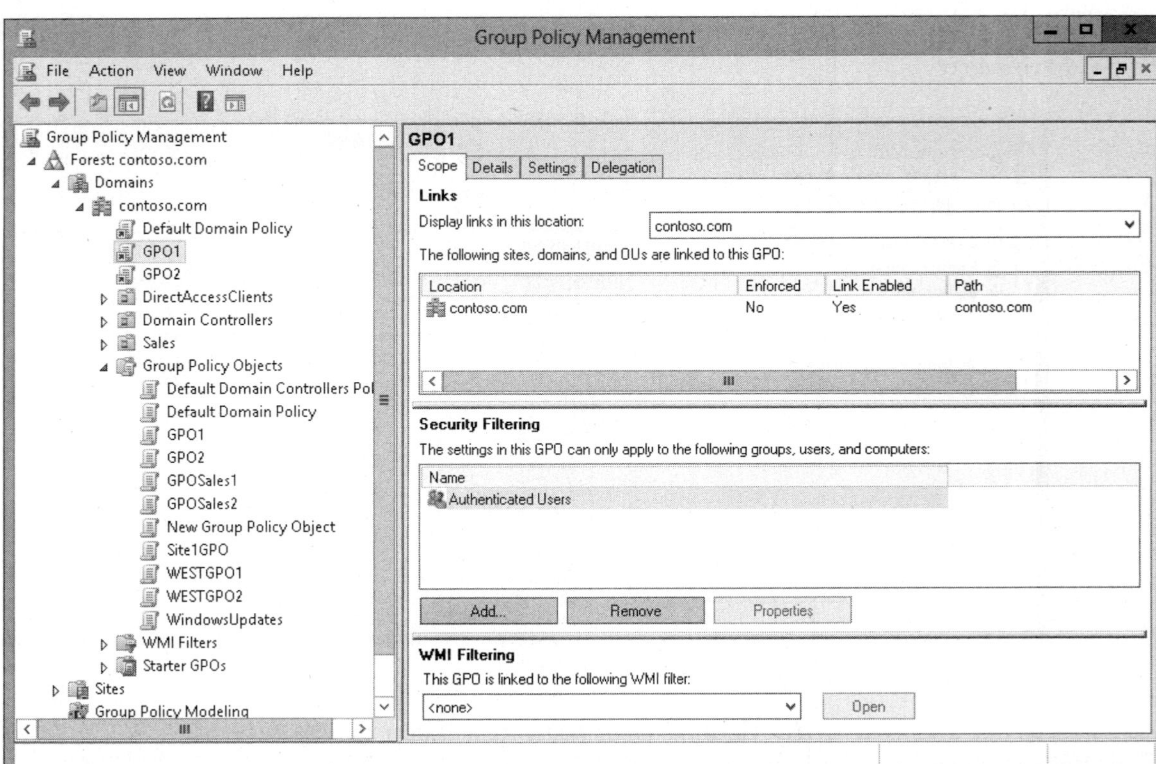

- To delete a link to a container for a GPO without deleting the GPO, you can right-click the GPO for a container and click *Delete*. When it asks whether you want to delete the link, you click *OK*.
- Alternatively, you can disable the link or delete a link for a container by right-clicking the container in the Scope tab and clicking the *Link Enabled* option or the *Delete Link(s)* option, respectively.

You can disable the user configuration settings, computer configuration settings, or both settings by right-clicking the GPO under the Group Policy Objects and select *GPO Status* (see Figure 19-5). You can then choose the appropriate option. However, note that when you change the GPO status, it affects all containers that the GPO is linked to.

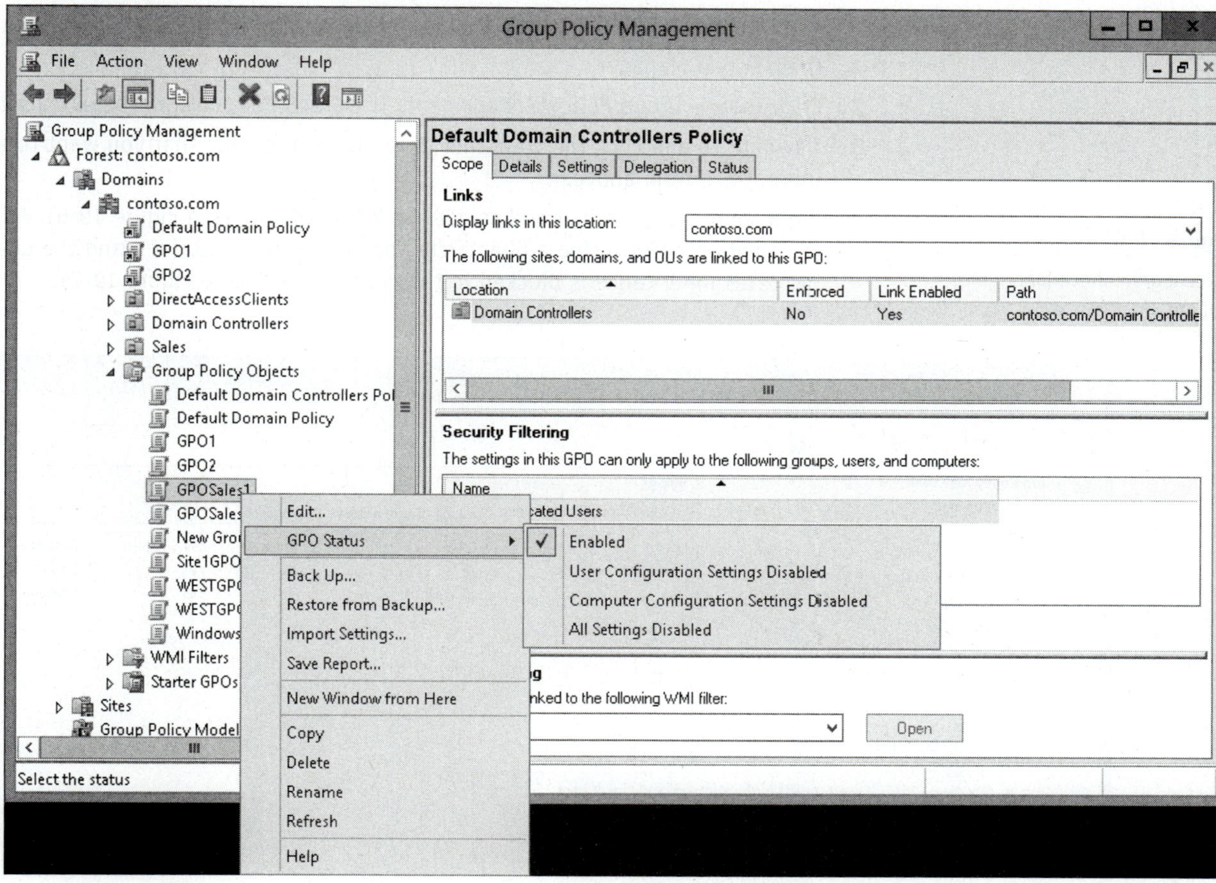

Figure 19-5

Configuring the GPO status

Using Filtering with Group Policies

As mentioned previously, group policies flow down from the upper containers to the lower objects. However, you might want to define a group policy and not want them to be overwritten by other GPOs, or you might not want the GPO to flow down to lower containers.

The exceptions to the processing of group policies can be modified with the following options:

- Block policy inheritance
- Enforce option

CONFIGURING BLOCKING OF INHERITANCE

CERTIFICATION READY
Configure blocking of inheritance.
Objective 6.1

By default, group policies flow down to the lower containers and objects. You can prevent the inheritance of policy settings by blocking all Group Policy settings from the GPOs linked to parent containers in the Group Policy hierarchy. GPOs linked directly to the container and GPOs linked to lower containers are unaffected.

BLOCK THE INHERITANCE OF GPOs

GET READY. To block the inheritance of GPOs, perform the following steps:

1. Open Server Manager.
2. Click Tools > Group Policy Management. The *Group Policy Management console* opens.
3. Navigate to and click the container (site, domain, or OU) that you want to stop inheritance from above.
4. Right-click the container and select Block Inheritance (see Figure 19-6). An exclamation point inside a blue circle appears for the container, and the checkmark indicates inheritance is blocked in the context menu (see Figure 19-7).

Figure 19-6

Selecting the Block Inheritance option

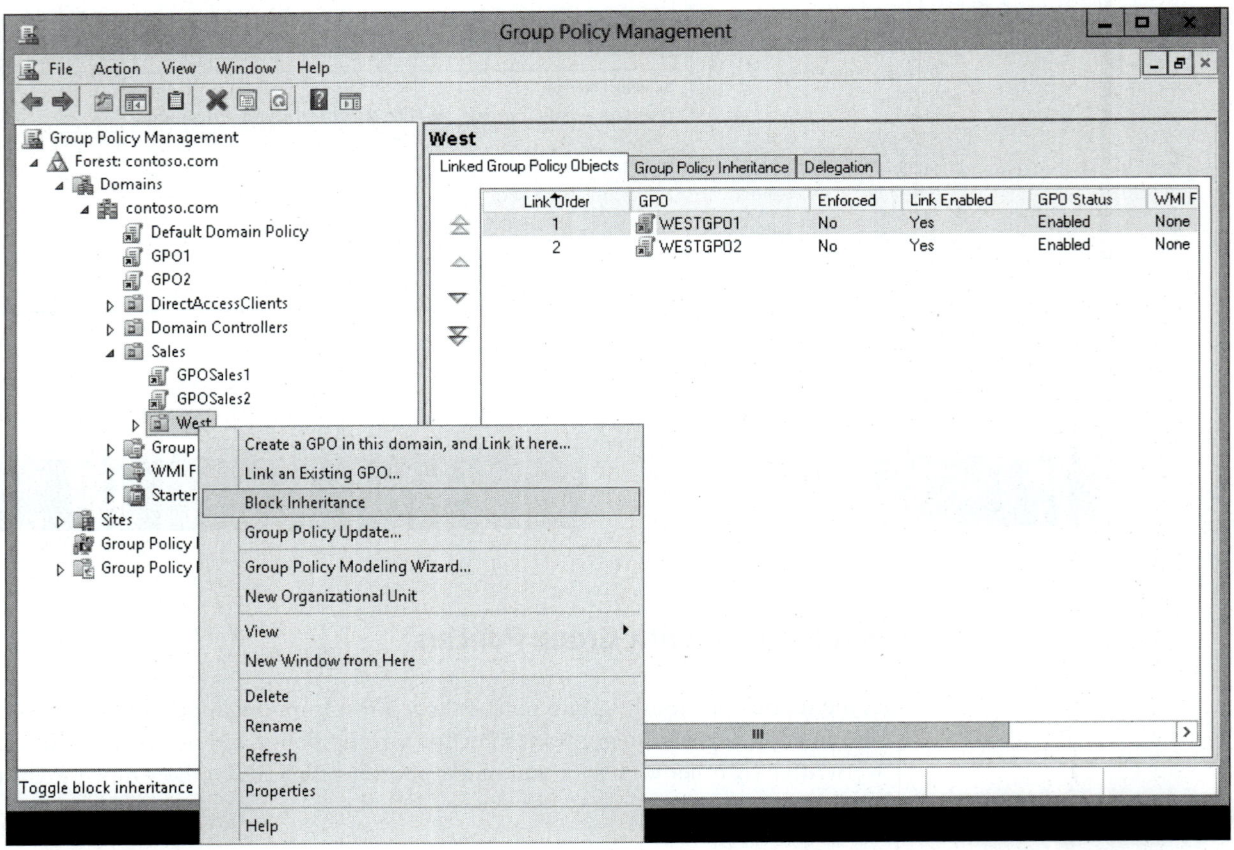

Figure 19-7

Showing that a GPO has the Block Inheritance option enabled

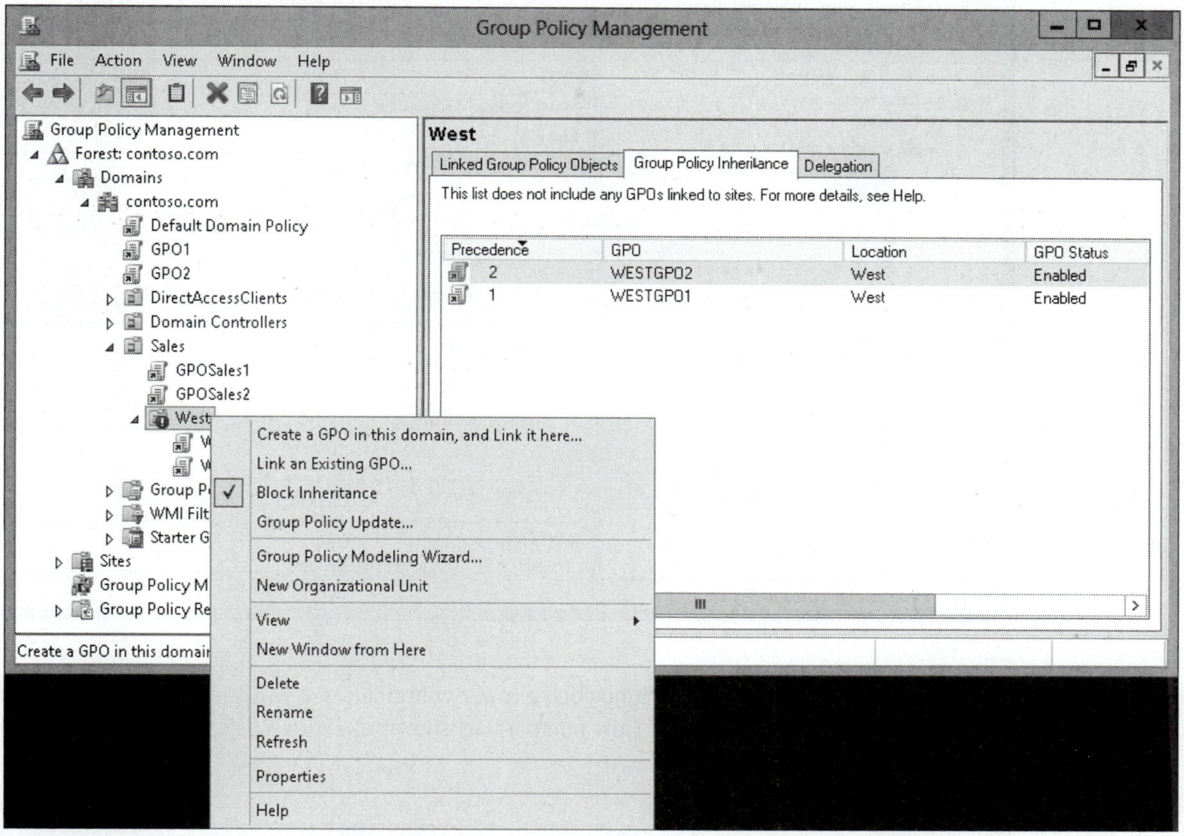

5. Close the *Group Policy Management console*.

You should use block inheritance sparingly. Instead, you can use security group filtering to control what group policies.

CONFIGURING ENFORCED POLICIES

CERTIFICATION READY
Configure enforced policies.
Objective 6.1

Let's say that you want to apply a GPO, and you do not want that GPO to be overridden by a GPO that is executed later. By enforcing a GPO link, the GPO takes the highest precedence, which will prevail over any conflicting policy settings in other GPOs. In addition, an enforced link applies to child containers even when those containers are set to Block Inheritance.

ENFORCE A GPO

GET READY. To enforce a GPO, perform the following steps:

1. Open Server Manager.
2. Click Tools > Group Policy Management. The *Group Policy Management console* opens.
3. Navigate to and click the GPO in the desired container.
4. Right-click the GPO and click Enforced (see Figure 19-8).

Figure 19-8

Enforcing a GPO

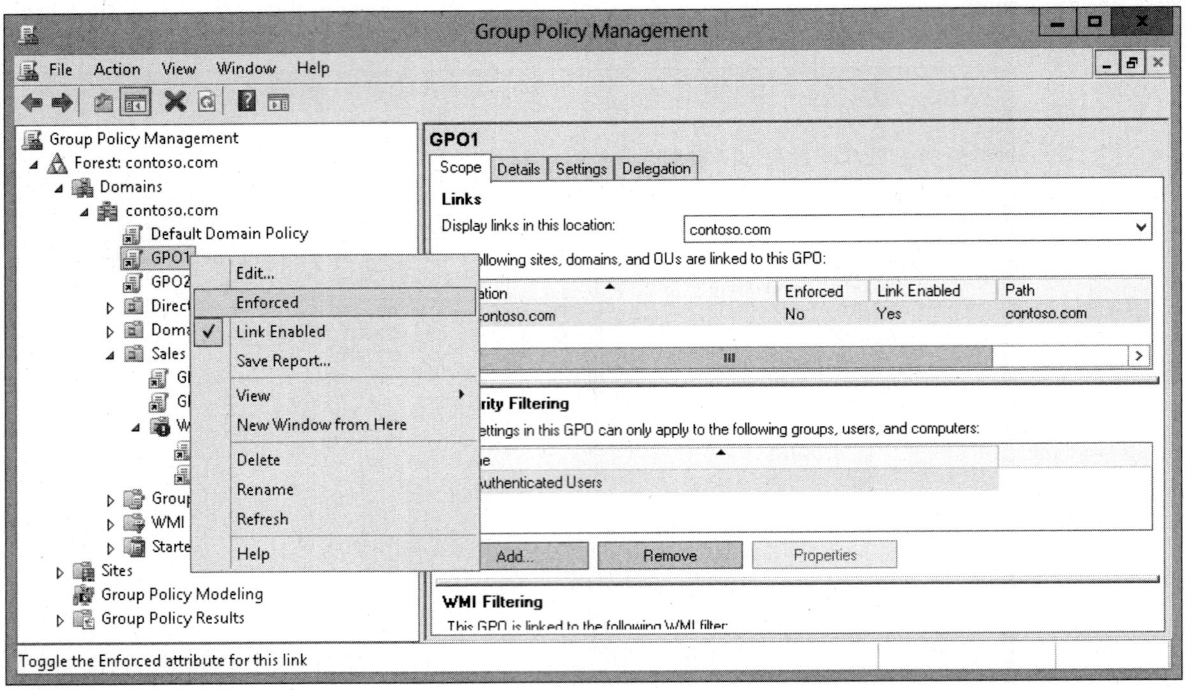

5. When you right-click a lower container, you will see that the enforced GPO has a high precedence (low number), as shown in Figure 19-9.

Figure 19-9

Showing the effect of enforcing a GPO

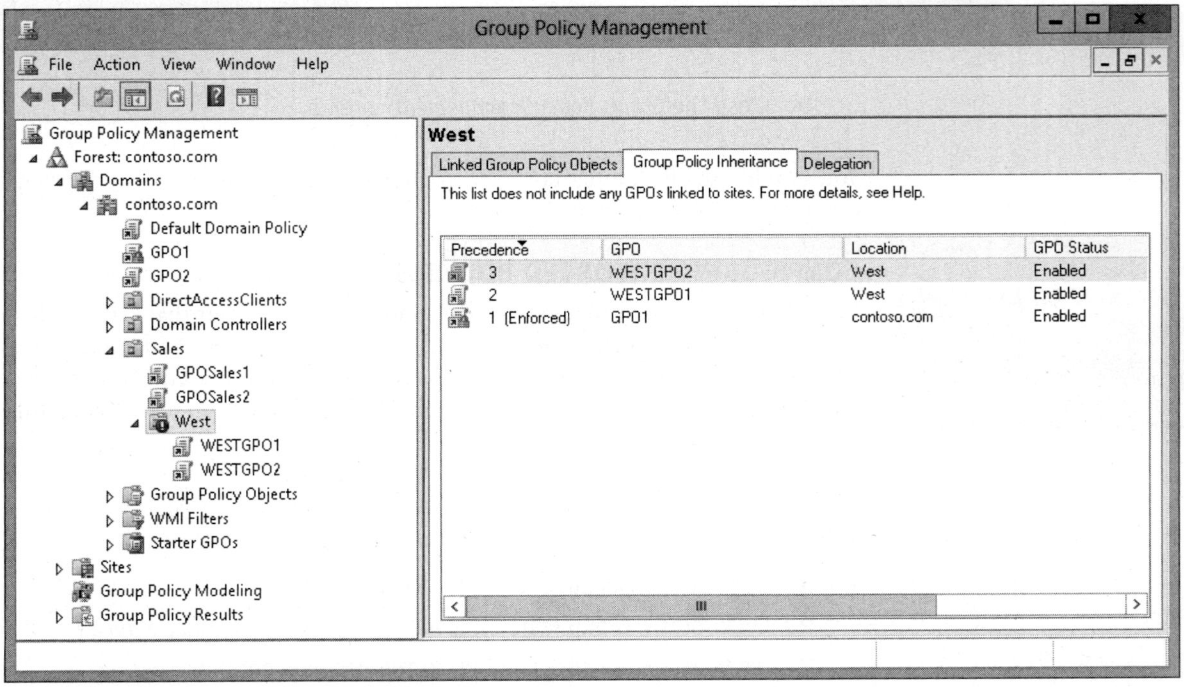

6. Close the *Group Policy Management console*.

Configuring Security Filtering and WMI Filtering

By default, Group Policy settings are applied to all child objects within the container to which they are linked to. Although you need to organize your OUs to help you manage your resources, you sometimes need to have granular control that allows you to specify which clients (computers and users) that the group policy applies to.

CERTIFICATION READY
Configure security filtering and WMI filtering.
Objective 6.1

To give you granular control of whom or what receives a group policy, you can use the following filters:

- **Security group filtering:** Uses a security access list (ACL) to determine who can modify or read a policy and who or what a GPO is applied to.
- **WMI filtering:** Uses the WMI Query Language (WQL) to control who or what a GPO is applied to.

USING SECURITY FILTERING

Security group filtering specifies which users, computers, or groups based on ACL receive a GPO. For example, let's say you have a GPO that locks down a computer so that the user cannot access certain Control Panel applets on his or her computer. However as an administrator, or technical support person, a user might need to have access to those applets to perform his or her job, reconfigure a system, or troubleshoot a problem. Therefore, you can use security group filtering to apply to some and not others.

For a user to receive GPO settings, a user must have Allow Read and Allow Apply Group Policy permissions to the GPO. By default, the Authenticated Users give the Apply Group Policy permissions. To all new GPOs, this means that all users and computers are affected by the container that the GPO is linked to and the user and computer is a member of.

The ways to filtering GPO scopes are to perform one of the following:

- Remove the Allow Apply group policy permissions to a group such as Authenticated Users.
- Remove the Authenticated Users group access control entry (ACE), add other groups or user, and assign the Allow Apply group policy permissions.
- Add ACE for another group, user, or computer assign the Deny Apply group policy permissions. Similar to NTFS permissions, the Deny settings always supersede any Allow settings that are granted to a user through member to another group or the user directly.

Although the Domain Admins group has Full Control permissions to a GPO, the Domain Admins are not directly assigned the Apply group policy permission. Instead, the Domain Admins receive the Allow Apply group policy that is assigned to the Authenticated Users group. The Allow Full Control permission for a GPO allows the group or user to manage the GPO.

CONFIGURE A SECURITY GROUP FILTERING

GET READY. To configure a security group filtering, perform the following steps:

1. Open Server Manager.
2. Click Tools > Group Policy Management. The *Group Policy Management console* opens.
3. Navigate and click the GPO you want to modify.

4. Click the Delegation tab (see Figure 19-10) and click Advanced. The *GPO Security Settings* dialog box opens (see Figure 19-11).

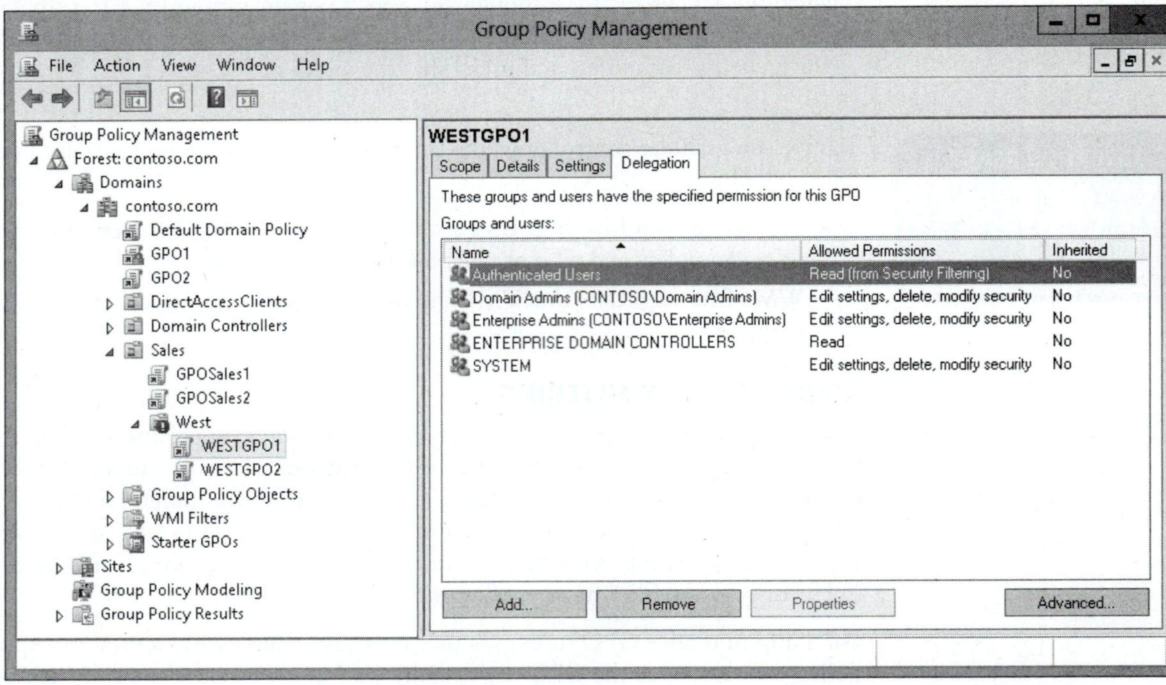

Figure 19-10

Showing current groups and users that permissions to a GPO

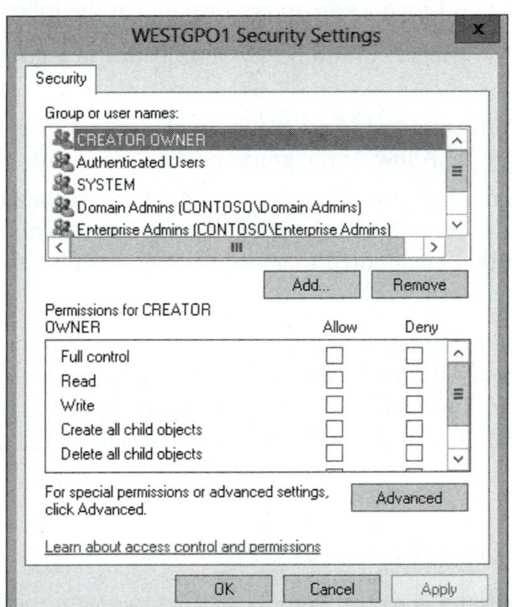

Figure 19-11

Showing the ACL for a GPO

5. If the Administrators group is not listed in the *Group or User Names* window, click Add and type Administrators in the *Enter Object Names to Select* dialog box. Click OK.
6. Make sure that Administrators is selected. Then click the Deny checkbox for the Apply Group Policy permission (see Figure 19-12).

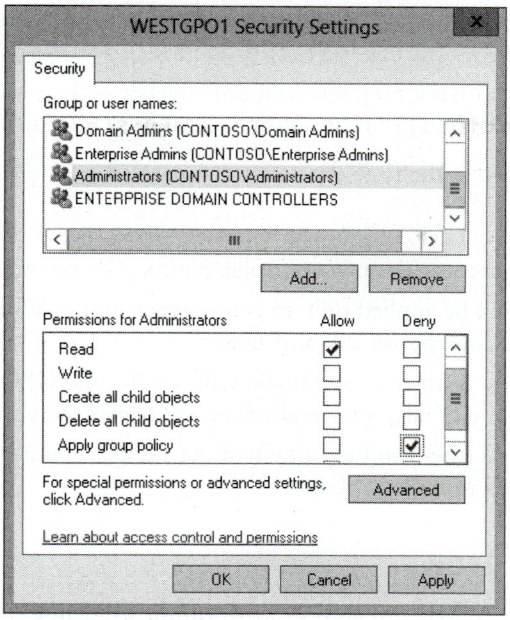

Figure 19-12

Clicking the Deny Apply Group Policy permission

7. Click OK to close the *GPO Security Settings* dialog box. When it states that Deny entries take precedence and asks whether you want to continue, click Yes.
8. Close the *Group Policy Management console*.

Unfortunately, when you exclude a group, the exclusion is not shown in the Security Filtering section of the Scope tab. Instead, you need to use the Advanced options to see the Deny permissions. Because it cannot be easily seen, it is recommended to use the Deny permissions sparingly.

USING WMI FILTERING

Windows Management Instrumentation (WMI) is a component that extends the Windows Driver Model to provide an interface to the operating system to provide information and notification on hardware, software, operating systems, and services. ***WMI filtering*** configures a GPO to be applied to certain users or computers based on specific hardware, software, operating systems, and services. For example:

- Computers running Windows XP Professional only (`Select * from Win32_OperatingSystem where Caption = " Microsoft Windows XP Professional"`)
- Computers running Windows XP Professional with SP3 only (`Select * from Win32_OperatingSystem WHERE Caption="Microsoft Windows XP Professional" AND CSDVersion="Service Pack 3"`)
- Computers that are 32-bit machines only (`Select * from Win32_Processor where AddressWidth ='32'`)
- Computers that have 500 MB free item installed (`SELECT * FROM Win32_LogicalDisk WHERE (Name = " C:") AND DriveType = 3 AND FreeSpace > 500000000 AND FileSystem = " NTFS"`)
- A certain type of computer, such as a Toshiba Tecra 800 or 810 (`Select * from Win32_ComputerSystem where manufacturer = "Toshiba" and Model = "Tecra 800" OR Model = "Tecra 810"`)
- A certain software package (MSIPackage1 or MSIPackage2) installed (`Select * from Win32_Product where name = "MSIPackage1" OR name = "MSIPackage2"`)

- A mobile computer based on the presence of a battery (`Select * from Win32_Battery WHERE (BatteryStatus <> 0)`
- A computer that has a ping low round trip delay, such as less than 3 ms (`Select * from PingProtocolStatus where address = 'Server1' AND hops < 3)`

The filter is evaluated at the time the policy is processed.

To use WMI filters:

- You need to have one domain controller running Windows Server 2003 or higher.
- WMI filters will be applied only to computers running Windows XP Professional or newer, or Windows Server 2003 or newer.
- All filter criteria must have an outcome of true for the GPO to be applied. Any criteria with an outcome of false after evaluation will negate the application of the GPO.
- Only one WMI filter can be configured per GPO. After a WMI filter has been created, it can be linked to multiple GPOs.

USE WMI WITH GPOs

GET READY. To use WMI with a GPO, perform the following steps:

1. Open Server Manager.
2. Click Tools > Group Policy Management. The *Group Policy Management console* opens.
3. Navigate to and click the WMI filters. Figure 19-13 shows the WMI Filters folder.

Figure 19-13

Opening the WMI Filters node

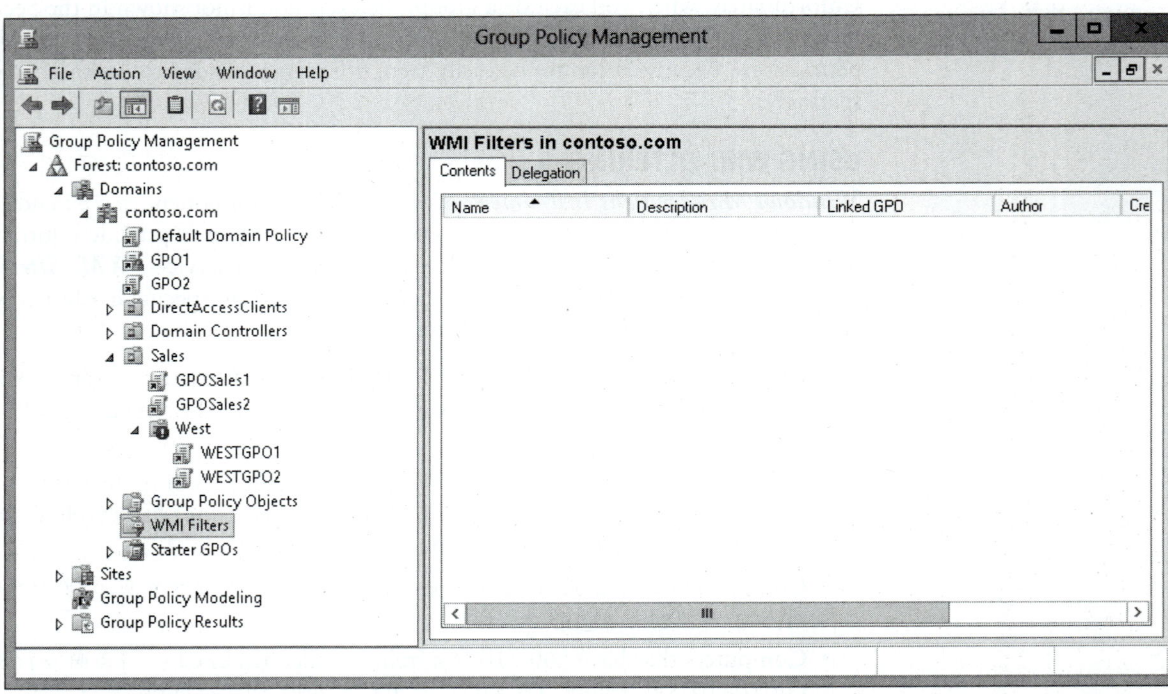

4. Right-click the WMI Filters node and click New. The *New WMI Filter* dialog box opens (see Figure 19-14).

Figure 19-14

Opening the New WMI Filter dialog box

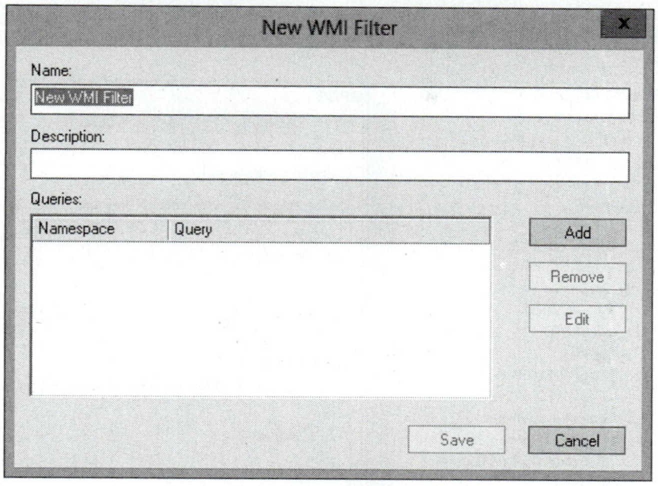

5. In the *Name and Description* fields, enter a name and description for the new WMI filter.
6. In the *Queries* section, click Add. The *WMI Query* dialog box opens (see Figure 19-15).

Figure 19-15

Opening the WMI Query dialog box

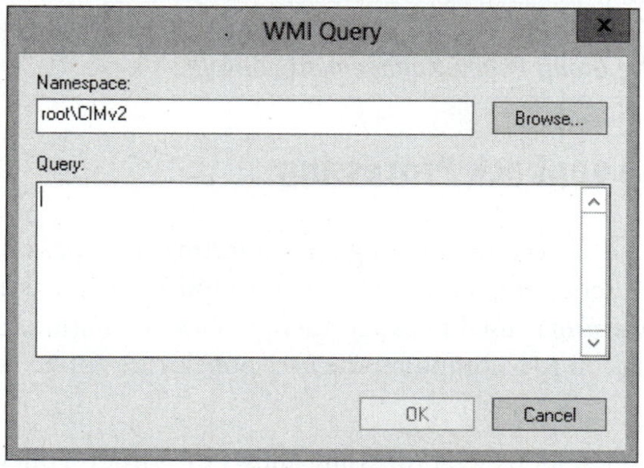

7. Enter the desired query information and click OK to close the *WMI Query* dialog box.
8. Click Save to create the WMI filter.
9. Navigate to the *Group Policy Objects* node and click the GPO to be assigned the WMI filter.
10. On the Scope tab, select the name of the WMI filter you just created from the WMI Filtering drop-down box (see Figure 19-16). Click Yes to confirm your changes.

Figure 19-16

Opening the WMI Query dialog box

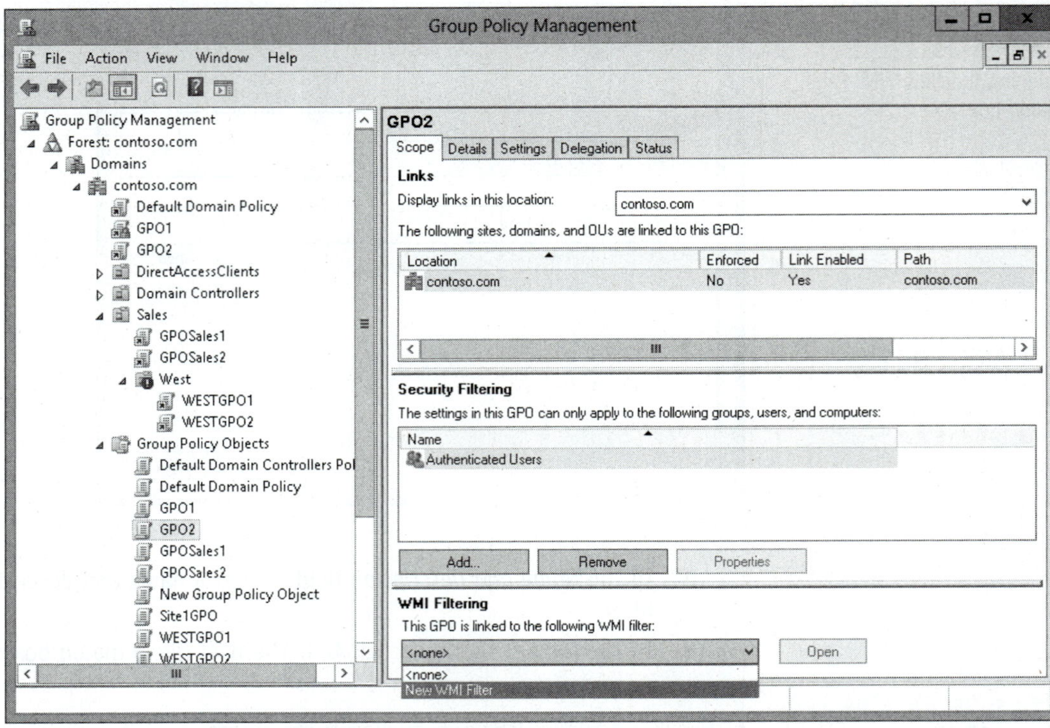

11. Close the *Group Policy Management console*.

Configuring Loopback Processing

As you recall, GPO computer configuration settings are applied when a computer starts up, and GPO user configuration settings are applied when a user logs on. Group Policy ***loopback processing*** is used to assign user policies to computer objects. Therefore, no matter who logs on to a computer, the user policies are applied to the computer.

CERTIFICATION READY
Configure loopback processing.
Objective 6.1

As the name implies, loopback processing allows the Group Policy processing order to circle back and reapply the computer policies after all user policies and logon scripts run. It is intended to keep the configuration of the computer the same regardless of who logs on.

The loopback policy is enabled using the Group Policy Management Editor, specifically the Computer Configuration\Policies\Administrative Templates\System\Group Policy\Configure user Group Policy Loopback processing mode (see Figure 19-17). After you enable the setting, you have two modes to choose from that specify the loopback processing mode:

- ***Replace mode:*** The user settings defined in the computer's GPO replace the user settings normally applied to the user. The Replace mode is useful in a situation such as a kiosk, classroom, or public library, where users should receive a standard configuration.
- ***Merge mode:*** The user settings defined in the computer's GPOs and user settings normally applied to the user are combined. If the settings conflict, the user settings in the computer's GPO take precedence over the user's normal settings. This mode is useful to apply additional settings to users' typical configurations, such as mapping additional printers, replacing the wallpaper on a computer, or disabling certain applications or devices in a conference room or reception area.

Figure 19-17

Configuring the Group Policy loopback processing mode

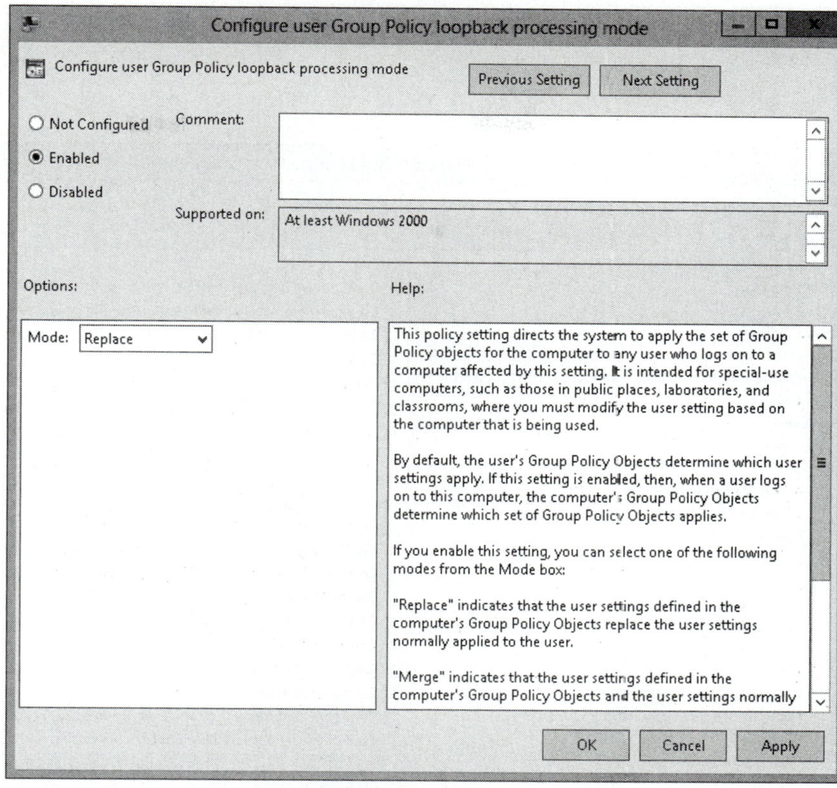

For computers that are shared by more than one user (such as a kiosk, classroom, or public library), you can use the Replace option to reduce the need to undo actions that are applied by the settings for the user logging on.

Configuring Client-Side Extension Behavior

Group policies are client driven, which means that the Group Policy client pulls the GPOs from the domain, which triggers processes called ***client-side extensions (CSEs)*** that interrupt the settings in a GPO and make the changes to the local computer or the currently logged-on user.

CERTIFICATION READY
Configure client-side extension (CSE) behavior.
Objective 6.1

Each major category of policy setting has CSEs. For example, the Security CSE applies security changes, while the script CSE applies startup and logon scripts. Each version of Windows has added CSEs to extend the functional reach of Group Policy. Figure 19-18 shows some of the CSE that can be configured using group policies.

You can configure the behavior of CSEs by using Group Policy, specifically \Computer Configuration\Policies\Administrative Template\System\Group Policy\. Most CSEs apply settings in a GPO only if that GPO has changed, which reduces the processing that needs to be done. Settings managed by the Security CSE are an important exception to the default policy processing settings. Security settings are reapplied every 16 hours even if a GPO has not changed.

If you open the Configure a particular CSE processing, you can configure the CSE to process the group policies even if the GPO has not changed by selecting the Process even if the Group Policy objects have not changed (see Figure 19-19).

To manually refresh a group policy, you use the GPUpdate command. The `gpupdate /force` command causes the system to reapply all settings in all GPOs scoped to the user or computer, because some policies settings require a logoff or a reboot. For these settings, you can use the `gpupdate /force /logoff /boot`.

Figure 19-18

Displaying some of the client-side extensions that are available

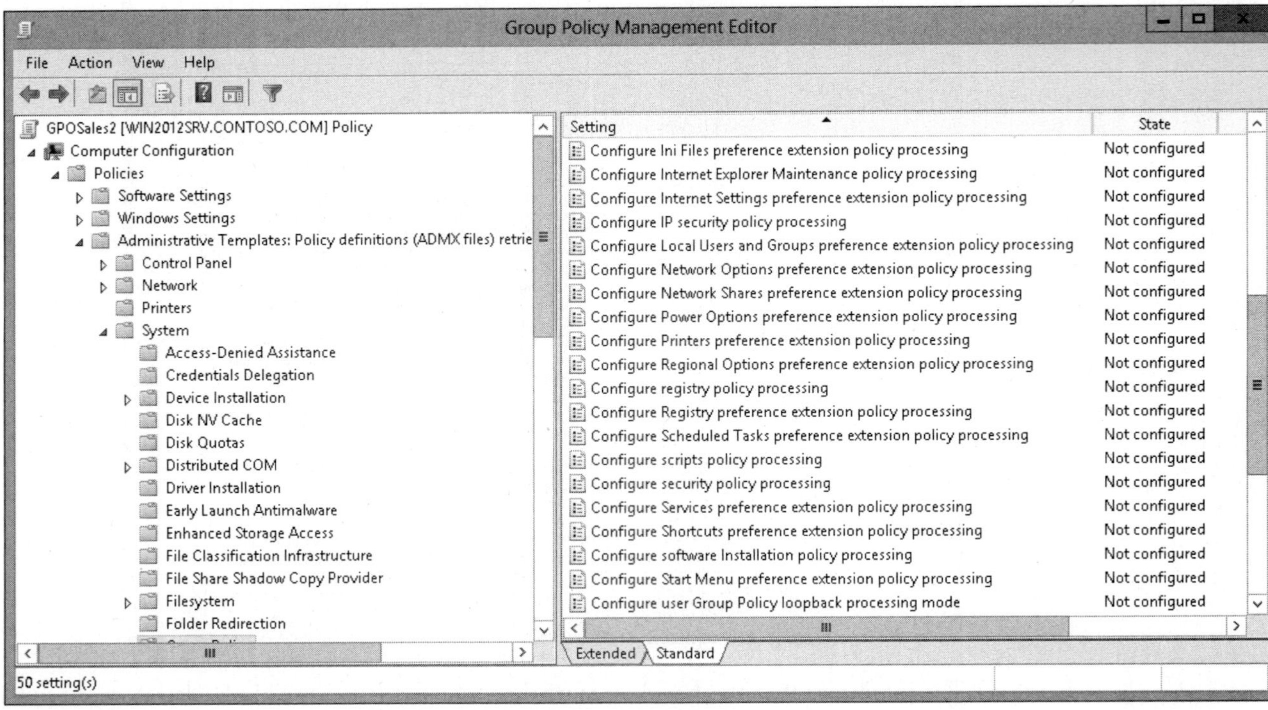

Figure 19-19

Configuring scripts policy processing

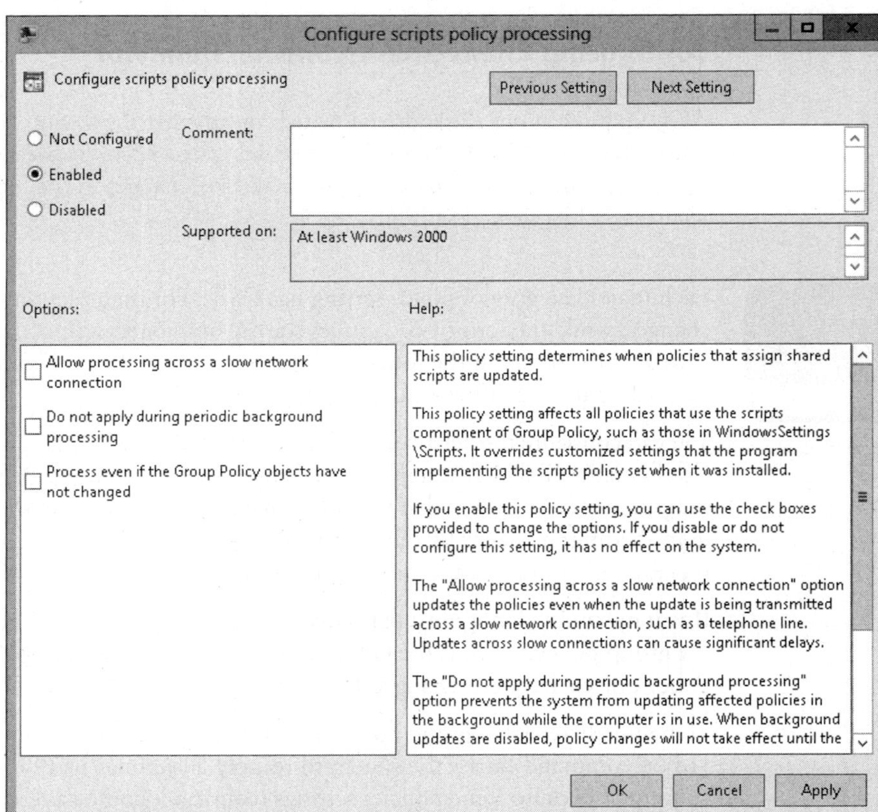

Starting with Windows 8 and Windows Server 2012, you can remotely refresh Group Policy settings for all computers in an OU using the Group Policy Management console or by using the Windows PowerShell `Invoke-GPUpdate` cmdlet. To refresh Group Policy settings using the Group Policy Management console, right-click the OU and select *Group Policy Update*. While you will not able to refresh policies on the Computer OU, you can refresh policies with the `Invoke-GPUpdate` cmdlet.

LOOKING AT GPOs AND DISCONNECTED COMPUTERS

If a computer is disconnected from the network, the settings previously applied by Group Policies continue to take effect. If you are not connected to the network, logon, logoff, and shutdown scripts will not run, because they might rely on other servers to execute.

CONFIGURING AND MANAGING SLOW-LINK PROCESSING

CERTIFICATION READY
Configure and manage slow-link processing.
Objective 6.1

Sometimes when using group policies to perform certain tasks, group policies being executed over slow network links can affect the performance of the client computer or between a site and the corporate office of a site or the computer being configured via a GPO. By default, a link is considered slow if the link is less than 500 kilobits per second (kbps). You can change the slow-link policy processing behavior of each client-side extension by using policy settings located in Computer Configuration\Policies\Administrative Templates\System\Group Policy. The Configure Group Policy slow-link detection (see Figure 19-20) is used to define what is considered a slow-link connection. You can then use other settings with the Group Policy folder to modify the behavior of client-side extensions such as scripts or software installation so that it does or does not process policies over a slow link.

Figure 19-20
Defining the maximum speed of a slow link

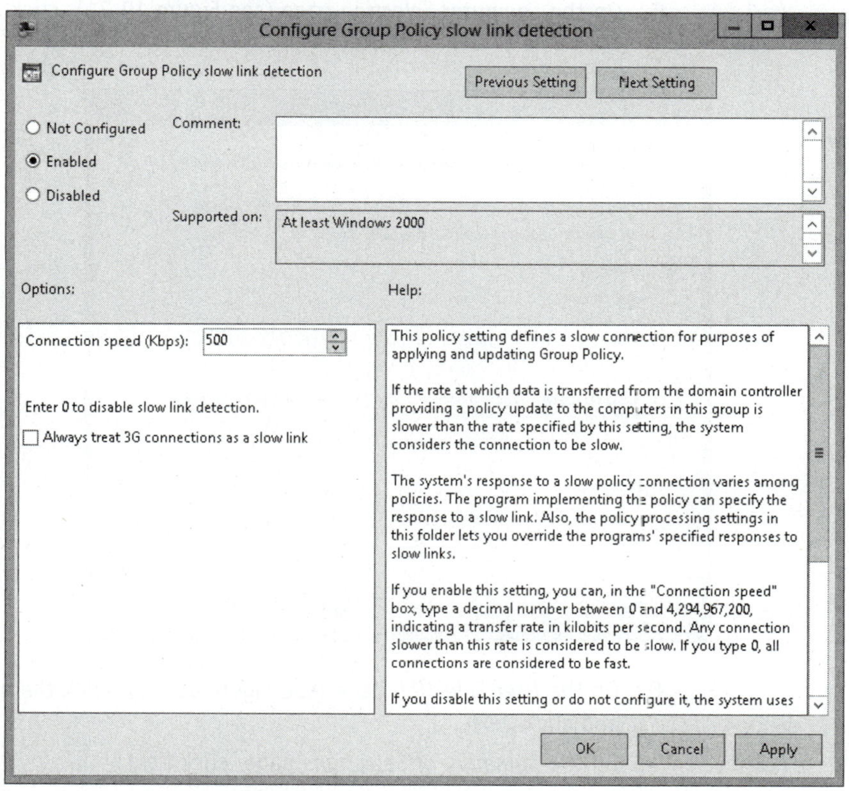

Troubleshooting GPOs

The ***Result Set of Policy (RSoP)*** is the actual policies that are applied to a computer and the user that logs into that computer.

Windows Server 2012 provides the following tools for performing RSoP analysis:

- The Group Policy Results Wizard
- The GPResult.exe command
- The Group Policy Modeling Wizard

To help you analyze the cumulative effect of GPOs and policy settings on a user or computer in your organization, you can run the ***Group Policy Results Wizard***. To run the Group Policy Results Wizard, the following must be true:

- The target computer must be online.
- You must have administrative credentials on the target computer.
- The target computer must run Windows XP or newer.
- WMI must be running on the target computer, and ports 135 and 445 must be available to access WMI on the target computer.

RUN THE GROUP POLICY RESULTS WIZARD

GET READY. To run the Group Policy Results Wizard, perform the following steps:

1. Open Server Manager.
2. Click Tools > Group Policy Management. The *Group Policy Management console* opens.
3. Navigate to and right-click the Group Policy Results and click Group Results Group Policy Results Wizard.
4. When the *Group Policy Results Wizard* starts, click Next.
5. On the *Computer Selection* page (see Figure 19-21), click Another Computer and type the name of the computer in the text box. Click Next.

Figure 19-21

Viewing the *Computer selection* page

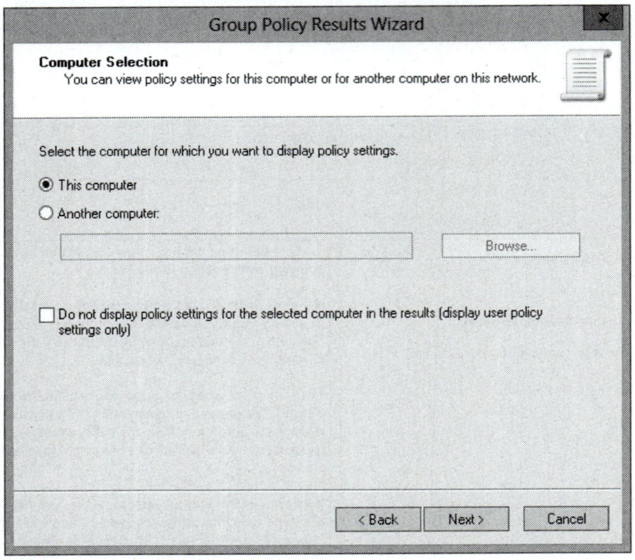

6. On the *User Selection* page (see Figure 19-22), click the user that you want to check, and click Next.
7. On the *Summary of Selections* page, click Next.
8. On the *Completing the Group Policy Results Wizard*, click Finish.
9. Under the *Group Policy Results* node, click the desired user on computer.
10. Click the Details tab. As shown in Figure 19-23, the settings are applied and the GPO where the settings come from. It also displays the applied GPOs and the list of the Denied GPOs.
11. Close the *Group Policy Management console*.

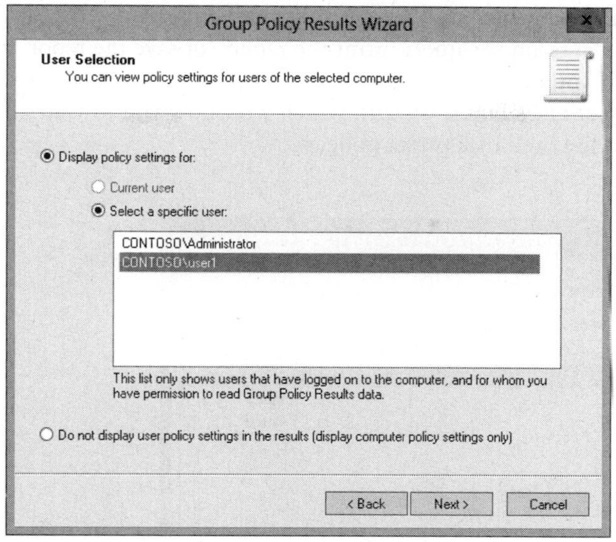

Figure 19-22

Viewing the User Selection page

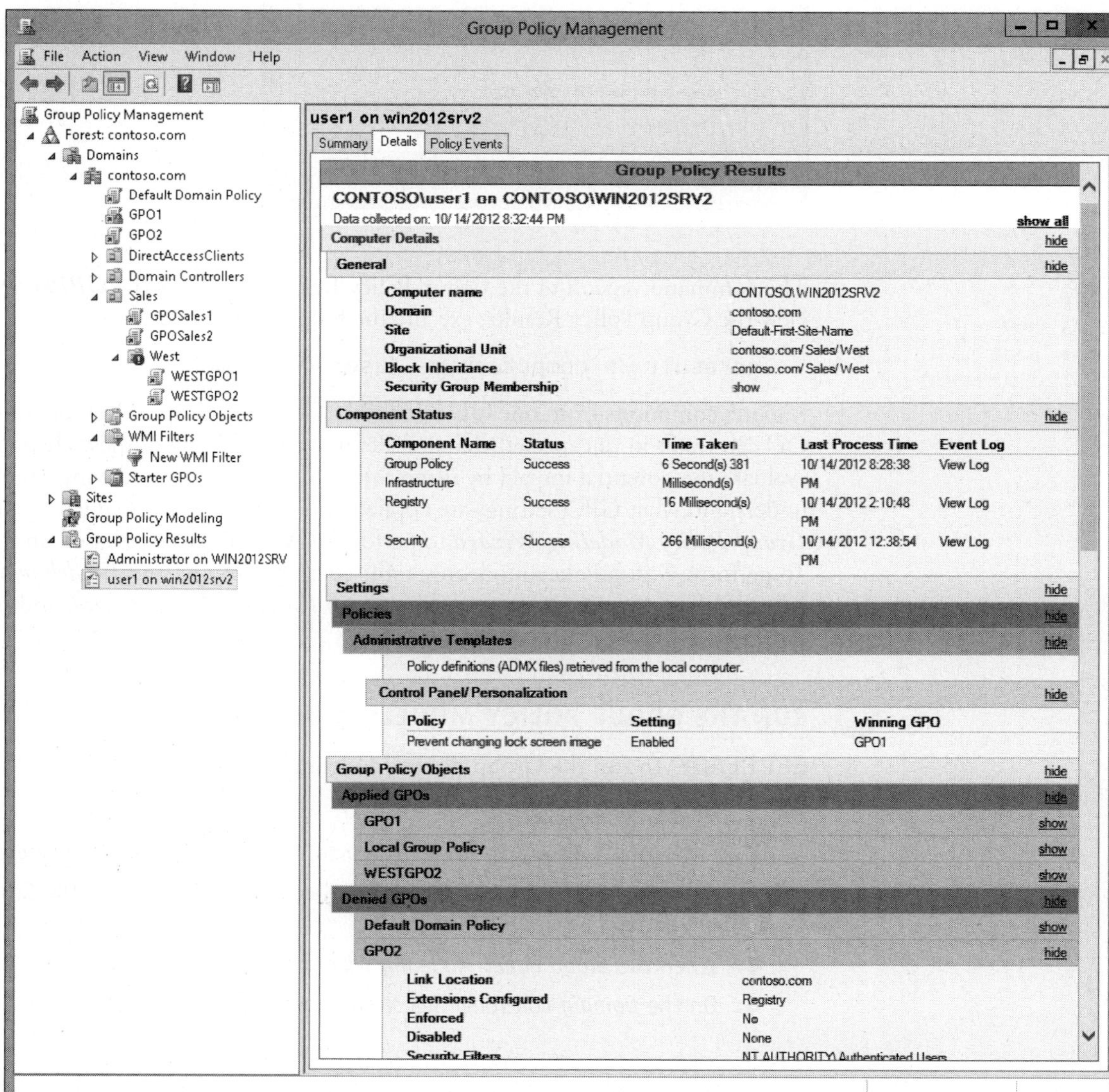

Figure 19-23

Viewing the Details tab for Group Policy Results

After you generate an RSoP report with the Group Policy Results Wizard, you can right-click the report to rerun the query, print the report, or save the report as either an XML file or an HTML. If you open the Action menu and click *Advanced View*, the Resultant Set of Policy snap-in opens (see Figure 19-24), which will allow you to view all applied settings, including IPsec, wireless, and disk quota policies.

Figure 19-24

Using the Resultant Set of Policy console

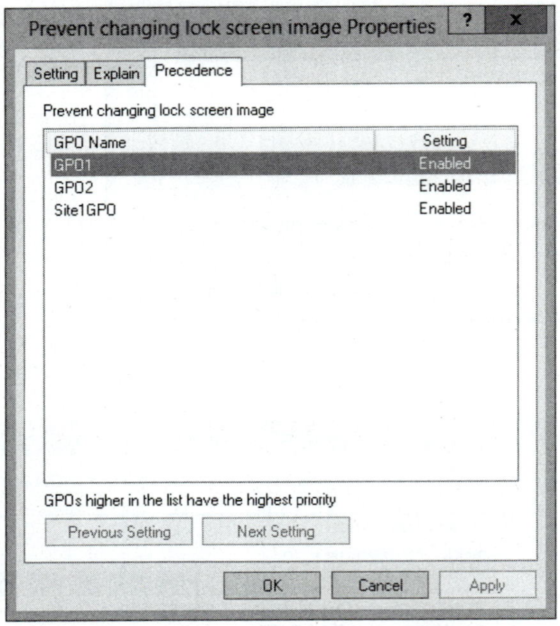

The command version of the Group Policy Results Wizard is the ***GPResult.exe*** command. To view the Group Policy Results, execute the following command:

```
gpresult /s computername /user username /r
```

Moving computers from one OU to another OU, changing a GPO, or adding or removing an OU can result in unexpected changes. Before you make any of these changes, you should evaluate the potential impact by using the RSoP for the user and computer to make sure you understand what GPO settings are applied and where they are applied to, and then use the ***Group Policy Modeling Wizard*** to perform a What-if Analysis based on the desired change. To perform Group Policy modeling, right-click the *Group Policy Modeling* node in the Group Policy Management console tree, click *Group Policy Modeling Wizard*, and then perform the steps in the wizard.

RUN THE GROUP POLICY MODELING WIZARD

GET READY. To run the Group Policy Modeling Wizard, perform the following steps:

1. Open Server Manager.
2. Click Tools > Group Policy Management. The *Group Policy Management console* opens.
3. Navigate to and right-click Group Policy Modeling and click the Group Policy Modeling Wizard.
4. When the *Group Policy Modeling Wizard* starts, click Next.
5. On the *Domain Controller Selection* page (see Figure 19-25), click Next.

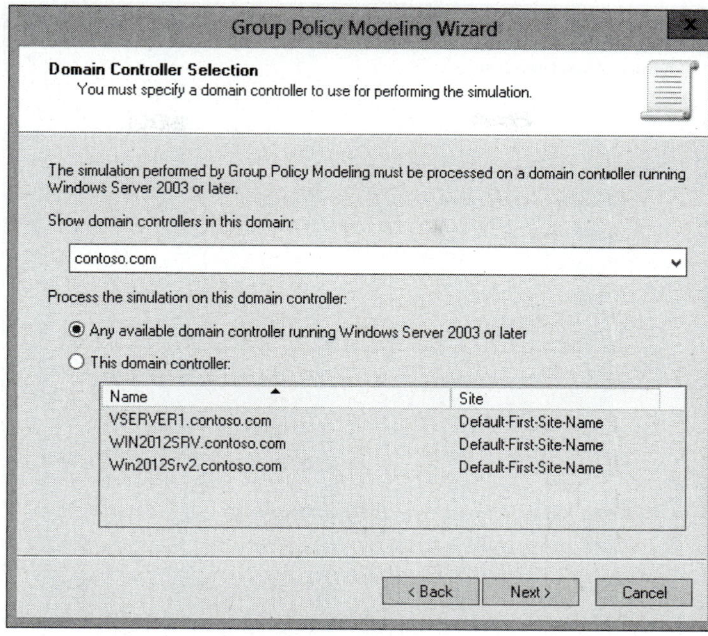

Figure 19-25

Selecting the domain controller

6. On the *User and Computer Selection* page (see Figure 19-26), click Browse in the *User information* section. When the *Choose User Container* dialog box opens, navigate to the OU where you want to place the user and click OK.

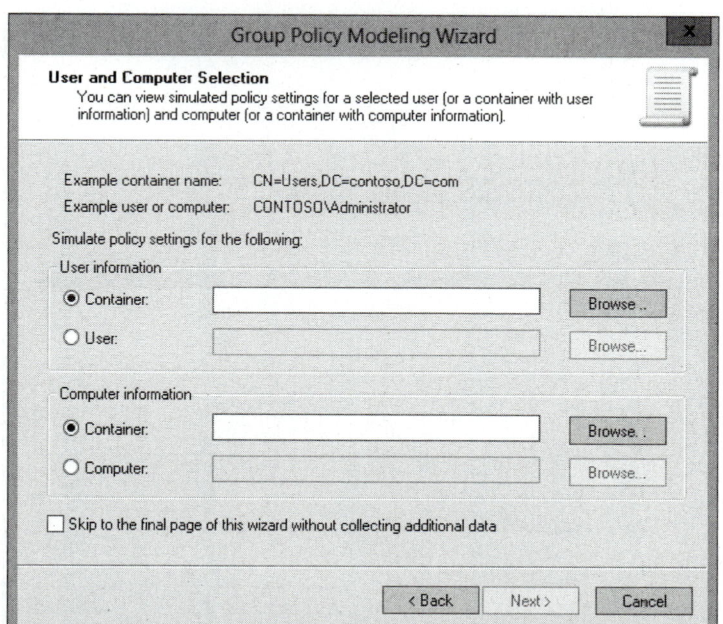

Figure 19-26

Selecting the user and computer to model

7. Click Browse in the *Computer information* section. When the *Choose Computer Container* dialog box opens, navigate to the OU where you want to place the computer and click OK. Click Next.
8. On the *Advanced Simulation Options* page (see Figure 19-27), if desired, select Slow network connection and/or, Loopback processing. You can also specify the site from the pull-down menu. Click Next.

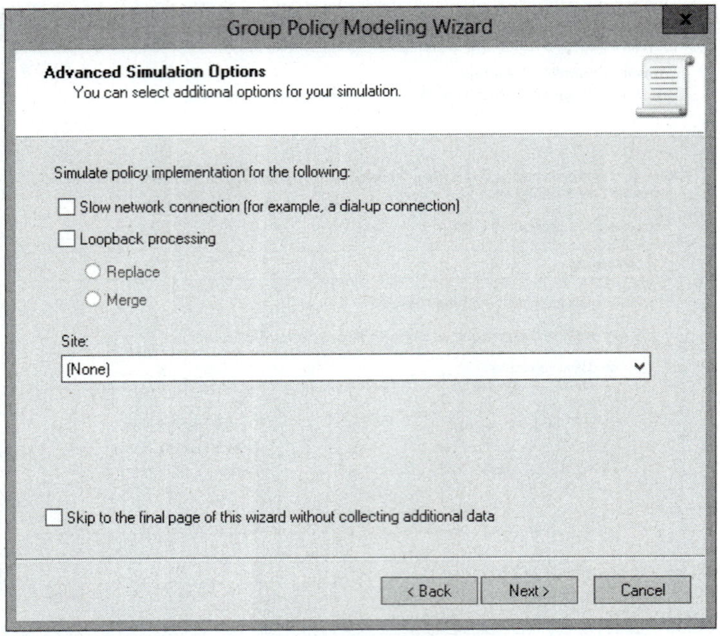

Figure 19-27

Selecting advanced options

9. On the *User Security Groups* page (see Figure 19-28), the current groups for the user is displayed. You can use the Add button to include additional groups, and click a group and use the Remove button to remove the group. Click Next.

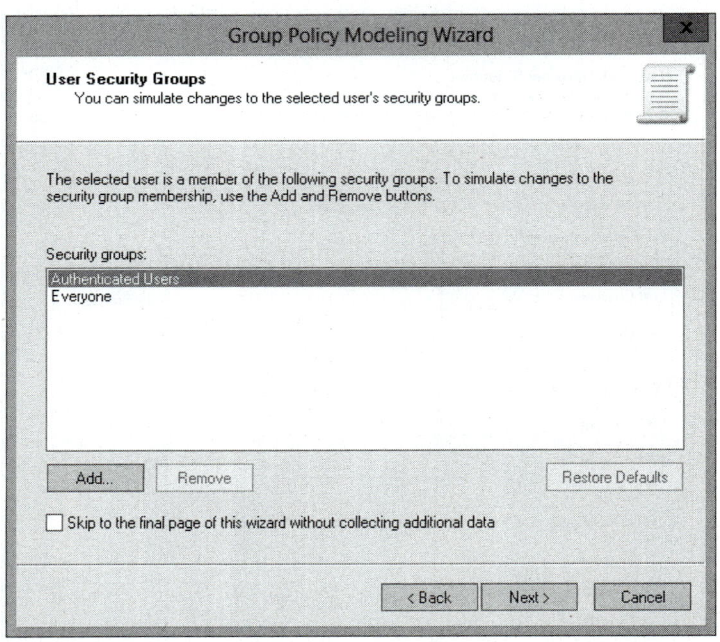

Figure 19-28

Changing the user security groups

10. On the *Computer Security Groups* page (see Figure 19-29), the current groups for the computer is displayed. You can use the Add button to add additional groups, and click a group and use the Remove button to remove the group. Click Next.

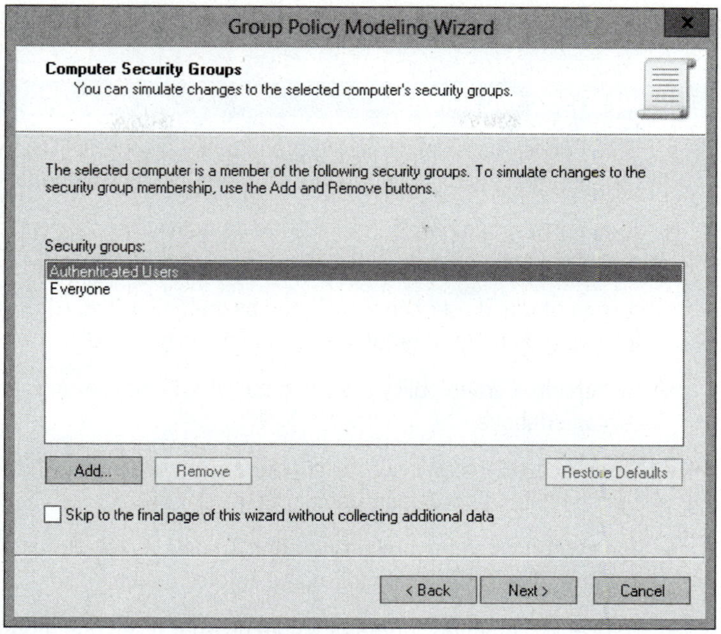

Figure 19-29

Changing the computer security groups

11. On the *WMI Filters for Users* page (see Figure 19-30), you can use All linked filters (default), or you can select Only these filters, use the List Filters button to display the WMI filters that are linked to the GPO, and remove the WMI link. Click Next.

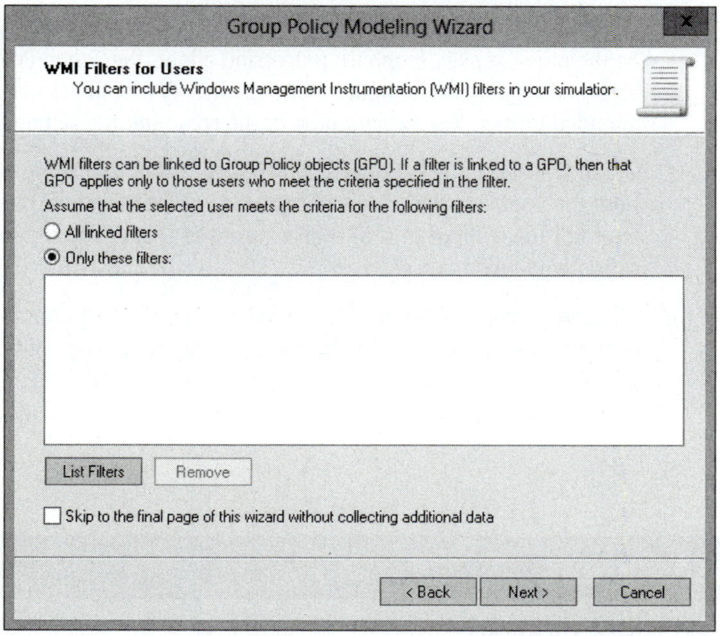

Figure 19-30

Changing the WMI filters used

12. On the *Summary of Selections* page, click Next.
13. When the wizard completes, click Finish.
14. Click the Details tab to view the GPOs and GPO settings that are applied.
15. Close the *Group Policy Management console*.

SKILL SUMMARY

IN THIS LESSON, YOU LEARNED:

- Group policies are defined using group policy objects (GPOs), which are the collection of configuration instructions that are processed by the computer.
- To assign a group policy, it is linked to an Active Directory container (site, domain, or organizational unit).
- A computer and user can be affected by multiple GPOs. GPOs are processed in the following order: local group policy, site, domain, and OU.
- By default, a group policy uses inheritance, whereas settings are inherited from the container above.
- When Active Directory is installed, there are two domain GPOs created by default: Default Domain Policy and Default Domain Controller Policy.
- The exceptions to the processing of group policies can be modified with the following options: Block policy inheritance and Enforce option.
- To give you granular control of whom or what receives a group policy, you can use security group filtering and WMI filtering.
- Windows Management Instrumentation (WMI) is a component that extends the Windows Driver Model to provide an interface to the operating system to provide information and notification on hardware, software, operating systems, and services.
- WMI filtering configures a GPO to be applied to certain users or computers based on specific hardware, software, operating systems, and services.
- As the name implies, loopback processing allows the Group Policy processing order to circle back and reapply the computer policies after all user policies and logon scripts run. It is intended to keep the configuration of the computer the same regardless of who logs on.
- Group Policies are client driven, which means that the Group Policy client pulls the GPOs from the domain, which triggers processes called client-side extensions (CSEs) that interrupt the settings in a GPO and make the changes to the local computer or the currently logged-on user.
- Windows Server 2012 provides the following tools for performing RSoP analysis: the Group Policy Results Wizard, the GPResult.exe command, and the Group Policy Modeling Wizard.

■ Knowledge Assessment

Multiple Choice

Select the correct answer for each of the following questions.

1. What are the two default group policies that are already created in Active Directory? (Choose two answers)
   a. Default Domain Controller Policy
   b. Default Computer profile
   c. Default User Profile
   d. Default Domain Policy

2. GPOs are assigned to users by which of the following?
   a. Being linked to a container in Active Directory
   b. Being assigned to a security group
   c. Being assigned to the user
   d. Being assigned to a computer

3. You assign a GPO at the domain. How do you ensure that it is not overridden by another GPO?
   a. Use a block policy inheritance.
   b. Use the Enforce option.
   c. Use loopback.
   d. Use the No override option.

4. You have 20 users assigned to an OU. You want 10 of those users to be affected by a GPO and 10 others not to be affected by a GPO. What should you do?
   a. Use a block policy inheritance.
   b. Use an enforce list.
   c. Use a security filter.
   d. Use a group assignment.

5. Which do you use if you want to apply a group policy that affects only laptops?
   a. WMI filtering
   b. Security group filtering
   c. Enforce options
   d. loopback option

6. How many WMI filters can you configure per GPO?
   a. One per GPO
   b. One per GPO setting
   c. Four
   d. Unlimited

7. Which two modes are used in loopback processing?
   a. Enforce mode
   b. Replace mode
   c. No bar mode
   d. Merge mode

8. Which command is used to force a computer to download GPO settings after a GPO has been modified?
   a. `gpdownload /force`
   b. `gpdownload /now`
   c. `gpresults /now`
   d. `gpupdate /force`

9. By default, what speed is considered a slow link when using slow-link processing?
   a. 128 kbps
   b. 500 kbps
   c. 512 kbps
   d. 1,024 kbps

10. Which tool is used to order GPO precedence when assigning multiple GPOs to an OU?
    a. Group Policy Editor
    b. Group Policy Management console
    c. Active Directory Users and Computers
    d. GPResults.exe

Best Answer

Choose the letter that corresponds to the best answer. More than one answer choice may achieve the goal. Select the BEST answer.

1. What do you call settings that flow from one container to a child container?
   a. Filtering
   b. Enforcement
   c. Loopback
   d. Inheritance

2. What happens when you have two GPOs assigned to the same OU?
   a. The GPO that was created first has higher precedence.
   b. The GPO that was created last has higher precedence.
   c. The GPO with the lowest priority number assigned has higher precedence.
   d. The GPO with the highest priority number assigned has higher precedence.

3. What tool is best to determine which GPO is assigning a particular GPO setting?
   a. Group Policy Results Wizard
   b. Group Policy Modeling Wizard
   c. Gpupdate.exe
   d. Group Policy Editor

4. Which GPO is best to assign auditing of domain users logging in using his or her domain account?
   a. Default Domain Policy
   b. Default Domain Controller Policy
   c. An OU GPO
   d. Default Site Policy

5. You create a Server OU. You want to isolate the Server OU so that it will not be affected by any of the domain GPOs. What should you do?
   a. Use the enforce option.
   b. Use block policy inheritance.
   c. Use a WMI filter.
   d. Use a security group filter.

Matching and Identification

1. Which of the following are client-side extensions?
   _______ a) security
   _______ b) Internet Settings
   _______ c) registry
   _______ d) FAT
   _______ e) scripts
   _______ f) Active Directory
   _______ g) Internet Explorer Maintenance
   _______ h) domain user
   _______ i) folder preferences
   _______ j) EFS recovery
   _______ k) keyboard

Build a List

1. Identify the correct order in which policies are processed? Not all steps will be used.
   _____ Default
   _____ Local group policy
   _____ Template
   _____ OU
   _____ User-Defined
   _____ Site
   _____ Domain

2. Identify the steps in order in which group policies are processed.
   _____ Establishes a secure link between the computer and a domain controller.
   _____ Apply user configuration from GPOs.
   _____ Apply computer configuration from GPOs.
   _____ Displays Login dialog box.
   _____ Obtains a list of user-based GPOs from the client computer.
   _____ Obtains a list of computer-based GPOs for the client computer.
   _____ User logs into system.
   _____ Displays User Desktop

3. Identify the steps in order to use a WMI filter. Not all steps will be used.
   _____ Create the GPO.
   _____ Select the WMI filter.
   _____ Create the WMI filter.
   _____ Link the WMI filter to the OU.
   _____ Link the OU to the WMI.

4. Client-side extensions (CSEs) are managed using a group policy. Identify the path in order with the GPO from top to bottom to the CSE settings.
   _____ Administrative Template
   _____ Administration
   _____ Computer Configuration
   _____ User Configuration
   _____ Windows Security
   _____ GPOs
   _____ Policies
   _____ System
   _____ Group Policy
   _____ CSE

Business Case Scenarios

Scenario 19-1: Placing the GPOs

You are an administrator of the Contoso Corporation. The Contoso Corporation has a domain called *contoso.com*. At the top level, you have the following OUs:

- Sales
- Marketing
- Support
- Manufacturing
- Engineering

Under each OU, you have additional OUs: North, South, East, and West. You need to implement the following GPO settings:

- Have strong passwords and a minimum of eight characters.
- The Sales team should have passwords with a minimum of 10 characters.
- All computers should have the company logo desktop picture, without exception.
- All computers in the Sales OU should have the widget.msi program installed.
- All computers in the Manufacturing and Engineering departments should have the widget2.msi program installed.
- All computers except Support should have the screen saver enabled.

What do you recommend?

Scenario 19-2: Configure a Library Computer

You are setting up a library for the Contoso University. You want to configure the library computer to have a standard desktop screen, color scheme, programs available, and proxy settings. You need to ensure that no matter who logs on, the computer will have the same settings. What should you do?

Configuring Group Policy Settings

LESSON 20

70-411 EXAM OBJECTIVE

Objective 6.2 – Configure Group Policy settings. This objective may include but is not limited to: configure settings, including software installation, folder redirection, scripts, and administrative template settings; import security templates; import custom administrative template files; convert administrative templates using ADMX Migrator; configure property filters for administrative templates.

Lesson Heading	Exam Objective
Configuring Group Policy Settings	Configure Group Policy Settings
Performing Software Installation Using Group Policies	Configure settings including software installation
Using Folder Redirection	Configure settings including folder redirection
Using Scripts with Group Policies	Configure settings including scripts
Using Administrative Templates	Configure settings including administrative template settings
Using Security Templates	Import security templates
Using Custom Administrative Template Files	Import custom administrative template files
Converting Administrative Templates Using ADMX Migrator	Convert administrative templates using ADMX Migrator
Configuring Property Filters for Administrative Templates	Configure property filters for administrative templates

KEY TERMS

ADM files
Administrative Templates
Administrative Templates Property Filters
ADML files
ADMX files
ADMX Migrator
assign software to a computer
assign software to a user
Central Store
folder redirection
logoff script
logon script
Microsoft Software Installation (MSI) file
Microsoft Windows Script Hosts (WSH)
MSI Patch files
MSI Transform files
publish software to a user
script
security template
shutdown script
Software Settings
startup script
Windows Installer
Windows Settings

■ Configuring Group Policy Settings

THE BOTTOM LINE

One of the most powerful tools available with Active Directory is group policies that allow you to control the working environment of the computers and users of the organizations. It provides the centralized management and configuration of operating systems, applications, and user settings.

CERTIFICATION READY
Configure Group Policy settings.
Objective 6.2

There are thousands of settings available with group policies. In addition, as each version of Windows is released, new settings are added to allow administrators to configure new technology that has been added to Windows, give control that was not available previously, or to give more granular control.

As discussed, group policies are broken down to computer settings (contained in the Computer Configuration node) and user settings (contained in the User Configuration node). The ***Computer Configuration*** node contains settings that are applied to the computer regardless of who logs on to the computer. By default, computer settings are applied when the computer is started. ***User Configuration*** node contains settings that are applied when the user logs on. Group policy settings are refreshed every 90 minutes with a random delay of 30 minutes (giving a random range between 90 minutes and 120 minutes). On domain controllers, group policies get refreshed every five minutes.

Starting with Windows Server 2008, the Computer Configuration and User Configuration nodes are divided into Policies and Preferences nodes (see Figure 20-1). Policies include the

Figure 20-1

Viewing the Group Policy Object (GPO) node structure

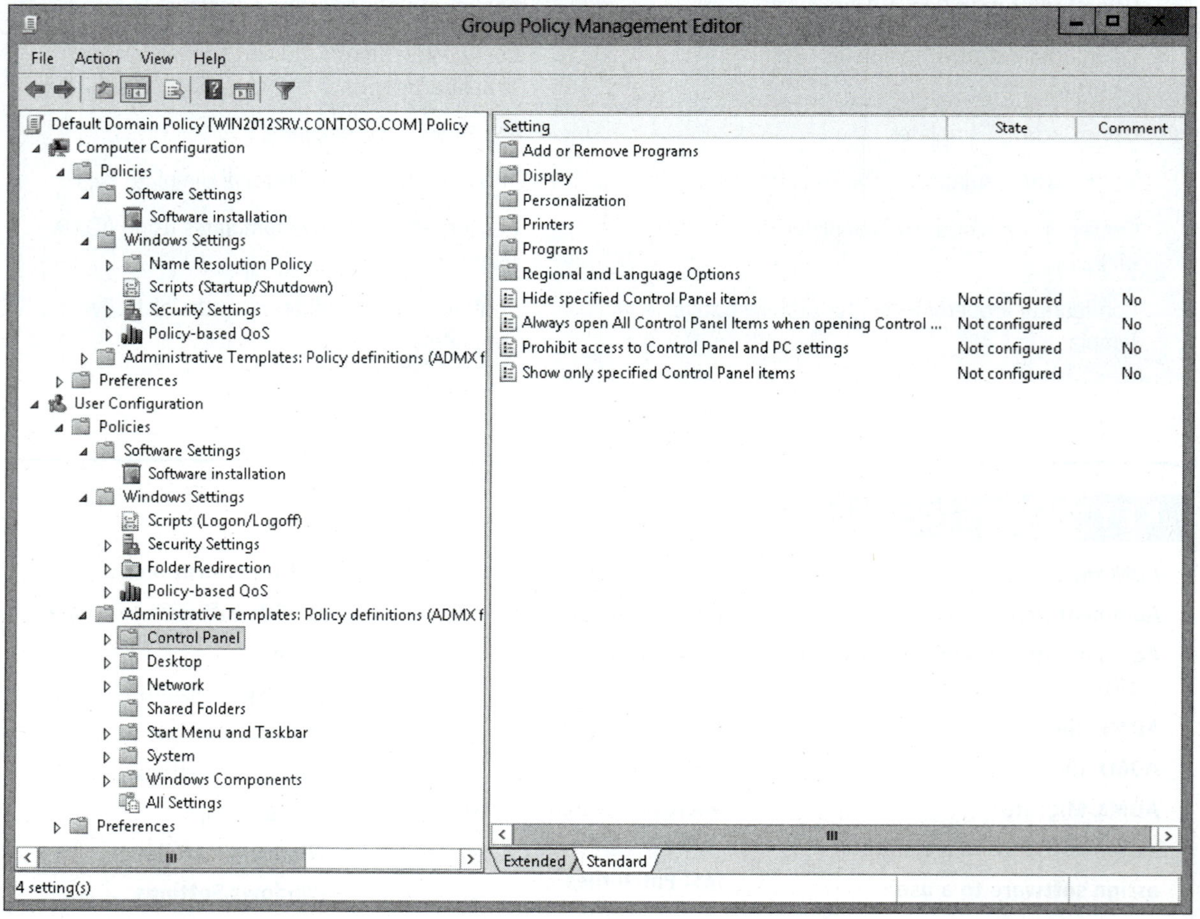

traditional settings that were available with earlier versions of Windows, but also have many new settings that were not available previously. Preferences allow you to configure additional Windows settings that were not available previously and they allow more control on how the settings are applied to the clients. Preferences are discussed in Lesson 22, "Configuring Group Policy Settings."

Computer Configuration\ Policies can be divided into the following nodes:

- ***Software Settings:*** Contains only one node, Software installation, which allows you to install and maintain software within your organization.
- ***Windows Settings:*** Allows you to configure Windows settings, including Name Resolution Policy, Scripts (Startup/Shutdown), Security Settings, and Policy-Based QoS nodes.
- ***Administrative Templates:*** Contains registry-based Group Policy settings that are used to configure the computer environment, such as the Control Panel, Printers, System, and Windows components.

Software Configuration\Policies can be divided into the following nodes:

- **Software Settings:** Contains only one node, Software installation, which allows you to install and maintain software within your organization.
- **Windows Settings:** Allows you to configure Windows settings, including Scripts (Logon/Logoff), Security Settings, Folder Redirection, and Policy-Based QoS nodes.
- **Administrative Templates:** Contains registry-based Group Policy settings that are used to configure the user environment, such as the Control Panel, Printers, System, and Windows components.

Performing Software Installation Using Group Policies

Most experienced Windows users know how to install an application. You insert a CD or DVD in a drive and the application installation automatically starts, or you double-click an installation file (such as file that has an .exe or .msi filename extension). If you need to deploy software to hundreds of computers within your organization can be a chore. However, if all of the computers are connected to a network, you can use group policies to install, manage, and maintain software for your organization.

CERTIFICATION READY
Configure Settings including software installation.
Objective 6.2

The ***Windows Installer*** is a software component used for the installation, maintenance, and removal of software on Windows. The installation information for software is stored in a ***Microsoft Software Installation (MSI) file*** in a database installation file that has an .msi filename extension. Besides performing installation, msi files can be used in self-healing for damaged applications and to remove an application cleanly.

Besides installing MSI files with group policies, you can also install MSI transform files (.mst) and MSI patch files (.msp). ***MSI Transform files*** are used to deploy customized MSI files. For example, you can install Microsoft Office, which consists of multiple applications. You can create a transform file using the Custom Installation Wizard that is included with Microsoft Office so that you can install all the applications except Microsoft Access.

MSI Patch files are used to apply service packs and hot fixes to installed software. Rather than having a complete database found with MSI files, a patch file contains a minimum of a database transform procedure that adds patching information to the target installation package database.

Windows Installer cannot install .exe files. To distribute a software package that installs with an .exe file, you must convert the .exe file to an .msi file by using a third-party utility or you will need to define a ZAP file (file with a .ZAP filename extension). ZAP files are created with a text editor, such as Notepad and they can be only published (not assigned).

ASSIGNING OR PUBLISHING A PACKAGE

To deploy software with group policies, you need to take the following steps:

1. Create a distribution point on the publishing server.
2. Create a GPO to use to distribute the software package.
3. Assign or publish a package to a user or computer.

To create a distribution point on a server, you first create a shared network folder where you will put the Microsoft Windows Installer package and any related files that you need for the installation to succeed. Next, you set permissions on the share to allow access to the distribution package. Then copy or install the package to the distribution point. For most packages, you just copy the installation files to the shared folders. For other packages such as Microsoft Office, you install the software to the distribution point (sometimes referred to as an administrative install), which allows for faster installations and customization. You need to contact the vendor or search the vendor's website to determine whether you should perform an administrative install.

You should next create a separate GPO to deploy the software. By using a separate GPO, you can disable the GPO or delete the GPO, and only the deployment of the software will be affected.

When you deploy the installation via group policies, you can deploy the software to the user or the computer. Software that is installed for a user is not available for other users unless the software is also installed for the other users. When you install to a computer, the software is available to all users.

When you install to a user or computer, you have the option to assign software or publish software:

- ***Assign software to a user:*** The software is available on the user's Start menu when the user logs on. However, the installation does not occur unless the user clicks the application icon on the Start menu or a file that is associated with the application (for example, .docx then installs Microsoft Word) is opened.
- ***Assign software to a computer:*** The application is installed the next time that the computer starts.
- ***Publish software to a user:*** A program shortcut will be available in the Control Panel's Programs applet, or you can configure the application to be installed when a file that is associated with the application is opened.

An application cannot be published to a computer.

When configuring Group Policy to deploy applications, they must be mapped to UNC paths. If you use local paths, the deployment will fail. In addition, you need to be careful where you place the deployment servers and when the deployment will actually occur. Large applications can generate a lot of network traffic, which might affect local traffic and can greatly affect slower WAN links for remote sites. Lastly, assuming that slow link is enabled (which is enabled by default) as discussed in Lesson 19, "Configuring Group Policy Processing," the CSE will not deliver the software over a slow link.

When the software is installed using group policies, which uses the Windows Installer service, the service runs with elevated privileges. Therefore, no matter who is logged onto the system, the software will still be installed as long as the user has read access to the software distribution point.

When software is installed with group policies, the applications are resilient. If an application becomes corrupted, the installer will detect and reinstall or repair the application.

CREATE A NEW SOFTWARE INSTALLATION PACKAGE

GET READY. To create a new Windows Installer Package within a GPO, perform the following steps:

1. Open the Group Policy Management Editor for the GPO you want to configure.
2. Navigate to Software Settings under the *Computer Configuration or User Configuration* node, and open \Policies\Software Settings (see Figure 20-2).

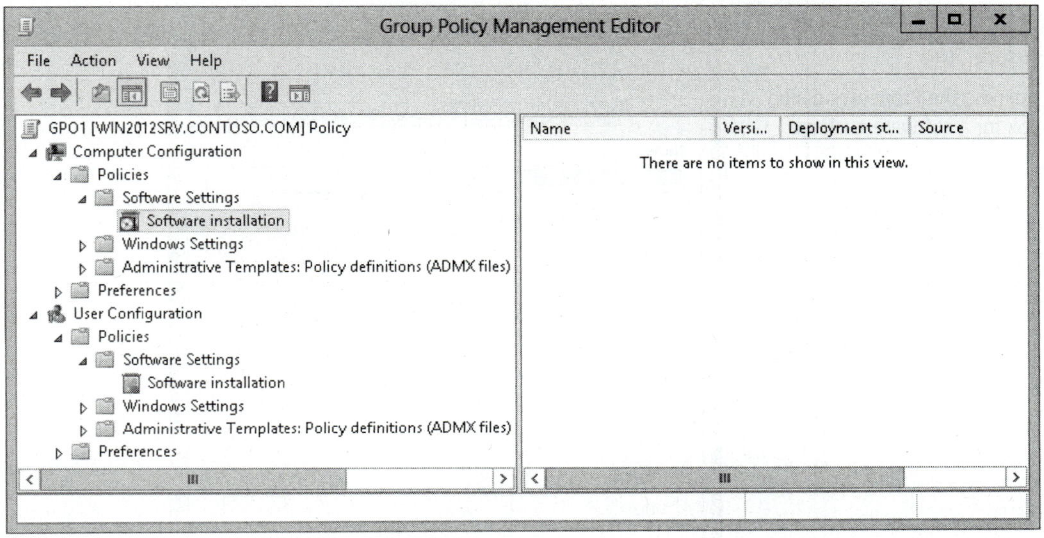

Figure 20-2
Opening the Software Installation node

3. Right-click the Software Installation node, select New, and then click Package. The *Open* dialog box opens.
4. Navigate to the UNC path of the software distribution point for the Windows Installer packages (.msi file), and then click Open.
5. When the *Deploy Software* dialog box opens (see Figure 20-3), select one of the following:
   - Published
   - Assigned
   - Advanced

   The Advanced option is used to set properties for the Windows Installer package, including published or assigned options and modifications.

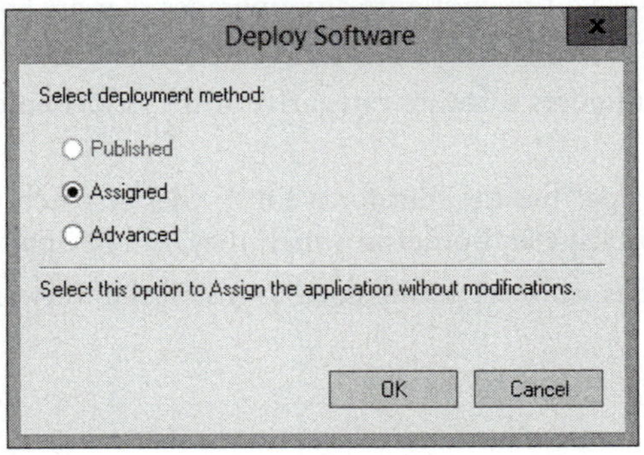

Figure 20-3
Selecting the deployment method

6. Click OK.
7. If you selected *Published* or *Assigned*, the Windows Installer package is added to the GPO. If you selected *Advanced*, the *Properties* dialog box for the Windows Installer package opens to permit you to set properties for the Windows Installer package, including deployment options and modifications. Make the necessary modification and click OK.
8. Close the *Group Policy Management Editor* window.

If you selected the Advanced options when you created the installation package or if you right-click the package and select *Properties*, the Properties dialog box opens (see Figure 20-4).

Figure 20-4

Opening the Properties dialog box for a software package

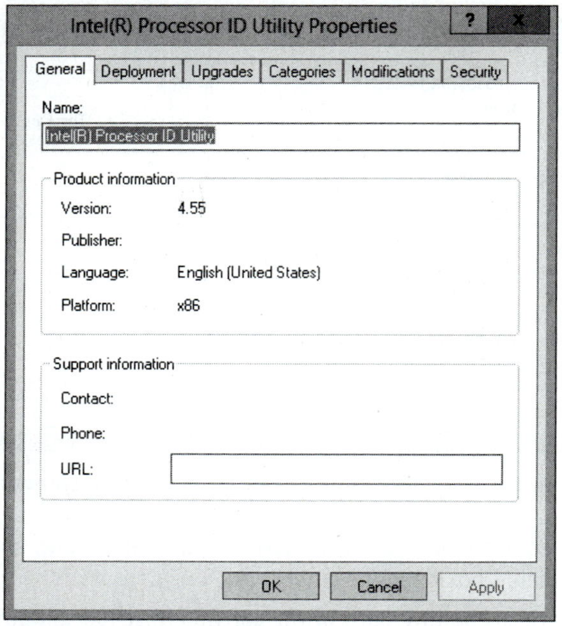

You can further configure the package with the following tabs:

- **General:** Allows you to change the default name of the package, and to specify a URL that points to a support web page.
- **Deployment:** Allows you to change the Deployment Type, Deployment Options, and Installation User Interface Options (Basic or Maximum) (see Figure 20-5). The Advanced button contains additional deployment information, such as advanced deployment options and diagnostics information.
- **Upgrades:** Allows you to configure any upgrades that are applied to a package (see Figure 20-6).
- **Categories:** Configures software categories in the Add/Remove Programs option of Control Panel.
- **Modifications:** Specifies the transform (.mst) files or patch (.msp) files that are to be applied to the package and order in which they will be applied.
- **Security:** Specifies who has permissions to install the software using this package.

Figure 20-5

Changing the deployment type and deployment options

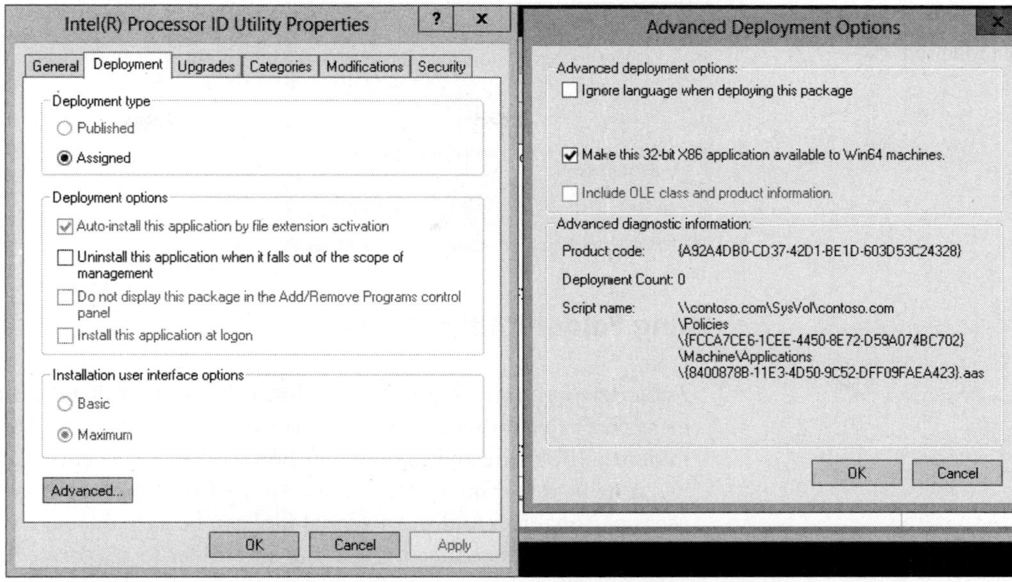

Figure 20-6

Upgrading a software package

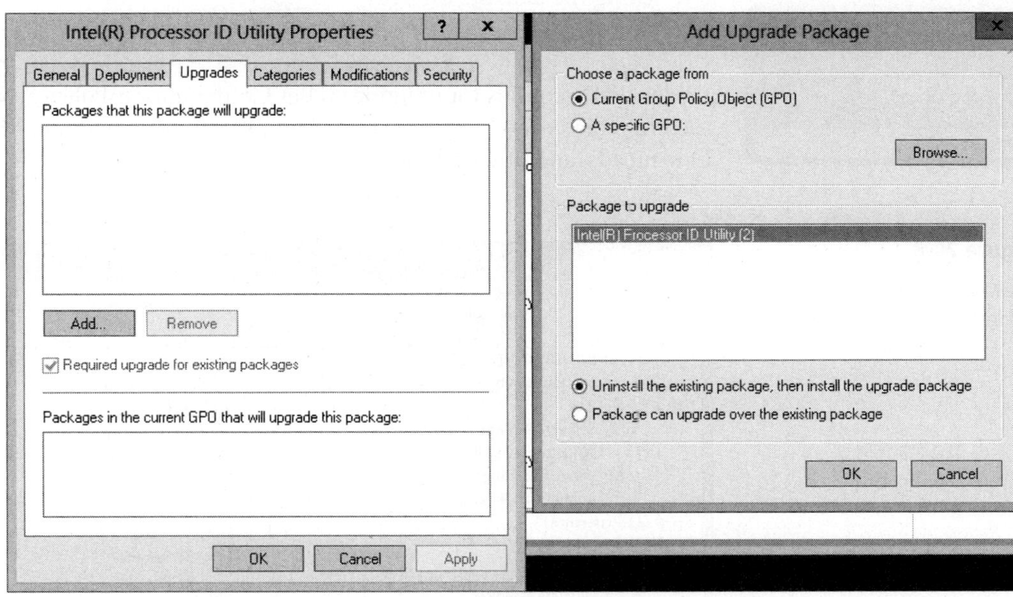

REDEPLOYING AN APPLICATION

After a computer has installed an application, and you choose to change the software package, you can then choose to redeploy the software. To redeploy the software, you right-click the package in the GPO, click *All Tasks*, and click *Redeploy Application*.

UNINSTALLING A PACKAGE

From time to time, you might choose to remove an application that has been deployed with a software package. To remove an application, you right-click the package, click *All Tasks*, and then click *Remove*. When the Remove Software dialog box opens (see Figure 20-7), you can choose one of the following options:

- Immediately Uninstall The Software From Users And Computers
- Allows Users To Continue To Use The Software, But Prevents New Installations

Figure 20-7

Removing software

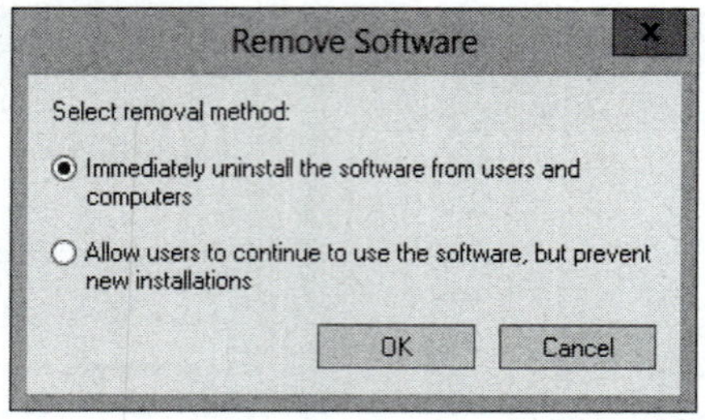

Using Folder Redirection

Folder redirection allows you to redirect the content of a certain folder to a network location or to another location on the user's local computer. For example, the Documents folder can be redirected to the user's home folder on a centralized server. By having the Documents folder on a centralized server, you can perform a centralized backup of all user's personal files and the personal files can be available no matter what client computer they log on to. By redirecting a folder and folder to a separate drive on the locating computer, you can separate the data files from the operating system files, so that when you have to reinstall a computer, you need to reinstall only the operating system drive without touching the data file drive.

CERTIFICATION READY
Configure Settings including folder redirection.
Objective 6.2

Folder Redirection is found under \User Configuration\Policies\Windows Settings. It can be used to redirect the Desktop, Start Menu, Documents, Picture, Music, Videos, Favorites, Downloads, and other related folders (see Figure 20-8).

Figure 20-8

Viewing the Folder Redirection folders

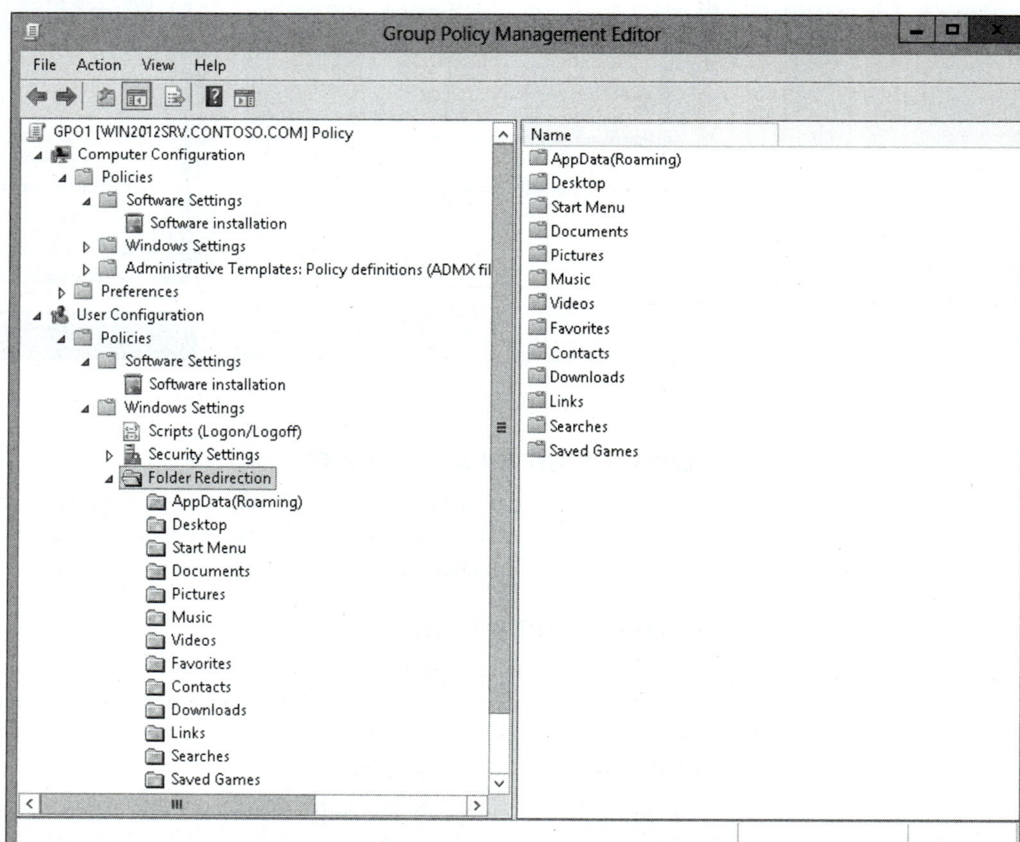

CONFIGURE FOLDER REDIRECTION

GET READY. To configure folder redirection, perform the following steps:

1. Open the Group Policy Management Editor for the GPO you want to configure.
2. Navigate to the \User Configuration\Policies\Windows Settings\Folder Redirection node.
3. Right-click the Documents folder in the left window pane and select Properties. The *Documents Properties* dialog box opens (see Figure 20-9).

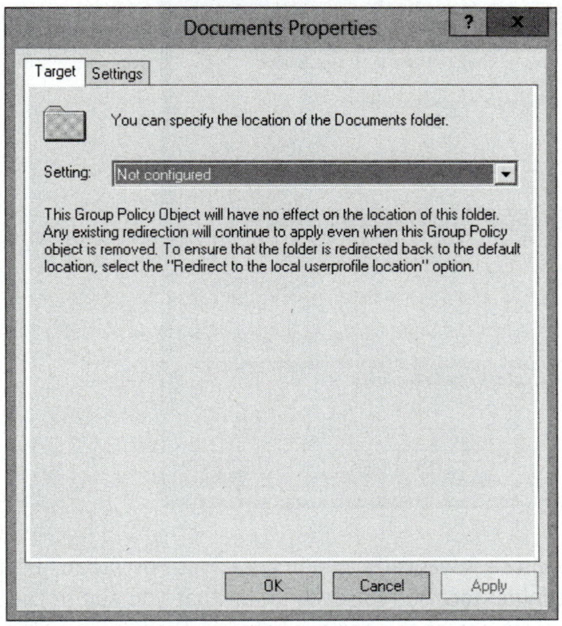

Figure 20-9

Configuring the Documents Properties

4. Open the Settings dialog box and select one of the following options:
   - **Basic—Redirect everyone's folder to the same location:** Redirects the Documents folder to the location you specify.
   - **Advanced—Specify locations for various user groups:** Redirects the Documents folder to a different place depending on a particular user's group membership.
   - **Not configured**—The folder will not be redirected.
5. If you chose Basic-Redirect Everyone's Folder To The Same Location (see Figure 20-10), specify the Target folder location using a UNC in the *Settings* dialog box. Choose from the following options:
   - **Redirect to the user's home directory:** Redirects the Documents folder to the user's home directory, specified in their Active Directory account tab for the user. This option is available only if you are redirecting the Documents folder. By allowing the system to create the subfolder structure automatically, the system will automatically create assign appropriate permissions on the shared folder.
   - **Create a folder for each user under the root path:** Allows you to specify the path to a folder, whereas the group policy creates a subfolder for each user based on the %username% variable and the folder name of the redirected folder (such as Documents or Music), and redirects the appropriate folder there.

- **Redirect to the following location:** Allows you to redirect a folder to a specific folder, which is the same for all users. You might use this if you want the same items to appear for every user.
- **Redirect to the local userprofile location:** Redirects to the user's local profile located on the local computer and copies the contents of the redirected folder back to the user profile location. The redirected folder contents are not deleted.

Figure 20-10

Redirecting to the user's home directory

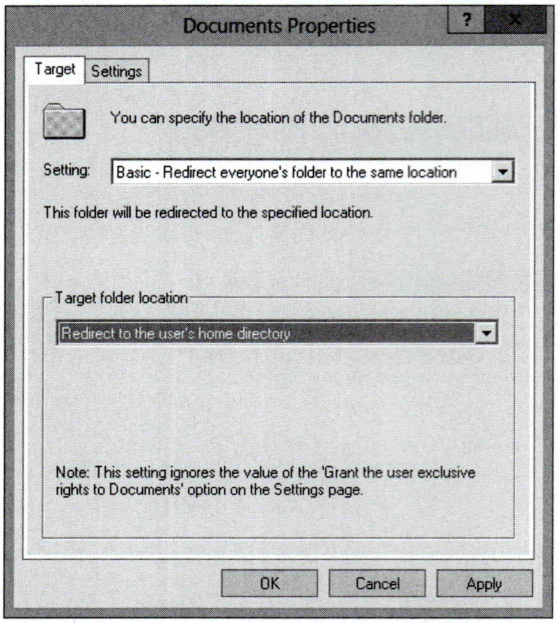

6. If you chose Advanced–Specify Locations For Various User Groups, you specify the target folder location for each group that you add in the *Settings* dialog box. You will then select one of the options listed in the previous step. Click Add to select the groups and choose the target folder location for redirected files. The *Specify Group and Location* dialog box opens (see Figure 20-11). Click OK to close the *Specify Group and Location* dialog box.

Figure 20-11

Specifying the security group membership when using Advanced mode

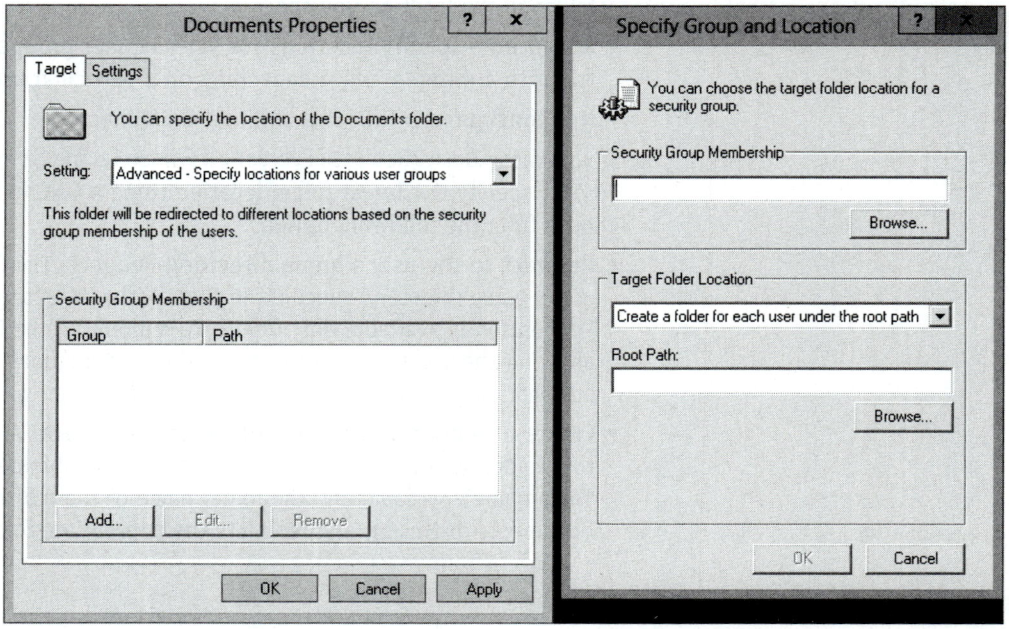

7. Click the Settings tab (see Figure 20-12).

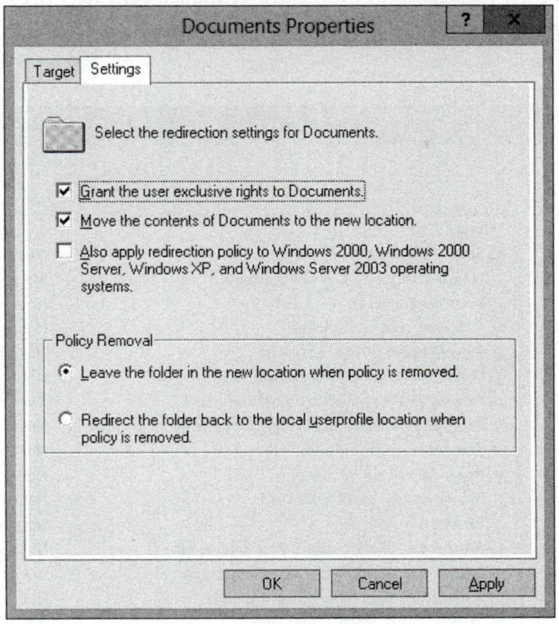

Figure 20-12

Configuring settings when using Advanced mode

8. Click to enable the Grant the user exclusive rights to Documents checkbox, to automatically configure the permissions for the user to access the folder.
9. Click to enable the Move the contents of Documents to the new location checkbox if you need to move the current content of the Documents to the new location.
10. If you will be supporting down-level clients such as Windows XP, select Also apply redirection policy to Windows 2000, Windows 2000 Server, Windows XP, and Windows Server 2003 operating systems.
11. To configure the Policy Removal settings, select one of the following options:
    - Leave the folder in the new location when policy is removed.
    - Redirect the folder back to the local userprofile location when policy is removed.
12. Click OK to close the *Documents Properties* dialog box.
13. Close the *Group Policy Management Editor* window.

When you plan and implement redirected folders, be sure to test the redirected folders before you reconfigure everyone within an organization. In addition, you will need to ensure that you have enough space on the server or servers that will hold the redirected folders. If you chose to disable offline files for security reasons, you should consider making the file server highly available using DFS or clustering. Lastly, some users might see slow logon times the first time they log into their computers after Folder Redirection is implemented, while the files are being copied to the new location. You need to watch the amount of traffic that the transfer might generate, especially if it has to go over slower WAN links.

Redirected folders are often used with offline files so that users can access the files from his or her own computer and the files will be synchronized to the file server. In addition, laptop users can still access their files when not connected to the network.

Most of the time, the default settings for offline files are sufficient. To modify the settings for offline files for your organization, you can use group policies. The offline file settings are located at Computer Configuration\Policies\Administrative Templates\Network\Offline Files and User Configuration\Policies\Administrative Templates\Network\Offline Files (see Figure 20-13). By default, Redirected Folders are available offline. However, you can disable Offline Files by setting *Prevent use of Offline Files* to *Enabled.*

Figure 20-13

Using group policies to configure offline files

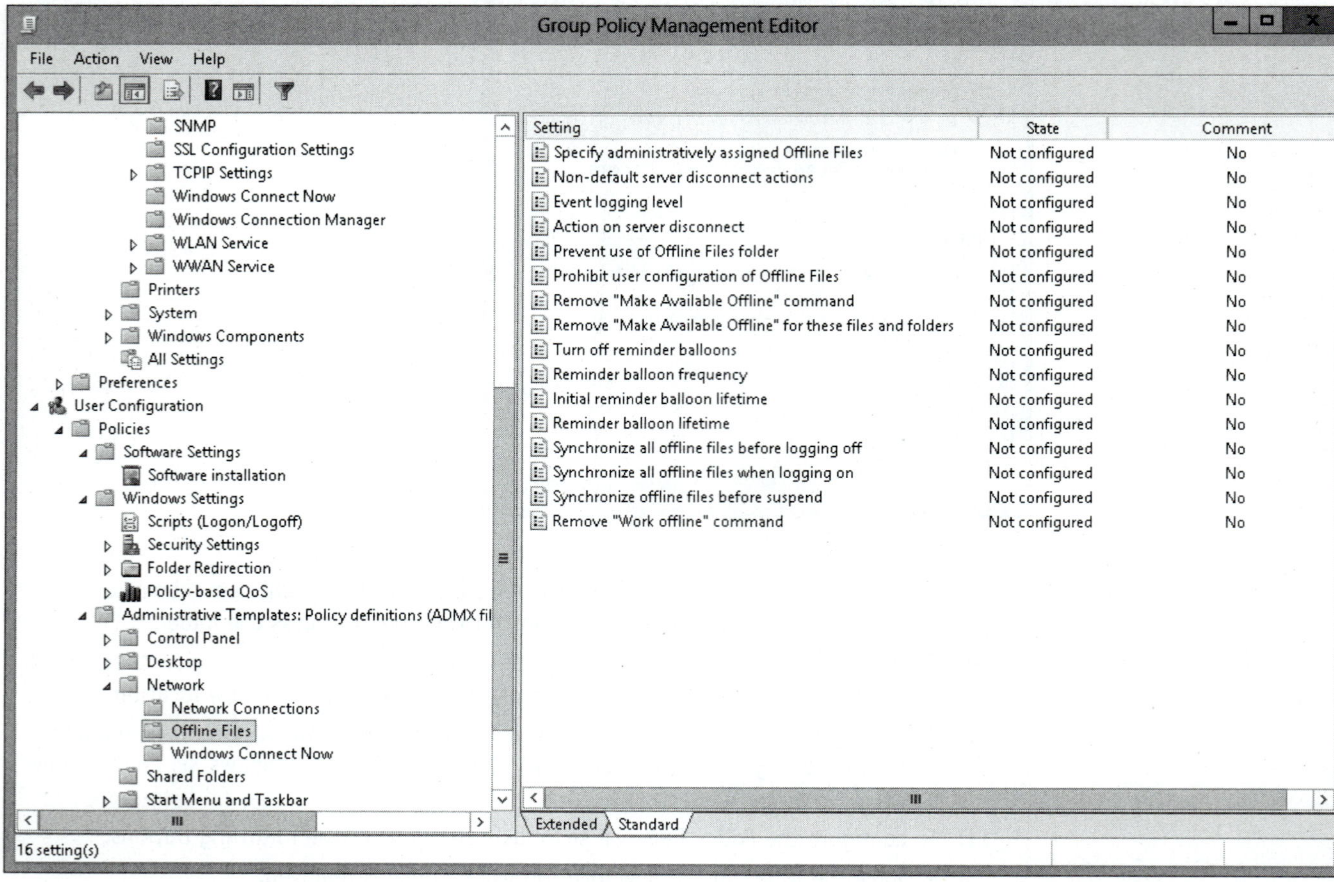

Using Scripts with Group Policies

A ***script*** is a list of commands that can be executed within a single file, which can perform repetitive tasks. You can use group policies to execute login/logoff scripts and startup/shutdown scripts. Some of the uses include cleaning up desktops when users log off and shut down computers, deleting the contents of temporary directories, mapping drives and printers, and setting environment variables.

CERTIFICATION READY
Configure settings including scripts.
Objective 6.2

The ***Microsoft Windows Script Hosts (WSH)*** is the component that provides scripting capabilities to Windows. Besides running batch files, it can also run JScripts and VBScripts. When creating scripts for the computer or user that are implemented through group policies, you can execute batch files, JScripts, VBScripts, and Windows PowerShell scripts.

To use scripts, perform the following steps:

1. Create the login script.
2. Execute the script manually to make sure that the script runs and performs as planned.

TAKE NOTE*

The writing of scripts is beyond the scope of this course and exam. However, you can find an abundant amount of information on writing scripts on the Internet.

3. Copy the script to the c:\Windows\Sysvol\Sysvol\Domain Name\Scripts folder on a domain controller. The content of SYSVOL volume is automatically replicated to the other domain controllers within the domain.
4. Configure a GPO to execute the script during startup, shutdown, logon, or logoff.

For computers, you can assign a ***startup scripts*** and ***shutdown scripts***. These are configured using the GPOs Computer Configuration\Policies\Windows Settings\Scripts (Startup/Shutdown). For users, you can assign a ***logon scripts*** and ***logoff scripts***. These are configured using the GPOs User Configuration\Policies\Windows Settings\Scripts (Logon/Logoff) as shown in Figure 20-14.

Figure 20-14

Viewing the user scripts

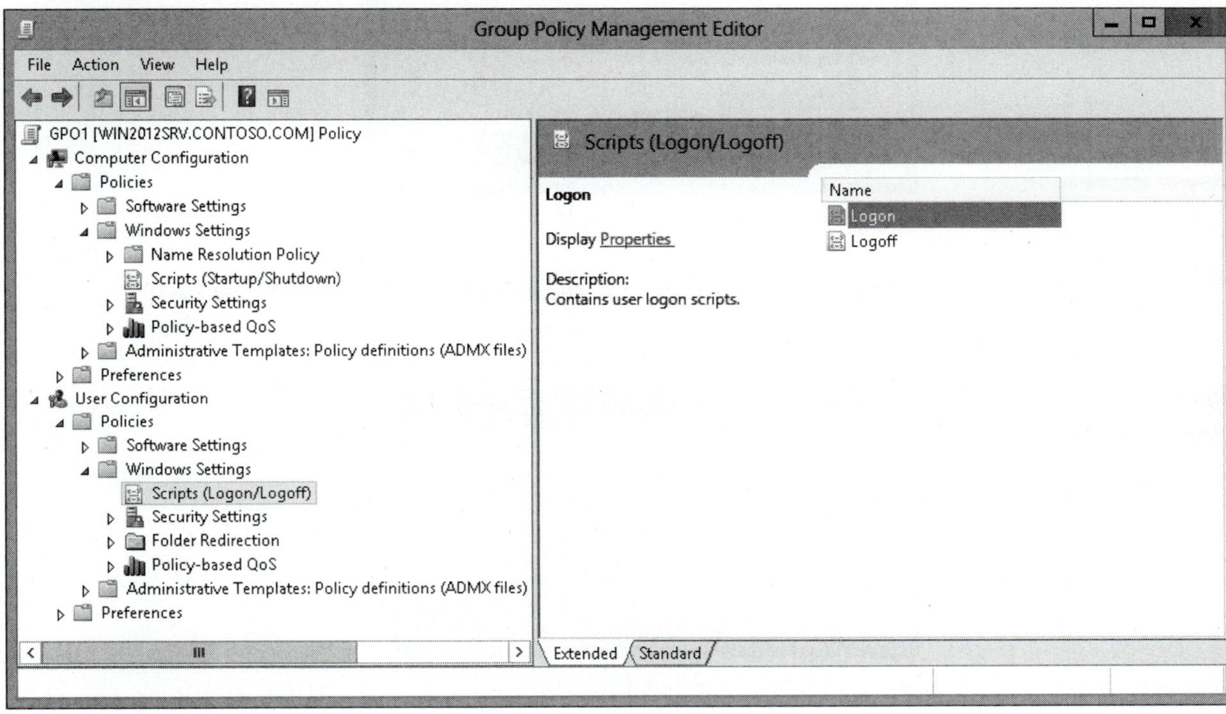

IMPLEMENT A LOGIN SCRIPT USING GROUP POLICIES

GET READY. To implement a login script using group policies, perform the following steps:

1. Open the Group Policy Management Editor for the GPO you want to configure.
2. Navigate to User Configuration\Policies\Windows Settings\Scripts (Logon/Logoff).
3. Double-click Logon to open the *Logon Properties* dialog box (see Figure 20-15).

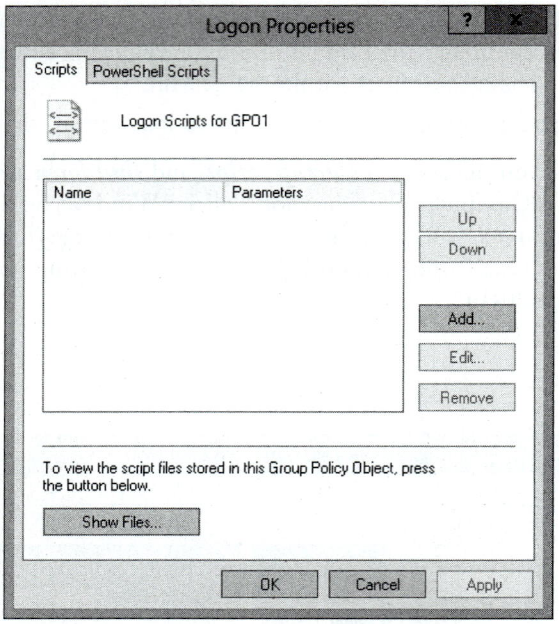

Figure 20-15

Opening the Logon Properties dialog box

4. Click Add to open the *Add a Script* dialog box (see Figure 20-16).

Figure 20-16

Adding a script to a GPO

5. In the *Script Name* text box, type the path to the script, or click Browse to navigate to the script file in the *Netlogon* shared folder on the domain controller.
6. If necessary, type any parameters that are required by the script.
7. Click OK to close the *Logon Properties* dialog box.
8. Close the *Group Policy Management Editor* window.

You use the *Edit* button to edit a selected script. You can use the *Remove* button to remove the script from the GPO. You can use the *Show Files* button to open the \SysVol*.domain name*,\Policies\{*GPO_GUID*}\User\Scripts\Logon folder to see a list of all scripts associated with the GPO.

If you assign multiple scripts, the scripts are processed in the order that you specify. To change the order, click to select the script and use the Up and Down buttons.

Using Administrative Templates

Windows Server 2012 includes thousands of Administrative Template policies, which contains registry-based policy settings that are used to configure the user and computer environment. For example, to configure the user's desktop image or a default screen saver, you use an Administrative Template policy.

CERTIFICATION READY
Configure settings including administrative template settings.
Objective 6.2

Traditionally, ***ADM files*** have been used to define the settings that an administrator can configure through Group Policy. ADM files use their own markup language, which made it difficult to customize ADM files. The ADM templates are located in the %SystemRoot%\Inf folder.

Windows Vista and Windows Server 2008 introduced ***ADMX files***, which are based on eXtensible Markup Language (XML). ADMX files can be stored in a single location called the *Central Store* in the SYSVOL directory. Unlike ADM files, ADMX files are not stored in individual GPOs. The Group Policy Management Editor automatically reads and displays settings from the local ADMX file store. By default, ADMX files are stored in the Windows\PolicyDefinitions folder, but they can be stored in a central location in the SYSVOL label.

ADMX files are language neutral. The descriptions of the settings are not part of the ADMX files. Instead, they are stored in language-specific ***ADML files***. ADML files are stored in a subfolder of the PolicyDefinitions folder. By default, only the ADML language files for the language of the installed operating system are added.

MANAGING ADMINISTRATIVE TEMPLATES

Administrative Templates appear under both Computer Configuration and User Configuration. The requirements for an Administrative Template setting, such as which operating system supports the setting and the description of the feature, are displayed:

- On the Extended tab when you click to select an Administrative Template setting (see Figure 20-17)
- When you double-click an Administrative Template setting (see Figure 20-18)

Figure 20-17

Selecting an Administrative Template

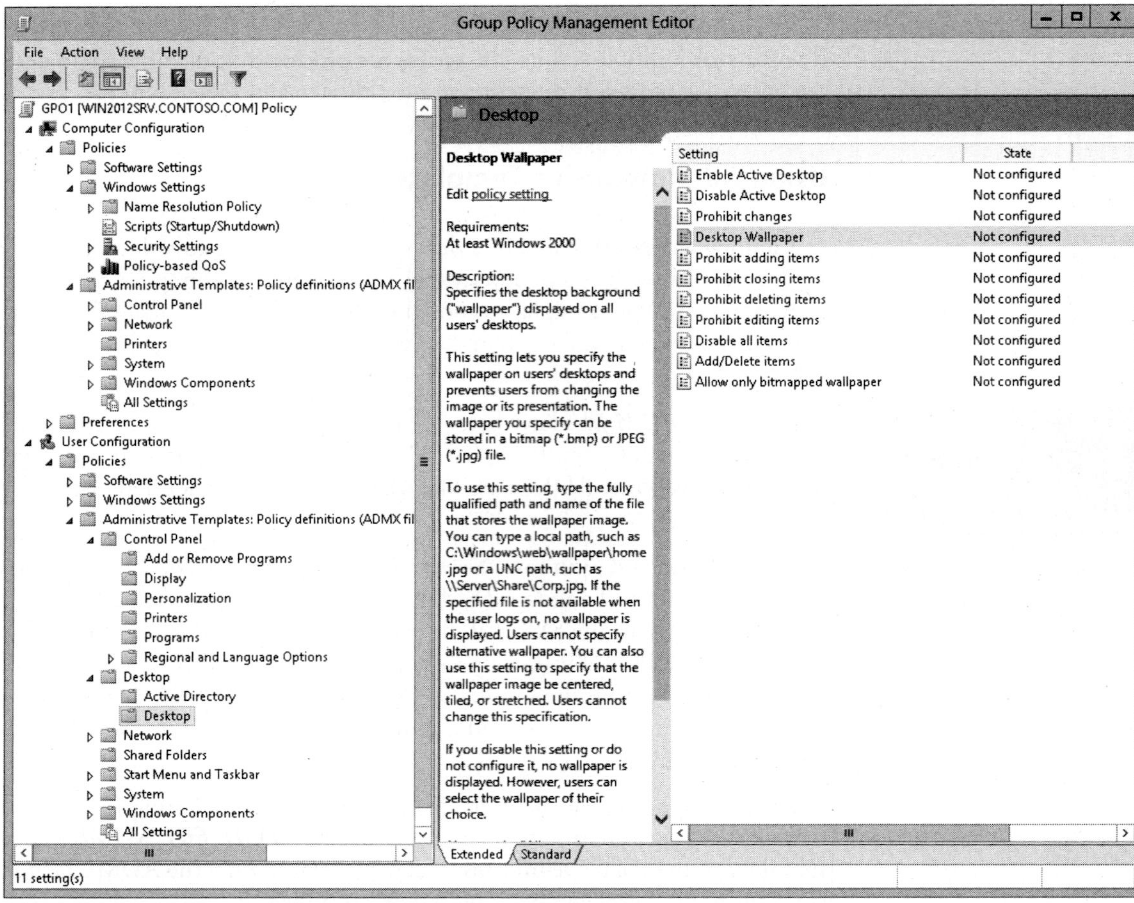

Figure 20-18

Viewing the Settings dialog box

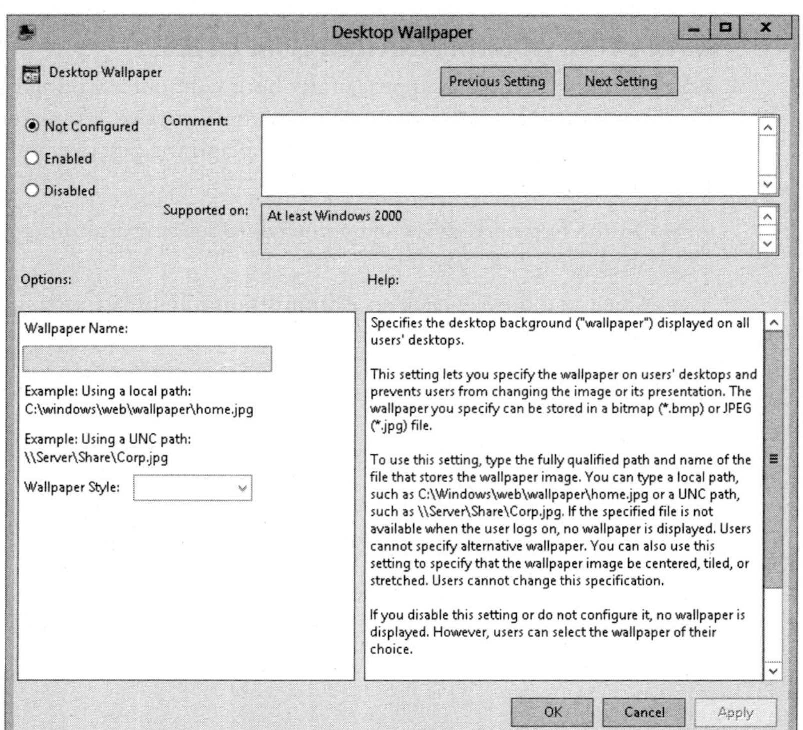

When configuring Administrative Templates, there are three states:

- **Not Configured:** The registry key is not modified or overwritten.
- **Enabled:** The registry key is modified by this setting.
- **Disabled:** The Disabled settings undo a change made by a prior Enabled setting.

If you want to undo the group policy, removing the group policy does not necessarily remove the setting from a computer that has the setting configured with a GPO. In these cases, you need to change the policy to Disabled (or create a second policy) and is applied to the computer and/or user. After the policy is applied, the policy can be removed. The policy can also be manually removed using the registry editor (HKEY_CURRENT_USER\Software\Microsoft\Windows\CurrentVersion\Policies and HKEY_LOCAL_MACHINE\Software\Microsoft\Windows\CurrentVersion\Policies).

Some Administrative Templates will be used to configure a setting, such as specifying a desktop image or specifying a screen saver. Although these settings are configured with group policies, some of these settings can be changed while the computer is running. However, when the group policy is reapplied, the setting will revert back to the setting defined with the GPO. Other settings will be used to lock down a computer so that users cannot modify a setting or hide the setting from the user.

CONFIGURE THE DESKTOP BACKGROUND IMAGE WITH GROUP POLICIES

GET READY. To configure the desktop background image with group policies, perform the following steps:

1. Open the Group Policy Management Editor for the GPO you want to configure.
2. Navigate to User Configuration\Policies\Administrative Templates\Desktop\Desktop.
3. Double-click Desktop Wallpaper. The *Desktop Wallpaper* dialog box opens.
4. Click Enabled.
5. In the *Wallpaper Name* text box, type the path and name of an image file.
6. Click OK to close the *Desktop Wallpaper* dialog box. The *Desktop Wallpaper* shows as *Enabled*.
7. Close the *Group Policy Management Editor* window.

CREATING A CENTRAL STORE

The ***Central Store*** is a folder structure created in the SYSVOL directory on the domain controllers in each domain in your organization. You have to create only the Central Store on a single domain controller for each domain, because the content of the SYSVOL will be replicated to the other domain controllers.

When there is no Central Store, the Group Policy Object Editor reads the local versions of the ADMX files used by the local GPO on the Windows machine stored in the %systemroot%\PolicyDefinitions\ folder (which is typically the C:\Windows\PolicyDefinitions folder).

To create the Central Store, follow these steps:

1. Create a PolicyDefinitions folder in the %systemroot%\sysvol\domain\policies\ folder.
2. The PolicyDefinitions folder stores all of the language-neutral ADMX files. Therefore, copy all files from the %systemroot%\PolicyDefinitions* folder to the %systemroot%\sysvol\domain\policies\ folder.
3. Copy all the language folders and files to the %systemroot%\sysvol\domain\policies\PolicyDefinitions. For example, if you use the US English files, you copy the files from the %systemroot%\PolicyDefinitions\EN-US* folder to the %systemroot%\sysvol\domain\policies\PolicyDefinitions\EN-US\ folder.

The Group Policy Object Editor automatically reads all ADMX files stored in the Central Store.

Using Security Templates

Group Policies are often used to make a computer more secure. By using security templates, you can implement security settings quickly and efficiently, you can copy and apply security settings from one computer to another, and you can check the security settings based on a security template.

CERTIFICATION READY
Import security templates.
Objective 6.2

Each computer running Windows 7 and 8 and any computer running Windows Server 2008 R2 and Windows Server 2012 maintains a collection of security settings that can be managed by using the local group policies. These settings can be configured using the Group Policy Object Editor snap-in with the Local Computer object selected, or the Local Security Policy console (see Figure 20-19) found in Administrative Tools. Of course, if you want to configure all computers for your organization, you should use non-local group policies.

Figure 20-19

Using the Local Security Policy console

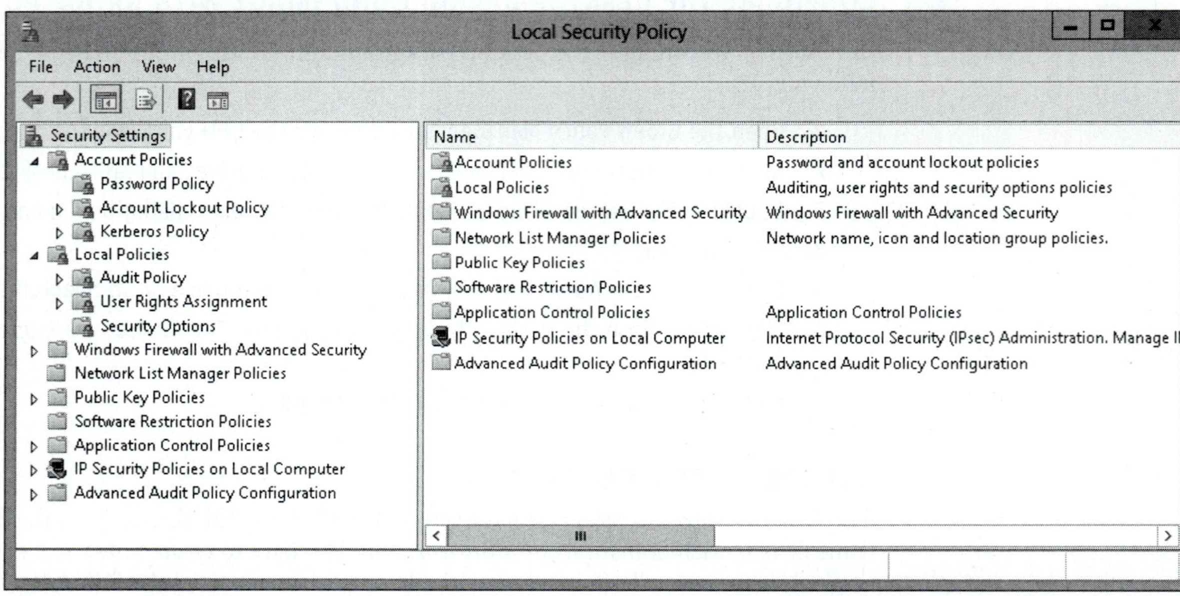

A ***security template*** is a collection of configuration settings stored in a text file with the .inf extension. They can be used for the following:

- Save the security configuration to a file.
- Deploy the security settings to a computer or group policy.
- Analyze compliance of a computer's current configuration against the desired configuration.

The Security template allows you to configure the following policies and settings:

- **Account Policies Specify:** Allows you to configure password restrictions, account lockout policies, and Kerberos policies.
- **Local Policies:** Allows you to configure audit policies, user rights assignments, and security options policies.

- **Event Log Policies**: Allows you to configure maximum event log sizes and rollover policies.
- **Restricted Groups**: Allows you to specify users who are allowed to be added to a specific group such as domain administrators.
- **System Services**: Allows you to specify the startup types and permissions for system services.
- **Registry Permissions**: Allows you to set access control permissions for specific registry keys.
- **File System Permissions**: Allows you to specify access control permissions for NTFS files and folders.

You can deploy security templates using the following:

- Active Directory group policy objects
- Security Configuration And Analysis snap-in

To manage security templates, you can use the Security Templates snap-in. Unfortunately, this snap-in is not included in Administrative Tools. Therefore, you need to open Microsoft Management Console (MMC) and manually add the snap-in.

OPEN THE SECURITY TEMPLATES SNAP-IN

GET READY. To open the security template snap-in, perform the following steps:

1. Right-click the Start menu and select Command Prompt (Admin).
2. At the command prompt, execute the mmc command. An empty console opens.
3. Open the File menu, and click Add/Remove Snap-in.
4. When the *Add or Remove Snap-ins* dialog box opens, scroll down to and click Security Templates (see Figure 20-20). Click Add. Click OK. The Security Templates snap-in is available (see Figure 20-21).

Figure 20-20

Adding the Security Templates to MMC

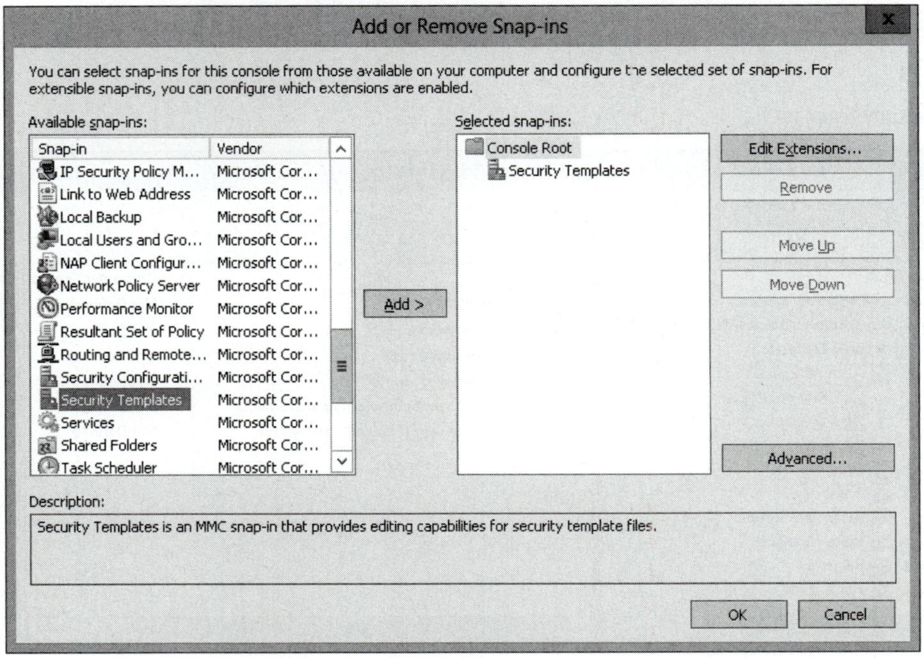

Figure 20-21

Viewing the Security Templates console

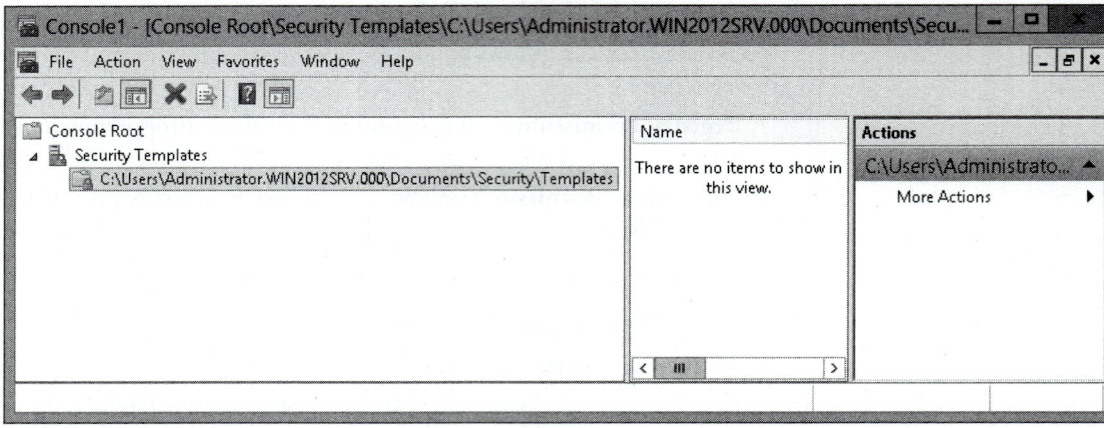

5. To create a new security template, right-click the node where you want to store the security template, and click New Template.
6. When the dialog box opens (see Figure 20-22), type a descriptive name in the *Template name* text box. Click OK. The security template is added in the console (see Figure 20-23).

Figure 20-22

Naming the security template

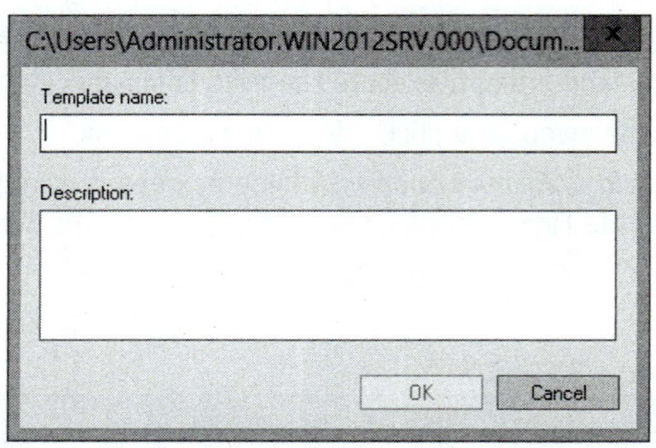

Figure 20-23

Viewing a security template

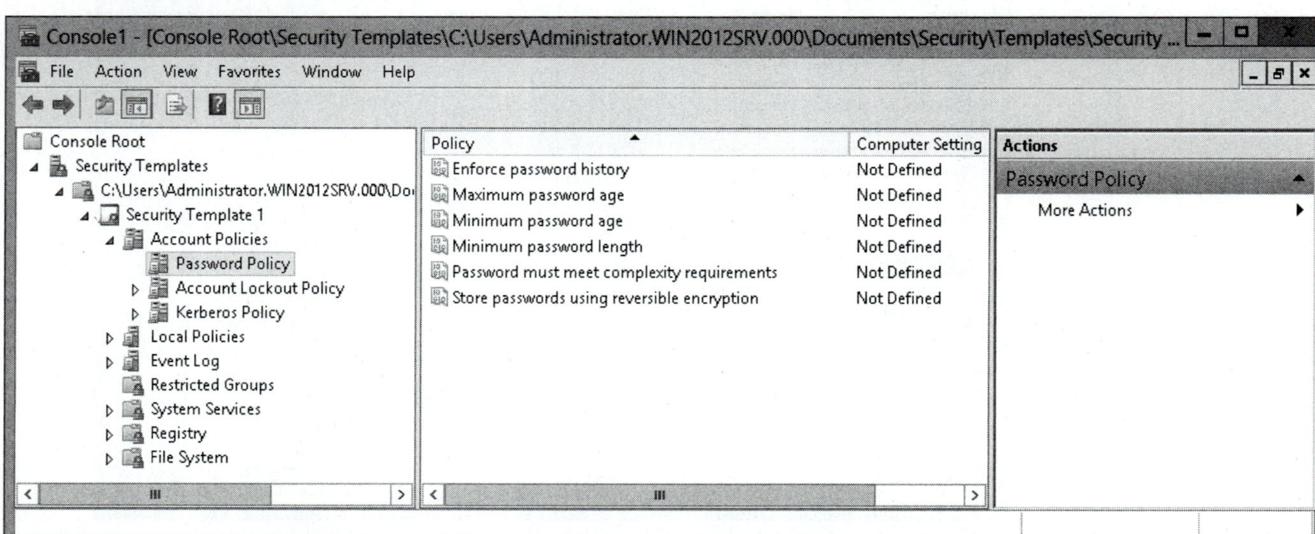

You configure settings the same way you configure a GPO. The only exception is when you add registry settings that are not already listed in the Local Policies\Security Option portion of the template. After you make your changes, right-click the template and click *Save*.

After a security template is created and saved, you can deploy those settings by importing the security template into the GPO for a domain, site, organization unit object, or a local computer. To import a security template into a GPO, open the GPO and right-click the *Security Settings* node and click *Import Policy*. If you select the *Clear This Database Before Importing* checkbox, all security settings in the GPO will be erased prior to importing the template settings, so the GPO's security settings will match the template's settings.

COMPARE SETTINGS WITH A SECURITY TEMPLATE

GET READY. To compare settings with a security template, perform the following steps:

1. Right-click the Start menu and select Command Prompt (Admin).
2. At the command prompt, execute the `mmc` command. An empty console opens.
3. Open the File menu, and click Add/Remove Snap-in.
4. When the *Add or Remove Snap-ins* dialog box opens, scroll down to and click Security Configuration and Analysis. Click Add. Click OK. The *Security Configuration and Analysis* console is available (see Figure 20-24).

Figure 20-24

Viewing the Security Configuration and Analysis console

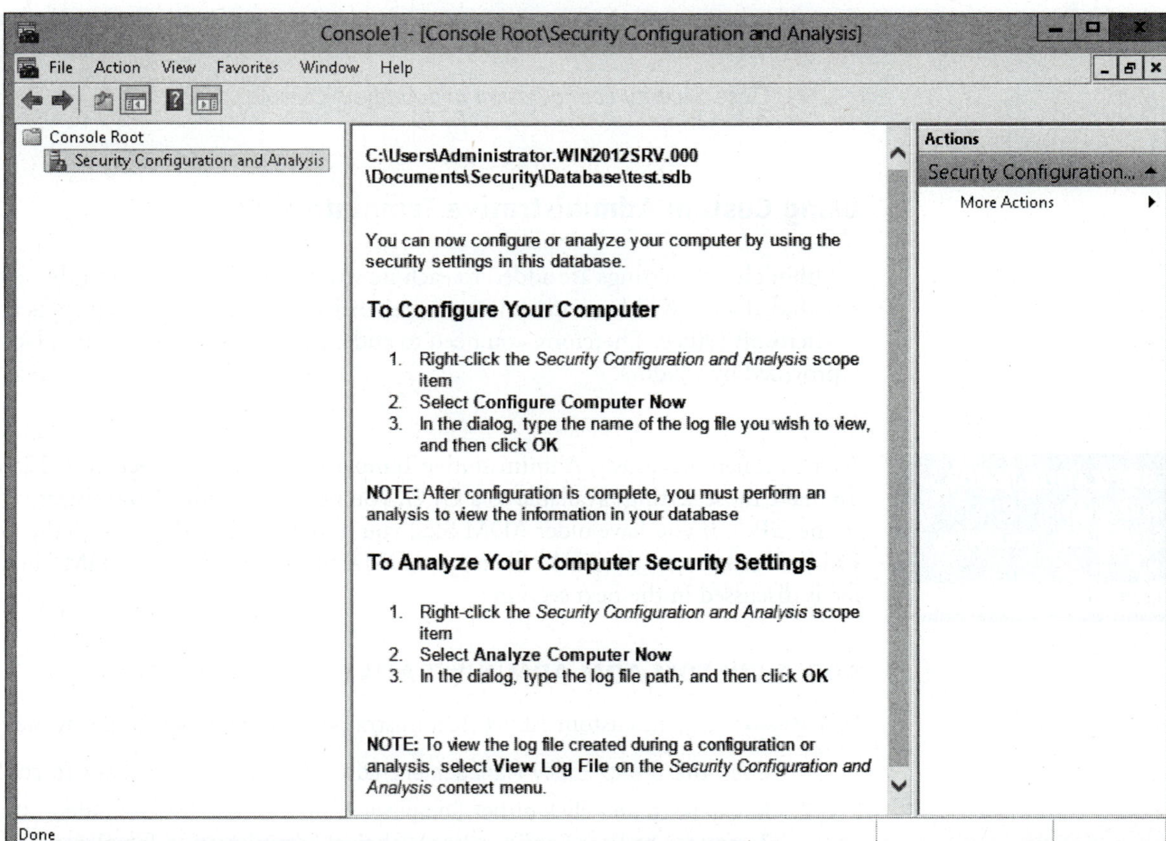

5. Right-click Security Configuration and Analysis and click Open Database.
6. To analyze a computer based on the security template, click Analyze Computer Now.
7. When the *Perform Analysis* dialog box opens, click OK.
8. When the analysis is done, check the settings looking for settings that are not compliant. For example, Figure 20-25 shows that the maximum password age is not compliant.

Figure 20-25

Comparing a security template with actual settings

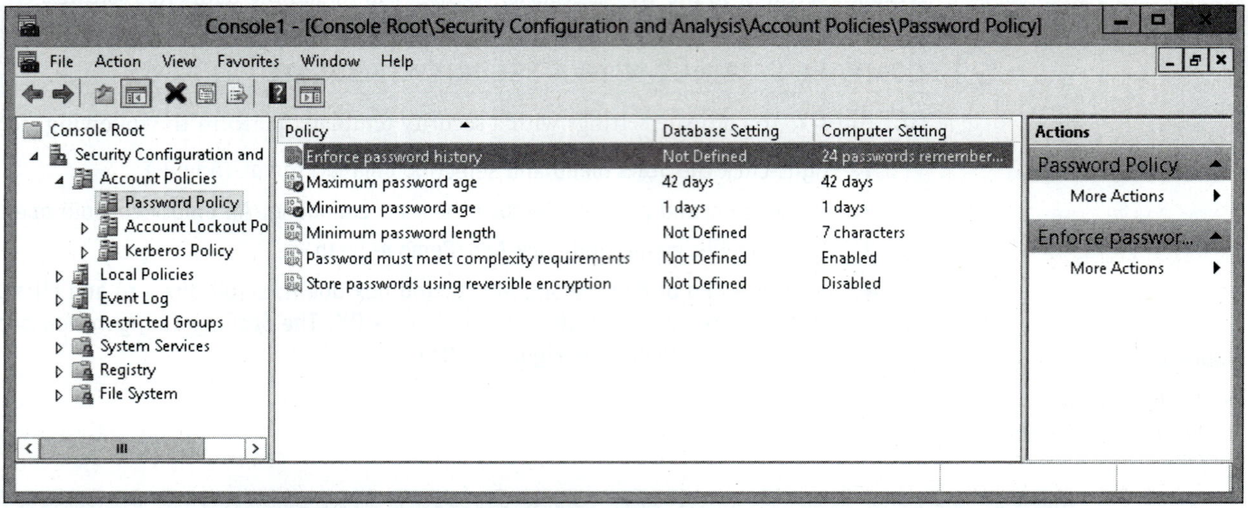

9. Close *Security Configuration and Analysis* console.

Using Custom Administrative Template Files

Although new settings are added to each new release of Windows, and the settings included with Windows are quite comprehensive, it does not support applications, such as Microsoft Office. Therefore, you need to add custom administrative template files that are provided by vendors.

CERTIFICATION READY
Import custom administrative template files.
Objective 6.2

As mentioned previously, Administrative Templates for Windows Server 2012 are ADMX files. To make those settings available to a GPO, you need to add the Administrative Templates file to the GPO. If you have older ADM files, you have to either add them to the GPO, or you will have to convert the ADM file to an ADMX file. Converting an ADM file to the ADMX file is discussed in the next section.

ADD A CUSTOM ADM ADMINISTRATIVE TEMPLATE FILES

GET READY. To add custom ADM Administrative Template files, perform the following steps:

1. Open the Group Policy Management Editor for the GPO you want to configure.
2. Navigate to and click either Computer Configuration\Policies\Administrative Templates or User Configuration\Policies\Administrative Templates.
3. Right-click Administrative Templates and Add/Remove Templates. The *Add/Remove Templates* dialog box opens (see Figure 20-26).

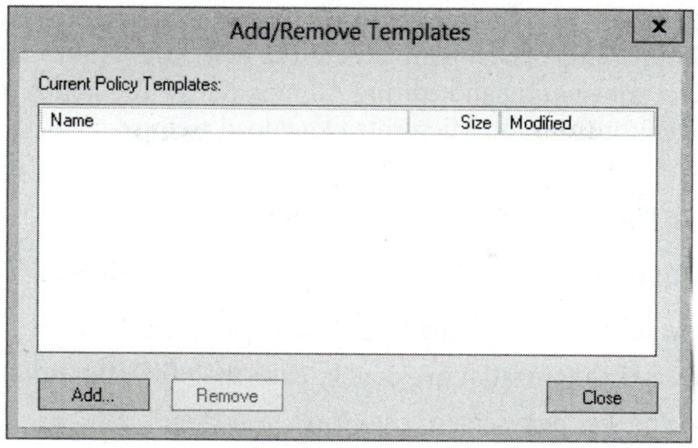

Figure 20-26

Opening the Add/Remove Templates dialog box

4. Click Add. The *Policy Templates* dialog box opens.
5. Navigate to the custom Administrative Templates and click Open (see Figure 20-27). Click Close to close the *Add/Remove Templates* dialog box.

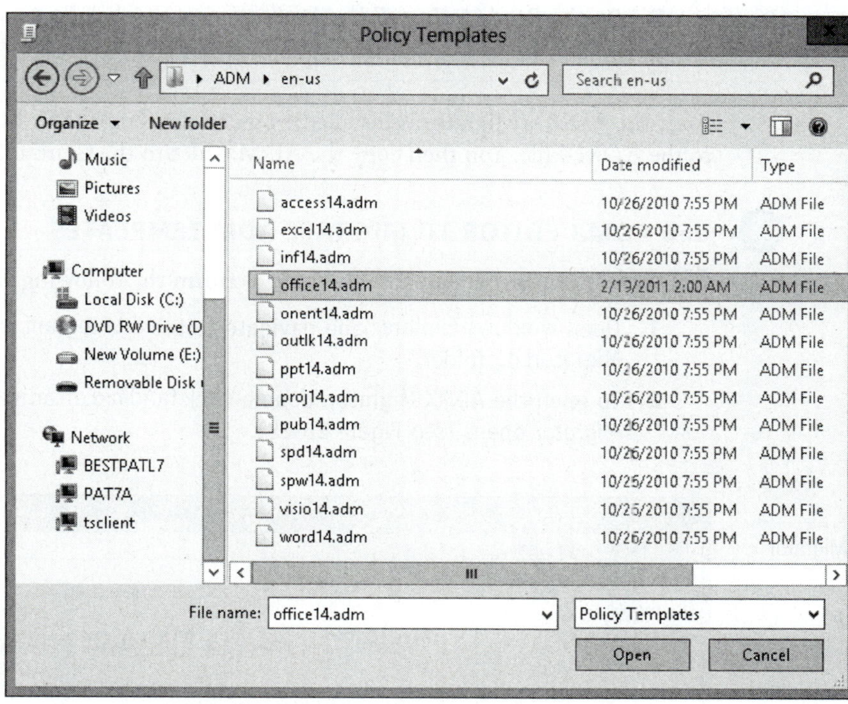

Figure 20-27

Navigating and opening an ADM file

6. Close the *Group Policy Management Editor* window.

Converting Administrative Templates Using ADMX Migrator

CERTIFICATION READY
Convert administrative templates using ADMX Migrator.
Objective 6.2

Although Windows XP and Windows Server 2003/Windows Server 2003 R2 use ADM files, Windows Vista, Windows 7, Windows 8, Windows Server 2008/Windows Server 2008 R2, and Windows Server 2012 users use ADMX files. The Central Store allows you to store ADMX files so that you don't need to copy the ADMX into every GPO. However, because the Central Store cannot make use of ADM, you need to convert the ADM files to ADMX.

ADMX Migrator is a snap-in for the MMC that simplifies the process of converting your existing Group Policy ADM templates to the new ADMX format and provides a graphical user interface for creating and editing Administrative Templates. You can download the ADMX Migrator from the Microsoft Download website.

INSTALL ADMX MIGRATOR

GET READY. To install ADMX Migrator, perform the following steps:

1. Download and store the ADMXMigrator.msi file.
2. To start the installation, double-click the ADMXMigrator.msi file.
3. On the *Welcome* screen, click Next.
4. On the *License Agreement* page, click I accept the license agreement option and click Next.
5. On the *User Information* page, click Next.
6. On the *Destination Folder* page, click Next.
7. Specify an installation folder, and then click Next.
8. On the *Ready to Install the Application* page, click Next.
9. When the installation is complete, click Finish.

After the ADMX Migrator is installed, you can use the ADMX Editor to migrate an ADM file to the ADMX file. You then copy the ADMX files to the Central Store.

USE ADMX EDITOR TO MIGRATE ADM TEMPLATES

GET READY. To install ADMX Migrator, perform the following steps:

1. Open Windows Explorer and navigate to the C:\Program Files (x86)\FullArmor\ADMX MigratorLog folder.
2. To open the ADMX Migrator, double-click faAdmxEditor.msc. The *FullArmor ADMX Migrator* opens (see Figure 20-28).

Figure 20-28

Opening the ADMX Migrator

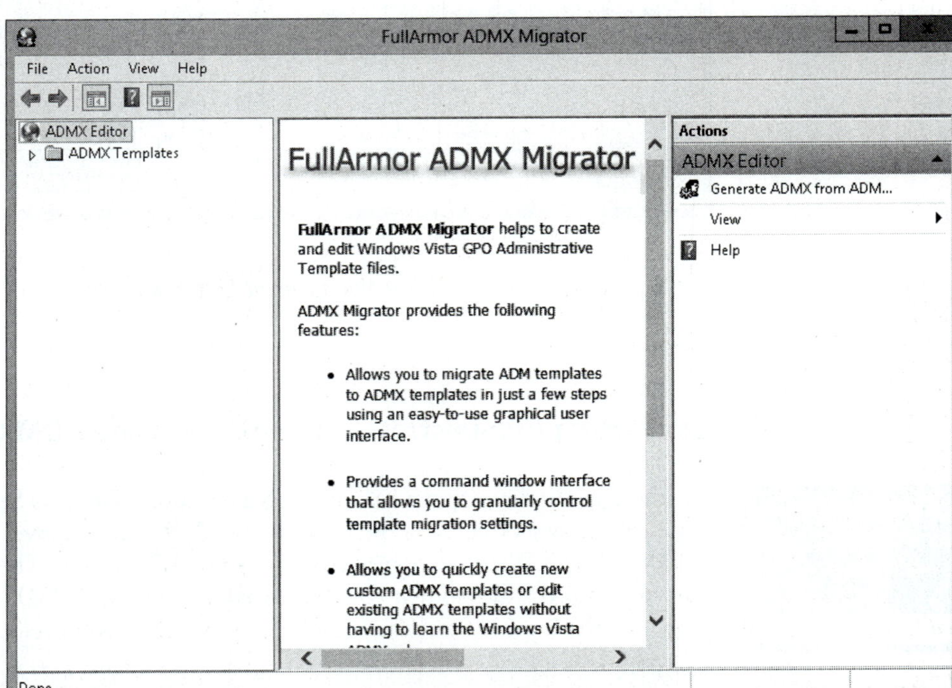

3. Click the ADMX Editor node.
4. Open the *Action* menu and click Generate ADMX from ADM.
5. When the *Open* dialog box opens, navigate to the ADM file and click Open.
6. When the *ADM to ADMX Conversion Results* dialog box opens, click Close.
7. When it asks whether you want to load the template into ADMX Editor, click Yes.
8. In the tree pane, expand ADMX Templates. ADMX Editor displays the new ADMX template in the results pane.
9. Close the *ADMX Migrator*.

Configuring Property Filters for Administrative Templates

By default, all policy settings are displayed. To narrow down the displayed list of settings, you can use ***Administrative Templates Property Filters***.

CERTIFICATION READY
Configure property filters for administrative templates.
Objective 6.2

To filter the settings displayed, you can select or deselect the following filter options:

- Managed or Non-Managed settings
- Configured or Not Configured
- Keyword Filters
- Requirements Filters

To configure the Filters, right-click *Administrative Templates* under Computer Configuration or User Configuration and click *Filter Options* (see Figure 20-29).

Figure 20-29

Configuring the Administrative Templates Property Filters

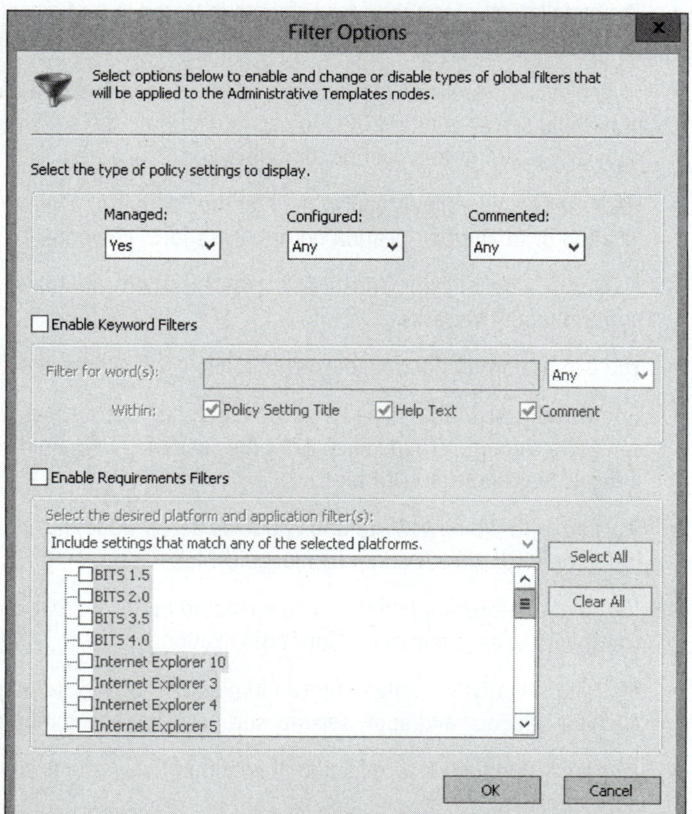

Administrative Templates can be divided into managed and non-managed and configured and not-configured. Managed policy settings and remove a policy setting when it is no longer within the scope of the user or computer. To display only the Managed settings, you select *Yes* under the Managed section. The default option is Yes.

When opening a GPO, most settings are not configured. Therefore, if you want to show only the Configured settings, select *Yes* in the Configured section. The default setting is Any.

There are hundreds of settings located within the Administrative Templates. Therefore, to help you find a setting, you can select the Enable keyword filters and then specify a keyword.

Lastly, if you want to show only settings that will run on a certain operating system or other component such as a certain version of Internet Explorer, you will enable the *Enable Requirements Filters* option and specify which settings based on the requirement you want to display.

SKILL SUMMARY

IN THIS LESSON, YOU LEARNED:

- One of the most powerful tools available with Active Directory is Group Policies that allow you to control the working environment of the computers and users of the organizations. It provides the centralized management and configuration of operating systems, applications, and user settings.
- Group policy settings are refreshed every 90 minutes with a random delay of 30 minutes (giving a random range between 90 minutes and 120 minutes).
- The Windows Installer is a software component used for the installation, maintenance, and removal of software on Windows.
- The installation information for software is stored in a Microsoft Software Installation (MSI) file in a database installation file that has an MSI filename extension.
- To deploy software with group policies, you need to create a distribution point on the publishing server, create a GPO to use to distribute the software package, and assign or publish a package to a user or computer.
- Folder redirection allows you to redirect the content of a certain folder to a network location or to another location on the user's local computer.
- A script is a list of commands that can be executed within a single file, which are used to perform repetitive tasks.
- You can use group policies to execute login/logoff scripts and startup/shutdown scripts.
- Traditionally, ADM files have been used to define the settings that an administrator can configure through Group Policy. ADM files use their own markup language, which made it difficult to customize ADM files.
- Starting with Windows Vista and Windows Server 2008 introduced ADMX files, which are based on eXtensible Markup Language (XML).
- The Central Store is a folder structure created in the SYSVOL directory on the domain controllers in each domain in your organization.
- By using security templates, you can implement security settings quickly and efficiently, and you can copy and apply security settings from one computer to another.
- A security template is a collection of configuration settings stored in a text file with the .inf extension.

- ADMX Migrator is a snap-in for the Microsoft Management Console (MMC) that simplifies the process of converting your existing Group Policy ADM templates to the new ADMX format and provides a graphical user interface for creating and editing Administrative Templates.
- By default, all policy settings are displayed. To narrow down the displayed list of settings, you can use Administrative Templates Property Filters.

Knowledge Assessment

Multiple Choice

Select the correct answer for each of the following questions.

1. How often do group policies get refreshed on client PCs?
   - **a.** Every 5 minutes
   - **b.** Every hour
   - **c.** Every 90 to 120 minutes
   - **d.** Every 4 hours
2. Which filename extension patches files for Microsoft Software Installation (MSI) files?
   - **a.** .msi
   - **b.** .exe
   - **c.** .msp
   - **d.** .zap
3. Which type of software installation would you perform if you want to add an icon to the user's control panel?
   - **a.** Assign software to a user
   - **b.** Assign software to a computer
   - **c.** Publish software to a user
   - **d.** Publish software to a computer
4. Which type of software supports self-healing?
   - **a.** .hlp
   - **b.** .zap
   - **c.** .exe
   - **d.** .msi
5. Which option would you use to repoint the Documents folder to the user's home folder?
   - **a.** Folder Placement
   - **b.** Folder Redirection
   - **c.** Folder shortcut
   - **d.** Folder Sync
6. Which type of folder redirection would you use to redirect the user's home directory to a location based on the group that the user is a member of?
   - **a.** Basic
   - **b.** Advanced
   - **c.** Specific
   - **d.** Customized

7. Most of the time, why do laptop users use folder redirection?
   a. Folder caching
   b. Folder syncing
   c. Mobile folders
   d. Offline folders

8. Where is the Central Store located?
   a. C:\Windows\PolicyDefinitions
   b. C:\Windows\SYSVOL\domain\Policies\PolicyDefinitions
   c. C:\Windows\Central
   d. C:\Windows\Store

9. Which is used to convert an .adm file to an .admx file?
   a. ADMX Migrator
   b. ADMX Converter
   c. ADMX Migration Tool
   d. GPMC

10. What is used to display only the Administrative Templates that are being used?
    a. Display viewer
    b. GPO attributes
    c. Attribute filter
    d. Property filters

Best Answer

Choose the letter that corresponds to the best answer. More than one answer choice may achieve the goal. Select the BEST answer.

1. You have an application that needs to be installed on 250 computers. The application should modify the registry on each target computer. The vendor provides a file with an .adm extension. How can you deploy the registry setting?
   a. Import the .adm file into a GPO and edit the GPO to modify the registry setting. Link the GPO to the OU of the computers that need the application.
   b. Use Windows PowerShell to copy the .adm file to the C:\Windows\Registry folder.
   c. Schedule a script that uses the `regedit` command to import the registry settings.
   d. Import the adm file into the Default Domain Policy OU and enable the registry settings in the GPO.

2. How do you determine whether a login script is replicated to all domain controllers?
   a. View the Group Policy status in the GPMC.
   b. Open the NTDS folder.
   c. Open the SoftwareDistribution folder.
   d. Open the SYSVOL folder.

3. You are an administrator for the Contoso Corporation. In Active Directory, you have a WebServer OU, which contains 10 web servers. You have been testing security settings for a server (called WebServer01) running IIS. How can you deploy the new security settings to the other web servers?
   a. Export the settings on the WebServer 01 to a security template. Use the secedit command to import the settings to each web server.
   b. Import the settings into the security.inf file template into a GPO and link the GPO to the WebServer OU.
   c. Export the settings on the WebServer01 to a security template. Then import the security settings into a GPO and link the GPO to the WebServer OU.
   d. Use the GPMC to export the security settings to the other servers.

4. Your domain is primarily based in the United States. Your company acquires an office in France. You need to ensure that the group policies that you have established support the French language. What do you need to do?
   a. Copy the DML files to the FR folder in the central store.
   b. Create a second set of GPOs with the French language.
   c. Load the French Language pack in the GPMC.
   d. Run the ADM migrator and convert the current GPOs to French.

5. What type of files do you install using Software Installation via group policies?
   a. .msi
   b. .exe
   c. .ins
   d. .adm

Matching and Identification

1. Match the GPO software installation option with its corresponding description
   _____ a) Assign software to user.
   _____ b) Assign software to a computer.
   _____ c) Publish software to a user.
   _____ d) Publish software to a computer.
   1. Installs the next time a computer is restarted.
   2. Creates a shortcut in the Control Panel to install the application.
   3. Installation begins when the program is picked from the Start menu or an associated file is opened.
   4. Not available.

Build a List

1. What are the steps, in order, to deploy software using group policies? Not all steps will be used.
   _____ Create a GPO to distribute the software package.
   _____ Assign or publish a package to a user or computer.
   _____ Create an MSI package.
   _____ Create a distribution point on the publishing server.
   _____ Add the software installation attribute.

2. What are the steps, in order, to deploy a script via a group policy? Not all steps will be used.
   _____ Create a login script.
   _____ Configure the GPO to execute the script.
   _____ Copy the script to the C:\Windows\Sysvol\Sysvol\Domain Name\Scripts folder.
   _____ Copy the script to the C:\Windows.
   _____ Copy the scripts to the shared folders called *Scripts*.
   _____ Create a shared folder called *Scripts*.
   _____ Test the script.
   _____ Link the script to an OU.

3. What are the steps, in order, to create a central store for GPOs?
   _____ Open the GPMC.
   _____ Open the ADM Migrator.
   _____ Copy the .adml files from the %systemroot%\PolicyDefinitions* folder to the %systemroot%\sysvol\domain\policies\ folder.
   _____ Copy the .admx files from the %systemroot%\PolicyDefinitions* folder to the %systemroot%\sysvol\domain\policies\ folder.
   _____ Copy all of the language folders and files to the %systemroot%\sysvol\domain\policies\PolicyDefintions folder.
   _____ Create a PolicyDefinitions folder in the %systemroot%\sysvol\domain\policies\ folder.
   _____ Select the Central Store tab and click the Create button.
4. Identify the path where the User's Administrative Templates is found in a GPO. Not all folders will be used.
   _____ HKEY_CURRENT_USER
   _____ HKEY_LOCAL_MACHINE
   _____ Windows
   _____ System
   _____ Microsoft
   _____ Software
   _____ Policies
   _____ CurrentVersion
   _____ Templates
   _____ Administrative Templates

Business Case Scenarios

Scenario 20-1: Standardizing a User's Work Environment

Many computers are shared among users and people often use different computers based on where they work. Therefore, you need to configure the following:

- Users must be able to access all documents that he or she stores in the Documents and Desktop folders.
- The users should also have the TimeClock.msi file installed so that he or she can clock in and out.

How can you accomplish this?

Scenario 20-2: Using an ADM File

You have an ADM file for the widget application. How do you implement the ADM settings into the Central Store and deploy the application so that it is fully installed and available for the users in the Sales OU?

Managing Group Policy Objects

LESSON 21

70-411 EXAM OBJECTIVE

Objective 6.3 – Manage Group Policy Objects (GPOs). This objective may include but is not limited to: back up, import, copy, and restore GPOs; create and configure a migration table; reset default GPOs; delegate Group Policy Management.

Lesson Heading	Exam Objective
Managing Group Policy Objects	Manage Group Policy Objects (GPOs)
Backing Up and Restoring GPOs	Back up, import, copy, and restore GPOs
Using a Migration Table	Create and configure a migration table
Resetting the Default GPOs	Reset default GPOs
Delegating Group Policy Management	Delegate Group Policy Management

KEY TERMS

Group Policy Container (GPC)
Group Policy Template (GPT)
DCGPOFix.exe
delegation
migration table

Managing Group Policy Objects

THE BOTTOM LINE

So far, we have discussed how to create Group Policy Objects (GPOs) and manage the settings within a GPO. But so far, managing of the GPOs themselves has not been discussed.

CERTIFICATION READY
Manage Group Policy Objects (GPOs).
Objective 6.3

Although Group Policy settings are configured using GPOs, GPOs are made of two components: ***Group Policy Container (GPC)*** and ***Group Policy Template (GPT)***. The GPC is an Active Directory object stored in the Group Policy Objects container with the domain naming content of the directory. The GPC defines basic attributes of the GPO, but it does not contain any of the settings.

The settings are contained in the GPT, a collection of files stored in the SYSVOL (%SystemRoot%\SYSVOL\<*Domain*>\Policies\<*GPOGUID*>) of each domain controller. Of course, as mentioned previously, this folder is replicated from one domain controller to another. The version of the GPO on a domain controller can be determined by looking at the \\{*servername*}\SYSVOL\{*domain*}\Policies\{*GUID*}\gpt.ini.

Backing Up and Restoring GPOs

CERTIFICATION READY
Back up, import, copy, and restore GPOs.
Objective 6.3

For most organizations, GPOs is an essential tool to help manage the user environment and to ensure security. If you back up a domain controller including the System State, you back up all GPOs. However, you can back up and restore GPOs using the Group Policy Management Console.

With the Group Policy Management Console, you can back up all GPOs or individual GPOs. Every time a backup is performed, a new backup version of the GPO is created.

BACK UP GPOs

GET READY. To back up GPOs, perform the following steps:

1. Open **Server Manager**.
2. Click **Tools > Group Policy Management**. The *Group Policy Management Console* opens.
3. Navigate to and click the **Group Policy Objects** container.
4. To back up all GPOs, right-click **Group Policy Objects** container and click **Back Up All**. The *Back Up Group Policy Object* dialog box opens (see Figure 21-1).

Figure 21-1
Opening the *Back Up Group Policy Object* dialog box

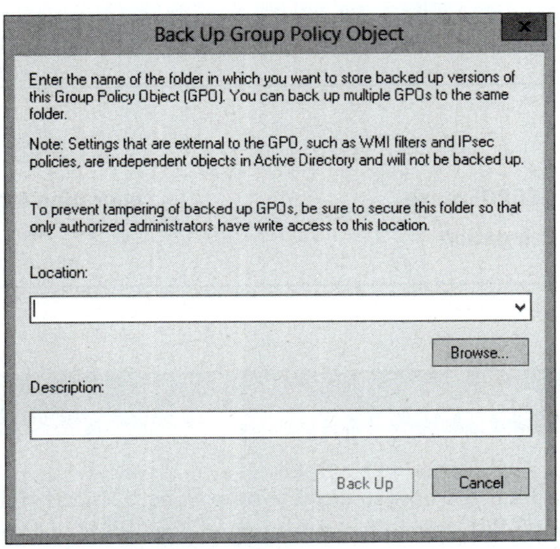

5. To back up a single GPO, right-click the GPO and click **Back Up**. The *Back Up Group Policy Object* dialog box opens.
6. In the *Location* text box, specify the location of where you want to store the backups and click **Back Up**.
7. When the backup is complete, click **OK**.
8. Close the *Group Policy Management Console*.

If a GPO gets deleted or corrupted, you can restore any of the historical versions of the GPO. The restore interface provides the ability for you to view the settings stored in the backed-up version before restoring it.

RESTORE A GPO

GET READY. To restore a GPO, perform the following steps:

1. Open Server Manager.
2. Click Tools > Group Policy Management. The *Group Policy Management Console* opens.
3. Navigate to and click the Group Policy Objects container.
4. To restore a GPO, right-click a GPO and click Restore from Backup.
5. When the *Restore Group Policy Object Wizard* opens, click Next.
6. On the *Backup location* page, specify the location of the backup folder in the *Backup folder* text box. Click Next.
7. On the *Source GPO* page (see Figure 21-2), click the GPO that you want to view and click the View Settings button to view the settings within the backed up GPO.

Figure 21-2

Restoring a GPO

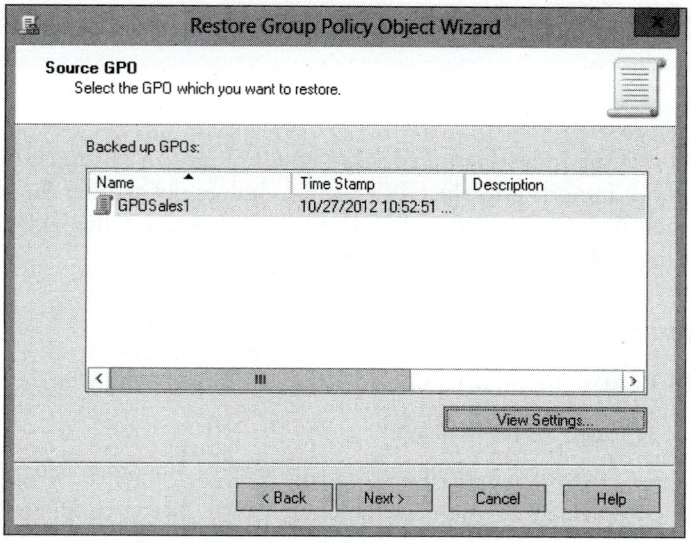

8. Select the GPO that you want to restore and click Next.
9. When the wizard is complete, click the Finish button.
10. When the restore is complete, click OK.
11. Close the *Group Policy Management Console*.

The Group Policy Management Console also has a Manage Backups feature. By using this feature, you can restore from backup, delete a backup, and view settings. To open the Manage Backups dialog box (see Figure 21-3), right-click *Group Policy Objects* container and click *Managed Backups*.

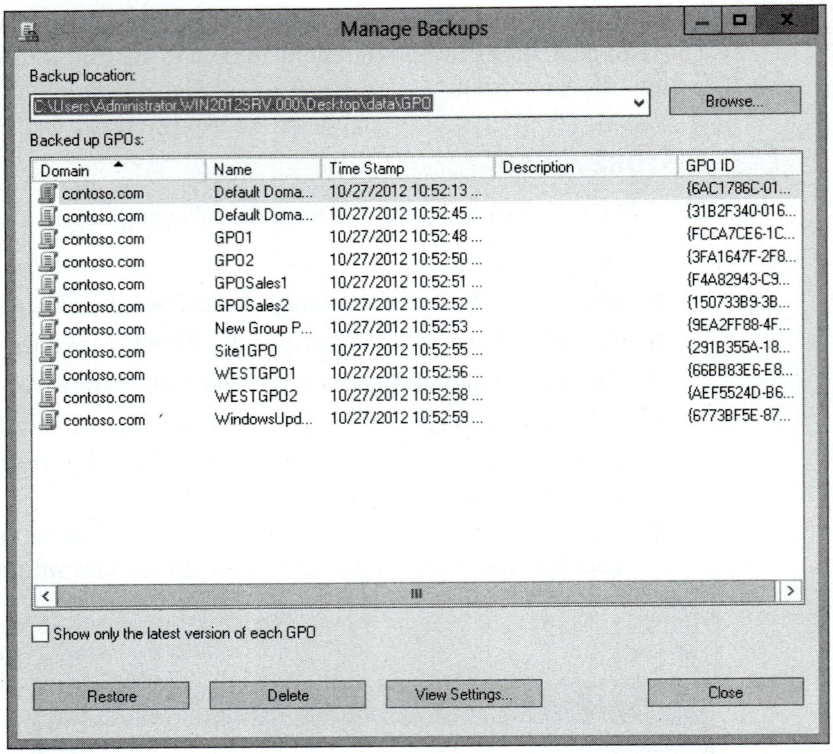

Figure 21-3

Managing GPO Backups

You can import settings of a backed up GPO into an existing GPO. When you import a GPO, it imports only the GPO settings. It does not transfer the security links or security principals assigned to the GPO. If you import settings into a GPO with settings, the imported settings will overwrite the existing settings.

IMPORT GPO SETTINGS

GET READY. To import a GPO setting, perform the following steps:

1. Open Server Manager.
2. Click Tools > Group Policy Management. The *Group Policy Management Console* opens.
3. Navigate to and click the Group Policy Objects container.
4. Right-click the target GPO and click Import Settings.
5. When the *Welcome* screen opens, click Next.
6. On the *Backup GPO* page, you can click Backup to back up the GPO before you import the settings. Click Next.
7. If you want to restore from a backup location, specify the location of the backups in the *Backup folder* text box and click Next.
8. Click the GPO that you want to copy from and click Next.
9. On the *Scanning Backup* page, click Next.
10. On the *Migrating References* page (see Figure 21-4), with the *Copying them identically from the source* selected, click Next.

Figure 21-4

Specifying how to transfer references to security principals

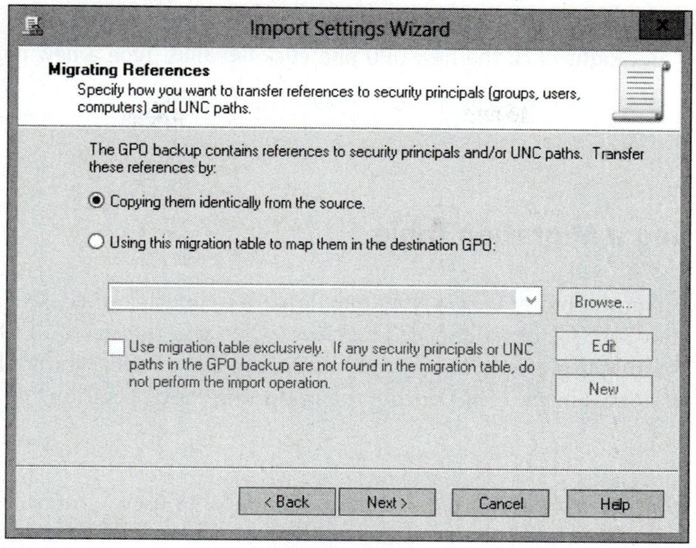

11. When the wizard is complete, click Finish.
12. When the import is complete, click OK.
13. Close the *Group Policy Management Console*.

Lastly, you can copy GPOs by using the Group Policy Management Console in the same domain and across domains. Similar to copy and paste used with files, the copy option copies the existing GPO. When you paste it to the Group Policy Objects container, it is named *copy of old_name*. You just have to rename a GPO to a more meaningful name. If you copy between domains, security principals will need to be redefined.

COPY A GPO

GET READY. To copy a GPO, perform the following steps:

1. Open Server Manager.
2. Click Tools > Group Policy Management. The *Group Policy Management Console* opens.
3. Navigate to and click the Group Policy Objects container.
4. Right-click a GPO and click Copy.
5. Right-click Group Policy Objects container and click Paste.
6. When the *Copy GPO* dialog box appears (see Figure 21-5), click Use the default permissions for the new GPOs or Preserve the existing permissions. Click OK.

Figure 21-5

Specifying how permissions are being copied or not

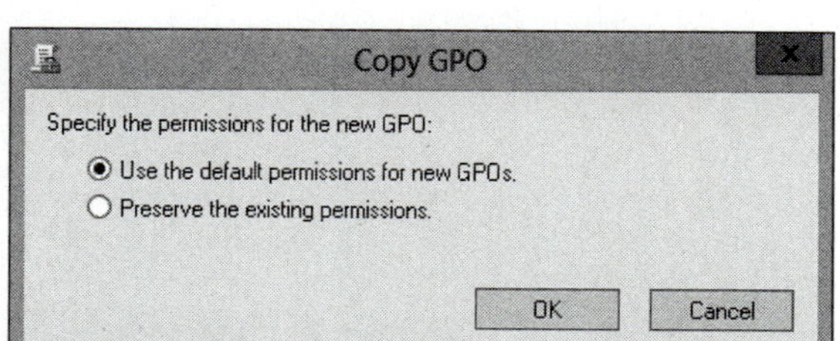

7. When the copy is complete, click OK.
8. Right-click the new GPO and click Rename. Type a new name and press the Enter key.
9. Close the *Group Policy Management Console*.

Using a Migration Table

When migrating GPOs from one domain to another, the GPO is specific to the domain where the GPO is defined. Therefore, when you transfer a GPO to a different domain, you might not want the same settings. You can use migration tables to modify these references in the GPO during the import or copy operation.

CERTIFICATION READY
Create and configure a migration table.
Objective 6.3

A ***migration table*** is a file that maps references to users, groups, computers, and UNC paths in the source GPO to new values in the destination GPO. A migration table consists of one or more mapping entries. When you specify a migration table while performing an import or copy, each reference in the source GPO will be replaced with a target reference. You can open the migration table when you import GPO settings or you can right-click *Domains* in the Group Policy Management Console and click *Open Migration Table Editor*.

USE A MIGRATION TABLE

GET READY. To use a migration table while importing GPO settings, perform the following steps:

1. Open Server Manager.
2. Click Tools > Group Policy Management. The *Group Policy Management Console* opens.
3. Navigate to and click the Group Policy Objects container.
4. Right-click a GPO and click Import.
5. When the *Import Settings Wizard* starts, click Next.
6. On the *Backup GPO* page, click Next.
7. On the *Backup location* page, specify the location of the backups in the *Backup folder* text box, click Next.
8. Click the GPO that you want to import and click Next.
9. On the *Scanning Backup* page, click Next.
10. On the *Migrating References* page, click Using this migration table to map them in the destination GPO option.
11. To create a new migration table, click New. The *Migration Table Editor – New* opens (see Figure 21-6).

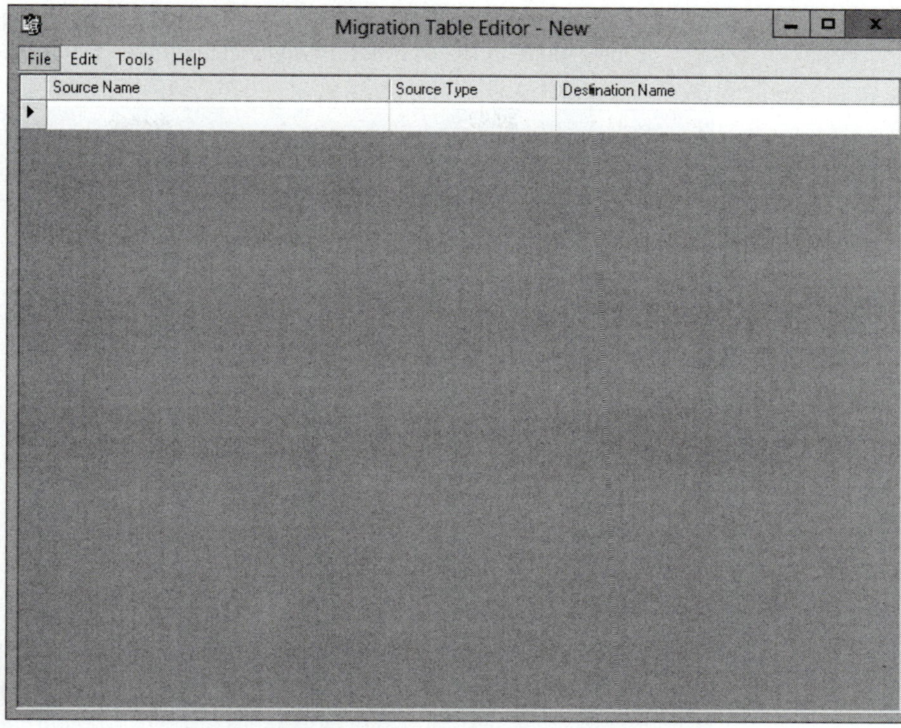

Figure 21-6

Creating a new migration table

12. Click Tools > Populate from Backup. Alternatively, you can also choose Populate from GPO.
13. On the *Select Backup* dialog box, click the GPO that you want to populate the migration table with and click OK. The migration table will populate (see Figure 21-7).

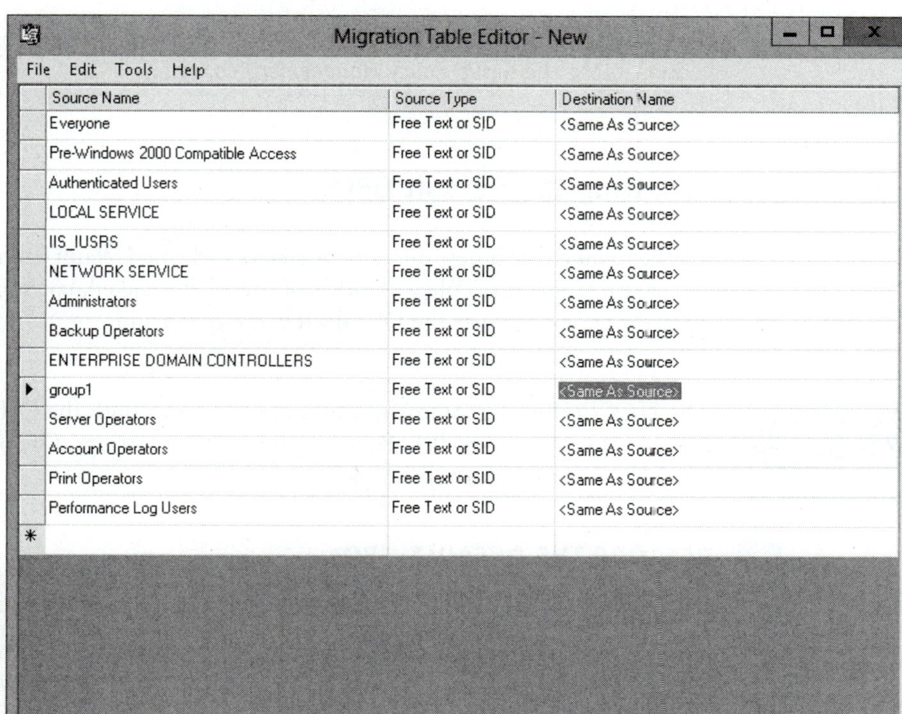

Figure 21-7

Populating the migration table

14. Review the Source Name. If you want the values to change for the target, type the new name in the *Destination Name* column (see Figure 21-8).

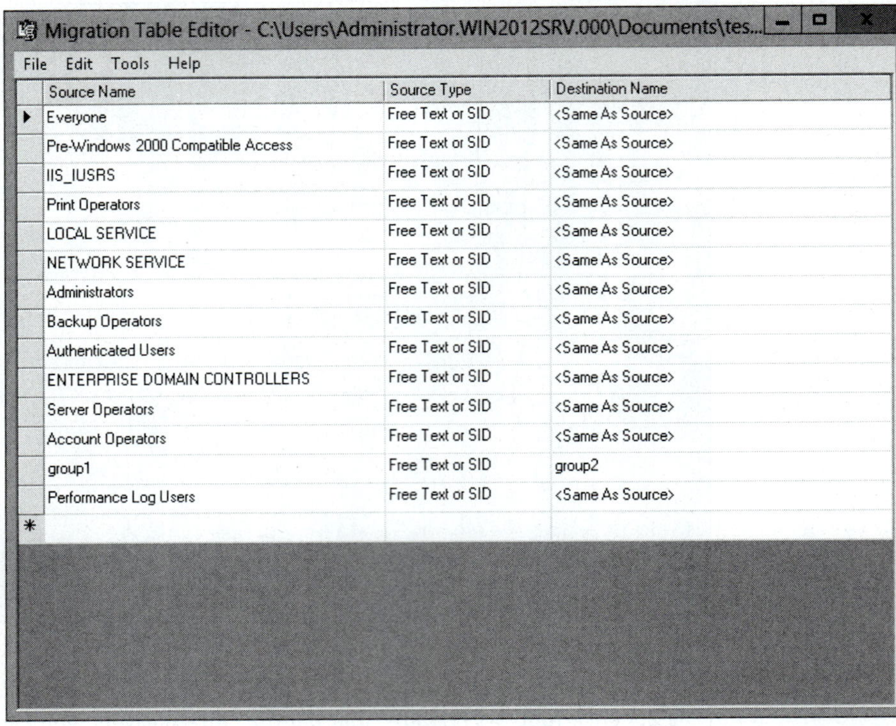

Figure 21-8

Specifying the changed destination value

15. Click File > Save. Specify a name in the *File name* text box and click Save.
16. Close the migration table.
17. On the *Migrating References* page, click Next.
18. When the wizard is complete, click Finish.
19. When the import is succeeded, click OK.
20. Close the *Group Policy Management Console*.

Resetting the Default GPOs

When you create a new domain, you start with the Default Domain Policy and Default Domain Controller Policy. If either of these gets deleted, corrupted, or you just want to start over, you can use the DCGPOFix.exe command.

CERTIFICATION READY
Reset default GPOs.
Objective 6.3

The ***DCGPOFix.exe*** command can restore either or both the Default Domain Policy and the Default Domain Controllers Policy to their default settings. Of course, you must be a domain administrator to perform this task.

RESTORE THE DEFAULT GPOs

GET READY. To restore the Default Domain Policy and the Default Domain Controllers Policy, perform the following steps:

1. Right-click the Start menu and select Command Prompt (Admin).
2. At the prompt, execute the `DcGPOFix` command.

3. When it warns that you are about to restore the Default Domain Policy and Default Domain Controller Policy, type Y for Yes and press the Enter key.
4. When it says that it will replace all User Rights Assignments, type Y for Yes and press the Enter key.
5. Close the command prompt.

Delegating Group Policy Management

In Active Directory, domain administrators are automatically granted permissions for performing Group Policy Management tasks. If you need to give other users permissions to manage group policies, you grant those permissions through ***delegation***.

CERTIFICATION READY
Delegate Group Policy Management.
Objective 6.3

When you grant a person or group to create GPOs, they also are granted permissions to manage the GPOs that they created. To delegate GPO permissions, you use the Group Policy Management Console.

SPECIFY WHO CAN CREATE GPOs

GET READY. To specify who can create GPOs, perform the following steps:

1. Open Server Manager.
2. Click Tools > Group Policy Management. The *Group Policy Management Console* opens.
3. Navigate to and click the Group Policy Objects container.
4. Click the Delegation tab. Figure 21-9 shows the Delegation tab.

Figure 21-9

Managing GPO delegates using the Delegation tab

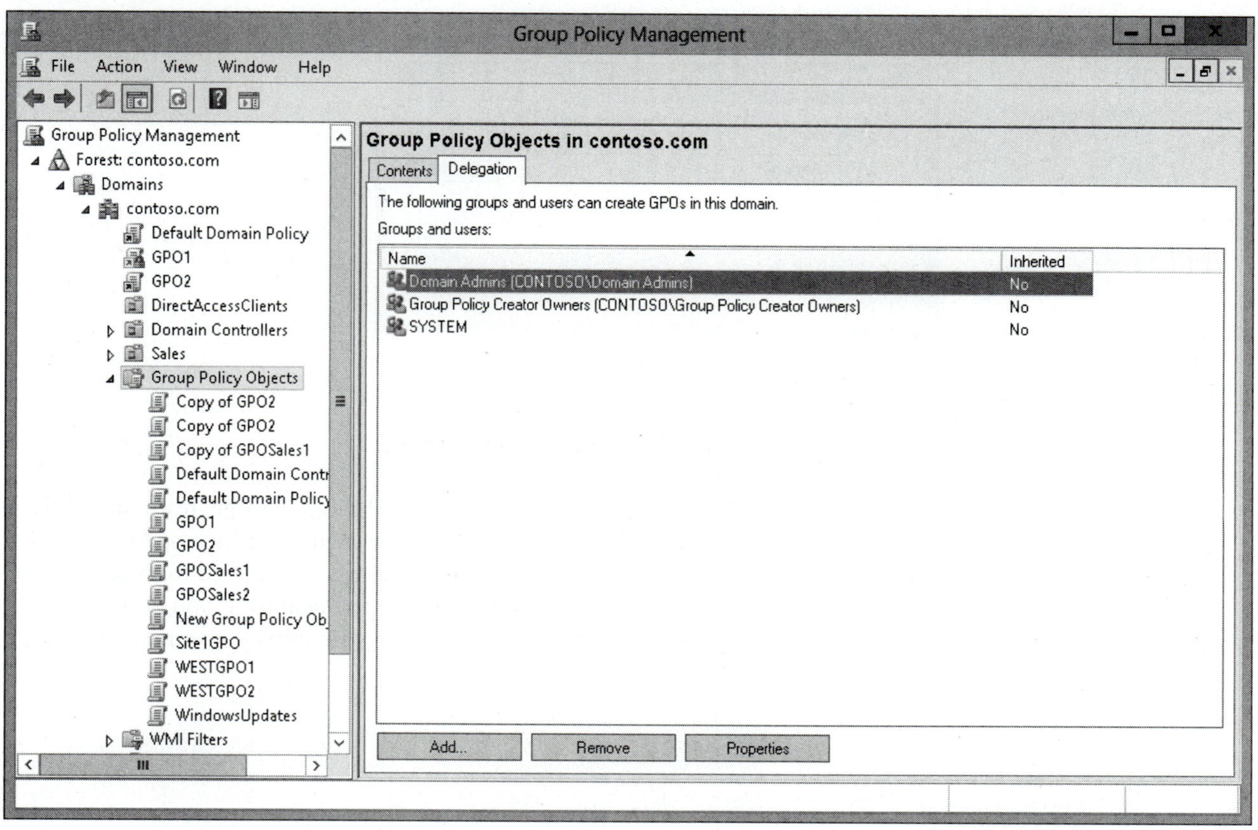

5. To add a user or group, click Add.
6. When the *Select User, Computer, or Group* dialog box opens, type the name of the user or group in the *Enter the object name to select* text box and click OK.
7. Close the *Group Policy Management Console*.

To give someone permission to manage a particular GPO, you use the Delegate tab of the individual GPO. When you add a user, you can then specify one of the following permissions:

- Read
- Edit settings
- Edit settings, delete, and modify security

SPECIFY WHO CAN MANAGE AN INDIVIDUAL GPO

GET READY. To specify who can manage an individual GPO, perform the following steps:

1. Open Server Manager.
2. Click Tools > Group Policy Management. The *Group Policy Management Console* opens.
3. Navigate to and click the Group Policy Objects container.
4. Right-click an individual GPO.
5. Click the Delegation tab.
6. To add a user or group, click Add.
7. When the *Select User, Computer, or Group* dialog box opens, type the name of the user or group in the *Enter the object name to select* text box and click OK.
8. When the *Add Group or User* dialog box opens (see Figure 21-10), assign the appropriate permission and click OK.

Figure 21-10

Assigning Permissions to a GPO

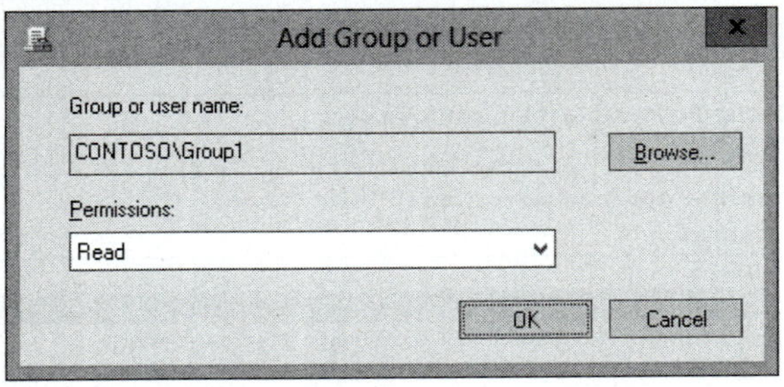

9. Close the *Group Policy Management Console*.

To give more granular control of users and groups who can manage, read, or are affected by a GPO, you click the *Advanced* button from the Delegation tab, which opens the GPO Security Settings dialog box (see Figure 21-11). For permissions to be applied to a user, the user must have the Allow Read and Allow Apply group policy permissions. If you don't want a GPO to apply, you can assign the Disallow Apply group policy permission to a user or group.

Figure 21-11

Managing security settings for a GPO

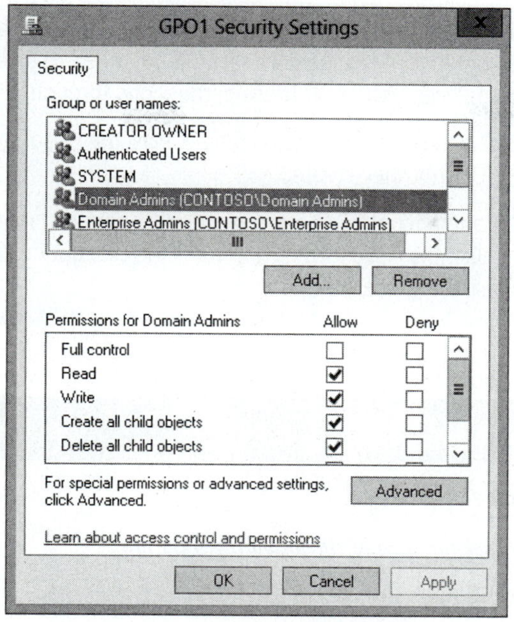

SKILL SUMMARY

IN THIS LESSON, YOU LEARNED:

- Although Group Policy settings are configured using GPOs, GPOs are made of two components: Group Policy Container (GPC) and Group Policy Template (GPT).
- The GPC is an Active Directory object stored in the Group Policy Objects container with the domain naming content of the directory.
- The settings are contained in the GPT, a collection of files stored in the SYSVOL (%SystemRoot%\SYSVOL\<Domain>\Policies\<GPOGUID>) of each domain controller.
- If you back up a domain controller including the System State, you will back up all GPOs. However, you can back up and restore GPOs using the Group Policy Management Console.
- The Group Policy Management Console also has a Manage Backups feature. By using this feature, you can restore from backup, delete a backup, and view settings.
- You can import settings from a backed up GPO into an existing GPO. When you import a GPO, it imports only the GPO settings. It does not transfer the security links or security principals.
- You can copy a GPOs by using the Group Policy Management Console in the same domain an across domains. Similar to copy and paste used with files, the copy option copies the existing GPO. When you paste it to the Group Policy Objects container, it is named copy of old_name.
- A migration table is a file that maps references to users, groups, computers, and UNC paths in the source GPO to new values in the destination GPO.
- The DCGPOFix.exe command can restore either or both the Default Domain Policy or the Default Domain Controllers Policy to their default settings.

(continued)

- In Active Directory, domain administrators are automatically granted permissions for performing Group Policy Management tasks. If you need to give other users permissions to manage group policies, you grant those permissions through delegation.
- When you grant a person or group to create GPOs, they also are granted permissions to manage the GPOs that they created.
- To give more granular control of users and groups who can manage, read, or are affected by a GPO, you click the Advanced button from the Delegation tab, which opens the GPO Security Settings dialog box.

Knowledge Assessment

Multiple Choice

Select the correct answer for each of the following questions.

1. Which two components make up a GPO?
  a. GPT
  b. GPMC
  c. GUID
  d. GPC

2. Which tool is used to back up only a GPO?
  a. Group Policy Management Console
  b. Security Analyze
  c. Windows Backup
  d. Group Policy Object Editor

3. Which feature allows you to restore from backup, delete a backup, and view the settings of a GPO?
  a. GPO Viewer
  b. Manage Backups
  c. Group Policy Object Editor
  d. Backup Manager

4. Which file maps references to users, groups, computers, and UNC paths when importing settings from one GPO to another GPO?
  a. sync settings
  b. conversion table
  c. redirect table
  d. migration table

5. Which command allows you to restore the Default Domain Policy or the Default Domain Controllers Policy to their default settings?
  a. GPORestore
  b. GPODef
  c. DCGPOFix
  d. ResetGPO

6. Which tab do you use in the GPMC that grants permissions to a user or group for a GPO?
  a. Permissions
  b. Delegation
  c. Advanced
  d. Groups and Users

7. Which of the following permissions can you grant to a group or user to manage a GPO? (Choose all that apply.)
   a. Edit settings
   b. Full Control
   c. Read
   d. Edit settings, delete, and modify security

8. Which button do you click on the Delegation tab that allows you to assign granular permissions to a GPO?
   a. Permissions
   b. Advanced
   c. All Permissions
   d. Manage

9. Which permission is necessary for a GPO to be applied to a group or user? (Choose all that apply.)
   a. Allow Apply group policy permission
   b. Allow Set permission
   c. Allow Read permission
   d. Allow Access permission

10. After you copy and paste a GPO, what is the last step that you have to do?
    a. Assign to the domain.
    b. Assign the manager of the GPO.
    c. Specify the users that the GPO is applied to.
    d. Rename the GPO.

Best Answer

Choose the letter that corresponds to the best answer. More than one answer choice may achieve the goal. Select the BEST answer.

1. Which feature do you use to copy the settings from one GPO to another GPO?
   a. Copy
   b. Backup
   c. Import
   d. Sync

2. Which feature allows you to copy the GPOs into a new GPO?
   a. Copy
   b. Backup
   c. Import
   d. Sync

3. What does not transfer when you import GPO settings? (Choose all that apply.)
   a. Security links
   b. Security settings
   c. Security principals
   d. Account settings

4. What needs to be redefined when you copy GPOs between domains?
   a. Account settings
   b. Password policy
   c. Security settings
   d. Security principals

5. When you give someone the permission to create GPOs, what else can the user do?
   a. Manage other GPOs.
   b. Manage other GPOs that the user created.
   c. Assign permissions to others for the Group Policies container.
   d. Allow Apply settings.

Build a List

1. Identify the path, in order of folders, of where the GPTs are stored? Not all folders will be used.
   _____ SYSVOL
   _____ Policies
   _____ System32
   _____ C:\Windows
   _____ GPO
   _____ Domain
   _____ INF

2. Identify the steps, in order, to import a GPO. Not all steps will be used.
   _____ Specify the source GPO.
   _____ Open GPMC.
   _____ Specify the migration table.
   _____ Specify the target GPO.
   _____ Right-click GPO and select Import Settings.
   _____ Rename the GPO.
   _____ Specify the backup location.

3. Identify the steps, in order, to copy a GPO. Not all steps will be used.
   _____ Specify the migration table.
   _____ Open GPMC.
   _____ Cut the GOP.
   _____ Copy the GPO.
   _____ Paste the GPO.
   _____ Rename the GPO.
   _____ Specify what happens to the permissions.

4. What steps are needed to stop a GPO to affect a group of users? Not all steps will be used.
   _____ Click Advanced button.
   _____ Click the GPO.
   _____ Click the Delegation tab.
   _____ Open the GPMC.
   _____ Add the group or user.
   _____ Select the Disallow Apply Group Policy.
   _____ Deselect the Allow Apply Group Policy.
   _____ Select the Disallow Read Group Policy.
   _____ Deselect the Allow Read Group Policy.

5. What steps are necessary to create a migration table? Not all steps will be used.
   _____ Right-click Domains and click Open Migration Table Editor.
   _____ Right-click a GPO and click Open Migration Table Editor.
   _____ Execute the MigTable.exe file.
   _____ After the changes have been made, open the File menu and click Save.
   _____ Open the GPMC.

Business Case Scenarios

Scenario 21-1: Copying GPOs to a Test Domain

You have multiple domains in your organization forest. In the primary corporate domain, you have created the multiple GPOs. You want to copy the GPOs to the test domain. However, you need to modify the primary corporate user groups to the primary test user groups and to change the production UNCs to the test UNC. What should you do?

Scenario 21-2: Allowing Others to Create GPOs

The developers need to create GPOs while allowing the developers to manage the GPOs that they create. In addition, you need to give administrative access to the Windows administrator team for all GPOs except the Default Domain Policy and Default Domain Controller Policy. What should you do to accomplish this while maintaining security?

22 LESSON

Configuring Group Policy Preferences

70-411 EXAM OBJECTIVE

Objective 6.4 – Configure Group Policy preferences. This objective may include but is not limited to: configure Group Policy Preferences (GPP) settings, including printers, network drive mappings, power options, custom registry settings, Control Panel settings, Internet Explorer settings, file and folder deployment, and shortcut deployment; configure item-level targeting.

Lesson Heading	Exam Objective
Using Group Policy Preferences	Configure Group Policy Preferences (GPP) settings, including printers, network drive mappings, power options, custom registry settings, Control Panel settings, Internet Explorer settings, file and folder deployment, and shortcut deployment
Configuring Preference Settings	
Configuring Windows Settings	
Configuring Control Panel Settings	
Configuring Item-Level Targeting	Configure item-level targeting

KEY TERMS

Group Policy Preferences (GPP) **item-level targeting** **targeting items**

■ Using Group Policy Preferences

THE BOTTOM LINE

Group Policies were expanded in Windows Server 2008 with the introduction of Group Policy Preferences. ***Group Policy Preferences (GPP)*** are made up of more than 20 new Group Policy client-side extensions (CSEs) that expand the range of configurable settings in a Group Policy object (GPO) that were not available before. Examples of the new GPP extensions include Folder Options, Drive Maps, Printers, Scheduled Tasks, Services, and Start Menu.

CERTIFICATION READY
Configure Group Policy Preferences (GPP) settings including printers, network drive mappings, power options, custom registry settings, Control Panel settings, Internet Explorer settings, file and folder deployment, and shortcut deployment.
Objective 6.4

The key difference between preferences and policy settings is enforcement. Although Group Policies settings cannot be modified, GPP writes preferences to the same locations in the registry that the application or operating system feature uses to store the setting. Although the group policy setting interface is usually disabled or grayed out, preference settings can still be changed.

By default, Group Policy refreshes preferences using the same interval as Group Policy settings. However, you can chose to prevent Group Policy from refreshing individual preferences by choosing to apply them only once. This allows you to assign a default value but allows the user to change to his or her liking.

GPP can be configured on domain controllers running Windows Server 2008 or higher. By default, GPP are supported by client computers running Windows Vista SP2, Windows 7 or higher, or Windows Server 2008 or higher. To support Windows XP SP3, Windows Vista SP1, or Windows Server 2003 client computers, you must install GPP Client Side Extensions from Microsoft Downloads or Windows Updates.

Configuring Preference Settings

When you create a GPO with preferences, the preferences options are configured much like you would in Windows such as using the Control Panel and Windows Explorer options. So when you need to configure Internet Options, the options that you configure will look exactly like the Internet Options found in the Windows Control Panel (see Figure 22-1).

Figure 22-1

Viewing GPP

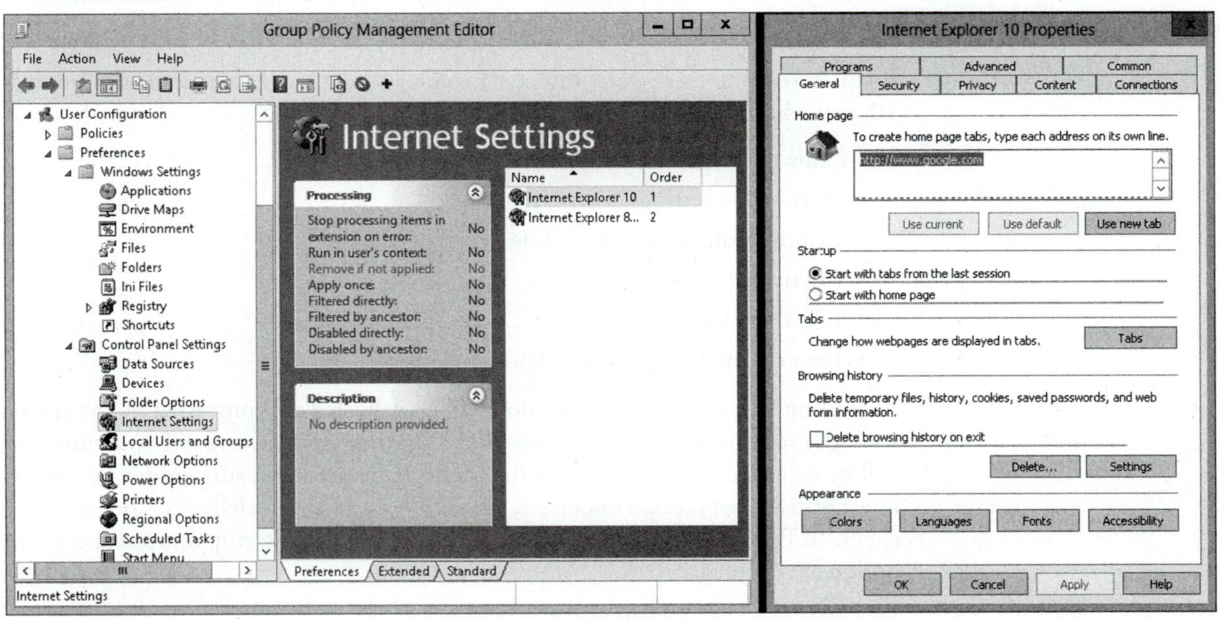

For most preferences settings, you right-click the option that you want to configure, select *New* and select the preference item that you want to create. For example, if you right-click Internet Settings (see Figure 22-2), you have the option to configure the following:

- Internet Explorer 5 and 6
- Internet Explorer 7
- Internet Explorer 8 and 9
- Internet Explorer 10

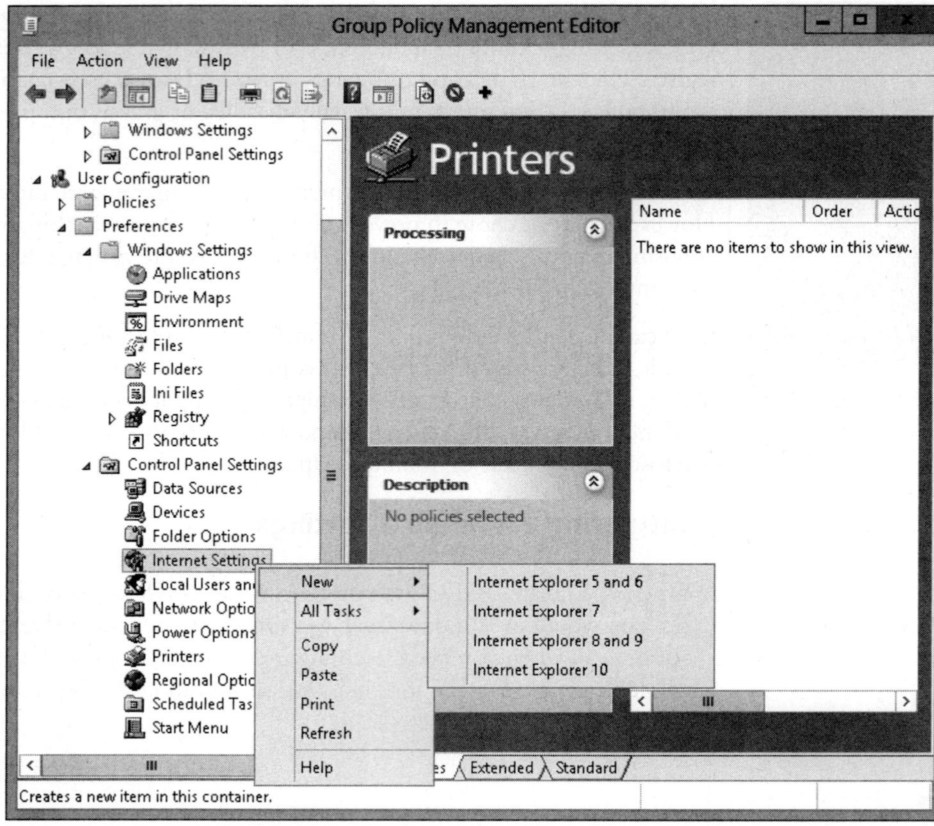

Figure 22-2

Creating a new preference

If you have some users using Internet Explorer 8 and 9 and some users using Internet Explorer 10, you will have to add entries for each one.

The following preferences support editing states:

- Start Menu settings
- Regional and Language settings
- Internet options
- Folder options
- Power options (to include Power Schemes)

An editing state specifies if the option will be delivered and processed by the client. If the setting is surrounded by a green box (solid lines) or has a green solid underline, the settings will be delivered and processed by the client. If the setting is surrounded by a red box (dashed lines) or has a red dashed underline, the settings will not be delivered and processed by the client. In Figure 22-1, the home page is disabled and the startup options and browsing history option are enabled.

To toggle the editing state, use the following keys:

- **F5:** Enable All
- **F6:** Enable Current
- **F7:** Disable Current
- **F8:** Disable All

Most preferences settings include the following Actions. Figure 22-3 shows the Environment preferences with the Action pull-down menu:

- **Create:** Create a new preference setting for the user or computer.
- **Replace:** Delete and recreate a preference setting for the user or computer. The result is that GPP replace all existing settings and files associated with the preference item.
- **Update:** Modify an existing preference setting for the user or computer.
- **Delete:** Remove an existing preference setting for the user or computer.

Figure 22-3

Selecting an action for a preference

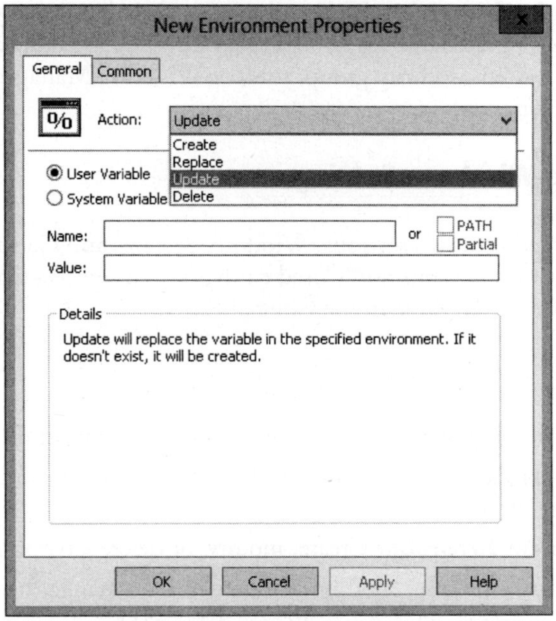

The last tab available for preference settings is the Common tab (see Figure 22-4), which allows you to control the behavior of the preference as follows:

- **Stop processing items in this extension if an error occurs:** When this option is selected, if an error occurs while processing a preference, no other preferences in this GPO will process.

Figure 22-4

Configuring common settings

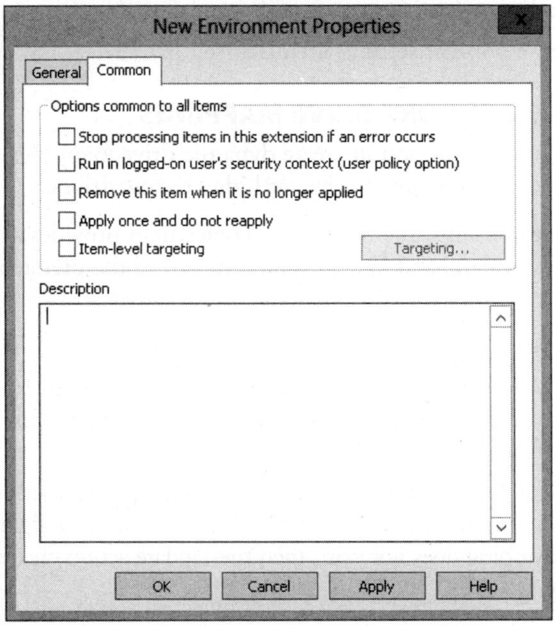

- **Run in logged-on user's security context:** By default, this option runs as the System account. If this option is selected, the logged-on user context is used.
- **Remove this item when it is no longer applied:** Unlike policy settings, preferences are not removed when the GPO that delivered it is removed. When the GPO is removed, the setting will be removed if this option is selected.
- **Apply once and do not reapply:** Normally, preferences are refreshed at the same interval as Group Policy settings. If this option is selected, this option will be applied only once on logon or startup.
- **Use Item-level targeting:** This option is used to determine which users or computers will receive a preference based on a criterion, such as computer name, IP address range, operating system, security group, user, or Windows Management Instrumentation (WMI) queries.

Configuring Windows Settings

GPP are divided into two sections: Windows Settings and Control Panel Settings. Windows Settings are commonly used configuration settings that are performed in Windows, but are not done in the Control Panel.

Preference extensions under Windows Settings include:

- **Applications Extension:** Configure settings for applications.
- **Drive Maps Extension:** Create, modify, or delete mapped drives, and configure the visibility of all drives.
- **Environment Extension:** Create, modify, or delete environment variables.
- **Files Extension:** Copy, modify, or delete files or change the attributes of the files.
- **Folders Extension:** Create, modify, or delete folders.
- **Ini Files Extension:** Add, replace, or delete sections or properties in configuration settings (.ini) or setup information (.inf) files.
- **Network Shares Extension:** Create, modify, or unshare shared folders.
- **Registry Extension:** Copy registry settings and apply them to other computers. Create, replace, or delete registry settings.
- **Shortcuts Extension:** Create, modify, or delete shortcuts.

Some of the more popular settings are discussed in the next few subsections.

CONFIGURING NETWORK DRIVE MAPPINGS

CERTIFICATION READY
Configure Group Policy Preferences (GPP) settings including network drive mappings.
Objective 6.4

Network drive maps allow you to create dynamic drive mappings to network shares, modify mapped drives, delete a mapped drive, or hide or show drives.

For Drive Map extensions, the type of preference item provides a choice of four actions: Create, Replace, Update, and Delete. The behavior of the preference item varies with the action selected and whether the drive letter already exists:

- **Create:** Create a new mapped drive for users.
- **Replace:** Delete and recreate mapped drives for users. If the drive mapping already exists, the drive mapping will be deleted. If the drive mapping does not exist, then the Replace action creates a new drive mapping.
- **Update:** Modify settings of an existing mapped drive for users. Only updates settings defined within the preference item. All other settings remain as configured on the mapped drive. If the drive mapping does not exist, then the Update action creates a new drive mapping.
- **Delete:** Remove a mapped drive for users.

CREATE A MAPPED DRIVE PREFERENCE ITEM

GET READY. To create a mapped drive preference item, perform the following steps:

1. Open the Group Policy Management Editor for the GPO you want to configure.
2. Navigate to and click Computer Configuration\Preferences\Windows Settings\Drive Maps or User Configuration\Preferences\Windows Settings\Drive Maps.
3. Right-click the Drive Maps node, click New, and select Mapped Drive. The *New Drive Properties* dialog box opens (see Figure 22-5).

Figure 22-5

Creating a new drive preference item

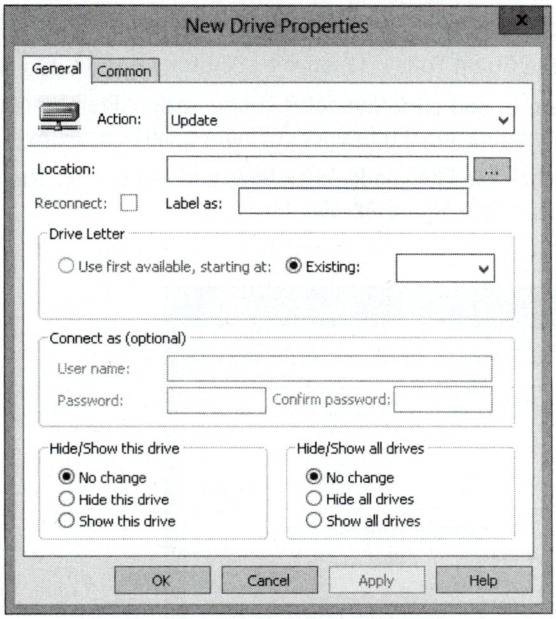

4. Select an Action for Group Policy to perform.
5. Specify the location of the remote drive using a Universal Naming Convention (UNC), the drive mapping, and the Connect as and the Hide/Show options.
6. Click the Common tab, and configure any of the Common options.
7. Click OK. The new preference item appears in the details pane.
8. Close the *Group Policy Management Editor*.

PERFORMING FILE AND FOLDER DEPLOYMENT

CERTIFICATION READY
Configure Group Policy Preferences (GPP) settings including file and folder deployment.
Objective 6.4

There might be times when you want to make sure that users have certain files available to them. Therefore, you can use the Files and Folders nodes under Windows Settings to copy, delete, or move files and folders.

File Preference item provides a choice of four actions: Create, Replace, Update, and Delete. The behavior of the preference item varies with the action selected and whether the file already exists:

- **Create:** Copy a file or files from a source location to a destination location if it does not already exist at the destination, and then configure the attributes of those files for computers or users.
- **Replace:** Delete a file or files, replace it with another file or files, and configure the attributes of those files for computers or users. If the file already exists, it will overwrite the file. If the file does not exist at the destination, then the Replace action copies the file from the source location to the destination.

- **Update:** Modify settings of an existing file or files for computers or users. Different from Replace, this option updates only the file attributes for the specified file or files. If the file does not exist, then the Update action copies the file from the source location to the destination.
- **Delete:** Remove a file or files for computers or users.

To copy, replace, update, or delete files, you can use the wildcard (* and ?) characters.

COPY, REPLACE, UPDATE, OR DELETE FILES

GET READY. To copy, replace, update, or delete files, perform the following steps:

1. Open the Group Policy Management Editor for the GPO you want to configure.
2. Navigate to and click Computer Configuration\Preferences\Windows Settings\Files or User Configuration\Preferences\Windows Settings\Files.
3. Right-click the Files node, click New, and select File. The *New File Properties* dialog box opens (see Figure 22-6).

Figure 22-6

Creating a new file preference item

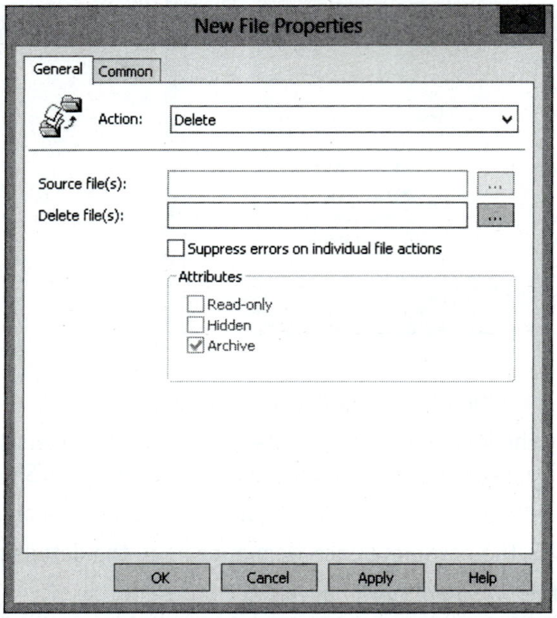

4. Select an Action for Group Policy to perform.
5. If you are copying, replacing, or updating files, specify the source files that you want to copy or replace in the *Source file(s)* text box. This option will be grayed out if you select the Delete action.
6. If you are copying, replacing, or updating files, specify the destination files in the Destination File.
7. If you are copying, replacing, or updating files, specify the file attributes.
8. If you are deleting files, specify the files in the *Delete file(s)* text box.
9. To allow multiple files to transfer even if one or more individual files fail to transfer, select the Suppress errors on individual file actions check box.
10. Click the Common tab, and configure any of the Common options.
11. Click OK. The new preference item appears in the details pane.
12. Close the *Group Policy Management Editor*.

Folder preference items provide a choice of four actions: Create, Replace, Update, or Delete folders and their contents:

- **Create:** Create a new folder for computers or users.
- **Replace:** Delete and recreate a folder for computers or users. If the folder does not exist, then the Replace action creates a new folder.
- **Update:** Modify an existing folder for computers or users. This action differs from Replace in that it updates only settings defined within the preference item. All other settings remain as configured on the folder. If the folder does not exist, then the Update action creates a new folder.
- **Delete:** Remove a folder for computers or users.

CREATE, REPLACE, UPDATE, AND DELETE FOLDERS AND THEIR CONTENT

GET READY. To create, replace, update, or delete a folder, perform the following steps:

1. Open the Group Policy Management Editor for the GPO you want to configure.
2. Navigate to and click Computer Configuration\Preferences\Windows Settings\Folders or User Configuration\Preferences\Windows Settings\Folders.
3. Right-click the Folders node, click New, and select Folder. The *New Folder Properties* dialog box opens (see Figure 22-7).

Figure 22-7

Creating a folder preference item

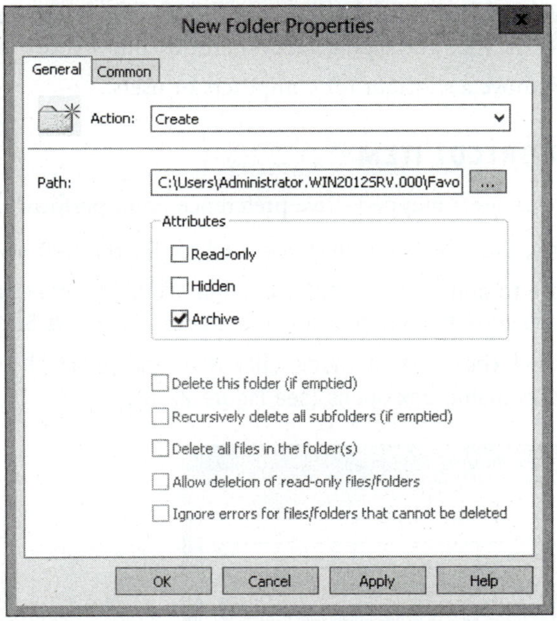

4. Select an Action for Group Policy to perform.
5. Specify the path of the folder in the *Path* text box.
6. If you need to delete folders that are not empty, enable the Delete this folder (if emptied) option.
7. If you need to delete all subfolders within the folder you are trying to delete, enable the Recursively delete all subfolders is selected option.
8. If you need to delete read-only file and folders, enable the Allow deletion of read-only files/folders option. If this option is selected, it also clears the read-only attribute of files and folders that this Folder item attempts to delete.
9. If you need to delete items within the folder that you are attempting to delete, you must enable the Delete all files in the folder(s) option.

10. If you want to suppress errors if the folder is not empty, a file that is open in the folder, a file or folder for which the user does not have permission, or any other file or folder that cannot be deleted, enable the Ignore errors for files/folders that cannot be deleted option.
11. Click the Common tab, and configure any of the Common options.
12. Click OK. The new preference item appears in the details pane.
13. Close the *Group Policy Management Editor*.

PERFORMING SHORTCUT DEPLOYMENT

CERTIFICATION READY
Configure Group Policy Preferences (GPP) settings including shortcut deployment.
Objective 6.4

Shortcut preference items allow you to configure a shortcut to a file system object (such as a file, folder, drive, share, or computer), a shell object (such as a printer, desktop item, or control panel item), or a URL (such as a web page or an FTP site).

This type of preference item provides a choice of four actions: Create, Replace, Update, and Delete. The behavior of the preference item varies with the action selected and whether the shortcut already exists.

- **Create:** Create a new shortcut for computers or users.
- **Replace:** Delete and recreate a shortcut for computers or users. If the shortcut already exists, it will be overwritten. If the shortcut does not exist, then the Replace action creates a new shortcut.
- **Update:** Modify settings of an existing shortcut for computers or users. If the shortcut does not exist, then the Update action creates a new shortcut.
- **Delete:** Remove a shortcut for computers or users.

CREATE A SHORTCUT ITEM

GET READY. To create a mapped drive preference item, perform the following steps:

1. Open the Group Policy Management Editor for the GPO you want to configure.
2. Navigate to and click Computer Configuration\Preferences\Windows Settings\Shortcuts or User Configuration\Preferences\Windows Settings\Shortcuts.
3. Right-click the Shortcuts node, click New, and select Shortcut. The *New Shortcut Properties* dialog box opens (see Figure 22-8).

Figure 22-8
Creating a shortcut preference item

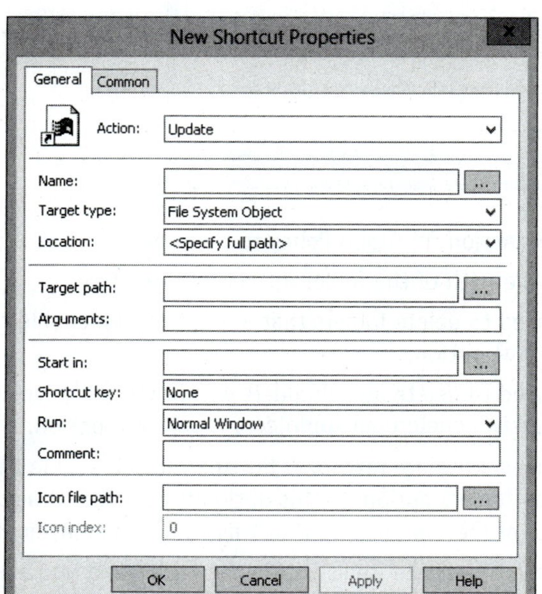

4. Select an Action for Group Policy to perform.
5. In the *Name* textbox, type in the name of the shortcut.
6. Using the *Target Type* pull-down menu, select File System Object, URL, or Shell Object.
7. Using the *Location* pull-down menu, select the location of the object such as Desktop, Start Menu, or Explorer Favorites.
8. In the *Target Path* text box, type a local path, UNC path, or drive letter that the shortcut will point to.
9. In the *Start in* text box, specify the working directory that contains files required by the target.
10. In the *Shortcut key* text box, type the key combinations to activate the shortcut. To remove the keyboard shortcut, press Delete or Backspace. This option is not available for Delete.
11. In the *Run* text box, select the size of the window on which to open the target of the shortcut.
12. In the *Comment* text box, which will be displayed as a tooltip, enter text describing the shortcut.
13. In the *Icon file path* text box, specify an icon for the shortcut.
14. Click the Common tab, and configure any of the Common options.
15. Click OK. The new preference item appears in the details pane.
16. Close the *Group Policy Management Editor*.

Configuring Control Panel Settings

The Control Panel Preferences allow you to configure the popular settings found within the Control Panel.

Preference extensions under Control Panel Settings include:

- **Data Sources Extension:** Create, modify, or delete Open Database Connectivity (ODBC) data source names.
- **Devices Extension:** Enable or disable hardware devices or classes of devices.
- **Folder Options Extension:** Configure folder options, such as creating, modifying, or deleting filename extension associations.
- **Internet Settings Extension:** Modify user-configurable Internet settings.
- **Local Users and Groups Extension:** Create, modify, or delete local users and groups.
- **Network Options Extension:** Create, modify, or delete virtual private networking (VPN) or dial-up networking connections.
- **Power Options Extension:** Modify power options and create, modify, or delete power schemes.
- **Printers Extension:** Create, modify, or delete TCP/IP, shared, and local printer connections.
- **Regional Options Extension:** Modify regional options.
- **Scheduled Tasks Extension:** Create, modify, or delete scheduled or immediate tasks.
- **Services Extension:** Modify services.
- **Start Menu Extension:** Modify Start Menu options.

CERTIFICATION READY
Configure Group Policy Preferences (GPP) settings including printers.
Objective 6.4

CONFIGURING PRINTER SETTINGS

Similar to adding a printer to Windows, you can add a shared printer, a TCP/IP printer, or a local printer.

The Printers preference extension allows you to create, configure, and delete local printers, TCP/IP printers, and Shared Printers Printer preference item. The next three exercises show you how to create these printers.

CREATE A NEW LOCAL PRINTER PREFERENCE ITEM

GET READY. To create a new local printer preference item, perform the following steps:

1. Open the Group Policy Management Editor for the GPO you want to configure.
2. Navigate to and click Computer Configuration\Preferences\Control Panel Settings\Printers or User Configuration\Preferences\Control Panel Settings\Printers.
3. Right-click the Printers node, click New, and select Local Printer. The *New Local Printer Properties* dialog box opens (see Figure 22-9).

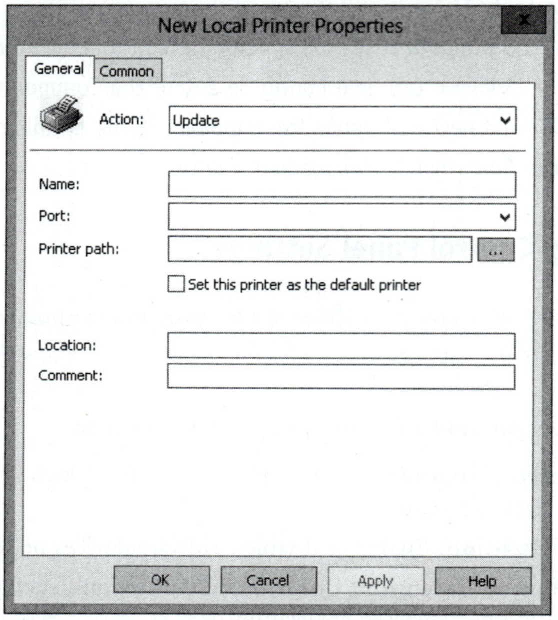

Figure 22-9
Creating a new local printer preference item

4. Select an Action for Group Policy to perform.
5. Specify the Name, port (Comx, LPTx, or USBx), and printer path for the printer. Then type a location and comments if desired.
6. Click the Common tab, and configure any of the Common options.
7. Click OK. The new preference item appears in the details pane.
8. Close the *Group Policy Management Editor*.

CREATE A NEW TCP/IP PRINTER PREFERENCE ITEM

GET READY. To create a new TCP/IP printer preference item, perform the following steps:

1. Open the Group Policy Management Editor for the GPO you want to configure.
2. Navigate to and click Computer Configuration\Preferences\Control Panel Settings\Printers or User Configuration\Preferences\Control Panel Settings\Printers.
3. Right-click the Printers node, click New, and select TCP/IP Printer. The *New TCP/IP Printer Properties* dialog box opens (see Figure 22-10).

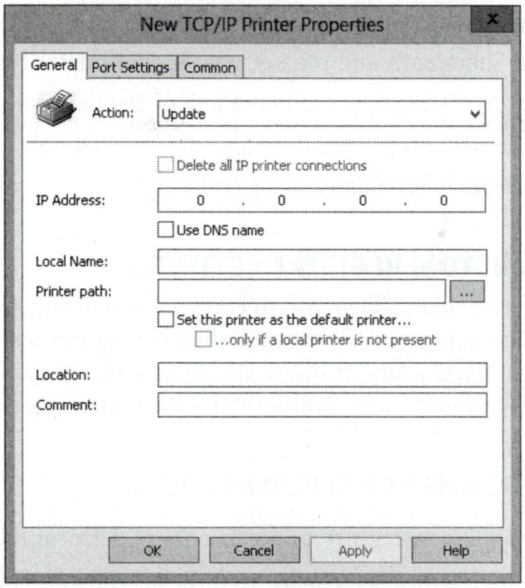

Figure 22-10

Creating a new TCP/IP printer preference item

4. Select an Action for Group Policy to perform.
5. Specify the IP Address, Local Name, and Printer Path for the printer. Then type a location and comments if desired.
6. Click the Common tab, and configure any of the Common options.
7. Click OK. The new preference item appears in the details pane.
8. Close the *Group Policy Management Editor*.

CREATE A NEW SHARED PRINTER PREFERENCE ITEM

GET READY. To create a new shared printer preference item, perform the following steps:

1. Open the Group Policy Management Editor for the GPO you want to configure.
2. Navigate to and click Computer Configuration\Preferences\Control Panel Settings\Printers or User Configuration\Preferences\Control Panel Settings\Printers.
3. Right-click the Printers node, click New, and select Shared Printer. The *New Shared Printer Properties* dialog box opens (see Figure 22-11).

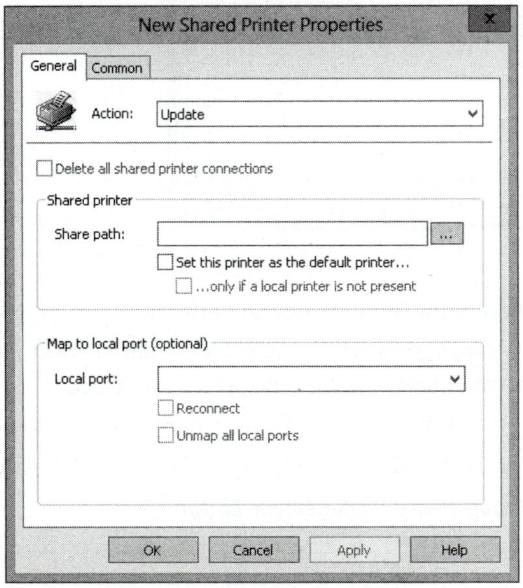

Figure 22-11

Creating a new shared printer preference item

4. Select an Action for Group Policy to perform.
5. Specify the Share path and the optional Local port for the printer.
6. Click the Common tab, and configure any of the Common options.
7. Click OK. The new preference item appears in the details pane.
8. Close the *Group Policy Management Editor*.

CERTIFICATION READY
Configure Group Policy Preferences (GPP) settings including custom registry settings.
Objective 6.4

CONFIGURING CUSTOM REGISTRY SETTINGS

Registry preference extension allows you to copy registry settings from one computer to another, and to create, replace, or delete an individual registry value. It also allows you to create an empty key, delete a key, or delete all values and subkeys in a key. Lastly, it allows you to create collections or folders to organize the Registry preference Items.

CREATE A NEW REGISTRY PREFERENCE ITEM

GET READY. To create a new registry preference item, perform the following steps:

1. Open the Group Policy Management Editor for the GPO you want to configure.
2. Navigate to and click Computer Configuration\Preferences\Windows Settings\Registry or User Configuration\Preferences\Windows Settings\Registry.
3. Right-click the Registry node, click New, and select Registry Item. The *Registry Properties* dialog box opens (see Figure 22-12).

Figure 22-12

Creating a new registry preference item

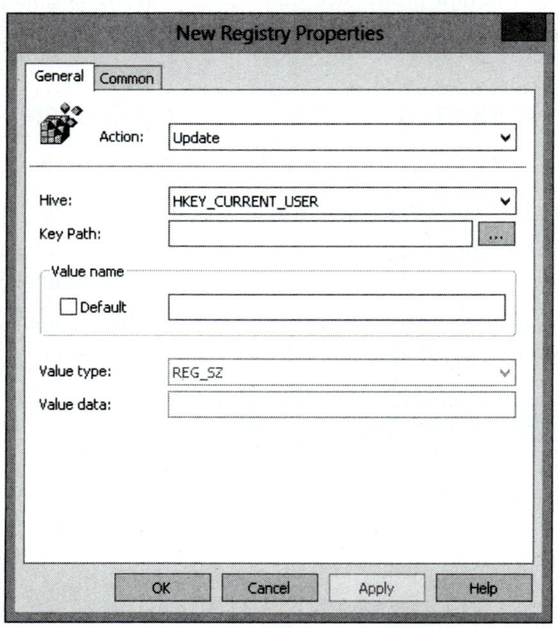

4. Select an Action for Group Policy to perform.
5. Specify the Hive such as HKEY_CURRENT_USER or HKEY_LOCAL_MACHINE. Then specify the value name, value type, and value data.
6. Click the Common tab, and configure any of the Common options.
7. Click OK. The new preference item appears in the details pane.
8. Close the *Group Policy Management Editor*.

To help you organize the registry settings, you can use collections, which act as folders to hold the registry settings. To create a collection, you just right-click *Registry* in the Group Policy Management Editor and select *Collection Item*. You then rename the collection to the desired name. After the collection is created, you can then add Registry items.

The last option under the Registry is the Registry Wizard, which allows you to create multiple Registry preference items based upon registry settings that you select on a computer. After you select the settings, you can modify the permissions after the entries are created. Lastly, the wizard organizes the registry items in a collection folder that mimics the structure of the registry.

CERTIFICATION READY
Configure Group Policy Preferences (GPP) settings including power options.
Objective 3.1

CONFIGURING POWER OPTIONS

The Power options extension allows you to create and configure Power Plan, Power Options, and Power Scheme preference items. The Power Options and Power Schemes are used with Windows XP and Windows Vista and Power Plan with Windows Vista and later.

CREATE A NEW POWER OPTIONS PREFERENCE ITEM

GET READY. To create a new power options preference item, perform the following steps:

1. Open the Group Policy Management Editor for the GPO you want to configure.
2. Navigate to and click Computer Configuration\Preferences\Control Panel Settings\Power Options or User Configuration\Preferences\Control Panel Settings\Power Options.
3. Right-click the Power Options node, click New, and select Power Options (Windows XP). The *New Power Options (Windows XP) Properties* dialog box opens (see Figure 22-13).

Figure 22-13

Creating a new power options (Windows XP) preference item

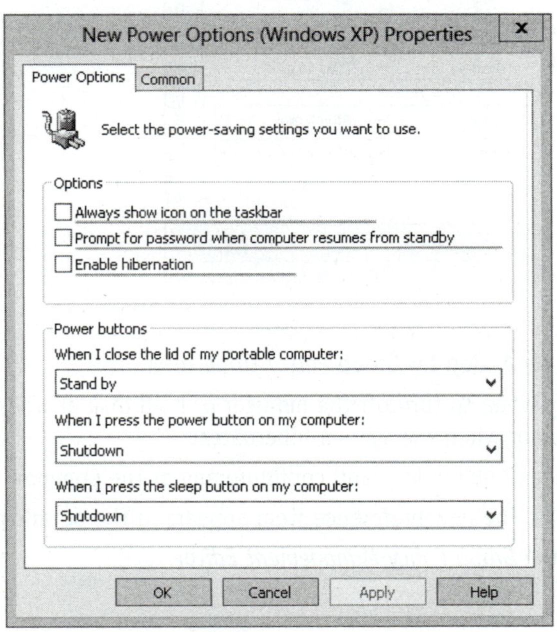

4. Select an Action for Group Policy to perform.
5. Specify whether the power icon shows on the taskbar, whether a password is required to resume from standby, and whether hibernation is enabled. You can also specify what happens when the laptop lid is closed, when the power button is pressed, and when the sleep button is pressed.

6. Click the Common tab, and configure any of the Common options.
7. Click OK. The new preference item appears in the details pane.
8. Close the *Group Policy Management Editor*.

CREATE A NEW POWER SCHEME PREFERENCE ITEM

GET READY. To create a power scheme preference item, perform the following steps:

1. Open the Group Policy Management Editor for the GPO you want to configure.
2. Navigate to and click Computer Configuration\Preferences\Control Panel Settings\Power Options or User Configuration\Preferences\Control Panel Settings\Power Options.
3. Right-click the Power Options node, click New, and select Power Scheme (Windows XP). The *New Power Scheme (Windows XP) Properties* dialog box opens (see Figure 22-14).

Figure 22-14

Creating a new power scheme preference item

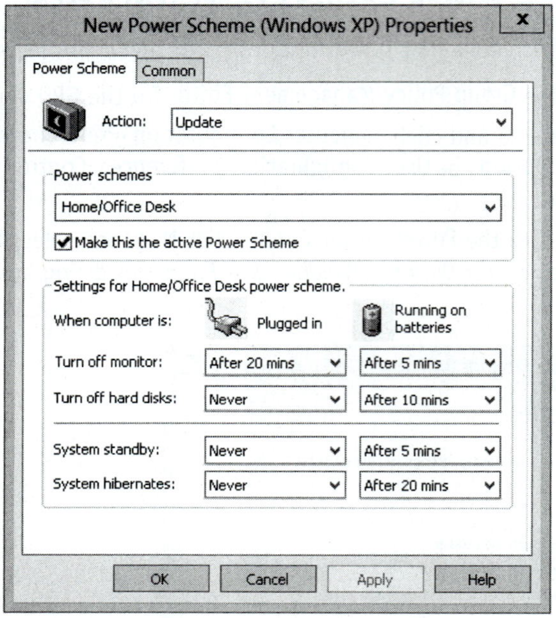

4. Select an Action for Group Policy to perform.
5. Specify when to turn off the monitor or hard disk or when the system goes into standby or when the system hibernates.
6. Click the Common tab, and configure any of the Common options.
7. Click OK. The new preference item appears in the details pane.
8. Close the *Group Policy Management Editor*.

CREATE A NEW POWER OPTIONS PREFERENCE ITEM

GET READY. To create a power options preference item, perform the following steps:

1. Open the Group Policy Management Editor for the GPO you want to configure.
2. Navigate to and click Computer Configuration\Preferences\Control Panel Settings\Power Options or User Configuration\Preferences\Control Panel Settings\Power Options.

3. Right-click the Power Options node, click New, and select Power Plan (At least Windows 7). The *New Power Scheme (At least Windows 7) Properties* dialog box opens (see Figure 22-15).

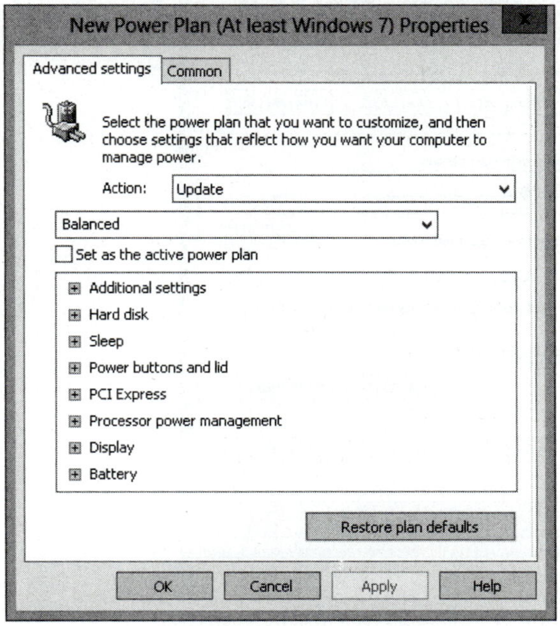

Figure 22-15

Creating a new power plan preference item

4. Select an Action for Group Policy to perform.
5. Specify which power plan to configure and modify the appropriate power options.
6. Click the Common tab, and configure any of the Common options.
7. Click OK. The new preference item appears in the details pane.
8. Close the *Group Policy Management Editor*.

CERTIFICATION READY
Configure Group Policy Preferences (GPP) settings including Internet Explorer settings.
Objective 6.4

CONFIGURING INTERNET EXPLORER SETTINGS

Group Policy includes the Internet Settings preference extension, which allows you to configure specific configuration of Internet settings or to configure an initial configuration of Internet settings, but allow end users to make changes.

CREATE AN INTERNET EXPLORER PREFERENCE ITEM

GET READY. To create an Internet Explorer preference item, perform the following steps:

1. Open the Group Policy Management Editor for the GPO you want to configure.
2. Navigate to and click User Configuration\Preferences\Control Panel Settings\Internet Settings.
3. Right-click the Internet Settings node, click New, and select Internet Explorer 10. The *New Internet Explorer 10 Properties* dialog box opens (see Figure 22-16).

Figure 22-16

Creating a new Internet settings preference item

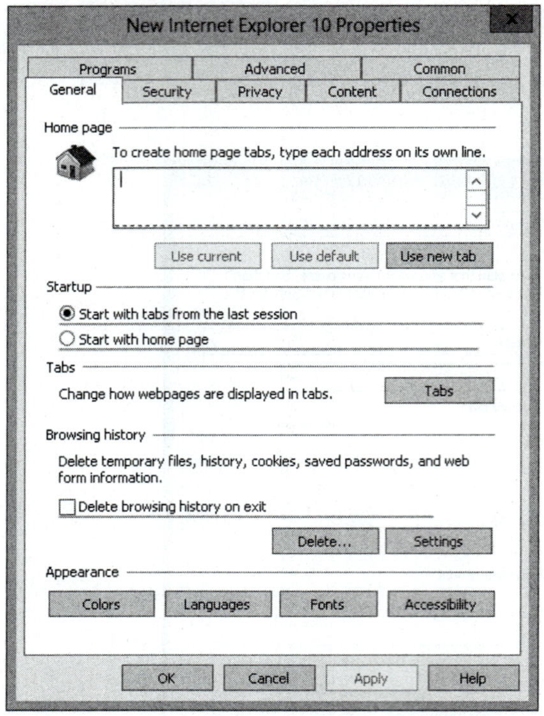

4. Under the General tab, specify a home, specify how tabs are displayed, and specify if Delete browsing history on exist.
5. On the Security tab (see Figure 22-17), specify the security level for each zone Internet, Local intranet, Trusted sites, and Restricted sites. You can also enable or disable Protected Mode. If necessary, click Custom Level to change individual settings for a zone.

Figure 22-17

Configuring Security zones

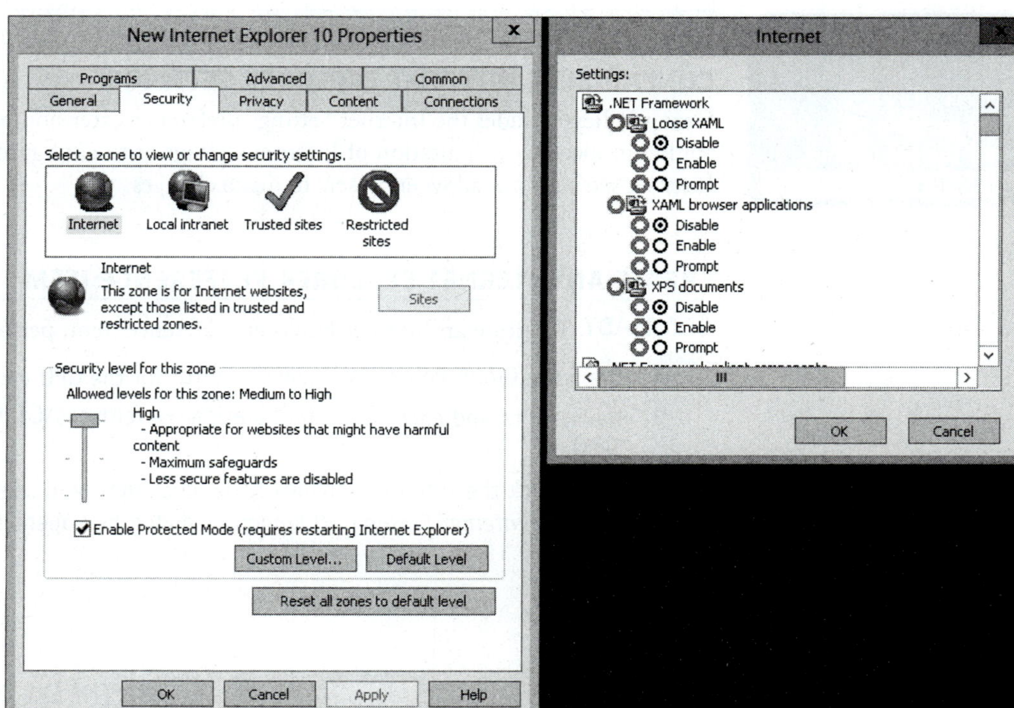

6. On the Privacy tab (see Figure 22-18), you can specify to turn on Pop-up blocker, configure the Pop-up Blocker by clicking Settings, or to configure InPrivate option.

Figure 22-18

Configuring Privacy settings

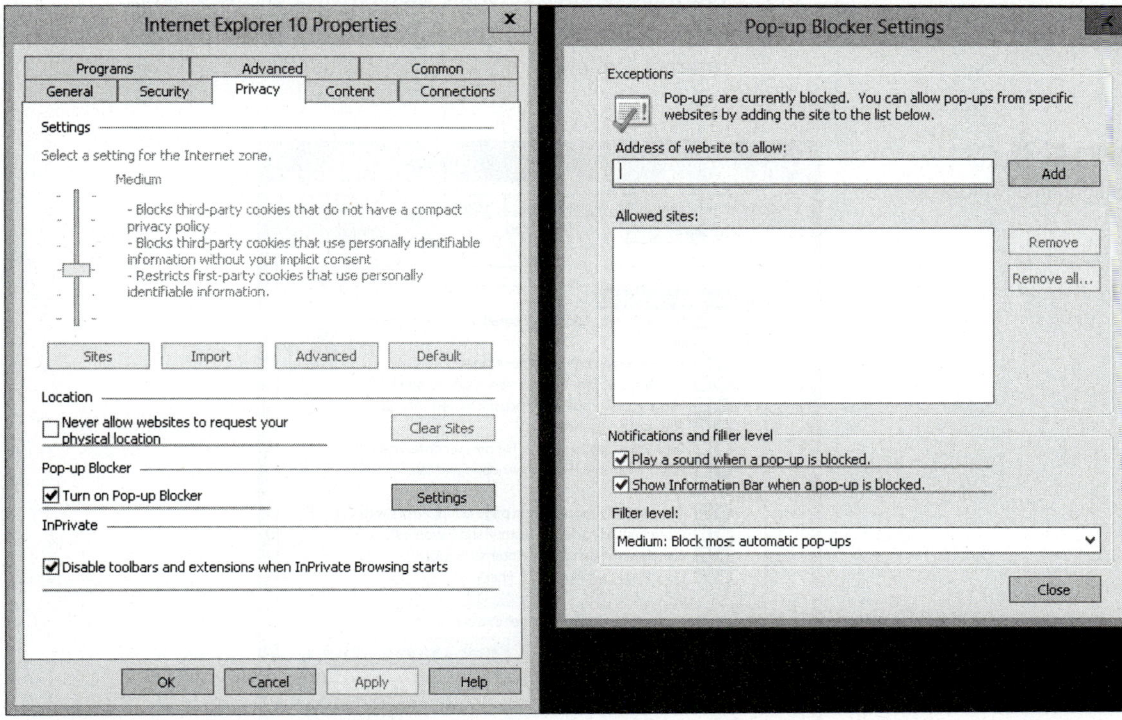

7. On the Content tab, you configure the AutoComplete settings and the Feeds and Web Slices settings.

8. On the Connections tab (see Figure 22-19), you can configure dial-up and Virtual Private Network settings and to configure LAN settings, which are necessary if your organization is using a proxy server.

Figure 22-19

Configuring Internet options

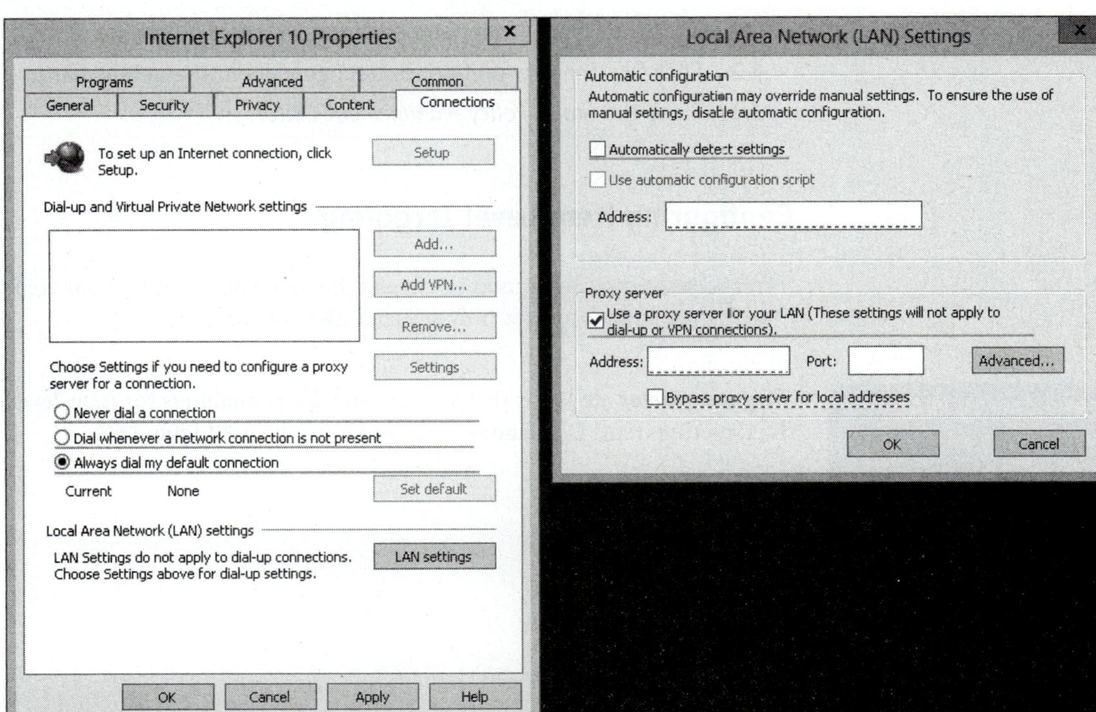

9. On the Programs tab, you can specify how Internet Explorer is open (on the desktop, in Internet Explorer, or let Internet Explorer decide). You can also specify whether you want to open Internet Explorer tiles on the desktop.
10. On the Advanced tab (see Figure 22-20), select individual Advanced settings for Internet Explorer.

Figure 22-20
Configuring advanced options

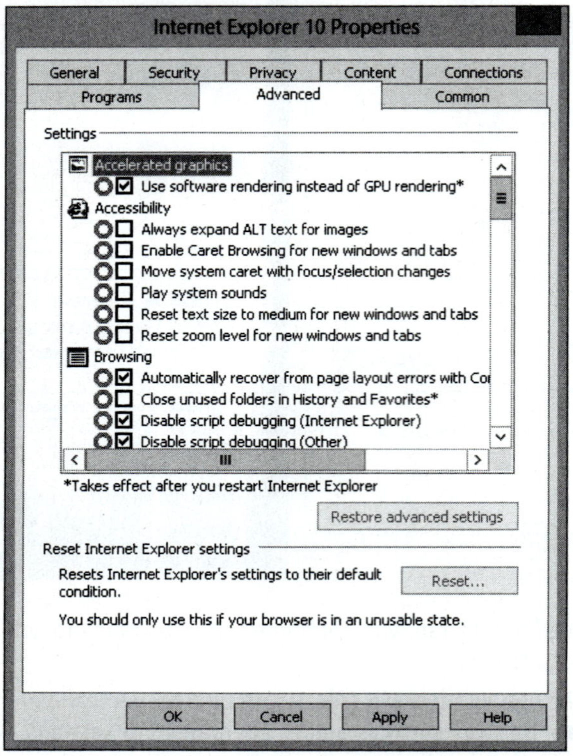

11. Click the Common tab, and configure any of the Common options.
12. Click OK. The new preference item appears in the details pane.
13. Close the *Group Policy Management Editor*.

Configuring Item-Level Targeting

Item-level targeting is used to change the scope of individual preference items so that the preference items apply to only selected users or computers.

CERTIFICATION READY
Configure item-level targeting.
Objective 6.4

Targeting items are items that you can specify as qualifiers for item-level targeting. Some of the targeting items (see Figure 22-21) that can be used include:

- Computer name
- CPU speed
- Date match
- Disk space
- Domain
- IP address range
- Network connection

- Operating system
- Portable computer
- RAM
- User
- Terminal session
- LDAP query
- Time range
- WMI query

Figure 22-21

Using item-level targeting

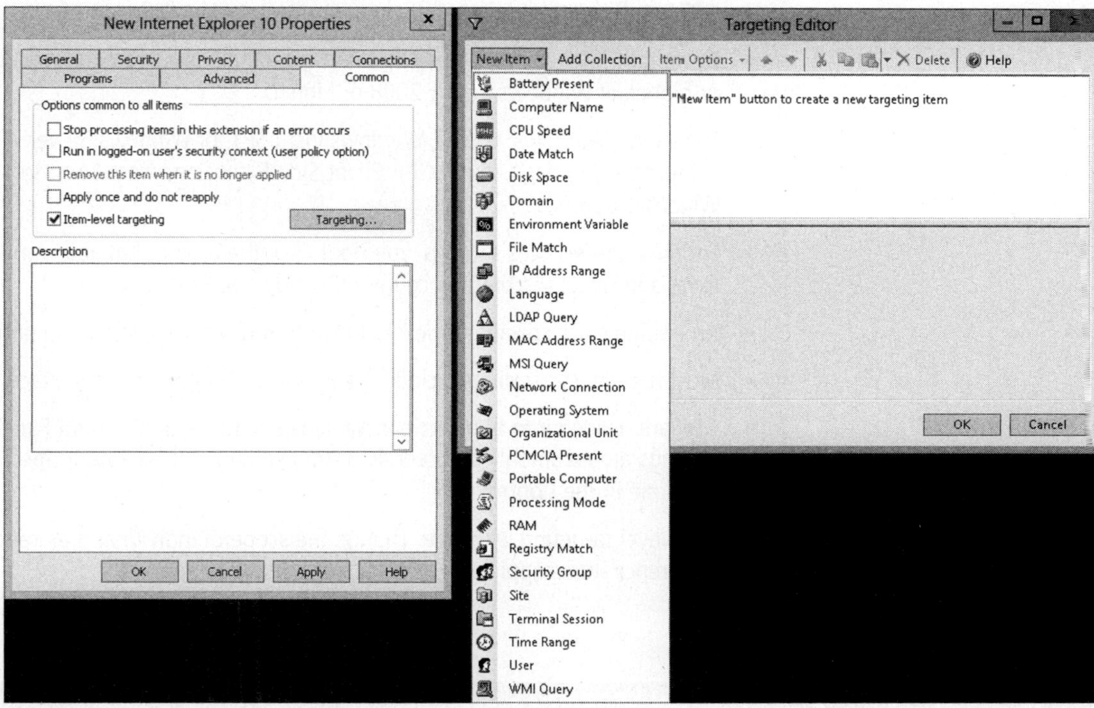

Each targeting item results in a value of either true or false. You can apply multiple targeting items to a preference item and select the logical operation (AND or OR) by which to combine each targeting item with the preceding one (see Figure 22-22). If the combined value is false, then the settings in the preference item are not applied to the user or computer.

Figure 22-22

Using the targeting editor

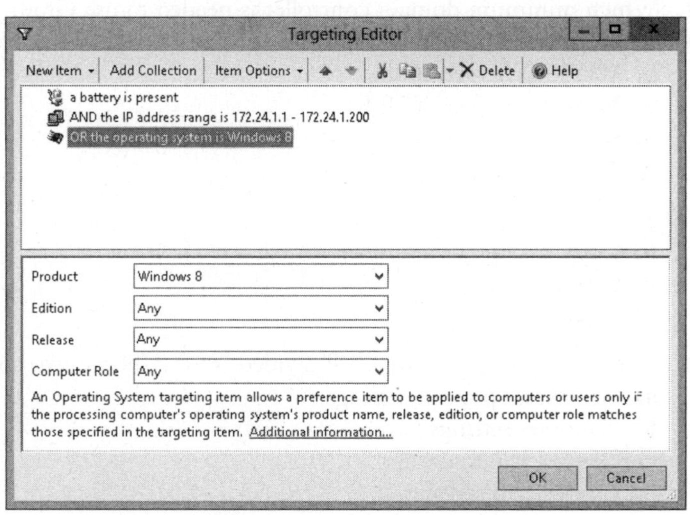

SKILL SUMMARY

IN THIS LESSON, YOU LEARNED:

- Group Policy Preferences (GPP) are made up of more than 20 new Group Policy client-side extensions (CSEs) that expand the range of configurable settings in a Group Policy object (GPO) that were not available before.
- Although Group Policies settings cannot be modified, GPP writes preferences to the same locations in the registry that the application or operating system feature uses to store the setting.
- GPP can be configured on domain controllers running Windows Server 2008 or higher.
- By default, GPP are supported by client computers running Windows Vista SP2, Windows 7 or higher, or Windows Server 2008 or higher.
- To support Windows XP SP3, Windows Vista SP1, or Windows Server 2003 client computers, you must install GPP Client Side Extensions from Microsoft Downloads or Windows Updates.
- For most preferences settings, you right-click the option that you want to configure, select New, and select the preference item that you want to create.
- An editing state specifies whether the option will be delivered and processed by the client.
- Most preferences settings include the following Actions: create, replace, update, and delete.
- GPP are divided into two sections: Windows Settings and Control Panel Settings. Windows Settings are commonly used configuration settings that are performed in Windows, but are not done in the Control Panel.
- Item-level targeting is used to change the scope of individual preference items so that the preference items apply only to selected users or computers.

Knowledge Assessment

Multiple Choice

Select the correct answer for each of the following questions.

1. Which minimum domain controller is needed to use Group Policy Preferences (GPP)?
   a. Windows Server 2003 R2
   b. Windows Server 2008
   c. Windows Server 2008 R2
   d. Windows Server 2012
2. Which of the following are Actions found in preferences? (Choose all that apply.)
   a. Delete
   b. Copy
   c. Create
   d. Replace
3. Which two categories are GPP divided into? (Choose two answers.)
   a. Command prompt settings
   b. Windows settings
   c. Control Panel settings
   d. User-owned settings

4. You create a Preference Item for Internet Explorer 10 and you configure the HTML editor option and it includes a red dashed underline. What should you do to enable this option?
   a. Press the F6 key.
   b. Press the F7 key.
   c. Press the F8 key.
   d. Press the F9 key.

5. Which of the following are Control Panel Settings options in GPP? (Choose all that apply.)
   a. Application extension
   b. Power Options extension
   c. Folders extensions
   d. Shortcuts extension

6. Which of the following are Windows Settings options in GPP? (Choose all that apply.)
   a. Folder Options
   b. Regional Options
   c. Network Shares
   d. Scheduled Tasks

7. You want to configure the default home page for Internet Explorer for your organization. You have Windows 7, Windows 8, Windows 9, and Windows 10. How many preference items do you need to create?
   a. 1
   b. 2
   c. 3
   d. 4

8. Which of the following preferences support Editing state for GPP? (Choose all that apply.)
   a. Network Shares
   b. Folder Options
   c. Regional and Language Settings
   d. Ini Files

9. Which printers are supported for GPP? (Choose all that apply.)
   a. TCP/IP printer
   b. Local printer
   c. Remote printer
   d. Shared printer

10. How do you include multiple targeting items when configuring GPP?
   a. Use a list.
   b. Configure an add-on.
   c. Add an attachment.
   d. Use logical operations.

Best Answer

Choose the letter that corresponds to the best answer. More than one answer choice may achieve the goal. Select the BEST answer.

1. Which of the following clients support GPP out of the box? (Choose all that apply.)
   a. Windows 7
   b. Windows 8
   c. Windows Server 2012
   d. Windows XP SP2
   e. Windows Vista SP1

2. What Group Policy Preference option would you select if you want to configure a default home page for Internet Explorer options?
   a. Set Default.
   b. Allow user to modify.
   c. Apply once and do not reapply.
   d. Use item-level targeting.

3. Where is GPP stored in the registry?
   a. In the Policy subkey
   b. The Preferences subkey
   c. The same location as the application or operating system feature uses to store the setting
   d. In the INI setting

4. You have Windows XP with SP3. What do you need to do support GPP?
   a. Install Client Side Extensions.
   b. Upgrade to SP4.
   c. Install the GPP Support Pack.
   d. Upgrade to Windows Vista.

5. You have users in the Engineering OU. You need to ensure that when a user logs off, he or she is automatically added to the local Administrators group. What should you do?
   a. Modify GPP.
   b. Configure GPP.
   c. Enable loopback processing in replace mode.
   d. Configure WMI filtering.

Matching and Identification

1. Identify which of the following are GPP Windows Settings.
   _______ a) Network Options Extension
   _______ b) Folder Extensions
   _______ c) Network Shares Extension
   _______ d) Power Options Extension
   _______ e) Registry Extension
   _______ f) Application Extension

2. Identify which of the following are GPP Control Panel Settings.
   _______ a) Local Users and Group Extension
   _______ b) Registry Extension
   _______ c) INI Files Extension
   _______ d) Printer Extension
   _______ e) Environment Extension
   _______ f) Regional Options Extension

Build a List

1. Identify the basic steps in order when configuring creating a data folder on the user's desktop. Not all steps will be used.
   _____ Right-click Computer Configuration\Preferences\Windows Settings\Folders.
   _____ Right-click User Configuration\Preferences\Windows Settings\Folders.
   _____ Specify the Make task.
   _____ Specify the Modify task.
   _____Specify the Create task.
   _____ Open GPMC.
   _____ Specify the path of the folder in the Path text box.
   _____ Click OK.

2. You want to clear out a C:\BAK folder if the C drive has less than 5 GB free. Identify the basic steps in order to perform this task.
   _____ Right-click Computer Configuration\Preferences\Windows Settings\Folders.
   _____ Right-click User Configuration\Preferences\Windows Settings\Folders.
   _____ Specify the Delete task.
   _____ Specify the Modify task.
   _____ Specify the Replace task.
   _____ Specify the conditional parameters.
   _____ Open GPMC.
   _____ Specify the path of the folder in the Path text box.
   _____ Click OK.
   _____ Specify the targeting item.

Choose an Option

1. You have an Active Directory domain called *contoso.com*. All client computers are running Windows 7 and 8. You need to enable Power Management so that every computer sleeps at night when not in use. Looking at the figure, what option should you choose?

Figure 22-23

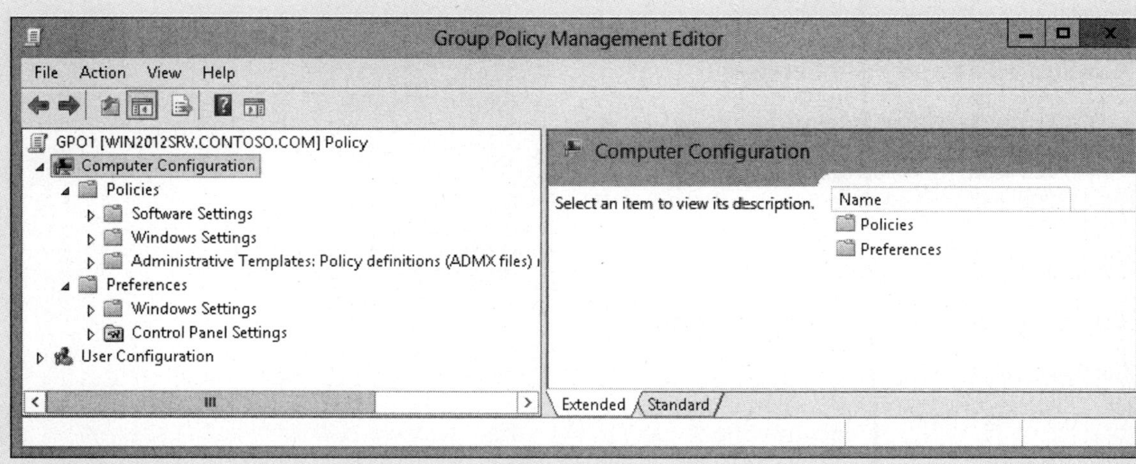

Business Case Scenarios

Scenario 22-1: Saving Power

You are an administrator for the Contoso Corporation. Your manager says that there is a need to save money when possible and he notices that at night, many computers are still on. He started to realize how much power all of these computers consume when they are not in use. Therefore, he wants you to come up with a solution to automatically put the computers to sleep when they are not being used. What do you propose?

Scenario 22-2: Adding Registry Settings

You are an administrator for the Contoso Corporation. You have a mix of Windows XP, Windows 7, and Windows 8 computers. For the Windows 8 computers, you need to add a registry setting. You do not want to add the registry settings for the Windows XP and Windows 7 clients. What should you do?

Appendix A
Exam 70-411 Administering Windows Server 2012

Exam Objective	Objective Number	Lesson Number
Deploy, Manage, and Maintain Servers		
Deploy and manage server images	1.1	1
Implement patch management	1.2	2
Monitor servers	1.3	3
Configure File and Print Services		
Configure Distributed File System (DFS)	2.1	4
Configure File Server Resource Manager (FSRM)	2.2	5
Configure file and disk encryption	2.3	6
Configure advanced audit policies	2.4	7
Configure Network Services and Access		
Configure DNS zones	3.1	8
Configure DNS records	3.2	9
Configure VPN and routing	3.3	10
Configure DirectAccess	3.4	11
Configure a Network Policy Server Infrastructure		
Configure Network Policy Server (NPS)	4.1	12
Configure NPS policies	4.2	13
Configure Network Access Protection (NAP)	4.3	14
Configure and Manage Active Directory		
Configure service authentication	5.1	15
Configure domain controllers	5.2	16
Maintain Active Directory	5.3	17
Configure account policies	5.4	18

(continued)

EXAM OBJECTIVE	OBJECTIVE NUMBER	LESSON NUMBER
Configure and Manage Group Policy		
Configure Group Policy processing	6.1	19
Configure Group Policy settings	6.2	20
Manage Group Policy Objects (GPOs)	6.3	21
Configure Group Policy preferences	6.4	22

Index

Note: Page number followed by "f" represent figure. Page number followed by "t" represent table.

D

E

F

G

H

I

K

L

M

X

Z